STUDENT TESTED, FACULTY APPROVED

THE ECON SOLUTION

Every 4LTR Press solution includes:

Visually Engaging Textbook

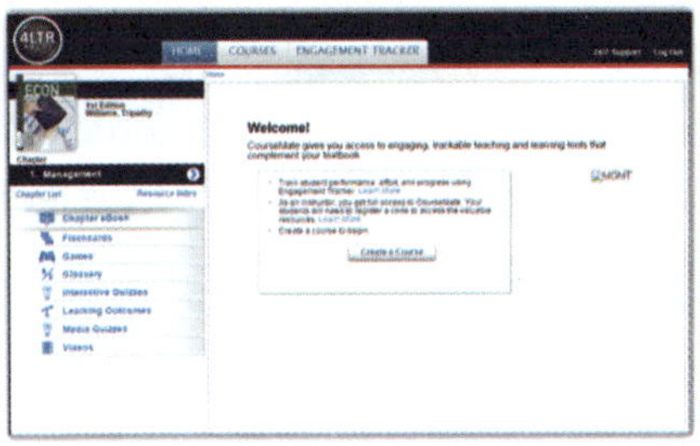

Online Study Tools

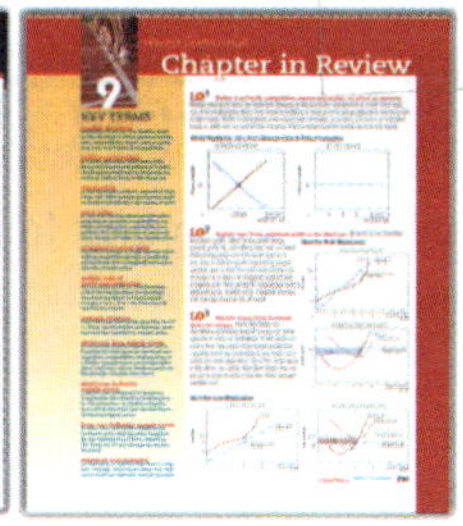

Review Pages

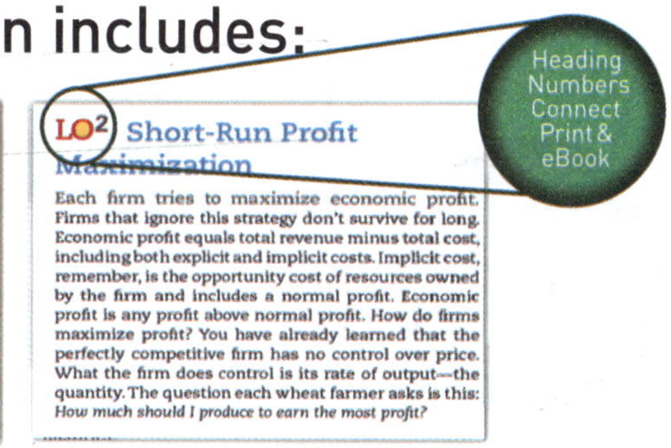

Interactive eBook

AF646118

STUDENT RESOURCES:

- Interactive eBook
- Flashcards
- Games
- Graphing Workshop
- Quizzes
- Videos

INSTRUCTOR RESOURCES:

- All Student Resources
- Engagement Tracker
- LMS Integration
- PowerPoint Slides
- Solution Manual
- Test Bank

Students sign in at www.cengagebrain.com

Instructors sign in at www.cengage.com/login

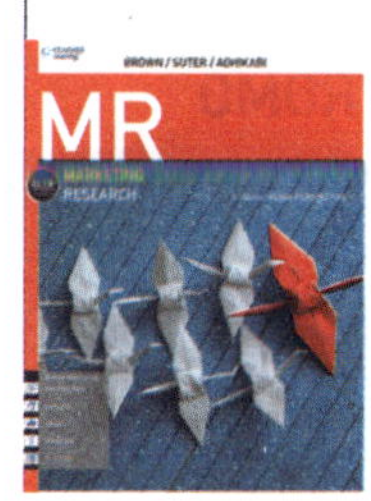

THE 4LTR PRESS PROCESS

Like all 4LTR Press solutions, Micro ECON begins and ends with student and faculty feedback. For the Principles of Microeconomics course, here's the process we used:

CONTINUOUSLY IMPROVING

MEET

Conduct research with students on their challenges and learning preferences.

Students taking Principles of Economics told us they needed contemporary relevent examples as well as interactive and convenient study tools.

SHOW

Develop the ideal product mix with students to address each course's needs.

For ECON we developed CourseMate, an interactive digital site with advanced study tools. The Graphing Workshop, found on CourseMate, helps students master graphs and equations to achieve success in economics.

TEST

Share student feedback and validate product mix with faculty.

Faculty have told us that tracking and assigning advanced study options is important, so we developed Engagement Tracker on CourseMate which enables them to do just that.

WORK

Publish, a Student-Tested, Faculty-Approved solution.

ECON makes Principles of Microeconomics relevent to students through a visually appealing format and puts course concepts in context with a broad array of print and digital resources.

PROMO FORTHCOMING

MM FORTHCOMING

CB FORTHCOMING

SELL FORTHCOMING

BSTAT FORTHCOMING

CFIN FORTHCOMING

GLOBAL FORTHCOMING

MICRO ECON

A South-Asian Prespective

William A. McEachern

University of Connecticut

Simrit Kaur

University of Delhi

CENGAGE

Australia • Brazil • India • Mexico • Singapore • United Kingdom • United States

CENGAGE

Micro ECON

William A. McEachern
Simrit Kaur

Cover Image: © iStockPhoto/ Thinkstock

© 2016 Cengage Learning India Pvt. Ltd.

Original Edition © 2010 South-Western, Cengage Learning

Micro ECON, 2e, SE Package, ISBN: 978-1-4390-3996-0

This edition is adapted by license from South-Western Cengage Learning, for sale in India, Pakistan, Bangladesh, Nepal and Sri Lanka only.

ALL RIGHTS RESERVED. No part of this work covered by the copyright herein may be reproduced, transmitted, stored, or used in any form or by any means graphic, electronic, or mechanical, including but not limited to photocopying, recording, scanning, digitizing, taping, Web distribution, information networks, or information storage and retrieval systems, without the prior written permission of the publisher.

For permission to use material from this text or product, submit all requests online at **www.cengage.com/permissions**

Further permission questions can be emailed to **India.permission@cengage.com**

ISBN-13: 978-81-315-2450-3
ISBN-10: 81-315-2450-7

Cengage Learning India Pvt. Ltd.
418, F.I.E., Patparganj
Delhi 110092

Cengage Learning is a leading provider of customized learning solutions with office locations around the globe, including Australia, Brazil, India, Mexico, Singapore, United Kingdom, United States. Locate your local office at:
www.cengage.com/global

Cengage Learning products are represented in Canada by Nelson Education, Ltd.

For product information, visit **www.cengage.co.in**

Printed in India
Fourth Impression 2019

MICRO **ECON**

Preface

4LTR Press, a Cengage Learning product, is a widely acclaimed concept of learning with a simple approach—creating an innovative teaching and learning solution built around today's learners and teachers. The idea behind bringing out this series of books is to introduce students and teachers in South Asia to an innovative concept in management studies. Since the launch, 4LTR Press has helped more than 1,800,000 college students at over 2,000 schools succeed worldwide. Every book in the series is built on the findings based on the inputs from discipline-specific focus groups, conversations, and surveys.

The books in this series present visually-engaging page layouts and succinct yet thorough topical coverage and are designed from the ground up to meet the needs of teachers and students. These books help increase students' classroom engagement and improve learning outcomes.

The books address a number of concerns, including the reality of the reading habits of the majority of today's students. 4LTR Press offers information in the formats students find engaging, while still providing the high-quality content instructors need. The chapters in these books are short and understandable. The text is easier to pay attention to, and the books are actually enjoyable to read. Everything is much more inviting than a regular textbook. The review sections at the end of each chapter serve a unique purpose: Students first go through the review section to preview the new concepts, then they read the chapter to understand the material, and finally they go through the review section again to make sure they have registered the key concepts.

We are sure that this series, a first of its kind in the South Asian market, will revolutionize the way students approach and become familiar with the concepts of business and economics.

MICRO

ECON Brief Contents

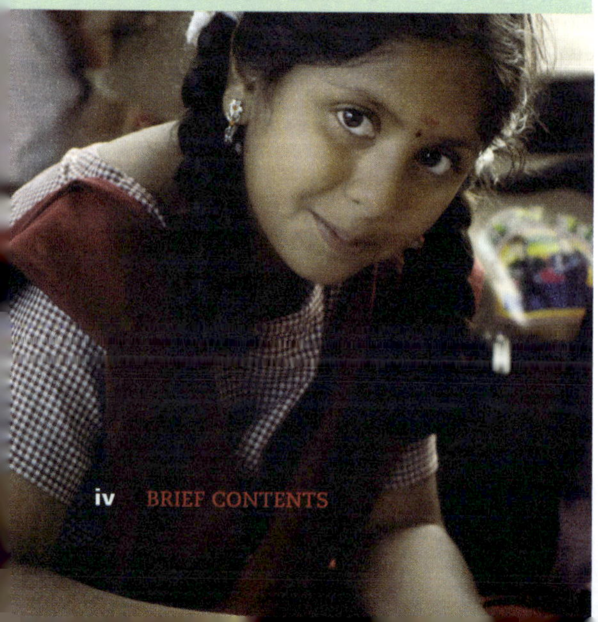

MICRO ECON

Contents

PART 1 Introduction to Economics

PART 2 Introduction to the Market System

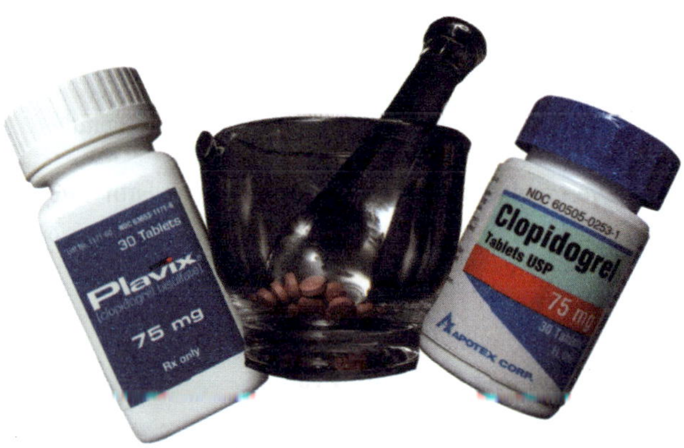

PART 3 Market Structure, Pricing, and Risk Analysis

PART 4 Resource Markets

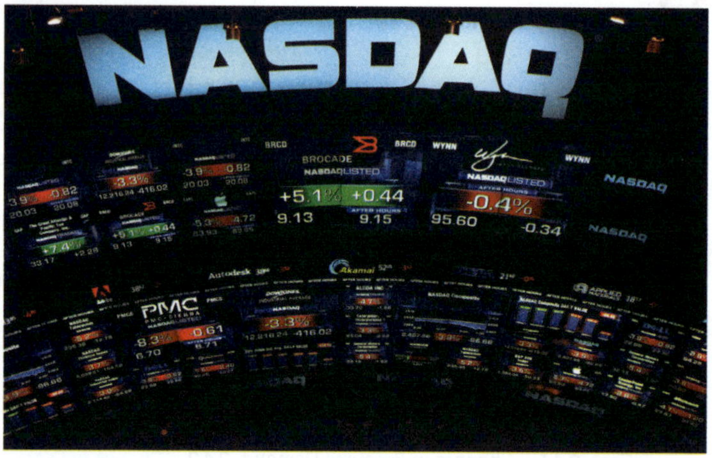
NASDAQ

PART 5 Market Failure and Public Policy

PART 6 International Microeconomics

CHAPTER 1

The Art and Science of Economic Analysis

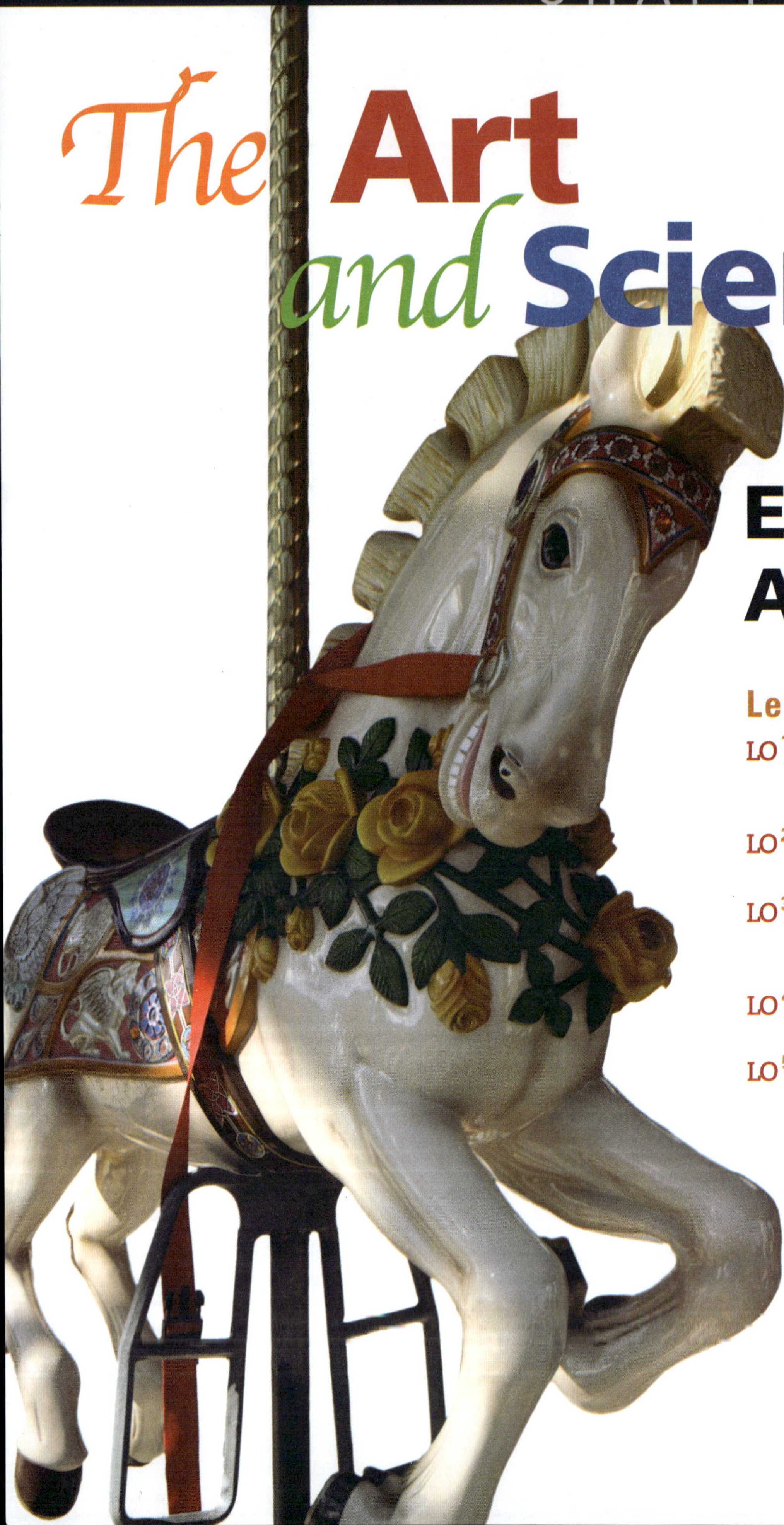

Learning Outcomes

- LO 1 Explain the economic problem of scarce resources and unlimited wants
- LO 2 Describe the forces that shape economic choices
- LO 3 Explain the relationship between economic theory and economic reality
- LO 4 Identify some pitfalls of economic analysis
- LO 5 Describe several reasons to study economics

“How can it be said that in economics ‘what goes around comes around’?”

Why do people want to participate in “Kaun Banega Crorepati”? Why is there no such thing as a free lunch? In what way are people who pound on vending machines relying on theory? What’s the big idea with economics? Finally, how can it be said that in economics “what goes around comes around”? These and other questions are answered in this chapter, which introduces the art and science of economic analysis.

You have been reading and hearing about economic issues for years—unemployment, inflation, poverty, government deficits, college tuition, airfares, stock prices, computer prices, petrol prices. When explanations of these issues go into any depth, you may feel confused and get lost, the same way you do when the meteorological department forecaster tries to provide an in-depth analysis of high-pressure fronts colliding with moisture carried in from the coast.

What do you think?

Economics is a science, not an art.

Strongly Disagree					Strongly Agree	
1	2	3	4	5	6	7

What many people fail to realize is that economics is livelier than the dry accounts offered by the news media. Economics is about making choices, and you make economic choices every day—choices about whether to get a part-time job or focus on your studies, live in the hostel or rent a room outside campus, take a course in accounting or one in history, get married or stay single, pack a lunch or buy a sandwich. You already know much more about economics than you realize. You bring to the subject a rich personal experience, an experience that will be tapped throughout the book to reinforce your understanding of the basic ideas.

Topics discussed in Chapter 1 include:

- The economic problem
- Rational self-interest
- Marginal analysis
- Scientific method
- Normative versus positive analysis
- Pitfalls of economic thinking

© SHARON MEREDITH/ISTOCKPHOTO.COM

LO1 The Economic Problem: Scarce Resources, Unlimited Wants

Would you like a new car, a nicer home, better meals, more free time, a more interesting social life, more spending money, more leisure, more sleep? Who wouldn't? But even if you can satisfy some of these desires, others keep popping up. *The problem is that, although your wants, or desires, are virtually unlimited, the resources available to satisfy these wants are scarce.* A resource is *scarce* when it is not freely available—that is, when its price exceeds zero. Because resources are scarce, you must choose from among many wants, and whenever you choose, you must forgo satisfying some other wants. The problem of scarce resources but unlimited wants exists to a greater or lesser extent for each of the people on earth. Everybody—cab driver, farmer, brain surgeon, dictator, shepherd, student, politician—faces the problem. For example, a cab driver uses time and other scarce resources, such as the taxi, knowledge of the city, driving skills, and gasoline, to earn income. That income, in turn, buys housing, groceries, clothing, trips to Water World, and thousands of other goods and services that help satisfy some of the driver's unlimited wants. **Economics** examines how people use their scarce resources to satisfy their unlimited wants. Let's pick apart the definition, beginning with resources, then goods and services, and finally focus on the heart of the matter—economic choice, which arises from scarcity.

economics
the study of how people use their scarce resources to satisfy their unlimited wants

resources
the inputs, or factors of production, used to produce the goods and services that people want; resources consist of labor, capital, natural resources, and entrepreneurial ability

labor
the physical and mental effort used to produce goods and services

capital
the buildings, equipment, and human skills used to produce goods and services

natural resources
all "gifts of nature" used to produce goods and services; includes renewable and exhaustible resources

entrepreneurial ability
managerial and organizational skills needed to start a firm, combined with the willingness to take the risk of profit or loss

entrepreneur
a profit-seeking decision maker who starts with an idea, organizes an enterprise to bring that idea to life, and assumes the risk of the operation

Resources

Resources are the inputs, or factors of production, used to produce the goods and services that people want. *Goods and services are scarce because resources are scarce.* Resources sort into four broad categories: labor, capital, natural resources, and entrepreneurial ability. **Labor** is human effort, both physical and mental. Labor includes the effort of the cab driver and the brain surgeon. Labor itself comes from a more fundamental resource: *time*. Without time we can accomplish nothing. We allocate our time to alternative uses: we can *sell* our time as labor, or we can *spend* our time doing other things, like sleeping, eating, studying, playing sports, going online, watching TV, or just relaxing with friends.

Capital includes all human creations used to produce goods and services. Economists often distinguish between physical capital and human capital. *Physical capital* consists of factories, tools, machines, computers, buildings, airports, highways, and other human creations used to produce goods and services. Physical capital includes the cab driver's taxi, the surgeon's scalpel, and the building where your economics class meets. *Human capital* consists of the knowledge and skill people acquire to increase their productivity, such as the cab driver's knowledge of city streets, the surgeon's knowledge of human anatomy, and your knowledge of economics.

Natural resources are all *gifts of nature*, including bodies of water, trees, oil reserves, minerals, and even animals. Natural resources can be divided into renewable resources and exhaustible resources. A *renewable resource* can be drawn on indefinitely if used conservatively. Thus, timber is a renewable resource if felled trees are replaced to provide a steady supply. The air and rivers are renewable resources if they are allowed sufficient time to clean themselves of any pollutants. More generally, biological resources like fish, wildlife, forests, rivers, groundwater, grasslands, and soil are renewable if managed properly. An *exhaustible resource*—such as oil, coal, or copper ore—does not renew itself and so is available in a limited amount. Once burned, each barrel of oil or ton of coal is gone forever. The world's oil and coal deposits are exhaustible.

A special kind of human skill called **entrepreneurial ability** is the talent required to dream up a new product or find a better way to produce an existing one. This special skill comes from an entrepreneur. An **entrepreneur** is a profit-seeking decision maker who starts with an idea, then organizes an enterprise to bring that idea to life, and assumes the risk of operation. An entrepreneur pays resource owners for the opportunity to employ their resources in the firm. Every firm in the world today, such as Ford, Microsoft, Google, and Dell, began as an idea in the mind of an entrepreneur.

Resource owners are paid **wages** for their labor, **interest** for the use of their capital, and **rent** for the use of their natural resources. Entrepreneurial ability is rewarded by **profit**, which equals the *revenue* from items sold minus the cost of the resources employed to make those items. The word *profit* comes from the Latin *proficere,* which means "to benefit." The entrepreneur benefits from what's left over after paying other resource suppliers. Sometimes the entrepreneur suffers a loss. Resource earnings are usually based on the *time* these resources are employed. Resource payments therefore have a time dimension, as in a wage of $10 *per hour,* interest of 6 percent *per year,* rent of $600 *per month,* or profit of $10,000 *per year.*

There's no such thing as a free napkin.

© RANDY FARIS/CORBIS

Goods and Services

Resources are combined in a variety of ways to produce goods and services. A farmer, a tractor, 50 acres of land, seeds, and fertilizer combine to grow the good: wheat. One hundred musicians, musical instruments, chairs, a conductor, a musical score, and a recording studio combine to produce the music for a movie. Wheat is a **good** because it is something you can see, feel, and touch; it requires scarce resources to produce; and it satisfies human wants. The book you are now holding, the chair you are sitting in, the clothes you are wearing, and your next meal are all goods. The performance in a music festival is a **service** because it is intangible, yet it uses scarce resources to satisfy human wants. Lectures, movies, concerts, phone service, broadband connections, yoga lessons, dry cleaning, and haircuts are all services.

Because goods and services are produced using scarce resources, they are themselves scarce. *A good or service is scarce if the amount people desire exceeds the amount available at a zero price.* Because we cannot have all the goods and services we would like, we must continually choose among them. We must choose among more pleasant living quarters, better meals, nicer clothes, more reliable transportation, faster computers, and so on. Making choices in a world of **scarcity** means we must pass up some goods and services. But not everything is scarce. In fact some things we would prefer to have less of. For example, we would prefer to have less garbage, less spam email, and less pollution. Things we want none of even at a zero price are called *bads.* Think of a bad as the opposite of a good.

A few goods and services seem *free* because the amount available at a zero price exceeds the amount people want. For example, air and seawater often seem free because we can breathe all the air we want and have all the seawater we can haul away. Yet, despite the old saying "The best things in life are free," most goods and services are scarce, not free, and even those that appear to be free come with strings attached. For example, *clean air* and *clean* seawater have become scarce. *Goods and services that are truly free are not the subject matter of economics. Without scarcity, there would be no economic problem and no need for prices.*

Sometimes we mistakenly think of certain goods as free because they involve no apparent cost to us. Napkins seem to be free at a restaurant. But you cannot take a handful of it. Supplying napkins, costs the restaurant and hence changed prices every year reflect that cost. Some restaurants make special efforts to keep napkin use down—such as packing them tightly into the dispenser or making you ask for them.

You may have heard the expression "There is no such thing as a free lunch." There is no free lunch because all goods and services involve a cost to someone. The lunch may seem free to us, but it draws scarce resources away from the production of other goods and services, and whoever provides a free lunch often expects something in return. A Russian proverb makes a similar point but with a bit more bite: "The only place you find free cheese is in a mousetrap." Albert Einstein once observed, "Sometimes one pays the most for things one gets for nothing."

wages
payment to resource owners for their labor

interest
payment to resource owners for the use of their capital

rent
payment to resource owners for the use of their natural resources

profit
reward for entrepreneurial ability; sales revenue minus resource cost

good
a tangible product used to satisfy human wants

service
an activity, or intangible product, used to satisfy human wants

scarcity
occurs when the amount people desire exceeds the amount available at a zero price

Economic Decision Makers

There are four types of decision makers in the economy: households, firms, governments, and the rest of the world. Their interaction determines how an economy's resources are allocated. *Households* play the starring role. As consumers, households demand the goods and services produced. As resource owners, households supply labor, capital, natural resources, and entrepreneurial ability to firms, governments, and the rest of the world. *Firms, governments,* and *the rest of the world* demand the resources that households supply and then use these resources to supply the goods and services that households demand. The rest of the world includes foreign households, firms, and governments that supply resources and products to U.S. markets and demand resources and products from U.S. markets.

Markets are the means by which buyers and sellers carry out exchange. By bringing together the two sides of exchange, markets determine price and quantity. Markets are often physical places, such as supermarkets, department stores, shopping malls, or yard sales. But markets also include other mechanisms by which buyers and sellers communicate, such as classified ads, radio and television ads, telephones, bulletin boards, online sites, and face-to-face bargaining. These market mechanisms provide information about the quantity, quality, and price of products offered for sale. Goods and services are bought and sold in **product markets**. Resources are bought and sold in **resource markets**. The most important resource market is the labor, or job, market. Think about your own experience looking for a job, and you get some idea of that market.

market
a set of arrangements by which buyers and sellers carry out exchange at mutually agreeable terms

product market
a market in which a good or service is bought and sold

resource market
a market in which a resource is bought and sold

circular-flow model
a diagram that traces the flow of resources, products, income, and revenue among economic decision makers

A Simple Circular-Flow Model

Now that you have learned a bit about economic decision makers, consider how they interact. Such a picture is conveyed by the **circular-flow model**, which describes the flow of resources, products, income, and revenue among economic decision makers. The simple circular-flow model focuses on the primary interaction in a market economy—that between households and firms. Exhibit 1 shows households on the left and firms on the right; please take a look.

Exhibit 1

The Simple Circular-Flow Model for Households and Firms

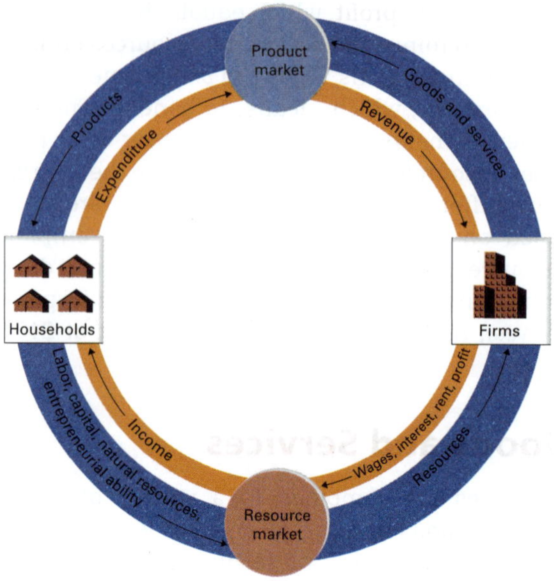

Households supply labor, capital, natural resources, and entrepreneurial ability to firms through resource markets, shown in the lower portion of the exhibit. In return, households demand goods and services from firms through product markets, shown on the upper portion of the exhibit. Viewed from the business end, firms demand labor, capital, natural resources, and entrepreneurial ability from households through resource markets, and firms supply goods and services to households through product markets.

The flows of resources and products are supported by the flows of income and expenditure—that is, by the flow of money. So let's add money. The demand and supply of resources come together in resource markets to determine what firms pay for resources. These resource prices—wages, interest, rent, and profit—flow as *income* to households. The demand and supply of products come together in product markets to determine what households pay for goods and services. These product prices of goods and services flow as *revenue* to firms. Resources and products flow in one direction—in this case, counterclockwise—and the corresponding payments flow in the other direction—clockwise. What goes around comes around. Take a little time now to trace the logic of the circular flows.

LO2 The Art of Economic Analysis

An economy results from the choices that millions of individuals make in attempting to satisfy their unlimited wants. Because these choices lie at the heart of the economic problem—coping with scarce resources but unlimited wants—they deserve a closer look. Learning about the forces that shape economic choice is the first step toward mastering the art of economic analysis.

Rational Self-Interest

A key economic assumption is that individuals, in making choices, rationally select alternatives they perceive to be in their best interests. By *rational,* economists mean simply that people try to make the best choices they can, given the available information. People may not know with certainty which alternative will turn out to be the best. They simply select the alternatives they *expect* will yield the most satisfaction and happiness. In general, **rational self-interest** means that individuals try to maximize the expected benefit achieved with a given cost or to minimize the expected cost of achieving a given benefit.

Rational self-interest should not be viewed as blind materialism, pure selfishness, or greed. For most of us, however, self-interest often includes the welfare of our family, our friends, and perhaps the poor of the world. Even so, our concern for others is influenced by the cost of that concern. We may readily volunteer to drive a friend to the airport on Saturday afternoon but are less likely to offer a ride if the plane leaves at 6:00 A.M. When we donate clothes to an organization such as Helpage, they are more likely to be old and worn than brand new. People tend to give more to charities when their contributions are tax deductible. TV stations are more likely to donate airtime for public-service announcements during the dead of night than during prime time. In Asia some people burn money to soothe the passage of a departed loved one. But they burn fake money, not real money. The notion of self-interest does not rule out concern for others; it simply means that concern for others is influenced by the same economic forces that affect other economic choices. *The lower the personal cost of helping others, the more help we offer.*

An economy results from the choices that millions of individuals make in attempting to satisfy their unlimited wants.

Choice Requires Time and Information

Rational choice takes time and requires information, but time and information are scarce and therefore valuable. If you have any doubts about the time and information required to make choices, talk to someone who recently purchased a home, a car, or a personal computer. Talk to a corporate official trying to decide whether to introduce a new product, sell online, build a new factory, or buy another firm. Or think back to your own experience of choosing a college. You probably talked to friends, relatives, teachers, and guidance counselors. You likely used school catalogs, college guides, and Web sites. You may have visited some campuses to see the admissions staff and anyone else willing to talk. The decision took time and money, and it probably involved aggravation and anxiety.

Because information is costly to acquire, we are often willing to pay others to gather and digest it for us. College guidebooks, stock analysts, travel agents, real estate brokers, career counselors, restaurant critics, movie reviewers, and specialized Web sites, attest to our willingness to pay for information that improves our choices. As we'll see next, *rational decision makers continue to acquire information as long as the additional benefit expected from that information exceeds the additional cost of gathering it.*

Economic Analysis Is Marginal Analysis

Economic choice usually involves some adjustment to the existing situation, or status quo. Amazon.com must decide whether to add an additional line of products. The school superintendent must decide whether to hire another teacher. Your favorite jeans are on sale, and you must decide whether to buy another pair. You are wondering whether to carry

rational self-interest individuals try to maximize the expected benefit achieved with a given cost or to minimize the expected cost of achieving a given benefit

© JUSTIN SULLIVAN/GETTY IMAGES NEWS/GETTY IMAGES

> > **After armed guards escorted the shipment of *Harry Potter and the Deathly Hallows* to Amazon, the online retailer, it deposited the top-secret books in a guarded security zone. The zone had one entrance, and employees required a special badge to enter. Only longtime employees were allowed to pack the books, and counts were taken multiple times a day to ensure that no copies "went missing." The marginal cost for distributing such a hot title were certainly not insignificant.**

an extra course next term. You just finished lunch and are deciding whether to have dessert.

Economic choice is based on a comparison of the *expected marginal benefit* and the *expected marginal cost* of the action under consideration. **Marginal** means incremental, additional, or extra. Marginal refers to a change in an economic variable, a change in the status quo. *A rational decision maker changes the status quo if the expected marginal benefit from the change exceeds the expected marginal cost.* For example, Amazon.com compares the marginal benefit expected from adding a new line of products (the additional sales revenue) with the marginal cost (the additional cost of the resources required). Likewise, you compare the marginal benefit you expect from eating dessert (the additional pleasure or satisfaction) with its marginal cost (the additional money, time, and calories).

marginal incremental, additional, or extra; used to describe a change in an economic variable

microeconomics the study of the economic behavior in particular markets, such as that for computers or unskilled labor

macroeconomics the study of the economic behavior of entire economies

Typically, the change under consideration is small, but a marginal choice can involve a major economic adjustment, as in the decision to quit school and find a job. For a firm, a marginal choice might mean building a plant in Mexico or even filing for bankruptcy. By focusing on the effect of a marginal adjustment to the status quo, the economist is able to cut the analysis of economic choice down to a manageable size. Rather than confront a bewildering economic reality head-on, the economist begins with a marginal choice to see how this choice affects a particular market and shapes the economic system as a whole. Incidentally, to the noneconomist, *marginal* usually means relatively inferior, as in "a movie of marginal quality." Forget that meaning for this course and instead think of *marginal* as meaning incremental, additional, or extra.

Microeconomics and Macroeconomics

Although you have made thousands of economic choices, you probably seldom think about your own economic behavior. For example, why are you reading this book right now rather than doing something else? **Microeconomics** is the study of your economic behavior and the economic behavior of others who make choices about such matters as how much to study and how much to party, how much to borrow and how much to save, what to buy and what to sell. Microeconomics examines individual economic choices and how markets coordinate the choices of various decision makers. Microeconomics explains how price and quantity are determined in individual markets—the market for breakfast cereal, sports equipment, or used cars, for instance.

You have probably given little thought to what influences your own economic choices. You have likely given even less thought to how your choices link up with those made by millions of others in the U.S. economy to determine economy-wide measures such as total production, employment, and economic growth. **Macroeconomics** studies the performance of the economy as a whole. Whereas microeconomics studies the individual pieces of the economic puzzle, as reflected in particular markets, macroeconomics puts all the pieces together to focus on the big picture.

To review: The art of economic analysis focuses on how people use their scarce resources in an attempt to satisfy their unlimited wants. Rational self-interest guides individual choice. Choice requires time and information and involves a comparison of the marginal benefit and marginal cost of alternative actions. Microeconomics looks at the individual pieces of the economic puzzle; macroeconomics fits the pieces together to shape the big picture.

LO3 The Science of Economic Analysis

Economists use scientific analysis to develop theories, or models, that help explain economic behavior. An **economic theory**, or **economic model**, is a simplification of economic reality that is *used to make predictions about the real world*. A theory, or model, such as the circular-flow model, captures the important elements of the problem under study but need not spell out every detail and interrelation. In fact, adding more details may make a theory more unwieldy and, therefore, less useful. For example, a wrist watch is a model that tells time, but a watch festooned with extra features is harder to read at a glance and is therefore less useful as a time-telling model. The world is so complex that we must simplify to make sense of things. Store mannequins simplify the human form (some even lack arms and heads). Comic strips simplify characters—leaving out fingers or a mouth, for instance. You might think of economic theory as a stripped-down, or streamlined, version of economic reality.

A good theory helps us understand a messy and confusing world. Lacking a theory of how things work, our thinking can become cluttered with facts, one piled on another as in a messy closet. You could think of a good theory as a closet organizer for the mind. A good theory offers a helpful guide to sorting, saving, and understanding information.

© DAVID LEAHY/TAXI/GETTY IMAGES

A good theory can act like a closet organizer for your mind, helping you understand a messy and confusing world.

The Role of Theory

Most people don't understand the role of theory. Perhaps you have heard, "Oh, that's fine in theory, but in practice it's another matter." The implication is that the theory in question provides little aid in practical matters. People who say this fail to realize that they are merely substituting their own theory for a theory they either do not believe or do not understand. They are really saying, "I have my own theory that works better."

All of us employ theories, however poorly defined or understood. Someone who pounds on the PCO (Public call office or the local public phone) that just ate a two rupee coin has a crude theory about how that machine works. One version of that theory might be "The coin drops through a series of whatchamacallits, but sometimes it gets stuck. *If* I pound on the machine, *then* I can free up the coin and send it on its way." Evidently, this theory is widespread enough that people continue to pound on machines that fail to perform (a real problem for the machine industry and one reason newer machines are fronted with glass). Yet, if you were to ask these mad pounders to explain their "theory" about how the machine operates, they would look at you as if you were crazy.

The Scientific Method

To study economic problems, economists employ a process of theoretical investigation called *the scientific method*, which consists of four steps, as outlined in Exhibit 2.

Step One: Identify the Question and Define Relevant Variables

The scientific method begins with curiosity: Someone wants to answer a question. Thus, the first step is to identify the economic question and define the variables relevant to a solution. For example, the question might be "What is the relationship between the price of Pepsi and the quantity of Pepsi purchased?" In this case, the relevant variables are price and quantity. A **variable** is a measure that can take on different values at different times. The variables of concern become the elements of the theory, so they must be selected with care.

Step Two: Specify Assumptions

The second step is to specify the assumptions under which the theory is to apply. One major category of

economic theory (economic model)
a simplification of reality used to make predictions about cause and effect in the real world

variable
a measure, such as price or quantity, that can take on different values at different times

Exhibit 2

The Scientific Method: Step by Step

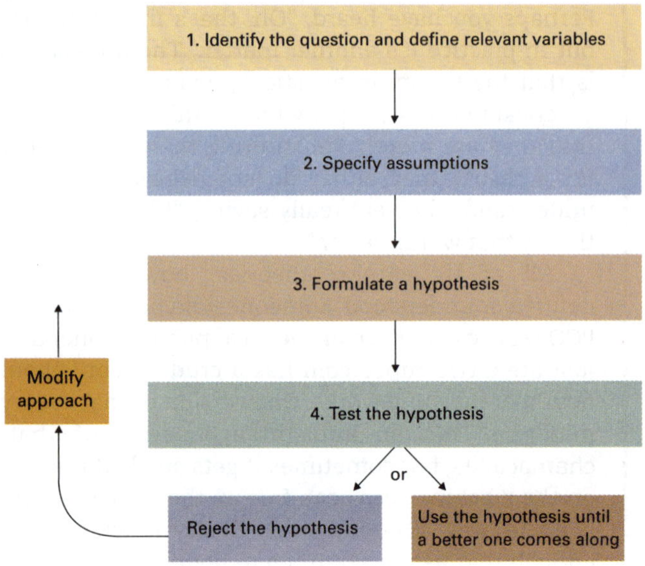

assumptions is the other-things-constant assumption—in Latin, the *ceteris paribus* assumption. The idea is to identify the variables of interest and then focus exclusively on the relationships among them, assuming that nothing else important changes—that other things remain constant. Again, suppose we are interested in how the price of Pepsi influences the amount purchased. To isolate the relation between these two variables, we assume that there are no changes in other relevant variables such as consumer income, the average temperature, or the price of Coke.

We also make assumptions about how people behave; these are called behavioral assumptions. The primary behavioral assumption is rational self-interest. Earlier we assumed that individual decision makers pursue self-interest rationally and make choices accordingly. Rationality implies that each consumer buys the products expected to maximize his or her level of satisfaction. Rationality also implies that each firm supplies the products expected to maximize the firm's profit. These kinds of assumptions are called behavioral assumptions because they specify how we expect economic decision makers to behave—what makes them tick, so to speak.

other-things-constant assumption the assumption, when focusing on the relation among key economic variables, that other variables remain unchanged; in Latin, *ceteris paribus*

behavioral assumption an assumption that describes the expected behavior of economic decision makers—what motivates them

hypothesis a theory about how key variables relate

positive economic statement a statement that can be proved or disproved by reference to facts

normative economic statement a statement that reflects an opinion, which cannot be proved or disproved by reference to the facts

© MARTIN LEE/MEDIABLITZIMAGES (UK) LIMITED/ALAMY

Step Three: Formulate a Hypothesis

The third step in the scientific method is to formulate a hypothesis, which is a theory about how key variables relate to each other. For example, one hypothesis holds that if the price of Pepsi goes up, other things constant, then the quantity purchased declines. The hypothesis becomes a prediction of what happens to the quantity purchased if the price increases. *The purpose of this hypothesis, like that of any theory, is to help make predictions about cause and effect in the real world.*

Step Four: Test the Hypothesis

In the fourth step, by comparing its predictions with evidence, we test the validity of a hypothesis. To test a hypothesis, we must focus on the variables in question, while carefully controlling for other effects assumed not to change. The test leads us either to (1) reject the hypothesis, or theory, if it predicts worse than the best alternative theory or (2) use the hypothesis, or theory, until a better one comes along. If we reject the hypothesis, we can go back and modify our approach in light of the results. Please spend a moment now reviewing the steps of the scientific method in Exhibit 2.

Normative Versus Positive

Economists usually try to explain how the economy works. Sometimes they concern themselves not with how the economy *does* work but how it *should* work. Compare these two statements: "The Indian unemployment rate is 9.5 percent" and "The Indian unemployment rate should be lower." The first, called a positive economic statement, is an assertion about economic reality that can be supported or rejected by reference to the facts. Positive economics, like physics or biology, attempts to understand the world around us. The second, called a normative economic statement, reflects an opinion. And an opinion is merely that—it cannot be shown to be true or false by reference to the facts. Positive statements concern what is; normative statements concern what, in someone's opinion, *should be*. Positive statements need not necessarily be true, but they must be subject to verification or refutation by reference to the facts. Theories are expressed as positive statements such as "If the price of Pepsi increases, then the quantity demanded decreases."

Most of the disagreement among economists involves normative debates—such as the appropriate role of government—rather than statements of positive analysis. To be sure, many theoretical issues remain unresolved, but economists generally agree on most fundamental theoretical principles—that is, about positive economic analysis. For example, in a survey of 464 U.S. economists, only 6.5 percent disagreed with the statement "A ceiling on rents reduces the quantity and quality of housing available." This is a positive statement because it can be shown to be consistent or inconsistent with the evidence. In contrast, there was much less agreement on normative statements such as "The distribution of income in the United States should be more equal." Half the economists surveyed "generally agreed," a quarter "generally disagreed," and a quarter "agreed with provisos."[1]

Normative statements, or value judgments, have a place in a policy debate such as the proper role of government, provided that statements of opinion are distinguished from statements of fact. In such policy debates, you are entitled to your own opinion, but you are not entitled to your own facts.

Economists Tell Stories

Despite economists' reliance on the scientific method for developing and evaluating theories, economic analysis is as much art as science. Formulating a question, isolating the key variables, specifying the assumptions, proposing a theory to answer the question, and devising a way to test the predictions all involve more than simply an understanding of economics and the scientific method. Carrying out these steps requires good intuition and the imagination of a storyteller. Economists explain their theories by telling stories about how they think the economy works. To tell a compelling story, an economist relies on case studies, anecdotes, parables, the personal experience of the listener, and supporting data. Throughout this book, you'll hear stories that bring you closer to the ideas under consideration. The stories, such as the one about the Pepsi machine, breathe life into economic theory and help you personalize abstract ideas.

> "Economists explain their theories by telling stories about how they think the economy works."

Predicting Average Behavior

The goal of an economic theory is to predict the impact of an economic event on economic choices and, in turn, the effect of these choices on particular markets or on the economy as a whole. Does this mean that economists try to predict the behavior of particular consumers or producers? Not necessarily, because a specific individual may behave in an unpredictable way. But the unpredictable actions of numerous individuals tend to cancel one another out, so the *average behavior* of groups can be predicted more accurately. For example, if the federal government cuts personal income taxes, certain households may decide to save the entire tax cut. On average, however, household spending increases. Likewise, if McDonald's cuts the price of burgers, the manager can better predict how much sales will increase than how a specific customer coming through the door will respond. *The random actions of individuals tend to offset one another, so the average behavior of a large group can be predicted more accurately than the behavior of a particular individual.* Consequently, economists tend to focus on the average, or typical, behavior of people in groups—for example, as average taxpayers or average burger consumers—rather than on the behavior of a specific individual.

LO4 Some Pitfalls of Faulty Economic Analysis

Economic analysis, like other forms of scientific inquiry, is subject to common mistakes in reasoning that can lead to faulty conclusions. Here are three sources of confusion.

The Fallacy That Association Is Causation

In the last two decades, the number of physicians specializing in cancer treatment increased sharply. At the same time, the incidence of some cancers increased. Can we conclude that physicians cause cancer? No. To assume that event A caused event

1. Richard M. Alston et al., "Is There a Consensus Among Economists in the 1990s?" *American Economic Review* 82 (May 1992): pp. 203–209, Table 1.

B simply because the two are associated in time is to commit the **association-is-causation fallacy**, a common error. The fact that one event precedes another or that the two events occur simultaneously does not necessarily mean that one causes the other. Remember: Association is not necessarily causation.

The Fallacy of Composition

Perhaps you have been to a rock concert where everyone stands to get a better view. At some concerts, most people even stand on their chairs. But even standing on chairs does not improve the view if others do the same. Likewise, arriving early to buy game tickets does not work if many others have the same idea. These are examples of the **fallacy of composition**, which is an erroneous belief that what is true for the individual, or the part, is also true for the group, or the whole.

The Mistake of Ignoring the Secondary Effects

In many cities, public officials have imposed rent controls on apartments. The primary effect of this policy, the effect policy makers focus on, is to keep rents from rising. Over time, however, fewer new apartments get built because renting them becomes less profitable. Moreover, existing rental units deteriorate because owners have plenty of customers anyway. Thus, the quantity and quality of housing may decline as a result of what appears to be a reasonable measure to keep rents from rising. The mistake was to ignore the **secondary effects**, or the unintended consequences, of the policy. Economic actions have secondary effects that often turn out to be more important than the primary effects. Secondary effects may develop more slowly and may not be immediately obvious, but good economic analysis tries to anticipate them and take them into account.

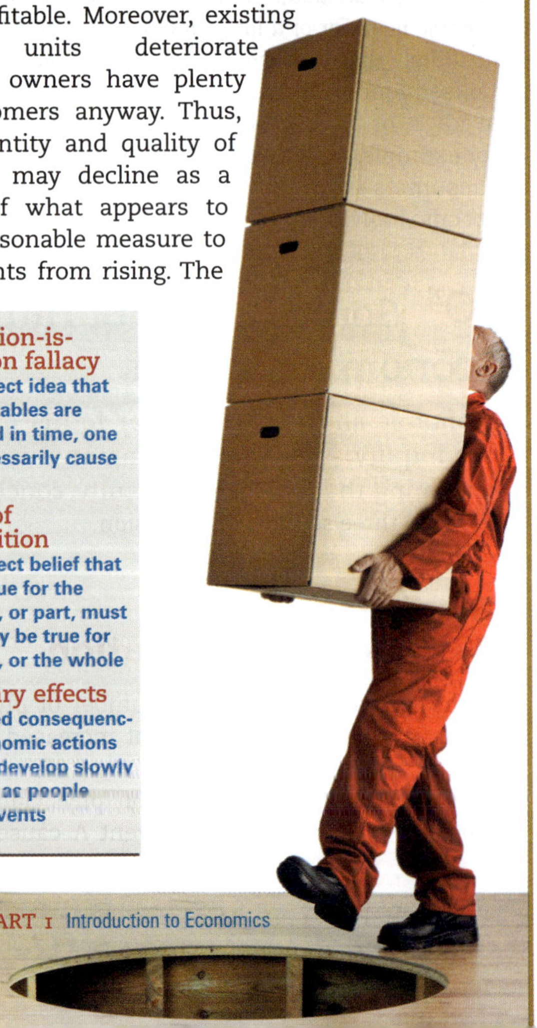
© DIAMOND SKY IMAGES/DIGITAL VISION/GETTY IMAGES

association-is-causation fallacy
the incorrect idea that if two variables are associated in time, one must necessarily cause the other

fallacy of composition
the incorrect belief that what is true for the individual, or part, must necessarily be true for the group, or the whole

secondary effects
unintended consequences of economic actions that may develop slowly over time as people react to events

LO5 Why Study Economics

The change in economic policy and the reforms in India from 1990 onwards is attributed to the toughtful leadership of Manmohan Singh, who was then the Finance Minister in the Cabinet of P.V. Narashimha Rao. Economists have been appointed to ministerial cabinet posts, planning commission, finance commission, Reserve Bank of India and work in the Indian Economic Service. Economics is the only social science and the only business discipline for which the prestigious Nobel Prize is awarded, and pronouncements by economists are reported in the media daily. *The Economist*, a widely respected news weekly from London, has argued that economic ideas have influenced policy "to a degree that would make other social scientists drool."[2]

The economics profession thrives because its models usually do a better job of making economic sense out of a confusing world than do alternative approaches. But not all economists are wealthy, nor is personal wealth the goal of the discipline. In a similar vein, not all doctors are healthy (some even smoke), not all carpenters live in perfectly built homes, not all marriage counselors are happily married, and not all child psychologists have well-adjusted children. Still, those who study economics do reap financial rewards.

Among college graduates, all kinds of factors affect earnings, such as general ability, occupation, college attended, college major, and highest degree earned. To isolate the effects of the college major on earnings, a National Science Foundation study surveyed people in specific age groups who worked full time and had earned a bachelor's as their highest degree. Exhibit 3 shows the median earnings by major for men and women ages 35 to 44. As a point of reference, the *median* annual earnings for men was $43,199 (half earned more and half earned less). The median earnings for women was $32,155, only

2. "The Puzzling Failure of Economics," *The Economist*, 23 August 1997, p. 11.

Indian Economists

The earliest of the study of National Income of India was done by V.K.R.V. Rao in 1936. He was instrumental in the growth and study of economics in India. He established the Institute of Economic Growth, New Delhi, the Delhi School of Economics, and the Institute for Social and Economic Change, Bangalore, which has helped in setting the foundation for social science research in India.

The other famous economist of Indian origin is Amartya Sen, who was awarded the Nobel Prize for Economics in 1998 for his contributions to welfare economics—studies of social choice, welfare measurement and poverty.

The other well known economists who have influenced the thinking in the Indian economy in recent times include Prime Minister, Manmohan Singh, the former Governor of Reserve Bank of India, Y.V. Reddy, and Chief Economic Advisor to the Ministry of Finance Kaushik Basu.

Famous Economics Majors

© AP IMAGES

Are you the next successful economics major?

A number of world leaders majored in economics, including three of the last seven U.S. presidents, Philippines President Gloria Macapagal-Arroyo, who earned a Ph.D. in the subject, U.S. Supreme Court Justices Steven Breyer and Anthony Kennedy, and former Justice Sandra Day O'Connor. Other economics majors include billionaire Donald Trump, former eBay President (and billionaire) Meg Whitman, Microsoft chief executive officer (and billionaire) Steve Ballmer, CNN founder (and billionaire) Ted Turner, Intel President Paul Otellini, NFL Patriot's coach Bill Belichick, Governor Arnold Schwarzenegger, high-tech guru Esther Dyson, and Scott Adams, creator of Dilbert, the mouthless wonder.

SOURCE: "The World's Billionaires," *Forbes,* 11 March 2009.

74 percent that of men. Among men, the top pay was the $53,286 median earned by engineering majors; that pay was 23 percent above the median for all men surveyed. Among women, the top pay was the $49,170 median earned by economics majors; that pay was 53 percent above the median for all women surveyed.

Incidentally, men who majored in economics earned a median of $49,377, ranking them seventh among 27 majors and 14 percent above the median for all men surveyed. Thus, even though the median pay for all women was only 74 percent of the median pay for all men, women who majored in economics earned about the same as men who majored in economics. We can say that *economics majors earned more than most, and they experienced no pay difference based on gender.*

Note that among both men and women, the majors ranked toward the top of the list tend to be more quantitative and analytical. According to the study's author, "Employers may view certain majors as more difficult and may assume that graduates in these fields are more able and hard working, whereupon they offer them higher salaries."[3] The selection of a relatively more challenging major such as economics sends a favorable signal to future employers.

The study also examined the kinds of jobs different majors actually found. Those who majored in economics became mid- and top-level managers, executives, and administrators. They also worked in sales, computer fields, financial analysis, and economic analysis. Remember, the survey was limited to those whose highest degree was the baccalaureate, so it excluded the many economics majors who went on to pursue graduate studies in law, business administration, economics, public administration, journalism, and other fields.[4]

Final Word

This textbook describes how economic factors affect individual choices and how all these choices come together to shape the economic system. Economics

3. Daniel E. Hecker, "Earnings of College Graduates, 1993," *Monthly Labor Review* (December 1995): p. 15.

4. For a survey of employment opportunities, go to the U.S. Labor Department's Occupational Outlook Handbook at http://www.bls.gov/oco/.

Exhibit 3

Median Annual Earnings of 35- to 44-Year-Olds with Bachelor's as Highest Degree, by Major

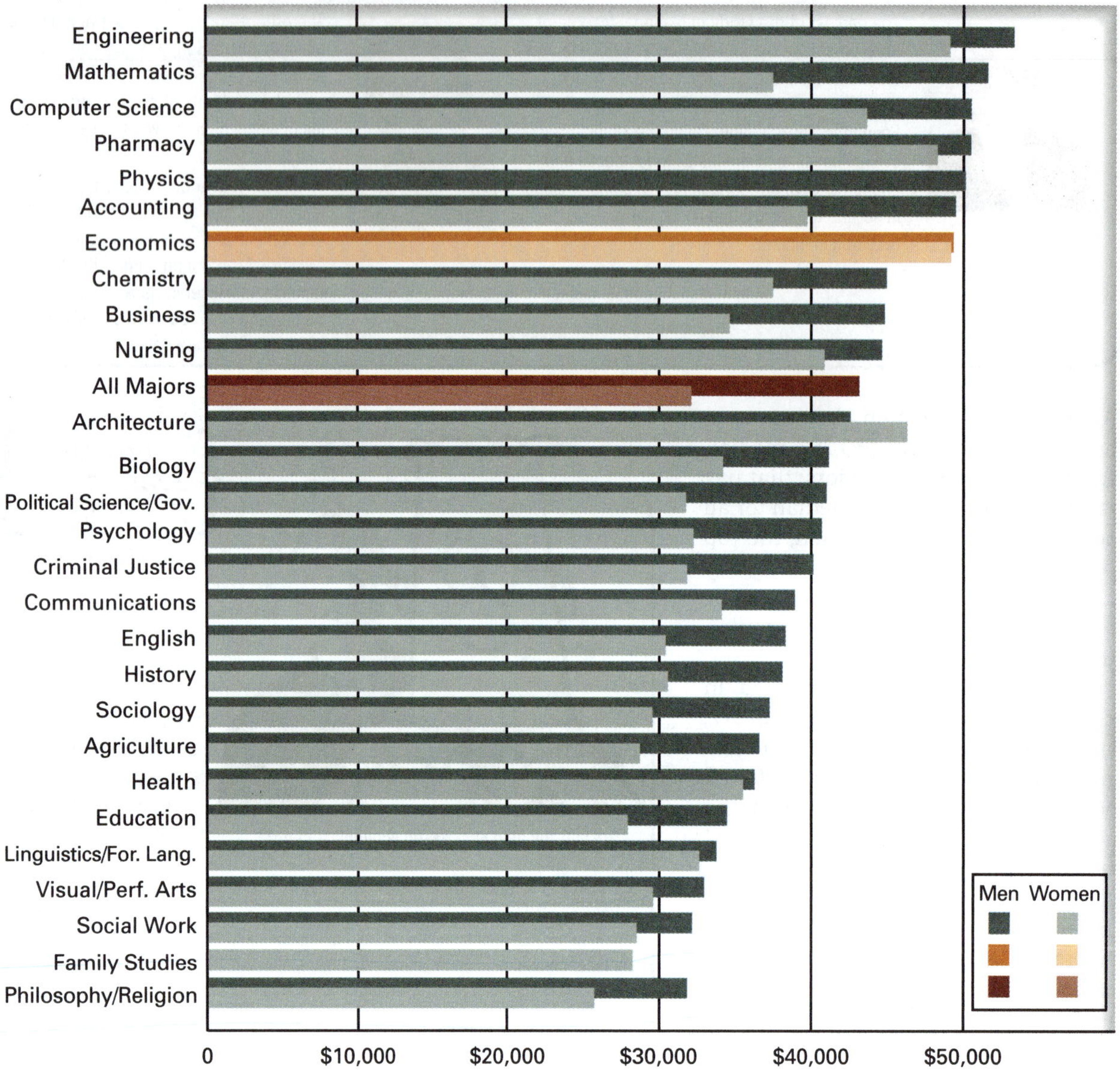

SOURCE: Earnings are for 1993 based on figures reported by Daniel Hecker in "Earnings of College Graduates, 1993." *Monthly Labor Review* (December 1995): pp. 3–17.

is not the whole story, and economic factors are not always the most important. But economic considerations have important and predictable effects on individual choices, and these choices affect the way we live.

Sure, economics is a challenging discipline, but it is also an exciting and rewarding one. The good news is that you already know a lot about economics. To use this knowledge, however, you must cultivate the art and science of economic analysis. You must be able to simplify the world to formulate questions, isolate the relevant variables, and then tell a persuasive story about how these variables relate.

An economic relation can be expressed in words, represented as a table of quantities, described by a mathematical equation, or illustrated as a graph. The appendix to this chapter introduces graphs. You may find this unnecessary. If you are already familiar with relations among variables, slopes, tangents, and the like, you can probably just browse. But if you have little recent experience with graphs, you might benefit from a more careful reading with pencil and paper in hand.

The next chapter introduces key tools of economic analysis. Subsequent chapters use these tools to explore economic problems and to explain economic behavior that may otherwise seem puzzling. You must walk before you can run, however, and in the next chapter, you take your first wobbly steps.

© CHAPEL HOUSE PHOTOGRAPHY

Appendix

Understanding Graphs

Take out a pencil and a blank piece of paper. Go ahead. Put a point in the middle of the paper. This is your point of departure, called the **origin**. With your pencil at the origin, draw a straight line off to the right. This line is called the **horizontal axis**. The value of the variable *x* measured along the horizontal axis increases as you move to the right of the origin. Now mark off this line from 0 to 20, in increments of 5 units each. Returning to the origin, draw another line, this one straight up. This line is called the **vertical axis**. The value of the variable *y* measured along the vertical axis increases as you move upward. Mark off this line from 0 to 20, in increments of 5 units each.

Within the space framed by the two axes, you can plot possible combinations of the variables measured along each axis. Each point identifies a value measured along the horizontal, or *x*, axis *and* a value measured along the vertical, or *y*, axis. For example, place point *a* in your graph to reflect the combination where *x* equals 5 units and *y* equals 15 units. Likewise, place point *b* in your graph to reflect 10 units of *x* and 5 units of *y*. Now compare your results with the points shown in Exhibit 4.

A **graph** is a picture showing how variables relate, and a picture can be worth a thousand words. Take a look at Exhibit 5, which shows the annual U.S. unemployment rate since 1900. The years are measured along the horizontal axis and the unemployment rate is measured as a percentage along the vertical axis. Exhibit 5 is a *time-series graph*, which shows the value of a variable, in this case the percentage of the labor force unemployed, over time. If you had to describe the information presented in Exhibit 5 in words, the explanation could take many words. The picture shows not only how one year compares to the next but also how one decade compares to another and how the rate trends over time. The sharply higher unemployment rate during the Great Depression of the 1930s is unmistakable. *Graphs convey information in a compact and efficient way.*

Exhibit 4

Basics of a Graph

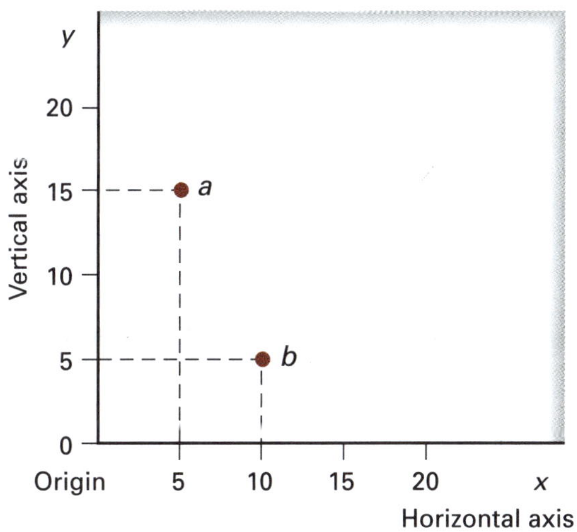

This appendix shows how graphs express a variety of possible relations among variables. Most graphs of interest in this book reflect the relationship between two economic variables, such as the unemployment rate and the year, the price of a product and the quantity demanded, or the price of production and the quantity supplied. Because we focus on just two variables at a time, we usually assume that other relevant variables remain constant.

One variable often depends on another. The time it takes you to drive home depends on your average speed. Your weight depends on how much you eat. The amount of Pepsi people buy depends on its price. A *functional relation* exists between two variables when the value of one variable *depends* on the value of another variable. The value of the **dependent variable** depends on the value of the **independent variable**. The task of the economist is to isolate economic relations and determine the direction of causality, if any. Recall that one of the pitfalls of economic thinking is the erroneous belief that association is causation. We cannot conclude that, simply because two events relate in time, one causes the other. There may be no relation between the two events.

origin on a graph depicting two-dimensional space, the zero point

horizontal axis line on a graph that begins at the origin and goes to the right and left; sometimes called the *x* axis

vertical axis line on a graph that begins at the origin and goes up and down; sometimes called the *y* axis

graph a picture showing how variables relate in two-dimensional space; one variable is measured along the horizontal axis and the other along the vertical axis

dependent variable a variable whose value depends on that of the independent variable

independent variable a variable whose value determines that of the dependent variable

Drawing Graphs

Let's begin with a simple relation. Suppose you are planning to drive across country and want to determine how far you will travel each day. You plan to average 50 miles per hour. Possible combinations of driving time and distance traveled per day appear in Exhibit 6. One column lists the hours driven per day, and the next column lists the number of

Exhibit 5

U.S. Unemployment Rate Since 1900

A time-series graph depicts the behavior of some economic variable over time.

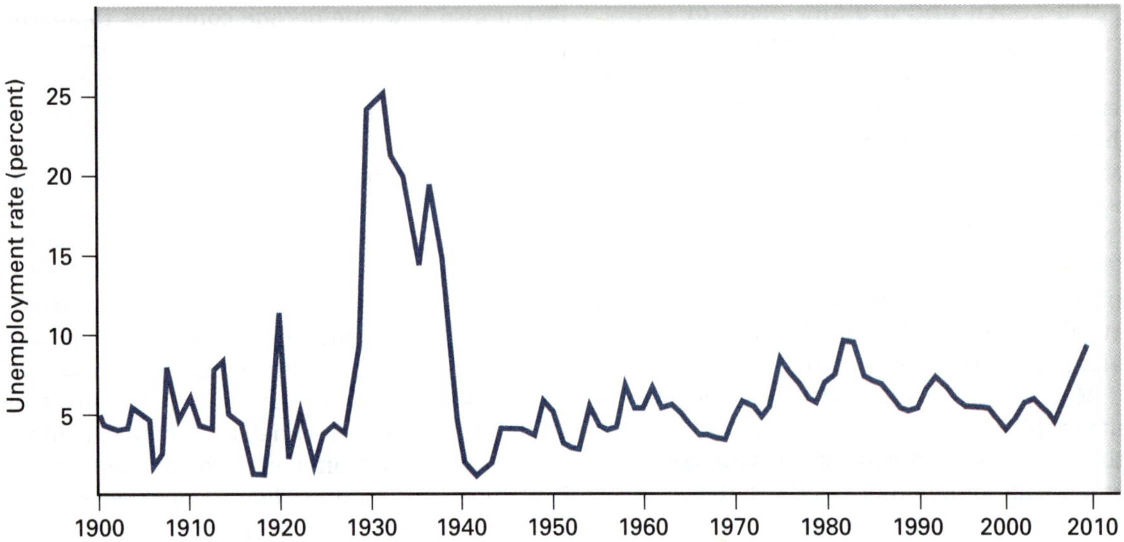

SOURCE: *Bicentennial Edition: Historical Statistics of the United States, Colonial Times to 1970,* U. S. Census Bureau, and *The Economic Report of the President, 2009.*

miles traveled per day, assuming an average speed of 50 miles per hour. The distance traveled, the *dependent* variable, depends on the number of hours driven, the *independent* variable. Combinations of hours driven and distance traveled are shown as *a, b, c, d,* and *e*. Each combination of hours driven and distance traveled is represented by a point in Exhibit 7. For example, point *a* shows that if you drive for 1 hour, you travel 50 miles. Point *b* indicates that if you drive for 2 hours, you travel 100 miles. By connecting the points, or possible combinations, we create a line running upward and to the right. This makes sense, because the longer you drive, the farther you travel. Assumed constant along this line is your average speed of 50 miles per hour.

Types of relations between variables include the following:

1. As one variable increases, the other increases—as in Exhibit 7; this is called a **positive**, or **direct**, **relation** between the variables.
2. As one variable increases, the other decreases; this is called a **negative**, or **inverse**, **relation**.
3. As one variable increases, the other remains unchanged; the two variables are said to be *independent*, or *unrelated*. One of the advantages of graphs is that they easily convey the relation between variables. We do not need to examine the particular combinations of numbers; we need only focus on the shape of the curve.

positive relation (direct relation) occurs when two variables increase or decrease together; the two variables move in the same direction

negative relation (inverse relation) occurs when two variables move in opposite directions; when one increases, the other decreases

Exhibit 6

Schedule Relating Distance Traveled to Hours Driven

The distance traveled per day depends on the number of hours driven per day, assuming an average speed of 50 miles per hour. This table shows combinations of hours driven and distance traveled. These combinations are shown as points in Exhibit 7.

	Hours Driven per Day	Distance Traveled per Day (miles)
a	1	50
b	2	100
c	3	150
d	4	200
e	5	250

© IMAGE SOURCE

Exhibit 7

Graph Relating Distance Traveled to Hours Driven

Points *a* through *e* depict different combinations of hours driven per day and the corresponding distances traveled. Connecting these points graphs a line.

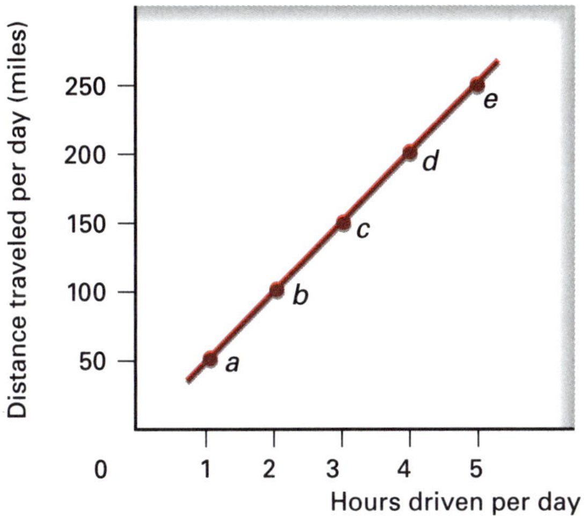

The Slopes of Straight Lines

A more precise way to describe the shape of a curve is to measure its slope. The **slope of a line** indicates how much the vertical variable changes for a given increase in the horizontal variable. Specifically, the slope between any two points along any straight line is the vertical change between these two points divided by the horizontal increase, or

$$\text{Slope} = \frac{\text{Change in the vertical distance}}{\text{Increase in the horizontal distance}}$$

Each of the four panels in Exhibit 8 indicates a vertical change, given a 10-unit increase in the horizontal variable. In panel (a), the vertical distance increases by 5 units when the horizontal distance increases by 10 units. The slope of the

slope of a line a measure of how much the vertical variable changes for a given increase in the horizontal variable; the vertical change between two points divided by the horizontal increase

Exhibit 8

Alternative Slopes for Straight Lines

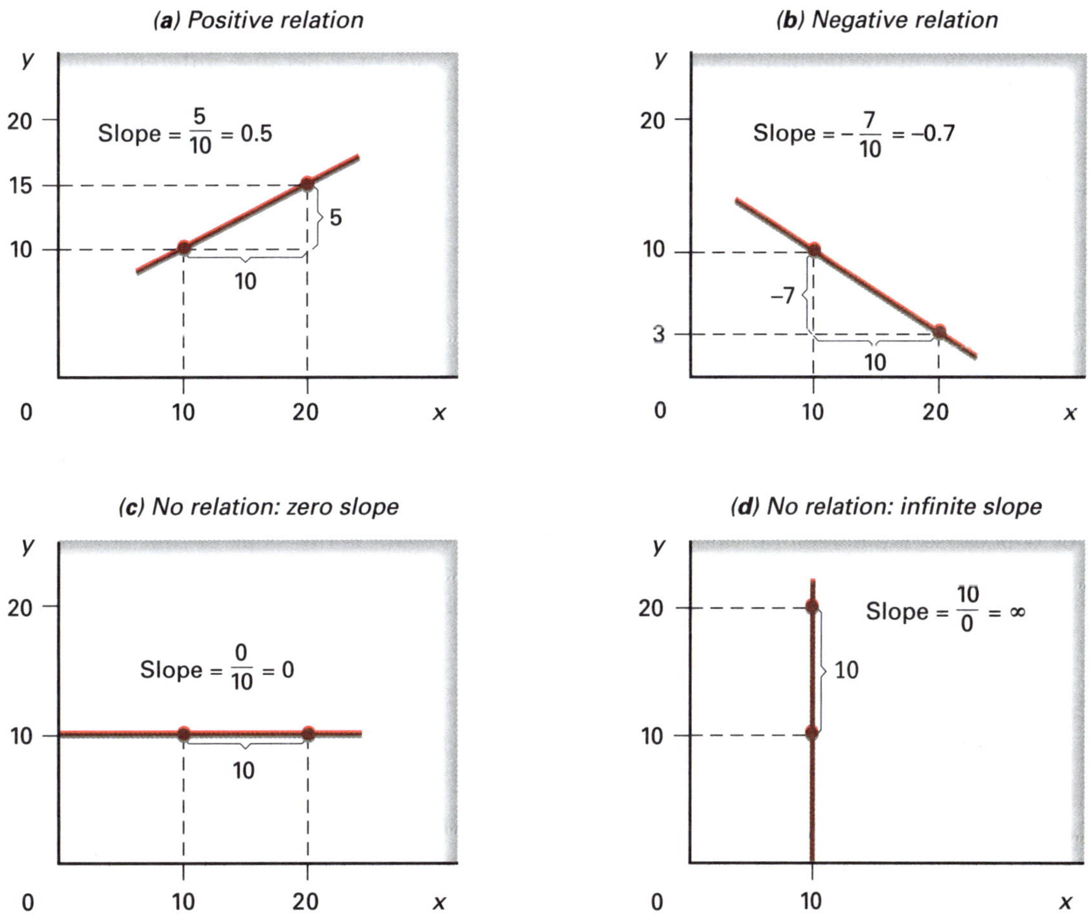

Exhibit 9

Slope Depends on the Unit of Measure

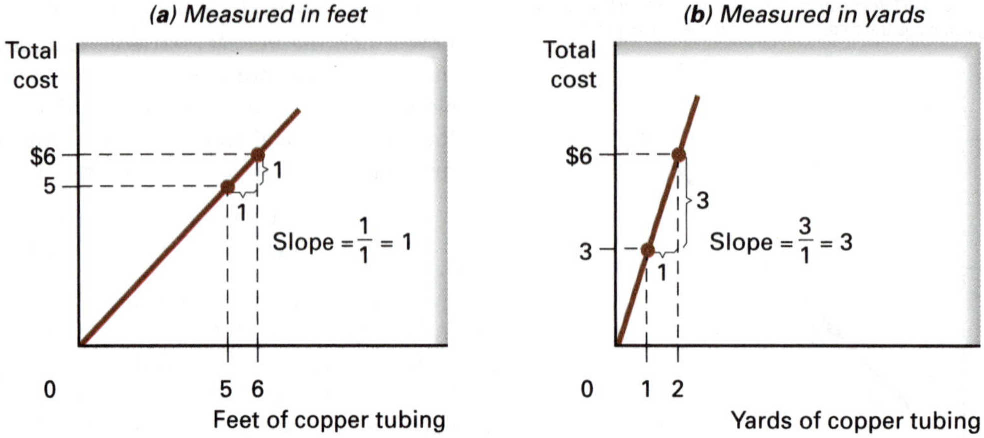

line is therefore 5/10, or 0.5. Notice that the slope in this case is a positive number because the relation between the two variables is positive, or direct. This slope indicates that for every 1-unit increase in the horizontal variable, the vertical variable increases by 0.5 units. The slope, incidentally, does not imply causality; the increase in the horizontal variable does not necessarily *cause* the increase in the vertical variable. The slope simply measures the relation between an increase in the horizontal variable and the associated change in the vertical variable.

In panel (b) of Exhibit 8, the vertical distance declines by 7 units when the horizontal distance increases by 10 units, so the slope equals –7/10, or –0.7. The slope in this case is a negative number because the two variables have a negative, or inverse, relation. In panel (c), the vertical variable remains unchanged as the horizontal variable increases by 10, so the slope equals 0/10, or 0. These two variables are not related. Finally, in panel (d), the vertical variable can take on any value, although the horizontal variable remains unchanged. Again, the two variables are not related. In this case, any change in the vertical measure, for example a 10-unit change, is divided by 0, because the horizontal value does not change. Any change divided by 0 is infinitely large, so we say that the slope of a vertical line is infinite.

The Slope, Units of Measurement, and Marginal Analysis

The mathematical value of the slope depends on the units measured on the graph. For example, suppose copper tubing costs $1 a foot. Graphs depicting the relation between total cost and quantity purchased are shown in Exhibit 9. In panel (a), the total cost increases by $1 for each 1-foot increase in the amount of tubing purchased. Thus, the slope equals 1/1, or 1. If the cost per foot remains the same but units are measured not in *feet* but in *yards*, the relation between total cost and quantity purchased is as depicted in panel (b). Now total cost increases by $3 for each 1-*yard* increase in output, so the slope equals 3/1, or 3. Because different units are used to measure the copper tubing, the two panels reflect different slopes, even though the cost is $1 per foot in each panel. Keep in mind that *the slope depends in part on the units of measurement.*

Economic analysis usually involves *marginal analysis*, such as the marginal cost of one more unit of output. The slope is a convenient device for measuring marginal effects because it reflects the change in total cost, measured along the vertical axis, for each 1-unit change in output, measured along the horizontal axis. For example, in panel (a) of Exhibit 9, the marginal cost of another *foot* of copper tubing is $1, which also equals the slope of the line. In panel (b), the marginal cost of another *yard* of tubing is $3, which again is the slope of that line. Because of its applicability to marginal analysis, the slope has special relevance in economics.

The Slopes of Curved Lines

The slope of a straight line is the same everywhere along the line, but the slope of a curved line differs along the curve, as shown in Exhibit 10. To find the slope of a curved line at a particular point, draw a straight line that just touches the curve at that point but does not cut or cross the curve. Such a line is

Exhibit 10

Slope at Different Points on a Curved Line

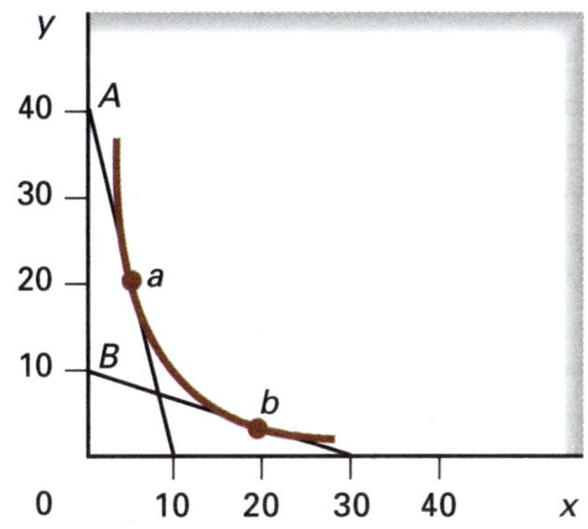

called a tangent to the curve at that point. The slope of the tangent gives the slope of the curve at that point. Look at line A, which is tangent to the curve at point *a*. As the horizontal value increases from 0 to 10, the vertical value drops along A from 40 to 0. Thus, the vertical change divided by the horizontal change equals –40/10, or –4, which is the slope of the curve at point *a*. This slope is negative because the vertical value decreases as the horizontal value increases. Line B, a line tangent to the curve at point *b*, has the slope –10/30, or –0.33. As you can see, the curve depicted in Exhibit 10 gets flatter as the horizontal variable increases, so the value of its slope approaches zero.

Other curves, of course, will reflect different slopes as well as different changes in the slope along the curve. Downward-sloping curves have negative slopes, and upward-sloping curves, positive slopes. Sometimes curves, such as those in Exhibit 11, are more complex, having both positive and negative ranges, depending on the horizontal value. In the hill-shaped curve, for small values of *x*, there is a positive relation between *x* and *y*, so the slope is positive. As the value of *x* increases, however, the slope declines and eventually becomes negative. We can divide the curve into two segments: (1) the segment between the origin and point *a*, where

Exhibit 11

Curves with Both Positive and Negative Slopes

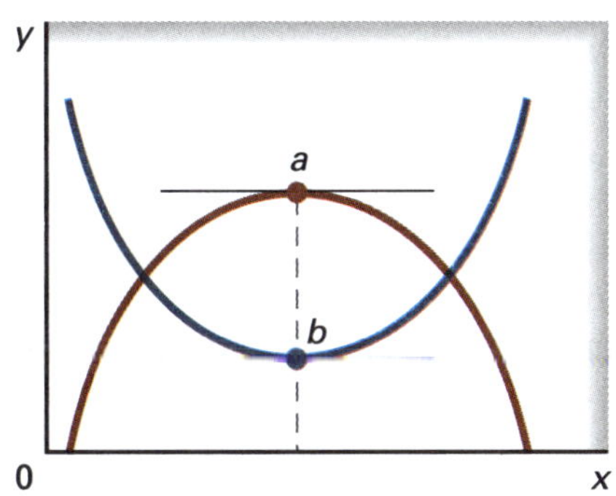

Exhibit 12

Shift of Line Relating Distance Traveled to Hours Driven

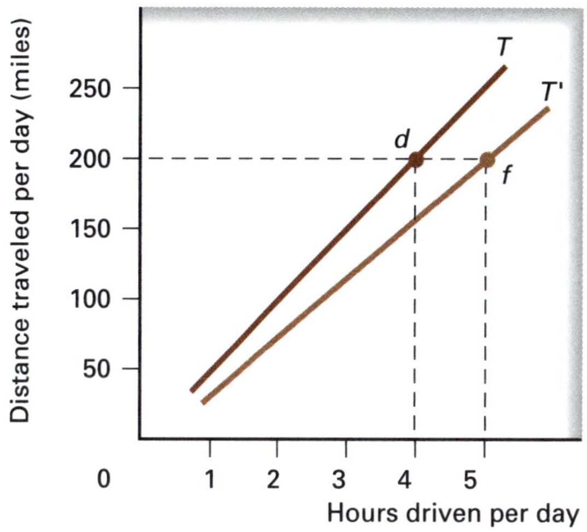

the slope is positive, and (2) the segment of the curve to the right of point *a*, where the slope is negative. The slope of the curve at point *a* is 0. The U-shaped curve in Exhibit 11 represents the opposite relation: *x* and *y* are negatively related until point *b* is reached; thereafter, they are positively related. The slope equals 0 at point *b*.

Line Shifts

Let's go back to the example of your cross-country trip, where we were trying to determine how many miles you would travel per day. Recall that we measured hours driven per day on the horizontal axis and miles traveled per day on the vertical axis, assuming an average speed of 50 miles per hour. That same relation is shown as line T in Exhibit 12. What happens if the average speed is 40 miles per hour? The entire relation between hours driven and distance traveled would change, as shown by the shift to the right of line T to T′. With a slower average speed, any distance traveled per day now requires more driving time. For example, 200 miles traveled requires 4 hours of driving when the average speed is 50 miles per hour (as shown by point *d* on curve T), but 200 miles takes 5 hours when your speed averages 40 miles per hour (as shown by point *f* on curve T′). Thus, *a change in the assumption about average speed changes the relationship between the two variables observed.* This changed relationship is expressed by a shift of the line that shows how the two variables relate.

That ends our once-over of graphs. Return to this appendix when you need a review.

tangent
a straight line that touches a curve at a point but does not cut or cross the curve; used to measure the slope of a curve at a point

Multiple Choice Questions

1. In economics, money is an example of capital.
   a. True
   b. False
2. Which of the following are the four categories of resources?
   a. human effort, human capital, money, and natural resources
   b. labor, physical capital, money, and entrepreneurial ability
   c. labor, entrepreneurial ability, capital, and money
   d. labor, entrepreneurial ability, capital, and natural resources
   e. human effort, money, entrepreneurial ability, and natural resources
3. Which of the following is an example of human capital?
   a. a pizza oven
   b. college education
   c. labor
   d. bulldozer
   e. stocks and bonds
4. Scarcity
   a. exists because people have wants that are unlimited relative to the availability of resources to satisfy those wants
   b. applies when a resource is not freely available
   c. means that each society and each individual must make choices
   d. exists in all societies
   e. all of the above are true
5. Some individuals or families can become completely saturated with a service such as television. This suggests that
   a. wants are limited
   b. desires for a single commodity can be satisfied but then the focus will switch to other goods and services
   c. a highly productive economy may someday be able to satisfy all human desires
   d. resources are not truly fixed in supply as we generally assume
   e. scarcity does not exist
6. Which of the following is the best definition of economics?
   a. An investigation of the quantities and prices of the various goods produced by the nations of the world.
   b. A study of why inflation and unemployment periodically plague the U.S. economy.
   c. An analysis of how individuals and societies deal with the problem of scarcity.
   d. An examination of the role that money plays in the economy.
   e. A study of how goods and services are distributed throughout the world.
7. Economists classify all of the following as capital, except one. Which one is *not* capital?
   a. a $20 bill in a firm's petty cash drawer
   b. the building where our economics class meets
   c. a plumber's wrench
   d. a railroad car
   e. a factory
8. When economists refer to capital, they might mean
   a. money
   b. human skills used in production
   c. stocks
   d. bonds
   e. bank loans
9. Which of the following is an example of capital?
   a. pizza ovens
   b. bulldozers
   c. a college education
   d. carpentry skills
   e. all of the above
10. If a business produces and sells only one unit of a good, its profit would be the
    a. price received for the good
    b. price of the product minus the cost of the resources used to produce the product
    c. return paid to the firm's bank on its outstanding loans
    d. price of the product minus the wages paid for the labor used to produce it
    e. wages paid for the labor used to produce the product minus the price
11. An entrepreneur is a(n)
    a. individual who has much education
    b. organizer who seeks profitable opportunities and is willing to accept risks
    c. business organization that uses inputs to produce output

d. administrator who runs an enterprise without accepting any risk of financial loss
e. depot or storehouse for commercial products

12. The difference between a good and a service is that
    a. a good helps satisfy unlimited wants; a service does not
    b. a service helps satisfy unlimited wants; a good does not
    c. a services is available in unlimited quantities; a good is not
    d. a good is available in unlimited quantities; a service is not
    e. a good is tangible; a service is not

13. The expression "There's no such thing as a free lunch" means
    a. that even if the lunch is free, we pay for it in extra calories
    b. that resources used up in producing the lunch are not available to satisfy other wants
    c. the same thing as "The best things in life are free"
    d. you can eat only if you work first
    e. neither sea water nor air is free

14. The assumption of rational self-interest does not rule out the possibility of concern for other individuals.
    a. True
    b. False

15. Mike wants to buy a used car from Jim. Jim wants to sell his car for $5,600. Before buying the car, Mike wants to take the car to a mechanic, for a complete inspection. Mike estimates the costs for this inspection at $50 and his expected benefits at $60. What should Mike do and why?
    a. Take the car to the mechanic because the expected benefit is lower than the expected cost.
    b. Buy the car because Jim is a friend and he would never sell a 'lemon'
    c. Don't take the car to the mechanic because expected benefit is lower than the expected cost.
    d. Take the car to the mechanic because the expected benefit is greater than the expected cost.
    e. Don't take the car to the mechanic because expected benefit is greater than the expected cost

16. To say that people make marginal decisions means that
    a. they usually wait until the last minute before making a decision to buy
    b. they weigh the additional costs and additional benefits of various activities before they make a decision
    c. most people just barely get by on the incomes they earn and live from day to day on the very edge of subsistence
    d. given a choice, most people would prefer to make their own decisions concerning the things that affect their lives
    e. they consider the total cost and benefit of various activities before they make a purchase

17. When constructing an economic model, economists
    a. rely mostly on their own value judgments and ignore the far more complex world of facts
    b. always try to duplicate reality by including all available information
    c. use assumptions that are true for the individual but never true for the whole economy
    d. must rely on simplifying assumptions that abstract from the complexity of the real world
    e. are primarily concerned with making realistic assumptions

18. Which of the following is a positive statement?
    a. An unemployment rate of 7 percent or higher is a national disgrace.
    b. Unemployment is a less important problem than inflation.
    c. When the national unemployment rate is 7 percent, the unemployment rate for inner-city youth is often close to 40 percent.
    d. Unemployment and inflation are equally important problems.
    e. An inflation rate of 7 percent is too high.

19. The fallacy of composition is the error of believing a cause-effect relationship exists between two events that are associated in time.
    a. True
    b. False

20. Someone who commits the fallacy of composition is likely to assume that
    a. the simplest model is the best predictor
    b. event B, which follows event A, was caused by event A
    c. event B, which follows event A, was not necessarily caused by event A

d. what is true for the individual is also true for the group

e. what is true for the individual is not necessarily true for the group

Answers

1. b 2. d 3. b 4. e 5. b 6. c 7. a 8. b 9. e 10. b

11. b 12. e 13. b 14. a 15. d 16. b 17. d 18. c 19. b 20. d

Long Answer Questions

LO1 Explain the economic problem of scarce resources and unlimited wants

1.1. *(Definition of Economics)* What determines whether or not a resource is scarce? Why is the concept of scarcity important to the definition of economics?

LO2 Describe the forces that shape economic choices

2.1. *(Rational Self-Interest)* Discuss the impact of rational self-interest on each of the following decisions:
   a. Whether to attend college full time or enter the workforce full time
   b. Whether to buy a new textbook or a used one
   c. Whether to attend a local college or an out-of-town college

2.2. *(Rational Self-Interest)* If behavior is governed by rational self-interest, why do people make charitable contributions of time and money?

2.3. *(Marginal Analysis)* The owner of a small pizzeria is deciding whether to increase the radius of delivery area by one mile. What considerations must be taken into account if such a decision is to increase profitability?

2.4. *(Time and Information)* It is often costly to obtain the information necessary to make good decisions. Yet your own interests can be best served by rationally weighing all options available to you. This requires informed decision making. Does this mean that making uninformed decisions is irrational? How do you determine how much information is the right amount?

2.5 Which problems of an economy constitute the subject matter of micro-economics and macro-economics?

LO3 Explain the relationship between economic theory and economic reality

3.1. *(Role of Theory)* What good is economic theory if it can't predict the behavior of a specific individual?

3.2 To study economic problems, economists usually employ a process of theoretical investigation called the scientific method, which consists of four steps. Explain each of these steps.

3.3 Which of the following statements are positive and which are normative?
   a. The poor people are relatively unhealthy as compared to the wealthy people.
   b. Rich countries should provide medicine more cheaply to the poor nations.
   c. Protectionist policies should be abolished.

3.4 Why does the distinction between positive and normative statements matter for economics?

LO4 Identify some pitfalls of economic analysis

4.1. *(Pitfalls of Economic Analysis)* Review the discussion of pitfalls in economic thinking in this chapter. Then identify the fallacy, or mistake in thinking, in each of the following statements:
   a. Raising taxes always increases government revenues.
   b. Whenever there is a recession, imports decrease. Therefore, to stop a recession, we should increase imports.
   c. Raising the tariff on imported steel helps the U.S. steel industry. Therefore, the entire economy is helped.
   d. Gold sells for about $900 per ounce. Therefore, the U.S. government could sell all the gold in Fort Knox at $900 per ounce and reduce the national debt.

4.2. *(Association Versus Causation)* Suppose I observe that communities with lots of doctors tend to have relatively high rates of illness. I conclude that doctors cause illness. What's wrong with this reasoning?

LO5 Describe several reasons to study economics

5.1. *(Studying Economics)* According to the text, economics majors on average make more money than most other majors and have more job opportunities. Are these the primary motivations one might have for studying economics? What are your motivations for studying economics?

Appendix

A.1 Draw graphs of the following relationships, where Y is on the vertical axis and X on the horizontal axis:
   a. $Y = X$
   b. $Y = 100 - 3X$
   c. $Y = (-)100 + 4X$

THE ART AND SCIENCE OF ECONOMIC ANALYSIS

Chapter in Review

KEY TERMS

economics
the study of how people use their scarce resources to satisfy their unlimited wants

resources
the inputs, or factors of production, used to produce the goods and services that people want; resources consist of labor, capital, natural resources, and entrepreneurial ability

labor
the physical and mental effort used to produce goods and services

capital
the buildings, equipment, and human skills used to produce goods and services

natural resources
so-called "gifts of nature" used to produce goods and services; includes renewable and exhaustible resources

entrepreneurial ability
managerial and organizational skills needed to start a firm, combined with the willingness to take the risk of profit or loss

entrepreneur
a profit-seeking decision maker who starts with an idea, organizes an enterprise to bring that idea to life, and assumes the risk of the operation

wages
payment to resource owners for their labor

interest
payment to resource owners for the use of their capital

rent
payment to resource owners for the use of their natural resources

profit
reward for entrepreneurial ability; sales revenue minus resource cost

good
a tangible product used to satisfy human wants

service
an activity, or intangible product, used to satisfy human wants

scarcity
occurs when the amount people desire exceeds the amount available at a zero price

market
a set of arrangements by which buyers and sellers carry out exchange at mutually agreeable terms

product market
a market in which a good or service is bought and sold

resource market
a market in which a resource is bought and sold

circular-flow model
a diagram that traces the flow of resources, products, income, and revenue among economic decision makers

LO1 Explain the economic problem of scarce resources and unlimited wants. The problem is that, although your wants, or desires, are virtually unlimited, the resources available to satisfy these wants are scarce. Because resources are scarce, you must choose from among your many wants, and whenever you choose, you must forgo satisfying some other wants. Without scarcity, there would be no economic problem and no need for prices.

The Simple Circular-Flow Model for Households and Firms

Households earn income by supplying resources to the resource market, as shown in the lower portion of the model. Firms demand these resources to produce goods and services, which they supply to the product market, as shown in the upper portion of the model. Households spend their income to demand these goods and services. This spending flows through the product market as revenue to firms.

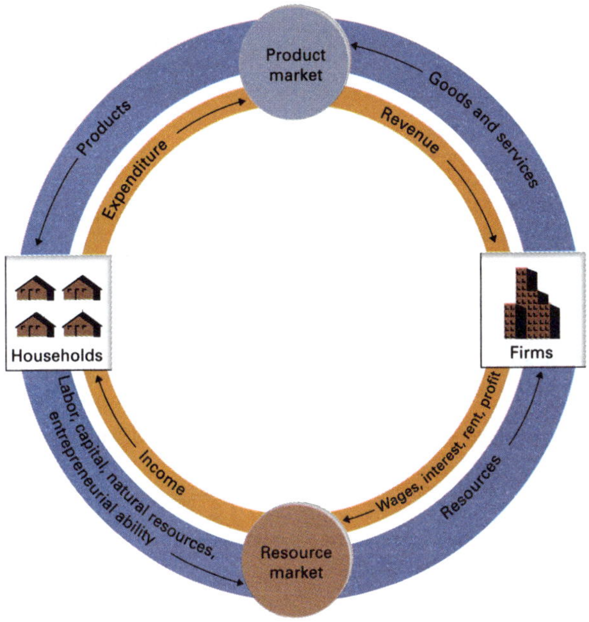

LO2 Describe the forces that shape economic choices. An economy results from the choices that millions of individuals make in attempting to satisfy their unlimited wants. A key economic assumption is that individuals, in making choices, rationally select alternatives they perceive to be in their best interests. Economic choice is based on a comparison of the expected marginal benefit and the expected marginal cost of the action under consideration.

LO3 Explain the relationship between economic theory and economic reality. An economic theory is a simplification of economic reality that is used to make predictions about the real world. A theory, or model, captures the important elements of the problem under study but need not spell out every detail and interrelation. You might think of economic theory as a streamlined version of economic reality.

rational self-interest
individuals try to maximize the expected benefit achieved with a given cost or to minimize the expected cost of achieving a given benefit

marginal
incremental, additional, or extra; used to describe a change in an economic variable

microeconomics
the study of the economic behavior in particular markets, such as that for computers or unskilled labor

macroeconomics
the study of the economic behavior of entire economies

economic theory (economic model)
a simplification of reality used to make predictions about cause and effect in the real world

variable
a measure, such as price or quantity, that can take on different values at different times

other-things-constant assumption
the assumption, when focusing on the relation among key economic variables, that other variables remain unchanged; in Latin, *ceteris paribus*

behavioral assumption
an assumption that describes the expected behavior of economic decision makers, what motivates them

hypothesis
a theory about how key variables relate

positive economic statement
a statement that can be proved or disproved by reference to facts

normative economic statement
a statement that reflects an opinion, which cannot be proved or disproved by reference to the facts

association-is-causation fallacy
the incorrect idea that if two variables are associated in time, one must necessarily cause the other

fallacy of composition
the incorrect belief that what is true for the individual, or part, must necessarily be true for the group, or the whole

secondary effects
unintended consequences of economic actions that may develop slowly over time as people react to events

The Scientific Method: Step by Step

The steps of the scientific method are designed to develop and test hypotheses about how the world works. The objective is a theory that predicts outcomes more accurately than the best alternative theory. A hypothesis is rejected if it does not predict as accurately as the best alternative. A rejected hypothesis can be modified in light of the test results.

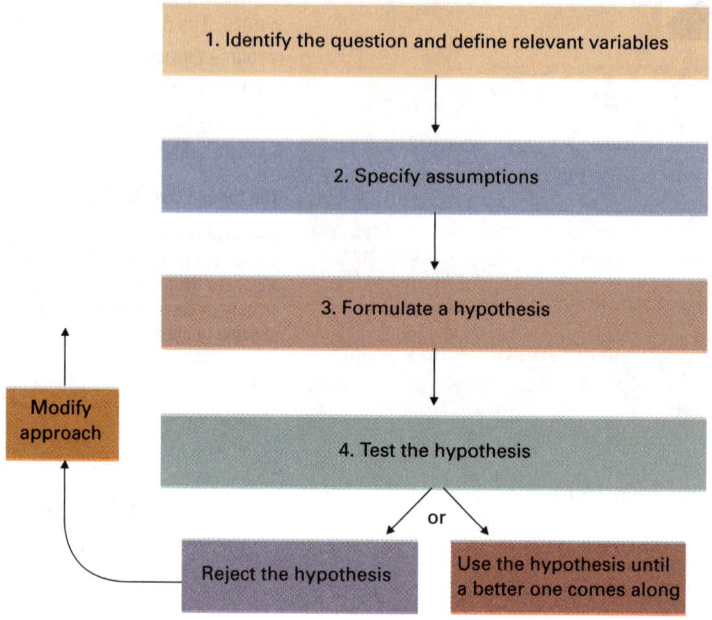

LO4 Identify some pitfalls of economic analysis. Economic analysis, like other forms of scientific inquiry, is subject to common mistakes in reasoning that can lead to faulty conclusions. Three sources of confusion are the fallacy that association is causation, the fallacy of composition, and the mistake of ignoring secondary effects.

LO5 Describe several reasons to study economics. The economics profession thrives because its models usually do a better job of making economic sense out of a confusing world than do alternative approaches. Studies show that economics majors earn more than most and they experience no pay difference based on gender.

APPENDIX TERMS

origin
on a graph depicting two-dimensional space, the zero point

horizontal axis
line on a graph that begins at the origin and goes to the right and left; sometimes called the *x* axis

vertical axis
line on a graph that begins at the origin and goes up and down; sometimes called the *y* axis

graph
a picture showing how variables relate in two-dimensional space; one variable is measured along the horizontal axis and the other along the vertical axis

dependent variable
a variable whose value depends on that of the independent variable

independent variable
a variable whose value determines that of the dependent variable

positive relation (direct relation)
occurs when two variables increase or decrease together; the two variables move in the same direction

negative relation (inverse relation)
occurs when two variables move in opposite directions; when one increases, the other decreases

slope of a line
a measure of how much the vertical variable changes for a given increase in the horizontal variable; the vertical change between two points divided by the horizontal increase

tangent
a straight line that touches a curve at a point but does not cut or cross the curve; used to measure the slope of a curve at a point

CHAPTER

2

Learning Outcomes

- LO 1 Describe the impact of choice on opportunity
- LO 2 Explain how comparative advantage, specialization, and exchange affect economic outcomes (output)
- LO 3 Outline how economies function as production systems
- LO 4 Describe different economic systems and the decision-making rules that define them

Economic Tools *and* Economic Systems

> “What goods and services should different economies produce, how should they produce them, and for whom should they produce them?”

Why are you reading this book right now rather than doing something else? What is college costing you? Why will you eventually major in one subject rather than continue to take courses in different ones? Why is fast food so fast? Why is there no sense crying over spilt milk? These and other questions are addressed in this chapter, which introduces some tools of economic analysis—some tools of the trade.

Chapter 1 introduced the idea that scarcity forces us to make choices, but the chapter said little about how to make economic choices. This chapter develops a framework for evaluating economic alternatives. First, we consider the cost involved in selecting one alternative over others. Next, we develop tools to explore the choices available to individuals and to the economy as a whole. Finally, we examine the questions that different economies must answer—questions about what goods and services to produce, how to produce them, and for whom to produce them.

What do you think?

I have more stuff than I have opportunity to make use of.

Strongly Disagree						*Strongly Agree*
1	2	3	4	5	6	7

Topics discussed in Chapter 2 include:

- Opportunity cost
- Comparative advantage
- Division of labor
- Specilization
- Production possibilities frontier
- Three economic questions
- Economic systems

LO1 Choice and Opportunity Cost

Think about a decision you just made: the decision to begin reading this chapter right now rather than use the time to study for another course, play sports, watch TV, go online, get some sleep, hang with friends, or do something else. Suppose your best alternative to reading right now is getting some sleep. The cost of reading is passing up the opportunity of sleep. Because of scarcity, whenever you make a choice, you must pass up another opportunity; you must incur an *opportunity cost*.

© ISTOCKPHOTO/THINKSTOCK

Opportunity Cost

What do we mean when we talk about the cost of something? Isn't it what we must give up—must forgo—to get that thing? The opportunity cost of the chosen item or activity is *the value of the best alternative that is forgone*. You can think of opportunity cost as the *opportunity lost*. Sometimes opportunity cost can be measured in terms of money, although, as we shall see, money is usually only part of opportunity cost.

How many times have you heard people say they did something because they "had nothing better to do"? They actually mean they had nothing else going on. Yet, according to the idea of opportunity cost, people *always* do what they do because they have nothing better to do. The choice selected seems, at the time, preferable to any other possible alternative. You are reading this chapter right now because you have nothing better to do. In fact, you are attending college for the same reason: College appears more attractive than your best alternative.

The Opportunity Cost of Change

Consider the following major challenges that Prime Minister Manmohan Singh has spelled out in his 2012 New Year's message to the Nation and what they might cost to address:

First, there is the urgent challenge of eradicating poverty, hunger and illiteracy, and providing gainful employment to all. This is the challenge of livelihood security.

The second challenge that demands attention is economic security. Economic security comes from having an economy that can produce the material, output required to achieve, desired consumption levels for the people, and one that can generate the productive jobs needed to satisfy the aspirations of the workforce.

The third challenge is that of energy security. Energy is essential for development because higher levels of production inevitably involve larger energy use.

A fourth important challenge in the years ahead is the challenge of ecological security. Economic growth is essential for the well being of people, but cannot be pursued in a manner which damages the environment.

Finally, and most importantly, democracy faces threats to internal and external security which can be viewed as the challenge of national security.

SOURCE: "Five Key Challenges", New Year Message to Nation, December 31, 2011, www.outlookindia.com.

Opportunity Cost Is Subjective

Like beauty, opportunity cost is in the eye of the beholder. It is subjective. Only the individual making the choice can identify the most attractive alternative. But the chooser seldom knows the actual value of the best alternative forgone, because that alternative is "the road not taken." If you give up an evening of pizza and conversation with friends to work on a term paper, you will never know exactly what you gave up. You know only what you *expected*. Evidently, you expected the value of working on that paper to exceed the value of the best alternative. (Incidentally, focusing on the best alternative forgone makes all lesser alternatives irrelevant.)

Calculating Opportunity Cost Requires Time and Information

Economists assume that people rationally choose the most valued alternative. This does not mean you exhaustively assess the value of all possibilities. You assess alternatives as long as the expected marginal benefit of gathering more information about your options exceeds the expected marginal cost (even if you are not aware of making such conscious calculations). In other words, you do the best you can for yourself.

opportunity cost the value of the best alternative forgone when an item or activity is chosen

Because learning about alternatives is costly and time consuming, some choices are based on limited or even wrong information. Indeed, some choices may turn out badly (you went for a picnic but it rained; the movie you rented stank; your new shoes pinch; your new exercise equipment gets no exercise; the share you bought tanked). At the time you made the choice, however, you thought you were making the best use of all your scarce resources, including the time required to gather and evaluate information about your alternatives.

Time: The Ultimate Constraint

The Sultan of Brunei is among the richest people on earth, with wealth topping $20 billion based on huge oil revenues that flow into his tiny country. He and his royal family (which has ruled for six centuries) live in a palace with 1,788 rooms, 250 toilets, and a throne room the size of a football field. The family owns hundreds of cars, including dozens of Rolls-Royces. Supported by such wealth, the Sultan would appear to have overcome the economic problem of scarcity. Though he can buy just about whatever he wants, he lacks the time to enjoy his stuff. If he pursues one activity, he cannot at the same time do something else. Each activity involves an opportunity cost. Consequently, the Sultan must choose from among the competing uses of his scarcest resource, time. Although your alternatives are less exotic, you too face time constraints, especially toward the end of the college term.

© AP IMAGES

Opportunity Cost Varies with Circumstance

Opportunity cost depends on your alternatives. This is why you are more likely to study on a Tuesday night than on a Saturday night. On a Tuesday night, the opportunity cost of studying is lower because your alternatives are less attractive than on a Saturday night, when more is happening. Suppose you go to a movie on Saturday night. Your opportunity cost is the value of your best alternative forgone, which might be attending a college game. For some of you, studying on Saturday night may be well down the list of alternatives—perhaps ahead of reorganizing your closet but behind doing your laundry.

Opportunity cost is subjective, but in some cases, money paid for goods and services is a reasonable approximation. For example, the opportunity cost of the new DVD player you bought is the value of spending that $100 on the best forgone alternative. The money measure may leave out some important elements, however, particularly the value of the time involved. For example, renting a movie costs you not just the $4 rental fee but the time and travel required to get it, watch it, and return it.

Sunk Cost and Choice

Suppose you have just finished grocery shopping and are wheeling your cart toward the payment counters. How do you decide which line to join? Easy. You pick the shortest one. Suppose that it barely moves for 10 minutes, when you notice that a cashier has opened a new line and invites you to check out. Do you switch to the open cashier, or do you think, "Since I've already spent 10 minutes in this line, I'm staying put"? The 10 minutes you waited represents a **sunk cost**, which is a cost that has already been incurred and cannot be recovered, regardless of what you do next. You should ignore sunk cost in making economic choices. Hence, you should switch. *Economic decision makers should consider only those costs that are affected by the choice. Sunk costs have already been incurred and are not affected by the choice, so they are irrelevant.* Likewise, you should walk out on a bad movie, even if you spent $10 to get in. Your $10 is gone, and sitting through that stinker only makes you worse off. The irrelevance of sunk costs is underscored by proverbs such as "Don't throw good money after bad," "Let bygones be bygones," "That's water over the dam," and "There's no sense crying over spilt milk." The milk has already spilled, so whatever you do now cannot change that.

> You should ignore sunk cost in making economic choices.

Now that you have some idea about opportunity cost, let's see how it helps solve the economic problem.

LO2 Comparative Advantage, Specialization, and Exchange

Suppose you live in a hostel. You and your roommate have such tight schedules that you each can spare only about an hour a week for mundane tasks like ironing shirts and typing papers (granted, in reality you may not iron shirts or type papers, but this example will help you understand some important principles). Each of you must turn in a typed three-page paper every week, and you each prefer ironed shirts when you have the time. Let's say it takes you a half hour to type a handwritten paper. Your roommate on the other hand takes about an hour. But your roommate is a talented ironer and can iron a shirt in 5 minutes flat (or should that be, iron it flat in 5 minutes?). You take twice as long, or 10 minutes, to iron a shirt.

During the hour set aside each week for typing and ironing, typing takes priority. If you each do your own typing and ironing, you type your paper in a half hour

sunk cost a cost that has already been incurred, cannot be recovered, and thus is irrelevant for present and future economic decisions and iron three shirts in the remaining half hour. Your roommate takes the entire hour typing the paper, leaving no time for ironing. Thus, if you each do your own tasks, the combined output is two typed papers and three ironed shirts.

The Law of Comparative Advantage

Before long, you each realize that total output would increase if you did all the typing and your roommate did all the ironing. In the hour available for these tasks, you type both papers and your roommate irons 12 shirts. As a result of specialization, total output increases by 9 shirts! You strike a deal to exchange your typing for your roommate's ironing, so you each end up with a typed paper and 6 ironed shirts. Thus, *each of you is better off as a result of specialization and exchange.* By specializing in the task that you each do better, you are using the **law of comparative advantage**, which states that the individual with the lower opportunity cost of producing a particular output should specialize in producing that output. You face a lower opportunity cost of typing than does your roommate, because in the time it takes to type a paper, you could iron 3 shirts whereas your roommate could iron 12 shirts in the time it takes your roommate to type the paper. And if you face a lower opportunity cost of typing, your roommate must face a lower opportunity cost of ironing (try working that out).

Absolute Advantage Versus Comparative Advantage

The gains from specialization and exchange so far are obvious. A more interesting case is if you are faster at both tasks. Suppose the example changes only in one respect: your roommate takes 12 minutes to iron a shirt compared with your 10 minutes. You now have an *absolute advantage* in both tasks, meaning each task takes you less time than it does your roommate. More generally, having an **absolute advantage** means making something using fewer resources than other producers require.

Does your absolute advantage in both activities mean specialization is no longer a good idea? Recall that the law of comparative advantage states that the individual with the *lower opportunity cost* of producing a particular good should specialize in that good. You still take 30 minutes to type a paper and 10 minutes to iron a shirt, so your opportunity cost of typing the paper remains at three ironed shirts. Your roommate takes an hour to type a paper and 12 minutes to iron a shirt, so your roommate could iron five shirts in the time it takes to type a paper. Your opportunity cost of typing a paper is ironing three shirts; for your roommate it's ironing five shirts. *Because your opportunity cost of typing is lower than your roommate's, you still have a comparative advantage in typing.* Consequently, your roommate must have a comparative advantage in ironing (again, try working this out to your satisfaction). Therefore, you should do all the typing and your roommate, all the ironing. Although you have an absolute advantage in both tasks, your **comparative advantage** calls for specializing in the task for which you have the lower opportunity cost—in this case, typing.

If neither of you specialized, you could type one paper and iron three shirts. Your roommate could still type just the one paper. Your combined output would be two papers and three shirts. If you each specialized according to comparative advantage, in an hour you could type both papers and your roommate

© STOCKBYTE/GETTY IMAGES / © C SQUARED STUDIOS/PHOTODISC/GETTY IMAGES / © IMAGE SOURCE BLACK/JUPITERIMAGES

law of comparative advantage the individual, firm, region, or country with the lowest opportunity cost of producing a particular good should specialize in that good

absolute advantage the ability to make something using fewer resources than other producers use

comparative advantage the ability to make something at a lower opportunity cost than other producers face

"Does your absolute advantage in both activities mean specialization is no longer a good idea?"

SPECIALIZATION

could iron five shirts. Thus, specialization increases total output by two ironed shirts. Even though you are better at both tasks than your roommate, you are comparatively better at typing. Put another way, your roommate, although worse at both tasks, is not quite as bad at ironing as at typing.

Don't think that this is just common sense. Common sense would lead you to do your own ironing and typing, because you are better at both. *Absolute advantage focuses on who uses the fewest resources, but comparative advantage focuses on what else those resources could produce—that is, on the opportunity cost of those resources.* Comparative advantage is the better guide to who should do what.

The law of comparative advantage applies not only to individuals but also to firms, regions of a country, and entire nations. Individuals, firms, regions, or countries with the lowest opportunity cost of producing a particular good should specialize in producing that good. Because of such factors as climate, workforce skills, natural resources, and capital stock, certain parts of the country and certain parts of the world have a comparative advantage in producing particular goods. From Washington State apples to Florida oranges, from software in India to hardware in Taiwan—*resources are allocated most efficiently across the country and around the world when production and trade conform to the law of comparative advantage.*

Specialization and Exchange

In the previous example, you and your roommate specialized and then exchanged output. No money was involved. In other words, you engaged in **barter**, where products are traded directly for other products. Barter works best in simple economies with little specialization and few traded goods. But for economies with greater specialization, *money* facilitates exchange. Money—coins, bills, cheques, and debit cards—is a *medium of exchange* because it is the one thing that everyone accepts in return for goods and services.

Because of specialization and comparative advantage, most people consume little of what they produce and produce little of what they consume. Each individual specializes, then exchanges that product for money, which in turn is exchanged for goods and services. Did you make anything you are wearing? Probably not. Think about the degree of specialization that went into your cotton shirt. A farmer in a warm climate grew the cotton and sold it to someone who spun it into thread, who sold it to someone who wove it into fabric, who sold it to someone who sewed the shirt, who sold it to a wholesaler, who sold it to a retailer, who sold it to you. Many specialists created that shirt.

> "The degree of specialization is limited by the extent of the market."

Evidence of specialization is all around us. Shops at the mall specialize in products ranging from luggage to furnishings. Restaurants range from subs to sushi. Or let your fingers do the walking through the help-wanted ads or *Yellow Pages*, where you will find thousands of specializations. Without moving a muscle, you can observe the division of labor within a single industry by watching the credits roll at the end of a movie. The credits show scores of specialists—from gaffer (lighting electrician) to assistant location scout. TV is no different. A typical TV drama, such as *Friends*, requires hundreds of specialists.

Some specialties may seem odd. For example, professional mourners in Taiwan are sometimes hired by grieving families to scream, wail, and otherwise demonstrate the deep anguish befitting a proper funeral. The degree of specialization is perhaps most obvious online, where the pool of potential customers is so vast that individual sites become sharply focused. For example, you can find sites specializing in musical bowls, tongue studs, and toe rings—Just to name a few of the hundreds of thousands of specialty sites. You won't find such precise specialization at the mall. Adam Smith said the degree of specialization is limited by the extent of the market. Online sellers draw on the broadest customer base in the world to find a market niche.

Division of Labor and Gains from Specialization

Picture a visit to McDonald's: "Let's see, I'll have a Big Mac, an order of fries, and a chocolate shake." Less than a minute later your order is ready. It would take you much longer to make a homemade version of this meal. Why is the McDonald's meal faster, cheaper, and—for some people—tastier than one you could make yourself? Why is fast food so fast? McDonald's takes advantage of the gains resulting from the **division of labor**. Each worker, rather than preparing an entire meal, specializes in separate tasks. This division of labor allows the group to produce much more.

barter the direct exchange of one good for another without using money

division of labor breaking down the production of a good into separate tasks

> Adam Smith said the degree of specialization is limited by the extent of the market.

How is this increase in productivity possible? First, the manager can assign tasks according to *individual preferences and abilities*—that is, according to the law of comparative advantage. The worker with the toothy smile and pleasant personality can handle the customers up front; the one with the strong back but few social graces can handle the heavy lifting out back. Second, a worker who performs the same task again and again gets better at it (experience is a good teacher). The worker filling orders at the drive-through, for example, learns to deal with special problems that arise. As another example, consider the experience gained by someone screening bags at the airport. Experience helps the screener distinguish the harmful from the harmless. Third, specialization means no time is lost moving from one task to another. Finally, and perhaps most importantly, the **specialization of labor** allows for the introduction of more sophisticated production techniques—techniques that would not make sense on a smaller scale. For example, McDonald's large shake machine would be impractical in the home. *Specialized machines make workers more productive.*

> ONLINE SELLERS DRAW ON THE BROADEST CUSTOMER BASE IN THE WORLD TO FIND A MARKET NICHE.

To review: The specialization of labor (1) takes advantage of individual preferences and natural abilities, (2) allows workers to develop more experience at a particular task, (3) reduces the need to shift between different tasks, and (4) permits the introduction of laborsaving machinery. Specialization and the division of labor occur not only among individuals but also among firms, regions, and indeed entire countries. The cotton shirt mentioned earlier might involve growing cotton in one country, turning it into cloth in another, making the shirt in a third, and selling it in a fourth.

We should also acknowledge the downside of specialization. Doing the same thing all day can become tedious. Consider, for example, the assembly-line worker whose sole task is to tighten a particular bolt. Such a job could drive that worker bonkers or lead to repetitive motion injury. Thus, the gains from dividing production into individual tasks must be weighed against any problems caused by assigning workers to repetitive, tedious, and potentially harmful jobs. Fortunately, many routine tasks, particularly on assembly lines, can be turned over to robots.

specialization of labor focusing work effort on a particular product or a single task

production possibilities frontier (PPF) a curve showing alternative combinations of goods that can be produced when available resources are used efficiently; a boundary line between inefficient and unattainable combinations

LO3 The Economy's Production Possibilities

The focus to this point has been on how individuals choose to use their scarce resources to satisfy their unlimited wants or, more specifically, how they specialize based on comparative advantage. This emphasis on the individual has been appropriate because the economy is shaped by the choices of individual decision makers, whether they are consumers, producers, or public officials. Just as resources are scarce for the individual, they are also scarce for the economy as a whole (no fallacy of composition here). An economy has millions of different resources that can be combined in all kinds of ways to produce millions of different goods and services. This section steps back from the immense complexity of the real economy to develop another model, which explores the economy's production options.

Efficiency and the Production Possibilities Frontier

Let's develop a model to get some idea of how much an economy can produce with the resources available. What are the economy's production capabilities? Here are the model's assumptions:

1. To simplify matters, output is limited to just two broad classes of products: consumer goods and capital goods.
2. The focus is on production during a given period—in this case, a year.
3. The economy's resources are fixed in both quantity and quality during that period.
4. Society's knowledge about how these resources combine to produce output—that is, the available *technology*—does not change during the year.
5. Also assumed fixed during the period are the "rules of the game" that facilitate production and exchange. These include such things as the legal system, property rights, tax laws, patent laws, and the manners, customs, and conventions of the market.

The point of these simplifying assumptions is to freeze in time the economy's resources, technology, and rules of the game so we can focus on the economy's production options.

Given the resources, technology, and rules of the game available in the economy, the **production possibilities frontier**, or **PPF**, identifies possible combinations of the two types of goods that can be produced when all available resources are employed efficiently. *Resources are employed efficiently when there is no change that could increase the production of one good without decreasing the production of the other good.* **Efficiency** involves getting the most from available resources.

The economy's PPF for consumer goods and capital goods is shown by the curve AF in Exhibit 1. Point A identifies the amount of consumer goods produced per year if all the economy's resources are used efficiently to produce consumer goods. Point F identifies the amount of capital goods produced per year if all the economy's resources are used efficiently to produce capital goods. Points along the curve between A and F identify possible combinations of the two goods that can be produced when *all* the economy's resources *are used efficiently*.

Inefficient and Unattainable Production

Points inside the PPF, such as *I* in Exhibit 1, identify combinations that do not employ resources efficiently. Note that point C yields more consumer goods and no fewer capital goods than *I*. And point E yields more capital goods and no fewer consumer goods than *I*. Indeed, any point along the PPF between C and E, such as point *D*, yields both more consumer goods and more capital goods than *I*. Hence, point *I* is *inefficient*. By using resources more efficiently, the economy can produce more of at least one good without reducing the production of the other good. Points outside the PPF, such as *U* in Exhibit 1, identify *unattainable* combinations, given the availability of resources, technology, and rules of the game. Thus, *the PPF not only shows efficient combinations of production but also serves as the boundary between inefficient combinations inside the frontier and unattainable combinations outside the frontier.*

The Shape of the Production Possibilities Frontier

Focus again on point A in Exhibit 1. Any movement along the PPF involves giving up some of one good to get more of the other. Movements down along the curve indicate that the opportunity cost of more capital goods is fewer consumer goods. For example, moving from point A to point B *increases* capital production from none to 10 million units but *reduces* consumer units from 50 million to 48 million. Increasing capital to 10 million units reduces consumer goods only a little. Capital production initially employs resources (such as heavy machinery used to build factories) that add few consumer units but are quite productive in making capital.

As shown by the dashed lines in Exhibit 1, each additional 10 million capital units reduces consumer units by a successively larger amount. The resources used to produce more capital were increasingly better suited to producing consumer goods. *The opportunity cost of making more capital goods inceases, because resources in the economy are not all perfectly adaptable to the production of both types of goods.* The shape of the production possibilities frontier reflects the **law of increasing opportunity cost**. If the economy uses all resources efficiently, the law of increasing opportunity cost states that each additional increment of one good requires the economy to sacrifice successively larger and larger increments of the other good.

The PPF derives its bowed-out shape from the law of increasing opportunity cost. For example, whereas the first 10 million units of capital have an opportunity cost of only 2 million consumer units, the final 10 million units of capital—that is, the increase from point E to point F—have an opportunity cost of 20 million consumer units. Notice that the slope of the PPF shows the opportunity cost of an increment of capital. As the economy moves down the curve, the curve becomes steeper, reflecting the higher opportunity cost of capital goods in terms of forgone consumer goods. The law of increasing opportunity cost also applies when moving from the production of capital goods to the production of consumer goods. If resources were perfectly adaptable to alternative uses, the PPF

Exhibit 1

The Economy's Production Possibilities Frontier

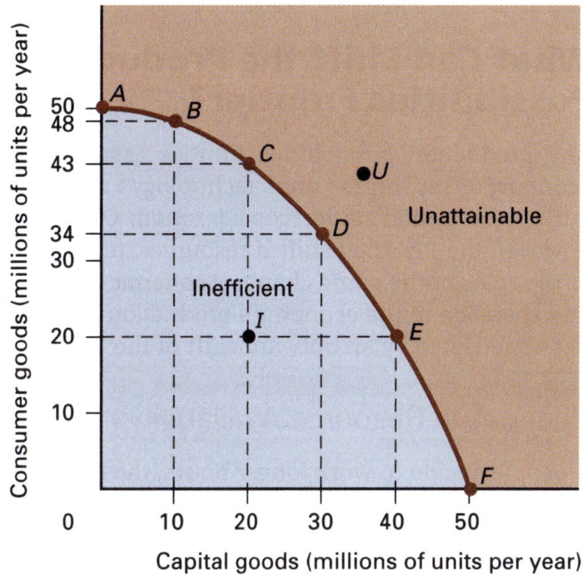

efficiency the condition that exists when there is no way resources can be reallocated to increase the production of one good without decreasing the production of another; getting the most from available resources

law of increasing opportunity cost to produce more of one good, a successively larger amount of the other good must be sacrificed would be a straight line, reflecting a constant opportunity cost along the PPF.

What Can Shift the Production Possibilities Frontier?

Any production possibilities frontier assumes the economy's resources and technology are fixed during the period under consideration. Over time, however, the PPF may shift if resources, technology, or the rules of the game change. **Economic growth** is an expansion in the economy's production possibilities as reflected by an outward shift of the PPF.

Changes in Resource Availability

If people decide to work longer hours, the PPF shifts outward, as shown in panel (a) of Exhibit 2. An increase in the size or health of the labor force, an increase in the skills of the labor force, or an increase in the availability of other resources, such as new oil discoveries, also shifts the PPF outward. In contrast, a decrease of resources shifts the PPF inward, as depicted in panel (b). For example, in 1990 Iraq invaded Kuwait, setting oil fields ablaze and destroying much of Kuwait's physical capital. In West Africa, the encroaching sands of the Sahara destroy thousands of square miles of farmland each year. And in northwest China, a rising tide of wind-blown sand has claimed grasslands, lakes, and forests and swallowed entire villages, forcing tens of thousands of people to flee.

The new PPFs in panels (a) and (b) appear to be parallel to the original ones, indicating that the resources that changed could produce both capital goods and consumer goods. For example, an increase in electrical power can enhance the production of both, as shown in panel (a). If a resource such as farmland benefits just consumer goods, then increased availability or productivity of that resource shifts the PPF more along the consumer goods axis, as shown in panel (c). Panel (d) shows the effect of an increase in a resource such as construction equipment that is suited only to capital goods.

Increases in the Capital Stock

An economy's PPF depends in part on the stock of human and physical capital. The more capital an economy produces during one period, the more output can be produced in the next period. Thus, producing more capital goods this period (for example, more machines in the case of physical

economic growth
an increase in the economy's ability to produce goods and services; reflected by an outward shift of the economy's production possibilities frontier

Exhibit 2

Shifts of the Economy's Production Possibilities Frontier

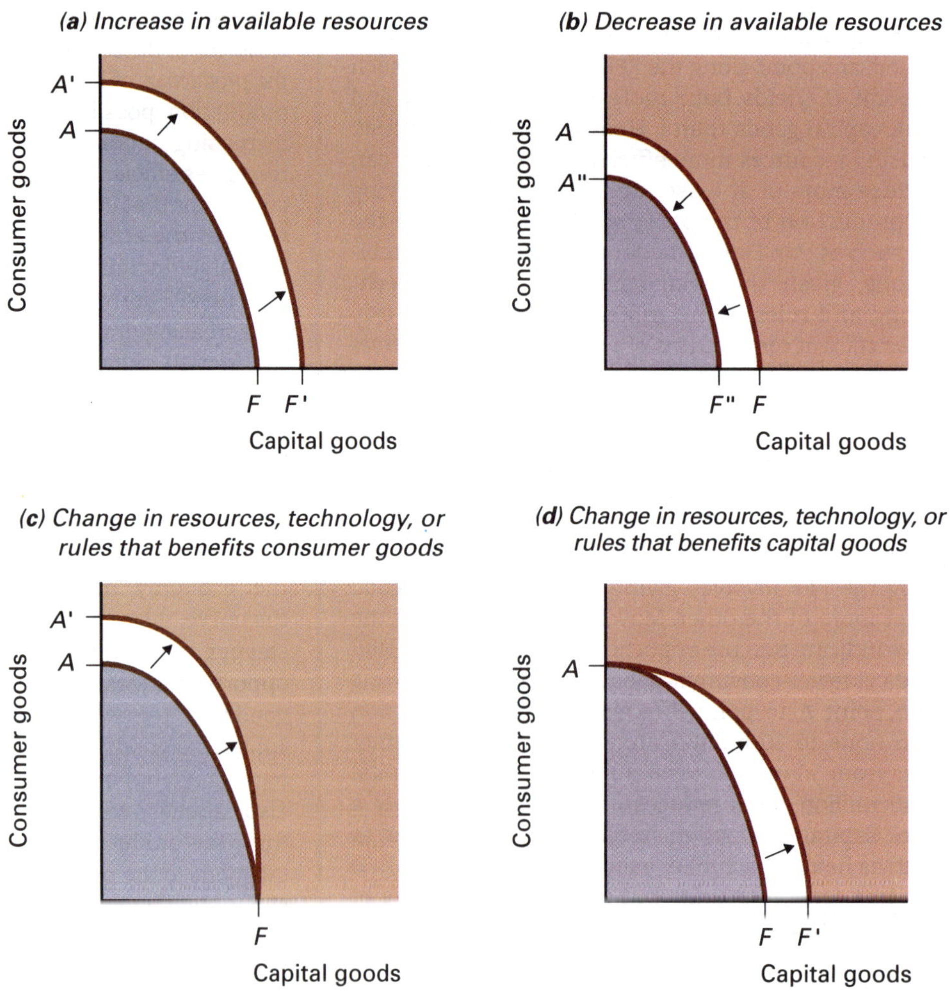

Disasters cause an inward shift or retraction of the PPF.

© REUTERS/LANDOV

if they are more confident that their investment will not be appropriated by government, stolen by thieves, destroyed by civil unrest, or blown up by terrorists. Improvements in the rules of the game shift the economy's PPF outward. On the other hand, greater instability reduces the economy's productive capacity, as reflected by in inward shift of the PPF. Rankings like the ones in Exhibit 3 illustrate how rules of the game of a particular country affect how easy it is to conduct business there.

capital or more education in the case of human capital) shifts the economy's PPF outward the next period. The choice between consumer goods and capital goods is really the choice between present consumption and future production. Again, the more capital goods produced this period, the greater the economy's production possibilities next period.

Technological Change

A technological discovery that employs resources more efficiently could shift the economy's PPF outward. Some discoveries enhance the production of both consumer goods and capital goods, as shown in panel (a) of Exhibit 2. For example, the Internet has increased each firm's ability to identify available resources. A technological discovery that benefits consumer goods only, such as more disease resistant crops, is reflected by a rotation outward of the PPF along the consumer goods axis, as shown in panel (c). Note that point F remains unchanged because the breakthrough does not affect the production of capital goods. Panel (d) shows a technological advance in the production of capital goods, such as better software for designing heavy machinery.

Improvements in the Rules of the Game

The **rules of the game** are the formal and informal institutions that support the economy—the laws, customs, manners, conventions, and other institutional underpinnings that encourage people to pursue productive activity. A more stable political environment and more reliable property rights increase the incentive to work and to invest, and thus help the economy grow. For example, people have more incentive to work if taxes claim less of their paycheques. People have more incentive to invest

Exhibit 3

Best 10 and Worst 10 Among 183 Countries Based on Ease of Doing Business, According to the World Bank

Best 10	Ease of Doing Business Rank (Top 10)	Bottom 10	Ease of Doing Business Rank (Bottom Ten)
Singapore	1	Haiti	174
Hong Kong SAR, China	2	Benin	175
New Zealand	3	Guinea-Bissau	176
United States	4	Venezuela, RB	177
Denmark	5	Congo, Dem. Rep.	178
Norway	6	Guinea	179
United Kingdom	7	Eritrea	180
Korea, Rep.	8	Congo, Rep.	181
Iceland	9	Central African Republic	182
Ireland	10	Chad	183

SOURCE: Doing Business, World Bank (2011), http://doingbusiness.org/rankings.

What We Learn from the PPF

The PPF demonstrates several ideas introduced so far. The first is *efficiency*: The PPF describes efficient combinations of outputs, given the economy's resources, technology, and rules of the game. The second idea is *scarcity*: Given the resources, technology, and rules of the game, the economy can produce only so much. The

rules of the game the formal and informal institutions that support the economy—the laws, customs, manners, conventions, and other institutional underpinnings that encourage people to pursue productive activity

PPF slopes downward, so more of one good means less of the other good, thus demonstrating *opportunity cost*. The PPF's bowed-out shape reflects the *law of increasing opportunity cost*, which arises because some resources are not perfectly adaptable to the production of each good. And a shift outward in the PPF reflects *economic growth*.

Finally, because society must somehow select a specific combination of output—a single point—along the PPF, the PPF also underscores the need for *choice*. Selecting a particular combination determines not only consumer goods available this period but also the capital stock available next period. One thing the PPF does not tell us is which combination to choose. The PPF tells us only about the costs, not the benefits, of the two goods. To make a selection, we need to know about both costs *and* benefits. How society goes about choosing a particular combination depends on the nature of the economic system, as you will see next.

LO4 Economic Systems

Each point along the economy's production possibilities frontier is an efficient combination of outputs. Whether the economy produces efficiently and how the economy selects the most preferred combination depends on the decision-making rules employed. But regardless of how decisions are made, each economy must answer three fundamental questions.

Three Questions Every Economic System Must Answer

What goods and services are to be produced? How are they to be produced? And for whom are they to be produced? An **economic system** is the set of mechanisms and institutions that resolve the *what, how*, and *for whom* questions. Some criteria used to distinguish among economic systems are (1) who owns the resources, (2) what decision-making process is used to allocate resources and products, and (3) what types of incentives guide economic decision makers.

What Goods and Services Are to Be Produced?

economic system the set of mechanisms and institutions that resolve the what, how, and for whom questions

Most of us take for granted the incredible number of choices that go into deciding what gets produced—everything from which new kitchen appliances are introduced, which roads get built, to which movies are made. Although different economies resolve these and millions of other questions using different decision-making rules and mechanisms, all economies must somehow make such choices.

How Are Goods and Services to Be Produced?

The economic system must determine how output gets produced. Which resources should be used, and how should they be combined to produce each product? How much labor should be used and at what skill levels? What kinds of machines should be used? What new technology should be incorporated into the latest video games? Should the office complex be built in the city or closer to the interstate highway? Millions of individual decisions determine which resources are employed and how these resources are combined.

For Whom Are Goods and Services to Be Produced?

Who will actually consume the goods and services produced? The economic system must determine how to allocate the fruits of production among the population. Should everyone receive equal shares? Should the weak and the sick get more? Should those willing to wait in line get more? Should goods be allocated according to height? Weight? Religion? Age? Gender? Race? Looks? Strength? Political connections? The value of resources supplied? The question "For whom are goods and services to be produced?" is often referred to as the *distribution question*.

Although the three economic questions were discussed separately, they are closely related. The answer to one depends on the answers to the others. For example, an economy that distributes goods and services uniformly to all will, no doubt, answer the what-will-be-produced question differently than an economy that somehow allows more personal choice. As we have seen, laws about resource ownership and the role of government determine the "rules of the game"—the set of conditions that shape individual incentives and constraints. Along a spectrum ranging from the freest to the most regimented types of economic systems, *pure capitalism* would be at one end and the *pure command system* at the other.

Pure Capitalism

Under **pure capitalism**, the rules of the game include the private ownership of resources and the market distribution of products. Owners have *property rights* to the use of their resources and are therefore free to supply those resources to the highest bidder. **Private property rights** allow individuals to use resources or to charge others for their use. Any income derived from supplying labor, capital, natural resources, or entrepreneurial ability goes to the individual resources owners. Producers are free to make and sell whatever they think will be profitable. Consumers are free to buy whatever goods they can afford. All this voluntary buying and selling is coordinated by unrestricted markets, where buyers and sellers make their intentions known. Market prices guide resources to their most productive use and channel goods and services to the consumers who value them the most.

Under pure capitalism, markets answer the what, how, and for whom questions. That's why capitalism is also referred to as a *market system*. Markets transmit information about relative scarcity, provide individual incentives, and distribute income among resource suppliers. No individual or small group coordinates these activities. Rather, it is the voluntary choices of many buyers and sellers responding only to their individual incentives and constraints that direct resources and products to those who value them the most.

According to Adam Smith (1723–1790), market forces allocate resources as if by an "invisible hand"—an unseen force that harnesses the pursuit of self-interest to direct resources where they earn the greatest payoff. According to Smith, *although each individual pursues his or her self-interest, the "invisible hand" of markets promotes the general welfare.* Capitalism is sometimes called *laissez-faire;* translated from the French, this phrase means "to let do," or to let people do as they choose without government intervention. Thus, under capitalism, voluntary choices based on rational self-interest are made in unrestricted markets to answer the questions what, how, and for whom.

As we will see in later chapters, pure capitalism has its flaws. The most notable market failures are:

1. No central authority protects property rights, enforces contracts, and otherwise ensures that the rules of the game are followed.
2. People with no resources to sell could starve.
3. Some producers may try to monopolize markets by eliminating the competition.
4. The production or consumption of some goods involves side effects that can harm or benefit people not involved in the market transaction.
5. Private firms have no incentive to produce so-called *public goods,* such as national defense, because private firms cannot prevent nonpayers from enjoying the benefits of public goods.

Because of these limitations, countries have modified pure capitalism to allow some role for government. Even Adam Smith believed government should play a role. The United States is among the most market-oriented economies in the world today.

Pure Command System

In a **pure command system**, resources are directed and production is coordinated not by market forces but by the "command," or central plan, of government. In theory at least, instead of private property, there is public, or *communal,* ownership of property. That's why central planning is sometimes called *communism.* Government planners, as representatives of all the people, answer such questions through *central plans* spelling out how much steel, how many cars, and how much housing to produce. They also decide how to produce these goods and who gets them.

In theory, the pure command system incorporates individual choices into collective choices, which, in turn, are reflected in the central plans. In fact, command economies often have names that focus on collective choice, such as the People's Republic of China and the Democratic People's Republic of Korea (North Korea). In practice, the pure command system also has flaws, most notably:

1. Running an economy is so complicated that some resources are used inefficiently.
2. Because nobody in particular owns resources, each person has less incentive to employ them in their highest-valued use, so some resources are wasted.
3. Central plans may reflect more on the preferences of central planners than those of society.
4. Because government is responsible for all production, the variety of products tends to be more limited than in a capitalist economy.

pure capitalism
an economic system characterized by the private ownership of resources and the use of prices to coordinate economic activity in unregulated markets

private property rights
an owner's right to use, rent, or sell resources or property

pure command system
an economic system characterized by the public ownership of resources and centralized planning

Common ownership often leads to common neglect.

© NORTH WIND/NORTH WIND PICTURE ARCHIVES/ALL RIGHTS RESERVED.

5. Each individual has less personal freedom in making economic choices.

Because of these limitations, countries have modified the pure command system to allow a role for markets. North Korea is perhaps the most centrally planned economy in the world today.

Mixed and Transitional Economies

No country on earth exemplifies either type of economic system in its pure form. Economic systems have grown more alike over time, with the role of government increasing in capitalist economies and the role of markets increasing in command economies. India represents a **mixed system**, where government is also directly involved in economic activity. What's more, government regulates the private sector in a variety of ways. For example, the industrial policy in each state determines the types of industries allowed. Government agencies and departments regulate workplace safety, environmental quality, competitive fairness, food and drug quality, and many other activities.

mixed system
an economic system characterized by the private ownership of some resources and the public ownership of other resources; some markets are regulated by government

Although both ends of the spectrum have moved toward the center, capitalism has gained the most converts in recent decades. Perhaps the benefits of markets are no better illustrated than where a country, as a result of war or political upheaval, became divided by ideology into a capitalist economy and a command economy, such as with Taiwan and China or South Korea and North Korea. In each case, the economies began with similar human and physical resources, but once they went their separate ways, economic growth diverged sharply, with the capitalist economies outperforming the command economies. For example, Taiwan's production per capita in 2006 was four times that of China, and South Korea's production per capita was 12 times that of North Korea.

Consider the experience of the pilgrims in 1620 while establishing Plymouth Colony. They first tried communal ownership of the land. That turned out badly. Crops were neglected and food shortages developed. After three years of near starvation, the system was changed so that each family was assigned a private plot of land and granted the fruits of that plot. Yields increased sharply. The pilgrims learned that people take better care of what they own individually; common ownership often leads to common neglect. However, in contrast, we have the experience of common property resource—the sacred groves seen in the North Eastern States of

India, which has helped in protecting the local flora and fauna.

Recognizing the incentive power of property rights and markets, some of the most die-hard central planners are now allowing a role for markets. For example, about one-fifth of the world's population lives in China, which grows more market oriented each day, even going so far as to give private property constitutional protection on a par with state property. In a poll of Chinese citizens, 74 percent agreed that "the free enterprise system is the best system on which to base the future of the world." Among Americans polled, 71 percent agreed with that statement.[2] More than a decade ago, the former Soviet Union dissolved into 15 independent republics; most converted state-owned enterprises into private firms. From Moscow to Beijing, from Hungary to Mongolia, the transition to mixed economies now under way in former command economies will shape the world for decades to come.

2. As reported in "Capitalism, Comrade," *Wall Street Journal,* 18 January 2006.

Economies Based on Custom or Religion

Finally, some economic systems are molded largely by custom or religion. For example, caste systems in India and elsewhere restrict occupational choices. Charging interest is banned under Islamic law. Family relations also play significant roles in organizing and coordinating economic activity. Even in the United States, some occupations are still dominated by women, others by men, largely because of tradition. Your own pattern of consumption and choice of occupation may be influenced by some of these considerations.

Final Word

Although economies can answer the three economic questions in a variety of ways, this book focuses primarily on the mixed market system, such as exists in India and the United States. This type of economy blends *private choice,* guided by the price system in competitive markets, with *public choice,* guided by democracy in political markets. The study of mixed market systems grows more relevant as former command economies try to develop markets. The next chapter focuses on the economic actors in a mixed economy and explains why government gets into the act.

Multiple Choice Questions

1. Opportunity cost exists because
   a. technology is fixed at any point in time
   b. the law of comparative advantage is working
   c. resources are scarce but wants are unlimited
   d. the value of lost opportunities varies from person to person
   e. efficiency is measured by the monetary cost of an activity
2. Opportunity cost is defined
   a. only in terms of money spent
   b. as the value of all alternatives not chosen
   c. as the value of the best alternative not chosen
   d. as the difference between the benefits from a choice and the benefits from the next best alternative
   e. as the difference between the benefits from a choice and the costs of that choice
3. A test was scheduled for Monday morning, but you went to a party on Saturday night. If you hadn't attended the party, you could have studied for the test or gone to a movie. Which of the following is true?
   a. The opportunity cost of going to the movie is studying for the test.
   b. The opportunity cost of going to the party is the movie.
   c. The opportunity cost of going to the party is both the movie and the study time.
   d. Because you could go to the party only that night but could go to a movie any time, the opportunity cost of the party is the study time.
   e. From the above information, it's not possible to determine the opportunity cost of attending the party.
4. Congratulations, you have been admitted to the Blue-and-Blue College. Your annual expenses are as follows: $19,000 for tuition, $1,000 for fees and books, and $4,000 for room and board. You are also receiving a scholarship of $7,500. The next best alternative to going to college is to get a full-time job that pays $24,000 a year (after taxes). What is your opportunity cost of going to college?
   a. $40,500
   b. $44,000
   c. $32,500
   d. $36,500
   e. I don't have enough information to calculate the opportunity cost of going to college.
5. You can either go to see a movie with your friends or go to the library and study for tomorrow's Economics test. Usually, you enjoy going at the movies just as much as you enjoy studying for Economics. However, tomorrow's test will determine your final grade and you need an A for the class, otherwise you'll be losing your scholarship. Which of the following is correct?
   a. The opportunity cost of studying is high because if you study you'll get an A for the class.
   b. The opportunity cost of going to see the movie is high because if you don't study you'll fail the class and lose your scholarship.
   c. The opportunity cost of studying is low because you like going at the movies.
   d. The opportunity cost of going to see the movie is low because if you don't study you'll fail the class and lose your scholarship.
   e. The opportunity cost of studying is low because if you don't study you'll fail the class and lose your scholarship.
6. The law of comparative advantage says that a person should produce a good if she
   a. has the greatest desire to consume that good
   b. has the lowest opportunity cost of producing that good
   c. has an absolute advantage in a related activity
   d. has a comparative advantage in a related activity
   e. is equally good at producing this good as someone else is
7. John can clean the house in 3 hours and paint the basement in 3 hours, whereas Mike can clean the house in 5 hours and paint the basement in 4 hours. Which of the following statements are correct?
   a. John has absolute advantage only in painting the basement.
   b. John has absolute advantage only in cleaning the house

c. Mike has absolute advantage in cleaning the house
d. Mike has absolute advantage in both cleaning the house and painting the basement
e. John has absolute advantage in both cleaning the house and painting the basement

8. If Jeremy has an absolute advantage in cooking and Margaret has an absolute advantage in cleaning, then
   a. Jeremy has a comparative advantage in cooking, and Margaret has a comparative advantage in cleaning
   b. Jeremy has a comparative advantage in cleaning, and Margaret has a comparative advantage in cooking
   c. we can conclude nothing about comparative advantage
   d. Jeremy has a comparative advantage in cooking, but we can conclude nothing about Margaret
   e. Margaret has a comparative advantage in cleaning, but we can conclude nothing about Jeremy

9. If Daniel produces one pair of shoes in 4 hours and Sarah produces one pair of shoes in 3 hours, then
   a. Sarah has a comparative advantage in shoemaking
   b. Daniel has a comparative advantage in shoemaking
   c. Sarah has an absolute and a comparative advantage in shoemaking
   d. Daniel has an absolute and a comparative advantage in shoemaking
   e. Sarah has an absolute advantage in shoemaking

10. Given the information in Exhibit 4, which product should Friday (an individual) make?

Exhibit 4

	Robinson Crusoe	Friday
Fishhooks per day	30	60
Fishing poles per day	2	10

   a. fishhooks because he can make 30 more per day than Crusoe but only 8 more fishing poles
   b. both because he is better at both
   c. fishing poles because that is where his comparative advantage lies
   d. neither because Crusoe is better at both
   e. we cannot tell from the given information

11. The production possibilities frontier represents all desirable combinations of outputs.
   a. True
   b. False

12. Society's production possibilities frontier
   a. helps explain the immense complexity of the real economy
   b. demonstrates that, although resources are scarce for individuals, there is no problem of scarcity for society as a whole
   c. is based on unrealistic assumptions and therefore has no value as an economic tool
   d. is based on simplifying assumptions, but is still useful for illustrating scarcity, opportunity cost, and economic growth
   e. is based on the assumption that technology is constantly changing

13. Points inside the production possibilities frontier represent
   a. full and efficient use of all resources
   b. inefficiency or unemployment (or both)
   c. currently unattainable combinations of outputs
   d. currently unattainable combinations of resources
   e. the most desirable combinations of outputs

14. The typical concave (i.e., bowed-out) shape of the production possibilities frontier reflects the law of increasing opportunity cost.
   a. True
   b. False

15. Exhibit 5 represents two production possibilities frontiers for the country of Toyland. Currently, the country produces at point C. Which of the following would move the economy at point M where the same number of pizzas but fewer iPods are produced?
   a. Using the existing resources more efficiently
   b. A decrease in the quality of a resource used in the production of both pizzas and iPods
   c. The discovery of a better technology that helps mostly the production of pizzas
   d. An increase in the quantity of a resource that is used only in the production of iPods
   e. A decrease in the quantity of a resource that is used only in the production of iPods

16. Exhibit 5 represents two production possibilities frontiers for the country of

Toyland. Currently, the country produces at point C. Which of the following would move the economy at point D where fewer pizzas but more iPods are produced?

Exhibit 5

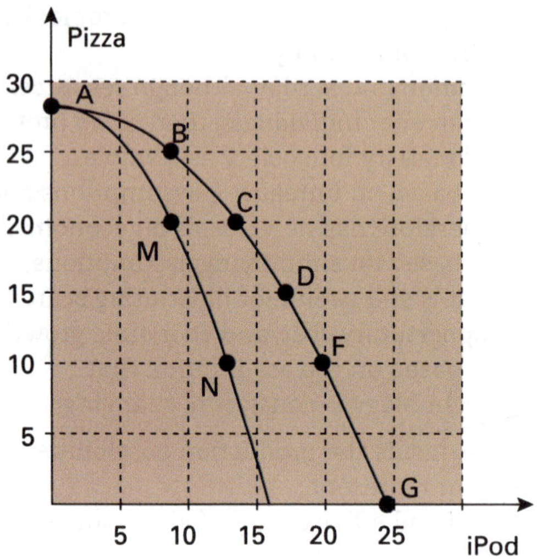

a. Using the existing resources more efficiently
b. A decrease in the quality of a resource used in the production of both pizzas and iPods
c. An increase in the quantity of a resource that is used only in the production of iPods
d. The country's desire to produce more iPods
e. Discovery and implementation of a better technology that increases workers' productivity

17. If the production possibilities curve is a downward-sloping straight line, that would indicate
    a. that society cannot decide which good it prefers
    b. an absence of scarcity
    c. constant opportunity cost
    d. inefficiency
    e. specialization

18. A production possibilities frontier can shift outward for all of the following reasons *except one*. Which is the exception?
    a. a decrease in the unemployment rate
    b. an improvement in labor skills
    c. an improvement in technology
    d. a larger work force
    e. a larger capital stock

19. A production possibilities frontier can shift inward if there is
    a. an increase in the unemployment rate
    b. mandatory retirement at age 55
    c. an improvement in technology
    d. a larger work force
    e. a larger capital stock

20. The "invisible hand" described by Adam Smith refers to the
    a. allocative role of markets and market forces
    b. importance of government intervention and central planning
    c. actions of successful entrepreneurs in directing the economy
    d. role of monopolized industries in leading the nation
    e. value of religious belief in creating an ideal economy

Answers

1. c 2. c 3. e 4. d 5. b 6. b 7. e 8. c 9. e 10. c
11. b 12. d 13. b 14. a 15. d 16. d 17. c 18. a 19. b 20. a

Long Answer Questions

LO1 Describe the impact of choice on opportunity

1.1. *(Sunk Cost and Choice)* Suppose you go to a restaurant and buy an expensive meal. Halfway through, despite feeling quite full, you decide to clean your plate. After all, you think, you paid for the meal, so you are going to eat all of it. What's wrong with this thinking?

1.2. *(Opportunity Cost)* You can either spend spring break working at home for $80 per day for five days or go to Florida for the week. If you stay home, your expenses will total about $100. If you go to Florida, the airfare, hotel, food, and miscellaneous expenses will total about $700. What's your opportunity cost of going to Florida?

1.3. Explain the concept of opportunity cost and discuss how it relates to the problem of choice between scarce alternatives.

1.4. What is the opportunity cost to you of each of the following:
   a. Going for a vacation for two days during weekdays.
   b. Going for a vacation for two days during weekend.
   c. Working at McDonald's during vacation.

LO2 Explain how comparative advantage, specialization, and exchange affect economic outcomes (output)

2.1. *(Absolute and Comparative Advantage)* You have the following information concerning the production of wheat and cloth in the United States and the United Kingdom:

	Labor Hours Required to Produce One Unit	
	United Kingdom	**United States**
Wheat	2	1
Cloth	6	5

a. What is the opportunity cost of producing a unit of wheat in the United Kingdom? In the United States?
b. Which country has an absolute advantage in producing wheat? In producing cloth?
c. Which country has a comparative advantage in producing wheat? In producing cloth?
d. Which country should specialize in producing wheat? In producing cloth?

2.2. *(Specialization)* Provide some examples of specialized markets or retail outlets. What makes the Web so conducive to specialization?

LO3 Outline how economies function as production systems

3.1. *(Shape of the PPF)* Suppose a production possibilities frontier includes the following combinations:

Cars	Washing Machines
0	1,000
100	600
200	0

a. Graph the PPF, assuming that it has no curved segments.
b. What is the cost of producing an additional car when 50 cars are being produced?
c. What is the cost of producing an additional car when 150 cars are being produced?
d. What is the cost of producing an additional washing machine when 50 cars are being produced? When 150 cars are being produced?
e. What do your answers tell you about opportunity costs?

3.2. *(Production Possibilities)* Suppose an economy uses two resources (labor and capital) to produce two goods (wheat and cloth). Capital is relatively more useful in producing cloth, and labor is relatively more useful in producing wheat. If the supply of capital falls by 10 percent and the supply of labor increases by 10 percent, how will the PPF for wheat and cloth change?

3.3. *(Production Possibilities)* There's no reason why a production possibilities frontier could not be used to represent the situation facing an individual. Imagine your own PPF. Right now—today—you have certain resources—your time, your skills, perhaps some capital. And you can produce various outputs. Suppose you can produce combinations of two outputs, call them studying and partying.

a. Draw your PPF for studying and partying. Be sure to label the axes of the diagram appropriately. Label the points where the PPF intersects the axes, as well as several other points along the frontier.
b. Explain what it would mean for you to move upward and to the left along your personal PPF. What kinds of adjustments would you have to make in your life to make such a movement along the frontier?
c. Under what circumstances would your personal PPF shift outward? Do you think the shift would be a "parallel" one? Why, or why not?

3.4. *(Shifting Production Possibilities)* Determine whether each of the following would cause the economy's PPF to shift inward, outward, or not at all:

a. An increase in average length of annual vacations
b. An increase in immigration
c. A decrease in the average retirement age
d. The migration of skilled workers to other countries

3.5. What is a production possibility curve/frontier? Why is it important to distinguish between:

a. A movement from a point within the PPF to a point on the PPF?
b. A movement from one point on the PPF to another point on the PPF?

3.6. Does the shape of the PPF depend upon the Returns to Scale? Explain.

LO4 Describe different economic systems and the decision-making rules that define them

4.1. *(Economic Systems)* The United States is best described as having a mixed economy. What are some elements of command in the U.S. economy? What are some elements of tradition?

4.2. What are the basic central problems of an economy?

4.3. How is a pure command system different from pure capitalism? What are some of the flaws related to each type of market system?

Chapter in Review

2

KEY TERMS

opportunity cost
the value of the best alternative forgone when an item or activity is chosen

sunk cost
a cost that has already been incurred, cannot be recovered, and thus is irrelevant for present and future economic decisions

law of comparative advantage
the individual, firm, region, or country with the lowest opportunity cost of producing a particular good should specialize in that good

absolute advantage
the ability to make something using fewer resources than other producers use

comparative advantage
the ability to make something at a lower opportunity cost than other producers face

barter
the direct exchange of one good for another without using money

division of labor
breaking down the production of a good into separate tasks

specialization of labor
focusing work effort on a particular product or a single task

production possibilities frontier (PPF)
a curve showing alternative combinations of goods that can be produced when available resources are used efficiently; a boundary line between inefficient and unattainable combinations

efficiency
the condition that exists when there is no way resources can be reallocated to increase the production of one good without decreasing the production of another; getting the most from available resources

law of increasing opportunity cost
to produce more of one good, a successively larger amount of the other good must be sacrificed

economic growth
an increase in the economy's ability to produce goods and services; reflected by an outward shift of the economy's production possibilities frontier

rules of the game
the formal and informal institutions that support the economy—laws, customs, manners, conventions, and other institutional underpinnings that encourage people to pursue productive activity

economic system
the set of mechanisms and institutions that resolve the what, how, and for whom questions

LO1 Describe the impact of choice on opportunity. Resources are scarce, but human wants are unlimited. Because you cannot satisfy all your wants, you must choose, and whenever you choose, you must forgo some option. Choice involves an opportunity cost. The opportunity cost of the selected option is the value of the best alternative forgone.

LO2 Explain how comparative advantage, specialization, and exchange affect economic outcomes (output). The law of comparative advantage says that the individual, firm, region, or country with the lowest opportunity cost of producing a particular good should specialize in that good. Specialization according to the law of comparative advantage promotes the most efficient use of resources. The specialization of labor increases efficiency by (a) taking advantage of individual preferences and natural abilities, (b) allowing each worker to develop expertise and experience at a particular task, (c) reducing the need to shift between different tasks, and (d) allowing for the introduction of more specialized machines and large-scale production techniques.

LO3 Outline how economies function as production systems. The production possibilities frontier, or PPF, shows the productive capabilities of an economy when all resources are used efficiently. The frontier's bowed-out shape reflects the law of increasing opportunity cost, which arises because some resources are not perfectly adaptable to the production of different goods. Over time, the frontier can shift in or out as a result of changes in the availability of resources, in technology, or in the rules of the game. The frontier demonstrates several economic concepts, including efficiency, scarcity, opportunity cost, the law of increasing opportunity cost, economic growth, and the need for choice.

The Economy's Production Possibilities Frontier

If the economy uses its available resources and technology efficiently in producing consumer goods and capital goods, that economy is on its production possibilities frontier, *AF*. The *PPF* is bowed out to reflect the law of increasing opportunity cost: additional units of capital goods require the economy to sacrifice more and more units of consumer goods. Note that more consumer goods must be given up in moving from *E* to *F* than in moving from *A* to *B*, although in each case the gain in capital goods is 10 million units. Points inside the *PPF*, such as *I*, represent inefficient use of resources. Points outside the *PPF*, such as *U*, represent unattainable combinations.

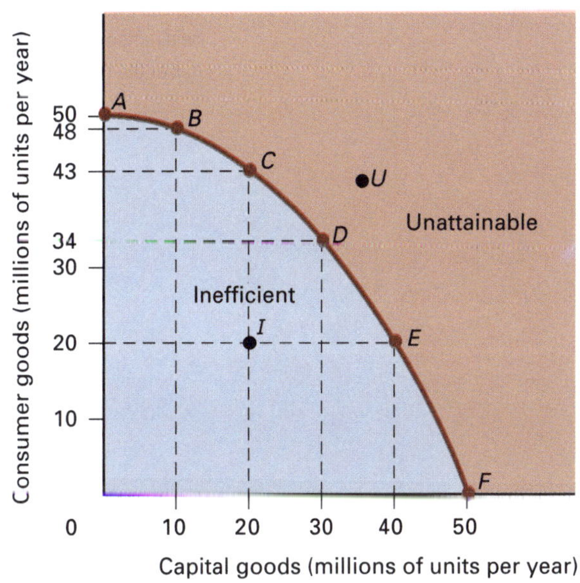

pure capitalism
an economic system characterized by the private ownership of resources and the use of prices to coordinate economic activity in unregulated markets

private property rights
an owner's right to use, rent, or sell resources or property

pure command system
an economic system characterized by the public ownership of resources and centralized planning

mixed system
an economic system characterized by the private ownership of some resources and the public ownership of other resources; some markets are regulated by government

Shifts of the Economy's Production Possibilities Frontier

When the resources available to an economy change, the *PPF* shifts. If more resources become available or if technology improves, the *PPF* shifts outward, as in panel (a), indicating that more output can be produced. A decrease in available resources causes the *PPF* to shift inward, as in panel (b). Panel (c) shows a change affecting consumer goods production. More consumer goods can now be produced at any given level of capital goods. Panel (d) shows a change affecting capital goods production.

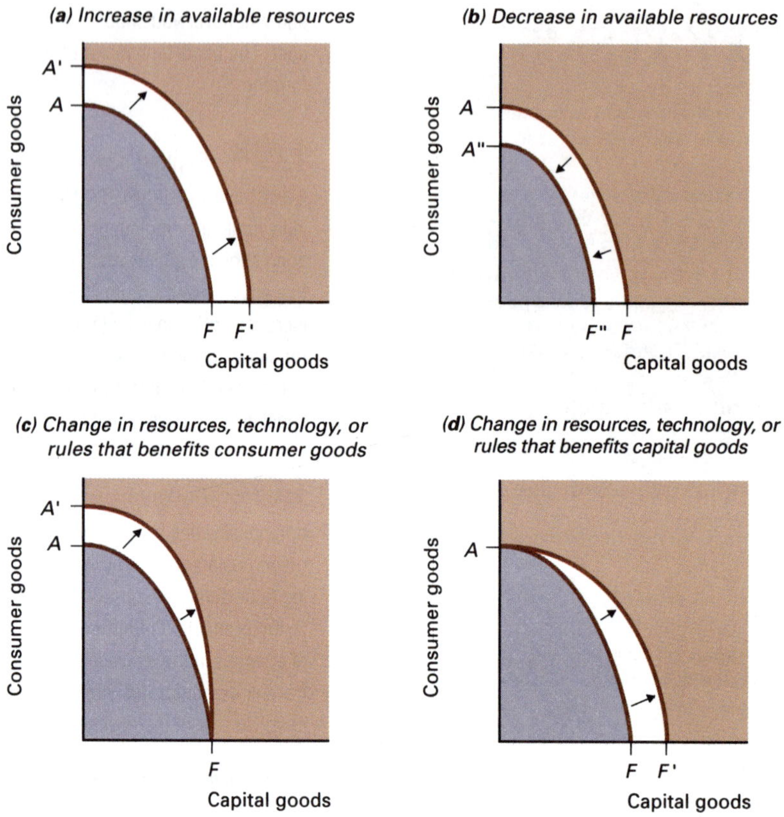

LO4 Describe different economic systems and the decision-making rules that define them. All economic systems, regardless of their decision-making processes, must answer three basic questions: What is to be produced? How is it to be produced? And for whom is it to be produced? Economies answer the questions differently, depending on who owns the resources and how economic activity is coordinated. Economies can be directed by market forces, by the central plans of government, or, in most cases, by a mix of the two.

CHAPTER 3

Economic Decision Makers

Learning Outcomes

LO 1 Explain the role of the household in an economic system

LO 2 Identify the different types of firms and describe their roles in the economy

LO 3 Outline the ways governments affect their economies

LO 4 Outline the international influences on an economy

© POLKA DOT/THINKSTOCK

“What happens to personal income once it comes into the household?”

If we live in the age of specialization, then why haven't specialists taken over all production? For example, why do most of us still do our own laundry and perform dozens of other tasks for ourselves? In what sense has production moved from the household to the firm and then back to the household? If the “invisible hand” of competitive markets is so efficient, why does government get into the act? Answers to these and other questions are addressed in this chapter, which discusses the four economic decision makers: households, firms, governments, and the rest of the world.

To develop a better feel for how the economy works, you must get more acquainted with the key players. You already know more about them than you may realize. You grew up in a household. You have dealt with firms all your life, from Sony to Subway. You know much about governments, from taxes to public schools. And you have a growing awareness of the rest of the world, from online sites, to imports, to foreign travel. This chapter draws on your abundant personal experience with economic decision makers to consider their makeup and objectives.

What do you think?

If I could afford it, I would hire a housekeeper.

Strongly Disagree 1 2 3 4 5 6 7 *Strongly Agree*

Topics discussed in Chapter 3 include:

- Evolution of the household
- Evolution of the firm
- Types of firms
- Market failures and government remedies
- Taxing and public spending
- International trade and finance

LO1 The Household

Households play the starring role in a market economy. Their demand for goods and services determines what gets produced. And their supplies of labor, capital, natural resources, and entrepreneurial ability produce that output. As demanders of goods and services and suppliers of resources, households make all kinds of choices, such as what to buy, how much to save, where to live, and where to work. Although a household usually consists of several individuals, we will view each household as acting like a single decision maker.

The Evolution of the Household

In earlier times, when the economy was primarily agricultural, a farm household was largely self-sufficient. Each family member specialized in a specific farm task—cooking meals, making clothes, tending livestock, planting crops, and so on. These early households produced what they consumed and consumed what they produced. With the introduction of new seed varieties, better fertilizers, and laborsaving machinery, farm productivity increased sharply. Fewer farmers were needed to grow enough food to feed a nation. At the same time, the growth of urban factories increased the demand for factory labor. As a result, workers moved from farms to cities, where they became more specialized but less self-sufficient.

Households evolved in other ways. For example, even in the industrialized nations only a very small percentage of married women with young children were in the labor force in 1950s. Since then, higher levels of education among women and a growing demand for their labor increased women's earnings, thus raising their opportunity cost of working in the home. This higher opportunity cost contributed to their growing labor force participation. Today in U.S.A, 70 percent of women with children under 18 are in the labor force.

utility the satisfaction received from consumption; sense of well-being

The rise of two-earner households has affected the family as an economic unit. Households produce less for themselves and demand more from the market. For example, child-care services and fast-food restaurants have displaced some household production. The rise in two-earner families has reduced specialization within the household—a central feature of the farm family. Nonetheless, some production still occurs in the home, as we'll explore later.

Households Maximize Utility

There are nearly 194 million households in India with 1028 million people. All those who live together under one roof are considered part of the same household. What exactly do households attempt to accomplish in making decisions? Economists assume that people try to maximize their level of satisfaction, sense of well-being, happiness, and overall welfare. In short, households attempt to maximize **utility**. Households, like other economic decision makers, are viewed as rational, mean-

India's Working Women

Women's work participation rate is quite low in India as compared to other countries. Traditionally much of the economic activity of women, whether domestic or otherwise, has not been fully recognized. In fact, many times women's work is not counted at all due to various social reasons. Marginalization of women in employment, though recognized from 1970s has not really improved over the passing years.

The National Sample Survey (NSS) of 2009-10 has shown that the total female employment has actually declined at an annual rate of 1.72 percent between 2004-05 and 2009-10. The female participation rates in rural areas are three times that of urban areas.

As can be seen, a larger proportion of women are self-employed, with a large share of unpaid labor. In the urban areas, there has been an increase in regular employment on account of increase in education. But there has also been an increase in the form of domestic service—as maids, helpers.

Studies have shown that economic growth has still not generated any great diversification of employment for women.

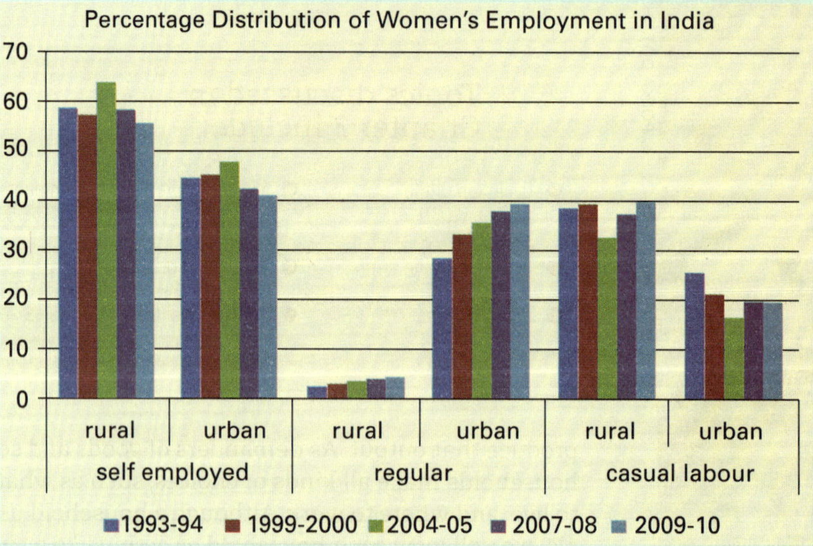

SOURCE: Computed from data taken from Employment and Unemployment Reports of NSS, for the four rounds of 1993-94, 1999-2000, 2004-05, 2007-08 and 2009-10. Availabe at http://mospi.nic.in.

ing that they try to act in their best interests and do not deliberately make themselves less happy. Utility maximization depends on each household's subjective goals, not on some objective standard. For example, some households maintain neat homes with well-groomed lawns; others pay little attention to their homes and use their lawns as junkyards.

Households as Resource Suppliers

Households use their limited resources—labor, capital, natural resources, and entrepreneurial ability—in an attempt to satisfy their unlimited wants. They can use these resources to produce goods and services in their homes. For example, they can prepare meals, do their own laundry, mow the lawn, and fix a leaky tap. They can also sell these resources in the resource market and use the income to buy goods and services in the product market. The most valuable resource sold by most households is labor.

Panels (a) and (b) of Exhibit 1 show the different sources of personal incomes of Indian households in rural and urban areas in 2009-10. The nature and type of work from which a household derives its major income is an important indicator of the activity pattern of its members. In rural India, 47% of the households are self-employed. In urban India, 35% are self employed and 40% of the households are regular wage/salaried.

Self-employed persons are those who operate their own farm or non-farm enterprises or are engaged independently in a profession or trade on own-account or with one or a few partners who are treated as self-employed in household enterprises. The essential feature of the self-employed is that they have *autonomy* (decide how, where, and when to produce) and *economic independence* (in respect of choice of market, scale of operation, and finance) for carrying out their operation. A **regular wage/salaried employee** is that person who works in others' farm or non-farm enterprises (both household and non-household) and, in return, receives salary or wages on a regular basis (i.e., not on the basis of daily or periodic renewal of work contract). A person, who is casually engaged in others' farm or nonfarm enterprises (both household and non-household) and, in return, receives wages according to the terms of the daily or periodic work contract, is a **casual wage laborer**.

Because of poor education, disability, discrimination, time demands of caring for small children, or bad luck, some households have few resources that are valued in the market. In developed countries, society has made the political decision that individuals in such circumstances should receive short-term public assistance. Consequently, the government gives some households **transfer payments**, which are outright grants. *Cash transfers* are monetary payments, such as welfare benefits, Social Security, unemployment compensation, and disability benefits. *In-kind transfers* provide for specific goods and services, such as food stamps, health care, and housing. Such schemes for cash transfers are under discussion in India, but not yet implemented.

Households as Demanders of Goods and Services

What happens to personal income once it comes into the household? Most goes to personal consumption, which sorts into three broad spending categories: (1) *durable goods*—that is, goods expected to last three or more years—such as an automobile or a refrigerator; (2) *nondurable goods*, such as food, clothing, and petrol or kerosene; and (3) *services*, such as haircuts, air travel, and medical care. The panels (c) and (d) in Exhibit 1 show the spending of personal income of the average rural and urban households in India.

The major proportion of the income both in urban and rural households is spent on nondurable goods, mainly food. The interesting point is the low levels of taxes paid by the average rural and urban households in India. However, services account for a substantial proportion of expenditure, because many services, such as child care, and other support services are shifting from do-it-yourself home production to market production.

Self-employed
person who operate their own farm or non-farm enterprises or are engaged independently in a profession or trade on own-account or with one or a few partners who are treated as self-employed in household enterprises

regular wage/salaried employee
is that person who works in others' farm or non-farm enterprises (both household and non-household) and, in return, receives salary or wages on a regular basis (i.e., not on the basis of daily or periodic renewal of work contract)

casual wage laborer
a person, who is casually engaged in others' farm or nonfarm enterprises (both household and non-household) and, in return, receives wages according to the terms of the daily or periodic work contract

transfer payments
cash or in-kind benefits given to individuals as outright grants from the government

Exhibit 1

Rural and Urban Household Types in India: Categorized by Major Source of Income and Average Monthly Per Capita Expenditure (2009–10)

Panel (a) Nearly one-third of rural households are self-employed in agricultural activities

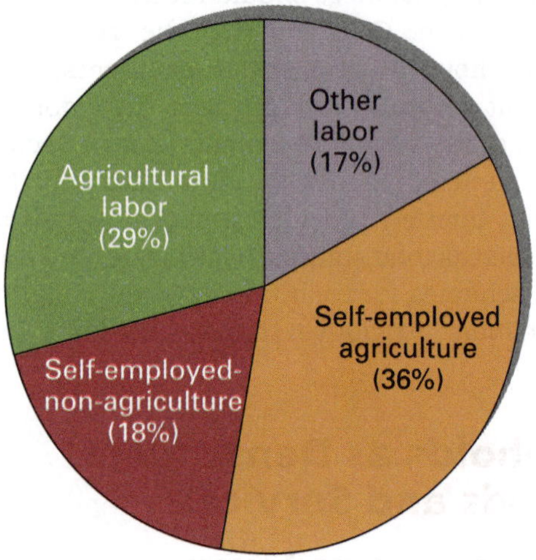

Panel (b) Nearly 40 percent of urban households are regular wage earning or salaried class

Panel (c) An average rural household spends nearly 74 percent of its consumption expenses toward nondurable goods, of which food is nearly takes up 57 percent.

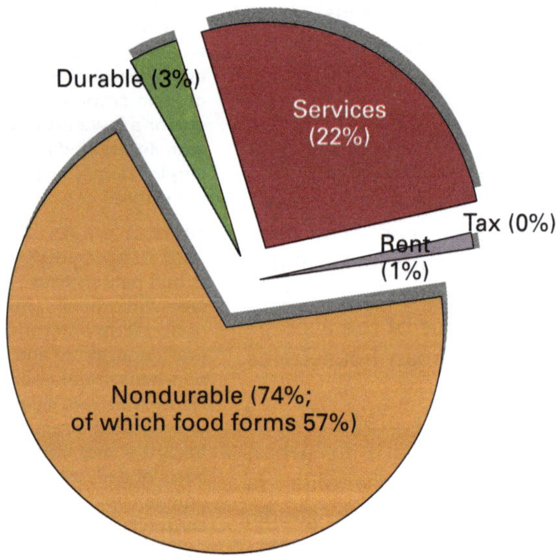

Panel (b) An average urban household spends nearly 58 percent of its consumption expenses towards nondurables, of which food nearly takes up 44 percent.

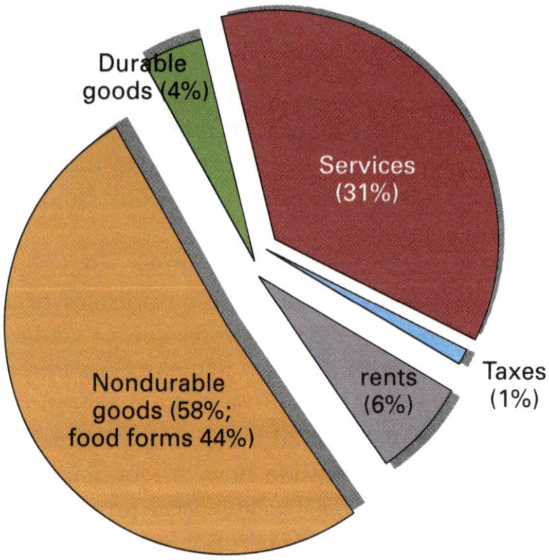

SOURCE: Computed using data from NSS Report No.537: Employment and Unemployment Situation in India, 2009-10 and NSS Report No.538: Level and Pattern of Consumption Expenditure, 2009-10.

LO² The Firm

Household members once built their own homes, made their own clothes and furniture, grew their own food, and amused themselves with books, games, and hobbies. Over time, however, the efficiency arising from comparative advantage resulted in a greater specialization among resource suppliers. This section takes a look at firms, beginning with their evolution.

The Evolution of the Firm

> SPECIALIZATION AND COMPARATIVE ADVANTAGE EXPLAIN WHY HOUSEHOLDS ARE NO LONGER SELF-SUFFICIENT.

Specialization and comparative advantage explain why households are no longer self-sufficient. But why is a firm the natural result? For example, rather than make a woolen sweater from scratch, couldn't a consumer take advantage of specialization by negotiating with someone who produced the wool, another who spun the wool into yarn, and a third who knitted the yarn into a sweater? Here's the problem with that model: If the consumer had to visit each of these specialists and strike an agreement, the resulting *transaction costs* could easily erase the gains from specialization. Instead of visiting and bargaining with each specialist, the consumer can pay someone to do the bargaining—an entrepreneur, who hires all the resources necessary to make the sweater. *An entrepreneur, by contracting for many sweaters rather than just one, is able to reduce the transaction costs per sweater.*

© PHOTOS.COM/JUPITERIMAGES

For about two hundred years, profit-seeking entrepreneurs relied on "putting out" raw material, like wool and cotton, to rural households that turned it into finished products, like woolen goods made from yarn. The system developed in the British Isles, where workers' cottages served as tiny factories, especially during winter months, when farming chores were light (so the opportunity cost was low). This approach, which came to be known as the *cottage industry system*, still exists in some parts of the world. You might think of this system as part way between household self-sufficiency and the modern firm.

As the British economy expanded in the 18th century, entrepreneurs began organizing the stages of production under one roof. Technological developments, such as waterpower and later steam power, increased the productivity of each worker and contributed to the shift of employment from rural areas to urban factories. *Work, therefore, became organized in large, centrally powered factories that (1) promoted a more efficient division of labor, (2) allowed for the direct supervision of production, (3) reduced transportation costs, and (4) facilitated the use of machines far bigger than anything used in the home.* The development of large-scale factory production, known as the **Industrial Revolution**, began in Great Britain around 1750 and spread to the rest of Europe, North America, and Australia.

Production, then, evolved from self-sufficient rural households to the cottage industry system, where specialized production occurred in the household, to production in a firm. Today, entrepreneurs combine resources in firms such as factories, mills, offices, stores, and restaurants. **Firms** are economic units formed by profit-seeking entrepreneurs who combine labor, capital, and natural resources to produce goods and services. Just as we assume that households try to maximize utility, we assume that firms try to *maximize profit*.[1] Profit, the entrepreneur's reward, equals sales revenue minus the cost of production.

Types of Firms

There are about 30 million for-profit businesses in the United States. Two-thirds are small retail businesses, small service operations, part-time home-based businesses, and small farms. Each year more than a million new businesses start up and many fail. Firms are organized in one of three ways: as a sole proprietorship, as a partnership, or as a corporation.

Sole Proprietorships

The simplest form of business organization is the **sole proprietorship**, a single-owner firm. Examples are self-employed plumbers, farmers, and dentists. Most sole proprietorships consist of just the self-employed proprietor—there are no hired employees. To organize a sole proprietorship, the owner simply opens his business by, for example, taking out a classified ad announcing availability for plumbing or

1. This assumption is relaxed in Part 3 of the textbook.

Industrial Revolution development of large-scale factory production that began in Great Britain around 1750 and spread to the rest of Europe, North America, and Australia

firms economic units formed by profit-seeking entrepreneurs who employ resources to produce goods and services for sale

sole proprietorship a firm with a single owner who has the right to all profits but who also bears unlimited liability for the firm's losses and debts whatever. The owner is in complete control. But he or she faces unlimited liability and could lose everything, including a home and other personal assets, to settle business debts or other claims against the business. Also, since the sole proprietor has no partners or other financial backers, raising enough money to get the business going can be a challenge. One final disadvantage is that a sole proprietorship usually goes out of business when the proprietor dies or leaves the business. In the U.S., a sole proprietorship is still the most common type of business, accounting most recently for 72 percent of all U.S. businesses, generating only 4 percent of the U.S. business sales.

Partnerships

A more complicated form of business is the **partnership**, which involves two or more individuals who agree to combine their funds and efforts in return for a share of the profit or loss. Law, accounting, and medical partnerships typify this business form. Partners have strength in numbers and often find it easier than sole proprietors to raise enough funds to get the business going. But partners may not always agree. Also, each partner usually faces unlimited liability for any debts or claims against the partnership, so one partner could lose everything because of another's mistake. Finally, the death or departure of one partner can disrupt the firm's continuity and require a complete reorganization.

Corporations

By far the most influential form of business is the corporation. A **corporation** is a legal entity established through articles of incorporation. Shares of stock confer corporate ownership, thereby entitling stockholders to a claim on any profit. A major advantage of the corporate form is that many investors—hundreds, thousands, even millions—can pool their funds, so incorporating represents the easiest way to amass large sums to finance the business. Also, stockholder liability for any loss is limited to the value of their stock, meaning stockholders enjoy *limited liability*. A final advantage of this form of organization is that the corporation has a life apart from its owners. The corporation survives even if ownership changes hands, and it can be taxed, sued, and even charged with a crime as if it were a person.

partnership
a firm with multiple owners who share the profits and bear unlimited liability for the firm's losses and debts

corporation
a legal entity owned by stockholders whose liability is limited to the value of their stock ownership

cooperative
an organization consisting of people who pool their resources to buy and sell more efficiently than they could individually

The corporate form has some disadvantages as well. A stockholder's ability to influence corporate policy is limited to voting for a board of directors, which oversees the operation of the firm. Each share of stock usually carries with it one vote. The typical stockholder of a large corporation owns only a tiny fraction of the shares and thus has little say. Whereas the income from sole proprietorships and partnerships is taxed only once, corporate income gets whacked twice—first as corporate profits and second as stockholder income, either as corporate dividends or as realized capital gains. A *realized capital gain* is any increase in the market price of a share that occurs between the time the share is purchased and the time it is sold.

Panel (a) of Exhibit 2 shows the percentage of each of various types of firms In India. The corporate sector makes up 37 percent of all the Indian businesses. It is made up of public limited companies, private limited companies, government department enterprises, and public corporations. The most common form of business is the partnership firms which make up for 30 per cent of the Indian firms. The kinds of factories included under others are khadi and village industries, handloom enterprises, cooperative societies.

Panel (b) shows the total output of the various firms. Total output is the total ex-factory value of products and by-products manufactured as well as other receipts such as receipts from non-industrial services rendered to others, work done for others on material supplied by them, value of electricity produced and sold, sale value of goods sold in the same condition as purchased, addition in stock of semi-finished goods and own construction.

Cooperatives

A **cooperative**, or "co-op" for short, is a group of people who cooperate by pooling their resources to buy and sell more efficiently than they could independently. Cooperatives try to minimize costs and operate with limited liability of members. The government grants most cooperatives tax-exempt status. There are two types: consumer cooperatives and producer cooperatives.

Consumer Cooperatives

A *consumer cooperative* is a retail business owned and operated by some or all of its customers in order to reduce costs. Some cooperatives require members to pay an annual fee and others require them to work a certain number of hours each year. Members sometimes pay lower prices than other customers or

Exhibit 2

Type of Firms in India and Their Total Output (2009–2010)

Panel (a) Type of firms in India (2009-10) *Panel (b) Total output by type of firms (2009-10)*

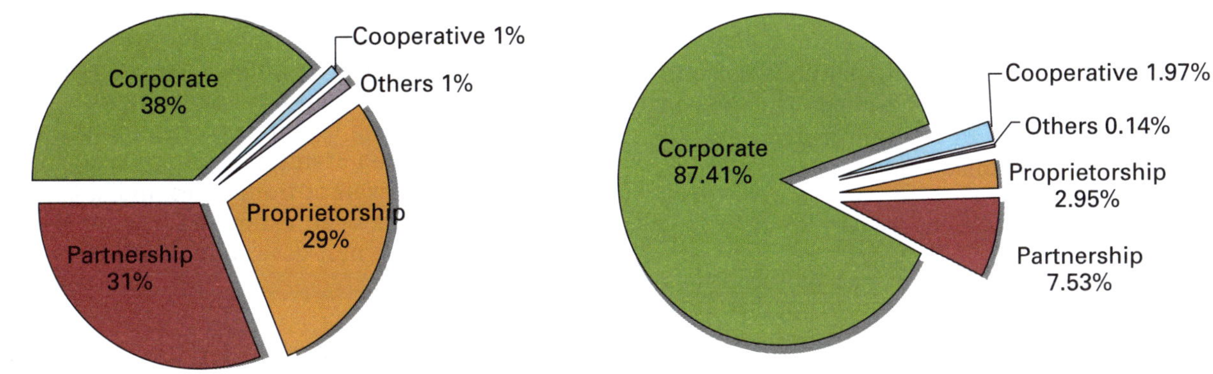

SOURCE: Based upon data from Annual Survey of Industries, 2009-2010. Available at http://mospi.nic.in.

Amul an Extremely Successful Dairy Cooperative in India

Amul (based in Anand, Gujarat) is an example of an extremely successful dairy cooperative in India. Formed in 1946, it is a brand name managed by an Indian cooperative organization, Gujarat Co-operative Milk Marketing Federation Ltd. (GCMMF), which today is jointly owned by 3.03 million milk producers in Gujarat. Amul spurred the White Revolution in India which in turn made India the largest producer of milk and milk products in the world. It is also the world's largest producer of vegetarian cheese brand. Dr Verghese Kurien, former chairman of the GCMMF, is recognized as a key person behind the success of Amul.

History: The Kaira District Co-operative Milk Producers' Union was registered on December 01, 1946 as a response to exploitation of marginal milk producers by traders or agents of existing dairies in the small town named Anand (in Kaira District of Gujarat). Milk producers had to travel long distances to deliver milk to the only dairy, the Polson Dairy in Anand that at that time had monopoly rights to collect milk from Anand and supply it to Bombay city in turn. Angered by the unfair and manipulative trade practices, the farmers of Kaira District approached Sardar Vallabhbhai Patel (who later became the first Deputy Prime Minister and Home Minister of free India) who advised the farmers to form a cooperative and supply milk directly to the Bombay Milk Scheme instead of selling it to Polson (who did the same but gave low prices to the producers). He sent Morarji Desai (who later became Prime Minister of India) to organize the farmers. In 1946, the farmers of the area went on a milk strike refusing to be further oppressed. Thus, the Kaira District Cooperative was established to collect and process milk in the District of Kaira in 1946. Milk collection was also decentralized. Village level cooperatives were established to organize the marginal milk producers in each of these villages.

Impressed with the development of dairy cooperatives in Kaira District and its success, Lal Bahadur Shastri, the then Prime Minister of India during his visit to Anand in 1964, asked Dr. Kurien to replicate the Anand type dairy cooperatives all over India. Thus, the National Dairy Development Board was formed and Operation Flood Programme was launched for replication of the Amul Model all over India.

The Amul Model is a three-tier cooperative structure. This structure consists of a Dairy Cooperative Society at the village level affiliated to a Milk Union at the District level which in turn is further federated into a Milk Federation at the State level. The above three-tier structure was set up in order to delegate various functions. Milk collection is done at the Village Dairy Society, Milk Procurement & Processing at the District Milk Union and Milk & Milk Products Marketing at the State Milk Federation. This helps in eliminating not only internal competition but also ensuring that economies of scale are achieved. As the above structure was first evolved at Amul in Gujarat and thereafter replicated all over the country under the Operation Flood Programme, it is known as the "Amul Model" or "Anand Pattern" of Dairy Cooperatives.

SOURCE: http://en.wikipedia.org/wiki/Amul.

may share in any revenues that exceed costs. In the United States, consumer cooperatives operate credit unions, electric-power facilities, health plans, apartment buildings, and grocery stores, among other businesses. Many college bookstores are cooperatives. In India, the best examples of consumer cooperatives include Kendriya Bhandar, Sahkar Bhandar, and Apna Bazaar. They primarily help the consumers to buy products at reasonable prices. They help in eliminating middlemen in the transactions between the producer and the consumer.

Producer Cooperatives

In a *producer cooperative,* producers join forces to buy supplies and equipment and to market their output. Each producer's objective is to reduce costs and increase profits. U.S. legislation allows farmers to cooperate without violating antitrust laws. Firms in other industries could not do this legally. Farmers pool their funds to purchase machinery and supplies, provide storage and processing facilities, and transport goods to market. Sunkist, for example, in U.S. is a farm cooperative owned and operated by 6,500 citrus growers in California and Arizona. The best examples in India are Boyanika (Odisha), Haryana Handlooms, which protect the smallest producers to buy raw materials. One of the most well known of India's products, the Amul Butter is from a cooperative marketing society, where the producers have come together to sell their products, under the Gujarat cooperative Milk Marketing Federation. Similarly, cooperative farming societies and housing cooperative societies are quite common in India.

"Although you wouldn't hire someone to brush your teeth, dental work is not for amateurs"

Not-for-Profit Organizations

So far, you have learned about organizations that try to maximize profits or, in the case of cooperatives, to minimize costs. Some organizations have neither as a goal. Not-for-profit organizations engage in charitable, educational, humanitarian, cultural, professional, and other activities, often with a social purpose. Government agencies do not have profit as a goal either, but governments are not included in this definition of not-for-profit organizations.

not-for-profit organizations
groups that do not pursue profit as a goal; they engage in charitable, educational, humanitarian, cultural, professional, or other activities, often with a social purpose

Like businesses, not-for-profit organizations evolved to help people accomplish their goals. Examples include nonprofit hospitals, private schools and colleges, religious organizations, the Red Cross, charitable foundations, museums, labor unions, and professional organizations. But even not-for-profit organizations must somehow pay the bills. Revenues typically include some combination of voluntary contributions and service charges, such as college tuition and hospital charges. In India also just as in the United States, not-for-profit organizations are usually exempt from taxes. India, according to a study, has been estimated to have nearly 3.3 million active non-government, not-for-profit organizations.[2]

Why Does Household Production Still Exist?

If firms are so efficient at reducing transaction and production costs, why don't they make everything? Why do households still perform some tasks, such as cooking and cleaning? *If a household's opportunity cost of performing a task is below the market price, then the household usually performs that task.* People with a lower opportunity cost of time do more for themselves. For example, housewives are more likely to cook their food than high profile professional women. Let's look at some reasons for household production.

No Skills or Special Resources Are Required

Some activities require so few skills or special resources that householders find it cheaper to do the jobs themselves. Sweeping the kitchen floor requires only a broom and some time, so it's usually performed by household members. Sanding a wooden floor, however, involves special machinery and expertise, so this service is usually left to professionals. Similarly, although you wouldn't hire someone to brush your teeth, dental work is not for amateurs. *Households usually perform domestic chores that demand neither expertise nor special machinery.*

Household Production Avoids Taxes

Suppose you are deciding whether to pay someone $3,000 to paint your house or to do it yourself. If the

2. First official estimate: An NGO for every 400 people in India, "http://www.Indianexpress.com" www.Indianexpress.com.

income tax rate is one-third, you must earn $4,500 before taxes to have the $3,000 after taxes to pay for the job. And the painter who charges you $3,000 nets only $2,000 after paying $1,000 in taxes. Thus, you must earn $4,500 so that the painter can take home $2,000. If you paint the house yourself, no taxes are involved. The tax-free nature of do-it-yourself activity favors household production over market transactions.

Household Production Reduces Transaction Costs

Getting estimates, hiring a contractor, negotiating terms, and monitoring job performance all take time and require information. Doing the job yourself reduces these transaction costs. Household production also allows for more personal control over the final product than is usually available through the market. For example, some people prefer home-cooked meals, because they can season home-cooked meals to individual tastes.

Technological Advances Increase Household Productivity

Technological breakthroughs are not confined to market production. Vacuum cleaners, washers and dryers, dishwashers, microwave ovens, and other modern appliances reduce the time and often the skill required to perform household tasks. Also, new technologies

© COMSTOCK IMAGES/JUPITERIMAGES

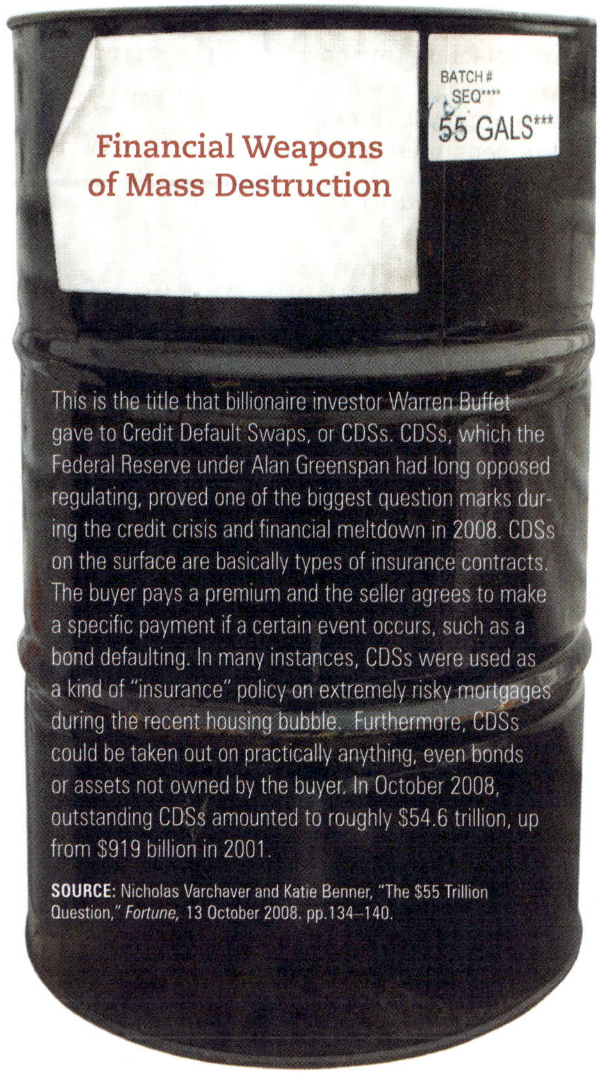

© ISTOCKPHOTO.COM

such as DVD players, HDTV, broadband downloads, and computer games enhance home entertainment. Indeed, microchip-based technologies have shifted some production from the firm back to the household.

LO3 The Government

You might think that production by households and firms could satisfy all consumer wants. Why must yet another economic decision maker get into the act? After all, governments play some role in every nation on earth.

The Role of Government

Sometimes the unrestrained operation of markets yields undesirable results. Too many of some goods and too few of other goods get produced. This section discusses the sources of **market failure** and how society's overall welfare may be improved through government intervention.

> THE SUPPLIER OF A PRIVATE GOOD CAN EASILY EXCLUDE THOSE WHO FAIL TO PAY.

Establishing and Enforcing the Rules of the Game

Market efficiency depends on people like you using your resources to maximize your utility. But what if you were repeatedly robbed of your paycheck on your way home from work? Or what if, after you worked two weeks in a new job, your boss is not happy and said you wouldn't get paid? Why bother working? The market system would break down if you could not safeguard your private property or if you could not enforce contracts. Governments safeguard private property through police protection and enforce contracts through a judicial system. More generally, governments try to make sure that market participants abide by the rules of the game. These rules are established through government laws and regulations and also through the customs and conventions of the marketplace.

Promoting Competition

Although the "invisible hand" of competition usually promotes an efficient allocation of resources, some firms try to avoid competition through *collusion*, which is an agreement among firms to divide the market and fix the price. Or an individual firm may try to eliminate the competition by using unfair business practices. For example, to drive out local competitors, a large firm may temporarily sell at a price below cost. Government antitrust laws try to promote competition by prohibiting collusion and other anticompetitive practices.

market failure
a condition that arises when the unregulated operation of markets yields socially undesirable results

monopoly
a sole supplier of a product with no close substitutes

natural monopoly
one firm that can supply the entire market at a lower per-unit cost than could two or more firms

private good
a good that is both rival in consumption and exclusive, such as pizza

public good
a good that, once produced, is available for all to consume, regardless of who pays and who doesn't; such a good is nonrival and nonexclusive, such as a safer community

Regulating Natural Monopolies

Competition usually keeps the product price below what it would be without competition—that is, below the price charged by a **monopoly**, a sole supplier to the market. In rare instances, however, a monopoly can produce and sell the product for less than could competing firms. For example, electricity is delivered more efficiently by a single firm that wires the community than by competing firms each stringing its own wires. When it is cheaper for one firm to serve the market than for two or more firms to do so, that one firm is called a **natural monopoly**. Since a natural monopoly faces no competition, it maximizes profit by charging a higher price than would be optimal from society's point of view. A lower price and greater output would improve social welfare. Therefore, the government usually regulates the natural monopoly, forcing it to lower its price and increase output.

Providing Public Goods

So far this book has been talking about private goods, which have two important features. First, private goods are *rival* in consumption, meaning that the amount consumed by one person is unavailable for others to consume. For example, when you and some friends share a pizza, each slice they eat is one less available for you. Second, the supplier of a private good can easily exclude those who fail to pay. Only paying customers get pizza. Thus, private goods are said to be *exclusive*. So **private goods**, such as pizza, are both rival in consumption and exclusive. In contrast, **public goods** are *nonrival* in consumption. For example, your family's benefit from a safer neighborhood does not reduce your neighbor's benefit. What's more, once produced, public goods are available to all. Suppliers cannot easily prevent consumption by those who fail to pay. For example, reducing terrorism is *nonexclusive*. It benefits all in the community, regardless of who pays for it and who doesn't. Because public goods are *nonrival* and *nonexclusive*, private firms cannot sell them profitably. The government, however, has the authority to enforce tax collections for public goods. Thus, the government provides public goods and funds them with taxes.

Dealing with Externalities

Market prices reflect the private costs and private benefits of producers and consumers. But sometimes production or consumption imposes costs or benefits on third parties—on those who are neither suppliers nor demanders in a market transaction. For example, a paper mill fouls the air breathed by nearby residents, but the price of paper fails to reflect such costs. Because these pollution costs are outside, or external to, the market, they are called *externalities*.

An **externality** is a cost or a benefit that falls on a third party. A negative externality imposes an external cost, such as factory pollution or auto emissions. A positive externality confers an external benefit, such as getting a good education or driving carefully. Because market prices do not reflect externalities, governments often use taxes, subsidies, and regulations to discourage negative externalities and encourage positive externalities. For example, a polluting factory often faces taxes and regulations aimed at curbing that pollution. And because more educated people can read road signs and have options that pay better than crime, governments try to encourage education with free public schools and subsidized higher education and by keeping people in school until their 16th birthdays.

A More Equal Distribution of Income

As mentioned earlier, some people, because of poor education, mental or physical disabilities, or perhaps the need to care for small children, are unable to support themselves and their families. Because resource markets do not guarantee even a minimum level of income, transfer payments reflect society's attempt to provide a basic standard of living to all households. Most citizens agree that government should redistribute income to the poor (note the normative nature of this statement). Opinions differ about who should receive benefits, how much they should get, what form benefits should take, and how long benefits should last.

Full Employment, Price Stability, and Economic Growth

Perhaps the most important responsibility of government is fostering a healthy economy, which benefits just about everyone. The government—through its ability to tax, to spend, and to control the money supply—attempts to promote full employment, price stability, and economic growth. Pursuing these objectives by taxing and spending is called **fiscal policy**. Pursuing them by regulating the money supply is called **monetary policy**. Macroeconomics examines both policies.

Government's Structure and Objectives

India has a *federal system* of government, meaning that responsibilities are shared across levels of government. State governments grant some powers to local governments and surrender some powers to the national, or federal, government. As the system has evolved, the federal government has primary responsibility for national security, economic stability, and market competition. State governments fund public higher education, prisons, and—with aid from the federal government—highways and welfare. Local governments provide primary and secondary education with aid from the state, plus police and fire protection. Here are some distinguishing features of government.

Roles of Government

Here's a quick review of beneficial government interventions in markets:

- Establishing and enforcing the rules of the game
- Promoting competition
- Regulating natural monopolies
- Providing public goods
- Dealing with externalities
- Distributing income more equally
- Pursuing full employment, price stability, and economic growth

Difficulty in Defining Government Objectives

We assume that households try to maximize utility and firms try to maximize profit, but what about governments—or, more specifically, what about government decision makers? What do they try to maximize? The federal government relies on offsetting, or countervailing, powers across the executive, legislative, and judicial branches. Government does not act as a single, consistent decision maker. Even within the federal executive branch, there are so many agencies and bureaus that at times they seem to work at cross-purposes. For example, the ongoing debate about the goods and services tax (GST) in India. Though the states in principle agree to a single format they are not fully ready to accept and implement the rules. It is seen that elected officials are vote maximizers. In this

externality a cost or a benefit that affects neither the buyer or seller, but instead affects people not involved in the market transaction

fiscal policy the use of government purchases, transfer payments, taxes, and borrowing to influence economy-wide variables such as inflation, employment, and economic growth

monetary policy regulation of the money supply to influence economy-wide variables such as inflation, employment, and economic growth theory, vote maximization guides the decisions of elected officials who, in turn, oversee government employees.

Voluntary Exchange Versus Coercion

Market exchange relies on the voluntary behavior of buyers and sellers. Don't you like a product? No problem—don't buy it. But in political markets, the situation is different. Any voting rule except unanimous consent must involve some government coercion. Public choices are enforced by the police power of the state. Those who fail to pay their taxes could be penalized, even though they may object to some programs those taxes support, such as the costs of security in troubled states or capital punishment.

No Market Prices

Another distinguishing feature of governments is that public output is usually offered at either a zero price or at a price below the cost of providing it. If you now study in a premier institution of the government, your tuition probably covers only about half the state's cost of providing your education. Because the revenue side of the government budget is usually separate from the expenditure side, there is no necessary link between the cost of a program and the benefit. In the private sector, the expected marginal benefit is at least as great as marginal cost; otherwise, market exchange would not occur.

The Size and Growth of Government

One way to track the impact of government over time is by measuring government outlays relative to the *gross domestic product*, or *GDP*, which is the total value of all final goods and services produced in the country. In the U.S. in 1929, the year the Great Depression began, all government outlays, mostly by state and local governments, totaled about 10 percent of GDP. At the time, the federal government played a minor role. In fact, during the nation's first 150 years, federal outlays, except during war years, never exceeded 3 percent relative to GDP.

The Great Depression, World War II, and a change in macroeconomic thinking boosted the share of government outlays to 38 percent of GDP in 2008, with about two-thirds of that by the federal government. In comparison, government outlays relative to GDP were 36 percent in Japan; 39 percent in Canada; 43 percent in Germany; 45 percent in the United Kingdom; 49 percent in Italy; and 52 percent in France. Government outlays by the 28 largest industrial economies averaged 41 percent of GDP in 2009.[3] Thus, government outlays in the United States relative to GDP are below those of most other advanced economies.

© IMAGE SOURCE PINK/JUPITERIMAGES

Let's look briefly at the composition of the outlays of the central government in India. Panel (a) of Exhibit 3 shows the major components of government spending between 1972-73 and 2010-11. Defence, subsidies, and interest payments are three important expenditure items in the overall government spending, which have always been higher than other outlays over the years, except in the recent past. Government is borrowing to spend on various activities.

The panel (b) of Exhibit 3 shows the share of outlays between the development and non-development expenditure of the central government in India. The development expenditure includes the amounts spent on social services and economic services. Social services include amounts spent on education, medical and public health, family welfare, water supply and sanitation, housing and nutrition. The amounts spent on agriculture and allied activities, rural development, irrigation and flood control, energy, industry and minerals and transport and communication are considered under the head of economic services. The exhibit clearly shows the falling share of development expenditure in the country.

Sources of Government Revenue

Taxes provide the bulk of revenue at all levels of government. The federal government relies primarily on

3. The Organization of Economic Cooperation and Development, OECD *Economic Outlook* (June 2008): Annex Table 25.

Exhibit 3

Outlays of the Central Government of India

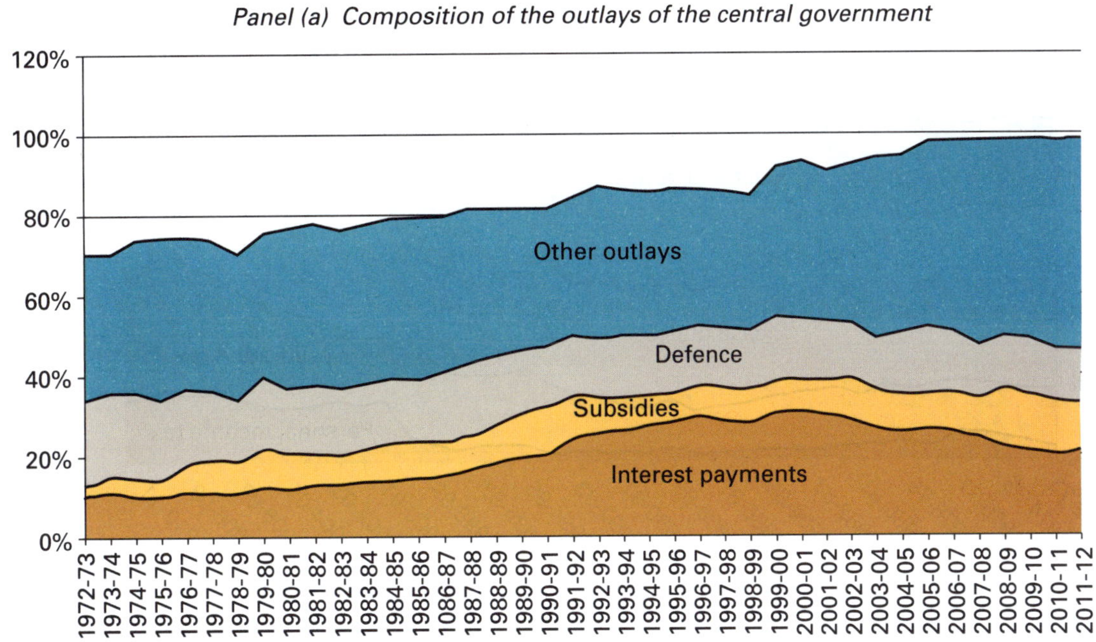

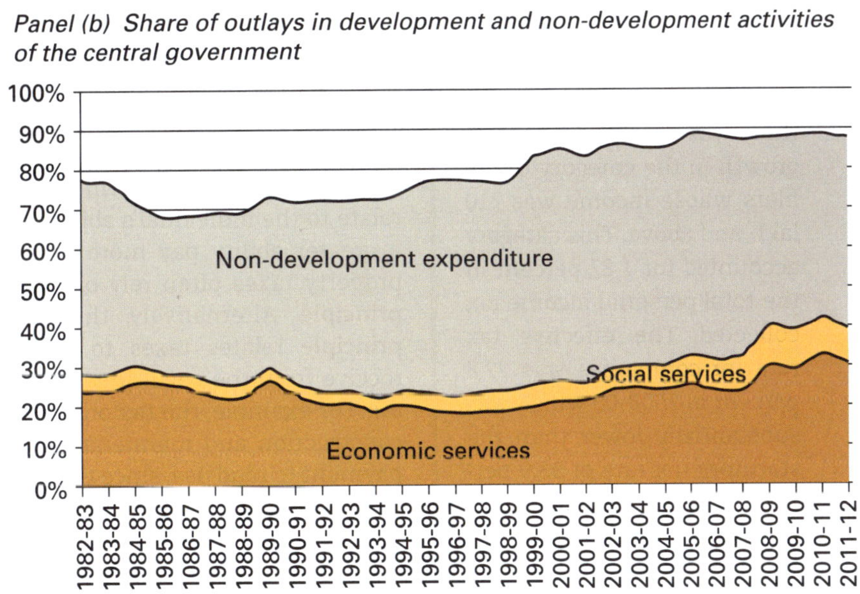

SOURCE: Computed using tables from the Handbook of Statistics on Indian Economy, 2010-11. Available at www.rbi.org.in.

the individual income tax, state governments rely on income and sales taxes, and local governments rely on the property tax. Other revenue sources include user charges, such as highway tolls, and borrowing. For additional revenue, some states also monopolize certain markets, such as for lottery tickets and liquor.

Exhibit 4 focuses on the composition of the revenues of the central government since 1972-73 in India. The two major sources of income is the direct and indirect taxes. The direct taxes levied by the Parliament mainly comprise of personal income tax and the corporation tax, which constitutes nearly 64.5 percent of direct tax collection. In 2010-11, personal income tax was required to be paid if the income level reached above ₹1.6 lakhs. It is seen that in case of personal income taxes, as of 2006-07,

Exhibit 4

Tax receipts of Central Government

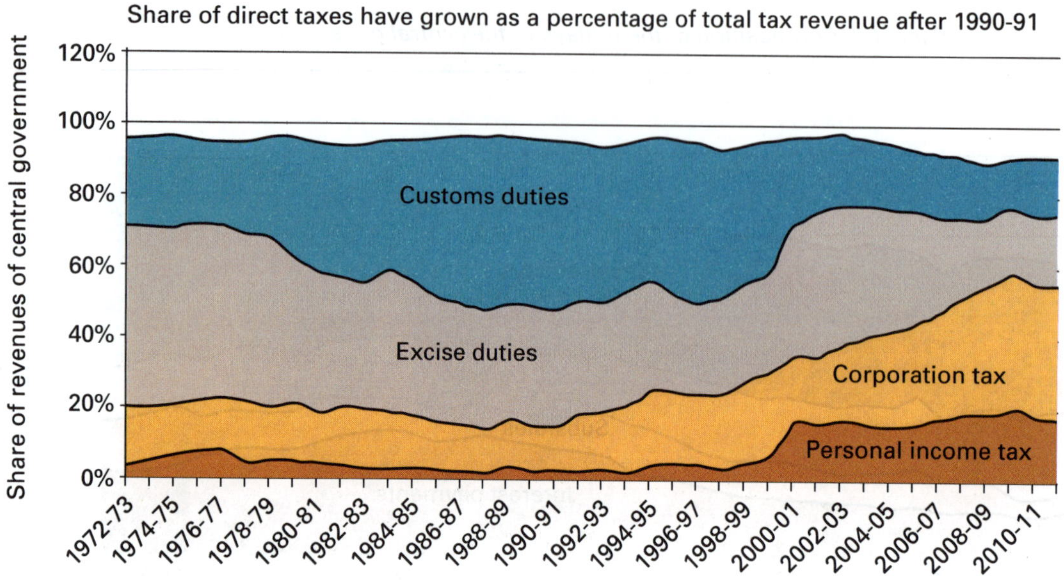

SOURCE: The figure is computed using tables from the Handbook of Statistics on Indian Economy, 2010-11. Available at www.rbi.org.in.

ability-to-pay tax principle those with a greater ability to pay, such as those earning higher incomes or those owning more property, should pay more taxes

benefits-received tax principle those who get more benefits from the government program should pay more taxes

tax incidence the distribution of tax burden among taxpayers; who ultimately pays the tax

proportional taxation the tax as a percentage of income remains constant as income increases; also called a flat tax

progressive taxation the tax as a percentage of income increases as income increases

nearly 88 percent of those who filed taxes were in the category whose income was below ₹2 lakh[4]. However, between 2002-03 and 2006-07, there was nearly a 60 percent growth in the category of tax filers whose income was ₹10 lakh and above. This category accounted for 1.87 percent in the total personal income tax collected. The effective tax rate for companies was 22.8 percent in 2008-09 which was substantially lower than the statutory tax rate of 33.9 percent, because of the many tax concessions that the companies availed of.[5]

The excise duties and customs form the indirect taxes whose share has come down over the years. This reflects the growth in the incomes of citizens due to the opening of the economy to the outside world through the liberalization process.

Tax Principles and Tax Incidence

The structure of a tax is often justified on the basis of one of two general principles. First, a tax could relate to the individual's ability to pay, so those with a greater ability pay more taxes. Income taxes or property taxes often rely on this **ability-to-pay tax principle**. Alternatively, the **benefits-received tax principle** relates taxes to the benefits taxpayers receive from the government activity funded by the tax. For example, the tax on gasoline funds highway construction and maintenance, thereby linking tax payment to road use, since those who drive more pay more gas taxes.

Tax incidence indicates who actually bears the burden of the tax. One way to evaluate tax incidence is by measuring the tax as a percentage of income. Under **proportional taxation**, taxpayers at all income levels pay the same percentage of their income in taxes. A proportional income tax is also called a flat tax, since the tax as a percentage of income remains constant, or flat, as income increases. Note that under proportional taxation, although taxes remain constant as a percentage of income, the dollar amount of taxes increases as income increases.

Under **progressive taxation**, the percentage of income paid in taxes increases as income increases.

4. 1 lakh = 1,00,000

5. Report No. CA 8 of 2008 (Direct Taxes) for period ended March 2007; Report No.2 of 2010-11(Direct Taxes) for the period ended March 2010, http://saiindia.gov.in.

The **marginal tax rate** indicates the percentage of each additional dollar of income that goes to taxes. Because high marginal rates reduce the after-tax return from working or investing, high marginal rates can reduce people's incentives to work and invest. In 1953, the report of the Taxation Enquiry Commission, helped set up the tax system in India. The personal income tax rates were extraordinarily high during the period 1950-80. In 1970-71, the personal income tax had 11 brackets with the tax rates progressively rising from 10 to 85%. These high taxes forced people to evade taxes. Hence on the recommendation of the Direct Taxes Enquiry Committee, 1971 the tax rates were brought down to 77% in 1974-75. From then onwards, attempts were made to progressively reduce the marginal rates further over a period of time. In 1976-77, the marginal rate was further reduced to 66 percent. In a major initiative in 1985-86, the number of tax brackets were further reduced from eight to four and the highest marginal rate was brought down to 50 percent. In 1991 on the basis of the recommendation of the Tax Reform Committee, the tax rates were considerably simplified to have only three tax brackets of 20, 30, 40 percent in 1992-93. Further they were brought down to 10,20, 30 percent in 1997-98. The personal income tax rates have remained stable since then, with some changes in the tax slabs.

International trade occurs because the opportunity cost of producing specific goods differs across countries.

Finally, under **regressive taxation**, the percentage of income paid in taxes decreases as income increases, so the marginal tax rate declines as income increases. Most U.S. payroll taxes are regressive, because they impose a flat rate up to a certain level of income, above which the marginal rate drops to zero. For example, Social Security taxes were levied on the first $106,800 of workers' pay in 2009. Half of the 12.4 percent tax is paid by employers and half by employees (the self-employed pay the entire 12.4 percent).

Taxes often do more than fund public programs. Some taxes discourage certain activity. For example, a pollution tax can help clean the air. A tax on gasoline can encourage people to work at home, carpool, or use public transportaion. Some taxes have unintended consequences. For example, in Egypt a property tax is not imposed until a building is complete. To avoid such taxes, builders never finish the job; multistory dwellings are usually missing the top floor. As another example of how taxes can distort the allocation of resources, property taxes in Amsterdam and Vietnam were originally based on the width of the building. As a result, buildings in those places are extremely narrow.

This discussion of revenue sources brings to a close, for now, our examination of the role of government in the economy. Government has a pervasive influence on the economy, and its role is discussed throughout the book.

LO4 The Rest of the World

So far, the focus has been on institutions within the country—that is, on *domestic* households, firms, and governments. This focus is appropriate because our primary objective is to understand the workings of the economy. But the rest of the world affects what the country's households consume and what firms produce. For example, Japan and China supply us with all kinds of manufactured goods, thereby affecting prices, wages, and profits. Likewise, political events in the Persian Gulf can affect what consumers pay for oil. Foreign decision makers, therefore, influence the country's economy—what we produce and what we consume. The *rest of the world* consists of the households, firms, and governments in the two hundred or so sovereign nations throughout the world.

International Trade

In the previous chapter, you learned about comparative advantage and the gains from specialization. These gains explain why householders stopped doing everything for themselves and began to specialize. *International trade arises for the same reasons. International trade occurs because the opportunity cost of producing specific goods differs across countries.* Americans import raw materials like crude oil, diamonds, and coffee beans and finished goods like cameras, DVD players, and automobiles. U.S. producers export sophisticated products like computer software, aircraft, and movies, as well as agricultural products like wheat and corn.

For example, trade between the United States and the rest of the world has increased in recent decades. In 1970, U.S. exports of goods and services amounted to only 6 percent of the gross domestic product. That has increased to 12 percent. The top 10 destinations for U.S.

marginal tax rate the percentage of each additional dollar of income that goes to the tax

regressive taxation the tax as a percentage of income decreases as income increases

exports in order of importance are Canada, Mexico, Japan, China, United Kingdom, Germany, South Korea, Netherlands, France, and Taiwan. In contrast, India's share in the world export market is just about one percent.

The **merchandise trade balance** equals the value of exported goods minus the value of imported goods. Goods in this case are distinguished from services, which show up in another trade account. For the last quarter century, the United States has imported more goods than it has exported, resulting in a merchandise trade deficit. Just as a household must pay for its spending, so too must a nation. The merchandise trade deficit must be offset by a surplus in one or more of the other *balance-of-payments* accounts. A nation's **balance of payments** is the record of all economic transactions between its residents and residents of the rest of the world.

merchandise trade balance
the value during a given period of a country's exported goods minus the value of its imported goods

balance of payments
a record of all economic transactions during a given period between residents of one country and residents of the rest of the world

foreign exchange
foreign money needed to carry out international transactions

tariff
a tax on imports

quota
a legal limit on the quantity of a particular product that can be imported

Exchange Rates

The lack of a common currency complicates trade between countries. How many U.S. dollars buy a Porsche? An American buyer cares only about the dollar cost; the German carmaker cares only about the *euros* (€) received (the common currency of 16 European countries). To facilitate trade funded by different currencies, a market for foreign exchange has developed. **Foreign exchange** is foreign currency needed to carry out international transactions. The supply and demand for foreign exchange comes together in *foreign exchange markets* to determine the exchange rate. The *exchange rate* measures the price of one currency in terms of another. For example, the exchange rate between the euro and the dollar might indicate that one euro exchanges for $1.20. At that exchange rate, a Porsche selling for €100,000 costs $120,000. The exchange rate affects the prices of imports and exports and thus helps shape the flow of foreign trade.

Trade Restrictions

Despite clear gains from international specialization and exchange, nearly all nations restrict trade to some extent. These restrictions can take the form of (1) **tariffs**, which are taxes on imports; (2) **quotas**, which are limits on the quantity of a particular good that can be imported from a country; and (3) other trade restrictions. If specialization according to comparative advantage is so beneficial, why do most countries restrict trade? Restrictions benefit certain domestic producers that lobby their governments for these benefits. For example, U.S. growers of sugar cane have benefited from legislation restricting imports, thereby raising U.S. sugar prices. These higher prices hurt domestic consumers, but consumers are usually unaware of this harm. Trade restrictions interfere with the free flow of products across borders and tend to hurt the overall economy.

© JOSE LUIS PELAEZ, INC./IMAGE SOURCE/JUPITERIMAGES / © DYNAMIC GRAPHICS/CREATAS IMAGES/JUPITERIMAGES

Final Word

This chapter examined the four economic decision makers: households, firms, governments, and the rest of the world. Domestic households are by far the most important, for they supply resources and demand goods and services.

If you were to stop reading right now, you would already know more economics than most people. But to understand market economics, you must learn how markets work. The next chapter introduces demand and supply.

Multiple Choice Questions

1. Harold, a delivery man, washes and irons his own shirts. Sarah, his boss, sends her clothes to a laundry. Which is the most plausible economic explanation for this difference?
   a. Harold must enjoy ironing more than Sarah does.
   b. Harold must be better at ironing than Sarah is.
   c. The opportunity cost of ironing is greater for Harold.
   d. Harold probably has an absolute advantage in ironing.
   e. Sarah has a higher opportunity cost of laundering her clothes than Harold does.
2. Rationality in the household decision-making process means that
   a. all households make the same decisions
   b. everyone in the household agrees on all decisions
   c. households act in their own best interests
   d. households want to earn as much income as possible
   e. all households would make the same decisions given the same information on products qualities and prices
3. A cottage industry is one that
   a. produces rural housing
   b. takes advantage of the division of labor
   c. uses highly specialized resources in a complex production process
   d. produces cottage cheese
   e. carries out production in workers' homes
4. A large number of businesses are organized as sole proprietorships because it is easy for them to acquire large sums of financing.
   a. True
   b. False
5. Suppose you own a proprietorship that is in serious financial difficulty. The assets of the company are $100,000, but liabilities are $175,000. You also have, however, stock in General Motors worth $200,000. If you file bankruptcy, what amount of personal assets do you stand to lose?
   a. $100,000
   b. $75,000
   c. $200,000
   d. $275,000
   e. $375,000
6. A realized capital gain is
   a. the difference between the price of a share of stock and what the investor paid for it (i.e., the broker's fee)
   b. the difference between the original value of a piece of equipment and its depreciated value
   c. an increase in the net worth of a sole proprietorship or partnership
   d. an increase in the market value of a share of stock held by an individual
   e. the difference between the selling price and the purchase price of a share of stock
7. One reason why Jim mows his own lawn instead of hiring Mike to mow the lawn is:
   a. It is cheaper to hire Mike to mow Jim's lawn
   b. Jim has a lower opportunity cost of his time
   c. Mike has a lower opportunity cost of his time
   d. Mike lawnmower is better than Mike's lawnmower
   e. Jim has a higher opportunity cost of his time
8. Household production is more likely to occur when
   a. it requires many specialized resources
   b. technology makes it more costly than market production
   c. tax avoidance is undesirable
   d. less control over the final product is desirable
   e. the opportunity cost of household work is relatively small
9. Natural monopolies occur when
   a. government antitrust laws are too weak or not enforced
   b. negative externalities are present
   c. firms collude to set prices and divide the market among themselves
   d. one firm can service the market more cheaply than two or more firms can
   e. a public good is produced by a private firm
10. Which of the following is a defining characteristic of a public good?
   a. It is produced and distributed by the government.
   b. The decision to produce it is made by the public through the voting process.

c. It is produced and distributed by private firms according to government regulations.
d. It is freely available to everyone once it is produced.
e. It is purchased by one government agency from another government agency.

11. The funds to pay for police protection are usually raised through taxation because
    a. police protection would be hard to provide exclusively to those who voluntarily pay for it
    b. people would not voluntarily pay salaries to officials who might arrest them
    c. police protection is a basic necessity
    d. goods financed through taxation can be guaranteed to all who pay for it
    e. the government believes that those who receive the benefits from the service should pay for it
12. A public good is one that is supplied to
    a. only people who pay for it
    b. only people who do not pay for it
    c. all people, regardless of whether they pay or not
    d. the government from private firms
    e. foreign governments from our federal government
13. What is the rationale for government provision of education?
    a. Not all incomes are equal, but everyone has the right to education regardless of wealth.
    b. Potential students consider only their personal benefits gained from education, but the rest of society benefits, too.
    c. No education would be provided in the absence of government provision because everyone would consume it without paying.
    d. The cost of providing education for the entire public is too large.
    e. The government can provide education at a much lower cost than the private sector.
14. Externalities are defined as
    a. any transaction external to the firm
    b. costs or benefits that fall on third parties
    c. policies that firms undertake to sell products outside the country
    d. managers' dealings with stockholders outside the firm
    e. costs of maintaining plant and equipment to avoid the scrutiny of external auditors
15. Which of the following is *not* a government transfer program?
    a. unemployment compensation
    b. Social Security
    c. food stamps
    d. Medicare
    e. movement of soldiers to a different military base
16. Government policies are coercive, whereas markets are not. This implies that
    a. government activity will always be less efficient than market activity
    b. households cannot maximize utility if they consume any government goods and services
    c. market transactions result in an equal number of gainers and losers
    d. self-interest and public interest are always in conflict
    e. government can provide some goods and services when private markets fail to do so
17. Bradley earns $150,000 a year. For the first $50,000 he earns, the tax rate is 10%. For the next $50,000 he earns, Bradley has to pay a tax rate of 8%, and for the last $50, 000 he earns the tax rate is 5%. Based on this information, which of the following is correct?
    a. The tax system is proportional
    b. Bradley pays $25,000 in taxes each year
    c. The tax system is progressive
    d. The tax system is regressive
    e. Bradley pays too much tax
18. A tax is said to be progressive if
    a. the absolute size of the tax (in dollars) increases as income increases
    b. the wealthy pay a smaller percentage of their income than the poor
    c. the average tax rate falls as income rises
    d. the proportion of income paid as taxes increases as income increases
    e. the proceeds are used to pay for liberal political programs
19. A tax collects $3,000 per year from a family with an income of $25,000 and takes $4,000 per year from a family with an income of $50,000. This tax plan is
    a. regressive
    b. proportional
    c. progressive
    d. based on the ability-to-pay principle
    e. impossible to determine with the information provided

20. Katie had a before-tax income of $40,000 and paid taxes of $6,000. Rinji had a before-tax income of $35,000 and paid taxes of $5,250. Based on this information, the tax system is
    a. There is insufficient information to answer the question.
    b. progressive
    c. based on the benefits received
    d. regressive
    e. proportional

Answers

1. e 2. c 3. e 4. b 5. b 6. e 7. b 8. e 9. d 10. d
11. a 12. c 13. b 14. b 15. e 16. e 17. d 18. d 19. a 20. e

LONG ANSWER QUESTIONS

LO1 Explain the role of the household in an economic system

1.1. *(Evolution of the Household)* Determine whether each of the following would increase or decrease the opportunity costs for mothers who choose not to work outside the home. Explain your answers.
   a. Higher levels of education for women
   b. Higher unemployment rates for women
   c. Higher average pay levels for women
   d. Lower demand for labor in industries that traditionally employ large numbers of women

1.2. *(Household Production)* Many households supplement their food budget by cultivating small vegetable gardens. Explain how each of the following might influence this kind of household production:
   a. Both husband and wife are professionals who earn high salaries.
   b. The household is located in a city rather than in a rural area.
   c. The household is located in a region where there is a high sales tax on food.
   d. The household is located in a region that has a high property tax rate.

1.3. *(Household Production)* What factors does a householder consider when deciding whether to produce a good or service at home or buy it in the marketplace?

1.4. *(Objectives of the Economic Decision Makers)* In economic analysis, what are the assumed objectives of households, firms, and the government?

LO2 Identify the different types of firms and describe their roles in the economy

2.1. *(Corporations)* How did the institution of the firm get a boost from the advent of the Industrial Revolution? What type of business organization existed before this?

2.2. *(Sole Proprietorships)* What are the disadvantages of the sole proprietorship form of business?

2.3. *(Cooperatives)* How do cooperatives differ from typical businesses?

2.4. *(Evolution of the Firm)* Explain how production after the Industrial Revolution differed from production under the cottage industry system.

LO3 Outline the ways governments affect their economies

3.1. *(Government)* Complete each of the following sentences:
   a. When the private operation of a market leads to overproduction or underproduction of some good, this is known as a(n) ________.
   b. Goods that are nonrival and nonexcludable are known as ________.
   c. ________ are cash or in-kind benefits given to individuals as outright grants from the government.
   d. A(n) ________ confers an external benefit on third parties that are not directly involved in a market transaction.
   e. ________ refers to the government's pursuit of full employment and price stability through variations in taxes and government spending.

3.2. *(Tax Rates)* Suppose taxes are related to income level as follows:

Income	Taxes
$1,000	$200
$2,000	$350
$3,000	$450

   a. What percentage of income is paid in taxes at each level?
   b. Is the tax rate progressive, proportional, or regressive?
   c. What is the marginal tax rate on the first $1,000 of income? The second $1,000? The third $1,000?

3.3. *(Government Revenue)* What are the sources of government revenue in the United States? Which types of taxes are most important at each level of government? Which two taxes provide the most revenue to the federal government?

3.4. *(Externalities)* Suppose there is an external cost, or negative externality, associated with production of a certain good. What's wrong with letting the market determine how much of this good will be produced?

3.4 Mention some of the sources of market failure. Under such circumstances, can the society's welfare be improved by government intervention?

3.5 State and explain the different ways in which government intervention may improve efficiency. In this context, explain in detail how governments deal with externalities?

3.6 How is proportional taxation different from progressive taxation? What do you understand by the term 'regressive' taxation?

LO4 Outline the international influences on an economy

4.1. *(International Trade)* Why does international trade occur? What does it mean to run a deficit in the merchandise trade balance?

4.2. *(International Trade)* Distinguish between a tariff and a quota. Who benefits from and who is harmed by such restrictions on imports?

4.3 Explain the difference between 'trade balance' and 'balance of payment'? What are the different ways in which trade restrictions may be imposed?

ECONOMIC DECISION MAKERS

Chapter in Review

3

KEY TERMS

utility
the satisfaction received from consumption; sense of well-being

Self-employed
person who operate their own farm or non-farm enterprises or are engaged independently in a profession or trade on own-account or with one or a few partners who are treated as self-employed in household enterprises

regular wage/salaried employee
is that person who works in others' farm or non-farm enterprises (both household and non-household) and, in return, receives salary or wages on a regular basis (i.e., not on the basis of daily or periodic renewal of work contract)

casual wage laborer
a person, who is casually engaged in others' farm or nonfarm enterprises (both household and non-household) and, in return, receives wages according to the terms of the daily or periodic work contract

transfer payments
cash or in-kind benefits given to individuals as outright grants from the government

Industrial Revolution
development of large-scale factory production that began in Great Britain around 1750 and spread to the rest of Europe, North America, and Australia

firms
economic units formed by profit-seeking entrepreneurs who employ resources to produce goods and services for sale

sole proprietorship
a firm with a single owner who has the right to all profits but who also bears unlimited liability for the firm's losses and debts

partnership
a firm with multiple owners who share the profits and bear unlimited liability for the firm's losses and debts

corporation
a legal entity owned by stockholders whose liability is limited to the value of their stock ownership

cooperative
an organization consisting of people who pool their resources to buy and sell more efficiently than they could individually

not-for-profit organizations
groups that do not pursue profit as a goal; they engage in charitable, educational, humanitarian, cultural, professional, or other activities, often with a social purpose

LO1 Explain the role of the household in an economic system.

Households play the starring role in a market economy. Their demand for goods and services determines what gets produced and their supplies of labor, capital, natural resources, and entrepreneurial ability produce that output. As demanders of goods and services and suppliers of resources, households make all kinds of choices in an attempt to maximize utility.

Rural and Urban Household Types in India: Categorized by Major Source of Income and Average Monthly Per Capita Expenditure (2009–10)

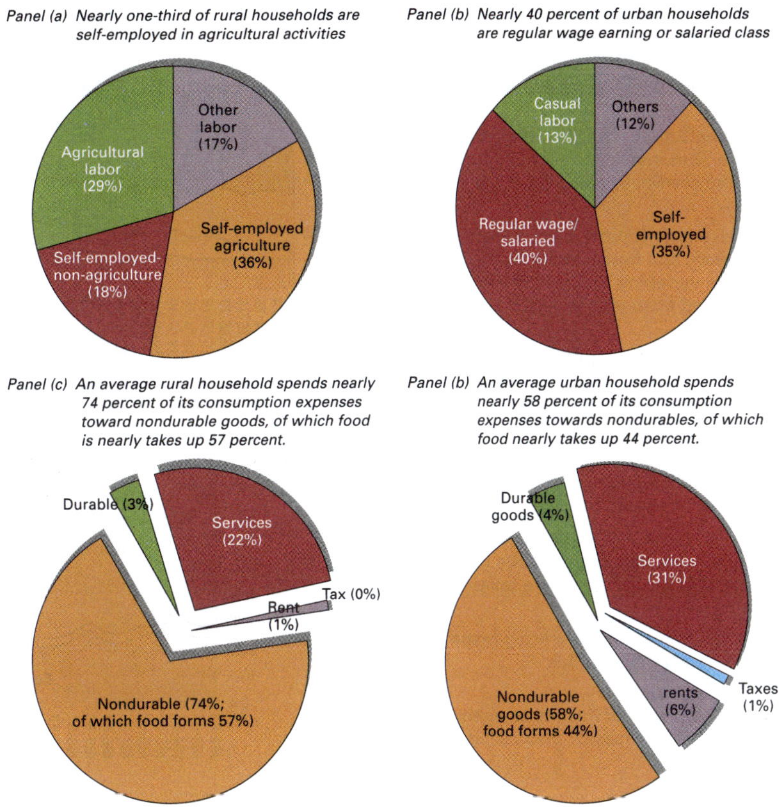

LO2 Identify the different types of firms and describe their roles in the economy.

Firms are economic units formed by entrepreneurs who combine labor, capital, and natural resources to produce goods and services in an attempt to maximize profit. For-profit firms organize in one of three ways: as a sole proprietorship, as a partnership, or as a corporation. Not-for-profit organizations engage in activities that often have a social purpose, while cooperatives are groups that organize with the goal of minimizing costs.

Type of Firms in India and Their Total Output (2009–2010)

Panel (a) Type of firms in India (2009-10)   Panel (b) Total output by type of firms (2009-10)

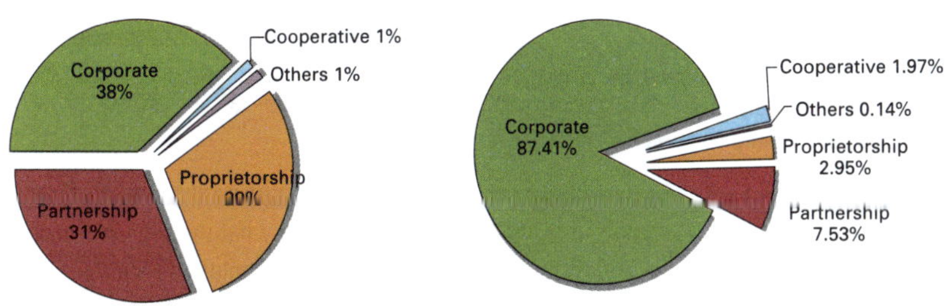

SOURCE: Based upon data from Annual Survey of Industries, 2009-2010. Available at http://mospi.nic.in.

market failure
a condition that arises when the unregulated operation of markets yields socially undesirable results

monopoly
a sole supplier of a product with no close substitutes

natural monopoly
one firm that can supply the entire market at a lower per-unit cost than could two or more firms

private good
a good that is both rival in consumption and exclusive, such as pizza

public good
a good that, once produced, is available for all to consume, regardless of who pays and who doesn't; such a good is nonrival and nonexclusive, such as a safer community

externality
a cost or a benefit that affects neither the buyer or seller, but instead affects people not involved in the market transaction

fiscal policy
the use of government purchases, transfer payments, taxes, and borrowing to influence economy-wide variables such as inflation, employment, and economic growth

monetary policy
regulation of the money supply to influence economy-wide variables such as inflation, employment, and economic growth

ability-to-pay tax principle
those with a greater ability to pay, such as those earning higher incomes or those owning more property, should pay more taxes

benefits-received tax principle
those who get more benefits from the government program should pay more taxes

tax incidence
the distribution of tax burden among taxpayers; who ultimately pays the tax

proportional taxation
the tax as a percentage of income remains constant as income increases; also called a flat tax

progressive taxation
the tax as a percentage of income increases as income increases

marginal tax rate
the percentage of each additional dollar of income that goes to the tax

regressive taxation
the tax as a percentage of income decreases as income increases

merchandise trade balance
the value during a given period of a country's exported goods minus the value of its imported goods

balance of payments
a record of all economic transactions during a given period between residents of one country and residents of the rest of the world

foreign exchange
foreign money needed to carry out international transactions

tariff
a tax on imports

quota
a legal limit on the quantity of a particular product that can be imported

LO3 **Outline the ways governments affect their economies.** Governments attempt to improve society's overall welfare by intervening in cases of market failure. Beneficial government interventions in markets include establishing and enforcing the rules of the game, promoting competition, regulating natural monopolies, providing public goods, dealing with externalities, more equally distributing income, and pursuing full employment, price stability, and economic growth.

Outlays of the Central Government of India

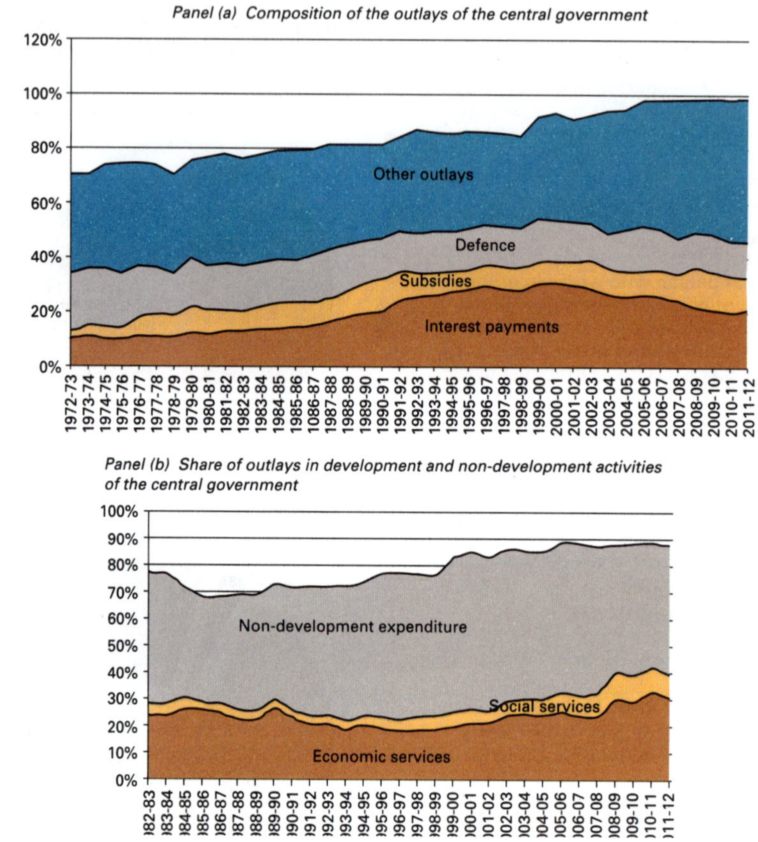

Tax receipts of Central Government

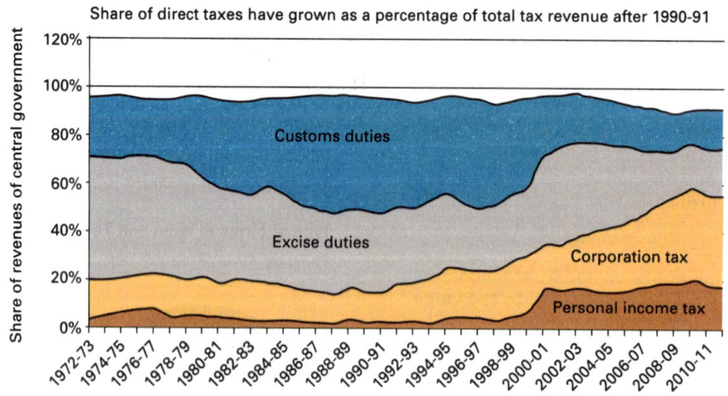

LO4 **Outline the international influences on an economy.** The rest of the world affects what the country's households consume and what firms produce. The country's households and firms are consumers and suppliers of manufactured goods and raw materials from and to foreign economies, and these transactions impact the country's prices, wages, and profits. International trade, exchange rates, and trade restrictions all affect the country's economy.

CHAPTER

4

Demand, Supply, *and* Markets

Learning Outcomes

- LO 1 Explain how the law of demand affects market activity
- LO 2 Explain how the law of supply affects market activity
- LO 3 Describe how the interaction between supply and demand creates markets
- LO 4 Describe how markets reach equilibrium
- LO 5 Explain how markets react during periods of disequilibrium

© STOCKBYTE/GETTY IMAGES

"Why do roses cost more on Valentine's Day than during the rest of the year?"

Why do roses cost more on Valentine's Day than during the rest of the year? Why do TV ads cost more airing them during a popular sport than during normal course of performance? Why do hotels in hill stations charge more in summers than in winters? Why do surgeons earn more than butchers? Why do cricket pros earn more than hockey pros? Answers to these and most economic questions boil down to the workings of demand and supply—the subject of this chapter.

This chapter introduces demand and supply and shows how they interact in competitive markets. *Demand and supply are the most fundamental and the most powerful of all economic tools*—important enough to warrant a chapter. Indeed, some believe that if you program a computer to answer "demand and supply" to every economic question, you could put many economists out of work. An understanding of the two ideas will take you far in mastering the art and science of economic analysis. This chapter uses graphs, so you may need to review the Chapter 1 appendix as a refresher.

What do you think?

Professional athletes should earn comparable salaries regardless of the sport they play.

Strongly Disagree					*Strongly Agree*	
1	2	3	4	5	6	7

Topics discussed in Chapter 4 include:

- Demand and quantity demanded
- Movement along a demand curve
- Shift of a demand curve
- Supply and quantity supplied
- Movement along a supply curve
- Shift of a supply curve
- Markets and equilibrium
- Disequilibrium

LO1 Demand

How many Pepsi can will one buy each month at a price of ₹15? What if the price is ₹10? What if it's ₹20? The answers reveal the relationship between the price of Pepsi and the quantity demanded. Such a relationship is called the *demand* for Pepsi. **Demand** indicates the quantity consumers are both *willing and able* to buy at each possible price during a given time period, other things constant. Because demand pertains to a specific

demand
a relation between the price of a good and the quantity that consumers are willing and able to buy per period, other things constant

period—a day, a week, a month—think of demand as the *amounts purchased per period* at each possible price. Also, notice the emphasis on *willing and able*. You may be *able* to buy a new Harley-Davidson XL 883 Sportster for $6,999 because you can afford one, but you may not be *willing* to buy one if motorcycles don't interest you. Similarly, you may be willing to buy a yacht but you may not be able to buy it for lack of resources. Thus, in order for something to be demanded, the consumer must be both willing and able to buy the commodity.

Sell for less, and the world will beat a path to your door.

The Law of Demand

In 1962, Sam Walton opened his first store in Rogers, Arkansas, with a sign that read "Wal-Mart Discount City. We sell for less." Wal-Mart now sells more than any other retailer in the world because prices are among the lowest around. As a consumer, you understand why people buy more at a lower price. Sell for less, and the world will beat a path to your door. Wal-Mart, for example, sells on average over 20,000 pairs of shoes *an hour*. This relation between the price and the quantity demanded is an economic law. The **law of demand** says that quantity demanded varies inversely with price, other things constant. Thus, the higher the price, the smaller the quantity demanded; the lower the price, the greater the quantity demanded.

law of demand
the quantity of a good that consumers are willing and able to buy per period relates inversely, or negatively, to the price, other things constant

substitution effect of a price change
when the price of a good falls, that good becomes cheaper compared to other goods so consumers tend to substitute that good for other goods

money income
the number of dollars a person receives per period, such as $400 per week

real income
income measured in terms of the goods and services it can buy; real income changes when the price changes

Demand, Wants, and Needs

Consumer demand and wants are not the same. As we have seen, wants are unlimited. You may want a new Mercedes SL600 Roadster convertible, but the $139,975 price tag is likely beyond your budget (that is, the quantity you demand at that price is zero). Nor is demand the same as need. You may need a new muffler for your car, but a price of $300 is just too high for you. If, however, the price drops enough—say, to $200—then you become both willing and able to buy one.

The Substitution Effect of a Price Change

What explains the law of demand? Why, for example, is more demanded at a lower price? The explanation begins with unlimited wants confronting scarce resources. Many goods and services could satisfy particular wants. For example, you can satisfy your hunger with pizza, burgers, chicken, or hundreds of other foods. Similarly, you can satisfy your desire for warmth in the winter with warm clothing, a home-heating system, a trip to Goa, or in many other ways. Clearly, some alternatives have more appeal than others (a trip to Goa is more fun than warm clothing). In a world without scarcity, everything would be free, so you would always choose the most attractive alternative. Scarcity, however, is a reality, and the degree of scarcity of one good relative to another helps determine each good's relative price.

Notice that the definition of *demand* includes the other-things-constant assumption. Among the "other things" assumed to remain constant are the prices of other goods. For example, if the price of pizza declines while other prices remain constant, pizza becomes relatively cheaper. Consumers are more *willing* to purchase pizza when its relative price falls; they substitute pizza for other goods. This principle is called the **substitution effect of a price change**. On the other hand, an increase in the price of pizza, other things constant, increases the opportunity cost of pizza. This higher opportunity cost causes consumers to substitute other goods for the now higher-priced pizza, thus reducing their quantity of pizza demanded. Remember that it *is the change in the relative price—the price of one good relative to the prices of other goods—that causes the substitution effect*. If all prices changed by the same percentage, there would be no change in relative prices and no substitution effect.

The Income Effect of a Price Change

A fall in the price increases the quantity demanded for a second reason. Suppose you earn $30 a week from a part-time job, so $30 is your money income. **Money income** is simply the number of dollars received per period, in this case, $30 per week. Suppose you spend all that income on pizza, buying three a week at $10 each. What if the price drops to $6? At the lower price you can now afford five pizzas a week. Your money income remains at $30 per week, but the decrease in the price has increased your **real income**—that is, your income measured in terms of what it can buy. The price reduction, other things constant, increases the purchasing power of your income, thereby increasing your ability to buy pizza. The quantity of pizza you demand will likely increase because of this income effect of a price change. You may not increase your quantity demanded to five pizzas, but you could. If you decide to purchase four pizzas a week when the price drops to $6, you would still have $6 remaining to buy other goods. Thus, the income effect of a lower price increases your real income and thereby increases your ability to purchase all goods. Because of the income effect, consumers typically increase their quantity demanded when the price declines.

Conversely, an increase in the price of a good, other things constant, reduces real income, thereby reducing the *ability* to purchase all goods. Because of the income effect, consumers typically reduce their quantity demanded when the price increases. Again, note that money income, not real income, is assumed to remain constant along a demand curve. A change in price changes your real income, so real income varies along a demand curve. The lower the price, the greater your real income.

The Demand Schedule and Demand Curve

Demand can be expressed as a *demand schedule* or as a *demand curve*. Exhibit 1a shows a hypothetical demand schedule for pizza. In describing demand, we must specify the units measured and the period

Exhibit 1a

The Demand Schedule for Pizza

	Price per Pizza	Quantity Demanded per Week (millions)
a	$15	8
b	12	14
c	9	20
d	6	26
e	3	32

© THINKSTOCK IMAGES/JUPITERIMAGES

considered. In our example, the unit is a 12-inch regular pizza and the period is a week. The schedule lists possible prices, along with the quantity demanded at each price. At a price of $15, for example, consumers demand 8 million pizzas per week. As you can see, the lower the price, other things constant, the greater the quantity demanded. Consumers substitute pizza for other foods. And as the price falls, real income increases, causing consumers to increase the quantity of pizza they demand. If the price drops as low as $3, consumers demand 32 million per week.

The demand schedule in Exhibit 1a appears as a demand curve in Exhibit 1b, with price measured on the vertical axis and the quantity demanded per week on the horizontal axis. Each price-quantity combination listed in the demand schedule in Exhibit 1a becomes a point in Exhibit 1*b*. Point *a*, for example, indicates that if the price is $15, consumers demand 8 million pizzas per week. These points connect to form the demand curve for pizza, labeled *D*. (By the way, some demand curves are straight lines, some are curved lines, and some are even jagged lines, but all are called demand *curves*.)

Exhibit 1b

The Demand Curve for Pizza

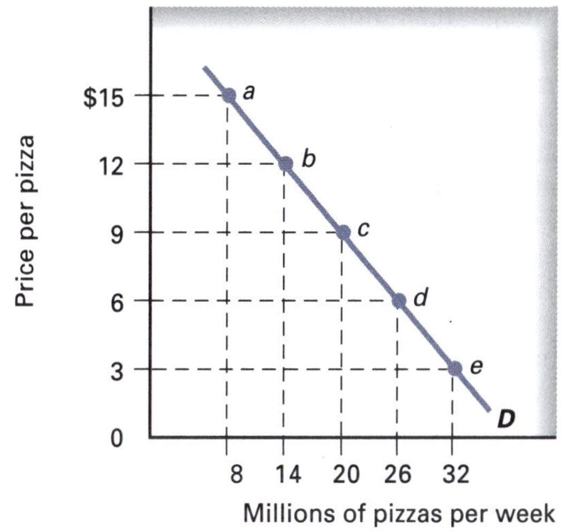

A demand curve slopes downward, reflecting the *law of demand*: Price and quantity demanded are inversely related, other things constant. Besides money income, also assumed constant along the demand curve are the prices of other goods. Thus, along the demand curve for pizza, the price of pizza changes *relative to the prices of other goods*. The demand curve shows the effect of a change in the *relative price* of pizza—that is, relative to other prices, which do not change.

Take care to distinguish between *demand* and *quantity demanded*. The *demand* for pizza is not a specific amount, but rather the *entire relationship* between

income effect of a price change
a fall in the price of a good increases consumers' real income, making consumers more able to purchase goods; for a normal good, the quantity demanded increases

demand curve
a curve showing the relation between the price of a good and the quantity consumers are willing and able to buy per period, other things constant

price and quantity demanded—represented by the demand schedule or the demand curve. An individual point on the demand curve indicates the **quantity demanded** at a particular price. For example, at a price of \$12, the quantity demanded is 14 million pizzas per week. If the price drops from \$12 to, say, \$9, this is shown in Exhibit 1b by *a movement along the demand curve*—in this case from point *b* to point *c*. Any movement along a demand curve reflects a *change in quantity demanded*, not a change in demand.

The law of demand applies to the millions of products sold in grocery stores, department stores, clothing stores, shoe stores, drugstores, music stores, bookstores, hardware stores, travel agencies, and restaurants, as well as through mail-order catalogs, the Yellow Pages, classified ads, online sites, stock markets, real estate markets, job markets, flea markets, and all other markets. The law of demand applies even to choices that seem more personal than economic, such as whether or not to own a pet. For example, after New York City passed an anti-dog-litter law, law-abiding owners had to follow their dogs around the city with scoopers, plastic bags—whatever would do the job. Because the law raised the personal cost of owning a dog, the quantity of dogs demanded decreased. Some owners simply abandoned their dogs, raising the number of strays in the city. The number of dogs left at animal shelters doubled. The law of demand predicts this inverse relation between cost, or price, and quantity demanded.

It is useful to distinguish between **individual demand**, which is the demand of an individual consumer, and **market demand**, which is the sum of the individual demands of all consumers in the market. In most markets, there are many consumers, sometimes millions. Unless otherwise noted, when we talk about demand, we are referring to market demand, as shown in Exhibit 1.

quantity demanded the amount of a good consumers are willing and able to buy per period at a particular price, as reflected by a point on a demand curve

individual demand a relation between the price of a good and the quantity purchased by an individual consumer per period, other things constant

market demand the relation between the price of a good and the quantity purchased by all consumers in the market during a given period, other things constant; sum of the individual demands in the market

© RADIUS IMAGES/JUPITERIMAGES

Shifts of the Demand Curve

A demand curve isolates the relation between the price of a good and quantity demanded when other factors that could affect demand remain unchanged. What are those other factors, and how do changes in them affect demand? Variables that can affect market demand are (1) the money income of consumers, (2) prices of other goods, (3) consumer expectations, (4) the number or composition of consumers in the market, (5) consumer tastes, and (6) advertising outlay. How do changes in each affect demand?

Changes in Consumer Income

Exhibit 2 shows the market demand curve *D* for pizza. This demand curve assumes a given level of money income. Suppose consumer income increases. Some consumers will then be willing and able to buy more pizza at each price, so market demand increases. The demand curve shifts to the right from *D* to *D*′. For example, at a price of \$12, the amount of pizza demanded increases from 14 million to 20 million per week, as indicated by the movement from point *b* on demand curve *D* to point *f* on demand curve *D*′. In short, *an increase in demand—that is, a rightward shift of the demand curve—means that consumers are willing and able to buy more pizza at each price.*

Exhibit 2

An Increase in the Market Demand for Pizza

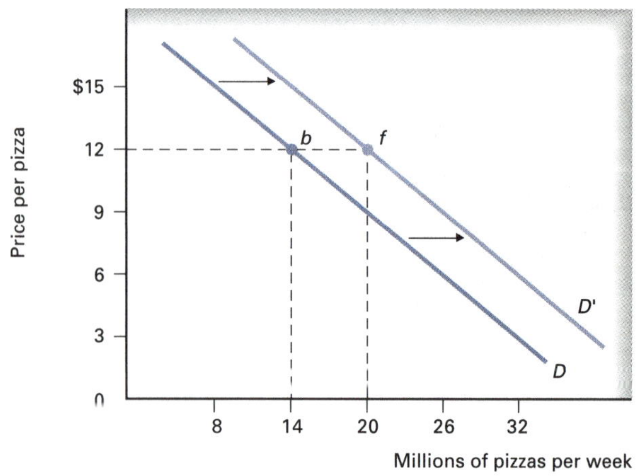

© THINKSTOCK IMAGES/JUPITERIMAGES

Goods are classified into two broad categories, depending on how demand responds to changes in money income. The demand for a normal good increases as money income increases. Because pizza is a normal good, its demand curve shifts rightward when money income increases. Most goods are normal. In contrast, demand for an inferior good actually decreases as money income increases, so the demand curve shifts leftward. Examples of inferior goods include low quality food grain, used furniture, and used clothing. As money income increases, consumers tend to switch from these inferior goods to normal goods (such as better quality food grain, new furniture, and new clothing).

Changes in the Prices of Other Goods

Again, the prices of other goods are assumed to remain constant along a given demand curve. Now let's bring these other prices into play. Consumers have various ways of trying to satisfy any particular want. Consumers choose among substitutes based on relative prices. For example, pizza and sandwiches are substitutes, though not perfect ones. An increase in the price of sandwiches, other things constant, reduces the quantity of sandwiches demanded along a given sandwiches demand curve. An increase in the price of sandwiches also increases the demand for pizza, shifting the demand curve for pizza to the right. Two goods are considered substitutes if an increase in the price of one shifts the demand for the other rightward and, conversely, if a decrease in the price of one shifts demand for the other leftward.

Goods used in combination are called *complements*. Examples include Coke and pizza, milk and cookies, computer software and hardware, and airline tickets and rental cars. Two goods are considered complements if an increase in the price of one decreases the demand for the other, shifting that demand curve leftward. For example, an increase in the price of pizza shifts the demand curve for Coke leftward. But most pairs of goods selected at random are *unrelated*—for example, pizza and housing, or milk and petrol. Still, an increase in the price of an unrelated good reduces the consumer's real income and can reduce the demand for pizza and other goods. For example, a sharp increase in petrol prices reduces the amount of income people have to spend on other goods, such as pizza.

Changes in Consumer Expectations

Another factor assumed constant along a given demand curve is consumer expectations about factors that influence demand, such as incomes or prices. A change in consumers' *income expectations* can shift the demand curve. For example, a consumer who learns about a pay raise might increase demand well before the raise takes effect. A college senior who lands that first real job may buy a new car even before graduation. Likewise, a change in consumers' *price expectations* can shift the demand curve. For example, if you expect the price of pizza to jump next week, you may buy an extra one today for the freezer, shifting this week's demand for pizza rightward. Or if consumers come to believe that home prices will climb next month, some will increase their demand for housing now, shifting this month's demand for housing rightward. On the other hand, if housing prices are expected to fall next month, some consumers will postpone purchases, thereby shifting this month's housing demand leftward.

Changes in the Number or Composition of Consumers

As mentioned earlier, the market demand curve is the sum of the individual demand curves of all consumers in the market. If the number of consumers changes, the demand curve will shift. For example, if the population grows, the demand curve for pizza will shift rightward. Even if total population remains unchanged, demand could shift with a change in the composition of the population. For example, a bulge in the teenage population could shift pizza demand rightward. A baby boom would shift rightward the demand for car seats and baby food. A growing student population would affect the demand for fast foods.

Changes in Consumer Tastes

What kind of toppings do you like on your pizza?

normal good
a good, such as new clothes, for which demand increases, or shifts rightward, as consumer income rises

inferior good
a good, such as used clothes, for which demand decreases, or shifts leftward, as consumer income rises

substitutes
goods, such as Coke and Pepsi, that relate in such a way that an increase in the price of one shifts the demand for the other rightward

complements
goods, such as milk and cookies, that relate in such a way that an increase in the price of one shifts the demand for the other leftward

Are you into tattoos and body piercings? Is music to your ears more likely to be rock, country, hip-hop, reggae, R&B, jazz, funk, Latin, gospel, new age, or classical? Choices in food, body art, music, clothing, books, movies, TV—indeed, all consumer choices—are influenced by consumer tastes. **Tastes** are nothing more than your likes and dislikes as a consumer. What determines tastes? Your desires for food when hungry and drink when thirsty are largely biological. So too is your desire for comfort, rest, shelter, friendship, love, status, personal safety, and a pleasant environment. Your family background affects some of your tastes—your taste in food, for example, has been shaped by years of home cooking. Other influences include the surrounding culture, peer pressure, and religious convictions. So economists can say a little about the origin of tastes, but they claim no special expertise in understanding how tastes develop and change over time. Economists recognize, however, that tastes have an important impact on demand. For example, although pizza is popular, some people just don't like it, and those who are lactose intolerant can't stomach the cheese topping. Thus, most people like pizza but some don't.

In our analysis of consumer demand, *we will assume that tastes are given and are relatively stable.* Tastes are assumed to remain constant along a given demand curve. A change in the tastes for a particular good would shift that good's demand curve. For example, a discovery that the tomato sauce and cheese combination on pizza promotes overall health could change consumer tastes, shifting the demand curve for pizza to the right. But because a change in tastes is so difficult to isolate from other economic changes, we should be reluctant to attribute a shift of the demand curve to a change in tastes. We try to rule out other possible reasons for a shift of the demand curve before accepting a change in tastes as the explanation.

tastes
consumer preferences; likes and dislikes in consumption; assumed to remain constant along a given demand curve

movement along a demand curve
change in quantity demanded resulting from a change in the price of the good, other things constant

shift of a demand curve
movement of a demand curve right or left resulting from a change in one of the determinants of demand other than the price of the good

supply
a relation between the price of a good and the quantity that producers are willing and able to sell per period, other things constant

law of supply
the amount of a good that producers are willing and able to sell per period is usually directly related to its price, other things constant

supply curve
a curve showing the relation between the price of a good and the quantity producers are willing and able to sell per period other things constant

That wraps up our look at changes in demand. Before we turn to supply, you should remember the distinction between a **movement along a given demand curve** and a **shift of a demand curve**. A change in *price*, other things constant, causes a *movement along a demand curve*, changing the quantity demanded. A change in one of the determinants of demand other than price causes a *shift of a demand curve*, changing demand.

LO2 Supply

Just as demand is a relation between price and quantity demanded, supply is a relation between price and quantity supplied. **Supply** indicates how much producers are *willing* and *able* to offer for sale per period at each possible price, other things constant. The **law of supply** states that the quantity supplied is usually directly related to its price, other things constant. Thus, the lower the price, the smaller the quantity supplied; the higher the price, the greater the quantity supplied.

© THINKSTOCK IMAGES/JUPITERIMAGES

The Supply Schedule and Supply Curve

Exhibit 3 presents the market *supply schedule* and market **supply curve** S for pizza. Both show the quantities supplied per week at various possible prices by the thousands of pizza makers in the economy. As you can see, price and quantity supplied are directly, or positively, related. Producers offer more at a higher price than at a lower price, so the supply curve slopes upward.

Exhibit 3a

The Supply Schedule for Pizza

Price per Pizza	Quantity Supplied per Week (millions)
$15	28
12	24
0	20
6	16
3	12

There are two reasons why producers offer more for sale when the price rises. First, as the price increases, other things constant, a producer becomes more *willing* to supply the good. Prices act as signals to existing and potential suppliers about the rewards for producing various goods. A higher pizza price attracts resources from lower-valued uses. *A higher price makes producers more willing to increase quantity supplied.*

Higher prices also increase the producer's *ability* to supply the good. The law of increasing opportunity cost, as noted in Chapter 2, states that the opportunity cost of producing more of a particular good rises as output increases—that is, the *marginal cost* of production increases as output increases. Because producers face a higher marginal cost for additional output, they need to get a higher price for that output to be *able* to increase the quantity supplied. *A higher price makes producers more able to increase quantity supplied.* As a case in point, a higher price for gasoline increases oil companies' ability to extract oil from tar sands, to drill deeper, and to explore in less accessible areas, such as the remote jungles of the Amazon, the stormy waters of the North Sea, and the frozen tundra above the Arctic Circle.

>> Higher gasoline prices increase a company's ability to explore and drill in less accessible areas.

© PETER & GEORGINA BOWATER/STOCK CONNECTION/JUPITERIMAGES

Exhibit 3b

The Supply Curve for Pizza

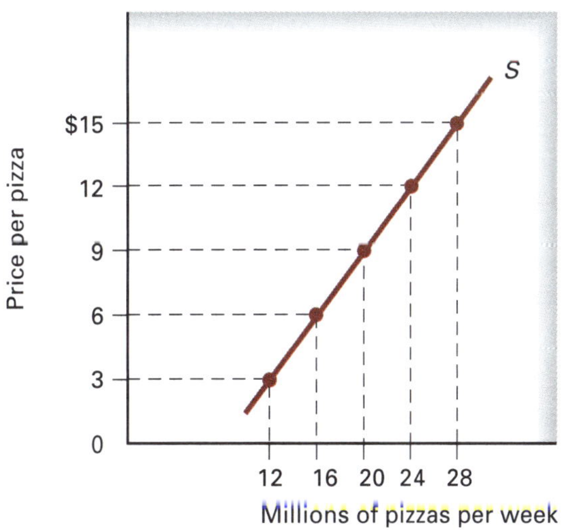

Thus, a higher price makes producers more *willing* and more *able* to increase quantity supplied. Producers are more *willing* because production becomes more profitable than other uses of the resources involved. Producers are more *able* because they can afford to cover the higher marginal cost that typically results from increasing output.

As with demand, we distinguish between *supply* and **quantity supplied**. *Supply* is the entire relationship between prices and quantities supplied, as reflected by the supply schedule or supply curve. *Quantity supplied* refers to a particular amount offered for sale at a particular price, as reflected by a point on a given supply curve. We also distinguish between **individual supply**, the supply of an individual producer, and **market supply**, the sum of individual supplies of all producers in the market. Unless otherwise noted, the term *supply* refers to market supply.

quantity supplied the amount offered for sale per period at a particular price, as reflected by a point on a given supply curve

individual supply the relation between the price of a good and the quantity an individual producer is willing and able to sell per period, other things constant

market supply the relation between the price of a good and the quantity all producers are willing and able to sell per period, other things constant

Shifts of the Supply Curve

The supply curve isolates the relation between the price of a good and the quantity supplied, other things constant. Assumed constant along a supply curve are the determinants of supply other than the price of the good, including (1) the state of technology, (2) the prices of relevant resources, (3) the prices of alternative goods, (4) producer expectations, and (5) the number of producers in the market. Let's see how a change in each affects the supply curve.

Changes in Technology

Recall from Chapter 2 that the state of technology represents the economy's knowledge about how to combine resources efficiently. Along a given supply curve, technology is assumed to remain unchanged. If a better technology is discovered, production costs will fall, so suppliers will be more willing and able to supply the good at each price. Consequently, supply will increase, as reflected by a rightward shift of the supply curve. For example, suppose a new high-tech oven that costs the same as existing ovens bakes pizza in half the time. Such a breakthrough would shift the market supply curve rightward, as from S to S′ in Exhibit 4, where more is supplied at each possible price. For example, at a price of \$12, the amount supplied increases from 24 million to 28 million pizzas, as shown in Exhibit 4 by the movement from point *g* to point *h*. In short, *an increase in supply—that is, a rightward shift of the supply curve—means that producers are willing and able to sell more pizza at each price.*

© THINKSTOCK IMAGES/JUPITERIMAGES

Changes in the Prices of Relevant Resources

Relevant resources are those employed in the production of the good in question. For example, suppose the price of mozzarella cheese falls. This price decrease reduces the cost of making pizza, so producers are more willing and better able to supply it. The supply curve for pizza shifts rightward, as shown in Exhibit 4. On the other hand, an increase in the price of a relevant resource reduces supply, meaning a shift of the supply curve leftward. For example, a higher price of mozzarella increases the cost of making pizza. Higher production costs decrease supply, as reflected by a leftward shift of the supply curve.

relevant resources resources used to produce the good in question

alternative goods other goods that use some or all of the same resources as the good in question

Exhibit 4

An Increase in the Supply of Pizza

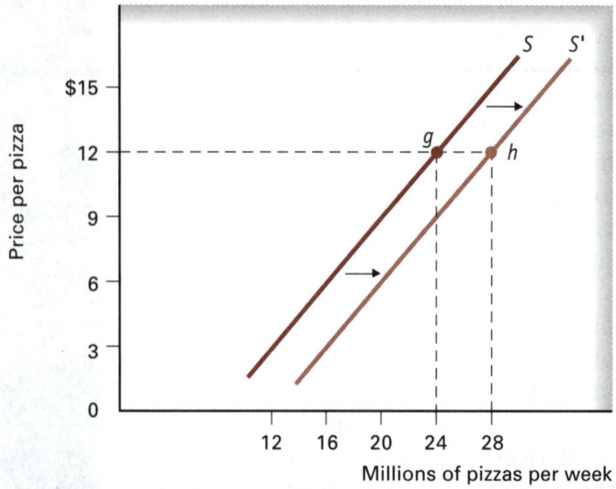

Changes in the Prices of Alternative Goods

Nearly all resources have alternative uses. The labor, building, machinery, ingredients, and knowledge needed to run a pizza business could produce other baked goods. **Alternative goods** are those that use some of the same resources employed to produce the good under consideration. For example, a decrease in the price of Italian bread reduces the opportunity cost of making pizza. As a result, some bread makers become pizza makers so the supply of pizza increases, shifting the supply curve of pizza rightward as in Exhibit 4. On the other hand, if the price of an alternative good, such as Italian bread, increases, supplying pizza becomes relatively less attractive compared to supplying Italian bread. As resources shift from pizza to bread, the supply of pizza decreases, or shifts to the left.

Changes in Producer Expectations

Changes in producer expectations can shift the supply curve. For example, a pizza maker expecting higher pizza prices in the future may expand his or her pizzeria now, thereby shifting the supply of pizza rightward. When a good can be easily stored (crude oil, for example, can be left in the ground), expecting higher prices in the future might prompt some producers to *reduce* their current supply while awaiting the higher price. Thus, an expectation of higher prices in the future could either increase or decrease current supply, depending on the good. More generally, any change affecting future profitability, such as a change in business taxes, could shift the supply curve now.

Changes in the Number of Producers

Because market supply sums the amounts supplied at each price by all producers, market supply depends on the number of producers in the market. If that number increases, supply will increase, shifting supply to the right. If the number of producers decreases, supply will decrease, shifting supply to the left. As an example of increased supply, the number of Café coffee day shops has increased, shifting the supply curve of coffee to the right.

Finally, note again the distinction between a **movement along a supply curve** and a **shift of a supply curve**. A change in *price*, other things constant, causes *a movement along a supply curve*, changing the quantity supplied. A change in one of the determinants of supply other than price causes a *shift of a supply curve*, changing supply.

You are now ready to bring demand and supply together.

LO3 Demand and Supply Create a Market

Demanders and suppliers have different views of price. Demanders pay the price and suppliers receive it. Thus, a higher price is bad news for consumers but good news for producers. As the price rises, consumers reduce their quantity demanded along the demand curve and producers increase their quantity supplied along the supply curve. How is this conflict between producers and consumers resolved?

Markets

A market sorts out differences between demanders and suppliers. A *market*, as you know from Chapter 1, includes all the arrangements used to buy and sell a particular good or service. Markets reduce **transaction costs**—the costs of time and information

© JOHN FOXX/STOCKBYTE/GETTY IMAGES

required for exchange. For example, suppose you are looking for a summer job. One approach might be to go from employer to employer looking for openings. But this could have you running around for days or weeks. A more efficient strategy would be to pick up a copy of the local newspaper or go online and look for openings. Classified ads and Web sites, which are elements of the job market, reduce the transaction costs of bringing workers and employers together.

The coordination that occurs through markets takes place not because of some central plan but because of Adam Smith's "invisible hand." For example, the auto dealers in your community tend to locate together, usually on the outskirts of town, where land is cheaper. The dealers congregate not because they all took an economics course or because they like one another's company but because together they become a more attractive destination for car buyers. A dealer who makes the mistake of locating away from the others misses out on a lot of business. Similarly, stores locate together so that more shoppers will be drawn by the call of the mall. From Orlando theme parks to Broadway theaters to Las Vegas casinos, suppliers congregate to attract demanders.

Market Equilibrium

To see how a market works, let's bring together market demand and supply. Exhibit 5 shows the market

movement along a supply curve
change in quantity supplied resulting from a change in the price of the good, other things constant

shift of a supply curve
movement of a supply curve left or right resulting from a change in one of the determinants of supply other than the price of the good

transaction costs
the costs of time and information required to carry out market exchange

Exhibit 5

Equilibrium in the Pizza Market

(a) Market schedules

	Millions of Pizzas per Week			
Price per Pizza	**Quantity Demanded**	**Quantity Supplied**	**Surplus or Shortage**	**Effect on Price**
$15	8	28	Surplus of 20	Falls
12	14	24	Surplus of 10	Falls
9	20	20	Equilibrium	Remains the same
6	26	16	Shortage of 10	Rises
3	32	12	Shortage of 20	Rises

(b) Market curves

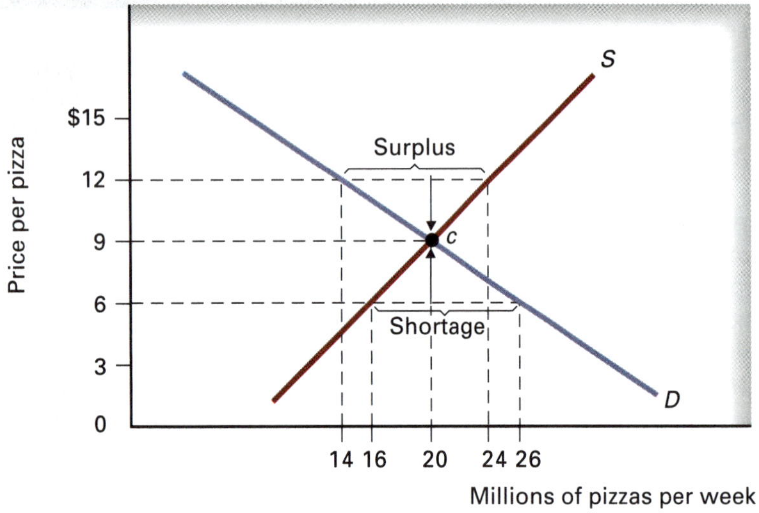

for pizza, using schedules in panel (a) and curves in panel (b). Suppose the price initially is $12. At that price, producers supply 24 million pizzas per week, but consumers demand only 14 million, resulting in an *excess quantity supplied*, or a **surplus**, of 10 million pizzas per week. Suppliers don't like getting stuck with unsold pizzas. Their desire to eliminate the surplus puts downward pressure on the price, as shown by the arrow pointing down in the graph. As the price falls, producers reduce their quantity supplied and consumers increase their quantity demanded. The price continues to fall as long as quantity supplied exceeds quantity demanded.

surplus at a given price, the amount by which quantity supplied exceeds quantity demanded; a surplus usually forces the price down

shortage at a given price, the amount by which quantity demanded exceeds quantity supplied; a shortage usually forces the price up

equilibrium the condition that exists in a market when the plans of buyers match those of sellers, so quantity demanded equals quantity supplied and the market clears

Alternatively, suppose the price initially is $6. You can see from Exhibit 5 that at that price, consumers demand 26 million pizzas but producers supply only 16 million, resulting in an *excess quantity demanded*, or a **shortage**, of 10 million pizzas per week. Producers quickly notice that they have sold out and those customers still demanding pizzas are grumbling. Profit-maximizing producers and frustrated consumers create market pressure for a higher price, as shown by the arrow pointing up in the graph. As the price rises, producers increase their quantity supplied and consumers reduce their quantity demanded. The price continues to rise as long as quantity demanded exceeds quantity supplied.

Thus, *a surplus creates downward pressure on the price, and a shortage creates upward pressure.* As long as quantity demanded differs from quantity supplied, this difference forces a price change. Note that a shortage or a surplus depends on the price. There is no such thing as a general shortage or a general surplus, only a shortage or a surplus at a particular price.

A market reaches equilibrium when the quantity demanded equals quantity supplied. In **equilibrium**, the independent plans of both buyers and sellers exactly match, so market forces exert no pressure for change. In Exhibit 5, the demand and supply curves intersect at the *equilibrium point*, identified as point *c*. The *equilibrium price* is $9 per pizza, and the *equilibrium quantity* is 20 million per week. At that price and quantity, the market *clears*. Because there is no shortage or surplus, there is no pressure for the price to change. The demand and supply curves form an "x" at the intersection. The equilibrium point is found where "x" marks the spot.

A market finds equilibrium through the independent actions of thousands, or even millions, of buyers and sellers. In one sense, the market is personal because each consumer and each producer makes a personal decision about how much to buy or sell at a given price. In another sense, the market is impersonal because it requires no conscious communication or coordination among consumers or producers. The price does all the talking. *Impersonal market forces synchronize the personal and independent decisions of many individual buyers and sellers to achieve equilibrium price and quantity.*

LO4 Changes in Equilibrium Price and Quantity

Equilibrium occurs when the intentions of demanders and suppliers exactly match. Once a market reaches equilibrium, that price and quantity prevail until something happens to demand or supply. A change in any determinant of demand or supply usually changes equilibrium price and quantity in a predictable way, as you'll see.

Shifts of the Demand Curve

In Exhibit 6, demand curve *D* and supply curve *S* intersect at point *c* to yield the initial equilibrium price of $9 and the initial equilibrium quantity of 20 million 12-inch regular pizzas per week. Now suppose that one of the determinants of demand changes in a way that increases demand, shifting the demand curve to the right from *D* to *D*′. Any of the following could shift the demand for pizza rightward: (1) an increase in the money income of consumers (because pizza is a normal good); (2) an increase in the price of a substitute, such as tacos, or a decrease in the price of a complement, such as Coke; (3) a change in consumer expectations that causes people to demand more pizzas now; (4) a growth in the number of pizza consumers; or (5) a change in consumer tastes—based, for example, on a discovery that the tomato sauce on pizza has antioxidant properties that improve overall health.

After the demand curve shifts rightward to *D*′ in Exhibit 6, the amount demanded at the initial price of $9 is 30 million pizzas, which exceeds the amount supplied of 20 million by 10 million pizzas. This shortage puts upward pressure on the price. As the price increases, the quantity demanded decreases along the new demand curve *D*′, and the quantity supplied increases along the existing supply curve *S* until the two quantities are equal once again at equilibrium point *g*. The new equilibrium price is $12, and the new equilibrium quantity is 24 million pizzas per week. Thus, given an upward-sloping supply curve, an increase in demand increases both equilibrium price and quantity. A decrease in demand would lower both equilibrium price and quantity. These results can be summarized as follows: *Given an upward-sloping supply curve, a rightward shift of the demand curve increases both equilibrium price and quantity and a leftward shift decreases both equilibrium price and quantity.*

© THINKSTOCK IMAGES/JUPITERIMAGES

Exhibit 6

Effects of an Increase in Demand

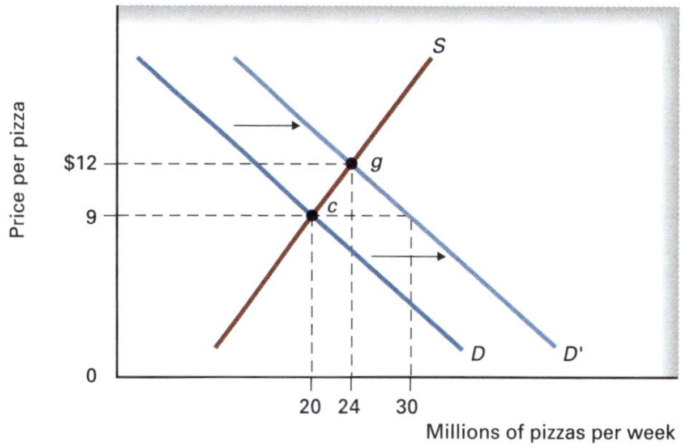

Shifts of the Supply Curve

Let's consider shifts of the supply curve. In Exhibit 7, as before, we begin with demand curve *D* and supply curve *S* intersecting at point *c* to yield an equilibrium price of $9 and an equilibrium quantity of 20 million pizzas per week. Suppose one of the determinants of supply changes, increasing supply from *S* to *S*′. Changes that could shift the supply curve rightward include (1) a technological breakthrough in pizza ovens; (2) a reduction in the price of a relevant resource, such as mozzarella cheese; (3) a decline in the price of an alternative good, such as Italian bread; (4) a change in expectations that encourages pizza makers to expand production now; or (5) an increase in the number of pizzerias.

After the supply curve shifts rightward in Exhibit 7, the amount supplied at the initial price of $9 increases from 20 million to 30 million, so produc-

Exhibit 7

Effects of an Increase in Supply

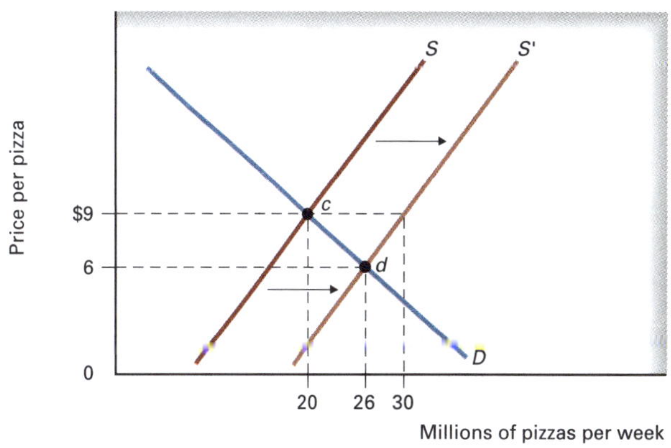

ers now supply 10 million more pizzas than consumers demand. This surplus forces the price down. As the price falls, the quantity supplied declines along the new supply curve but the quantity demanded increases along the existing demand curve until a new equilibrium point *d* is established. The new equilibrium price is $6, and the new equilibrium quantity is 26 million pizzas per week. In short, an increase in supply reduces the price and increases the quantity. On the other hand, a decrease in supply increases the price but decreases the quantity. Thus, *given a downward-sloping demand curve, a rightward shift of the supply curve decreases price but increases quantity, and a leftward shift increases price but decreases quantity.*

Exhibit 8

Indeterminate Effect of an Increase in Both Demand and Supply

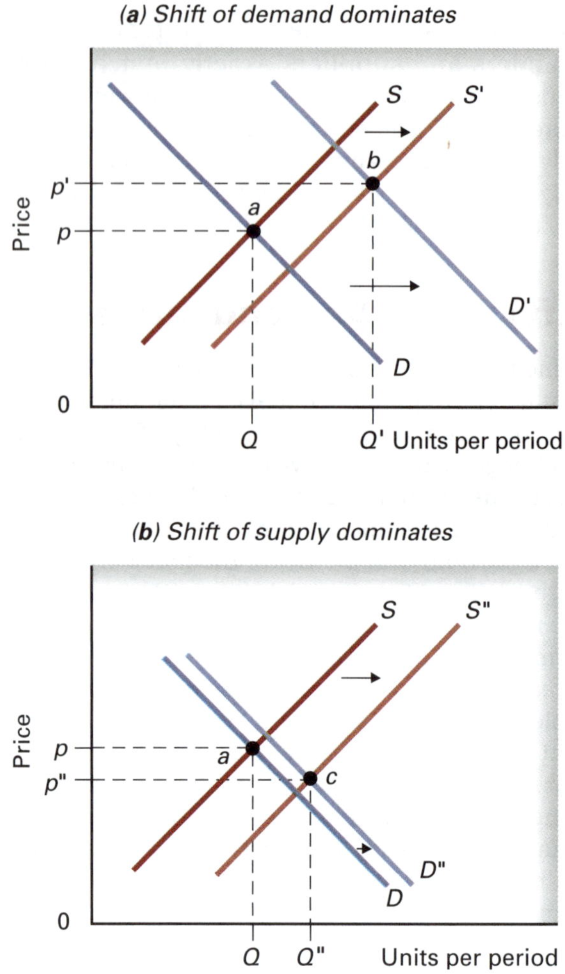

Simultaneous Shifts of Demand and Supply Curves

As long as only one curve shifts, we can say for sure how equilibrium price and quantity will change. If both curves shift, however, the outcome is less obvious. For example, suppose both demand and supply increase, or shift rightward, as in Exhibit 8. Note that in panel (a), demand shifts more than supply, and in panel (b), supply shifts more than demand. In both panels, equilibrium quantity increases. The change in equilibrium price, however, depends on which curve shifts more. If demand shifts more, as in panel (a), equilibrium price increases. For example, between 1995 and 2005, the demand for housing in the U.S. increased more than the supply, so both price and quantity increased. But if supply shifts more, as in panel (b), equilibrium price decreases. For example, in the last decade, the supply of personal computers has increased more than the demand, so price has decreased and quantity increased.

Conversely, if both demand and supply decrease, or shift leftward, equilibrium quantity decreases. But, again, we cannot say what will happen to equilibrium price unless we examine relative shifts. (You can use Exhibit 8 to consider decreases in demand and supply by viewing D' and S' as the initial curves.) If demand shifts more, the price will fall. If supply shifts more, the price will rise.

© THINKSTOCK IMAGES/JUPITERIMAGES

If demand and supply shift in opposite directions, we can say what will happen to equilibrium price. Equilibrium price will increase if demand increases and supply decreases. Equilibrium price will decrease if demand decreases and supply increases. Without reference to particular shifts, however, we cannot say what will happen to equilibrium quantity.

These results are no doubt confusing, but Exhibit 9 summarizes the four possible combinations of changes. Using Exhibit 9 as a reference, please take the time right now to work through some changes in demand and supply to develop a feel for the results.

LO5 Disequilibrium

A surplus exerts downward pressure on the price, and a shortage exerts upward pressure. Markets, however, don't always reach equilibrium quickly. During the time required to adjust, the mar-

Exhibit 9

Effects of Shifts of Both Demand and Supply

Change in supply \ Change in demand	Demand increases	Demand decreases
Supply increases	Equilibrium price change is indeterminate. Equilibrium quantity increases.	Equilibrium price falls. Equilibrium quantity change is indeterminate.
Supply decreases	Equilibrium price rises. Equilibrium quantity change is indeterminate.	Equilibrium price change is indeterminate. Equilibrium quantity decreases.

Rare talent alone doesn't command high pay. Only the 300 or so top riders can earn a living. Only the top 50 or so make more than $100,000.

© HANS-PETER MERTEN/MAURITIUS DIE BILDAGENTUR GMBH/PHOTOLIBRARY

ket is said to be in disequilibrium. **Disequilibrium** is usually temporary as the market gropes for equilibrium. But sometimes, often as a result of government intervention, disequilibrium can last a while, perhaps decades, as we will see next.

Price Floors

Sometimes public officials set prices above their equilibrium levels. For example, the state government regulates some agriculture prices in an attempt to ensure farmers a higher and more stable income than they would otherwise earn. To achieve higher prices, the state government sets a **price floor**, or a *minimum* selling price that is above the equilibrium price. Exhibit 10a shows the effect of a $2.50 per gallon price floor for milk. At that price, farmers supply 24 million gallons per week, but consumers demand only 14 million gallons, yielding a surplus of 10 million gallons. This surplus milk will pile up on store shelves, eventually souring. To take it off the market, the government usually agrees to buy the surplus milk. The state government, in fact, spends billions buying and storing surplus agricultural products. Note, to have an impact, a price floor must be set above the equilibrium price. A price floor set at or below the equilibrium price would be nonbinding (how come?). Price floors distort markets and reduce economic welfare.

disequilibrium the condition that exists in a market when the plans of buyers do not match those of sellers; a temporary mismatch between quantity supplied and quantity demanded as the market seeks equilibrium

price floor a minimum legal price below which a product cannot be sold; to have an impact, a price floor must be set above the equilibrium price

Why did Milk Prices Soar when Ganesha Started Drinking Milk?

The **Hindu milk miracle** was a phenomenon, considered by many Hindus as a miracle, which occurred on September 21, 1995. Before dawn, a Hindu worshipper at a temple in New Delhi made an offering of milk to a statue of Ganesha. When a spoonful of milk from the bowl was held up to the trunk of the statue, the liquid was seen to disappear, apparently taken in by the idol. Word of the event spread quickly, and by mid-morning it was found that statues of the entire Hindu pantheon in temples all over North India were taking in milk.

By noon the news had spread beyond India, and Hindu temples in Britain, Canada, Dubai, and Nepal among other countries had successfully replicated the phenomenon, and the Vishva Hindu Parishad had announced that a miracle was occurring.

On this day, many stores in areas with significant Hindu communities saw a massive jump in sales of milk. Overall milk sales in New Delhi jumped over 30 percent. Since supplies could not adjust to the increased demand, instantaneously milk shortages were reported. The market adjusted with the price of milk soaring on this day. Several cafes (e.g., in Calcutta) stopped offering customers tea with milk. They instead preferred to sell milk for 10 times the normal price.

© THINKSTOCK IMAGES/JUPITERIMAGES

Price Ceilings

Sometimes public officials try to keep a price below the equilibrium level by setting a **price ceiling**, or a *maximum* selling price. Concern about the rising cost of rental housing in some cities has prompted city officials to impose rent ceilings. Exhibit 10b depicts the demand and supply of rental housing. The vertical axis shows monthly rent, and the horizontal axis shows the quantity of rental units. The equilibrium, or market-clearing, rent is $1,000 per month, and the equilibrium quantity is 50,000 housing units. Suppose city officials set a maximum rent of $600 per month. At that ceiling price, 60,000 rental units are demanded, but only 40,000 supplied, resulting in a housing shortage of 20,000 units. Because of the price ceiling, the rental price no longer rations housing to those who value it the most. Other devices emerge to ration housing, such as long waiting lists, personal connections, and the willingness to make under-the-table payments, such as "key fees," "finder's fees," high security deposits, and the like. To have an impact, a price ceiling must be set below the equilibrium price. A price ceiling set at or above the equilibrium level would be nonbinding. Price floors and ceilings distort markets and reduce economic welfare.

price ceiling
a maximum legal price above which a product cannot be sold; to have an impact, a price ceiling must be set below the equilibrium price

Government intervention is not the only source of market disequilibrium. Sometimes, when new products are introduced or when demand suddenly changes, it takes a while to reach equilibrium. For example, popular toys, best-selling books, and chart-busting CDs sometimes sell out. On the other hand, some new products attract few customers and pile up unsold on store shelves, awaiting a "clearance sale."

Final Word

Demand and supply are the building blocks of a market economy. Although a market usually involves the interaction of many buyers and sellers, few markets are consciously designed. Just as the law of gravity works whether or not we understand Newton's principles, market forces operate whether or not participants understand demand and supply. These forces arise naturally, much the way car dealers cluster on the outskirts of town to attract more customers.

Markets have their critics. Some observers may be troubled, for example, that an NBA star like Kevin Garnett earns a salary that could pay for 500 new schoolteachers, or that movie stars earn enough to pay for 1,000 new schoolteachers, or that U.S. con-

Exhibit 10a

Price Floors for Milk

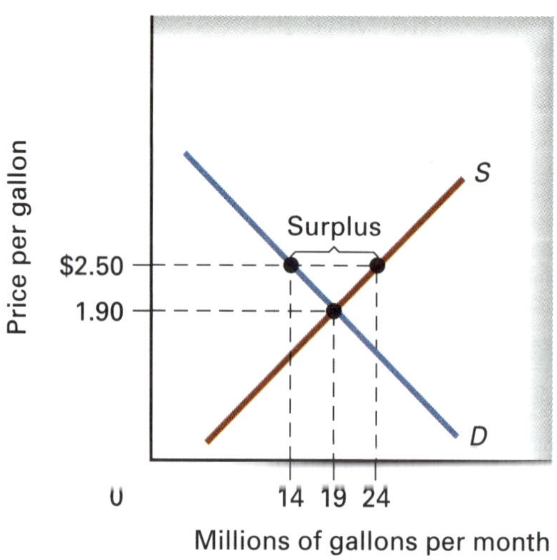

Exhibit 10b

Price Ceilings for Rent

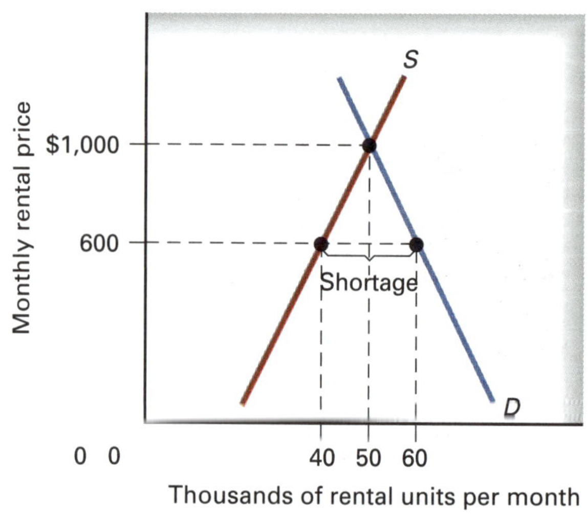

sumers spend over $40 billion on their pets. On your next trip to the supermarket, notice how much shelf space goes to pet products—often an entire aisle. PetSmart, a chain store, sells over 12,000 pet items. Veterinarians offer cancer treatment, cataract removal, root canals, even acupuncture. Kidney dialysis for a pet can cost over $75,000 per year.

In a market economy, consumers are kings and queens. Consumer sovereignty rules, deciding what gets produced. Those who don't like the market outcome usually look to government for a solution through price ceilings and price floors, regulations, income redistribution, and public finance more generally.

MULTIPLE CHOICE QUESTIONS

1. The law of demand says that as the price of a good rises,
   a. buyers recognize that price may be even higher in the future, and so they buy now
   b. buyers purchase less in hopes that the price will fall in the future
   c. buyers purchase less, in part because their real income has fallen
   d. buyers purchase more, in part because the price of a substitute has risen
   e. buyers purchase more, in part because it has higher status at a higher price
2. Movements along a demand curve are called changes in
   a. Demand
   b. opportunity costs
   c. quantity demanded
   d. the substitution effect
   e. preferences
3. The substitution effect of a change in the price of bananas refers to the way in which a change in the
   a. price of a substitute affects the demand for bananas
   b. price of bananas affects the ability to buy them
   c. relative price of bananas changes demand for them
   d. relative price of bananas changes the quantity demanded of bananas
   e. price of a substitute affects the quantity demanded of bananas
4. If pretzels are a normal good, the income effect of a price change means that
   a. as income increases, the quantity demanded increases along the demand curve for pretzels
   b. as income increases, the demand curve for pretzels shifts rightward
   c. as income increases, the demand curve for pretzels shifts leftward
   d. as the price of pretzels increases, the real income of individuals who demand pretzels decreases, so the quantity demanded of pretzels decreases
   e. as the price of pretzels increases, income increases
5. Which of the following will *not* shift the demand curve for movie tickets?
   a. a change in the cost of babysitting services
   b. a change in the price of movie tickets
   c. a change in the quality of television programs
   d. a change in the income of movie-goers
   e. a change in the number of consumers
6. The difference between normal and inferior goods is that
   a. normal goods are of better quality than inferior goods
   b. an increase in price will shift the demand curve for a normal good rightward and the demand curve for an inferior good leftward
   c. if the price of a normal good increases, individuals who buy it are poorer; for inferior goods, the opposite is true
   d. an inferior good is something that will not be demanded until quantities of the normal good have been exhausted
   e. an increase in income will shift the demand curve for a normal good rightward and the demand curve for an inferior good leftward
7. An increase in the demand for peanut butter could be caused by a(n)
   a. decrease in consumer income
   b. increase in the supply of peanut butter
   c. decrease in the price of bread
   d. drought in Georgia that destroyed 30 percent of the peanut crop
   e. decrease in the price of bologna
8. Supply curves generally slope upward because of all of the following reasons *except one*. Which is the exception?
   a. Producers are willing to offer more of a good at higher prices.
   b. A higher price attracts resources from less-valued uses.
   c. Producers must be compensated for the rising opportunity cost of additional output.
   d. Producers have a greater incentive to sell more as the price increases.
   e. The price of a good usually must fall to induce an increase in quantity supplied.
9. Which of the following is the reason supply curves typically slope upward?
   a. Opportunity cost of production increases as quantity supplied increases.
   b. Supply increases as opportunity cost decreases.

c. Price increases as supply decreases.
d. Quantity supplied is unrelated to price.
e. The income and substitution effects of a price change.

10. If the supply curves for the following goods were plotted, they all would slope upward *except one*. Which is the exception?
a. red Corvettes
b. yogurt
c. diamond rings
d. original copies of the Mona Lisa
e. wine from Greece

11. An improvement in technology would shift
a. the demand curve leftward
b. the demand curve rightward
c. the supply curve leftward
d. neither the supply nor the demand curve; instead, there is movement along both of them
e. the supply curve rightward

12. Which of the following will *not* shift the market supply curve for corn?
a. a change in the price of corn
b. a change in the price of soybeans
c. a change in the price of herbicides and pesticides
d. a change in storage technology
e. a change in the number of acres planted in corn

13. Economists emphasize the importance of equilibrium in markets because
a. trading in markets can only occur at the equilibrium price and quantity
b. the behavior of buyers and sellers will automatically guide the market toward the equilibrium price and quantity
c. all buyers and sellers are better off at the equilibrium point than any other price and quantity combination
d. it represents a compromise between sellers hoping for low prices and buyers searching for high prices
e. it is the only price-quantity combination that guarantees that the poorest members of society can purchase the good or service

14. Saccharin and aspartame are both low-calorie substitutes for sugar. If saccharin is found to cause cancer,
a. the price of aspartame will increase
b. the price of sugar will decrease
c. the price of saccharin will increase
d. the demand curves for aspartame and sugar will shift leftward
e. aspartame and sugar will be complements

15. Velcro is becoming more and more popular for a variety of uses, including as fasteners for shoes. What should happen to the equilibrium price and quantity for shoelaces as a result?
a. Both price and quantity should increase.
b. Both price and quantity should decrease.
c. Price should increase and quantity decrease.
d. Price should decrease and quantity increase.
e. Nothing.

16. Attempts are being made to develop a biodegradable plastic using agricultural produce such as potatoes. If these attempts are successful, what will happen to the equilibrium price and quantity of potatoes?
a. Price will increase and quantity decrease.
b. Price will increase and quantity increase.
c. Price will decrease and quantity increase.
d. Price will decrease and quantity decrease.
e. No change in equilibrium price and quantity will occur.

17. The market for chewing gum is competitive with a current price of 50 cents per pack and quantity of 100,000 packs. Which of the following events would lead to a new equilibrium price of 40 cents and quantity of 80,000 packs?
a. an increase in the price of other kinds of candy
b. an increase in the price of the ingredients used to make chewing gum
c. a decrease in the number of young people in the population
d. an agreement by workers in the chewing gum industry to work for lower wages
e. an improvement in chewing gum production technology

18. A new hormone will increase the amount of milk each cow produces. If this hormone is adopted by many dairies, what will be the effect on the milk market?
a. an increase in supply, higher equilibrium price, and lower equilibrium quantity
b. a decrease in supply, lower equilibrium price, and lower equilibrium quantity
c. an increase in supply, lower equilibrium price, and higher equilibrium quantity
d. an increase in supply, higher equilibrium price, and higher equilibrium quantity
e. a decrease in supply, lower equilibrium price, and higher equilibrium quantity

19. If demand increases and supply decreases,
    a. equilibrium price will fall and equilibrium quantity will rise
    b. equilibrium price and quantity will both rise
    c. equilibrium quantity will rise; equilibrium price will either rise or fall
    d. equilibrium price will fall; equilibrium quantity will either rise or fall
    e. equilibrium price will rise; equilibrium quantity will either rise, fall, or remain unchanged

20. Suppose a market is in equilibrium and then a price floor is established below the equilibrium price. Which of the following will happen?
    a. quantity demanded will increase
    b. a surplus will develop
    c. a shortage will develop
    d. the quantity sold will rise
    e. the market will remain in equilibrium

Answers

1. c	2. c	3. d	4. d	5. b	6. e	7. c	8. e	9. a	10. d
11. e	12. a	13. b	14. a	15. b	16. b	17. c	18. c	19. e	20. e

Long Answer Questions

LO1 Explain how the law of demand affects market activity

1.1. *(Shifting Demand)* Using demand and supply curves, show the effect of each of the following on the market for cigarettes:
   a. A cure for lung cancer is found.
   b. The price of cigars increases.
   c. Wages increase substantially in states that grow tobacco.
   d. A fertilizer that increases the yield per acre of tobacco is discovered.
   e. There is a sharp increase in the price of matches, lighters, and lighter fluid.
   f. More states pass laws restricting smoking in restaurants and public places.

1.2. *(Substitutes and Complements)* For each of the following pair of goods, determine whether the goods are substitutes, complements, or unrelated:
   a. Peanut butter and jelly
   b. Private and public transportation
   c. Coke and Pepsi
   d. Alarm clocks and automobiles
   e. Golf clubs and golf balls

1.3 How will each of the following affect the position of the demand curve for DVD players?
   a. An increase in the price of film DVDs.
   b. A decrease in the price of DVD players.
   c. An increase in per capita income.
   d. A decrease in the price of cinema tickets.

1.4 What is meant by market demand curve? On what factors does the market demand function of a commodity depend?

1.5 Which of the following pairs of goods are substitutes and which are complements? Explain.
   a. Insulation and heating oil
   b. Hot dogs and mustard
   c. Television sets and videocassette recorders

LO2 Explain how the law of supply affects market activity

2.1. *(Supply)* What is the law of supply? Give an example of how you have observed the law of supply at work. What is the relationship between the law of supply and the supply curve?

LO3 Describe how the interaction between supply and demand creates markets

3.1. *(Demand and Supply)* How do you think each of the following affected the world price of oil? (Use demand and supply analysis.)
   a. Tax credits were offered for expenditures on home insulation.
   b. The Alaskan oil pipeline was completed.
   c. The ceiling on the price of oil was removed.
   d. Oil was discovered in the North Sea.
   e. Sport utility vehicles and minivans became popular.
   f. The use of nuclear power declined.

3.2. *(Demand and Supply)* What happens to the equilibrium price and quantity of ice cream in response to each of the following? Explain your answers.
   a. The price of dairy cow fodder increases.
   b. The price of beef decreases.
   c. Concerns arise about the fat content of ice cream. Simultaneously, the price of sugar (used to produce ice cream) increases.

LO4 Describe how markets reach equilibrium

4.1. *(Equilibrium)* "If a price is not an equilibrium price, there is a tendency for it to move to its equilibrium level. Regardless of whether the price is too high or too low to begin with, the adjustment process will increase the quantity of the good purchased." Explain, using a demand and supply diagram.

4.2 *(Equilibrium)* Assume the market for corn is depicted as in the table that appears below.

a. Complete the table below.
b. What market pressure occurs when quantity demanded exceeds quantity supplied? Explain.
c. What market pressure occurs when quantity supplied exceeds quantity demanded? Explain.
d. What is the equilibrium price?
e. What could change the equilibrium price?
f. At each price in the first column of the table below, how much is sold?

Price per Bushel	Quantity Demanded (millions of bushels)	Quantity Supplied (millions of bushels)	Surplus/ Shortage	Will Price Rise or Fall?
$1.80	320	200	______	______
2.00	300	230	______	______
2.20	270	270	______	______
2.40	230	300	______	______
2.60	200	330	______	______
2.80	180	350	______	______

4.3. *(Market Equilibrium)* Determine whether each of the following statements is true, false, or uncertain. Then briefly explain each answer.
a. In equilibrium, all sellers can find buyers.
b. In equilibrium, there is no pressure on the market to produce or consume more than is being sold.
c. At prices above equilibrium, the quantity exchanged exceeds the quantity demanded.
d. At prices below equilibrium, the quantity exchanged is equal to the quantity supplied

4.4. *(Changes in Equilibrium)* What are the effects on the equilibrium price and quantity of steel if the wages of steelworkers rise and, simultaneously, the price of aluminum rises?

LO5 Explain how markets react during periods of disequilibrium.

5.1. *(Price Floor)* There is considerable interest in whether the minimum wage rate contributes to teenage unemployment. Draw a demand and supply diagram for the unskilled labor market, and discuss the effects of a minimum wage. Who is helped and who is hurt by the minimum wage?

Numericals

1.1 In a certain fish market, there are suppliers with different time perspectives. As such, three market supply functions are estimated:
St = 10 ----------------Temporary period
Ss = 4+0.5 P ------------------ Short period
Sl = -20+ 2.5 P ------------------------Long period
Suppose that the market demand for fish suddenly changes from
D= 16 – 0.5 P to
D' = 24 – 0.5 P
Estimate exactly the effect of this change on
(i) market price, and
(ii) market output of fish corresponding to different time perspectives.
Show your results graphically also.

1.2 Assume the demand curve for gasoline is given by the following equation: P = 10 – 0.0005 Q, where P is the price per gallon and Q is the quantity of gasoline in gallons. Assume that the only supplier of gasoline in the region is General Gasoline Co. and that the marginal cost of production is constant at zero.
a. If the company is currently charging $4 a gallon, is it maximizing profit? If so, prove it. If not, find out the price that maximizes its profit, and compare the profits at the two prices.
b. Discuss the likely effect of the introduction of a fuel-efficient car in the region, i.e. what would happen to the equilibrium quantity. Show the changes on a graph that displays (you don't need to show actual numbers) General Gasoline's pricing solution and explain.

1.3 In Country Dreamland, cigarettes are forbidden, so people trade cigarettes in a black market. The cigarette demand is QD = 12 – P, and the cigarette supply is Qs = 2P.
a. Find the equilibrium price and quantity in the black market.
b. The government becomes aware of the black market and reinforces the police so that half of the cigarette supply would be seized and destroyed. Under this circumstance, what are the demand and supply functions? What is the new equilibrium price and quantity? Show the change by using a supply and demand diagram
c. How does the consumer surplus change between (a) and (b)?
d. Suppose that the government changes the policy and legalizes cigarette trade. Now cigarettes are traded in an open market. However, for every unit of cigarette purchased, the buyer has to pay tax T to the government. T is equal to the pre-tax price P. What are the demand and supply functions under this circumstance? What are the equilibrium price and quantity? What is the after-tax price paid by buyers?
e. Compare (b) and (d). Which policy do consumers prefer? Which policy does the government prefer and why?

1.4 Suppose you are a stock market analyst specializing in the stocks of theme parks, and you are examining Disneyland's stock. The Wall Street Journal reports that tourism has slowed down in the United States. At Six flags Magic Mountain in Valencia, California, a new Viper roller coaster is now operating and another new ride, is expected to open this year. Using demand and supply analysis, predict the impact of these events on ticket prices and attendance at Disneyland. As reported in The Wall Street Journal, Disneyland slashed ticket prices and admitted that attendance was somewhat lower. Is this consistent with your prediction using demand and supply analysis? In light of the fact that both price and output were falling at Disneyland, is the law of demand being violated in the world of fantasy?

1.5 Evaluate the following statements using graphical analysis. Provide a brief narrative explanation of your graph to support your evaluation. Make sure the axes and curves in your graphs are properly labeled.
a. "When demand for home heating oil increases, a shortage of heating oil will occur."
b. "A decrease in the supply of random access memory (RAM) chips for personal computers causes a shortage of RAM chips."

DEMAND, SUPPLY, AND MARKETS

Chapter in Review

4

KEY TERMS

demand
a relation between the price of a good and the quantity that consumers are willing and able to buy per period, other things constant

law of demand
the quantity of a good that consumers are willing and able to buy per period relates inversely, or negatively, to the price, other things constant

substitution effect of a price change
when the price of a good falls, that good become cheaper compared to other goods so consumers tend to substitute that good for other goods

money income
the number of dollars a person receives per period, such as $400 per week

real income
income measured in terms of the goods and services it can buy; real income changes when the price changes

income effect of a price change
a fall in the price of a good increases consumers' real income, making consumers more able to purchase goods; for a normal good, the quantity demanded increases

demand curve
a curve showing the relation between the price of a good and the quantity consumers are willing and able to buy per period, other things constant

quantity demanded
the amount of a good consumers are willing and able to buy per period at a particular price, as reflected by a point on a demand curve

individual demand
a relation between the price of a good and the quantity purchased by an individual consumer per period, other things constant

market demand
the relation between the price of a good and the quantity purchased by all consumers in the market during a given period, other things constant; sum of the individual demands in the market

normal good
a good, such as new clothes, for which demand increases, or shifts rightward, as consumer income rises

inferior good
a good, such as used clothes, for which demand decreases, or shifts leftward, as consumer income rises

substitutes
goods, such as Coke and Pepsi, that relate in such a way that an increase in the price of one shifts the demand for the other rightward

complements
goods, such as milk and cookies, that relate in such a way that an increase in the price of one shifts the demand for the other leftward

tastes
consumer preferences; likes and dislikes in consumption; assumed to remain constant along a given demand curve

LO1 Explain how the law of demand affects market activity.

Demand is a relationship between the price of a product and the quantity consumers are willing and able to buy per period, other things constant. According to the law of demand, quantity demanded varies negatively, or inversely, with the price. A demand curve slopes downward because a price decrease makes consumers (a) more willing to substitute this good for other goods and (b) more able to buy the good because the lower price increases real income.

The Demand Curve for Pizza

The market demand curve *D* shows the quantity of pizza demanded, at various prices, by all consumers. Price and quantity demanded are inversely related.

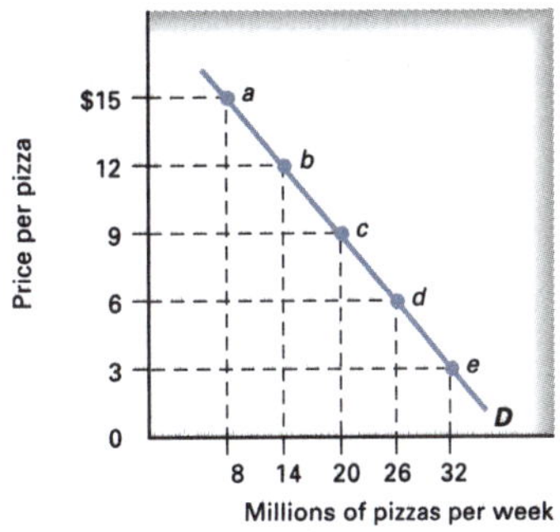

LO2 Explain how the law of supply affects market activity.

Supply is a relationship between the price of a good and the quantity producers are willing and able to sell per period, other things constant. According to the law of supply, price and quantity supplied are usually postitively, or directly, related, so the supply curve typically slopes upward. The supply curve slopes upward because higher prices make producers (a) more willing to supply this good rather than supply other goods that use the same resources and (b) more able to cover the higher marginal cost associated with greater output rates.

The Supply Curve for Pizza

Market supply curve *S* shows the quantity of pizza supplied, at various prices, by all pizza makers. Price and quantity supplied are directly related.

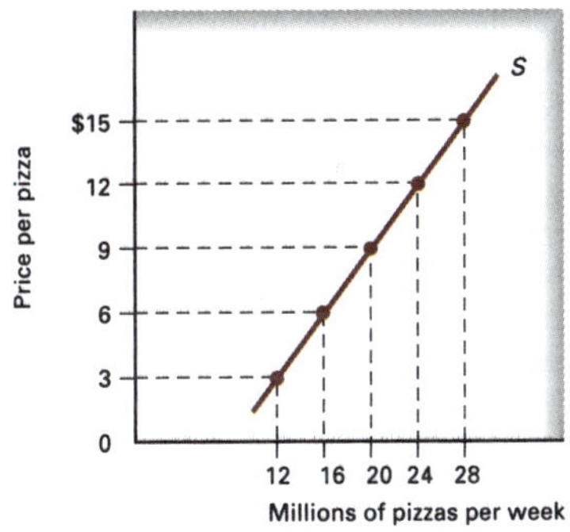

LO3 Describe how the interaction between supply and demand creates markets.

Demand and supply come together in the market for the good. A market provides information about the price, quantity, and quality of the good. In doing so, a market reduces the transaction costs of exchange—the costs of time and information required for buyers and sellers to make a deal. The interaction of demand and supply guides resources and products to their highest-valued use.

movement along a demand curve change in quantity demanded resulting from a change in the price of the good, other things constant

shift of a demand curve movement of a demand curve right or left resulting from a change in one of the determinants of demand other than the price of the good

supply a relation between the price of a good and the quantity that producers are willing and able to sell per period, other things constant

law of supply the amount of a good that producers are willing and able to sell per period is usually directly related to its price, other things constant

supply curve a curve showing the relation between price of a good and the quantity producers are willing and able to sell per period other things constant

quantity supplied the amount offered for sale per period at a particular price, as reflected by a point on a given supply curve

individual supply the relation between the price of a good and the quantity an individual producer is willing and able to sell per period, other things constant

market supply the relation between the price of a good and the quantity all producers are willing and able to sell per period, other things constant

relevant resources resources used to produce the good in question

alternative goods other goods that use some or all of the same resources as the good in question

movement along a supply curve change in quantity supplied resulting from a change in the price of the good, other things constant

shift of a supply curve movement of a supply curve left or right resulting from a change in one of the determinants of supply other than the price of the good

transaction costs the costs of time and information required to carry out market exchange

surplus at a given price, the amount by which quantity supplied exceeds quantity demanded; a surplus usually forces the price down

shortage at a given price, the amount by which quantity demanded exceeds quantity supplied; a shortage usually forces the price up

equilibrium the condition that exists in a market when the plans of buyers match those of sellers, so quantity demanded equals quantity supplied and the market clears

disequilibrium the condition that exists in a market when the plans of buyers do not match those of sellers; a temporary mismatch between quantity supplied and quantity demanded as the market seeks equilibrium

Equilibrium in the Pizza Market

Market equilibrium occurs at the price where quantity demanded equals quantity supplied. This is shown at point *c*. Price pressure occurs at all other points on the curves.

(a) Market schedules

Price per Pizza	Quantity Demanded (Millions of Pizzas per Week)	Quantity Supplied (Millions of Pizzas per Week)	Surplus or Shortage	Effect on Price
$15	8	28	Surplus of 20	Falls
12	14	24	Surplus of 10	Falls
9	20	20	Equilibrium	Remains the same
6	26	16	Shortage of 10	Rises
3	32	12	Shortage of 20	Rises

(b) Market curves

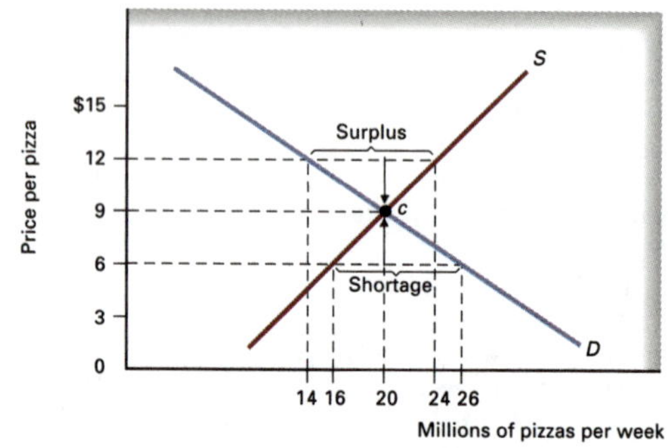

LO4 Describe how markets reach equilibrium.

Impersonal market forces reconcile the personal and independent plans of buyers and sellers. Market equilibrium, once established, will continue unless there is a change in a determinant that shapes demand or supply.

Effects of an Increase in Demand

An increase in demand is shown by a shift of the demand curve rightward from *D* to *D′*. Both price and quantity are higher following the rightward shift of the demand curve.

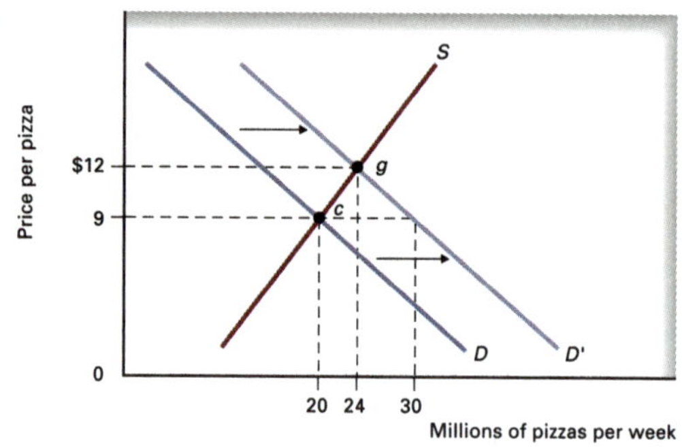

Effects of an Increase in Supply

An increase in supply is shown by a shift of the supply curve rightward, from *S* to *S′*. At the new equilibrium, quantity is greater and the price is lower than before the increase in supply.

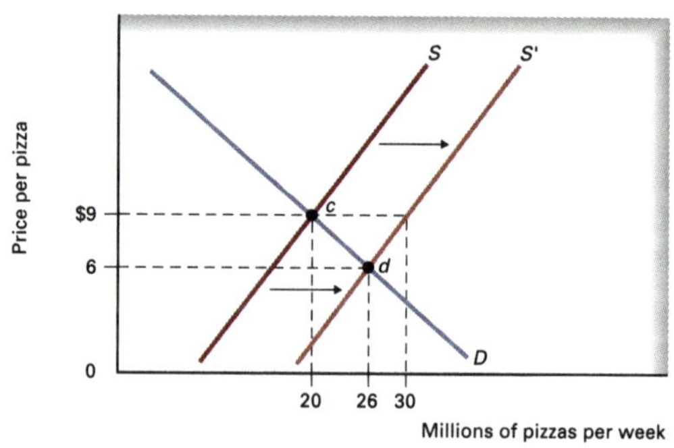

LO5 Explain how markets react during periods of disequilibrium.

Markets can't always achieve equilibrium quickly. Until they do, a period of disequilibrium occurs. Governments often impose price floors or price ceilings to manage the uncomfortable market effects of disequilibrium, like falling income or product surplus.

price floor a minimum legal price below which a product cannot be sold; to have an impact, a price floor must be set above the equilibrium price

price ceiling a maximum legal price above which a product cannot be sold; to have an impact, a price ceiling must be set below the equilibrium price

CHAPTER

5

Learning Outcomes

LO 1 Define and graph the price elasticity of demand

LO 2 Identify the determinants of the price elasticity of demand

LO 3 Define and graph the price elasticity of supply

LO 4 Describe other measures of elasticity

LO 5 Disuss the applications of theory of demand and supply

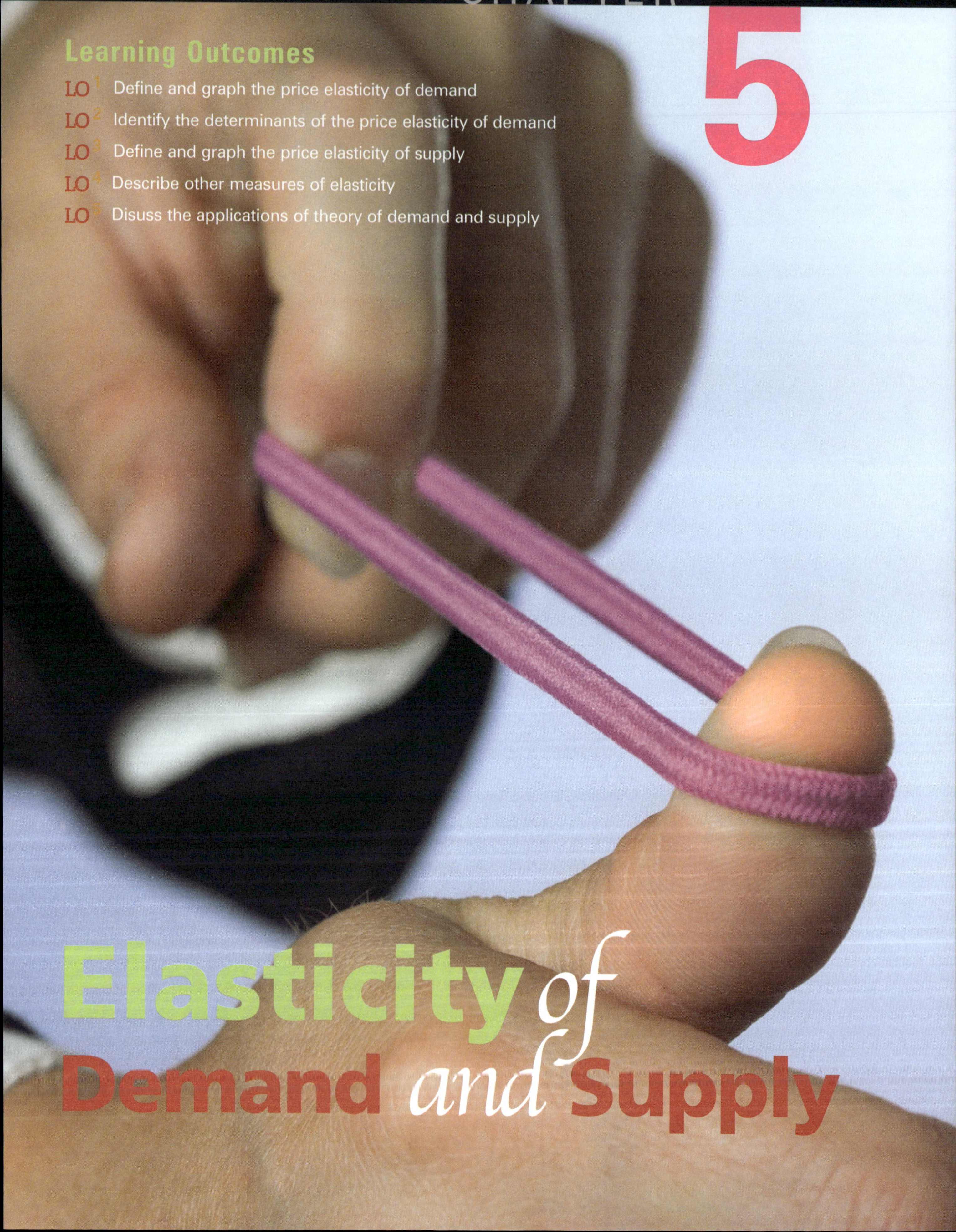

Elasticity *of* Demand *and* Supply

"What does the demand curve look like when price is no object?"

What does the demand curve look like when price is no criterion for purchase? What does the supply curve look like for Cadillacs once owned by Elvis Presley? Why do higher cigarette taxes cut smoking by teenagers more than by other age groups? Why are consumers more sensitive to the price of Pepsi than to the price of beverages more generally? Why does a good harvest often spell trouble for farmers? Answers to these and other questions are explored in this chapter, which takes a closer look at demand and supply.

What do you think?

If I were rich, I wouldn't shop at consignment stores.

Strongly Disagree					Strongly Agree	
1	2	3	4	5	6	7

As you learned in Chapter 1, macroeconomics concentrates on aggregate markets—on the big picture. But the big picture is a mosaic pieced together from individual decisions made by households, firms, governments, and the rest of the world. To understand how a market economy works, you must take a closer look at these individual decisions, especially at the role of prices. In a market economy, prices tell producers and consumers about the relative scarcity of products and resources.

A downward-sloping demand curve and an upward-sloping supply curve combine to form a powerful analytical tool. But to use this tool wisely, you need to learn more about demand and supply curves. The more you know, the better you can predict the effects of a change in the price on quantity. Decision makers are willing to pay dearly for such knowledge. For example, Taco Bell would like to know what happens to sales if taco prices change. Governments would like to know how a hike in cigarette taxes affects teenage smoking. Colleges would like to know how tuition increases affect enrollments. And subway officials would like to know how fare changes affect ridership. To answer such questions, you must learn how responsive consumers and producers are to price changes. This chapter introduces the idea of *elasticity*, a measure of *responsiveness*.

Topics discussed in Chapter 5 include:

- Price elasticity of demand
- Determinants of price elasticity
- Price elasticity and total revenue
- Price elasticity of supply
- Income elasticity of demand
- Cross-price elasticity of demand

© ISTOCKPHOTO/THINKSTOCK

LO1 Price Elasticity of Demand

Just before Thanksgiving 2006, Delta Airlines cut fares for some seats on more than 10,000 domestic flights. Was that a good idea? A firm's success or failure often depends on how much it knows about the demand for its product. For Delta's total revenue to increase, the gain in tickets sold would have to more than make up for the decline in ticket prices. Likewise, the operators of Taco Bell would like to know what happens to sales if the price drops from, say, \$1.10 to \$0.90 per taco. The law of demand tells us that a lower price increases quantity demanded, but by how much? How sensitive is quantity demanded to a change in price? After all, if quantity demanded increases enough, a price cut could be a profitable move for Taco Bell.

price elasticity of demand
measures how responsive quantity demanded is to a price change; the percentage change in quantity demanded divided by the percentage change in price

price elasticity formula
percentage change in quantity demanded divided by the percentage change in price; the average quantity and the average price are used as bases for computing percentage changes in quantity and in price

Calculating Price Elasticity of Demand

Let's get more specific about how sensitive changes in quantity demanded are to changes in price. Take a look at the demand curve in Exhibit 1. At the initial price of \$1.10 per taco, consumers demand 95,000 per day. If the price drops to \$0.90, quantity demanded increases to 105,000. Is such a response a little or a lot? The *price elasticity of demand* measures, in a standardized way, how responsive consumers are to a change in price. *Elasticity* is another word for *responsiveness*. In simplest terms, the **price elasticity of demand** measures the percentage change in quantity demanded divided by the percentage change in price, or:

Exhibit 1

Demand Curve for Tacos

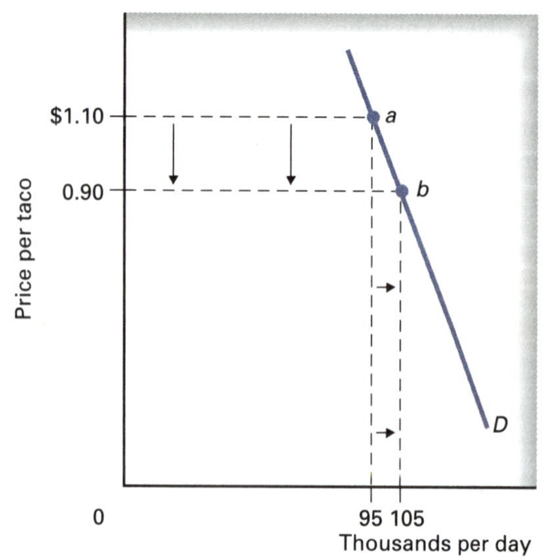

> *Elasticity* is another word for *responsiveness*.

$$\text{Price elasticity of demand} = \frac{\text{Percentage change in quantity demanded}}{\text{Percentage change in price}}$$

Thus, the price elasticity is a measure of the responsiveness of demand to changes in the commodity's own price. If the changes in price are very small, we use as a measure of the responsiveness of demand the point elasticity of demand. If the changes in price are not small, we use the arc elasticity of demand as the relevant measure.

The point elasticity of demand is defined as the proportionate change in the quantity demanded resulting from a very small proportionate change in price. Symbolically, we may write:

$$E_X = \frac{dQ}{Q} / \frac{dP}{P}$$

or

$$E_X = \frac{dQ}{dP} \times \frac{P}{Q}$$

If the demand curve is linear

$$Q = b_0 - b_1P$$

It can be re-written as

$$P = a_0 - a_1Q$$

where $a_0 = b_0/b_1$ and $a_1 = 1/b_1$

The slope of this demand curve is $dP/dQ = -a_1$. Substituting in the elasticity formula we obtain:

$$E_X = \frac{dQ}{dP} \times \frac{P}{Q}$$

$$E_X = (1/\text{slope}) \times \frac{P}{Q}$$

This implies that the elasticity for a linear demand curve (by definition having a constant slope) changes at various points along the demand curve. Also to be noted is that since P and Q are inversely related, E_X is expected to be negative. To avoid interpreting a negative price elasticity, in most of the textbooks, therefore, formula for price elasticity of demand is pre-multiplied by minus to get a positive value.

Thus, E_x is generally written as

$$Ex = -\frac{dQ}{dP} \times \frac{P}{Q}$$

Graphically the point elasticity of a linear-demand curve is shown by the ratio of the segments of the line to the right and to the left of the particular point. In Exhibit 2, the elasticity of the linear-demand curve at point R is the ratio:

$$\frac{RB}{AR} = \frac{Q_1B}{oQ_1} = \frac{P_1o}{AP_1}$$

Exhibit 2

Linear Demand Curve and its Elasticity

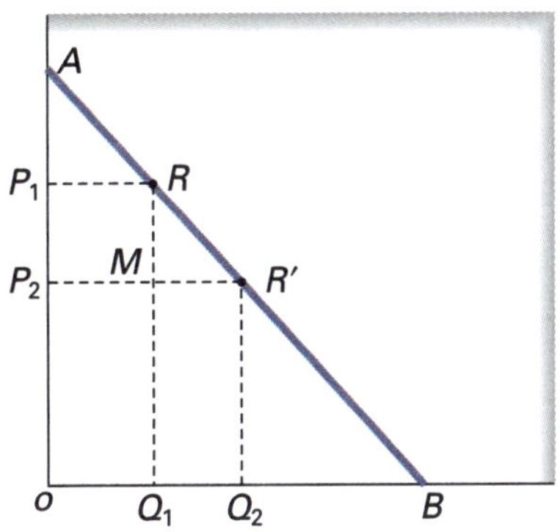

Proof
Exhibit 2 represents

$$\Delta P = P_1P_2 = MR$$
$$\Delta Q = Q_1Q_2 = MR'$$
$$P = oP_1$$
$$Q = oQ_1$$

If we consider very small changes in P and Q, then $\Delta P \approx dP$ and $\Delta Q \approx dQ$. Thus, substituting in the formula for the point elasticity, we obtain

$$E_x = \frac{dQ}{dP} \times \frac{P}{Q} = \frac{Q_1Q_2}{P_1P_2} \times \frac{oP_1}{oQ_1} = \frac{MR'}{MR} \times \frac{oP_1}{oQ_1}$$

Exhibit 2 indicates that triangles RMR' and RQ_1B are similar (because each corresponding angle is equal). Hence

$$\frac{MR'}{MR} = \frac{Q_1B}{RQ_1} = \frac{Q_1B}{Q_1R} = \frac{Q_1B}{oP_1}$$

$$\frac{Q_1B}{OP_1} \times \frac{oP_1}{oQ_1} = \frac{Q_1B}{oQ_1}$$

Further, triangles AP_1R and RQ_1B are also similar, so that

$$\frac{Q_1B}{RB} = \frac{P_1R}{RA} = \frac{oQ_1}{AR}$$

Rearranging we obtain:

$$\frac{Q_1B}{oQ_1} = \frac{RB}{RA}$$

Thus, the price elasticity at point R is:

$$E_x = \frac{Q_1B}{oQ_1} = \frac{RB}{AR}$$

We can also prove that

$$E_x \text{ at } R = \frac{Q_1B}{oQ_1} = \frac{RB}{AR} = \frac{P_1o}{AP_1}$$

Given this graphical measurement of point elasticity, it is obvious that at the mid-point of a linear-demand curve $E_x = 1$.

But what's the price elasticity of demand when the price of tacos falls from \$1.10 to \$0.90—that is, what's the price elasticity of demand between points *a* and *b* in Exhibit 1? For price elasticity to be a clear and reliable measure, we should get the same result between points *a* and *b* as we get between points *b* and *a*. To ensure that consistency, we must take the average of the initial price and the new price and use that as the base for computing the percentage change in price. For example, in Exhibit 1, the base used to calculate the percentage change in price is the average of \$1.10 and \$0.90, which is \$1.00. The percentage change in price is therefore the change in price, −\$0.20, divided by \$1.00, which works out to be −20 percent.

The same holds for changes in quantity demanded. In Exhibit 1, the base used for computing the percentage change in quantity demanded is the average of 95,000 and 105,000, which is 100,000. So the percentage increase in quantity demanded is the change in quantity demanded, 10,000, divided by 100,000, which works out to be 10 percent. So the resulting price elasticity of demand between points *a* and *b* (and between points *b* and *a*) is the percentage increase in quantity demanded, 10 percent, divided by the percentage decrease in price, −20 percent, which is −0.5 (=10%/−20%).

Let's generalize the **price elasticity formula**. If the price changes from *p* to *p*′, other things constant, the quantity demanded changes from *q* to *q*′. The change in price can be represented as Δp and the change in quantity as Δq. The formula for

© CIARAN GRIFFIN/STOCKBYTE/GETTY IMAGES

calculating the price elasticity of demand E_D between the two points is the percentage change in quantity demanded divided by the percentage change in price, or:

$$E_X = \frac{\Delta q}{(q + q')/2} \div \frac{\Delta p}{(p + p')/2}$$

Again, because the average quantity and average price are used as the bases for computing percentage change, the same elasticity results whether going from the higher price to the lower price or the other way around.

In general, if the demand curve is not linear, but convex to the origin (refer Exhibit 3a), then the arc elasticity is a measure of the average elasticity, that is, the elasticity at the mid-point of the chord that connects the two points (A and B) on the demand curve. The two points are defined by the initial and the new price levels. It should be clear that the measure of the arc elasticity is an approximation of the true elasticity. This is because while we are to estimate the elasticity at the mid-point of the arc AB (given by point G), by averaging the original and final prices and outputs we actually estimate the elasticity over the mid-point of the chord AB (given by point H). Since we do not know the intermediate prices and quantities, this approximation will remain. In addition, it may be noted that the more convex to the origin the demand curve is, the greater the linear approximation attained by the arc elasticity formula, and hence poorer will be the estimate. For instance, in Exhibit 3b, demand curve 2 is more convex than demand curve 1. It is also clear from the exhibit that point T on demand curve 2 lies farther away from point H (mid-point of the chord) than point M on demand curve 1. However, since points A and B are common to both the demand curves, arc elasticity estimation will be same for both the curves, irrespective of their curvatures.

Exhibit 3

Arc Elasticity: An Approximation of True Elasticity

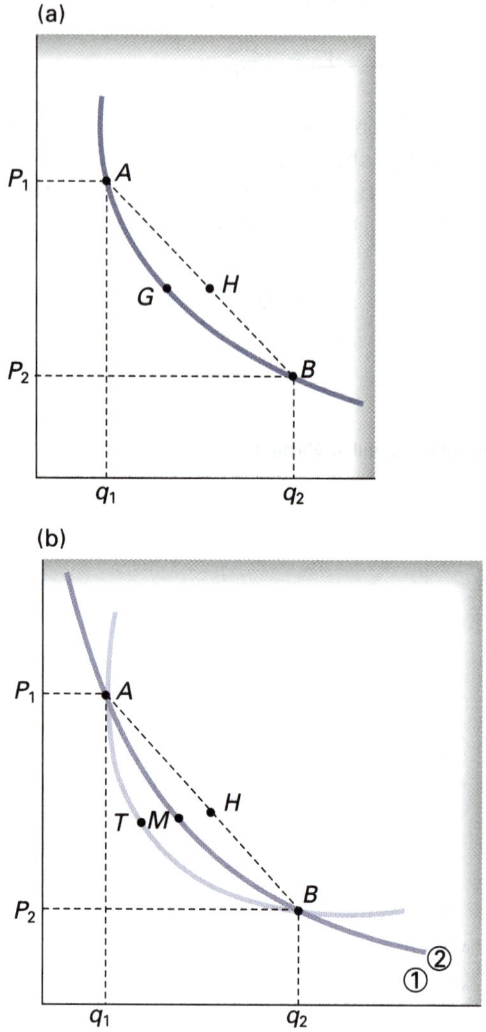

Elasticity expresses a relationship between two amounts: the percentage change in quantity demanded and the percentage change in price. Because the focus is on the *percentage change,* we don't need to be concerned with how output or price is measured. For example, suppose the good in question is apples. It makes no difference in the elasticity formula whether we measure apples in pounds, bushels, or even tons. All that matters is the percentage change in quantity demanded. Nor does it matter whether we measure price in U.S. dollars, Mexican pesos, Zambian kwacha, or Indonesian rupiah. All that matters is the percentage change in price.

$$E_x = \frac{\Delta q}{(q + q')/2} \div \frac{\Delta p}{(p + p')/2}$$

Finally, the law of demand states that price and quantity demanded are inversely related, so the change in price and the change in quantity demanded move in opposite directions. In the elasticity formula, the numerator and the denominator have opposite signs, leaving the price elasticity of demand with a negative sign. Because constantly referring to elasticity as a negative number gets old fast, from here on we treat the price elasticity of demand as an absolute value, or as a positive number. For example, the absolute value of the elasticity measured in Exhibit 1 is 0.5. Still, from time to time, you will be reminded that we are discussing absolute values.

Categories of Price Elasticity of Demand

As you'll see, the price elasticity of demand usually varies along a demand curve. Ranges of elasticity can be divided into three categories, depending on how responsive quantity demanded is to a change in price. If the percentage change in quantity demanded is smaller than the percentage change in price, the resulting elasticity has an absolute value between 0 and 1.0. That portion of the demand curve is said to be inelastic, meaning that quantity demanded is relatively *unresponsive* to a change in price. For example, the elasticity derived in Exhibit 1 between points *a* and *b* was 0.5, so that portion of the demand curve is inelastic. If the percentage change in quantity demanded just equals the percentage change in price, the resulting elasticity has an absolute value of 1.0, and that portion of a demand curve is unit-elastic. Finally, if the percentage change in quantity demanded exceeds the percentage change in price, the resulting elasticity has an absolute value exceeding 1.0, and that portion of a demand curve is said to be elastic. In summary, *the price elasticity of demand is inelastic if its absolute value is between 0 and 1.0, unit elastic if equal to 1.0, and elastic if greater than 1.0.*

The range of values of the elasticity thus varies between zero and infinity. That is:

$$\text{Zero} \leq E_X \leq \text{Infinity}$$

To generalize:

If $E_X = 0$, the demand is perfectly inelastic
If $E_X = 1$, the demand has unitary elasticity
If $E_X =$ infinite, the demand is perfectly elastic
If $0 < E_X < 1$, we say that the demand is inelastic
If $1 < E_X <$ infinite, we say that the demand is elastic

Elasticity and Total Revenue

Knowledge of price elasticity of demand is especially valuable to producers, because it indicates the effect of a price change on total revenue. Total revenue (TR) is the price (*p*) multiplied by the quantity demanded (*q*) at that price, or TR = *p* × *q*. What happens to total revenue when price decreases? Well, according to the law of demand, a lower price increases quantity demanded, which tends to increase total revenue. But, a lower price means producers get less for each unit sold, which tends to decrease total revenue. The overall impact of a lower price on total revenue therefore depends on the net result of these opposite effects. *If the positive effect of a greater quantity demanded more than offsets the negative effect of a lower price, then total revenue rises.* More specifically, if demand is *elastic*, the percentage increase in quantity demanded exceeds the percentage decrease in price, so total revenue increases. If demand is *unit elastic*, the percentage increase in quantity demanded just equals the percentage decrease in price, so total revenue remains unchanged. Finally, if demand is *inelastic*, the percentage increase in quantity demanded is less than the percentage decrease in price, so total revenue decreases.

$$TR = p \times q$$

Price Elasticity and the Linear Demand Curve

A look at elasticity along a particular type of demand curve, the linear demand curve, ties together the ideas discussed so far. A linear demand curve is simply a straight-line demand curve, as in panel (a) of Exhibit 4. Panel (b) shows the total revenue generated by each price-quantity combination along the demand curve in panel (a). Recall that total revenue equals price times quantity. Please take a moment to see how the demand curve and total revenue curve relate.

Because the demand curve is linear, its slope is constant, so a given decrease in price always causes the same unit increase in quantity demanded. For example, along the demand curve in Exhibit 4, a $10 drop in price always increases quantity demanded by 100 units. But the price elasticity of demand is larger on the higher-price end of the demand curve than on the lower-price end. Here's why. Consider a movement from point *a* to point *b* on the upper end of

inelastic demand
a change in price has relatively little effect on quantity demanded; the percentage change in quantity demanded is less than the percentage change in price; the resulting price elasticity has an absolute value less than 1.0

unit-elastic demand
the percentage change in quantity demanded equals the percentage change in price; the resulting price elasticity has an absolute value of 1.0

elastic demand
a change in price has a relatively large effect on quantity demanded; the percentage change in quantity demanded exceeds the percentage change in price; the resulting price elasticity has an absolute value exceeding 1.0

total revenue
price multiplied by the quantity demanded at that price

linear demand curve
a straight-line demand curve; such a demand curve has a constant slope but usually has a varying price elasticity

the demand curve in Exhibit 4. The $10 price drop is a percentage change of 10/85, or 12 percent. The 100-unit increase in quantity demanded is a percentage change of 100/150, or 67 percent. Therefore, the price elasticity of demand between points *a* and *b* is 67%/12%, which equals 5.6. Between points *d* and *e* on the lower end, however, the $10 price decrease is a percentage change of 10/15, or 67 percent, and the 100-unit quantity increase is a percentage change of 100/850, or only 12 percent. The price elasticity of demand is 12%/67%, or 0.2. In other words, *if the demand curve is linear, consumers are more responsive to a given price change when the initial price is high than when it's low.*

Exhibit 4

Demand, Price Elasticity, and Total Revenue

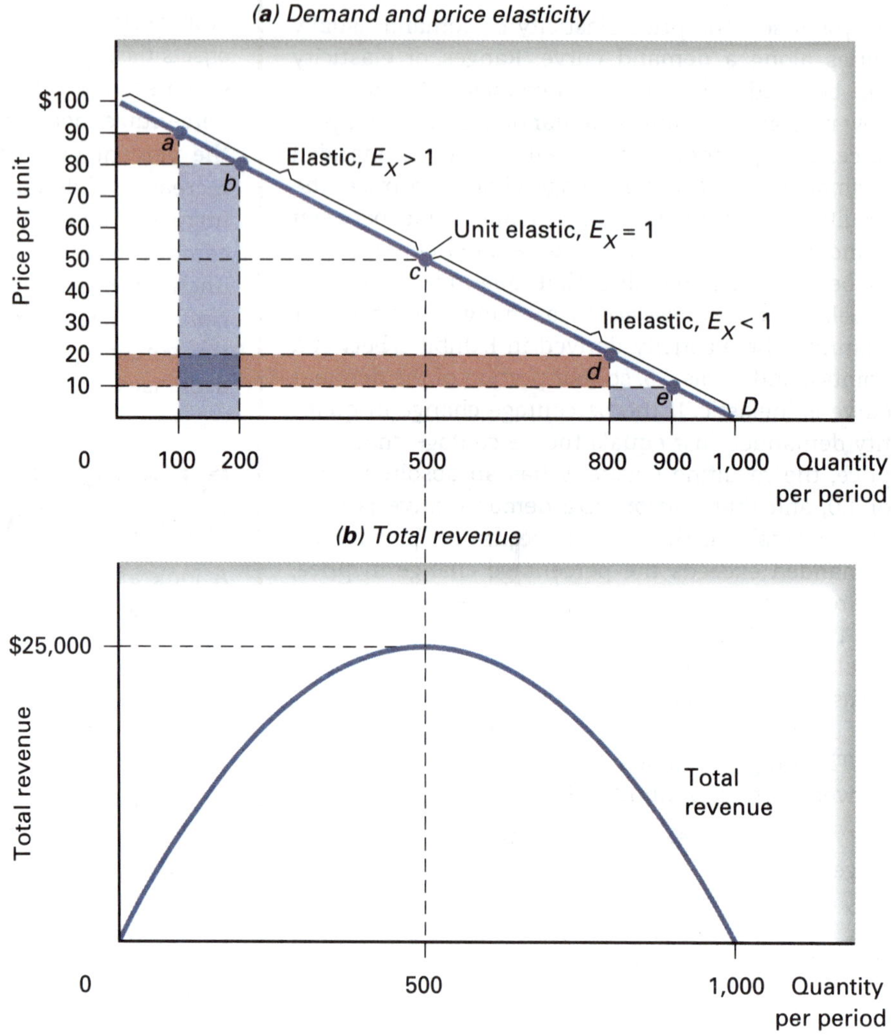

Demand becomes less elastic as we move down the curve. At a point halfway down the linear demand curve in Exhibit 4, the elasticity is 1.0. *This halfway point divides a linear demand curve into an elastic upper half and an inelastic lower half.* You can observe a clear relationship between the elasticity of demand in panel (a) and total revenue in panel (b). Notice that where demand is elastic, a decrease in price increases total revenue because the gain in revenue from selling more units (represented by the large blue rectangle) exceeds the loss in revenue from selling all units at the lower price (the small pink rectangle). But where demand is inelastic, a price decrease reduces total revenue because the gain in revenue from selling more units (the small blue rectangle) is less than the loss in revenue from selling all units at the lower price (the large pink rectangle). And where demand is unit elastic, the gain and loss of revenue exactly cancel each other out, so total revenue at that point remains constant (thus, total revenue peaks in the lower panel).

To review, total revenue increases as the price declines until the midpoint of the linear demand curve is reached, where total revenue peaks. In Exhibit 4, total revenue peaks at $25,000 where quantity demanded equals 500 units. To the right of the midpoint of the demand curve, total revenue declines as the price falls. More generally, regardless of whether demand is straight or curved, there is a consistent relationship between the price elasticity of demand and total revenue: *A price decline increases total revenue if demand is elastic, has no effect on total revenue if demand is unit elastic, and decreases total revenue if demand is inelastic.* Finally, note that a downward-sloping linear demand curve has a constant slope but a varying elasticity, so *the slope of a demand curve is not the same as the price elasticity of demand.*

Mathematical Relationship: Total Revenue, Marginal Revenue, and Average Revenue

From the market-demand curve, we can derive the total expenditure of the consumers, which forms the total revenue of the firms selling the particular commodity.

The total revenue is the product of the quantity sold and the price.

$$TR = P \times Q$$

The marginal revenue is the change in total revenue resulting from selling an additional unit of the commodity. Graphically, the marginal revenue is the slope of the total revenue curve at any one level of output. Mathematically, MR is the derivative of the TR function:

$$MR = \frac{d(TR)}{dQ} = \frac{d(PQ)}{dQ}$$

or

$$MR = P + Q \times \frac{dP}{dQ}$$

If the demand curve is linear, its equation is

$$Q = b_0 - b_1 P$$

or solving for P,

$$P = a_0 - a_1 Q$$

where

$$a_0 = \frac{b_0}{b_1} \quad \text{and} \quad a_1 = \frac{1}{b_1}$$

Substituting P in the total revenue funtion we get

$$TR = PQ = a_0 Q - a_1 Q^2$$

$$MR = \frac{d(TR)}{dQ} = a_0 - 2a_1 Q$$

This proves that the MR curve has the same intercept as the AR curve. In other words, MR starts from the same point (a_0) as the demand curve. Further, while the slope of the AR curve is (–)a_1, the MR curve is twice as steep as the AR curve with its slope being (–)$2a_1$. Thus, for a linear demand curve, the MR curve is also linear with a negative slope twice as steep as the slope of the demand curve (AR curve).

Mathematical Relationship: Total Revenue, Marginal Revenue, Average Revenue, and the Price Elasticity of Demand

The marginal revenue is related to the average revenue and the price elasticity of demand with the formula:

$$MR = AR\left(1 - \frac{1}{Ex}\right)$$

Since AR = P, we can re-write the equation as:

$$MR = P\left(1 - \frac{1}{Ex}\right)$$

Proof:

Assume that the demand function is $P = f(Q)$

The total revenue is $TR = PQ = [f(Q)]Q$

MR is

$$MR = \frac{d(PQ)}{dQ} = P\frac{dQ}{dQ} + \frac{dP}{dQ} = P + Q\frac{dP}{dQ}$$

The price elasticity of demand is defined as

$$Ex = -\frac{dQ}{dP} \times \frac{P}{Q}$$

Rearranging we obtain

$$-Ex\frac{Q}{P} = \frac{dQ}{dP}$$

$$-\frac{P}{ExQ} = \frac{dP}{dQ}$$

Substituting dP/dQ in the expression of the MR we find

$$MR = P + Q\frac{dP}{dQ} = P - Q\frac{P}{ExQ} = P - \frac{P}{Ex}$$

or

$$MR = P\left(1 - \frac{1}{Ex}\right)$$

We now examine the relationship between total revenue and price elasticity of demand. We know that if the demand curve is falling, the TR curve initially increases, reaches a maximum, and then starts declining. We can use the earlier derived relationship between MR, P, and E_X to establish the shape of the total revenue curve. The total revenue curve reaches its maximum level at the point where $E_X = 1$. This is because at this point of its slope, the marginal revenue, is equal to zero.

- Thus, if $E_x = 1$, marginal revenue is zero. Further, when MR = 0, TR reaches its maximum.

$$MR = P\left(1 - \frac{1}{1}\right) = 0$$

- If $E_x > 1$, marginal revenue is positive for $P > 0$. Since $MR > 0$, it implies that the total revenue is increasing. That is:

$$P > 0 \text{ and } \left(1 - \frac{1}{Ex}\right) > 0; \text{ hence } MR > 0$$

- If $E_x < 1$, marginal revenue is negative for $P > 0$. Since $MR < 0$, it implies that the total revenue is decreasing. That is:

$$P > 0 \text{ and } \left(1 - \frac{1}{Ex}\right) < 0; \text{ hence } MR < 0$$

The relationship is given in Exhibit 5.

We may summarize these results as follows:

1. If the demand is inelastic ($E_x < 1$), an increase in price leads to an increase in total revenue, and a decrease in price leads to fall in total revenue. That is P and TR move in the same direction.

2. If the demand is elastic ($E_x > 1$), an increase in price will result in the decrease of the total revenue, while a decrease in price will result in an increase in the total revenue. That is P and TR move in opposite direction.
3. If the demand has unitary elasticity, total revenue is not affected by changes in price.

THE SLOPE OF A DEMAND CURVE IS NOT THE SAME AS THE PRICE ELASTICITY OF DEMAND.

Exhibit 5

Relationship Between *AR*, *MR*, *TR*, and Elasticity

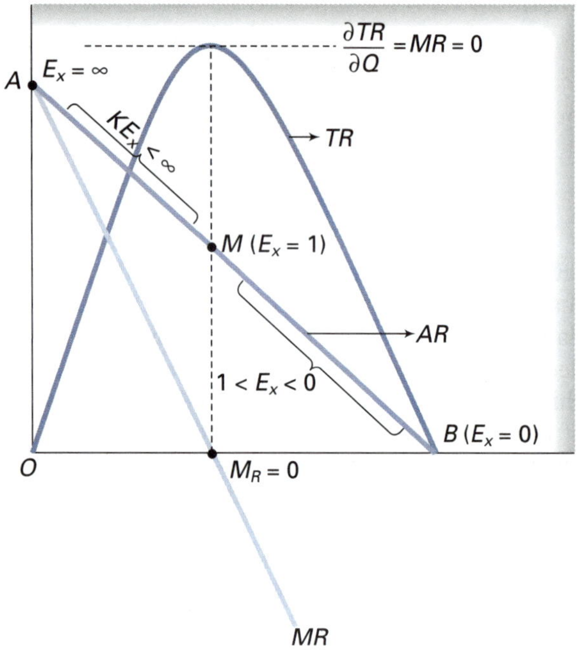

Constant-Elasticity Demand Curves

Again, price elasticity measures the responsiveness of consumers to a change in price. The shape of the demand curve for a firm's product is key in the pricing and output decision. This responsiveness varies along a linear demand curve unless the demand curve is horizontal or vertical, as in Exhibits 6a and 6b. These two demand curves, along with the special demand curve in Exhibit 6c, are all called *constant-elasticity demand curves* because the elasticity does not change along the curves.

perfectly elastic demand curve a horizontal line reflecting a situation in which any price increase would reduce quantity demanded to zero; the elasticity has an absolute value of infinity

Perfectly Elastic Demand Curve

The horizontal demand curve in Exhibit 6a indicates that consumers demand all that is offered for sale at the given price *p* (the quantity actually demanded depends on the amount supplied at that price). If the price rises above *p*, however, quantity demanded drops to zero. This is a **perfectly elastic demand curve**, and its elasticity value is infinity, a number too large to be defined. You may think this an odd sort of demand curve: Consumers, as a result of a small increase in price, go from demanding as much as is supplied to demanding none of the good. Consumers are so sensitive to price changes that they tolerate no price increase. As you will see in a later chapter, this behavior reflects the demand for the output of any individual producer when many producers supply identical products at the market price of *p*.

Exhibit 6a

Constant-Elasticity Demand Curves: Perfectly Elastic

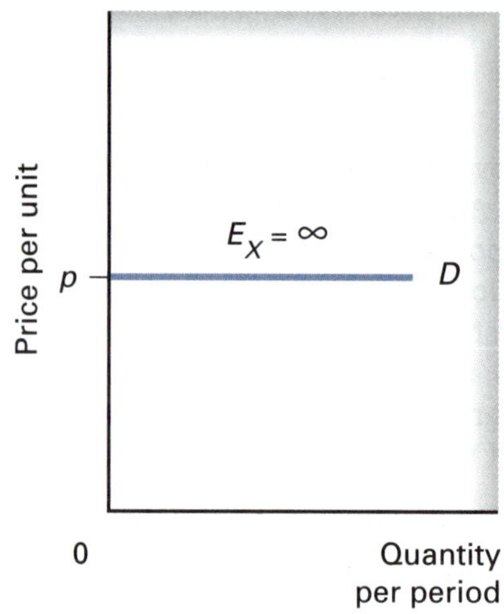

Perfectly Inelastic Demand Curve

Along the vertical demand curve in Exhibit 6b, quantity demanded does not vary when the price changes. This demand curve expresses consumer sentiment when "price is no object." For example, if you are extremely rich and need insulin to survive, price would be no object. No matter how high the price, you would continue to demand whatever it takes. And if the price of insulin should drop, you would not increase your quantity demanded. Because the percentage change in quantity demanded is zero

Exhibit 6b

Constant-Elasticity Demand Curves: Perfectly Inelastic

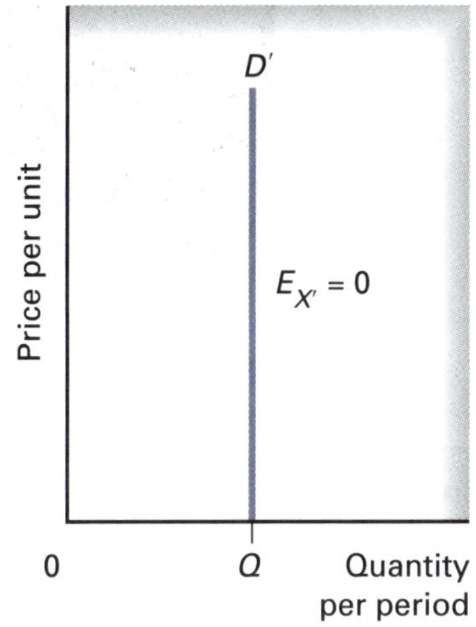

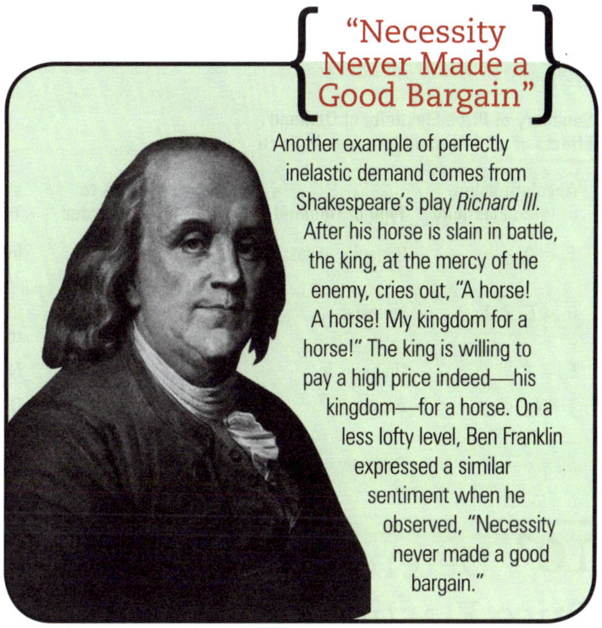

© CLASSICSTOCK/ALAMY

for any given percentage change in price, the numerical value of the price elasticity is zero. A vertical demand curve is called a **perfectly inelastic demand curve**.

Unit-Elastic Demand Curve: Rectangular Hyperbola

Exhibit 6c presents a demand curve that is unit elastic everywhere. Along a **unit-elastic demand curve**, any percentage change in price causes an exact opposite percentage change in quantity demanded. Because changes in price and in quantity demanded are offsetting, total revenue remains constant for every price-quantity combination along the curve.

Exhibit 6c

Constant-Elasticity Demand Curves: Unit Elastic

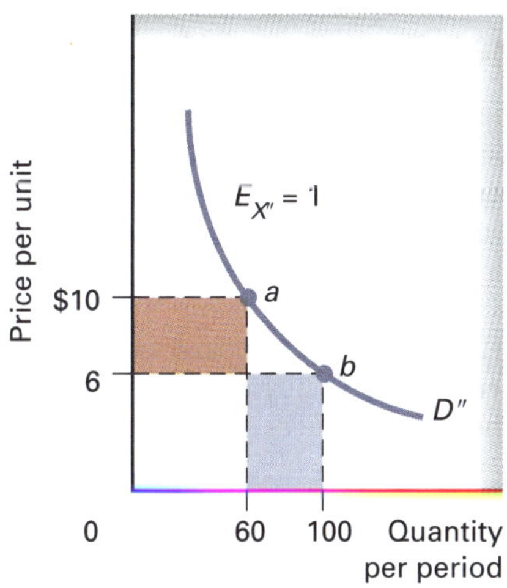

For example, when the price falls from $10 to $6, the quantity demanded increases from 60 to 100 units. The price drops by $4/$8, or 50 percent, and the quantity increases by 40/80, or 50 percent. The pink shaded rectangle shows the loss in total revenue from cutting the price; the blue shaded rectangle shows the gain in total revenue from selling more at the lower price. Because the demand curve is unit elastic, the revenue gained from selling more just offsets the revenue lost from lowering the price, so total revenue remains unchanged at $600.

Each demand curve in Exhibit 6 is called a **constant-elasticity demand curve** because the elasticity is the same all along the curve. In contrast, the downward-sloping linear demand curve examined earlier had a different elasticity value at each point along the curve. Exhibit 7 lists the absolute values for the five categories of price elasticity we have discussed, summarizing the effects of a 10 percent price increase on quantity demanded and on total revenue. Give this exhibit some thought now, and see if you can draw a demand curve for each category of elasticity.

perfectly inelastic demand curve
a vertical line reflecting a situation in which any price change has no effect on the quantity demanded; the elasticity value is zero

unit-elastic demand curve
everywhere along the demand curve, the percentage change in price causes an equal but offsetting percentage change in quantity demanded, so total revenue remains the same; the elasticity has an absolute value of 1.0

constant-elasticity demand curve
the type of demand that exists when price elasticity is the same everywhere along the curve; the elasticity value is unchanged

Exhibit 7

Summary of Price Elasticity of Demand Effects of a 10 Percent Increase in Price

Absolute Value of Price Elasticity	Type of Demand	What Happens to Quantity Demanded	What Happens to Total Revenue
$E_D = 0$	Perfectly inelastic	No change	Increases by 10 percent
$0 < E_D < 1$	Inelastic	Drops by less than 10 percent	Increases by less than 10 percent
$E_D = 1$	Unit elastic	Drops by 10 percent	No change
$1 < E_D < \infty$	Elastic	Drops by more than 10 percent	Decreases
$E_D = \infty$	Perfectly elastic	Drops to 0	Drops to 0

© JB REED/BLOOMBERG NEWS/LANDOV

LO2 Determinants of the Price Elasticity of Demand

So far we have explored the technical properties of demand elasticity and discussed why price elasticity varies along a downward-sloping demand curve. But we have yet to consider why price elasticities of demand are different for different goods. Several factors influence the price elasticity of demand for a good.

Availability of Substitutes

As we saw in Chapter 4, your particular wants can be satisfied in a variety of ways. A rise in the price of pizza makes other food relatively cheaper. If close substitutes are available, an increase in the price of pizza prompts some consumers to buy substitutes. But if nothing else satisfies like pizza, the quantity of pizza demanded does not decline as much. *The greater the availability of substitutes and the more similar these substitutes are to the good in question, the greater that good's price elasticity of demand.*

The number and similarity of substitutes depend on how the good is defined. *The more narrow the definition, the more substitutes and, thus, the more elastic the demand.* For example, the demand for Post Raisin Bran is more elastic than the demand for raisin bran more generally because there are more substitutes for Post Raisin Bran, including Kellogg's Raisin Bran and Total Raisin Bran, than for raisin bran more generally. The demand for raisin bran, however, is more elastic than the demand for breakfast cereal more generally because the consumer has many substitutes for raisin bran, such as cereals made from corn, rice, wheat, or oats, and processed with or without honey, nuts, fruit, or chocolate. To give you some idea of the range of elasticities, the price elasticity of demand for Post Raisin Bran has been estimated to be −2.5 versus −0.9 for all breakfast cereal.[1]

Certain goods—some prescription drugs, for instance—have no close substitutes. The demand for such goods tends to be less elastic than for goods with close substitutes, such as Bayer aspirin. Much advertising is aimed at establishing in the consumer's mind the uniqueness of a particular product—an effort to convince consumers "to accept no substitutes." Why might a firm want to make the demand for its product less elastic?

As an example of the impact of substitutes on price elasticity, consider the timing of commercial breaks during network TV movies. When the movie begins, viewers have several substitutes available, including other shows and perhaps movies on other networks. To keep viewers from switching channels, the first movie segment is longer than usual, perhaps 20 or 25 minutes before a commercial break. But once viewers get interested in the movie, shows on other channels are no longer good substitutes, so broadcasters inject commercials more often with less fear of losing viewers. Toward the end of the movie, networks insert commercials with even greater frequency, confident that viewers will hang on to see how things turn out.

Share of the Consumer's Budget Spent on the Good

Recall that a higher price reduces quantity demanded in part because a higher price reduces the real spending power of consumer income. Because spending on some goods claims a large share of the consumer's budget, a change in the price of such a good has a substantial impact on the consumer's *ability* to buy it. An increase in the price of housing, for example, reduces consumers' ability to buy housing. The income effect of a higher price reduces the quantity demanded. In

1. See Jerry A. Hausman "The Price Elasticity of Demand for Breakfast Cereal," in *The Economics of New Goods,* T. F. Bresnahan and J. J. Gordon, eds. (University of Chicago Press, 1997).

contrast, the income effect of an increase in the price of, say, paper towels is trivial because paper towels represent such a tiny share of any budget. *The more important the item is as a share of the consumer's budget, other things constant, the greater is the income effect of a change in price, so the more price elastic is the demand for the item.* Hence, the quantity of housing demanded is more responsive to a given percentage change in price than is the quantity of paper towels demanded.

> "Consumers can substitute lower-priced goods for higher-priced goods, but finding substitutes usually takes time."

Length of Adjustment Period

Consumers can substitute lower-priced goods for higher-priced goods, but finding substitutes usually takes time. Suppose your college announces a sharp increase in room and board fees, effective next term. Some students will move off campus before the next term begins; others may wait until the next academic year. Over time, the college may get fewer applicants for room and board and more incoming students will choose off-campus housing. The longer the adjustment period, the greater the consumers' ability to substitute away from relatively higher-priced products toward lower-priced substitutes. Thus, *the longer the period of adjustment, the more responsive the change in quantity demanded is to a given change in price.* Here's another example: Between 1973 and 1974, OPEC (Organization of the Petroleum Exporting Countries) raised gasoline prices 45 percent, but the quantity demanded initially decreased only 8 percent. As more time passed, however, people bought smaller cars and made greater use of public transportation. They also bought more energy-efficient appliances and added more insulation to their homes. Thus, the percentage change in quantity demanded was greater the longer consumers adjusted to the price hike.

Exhibit 8

Demand Becomes More Elastic over Time

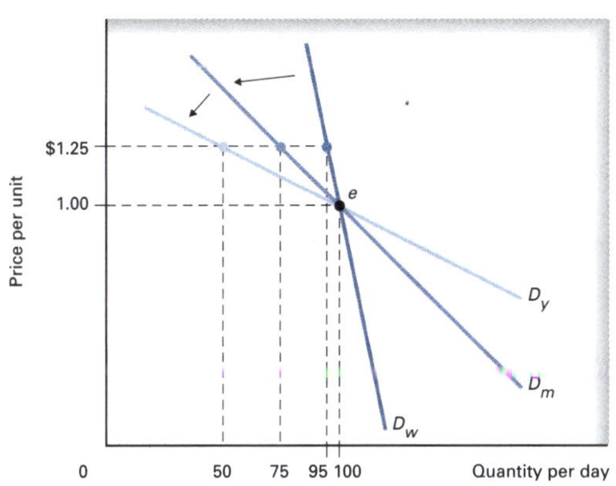

Exhibit 8 shows how demand becomes more elastic over time. Given an initial price of $1.00 at point *e*, let D_w be the demand curve one week after a price change; D_m, one month after; and D_y, one year after. Suppose the price increases to $1.25. The more time consumers have to respond to the price increase, the greater the reduction in quantity demanded. The demand curve D_w shows that one week after the price increase, the quantity demanded has not declined much—in this case, from 100 to 95 per day. The demand curve D_m indicates a reduction to 75 per day after one month, and demand curve D_y shows a reduction to 50 per day after one year. Notice that among these demand curves and over the range starting from point *e*, the flatter the demand curve, the more price elastic the demand. Here, elasticity seems linked to the slope because we begin from a common point—the price-quantity combination at point *e*.

Elasticity Estimates

Let's look at some estimates of the price elasticity of demand for particular goods and services. Remember, finding alternatives when the price increases takes time. Thus, when estimating price elasticity, economists often distinguish between a period during which consumers have little time to adjust—let's call it the

Exhibit 9

Selected Price Elasticities of Demand (absolute values)

Product	Short Run	Long Run
Cigarettes (among adults)	—	0.4
Electricity (residential)	0.1	1.9
Air travel	0.1	2.4
Medical care and hospitalization	0.3	0.9
Gasoline	0.4	1.5
Milk	0.4	—
Fish (cod)	0.5	—
Wine	0.7	1.2
Movies	0.9	3.7
Natural gas (residential)	1.4	2.1
Automobiles	1.9	2.2
Chevrolets	—	4.0

SOURCES: F. Chaloupka, "Rational Addictive Behavior and Cigarette Smoking," *Journal of Political Economy* (August 1991); Hsaing-tai Cheng and Oral Capps, Jr., "Demand for Fish," *American Journal of Agricultural Economics* (August 1998); J. Johnson et al., "Short-Run and Long-Run Elasticities for Canadian Consumption of Alcoholic Beverages," *Review of Economics and Statistics* (February 1992); Douglas Young et al., "Alcohol Consumption, Measurement Error, and Beverage Prices," *Journal of Studies on Alcohol* (March 2003); J. Griffin, *Energy Conservation in the OECD, 1980–2000* (Cambridge, Mass.: Balinger, 1979); H. Houthakker and L. Taylor, *Consumer Demand in the United States: Analysis and Projections,* 2nd ed. (Cambridge, Mass.: Harvard University Press, 1970); and G. Lakshmanan and W. Anderson, "Residential Energy Demand in the United States," *Regional Science and Urban Economics* 10 (August 1980).

© BRIAN HAGIWARA/FOODPIX/JUPITERIMAGES

{Smoke Out}

There are no close substitutes for cigarettes, even in the long run, so the demand for cigarettes among adults is price inelastic. For teens, however, demand for cigarettes is more price elastic. Why are teenagers more sensitive to price changes than adults?

1. Because teen income is relatively low, the share spent on cigarettes usually exceeds the share spent by adult smokers.
2. Peer pressure shapes a young person's decision to smoke more than an adult's decision to continue smoking (if anything, adults face negative peer pressure for smoking). Thus, the effect of a higher price gets magnified among young smokers because that higher price also reduces smoking by peers. With fewer peers smoking, teens face less pressure to smoke, and so on.
3. Young people not yet addicted to nicotine are more sensitive to price increases than are adult smokers, who are more likely to be already hooked. Increasing taxes on cigarettes, then, can have a significant impact on teen smoking. A large tax increase on cigarettes in Canada cut youth smoking by two-thirds.

SOURCES: John Tauras, "An Empirical Analysis of Adult Cigarette Demand," *Eastern Economic Journal* 31(3) (Summer 2005): pp. 361–375; Phillip Cook and Rebecca Hutchinson, "Smoke Signals: Adolescent Smoking and School Continuation," *NBER Working Paper* 12462 (August 2006); and Hana Ross and Frank Chaloupka, "The Effects of Public Policies and Prices on Youth Smoking," *Southern Economic Journal* (April 2004).

short run—and a period during which consumers can more fully adjust to a price change—let's call it the *long run*. Exhibit 6 provides some short-run and long-run price elasticity estimates for selected products.

The price elasticity of demand is greater in the long run because consumers have more time to adjust. For example, if the price of electricity rose today, consumers in the short run might cut back a bit in their use of electrical appliances, and those in homes with electric heat might lower the thermostat in winter. Over time, however, consumers would switch to more energy-efficient appliances, insulate their homes better, and perhaps switch from electric heat. So the demand for electricity is more elastic in the long run than in the short run, as shown in Exhibit 8. In fact, in every instance where estimates for both the short run and the long run are listed, demand is more elastic in the long run than the short run. Notice also that the demand for Chevrolets is more elastic than the demand for automobiles more generally. Chevrolets have many more substitutes than do automobiles in general.

We now develop a number of theorems related to price elasticity of demand.

Theorem 1

The price elasticity of demand for a linear demand curve varies from infinity at the price axis, to zero at the quantity axis.

Proof

Refer to Exhibit 10

Exhibit 10

Price Elasticity of Demand for a Linear Demand Curve

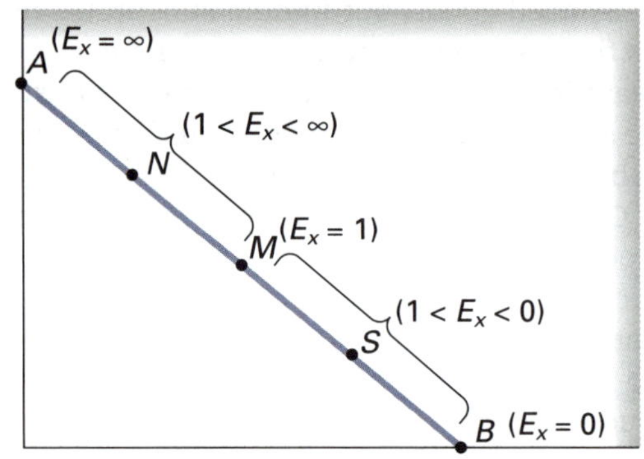

We have already proved that the elasticity of a linear demand curve is given by the ratio of segments to the right and left of the point.

Thus:

$$E_x \text{ at A } = \frac{AB}{O} = \infty$$

$$E_x \text{ at N } = \frac{NB}{AN} > 1 \text{ (Since N lies to the left of midpoint)}$$

$$E_x \text{ at M } = \frac{MB}{AM} = 1 \text{ (Since M is the midpoint)}$$

$$E_x \text{ at S } = \frac{SB}{AS} < 1 \text{ (Since S lies to the right of midpoint)}$$

$$E_x \text{ at B } = \frac{O}{AB} = 0$$

Theorem 2

Comparing two linear demand curves with the same slope, the one farther away from the origin has lower elasticity at any given price.

Proof

Let the two demand curves be represented by AB and RS. Since the demand curves are parallel, they have common slope.

Exhibit 11

Two Demand Curve with Same Slope But Different Elasticities

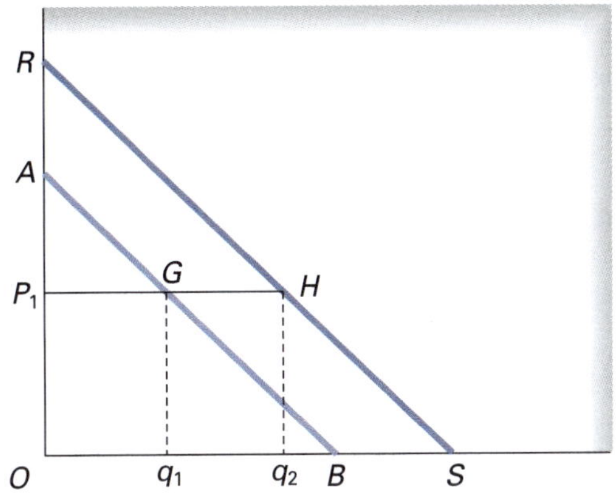

Now:

$$E_x \text{ at } G = \frac{\partial q}{\partial P} \times \frac{P}{q} = \frac{\partial q}{\partial P} \times \frac{OP_1}{Oq_1}$$

$$E_x \text{ at } H = \frac{\partial q}{\partial P} \times \frac{P}{q} = \frac{\partial q}{\partial P} \times \frac{OP_1}{Oq_2}$$

It may be noted that $\frac{\partial q}{\partial P}$ is common to both. Further, $oq_2 > oq_1$. Thus $\frac{OP_1}{Oq_1} > \frac{OP_1}{Oq_2}$.

Therefore E_x at G is greater than. E_x at H.

Theorem 3

For two intersecting demand curves, the flatter curve has higher elasticity.

Proof

Let the two demand curves be *CD* and *AB*.

Exhibit 12

Flatter Demand Curve as Higher Elasticity

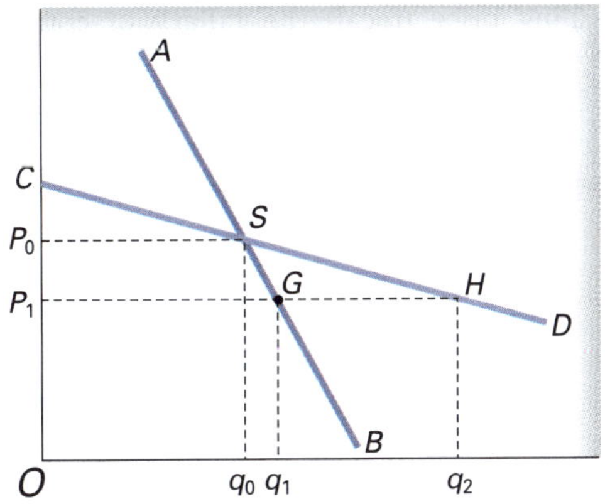

Elasticity is defined as:

$$E_x = \frac{\Delta q}{\Delta P} \times \frac{P}{q}$$

At the point of intersection (s), $\frac{P}{q}$ is common for both the demand curves. Thus, elasticity varies with $\frac{\Delta q}{\Delta P}$.

Now $\Delta q = q_0q_1$ for demand curve *AB*, while
$\Delta q = q_0q_2$ for demand curve *CD*.

Since $q_0q_2 > q_0q_1$,

$\frac{\Delta q}{\Delta P}$ is greater for demand curve *CD*, so that its elasticity is higher.

Theorem 4

Two demand curves with different slopes can have same elasticity for any given price.

Proof

Let the two demand curves be *AB* and *AC*. They have a common intercept on the vertical axis.

Now,

$$E_x \text{ at } G = \frac{GB}{AG} = \frac{q_1B}{Oq_1} = \frac{P_0O}{AP_0}$$

Similarly,

$$E_x \text{ at } H = \frac{HC}{AH} = \frac{q_2C}{Oq_2} = \frac{P_0O}{AP_0}$$

Exhibit 13

Iso-Elastic Demand Curves

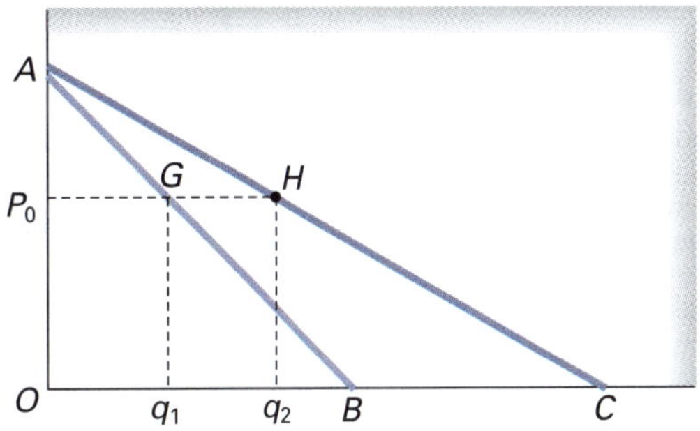

Since the ratio $\frac{P_0O}{AP_0}$ is common for both the demand curves, E_x at G is the same as E_x at *H*. Such demand curves, with same elasticities at any given price are said to be "isoelastic" demand curves.

LO3 Price Elasticity of Supply

Prices signal both sides of the market about the relative scarcity of products. Higher prices discourage consumption but encourage production. Lower prices encourage consumption but discourage production. The price elasticity of demand measures how responsive consumers are to a price change. Likewise, the **price elasticity of supply** measures how responsive producers are to a price change. Supply elas-

price elasticity of supply
a measure of the responsiveness of quantity supplied to a price change; the percentage change in quantity supplied divided by the percentage change in price

$$E_s = \frac{\Delta q}{(q + q')/2} \div \frac{\Delta p}{(p + p')/2}$$

ticity is calculated in the same way as demand elasticity. In simplest terms, the price elasticity of supply equals the percentage change in quantity supplied divided by the percentage change in price. Because a higher price usually increases quantity supplied, the percentage change in price and the percentage change in quantity supplied move in the same direction, so the price elasticity of supply is usually a positive number.

Exhibit 14 depicts a typical upward-sloping supply curve. As you can see, if the price increases from p to p', the quantity supplied increases from q to q'. Price and quantity supplied move in the same direction. Let's look at the arc elasticity formula for the supply curve. The price elasticity of supply is:

$$E_S = \frac{\Delta q}{(q + q')/2} \div \frac{\Delta p}{(p + p')/2}$$

where Δq is the change in quantity supplied and Δp is the change in price. This is the same formula used to compute the price elasticity of demand except that q here is quantity supplied, not quantity demanded. The terminology for supply elasticity is the same as for demand elasticity: If supply elasticity is less than 1.0, supply is inelastic; if it equals 1.0, supply is unit elastic; and if it exceeds 1.0, supply is elastic.

inelastic supply a change in price has relatively little effect on quantity supplied; the percentage change in quantity supplied is less than the percentage change in price; the price elasticity of supply has a value less than 1.0

unit-elastic supply the percentage change in quantity supplied equals the percentage change in price; the price elasticity of supply equals 1.0

elastic supply a change in price has a relatively large effect on quantity supplied; the percentage change in quantity supplied exceeds the percentage change in price; the price elasticity of supply exceeds 1.0

perfectly elastic supply curve a horizontal line reflecting a situation in which any price decrease drops the quantity supplied to zero; the elasticity value is infinity

Constant-Elasticity Supply Curves

Again, price elasticity of supply measures the responsiveness of producers to a change in price. This responsiveness varies along a linear supply curve unless the curve is horizontal or vertical, as in Exhibits 15a and 15b, or passes through the origin, as in Exhibit 15c. These three supply curves are called *constant-elasticity supply curves* because the elasticity does not change along the curves.

Exhibit 14

Price Elasticity of Supply

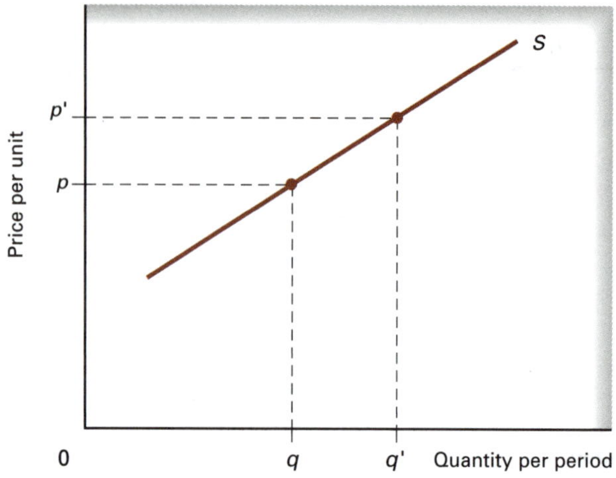

Perfectly Elastic Supply Curve

At one extreme is the horizontal supply curve, such as supply curve S in Exhibit 15a. In this case, producers supply none of the good at a price below p but supply any amount at price p (the quantity actually supplied at price p depends on the amount demanded at that price). Because a tiny increase from a price just below p to a price of p results in an unlimited quantity supplied, this is called a perfectly elastic supply curve, which has a numerical value of infinity. As individual consumers, we typically face perfectly elastic supply curves. When we go to the supermarket, we usually can buy as much as we want at the prevailing price but none at a lower price. Obviously all consumers together could not buy an unlimited amount at the prevailing price (recall the fallacy of composition from Chapter 1).

Exhibit 15a

Constant-Elasticity Supply Curves: Perfectly Elastic

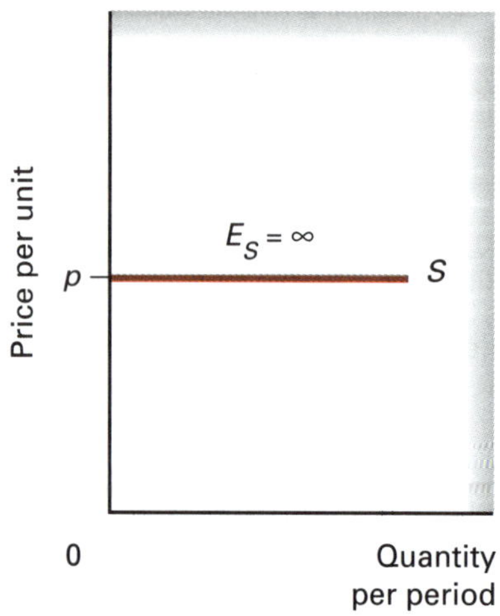

Perfectly Inelastic Supply Curve

The least responsive relationship is where there is no change in the quantity supplied regardless of the price, as shown by the vertical supply curve S′ in Exhibit 15b. Because the percentage change in quantity supplied is zero, regardless of the change in price, the price elasticity of supply is zero. This is a **perfectly inelastic supply curve**. Any good in fixed supply, such as Picasso paintings, 1995 Dom Perignon champagne, or Cadillacs once owned by Elvis Presley, has a perfectly inelastic supply curve.

Exhibit 15b

Constant-Elasticity Supply Curves: Perfectly Inelastic

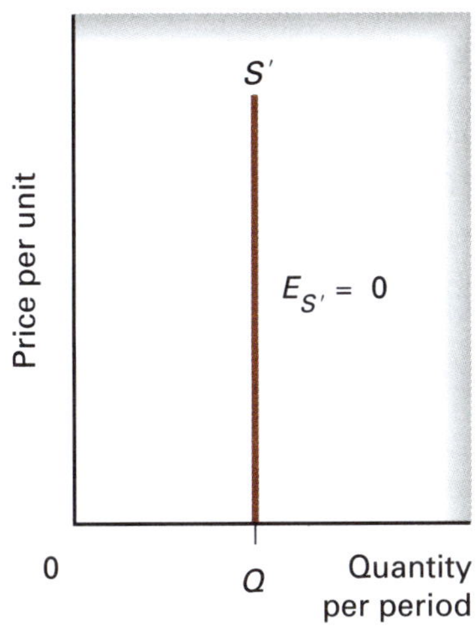

Unit-Elastic Supply Curve

Any supply curve that is a straight line from the origin—such as S″ in Exhibit 15c—is a **unit-elastic supply curve**. This means a percentage change in price always generates an identical percentage change in quantity supplied. For example, along S″ a doubling of the price results in a doubling of the quantity supplied. Note that unit elasticity is based not on the slope of the line but on the fact that the linear supply curve is a ray from the origin.

Exhibit 15c

Constant-Elasticity Supply Curves: Unit Elastic

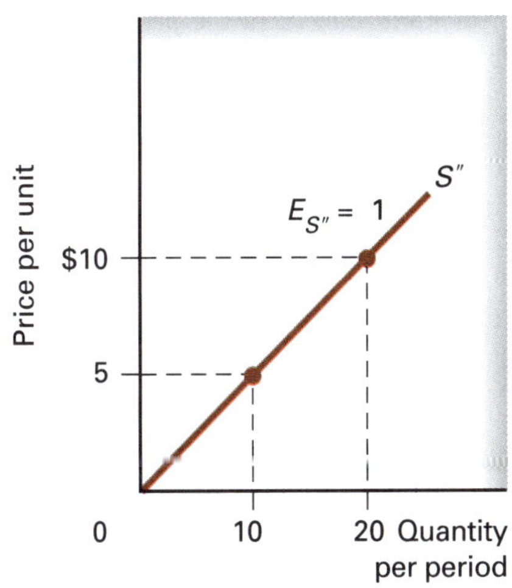

Proof: Any straight line supply curve from the origin has unitary elasticity.

Exhibit 16

Unitary Elastic Supply Curve: The Proof

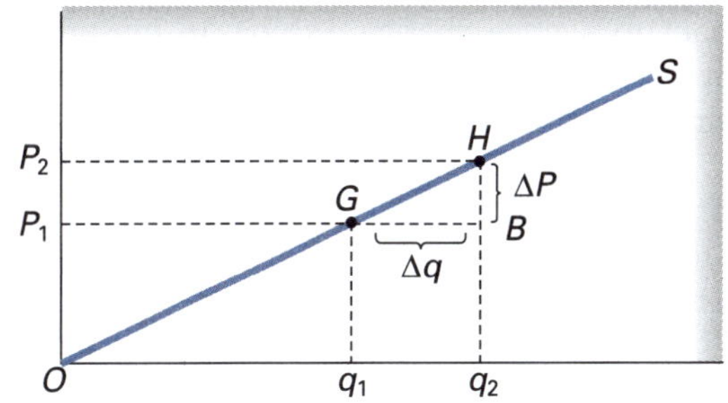

In Exhibit 16 consider triangles HBG and Hq2O. Clearly these are similar triangles. Thus, ratio of any two sides of one triangle will be equal to the ratio of corresponding two sides of the other triangle.

Now $$\frac{HB}{GB} = \frac{Hq_2}{Oq_2}$$

$$Ex = \frac{\Delta q}{\Delta P} \times \frac{P}{q}$$

But $$\frac{\Delta q}{\Delta P} = \frac{GB}{HB} \left(= \frac{Oq_2}{Hq_2} \right)$$

and $$\frac{P}{q} = \frac{Hq_2}{Oq_2}$$

Re-writing

$$Ex = \frac{GB}{HB} \times \frac{Hq_2}{Oq_2}$$

$$= \frac{Oq_2}{Hq_2} \times \frac{Hq_2}{Oq_2}$$

$$Ex = 1$$

Determinants of Supply Elasticity

The elasticity of supply indicates how responsive producers are to a change in price. Their response depends on how easy it is to alter quantity supplied when the price changes. If the cost of supplying additional units rises sharply as output

perfectly inelastic supply curve
a vertical line reflecting a situation in which a price change has no effect on the quantity supplied; the elasticity value is zero

unit-elastic supply curve
a percentage change in price causes an identical percentage change in quantity supplied; depicted by a supply curve that is a straight line from the origin; the elasticity value equals 1.0

expands, then a higher price causes little increase in quantity supplied, so supply tends to be inelastic. But if the marginal cost rises slowly as output expands, the lure of a higher price prompts a large increase in quantity supplied. In this case, supply is more elastic.

One determinant of supply elasticity is the length of the adjustment period under consideration. Just as demand becomes more elastic over time as consumers adjust to price changes, supply also becomes more elastic over time as producers adjust to price changes. The longer the adjustment period under consideration, the more able producers are to adapt to a price change. Exhibit 16 presents different supply curves for each of three periods. S_w is the supply curve when the period of adjustment is a week. As you can see, a higher price generates little response in quantity supplied because firms have little time to adjust. This supply curve is inelastic between $1.00 to $1.25.

Exhibit 16

Supply Becomes More Elastic over Time

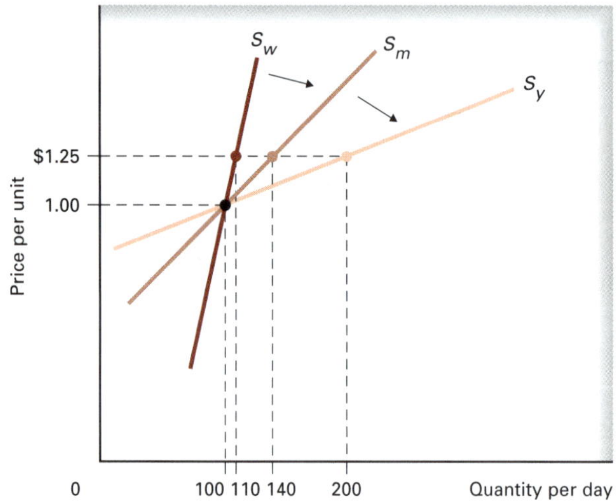

S_m is the supply curve when the adjustment period under consideration is a month. Firms have more time to vary output. Thus, supply is more elastic when the adjustment period is a month than when it's a week. Supply is yet more elastic when the adjustment period is a year, as is shown by S_y. As the adjustment period lengthens, the supply response increases. For example, if the price of oil increases, oil producers in the short run can try to pump more from existing wells, but in the long run, a higher price stimulates more exploration. Research confirms the positive link between the price elasticity of supply and the length of the adjustment period. *The elasticity of supply is typically greater the longer the period of adjustment.*

The ability to increase quantity supplied in response to a higher price differs across industries. For example, oil was discovered on Alaska's north slope in 1967; but oil did not begin to flow south until a decade later. More generally, the response time is slower for suppliers of oil, electricity, and timber (where expansion may take years, if not decades) than for suppliers of window-washing service, lawn maintenance, and hot-dog vending (where expansion may take only days).

income elasticity of demand
the percentage change in demand divided by the percentage change in consumer income; the value is positive for normal goods and negative for inferior goods

LO4 Other Elasticity Measures

Price elasticities of demand and supply are frequently used in economic analysis, but three other elasticity measures also provide valuable information.

Income Elasticity of Demand

What happens to the demand for new cars, fresh vegetables, or computer software if consumer income increases by, say, 10 percent? The answer is of great interest to producers because it helps them predict the effect of changing consumer income on quantity sold and on total revenue. The **income elasticity of demand** measures how responsive demand is to a change in consumer income. Specifically, *the income elasticity of demand measures the percentage change in demand divided by the percentage change in income that caused it.*

Symbolically, we may write point income elasticity as:

$$E_I = \frac{dQ}{Q} \Big/ \frac{dI}{I} = \frac{dQ}{dI} \times \frac{I}{Q}$$

Similarly, arc income elasticity may be calculated as:

$$E_I = \frac{\Delta Q}{\Delta I} \times \frac{\frac{I_1 + I_2}{2}}{\frac{Q_1 + Q_2}{2}} = \frac{\Delta Q}{\Delta I} \times \frac{I_1 + I_2}{Q_1 + Q_2}$$

© MARK CASS/BRAND X PICTURES/JUPITERIMAGES

© AP IMAGES

Fast Facts—Economic Recession and Automotive Sales

1.9 million—nonfarm job losses January–November 2008.

6.7%—November 2008 unemployment rate

$3.6 billion—October 2008 decline in outstanding consumer credit charges

0.5%—decline in U.S. GDP during 3Q08

746,789—November 2008 U.S. new-vehicle sales

37%—November 2008 decline in U.S. new-vehicle sales

$60 billion—accumulated debt of General Motors Corp.

2011—estimated time that Ford Motor Co. will break even or return to profitability

Now consider this: Are automobiles normal goods or inferior goods?

SOURCE: Sudeep Reddy, Ray A. Smith, and Kris Maher, "Job Losses Worst Since '74: 533,000 Shed in November," *Wall Street Journal,* 6 December 2008. Available at http://online.wsj.com/article/SB122848262764182657.html (accessed 11 December 2008); Jeff Bater, "Consumer Borrowing Declined in November," Real Time Economics Blog, posted 5 December 2008. Available at http://blogs.wsj.com/economics/2008/12/05/consumer-borrowing-declined-in-november/ (accessed 11 December 2008); John D. Stoll, Matthew Dolan, Jeffrey McCracken, and Josh Mitchell, "Big Three Seek $34 Billion Aid," *Wall Street Journal,* 3 December 2008. Available at http://online.wsj.com/article/SB122823078705672467.html (accessed 11 December 2008).

As noted in Chapter 4, the demand for some products, such as used furniture and used clothing, actually declines, or shifts leftward, as income increases. Thus, the income elasticity of demand for such goods is negative. Goods with income elasticities less than zero are called *inferior goods*. But the demand for most goods increases, or shifts rightward, as income increases. These are called *normal goods* and have income elasticities greater than zero.

Let's take a closer look at normal goods. Suppose demand increases as income increases but by a smaller percentage than income increases. In such cases, the income elasticity is greater than 0 but less than 1. For example, people buy more food as their incomes rise, but the percentage increase in demand is less than the percentage increase in income. Normal goods with income elasticities less than 1 are called *income inelastic. Necessities* such as food, housing, and clothing often have income elasticities less than 1. Goods with income elasticity greater than 1 are called *income elastic. Luxuries* such as high-end cars, vintage wines, and meals at upscale restaurants have income elasticities greater than 1. By the way, the terms *inferior goods, necessities,* and *luxuries* are not value judgments about the merits of particular goods; these terms are simply convenient ways of classifying economic behavior.

The main determinants of income elasticity are:

1. The nature of the need that the commodity covers: the percentage of income spent on food declines as income increases (this is known as Engel's Law and has sometimes been used as a measure of welfare and of the development stage of an economy).
2. The initial level of income of a country: For example, a TV set is a luxury in an underdeveloped, poor country while it is a "necessity" in a country with high per capita income.
3. The time period: Because consumption patterns adjust with a time-lag to changes in income.

Exhibit 17 presents income elasticity estimates for some goods and services. The figures indicate, for example, that as income increases, consumers spend proportionately more on wine, restaurant meals, and owner-occupied housing. Spending on food and rental housing also increases as income increases, but less than proportionately. Spending on beer declines with rising income. So as income rises, the demand for restaurant meals increases more in percentage terms than does the demand for food, and the demand for owner-occupied housing increases more in percentage terms than does the demand for rental housing. The demand for wine increases sharply, while the demand for beer declines. Flour also has negative income elasticity. According to these estimates, beer and flour are inferior goods.

Cross-Price Elasticity of Demand

A firm that produces an entire line of products has a special interest in how a change in the price of one item affects the demand for another. For example, the Coca-Cola Company needs to know how changing the price of Cherry Coke affects sales of Classic Coke. The company also needs to know the relationship between the price of Coke and the demand for Pepsi and vice versa. The responsiveness of the

Exhibit 17

Selected Income Elasticities of Demand

Product	Income Elasticity	Product	Income Elasticity
Wine	5.03	Physicians' services	0.75
Private education	2.46	Coca-Cola	0.68
Automobiles	2.45	Beef	0.62
Owner-occupied housing	1.49	Food	0.51
Furniture	1.48	Coffee	0.51
Dental service	1.42	Cigarettes	0.50
Restaurant meals	1.40	Gasoline and oil	0.48
Spirits ("hard" liquor)	1.21	Rental housing	0.43
Shoes	1.10	Pork	0.18
Chicken	1.06	Beer	−0.09
Clothing	0.92	Flour	−0.36

SOURCES: Ivan Bloor, "Food for Thought," *Economic Review* (September 1999); F. Gasmi et al., "Econometric Analysis of Collusive Behavior in a Soft-Drink Market," *Journal of Economics and Management Strategy* (Summer 1992); X. M. Gao et al., "A Microeconomic Model Analysis of U.S. Consumer Demand for Alcoholic Beverages," *Applied Economics* (January 1995); H. Houthakker and L. Taylor, *Consumer Demand in the United States: Analyses and Projections,* 2nd ed. (Cambridge, Mass.: Harvard University Press, 1970); C. Huang et al., "The Demand for Coffee in the United States, 1963–1977," *Quarterly Review of Economics and Business* (Summer 1980); and G. Brester and M. Wohlgenant, "Estimating Interrelated Demands for Meats Using New Measures for Ground and Table Cut Beef," *American Journal of Agricultural Economics* (November 1991).

© IMAGE SOURCE

demand for one good to changes in the price of another good is called the **cross-price elasticity of demand**. This is defined as the percentage change in the demand of one good divided by the percentage change in the price of another good.

> "As income rises, the demand for restaurant meals increases more in percentage terms than does the demand for food, and the demand for owner-occupied housing increases more in percentage terms than does the demand for rental housing."

Symbolically we may write point cross price elasticity as:

$$E_{xy} = \frac{dQ_x}{Q_x} \Big/ \frac{dP_x}{P_x} = \frac{dQ_x}{dP_y} \times \frac{P_y}{Q_x}$$

Similarly, arc cross price elasticity may be calculated as:

$$E_{xy} = \frac{\Delta Q_x}{\Delta P_y} \times \frac{\frac{P_{y1} + P_{y2}}{2}}{\frac{Q_{x1} + Q_{x2}}{2}} = \frac{\Delta Q_x}{\Delta P_y} \times \frac{P_{y1} + P_{y2}}{Q_{x1} + Q_{x2}}$$

cross-price elasticity of demand the percentage change in the demand of one good divided by the percentage change in the price of another good; it's positive for substitutes, negative for complements, and zero for unrelated goods

Its numerical value can be positive, negative, or zero, depending on whether the two goods in question are substitutes, complements, or unrelated, respectively.

The higher the value of the cross price elasticity between two goods, the stronger will be the degree of substitutability or complementarily between x and y.

The main determinant of cross price elasticity is the nature of the commodities relative to their uses. If two commodities can satisfy equally well the same need, the cross price elasticity is high and vice-versa.

Substitutes

If an increase in the price of one good leads to an increase in the demand for another good, their cross-price elasticity is positive and the two goods are *substitutes*. For example, an increase in the price of Coke, other things constant, shifts the demand for Pepsi rightward, so the two are substitutes. The cross-price elasticity between Coke and Pepsi has been estimated at about 0.7, indicating that a 10 percent increase in the price of one increases the demand for the other by 7 percent.[2]

Complements

If an increase in the price of one good leads to a decrease in the demand for another, their cross-price elasticity is negative and the goods are *complements*. For example, an increase in the price of gasoline, other things constant, shifts the demand for tires leftward because people drive less and replace their tires less frequently. Gasoline and tires have a negative cross-price elasticity and are complements.

In summary: *The cross-price elasticity of demand is positive for substitutes and negative for complements.* Most pairs of goods selected at random are unrelated, so their cross-price elasticity is zero.

The Promotional or Advertisement Elasticity of Demand

Advertising elasticity of demand measures the sensitivity of sales (quantity demanded) to changes in expenditure for advertising and promotion. The point formula is

$$e_A = \frac{dQ_x}{Q_x} \Big/ \frac{dA}{A} = \frac{dQ_x}{dA} \times \frac{A}{Q_x}$$

where Q_x = the quantity sold or total revenue from sales and A denotes advertising expenditure. Arc elasticity is measured as:

$$E_A = \frac{\Delta Q}{\Delta A} \times \frac{\frac{A_1 + A_2}{2}}{\frac{Q_1 + Q_2}{2}} = \frac{\Delta Q}{\Delta A} \times \frac{A_1 + A_2}{Q_1 + Q_2}$$

Combined Effect of Demand Elasticities

As we said earlier, every factor that affects demand has a corresponding elasticity. When all factors are allowed to change simultaneously, their combined influence of demand is simply the sum of their individual elasticities. For example, suppose a firm is producing a luxury good and enjoys annual sales of 100,000 units. Currently the sales price per unit is twice the direct cost of manufacture. The firm's management estimates that the price elasticity of demand for this product, E_X is about –1.3, and the income elasticity of demand for it E_I is about 2.0. Economic forecasters expect real disposable income to increase by 6 per cent in the coming year. The company has just signed a labor contract that will increase direct manufacturing costs by 10 per cent. If the company follows its current pricing policy next year, how many units can it expect to sell?

The quantity demanded next year, Q_1, will be the current demand, plus the change in Q_0 caused by the price increase, Q_0, plus the change caused by the rise in income, i.e.,

$$Q_1 = Q_0 + Q_0\left(\frac{\Delta P}{P}\right)E_X + Q_0\left(\frac{\Delta I}{I}\right)E_I$$

$$= Q_0\left(I + \frac{\Delta P}{P}E_X + \frac{\Delta I}{I}E_I\right)$$

where

Q_0 = Quantity demanded in year 0 (this year)
Q_1 = Quantity demanded in year 1 (next year)
$\Delta P/P$ = Proportionate change in price
E_x = Price elasticity of demand
$\Delta I/I$ = Proportionate change in income
E_I = Income elasticity of demand

Hence,

$$Q_1 = 100{,}000\,[1 + (0.10)(-1.3) + (0.06)(2.0)] = 99{,}000$$

That is to say, the effect of the price increase will more than offset the effect of the increase in income. The net result will be a loss in sales if we assume that all other factors, such as advertising and competitor's prices, remain the same.

LO5 Applications: Theory of Demand and Supply

Application 1: Is Drug Interdiction Better Than Drug Education

In the present scenario, most nations are plagued by drug abuse. This is one of the most challenging issues faced by any country. Drug addiction not only poses a threat to the health of the youth in the country, but it also gives rise to drug related crimes. Hence, it is crucial that governments take appropriate steps to curb usage of drugs (refer Exhibit 18).

Exhibit 18a

Drug Interdiction Shifts Supply Curve Leftwards

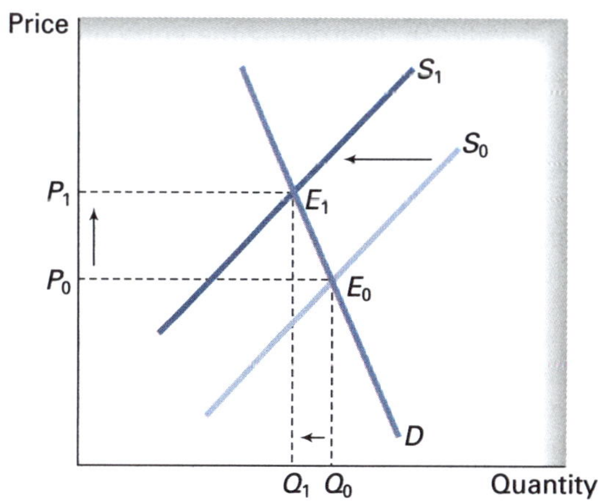

2. F. Gasmi, J. Laffont, and Q. Vuong, "Econometric Analysis of Collusive Behavior in a Soft-Drink Market," *Journal of Economics and Management Strategy* (Summer 1992).

Why Good Harvests . . . Spell Trouble for Farmers

© ANDY SACKS/STONE/GETTY IMAGES

Many of the forces that determine farm production are beyond a farmer's control. Temperature, rainfall, pests, and other natural forces affect crop size and quality. For example, favorable weather boosted crop production 16 percent in one recent year. Such increases create special problems for farmers because the demand for most farm crops, such as milk, eggs, corn, potatoes, oats, sugar, and beef, is price inelastic.

Demand for food is *income* inelastic, and it also tends to be *price* inelastic. As household incomes grow over time, spending on food may increase because consumers substitute prepared foods and restaurant meals for home cooking. But this switch has little effect on the total demand for farm products. (This modest increase in demand from *D* to *D'* is reflected in Exhibit 19.)

Because of technological improvements in production, however, the supply of farm products has increased sharply. Developments such as more sophisticated machines, better fertilizer, and healthier seeds have increased farm output per hour of labor 11-fold since 1950. Exhibit 19 shows a big increase in the supply of grain from *S* to *S'*. Because the supply increase exceeds the demand increase, the price declines. And because the demand for grain is price inelastic, the percentage drop in price exceeds the percentage increase in output. The combined effect in our example is lower total revenue.

Thus, we conclude that "**good news for farming can be bad news for farmers**".

However, even though such factors make the farmers worse off, they still adopt new hybrids or techniques of farming. This is because the agricultural market is a perfectly competitive market and each producer is a price taker. Therefore, at any given price, farmers consider it better to produce and sell more.

Exhibit 19

The Effect of Increases in Demand and Supply on Farm Revenue

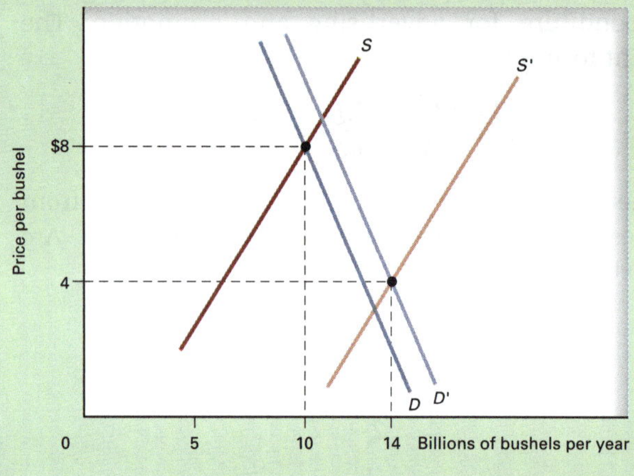

SOURCES: Bruce L. Gardner, "Changing Economic Perspective on the Farm Problem," *Journal of Economic Literature* 30 (March 1992): 62–105; and *Economic Report of the President,* February 2007, Tables B-99 at http://www.gpoaccess.gov/eop/. For current economic research at the U.S. Department of Agriculture, go to http://www.ers.usda.gov/.

In this regard, there are two contrasting methods that a country can adopt.

(i) *Drug Interdiction:* Restricting the entry of drugs in a country to reduce the circulation and supply of drugs.

(ii) *Drug Education:* Educating the youth about the ill effects of drugs. This helps in creating awareness and sensitising youth to work against drug abuse. As a result, the demand for drugs is reduced.

Policy makers have conflicting opinion about the success of the two strategies. In order to understand the effect of these strategies, we must first examine how they impact the forces of demand and supply.

Drug Interdiction: Although the purpose of drug interdiction is to reduce drug abuse, its direct impact is on the sellers. In order to check drug abuse, the government restricts the entry of drugs in the country and arrests more and more smugglers. This increases the cost of selling drugs. Therefore, the quantity of drugs sold at any given price decreases. This shifts the supply curve to the left from S_0 to S_1, keeping the demand curve constant. (Refer Exhibit 18a)

Now, drug addicts are unlikely to change their habits due to increase in drug prices. We can, thus, consider the demand for drugs to be inelastic in nature. As shown in Exhibit 18a, the percentage increase in price is higher than the percentage decrease in quantity demanded. Therefore, the total revenue from sale of drugs will increase. This implies that the drug addicts now have to pay more to buy drugs. They are thus more likely to engage in violence related crime to meet this requirement. Therefore, drug interdiction may result in increasing drug related crimes.

Drug Education: Drug education helps sensitize people against drug abuse. Unlike interdiction, drug education affects the demand for drugs. As more and more awareness is created, the demand for drugs decreases, thus, shifting the demand curve to the left

Exhibit 18b

Drug Education Shifts the Demand Curve Leftwards

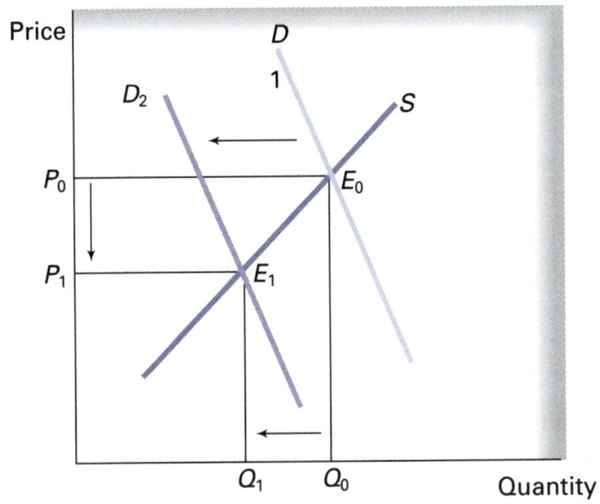

from D_1 to D_2 (refer Exhibit 18b). However, the supply remains the same. Now, we see that as a result of leftward shift of the demand curve, the quantity demanded drops from Q_0 to Q_1 and the price falls from P_0 to P_1. As a result of this, the total revenue also decreases from $OP_0E_0Q_0$ to $OP_1E_1Q_1$.

Therefore, we can conclude that drug education is a better tool than drug interdiction. It not only reduces the quantity of drugs demanded, but also reduces drug abuse related violence.

Application 2: Why Did OPEC Fail to Keep the Oil Prices High in the Long Run

The Organisation of Petroleum Exporting Countries (OPEC) functions like a cartel of petroleum exporters in the world. In the 1970s, the OPEC members decided to raise the oil prices to increase their profits. In order to do so, they decided to reduce the supply of oil, thus, shifting the supply curve to the left.

Now, we know that the response to a change in supply of oil depends on the time horizon.

In the short run, both the demand and supply of oil are inelastic (refer Exhibit 20). This is because the quantity of known oil reserves and the capacity for oil extraction cannot be changed in the short run. In addition, the consumption habits of the buyers can't be adjusted immediately.

As a result, a decrease in supply from S_0 to S_1 results in a marginal decrease in the quantity demanded from Q_0 to Q_1. However, the price increases sharply from P_0 to P_1. This leads to an increase in the total revenue (TR = PxQ), thus, increasing the profits of the sellers in the short run.

Exhibit 20

Short-Run Equilibrium

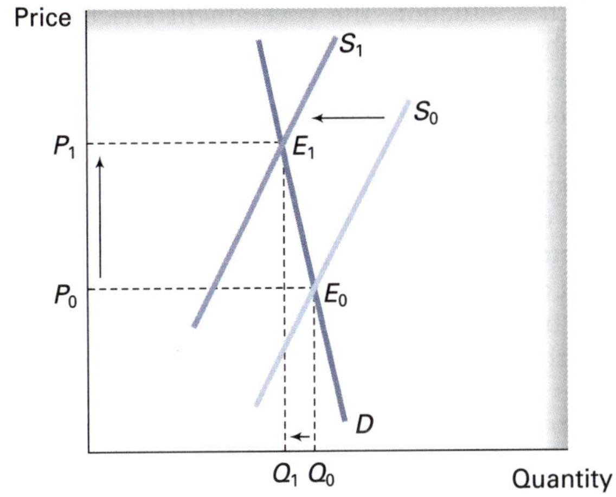

However, in the long run, the supply and demand of oil is relatively elastic (refer Exhibit 21). This is because producers outside of OPEC respond to price hike by building their supply capacity and undertaking new explorations. Also, the consumers respond by decreasing consumption. Hence, even though the supply curve shifts from S_0 to S_1, the price increases only marginally from P_0 to P_1 whereas, the quantity demanded falls from Q_0 to Q_1. In the long run the percentage increase in price is less than the percentage decrease in quantity demanded. This results in a decline in the total revenue and subsequently the profits of oil producers.

Therefore, the OPEC failed to keep the oil prices high in the long run.

Exhibit 21

Long-Run Equilibrium

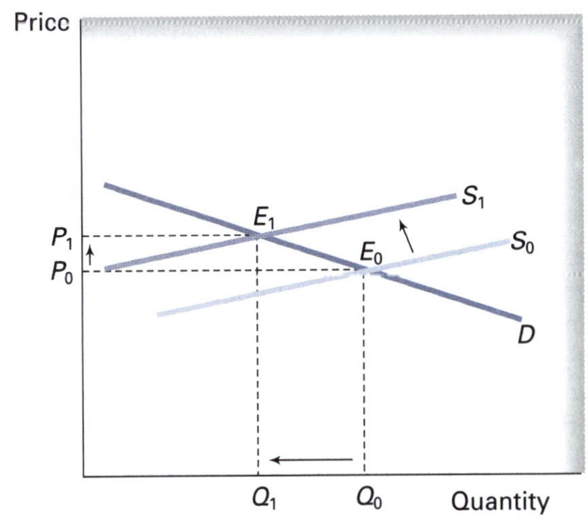

Application 3: Short-Run and Long-Run Effect of Rent Control

In such a situation, the government enacts a law whereby rent ceilings are imposed. The landlords by law cannot charge their tenants a rent above this ceiling. The intention of the government is to help the poor by placing price ceiling on the rents. Economists often criticize rent control, arguing that it is a highly inefficient way to help the poor raise their standard of living. However, the adverse effects of rent control are less apparent to the general population because these effects occur over many years.

In the short run, landlords have a fixed number of houses to rent, and they cannot adjust this number quickly as market conditions change (refer Exhibit 22). Moreover, the number of people searching for housing in a city may not be highly responsive to rents in the short run because people take time to adjust their housing arrangements. Therefore, the short-run supply and demand for housing are relatively inelastic. As with any price ceiling, rent control causes a shortage, if price ceiling is below the market clearing price. Yet, because supply and demand are inelastic in the short run, the initial shortage caused by rent control is small. The primary effect in the short run is to reduce rents.

Exhibit 22

Short-Run Effects of Rent Control

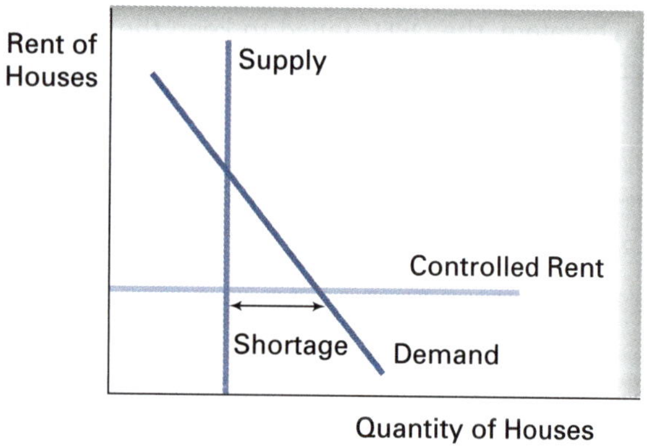

The long-run story is very different because the buyers and sellers of rental housing respond more to market conditions as time passes. On the supply side, landlords respond to low rents by not building new houses and by failing to maintain existing ones. On the demand side, low rents encourage people to find their own houses rather than sharing houses with roommates, etc. and induce more people to move into a city. Therefore, both supply and demand are more elastic in the long-run (refer Exhibit 23). When rent control depresses rents below the

Exhibit 23

Long-Run Effects of Rent Control

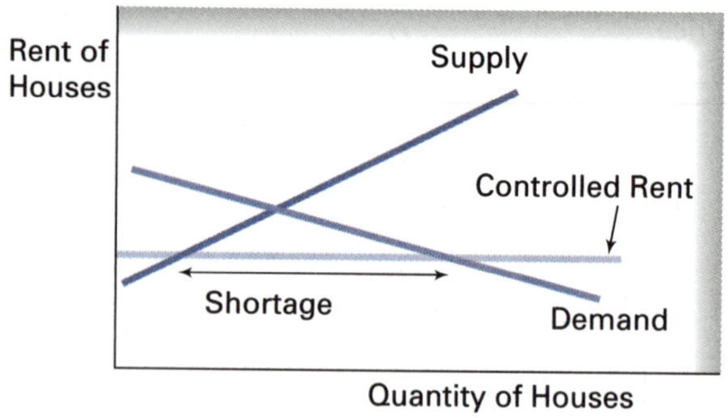

equilibrium level, the quantity of houses supplied falls substantially, and the quantity of houses demanded rises substantially. The result is a large shortage of housing. As illustrated in Exhibit 19, in the long run, the supply and demand for houses is more elastic, therefore, rent control causes a large shortage.

In cities with rent control, landlords use various mechanisms to ration housing. Sellers may discriminate among customers. Some give a preference to tenants without children. Still others discriminate on the basis of caste, creed, or religion. Sometimes, houses are allocated to those who are willing to offer under-the-table payments to house-owners. Further distortions also crop up. In free markets, landlords try to keep their buildings clean and safe because desirable houses command higher prices. By contrast, when rent control creates shortages and waiting lists, landlords lose their incentive to be responsive to tenants' concerns. In the end, tenants get lower rents, but they also get lower-quality housing.

Application 4: Per Unit Tax and its Distribution of Burden between Producer's and Consumer's

All governments levy taxes and occasionally increase the tax rates in order to generate revenues for various purposes. Several times, the tax is imposed on the commodity. Let us consider imposition of a per unit tax on the producer. Even though the tax is imposed on the producer, the question that arises is who ultimately bears the burden of this tax? Is it the producer or can the producer pass it on to the consumers. Alternatively, do both share the burden? If yes, then in what proportion? The answer to these questions mainly depends upon the price elasticity of demand and supply.

Let us consider an initial situation in which the demand curve D and the supply curve S intersect at the equilibrium point e (refer Exhibit 24). Now let the

Exhibit 24

Effect of a Per Unit Tax on Equilibrium Price and Quantity

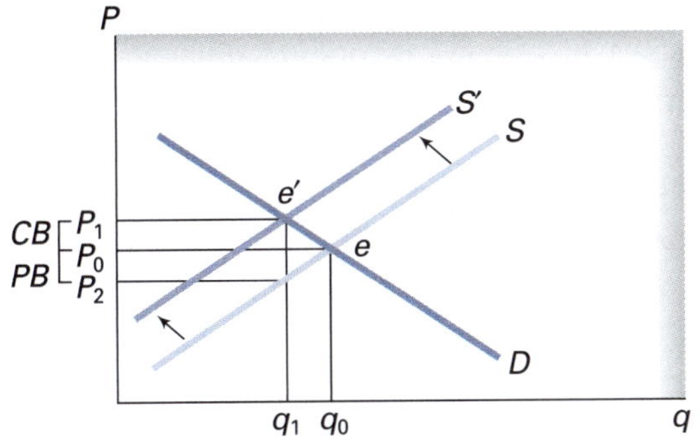

government impose a per unit tax on the producer/supplier. An increase in tax on suppliers means that they need to incorporate this increase in their cost. This results in a leftward shift of the supply curve from S to S′. In such a situation, since the imposition of tax is only on sellers, it leads to no change in the buyer's demand curve. Under the changed circumstances, the equilibrium point shifts from *e* to *e*′.

When this happens, there is a correspondingly change in price (which increases from P_0 to P_1) and in quantity demanded and supplied (which decreases from q_0 to q_1). Thus, we see that the additional price $P_1 - P_0$ is actually being paid by the consumer, even though the tax was levied upon the seller. This increase in price is known as the consumer's burden (CB). Similarly, the seller might be charging P_1 to the consumer but he does not get to keep the entire amount, as he has to pay tax to the government. The producer finally receives P_1 – Tax. This is given by P_2. Hence, due to imposition of a tax, the price the seller receives also goes down, from the original price of P_0 to the final price of P_2. Thus, the decrease in price received by the producer equal to $P_0 - P_2$ is known as the producer's burden (PB).

The total tax burden (TB) is, thus, CB plus PB. In our illustration, it is shared between both the producers and consumers.

$$TB = CB + PB$$
$$P_1P_2 = P_0P_1 + P_0P_2$$

Relation between Tax Incidence and Price Elasticity: We have concluded from the above discussion that the buyer and seller share the tax burden. But the question that remains unanswered is in what ratio is the tax burden shared? This question can be answered with the help of the concept of elasticity of demand and supply.

In general, it can be stated that:

1. CB > PB, when demand curve is relatively inelastic and supply curve is relatively elastic. That is, sellers are very responsive to the price of the good, whereas buyers are not very responsive. When a tax is imposed on a commodity with these elasticities, the price received by sellers does not fall much, so sellers bear only a small burden. By contrast, the price paid by buyers rises substantially, indicating that buyers bear most of the burden of the tax. This case is illustrated in Exhibit 25.

Exhibit 25

Distribution of Tax Burden with Relatively Inelastic Demand and Elastic Supply

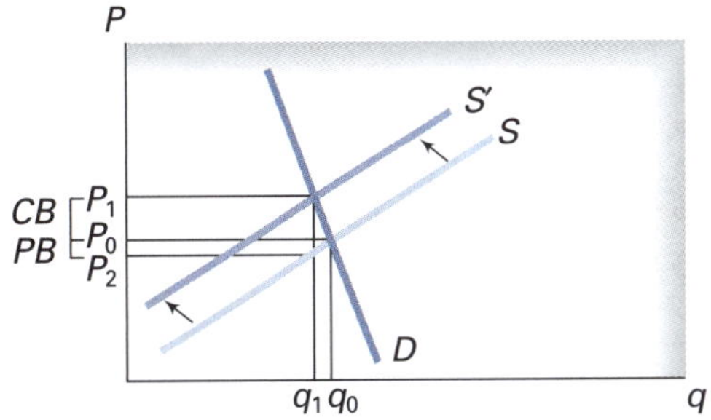

2. PB > CB, when supply curve is relatively inelastic and demand curve is relatively elastic. That is, sellers are not very responsive to the price of the good, whereas buyers are very responsive. When a tax is imposed on a commodity with these elasticities, the price paid by buyers does not rise much, while the price received by sellers falls substantially. Thus, sellers bear most of the burden of the tax. This case is illustrated in Exhibit 26.

Exhibit 26

Distribution of Tax Burden with Relatively Elastic Demand and Inelastic Supply

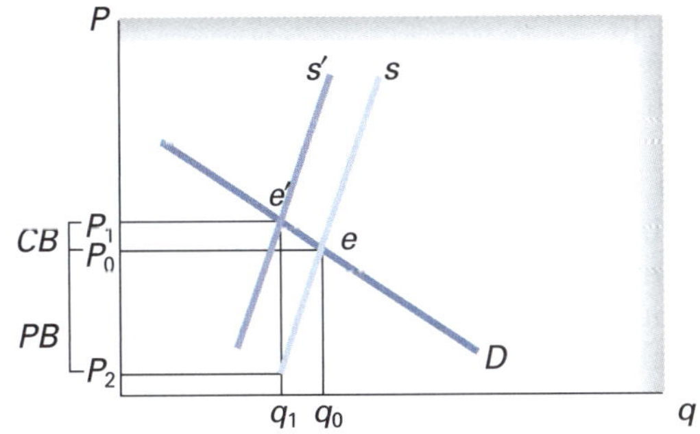

To generalize, it can be stated that the larger burden of the tax falls on the side which has the lower elasticity. This can be explained as follows. For example, the elasticity of demand is low. This means that the buyer has very few options to choose from. Similarly, if the elasticity of supply is low, it means that the seller has very few options to choose from. It can be logically accepted that the side with the fewer alternatives finds it more difficult to leave the market. Hence that side must bear the larger burden when the good is taxed.

Exhibit 27 illustrates a case to show that greater the elasticity of demand, lower is the CB and greater is the PB.

Exhibit 27

Distribution of Tax Burden

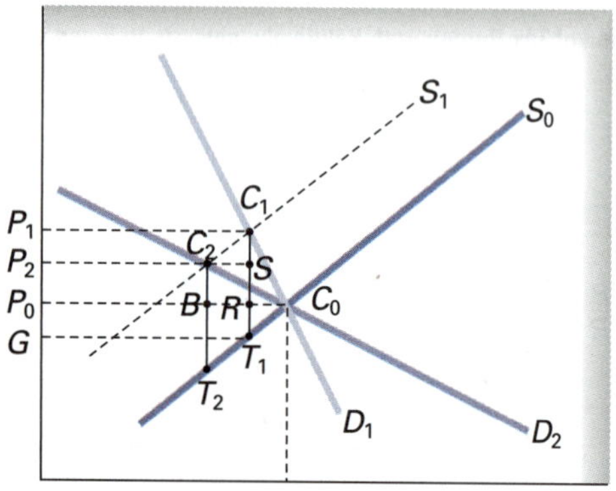

TB = e_1T_1 (along D_1) and e_2T_2 (along D_2). But $e_1 T_1 = e_2T_2$

CB along demand curve $D_1 = P_0P_1$

PB along $= P_0\,G = RT_1$

CB along demand curve $D_2 = P_2P_0$

PB D2 = B T2 = ST1

Sine $ST_1 > RT_1$, and $e_1T_1 = e_2T_2$

$\Rightarrow$ $(PB)_z > (PB)_1$

and

$(CB)_1 > (CB)_2$

Thus, CB is relatively more for the more inelastic demand curve.

Application 5: Effects of Agricultural Subsidy

Agricultural subsidies are a form of producer's subsidy in which the farmers are either directly subsidized (through cheaper loans/cash disbursal) or indirectly subsidized (subsidies for fertilizers, seeds, etc.). Subsidies are given by the government to encourage farmers to expand their production by decreasing the cost of production.

The demand curve for agricultural goods is relatively inelastic in the short run. As the production costs are reduced by the subsidies provided by the government, there is an increase in the supply due to the lower production costs. This causes the supply curve to shift outwards due to increased production. However, the demand curve is not affected and remains constant. As a result, there is an increase in the quantity of the agricultural goods demanded accompanied by a fall in the price (refer Exhibit 28).

As illustrated in the graph, the market equilibrium price of agricultural goods changes due to the shifting of the supply curve to the right. There is an increase in the quantity consumed (from Q_1 to Q_2) while there is a fall in the market equilibrium price (from P_1 to P_2). This is an artificial situation as the price is lowered due to the subsidies borne by the government.

Exhibit 28

Effect of Subsidy on Supply Curve

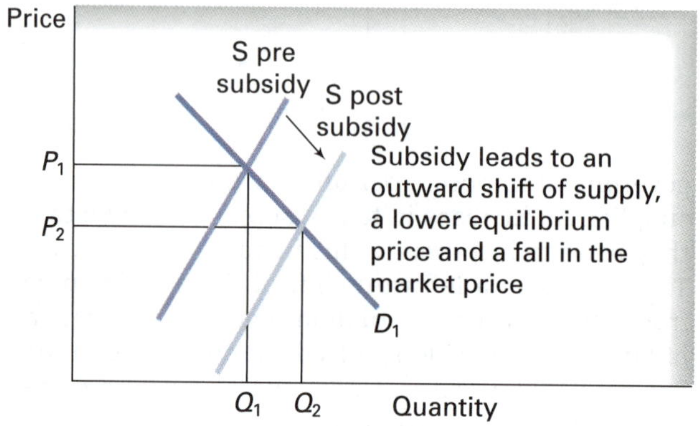

As illustrated in the exhibit, the subsidy causes a reduction in prices and hence benefits the end consumers. The gain to the consumer from the subsidy depends on the elasticity of the demand curve. When the demand is elastic, the effect of subsidy is an increase in the quantity of the goods with little decrease in the price. In such a case, the producer of the goods gains due to the subsidy. However, in case of inelastic demand, the subsidy results in a slight increase in the quantity of goods with a drastic decrease in price. Simply put, higher the inelasticity of the demand curve, higher is the consumer's gain. In the extreme case of perfectly inelastic demand, the consumer gains the entire subsidy as the market price reduces by an amount equal to the subsidy. This is shown in Exhibit 29.

Exhibit 29

Effect of Subsidy with Perfectly Inelastic Demand Curve

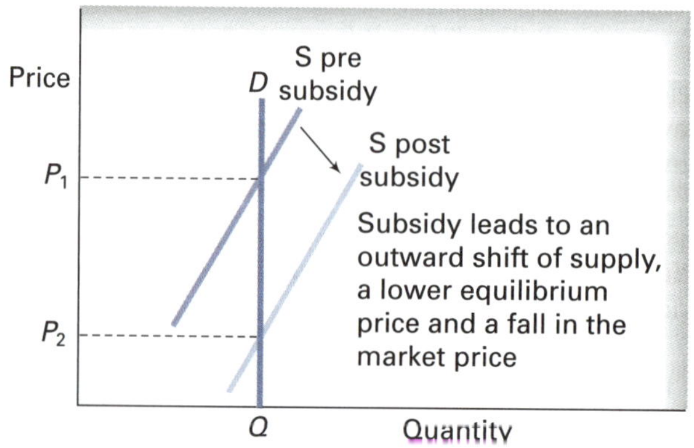

To summarize,

- Subsidies result in increased production due to lower production costs.
- In case of high elasticity of demand, the producer benefits more from the subsidy.
- In case of low elasticity of demand, the consumer gains a higher portion of the subsidy.

This necessitates the need for the government to have a better understanding of respective elasticities, for better execution of the subsidy programs to ensure that the intended group is the major beneficiary.

Final Word

Because this chapter has been more quantitative than earlier ones, the mechanics may have overshadowed the intuitive appeal and neat simplicity of elasticity. *Elasticity measures the willingness and ability of buyers and sellers to alter their behavior in response to changes in their economic circumstances.* Firms try to estimate the price elasticity of demand for their products. Governments also have an ongoing interest in various elasticities. For example, state governments want to know the effect of an increase in the sales tax on total tax receipts, and local governments want to know how an increase in income affects the demand for real estate and thus the revenue generated by a property tax. International groups are interested in elasticities; for example, OPEC is concerned about the price elasticity of demand for oil—in the short run and in the long run. Because a corporation often produces an entire line of products, it also has a special interest in certain cross-price elasticities. Some corporate economists estimate elasticities for a living.

MULTIPLE CHOICE QUESTIONS

1. If the value of the price elasticity of demand is –0.2, this means that a
   a. 20 percent decrease in price causes a 1 percent increase in quantity demanded
   b. 0.2 percent decrease in price causes a 1 percent increase in quantity demanded
   c. 5 percent decrease in price causes a 1 percent increase in quantity demanded
   d. 0.2 percent decrease in price causes a 0.2 percent increase in quantity demanded
   e. 100 percent decrease in price causes a 200 percent increase in quantity demanded
2. Elasticity is always
   a. measured in dollars
   b. measured in dollars per unit of quantity
   c. measured in units of quantity
   d. measured in units of quantity per dollar
   e. independent of the units of measurement
3. A new tax on beer will increase the price of beer by 35%. As a result, the quantity demanded of beer will decrease by 25%. Then, the demand for beer is:
   a. Elastic
   b. Inelastic
   c. Unit elastic
   d. Perfectly elastic
   e. Perfectly inelastic
4. The "Cherries for all" farm is selling cherries at $3 per pound and earns a total revenue of $300. The manager decides to increase the price to $4 per pound, but his decision reduces the total revenue to $240. Which of the following is a good explanation for what happened?
   a. The demand for cherries is inelastic
   b. The demand for cherries is perfectly inelastic
   c. The demand for cherries is perfectly elastic
   d. The demand for cherries is elastic
   e. The demand for cherries is unit elastic
5. Suppose that you allow yourself $50 per month to spend on compact disks. You spend exactly this much every month regardless of the price of compact disks. Therefore, your demand for CDs
   a. is elastic
   b. is inelastic
   c. is unit elastic
   d. cannot be characterized unless we know the price of a disk
   e. cannot be characterized unless we know the price and quantity of compact disks purchased
6. If demand is unit elastic, a price reduction will
   a. increase revenues
   b. reduce revenues
   c. reduce quantity demanded
   d. have no effect on revenues
   e. increase profits
7. Which of the following describes a situation in which demand must be inelastic?
   a. The price of pens rises by 10 cents, and quantity of pens demanded falls by 50.
   b. The price of pens rises by 10 cents, and total revenue rises.
   c. A 20 percent increase in the price of pens leads to a 20 percent decrease in the quantity of pens demanded.
   d. Total revenue does not change when the price of pens rises.
   e. Total revenue decreases when the price of pens rises.
8. One group of people uses New York City subways only during rush hour to travel to and from work. Another group uses them only in midday for leisure activity. If New York City wants to increase transit fares with the smallest possible reduction in revenue, for which group should it increase the fare?
   a. The rush-hour group because its demand for subway service is more elastic than that of the midday group.
   b. The rush-hour group because its demand for subway service is less elastic than that of the midday group.
   c. The midday group because its demand for subway service is more elastic than that of the rush-hour group.
   d. The midday group because its demand for subway service is less elastic than that of the rush-hour group.
   e. It doesn't matter because both groups have the same elasticity of demand.
9. Along a linear demand curve, as the price rises, demand becomes more
   a. steep
   b. elastic
   c. inelastic
   d. unit elastic
   e. variable

10. If the supply curve slopes upward and a $3 per unit tax on suppliers raises the profit-maximizing price by $3, demand must be perfectly inelastic.
    a. True
    b. False
11. For which of the following products is the consumer's demand curve most likely to be vertical?
    a. lobster, for a seafood lover
    b. cars, for high school students
    c. insulin, for a diabetic
    d. compact disks, for a music lover
    e. beef, for a food lover
12. The more broadly a good is defined,
    a. the more substitutes it has so the more elastic is its demand
    b. the fewer substitutes it has so the more elastic is its demand
    c. the more substitutes it has so the less elastic is its demand
    d. the fewer substitutes it has so the less elastic is its demand
    e. the more complements it has so the more elastic is its demand
13. The demand for flour is
    a. inelastic because there are few substitutes for flour and it represents a large percentage of a consumer's budget
    b. inelastic because there are many substitutes for flour and it represents a large percentage of a consumer's budget
    c. inelastic because there are few substitutes for flour and it represents a small percentage of a consumer's budget
    d. elastic because there are no substitutes for flour and it represents a large percentage of a consumer's budget
    e. elastic because there are many substitutes for flour and it represents a large percentage of a consumer's budget
14. Price elasticity of demand *and* price elasticity of supply are *both* influenced by
    a. the availability of close substitutes for the product
    b. the proportion of the consumer's budget spend on the product
    c. the length of the adjustment period considered
    d. technological conditions such as the additional costs of increasing production
    e. none of the above
15. Suppose the income elasticity of demand for a private college education is equal to 1.5. This means that
    a. every $1 increase in income provides an incentive for a $1.50 increase in expenditures on private college education
    b. every $1.50 increase in income provides an incentive for a $1 increase in expenditures on private college education
    c. a 10 percent increase in income causes a 15 percent increase in the demand for a private college education
    d. a 15 percent increase in income causes a 10 percent increase in the demand for a private college education
    e. a 10 percent decrease in private college tuition will have a large enough income effect to increase spending on private college education by 15 percent
16. Economists distinguish between normal and inferior goods using
    a. price elasticity of demand
    b. price elasticity of supply
    c. income elasticity of demand
    d. cross-price elasticity of demand
    e. tax incidence
17. Luxury goods are
    a. price inelastic
    b. income inelastic
    c. income elastic
    d. goods with negative income elasticity
    e. goods with positive price elasticity
18. The cross-price elasticity of demand between pancakes and waffles is positive. This indicates all of the following *except* one. Which is the exception?
    a. Pancakes and waffles are substitutes.
    b. An increase in the price of pancakes will shift the demand curve for waffles to the right.
    c. An increase in the price of waffles will shift the demand curve for pancakes to the right.
    d. A decrease in the supply of waffles will shift the demand curve for pancakes to the right.
    e. Pancake demand and waffle demand are price elastic.
19. In order to prove that Coca Cola and 7-Up are substitutes, one should test the _____ and get a _____.
    a. price elasticity of demand; number less than negative 1
    b. income elasticity; positive number
    c. cross-price elasticity; negative number

d. price elasticity of demand; number greater than negative 1
e. cross-price elasticity; positive number

20. To ensure that we get the same result for price elasticity no matter which direction we move on the demand curve, we must take the average of the
a. initial price and the initial quantity demanded and the average of the new price and the new quantity demanded
b. new price and the initial quantity demanded and the average of the new quantity demanded and the initial price
c. initial price and the new price and the average of the initial quantity demanded and the new quantity demanded
d. initial price and the new price only
e. new quantity demanded and the initial quantity demanded only

Answers

1. c	2. e	3. b	4. d	5. c	6. d	7. b	8. b	9. b	10. a
11. c	12. d	13. c	14. c	15. c	16. c	17. c	18. e	19. e	20. c

LONG ANSWER QUESTIONS

LO1 Define and graph the price elasticity of demand

1.1. *(Calculating Price Elasticity of Demand)* Suppose that 50 units of a good are demanded at a price of $1 per unit. A reduction in price to $0.20 results in an increase in quantity demanded to 70 units. Show that these data yield a price elasticity of 0.25. By what percentage would a 10 percent rise in the price reduce the quantity demanded, assuming price elasticity remains constant along the demand curve?

1.2. *(Price Elasticity and Total Revenue)* Fill in the blanks for each price-quantity combination listed in the following table. What relationship have you depicted?

P	Q	Price Elasticity	Total Revenue
$9	1	______	______
$8	2	______	______
$7	3	______	______
$6	4	______	______
$5	5	______	______
$4	6	______	______
$3	7	______	______
$2	8	______	______

1.3. *(Categories of Price Elasticity of Demand)* For each of the following absolute values of price elasticity of demand, indicate whether demand is elastic, inelastic, perfectly elastic, perfectly inelastic, or unit elastic. In addition, determine what would happen to total revenue if a firm raised its price in each elasticity range identified.

	Absolute Value	Elasticity	Effect of Price Increase
a	$E_D = 2.5$		
b	$E_D = 1.0$		
c	$E_D = \infty$		
d	$E_D = 0.8$		

LO2 Identify the determinants of the price elasticity of demand

2.1. *(Determinants of Price Elasticity)* Why is the price elasticity of demand for Coca-Cola greater than the price elasticity of demand for soft drinks generally?

2.2. *(Determinants of Price Elasticity)* Would the price elasticity of demand for electricity be more elastic over a shorter or a longer period of time?

LO3 Define and graph the price elasticity of supply

3.1. *(Price Elasticity of Supply)* Calculate the price elasticity of supply for each of the following combinations of price and quantity supplied. In each case, determine whether supply is elastic, inelastic, perfectly elastic, perfectly inelastic, or unit elastic.
a. Price falls from $2.25 to $1.75; quantity supplied falls from 600 units to 400 units.
b. Price falls from $2.25 to $1.75; quantity supplied falls from 600 units to 500 units.
c. Price falls from $2.25 to $1.75; quantity supplied remains at 600 units.
d. Price increases from $1.75 to $2.25; quantity supplied increases from 466.67 units to 600 units.

LO4 Describe other measures of elasticity

4.1. *(Cross-Price Elasticity)* Rank the following in order of increasing (from negative to positive) cross-price elasticity of demand with coffee. Explain your reasoning.

Bleach ______ Tea ______ Cream ______ Cola ______

4.2. *(Income Elasticity of Demand)* Calculate the income elasticity of demand for each of the following goods:

	Quantity Demanded When Income Is $10,000	Quantity Demanded When Income Is $20,000
Good 1	10	25
Good 2	4	5
Good 3	3	2

4.3. *(Other Elasticity Measures)* Complete each of the following sentences:

a. The income elasticity of demand measures, for a given price, the _________ in quantity demanded divided by the _________ income from which it resulted.

b. If a decrease in the price of one good causes a decrease in demand for another good, the two goods are _________.

c. If the value of the cross-price elasticity of demand between two goods is approximately zero, they are considered _________.

Numerical Questions

1. Paradise Lake, Inc., is a developer of mobile-home lots. Through statistical research, Paradise Lake has estimated the annual demand function for its lots to be as follows:

$$Q_L = 3{,}536 - 0.5P_L + 0.2P_C + 0.008I + 0.0001A$$

Where

Q_L = the number of Paradise Lake's lots purchased per year

P_L = the price of a Paradise Lake lot,

P_C = the price of a competing land company's lots,

I = average annual household income, and

A = the annual amount spent by Paradise Lake on advertising.

a. Find the income elasticity of demand for Paradise Lake's lots where P_L = $10,000; P_C = $8,000, I = $45,000, and A = $4,000.

b. Are these lots a normal good or an inferior good? Why?

c. Find the price elasticity of demand for Paradise Lake's properties at the same point as in part (a). Is the price elasticity of demand for Paradise Lake's properties elastic, inelastic, or unitary elastic? How do you know?

2. Suppose that the price of Product X falls from $25 to $20. In response, the demand in quantity of X increases from 100 to 120 units. The demand for Product Y increases from quantity of 200 to 300. Calculate the arc cross elasticity between Product Y and Product X. Is Y a substitute or complement for X? Explain. Does Product X follow the law of demand? Explain.

3. The following equation expresses the demand for product A as $Q_A = 400 - 5P_A + 3P_B$ and demand for product B is given by the function $Q_B = 300 - 2P_B + P_A$. The market prices and quantities for these goods are $P_A = 5$, $P_B = 2$, $Q_A = 481$, and $Q_B = 301$.

a. Suppose the price of product B increases to 3. What happens to the quantity demanded of both products?

b. Calculate the arc cross-elasticity between product A and product B using prices for product B of 2 and 3.

c. Are these goods substitutes or complements?

4. Let the demand function faced by the firm be multiplicative of the following form:

$$Q = aX_1^{b1} X_2^{b2} \ldots X_n^{bn}$$

Where '*a*' is a constant and 'b_i' is the known exponent associated with the i_{th} explanatory variable X_i, *i* = 1, ……*n*. Prove that b_i is the X_i variable's partial point elasticity of demand.

5. The Smithsonian uniform Co. has received a report from its consulting firm that the demand function for its model x revolutionary war uniform is:

$$Q_x = 10\, P_x^{-2.1}\, P_y^{2}\, P_z^{-1.5}\, I^{1.8} A^{0.9}$$

where Q_x is the quantity of uniforms demanded per time period, P_x is the price of model x uniforms per unit, P_y and P_z are prices of related goods, I is income and A is advertising.

i. Is the price elasticity of model x uniform elastic or inelastic? Why?

ii. What kind of relationship exists between Good x and Good z uniform? Why?

iii. Is the Smithsonian uniform Co.'s model x uniform an inferior good? Why?

iv. What factors would likely cause the coefficient of price elasticity of demand to be in the general range that the consulting firm has calculated?

6. The management of the Mini Mill Steel Company estimated the following elasticities for a special type of steel they sell: $E_p = -2$, $E_1 = 1$, and $E_{xy} = 1.5$, where *X* refers to steel and *Y* to aluminum. Next year, the firm would like to increase the price of the steel it sells by 6 per cent. The management of the firm forecasted that income will rise by 4 per cent next year, and the price of aluminium will fall by 2 per cent.

d. If the sales of the firm this year are 1,200 tons of the special type of steel, how many tons of steel can the firm expect to sell next year?

e. By what percentage must the firm change the price of steel to keep its sales at 1,200 tons next year?

7. Suppose the demand curve for personal computers is

$$Q = 8000 - 100\ \ P$$

Currently, P = $3,600

Calculate the point price elasticity. Is it elastic or inelastic? What will be the effect of a price decrease on total revenue?

8. Freshbake and Dreambake both sell wedding cakes. Assume current wedding cake sales to be $Q_F = 1{,}650$ and $Q_D = 620$. The demand curves for the two competitors are:

Freshbake: $P_F = 750 - .3Q_F$

Dreambake: $P_D = 700 - .5Q_D$

a. Calculate the point price elasticities for Freshbake and Dreambake.

b. Freshbake reduced the price of wedding cakes, thereby increasing sales from 1,650 to 1,734 units and reducing Dreambake' s sales to 610 units. What is the cross elasticity between Freshbake and Dreambake wedding cakes?

c. Does the price reduction by Freshbake make sense with regard to revenue?

9. Homespread department store sells household goods and clothing. As of now it is facing an oversupply of king size sheets and is contemplat-

ing putting them on sale in February. However, the next day, Comfort mattresses, a mattress shop next door put up its king size mattresses on sale for a period of one month.

a. Explain in words what effect, if any, this should have on the decision of Homespread department store about a sale on its king size sheets.

b. The cross price elasticity of mattress prices on sheet demand is –1.5. According to the advertisement for the mattress sale, the store is reducing the price on its king size mattress from $400 to $360. At $400 per mattress, the company was able to sell 50 king size mattresses last week. Homespread department store currently sells 100 sets of king size sheets per week at a price of $40 per set. How might the Homespread department store manager estimate what effect this sale will have on the demand for its king size sheets? Based on your calculations, what will be the effect on the quantity of sheets sold (You may assume that it is possible to buy fractions of sheets or mattresses)?

c. The price elasticity of supply for sheets is 2.5. Given your answer in part b), what will be the new price for king size sheets sold at Homespread department store? Use a diagram to help explain your answer.

Miscellaneous Questions

1. Fill in the blanks:
   a. The price elasticity of demand for a firm's product is equal to -1.5 over the range of prices being considered by the firm's manager. If the manager decreases the price of the product by 6 percent, the manager predicts the quantity demanded will ______________ (increase, decrease) by______________ percent.
   b. The price elasticity of demand for an industry's demand curve is equal to -1.5 for the range of prices over which supply increases. If total industry output is expected to increase by 30 percent as a result of the supply increase, managers in this industry should expect the market price of the good to ______________ (increase, decrease) by ____________ percent.
   c. When demand is elastic, an increase in price causes quantity demanded to ________________ and total revenue to ____________
   d. When demand is unitary elastic, an increase in price causes quantity demanded and total revenue to ______________
   e. If price falls and total revenue falls, demand must be ______________
2. Define price elasticity of demand, cross-price elasticity of demand and income elasticity of demand. Why is price elasticity a preferable indicator of how quantity demand of a commodity changes with regards to change in its price, as compared to slope of demand curve or its inverse? Is there any difference between point elasticity of demand and arc price elasticity of demand?
3. Imagine a firm having a negatively-sloped linear demand curve. Explain how the price elasticity of demand varies vis-à-vis total revenue of the firm along a linear demand curve.
4. Distinguish between normal and inferior goods. Is it true that a normal good must have an income elasticity that is more than one? Explain. Consider a situation where for four years in a row, income among consumers has increased. A machine tool company has had sales increases in each of these four years. Does the company produce inferior or normal goods? Forecasts predict that income will continue to rise in the future. Should the company anticipate that demand for its products will continue to rise? Explain.
5. How can cross-price elasticities of demand be used to help define the relevant firms in an industry? The cross elasticity between product A and product B is 8. Do you think that product A is likely to face an elastic or inelastic demand curve? Explain. Usually, what sign are the cross elasticities for complementary and substitute products?
6. What determines whether the producer's burden will be greater or smaller than the consumer's burden, when a per unit tax is imposed on the suppliers? Illustrate the same graphically.
7. Is drug education better than drug interdiction? Why?
8. What happens to wheat farmers and the market for wheat when University agronomists discover a new wheat hybrid that is more productive than existing varieties? Is it possible that good news for farming may be a bad news for farmers? Explain your answer with the help of demand and supply curves.
9. The famous Swedish economist Assar Lindbeck remarked in his book on rent controls, "Rent control appears to be the most efficient technique presently known to destroy a city—except for bombing." Rent controls place price ceilings on rents at levels below equilibrium rental rates for the stated purpose of making housing more affordable for low-income families. Using demand and supply analysis, answer the following questions:
   a. How does imposing rent controls affect the number of housing units available to low-income families in the short run? In the long run?
   b. Under rent controls, can all low-income families get rent-controlled housing?
   c. Why would Professor Lindbeck think rent controls are destructive?
10. A persistent problem facing our society is the use of illegal drugs. Suppose the government increases the number of agents devoted to the war on drugs. Comment on what happens in the market for illegal drugs.
11. Why would demand for natural gas be more inelastic in the short run than in the long run?
12. For each pair of price elasticities, which elasticity (in absolute value) is larger?
    a. The price elasticity for carbonated soft drinks or the price elasticity for Coca-Cola
    b. The price elasticity for socks (men's or women's) or the price elasticity for business suits (men's or women's).
    c. The price elasticity for electricity in the short run or the price elasticity for electricity in the long run.
13. In the 1970s, OPEC caused a dramatic increase in the price of oil. Why did OPEC fail to keep the price of oil high during the 1980s? Use diagrams to illustrate your point.

5

ELASTICITY OF DEMAND AND SUPPLY

Chapter in Review

KEY TERMS

price elasticity of demand measures how responsive quantity demanded is to a price change; the percentage change in quantity demanded divided by the percentage change in price

price elasticity formula percentage change in quantity demanded divided by the percentage change in price; the average quantity and the average price are used as bases for computing percentage changes in quantity and in price

inelastic demand a change in price has relatively little effect on quantity demanded; the percentage change in quantity demanded is less than the percentage change in price; the resulting price elasticity has an absolute value less than 1.0

unit-elastic demand the percentage change in quantity demanded equals the percentage change in price; the resulting price elasticity has an absolute value of 1.0

elastic demand a change in price has a relatively large effect on quantity demanded; the percentage change in quantity demanded exceeds the percentage change in price; the resulting price elasticity has an absolute value exceeding 1.0

total revenue price multiplied by the quantity demanded at that price

linear demand curve a straight-line demand curve; such a demand curve has a constant slope but usually has a varying price elasticity

perfectly elastic demand curve a horizontal line reflecting a situation in which any price increase would reduce quantity demanded to zero; the elasticity has an absolute value of infinity

perfectly inelastic demand curve a vertical line reflecting a situation in which any price change has no effect on the quantity demanded; the elasticity value is zero

unit-elastic demand curve everywhere along the demand curve, the percentage change in price causes an equal but offsetting percentage change in quantity demanded, so total revenue remains the same; the elasticity has an absolute value of 1.0

LO1 Define and graph the price elasticity of demand. The price elasticities of demand and supply show how responsive buyers and sellers are to changes in the price of a good. More elastic means more responsive. When the percentage change in quantity demanded exceeds the percentage change in price, demand is price elastic. If demand is price elastic, a price increase reduces total revenue and a price decrease increases total revenue. When the percentage change in quantity demanded is less than the percentage change in price, demand is price inelastic. If demand is price inelastic, a higher price increases total revenue and a lower price reduces total revenue. When the percentage change in quantity demanded equals the percentage change in price, demand is unit elastic; a price change does not affect total revenue.

Constant-Elasticity Demand Curves

The three panels show constant-elasticity demand curves, so named because the elasticity value does not change along the demand curve. Along the perfectly elastic, or horizontal, demand curve of panel (a), consumers will demand all that is offered for sale at price *p*, but demand nothing at a price above *p*. Along the perfectly inelastic, or vertical, demand curve of panel (b), consumers demand amount *Q* regardless of price. Along the unit-elastic demand curve of panel (c), total revenue is the same for each price-quantity combination.

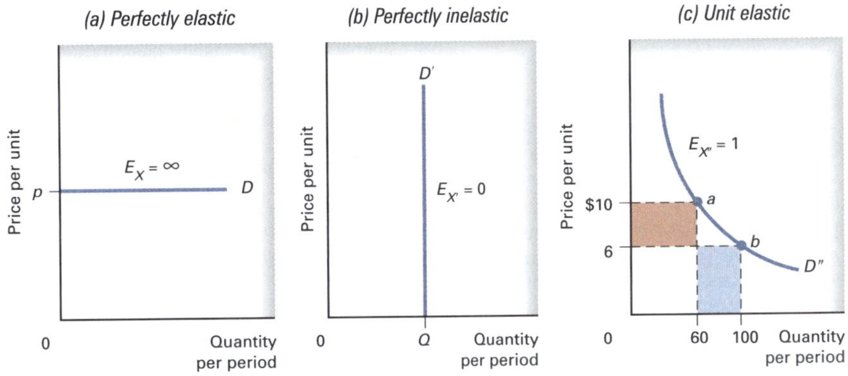

Summary of Price Elasticity of Demand Effects of a 10 Percent Increase in Price

Absolute Value of Price Elasticity	Type of Demand	What Happens to Quantity Demanded	What Happens to Total Revenue
$E_D = 0$	Perfectly inelastic	No change	Increases by 10 percent
$0 < E_D < 1$	Inelastic	Drops by less than 10 percent	Increases by less than 10 percent
$E_D = 1$	Unit elastic	Drops by 10 percent	No change
$1 < E_D < \infty$	Elastic	Drops by more than 10 percent	Decreases
$E_D = \infty$	Perfectly elastic	Drops to 0	Drops to 0

constant-elasticity demand curve the type of demand that exists when price elasticity is the same everywhere along the curve; the elasticity value is unchanged

price elasticity of supply a measure of the responsiveness of quantity supplied to a price change; the percentage change in quantity supplied divided by the percentage change in price

inelastic supply a change in price has relatively little effect on quantity supplied; the percentage change in quantity supplied is less than the percentage change in price; the price elasticity of supply has a value less than 1.0

unit-elastic supply the percentage change in quantity supplied equals the percentage change in price; the price elasticity of supply equals 1.0

elastic supply a change in price has a relatively large effect on quantity supplied; the percentage change in quantity supplied exceeds the percentage change in price; the price elasticity of supply exceeds 1.0

perfectly elastic supply curve a horizontal line reflecting a situation in which any price decrease drops the quantity supplied to zero; the elasticity value is infinity

perfectly inelastic supply curve a vertical line reflecting a situation in which a price change has no effect on the quantity supplied; the elasticity value is zero

unit-elastic supply curve a percentage change in price causes an identical percentage change in quantity supplied; depicted by a supply curve that is a straight line from the origin; the elasticity value equals 1.0

income elasticity of demand the percentage change in demand divided by the percentage change in consumer income; the value is positive for normal goods and negative for inferior goods

cross-price elasticity of demand the percentage change in the demand of one good divided by the percentage change in the price of another good; it's positive for substitutes, negative for complements, and zero for unrelated goods

CHAPTER EQUATIONS

$$E_D = \frac{\Delta q}{(q + q')/2} \div \frac{\Delta p}{(p + p')/2}$$

$$TR = p \times q$$

$$E_S = \frac{\Delta q}{(q + q')/2} \div \frac{\Delta p}{(p + p')/2}$$

LO2 Identify the determinants of the price elasticity of demand.

Demand is more elastic (a) the greater the availability of substitutes; (b) the more narrowly the good is defined; (c) the larger the share of the consumer's budget spent on the good; and (d) the longer the time period consumers have to adjust to a change in price.

Demand Becomes More Elastic over Time

D_w is the demand curve one week after a price increase from $1.00 to $1.25. Along this curve, quantity demanded per day falls from 100 to 95. One month after the price increase, quantity demanded has fallen to 75 along D_m. One year after the price increase, quantity demanded has fallen to 50 along D_y. At any given price, D_y is more elastic than D_m, which is more elastic than D_w.

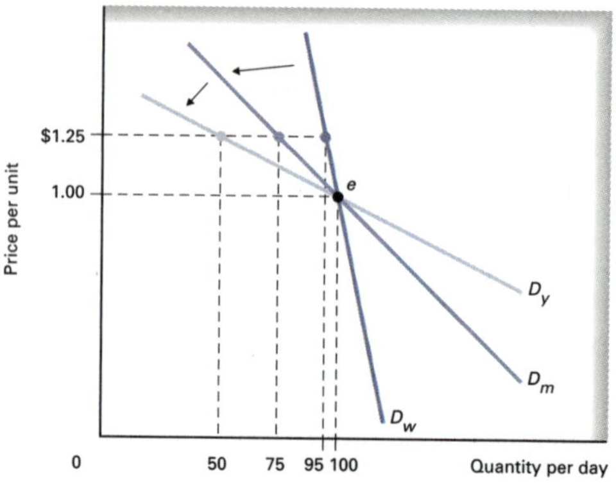

LO3 Define and graph the price elasticity of supply.

The price elasticity of supply measures the responsiveness of quantity supplied to price changes. Price elasticity of supply depends on how much the marginal cost of production changes as output changes. If marginal cost rises sharply as output expands, quantity supplied is less responsive to price increases and is thus less elastic. Also, the longer the time period producers have to adjust to price changes, the more elastic the supply.

Constant-Elasticity Supply Curves

The three panels show a constant-elasticity supply curve, so named because the elasticity value does not change along the curve. When supply is perfectly elastic, its curve S is horizontal. Along S, firms will supply any amount of output demanded at price p, but will supply none at prices below p. Supply curve S′ is perfectly inelastic, or vertical. S′ shows that the quantity supplied is independent of the price. In panel (c), S″, a straight line from the origin, is a unit-elastic supply curve. Any percentage change in price results in the same percentage change in quantity supplied.

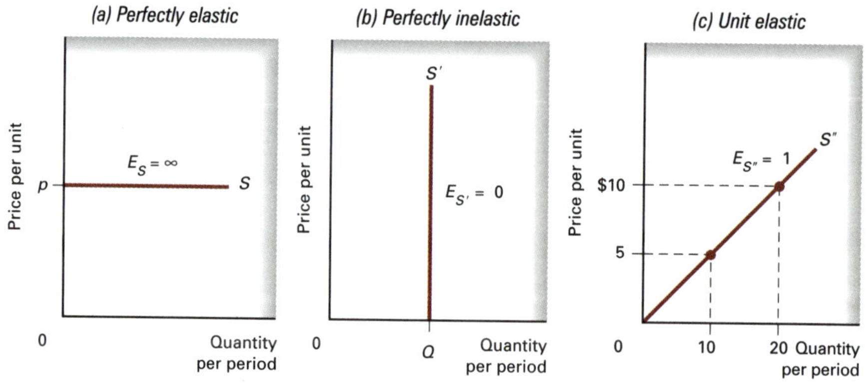

LO4 Describe other measures of elasticity.

Income elasticity of demand measures the responsiveness of demand to changes in consumer income. Income elasticity is positive for normal goods and negative for inferior goods. The cross-price elasticity of demand measures the impact of a change in the price of one good on the demand for another good. Two goods are defined as substitutes, complements, or unrelated, depending on whether their cross-price elasticity of demand is positive, negative, or zero, respectively.

LO5 Disuss the applications of theory of demand and supply

- Drug education is a better tool than drug interdiction. It not only reduces the quantity of drugs demanded, but also reduces drug abuse related violence.

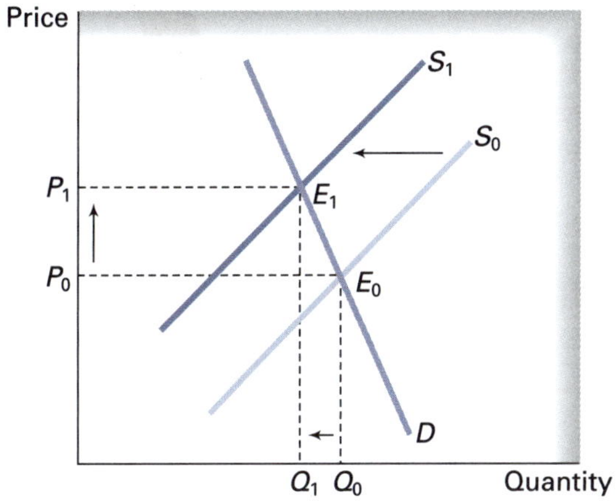

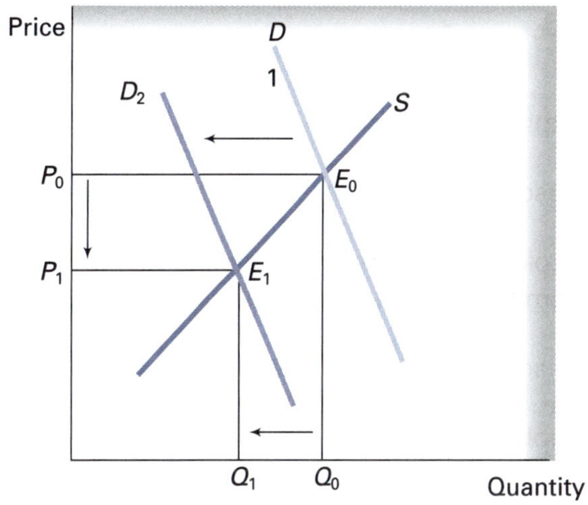

- OPEC cannot keep oil prices high in the long run.

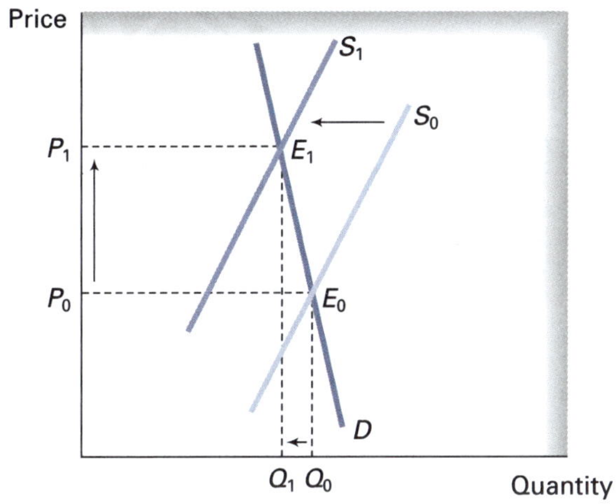

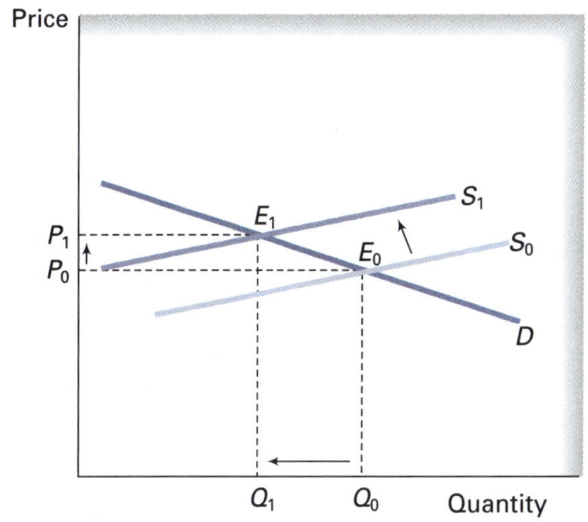

- The short-run supply and demand for housing are relatively inelastic. However, in the long run, the supply and demand for houses is more elastic. Therefore, rent control causes a larger shortage in the long-run than in the short-run.

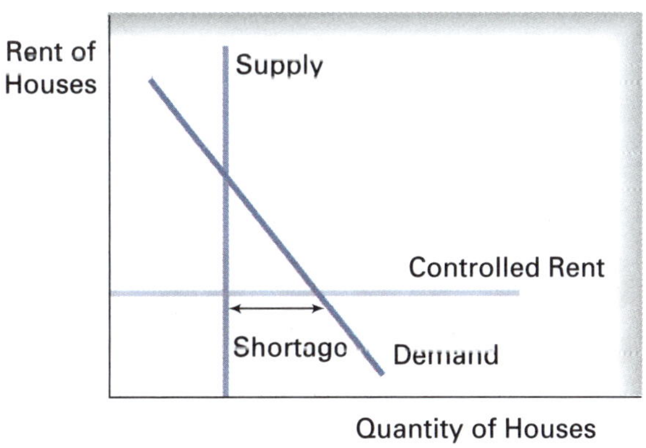

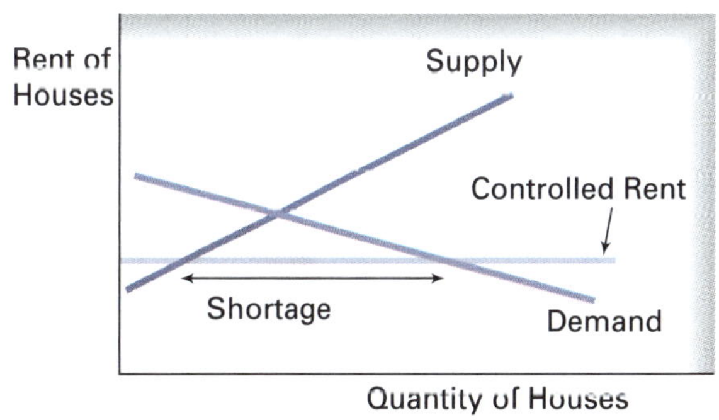

- The division of tax burden depends on elasticities of demand and supply. More inelastic the demand curve and more elastic the supply curve, the larger is the burden on consumer.

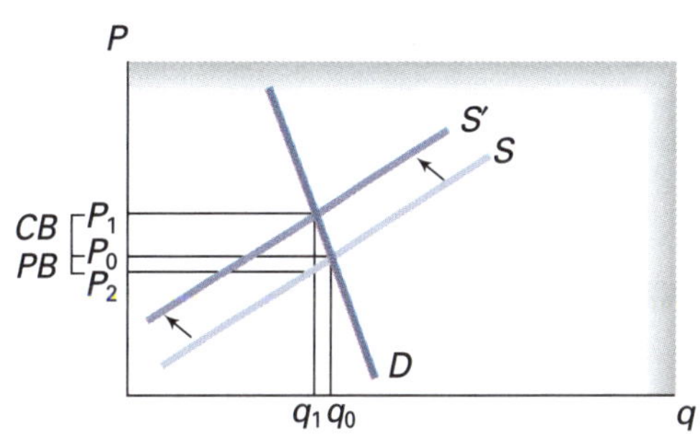

CHAPTER

6

Learning Outcomes

LO[1] Explain the basics of utility analysis

LO[2] Describe how to measure and maximize utility

LO[3] Explain how marginal utility and the law of demand can create consumer surplus

LO[4] Describe the role of time in demand

LO[5] Explain indifference curves theory of demand

Consumer Choice *and* Demand

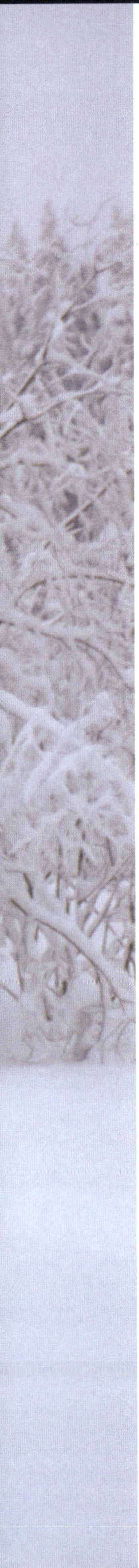

© KIM HART/ROBERT HARDING WORLD IMAGERY/JUPITERIMAGES

"What are cures for cabin fever and for spring fever?"

Why are newspapers sold in vending machines that allow you to take more than one? How much do you eat when you can eat all you want? Why don't restaurants allow doggie bags with their all-you-can-eat specials? What are cures for cabin fever and for spring fever? Why is water cheaper than diamonds even though water is essential to life and diamonds are simply bling? To answer these and other questions, we take a closer look at consumer demand, a key building block in economics.

You have already learned two reasons why demand curves slope downward. The first is the *substitution effect* of a price change. When the price of a good falls, consumers substitute that now-cheaper good for other goods. The second is the *income effect* of a price change. When the price of a good falls, real incomes increase, boosting consumers' ability to buy more.

Demand is so important that it needs more attention. This chapter develops the law of demand based on the utility, or satisfaction, of consumption. As usual, the assumption is that you and other consumers try to maximize utility, or satisfaction. Learning the theory behind your behavior will help you understand the implications of that behavior, making predictions more accurate.

What do you think?

I usually watch movies only once.

Strongly Disagree					*Strongly Agree*	
1	2	3	4	5	6	7

Topics discussed in Chapter 6 include:

- Total and marginal utility
- Law of diminishing marginal utility
- Measuring utility
- Utility-maximizing condition
- Consumer surplus
- Role of time in demand
- Time price of goods
- Indifference Curves
- Budget Line
- Slutcky Substitution Effect
- Hicks-Allen Substitution effect

LO1 Utility Analysis

Suppose you and a friend are dining out. After dinner, your friend asks how you liked your meal. You wouldn't say, "I liked mine twice as much as you liked yours."

Nor would you say, "It deserves a rating of 86 on the Consumer Satisfaction Index." The utility, or satisfaction, you derive from that meal cannot be compared with another person's experience, nor can your utility be measured based on some uniform standard. But you might say something such as, "I liked it better than my last meal here" or "I liked it better than campus food." More generally, you can say whether one of your experiences is more satisfying than another. Even if you say nothing about your likes and dislikes, we can draw conclusions about your preferences by observing your behavior. For example, we can conclude that you prefer apples to oranges if, when the two are priced the same, you buy apples every time.

"The utility you derive from a particular good, service, or activity depends on your *tastes and preferences.*"

Tastes and Preferences

As introduced in Chapter 3, *utility* is the sense of pleasure, or satisfaction, that comes from consumption. Utility is subjective. The utility you derive from a particular good, service, or activity depends on your *tastes and preferences*—your likes and dislikes in consumption. Some things are extremely appealing to you and others are not. You may not understand, for example, why someone would pay good money for sharks' fin soup, calves' brains, polka music, or martial arts movies. Why are most baby carriages sold in the United States navy blue, whereas they are yellow in Italy and chartreuse in Germany? And why do Australians favor chicken-flavored potato chips and chicken-flavored salt?

total utility
the total satisfaction you derive from consumption; this could refer to either your total utility of consuming a particular good or your total utility from all consumption

marginal utility
the change in your total utility from a one-unit change in your consumption of a good

law of diminishing marginal utility
the more of a good a person consumes per period, the smaller the increase in total utility from consuming one more unit, other things constant

As noted in Chapter 4, your desires for food and drink are largely biological, as is your desire for comfort, rest, shelter, friendship, love, status, personal safety, and a pleasant environment. Your family background shapes some of your tastes, such as food preferences. Other influences include your surrounding culture, peer pressure, and religious convictions. So economists can say something about the origin of tastes, but they claim no special expertise. Economists assume simply *that tastes are given and are relatively stable—that is, different people may have different tastes, but an individual's tastes are not constantly in flux.* However, tastes for some products do change over time.

Although some tastes do change over time, economists believe they are stable enough to allow us to examine relationships such as that between price and quantity demanded. If tastes were not relatively stable, then we could not reasonably make the other-things-constant assumption required for demand analysis. We could not even draw a demand curve.

The Law of Diminishing Marginal Utility

Suppose it's a hot summer day and you are extremely thirsty after jogging four miles. You pour yourself an 8-ounce glass of ice water. That first glass is wonderful, and it puts a serious dent in your thirst. The next glass is not quite as wonderful, but it is still pretty good. The third one is just fair; and the fourth glass you barely finish.

What can we say about the *utility*, or satisfaction, you get from water? Let's first distinguish between *total utility* and *marginal utility*. **Total utility** is the total satisfaction you derive from consumption. In this example, total utility is the total satisfaction you get from four glasses of water. **Marginal utility** is the change in total utility resulting from a one-unit change in consumption. For example, the marginal utility of a third glass of water is the change in total utility resulting from drinking that third glass.

Your experience with water reflects an economic law—the **law of diminishing marginal utility**. This law states that the more of a good you consume per period, other things constant, the smaller the increase in your total utility from additional consumption—that is, the smaller the marginal utility of each additional unit consumed. The marginal utility you derive from each additional glass of water declines as you drink more. You enjoy the first glass a lot, but each additional glass provides less and less marginal utility. If forced to drink a fifth glass, you wouldn't enjoy it; your marginal utility would be negative—you would experience *disutility*.

Diminishing marginal utility is a feature of all consumption. A second foot-long sub sandwich at one meal, for most people, would provide little or no

© MIKE KEMP/RUBBERBALL/JUPITERIMAGES

marginal utility. You might still enjoy a second movie on Friday night, but a third would probably be too much to take. In fact, almost anything repeated enough could become torture, such as being forced to watch the same movie or listen to the same song over and over and over. Yes, variety is the spice of life.

A long, cold winter spent cooped up inside can cause "cabin fever." Each additional cold day brings more disutility. But the fever breaks with the arrival of the first warm day of spring, which is something wonderful. That first warm, glorious day causes such delirious joy that this jump in marginal utility has its own fevered name—"spring fever." Spring fever is eventually "cured" by many warm days like the first. By the time many warm days pass by, you attach much less marginal utility to yet another warm day.

For some goods, the drop in marginal utility with additional consumption is greater. A second copy of the same daily newspaper would likely provide you no marginal utility (in fact, the design of newspaper vending machines relies on the fact that people will take no more than one).[1] Likewise, a second viewing of the same movie at one sitting usually yields no additional utility. More generally, expressions such as "Been there, done that" and "Same old, same old" convey the idea that, for many activities, things start to get old after the first time. Restaurants depend on the law of diminishing marginal utility when they hold all-you-can-eat specials—and no doggie bags allowed, because the deal is all you can eat now, not now and in the next few days.

1. This example appears in Marshall Jevons, *The Fatal Equilibrium* (Cambridge, Mass.: MIT Press, 1985).

LO2 Measuring Utility

So far, the description of utility has used such words as *wonderful, good,* and *fair*. The analysis can't be pushed very far with such subjective language. To predict consumer behavior, we need to develop a consistent way of viewing utility.

Units of Utility

Let's go back to the water example. Although there really is no objective way of measuring utility, if pressed, you could be more specific about how much you enjoyed each glass of water. For example, you might say the second glass was half as good as the first, the third was half as good as the second, the fourth was half as good as the third, and you passed up a fifth glass because you expected no positive utility. To get a handle on this, let's assign arbitrary numbers to the utility you get from water, so the pattern of numbers reflects your expressed level of satisfaction. Let's say the first glass provides you with 40 units of utility, the second glass with 20, the third with 10, and the fourth with 5. A fifth glass, if you were forced to drink it, would yield negative utility, or disutility—in this case, say, −2 units. *Developing numerical values for utility allows us to be more specific about the utility from consumption.* If it would help, you could think of these units more playfully as thrills, kicks, or jollies—as in, getting your kicks from consumption.

Each person has a uniquely subjective utility scale.

By attaching a numerical measure to utility, we can compare the total utility a particular consumer gets from different goods as well as the marginal utility that consumer gets from additional consumption. Thus, we can employ units of utility to evaluate a consumer's preferences. Note, however, that we cannot compare utility levels across consumers. *Each person has a uniquely subjective utility scale.*

The first column of Exhibit 1 lists possible quantities of water you might consume after running four miles on a hot day. The second column presents the total utility derived from that consumption, and the third column shows the marginal utility of each additional glass of water. Recall that marginal utility is the change in total utility from an additional unit of the good. You can see from the second column that total utility increases with each of the first four

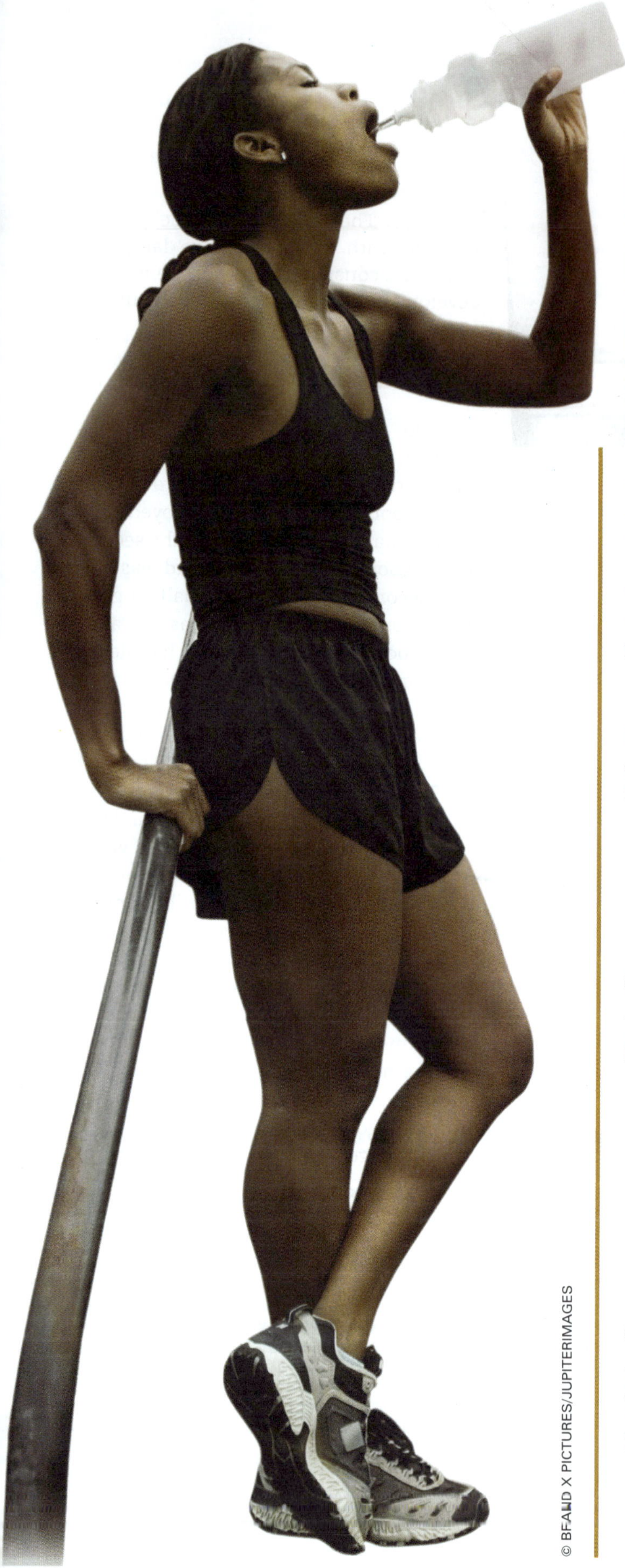

© BFALD X PICTURES/JUPITERIMAGES

Exhibit 1

Utility Derived from Drinking Water After Jogging Four Miles

Amount Consumed (8-ounce glasses)	Total Utility	Marginal Utility
0	0	—
1	40	40
2	60	20
3	70	10
4	75	5
5	73	−2

glasses but by smaller and smaller amounts. The third column shows that the first glass of water yields 40 units of utility, the second glass yields an additional 20 units, and so on. Marginal utility declines after the first glass of water, becoming negative with the fifth glass. *At any level of consumption, marginal utilities sum to total utility.* Total utility is graphed in panel (a) of Exhibit 2. Again, because of diminishing

Exhibit 2

Total Utility and Marginal Utility You Derive from Drinking Water after Jogging Four Miles

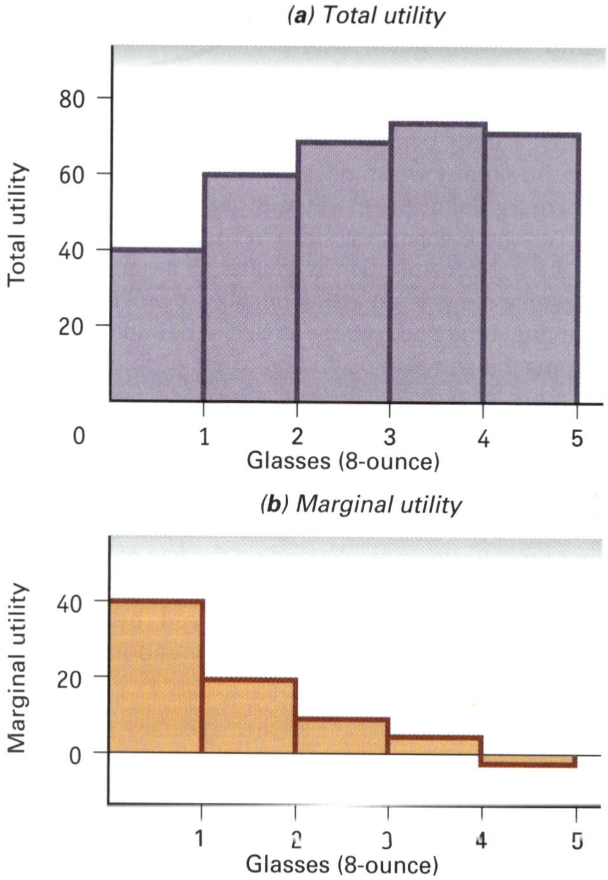

marginal utility, each additional glass of water adds less to total utility, so total utility increases for the first four glasses but at a decreasing rate. Panel (b) shows the law of diminishing marginal utility.

Utility Maximization in a World Without Scarcity

Economists assume that your purpose for drinking water, as with all consumption, is to *maximize your total utility.* So how much water do you consume? If the price of water is zero, you drink water as long as doing so increases total utility. Each of the first four glasses of water adds to your total utility. *If a good is free, you increase consumption as long as marginal utility is positive.* Let's broaden the analysis to a world of only two goods—pizza and video rentals. We continue to translate the satisfaction you receive from consumption into units of utility. Based on your tastes and preferences, suppose your total utility and marginal utility from consumption are as presented in Exhibit 3. The first four columns apply to pizza and the second four to video rentals. Please take a little time right now with each column.

Notice from columns (3) and (7) that each good shows diminishing marginal utility. Given this set of preferences, how much of each good would you consume per week? At a zero price, you would increase consumption as long as marginal utility is positive. Thus, you would consume at least the first six pizzas and first six videos because the sixth unit of each good yields marginal utility. Did you ever go to a party where the food and drinks were free to you? How much did you eat and drink? You ate and drank until you didn't want any more—that is, until the marginal utility of each additional bite and each additional sip fell to zero. Your consumption was determined not by prices or your income but simply by your tastes.

Utility Maximization in a World of Scarcity

Alas, goods are usually scarce, not free. Suppose the price of a pizza is $8, the rental price of a video is $4, and your part-time job pays $40 per week after taxes. Your utility is still based on your tastes, but you now buy goods with your limited income. How do you allocate your income between the two goods to maximize utility? To get the ball rolling, suppose you start off spending your entire budget of $40 on pizza, purchasing five pizzas a week, which yields a total of 142 units of utility. You quickly realize that if you buy one less pizza, you free up enough in your budget to rent two movies. Would total utility increase? Sure. You give up 12 units of utility, the marginal utility of the fifth pizza, to get 68 units of utility from the first two videos. Total utility zooms from 142 to 198. Then you notice that if you reduce purchases to three pizzas, you give up 18 units of utility from the fourth pizza but gain a total of 32 units of utility from the third and fourth videos. This is another utility-increasing move.

Further reductions in pizza, however, would reduce your total utility because you would give up 24 units of utility from the third pizza but gain only 14 units from the fifth and sixth videos. Thus, you quickly find that the utility-maximizing combination is three pizzas and four videos per week, for a total utility of 212. This means spending $24 on pizza and $16 on videos. *You are in equilibrium when consuming this combination because any affordable change would reduce your utility.*

Exhibit 3

Total and Marginal Utilities from Pizza and Videos

Pizza				Video Rentals			
(1) Consumed per Week	(2) Total Utility	(3) Marginal Utility	(4) Marginal Utility per Dollar if *p* – $8	(5) Viewed per Week	(6) Total Utility	(7) Marginal Utility	(8) Marginal Utility per Dollar if *p* = $4
0	0	—	—	0	0	—	—
1	56	56	7	1	40	40	10
2	88	32	4	2	68	28	7
3	**112**	**24**	**3**	3	88	20	5
4	130	18	2¼	**4**	**100**	**12**	**3**
5	142	12	1½	5	108	8	2
6	150	8	1	6	114	6	1½

© SANDIE HOWARD/ISTOCKPHOTO.COM

Utility-Maximizing Conditions

Once a consumer is in equilibrium, there is no way to increase utility by reallocating the budget. Any change in consumption decreases utility. But, wait, there's more: *In equilibrium, the last dollar spent on each good yields the same marginal utility.* Let's see how this works. Column (4) shows the marginal utility of pizza divided by its price of \$8. Column (8) shows the marginal utility of videos divided by its price of \$4. The equilibrium combination of three pizzas and four videos exhausts the \$40 budget and adds 3 units of utility for the last dollar spent on each good. **Consumer equilibrium** is achieved when the budget is exhausted and the last dollar spent on each good yields the same marginal utility. In equilibrium, pizza's marginal utility divided by its price equals video's marginal utility divided by its price. In short, the consumer gets the same bang from the last buck spent on each good. This equality can be expressed as:

$$\frac{MU_p}{p_p} = \frac{MU_v}{p_v}$$

where MU_P is the marginal utility of pizza, p_p is the price of pizza, MU_v is the marginal utility of videos, and p_v is the rental price. The consumer reallocates spending until the last dollar spent on each product yields the same marginal utility. Although this example considers only two goods, the logic of utility maximization applies to any number of goods.

In equilibrium, higher-priced goods must yield more marginal utility than lower-priced goods—enough additional utility to compensate for their higher price. Because a pizza costs twice as much as a video rental, the marginal utility of the final pizza purchased must, in equilibrium, be twice that of the final video rented. Indeed, the marginal utility of the third pizza, 24, is twice that of the fourth video, 12. Economists do not claim that you consciously equate the ratios of marginal utility to price, but they do claim that you act as if you had made such calculations. *Thus, you decide how much of each good to purchase by considering your tastes, market prices, and your income. Consumers maximize utility by equalizing the marginal utility from the last dollar spent on each good.*

$$\frac{MU_p}{p_p} = \frac{MU_v}{p_v}$$

consumer equilibrium
the condition in which an individual consumer's budget is spent and the last dollar spent on each good yields the same marginal utility; therefore, utility is maximized

Water for Diamonds

Q: Diamonds are bling—certainly not a necessity of life in any sense. Water is essential to life and has hundreds of valuable uses. For the price of a one-carat diamond, you could buy enough water to last a lifetime. So why are diamonds expensive and water cheap? How can something as useful as water cost so much less than something of such limited use as diamonds? The *diamonds-water paradox* discussed by Adam Smith in 1776 holds the answer.

:A Because water is essential to life, the total utility derived from water greatly exceeds the total utility derived from diamonds. Yet the market value of a good is based not on its total utility but its marginal utility. Because water is so abundant in nature, we consume it to the point where the marginal utility of the last gallon purchased is relatively low. Because diamonds are relatively scarce compared to water, the marginal utility of the last diamond purchased is relatively high. Thus, water is cheap and diamonds expensive. As Ben Franklin said, "We will only know the worth of water when the well is dry."

© HEMERA TECHNOLOGIES/PHOTOOBJECTS.NET/JUPITERIMAGES

© MIKE KEMP/RUBBERBALL/JUPITERIMAGES

LO3 Marginal Utility and the Law of Demand

How does utility analysis relate to your demand for pizza? The discussion so far yields a single point on your demand curve for pizza: At a price of \$8, you demand three pizzas per week. This is based on income of \$40 per week, a price of \$4 per video, and your tastes reflected by the utility tables in Exhibit 3. Knowing that three pizzas are demanded when the price is \$8 offers no clue about the shape of your demand curve for pizza.

Exhibit 4

Total and Marginal Utilities from Pizza and Videos After the Price of Pizza Decreases from $8 to $6

Pizza				Video Rentals			
(1) Consumed per Week	(2) Total Utility	(3) Marginal Utility	(4) Marginal Utility per Dollar if *p* = $6	(5) Viewed per Week	(6) Total Utility	(7) Marginal Utility	(8) Marginal Utility per Dollar if *p* = $4
0	0	—	—	0	0	—	—
1	56	56	9⅓	1	40	40	10
2	88	32	5⅓	2	68	28	7
3	112	24	4	3	88	20	5
4	**130**	**18**	**3**	**4**	**100**	**12**	**3**
5	142	12	2	5	108	8	2
6	150	8	1½	6	114	6	1½

To generate another point, let's see what happens to quantity demanded if the price of pizza changes, while keeping other things constant (such as tastes, income, and the price of video rentals). Suppose the price of a pizza drops from $8 to $6.

Exhibit 4 is the same as Exhibit 3, except the price per pizza is $6. Your original choice was three pizzas and four video rentals. At that combination and with the price of pizza now $6, the marginal utility per dollar spent on the third pizza is 4, while the marginal utility per dollar spent on the fourth video remains at 3. The marginal utilities of the last dollar spent on each good are no longer equal. What's more, the original combination of three pizzas and four videos now leaves $6 unspent. So you could still buy your original combination but have $6 left to spend (this, incidentally, shows the income effect of the lower price). You can increase utility by adjusting your consumption. Take a moment now to see if you can figure out what the new equilibrium should be.

In light of your utility schedules in Exhibit 4, you would increase your consumption to four pizzas per week. This strategy exhausts your budget and equates the marginal utilities of the last dollar expended on each good. Your video rentals remain the same. The marginal utility of the fourth pizza, 18, divided by the price of $6 yields 3 units of utility per dollar of expenditure, the same as you get from the fourth video. You are in equilibrium once again. Total utility increases by the 18 units you derive from the fourth pizza. Thus, you are clearly better off as a result of the price decrease.

We now have a second point on your demand curve for pizza—if the price of pizza is $6, you demand four pizzas. The two points are presented as *a* and *b* in Exhibit 5. We could continue to change the price of pizza and thereby generate additional points on the demand curve, but you can get some idea of the demand curve's downward slope from these two points. The shape of the demand curve for pizza matches our expectations based on the law of demand: Price and quantity demanded are inversely

Exhibit 5

Demand for Pizza Generated from Marginal Utility

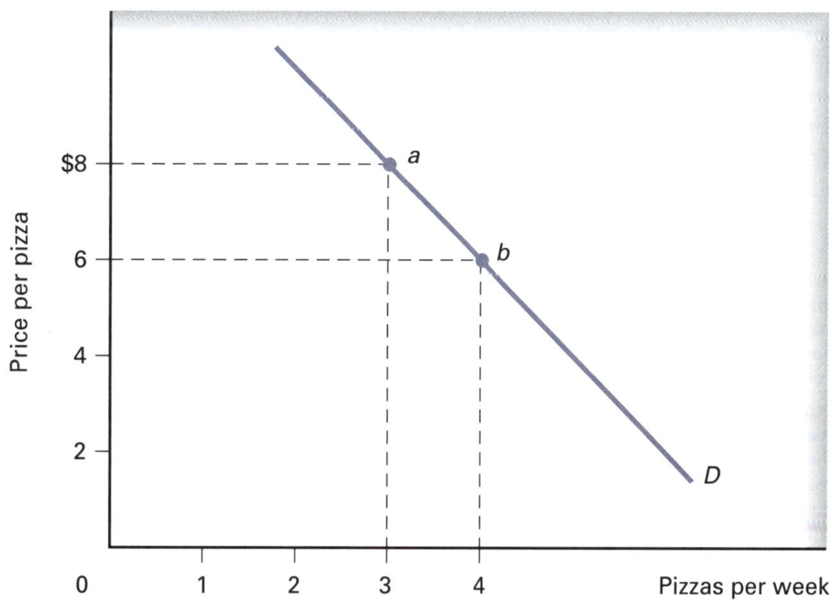

related. (Try estimating your price elasticity of demand between points a and b. Hint: What does your total spending on pizza tell you?)

We have gone to some lengths to see how you (or any consumer) maximize utility. Given prices and your income, your tastes and preferences naturally guide you to the best bundle. You are not even conscious of your behavior. The urge to maximize utility is like the force of gravity—both work whether or not you understand them. Even animal behavior seems consistent with the law of demand. Wolves, for example, exhibit no territorial concerns when game is plentiful. But when game becomes scarce, wolves carefully mark their territory and defend it against intruders. Thus, wolves appear to value game more when it is scarce.

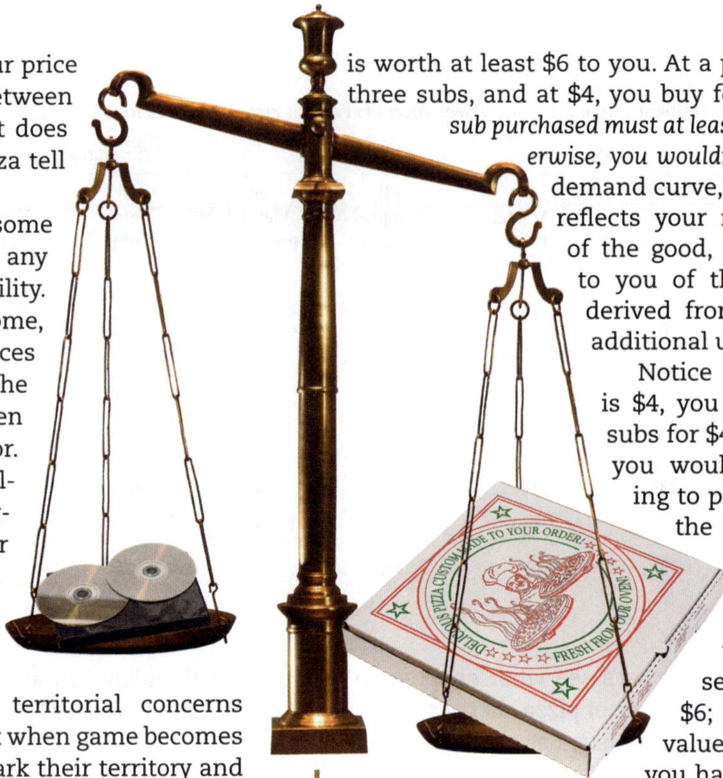

Now that you have some idea of utility, let's consider an application of utility analysis.

Consumer Surplus

In our earlier example, total utility increased when the price of pizza fell from $8 to $6. In this section, we take a closer look at how consumers benefit from a lower price. Suppose your demand for foot-long sub sandwiches is as shown in Exhibit 6. Recall that in constructing an individual's demand curve, we hold tastes, income, and the prices of related goods constant. Only the price varies. At a price of $8 or above, you find that the marginal utility of other goods that you could buy for $8 is higher than the marginal utility of a sub sandwich. Consequently, you buy no subs. At a price of $7, you are willing and able to buy one per month, so the marginal utility of that first sub exceeds the marginal utility you expected from spending that $7 on your best alternative—say, a movie ticket. A price of $6 prompts you to buy two subs a month. The second is worth at least $6 to you. At a price of $5, you buy three subs, and at $4, you buy four. *The value of the sub purchased must at least equal the price; otherwise, you wouldn't buy it.* Along the demand curve, therefore, the price reflects your **marginal valuation** of the good, or the dollar value to you of the marginal utility derived from consuming each additional unit.

marginal valuation the dollar value of the marginal utility derived from consuming each additional unit of a good

consumer surplus the difference between the most a consumer would pay for a given quantity of a good and what the consumer actually pays

Notice that if the price is $4, you can purchase four subs for $4 each, even though you would have been willing to pay more for each of the first three subs. The first sandwich provides marginal utility that you valued at $7; the second you valued at $6; and the third you valued at $5. In fact, if you had to, rather than go without subs, you would have been willing to pay $7 for the first, $6 for the second, and $5 for the third. The dollar value of the total utility of the first four sandwiches is $7 + $6 + $5 + $4 = $22 per month. But when the price is $4, you get four for a total of $16. Thus, a price of $4 confers a **consumer surplus**, or a consumer bonus, equal to the difference between the maximum amount you would have been willing to pay ($22) rather than go without subs altogether and what you actually pay ($16). When the price is $4, your consumer surplus is $22 − $16 = $6, as approximated by the six darker shaded blocks in Exhibit 6. Consumer surplus equals the value of the total utility you receive from con-

Exhibit 6

Consumer Surplus from Sub Sandwiches

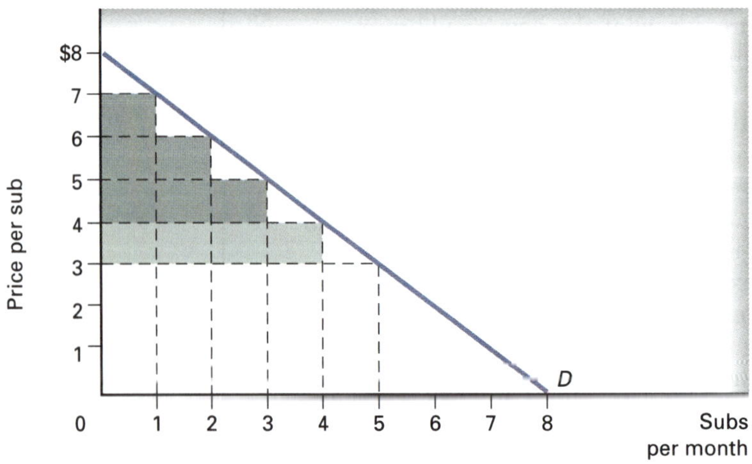

© HEMERA TECHNOLOGIES/PHOTOOBJECTS.NET/JUPITERIMAGES / © THINKSTOCK IMAGES/JUPITERIMAGES / © SANDIE HOWARD/ISTOCKPHOTO.COM

© CIARAN GRIFFIN/STOCKBYTE/GETTY IMAGES

suming the sandwiches minus your total spending on them. Consumer surplus is reflected by the area under the demand curve but above the price.

If the price falls to \$3, you buy five subs a month. Apparently, you feel that the marginal utility from the fifth one is worth at least \$3. The lower price means that you get all five for \$3 each, even though each except the fifth one is worth more to you than \$3. Your consumer surplus when the price is \$3 is the value of the total utility from the first five, which is \$7 + \$6 + \$5 + \$4 + \$3 = \$25, minus your cost, which is \$3 × 5 = \$15. Thus, your consumer surplus is \$25 − \$15 = \$10, as indicated by both the dark and the light shaded blocks in Exhibit 6. So if the price declines to \$3, your consumer surplus increases by \$4, as reflected by the four lighter-shaded blocks in Exhibit 6. You can see how consumers benefit from lower prices.

Incidentally, in some cases your consumer surplus is huge, such as from a bottle of water if you are dying of thirst, a winter coat if you are at risk of freezing, or a pair of glasses if you can't see without them.

Market Demand and Consumer Surplus

Let's talk now about the market demand for a good, assuming the market consists of you and two other consumers. *The market demand curve is simply the horizontal sum of the individual demand curves for all consumers in the market.* Exhibit 7 shows how the demand curves for three consumers in the market for sub sandwiches sum horizontally to yield the market demand. At a price of \$4, for example, you demand four subs per month, Brittany demands two, and Chris demands none. The market demand at a price of \$4 is therefore six sandwiches. At a price of \$2, you demand six per month, Brittany four, and Chris two, for a market demand of 12. *The market demand curve shows the total quantity demanded per period by all consumers at various prices.* Consumer surplus can be used to examine market demand as well as individual demand. *At a given price, consumer surplus for the market is the difference between the most consumers would pay for that quantity and the amount they do pay.*

Instead of just three consumers in the market, suppose there are many. Exhibit 8 presents market demand for a good with millions of consumers. If the price is \$2 per unit, each person adjusts his or her quantity demanded until the marginal valuation of the final unit purchased equals \$2. But each consumer gets to buy all other units for \$2 each as well. In Exhibit 8, the dark shading, bounded above by the demand curve and below by the price line at \$2, depicts the consumer surplus. The light shading shows the gain in consumer surplus if the price drops to \$1. Notice that if this good were given away, the consumer surplus would not be that much greater than when the price is \$1.

Consumer surplus is the net benefit consumers get from market exchange. It can be used to measure economic welfare and to compare the effects of different market structures, different tax structures, and different public programs.

Exhibit 7

Summing Individual Demand Curves to Derive the Market Demand for Sub Sandwiches

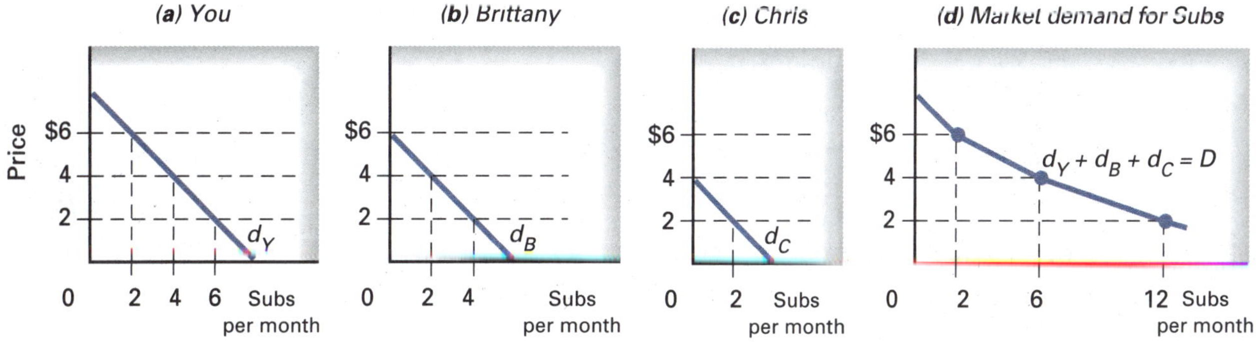

Exhibit 8

Market Demand and Consumer Surplus

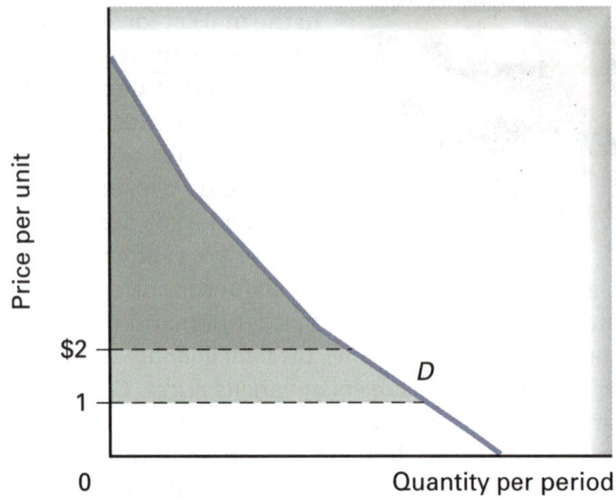

LO4 The Role of Time in Demand

Because consumption does not occur instantly, time plays a role in demand analysis. Consumption takes time and, as Ben Franklin said, "time is money"—time has a positive value for most people. Consequently, consumption has a *money price* and a *time price*. Goods are demanded because of the benefits they offer. It is not the microwave oven, personal computer, airline trip, or headache medicine that you value but the services they provide. Other things constant, you would gladly pay more to get the same benefit in less time, as with faster ovens, computers, airline trips, and headache relief. Likewise, you are willing to pay more for seedless grapes, seedless oranges, and seedless watermelon.

Your willingness to pay a premium for time-saving goods and services depends on the opportunity cost of your time. Differences in the value of time among consumers help explain differences in the consumption patterns observed in the economy. For example, a retired couple has more leisure time than a working couple and may clip discount coupons and search the newspapers for bargains, sometimes even going from store to store for particular grocery items on sale that week. The working couple tends to ignore the coupons and sales, eats out more often, and shops more at convenience stores, where they pay more for the "convenience." The retired couple is more inclined to drive to a vacation destination, whereas the working couple flies.

Just inside the gates at Disneyland, Disney World, and Universal Studios are boards listing the waiting times of each attraction and ride. At that point, the dollar cost of admission has already been paid, so the marginal dollar cost of each ride and attraction is zero. The waiting times offer a menu of the marginal *time costs* of each ride or attraction. Incidentally, people who were willing to pay up to $55 an hour at Disney World and $60 an hour at Disneyland (plus the price of admission), until recently, could take VIP tours that bypass the lines.[2] How much would you pay to avoid the lines?

© AP IMAGES

Differences in the opportunity cost of time among consumers shape consumption patterns and add another dimension to our analysis of demand.

LO5 Indifference Curves Theory of Demand

A household generally consumes a large variety of commodities, which we refer to as a commodity consumption bundle. As stated earlier, in order to meet its objective, the consumer maximizes his satisfaction given the constraint imposed by his budget and the prices of goods consumed. In this section we analyze consumer behavior when the satisfaction derived from a commodity cannot be measured cardinally. Only ordinal ranking is possible. In other words, while the consumer is able to rank different commodity bundles based on satisfaction received, he is unable to quantify the specific difference between satisfactions derived from different bundles. Keeping the assumption of cardinality in mind, in this section we shall explore some of the following questions: What are indifference curves? What is the substitution effect and income effect of a price change? How can consumer equilibrium be defined? Can we be sure that the demand curve is necessarily downward sloping?

Indifference Curves: An Alternate Approach to Study Consumer Behavior

In order to study consumer equilibrium, we need to understand the concept of indifference curves (IC) and budget constraint. An indifference curve represents various combinations of goods that provide the same level of satisfaction to the consumer. That is, satisfaction remains constant along an indifference curve. If we assume for simplicity, that a consumer spends all of his or her income on commodities Y and X, we can represent the tastes of the consumer in the indifference curves. An indifference curve then represents various combinations of commodity Y and commodity X that yield equal satisfaction to the consumer. In the indifference curve IC_1 in Exhibit 9, points A, B, and C represent various combinations of the commodities Y and X which give the consumer the same level of satisfaction. Thus, the satisfaction level remains the same as we move along any one indifference curve.

2. For example, see Nancy Keates, "Tourists Learn How to Mouse around Disney's Long Lines," *Wall Street Journal,* 27 March 1998.

Exhibit 9

An Indifference Curve

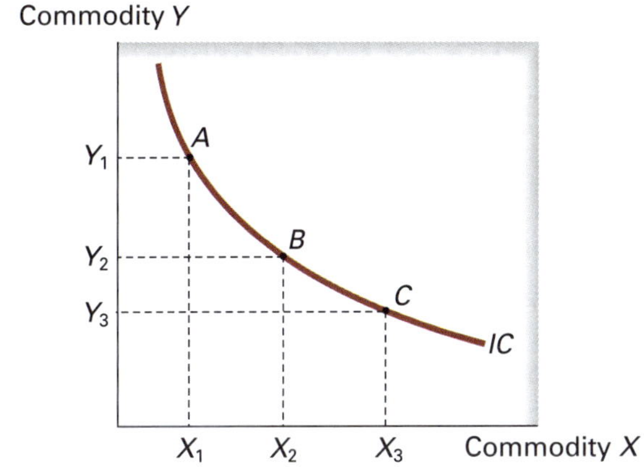

Slope of the Indifference Curve: Marginal Rate of Substitution (MRS_{xy})

The marginal rate of substitution is the rate at which a consumer is ready to give up one commodity in exchange for another commodity while maintaining the same level of satisfaction. It is represented by the slope at any given point on the indifference curve. Since the ICs may not be linear, it has to be noted that the value of marginal rate of substitution does not remain the same along any indifference curve. Thus, the rate at which a consumer would be willing to trade one commodity for another would depend upon the amount of the commodities that he is already consuming. So if the consumer has more of commodity X than Y, he would be willing to trade smaller amount of Y for an additional unit of X. On the other hand, if the consumer has less of X than Y, he would be willing to trade more of Y for an additional unit of X. Thus, MRS_{xy} keeps decreasing as we move downwards along an IC (in Exhibit 10,

Exhibit 10

Slope of Indifference Curve: MRS_{xy}

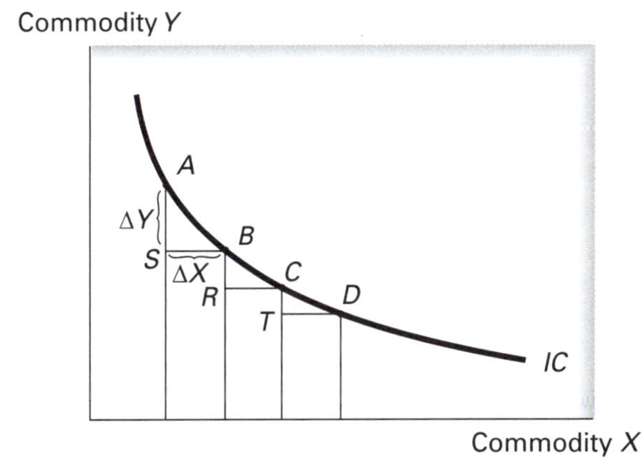

AS/SB > BR/RC > CT/TD, where SB = RC = TD). Alternatively, MRS_{yx} keeps increasing as we move leftwards along an *IC*.

Properties of Indifference Curves

The properties of indifference curves are discussed below:

Indifference Curves Are Negatively Sloped

The indifference curves must slope down from left to right. This means that an indifference curve is negatively sloped. It slopes downward because as the consumer increases the consumption of commodity X, he has to give up certain units of commodity Y in order to maintain the same level of satisfaction.

A Higher Indifference Curve Represents a Higher Level of Satisfaction

A higher indifference curve represents a higher level of satisfaction to the consumer, while any combination of goods X and Y that lie on a lower indifference curve yields a lower satisfaction. This is because consumers usually prefer more of something to less of it. In other words, we can say that the combination of goods which lies on a higher indifference curve will be preferred by a consumer to the combination which lies on a lower indifference curve. Thus, the satisfaction level at *H* will be higher than at *E* (refer Exhibit 11). Further, satisfaction level at E will be higher than at B or M. That is satisfaction at $IC_3 > IC_2 > IC_1$. Since indifference curves give ordinal measure of utility rather than cardinal measure, while we know that the level of satisfaction is more as the consumer moves to higher indifference curves, yet we are unable to know by how much the satisfaction increases as we move to a higher *IC*. Thus, while $IC_3 > IC_2 > IC_1$, one does not know by how much satisfaction at IC_3 is greater than IC_2 or IC_1.

Exhibit 11

An Indifference Map

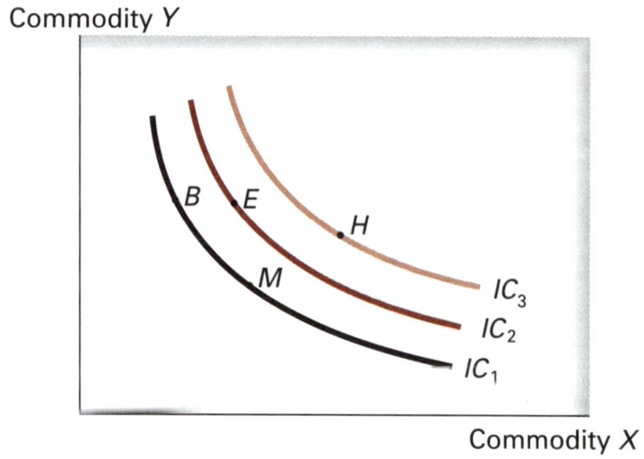

Indifference Curve Cannot Intersect Each Other

Two indifference curves cannot intersect each other at all. To understand why, let us consider that the two indifference curves intersect each other as shown in Exhibit 12. Let the two indifference curves IC_1 and IC_2 intersect at point *M*. Since the satisfaction level at each point along an indifference curve is the same, the utility level at points M and R should be the same as they lie on the same indifference curve IC_1. Similarly, the satisfaction level at points *M* and F will be equal as they lie on the same indifference curve IC_2. This would mean that the utility level at points R and F will also be equal. But this is not possible because at point F, the consumer has greater amount of the commodity Y as compared to point R for the same amount of X. Thus at point F, the consumer should be having greater amount of satisfaction than at point R. Thus, no two indifference curves can intersect each other.

Exhibit 12

Indifference Curves Cannot Intersect

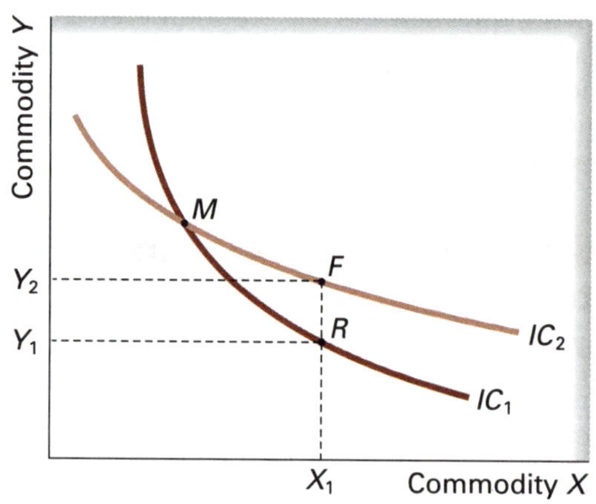

Indifference Curve Are Convex to the Origin

Indifference curves are convex to the origin (bowed inward). This is based on the assumption of diminishing marginal rate of substitution of X for Y.

Extreme Cases of Indifference Curves

The shape of an indifference curve tells us about the consumer's willingness to trade one good for the other. When the goods are easy to substitute for each other, the indifference curves are less convex; when the goods are difficult to substitute, the indifference curves are very convex. Taking the argument further, if the two goods are perfect substitutes, then the indifference curves will be straight lines since the marginal rate of substitution in this case will be constant. Examples of close substitutes are margarine and butter, tea and coffee, petroleum and natural gas. Classic example of perfect substitutes is 10 rupees coin and 5 rupees coin. A consumer would always substitute a 10 rupees coin for two 5 rupees coin. So the marginal rate of substitution will always remain the same along the indifference curve. On the other hand, if the goods are perfect complements then the indifference curves will be L-shaped, the two lines will be perpendicular to each other. An example would be a cake recipe that requires 4 cups flour and 1 cup sugar. No matter how much extra flour one has, one still cannot make more cakes without more sugar. Similarly, even if one has excess sugar, one cannot make more cakes unless one has enough flour. Another example of perfect complements could be a left shoe and a right shoe. The consumer is no better off having several right shoes if he has only one left shoe. Additional right shoes have zero marginal satisfaction without more left shoes. The marginal rate of substitution is either zero or infinite. Thus, the point of utilization is at the corner where both the perpendicular lines intersect. These are given by points R, S, or T in Exhibit 13(b). Indifference curves for perfect substitutes and perfect complements are given in Exhibit 13 (a) and (b).

Exhibit 13

Indifference Curves for Perfect Substitutes and Perfect Complements

(a)

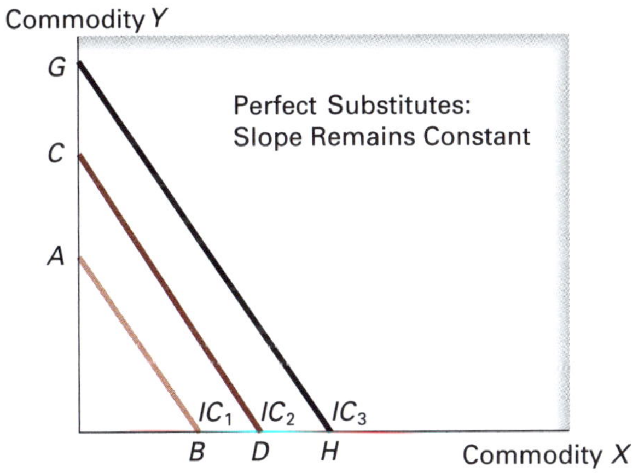

(b)

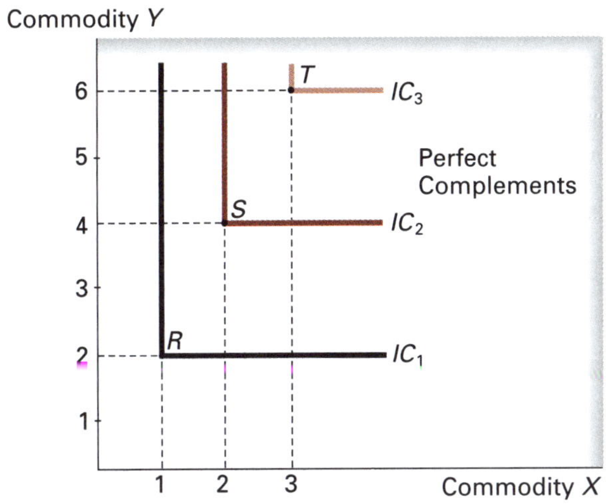

Budget Line

A budget line or price line represents various combinations of two goods, say X and Y, which the consumer can purchase with a given money income, price of X and price of Y. For example, a consumer has weekly income of $60. He purchases only two goods, packets of biscuits and packets of coffee. The price of each packet of biscuits (Y) is $6 and the price of each packet of coffee (X) is $12. Given the assumed income and the price of the two goods, the consumer can purchase various combinations of goods X and Y. Various combinations of goods that a consumer can buy with his available income of $60 can be 10Y and 0X; 6Y and 2X; 2Y and 4X or 0Y and 5X. Combination A in Exhibit 14 shows that if the whole amount of $60 is spent on the purchase of biscuits, then the consumer can buy 10 packets of biscuits at a price of $6 each. In this case, nothing is left to purchase coffee. Similarly, if the consumer spends the entire amount of $60 on the purchase of coffee, a maximum of 5 packets of coffee can be purchased at a price of $12 each. In this case, nothing is left for the purchase of biscuits. This is represented by combination *B*. Intermediate combinations, such as *M* and *N* show other combinations of biscuits and coffee that the consumer can buy, given that he has a budget of $60. The graphical representation of the budget line is provided in Exhibit 14. While the indifference curve shows people's preferences for the combination of two goods, the actual choices they make, however, depend on their budget constraint. The budget line is drawn as a continuous line. It identifies the options from which the consumer can choose the combination of goods.

Exhibit 14

Budget Line

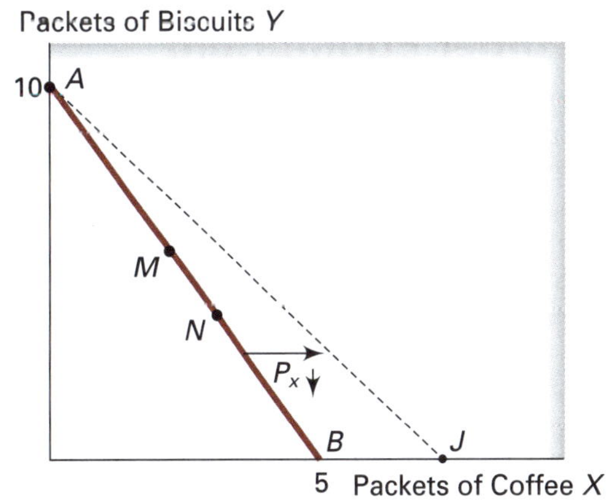

The budget line *AB* indicates all the combinations of packets of biscuits and packets of coffee which a consumer can buy given the assumed prices and income. In case, a consumer decides to purchase combination of goods inside the budget line, then it involves a total outlay that is smaller than the amount of $60 per week. However, if the consumer is assumed to exhaust all his income, then he must be on the budget line. Further, any point outside the budget line requires an outlay larger than the consumer's weekly income of $60 and thus represents an infeasible outlay.

The slope of the budget line indicates how many packets of biscuits a purchaser must give up to buy one more packet of coffee. Thus, the slope at any point on the budget line is given by $\Delta Y/\Delta X$ or two packets of biscuits = 1 packet of coffee. Since the budget line is a straight line, its slope remains constant.

An increase in income of the consumer makes the budget line to shift parallel to itself (to the right if income increases and to the left if income decreases, assuming prices remain constant). On the other hand, a change in the price of X or Y makes the budget line tilt. Let us consider that there is a change in the price of one good. The income of the consumer and price of other good is held constant. When there is a fall in the price of one good say commodity X, the consumer can purchase more of that good than before. A price change causes the budget line to rotate (tilt) about point A. This is shown by the dotted line in Exhibit 14. A flatter budget line means that the relative price of the good X on the horizontal axis is lower. In general, equation of the budget line can be written as:

$$M = P_xQ_x + P_yQ_y$$

This can be re-written as:

$$Q_y = \frac{M}{P_y} - \frac{P_x}{P_y}Q_x$$

where $\frac{M}{P_y}$ and $\frac{P_x}{P_y}$ represent the intercept and slope of the budget line, respectively.

Consumer Equilibrium

The term consumer's equilibrium refers to the amount of goods and services which the consumer may buy in the market given his income and given prices of goods in the market. When consumers make choices about the quantity of goods and services to consume, it is presumed that their objective is to **maximize total utility (satisfaction)**. In maximizing total utility, the consumer faces a number of constraints, the most important of which are

1. the consumer's *income* and
2. the *prices* of the goods and services that the consumer wishes to consume.

The consumer's effort is to maximize total utility, subject to these constraints. A consumer is said to be in equilibrium at a point where the budget line is tangent to the highest attainable indifference curve. Consumer equilibrium is represented in Exhibit 15. Specifically, two conditions must be met at equilibrium[3].

1. First: A given budget line should be tangent to an indifference curve. In other words, the marginal rate of substitution of commodity X for commodity Y (MRS_{xy}) must be equal to the ratio of the relative prices of X and Y. i.e.,
$$MRS_{xy} = Px / Py$$
2. Second: The second order condition is that indifference curves must be convex to the origin at the point of tangency.

Exhibit 15

Consumer Equilibrium

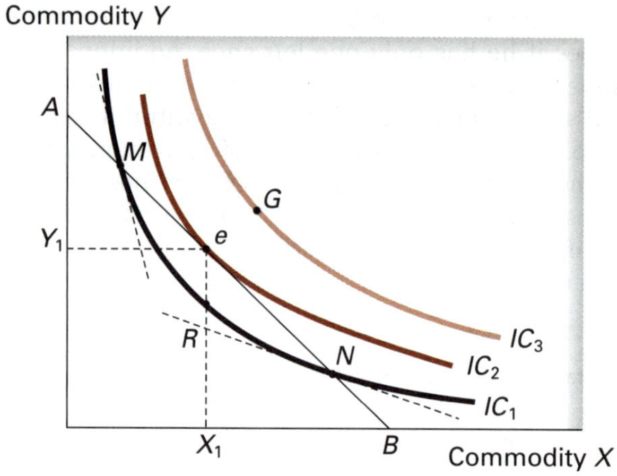

In Exhibit 15, there are three indifference curves IC_1, IC_2, and IC_3. The budget line *AB* is tangent to the indifference curve IC_2 at point "*e*". Therefore, the consumer is in equilibrium at point e, where the slope of *IC* equals the slope of the budget line. The consumer gets the maximum satisfaction by purchasing OY_1 units of commodity Y and OX_1 units of commodity X with the given money income.

At no other point on the indifference curve can the consumer be in equilibrium. For instance, at point M, the slope of the *IC* is greater than the slope of the *BL*. Similarly, at point N, the slope of *IC* is smaller than the slope of the *BL*. Also at both these points, while the consumer spends all his money income, his satisfaction remains at a lower *IC* given by IC_1. By moving to *e*, the consumer can enhance his satisfaction level. Similarly, while the consumer would like to be at point G on IC_3, it is not attainable

3. In addition, the following assumptions are made to determine the consumer's equilibrium position.

- Rationality: The consumer is rational. He wants to obtain maximum satisfaction given his income and prices.
- Utility is ordinal: It is assumed that the consumer can rank his preference according to the satisfaction of each combination of goods.
- Consistency of choice: It is also assumed that the consumer is consistent in the choice of goods.

as it lies beyond his budget constraint. Thus, the consumer's equilibrium position is only at point *e* where the price line is tangent to the highest attainable indifference curve IC_2. Geometrically, at tangency point *e*, the consumer's substitution ratio is equal to price ratio *Px/Py*. It implies that at equilibrium, what the consumer is willing to pay, i.e., his personal exchange rate between X and Y (MRS_{xy}) is equal to what he actually pays, i.e., the market exchange rate. So the equilibrium condition being satisfied at the point *e* is

Price of X / Price of Y = MRS of X for Y

The equilibrium condition given above states that the rate at which the individual is willing to substitute commodity X for commodity Y must equal the ratio at which he can substitute X for Y in the market at a given price. Also, when the consumer is in equilibrium, the indifference curve must be convex to the origin at the point of equilibrium. In other words, we can say that the *MRS* of X for Y must be diminishing at the point of equilibrium.

Some further thoughts on consumer equilibrium:

1. In case a commodity is an economic "good" up to certain point, and beyond which it becomes an economic "bad"; the indifference curves will be U shaped. Downward sloping until the point it is an economic good (point G, H, and R), and beyond which it becomes upward sloping (Refer Exhibit 16a).
2. In case both the commodities are "economic bads" (say pollution and noise or inflation and unemployment), the indifference curves will be downward sloping, concave to the origin (*MRS* will be increasing). Further, in this case a higher indifference curve will represent a lower preference (refer Exhibit 16b).
3. If there are two individuals A and B and two commodities X and Y, with individual A having a strong preference for good X and individual B a strong preference for good Y, then the indifference curves will be flatter for individual A and steeper for individual B (refer Exhibit 16c).
4. If the indifference curves are concave, maximization of utility will imply consuming only one of the two commodities. Also, equilibrium will not be at the point of tangency. Here, the consumer consumes either only X or only Y, depending on the shape of indifference curves and relative prices of X and Y. In panel A of Exhibit 16d, the equilibrium will be at point e_1,

Exhibit 16

Further Thoughts on Indifference Curves and Consumer Equilibrium

(a)

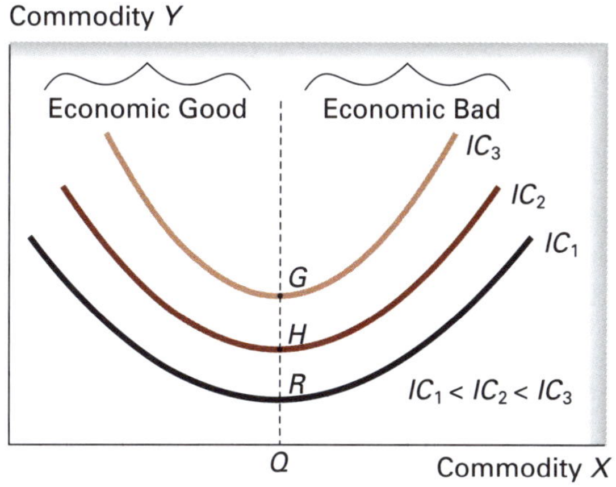

(b)

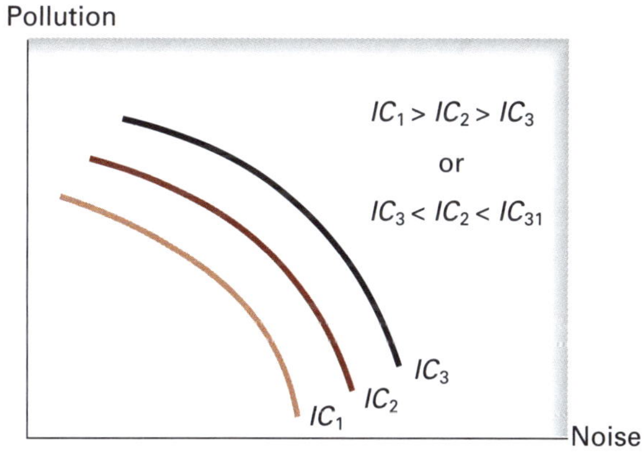

(c)

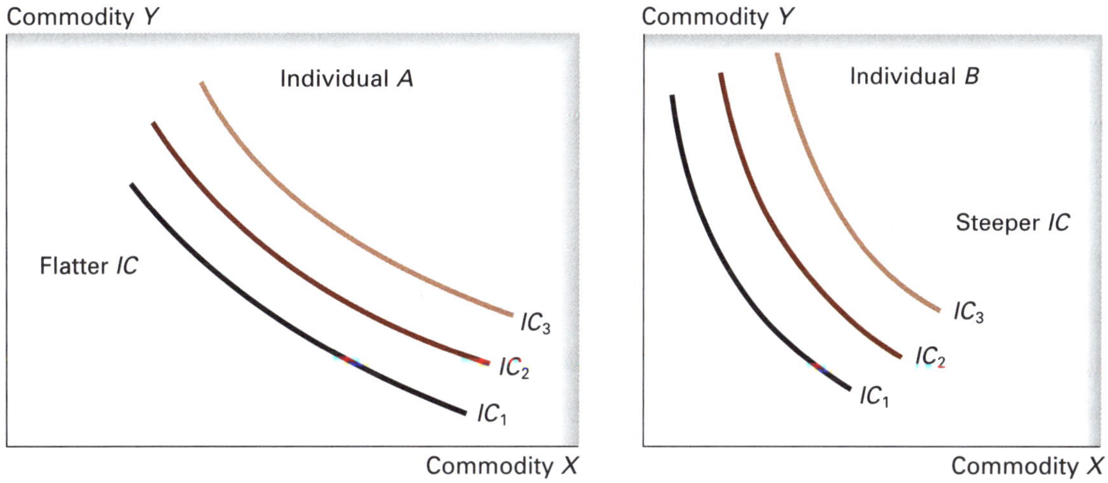

(d)

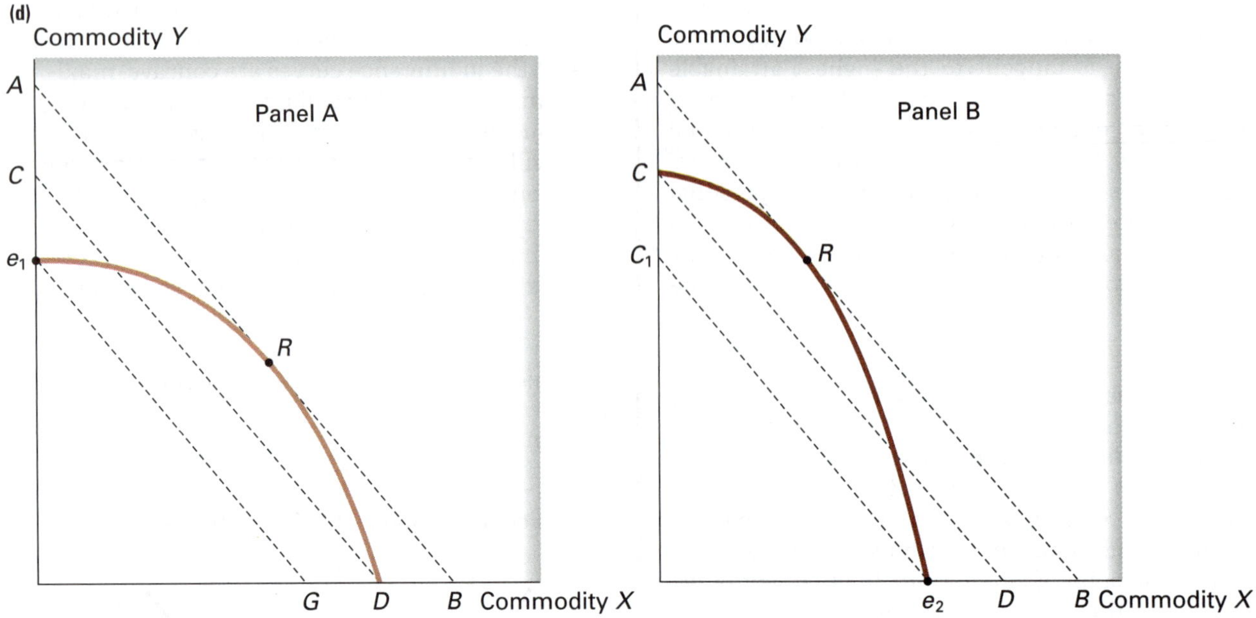

(e)

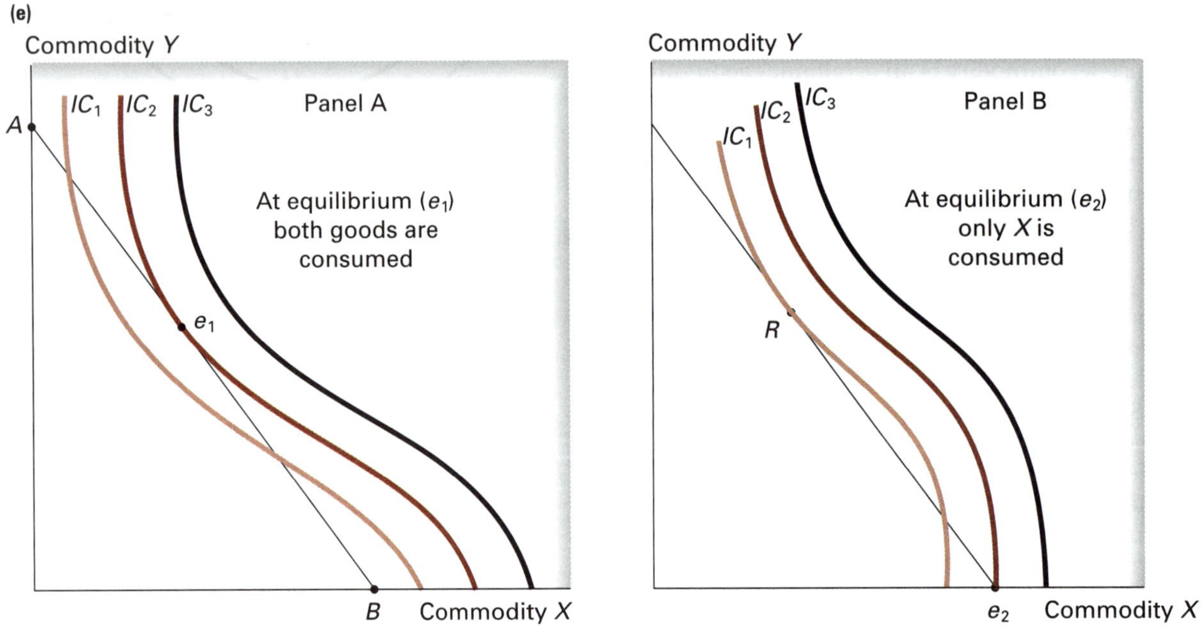

while in panel 2, the equilibrium is at e_2. As can be seen, these are not the respective points of tangency. In fact, the consumer can increase satisfaction by moving away from the point of tangency (R), to either e_1 or e_2 (refer Exhibit 16d). In one case, the consumer consumes only good Y (equilibrium at e_1), while in the other case he consumes only X (equilibrium at e_2).

5. If indifference curves have both convex and concave segments, then the consumer could be in equilibrium if he buys both the goods. Alternatively, equilibrium could also be a corner solution where only one of the two goods is consumed (refer Exhibit 16e). In the first panel, both the goods are purchased when the consumer is in equilibrium. This happens at point e_1. Here the consumer maximizes his utility at a point which lies in the convex portion of the indifference curve. However, in the second panel, the consumer maximizes utility by consuming only good X, and a corner solution exists at point e_2.

The Theory of Consumer Choice: Mathematical Representation

Suppose that a consumer spends all of his income

on two commodities, viz. X and Y. Equilibrium will be attained when the consumer maximizes utility (U) subject to his budget constraint (M). That is,

$$\text{Maximize } U = f(Q_X, Q_Y) \quad (1)$$

$$\text{Subject to } M = P_XQ_X + P_YQ_Y \quad (2)$$

Using the Lagrangian multiplier method, the constrained optimization problem can be solved.

To do so, we first form the Lagrangian function:

$$\phi = f(Q_X, Q_Y) + \lambda(M - P_XQ_X + P_YQ_Y) \quad (3)$$

Thereafter to maximize ϕ, we set the partial derivatives of ϕ with respect to Q_X, Q_Y and λ, equal to zero. That is,

$$\frac{\partial \phi}{\partial Q_X} = \frac{\partial f}{\partial Q_X} - \lambda P_X = 0 \quad (4)$$

$$\frac{\partial \phi}{\partial Q_Y} = \frac{\partial f}{\partial Q_Y} - \lambda P_Y = 0 \quad (5)$$

$$\frac{\partial \phi}{\partial \lambda} = M - P_XQ_X - P_YQ_Y = 0 \quad (6)$$

Solving equations 4 and 5 for λ and setting them equal to each other gives:

$$\lambda = \frac{\partial f/\partial Q_X}{P_X} = \frac{\partial f/\partial Q_Y}{P_Y} \quad (7)$$

$$\lambda = \frac{MU_X}{P_X} = \frac{MU_Y}{P_Y} \quad (8)$$

where MU_X is the marginal utility that the consumer gets from consuming the last unit of commodity X and MU_Y is the marginal utility of Y that the consumer gets from consuming the last unit of commodity X. Thus, equation 8 states that the consumer is in equilibrium when the marginal utility (MU) of the last dollar spent on X equals the marginal utility of the last dollar spent on Y. Thus, λ is the marginal utility of the last dollar spent on X and Y when the consumer is in equilibrium. From this equilibrium condition, we get one point on the individual's demand curves for commodity X and commodity Y. By changing the price of X and Y and repeating the process, we obtain other points of consumer equilibrium, and by joining these, we can derive the individual's demand curve for commodities X and Y.

Alternatively, the consumer's equilibrium condition can also be written as:

$$1/\lambda = \frac{MU_X}{MU_Y} = \frac{P_X}{P_Y} \quad (9)$$

Equation 9 implies that at equilibrium, the ratio of marginal utilities of the two commodities X and Y should be equal to the ratio of relative prices of goods X and Y.

Numerical Illustrations

Problem 1: A consumer has the utility function over goods x and y, $U(X, Y) = 12X^2Y^4$. Let the price of good X be given by P_x, and the price of good y be given by P_y. Let income be given by M. Based upon this information, comment on the following:

(a) What is the slope of the consumer's indifference curve at the consumption bundle, (1,1)?

(b) Derive the consumer's generalized demand function for goods x and y.

(c) If we have $P_x = \$2$, $P_y = \$2$, and M = 24, compute the utility maximizing consumption bundle for the consumer.

Solution:

(a) The slope of the indifference curve is given by the absolute value of marginal rate of substitution. The MRS is given by:

$$MRS = (\partial U/\partial X)/(\partial U/\partial Y) = (24XY^4) / (48X^2Y^3)$$
$$= Y/2X$$

When the consumption bundle is given by (1, 1), MRS can be estimated as 1/2. Therefore, the slope of the indifference curve is –1/2.

(b) To compute the utility maximizing consumption bundle, we set up the Lagrange function, ϕ, that maximizes consumers utility subject to budget constraint ($M = P_xX - P_yY$).

$$\phi = 12X^2Y^4 + \lambda(M - P_xX - P_yY)$$

By differentiating ϕ with respect to X, Y, and λ, and setting the derivatives equal to zero, yields the following:

$$\frac{\partial \phi}{\partial X} = 24XY^4 - \lambda P_x = 0 \quad (1)$$

$$\frac{\partial \phi}{\partial Y} = 48X^2Y^3 - \lambda P_y = 0, \text{ and} \quad (2)$$

$$\frac{\partial \phi}{\partial \lambda} = M - P_xX - P_yY = 0. \quad (3)$$

Solving the first two equations for λ and equating the expressions, we have

$$\lambda = 24XY^4/P_x = 48X^2Y^3/P_y \quad (4)$$

This can be solved for Y, yielding

$$Y = (2XP_x)/P_y \quad (5)$$

Substituting this expression into the budget equation, we have

$$0 = M - P_xX - [(P_y)(2XP_x)/P_y] = M - 3P_xX \quad (6)$$

Solving for X, we have the generalized demand function for X. That is:

$$X = M/3P_x \quad (7)$$

Plugging (7) into (5), we get the generalized demand for Y,

$$Y = \{2(M/3P_x) * P_x\}/P_y = 2M/3P_y$$

(c) By substituting $P_x = 2$, $P_y = 2$, and $M = 24$ into the generalized demand functions from part (b), we get $X = 4$ and $Y = 8$.

Substitution and Income Effect of a Fall in Price of a Product

As shown in Exhibit 17, if the price of product X falls, one end of the budget line tilts. Instead of AB, the new budget line is AJ. The consumer is now in equilibrium at e_3 instead of e_1. The consumer now maximizes his utility consuming X_3 of X and Y_3 of Y. The

Exhibit 17

The Price Effect

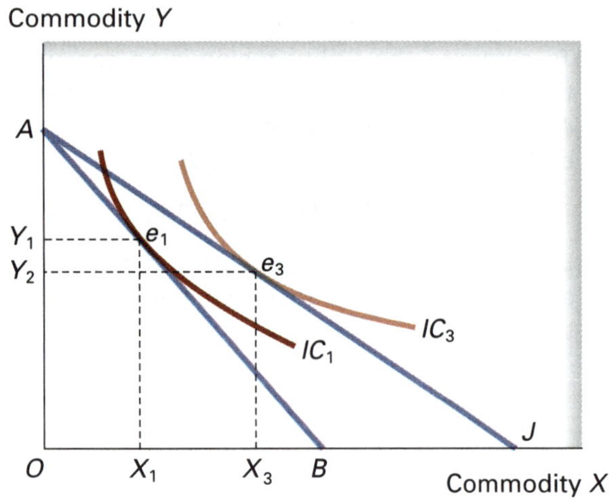

fall in the price of product X has led to an increase in quantity demanded of X by an amount X_1X_3.

The increase in quantity demanded of X by an amount X_1X_3 as a result of the fall in price is referred to as price effect. The price effect is made up of two effects: the substitution effect and the income effect. While a relative decrease in price of X motivates the consumer to buy more of X, there is also the possibility that an additional amount of X is being purchased on account of increase in purchasing power due to decrease in price of X. Our objective here is to distinguish these two effects.

Substitution Effect

The substitution effect shows the additional quantity of a commodity purchased due to it becoming relatively cheaper, real income of the consumer remaining constant.

There are two methods for observing the substitution effect. These are:

- The Hicks-Allen Substitution effect, and
- The Slutsky Substitution Effect.

The difference primarily lies in the way the two define "*real income of the consumer remaining constant*". In order to keep the real income constant, some amount of money income has to be taken away from the consumer. The Hicks substitution effect takes away from the consumer just enough money income to enable him get back to his old indifference curve. The Slutsky substitution effect, on the other hand, takes away from the consumer just enough money income to enable him get back to his old consumption basket. That is, in Hicks method we hold the satisfaction/utility constant, and hence the movement is along the original indifference curve, while in Slutsky method we hold the purchasing power constant in such a manner that the consumer can buy the original consumption bundle. We shall see later that this allows the consumer to reach a higher IC.

The Hicks-Allen Substitution effect: In the ***Hicksian method***, price change is accompanied by so much change in money income that the consumer is neither better off nor worse off than before in terms of satisfaction. The money income is changed by an amount which keeps the consumer on the same indifference curve. To elaborate, let the price of X fall and let the price of Y remain unchanged. With this fall in the price of good X, the real income of the consumer increases. To estimate the substitution effect, this increase in the real income of the consumer is so withdrawn that he is neither better off nor worse off than above. The amount by which the money income is reduced is called ***compensating variation in income***. Substitution effect thus captures the increase in quantity demanded of X, due to change in its relative price, real income of the consumer remaining constant.

The Hicksian substitution effect can be explained with the help of Exhibit 18. In this exhibit, the consumer with initial money income and given prices of two goods represented by price line AB is in equilibrium at point e_1 on indifference curve IC_1. He buys OX_1 quantity of good X and OY_1 quantity of good Y. We suppose now that the price of good X falls and the price of good Y remains the same. With the fall in the price of X, the budget line tilts from AB to AJ. Consumer's real income is raised because commodity X is now cheaper. This increase in the real income of the consumer is to be wiped out for finding out the substitution effect. The reduction in the money income of the consumer is to be made by an amount which keeps him on the original indifference curve IC_1. In case, the consumer's income is reduced by *AM* (in terms of Y) or *NJ* (in terms of X), the consumer will remain on the same indifference curve IC_1. *AM* or *NJ* is the compensating variation in income. At the new price line *AB*, the consumer is in equilibrium at point e_2. He now buys OX_2 of good X and OY_2 of good Y.

The increase in the purchase of good X by X_1X_2 and decrease in the purchase of good Y by Y_1Y_2 is due to the fall in the price of good X, real income remaining constant. The consumer has rearranged his purchase of good X and good Y as good X is now relatively cheaper and good Y is relatively dearer than before. The consumer has moved on the same indifference curve IC_1 from e_1 to point e_2, substituting the commodity that has become relatively cheaper for the one that has become relatively more expensive because of price change. The type of movement from point e_1 to e_2 on the same indifference curve represents the Hicks-Allen substitution effect. The substitution effect will always make the consumer to buy more of the relatively cheaper product.

Exhibit 18

The Hicks-Allen Substitution Effect

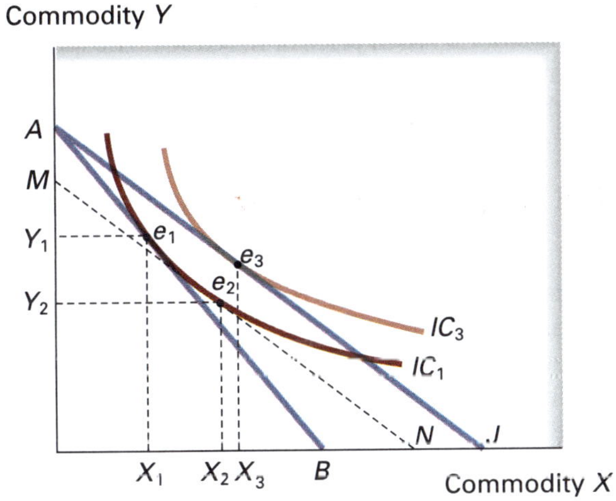

Slutsky Substitution Effect: In the Slutsky Substitution Effect, price change is accompanied by so much change in money income that the consumer is allowed to buy the previous commodity bundle (Exhibit 19). To elaborate, let point e_1 be the original optimizing bundle; it lies on IC_1 and the original budget constraint is denoted by *AB*. Now the price of X reduces, and thus his budget line tilts to *AJ*. Note that the Y intercept remains unchanged as the price of Y has not changed. In response to the decline in the price of good X, the consumer would choose point e_3. However, in order to separate the substitution effect from the price effect, we have to keep the

Exhibit 19

The Slutsky Substitution Effect

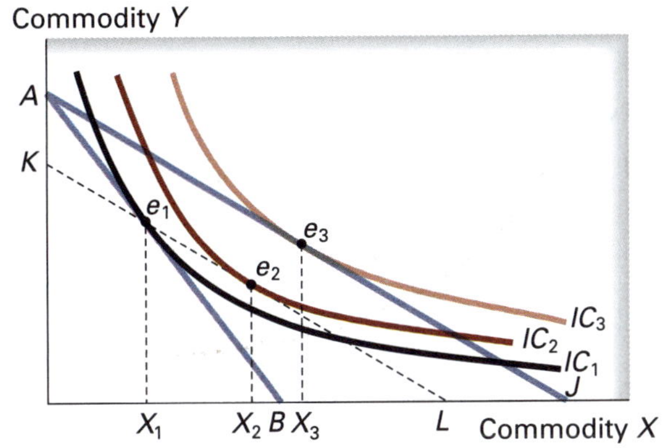

purchasing power constant. We therefore take back *AK* money income from the consumer in terms of good Y or *LJ* money income in terms of good X, to enable the consumer to purchase his original consumption bundle (given by point e_1). We thus get the new budget line *KL*. Given the new budget line, the consumer can become better off by moving to point e_2 on IC_2. This movement from e_1 to e_2 represents the Slutsky's substitution effect. The substitution effect will always make the consumer buy more of the relatively cheaper product.

The substitution effect is also known as the change in compensated demand. This name explicitly represents the fact that the consumer is compensated for a price fall/rise by adjusting income enough to purchase the old consumption bundle or to be on the original level of satisfaction. Uncompensated demand gives the total change in quantity demanded which is made up of both the substitution and the income effect. In the following sections, in general, substitution effect will be as given by Hicks-Allen.

Income Effect

The income effect is identified by shifting the budget line back outwards again. In this case, this leads to an increase in quantity demanded of good X by an amount X_2X_3 in Exhibit 18 and 19. The income effect shows the additional amount of commodity X purchased by the consumer, due to an increase in real income, relative prices remaining constant. However, it needs to be mentioned that the income effect can make the consumer buy more or less of X depending on whether X is a normal or an inferior good. In the case of a **normal good**, higher real income leads to an increase in quantity demanded of X; this complements the increase due to the substitution effect. This is shown in Exhibit 20.

Exhibit 20

Price Effect for a Normal Good

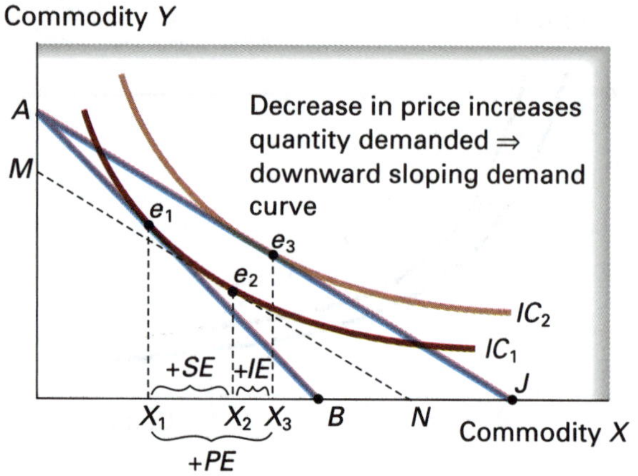

In the case of an inferior product the income effect leads to a fall in the quantity demanded of X, which works against the substitution effect. In Exhibit 21, the substitution effect is X_1X_2, and the income effect in minus X_2X_3. However, since the positive substitution effect outweighs the negative income effect, the overall price effect remains positive. The overall change in quantity demanded in X is an increase of X_1X_3. Thus, the quantity demanded of X rises with a fall in price of X. This

Exhibit 21

Price Effect for an Inferior Good

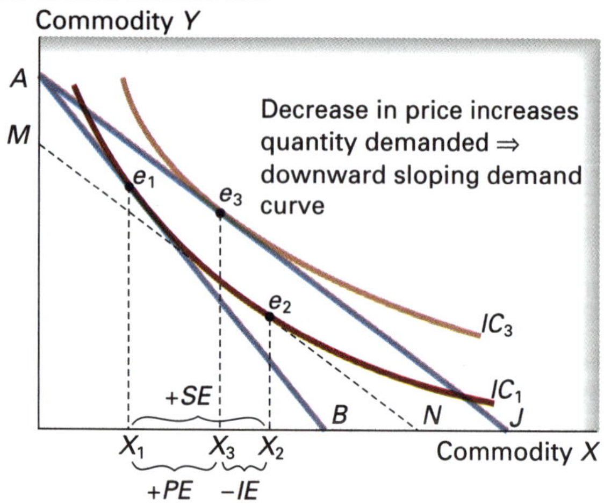

Exhibit 22

Price Effect for a Giffen Good

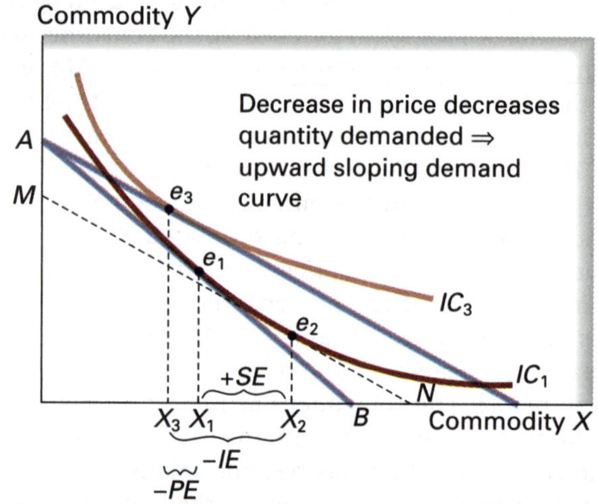

implies that the demand curve is downward sloping since a fall in price of X, increases the quantity demanded of X.

In the case of a **Giffen Good**, the income effect leads to a fall in the quantity demanded which works not only against the substitution effect, but also outweighs it. This means that following a price fall, the overall quantity demanded falls (Exhibit 22). This implies that the demand curve will be upward sloping since a fall in price of X, reduces the quantity demanded of X.

Exhibit 23 summarizes the above discussion.

The Impact of a Price Increase

A price increase can be analyzed in exactly the same way as a price decrease. Assume that the price of X increases. As shown in Exhibit 24, this leads to the budget line pivoting from AK. It now becomes AR. Equilibrium moves from e_1 to e_3. Given an increase in the price of a product X, the real income of the consumer falls, and his purchasing power reduces. To identify the substitution effect, we shift the budget line outwards and parallel until it is just tangent with the original indifference curve IC_1. This shows the substitution effect to be e_1e_2. The consumer is

Exhibit 23

Substitution Effect, Income Effect, and Price Effect of a Fall in Price

	Substitution Effect (*SE*)	Income Effect(*IE*)	Price Effect (*PE*)	Comment	Shape of Demand Curve
Normal good	Increases quantity demanded	Increases quantity demanded	Increases quantity demanded	*SE* and *IE* both in same direction	Downward sloping demand curve
Inferior good	Increases quantity demanded	Decreases quantity demanded	Increases quantity demanded	*SE* and *IE* in opposite direction but *SE* > *IE*	Downward sloping demand curve
Giffen good	Increases quantity demanded	Decreases quantity demanded	Decreases quantity demanded	*SE* and *IE* in opposite direction, and *SE* < *IE*	Upward sloping demand curve; Negates law of demand

Exhibit 24

Price Effect for a Rise in Price

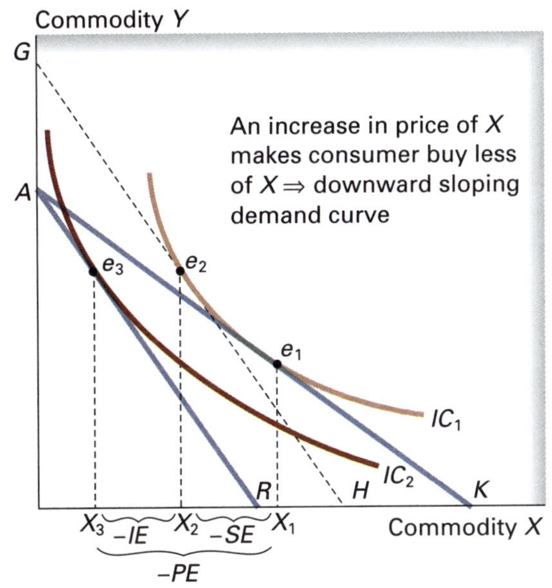

now buying less of X. Thus, consumers will always substitute away from the relatively more expensive product. In order to find the income effect, we take back the (hypothetical) money income that was given to the consumer. This can be shown by the effect of shifting the budget line back in and parallel to itself. In this case, the income effect is to further reduce the quantity demanded (which means it is a normal good) by X_2X_3. The overall decrease in quantity demanded is from X_1 to X_3. Since a rise in the price of X makes the consumer buy less of X, the demand curve will be downward sloping.

Understanding Substitutes and Complements using Indifference Curves

Indifference curve analysis also allows us to gauge whether two products X and Y are substitutes or complements. In Exhibit 25(a), a fall in the price of product X has led to a tilting of the budget line. Further, the equilibrium of the consumer moves from e_1 to e_3. As a result, more of X and less of Y is bought. We, therefore, conclude that X and Y are substitutes. The consumer has switched from product Y to product X. On the other hand, in Exhibit 25 (b), when the price of product X falls, it makes the consumer increase the quantity demanded of both X and Y (e_2). We, thus, conclude that the two products are complements. A lower price leads to more of both goods being purchased.

An Increase in Income

The effect on the demand for a product as a result of an increase in income can also be analyzed using indifference curve analysis. An increase in income shifts the budget line outwards parallel to itself. Since the relative prices have not changed, the slope of the budget line remains unchanged. The new combinations of products that maximize satisfaction can now be identified; from this the impact of income changes on the demand for a product can be analyzed. In Exhibit 26, the left panel shows that product X is a normal good. An increase in income

Exhibit 25 (a and b)

Indifference Curves: Understanding Substitutes and Complements

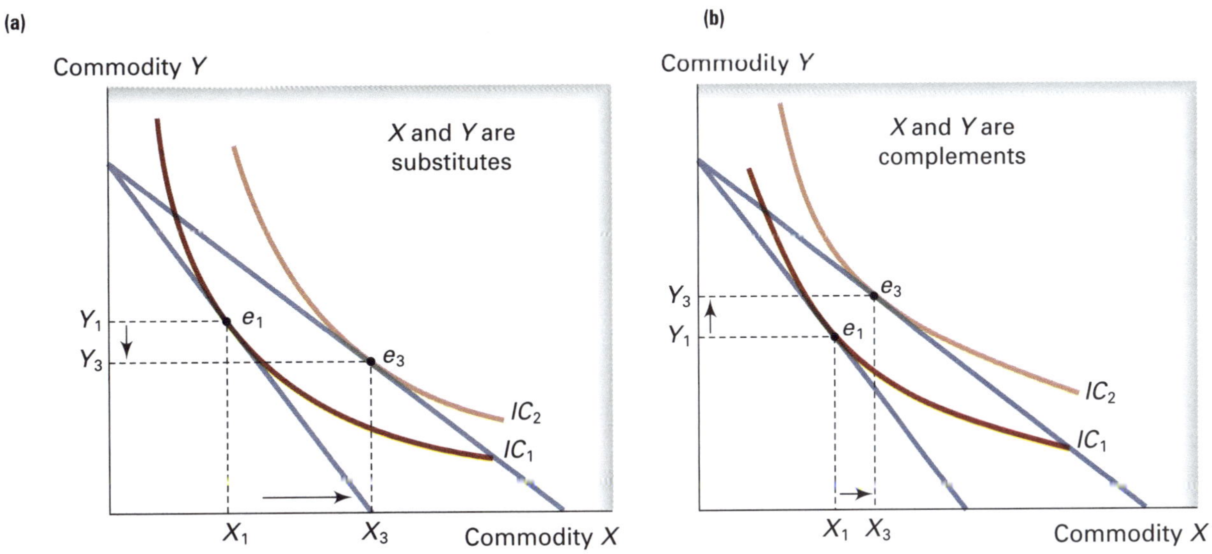

Exhibit 26

Income Effect for a Normal and an Inferior Good

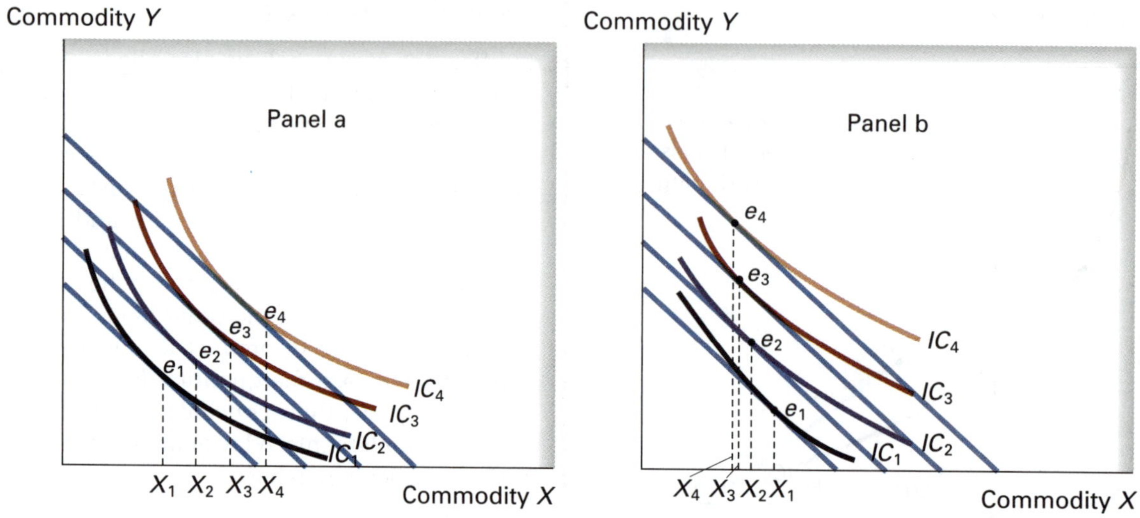

increases the quantity demanded of X. On the other hand, in the right panel, commodity X is an inferior good, as an increase in income reduces the quantity demanded.

Final Word

This chapter has analyzed consumer choice by focusing on utility, or satisfaction. We assumed that utility could be measured in some systematic (cardinal) way for a particular consumer, even though utility measures could not be compared across consumers. We then explored consumer equilibrium when satisfaction could not be measured, but could be only ranked (ordinal utility analysis). The goal in both the situations has been to explore utility satisfaction maximization and predict how consumers react to a change in price. We judge a theory not by the realism of its assumptions but by the accuracy of its predictions. Based on this criterion, the theory of consumer choice presented in this chapter has proven to be quite useful.

Again, to maximize utility, you or any other consumer do not need to understand the material presented in this chapter. Economists assume that the urge to maximize utility is natural and instinctive. In this chapter, we simply tried to analyze that process.

Multiple Choice Questions

1. Which of the following is true of units of utility?
   a. Each unit is worth $1.
   b. They cannot be compared across consumers.
   c. They apply to goods but not to services.
   d. They do not exist for very wealthy individuals.
   e. They are negative for inferior goods.
2. Which of the following statements cannot be made regarding consumer preferences?
   a. Pat enjoys her second cotton candy less than her first.
   b. Bill enjoys his second cotton candy as much as the first.
   c. Arnie enjoys two cotton candies more than one cotton candy.
   d. Arnie enjoys two cotton candies more than Pat enjoys one cotton candy.
   e. Bill and Arnie enjoy their second cotton candy less than they do their first.
3. Utility is
   a. the sense of pleasure or satisfaction derived from consuming goods and services
   b. the cost of acquiring goods and services
   c. the profit consumers earn from consuming goods and services
   d. the monetary value to consumers of goods and services
   e. the desire to consume goods and services
4. "I don't feel so good. I shouldn't have had that last doughnut." Which statement best describes this situation?
   a. The marginal utility of the last doughnut was positive.
   b. The marginal utility of doughnuts is still increasing.
   c. The total utility from eating doughnuts is negative.
   d. The marginal utility of the last doughnut was negative.
   e. The marginal utility of the next doughnut will be positive.
5. Joe the Economist tells his wife, Jane, that he wants to spend a weekend fishing with his friends. She replies, "You don't love me anymore." Just before she hits Joe with a croquet mallet, Joe explains to her that she has confused the concepts of
   a. marginal utility and price
   b. income and price
   c. marginal utility and total utility
   d. love and death
   e. consumer surplus and utility
6. Newspaper vending machines illustrate that publishers believe
   a. the average utility of two identical papers is zero or less
   b. the total utility from two identical newspapers is zero or less
   c. the marginal utility of a second identical newspaper is zero or less
   d. the marginal utility of a second identical newspaper is greater than the marginal utility of the first newspaper
   e. the total utility from two identical newspapers is less than the total utility from the first newspaper
7. If the marginal utility of each good a consumer buys does not diminish but remains constant, we should see consumers
   a. buying no goods at all
   b. spending all of their income on the good with the highest marginal utility
   c. buying one unit of each good
   d. buying only the least expensive good
   e. leaving the store in total confusion
8. Suppose Enid could increase her total utility by purchasing one more book and one less video rental. Which of the following is true?
   a. The marginal utility of video rentals exceeds the marginal utility of books.
   b. The marginal utility of books exceeds the marginal utility of video rentals.
   c. The marginal utility of video rentals is negative.
   d. The marginal utility per dollar spent on books exceeds that of video rentals.
   e. Total utility is at a maximum.
9. When a consumer spends income so that the ratio of marginal utilities (MUs) of all goods purchased equals the ratio of their prices, the consumer is
   a. maximizing marginal utility
   b. spending too much on all goods
   c. maximizing total utility
   d. beyond the point of diminishing marginal utility
   e. behaving in opposition to the principal of rational behavior
10. Sally is allocating her budget between two goods, A and B. If Sally has used up the budget on a combination of A and B for which

MU_A/P_A exceeds MU_B/P_B, she can increase total utility by buying

a. more A and less B
b. more B and less A
c. more A without changing her consumption of B
d. less B without changing her consumption of A
e. more B and more A

11. Along a consumer's demand curve, price reflects
    a. the costs of production
    b. the dollar value of the total utility from the good
    c. the dollar value of the marginal utility of each additional unit of the good
    d. the maximum quantity that could be purchased, given income
    e. non-rational decision making
12. Suppose you want to get to Orlando, Florida, for the week-long spring break. You can get there in two and one-half days by bus, and back in another two and one-half days. This will cost you $20 round-trip. You can fly there and back in four hours each way. This will cost $200. Which of the following is *not* true?
    a. It may be economically rational for you to go by plane rather than by bus.
    b. Depending on what else you can do that week, it may be economically rational for you to not go at all rather than to go by bus.
    c. The true cost of going to Orlando is either the time or the money you spend traveling, whichever it is you value more.
    d. The more you'd enjoy Orlando, the more economically rational it becomes for you to fly there instead of taking the bus.
    e. It is possible that it is rational for you to fly and rational for others to take the bus.
13. Which of the following must be true of an attorney who buys a portable computer so that she can work on trains and planes?
    a. She is engaging in conspicuous consumption.
    b. She gets utility from working.
    c. She thinks the opportunity cost of her time is higher than it really is.
    d. She thinks the opportunity cost of her time is lower than it really is.
    e. She is trying to reduce the opportunity cost of traveling.
14. After paying admission and entering King's Island Amusement Park near Cincinnati, Alan Fujiwara sees a list of waiting times for each attraction and ride. At this point, Alan's marginal dollar cost is
    a. zero and so are the marginal time costs of each attraction or ride
    b. zero, so he will base his next move on the marginal time costs of each attraction or ride
    c. greater than zero based on the admission price, so he will base his next move on the marginal time costs of each attraction or ride
    d. greater than zero based on the admission price, so he will ignore the marginal time costs of each attraction or ride
    e. less than zero and so are the marginal time costs of each attraction or ride
15. Which of the following statements about the substitution effect of a price change is true?
    a. It is caused by a change in relative prices.
    b. It affects the consumer's ability, rather than willingness, to purchase a good.
    c. It assumes that the consumer substitutes more expensive goods for cheaper ones when income increases.
    d. It is usually equal to the income effect.
    e. It may cause the consumer to buy less of the good when its price falls.
16. The substitution effect of a change in the price of bananas refers to the way in which a change in the
    a. price of a substitute affects the demand for bananas
    b. price of bananas affects the ability to buy them
    c. relative price of bananas changes demand for them
    d. relative price of bananas changes the quantity demanded of bananas
    e. price of a substitute affects the quantity demanded of bananas
17. Suppose there are only two goods, apples and oranges. What happens if the price of each good increases by 15 percent?
    a. The consumer will substitute apples for oranges.
    b. The consumer will substitute oranges for apples.
    c. There is no substitution effect because relative prices have remained constant.
    d. Demand for both goods increases.
    e. Demand for both goods decreases.
18. For a renter, the income effect of an increase in apartment rents will
    a. have a greater effect than the income effect of an increase in the price of chewing gum
    b. have no impact on the demand curve for apartments, because everything except price is assumed constant

c. have less of an effect than the income effect of an increase in the price of chewing gum
d. be almost negligible, because housing is a necessity
e. occur only when income increases

19. If pretzels are a normal good, the income effect of a price change means that
a. as income increases, the quantity demanded increases along the demand curve for pretzels
b. as income increases, the demand curve for pretzels shifts rightward
c. as income increases, the demand curve for pretzels shifts leftward
d. as the price of pretzels increases, the real income of individuals who demand pretzels decreases, so the quantity demanded of pretzels decreases
e. as the price of pretzels increases, income increases

20. The income effect of a *decrease in the price* of legal services (a normal good) is a(n)
a. decrease in the demand for legal services
b. decrease in the quantity demanded of legal services
c. increase in the demand for legal services
d. increase in the quantity demanded of legal services
e. new demand curve because everything else is no longer constant

Answers

1. b 2. d 3. a 4. d 5. c 6. c 7. b 8. d 9. c 10. a
11. c 12. c 13. e 14. b 15. a 16. d 17. c 18. a 19. d 20. d

Long Answer Questions

LO1 Explain the basics of utility analysis

1.1. *(Law of Diminishing Marginal Utility)* Some restaurants offer "all you can eat" meals. How is this practice related to diminishing marginal utility? What restrictions must the restaurant impose on the customer to make a profit?

1.2. *(Law of Diminishing Marginal Utility)* Complete each of the following sentences:
a. Your tastes determine the _______ you derive from consuming a particular good.
b. _______ utility is the change in _______ utility resulting from a(n) _______ change in the consumption of a good.
c. As long as marginal utility is positive, total utility is _______.
d. The law of diminishing marginal utility states that as an individual consumes more of a good during a given time period, other things constant, total utility _______.

1.3. *(Marginal Utility)* Is it possible for marginal utility to be negative while total utility is positive? If yes, under what circumstances is it possible?

LO2 Describe how to measure and maximize utility

2.1. *(Utility Maximization)* The following tables illustrate Eileen's utilities from watching first-run movies in a theater and from renting movies from a video store. Suppose that she has a monthly movie budget of $36, each movie ticket costs $6, and each video rental costs $3.

Movies in a Theater

Q	*TU*	*MU*	*MU/P*
0	0	____	____
1	200	____	____
2	290	____	____
3	370	____	____
4	440	____	____
5	500	____	____
6	550	____	____
7	590	____	____

Movies from a Video Store

Q	*TU*	*MU*	*MU/P*
0	0	____	____
1	250	____	____
2	295	____	____
3	335	____	____
4	370	____	____
5	400	____	____
6	425	____	____

a. Complete the tables.
b. Do these tables show that Eileen's preferences obey the law of diminishing marginal utility? Explain your answer.
c. How much of each good does Eileen consume in equilibrium?
d. Suppose the prices of both types of movies drop to $1 while Eileen's movie budget shrinks to $10. How much of each good does she consume in equilibrium?

2.2. *(Utility Maximization)* Suppose that a consumer has a choice between two goods, *X* and *Y*. If the price of *X* is $2 and the price of

Y is \$3, how much of X and Y does the consumer purchase, given an income of \$17? Use the following information about marginal utility:

Units	MU_X	MU_Y
1	10	5
2	8	4
3	2	3
4	2	2
5	1	2

LO3 Explain how marginal utility and the law of demand can create consumer surplus

3.1. *(The Law of Demand and Marginal Utility)* Daniel allocates his budget of \$24 per week among three goods. Use the following table of marginal utilities for good *A*, good *B*, and good *C* to answer the questions below:

Q_A	MU_A	Q_B	MU_B	Q_C	MU_C
1	50	1	75	1	25
2	40	2	60	2	20
3	30	3	40	3	15
4	20	4	30	4	10
5	15	5	20	5	7.5

a. If the price of *A* is \$2, the price of *B* is \$3, and the price of *C* is \$1, how much of each does Daniel purchase in equilibrium?

b. If the price of *A* rises to \$4 while other prices and Daniel's budget remain unchanged, how much of each does he purchase in equilibrium?

c. Using the information from parts (a) and (b), draw the demand curve for good *A*. Be sure to indicate the price and quantity demanded for each point on the curve.

3.2. *(Consumer Surplus)* Suppose the linear demand curve for shirts slopes downward and that consumers buy 500 shirts per year when the price is \$30 and 1,000 shirts per year when the price is \$25.

a. Compared to the prices of \$30 and \$25, what can you say about the marginal valuation that consumers place on the 300th shirt, the 700th shirt, and the 1,200th shirt they might buy each year?

b. With diminishing marginal utility, are consumers deriving any consumer surplus if the price is \$25 per shirt? Explain.

c. Use a market demand curve to illustrate the change in consumer surplus if the price drops from \$30 to \$25.

3.3. *(Consumer Surplus)* Suppose supply of a good is perfectly elastic at a price of \$5. The market demand curve for this good is linear, with zero quantity demanded at a price of \$25. Given that the slope of this linear demand curve is –0.25, draw a supply and demand graph to illustrate the consumer surplus that occurs when the market is in equilibrium.

LO4 Describe the role of time in demand

4.1. *(Role of Time in Demand)* In many amusement parks, you pay an admission fee to the park but you do not need to pay for individual rides. How do people choose which rides to go on?

LO5

5.1. Explain the difference between substitution effect and income effect of a price change?

5.2. What is a 'Giffen Good'? Illustrate using indifference curves.

5.3. Ceteris Paribus, if the price of good *X* rises, which of the following statements will be true:

a. The income effect alone will make the consumer buy more of *X* if *X* is a normal good.

b. The income effect alone will make the consumer buy less of *X* if *X* is an inferior good.

c. The substitution effect will make the consumer buy less of good *X* and it is irrelevant whether *X* is a normal or an inferior good.

NUMERICAL QUESTIONS

1. Reports suggest that consumption of tobacco among teens declined from 1975 to 2000. Between 1975 and 1981, there was a significant decline. In few years it increased and in others it decreased. The decline between 1975 and 1981 cannot be attributed to increase in cigarette prices. In fact, there was a decrease in price during that period. Research suggests that the increase in fuel prices over the period kept the teens away from smoking.

a. Discuss how a rise in fuel prices might affect the demand for cigarettes among teens.

b. Suppose there are two goods in the world, cigarettes and fuel. Draw a figure that shows how an increase in fuel prices can result in a decline in both fuel and cigarette consumption. Use the standard consumer behavior graph with budget lines and indifference curves. Label the figure appropriately.

c. In the late 1990s the price of cigarettes increased from \$2.50 per pack to \$3.25 per pack. In one community during this time period, the number of packs of cigarettes consumed by teenagers fell from 10,000 to 9,000. Assume that everything except cigarette prices remained the same. Calculate the arc price elasticity among teens between these price points.

d. Calculate the total expenditures on cigarettes by teens in part (c) both before and after the price increase. Did total revenue increase or fall? Discuss how this answer is implied by the arc elasticity that you calculated in part (c).

2. Determine the utility maximizing combination of *X* and *Y* when

$TU = 17X + 20Y^2 - 2X^2 - Y^2$

Price of X = \$3

Price of Y = \$4

Money Income = \$22

KEY TERMS

total utility
the total satisfaction you derive from consumption; this could refer to either your total utility of consuming a particular good or your total utility from all consumption

marginal utility
the change in your total utility from a one-unit change in your consumption of a good

law of diminishing marginal utility
the more of a good a person consumes per period, the smaller the increase in total utility from consuming one more unit, other things constant

consumer equilibrium
the condition in which an individual consumer's budget is spent and the last dollar spent on each good yields the same marginal utility; therefore, utility is maximized

marginal valuation
the dollar value of the marginal utility derived from consuming each additional unit of a good

consumer surplus
the difference between the most a consumer would pay for a given quantity of a good and what the consumer actually pays

CHAPTER EQUATION

Consumer Equilibrium

$$\frac{MU_p}{p_p} = \frac{MU_v}{p_v}$$

LO1 Explain the basics of utility analysis. Utility is the sense of pleasure, or satisfaction, that comes from consumption. Utility is subjective. Marginal utility is the change in total utility resulting from a one-unit change in consumption. The law of diminishing marginal utility states that the more of a good you consume per period, all other things constant, the smaller the increase in your total utility from additional consumption.

Total Utility and Marginal Utility You Derive from Drinking Water After Jogging Four Miles

Total utility, shown in panel (a), increases with each of the first four glasses of water consumed but by smaller and smaller amounts. The fifth glass causes total utility to fall, implying that marginal utility is negative, as shown in panel (b).

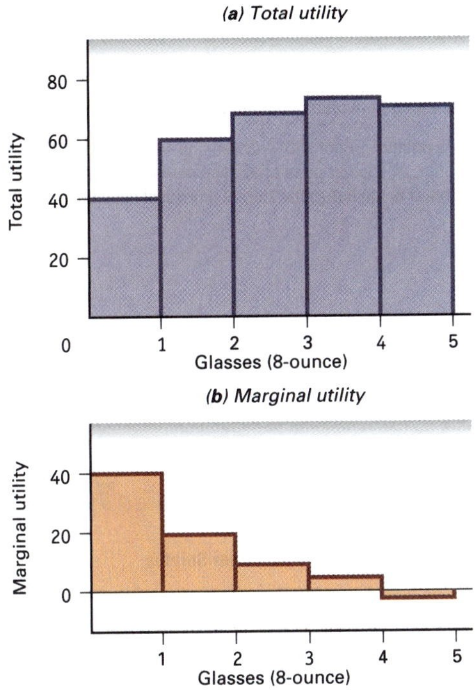

LO2 Describe how to measure and maximize utility. By attaching a numerical measure to utility, we can compare the total utility a particular consumer gets from different goods as well as the marginal utility that consumer gets from additional consumption. Economists assume that the purpose of consumption is to maximize your total utility. You decide how much of each good to purchase by considering your tastes, market prices, and your income. Consumers maximize utility by equalizing the marginal utility from the last dollar spent on each good.

LO3 Explain how marginal utility and the law of demand can create consumer surplus. Utility analysis can be used to construct an individual consumer's demand curve. The consumer's objective is to maximize utility within the limits imposed by income and prices. In a world without scarcity, utility is maximized by consuming a good until its marginal utility reaches zero. In the real world—a world shaped by scarcity as reflected by prices—utility is maximized when the budget is exhausted and the marginal utility of the final unit consumed divided by that good's price is identical for each different good. Consumer surplus is the difference between the maximum amount consumers would pay for a given quantity of the good and the amount they actually pay. Consumer surplus increases as the price declines. Consumer surplus equals the value of the total utility you receive from consumption less your total spending.

Demand for Pizza Generated from Marginal Utility

At a price of \$8 per pizza, the consumer is in equilibrium when consuming three pizzas per week (point *a*). Marginal utility per dollar is the same for all goods consumed. If the price falls to \$6, the consumer increases consumption to four pizzas (point *b*). Points *a* and *b* are two points on this consumer's demand curve for pizza.

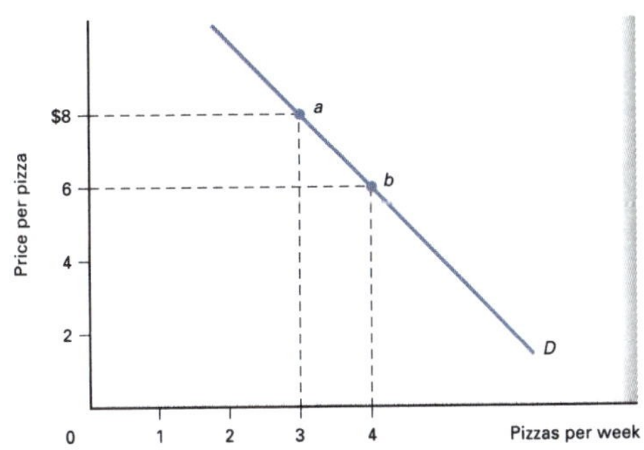

Consumer Surplus from Sub Sandwiches

At a given quantity of sub sandwiches, the height of the demand curve shows the value of the last one purchased. The area under the demand curve for a specific quantity shows the total value a consumer attaches to that quantity. At a price of $4, the consumer purchases four subs. The first one is valued at $7, the second at $6, the third at $5, and the fourth at $4. The consumer values four at $22. Because the consumer pays $4 per sub, all four can be purchased for $16. The difference between what the consumer would have been willing to pay ($22) and what the consumer actually pays ($16) is called consumer surplus. When the price is $4, the consumer surplus is $6, as represented by the dark shaded area under the demand curve above $4. When the price of per sub falls to $3, consumer surplus increases by $4, as reflected by the lighter shaded area.

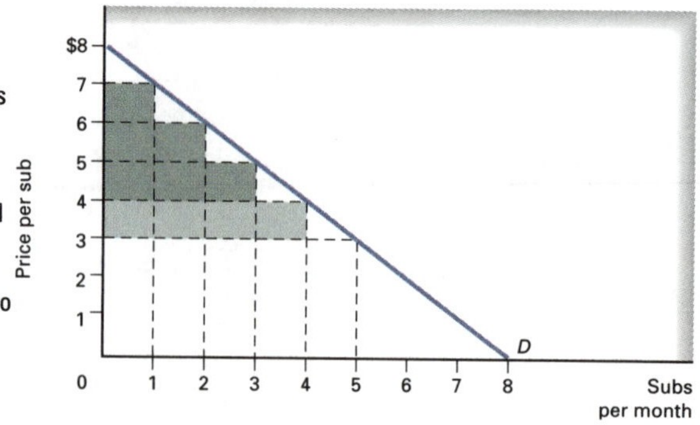

Summing Individual Demand Curves to Derive the Market Demand for Sub Sandwiches

At a price of $4 per sub, you demand 4 per month, Brittany demands 2, and Chris demands 0. Quantity demanded at a price of $4 is $4 + 2 + 0 = 6$ subs per month. At a lower price of $2, you demand 6, Brittany demands 4, and Chris demands 2. Quantity demanded at a price of $2 is 12 subs. The market demand curve D is the horizontal sum of individual demand curves d_Y, d_B, and d_C.

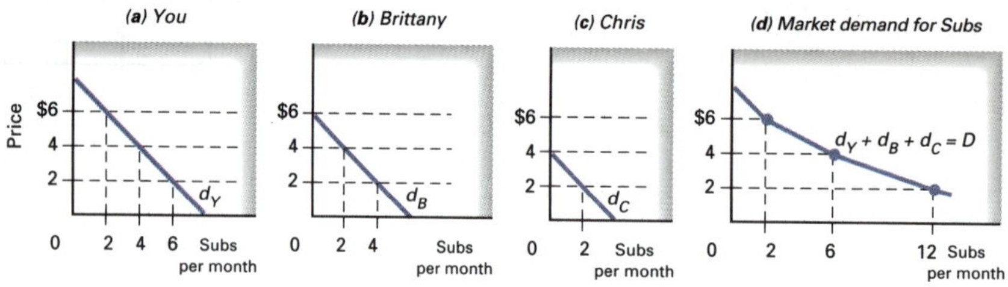

Market Demand and Consumer Surplus

Consumer surplus at a price of $2 is shown by the darker area. If the price falls to $1, consumer surplus increases to include the lighter area. At a zero price, consumer surplus increases to include the entire area under the demand curve.

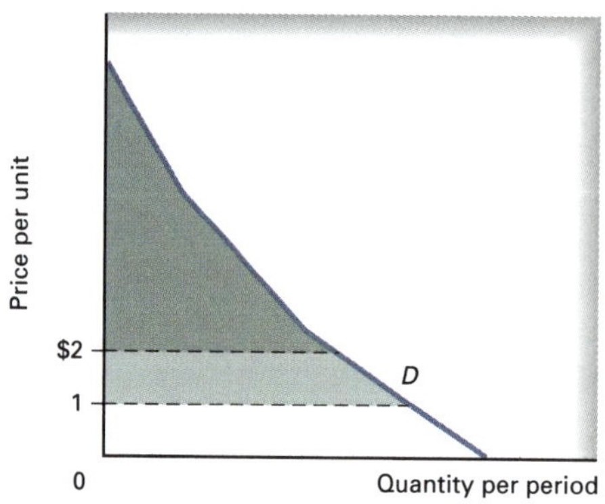

LO4 Describe the role of time in demand. Because consumption does not occur instantly, time plays a role in demand analysis. Consumption takes time, and time has a positive value for most people. Consequently, consumption has a money price and a time price. Your willingness to pay a premium for time-saving goods and services depends on the opportunity cost of your time.

LO5 Explain indifference curves theory of demand. A household generally consumes a large variety of commodities, which we refer to as a commodity consumption bundle. As stated earlier, in order to meet its objective, the consumer maximizes his satisfaction given the constraint imposed by his budget and the prices of goods consumed. We analyze consumer behavior when the satisfaction derived from a commodity cannot be measured cardinally. Only ordinal ranking is possible. In other words, while the consumer is able to rank different commodity bundles based on satisfaction received, he is unable to quantify the specific difference between satisfactions derived from different bundles. An indifference curve represents various combinations of goods that provide the same level of satisfaction to the consumer. That is, satisfaction remains constant along an indifference curve.

CHAPTER

7

Learning Outcomes

LO 1 Explain the relationship between cost and profit

LO 2 Identify the elements that affect production in the short term

LO 3 Identify the elements that affect production in the long run

LO 4 Explain how the costs of production vary with output in the short run

LO 5 Describe how firms use the long-run average cost curve to make choices about production

Theory *of* Production *and* Cost

© HUCHEN LU/ISTOCKPHOTO.COM

"Why do too many cooks spoil the broth?"

Why do too many cooks spoil the broth? Why do movie theaters have so many screens? Why don't they add even more? If you go into business for yourself, how much must you earn just to break even? Why might your grade point average fall even though you improved from the previous term? Answers to these and other questions are discovered in this chapter, which introduces production and cost in the firm.

The previous chapter explored the consumer behavior shaping the demand curve. You were asked to think like a consumer, or demander. This chapter examines the producer behavior shaping the supply curve. You must now think like a producer, or supplier. You may feel more natural as a consumer (after all, you *are* one), but you already know a lot more about producers than you may realize. They all have the same goal—they try to maximize profit, which is revenue minus cost. This chapter introduces the cost side of the profit equation.

What do you think?

I'd rather go to a movie theater with lots of screens than to a one-screen movie house.

Strongly Disagree					Strongly Agree	
1	2	3	4	5	6	7

Topics discussed in Chapter 7 include:

- Explicit and implicit costs
- Economic and normal profit
- Increasing and diminishing returns
- Production function
- Ridge lines
- Short-run costs
- Long run costs
- Economies and diseconomies of scale
- Isoquant
- Isocosts

LO1 Cost and Profit

With demand, we assume that consumers try to maximize utility, a goal that motivates their behavior. With supply, we assume that producers try to maximize *profit,* and this goal motivates their behavior. *Firms try to earn a profit by transforming resources into salable products.* Over time, firms that survive and grow are those that are more profitable. Unprofitable firms eventually fail. Each year, millions of new firms enter the marketplace and many leave. The firm's decision makers must choose what goods and services to produce and what resources to employ. They must make plans while confronting uncertainty about consumer demand, resource availability, and the intentions of other firms in the market. *The lure of profit is so strong, however, that eager entrepreneurs are always ready to pursue their dreams.*

Explicit and Implicit Costs

To hire a resource, a firm must pay at least the resource's *opportunity cost*—that is, at least what the resource could earn in its best alternative use. For most resources, a cash payment approximates the opportunity cost. For example, the $3 per pound that Domino's Pizza pays for cheese must at least equal the cheese producer's opportunity cost of supplying it. Firms do not make direct cash payments for resources they own. For example, a firm pays no rent to operate in a company-owned building. Similarly, small-business owners usually don't pay themselves an hourly wage. Yet these resources are not free. *Whether hired in resource markets or owned by the firm, all resources have an opportunity cost.* Company-owned buildings can be rented or sold; small-business owners can find other work.

A firm's **explicit costs** are its actual cash payments for resources: wages, rent, interest, insurance, taxes, and the like. In addition to these direct cash outlays, or explicit costs, the firm also incurs **implicit costs**, which are the opportunity costs of using resources owned by the firm or provided by the firm's owners. Examples include the use of a company-owned building, use of company funds, or the time of the firm's owners. Like explicit costs, implicit costs are opportunity costs. But unlike explicit costs, implicit costs require no cash payment and no entry in the firm's *accounting statement,* which records its revenues, explicit costs, and accounting profit.

explicit cost
opportunity cost of resources employed by a firm that takes the form of cash payments

implicit cost
a firm's opportunity cost of using its own resources or those provided by its owners without a corresponding cash payment

accounting profit
a firm's total revenue minus its explicit costs

economic profit
a firm's total revenue minus its explicit and implicit costs

Alternative Measures of Profit

An example may help clarify the distinction between explicit and implicit costs. Linda Wheeler earns $50,000 a year as an aeronautical engineer with the Skyhigh Aircraft Corporation. On her way home from work one day, she gets an idea for a rounder, more friction-resistant airplane wheel. She decides to quit her job and start a business, which she calls Wheeler Dealer. To buy the necessary machines and equipment, she withdraws $20,000 from a savings account earning interest of $1,000 a year. She hires an assistant and starts producing the wheel using the spare space in her condominium's parking garage, which she had been renting to a neighbor for $100 a month.

Sales are slow at first—people keep telling her she is just trying to reinvent the wheel—but her wheel eventually gets rolling. When Wanda reviews the firm's performance after the first year, she is pleased. As you can see in the top portion of Exhibit 1, company revenue in 2010 totaled $105,000. After paying her assistant and for materials and equipment, the firm shows an accounting profit of $64,000. **Accounting profit** equals total revenue minus explicit costs. Accountants use this profit to determine a firm's taxable income.

© IMAGE SOURCE

Exhibit 1

Wheeler Dealer Accounts, 2010

Total revenue		$105,000
Less explicit costs:		
Assistant's salary	−$21,000	
Material and equipment	−$20,000	
Equals accounting profit		$64,000
Less implicit costs:		
Wanda's forgone salary	−$50,000	
Forgone interest on savings	−$1,000	
Forgone garage rental	−$1,200	
Equals economic profit		$11,800

But accounting profit ignores the opportunity cost of Linda's own resources used in the firm. First is the opportunity cost of her time. Remember, she quit a $50,000-a-year job to work full time on her business, thereby forgoing that salary. Second is the $1,000 in annual interest she passes up by funding the operation with her own savings. And third, by using the spare bay in the garage for the business, she forgoes $1,200 per year in rental income. The forgone salary, interest, and rental income are implicit costs because she no longer earns income from the best alternative uses of these resources.

Economic profit equals total revenue minus all costs, both implicit and explicit; *economic profit takes* *into account the opportunity cost of all resources used in production*. In Exhibit 1, accounting profit of $64,000 less implicit costs of $52,200 yields an economic profit of $11,800. What would happen to the accounting statement if Linda decided to pay herself a salary of $50,000 per year? Explicit costs would increase by $50,000, and implicit costs would decrease by $50,000. Thus, accounting profit would decrease by $50,000, but economic profit would not change because it already reflects both implicit and explicit costs.

© MINT PHOTOGRAPHY/ALAMY

There is one other profit measure to consider. The accounting profit just sufficient to ensure that all resources used by the firm earn their opportunity cost is called a **normal profit**. Wheeler Dealer earns a normal profit when accounting profit equals implicit costs—the sum of the salary Linda gave up at her regular job ($50,000), the interest she gave up by using her own savings ($1,000), and the rent she gave up on her garage ($1,200). Thus, if the accounting profit is $52,200 per year—the opportunity cost of resources Linda supplies to the firm—the company earns a normal profit. *Any accounting profit in excess of a normal profit is economic profit*. If accounting profit is large enough, it can be divided into normal profit and economic profit. The $64,000 in accounting profit earned by Linda's firm consists of (1) a normal profit of $52,200, which covers her implicit costs—the opportunity cost of resources she supplies the firm, and (2) an economic profit of $11,800, which is over and above what these resources, including Linda's time, could earn in their best alternative use.

As long as economic profit is positive, Linda is better off running her own firm than working for Skyhigh Aircraft. If total revenue had been only $50,000, an accounting profit of only $9,000 would cover less than one-fifth of her salary, to say nothing of her forgone rent and interest. Because Linda would not have covered her implicit costs, she would not be earning even a normal profit and would be better off back in her old job.

To understand profit maximization, you must develop a feel for both revenue and cost. In this chapter, you begin learning about the cost of production, starting with the relationship between inputs and outputs.

LO2 Production in the Short Run

We shift now from a discussion of profit, which is why firms exist, to a discussion of how firms operate. Suppose a new McDonald's just opened in your neighborhood and business is booming far beyond expectations. The manager responds to the unexpected demand by quickly hiring more workers. But cars are still backed up into the street waiting for a parking space. The solution is to add a drive-through window, but such an expansion takes time. What to do?

Fixed and Variable Resources

Some resources, such as labor, are called **variable resources** because they can be varied quickly to change the output rate. But adjustments in other resources take more time. Resources that cannot be altered easily—the size of the building, for example—are called **fixed resources**. When considering the time required to change the quantity of resources employed, economists distinguish between the short run and the long run. In the **short run**, at least one resource is fixed. In the **long run**, no resource is fixed.

Output can be changed in the short run by adjusting variable resources, but the size, or scale, of the firm is fixed in the short run. In the long run, all resources can be varied. The length of the long run differs from industry to industry because the nature of production differs. For example, the size of a McDonald's outlet can be increased more quickly than can the size of an auto plant. Thus, the long run for that McDonald's is shorter than the long run for an automaker.

normal profit the accounting profit earned when all resources earn their opportunity cost

variable resource any resource that can be varied in the short run to increase or decrease production

fixed resource any resource that cannot be varied in the short run

short run a period during which at least one of a firm's resources is fixed

long run a period during which all resources under the firm's control are variable

The Law of Diminishing Marginal Returns

Let's focus on the short-run link between resource use and the rate of output by considering a hypothetical moving company called Smoother Mover. Suppose the company's fixed resources, such as a warehouse, are already in place and that labor is the only variable resource. Exhibit 2 relates the amount of labor employed to the amount of output produced. Labor is measured in worker-days, which is one worker for one day, and output is measured in tons of furniture moved per day. The first column shows the amount of labor employed, which ranges from 0 to 8 worker-days. The second column shows the tons of furniture moved per day, or the **total product**, at each level of employment. The relationship between the amount of resources employed and total product is called the firm's **production function**. The third column shows the **marginal product** of each worker—that is, the change in total product resulting from an additional unit of labor, assuming other resources remain unchanged. Spend a little time now getting acquainted with the three columns.

total product
a firm's total output

production function
the relationship between the amount of resources employed and a firm's total product

marginal product
the change in total product that occurs when the use of a particular resource increases by one unit, all other resources constant

increasing marginal returns
the marginal product of a variable resource increases as each additional unit of that resource is employed

law of diminishing marginal returns
as more of a variable resource is added to a given amount of a fixed resource, marginal product eventually declines and could become negative

Exhibit 2

The Short-Run Relationship Between Units of Labor and Tons of Furniture Moved

Units of the Variable Resource (worker-days)	Total Product (tons moved per day)	Marginal Product (tons moved per day)
0	0	—
1	2	2
2	5	3
3	9	4
4	12	3
5	14	2
6	15	1
7	15	0
8	14	−1

Increasing Marginal Returns

Without labor, nothing gets moved, so total product is 0. If one worker is hired, that worker must do all the driving, packing, crating, and moving. Some of the larger items, such as couches and major appliances, cannot easily be moved by a single worker. Still, in our example one worker moves 2 tons of furniture per day. When a second worker is hired, some division of labor occurs, and two together can move the big stuff more easily, so production more than doubles to 5 tons per day. The marginal product of the second worker is 3 tons per day. Adding a third worker allows for a finer division of labor. For example, one worker can pack fragile items while the other two do the heavy lifting. Total product is 9 tons per day, 4 tons more than with two workers. Because the marginal product increases, the firm experiences **increasing marginal returns** from labor as each of the first three workers is hired.

Diminishing Marginal Returns

A fourth worker's marginal product is less than that of a third worker. Hiring still more workers increases total product by successively smaller amounts, so the marginal product declines after three workers. With that fourth worker, the **law of diminishing marginal returns** takes hold. This law states that as more of a variable resource is combined with a given amount of another resource, marginal product eventually

© RUBBERBALL/JUPITERIMAGES / © GOODSHOOT/JUPITERIMAGES

declines. *The law of diminishing marginal returns is the most important feature of production in the short run.* As more labor is hired, marginal product could turn negative, so total product would decline. For example, when Smoother Mover hires an eighth worker, workers start getting in each other's way, and workers take up valuable space in the moving van. As a result, an eighth worker actually subtracts from total output, yielding a negative marginal product. Likewise, a McDonald's outlet can hire only so many workers before congestion and confusion in the work area cut total product ("too many cooks spoil the broth").

Exhibit 3

The Total and Marginal Product of Labor

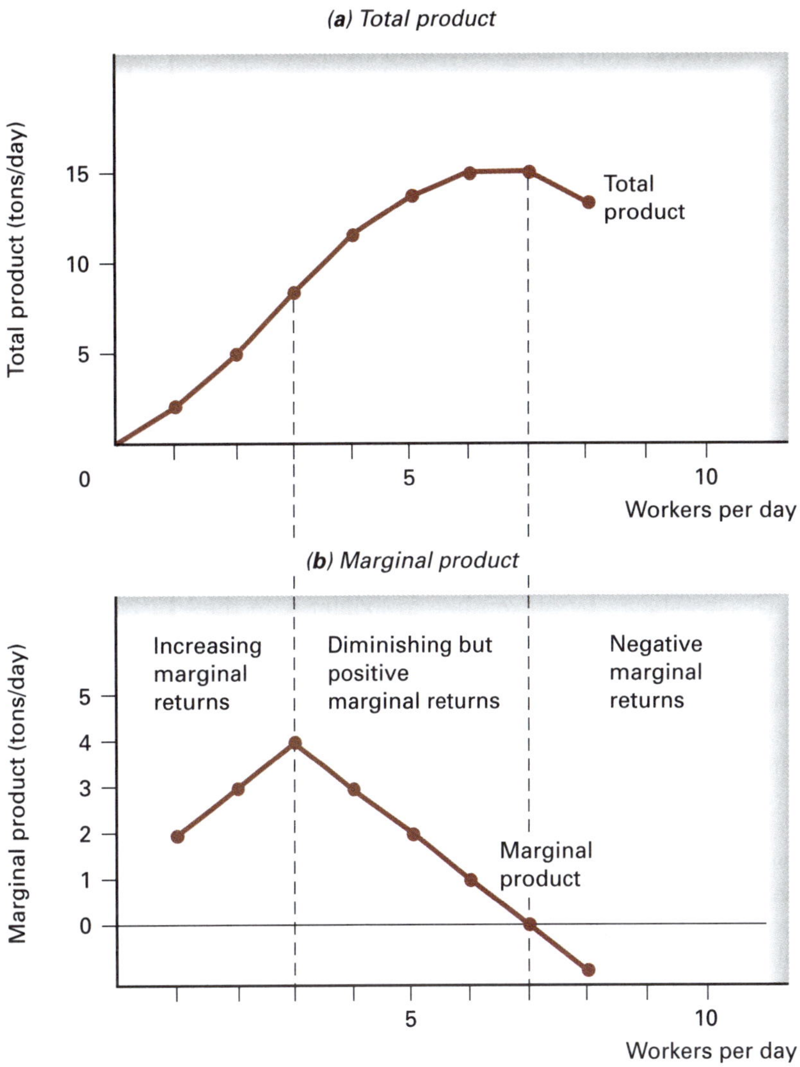

The Total and Marginal Product Curves

Exhibit 3 illustrates the relationship between total product and marginal product, using data from Exhibit 2. Note that because of increasing marginal returns, marginal product in panel (b) increases with each of the first three workers. With marginal product increasing, total product in panel (a) increases at an increasing rate (although this is hard to see in Exhibit 3). But once decreasing marginal returns set in, which begins with the fourth worker, marginal product declines. Total product continues to increase but at a decreasing rate. As long as marginal product is positive, total product increases. Where marginal product turns negative, total product starts to fall. Exhibit 3 summarizes all this by sorting production into three ranges: increasing marginal returns, diminishing but positive marginal returns, and negative marginal returns. These ranges for marginal product correspond with total product that increases at an increasing rate, increases at a decreasing rate, and declines.

The Production Analysis: Short Run

A production function is simply an input–output relationship. The expression of the production function is $Q = f(X_1, X_2 \ldots X_n)$, where Q, a specific output, is a function of the input factors, $X_1, X_2, \ldots, X_n$, each of which represents a well-defined homogeneous class. All of these factors of production (such as land, labor, capital, and entrepreneur) are commonly aggregated into the two basic factors of capital (*K*), and labor (*L*), so that in general $Q = f(K, L)$.

It is important to remember that a production function relates to some given level of technology. Production functions can be for either the short run or long run. Here we discuss the short run single variable factor production function.

The Law of Variable Proportions

The operation of the law of variable proportions, also known as the law of diminishing returns, shows that in a given state of technology and keeping other productive factors constant, additional units of a particular variable input will yield increasing returns of the variable factor up to a point. Eventually, a point is reached beyond which further additions of the variable factor yield diminishing returns per unit of input. That is to say, marginal product increases over a certain range of input up to a point, after which it decreases and eventually becomes negative. The law of diminishing return applies to virtually all types of production functions, ranging from those that characterize agriculture and automobile production to those that emerge in retailing, textile operation, zinc mining, and manufacturing of zippers. It is thus a phenomenon of great significance and generality.

The Total, Marginal, and Average Relationship

As long as the MP_X curve is rising, the total product curve increases at an increasing rate and is convex to the X-axis. The point on the X-axis at which the TP_X curve changes its curvature (point of inflection) corresponds precisely to the point at which MP_X curve peaks, as shown by broken line in Exhibit 4. In the law of variable proportions stated above, it is the peak of the marginal product curve that is referred to as point of diminishing (marginal) return. For points prior to this, there are increasing returns to the variable factor and for points beyond this there are decreasing returns.

The average product is the total product divided by the total variable input. Graphically, it is represented by constructing a ray from the origin to the point on the TP_X curve, for any given level of variable input. The AP_X too first rises, reaches a peak and diminishes thereafter. However, so long as TP_X remains positive, AP_X too remains positive and never becomes zero or negative. The peak of the average product curve represents the point of diminishing average return.

When the total product curve reaches its maximum, the total product is neither rising nor falling. Hence, its slope is zero. Since the slope of the TP_X curve represents the MP_X, it follows that when TP is maximum, MP_X is zero. Beyond its maximum, the total product declines; its graph must have a negative slope. The marginal product also must be negative. In summary, increasing returns to the variable factor exist when MP_X is positive and rising; decreasing returns occur when MP_X is positive and falling; negative returns are realized when MP_X is negative and falling.

The Average-Marginal Relationship: As long as the marginal product exceeds the average product, the average productivity of the variable factor increases as input increases. When the marginal product is less than the average product, the average product decreases as input increases. When the average product is at a maximum, the marginal product is equal to it.

The Three Stages of Production and the Elasticity of Production

We now define the three stages of production (Stage 1, 2, and 3) for a short run production function.

Stage 1: This stage extends from zero input of the variable factor to the level of input where the average product is maximum. In this stage, the fixed factors are excessive relative to the variable input. Consequently, output can be increased by increasing the variable input relative to the fixed input.

Stage 2: This stage extends from the end of Stage 1 (the point where the marginal product and the average product are equal and average product is at its peak) to the point where the marginal product is zero and the total product is maximum.

Stage 3: In this stage, which lies beyond Stage 2, the variable factor is excessive relative to the fixed factors, the marginal product is negative, and the total product is falling. It is completely irrational to produce in this stage.

We now define the elasticity of production. It is defined as the percentage change in output due to a percentage change in variable input. Mathematically, it is given by:

$$E_\rho = \frac{\Delta Q}{\Delta X} \cdot \frac{X}{Q}$$

Since $MP_X = \Delta Q/\Delta X$ and $AP_X = Q/X$, we can re-write production elasticity as:

$$E_\rho = \frac{\Delta Q}{\Delta X} \cdot \frac{X}{Q} = \frac{MP_X}{AP_X}$$

In Stage 1, the elasticity coefficient is greater than unity (written $E_\rho > 1$) because $MP_X > AP_X$. This means that a one percent change in the input causes more than a one percent change in the output. Therefore, it would pay to keep increasing the input at this stage.

At the beginning of Stage 2, $MP_X = AP_X$. Hence $E_\rho = 1$, which means that a one percent change in input causes a one percent change in output. Throughout the rest of Stage 2, the marginal product is less than the average product, but it is not negative. Therefore, the percentage change in output is less than the percentage changes in input, but it is greater than or equal to zero; that is, $0 \le E_\rho \le 1$.

In Stage 3, the marginal product is negative, hence elasticity is also negative, that is, $E_\rho < 0$. This means that the percentage change in output is negative with respect to any increase in input, implying that no profit maximizing producer should ever operate in this range.

Exhibit 4

Three Stages of Production

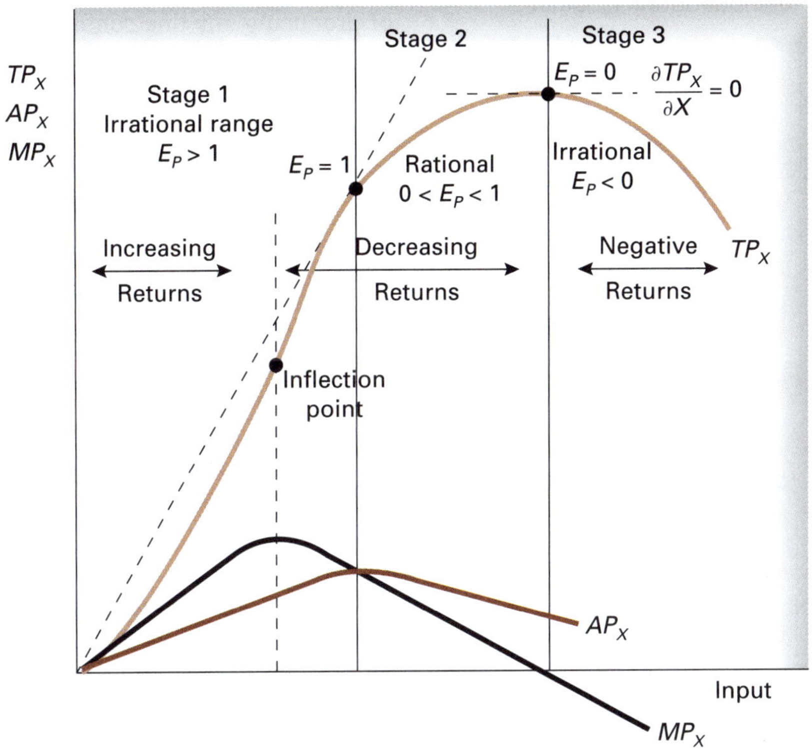

Optimal Relationships: Equilibrium of the Producer

In the previous discussion of the average-marginal relationship, it was noted that although peak efficiency occurs at the beginning of Stage 2, where $MP_X = AP_X$, this is not necessarily the point of maximum profit. To determine the optimum input-output relationship for maximum profit, we must shift the analysis from physical productivity to economic productivity.

Profit is maximum when the marginal revenue product (MRP_X) equals the marginal factor cost (MFC_X) or marginal resource cost (MRC_X). Marginal revenue product is the marginal product of input (X) multiplied by the marginal revenue by selling the output (Q). Mathematically, it is given by:

$$MRP_X = MP_X{*}MR_Q$$

Therefore, at equilibrium we have:

$$MRP_X = MP_X{*}MR_Q = MFC_X$$

Assuming that the marginal revenue by selling the output (Q), is given by its price (P_Q), and the marginal factor cost is the price of the factor (say, the wage rate of labor, P_L), then the equilibrium condition may be denoted as:

$$MRP_X = MP_X{*}P_Q$$

i.e., if the price of the input factor is known; the price of the output is known; and the production function is known, then the marginal product and marginal revenue product can be calculated. The profit maximizing firm will employ additional input up to the point at which marginal revenue product of that input is equal to its price or *MFC*. The optimal input employed by a profit maximizing firm is represented in Exhibit 5. For example, suppose that each unit of output sells for \$2 and that each unit of input costs \$20. Optimal production occurs when

$$MRP_X = MP_X{*}P_Q$$
$$\$2{*}MP_X = \$20$$
$$MP_X = \$10$$

Thus, the firm will continue to increase production as long as the marginal product exceeds 10, and will stabilize production at the level where the marginal product equals 10.

Exhibit 5

Optimal Use of Input

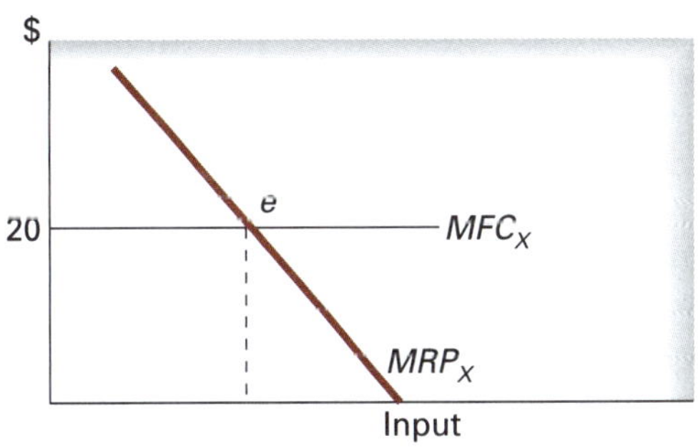

LO3 Production in the Long Run

In the long run, all factors of production can be varied. Assuming a two factor long run production function (*L* and *K*), the equilibrium of the producer is determined where the isoquants are tangent to the isocosts (provided isoquants are convex to the origin). An *isoquant* includes (is the locus of) all the

Exhibit 6

Isoquants: Various Shapes

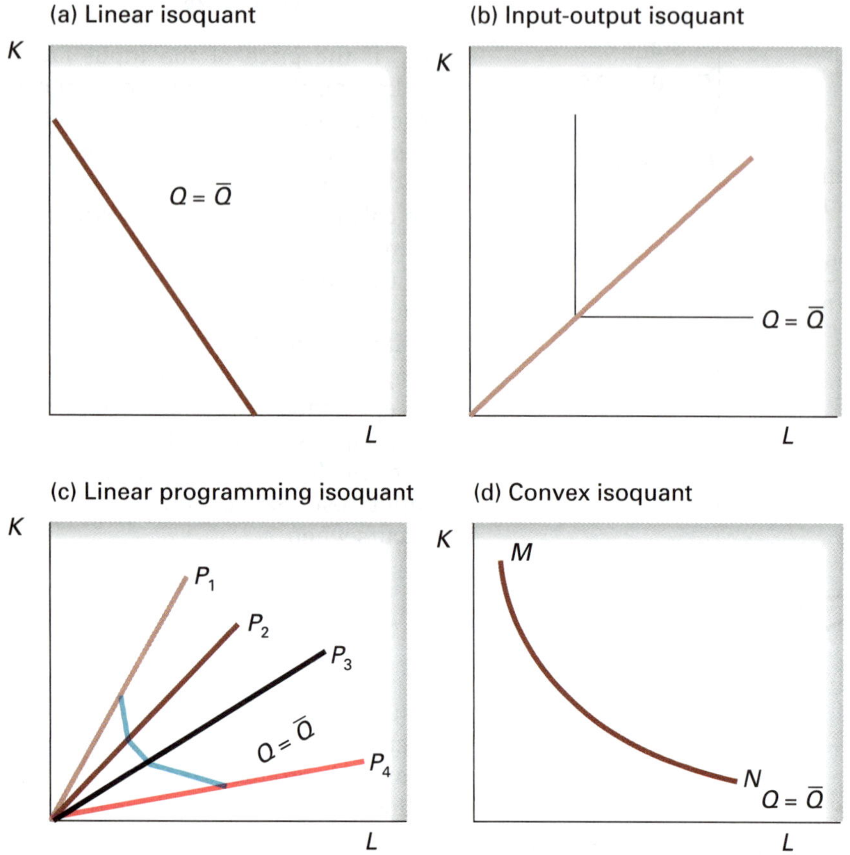

technically efficient methods (or all the combinations of factors of production, L and K) for producing a given level of output. The isocost represents various combinations of L and K that the producer can purchase given his budget, and prices of factors of production.

The production isoquant may assume various shapes depending on the degree of substitutability between factors.

Linear isoquant: This type of isoquant assumes perfect substitutability of factors of production: a given commodity may be produced by using only capital, or only labor, or by an infinite combination of K and L (Exhibit 6a).

Input-output isoquant: This assumes strict complementarity (that is zero substitutability) of the factors of production. There is only one method of production of any one commodity. The isoquant takes the shape of a right angle (Exhibit 6a). This type of isoquant is also called "Leontief isoquant" after Leontief, who invented the input-output analysis.

An isoquant includes (is the locus of) all the technically efficient methods (or all the combinations of factors of production, L and K) for producing a given level of output.

Kinked isoquant: This assumes limited substitutability of K and L. There are only a few processes of producing any one commodity. Substitutability of the factors is possible only at the kinks (Exhibit 6c). This form is also called "activity analysis isoquant" or "linear programming isoquant", because it is basically used in linear programming.

Smooth, convex isoquant: This form assumes continuous substitutability of K and L only over a certain range, beyond which factors cannot substitute each other. The isoquant appears as smooth curve, convex to the origin (Exhibit 6d).

It should be noted that kinked isoquants are more realistic. Engineers, managers, and production executives consider the production processes as discrete rather than as continuous. However, traditional economic theory generally assumes continuous isoquants, because they are simpler to handle mathematically. We too shall assume isoquants to be continuous. It may be noted that this is considered as an approximation to the more realistic form of kinked isoquant. This is because as we increase the number of processes, the kinks come closer and closer, until at the limit (as the number of processes becomes infinite) the isoquant becomes a smooth curve.

In Exhibit 7, the production function is depicted in the form of a set of isoquants. By construction, the higher and to the right an isoquant, the higher the level of output it depicts. By assumption, isoquants cannot intersect. While the isoquants have been shown to be downward sloping within the upper and lower ridge lines, as depicted by curves OM and ON beyond these the isoquants are upward sloping. An efficient range of the isoquant is represented by the range when it is downward sloping. In the efficient range, the marginal production of factors is dimin-

Exhibit 7

Ridge Lines and the Relevant Portion of Isoquants

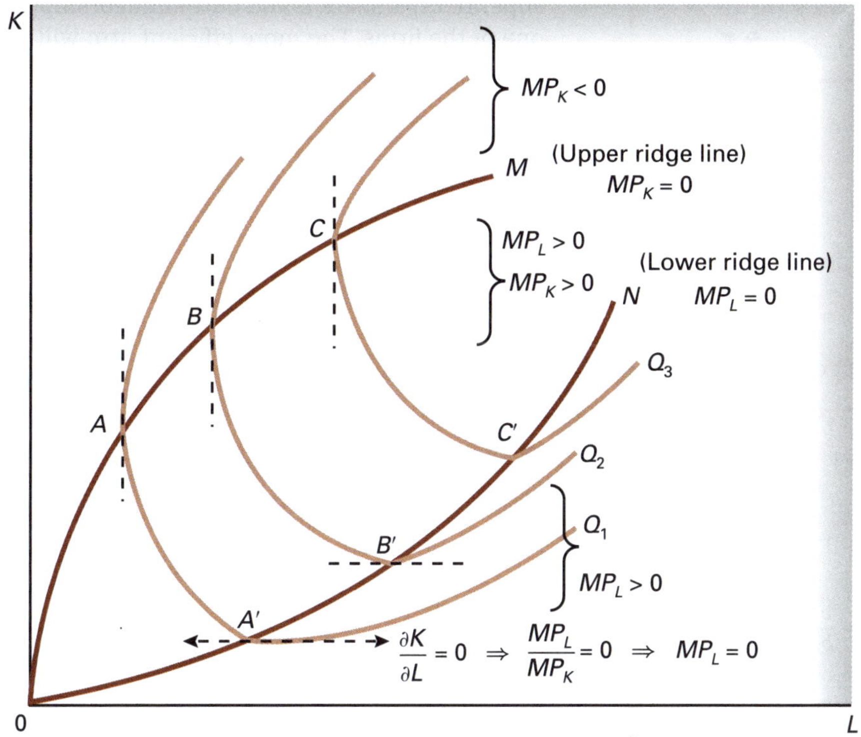

RIDGE LINES DEMARCATE THE EFFICIENT RANGE OF PRODUCTION FROM THE INEFFICIENT RANGE

ishing but positive. Inefficient range of isoquant is represented when isoquants are upward sloping. Ridge lines demarcate the efficient range of production from the inefficient range. The locus of points of isoquants where the marginal products of the factors (L and K) are zero form the ridge lines. The upper ridge line implies that MP_K is zero. The lower ridge line implies that MP_L is zero. Production techniques are technically efficient only inside the ridge lines. Outside the ridge lines, the marginal products of factors are negative and the methods of production are inefficient, since they require more quantity of both factors for producing a given level of output. Such inefficient methods are not considered by the theory of production, since they imply irrational behavior of the firm. The condition of positive but declining marginal products of the factors defines the range of efficient production (the range of isoquants over which they are convex to the origin).

The slope of isoquant ($\partial K/\partial L$) defines degree of substitutability of the factors of production, and is termed as marginal rate of technical substitution (*MRS*) of the factors. Since, isoquants are downward sloping in the relevant region, *MRS* is typically negative.

$$\frac{\partial K}{\partial L} = MRS_{LK}$$

It can be proved that the MRS is equal to the ratio of the marginal products of the factors:

$$MRS_{LK} = \frac{\partial K}{\partial L} = \frac{\partial Q/\partial L}{\partial Q/\partial K} = \frac{MP_L}{MP_K}$$

While MRS is an important concept, it has a serious defect. It depends on the units of measurement of the factors. A better measure of the ease of factor substitution is provided by the elasticity of substitution. The elasticity of substitution is defined as the percentage change in the capital-labor ratio, divided by the percentage change in the rate of technical substitution. Since both the numerator and denominator are measured in the same unit, the elasticity of substitution is a pure number.

$$\sigma = \frac{\text{percentage change in } K/L}{\text{percentage change in MRS}}$$

$$\sigma = \frac{d(K/L)/(K/L)}{d(MRS)/(MRS)}$$

We now illustrate the above concepts with a specific form of production function, known as the Cobb-Douglas production function. Empirical studies generally rely on this form of the production function. It has several properties, some of which are discussed below.

The Cobb-Douglas function is of the form:

$$Q = b_0 \cdot L^{b1} \cdot K^{b2}$$

1. The marginal product of factors
   (a) MP_L

> **The Cobb-Douglas function is of the form: $Q = b_0 \cdot L^{b1} \cdot K^{b2}$**

$$MP_L = \frac{\partial Q}{\partial L} = b_1 \cdot b_0 \cdot L^{b1-1} \cdot K^{b2}$$
$$= b_1(b_0 \cdot L^{b1}K^{b2})L^{-1}$$
$$= b_1 \cdot \frac{Q}{L} = b_1(AP_L)$$

where AP_L = the average product of labor

(b) Similarly,

$$MP_K = b_2 \cdot \frac{Q}{K} = b_2(AP_K)$$

2. The marginal rate of substitution

$$MRS_{LK} = \frac{\partial Q/\partial L}{\partial Q/\partial K} = \frac{b_1\left(\frac{Q}{L}\right)}{b_2\left(\frac{Q}{K}\right)} = \frac{b_1}{b_2} \cdot \frac{K}{L}$$

3. The elasticity of substitution of a Cobb-Douglas production function equals 1

$$\sigma = \frac{d(K/L)/(K/L)}{d(MRS)/(MRS)}$$

Substituting the value of MRS as $\frac{b_1}{b_2} \cdot \frac{K}{L}$ we obtain:

$$\sigma = \frac{d(K/L)/(K/L)}{d\left(\frac{b_1}{b_2} \cdot \frac{K}{L}\right)/\left(\frac{b_1}{b_2} \cdot \frac{K}{L}\right)}$$
$$= \frac{d\left(\frac{K}{L}\right)/\left(\frac{b_1}{b_2}\right)}{\left(\frac{b_1}{b_2}\right)d\left(\frac{K}{L}\right)} = 1$$

4. In a Cobb-Douglas production function, the factor intensity is measured by the ratio b_1/b_2. The higher this ratio, the more labor intensive the technique. Similarly, the lower the ratio b_1/b_2, the more capital intensive the technique.
5. The efficiency of production in the organization of the factors of production is measured by the coefficient b_0. If two firms have the same K, L, b_1 and b_2 and still produce different quantities of output, the difference is attributable to the superior organization and entrepreneurship of one of the firms. The more efficient firm will have a larger b_0 than the less efficient one.
6. The returns to variable factor: In the Cobb-Douglas production function represented by $b_0 \cdot L^{b1} \cdot K^{b2}$ the power of L (b_1) represents the elasticity of output with respect to labor, and the power of K (b_2) represents the elasticity of output with respect to capital. The proof of same is given below:

$$Q = b_0 \cdot L^{b1} \cdot K^{b2}$$

Now,

$$\frac{\partial Q}{\partial L} = b_1 \cdot b_0 \cdot L^{b1-1} \cdot K^{b2}$$
$$E_L = \frac{\partial Q}{\partial L} \cdot \frac{L}{Q} = b_1 \cdot b_0 \cdot L^{b1-1} \cdot K^{b2}\left(\frac{L}{Q}\right)$$
$$= b_1 \cdot b_0 \cdot L^{b1-1} \cdot K^{b2}\left(\frac{L}{b_0 L^{b1} \cdot K^{b2}}\right)$$
$$= b_1$$

We can similarly prove that b_2 represents the output elasticity with respect to input capital.

7. The returns to scale: In a Cobb-Douglas production function, the returns to scale (a long run concept), are measured by the sum of the coefficients $b_1 + b_2$. The returns to scale are only a part of the economies of scale. While returns to scale are technical, economies of scale are both technical and financial.

To prove, let L and K increase by a factor λ. The new level of output is now given by:

$$Q^* = b_0 \cdot \lambda L^{b1} \cdot \lambda K^{b2}$$
$$= \lambda^{b1+b2}(b_0 \cdot L^{b1} \cdot K^{b2})$$
$$Q^* = \lambda^{b1+b2} Q$$

If $b_1 + b_2$ exceeds one, there are increasing returns to scale.

If $b_1 + b_2$ equals one, there are constant returns to scale.

If $b_1 + b_2$ is less than one, there are decreasing returns to scale.

> An isocost represents various combinations of L and K that the producer can purchase given his budget, and prices of factors of production.

We now explain the isocost curves. An isocost represents various combinations of L and K that the producer can purchase given his budget, and prices of factors of production.

Mathematically, it is denoted by:

$$\bar{C} = wL + rK$$

where C represents the budget constraint of the producer, w the price of labor, and r the price of capital. The slope of the isocost is given by the relative prices of factors of production. In our case, it is given by $P_L/P_K = w/r$.

The problem facing the firm is of constrained optimization. It may take either of the two forms:

1. Maximization of output, subject to cost constraint, or
2. Minimization of cost, subject to output constraint

Case 1: Maximization of Output Subject to Cost Constraint (Financial Constraint)

The firm is in equilibrium when it maximizes its output given its total cost outlay and the prices of the factors, w and r. In Exhibit 8, we see that the maximum level of output the firm can produce; given the cost constraint is Q_2, defined by the tangency of the isocost line, and the highest isoquant. The optimal combination of factors of production is K_2 and L_2, for prices w and r. Higher levels of output (to the right of e) are desirable but not attainable due to the cost constraint. Other points on AB or below it lie on a lower isoquant than Q_2. Hence Q_2 is the maximum output possible under the assumptions of given cost outlay, given production function, and given factor prices. At the point of tangency e, the slope of the isocost line (w/r) is equal to the slope of the isoquant (MP_L/MP_K). This constitutes the first condition for equilibrium. The second condition is that the

Exhibit 8

Maximization of Output Subject to Cost Constraint

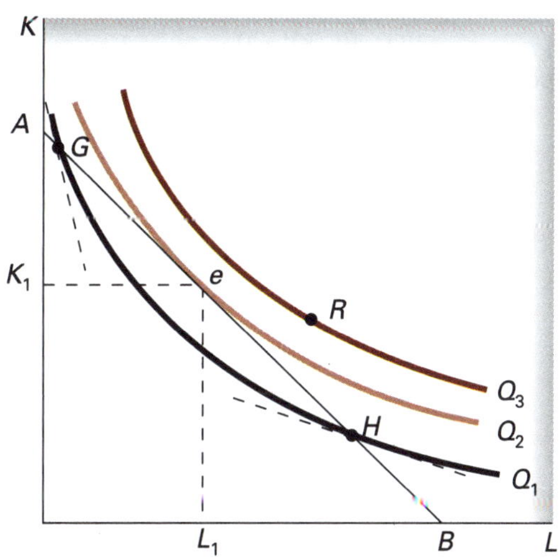

isoquants should be convex to the origin. In summary, the conditions for equilibrium of the firm are:

a. Slope of isoquant = Slope of isocost, or

$$\frac{MP_L}{MP_K} = \frac{\partial Q/\partial L}{\partial Q/\partial K} = MRS_{LK} = \frac{w}{r}$$

Exhibit 9

Corner Solution with Concave Isoquant

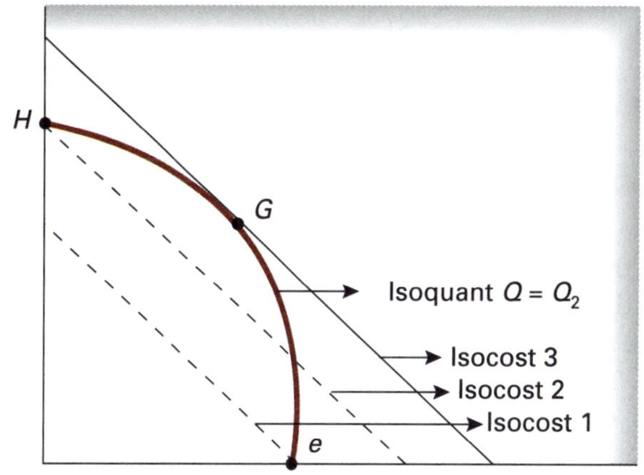

b. The isoquants must be convex to the origin. If the isoquant is concave, the point of tangency of the isocost and the isoquant curves does not define equilibrium position, because output Q_2 (depicted by the concave isoquant) can be produced with lower cost at e which lies on a lower isocost curve. Thus, with a concave isoquant we have a corner solution.

Mathematical derivation of the equilibrium condition

The objective function is now given by maximization of output, subject to cost constraint. This can be written as: Maximize: $Q = f(L, K)$; Subject to: $\bar{C} = wL + rK$ (cost constraint).

We solve this problem by using the Lagrangian multipliers. We first re-write the constraint in the form: $\bar{C} - wL - rK = 0$. And then multiply the constraint by a constant λ which is the Lagrangian multiplier: $\lambda(\bar{C} - wL - rK) = 0$. Thereafter, we form a composite objective function $\phi = Q + \lambda(\bar{C} - wL - rK) = 0$.

It can be shown that maximization of the objective function implies maximization of the output.

To solve the problem, we equate its partial derivatives with respect to L, K, and λ to zero.

$$\frac{\partial \phi}{\partial L} = \frac{\partial Q}{\partial L} + \lambda(-w) = 0 \quad (1)$$

$$\frac{\partial \phi}{\partial K} = \frac{\partial Q}{\partial K} + \lambda(-r) = 0 \quad (2)$$

$$\frac{\partial \phi}{\partial \lambda} = \bar{C} - wL - rK = 0 \quad (3)$$

Solving the first two equations for λ we obtain

$$\frac{\partial Q}{\partial L} = \lambda w \quad \text{or} \quad \lambda = \frac{\partial Q/\partial L}{w} = \frac{MP_L}{w} \tag{4}$$

and

$$\frac{\partial Q}{\partial L} = \lambda r \quad \text{or} \quad \lambda = \frac{\partial Q/\partial K}{r} = \frac{MP_K}{r} \tag{5}$$

Since we have λ in both the expressions, we equate equation 4 and 5 and get

$$\frac{\partial Q/\partial L}{w} = \frac{\partial Q/\partial K}{r}$$

or

$$= \frac{\partial Q/\partial L}{\partial Q/\partial K} = \frac{w}{r} \quad \Rightarrow \quad \frac{MP_L}{MP_K} = \frac{w}{r}$$

The firm is in equilibrium when it equates the ratio of the marginal productivities of factors to the ratio of the prices. Graphically, it implies that the slope of the isoquant is equated to the slope of the isocost.

The second-order condition (sufficient condition) for equilibrium of the firm requires that the marginal product curves of the two factors have a negative slope. The slope of the marginal product curve of labor is the second derivative of the production function:

$$\text{Slope of } MP_L \text{ curve} = \frac{\partial^2 Q}{\partial L^2}$$

Similarly for capital:

$$\text{Slope of } MP_K \text{ curve} = \frac{\partial^2 Q}{\partial K^2}$$

The second-order conditions are

$$\frac{\partial^2 Q}{\partial L^2} < 0 \quad \text{and} \quad \frac{\partial^2 Q}{\partial K^2} < 0$$

and

$$\left(\frac{\partial^2 Q}{\partial L^2}\right)\left(\frac{\partial^2 Q}{\partial K^2}\right) > \left(\frac{\partial^2 Q}{\partial L \partial K}\right)^2$$

These conditions are sufficient for establishing the convexity of the isoquants.

Case 2: Minimization of Cost for a Given Level of Output

Graphically, the equilibrium is still defined by the tangency of the isocost line, with the isoquant. However, here we have several isocosts and only one isoquant, though the conditions for equilibrium of the firm are formally the same as earlier. That is, there must be tangency of the given isoquant and the lowest possible isocost curve, and the isoquant must be convex. Isocost curves closer to the origin show a lower total-cost outlay. The isocost lines are parallel because they are drawn on the assumption of constant prices of factors: since w and r do not change, all the curves have the same slope w/r.

Exhibit 10

Minimization of Cost Subject to Output Constraint

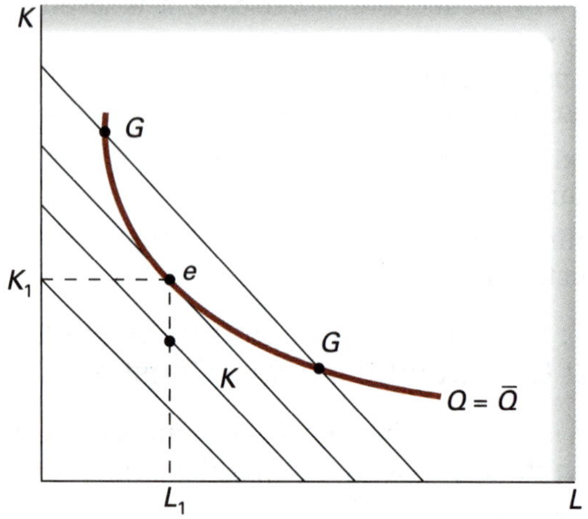

The firm minimizes its costs by employing the combination of K and L determined by the point of tangency of the $\bar{Q}$ isoquant with the lowest isocost line. Points below *e* are desirable because they show lower cost but are not attainable for output $\bar{Q}$. Points above *e* show higher costs. Hence, point *e* is the least-cost point, the point denoting the least-cost combination of the factors K and L for producing $\bar{Q}$.

Mathematical derivation of the equilibrium condition

The objective function is now given by minimization of cost, subject to output constraint. Formally, this can be written as:

Minimize $\quad C = f(Q) = wL + rK$

Subject to $\quad \bar{Q} = f(L, K)$

We re-write the constraint as $\quad \bar{Q} - f(L, K) = 0$

Thereafter, we premultiply the constraint by the Lagrangian multiplier λ.

$$\lambda\{\bar{Q} - f(L, K)\} = 0$$

The composite function is now given as:

$$\phi = C - \lambda\{\bar{Q} - f(L, K)\}$$

or

$$\phi = wL + rK - \lambda\{\bar{Q} - f(L, K)\}$$

To solve the problem, we equate its partial derivatives with respect to L, K, and λ to zero.

$$\frac{\partial \phi}{\partial L} = w - \lambda\frac{\partial f(L, K)}{\partial L} = 0 = w - \lambda\left(\frac{\partial Q}{\partial L}\right)$$

$$\frac{\partial \phi}{\partial K} = r - \lambda\frac{\partial f(L, K)}{\partial K} = 0 = r - \lambda\left(\frac{\partial Q}{\partial K}\right)$$

$$\frac{\partial \phi}{\partial \lambda} = -[\bar{Q} - f(L, K)] = 0$$

From the first two expressions we obtain

$$w = \lambda\left(\frac{\partial Q}{\partial L}\right)$$

$$r = \lambda\left(\frac{\partial Q}{\partial K}\right)$$

Dividing through these expressions we find

$$\frac{w}{r} = \frac{\partial Q/\partial L}{\partial Q/\partial K} = MRS_{LK}$$

This equilibrium condition is the same as in Case 1. The second order (sufficient) condition requires the isoquant to be convex at the point of equilibrium. Mathematically, it implies that marginal product of factors must have negative slopes. That is

$$\frac{\partial^2 Q}{\partial L^2} < 0 \quad \text{and} \quad \frac{\partial^2 Q}{\partial K^2} < 0$$

and

$$\left(\frac{\partial^2 Q}{\partial L^2}\right)\left(\frac{\partial^2 Q}{\partial K^2}\right) > \left(\frac{\partial^2 Q}{\partial L \partial K}\right)^2$$

Numerical Illustrations: Constrained Optimization

Problem 1: Given: $Q = 100K^{0.5}L^{0.5}$, $C^* = \$1{,}000$, $w = \$30$, and $r = \$40$. Determine the amount of labor and capital that the firm should use in order to maximize output. What is this level of output?

Solution: Maximize $Q = f(L, K)$ subject to $C^* = wL + rK$

The Lagrangian function is given by:

$$\phi = f(L, K) + \lambda(C^* - wL - rK)$$

If ϕ has to be maximized, partial derivatives of ϕ with respect to L, K, and λ have to be zero. That is:

i. $\partial\phi/\partial L = \partial f/\partial L - \lambda w = 0$

ii. $\partial\phi/\partial K = \partial f/\partial K - \lambda r = 0$

iii. $\partial\phi/\partial\lambda = C^* - wL - rK = 0$

The ϕ function in this case is given by:

$\phi = 100K^{0.5}L^{0.5} + \lambda(1000 - 30L - 40K)$

$$\frac{\partial\phi}{\partial L} = 0 \Rightarrow (0.5)\,100K^{0.5}L^{-0.5} - 30\lambda = 0$$

$$\Rightarrow 50\frac{\sqrt{K}}{\sqrt{L}} = 30\lambda = 0$$

$$\Rightarrow \frac{50}{30}\frac{\sqrt{K}}{\sqrt{L}} = \lambda \quad (1)$$

$$\frac{\partial\phi}{\partial K} = 0 \Rightarrow (0.5)\,100\frac{\sqrt{L}}{\sqrt{K}} - 40\lambda = 0$$

$$\Rightarrow 50\frac{\sqrt{L}}{\sqrt{K}} = 40\lambda$$

$$\Rightarrow \frac{50}{40}\frac{\sqrt{L}}{\sqrt{K}} = \lambda \quad (2)$$

$$\frac{\partial\phi}{\partial\lambda} = 0 \Rightarrow 1000 - 30L - 40K = 0 \quad (3)$$

Equating (1) and (2) yields:

$$\frac{50}{30}\frac{\sqrt{K}}{\sqrt{L}} = \frac{50}{40}\frac{\sqrt{L}}{\sqrt{K}}$$

$\Rightarrow 40K = 30L$ or $4K = 3L$

$$\Rightarrow K = \frac{3}{4}L \quad (4)$$

Substituting the value of 4 in 3 yields:

$$1000 - 30L - 40\left(\frac{3}{4}\right)L = 0$$

$$\Rightarrow 1000 = 60L$$

$$L = 16.66$$

and $K = 12.5$

Now maximum output $Q = 100K^{0.5}L^{0.5}$

$= 100 * \sqrt{12.5}\sqrt{16.66}$

$= 1{,}438$ Units

Problem 2: Given: $Q = 100K^{0.5}L^{0.5}$, $w = \$50$, and $r = \$40$. Show how to determine the amount of labor and capital that the firm should use in order to minimize the cost of producing 1, 118 units of output. What is this minimum cost?

Solution: Minimize $C = wL + rK$ subject to $Q^* = f(L, K)$

The Lagrangian function is given by:

$$\phi' = wL + rK + \lambda'\{Q^* - f(L, K)\}$$

If ϕ has to be maximized, partial derivatives of ϕ with respect to L, K, and λ have to be zero.

i. $\partial\phi'/\partial L = w - \lambda'(\partial f/\partial L) = 0$

ii. $\partial\phi'/\partial K = r - \lambda'(\partial f/\partial K) = 0$

iii. $\partial\phi'/\partial\lambda' = Q^* - f(L, K) = 0$

$\phi' = 50L + 40K + \lambda'\,(1118 - 100K^{0.5}\cdot L^{0.5})$

$$\frac{\partial\phi'}{\partial L} = 0 \Rightarrow 50 - \frac{100}{2}\frac{K^{0.5}}{L^{0.5}}\lambda' = 0$$

$$\Rightarrow 50 - 50\frac{\sqrt{K}}{\sqrt{L}}\lambda' = 0$$

$$\Rightarrow \frac{50}{50}\frac{\sqrt{L}}{\sqrt{K}} = \lambda'$$

$$\Rightarrow \frac{\sqrt{L}}{\sqrt{K}} = \lambda' \quad (1)$$

$$\frac{\partial\phi'}{\partial K} = 40 - 50\frac{\sqrt{L}}{\sqrt{K}}\lambda' = 0$$

$$\Rightarrow 40 = 50\frac{\sqrt{L}}{\sqrt{K}}\lambda' = 0$$

$$\Rightarrow \frac{4}{5}\frac{\sqrt{K}}{\sqrt{L}} = \lambda' \quad (2)$$

$$\frac{\partial\psi'}{\partial\lambda'} = 1118 - 100K^{0.5}L^{0.5} = 0 \quad (3)$$

$$\frac{\sqrt{L}}{\sqrt{K}} = \frac{4}{5}\frac{\sqrt{K}}{\sqrt{L}}$$

$$\Rightarrow \quad 5L = 4K$$

$$L = \frac{4}{5}K \qquad (4)$$

Substituting (4) in (3) yields:

$$1118 - 100\sqrt{K}\sqrt{\left(\frac{4}{5}\right)K}$$

$$1118 = 100 * \sqrt{K}\sqrt{L} \qquad (5)$$

Substitute equation (4) in (5)

$$1118 = 100 * \sqrt{K}\sqrt{\left(\frac{4}{5}\right)K}$$

$K = 11.18 * 0.5 * 2.23$

$K = 12.46$, and

$L = 9.97$

Now minimizing the cost $C = wL + rK$

$= 50 * 12.46 + 40 * 9.97$

$= 623 + 398.8$

$= \$1{,}021.8$

Problem 3: Given the firm's production function:

$$Q = 2 \log L + 4 \log K$$

And the input prices $P_L = 4$ and $P_K = 12$

Find out the firm's

a. Expansion path
b. Supply function
c. Derived demand function

Solution: a. Expansion path:

The objective is to maximize output subject to cost constraint.

$$\phi = 2\log L + 4 \log K + \lambda(4L + 12K - C)$$

Taking partial derivatives, we get:

$$\frac{\partial\phi}{\partial L} = \frac{2}{L} + 4\lambda = 0 : \lambda = \frac{-2}{4L} \qquad (1)$$

$$\frac{\partial\phi}{\partial K} = \frac{4}{K} + 12\lambda = 0 : \lambda = \frac{-4}{12K} \qquad (2)$$

$$\frac{\partial\phi}{\partial\lambda} = 4L + 12K - C = 0 \qquad (3)$$

Equating (1) and (2) yields

$$\frac{-2}{4L} = \frac{-4}{12K} \Leftrightarrow \frac{1}{2L} = \frac{1}{3K} \text{ or } 2L = 3 \text{ or } L = \frac{3}{2}K \qquad (4)$$

Direct substitution in the cost function gives:

$$K = \frac{C}{18};\; L = \frac{C}{12};\; \lambda = \frac{-6}{C}$$

This constitutes the required expansion path relationships giving the amount of each input purchased as a function of total outlay, C.

b. Supply function:

The supply schedule gives the quantities of a good that a firm is willing and able to supply at various prices, other things remaining the same. Assuming that the firm maximizes its profit,

$$\pi = PQ - 4L - 12K$$

Subject to the constraint imposed by the company's production function gives the following Lagrangian function:

$$\phi_1 = PQ - 4L - 12K + \lambda(Q - 2 \log L - 4 \log K)$$

The partial derivatives with respect to Q, L, and K are

$$\frac{\partial\phi_1}{\partial Q} = P + \lambda = 0 \Leftrightarrow P = -\lambda$$

$$\frac{\partial\phi_1}{\partial L} = -4 - \frac{2\lambda}{L} = 0 \Leftrightarrow -4 = \frac{2\lambda}{L} \Leftrightarrow -4 = \frac{-2P}{L}$$

OR

$$\frac{\partial\phi_1}{\partial K} = -12 - \frac{4\lambda}{K} = 0 \Leftrightarrow -12 = \frac{4\lambda}{K} \Leftrightarrow K = \frac{P}{3}$$

$$\frac{\partial\phi_1}{\partial\lambda} = Q - 2\log L - 4\log K = 0$$

Plugging in the values of L and K in the production function, we get the supply function.

$$Q = 2\log\frac{P}{2} + 4\log\frac{P}{3}$$

c. Derived demand functions:

We have also got the derived demand functions for two inputs L and K as a function of price of the output which is produced with the help of labor and capital.

Testing Production Functions for Returns to Scale

Returns to scale is defined as the ratio of percentage change in output due to percentage change in inputs. It is a long run concept as all factors are allowed to vary. It thus represents the long run elasticity of production. For increasing returns to scale, $E_\rho > 1$; for constant returns to scale, $E_\rho = 1$; and for decreasing returns to scale, $E_\rho < 1$.

When the production function is known, it can be analyzed algebraically for returns to scale. Suppose we have the production function

$$Q = f(X_1, X_2, X_3)$$

Now suppose we increase each input factor by the proportion Ω. Output will then increase by some proportion, h, resulting in

$$hQ = f(\Omega X_1, \Omega X_2, \Omega X_3)$$

If $h > \Omega$, there are increasing returns to scale.
If $h = \Omega$, there are constant returns to scale.
If $h < \Omega$, there are decreasing returns to scale. For example, suppose we have the production function

$$Q = f(5X_1, 3X_2, 0.5X_3)$$

With initial inputs $X_1 = 3$, $X_2 = 1$, $X_3 = 2$. Total output, therefore, is

$$Q_1 = 5(3) + 3(1) + 0.5(2) = 19$$

Now we double the inputs to $X_1 = 6$, $X_2 = 2$, $X_3 = 4$. Output is then

$$Q_2 = 5(6) + 3(2) + 0.5(4) = 38$$

Doubling the inputs ($\Omega = 2$) has doubled the output ($h = 2$). Therefore, there are constant returns to scale, since $h = \Omega$.

Homogeneous Functions: If the constant term, Ω can be factored out, the function is said to be homogeneous of degree *n*. For example, when the function

$$Q = 5X_1 + 6X_2 + X_3$$

is scaled up, we get

$$hQ = 5(\Omega X_1) + 6(\Omega X_2) + \Omega X_3$$
$$hQ = \Omega(5X_1 + 6X_2 + X_3)$$

The exponent of Ω is 1, therefore, $h = \Omega$, and the function yields constant returns to scale.

As an example, suppose we have the following production function

$$Q = 2.1X_1^{0.6}X_2^{0.4}X_3^{0.2}$$

We get

$$hQ = 2.1(\Omega X_1)^{0.6}(\Omega X_2)^{0.4}(\Omega X_3)^{0.2}$$
$$Q = 2.1\Omega^{1.2}X_1^{0.6}X_2^{0.4}X_3^{0.2}$$

Since 1.2, the exponent of Ω, is greater than 1, $h > \Omega$, the function exhibits increasing returns to scale. In general, the degree of homogeneity (indicated by the exponent of Ω, as given by γ) indicates returns to scale:

1. If $\gamma > 1$, it implies increasing returns to scale.
2. If $\gamma = 1$, it implies constant returns to scale.
3. If $\gamma < 1$, it implies decreasing returns to scale.

Non-homogeneous Functions: When the production function is non-homogeneous because the scaling constant Ω cannot be factored out, the function can still be tested by employing the equation

$$hQ = f(\Omega X_1, \Omega X_2, \Omega X_3)$$

and by assigning numerical values to the variables. For example, we have the production function

$$Q = 10L + 0.6LCM + 2.1L^{0.4}C^{0.3}M^{0.2}$$

Examining this equation term by term, we see that each term has different returns to scale. The first term, $10L$, would yield constant returns to scale. The second term, $0.6LCM$, would yield increasing returns to scale. The third term, $2.1L^{0.4}C^{0.3}M^{0.2}$, would yield decreasing returns to scale. The overall returns to scale would thus depend upon which term would exert the strongest influence when scaled up. To test this function for returns to scale, we need to select some set of reasonable values for the variables, then scale up and see what happens. Suppose we let $L = 10$, $C = 5$, $M = 2$. Then substituting in equation above,

$$Q = 10(10) + 0.6(10)(5)(2) + 2.1(10)^{0.4}(5)^{0.3}(2)^{0.2}$$
$$= 169.8$$

Now suppose we double the inputs, i.e., $\Omega = 2$. Then the value of h turns out to be 4.1. Since, $h > \Omega$, we conclude that the function exhibits increasing returns to scale.

LO4 Costs in the Short Run

Now that we have examined the relationship between the amount of resources used and the rate of output, let's consider how the cost of production varies as output varies. There are two kinds of costs in the short run: fixed and variable. Fixed cost pays for fixed resources and variable cost pays for variable resources. A firm must pay a **fixed cost** even if no output is produced. Even if Smoother Mover hires no labor and moves no furniture, it incurs property taxes, insurance, vehicle registration, plus any opportunity cost for warehouse and equipment. By definition, fixed cost is just that: fixed—it does not vary with output in the short run. Suppose the firm's *fixed cost* is $200 per day.

Variable cost, as the name implies, is the cost of variable resources—in this case, labor. When no labor is employed, output is zero, as is variable cost. As workers are hired, output increases, as does variable cost. Variable cost depends on the amount of labor employed and on the wage. If the wage is $100 per day, *variable* cost equals the number of workers hired times $100.

Total Cost and Marginal Cost in the Short Run

Exhibit 11 offers cost data for Smoother Mover. The table lists the cost of production associated with alternative rates of output. Column (1) shows possible rates of output in the short run, measured in tons of furniture moved per day.

Total Cost

Column (2) shows the fixed cost (FC) at each rate of output. Note that fixed cost, by definition, remains constant at $200 per day regardless of output. Column (3) shows the labor needed to

fixed cost any production cost that is independent of the firm's rate of output

variable cost any production cost that changes as the rate of output changes produce each rate of output based on the productivity figures reported in Exhibits 2 and 3. For example, moving 2 tons a day requires one worker, 5 tons requires two workers, and so on. Only the first six workers are listed because additional workers would add nothing to output and would not be hired. Column (4) lists variable cost (VC) per day, which equals $100 times the number of workers employed. For example, the variable cost of moving 9 tons of furniture per day is $300 because this output rate requires three workers. Column (5) lists the **total cost** (TC), the sum of fixed cost and variable cost: $TC = FC + VC$. As you can see, when output is zero, variable cost is zero, so total cost consists entirely of the fixed cost of $200. Incidentally, because total cost is the opportunity cost of all resources used by the firm, total cost includes a normal profit but not an economic profit. Think about that.

$TC = FC + VC$

$MC = \Delta TC/\Delta q$

Marginal Cost

Of special interest to the firm is how total cost changes as output changes. In particular, what is the marginal cost of producing another unit? The **marginal cost** (MC) of production listed in column (6) of Exhibit 11 is simply the change in total cost divided by the change in output, or $MC = \Delta TC/\Delta q$, where Δ means "change in." For example, increasing output from 0 to 2 tons increases total cost by $100 (= $300 − $200). The marginal cost of each of the first 2 tons is the change in total cost, $100, divided by the change in output, 2 tons, or $100/2, which equals $50. The marginal cost of each of the next 3 tons is $100/3, or $33.33.

Notice in column (6) that marginal cost first decreases, then increases. *Changes in marginal cost reflect changes in the marginal productivity of the variable resource.* Because of increasing marginal returns, each of the first three workers produces more than the previous one. This greater productivity results in a falling marginal cost for the first 9 tons moved. Beginning with the fourth worker, the firm experiences diminishing marginal returns from labor, so the marginal cost of output increases. *When the firm experiences increasing marginal returns, the marginal cost of output falls; when the firm experiences diminishing marginal returns, the marginal cost of output increases.* Thus, marginal cost in Exhibit 11 first falls and then rises, because marginal returns from labor first increase and then diminish.

Total and Marginal Cost Curves

Exhibits 12 shows cost curves for the data in Exhibit 11. Because fixed cost does not vary with output, the fixed cost curve is a horizontal line at the $200 level in panel (a). Variable cost is zero when output is zero, so the *variable cost curve* starts from the origin. The *total cost curve* sums the fixed cost curve and the variable cost curve. Because a constant fixed cost is added to variable cost, the total cost curve is simply the variable cost curve shifted vertically by the fixed cost.

In panel (b) of Exhibit 12, marginal cost declines until the ninth unit of output and then increases, reflecting labor's increasing and then diminishing marginal returns. There is a relationship between the two panels because the change in total cost resulting from a one-unit change in production equals the marginal cost. With each successive unit of output, total cost increases by the marginal cost of that unit. Thus, *the slope of the total cost curve at each rate of output equals the marginal cost at that rate of output.* The total cost curve can be divided into two sections, based on what happens to marginal cost:

1. Because of increasing marginal returns from labor, marginal cost at first declines, so total

total cost
the sum of fixed cost and variable cost, or $TC = FC + VC$

marginal cost
the change in total cost resulting from a one-unit change in output; the change in total cost divided by the change in output, or $MC = \Delta TC/\Delta q$

Exhibit 11

Short-Run Total and Marginal Cost Data for Smoother Mover

(1) Tons Moved per Day (*q*)	(2) Fixed Cost (*FC*)	(3) Workers per Day	(4) Variable Cost (*VC*)	(5) Total Cost ($TC = FC + VC$)	(6) Marginal Cost ($MC = \Delta TC/\Delta q$)
0	$200	0	$ 0	$200	—
2	200	1	100	300	$ 50.00
5	200	2	200	400	33.33
9	200	3	300	500	25.00
12	200	4	400	600	33.33
14	200	5	500	700	50.00
15	200	6	600	800	100.00

Exhibit 12

Total and Marginal Cost Curves for Smoother Mover

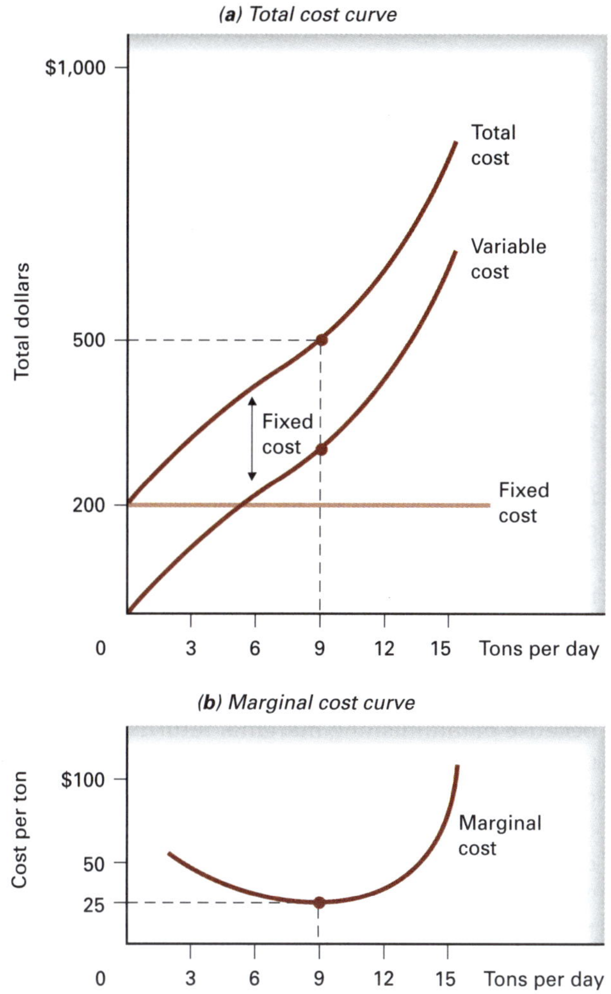

cost initially increases by successively smaller amounts and the total cost curve becomes less steep.

2. Because of diminishing marginal returns from labor, marginal cost starts increasing after the ninth unit of output, so total cost increases by successively larger amounts and the total cost curve becomes steeper.

Keep in mind that economic analysis is marginal analysis. Marginal cost is the key to economic decisions. *Marginal cost indicates how much total cost increases if one more unit is produced or how much total cost drops if production declines by one unit.*

Average Cost in the Short Run

Although marginal cost is of most interest, the average cost per unit of output is also useful. We can distinguish between average variable cost and average total cost. These measures appear in columns (5) and (6) of Exhibit 13. Column (5) lists **average variable cost**, or *AVC*, which equals variable cost divided by output, or $AVC = VC/q$. The final column lists **average total cost**, or ATC, which equals total cost divided by output, or $ATC = TC/q$. Each measure of average cost first declines as output expands and then increases (except average fixed cost (AFC), which continuously declines).

The Relationship Between Marginal Cost and Average Cost

To understand the relationship between marginal cost and average cost, let's begin with an example of college grades. Think about how your grades each term affect your grade point average (GPA). Suppose you do well your first term, starting

average variable cost variable cost divided by output, or $AVC = VC/q$

average total cost total cost divided by output, or $ATC = TC/q$; the sum of average fixed cost and average variable cost, or $ATC = AFC + AVC$

Exhibit 13

Short-Run Total, Marginal, and Average Cost Data for Smoother Mover

Marginal cost first falls then increases because of increasing then diminishing marginal returns from labor. As long as marginal cost is below average cost, average cost declines. Once marginal cost exceeds average cost, average cost increases. Columns (4), (5), and (6) show the relation between marginal and average costs.

(1) Tons Moved per Day (q)	(2) Variable Cost (VC)	(3) Total Cost ($TC = FC + VC$)	(4) Marginal Cost ($MC = \Delta TC/\Delta q$)	(5) Average Variable Cost ($AVC = VC/q$)	(6) Average Total Cost ($ATC = TC/q$)
0	$ 0	$200	$ 0	$ —	∞
2	100	300	50.00	50.00	$150.00
5	200	400	33.33	40.00	80.00
9	300	500	25.00	33.33	55.55
12	400	600	33.33	33.33	50.00
14	500	700	50.00	35.71	50.00
15	600	800	100.00	40.00	53.33

$AVC = VC/q$
$ATC = TC/q$
$AFC = FC/q$

© DIGITAL VISION/GETTY IMAGES

your college career with a 3.4 (out of 4.0). Your grades for the second term drop to 2.8, reducing your GPA to 3.1. You slip again in the third term to a 2.2, lowering your GPA to 2.8. Your fourth-term grades improve a bit to 2.4, but your GPA continues to slide to 2.7. In the fifth term, your grades improve to 2.7, leaving your GPA unchanged at 2.7. And in the sixth term, you get 3.3, pulling your GPA up to 2.8. Notice that when your term grades are below your GPA, your GPA falls. Even when your term performance improves, your GPA does not improve until your term grades exceed your GPA. Your term grades first pull down your GPA and then eventually pull it up.

Let's now take a look at the relationship between marginal cost and average cost. In Exhibit 6, marginal cost has the same relationship to average cost as your term grades have to your GPA. You can observe this marginal-average relationship in columns (4) and (5). Because of increasing marginal returns from the first three workers, the marginal cost falls for the first 9 tons of furniture moved. Because marginal cost is below average cost, marginal cost pulls down average cost. Marginal cost and average cost are equal when output equals 12 tons, and marginal cost exceeds average cost when output exceeds 12 tons, so marginal cost pulls up average cost.

Exhibit 14 shows the same marginal cost curve first presented in Exhibit 12, along with average cost curves based on data in Exhibit 13. At low rates of output, marginal cost declines as output expands because of increasing marginal returns from labor. As long as marginal cost is below average cost, marginal cost pulls down average cost as output expands. At higher rates of output, marginal cost increases because of diminishing marginal returns from labor. Once marginal cost exceeds average cost, marginal cost pulls up average cost. The fact that marginal cost first pulls average cost down and then pulls it up explains why the average cost curves have a U shape. The shapes of the average variable cost curve and the average total cost curve are determined by the shape of the marginal cost curve, so each is shaped by increasing then diminishing marginal returns.

Exhibit 14

Average and Marginal Cost Curves for Smoother Mover

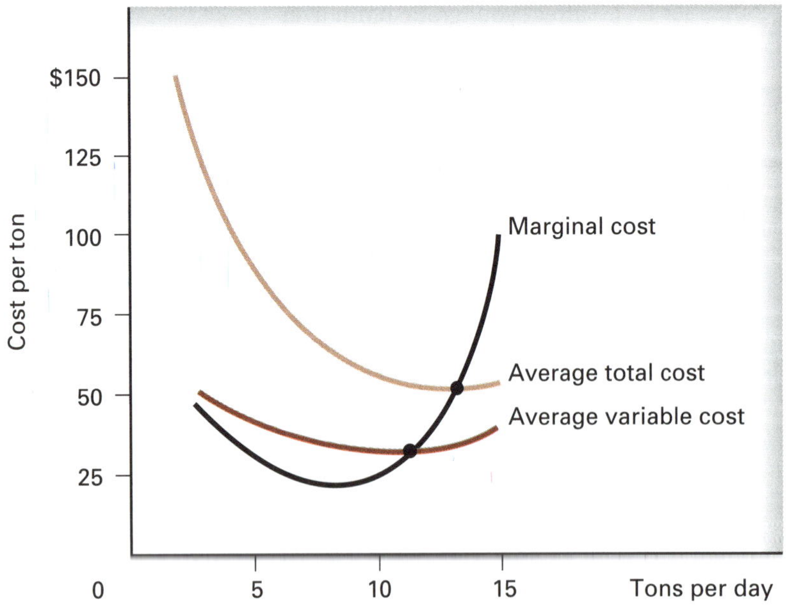

Notice also that the rising marginal cost curve intersects both the average variable cost curve and the average total cost curve where these average curves reach their minimum. This occurs because the marginal pulls down the average where the marginal is below the average and pulls up the average where the marginal is above the average. One more thing: The distance between the average variable cost curve and the average total cost curve is *average fixed cost*, which gets smaller as the rate of output increases. (Why does average fixed cost get smaller?)

The law of diminishing marginal returns determines the shapes of short-run cost curves. When the marginal product of labor increases, the marginal cost of output falls. Once diminishing marginal returns take hold, the marginal cost of output rises. Thus, marginal cost first falls and then rises. And the marginal cost curve dictates the shapes of the average cost curves. When marginal cost is less than average cost, average cost declines. When marginal cost is above average cost, average cost increases. Got it? If not, please reread this paragraph.

We now provide a mathematical proof of the same.

Relationship between TC and MC

$$TC = AC \times q \quad (1)$$

$$MC = \frac{\partial TC}{\partial q} = AC\frac{\partial q}{\partial q} + q\frac{AC}{\partial q} \quad \text{(using product rule)}$$

$$MC = AC + q\frac{\partial AC}{\partial q} \quad (2)$$

But $\frac{\partial AC}{\partial q}$ represents the slope of the AC curve.

Since AC is "U" shaped, its slope can be negative, positive, or zero.

1. If AC is falling, then $\frac{\partial AC}{\partial q} < 0$

   and MC < AC, i.e. MC lies below AC, when AC is falling.
2. If AC is rising, then $\frac{\partial AC}{\partial q} > 0$

   and MC > AC, i.e. MC lies above AC, when AC is rising.
3. If AC is at its minimum, $\frac{\partial AC}{\partial q} = 0$

   and MC = AC, i.e. MC equals AC, when AC is at its minimum. A similar relationship can be derived between AVC and MC.

LO5 Costs in the Long Run

So far, the analysis has focused on how costs vary as the rate of output expands in the short run for a firm of a given size. In the long run, all inputs that are under the firm's control can be varied, so there is no fixed cost. The long run is not just a succession of short runs. The long run is best thought of as a *planning horizon.* In the long run, the choice of input combinations is flexible. But once the size of the plant has been selected and the concrete has been poured, the firm has fixed costs and is operating in the short run. Firms plan for the long run, but they produce in the short run. We turn now to long-run costs.

Economies of Scale

Like short-run average cost curves, the firm's long-run average cost curve is U-shaped. Recall that the shape of the short-run average total cost curve is determined primarily by increasing and diminishing marginal returns of the variable resource. A different principle shapes the long-run cost curve. If a firm experiences **economies of scale**, long-run average cost falls as output expands. Consider some sources of economies of scale. *A larger size often allows for larger, more specialized machines and greater specialization of labor.* For example, compare the household-size kitchen of a small restaurant with the kitchen at a McDonald's. At low rates of output, the smaller kitchen produces meals at a lower average cost than does McDonald's. But if production in the smaller kitchen increases beyond, say, 100 meals per day, a kitchen on the scale of McDonald's would make meals at a lower average cost. Thus, because of economies of scale, the long-run average cost for a restaurant may fall as size increases. As an example, the idea for McDonald's snack wrap started when a franchisee suggested that the company find more uses for the strips of chicken served with dipping sauce. Selling more chicken allowed each restaurant to cook new batches more frequently, which meant customers got a fresher product.[1]

A larger scale of operation allows a firm to use larger, more efficient machines and to assign workers to more specialized tasks. Production techniques such as the assembly line can be introduced only if the rate of output is suffiently large. Typically, as the scale of firm increases, capital substitutes for labor and complex machines substitute for simpler machines.

In addition to economies associated with factor labor (due to better division and specialization of labor activities), and capital (due to indivisibility of capital), economies of scale may also be reaped due to the following:

1. Economies on account of transportation cost
2. Economics on account of marketing and advertising costs.
3. Economies associated with finance
   - Discounts that are made available on bulk purchase
   - Easier and cheaper access to raise credit from market due to large size of firm
4. Managerial economics of scale

economies of scale forces that reduce a firm's average cost as the scale of operation increases in the long run

1. As reported by Janet Adamy, "For McDonald's It's a Wrap," *Wall Street Journal,* 30 January 2007.

© DANIEL BARRY/BLOOMBERG NEWS/LANDOV

Diseconomies of Scale

Often another force, called **diseconomies of scale**, may eventually take over as a firm expands its plant size, increasing long-run average cost as output expands. As the amount and variety of resources employed increase, so does the *task of coordinating all these inputs*. As the workforce grows, additional layers of management are needed to monitor production. In the thicket of bureaucracy that develops, communications may get mangled. Top executives have more difficulty keeping in touch with the factory floor because information is distorted as it moves up and down the chain of command. Indeed, in large organizations, rumors may become a primary source of information, reducing efficiency and increasing average cost. Note that *diseconomies of scale result from a larger firm size, whereas diminishing marginal returns result from using more variable resources in a firm of a given size.*

The Long-Run Average Cost Curve

Because of the special nature of technology in the industry, suppose a firm must choose from among three possible plant sizes: small, medium, and large. Exhibit 15 presents this simple case. The average cost curves for the three sizes are *SS′*, *MM′*, and *LL′*. Which size should the firm build to minimize average cost? The appropriate size, or scale, for the firm depends on how much output the firm wants to produce. For example, if q is the desired output, average cost is lowest with a small plant size. If the desired output is q', the medium plant size offers the lowest average cost. With the medium plant, the firm experiences economies of scale. With the large plant, the firm experiences diseconomies of scale.

More generally in Exhibit 15, for output less than q_a, average cost is lowest when the plant is small. For output between q_a and q_b, average cost is lowest for the medium plant. And for output that exceeds q_b, average cost is lowest when the plant is large. The **long-run average cost curve**, or *LRAC* curve, sometimes called the firm's *planning curve*, connects portions of the three short-run average cost curves that are lowest for each output rate. In Exhibit 15, that curve consists of the line segments connecting *S*, *a*, *b*, and *L′*. So even though the firm experiences diseconomies of scale with the largest plant size, the large firm is the one to build if the firm needs to produce more than q_b.

diseconomies of scale
forces that may eventually increase a firm's average cost as the scale of operation increases in the long run

long-run average cost curve
a curve that indicates the lowest average cost of production at each rate of output when the size, or scale, of the firm varies; also called the planning curve

Exhibit 15

Short-Run Average Total Cost Curves Form the Long-Run Average Cost Curve, or Planning Curve

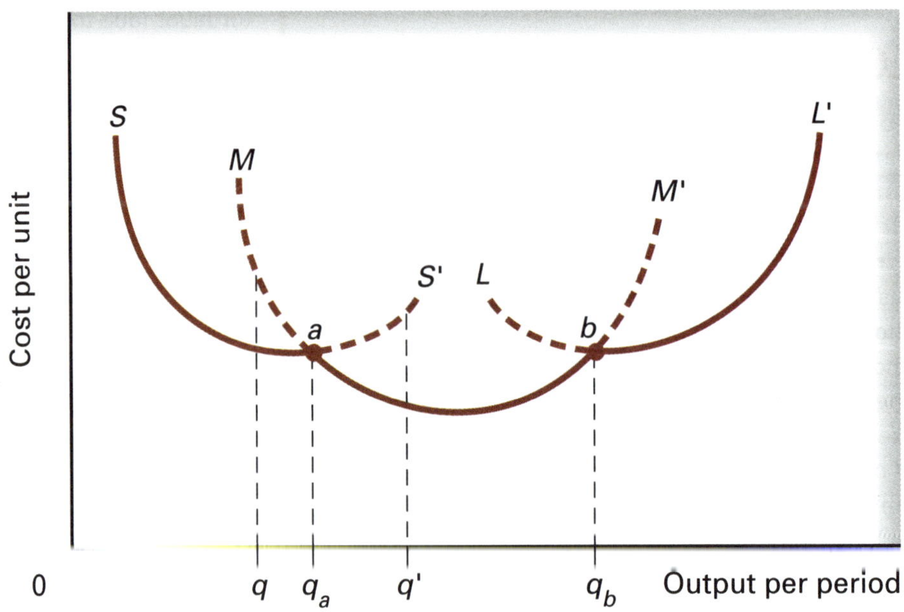

Exhibit 16

Many Short-Run Average Total Cost Curves Form a Firm's Long-Run Average Cost Curve, or Planning Curve

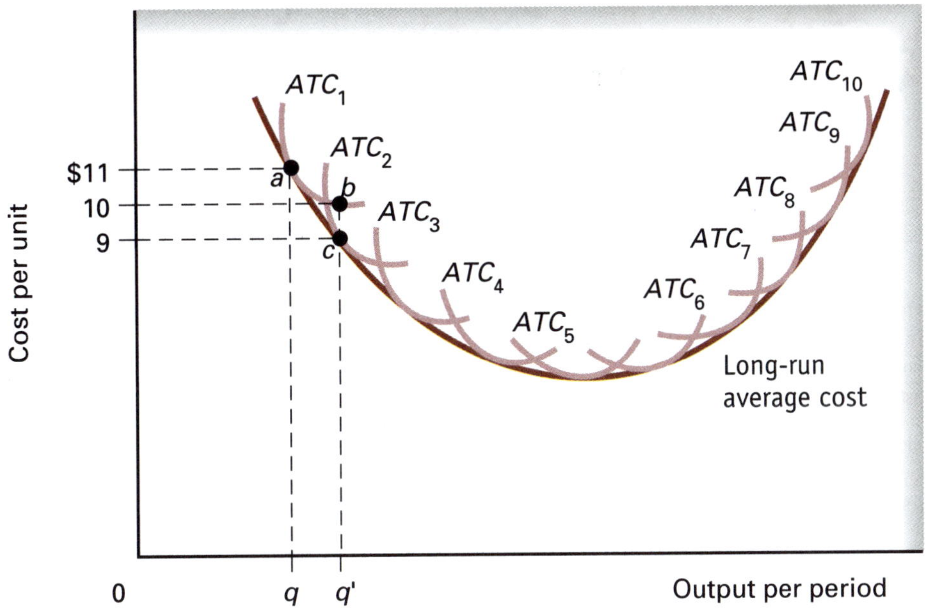

Now suppose there are many possible plant sizes. Exhibit 16 presents a sample of short-run cost curves shown in pink. The long-run average cost curve, shown in red, is formed by connecting the points on the various short-run average cost curves that represent the lowest per-unit cost for each rate of output. Each of the short-run average cost curves is tangent to the long-run average cost curve, or *planning curve*. If we could display enough short-run cost curves, we would have a different plant size for each rate of output. *These points of tangency represent the least-cost way of producing each particular rate of output, given resource prices and the technology.* For example, the short-run average total cost curve ATC_1 is tangent to the long-run average cost curve at point *a*, where $11 is the lowest average cost of producing output *q*. Note, however, that other output rates along ATC_1 have a lower average cost. For example, the average cost of producing *q*′ is only $10, as identified at point *b*. Point *b* depicts the lowest average cost along ATC_1. So, while the point of tangency reflects the least-cost way of producing a particular rate of output, that tangency point does not reflect the minimum average cost for this particular plant size.

If the firm decides to produce *q*′, which size plant should it choose to minimize the average cost of production? Output rate *q*′ could be produced at point *b*, which represents the minimum average cost along ATC_1. But average cost is lower with a larger plant. With the plant size associated with ATC_2, the average cost of producing *q*′ would be minimized at $9 per unit at point *c*. *Each point of tangency between a short-run average cost curve and the long-run average cost curve represents the least-cost way of producing that particular rate of output.*

In the long run, a firm can vary the inputs under its control. Some resources, however, are not under the firm's control, and the inability to vary them may contribute to diseconomies of scale.

It is possible for average cost to neither increase nor decrease with changes in firm size. If neither economies of scale nor diseconomies of scale are apparent over some range of output, a firm experiences **constant long-run average cost**. Perhaps economies and diseconomies of scale exist simultaneously in the firm but have offsetting effects. Exhibit 17 presents a firm's long-run average cost curve, or *LRAC* curve, which is divided into output segments reflecting economies of scale, constant long-run

Exhibit 17

A Firm's Long-Run Average Cost Curve

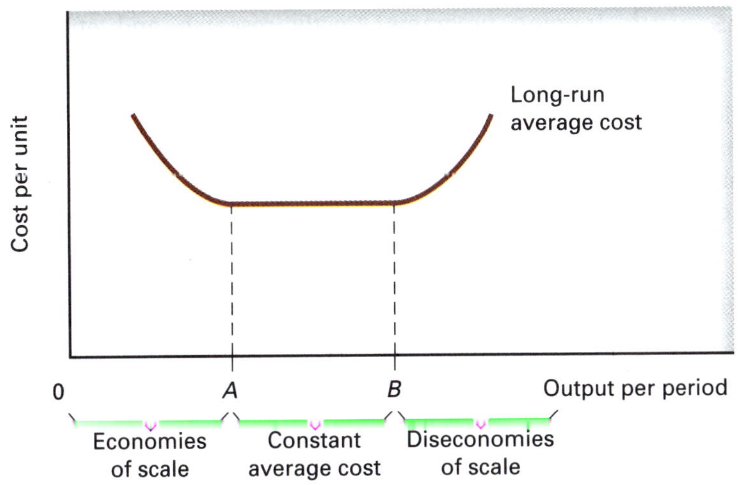

constant long-run average cost a cost that occurs when, over some range of output, long-run average cost neither increases nor decreases with changes in firm size

Economics at the Movies

Movie theaters add screens to achieve economies of scale. Consider this: A theater with one screen needs three people to run it: one person to sell tickets, one to sell popcorn (concession stand sales account for well over half the profit at most theaters), and one to operate the movie projector. But if a second screen is added, the same staff of three can perform these tasks for both screens (an increase in productivity). Other factors that further increase **economies of scale**:

- construction costs per screen are reduced because only one lobby and one set of rest rooms are required;
- the theater may get a better deal from movie distributors;
- the theater can run bigger, more noticeable newspaper ads;
- and the theater can spread the cost over more films.

If adding more screens is good, then adding many more screens is better, right? But why stop at, say, 10 or even 20 screens per theater? Why not 30 screens, particularly in thickly populated areas with sufficient demand? The answer is simple: **diseconomies of scale**.

- Traffic congestion around the theater grows with the number of screens at that location. Public roads are a resource the theater cannot control.
- The supply of popular films may not be large enough to fill so many screens.
- Time itself is a resource that the firm cannot easily control. Only certain hours are popular with moviegoers. Scheduling becomes more difficult because the manager must space out starting and ending times to avoid the crush that occurs when too many customers come and go at the same time. No more "prime time" can be created. (To spread out the customers, theaters offer discounts for morning or early afternoon showings.)

Thus, theater owners lack control over such inputs as the public roads, the supply of films, and the amount of "prime time" in the day. These factors contribute to diseconomies of scale.

SOURCES: Shirley Won, "Cineplex Sees Past the Big Picture," *Globe and Mail,* 8 February 2007; Scott Bowles, "ShoWest: Movie Theaters Look to Keep the Streak Alive," *USA Today,* 12 March 2007; Sandy Cohen, "Movie Fans Prefer the Theater Experience," *Forbes,* 7 March 2007; and *Statistical Abstract of the United States: 2007,* U.S. Census Bureau, http://www.census.gov/compendia/statab/.

© DYNAMIC GRAPHICS/CREATAS IMAGES/JUPITERIMAGES

average costs, and diseconomies of scale. Output must reach quantity *A* for the firm to achieve the **minimum efficient scale**, which is the lowest rate of output at which long-run average cost is at a minimum.

Economies and Diseconomies of Scale at the Firm Level

Our discussion so far has referred to a particular plant—a movie theater or a restaurant, for example. But a firm could also be a collection of plants, such as the hundreds of movie theaters in a chain or the thousands of McDonald's restaurants. More generally, we can distinguish between economies and diseconomies of scale at the *plant level*—that is, at a particular location—and at the *firm level*, where the firm is a collection of plants.

minimum efficient scale
the lowest rate of output at which a firm takes full advantage of economies of scale

McDonald's experiences economies of scale at the plant, or restaurant, level because of its specialization of labor and machines, but it also benefits from economies of scale at the firm level. Experience gained from decades of selling hamburgers can be shared with new managers through centralized training programs. Costly research and efficient production techniques can also be shared across thousands of locations. For example, McDonald's took three years to decide on the exact temperature of the holding cabinets for its hamburger patties. What's more, the cost of advertising and promoting McDonald's through sponsorship of world events such as the Olympics can be spread across 30,000 restaurants in more than 100 countries.

Some diseconomies may also arise in such large-scale operations. The fact that the menu must be reasonably uniform across thousands of locations means that if customers in some parts of the country or the world do not like a product, it may not get on the menu, even though it might be popular elsewhere. Another problem with a uniform menu is that the ingredients must be available around the world and cannot be subject to droughts or sharp swings in price. For example, McDonald's considered adding a shrimp salad to the menu but decided not to when advised the move could deplete the nation's shrimp supply.[2]

Other large firms do what they can to reduce diseconomies of scale at the firm level. For example, IBM undertook a massive restructuring program to decentralize into six smaller decision-making groups. Some big corporations have even spun off parts of their operation to form new corporations. For example, Hewlett-Packard split off Agilent Technologies, AT&T created Lucent Technologies, and DaimlerChrysler, the international automaker sold its Chrysler side of the business to a private equity group (a group that has since required a federal bailout to stay afloat).

2. Janet Adamy, "For McDonald's It's a Wrap," *Wall Street Journal,* 30 January 2007; Andrew Martin, "McDonald's Says Latest Results Are Strongest in 30 Years," *New York Times,* 25 January 2007; James L. Watson, ed., *Golden Arches East: McDonald's in East Asia* (Palo Alto, Calif.: Stanford University Press, 1998); and McDonald's Web site at http://www.mcdonalds.com/.

Final Word

By considering the relationship between production and cost, we have developed the foundation for a theory of firm behavior. Despite what may appear to be a tangle of short-run and long-run cost curves, *only two relationships between resources and output underlie all the curves. In the short run, it's increasing and diminishing returns from the variable resource. In the long run, it's economies and diseconomies of scale.* If you understand the sources of these two phenomena, you grasp the central ideas of the chapter. Our examination of production and cost in the short run and long run lays the groundwork for a firm's supply curve, to be covered in a later chapter.

MULTIPLE CHOICE QUESTIONS

1. Which of the following is not an explicit cost?
   a. Payment for raw materials
   b. The value of the firm's owner own time
   c. Wages for the workers
   d. Insurance cost
   e. Utilities payment
2. Marge opens an oxygen bar in a building she owns. She used to rent the building to her brother in law for $10,000 a year. To open the oxygen bar, Marge quit her job as a physician assistant, which paid $80,000 a year. As a bar owner, Marge has to pay $40,000 a year wages for her bartender, spend $25,000 a year for supplies, and the utilities bill is $9,500 a year. To cover the start-up costs, she used up all of her savings which earned $4,600 in interest. What are her implicit costs?
   a. $10,000
   b. $90,000
   c. $84,600
   d. $94,600
   e. $74,500
3. Marge opens an oxygen bar in a building she owns. She used to rent the building to her brother in law for $10,000 a year. To open the oxygen bar, Marge quit her job as a physician assistant, which paid $80,000 a year. As a bar owner, Marge has to pay $40,000 a year wages for her bartender, spend $25,000 a year for supplies, and the utilities bill is $9,500 a year. To cover the start-up costs, she used up all of her savings which earned $4,600 in interest. What are her explicit costs?
   a. $40,000
   b. $49,500
   c. $84,600
   d. $94,600
   e. $74,500
4. Amanda, age 6, opens a lemonade stand. She makes all the lemonade from a mix she found in her parents' pantry. Her stand is an old box she found in the garage. The pitcher and paper cups were taken from the kitchen. Which of the following is true?
   a. The opportunity cost of the lemonade is zero.
   b. The only opportunity cost of the lemonade is Amanda's time.
   c. Amanda's explicit costs are zero.
   d. The implicit costs of Amanda's lemonade are zero.
   e. Whatever revenue Amanda gets will be pure economic profit.
5. Maryann and Don want to open their own deli. To do so, Maryann must give up her job, at which she earns $20,000 per year, and Don must give up his part-time job, at which he earns $10,000 per year. They must liquidate their money market fund, which earns $1,000 interest annually. The rent on the building is $10,000 per year, and expenses for such necessities as utilities, corned beef, and pickles are $35,000 annually. What minimum amount of revenue per year would make it worthwhile, financially, for Maryann and Don to operate the deli?
   a. $10,000
   b. $35,000
   c. $45,000
   d. $31,000
   e. $76,000
6. Suppose Ernie gives up his job as financial advisor for P.E.T.S., at which he earned $30,000 per year, to open up a store selling spot remover to Dalmatians. He invested $10,000 in the store, which had been in savings earning 5 percent interest. This year's revenues in the new business were $50,000, and explicit costs were $10,000. Calculate Ernie's accounting profit.
   a. $10,000
   b. $50,000
   c. $20,000
   d. $40,000
   e. $9,500
7. Normal profit is defined as
   a. accounting profit
   b. economic profit
   c. profit necessary to ensure that opportunity costs are covered
   d. accounting profit minus economic profit
   e. economic profit minus accounting profit
8. Suppose a professor gives up her teaching job to devote her time to writing textbooks. If salaries of professors rise,
   a. her accounting profit will rise
   b. her accounting profit will fall
   c. her explicit costs will rise
   d. her economic profit from textbooks will fall
   e. her economic profit from textbooks will rise

9. The short run is a period of time
   a. less than one year
   b. greater than one year
   c. during which all resources are variable
   d. during which at least one resource is fixed
   e. during which at least one resource is variable

10. Which of the following is true of marginal product?
   a. The firm should produce where marginal product is greatest.
   b. The firm should produce where marginal product is increasing.
   c. When marginal product is falling, total product is falling.
   d. The firm should produce where marginal product is zero.
   e. When marginal product is increasing, total product is increasing by increasing amounts.

11. Jerry's ice-cream parlor is hosting Andrew's birthday party in one week. Overall, 25 to 30 people will attend the party and Andrew's costs are as follows: \$200 for rent, \$150 for the cake, \$3 per person for customized invitations, \$15 per person for the meal, \$50 for decorations, and \$8 per person for party favors. For simplicity, assume that Andrew is considered one of the guests and he receives an invitation too. Assuming that 25 people attend the party, the fixed cost of the party is:
   a. \$400
   b. \$1,050
   c. \$650
   d. \$350
   e. \$250

12. What is true of marginal cost when marginal returns are increasing?
   a. It is negative and increasing.
   b. It is negative and decreasing.
   c. It is positive and increasing.
   d. It is positive and decreasing.
   e. It is positive and has a constant slope.

13. Which of the following correctly describes the relationship between the marginal cost and average variable cost curves?
   a. MC is everywhere above AVC
   b. AVC is everywhere above MC
   c. MC crosses AVC at AVC's minimum point
   d. MC crosses AVC at MC's minimum point
   e. both AVC and MC first rise and then fall

14. LAC is tangent to SAC, when SAC is at its minimum.
   a. True
   b. False

15. If the isoquant is given by X + Y = 10, then the marginal rate of technical substitution between X and Y is:
   a. +1.
   b. zero.
   c. infinity.
   d. negative and then positive.

16. Given the production function $Q = 2X^5Y^5$, the isoquant for Q = 4 is given by
   a. Y = 4X.
   b. $Y = \sqrt{X}$.
   c. Y = 1/4X.
   d. $Y^2 = X$.
   e. none of the above.

17. When the isoquant is linear it indicates that the ratio of the price per unit of each of the two inputs is:
   a. increasing with the input quantity.
   b. decreasing with the input quantity.
   c. constant.
   d. increasing with one input and therefore decreasing with the other input, both at the same rate.
   e. none of the above.

18. Given the linear isocost function 10X + 20Y = 1,000, if the price of X rises to \$11 per unit but the price of Y and the budget remain unchanged, the new isocost function:
   a. is above and parallel to the previous isocost.
   b. is below and parallel to the previous isocost.
   c. coincides with the previous isocost, throughout.
   d. is above and crossing the previous isocost.
   e. none of the above.

19. Given the production function Q = 4X + 6Y + XY subject to the budget constraint 4X + 6Y = 2400, the optimal inputs are:
   a. X = Y = 200
   b. X = 300; Y = 200.
   c. X = 50; Y = 200.
   d. X = 125; Y = 250.
   e. none of the above.

20. A production process uses two inputs, X and Y. At a given level of output Q = 50, the following data are pertinent: $MP_X = 10$, $MP_Y = 15$, $C_X = \$2$, and $C_Y = \$5$. Which of the following best describes this situation:

a. $MRP_Y < MRP_X$.
b. too much X is being used and not enough Y is being used.
c. too much Y is being used and not enough X is being used.
d. there is not enough information to say what the situation is.
e. none of the above.

Answers

1. b 2. d 3. e 4. c 5. e 6. d 7. c 8. d 9. d 10. e
11. a 12. d 13. c 14. b 15. a 16. e 17. e 18. e 19. b 20. c

Long Answer Questions

LO1 Explain the relationship between cost and profit

1.1. *(Explicit and Implicit Costs)* Amos McCoy is currently raising corn on his 100-acre farm and earning an accounting profit of $100 per acre. However, if he raised soybeans, he could earn $200 per acre. Is he currently earning an economic profit? Why or why not?

1.2. *(Explicit and Implicit Costs)* Determine whether each of the following is an explicit cost or an implicit cost:
a. Payments for labor purchased in the labor market
b. A firm's use of a warehouse that it owns and could rent to another firm
c. Rent paid for the use of a warehouse not owned by the firm
d. The wages that owners could earn if they did not work for themselves

1.3. *(Alternative Measures of Profit)* Calculate the accounting profit or loss as well as the economic profit or loss in each of the following situations:
a. A firm with total revenues of $150 million, explicit costs of $90 million, and implicit costs of $40 million
b. A firm with total revenues of $125 million, explicit costs of $100 million, and implicit costs of $30 million
c. A firm with total revenues of $100 million, explicit costs of $90 million, and implicit costs of $20 million
d. A firm with total revenues of $250,000, explicit costs of $275,000, and implicit costs of $50,000

1.4. *(Alternative Measures of Profit)* Why is it reasonable to think of normal profit as a type of cost to the firm?

LO2 Identify the elements that affect production in the short term

2.1. *(Production in the Short Run)* Complete the following table. At what point does diminishing marginal returns set in?

Units of the Variable Resource	Total Product	Marginal Product
0	0	—
1	10	______
2	22	______
3	______	9
4	______	4
5	34	______

2.2. *(Costs in the Short Run)* Identify each of the curves in the following graph:

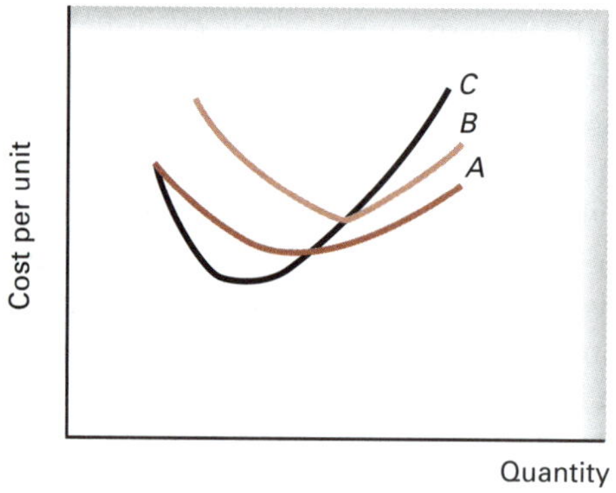

2.3 For a short run production function, graphically derive the marginal product and the average product curves of a variable input. Thereafter, discuss the relationship between the marginal product and the average product curves of a variable input.

2.4 What is meant by marginal resource cost and marginal revenue product of an input? How do they vary when more units of variable input are used?

2.5 Illustrate the Law of Diminishing Returns and the three stages of production, assuming that the production function has only one variable input. What is the optimal use of the variable input in Stage II., if the firm wants to maximize its profits?

LO3 Explain how the costs of production vary with output in the short run

3.1. *(Total Cost and Marginal Cost)* Complete the following table, assuming that each unit of labor costs $75 per day.

Quantity of Labor per Day	Output per Day	Fixed Cost	Variable Cost	Total Cost	Marginal Cost
0	_____	$300	$_____	$_____	$_____
1	5	_____	75	_____	15
2	11	_____	150	450	12.5
3	15	_____	_____	525	_____
4	18	_____	300	600	25
5	20	_____	_____	_____	37.5

a. Graph the fixed cost, variable cost, and total cost curves for these data.
b. What is the marginal product of the third unit of labor?
c. What is average total cost when output is 18 units per day?

3.2. *(Total Cost and Marginal Cost)* Complete the following table, where *L* is units of labor, *Q* is units of output, and *MP* is the marginal product of labor.

L	*Q*	*MP*	*VC*	*TC*	*MC*	*ATC*
0	0	_____	$ 0	$12	_____	_____
1	6	_____	$ 3	15	_____	_____
2	15	_____	$ 6	_____	_____	_____
3	21	_____	$ 9	_____	_____	_____
4	24	_____	$12	_____	_____	_____
5	26	_____	$15	_____	_____	_____

a. At what level of labor input do the marginal returns to labor begin to diminish?
b. What is the average variable cost when $Q = 24$?
c. What is this firm's fixed cost?
d. What is the wage rate per day?

3.3. *(Relationship Between Marginal Cost and Average Cost)* Assume that labor and capital are the only inputs used by a firm. Capital is fixed at 5 units, which cost $100 each. Workers can be hired for $200 each. Complete the following table to show average variable cost *(AVC)*, average total cost *(ATC)*, and marginal cost *(MC)*.

Quantity of Labor	Total Output	*AVC*	*ATC*	*MC*
0	0	_____	_____	_____
1	100	_____	_____	_____
2	250	_____	_____	_____
3	350	_____	_____	_____
4	400	_____	_____	_____
5	425	_____	_____	_____

1. Explain isoquants. What does the shape of isoquants signify? A company currently uses steel and aluminum in a production process. Steel costs $0.50 per kg, and aluminum costs $1.00 per kg. Suppose the government imposes a tax of $0.20 per kg on all metals. What affect will this have on the optimal input mix of the company? Represent the isoquants and isocost lines graphically as well.

3.5. Write notes on the following:
a. Ridge Lines.
b. Cobb Douglas Production Function

LO4 Describe how firms use the long-run average cost curve to make choices about production

4.1. *(Long-Run Costs)* Suppose the firm has only three possible scales of production as shown below:

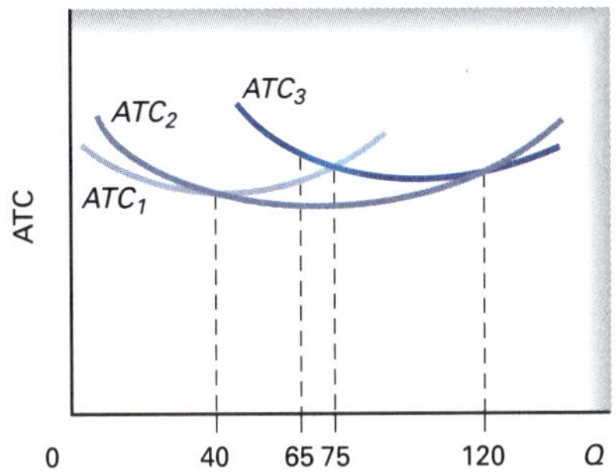

a. Which scale of production is most efficient when $Q = 65$?
b. Which scale of production is most efficient when $Q = 75$?
c. Trace out the long-run average cost curve on the diagram.

4.2 Draw the ATC, AVC and MC curve for a firm. Explain why the ATC curve reaches its lowest point after the AVC curve. Where does the MC curve intersect the AVC and ATC curves?

NUMERICAL QUESTIONS

1. Solve the following constrained maximization problem using the Lagrangian multiplier.
   $Q = f(L, K)$
   $C^* = wL + rK$
   Where w is the wage of labour and r is the rental price of capital.
2. A company producing soft drinks estimates its production function to be $Q = 400L^2K$, where Q is the quantity of soft drinks produced each week, L is the hours of labor required per week, and K is the number of machine hours required per week. It is known that each machine operates 120 hours every week. Cost of labour is $20/hour, and cost of machine is $1000 per week.
   a. If the firm has 20 machines and is currently producing at its optimal K/L ratio, how many people does the company employ? Assume each person works 40 hours a week.
   b. Constant technological innovation has led to a drop in the price of machines. The company now has the option to lease each machine for $800 a week. Will this have any impact on the optimal K/L ratio? Explain why.
3. Suppose a manufacturing company produces a single product. At its current input mix the marginal product of labor is 10 and the marginal product of capital is 20. The per unit price of labor and capital are $5 and $10, respectively. Is the company using an

optimal mix of labor and capital to produce its current output? If not, should it use more capital or labor? Explain.

4. Let the production function of a mobile phone manufacturer Metro Co. be given by $Q = 25LK$ where Q is the quantity of mobile phones produced in the month, L is the number of workers employed, and K is the number of machines used in the production. The monthly wage rate is given as $3,000 per worker and the monthly rental rate for a machine is $6,000. Currently Metro Co. employs 25 workers and 40 machines. Assume, in this case, perfect divisibility of labor and machines.
   a. What is the current average product of labor for Metro Co.? What is the current marginal product of machines? (Assume 1 unit increase in machines.)
   b. Does the company's production function display increasing, decreasing, or constant returns to scale? Explain.
   c. What is the total cost of the current production of Metro Inc for a month? What is the average cost to produce a mobile phone? Assuming the number of machines does not change, what is the marginal cost of producing one additional gun?
   d. What is the law of diminishing returns? Does this production display this characteristic? Explain.

5. Complete the following table, and also plot TC, TFC, TVC, MC, AC, AFC, and AVC against Q.

Q	TC	TFC	TVC	MC	AC	AFC	AVC
0							
1	500			80			
2				60			
3				50			
4				60			
5				75			
6				95			
7				120			
8				150			
9				185			

6. a. Suppose that you can sell as much of a product as you want at $100 per unit. Your marginal cost is: MC = 2Q. Your fixed cost is $50. What is the optimal output level? What is the optimal output, if your fixed cost is $60?
   b. Suppose that the marginal product of labor is: MP = 100 – L, where L is the number of workers hired. You can sell the product in the market for $50 per unit and the wage rate for labor is $100. How many workers should you hire?

7. Given the production function and input prices as:
   $Q = 6 \text{ Log } L + 12 \text{ Log } K$
   Price of labour = $12 per unit
   Price of capital = $36 per unit
   And assuming that the producer has only Rs.1944 to spend, derive the firm's optimal input combination of labour and capital.

8. Jupiter Products, Inc., has derived the following production function for its operation:
   $Q = 0.65L^{0.42}C^{0.38}M^{0.20}Z^{0.08}$
   Where Q = units of output per period of time, L = hours of labor, C = hours of machine services, M = hours of managerial input, and Z = miscellaneous resource services. Assuming that Jupiter's operations are sufficiently flexible to vary the usage of L, C, M, and Z, what kind of returns are indicated by this production function? Why?

9. Gamma Corporation, one of the firms that retains you as a financial analyst, is considering buying out Beta Corporation, a small manufacturing firm that is now barely operating at a profit. You recommend the buyout because you believe that new management could substantially reduce production costs, and thereby increase profits to a quite attractive level. You collect the following product information in order to convince the CEO at Gamma Corporation that Beta is indeed operating inefficiently.
   $MP_L = 10$
   $P_L = \$20$
   $MP_K = 15$
   $P_K = \$15$
   Explain how these data provide evidence of inefficiency. How could the new manager of Beta Corporation improve efficiency? Can you relate the information with graphical representation?

10. A production process uses two inputs, X and Y. At a given level of output $Q = 50$, the following data are pertinent: $MP_X = 10$, $MP_Y = 15$, $P_X = \$2$, and $P_Y = \$5$. Which of the following best describes this situation and WHY?
   a. $MRP_Y < MRP_X$.
   b. too much X is being used and not enough Y is being used.
   c. too much Y is being used and not enough X is being used.
   d. there is not enough information to say what the situation is.
   e. none of the above.

MISCELLANEOUS QUESTIONS

1. Distinguish between law of returns to variable factor and returns to scale.
2. Define short run and long run. Is the long-run the same calendar time for all firms? Explain.
3. Differentiate between economies of scale and economies of scope. What are learning curves and how do they differ from economies of scale?
4. Define the following and differentiate as well:
   a. Fixed cost and variable cost
   b. Acquisition cost and opportunity cost
   c. Explicit cost and implicit cost
   d. Marginal cost and incremental cost
5. Explain the economic significance of U-shape of the short-run and long-run average cost curves.

6. A personal digital assistant making company was one of the early leaders in the production of device. During the early period in development of the industry, the company decided to price the device substantially below its production costs. The decision led to high sales but resulted in near-term reductions in profits. Give the rationale behind company's decision. Will it eventually be of any help?
7. How does the concept of factors of production being substitutes or complementary help firms to allocate factors in an optimal manner? Do you think this problem is relevant to policy makers in taxing petrol to save energy and avoid pollution? How? Illustrate with examples and appropriate diagram.
8. 'Returns to scale' is linked to cost variation and technology of production (give diagrammatic presentation). Discuss cases where firms have really benefited by increasing returns to scale and captured a significant share of the market

Chapter in Review

KEY TERMS

explicit cost
opportunity cost of resources employed by a firm that takes the form of cash payments

implicit cost
a firm's opportunity cost of using its own resources or those provided by its owners without a corresponding cash payment

accounting profit
a firm's total revenue minus its explicit costs

economic profit
a firm's total revenue minus its explicit and implicit costs

normal profit
the accounting profit earned when all resources earn their opportunity cost

variable resource
any resource that can be varied in the short run to increase or decrease production

fixed resource
any resource that cannot be varied in the short run

short run
a period during which at least one of a firm's resources is fixed

long run
a period during which all resources under the firm's control are variable

total product
a firm's total output

production function
the relationship between the amount of resources employed and a firm's total product

marginal product
the change in total product that occurs when the use of a particular resource increases by one unit, all other resources constant

increasing marginal returns
the marginal product of a variable resource increases as each additional unit of that resource is employed

law of diminishing marginal returns
as more of a variable resource is added to a given amount of a fixed resource, marginal product eventually declines and could become negative

fixed cost
any production cost that is independent of the firm's rate of output

variable cost
any production cost that changes as the rate of output changes

LO1 Explain the relationship between cost and profit. Firms try to earn a profit by transforming resources into salable products. These resources, whether explicit or implicit, have an opportunity cost that must be accounted for. Accounting profit equals total revenue minus explicit costs. Economic profit equals total revenue minus all costs, both implicit and explicit.

Three Stages of Production

When total product increases by an increasing amount, marginal product is rising. When total product increases by a decreasing amount, marginal product is positive but declining. When total product is maximum, marginal product is zero. When total product is falling, marginal product is negative.

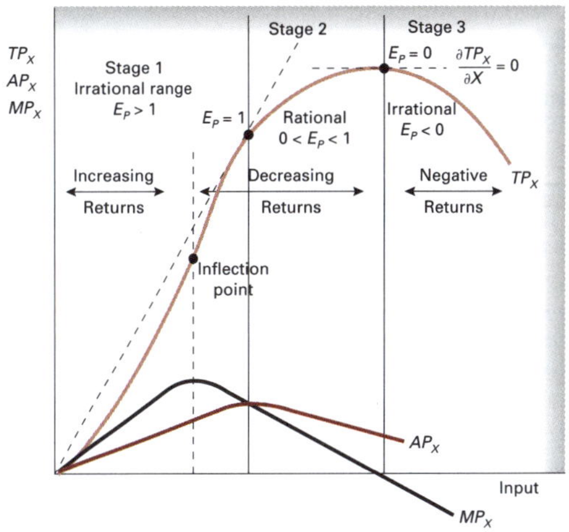

LO2 Identify the elements that affect production in the short term. Output can be changed in the short run by adjusting variable resources, such as labor, but the size, or scale, of the firm is fixed in the short run. Firms experience increasing marginal returns when increasing a variable resource, but only to a certain point. Eventually, the law of diminishing marginal returns takes hold, thus restricting a firm's ability to affect production in the short term.

LO3 Identify the elements that affect production in the long run. Production in the Long Run: Producer equilibrium in the long run can be of two kinds:

a) Maximization of output subject to cost constraint

b) Minimization of cost subject to output constraint.

In both the cases producer is in equilibrium when slope of isoquant equals the slope of isocost (provided the isoquants are convex to the origin).

Maximization of Output Subject to Cost Constraint

We see that the maximum level of output the firm can produce; given the cost constraint is Q_2, defined by the tangency of the isocost line, and the highest isoquant. The optimal combination of factors of production is K_2 and L_2, for prices w and r. Higher levels of output (to the right of e) are desirable but not attainable due to the cost constraint. Other points on AB or below it lie on a lower isoquant than Q_2. Hence Q_2 is the maximum output possible under the assumptions of given cost outlay, given production function, and given factor prices. At the point of tangency e, the slope of the isocost line (w/r) is equal to the slope of the isoquant (MP_L/MP_K). This constitutes the first condition for equilibrium. The second condition is that the isoquants should be convex to the origin.

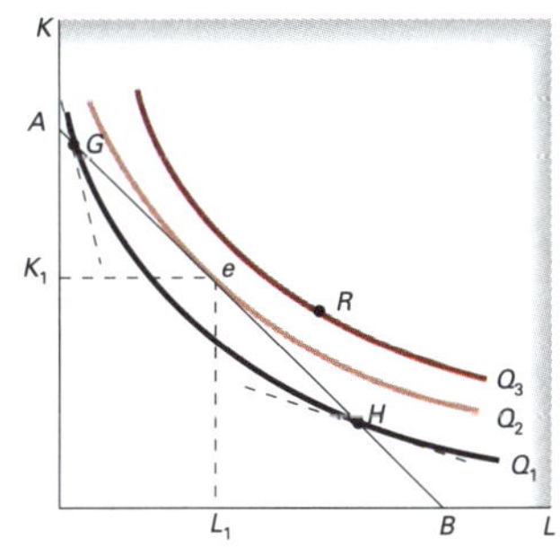

total cost
the sum of fixed cost and variable cost, or $TC = FC + VC$

marginal cost
the change in total cost resulting from a one-unit change in output; the change in total cost divided by the change in output, or $MC = \Delta TC/\Delta q$

average variable cost
variable cost divided by output, or $AVC = VC/q$

average total cost
total cost divided by output, or $ATC = TC/q$; the sum of average fixed cost and average variable cost, or $ATC = AFC + AVC$

economies of scale
forces that reduce a firm's average cost as the scale of operation increases in the long run

diseconomies of scale
forces that may eventually increase a firm's average cost as the scale of operation increases in the long run

long-run average cost curve
a curve that indicates the lowest average cost of production at each rate of output when the size, or scale, of the firm varies; also called the *planning curve*

constant long-run average cost
a cost that occurs when, over some range of output, long-run average cost neither increases nor decreases with changes in firm size

minimum efficient scale
the lowest rate of output at which a firm takes full advantage of economies of scale

CHAPTER EQUATIONS

Total Cost

$$TC = FC + VC$$

Marginal Cost

$$MC = \Delta TC/\Delta q$$

Average Variable Cost

$$AVC = VC/q$$

Average Total Cost

$$ATC = AFC + AVC$$
$$ATC = TC/q$$

Minimization of Cost Subject to Output Constraint

The firm minimizes its costs by employing the combination of K and L determined by the point of tangency of the $\bar{Q}$ isoquant with the lowest isocost line. Points below e are desirable because they show lower cost but are not attainable for output $\bar{Q}$. Points above e show higher costs. Hence, point e is the least-cost point, the point denoting the least-cost combination of the factors K and L for producing $\bar{Q}$.
Once again we observe that the producer is in equilibrium when slope of isoquant equals the slope of isocost (provided the isoquant is convex to the origin).

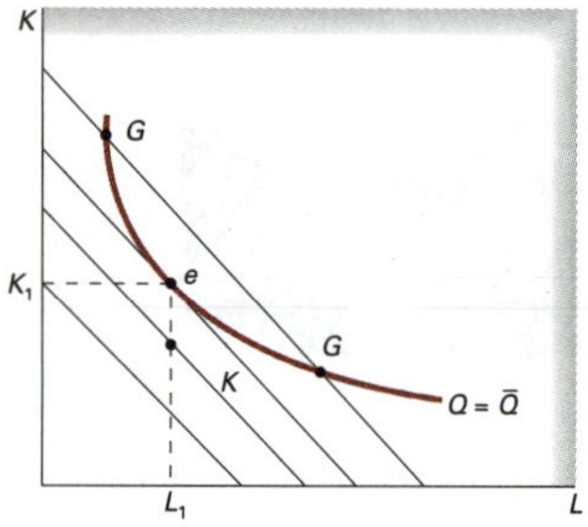

LO4 Explain how the costs of production vary with output in the short run. A fixed cost does not vary with output in the short run. Variable cost, is the cost of variable resources, such as labor, that do vary with output in the short run. When the firm experiences increasing marginal returns, the marginal cost of output falls; when the firm experiences diminishing marginal returns, the marginal cost of output increases.

Total and Marginal Cost Curves for Smoother Mover

In panel (a), fixed cost is \$200 at all levels of output. Variable cost starts from the origin and increases slowly at first as output increases. When the variable resource generates diminishing marginal returns, variable cost begins to increase more rapidly. Total cost is the vertical sum of fixed cost and variable cost. In panel (b), marginal cost first declines, reflecting increasing marginal returns from the variable resource (labor in this example), and then increases, reflecting diminishing marginal returns.

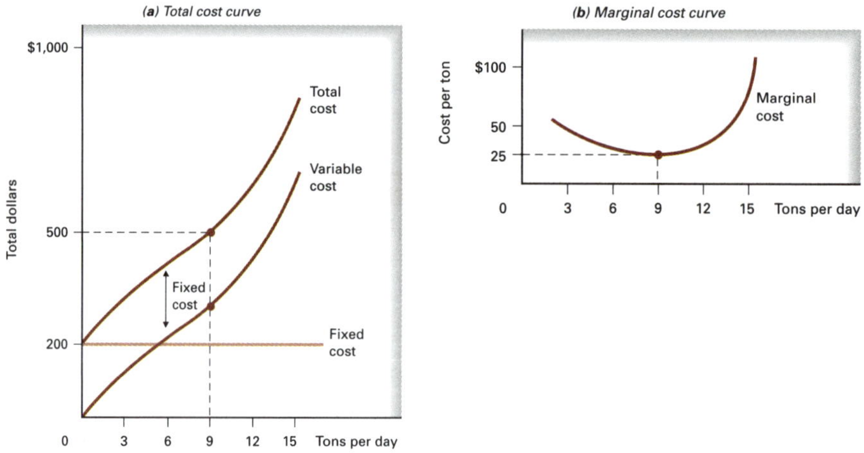

LO5 Describe how firms use the long-run average cost curve to make choices about production. For any given firm, the long-run average cost curve is formed by connecting the points on the various short-run average cost curves that represent the lowest per-unit cost for each rate of output. Each of the short-run average cost curves is tangent to the long-run average cost curve, or planning curve. These points of tangency represent the least-cost way of producing each particular rate of output.

If a firm experiences economies of scale, long-run average cost falls as output expands. A larger scale of operation allows a firm to use larger, more efficient techniques and machines and to assign workers to more specialized tasks. Diseconomies of scale may eventually take over as a firm expands its plant size, increasing long-run average cost as output expands.

Short-Run Average Total Cost Curves Form the Long-Run Average Cost Curve, or Planning Curve

Curves *SS'*, *MM'*, and *LL'* show short-run average total costs for small, medium, and large plants, respectively. For output less than q_a, average cost is lowest when the plant is small. Between q_a and q_b, average cost is lowest with a medium-size plant. If output exceeds q_b, the large plant offers the lowest average cost. The long-run average cost curve connects these low cost segments of each curve and is identified as *SabL'*.

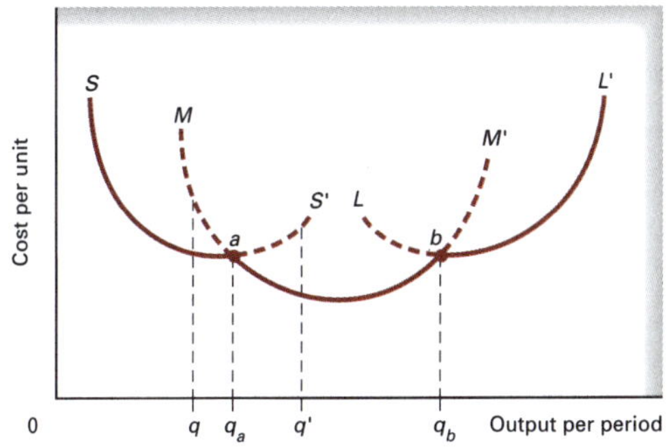

Many Short-Run Average Total Cost Curves Form a Firm's Long-Run Average Cost Curve, or Planning Curve

With many possible plant sizes, the long-run average cost curve is the envelope of portions of the short-run average cost curves. Each short-run curve is tangent to the long-run average cost curve. Each point of tangency represents the least-cost way of producing that level of output.

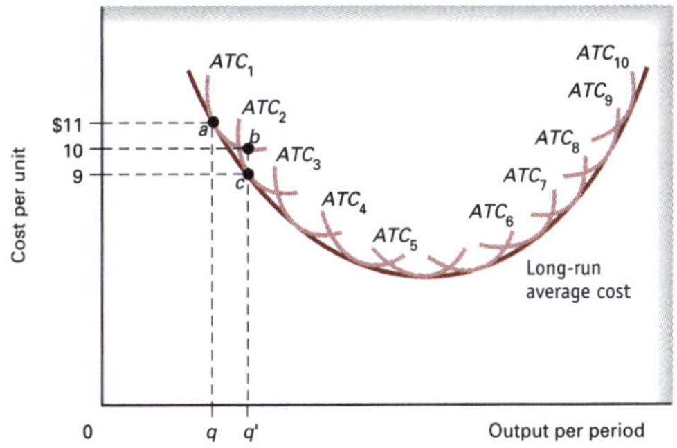

A Firm's Long-Run Average Cost Curve

Up to output level *A*, long-run average cost falls as the firm experiences economies of scale. Output level *A* is the minimum efficient scale—the lowest rate of output at which the firm takes full advantage of economies of scale. Between *A* and *B*, the average cost is constant. Beyond output level *B*, long-run average cost increases as the firm experiences diseconomies of scale.

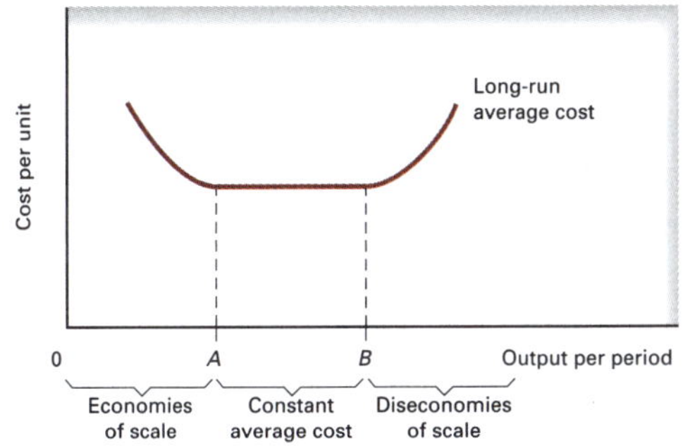

CHAPTER

8

Learning Outcomes

LO[1] Discuss the traditional theory of profit maximization

LO[2] Explain Baumol's theory of sales maximization: managerial theory of the firm

LO[3] Explain Marris's model of the managerial enterprise: managerial theory of the firm

LO[4] Explain Cyert and March's behavioral theory of a firm

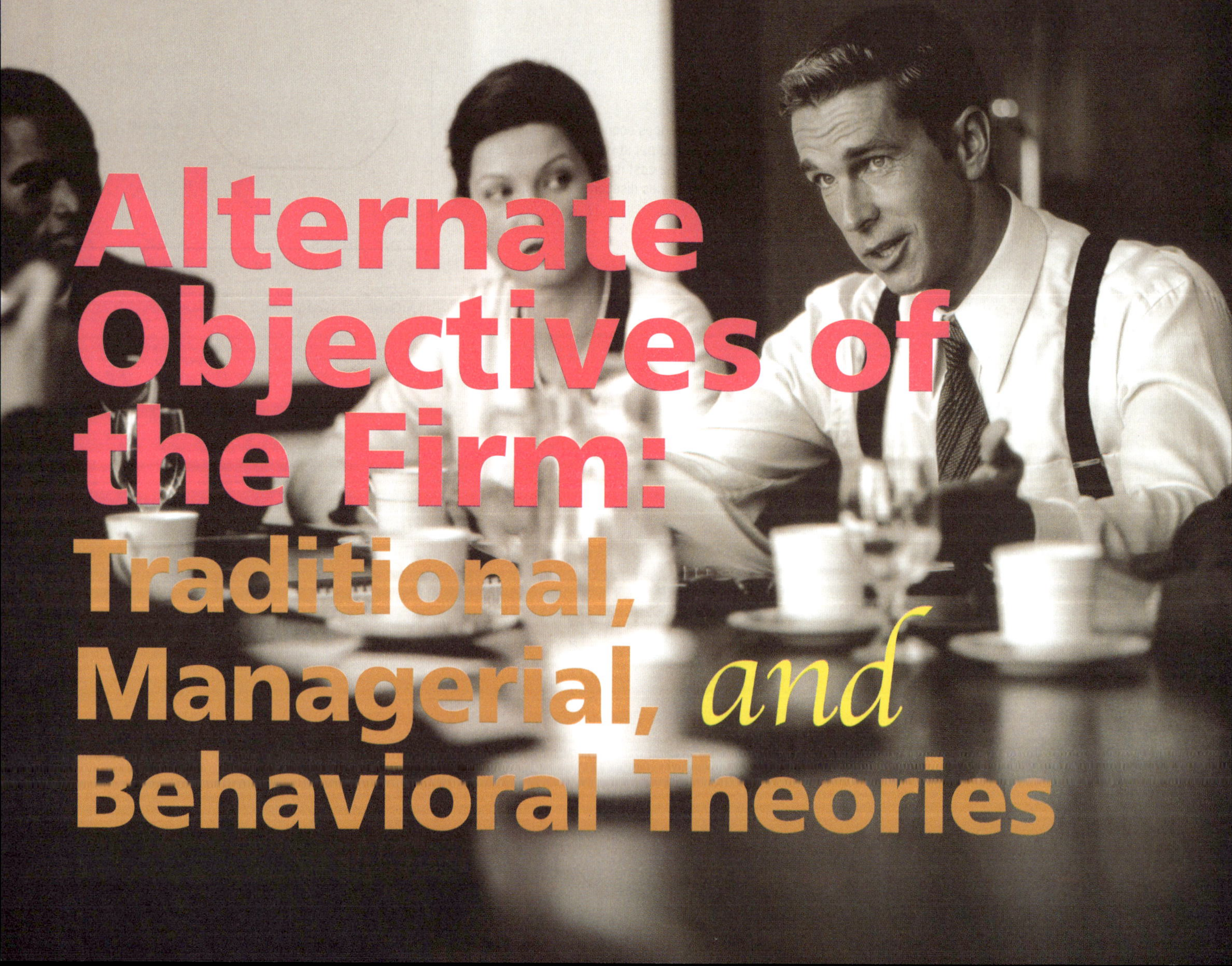

Alternate Objectives of the Firm: Traditional, Managerial, *and* Behavioral Theories

© STOCKBYTE/THINKSTOCK

“Why do some firms maximize output, while others may seek to maximize growth?”

Why do some firms maximize output, while others may seek to maximize growth? Why do some managers maximize their utility, while other firms try to satisfice? Why is it not possible to simultaneously maximize profits and sales and minimize costs? Why do some firms change price and output when fixed costs change, while others are unable to do so? What are the fundamental differences between the traditional and alternative theories of a firm? Answer to these and some other questions are explored in this chapter.

What do you think?

I shall be equally committed to my work, irrespective of whether I am allowed to reap the additional benefits of my work?

Strongly Disagree 1 2 3 4 5 6 7 *Strongly Agree*

Traditional economic theory assumes that the aim of the firm is to maximize profits in the short run by equating marginal revenue with marginal cost. This means that an additional unit of output will bring in as much money as it costs to produce it, so that its marginal profitability is zero. However, firms, in practice, lack the information to be profit maximizers in this way. Another criticism concerns the problem of deciding the time period over which the firm should be seeking to maximize profits. Selecting the price and output that maximizes profit in the short run may jeopardize profits in the future.

Topics discussed in Chapter 8 include:

- Traditional theory of profit maximization
- Behavioral theory of the firm
- Managerial theory of the firm
- Effective and ineffective profit constraints
- Satisficing theory
- Slack payments

In addition, firms do not necessarily aim to maximize profits even if they could. For instance, in public limited companies there is a separation between ownership and control of the business. Shareholders (principal) own the company but elect directors who in turn appoint management (agent). This results in a principal-agent problem. Since the managers are closer to the day to day operations of the firm they have more knowledge about the company than the owners. This information asymmetry (due to divorce of ownership from management) allows the management to pursue objectives that may be in variance with the owners. Unlike the owners, there aim may not be profit maximization. While this issue may be resolved by monitoring the performance of agents and offering incentives to them to act in the principal's interests, the same cannot be completely resolved. It is in response to such criticisms that the managerial and behavioral theories of the firm

traditional economic theory assumes that the aim of the firm is to maximize profits in the short run by equating marginal revenue with marginal cost

managerial and behavioral theory have been developed as an alternative to the traditional theory that assumes profit maximization to be the objective function of owners (who also manage the enterprise) have been developed as an alternative to the traditional theory that assumes profit maximization to be the objective function of owners (who also manage the enterprise).

Managerial theories conceive the firm as a coalition (of managers, workers, stockholders, customers, suppliers, tax collectors) whose members have conflicting goals that must be reconciled if the firm has to survive. The most important member of the coalition is the top management. This primarily is on account of two factors: (a) its power in decision making and (b) access to information. The basic objective of all managerial theories is that the managers maximize their own utility, subject to a minimum profit constraint that is imposed by the shareholder (owner). The managers meet this minimum profit constraint as otherwise their jobs would be in risk. In this chapter, we present two models of managerialism, viz., Baumol's model of "sales revenue maximization" and Marris's model of "managerial enterprise." These models have the same basic assumption, i.e., the maximization of manager's utility subject to a minimum profit constraint. They differ in terms of:

1. The factors which enter into the managerial utility function,
2. The key policy variables which the managers will use in attaining their goals, and
3. In their predictions of the consequences of changes in various parameters of the model.

Behavioral theories of the firm attempt to predict the actions of firms by studying the behavior of various groups of people within the firm and their interactions under conditions of potentially conflicting interests. In other words, behavioral theories are based on observations of how firms actually behave. An important idea in this context is that of profit satisficing where decision makers in a firm aim for a target level of profit rather than the maximum level. Complex behavioral theories suggest that firms are complex institutions involving different and competing management groups who may have conflicting aims. These aims in turn will be constrained by the interests of other stakeholders (groups of people who have an interest in a firm such as shareholders, customers, suppliers, workers, the local community, pressure groups, and the government). In case of conflicting targets, such conflict may be settled by a bargaining process between managers and/or stakeholders. A similar set of conflicting targets may be resolved differently in different firms depending on relative power, etc. However, firms with multiple goals will be satisfiers in the widest sense leading to conservative aspirations and organizational slack or x-inefficiency.

managerial theory the firm is conceived as a coalition (of managers, workers, stockholders, customers, suppliers, tax collectors) whose members have conflicting goals that must be reconciled if the firm has to survive. The most important member of the coalition is the top management.

behavioral theory predict the actions of firms by studying the behavior of various groups of people within the firm and their interactions under conditions of potentially conflicting interests. In other words, behavioral theories are based on observations of how firms actually behave

We now discuss each of these theories. We begin by discussing the traditional theory of profit maximization. Thereafter, we discuss the managerial and behavioral theories of a firm.

LO1 Traditional Theory of Profit Maximization

We first examine the conventional theory of the profit maximizing firm. For a profit-maximizing producer, the primary objective is to reach the point of production, where maximum profits are earned. That is, the producer keeps on producing till the marginal profitability of each extra unit of commodity produced is zero. Marginal profitability of zero implies that marginal revenue equals marginal cost (MR = MC). If this is not the case, then the producer can increase profits by altering production levels. Suppose the firm is producing at a suboptimal level of output, say at a point where the marginal cost is less than the marginal revenue. Now, if the firm increases production by an additional unit, MR would exceed MC. The marginal profitability would be positive which implies that total profits are rising.

Exhibit 1

The Profit Maximizing Firm: MR-MC Approach

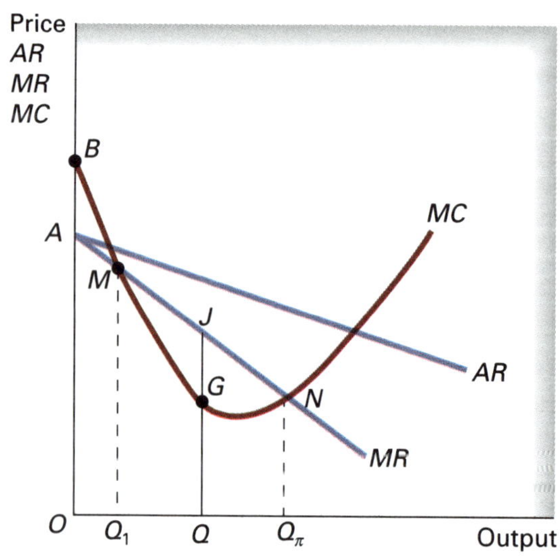

Thus, so long as marginal cost is less than marginal revenue, the firm can increase profit by producing more. On the other hand, if marginal revenue is less than the marginal cost, it pays the firm to reduce output. In this case, if the firm reduces production, the *MC* saved would exceed the *MR* lost. Thus, if marginal cost is greater than marginal revenue, the firm can raise profit by reducing production. We illustrate the profit maximizing equilibrium with the help of Exhibit 1. Before proceeding further, the students are advised to recall that area under *MR* represents *TR*, while the area under *MC* represents *TC*.

Thus, at any output, say *OQ*, total revenue is represented by the area under the marginal revenue curve given by *OAJQ*. Similarly, total cost is represented by the area under the marginal cost curve given by *OBGQ*. Now if the producer produces *OQ* units of the output, his total profit will be represented by *OAJQ* minus *OBGQ*. That is, the total profit is given by the difference between total revenue and total cost. Thus,

Total profit = *OAJQ* – *OBGQ* = *MJG* – *MAB*

A move to the right of Q will increase the size of the profit area *MJG*. In fact, only at output OQ_π will this area have reached its maximum size. Total profits will now be equal to area *MJNG* minus area *MAB*. At this output level profits are at their peak. At this level *MR* = *MC*. Also, when *MR* = *MC*, marginal profits are zero and total profits are at their peak. Thus, at the point of maximum profits, marginal costs and marginal revenues must be equal.

However, it is important to remember that while *MR* = *MC* is a necessary condition for profit maximization; it is not a sufficient condition. Here *MR* equals *MC* at point *M* also. However, at this point profits are not maximum. In fact, the producer ends up with a loss of Δ*BM*. A move in either direction from point Q_1 will help the firm. A leftward movement reduces its costs more than it reduces its revenues; while a rightward move adds more to its revenues than to its costs. Output OQ_1 is thus a point of minimum profits even though it meets the marginal profit-maximization condition, *MR* = *MC*. Thus, while at the point of maximum profits, marginal costs and marginal revenues must be equal; its converse is not true. In other words, each output level at which *MR* = *MC* is not necessarily the profit maximizing output.

Mathematical Representation of Profit Maximizing Condition

Maximize: $\pi = TR - TC$

First order condition for profit maximization is given by:

$$\frac{\partial \pi}{\partial q} = \frac{\partial TR}{\partial q} - \frac{\partial TC}{\partial q} = 0$$

$$\Rightarrow \quad \frac{\partial TR}{\partial q} = \frac{\partial TC}{\partial q}$$

$$\Rightarrow \quad MR = MC$$

This is the necessary condition for profit maximization.

Second order condition for profit maximization is given by:

$$\frac{\partial^2 \pi}{\partial q^2} = \frac{\partial^2 TR}{\partial q^2} - \frac{\partial^2 TC}{\partial q^2} < 0$$

$$= \frac{\partial MR}{\partial q} - \frac{\partial MC}{\partial q} < 0$$

Slope of *MR* < slope of *MC*

Diagrammatically, this implies that *MC* must cut *MR* from below. This is the sufficient condition for profit maximization.

Thus, there are two ways of interpreting a producers profit maximizing equilibrium.

1. The *TR-TC* Approach: This seeks to maximize the gap between *TR* and *TC*, or
2. The *MR-MC* Approach: This seeks to equate *MR* to *MC*, provided the sufficient condition is met.

Maximization of the gap between *TR* and *TC* yields the equilibrium condition *MR* = *MC*, *subject to MC cutting MR from below*. The same is illustrated in Exhibit 2. The point at which (i) *MR* equals *MC* and (ii) *MC* cuts *MR* from below is also the point where the gap between *TR* and *TC* is maximized. At this output level, the slope of *TR* (representing *MR*) equals the slope of *TC* (representing *MC*). Hence, the two slopes are parallel to each other.

LO2 Baumol's Theory of Sales Maximization: Managerial Theory of the Firm

In the early 1950s an American economist, W. Baumol, put forth an alternative model suggesting that firms often seek to maximize the money value of sales rather than profits. He recognized that firms cannot make a loss if they are to survive in the long term, so at least some profit must be made. Managers also need to make enough profit to satisfy their shareholders. As long as the firm continues to operate

Exhibit 2

Profit Maximizing Firm: TR-TC and MR-MC Approach

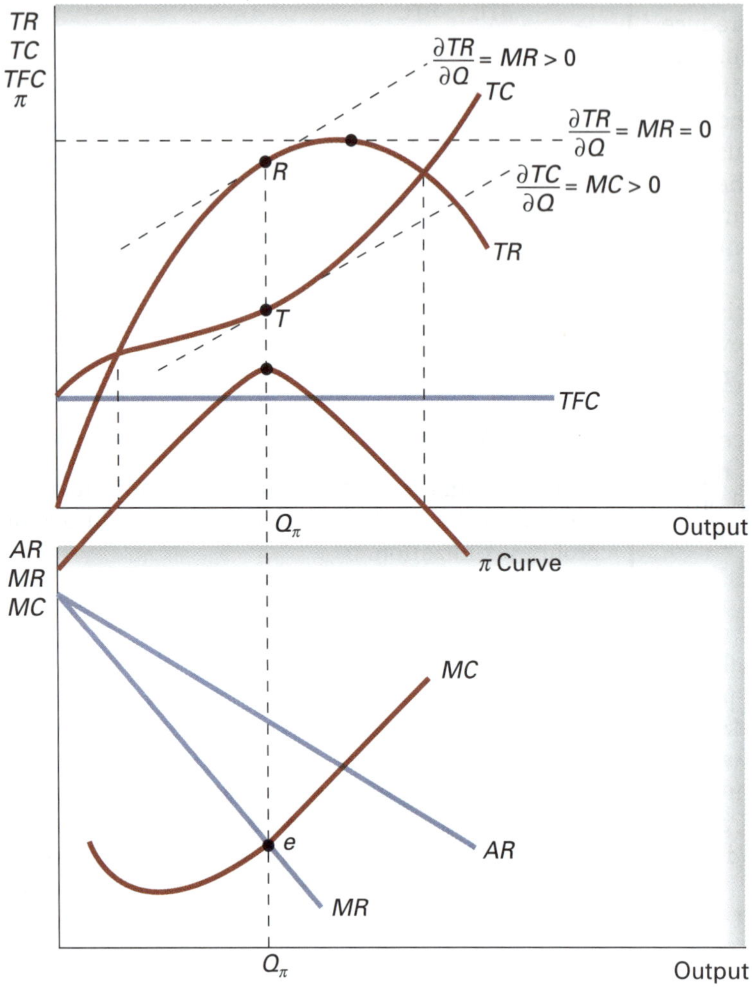

at an acceptable level of profits, the management will devote most of their resources to expansion of sales. Such objectives may be explained by a desire to maintain competitive position which is primarily dependent on market share of firms. In addition, sales maximization may be in the best interest of the management as their salaries and incentives may be dependent on the volume of sales revenue generated.

Sales maximization does not mean an attempt to obtain the largest possible physical volume of sales (which in a multi-product firm is difficult to define). Rather it refers to maximization of total revenue of sales. This happens when *TR* reaches its peak. It can be proved that the output level that maximizes total revenue implies that at this output *MR* equals zero. Further, when *MR* = 0 price elasticity of demand equals one. Thus, sales maximizing condition requires

sales maximization refers to maximization of total revenue of sales

MR = 0, (while profit maximization requires *MR* = *MC*, provided *MC* cuts *MR* from below). This happens at output level Q_s. Total profits earned at this output are BQ_s. A profit maximizer, on the other hand, produces $OQ\pi$ and earns a total profit of $AQ\pi$ (Exhibit 3).

However, if the sales maximizer faces a profit constraint, the equilibrium condition may change. While an ineffective profit constraint (profit constraint set at a level lower than BQ_s) leaves output unchanged, an effective profit constraint (profit constraint set at a level greater than BQ_s) makes the sales maximizer reduce output. In this case, though the money value of sales is not maximized, the firm does meet the profit requirement. Further, there are two output levels $OQ_{s\pi}$ and OQ_b, which satisfy the profit constraint. For reasons of being closer to maximization of sales, the producer chooses $OQ_{s\pi}$ over OQ_b. Thus, two types of equilibriums are possible: (i) pure sales maximization and (ii) constrained sales maximization. In turn, constrained sales maximization could be for an effective profit constraint or ineffective profit constraint. This is illustrated in Exhibit 3. It shows the firm's total revenue, total cost, and profit curves as indicated. The higher profit constraint is effective, while the lower one is ineffective.

The profit and sales maximizing outputs are, respectively, $OQ\pi$ and OQ_s. Now, if for example, the minimum required profit level is OG, then the sales maximizing output OQ_s will provide

© GOODSHOT/THINKSTOCK

Exhibit 3

Optimal Equilibrium Outputs Under Alternate Objectives

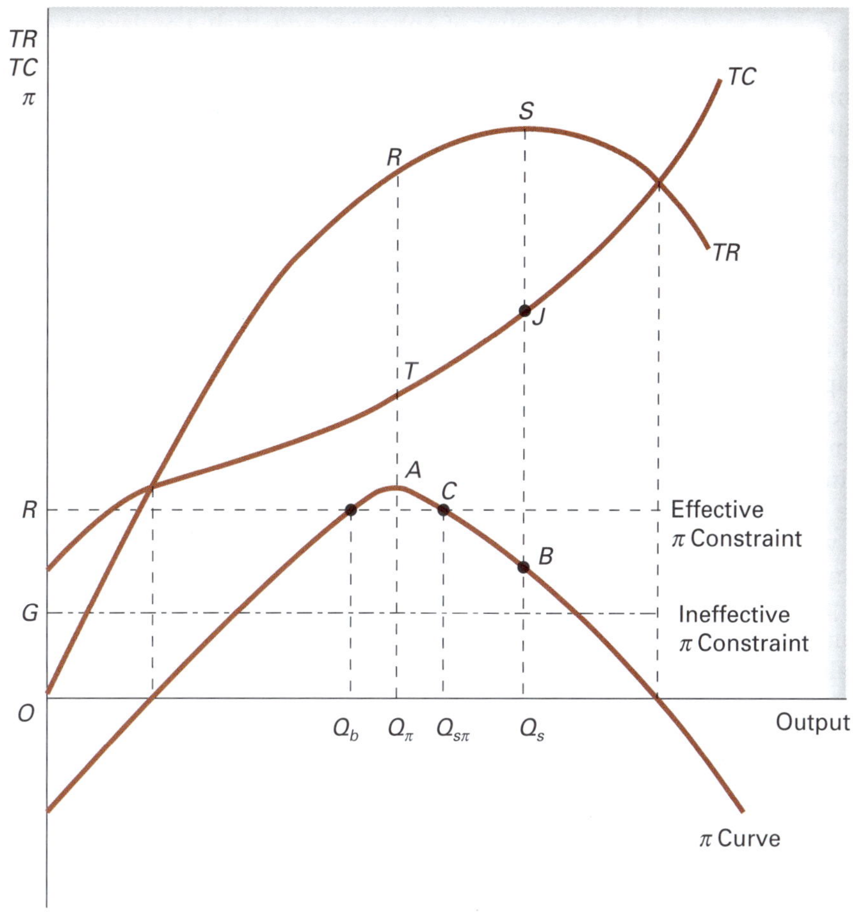

plenty of profit, and that is the amount it will pay the sales maximizer to produce. But if the producer's minimum required profit level is *OR*, then output OQ_s yields insufficient profit. Thus, the firm's output level will have to be reduced to level $OQ_{s\pi}$, which is just compatible with its profit constraint.

To be noted is the fact that a profit maximizer generally produces an output lower than either a pure sales maximizer or a constrained sales maximizer. This is because a profit maximizer equates *MR* to *MC*. Since *MC* is generally positive, a profit maximizer stops producing where *MR* is still positive. On the other hand, a pure sales maximizer stops where *MR* equals zero. Since *MR* is a downward sloping curve, the point at which *MR* equals zero lies to the right of the point where *MR* is still positive. This implies that a sales maximizer generally produces more than a profit maximizer. If, however, *MC* is zero, the two types of producers will produce the same level of output. We can, thus, conclude that lower the *MC* of production, lower will be the difference between outputs produced by a profit maximizer vis-a-vis the output produced by a sales maximizer.

It is important to appreciate that:

1. In general, the profit maximizer sells an output that is less than the output produced by the sales maximizer, while the price charged by the profit maximizer is generally higher than the price charged by a sales maximizer (with or without profit constraint). In the exceptional instance when *MC* equals zero, the two outputs will be the same. Additionally, as the *MC* becomes closer to zero, the difference between sales maximizing output and profit maximizing output keeps declining.
2. In addition, the output of a sales maximizer is generally greater than the output of a sales maximizer subject to profit constraint. However, if the profit constraint is the same as that of the profit made with pure sales maximization, then the two outputs would be the same.
3. A profit maximizer always produces in the elastic region of the demand curve, whereas a pure sales maximizer always produces where price elasticity of demand is unitary. Since output of a constrained sales maximizer lies between OQ_π and OQ_s, he too produces in the elastic region of the demand curve.
4. Normally, we do not experience firms to be pure sales maximizers. This is because the objective of maximizing revenue does not necessarily produce profits. Theoretically, the producer can always generate additional revenue by increasing marginal costs exorbitantly; say by continuous advertising of the product.

There are several important policy implications of Baumol's model. Two of these are discussed here. The first pertains to the role of advertising expenditure for a sales maximizing firm and the second pertains to the treatment of overhead costs and taxes. Each of these is discussed next.

Advertising Expenditure and Firm's Objective

How much a firm advertises is also a function of its objective function. In general, a sales maximizer advertises more than a profit maximizer. Baumol's single-product model with advertising is shown in Exhibit 4. The horizontal axis represents the magnitude of advertising expenditure and the vertical axis represents the total money value of sales and total profit. While advertising outlay is measured on the horizontal axis, the advertising function is shown as a 45 degree line. Production costs are assumed to be independent of advertising costs. As shown, the *TR* curve is drawn to be continuously upward sloping. This is because *TR* has been drawn to be a function of advertisement outlay and not of price. Further, it is assumed that increase in advertising expenditure can always increase physical volume of sales. Since more of the commodity can be sold with enhanced advertisement, *TR* need not fall. It may be recalled that while increase in output due to price reduction may or may not increase *TR* (depending upon the elasticity of demand: if demand is elastic, a reduction in price increases *TR*, while if demand is inelastic a reduction in price lowers *TR*), there is no reason to expect *TR* to fall when additional units are sold on account of enhanced advertising outlays at constant prices. Thus, the total revenue is an increasing function of advertising outlay. The assumed positive marginal return of advertising gives an insight as to why unconstrained sales maximization, in general cannot occur. It may also be noted that the *TR* curve has been constructed to increase at a diminishing rate because diminishing returns to advertisement are expected to set in. It may also be noted that *TR* has a positive intercept. This is because even with zero advertisement, some sales are expected. To get the total cost curve, we add all other costs (production and distribution) to advertising costs. We now get the line which depicts the firm's total (production, distribution, and selling) costs as a function of advertising outlay. Subtracting these total costs from the total revenues at each level of advertising outlay, we obtain the total profits curve (PP).

Exhibit 4 indicates that the profit maximizing expenditure on advertisement is OA_π, at which *PP* attains its maximum, R. If, however, the sales maxi-

Exhibit 4

Optimal Advertising Levels Under Alternate Objectives

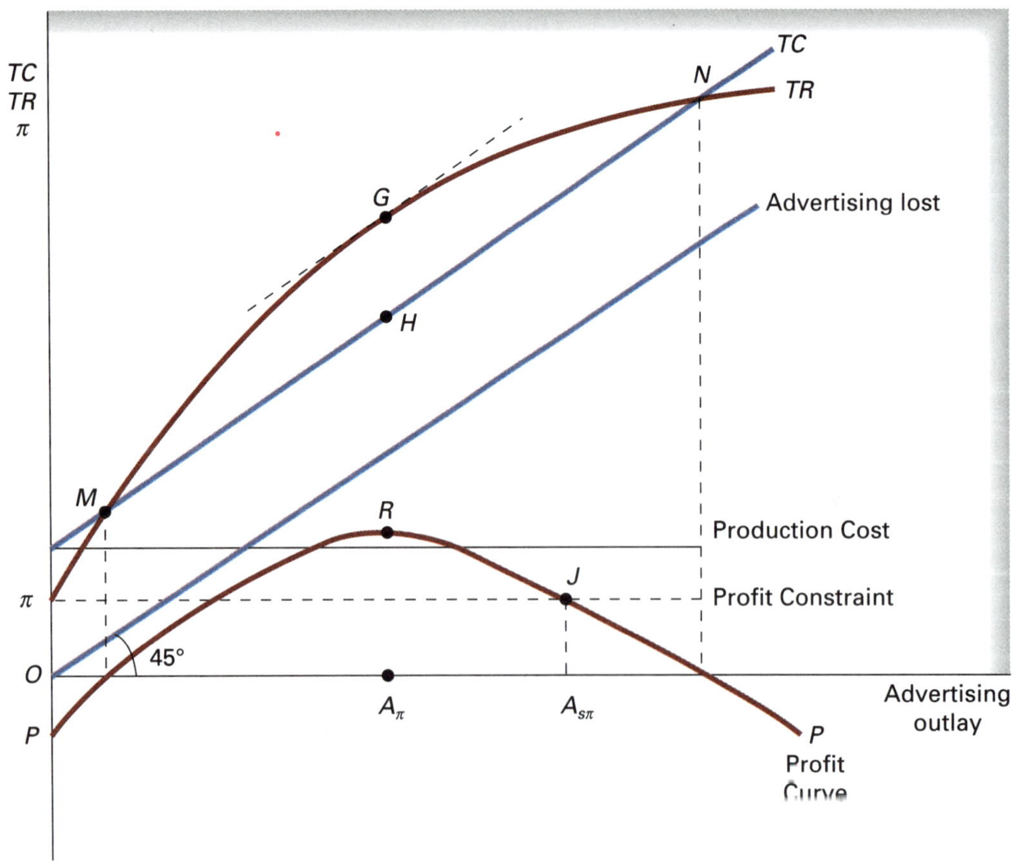

mizer's minimum acceptable profit level is $O\pi$, the constrained sales maximizing advertising budget level is $OA_{s\pi}$. It is to be noted that there is no possibility of an unconstrained sales maximum which is analogous to output OQ_s, as shown in Exhibit 3. For, by assumption, unlike a price reduction, increased advertising always increases total revenue. As a result, it will always pay the sales maximizer to increase his advertising outlay until he is stopped by the profit constraint. That is until profits have been reduced to the minimum acceptable level. This means that sales maximizers will normally advertise no less than and usually more than profit maximizers.

A major limitation of Baumol's analysis is that production costs are independent of advertising expenditure. This implies that total output is expected to remain unchanged even after advertising has taken place. With this assumption, an increase in money value of sales can take place only if prices increase post advertisement. However, Baumol later states that increase in advertisement *per se* does not involve a change in market price. If this is accounted for, then increase in *TR* due to enhanced advertisement is purely due to an increase in volume of sales. If this is true, then production costs cannot be assumed to be independent of advertisement outlay. In fact, each time more is produced, the production costs will have to rise given the positive marginal costs. Thus, Baumol's graphical illustration is inconsistent with his assumptions.

Exhibit 5

Changes in Fixed Costs and its Impact on Equilibrium Output

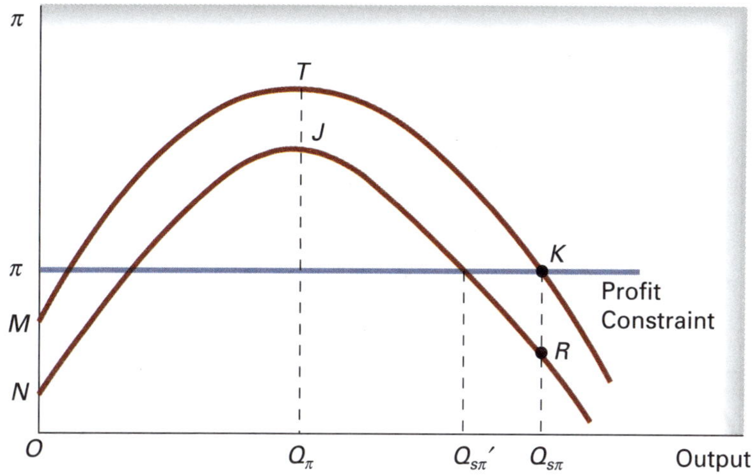

Pricing and Changes in Fixed Costs and Taxes

It is often taught to the students of economics that changes in fixed costs do not matter in decision making. However, real world scenario indicates that firms do respond to increases in fixed costs by reducing output and increasing price. This contrast between theory and practice is easily resolved if we allow for variations in the objective function of the firm. We will show that while a profit maximizer cannot do anything under rising fixed costs, a sales maximizing firm does respond by reducing output. Graphically, an increase in fixed costs means an upward shift of total cost curve and a uniform downward shift in the total profit curve by the amount by which fixed costs (or overhead expenses) have increased. Hence, if overheads rise by an amount equal to *MN* (refer Exhibit 5), then the profit maximizer leaves his output unchanged as the peak of the profit curve remains where it was. However, under constrained sales maximization hypothesis, output will fall from $OQ_{s\pi}$ to $OQ_{s\pi}'$, for at $OQ_{s\pi}$ profits will now be $RQ_{s\pi}$, which is less than the minimum acceptable level $KQ_{s\pi}$. Since firms in the real world do in fact change their output and price whenever overhead costs increase, Baumol states that the sales maximizing hypothesis has a better predictive performance than the traditional profit-maximizing hypothesis.

This result also has implications for tax policy. If a corporate profit tax is imposed on the profit maximising producer, then there is nothing a company can do to shift any part of the corporation tax on to the consumer or its employees. In other words, the profit maximizing firm can gain nothing by raising its prices or changing its outputs in response to a change in corporation tax rates, provided that these rates are so structured that the higher the firm's earnings are before taxes, the more it gets to keep after taxes. But if the firm wishes to maximize sales subject to a profit constraint, rather than maximizing profits, this conclusion does not hold. When taxes are raised, the firm will be motivated to increase its price (and, therefore, to reduce its output) in order to make up its lost profits. The possibility of shift in the incidence of tax occurs since the sales-maximizing firm has a reserve of profits (as it has not maximized profit) to which it can fall back on, when driven to do so by a rise in tax/costs. Thus, a **sales maximizer subject to profit constraint**, in response to an increase in corporate profit tax (increase

sales maximizer subject to profit constraint
in response to an increase in corporate profit tax (increase in fixed costs) the producer is induced to increase its price and reduce the quantities supplied

Exhibit 6

Imposition of a Specific Tax and its Impact on Equilibrium Output

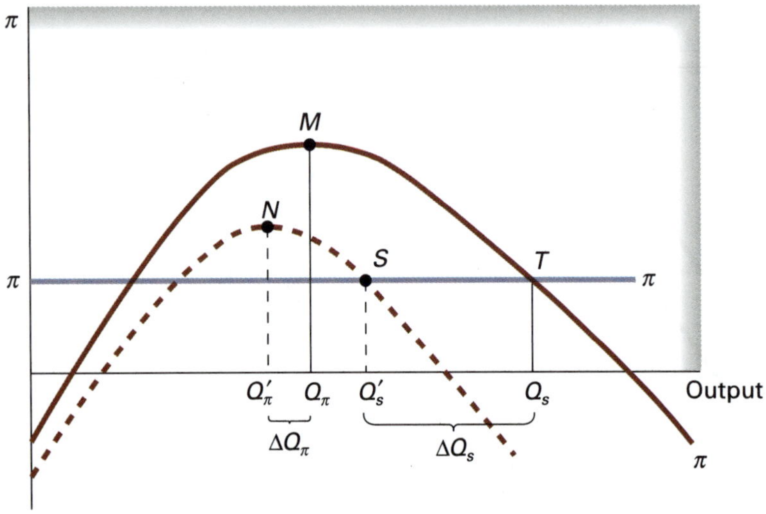

in fixed costs) is induced to increase its price and reduce the quantities supplied. To summarize, while profit maximizers are unable to shift the burden of the tax to the consumers, a sales maximizer (subject to profit constraint) is able to do so. Despite the theoretical simplicity of the profit maximizing model and the empirical appeal of the sales maximizing model, many economists believe that the firms tend to satisfice rather than maximize their objectives. This behavior of managers is discussed later.

The imposition of a specific tax (per unit of output) also shifts the profit curve inwards. However, the shift is not uniform. The downward shift is smaller for lower output levels and higher for larger output levels (refer Exhibit 6). In this case, while the constrained sales maximizer does lower the output and raise the price; even the profit maximizer does the same. He too reduces his output and raises the price, by passing a part of the tax to the consumers. However, the decrease in output and increase in price of the profit maximizer is less accentuated than the decrease in output and increase in price of the constrained sales maximizer. A similar result holds when variable costs change.

Numerical Illustration: Sales Maximization

Suppose that the demand function faced by an oligopolist is

$$Q = 100 - 10P \quad \text{or} \quad P = 10 - 0.1Q$$

So that the total revenue function is:

$$TR = PQ = (10 - 0.1Q)Q = 10Q - 0.1Q^2$$

If the total cost function of the firm is:

$$TC = 70 + 2Q$$

Then the total profit of the firm is:

$$\Pi = TR - TC = 10Q - 0.1Q^2 - 70 - 2Q$$

$$\Rightarrow \quad -70 + 8Q - 0.1Q^2$$

A profit maximizing firm maximizes profits when

$$d\Pi/dQ = 0$$

$$d\Pi/dQ = 8 - 0.2Q = 0$$

So that $Q\pi = 40$ and $P\pi = 10 - 0.1(40) = 6$

$$TR\pi = 10(40) - 0.1(40)^2 = 400 - 160 = 240$$

$$\Pi = -70 + 8(40) - 0.1(40)^2$$

$$\Rightarrow \quad -70 + 320 - 160$$

$$\Rightarrow \quad 90$$

On the other hand, a sales maximizer stops where

$$d(TR)/dQ = 0$$

$$d(TR)/dQ = 10 - 0.2Q = 0$$

$$\Rightarrow \quad Q_s = 50$$

Substituting the value of Q in demand function gives:

$$P_s = 10 - 0.1(50) = 5$$

$$TR_s = 10(50) - 0.1(50)^2 = 500 - 250 = 250$$

$$\Pi_s = -70 + 8(50) - 0.1(50)^2 = -70 + 400 - 250 = 80$$

To find Q_s, P_s, and TR_s if the minimum profit constraint of the firm is $\Pi = 85$, we proceed as follows:

$$\Pi = -70 + 8Q - 0.1Q^2 = 85$$

$$0.1Q^2 - 8Q + 155 = 0$$

Using the quadratic formula to find the roots of this equation, we have

$$Q_{s\pi} = \frac{-b \pm \sqrt{b^2 - 4ac}}{2a}$$

$$\Rightarrow \quad \frac{8 \pm \sqrt{8^2 - 4(.1)(155)}}{2 \times .1}$$

$$\Rightarrow \quad \frac{8 \pm \sqrt{2}}{2}$$

$$\Rightarrow \quad 47.07 \quad \text{or} \quad 32.93$$

Taking the larger of these two outputs, we have

$$P_{s\pi} = 10 - 0.1(47.04) = 5.29$$

And

$$TR_{s\pi} = 10(47.04) - 0.1(47.04)^2 = 470.70 - 221 = 249.14$$

So that

$$\Pi_{s\pi} = -70 + 8(47.07) - 0.1(47.07)^2 = -70 + 376.56 - 221.56 = 85 \text{ (The minimum } \Pi \text{ required)}$$

LO3 Marris's Model of the Managerial Enterprise: Managerial Theory of the Firm

The goal of the firm in Marris's model is the maximization of the balanced rate of growth of the firm, i.e., the maximization of the rate of growth of demand for the products of the firm and the growth of its capital supply (however, why shareholders may prefer growth to profit has not been stated).

$$\text{Maximize } g = g_D = g_c$$

where,

g = balanced growth rate

g_D = growth of demand for the products (it maximizes the utility of managers)

g_c = growth of supply of capital. It is assumed that the shareholders/owners aim at the maximization of the rate of growth of corporate capital, which is taken as the measure of the size of firm.

Corporate capital is defined as:

Corporate capital = fixed assets + inventories + short term assets + cash reserves

In pursuing this maximum balanced growth rate, the firm has two constraints:

1. Managerial constraint: set by the available managerial team and its skill.
2. Financial constraint: set by the desire of managers to achieve maximum job security.

Rationalization of goal is that by jointly maximizing the rate of growth of demand and capital, the managers achieve maximization of their own utility as well as the utility of shareholders.

Utility Functions of Managers and Shareholders

Utility function of owners includes variables such as profit, market share and capital, while the utility function of managers includes variables such as salaries, power, and job security. Specifically, the utility function of shareholders (owners) and managers and can be written as:

$$U_o = f\text{(Profit, Capital, Output, Market Share, Public Esteem)}$$

$$U_m = f\text{(Salary, Power, Status, Job Security)}$$

Marris argues that the difference between goals of managers and owners is not very wide; both of them are strongly correlated with a single variable: *the size of firm*. Furthermore, Marris argues that the managers do not maximize the absolute size of the firm, but the rate of growth (= *change of size*) of the firm.

© ISTOCKPHOTO/THINKSTOCK

The utility function of owners can be further written as:

$$U_o = f(g_c)$$

According to Marris, utility of managers is a function of growth rate of capital and not of profits (as the traditional theory of firm believes). Moreover, Marris further states that g_c and profits are not necessarily positively related to each other. In fact, under some circumstances they may become competing goals.

The utility function of managers can be written as:

$$U_m = f(g_D, s)$$

where,

g_D = growth rate of demand (Marris assumes that variables such as status, salaries, and power are positively related to g_D)

s = job security.

Marris argues that there is a constraint to g_D set by the managerial constraint and there is a constraint to "s" set by the financial constraint.

Marris's model the goal of the firm in Marris's model is the maximization of the balanced rate of growth of the firm

Marris treats "s" as an exogenously determined constraint by assuming that there is a saturation level of job security. Above the saturation level, the marginal utility from an increase in "s" is zero, while below the saturation level the marginal utility from an increase in "s" is infinite.

$$\frac{dU}{ds} = 0 \text{ (above the saturation level)}$$

$$\frac{dU}{ds} = \infty \text{ (below the saturation level)}$$

The objective of the managers is to have job security. They attach a disutility to the risk of being dismissed. They dislike policies which endanger their position by increasing the risk of their dismissal by owners. Marris suggests that job security is attained by adopting a prudent financial policy. The risk of dismissal of managers arises if their policies lead the firm towards financial failure or render the firm attractive to take-over raiders (because the new owners may decide to replace old management).

The managers avoid the risk of dismissal by:

1. Non-involvement with risky investment, i.e., by becoming risk avoiders
2. By adopting a "prudent financial policy", i.e., by choosing optimal levels of the following three financial ratios:
   i. Leverage or debt ratio

$$= \frac{\text{Value of Debts}}{\text{Total Assets}} = \frac{D}{A} = a_1$$

   ii. Liquidity Ratio $= \frac{\text{Liquid Assets}}{\text{Total Assets}} = \frac{L}{A} = a_2$

   iii. Retention Ratio $= \frac{\text{Retained Profit}}{\text{Total Profit}} = \frac{\pi_R}{\pi} = a_3$

It is assumed that managers do not want excessive debt, as it increases the probability of bankruptcy. Further, appropriate liquidity policy is equally important. While too high a ratio makes the firm attractive for take-overs, too low a liquidity ratio increases the probability of bankruptcy. The managers also need to have an adequate policy on the retention ratio. Retained profits, according to Marris are the most important source of finance for the growth of capital of the firm. However, the firm is not free to keep as much as it wants as the shareholders have to be satisfied with the distributed profits. In addition, if the distributed profits are low, existing shareholders may try to replace the existing management. This would put the job security of managers at risk.

financial security constraint
this is exogenously determined, by the risk attitude of the top management. Being subjective, it varies from manager to manager

The three financial ratios are combined into single parameter a, called the **financial security constraint**. This is exogenously determined, by the risk attitude of the top management. Being subjective, it varies from manager to manager. According to Marris, a is a weighted average of the three ratios, the weights depend on the subjective decisions of managers. The job security function may thus be written as:

$$a = f(a_1, a_2, a_3)$$

where a is positively related to a_1 and a_3, and negatively to a_2. In other words, a increases if either the liquidity is reduced, or the debt ratio is raised by increasing external finance, or the proportion of retained profits is increased (i.e., by reducing the distributed profits). Marris assumes "s" and "a" to be negatively related, i.e., as a increases, the position of the firm becomes more vulnerable to bankruptcy and/or takeovers and the job security of managers is reduced. Thus, a high value of a implies that managers are risk takers, while a low value of a implies that managers are risk-avoiders. The financial security constraint sets a limit to the rate of growth of capital supply (g_c).

The Model: Equilibrium of the Firm

The firm is in equilibrium when the maximum balanced growth rate between growth rate of demand and the rate of growth of capital supply is attained, i.e.,

$$g_D = g_C = g^* \text{ maximum}$$

According to Marris, g_D and g_C can be expressed in terms of two variables:

d = diversification rate

m = average profit (π) margin.

It is assumed that the firm first determines its financial policy (a), and consequently it chooses d and m, such that balanced growth rate g is maximized, i.e., ($g = g^*$). Marris assumes that price is a given parameter rather than a policy variable. Marris also assumes that costs are given. Only advertisement expenditure (A) and research and development (R&D) expenditure is assumed to be under the control of the firm. Marris's model by assuming average cost pricing rule gets:

$$\bar{P} = \bar{C} + A + (R\&D) + m$$

i.e., $m = \bar{P} - \bar{C} - (A) - (R\&D)$

Given $\bar{P}$ and $\bar{C}$, m is negatively related with (A) and (R&D). Thus, m is used as a proxy for the policy variables (A) and (R&D).

Thus, there are three policy variables:

1. a, the financial security coefficient
2. d, the rate of diversification
3. m, the average profit margin

The next step is to determine g_D and g_C in term of a.

The Rate of Growth of the Demand: g_D

It is assumed that firms grow by diversification and the rate of growth of demand for the products of the firm depends on the diversification rate, "d" and the percentage of successful new products, k, i.e.,

$$g_D = f(d, k)$$

Diversification could be:

i. By introducing a new product, i.e., differentiated diversification. It creates new demand.

ii. By introducing a product which has close substitutes available, i.e., imitative diversification.

k depends on :

$$k = f\,(A, R\&D, d)$$

Since

$$m = f\,(A, R\&D)$$

we can write:

$$k = f\,(m, d)$$

Explanation for negative relationship between k and d: higher is d, i.e., if too many new products are introduced too fast, the proportion of failures increases. Thus, although the rate of growth of demand g_D is positively correlated with d, g_D increases at a decreasing rate as d increases.

In summary: $g_D = f(d, m)$

Exhibit 7

The Rate of Growth of Demand

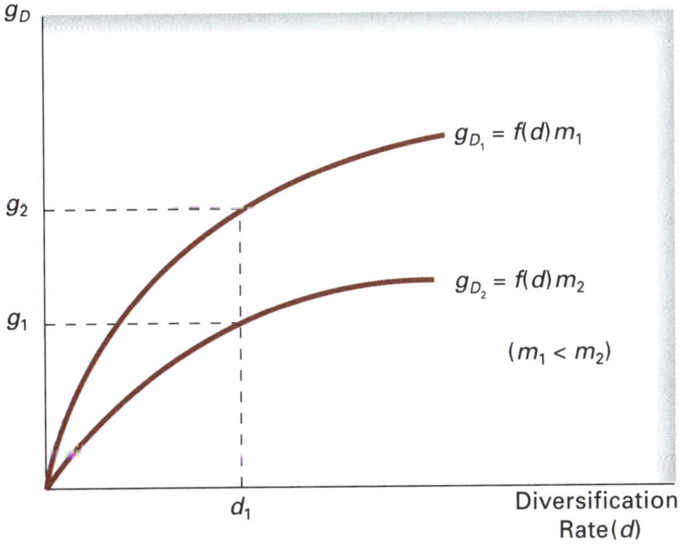

© ISTOCKPHOTO/THINKSTOCK

where $\dfrac{\partial g_D}{\partial d} > 0$ (but declining)

and $\dfrac{\partial g_D}{\partial m} < 0$

The g_D function is shown in Exhibit 7.

Along any curve, the average rate of profit is constant along any g_D curve. Also, as the profit margin increases, the g_D curve shifts down. Given d, lower is m, the larger is A and R&D and hence the larger the proportion of successful products and higher the growth of demand ($g_2 > g_1$).

The Rate of Growth of Supply of Capital: g_c

The rate of growth of corporate capital is financed from internal and external resources. The main source of the same is profits. Although profits are the main source of finance for growth, top management cannot retain as much profit as it would like; a satisfactory amount has to be distributed as dividends to the shareholders. Under Marris's assumptions, the rate of growth of capital supply is proportional to the level of profits. Since 'a' depends on retained profits, and retained profits effect the growth rate of capital g_c, we have,

$$g_c = a(\pi)$$

where, a = financial security coefficient
π = total profits

The next step is to express g_c in terms of policy variables d and m. The profits are a function of average rate of profit margin and efficiency of the firm, as reflected by the capital output (K/X) ratio. Thus,

$$\pi = f\left(m, \frac{K}{X}\right)$$

It is further assumed that the capital output ratio is a function of the diversification rate. Thus,

$$\frac{K}{X} = f(d)$$

Given K, the relation between X and d is up to a certain level of d positive, reaches a maximum, and then declines. Substituting,

$$\pi = f(m, d)$$

Further, substituting this value in $g_c = a(\pi)$ gives:

$$g_c = a[f(m, d)]$$

i.e., g_c depends on

i. financial policies of managers,
ii. average profit margin, and
iii. diversification rate.

As d keeps on increasing, eventually it will lead to fall in g_c. This is because:

A very high $d \Rightarrow$ hastening up of diversification process $\Rightarrow$ inefficient decisions $\Rightarrow$ fall in overall profit level $\Rightarrow$ low availability of internal finance $\Rightarrow$ lower g_c.

The relation between g_c and d, keeping a and m constant is given in Exhibit 8.

The complete form of Marris model may thus be summarized as:

$g_D = f(m, d)$: demand growth equation

$\pi = f(m, d)$: profit equation

$g_c = a\,[f(m, d)$: supply of capital equation

$a \le a^*$: a financial security constraint

$g_D = g_c$: condition for balanced growth equilibrium

equilibrium
the firm is in equilibrium when it reaches the highest point on the balanced growth curve (BGC)

Exhibit 8

The Rate of Growth of Capital Supply

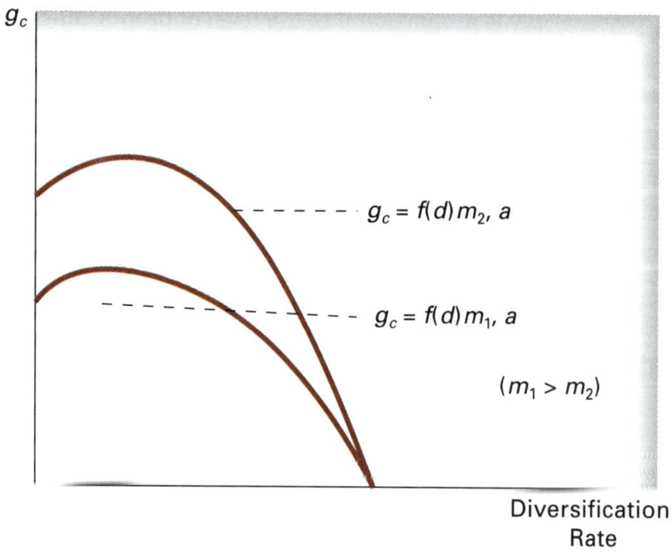

a is exogenously determined by risk attitude of managers, and

π is endogenously determined

m and d variables are policy instruments.

Equilibrium requires: $f(m, d) = a[f(m, d)]$

This gives us one equation in two unknown m and d (given a).

Equilibrium of the Firm

This model cannot be solved unless one of the variables "m" or "d" is determined by the managers. Once this is done, the equilibrium rate of growth can be determined.

The equilibrium of the firm is presented in Exhibit 9, formed by super-imposing Exhibits 7 and 8. Given their shapes, the g_D and g_c curves associated with a given profit rate intersect at some point. For example, the g_D and g_c curves corresponding to m_1 intersect at point A. Similarly, the g_D and g_c curves corresponding to m_2 intersect at point B, and so on. If we join all points of intersection of g_D and g_c curves corresponding to the same level of m, we form what Marris calls the balanced growth curve (BGC), given the financial constraint 'a'.

The firm is in **equilibrium** when it reaches the highest point on the balanced growth curve. In Exhibit 9, BGC corresponding to the financial constraint is *ABCD*. The balance growth rate g^* is defined by the highest point B of this BGC. In order to reach the equilibrium, the firm first decides its financial policy. Next it chooses a value of m or d. In the exhibit, BGC corresponding to the financial constraint is *ABCD*. The balanced growth rate (g^*) is defined as the highest point of this curve. This g^* is compatible with a unique pair of values of the policy variables, m^* and d^*.

LO4 Cyert and March's Behavioral Theory of a Firm

The behavioral theories of the firm started developing in the early 1950s. Few studies that contain some of the best scholarly writings that the research literature has to offer on the behavioral theory of the firm are Barnard's (1938) *The Functions of the Executive;* Simon's (1947) *Administrative Behavior;* March and Simon's (1958) *Organizations;* Cyert and March's (1963) *A Behavioral Theory of the Firm,* and Simon's (1982) *Models of Bounded Rationality: Behavioral*

Exhibit 9

Balanced Growth Curve

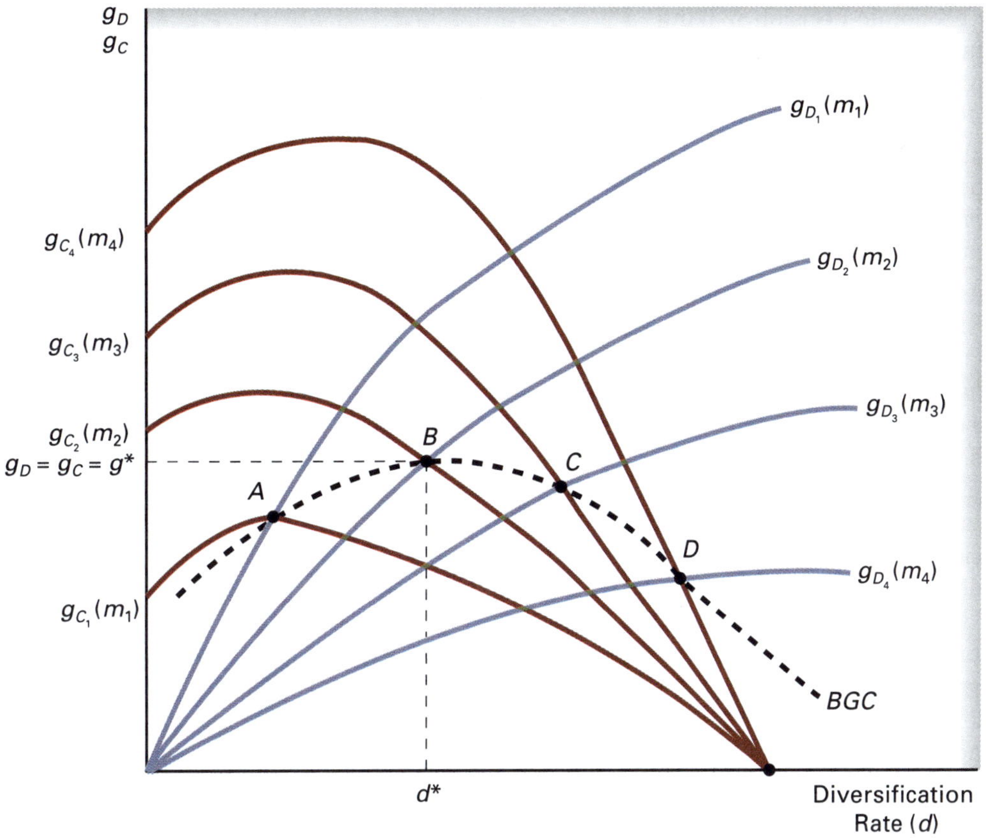

Economics and Business Organization. Simon's work titled *A Behavioral Model of Rational Choice* published in the Quarterly Journal of Economics (1955) is considered to be the seminal work in this area. Herbert Simon's work in the 1950s discussed behavior in situations of uncertainty, which argued that "people possess limited cognitive ability and so can exercise only bounded rationality when making decisions in complex, uncertain situations." Thus, individuals and groups tend to "satisfice", that is, attempt to attain realistic goals, rather than maximize a utility or profit function. This theory has subsequently been developed by Cyert and March. Cyert and March argued that the firm cannot be regarded as a monolith because different individuals and groups within it have their own aspirations and conflicting interests, and that the firm's behavior is the weighted outcome of these conflicts. Organizational mechanisms (such as "satisficing" and sequential decision-taking) exist to maintain conflict at levels that are not unacceptably detrimental. Compared to ideal state of productive efficiency, as per this theory, there is organizational slack (Leibenstein's X-inefficiency).

In this section, we briefly discuss the behavioral approach, as developed in particular by Richard Cyert and James G. March of the Carnegie School. Cyert and March (1963) emphasize the actual process of making business decisions and provide detailed observations of the ways in which organizations make these decisions. The behavioral theory of the firm, as developed by Cyert and March, *focuses on the decision making process of the large multi-product firm under uncertainty in an imperfect market*. It deals

© ISTOCKPHOTO/THINKSTOCK

with the large corporate managerial business in which ownership is divorced from management. The authors develop an empirically relevant, process-oriented general theory of economic decision making by a business firm. To build the behavioral theory of the firm, Cyert and March develop four major sub-theories concerning the following:

i. Organizational goals
ii. Organizational expectations/aspirations
iii. Organizational choice
iv. Organizational control

On *organizational goals* the theory considers how goals arise in an organization, how goals change over time, and how the organization attends to these goals. The theory views an organization as a coalition of stakeholders, with some of these stakeholders organized into sub-coalitions. In a business organization, the coalition members include managers, workers, stockholders, suppliers, customers, lawyers, tax collectors, regulatory agencies, and so on. The coalition members together decide on the goal and the goal-directed activity of the firm. These members have goals that often may conflict with each other and the challenge for the firm is to resolve these internal conflicts. Further, all resolutions of goals within the coalition are not made by money. Rather, many side payments are made to coalition members in the form of policy commitments. When goals are stated in the form of operational targets, it is possible to compare "aspirations" with "achievements." Periodic comparisons between the two help the coalition to revise goals and review its aspirations. Also, in general, the firm has multiple goals rather than a single goal. *Organizational expectations* assume that expectations of different member groups in an organization are generally dependent on hopes, wishes, past performance of the firm, and the internal bargaining needs of sub-units in the organization. Theory of *organizational choice* characterizes the process by which the alternatives available to the organization are ordered and selected. Organizational decisions depend on information estimates and expectations that ordinarily differ appreciably from reality. Further, organizations consider only a limited number of decision alternatives. Finally, organizations vary with respect to the amount of resources that such organizations devote to their organizational goals on the one hand and sub-organizational and individual goals on the other hand. The firm is considered to be an adaptively rational system in which the firm learns from experience. The theory of *organizational control* assumes that the firm has the following preventive measures:

1. Multiple, changing, acceptable-level goals that meet the demands (goals) of the coalition,
2. An approximate sequential consideration of alternatives that ensures that the first satisfactory alternative evoked is accepted, however, if failure occurs, search is intensified, and
3. Avoidance of uncertainty whereby the organization seeks to avoid uncertainty by following a policy of reacting to feedback rather than forecasting the environment.

As per the Cyert and March's model, the firm is conceived as a coalition of different groups which are connected with its activity in various ways: managers, workers, shareholders, customers, suppliers, bankers, tax inspectors, and so on. Each group has its own set of goals or demands. For example, workers want high wages, good pension schemes, etc. Managers want high salaries, power, and prestige. Shareholders want high profits, growing capital, and market size. The customers want low price and good quality, and so on. The goals of the firm are set ultimately by the top management. There are five main goals of the firm:

1. Production goal: It originates from the production department,
2. Inventory goal: It originates from the inventory department,
3. Sales goal: It originates from the sales department,
4. Share of the market goal: It originates from the sales department, and
5. Profit goal: It originates from the top management.

It may be noted that these goals change over time depending on the past history of the firm, as well as, on the conditions of the external environment, and on the changes of aspirations of groups within the organization.

The firm in behavioral theories seeks to satisfy, i.e., to attain a satisfactory level of overall performance; rather than to maximize profits, sales, or other magnitudes. The firm is a satisfying organization rather than a maximizing entrepreneur. The top management, responsible for the coordination of the activities of the various members of the firm, wishes to attain a satisfactory level of production, a satisfactory share of market, to earn a satisfactory level of profits, to acquire a satisfactory public image, and so on.

© ISTOCKPHOTO/THINKSTOCK

Means for Resolution of the Conflict

The most important means for the resolution of the conflict are primarily three. These are discussed below:

1. *Money Payments*: In the traditional theory, the entrepreneur resolves all demands by money payments, i.e., by paying to the factors their market prices. But in behavioral theory, payments of market prices to the owners of factors of production are not adequate for resolving the conflicting demands. Therefore, there are other means for the resolution of the conflicting demands.
2. *Side Payments*: For instance as given by *policy commitments*—for example, the top management in order to keep a good scientist in its research department, apart from paying him his salary (opportunity cost), must allocate certain funds for the development and conduct of the research plans (projects) of the scientist. These funds are money payments which do not go into the pocket of the scientist. They form a side payment for him, in the sense that they satisfy part of his demands which are associated with his research interests.
3. *Slack Payments*: Slack is defined as payments to the various groups of the coalition over and above those required for the efficient working of the firm. Slack may be earned by all groups of the coalition, e.g., workers may be paid higher wages, managers may be paid higher salaries or have other perquisites, shareholders may be paid higher dividends than the minimum required to satisfy their demands, customers may be given discounts which are not necessary to keep them tied to the firm, etc. In traditional economic theory, at least in equilibrium, such slack is often zero. However, in behavioral theory, slack is often positive and has an important role to play in resolving conflicts that may arise amongst coalition members. They also provide a cushion to absorb the shocks. They, thus, play a stabilizing and an adaptive role.

In managerial economics, only one type of slack is discussed, namely, the slack payments to mangers. The existence of slack has a stabilizing effect on the performance of the firm. It allows the firm to pursue its goal and have a steady performance in a changing environment, i.e., slack allows the firm to ignore to a large extent changes in its environment. In a period of bad business; the firm cuts the slack payments, thus, achieving a reduction in its cost, which makes it possible to the firm not to make other major downward readjustment in the aspiration levels. Similarly, in periods of flourishing business, slack payments increase, i.e., part of the realized profits is absorbed as a cost and hence profits appear as less than they would otherwise be, so that there is less room for an excessively optimistic upward adjustment of other aspiration levels. Thus, aspiration levels and the activity of the firm are more stable in a widely fluctuating environment, due to slack as a built in stabilizer.

Decision Making Process

Briefly, the decision-making process within the modern large corporations is made as follows (as outlined by Cohen and Cyert, 1965):

slack payments payments to the various groups of the coalition over and above those required for the efficient working of the firm

1. Firm forecasts the rival's reaction.

© ISTOCKPHOTO/THINKSTOCK

2. Firm forecasts the demand for its product.
3. The firm estimates its cost, including necessary slack payments.
4. The firm specifies its profit goal, based on revenue and cost calculations. The aspiration level of profits may be some average of past profits.
5. The actual performance is compared with the intended objectives. If achievement equals aspiration, the firm is satisfied; if not then firm starts a fresh decision-making process.
6. If profit goal is not attained, the firm re-examines its cost estimate, as the costs associated with slack expenses are under the direct control of the firm.
7. If new solution with downward cost adjustments leads to larger profits it is adopted.
8. If not, firm re-examines its demand estimates. It attempts to shift the demand by changing its sales strategy.
9. If new solution with revised costs and demand estimates attains the target profit, it is adopted.
10. If not then, firm readjusts downward its aspiration levels.

However, in actual practice, firms have multiple goals and not just a profit goal. These goals take the form of aspiration levels and the firm becomes a satisficer rather than a maximizer. These goals change over time depending on past achievements, aspirations, demands of groups, and expectations. The criterion of choice for goal setting is that where the selected alternative meets the demands (goals) of the coalition.

The Cyert and March theory is basically a short run theory. Despite the adaptive learning process, the firm does not seem to acquire the ability for long run planning.

Final Word

The firm is the micro-level decision making unit within an industry. Its decision making process is rather complex. Some economists believe that the decision making process is primarily driven by the motive of profit maximization. However, several others think alternatively. Quite a few hypotheses, such as the behavioral and managerial theories of a firm have been suggested as an alternative to the theory of profit maximization. Nevertheless, even the behavioral and managerial theories of a firm seem to supplement rather than substitute the traditional theory of profit maximization. Despite its limitations, the profit maximizing theory still remains fundamental and has a lot of applicability in real world business situations.

MULTIPLE CHOICE QUESTIONS

1. If $MR = MC$, then profits are maximized.
   a. True
   b. False
2. Why is the principal-agent problem less likely when getting a haircut than when getting a car repaired?
   a. Haircuts are less expensive than car repairs.
   b. There are no hidden actions when getting your hair cut.
   c. There are no hidden actions when getting your car repaired.
   d. Auto mechanics are less honest than hair stylists.
   e. There is no principal-agent relationship in car repair.
3. Which of the following will *not* reduce the likelihood of a principal-agent problem when getting your car repaired?
   a. asking to see the replaced parts
   b. staying to watch the repair being done
   c. gathering information on car repair
   d. not paying until after the repair job is finished
   e. persuading the mechanic you know a lot about cars
4. Copious Corp. is owned by 2 million stockholders who elect a board of directors that selects a management team responsible for hiring workers to serve customers by selling and repairing computer mice. Which of the following statements is true?
   a. In the principal-agent relationship between workers and customers, the customers are the agents.
   b. In the principal-agent relationship between workers and managers, the managers are the agents.
   c. In the principal-agent relationship between the stockholders and the board of directors, the stockholders are the agents.
   d. In the principal-agent relationship between the stockholders and the customers, the stockholders are the agents.
   e. In the principal-agent relationship between management and the board of directors, the managers are the agents.
5. A principal-agent problem arises when
   a. only less-qualified workers apply for a job
   b. a firm must find a proxy for unobservable qualities needed in employees
   c. potential employees have more information about their own productivity than do prospective employers
   d. a customer knows little about the service provided by a business
   e. a customer knows little about the service provided by a business and is, therefore, given poor service
6. If, as a firm increases its rate of output, total cost increases as well,
   a. profit cannot be maximized
   b. revenue cannot be maximized
   c. cost cannot be minimized
   d. marginal cost is increasing
   e. marginal cost is positive
7. Which point in the exhibit below indicates the quantity at which this firm will maximize profit?

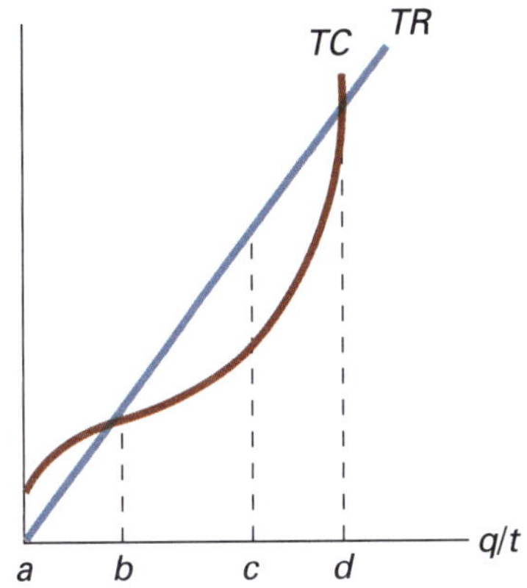

   a. point a
   b. point b
   c. point c
   d. point d
   e. either point b or point d
8.

Quantity of output	Total cost
0	$ 50
10	85
20	150
30	220
40	305
50	455

Consider the Exhibit above. If the market price is $8.50, what are the profit-maximizing output and profit?
   a. output = 40; profit = $35
   b. output = 40; profit = $0
   c. output = 0; profit = -$50

d. output and profit cannot be determined because marginal revenue cannot be calculated
e. output and profit cannot be determined because average variable cost cannot be calculated

9. Does Exhibit in Question 7 represent a long-run or a short-run situation?
a. long run because there is no fixed cost
b. short run because there is no equilibrium
c. long run because there is an equilibrium level of output
d. short run because there is fixed cost
e. long run because there is a normal profit

10. A sales maximizer maximizes total revenue at the quantity where marginal revenue equals zero.
a. True b. False

11. According to Cyert and March if the actual performance and achievements of a firm is much lower than expected aspirations and targets in that case
a. There will be a downward revision in the demands of various groups
b. There will be a negative revision in the demands of various groups
c. There will be upwards revision in the demands of various groups
d. There will be a normal revision in the demands of various groups

12. According to Cyert and March which of the following statements is incorrect?
a. There is need for harmonious and balanced blending of different objectives of an organization and multiple objectives of different groups
b. Making satisfactory levels of profit rather than maximum profits has become the slogan of the day.
c. The management has to accommodate as little as possible the demands of different groups with out sacrificing its own basic objective of making profits
d. Model highlights on satisfactory level of performance and achievements of its multiple objectives as maximization of different goals are not possible in a competitive world

13. Which of the following measure is adopted to over come conflicts of different groups and ensure smooth working of the organization by Cyert and March?
a. The management may follow the policy of sequential hearing of demand
b. Demands of each group may be seperated and separate attempts are made to fulfill them
c. The management may tackle the problem by decentralizing the decision making process
d. All the three methods

14. Which of the following will produce the maximum output?
a. A profit maximizer
b. A sales maximizer with a non operative profit constraint
c. A sales maximiser with an operative profit constraint
d. Cannot be determined without further information

15. What happens to the profit curve of a sales maximizer with the imposition of a per-unit tax?
a. Shifts downward to the left
b. Shifts downward to the right
c. Does not shift in the short run
d. Downward parallel shift

16. Which of the following is not an objective of the Marris model?
a. Maximizing growth of demand for products of the firm
b. Maximizing balanced growth rate of the firm
c. Maximizing growth rate of the profits of the firm
d. Maximizing growth of the supply of capital

17. According to the Marris's model of the managerial enterprise, which of the following is not a part of the financial security constraint?
a. Liquidity Ratio
b. Profitability Ratio
c. Leverage Ratio
d. Retention Ratio

18. According to which theory/model, sales revenue maximization is the most important goal of managers?
a. Baumol's theory
b. Marris Model
c. Willaimson's Model
d. Cyert & March Model

19. State True or False: "Marris model of managerial economics states that the firm's aim at balance rate of growth".
a. True b. False

20. Which of the following is not a principal-agent relationship?
    a. You hire a landscape specialist to plant trees in your front yard
    b. You hire a mechanic to fix your car
    c. You hire a carpenter to fix your kitchen cabinets
    d. You repair your own car
    e. You hire an electrician to fix your garbage disposal

Answers

1. b	2. b	3. d	4. e	5. e	6. e	7. c	8. a	9. d	10. a
11. a	12. c	13. d	14. b	15. a	16. c	17. b	18. a	19. a	20. d

Long Answer Questions

LO1 Discuss the traditional theory of profit maximization

1.1 Mathematically derive the necessary and sufficient conditions for profit maximization. Also illustrate the same using MR-MC approach.

LO2 Explain Baumol's theory of sales maximization: managerial theory of the firm

2.1 Illustrate and explain why a sales maximizer sells more than a profit maximizer? Under what circumstances, if any, will the sales maximizing output be the same as the profit maximizing output?

2.2 Do you agree with the view that the sales maximizer subject to profit constraint normally produces and advertises more that a profit maximizer? Why is it so?

2.3 Graphically illustrate that the output produced by a sales maximizer subject to profit constraint lies between the output produced by the profit maximizer and the output produced by the sales maximizer. Why is it so?

2.4 Explain Baumol's sales maximization model of firm. How is it different from the profit maximization model?

2.5 A sales maximizer subject to profit constraint changes his equilibrium price and output due to imposition of a lump sum tax. What is his level of profit in the changed scenario?

LO3 Explain Marris's model of the managerial enterprise: managerial theory of the firm

3.1 The Marris model is worth considering for the following reasons:

i. It is a model which tries to work out the implications of managerial objectives and contrast these with the implications of ownership objectives.

ii. The simplifying assumption of a steady-state growth path allows Marris to formulate a long-run equilibrium growth model in which the firm's rate of demand-side growth must balance its rate of supply-side growth, and in which factors can be identified that influence both sides.

In the light of the above statements, comment on Marris's Growth Model.

3.2 State and explain the limits to the growth of a firm.

3.3 How does the demand for a firm's product get affected by diversification over time?

3.4 In the context of the theory of the firm, compare and contrast Marris's model with that of Baumol.

LO4 Explain Cyert and March's behavioral theory of a firm

4.1 According to the Cyert and March model, the firm is a satisficing organisation rather than a maximising entrepreneur. Elucidate. Which is the most important means for the resolution of the conflict amongst the aspiration levels of the various groups in an organisation? Are there any examples of the applicability of Cyert and March in organization behavior/decision-making in current business scenario?

4.2 *"The existence of slack has a stabilizing effect on the performance of the firm. It allows the firm to pursue its goals and have a steady performance in a changing environment"*.
Analyse the above statement in the light of the behavioural model of Cyert and March.

Miscellaneous Questions

1. Mention some of the alternate theories of the firm.
2. Authors usually receive a fixed percentage of total revenue generated from sales of their books. It is the publisher who bears all the production costs and chooses the output level. Let the retail price of a book be fixed at \$40, the author receives \$10 per copy, while the publishing company receives the rest. The company is interested in maximizing its own profits. Do you think this model can create any friction between the author and the publisher? Does the selected output maximize the joint profits (for both the author and company) from the book?

Chapter in Review

KEY TERMS

traditional economic theory assumes that the aim of the firm is to maximize profits in the short run by equating marginal revenue with marginal cost

managerial and behavioral theory have been developed as an alternative to the traditional theory that assumes profit maximization to be the objective function of owners (who also manage the enterprise)

managerial theory the firm is conceived as a coalition (of managers, workers, stockholders, customers, suppliers, tax collectors) whose members have conflicting goals that must be reconciled if the firm has to survive. The most important member of the coalition is the top management.

behavioral theory predict the actions of firms by studying the behavior of various groups of people within the firm and their interactions under conditions of potentially conflicting interests. In other words, behavioral theories are based on observations of how firms actually behave

sales maximization refers to maximization of total revenue of sales

sales maximizer subject to profit constraint in response to an increase in corporate profit tax (increase in fixed costs) the producer is induced to increase its price and reduce the quantities supplied

Marris's model the goal of the firm in Marris's model is the maximization of the balanced rate of growth of the firm

financial security constraint this is exogenously determined, by the risk attitude of the top management. Being subjective, it varies from manager to manager

equilibrium in Marris Model the firm is in equilibrium when it reaches the highest point on the balanced growth curve (BGC)

slack payments payments to the various groups of the coalition over and above those required for the efficient working of the firm

LO1 **Discuss the traditional theory of profit maximization.** First order condition for profit maximization is given by:

$$\frac{\partial \pi}{\partial q} = \frac{\partial TR}{\partial q} - \frac{\partial TC}{\partial q} = 0$$

$$\Rightarrow \quad \frac{\partial TR}{\partial q} = \frac{\partial TC}{\partial q}$$

$$\Rightarrow \quad MR = MC$$

This is the necessary condition for profit maximization.

Second order condition for profit maximization is given by:

$$\frac{\partial^2 \pi}{\partial q^2} = \frac{\partial^2 TR}{\partial q^2} - \frac{\partial^2 TC}{\partial q^2} < 0$$

$$= \frac{\partial MR}{\partial q} - \frac{\partial MC}{\partial q} < 0$$

Slope of MR < slope of MC

Profit Maximizing Firm: TR-TC and MR-MC Approach

Maximization of the gap between *TR* and *TC* yields the equilibrium condition *MR = MC, subject to MC cutting MR from below*. The point at which (i) *MR* equals *MC* and (ii) *MC* cuts *MR* from below is also the point where the gap between *TR* and *TC* is maximized. At this output level, the slope of *TR* (representing *MR*) equals the slope of *TC* (representing *MC*). Hence, the two slopes are parallel to each other.

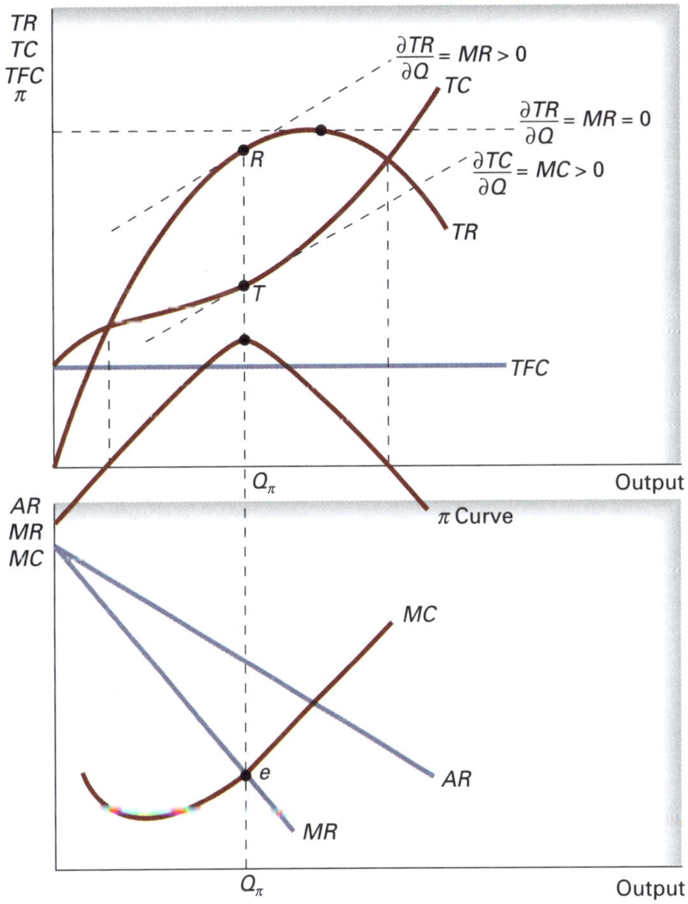

CHAPTER EQUATIONS

Marginal benefit = Marginal cost

$$TR = q \times p$$

$$AR = TR/q$$

Economic Profit or Loss = TR − TC

Market price = Marginal revenue = Average revenue

Diagrammatically, this implies that *MC* must cut *MR* from below. This is the sufficient condition for profit maximization.

Thus, there are two ways of interpreting a producers profit maximizing equilibrium.

1. The *TR-TC* Approach: This seeks to maximize the gap between *TR* and *TC*, or
2. The *MR-MC* Approach: This seeks to equate *MR* to *MC*, provided the sufficient condition is met.

LO2 Explain Baumol's theory of sales maximization: managerial theory of the firm. The profit and sales maximizing outputs are, respectively, $OQ\pi$ and OQ_s. Now, if for example, the minimum required profit level is *OG*, then the sales maximizing output OQ_s will provide plenty of profit, and that is the amount it will pay the sales maximizer to produce. But if the producer's minimum required profit level is *OR*, then output OQ_s yields insufficient profit. Thus, the firm's output level will have to be reduced to level $OQ_s\pi$, which is just compatible with its profit constraint.

To be noted is the fact that a profit maximizer generally produces an output lower than either a pure sales maximizer or a constrained sales maximizer. This is because a profit maximizer equates *MR* to *MC*. Since *MC* is generally positive, a profit maximizer stops producing where *MR* is still positive. On the other hand, a pure sales maximizer stops where *MR* equals zero. Since *MR* is a downward sloping curve, the point at which *MR* equals zero lies to the right of the point where *MR* is still positive. This implies that a sales maximizer generally produces more than a profit maximizer.

Optimal Equilibrium Outputs Under Alternate Objectives

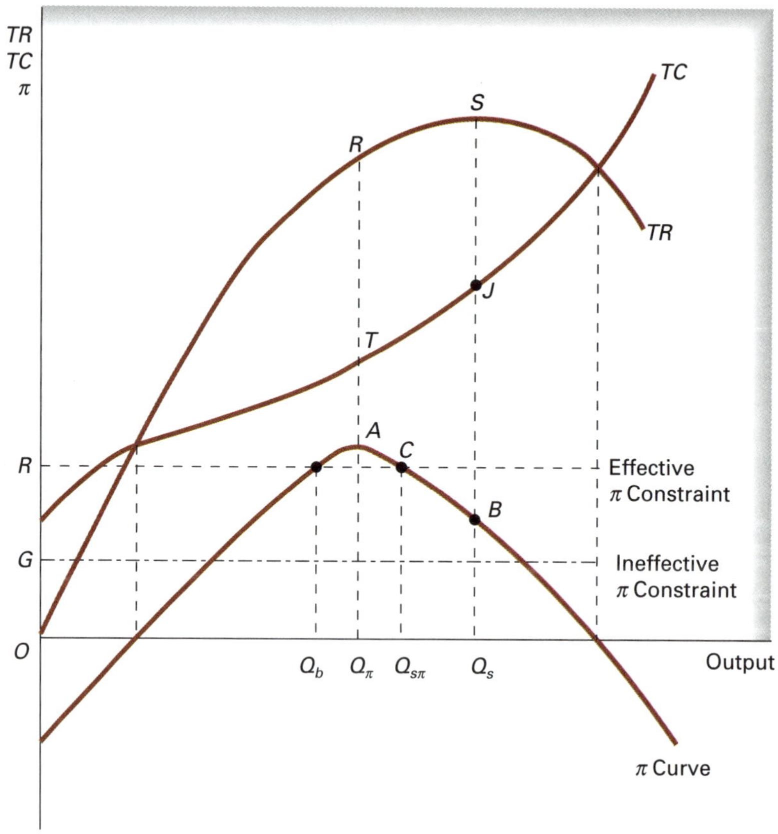

LO3 Explain Marris's model of the managerial enterprise: managerial theory of the firm. The goal of the firm in Marris's model is the maximization of the balanced rate of growth of the firm, i.e., the maximization of the rate of growth of demand for the products of the firm and the growth of its capital supply.

Balanced Growth Curve

The firm is in equilibrium when it reaches the highest point on the balanced growth curve (*BGC*). *BGC* corresponding to the financial constraint is *ABCD*. The balance growth rate g^* is defined by the highest point *B* of this *BGC*. In order to reach the equilibrium, the firm first decides its financial policy. Next it chooses a value of *m* or *d*. In the exhibit, *BGC* corresponding to the financial constraint is *ABCD*. The balanced growth rate (g^*) is defined as the highest point of this curve. This g^* is compatible with a unique pair of values of the policy variables, m^* and d^*.

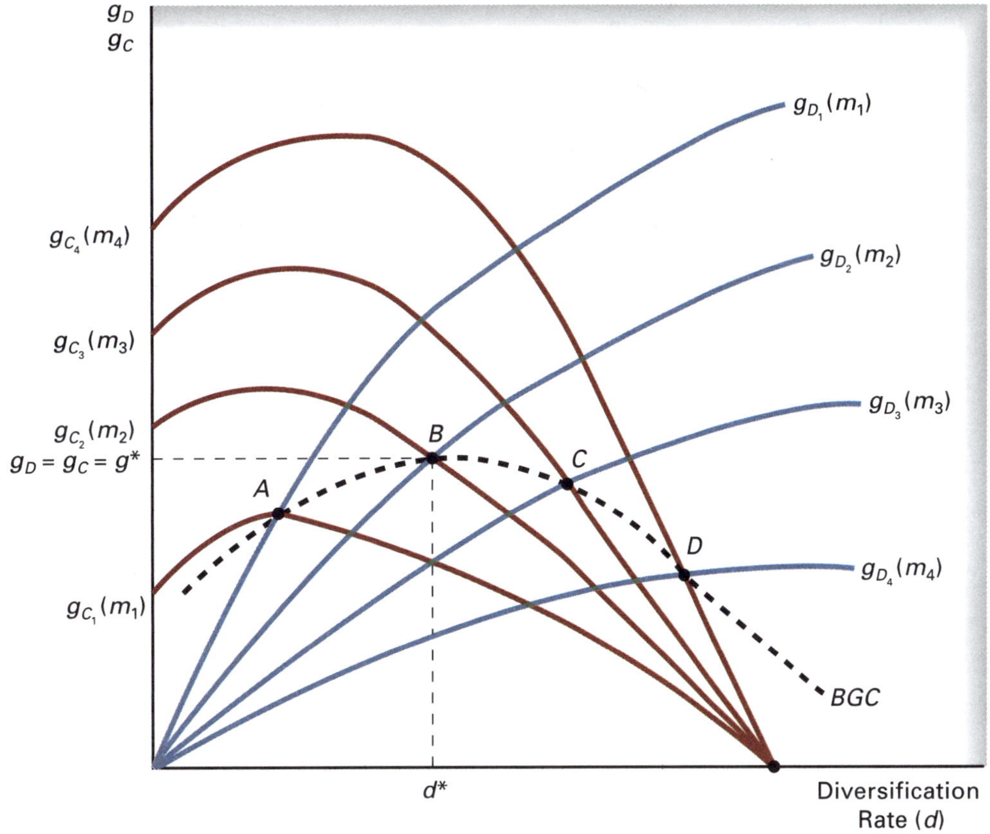

LO4 **Explain Cyert and March's behavioral theory of a firm.** Slack is defined as payments to the various groups of the coalition over and above those required for the efficient working of the firm. Slack may be earned by all groups of the coalition, e.g., workers may be paid higher wages, managers may be paid higher salaries or have other perquisites, shareholders may be paid higher dividends than the minimum required to satisfy their demands, customers may be given discounts which are not necessary to keep them tied to the firm, etc. In traditional economic theory, at least in equilibrium, such slack is often zero. However, in behavioral theory, slack is often positive and has an important role to play in resolving conflicts that may arise amongst coalition members. They also provide a cushion to absorb the shocks. They, thus, play a stabilizing and an adaptive role.

CHAPTER

9

Perfect Competition

Learning Outcomes

LO 1 Define a perfectly competitive market and explain its effect on demand LO 2 Explain how firms maximize profit in the short run LO 3 Identify ways firms minimize short-run losses LO 4 Explain how firms manage short-run supply LO 5 Describe how taking the long-run view affects economic factors LO 6 Describe how different cost structures influence an industry's long-run supply curve LO 7 Identify how concepts of efficiency are used to judge market performance

© SVEN HOPPE/ISTOCKPHOTO.COM

"What's so perfect about perfect competition?"

What do wheat and Google stock have in common? Why might a firm continue to operate even though it's losing money? Why do many firms fail to earn an economic profit? How can it be said that the more competitive the industry, the less individual firms compete with each other? What's the difference between making stuff right and making the right stuff? And what's so perfect about perfect competition? To answer these and other questions, we examine our first market structure—perfect competition.

The previous chapter developed cost curves for an individual firm in the short run and in the long run. In light of these costs, how much should a firm produce and what price should it charge? To discover the firm's profit-maximizing output and price, we revisit an old friend—demand. Demand and supply, together, guide the firm to maximum economic profit. In the next few chapters, we examine how firms respond to their economic environments in deciding what to supply, in what quantities, and at what price. We continue to assume that firms try to maximize profit.

What do you think?

The increasing demand for alternative fuel will create perfect competition among farmers.

Strongly Disagree						Strongly Agree
1	2	3	4	5	6	7

LO1 An Introduction to Perfect Competition

Market structure describes the important features of a market, such as the number of suppliers (are there many or few?), the product's degree of uniformity (do firms in the market supply identical products, or are there differences across firms?), the ease of entry into the market (can new firms enter easily or is entry blocked?), and the forms of competition among firms (do firms compete based only on price, or do they also compete through advertising and product differences?). Incidentally, the word *compete* derives from Latin words *cum,* which means "with," and *petere,* which means "to strive." A firm that competes strives with other firms to earn a profit by satisfying consumer wants. The various features will become clearer as we examine each market structure in the next few chapters. *A firm's decisions about how much to produce or what price to charge depend on the structure of the market.*

Topics discussed in Chapter 9 include:

- Market structure
- Price takers
- Marginal revenue
- Golden rule of profit maximization
- Loss minimization
- Short-run supply curve
- Long-run supply curve
- Competition and efficiency
- Producer surplus
- Gains from exchange

Before we get started, a few words about terminology. An *industry* consists of all firms that supply output to a particular *market,* such as the auto market, the shoe market, or the wheat market. The terms *industry* and *market* are used interchangeably throughout this chapter.

market structure important features of a market, such as the number of firms, product uniformity across firms, firms' ease of entry and exit, and forms of competition

Perfectly Competitive Market Structure

We begin with **perfect competition**, in some ways the most basic of market structures. A *perfectly competitive* market is characterized by (1) many buyers and sellers—so many that each buys or sells only a tiny fraction of the total amount in the market; (2) firms sell a **commodity**, which is a standardized product, such as a bushel of wheat, an ounce of gold, or a share of Google stock; such a product does not differ across suppliers; (3) buyers and sellers are fully informed about the price and availability of all resources and products; and (4) firms and resources are freely mobile—that is, over time they can easily enter or leave the industry without facing obstacles like patents, licenses, and high capital costs.

If these conditions exist in a market, an individual buyer or seller has no control over the price. Price is determined by market demand and supply. Once the market establishes the price, any individual firm is free to supply whatever quantity maximizes profit. *A perfectly competitive firm is so small relative to the market that the firm's supply decision does not affect the market price.* Examples of perfectly competitive markets include those for most agricultural products, such as wheat, corn, and livestock; markets for basic commodities, such as gold, silver, and copper; markets for widely traded stock, such as Google, ExxonMobil, and General Electric; and markets for foreign exchange, such as yen, euros, and pesos. Again, there are so many buyers and sellers that the actions of any one cannot influence the market price. For example, about 75,000 farmers in the United States raise hogs, and tens of millions of U.S. households buy pork products. The model of perfect competition allows us to make a number of predictions that hold up pretty well when compared to the real world. Perfect competition is also an important benchmark for evaluating the efficiency of other types of markets. Let's look at demand under perfect competition.

© ISTOCKPHOTO/THINKSTOCK

Demand Under Perfect Competition

Suppose the market in question is the world market for wheat and the firm in question is a wheat farm. In the world market for wheat, there are hundreds of thousands of farms, so any one supplies only a tiny fraction of market output. For example, the thousands of wheat farmers in Kansas together produce less than 3 percent of the world's supply of wheat. In Exhibit 1, the market price of wheat of $5 per bushel is determined in panel (a) by the intersection of the market demand curve D and the market supply curve S. Once the market determines the price, any farmer can sell all he or she wants to at that market price.

Each farm is so small relative to the market that each has no impact on the market price. Because all farmers produce an identical product—bushels of wheat, in this case—anyone who charges more than the market price sells no wheat. For example, a farmer charging $5.05 per bushel would find no

Exhibit 1

Market Equilibrium and a Firm's Demand Curve in Perfect Competition

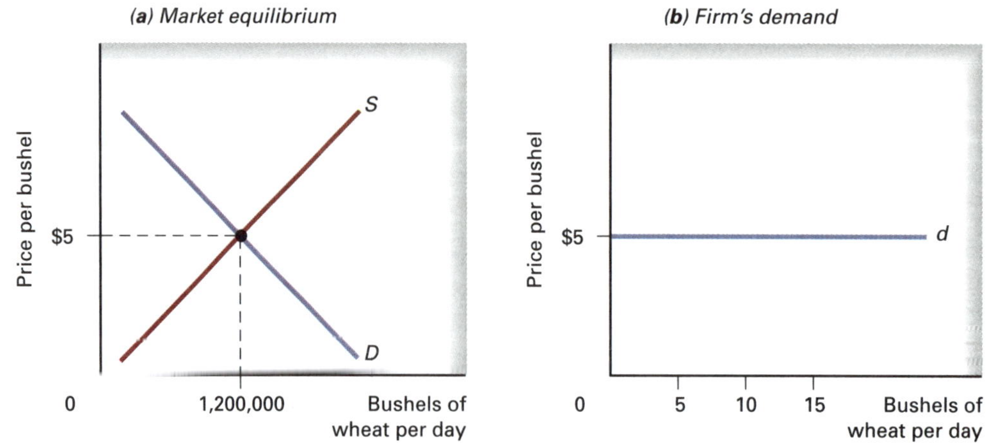

perfect competition
a market structure with many fully informed buyers and sellers of a standardized product and no obstacles to entry or exit of firms in the long run

commodity
a standardized product, a product that does not differ across producers, such as bushels of wheat or an ounce of gold

buyers. Of course, any farmer is free to charge less than the market price, but why do that when all wheat can be sold at the market price? Farmers aren't stupid (if they are, they don't last long). *The demand curve facing an individual farmer is, therefore, a horizontal line drawn at the market price.* In our example, the demand curve facing an individual farmer, identified as *d* in panel (b), is drawn at the market price of $5 per bushel. Thus, each farmer faces a horizontal, or a *perfectly elastic*, demand curve for wheat. A perfectly competitive firm is called a **price taker** because that firm must "take," or accept, the market price—as in "take it or leave it."

It has been said, "In perfect competition there is no competition." Ironically, two neighboring wheat farmers in perfect competition are not really rivals. They both can sell all they want at the market price. The amount one sells has no effect on the market price or amount the other can sell.

Exhibit 2

Short-Run Cost and Revenue for a Perfectly Competitive Firm

(1) Bushels of Wheat per Day (*q*)	(2) Marginal Revenue (Price) (*p*)	(3) Total Revenue ($TR = q \times p$)	(4) Total Cost (*TC*)	(5) Marginal Cost ($MC = \Delta TC/\Delta q$)	(6) Average Total Cost ($ATC = TC/q$)	(7) Economic Profit or Loss = $TR - TC$
0	—	$ 0	$15.00	—	—	−$15.00
1	$5	5	19.75	$4.75	$19.75	−14.75
2	5	10	23.50	3.75	11.75	−13.50
3	5	15	26.50	3.00	8.83	−11.50
4	5	20	29.00	2.50	7.25	−9.00
5	5	25	31.00	2.00	6.20	−6.00
6	5	30	32.50	1.50	5.42	−2.50
7	5	35	33.75	1.25	4.82	1.25
8	5	40	35.25	1.50	4.41	4.75
9	5	45	37.25	2.00	4.14	7.75
10	5	50	40.00	2.75	4.00	10.00
11	5	55	43.25	3.25	3.93	11.75
12	**5**	**60**	**48.00**	**4.75**	**4.00**	**12.00**
13	5	65	54.50	6.50	4.19	10.50
14	5	70	64.00	9.50	4.57	6.00
15	5	75	77.50	13.50	5.17	−2.50
16	5	80	96.00	18.50	6.00	−16.00

LO2 Short-Run Profit Maximization

Each firm tries to maximize economic profit. Firms that ignore this strategy don't survive for long. Economic profit equals total revenue minus total cost, including both explicit and implicit costs. Implicit cost, remember, is the opportunity cost of resources owned by the firm and includes a normal profit. Economic profit is any profit above normal profit. How do firms maximize profit? You have already learned that the perfectly competitive firm has no control over price. What the firm does control is its rate of output—the quantity. The question each wheat farmer asks is this: *How much should I produce to earn the most profit?*

Total Revenue Minus Total Cost

The firm maximizes economic profit by finding the quantity at which total revenue exceeds total cost by the greatest amount. The firm's total revenue is simply its output times the price. Column (1) in Exhibit 2 shows the farmer's output possibilities measured in bushels of wheat per day. Column (2) shows the market price of $5 per bushel, a price that does not vary with the the farmer's output. Column (3) shows the farmer's total revenue, which is output times price, or column (1) times column (2). And column (4) shows the farmer's total cost of supplying each quantity shown. Total cost already includes a normal profit, so total cost includes all opportunity costs. Although the table does not distinguish between fixed and variable costs, fixed cost must equal $15 per day, because total cost is $15 when output is zero. The presence of fixed cost tells us that at least one resource is fixed, so the farm must be operating in the short run.

At each output rate, total revenue in column (3) minus total cost in column (4) yields the farmer's economic profit or economic loss in column (7). As you can see, total revenue exceeds total cost at rates of output between 7 and 14 bushels, so the farm earns an *economic profit* at those output rates. Economic profit is maximized at $12 per day when the farm produces 12 bushels of wheat per day (the $12 and 12 bushels combination here is just a coincidence).

price taker
a firm that faces a given market price and whose quantity supplied has no effect on that price; a perfectly competitive firm that decides to produce must accept, or "take," the market price

These results are graphed in panel (a) in Exhibit 3, which shows the total revenue and total cost curves. As output increases by 1 bushel, total revenue increases by $5, so the farm's total revenue curve is a straight line emanating from the origin, with a slope of 5. The short-run total cost curve has the backward S shape introduced in the previous chapter, showing increasing and then diminishing marginal returns from the variable resource. Total cost always increases as more output is produced.

Subtracting total cost from total revenue is one way to find the profit-maximizing output. For output less than 7 bushels and greater than 14 bushels, total cost exceeds total revenue. The economic loss is measured by the vertical distance between the two curves. Between 7 and 14 bushels per day, total revenue exceeds total cost. The economic profit, again, is measured by the distance between the two curves. *Profit is maximized at the rate of output where total revenue exceeds total cost by the greatest amount.* Profit is greatest when 12 bushels are produced per day.

Exhibit 3

Short-Run Profit Maximization

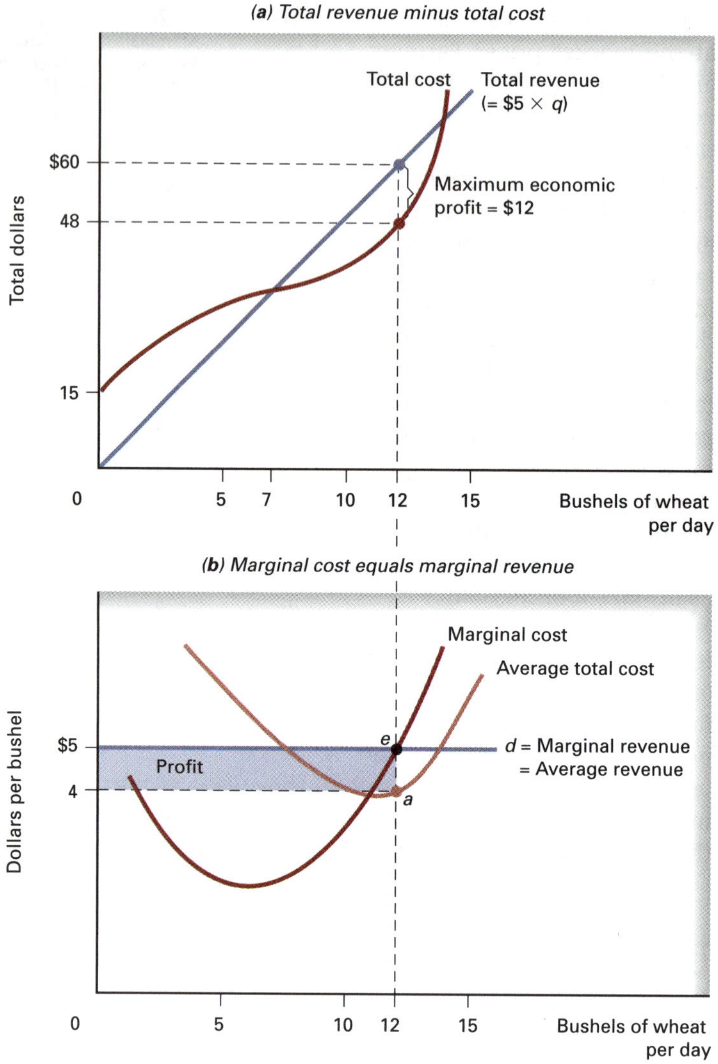

Marginal Revenue Equals Marginal Cost

Another way to find the profit-maximizing rate of output is to focus on marginal revenue and marginal cost. **Marginal revenue**, or **MR**, is the change in total revenue from selling another unit of output. In perfect competition, each firm is a price taker, so selling one more unit increases total revenue by the market price. Thus, *in perfect competition, marginal revenue is the market price*—in this example, $5. Column (2) of Exhibit 2 presents the farm's marginal revenue for each bushel of wheat.

marginal revenue (MR)
the firm's change in total revenue from selling an additional unit; a perfectly competitive firm's marginal revenue is also the market price

golden rule of profit maximization
to maximize profit or minimize loss, a firm should produce the quantity at which marginal revenue equals marginal cost; this rule holds for all market structures

In the previous chapter, you learned that *marginal cost* is the change in total cost from producing another unit of output. Column (5) of Exhibit 2 shows the farm's marginal cost for each bushel of wheat. Marginal cost first declines, reflecting increasing marginal returns in the short run as more of the variable resource is employed. Marginal cost then increases, reflecting diminishing marginal returns from the variable resource.

The firm increases production as long as each additional unit adds more to total revenue than to total cost—that is, as long as marginal revenue exceeds marginal cost. Comparing columns (2) and (5) in Exhibit 2, we see that marginal revenue exceeds marginal cost for each of the first 12 bushels of wheat. The marginal cost of bushel 13, however, is $6.50, compared with its marginal revenue of $5. Therefore, producing bushel 13 would reduce economic profit by $1.50. The farmer, as a profit maximizer, limits output to 12 bushels per day. More generally, a firm expands output as long as marginal revenue exceeds marginal cost and stops expanding before marginal cost exceeds marginal revenue. A shorthand expression for this approach is the **golden rule of profit maximization**, which says that a profit-maximizing firm produces where *marginal revenue equals marginal cost, provided marginal cost cuts marginal revenue from below.*

© F. SCHUSSLER/PHOTOLINK/PHOTODISC/GETTY IMAGES

Economic Profit in the Short Run

Per-unit revenue and cost data from Exhibit 2 are graphed in panel (b) in Exhibit 3. Because marginal revenue in perfect competition equals the market price, the marginal revenue curve is a horizontal line at the market price of $5, which is also the perfectly competitive firm's demand curve. At any quantity measured along the demand curve, marginal revenue is the price. Because the perfectly competitive firm can sell any amount for the same price per unit, marginal revenue is also **average revenue**, or *AR*. Average revenue equals total revenue divided by quantity, or $AR = TR/q$. Regardless of the output rate, therefore, the following equality holds along a perfectly competitive firm's demand curve:

Market price = Marginal revenue = Average revenue

The marginal cost curve intersects the marginal revenue curve at point *e*, where output is about 12 bushels per day. At lower rates of output, marginal revenue exceeds marginal cost, so the farm could increase profit by expanding output. At higher rates of output, marginal cost exceeds marginal revenue, so the farm could increase profit by reducing output. Profit itself appears as the shaded rectangle. The height of that rectangle, *ae*, equals the price (or average revenue) of $5 minus the average total cost of $4. Price minus average total cost yields an average profit of $1 per bushel. Profit per day, $12, equals the average profit per bushel, $1 (denoted by *ae*), times the 12 bushels produced.

Note that with the total cost and total revenue curves, we measure economic profit by the vertical *distance* between the two curves, as shown in panel (a) in Exhibit 3. But with the per-unit curves of panel (b) in Exhibit 3, we measure economic profit by an *area*—that is, by multiplying the average profit of $1 per bushel times the 12 bushels sold.

LO3 Minimizing Short-Run Losses

A firm in perfect competition has no control over the market price. Sometimes that price may be so low that a firm loses money no matter how much it produces. Such a firm can either continue to produce at a loss or temporarily shut down. But even if the firm shuts down, it cannot, *in the short run,* go out of business or produce something else. The short run is by definition a period too short to allow existing firms to leave the industry. In a sense, firms are stuck in their industry in the short run.

Fixed Cost and Minimizing Losses

When facing a loss, should a firm temporarily shut down? Intuition suggests the firm should. But keep in mind that the firm faces two types of cost in the short run: fixed cost, such as property taxes and fire insurance, which must be paid even if the firm produces nothing, and variable cost, such as labor, which depends on the amount produced. A firm that shuts down in the short run must still pay fixed cost. But, by producing, a firm's revenue may cover variable cost and a portion of fixed cost. A *firm produces rather than shuts down if total revenue exceeds the variable cost of production*. After all, if total revenue exceeds variable cost, that excess covers at least a portion of fixed cost.

Let's look at the same cost data presented in Exhibit 2, but now suppose the market price of wheat is $3 a bushel, not $5. This new situation is presented in Exhibit 4. Because of the lower price, total cost in column (4) exceeds total revenue in column (3) at all output rates. Each quantity thus yields a loss, as indicated by column (8). If the firm produces nothing, it loses the fixed cost of $15 per day. But, by producing anywhere from 6 and 12 bushels, the firm can cut that loss. From column (8), you can see that the loss is minimized at $10 per day where 10 bushels are produced. Compared to shutting down, producing 10 bushels adds $5 more to total revenue than to total cost. That $5 pays some of the firm's fixed cost.

Panel (a) of Exhibit 5 on page 115 presents the firm's total cost and total revenue

average revenue total revenue divided by quantity, or $AR = TR/q$; in all market structures, average revenue equals the market price

Exhibit 4

Minimizing Short-Run Losses

(1) Bushels of Wheat per Day (q)	(2) Marginal Revenue (Price) (p)	(3) Total Revenue ($TR = q \times p$)	(4) Total Cost (TC)	(5) Marginal Cost ($MC = \Delta TC/\Delta q$)	(6) Average Total Cost ($ATC = TC/q$)	(7) Average Variable Cost ($AVC = VC/q$)	(8) Economic Profit or Loss = $TR - TC$
0	—	$ 0	$15.00	—	—	—	−$15.00
1	$3	3	19.75	$4.75	$19.75	$4.75	−16.75
2	3	6	23.50	3.75	11.75	4.25	−17.50
3	3	9	26.50	3.00	8.83	3.83	−17.50
4	3	12	29.00	2.50	7.25	3.50	−17.00
5	3	15	31.00	2.00	6.20	3.20	−16.00
6	3	18	32.50	1.50	5.42	2.92	−14.50
7	3	21	33.75	1.25	4.82	2.68	−12.75
8	3	24	35.25	1.50	4.41	2.53	−11.25
9	3	27	37.25	2.00	4.14	2.47	−10.25
10	**3**	**30**	**40.00**	**2.75**	**4.00**	**2.50**	**−10.00**
11	3	33	43.25	3.25	3.93	2.57	−10.25
12	3	36	48.00	4.75	4.00	2.75	−12.00
13	3	39	54.50	6.50	4.19	3.04	−15.50
14	3	42	64.00	9.50	4.57	3.50	−22.00
15	3	45	77.50	13.50	5.17	4.17	−32.50
16	3	48	96.00	18.50	6.00	5.06	−48.00

curves for data in Exhibit 4. The total cost curve remains as in Exhibit 3. Because the price is $3, the total revenue curve now has a slope of 3, so it's flatter than at a price of $5. The total revenue curve now lies below the total cost curve for all output rates. The vertical distance between the two curves measures the loss at each output rate. If the farmer produces nothing, the loss is the fixed cost of $15 per day. The vertical distance between the two curves is minimized at 10 bushels, where the loss is $10 per day.

Marginal Revenue Equals Marginal Cost

We get the same result using marginal analysis. The per-unit data from Exhibit 4 are graphed in panel (b) of Exhibit 5. First we find the rate of output where marginal revenue equals marginal cost. Marginal revenue equals marginal cost at an output of 10 bushels per day. At that output, the market price of $3 exceeds the average variable cost of $2.50. Because price exceeds average variable cost, total revenue covers variable cost plus a portion of fixed cost. Specifically, $2.50 of the price pays the average variable cost, and the remaining $0.50 helps pay some of average fixed cost (average fixed cost equals average total cost of $4.00 minus average variable cost of $2.50). This still leaves a loss of $1 per bushel, which when multiplied by 10 bushels yields an economic loss of $10 per day, identified in panel (b) by the pink-shaded rectangle. *The bottom line is that the firm produces rather than shuts down if there is some rate of output where the price at least covers average variable cost.* (Why is the farmer in the short run better off operating at a loss rather than shutting down?)

Shutting Down in the Short Run

If total revenue exceeds variable costs, the farmer produces in the short run. You may have read or heard of firms reporting a loss; most continue to operate. In fact, many new firms lose money during the first few years of operations. Still, they hang on because they hope to be profitable eventually. But *if the average variable cost exceeds the price at all rates of output, the firm shuts down.* After all, why produce if doing so only increases the loss? For example, a wheat price of $2 would fall below the average variable cost at all rates of output. Faced with such a low price, a farmer would shut down and lose just fixed cost, rather than produce and lose both fixed cost plus some variable cost.

Exhibit 5

Short-Run Loss Minimization

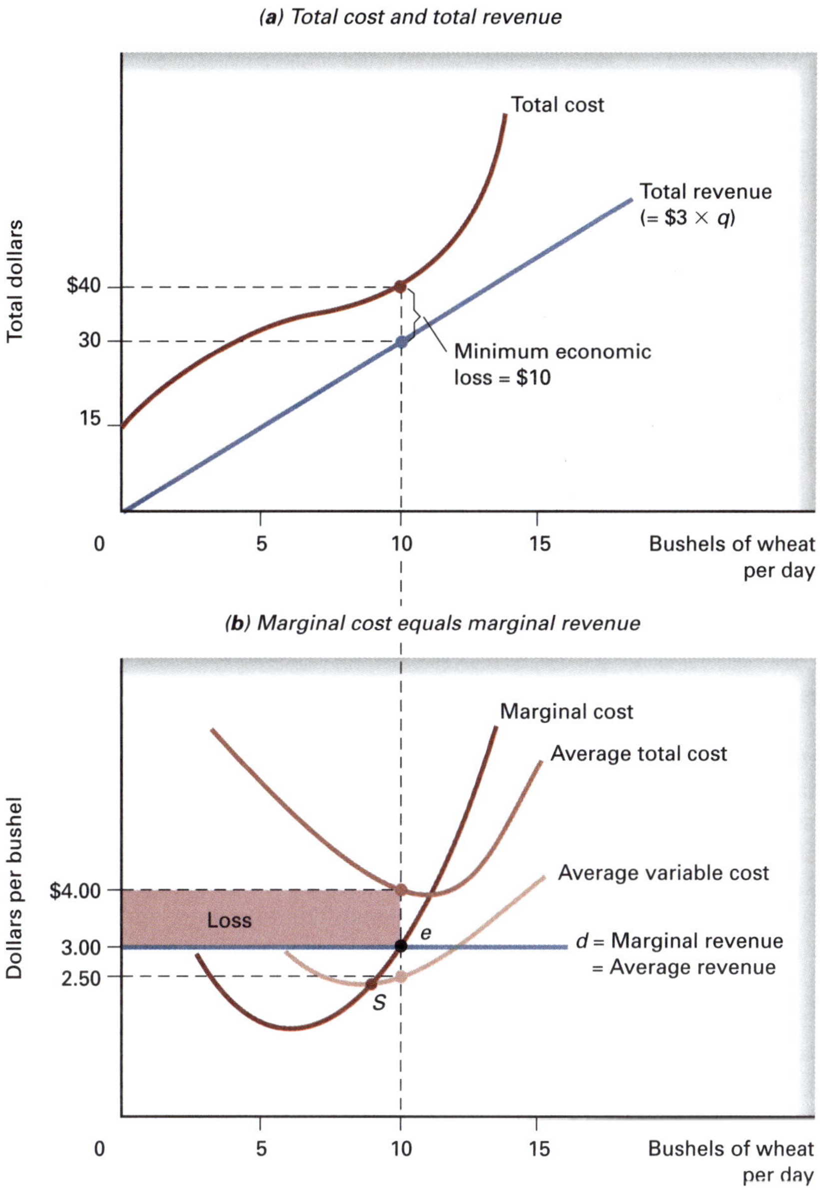

From column (7) of Exhibit 4, you can also see that the lowest price at which the farmer would just cover average variable cost is $2.47 per bushel given by point S, when output is 9 bushels per day. At this price, the farmer is indifferent between producing and shutting down, because either way the loss is the $15 per day in fixed cost. Any price above $2.47 allows the farmer, by producing, to also cover some fixed cost.

Shutting down is not the same as going out of business. In the short run, even a firm that shuts down keeps productive capacity intact—paying rent, insurance, and property taxes, keeping water pipes from freezing in the winter, and so on. For example, Dairy Queen shuts down for the winter in cooler climates, a business serving a college community may close during term breaks, and an auto plant responds to slack sales by temporarily halting production. These firms do not escape fixed cost by shutting down. When demand picks up again, production resumes. If the market outlook remains grim, the firm may decide to leave the market, but that's a long-run decision. The short run is defined as a period during which some costs are fixed, so a firm cannot escape those costs in the short run, no matter what it does. *Fixed cost is sunk cost in the short run, whether the firm produces or shuts down.*

Likewise, a concert promoter may cancel an event because of poor ticket sales even though the hall has been rented. And a movie producer may pull the plug on a nearly completed film that looks like a turkey to avoid sinking millions more on advertising. Concert promoters and movie producers want to cut their losses. They don't want to throw more good money after bad.

LO4 The Firm and Industry Short-Run Supply Curves

If average variable cost exceeds price at all output rates, the firm shuts down in the short run. But if price exceeds average variable cost, the firm produces the quantity at which marginal revenue equals marginal cost. As we'll see, a firm changes the rate of output if the market price changes.

The Short-Run Firm Supply Curve

The relationship between price and quantity is summarized in Exhibit 6. Points 1, 2, 3, 4, and 5 identify where the marginal cost curve intersects alternative marginal revenue, or demand, curves. At a price as low as p_1, the firm shuts down rather than produce at point 1 because that price is below average variable cost. So the loss-minimizing output rate at price p_1 is zero, as identified by q_1. At price p_2, the price just equals average variable cost, so the firm is indifferent between producing q_2 and shutting down; either way the firm loses fixed cost. Point 2 is called the *shutdown point*. If the price is p_3, the firm produces q_3 to minimize its loss (see if you can identify that loss in the diagram). At p_4, the firm produces q_4 to earn a normal profit, because price equals average total cost. Point 4 is called the *break-even point*. If the price rises to p_5, the firm earns short-run economic profit by producing q_5 (see if you can identify that economic profit in the diagram).

At prices below p_2, the firm shuts down in the short run. The quantity supplied when the price is p_2 or higher is determined by the intersection of the firm's marginal cost curve and its demand, or marginal revenue, curve. As long as the price covers average variable cost, the firm supplies the quantity at which the upward-sloping marginal cost curve intersects the marginal revenue, or demand, curve. Thus, that portion of the firm's marginal cost curve that intersects and rises above the lowest point on its average variable cost curve becomes the **short-run firm supply curve**. In Exhibit 6, the short-run supply curve is the upward-sloping portion of the marginal cost curve, beginning at point 2, the shutdown point. The solid portion of the short-run supply curve indicates the quantity the firm offers for sale at each price.

Farming: A Volatile Market

In 2008, farmers experienced unprecedented volatility in prices. For years, farmers could sell a bushel of corn for $2, often requiring federal subsidies to break even. Between expanding global demand and new energy laws increasing the use of ethanol in motor oil, corn prices over the summer of 2008 peaked, rising above $6 per bushel. Then, in September and October, the meltdown on Wall Street and a crunch on ethanol production drove demand back down. By the end of the year, corn prices sat closer to $4, but many farmers found that rising production costs outpaced the prices they could get for their crops. Furthermore, these prices were well above the levels that would have triggered federal subsidies. If the environment continues like this, farmers could reduce average variable costs and market supply by idling land, but the most indebted farmers could ultimately be driven out of business. How do you think the demand curve for an individual farmer changed each time market demand or market supply shifted in the volatile food markets?

SOURCE: Scott Kilman and Roger Thurow, "Bumpy Crop: Farming's Sudden Feasts and Famines," *Wall Street Journal*, 30 December 2008. Available at http://online.wsj.com/article/SB123059685167541039.html (accessed 30 December 2008).

© BRIAN HAGIWARA/BRAND X PICTURES/JUPITERIMAGES

The Short-Run Industry Supply Curve

Exhibit 7 presents examples of how supply curves for three firms with identical marginal cost curves can be summed *horizontally* to form the short-run industry supply curve (in perfect competition, there are many more firms). The **short-run industry supply curve** is the horizontal sum of all firms' short-run

Exhibit 6

Summary of Short-Run Output Decisions

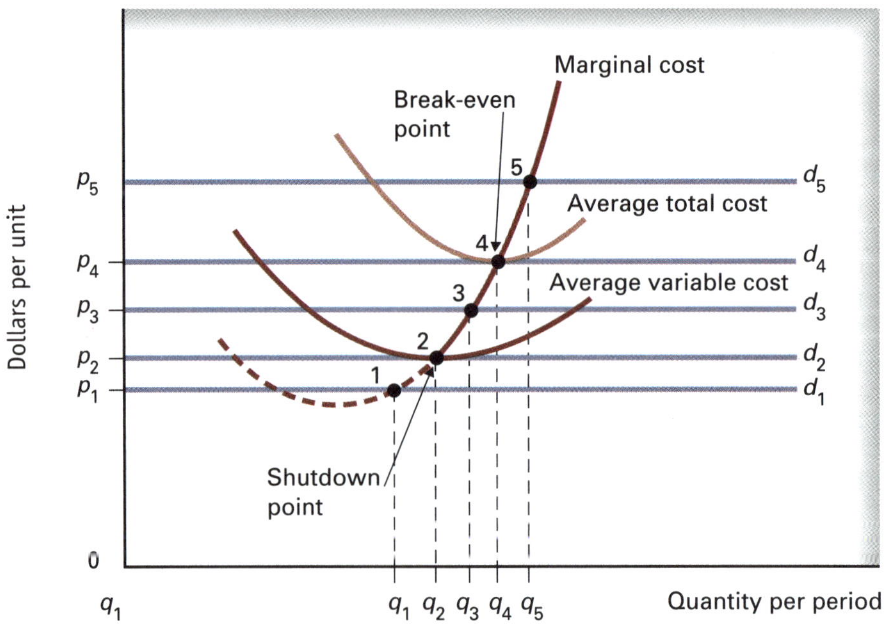

short-run firm supply curve a curve that shows how much a firm supplies at each price in the short run; in perfect competition, that portion of a firm's marginal cost curve that intersects and rises above the low point on its average variable cost curve

short-run industry supply curve a curve that indicates the quantity supplied by the industry at each price in the short run; in perfect competition, the horizontal sum of each firm's short-run supply curve

Exhibit 7

Aggregating Individual Supply to Form Market Supply

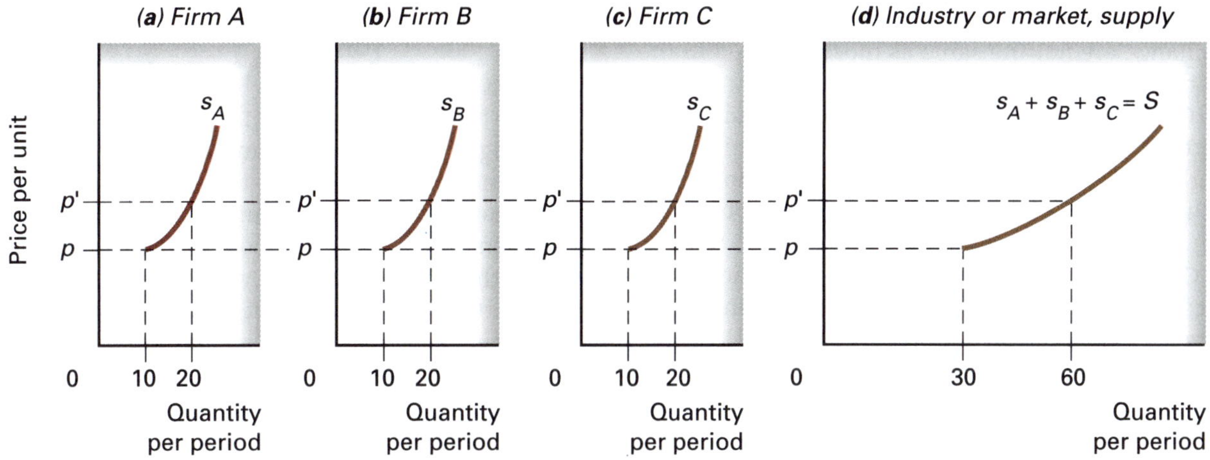

supply curves. At a price below *p*, no output is supplied. At price *p*, each of the three firms supplies 10 units, so the market supplies 30 units. At *p*′, which is above *p*, each firm supplies 20 units, so the market supplies 60 units.

Firm Supply and Market Equilibrium

Exhibit 8 shows the relationship between the short-run profit-maximizing output of the individual firm and market equilibrium price and quantity. Suppose there are 100,000 identical wheat farmers in this industry. Their individual supply curves (represented by the portions of the marginal cost curve at or rising above the average variable cost) are summed horizontally to yield the market, or industry, supply curve. The market supply curve appears in panel (b), where it intersects the market demand curve to determine the market price of $5 per bushel. At that price, each farmer supplies 12 bushels per day, as shown in panel (a), which sums to 1,200,000 bushels for the market, as shown in panel (b). Each farmer in the short run earns an economic profit of $12 per day, represented by the shaded rectangle in panel (a).

In summary: *A perfectly competitive firm supplies the short-run quantity that maximizes profit or minimizes loss. When confronting a loss, a firm either produces an output that minimizes that loss or shuts down temporarily. Given the conditions for perfect competition, the market converges toward the equilibrium price and quantity.*

Exhibit 8

Short-Run Profit Maximization and Market Equilibrium

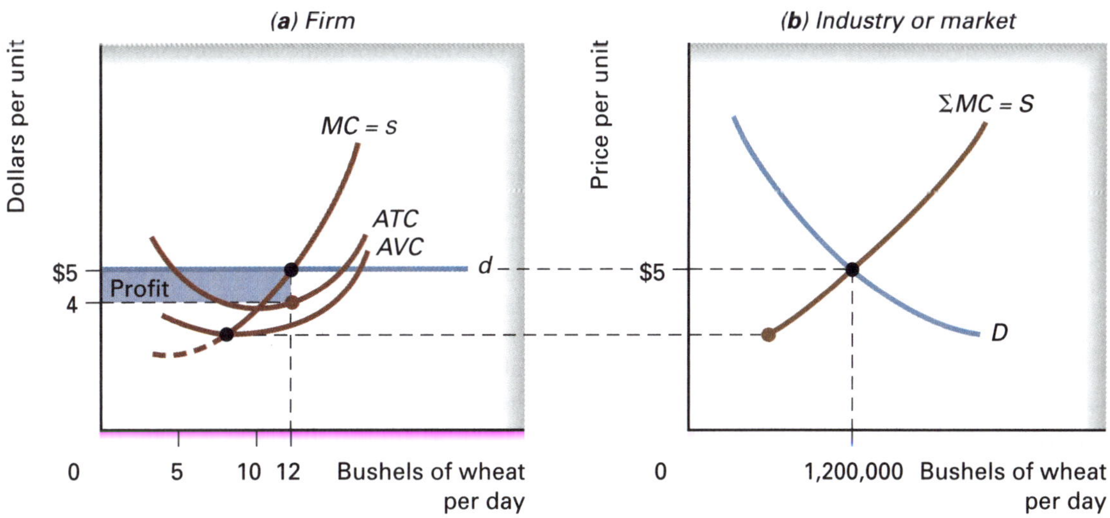

But how is that equilibrium actually reached? In the real world, markets operate based on customs and conventions, which vary across markets. For example, the rules acceptable on the New York Stock Exchange are not the same as those followed in the market for fresh fish.

One mechanism for reaching equilibrium is an auction. In a *Dutch auction,* prices start high and work down. Dutch auctions are more common when selling multiple lots of similar, though not identical, items, such as flowers in Amsterdam, tobacco in Canada, and fish in seaports around the world. Because there is some difference among the products for sale in a given market—for example, some flower lots are in better condition than others—this is not quite perfect competition because perfectly competitive markets sell identical products.

More common than the Dutch auction is the *English open outcry auction,* where bidding starts at a low price and moves up until only one buyer remains. Products sold this way include stocks, bonds, wine, art (think Sotheby's and Christie's), antiques, and livestock. On markets, such as the Chicago Board of Trade, prices for commodities such as wheat, gold, and coffee beans are continuously determined in the trading pits using variations of an open outcry auction.

The birth of the Internet has breathed new life into auctions. Web sites such as eBay, uBid, Yahoo!, and hundreds more hold online auctions for old maps, used computers, wine, airline tickets, antiques, military memorabilia, comic books, paperweights—you name it. As you can probably guess, eBay is the largest online auction and offers over 2,000 categories in a forum that mimics a live auction. Internet auctions allow specialized sellers to reach a world of customers. A listing on eBay, for example, could reach millions of people in more than 100 countries.

© F. SCHUSSLER/PHOTOLINK/PHOTODISC/GETTY IMAGES

LO5 Perfect Competition in the Long Run

In the short run, the quantity of variable resources can change, but other resources, which mostly determine firm size, are fixed. In the long run, however, a firm has time to enter and leave and to adjust its size—that is, to adjust its *scale* of operations. In the long run, there is no distinction between fixed and variable cost because all resources under the firm's control are variable.

Short-run economic profit, in the long run, encourages new firms to enter the market and may prompt existing firms to get bigger. Economic profit attracts resources from industries where firms are losing money or earning only a normal profit. This expansion in the number and size of firms shifts the industry supply curve rightward in the long run, driving down the price. New firms continue to enter a profitable industry and existing firms continue to expand as long as economic profit is greater than zero. Entry and expansion stop only when the resulting increase in supply drives down the price enough to erase economic profit. In the case of wheat farming, economic profit attracts new wheat farmers and may encourage existing wheat farmers to expand. *Short-run economic profit attracts new entrants in the long run and may cause existing firms to expand. Market supply thereby increases, driving down the market price until economic profit disappears.*

On the other hand, a short-run loss, in the long run, forces some firms to leave the industry or to reduce their scale of operation. In the long run, departures and reductions in scale shift the market supply curve to the left, thereby increasing the market price until remaining firms just break even—that is, earn a normal profit.

Zero Economic Profit in the Long Run

In the long run, firms in perfect competition earn just a normal profit, which means zero economic profit. Exhibit 9 shows a firm and the market in long-run equilibrium. Market supply adjusts as firms enter or leave or change their size. *This long-run adjustment continues until the market supply curve intersects the market demand curve at a price that corresponds to the lowest point on each firm's long-run average cost curve, or LRAC curve.* Because the long run is a period during which all resources under a firm's control are variable, a *firm in the long run is forced by competition to adjust its scale until average cost is minimized.* A firm that fails to minimize average cost will not survive in the long run. At point *e* in panel (a) of Exhibit 9, the firm is in equilibrium, producing *q* units per period

Exhibit 9

Long-Run Equilibrium for a Firm and the Industry

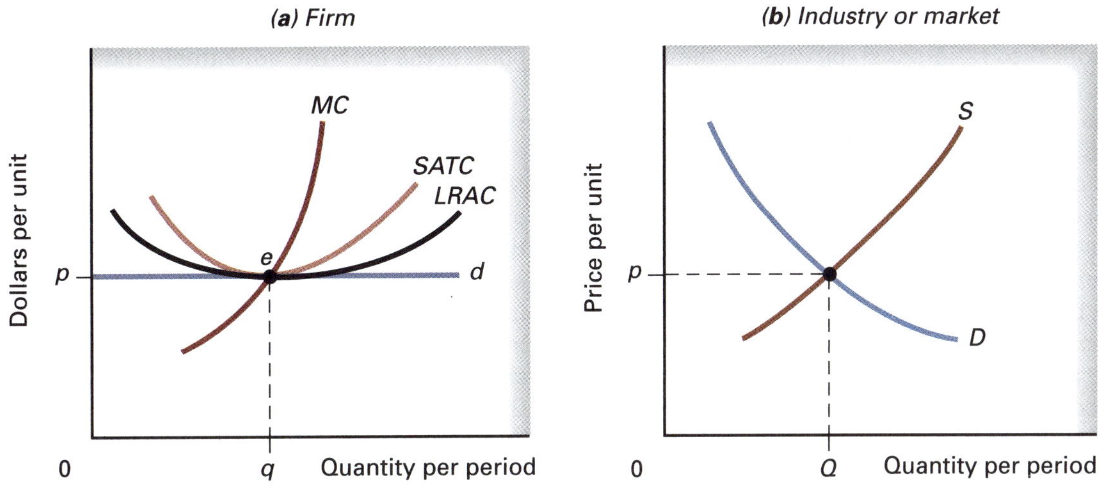

and earning just a normal profit. At point *e*, price, marginal cost, short-run average total cost, and long-run average cost are all equal. No firm in the market has any reason to change its output, and no outside firm has any incentive to enter this industry, because firms in this market are earning normal, but not economic, profit. In other words, resources employed in this industry earn their opportunity costs.

The Long-Run Adjustment to a Change in Demand

To explore the long-run adjustment process, let's consider how a firm and an industry respond to an increase in market demand. Suppose that the costs facing each firm do not depend on the number of firms in the industry (an assumption explained soon).

Effects of an Increase in Demand

Exhibit 10 shows a perfectly competitive firm and industry in long-run equilibrium, with the market supply curve intersecting the market demand curve at point *a* in panel (b). The market-clearing price is *p*, and the market quantity is Q_a. The firm, shown in panel (a), supplies q units at that market price, earning a normal profit. This representative firm produces where price, or marginal revenue, equals marginal cost, short-run average total cost, and long-run

Exhibit 10

Long-Run Adjustment to an Increase in Demand

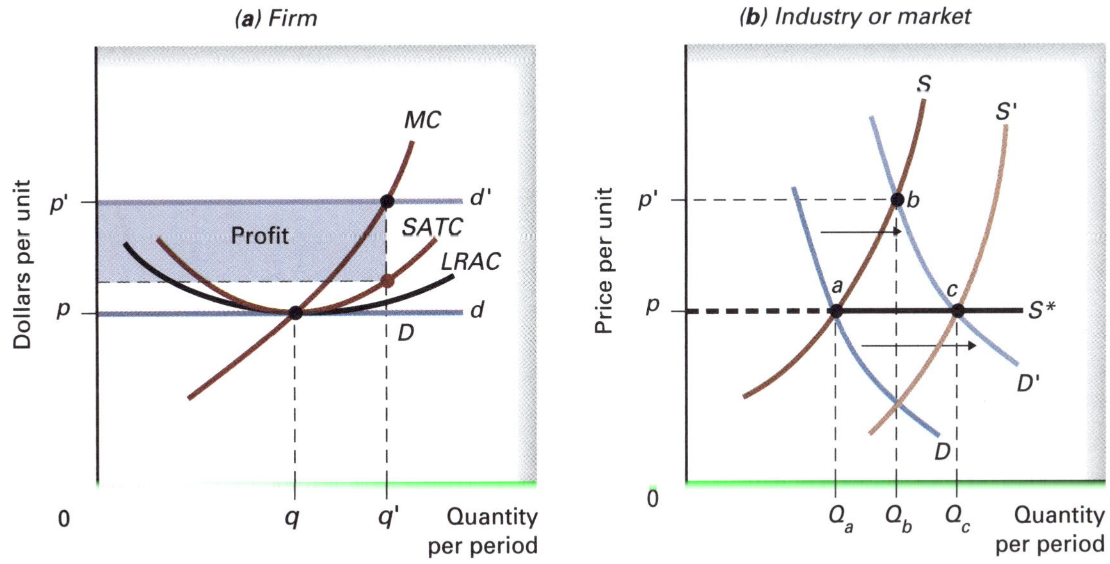

average cost. (Remember, a normal profit is included in the firm's average cost curves.)

Now suppose market demand increases, as reflected by a rightward shift of the market demand curve, from D to D' in panel (b), causing the market price to increase in the short run to p'. Each firm responds to the higher price by expanding output along its short-run supply, or marginal cost, curve until its quantity supplied increases to q', shown in panel (a) of Exhibit 10. At that output, the firm's marginal cost curve intersects the new marginal revenue curve, which is also the firm's new demand curve, d'. Note that in the short run, each firm now earns an economic profit, shown by the shaded rectangle. Because all firms increase their quantity supplied, industry quantity supplied increases to Q_b in panel (b).

Economic profit attracts new firms in the long run. Their entry shifts the market supply curve to the right, which forces the price down. Firms continue to enter as long as they can earn economic profit. The market supply curve eventually shifts out to S', where it intersects D' at point c, returning the price to its initial equilibrium level, p. The firm's demand curve drops from d' back down to d. As a result, each firm reduces output from q' back to q, and once again, each earns just a normal profit. Notice that although industry output increases from Q_a to Q_c, each firm's output returns to q. In this example, the additional output comes entirely from new firms drawn to the industry rather than from more output by existing firms (existing firms don't expand in this example because an increase in scale would increase average cost).

New firms are attracted to the industry by short-run economic profits resulting from the increase in demand. But this new entry shifts out market supply, forcing the market price down until economic profit disappears. In panel (b) of Exhibit 10, the short-run adjustment to increased demand is from point a to point b; the long-run adjustment moves to point c.

Effects of a Decrease in Demand

Next, let's trace the effects of a decrease of demand on the long-run market adjustment process. The initial long-run equilibrium in Exhibit 11 is the same as in Exhibit 10. Market demand and supply curves intersect at point a in panel (b), yielding an equilibrium price p and an equilibrium quantity Q_a. As shown in panel (a), each firm earns a normal profit in the long run by producing output rate q, where price, or marginal revenue, equals marginal cost, short-run average total cost, and long-run average cost.

Now suppose that market demand declines, as reflected in panel (b) by a leftward shift of the market demand curve, from D back to D''. In the short run, this forces the market price down to p''. With the market price lower, the demand curve facing each individual firm drops from d to d''. Each firm responds in the short run by reducing quantity supplied to q'' where the firm's marginal cost equals its now-lower marginal revenue, or price. Market output falls to Q_f. Because the lower market price is below average total cost, each firm operates at a loss. This loss is shown by the shaded rectangle in panel (a). Note, the price must still be above the average variable cost, because the firm's short-run supply curve, MC, is defined as that portion of the firm's marginal cost curve at or above its average variable cost curve.

Exhibit 11

Long-Run Adjustment to a Decrease in Demand

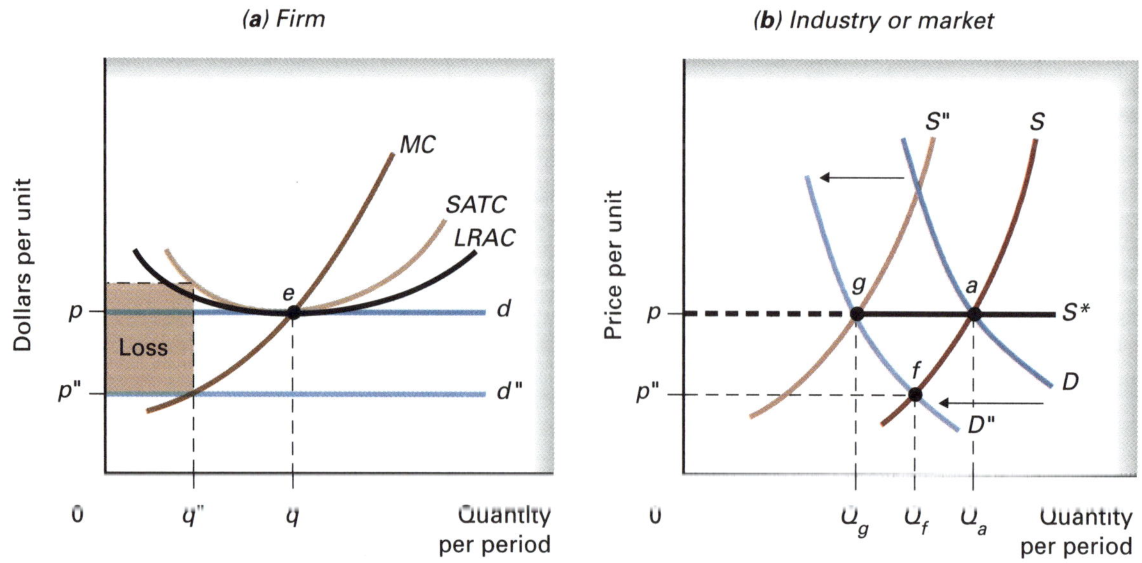

© COMSTOCK IMAGES/JUPITERIMAGES

A short-run loss forces some firms out of business in the long run. As firms exit, market supply decreases, or shifts leftward, so the price increases along market demand curve D''. Firms continue to leave until the market supply curve decreases to S'', where it intersects D'' at point g. Market output has fallen to Q_g, and price has returned to p. With the price back up to p, remaining firms once again earn a normal profit. When the dust settles, each remaining firm produces q, the initial equilibrium quantity. But, because some firms have left the industry, market output has fallen from Q_a to Q_g. Again, note that the adjustment involves the departure of firms from the industry rather than a reduction in the scale of firms, as a reduction in scale would increase each firm's long-run average cost.

LO6 The Long-Run Industry Supply Curve

Thus far, we have looked at a perfectly competitive firm's and industry's response to changes in demand, distinguishing between a short-run adjustment and a long-run adjustment. In the short run, a firm alters quantity supplied by moving up or down its marginal cost curves (that portion at or above average variable cost) until marginal cost equals marginal revenue, or price. If the price is too low to cover minimum average variable cost, a firm shuts down in the short run. An economic profit (or loss), in the long run, prompts some firms to enter (or leave) the industry or to adjust firm size until remaining firms earn a normal profit.

In Exhibits 10 and 11, we began with an initial long-run equilibrium point; then, in response to a shift of the demand curve, we found a new long-run equilibrium point. In each case, the price changed in the short run but not in the long run. Market output increased in Exhibit 10 and decreased in Exhibit 11. Connecting these long-run equilibrium points yields the *long-run industry supply curve,* labeled S^* in Exhibits 10 and 11. The **long-run industry supply curve** shows the relationship between price and quantity supplied once firms fully adjust to any short-term economic profit or loss resulting from a change in demand.

Constant-Cost Industries

The industry we have examined thus far is called **constant-cost industry** because each firm's long-run average cost curve does not shift up or down as industry output changes. In a constant-cost industry, each firm's per-unit costs are independent of the number of firms in the industry. The *long-run supply curve for a constant-cost industry is horizontal,* as is depicted by S^* in Exhibits 10 and 11. A constant-cost industry uses such a small portion of the resources available that increasing industry output does not bid up resource prices. For example, output in the pencil industry can expand without bidding up the prices of wood, graphite, and rubber, because the pencil industry uses such a tiny share of the market supply of these resources.

long-run industry supply curve
a curve that shows the relationship between price and quantity supplied by the industry once firms adjust in the long run to any change in market demand

constant-cost industry
an industry in which each firm's long-run average cost curve does not shift up or down as industry output changes

increasing-cost industries
industries in which firms encounter higher average costs as industry output expands in the long run

Increasing-Cost Industries

The firms in some industries encounter higher average costs as industry output expands in the long run. Firms in these **increasing-cost industries** find that expanding output bids up the prices of some resources or otherwise increases per-unit

© HAVENS STREANO/STOCK CONNECTION/JUPITERIMAGES

production costs, and these higher costs shift up each firm's cost curves. For example, a market expansion of oil production could bid up the prices of drilling rigs and the wages of petroleum engineers and geologists, raising per-unit production costs for each oil producer. Likewise, more housing construction could bid up what developers must pay for land, carpenters, lumber, and other building materials.

To illustrate the equilibrium adjustment process for an increasing-cost industry, we begin again in long-run equilibrium in Exhibit 12, with the firm shown in panel (a) and the industry in panel (b). Market demand curve *D* in panel (b) intersects short-run market supply curve *S* at equilibrium point *a* to yield market price p_a and market quantity Q_a. When the price is p_a, the demand (and marginal revenue) curve facing each firm is d_a as shown in panel (a). The firm supplies quantity *q*, where the price, or marginal revenue, equals marginal cost. At that output, average total cost equals the price, so the firm earns no economic profit in this long-run equilibrium.

Suppose an increase in the demand for this product shifts the market demand curve in panel (b) to the right from *D* to *D'*. The new demand curve intersects the short-run market supply curve *S* at point *b*, yielding the market price p_b and market quantity Q_b. With this price increase, each firm's demand curve shifts from d_a up to d_b. The firm's new short-run equilibrium occurs at point *b* in panel (a), where the marginal cost curve intersects the new demand curve, which is also the marginal revenue curve. Each firm produces output q_b. In the short run, each firm earns an economic profit equal to q_b times the difference between price p_b and the average total cost at that rate of output. So far, the sequence of events is the same as for a constant-cost industry.

Economic profit attracts new firms. Because this is an increasing-cost industry, new entrants drive up the cost of production, raising each firm's marginal and average cost curves. In panel (a) of Exhibit 12, *MC* and *ATC* shift up to *MC'* and *ATC'*. (We assume for simplicity that new average cost curves are vertical

Exhibit 12

An Increasing-Cost Industry

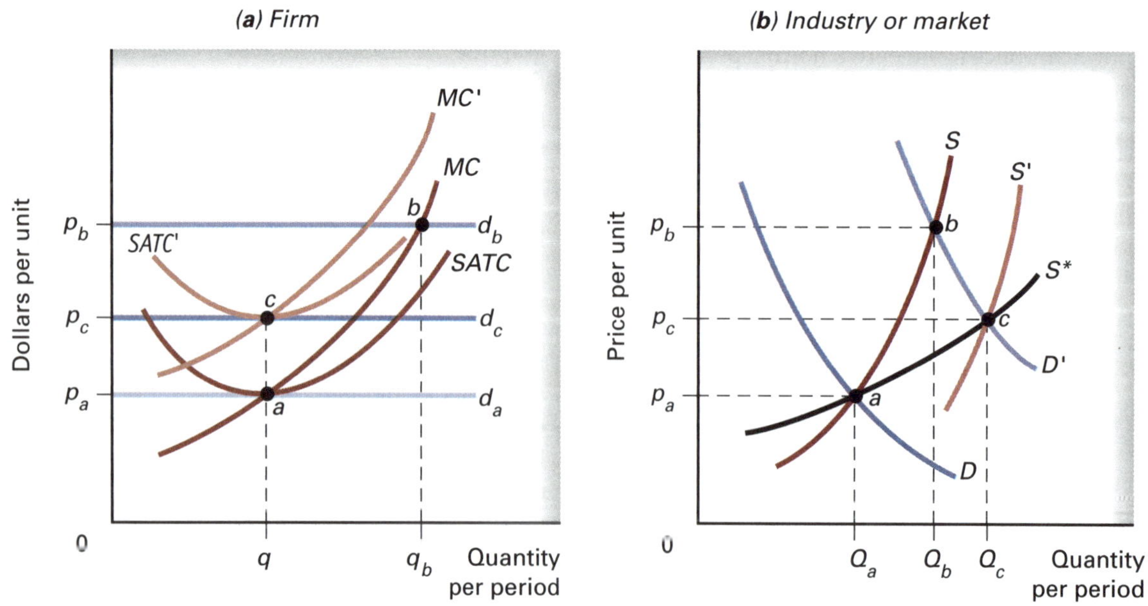

shifts of the initial ones, so the minimum efficient plant size remains the same.)

The entry of new firms also shifts the short-run industry supply curve to the right in panel (b), thus reducing the market price along D′. *New firms enter the industry until the combination of a higher production cost and a lower price squeezes economic profit to zero.* This long-run equilibrium occurs when the entry of new firms has shifted the short-run industry supply curve out to S′, which lowers the price until it equals the minimum on each firm's new average total cost curve. The market price does not fall back to the initial equilibrium level because each firm's average total cost curve has increased, or shifted up, with the expansion of industry output. The intersection of the new short-run market supply curve, S′, and the new market demand curve, D′, determines the new long-run market equilibrium point, *c*. Points *a* and *c* in panel (b) are on the *upward-sloping* long-run supply curve S* for this increasing-cost industry.

In constant-cost industries, each firm's costs depend simply on the scale of its plant and its rate of output. For increasing-cost industries, each firm's costs depend also on the number of firms in the market. By bidding up the price of resources, long-run expansion in an increasing-cost industry increases each firm's marginal and average costs. The long-run supply curve slopes upward, like S* in Exhibit 12.

To review: Firms in perfect competition can earn an economic profit, a normal profit, or an economic loss in the short run. But in the long run, the entry or exit of firms and adjustments in each firm's size force economic profit to zero. Competitive firms earn only a normal profit in the long run. This is true whether the industry in question experiences constant costs or increasing costs in the long run. Notice that, regardless of the nature of costs in the industry, the market supply curve is more elastic in the long run than in the short run. In the long run, firms can adjust all their resources, so they are better able to respond to changes in price. One final point: Firms in an industry could theoretically experience a lower average cost as output expands in the long run, resulting in a downward-sloping long-run industry supply curve. But such an outcome is considered so rare that we do not examine it.

As mentioned at the outset, perfect competition provides a useful benchmark for evaluating the efficiency of markets. Let's examine the qualities of perfect competition that make it so useful.

JUST BECAUSE *PRODUCTION* OCCURS AT THE LEAST POSSIBLE COST DOES NOT MEAN THAT THE *ALLOCATION* OF RESOURCES IS THE MOST EFFICIENT ONE POSSIBLE.

LO7 Perfect Competition and Efficiency

How does perfect competition stack up as an efficient user of resources? Two concepts of efficiency are used to judge market performance. The first, called *productive efficiency*, refers to producing output at the least possible cost. The second, called *allocative efficiency*, refers to producing the output that consumers value the most. *Perfect competition guarantees both productive efficiency and allocative efficiency in the long run.*

Productive Efficiency: Making Stuff Right

Productive efficiency occurs when the firm produces at the minimum point on its long-run average cost curve, so the market price equals the minimum average cost. The entry and exit of firms and any adjustment in the scale of each firm ensure that each firm produces at the minimum of its long-run average cost curve. Firms that do not reach minimum long-run average cost must, to avoid continued losses, either adjust their scale or leave the industry. Thus, *perfect competition produces output at minimum average cost in the long run.*

Allocative Efficiency: Making the Right Stuff

Just because *production* occurs at the least possible cost does not mean that the *allocation* of resources is the most efficient one possible. The products may not be the ones consumers want. This situation is akin to that of the airline pilot who informs passengers that there's good news and bad news: "The good news is that we're making record time. The bad news is that we're lost!" Likewise, firms may be producing goods efficiently but producing the wrong goods—that is, making stuff right but making the wrong stuff.

Allocative efficiency occurs when firms produce the output that consumers value most. How do we know that

productive efficiency the condition that exists when production uses the least-cost combination of inputs; minimum average cost in the long run

allocative efficiency the condition that exists when firms produce the output most preferred by consumers; marginal benefit equals marginal cost

<< The Egokast belt buckle is a 3.5″ LCD screen that displays videos you make and load into the buckle. Retailing for $289, the Egokast boasts a crystal clear picture (i.e., it's made right). If the unique buckle becomes popular, then marketers will have launched a successful new product (i.e., it's the right stuff).

© COURTESY OF SHAW KAAKE, EGOKAST

perfect competition guarantees allocative efficiency? The answer lies with the market demand and supply curves. Recall that the demand curve reflects the marginal value that consumers attach to each unit of the good, so the market price is the amount people are willing and able to pay for the final unit they consume. We also know that, in both the short run and the long run, the equilibrium price in perfect competition equals the marginal cost of supplying the last unit sold. Marginal cost measures the opportunity cost of resources employed to produce that last unit sold. Thus, the demand and supply curves intersect at the combination of price and quantity at which *the marginal value, or the marginal benefit, that consumers attach to the final unit purchased, just equals the opportunity cost of the resources employed to produce that unit.*

As long as marginal benefit equals marginal cost, the last unit produced is valued by consumers as much as, or more than, any other good those resources could have produced. There is no way to reallocate resources to increase the total value of all output in the economy. Thus, there is no way to reallocate resources to increase the total utility or total benefit consumers reap from production. *When the marginal benefit that consumers derive from a good equals the marginal cost of producing that good, that market is said to be allocatively efficient.*

Marginal benefit = Marginal cost

Firms not only are making stuff right, they are making the right stuff.

producer surplus a bonus for producers in the short run; the amount by which total revenue from production exceeds variable cost

What's So Perfect About Perfect Competition?

If the marginal cost of supplying a good just equals the marginal benefit to consumers, does this mean that market exchange confers no net benefits to participants? No. Market exchange usually benefits both consumers and producers. Recall that consumers enjoy a surplus from market exchange because the most they would be willing and able to pay for each unit of the good exceeds what they actually do pay. Exhibit 13 depicts a market in short-run equilibrium. *The consumer surplus* in this exhibit is represented by blue shading, which is the area below the demand curve but above the market-clearing price of $10.

Producers in the short run also usually derive a net benefit, or a surplus, from market exchange, because what they receive for their output exceeds the least they would accept to supply that quantity in the short run. Recall that the short-run market supply curve is the sum of each firm's marginal cost curve at or above its minimum average variable cost. Point *m* in Exhibit 13 is the minimum point on the market supply curve; it indicates that at a price of $5, quantity supplied is 100,000 units. At prices below $5, quantity supplied would be zero because firms could not cover average variable cost. A price of $5 just covers average variable cost.

If the market price rises to $6, quantity supplied increases until marginal cost equals $6. Market output increases from 100,000 to 120,000 units. Total revenue in this market increases from $500,000 to $720,000. Part of the higher revenue covers the higher marginal cost of production. But the rest provides a bonus to producers. After all, suppliers would have offered the first 100,000 units for only $5 each. If the price is $6, firms get to supply these 100,000 units for $6 each. Producer surplus at a price of $6 is the gold-shaded area between the prices of $5 and $6.

In the short run, **producer surplus** equals the total revenue producers are paid minus their variable cost of production. In Exhibit 13, the market-clearing price is $10 per unit, and producer surplus is depicted by the gold-shaded area between a price of $5 and the market price of $10. The most the firm can lose in the short run is to shut down. Any price that exceeds average variable cost, which is $5 in this example, reduces that short-run loss and generates

Exhibit 13

Consumer Surplus and Producer Surplus for a Competitive Market

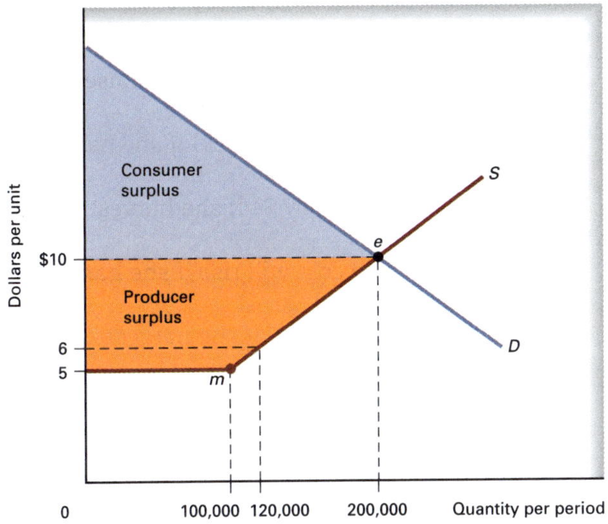

a producer surplus. A high enough price could yield economic profit.

The combination of consumer surplus and producer surplus shows the gains from voluntary exchange. Productive and allocative efficiency in the short run occurs at equilibrium point *e*, which also is the combination of price and quantity that maximizes the sum of consumer surplus and producer surplus, thus maximizing social welfare. **Social welfare** is the overall well-being of people in the economy. Even though marginal cost equals marginal benefit for the final unit produced and consumed, both producers and consumers usually derive a surplus, or a bonus, from market exchange.

Final Word

Let's review the assumptions of a perfectly competitive market and see how each relates to ideas developed in this chapter. *First*, there are many buyers and many sellers. This assumption ensures that no individual buyer or seller can influence the price (although recent experiments show that competition occurs even with few buyers and sellers). *Second*, firms produce a commodity, or a uniform product. If consumers could distinguish between the products of different suppliers, they might prefer one firm's product even at a higher price, so different producers could sell at different prices. In that case, not every firm would be a price taker—that is, each firm's demand curve would no longer be horizontal. *Third*, market participants have full information about all prices and all production processes. Otherwise, some producers could charge more than the market price, and some uninformed consumers would pay that higher price. Also, through ignorance, some firms might select outdated technology or fail to recognize opportunities for short-run economic profits. *Fourth*, all resources are mobile in the long run, with nothing preventing firms in the long run from entering profitable markets or leaving losing markets. If firms couldn't enter profitable markets, then some firms already in that market could earn economic profit in the long run.

Perfect competition is not the most common market structure observed in the real world. The markets for agricultural products, commodities such as gold and silver, widely traded stocks, and foreign exchange come close to being perfect. But even if not a single such industry could be found, the model would still be useful for analyzing market behavior. As you will see in the next two chapters, perfect competition provides a valuable benchmark for evaluating the efficiency of other market structures.

social welfare
the overall well-being of people in the economy; maximized when the marginal cost of production equals the marginal benefit to consumers

Multiple Choice Questions

1. Which of the following is *not* characteristic of perfect competition?
   a. many buyers and sellers
   b. brand name advertising
   c. standardized products
   d. fully informed buyers and sellers
   e. free entry and exit of firms
2. Which of the following is likely to be present in a perfectly competitive market?
   a. patents
   b. government licenses
   c. nonprice competition such as advertising
   d. high capital costs
   e. firms producing identical products
3. Suppose Thelma and Louise both sell fried green tomatoes in a perfectly competitive market. If Louise increases her output,
   a. Thelma must reduce output
   b. the price Thelma can charge falls
   c. the price Thelma can charge rises
   d. the price Thelma can charge is unaffected
   e. Thelma's profits must fall
4. The market for prunes is perfectly competitive with the equilibrium market price of $3 per pound. Farmer Joe wants a new tractor so he wants to sell his prunes at $3.50 a pound. Which of the following statements is correct?
   a. Farmer Joe will sell all his prunes at $3.50 per pound
   b. Farmer Joe will sell no prunes at $3.50 per pound
   c. Farmer Joe will sell no prunes at $2.50 per pound
   d. Farmer Joe will sell half of his prunes at $3.50 per pound
   e. Farmer Joe will sell half of his prunes at $3 per pound
5. In Connecticut, the apple market is perfectly competitive. Suppose that consumer tastes change so that the market demand for apples increases. In that case, the demand curves faced by individual firms will
   a. not change
   b. become less elastic
   c. shift upward
   d. shift leftward
   e. shift downward
6. Farmer Fanny sells her crops in a perfectly competitive market. If she produces 500 bushels for total revenue of $3,000 and if harvesting the 501st bushel would raise her total cost from $2,500 to $2,510, her
   a. revenue will increase by $4 if she harvests the 501st bushel
   b. revenue will fall by $4 if she harvests the 501st bushel
   c. average fixed cost will rise if she harvests the 501st bushel
   d. profit will fall by $10 if she harvests the 501st bushel
   e. profit will fall by $4 if she harvests the 501st bushel
7. The Hound Dog Bus Company contemplates expanding its New Mexico operations by offering service from Raton to Milk-of-Magnesia. The total cost of the trip would be $400, of which $150 is fixed cost, which it has already paid. The firm expects to earn $275 in revenue from the trip. The Hound Dog Bus Co. should
   a. offer this service because it will earn a positive economic profit
   b. not offer this service because the marginal revenue is less than the marginal cost
   c. offer this service because the revenue exceeds fixed cost
   d. not offer this service because the total cost exceeds the total revenue
   e. offer this service because the added revenue exceeds the added cost of this service
8. The Hound Dog Bus Company contemplates expanding its Virginia operations by offering service from Fairfax to Arlington. The total cost of the trip would be $120, of which $50 is fixed cost, which it has already paid. The firm expects to earn $60 in revenue from the trip. The Hound Dog Bus Company should
   a. offer this service because it will earn a positive economic profit
   b. not offer this service because the marginal revenue is less than the marginal cost
   c. offer this service because the revenue exceeds fixed cost
   d. not offer this service because the total cost exceeds the total revenue
   e. offer this service because the added revenue exceeds the added cost of this service

9. If the price-taking firm in Exhibit 15 is currently producing 6 units, then to maximize profit in the short run, it should
   a. keep producing 6 units
   b. increase production to 12 units
   c. increase production to 14 units
   d. increase production to 8 units
   e. shut down

Exhibit 15

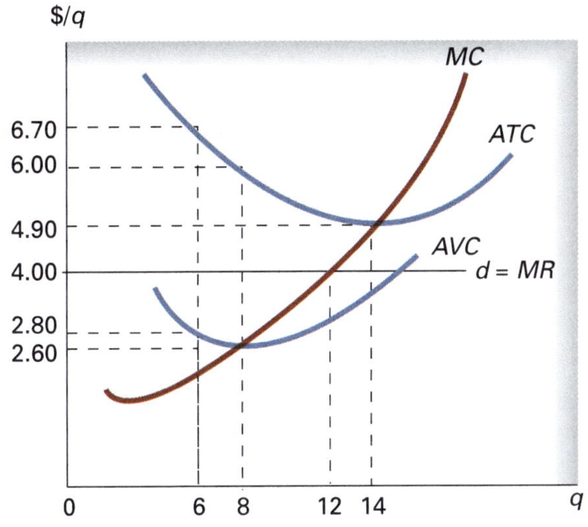

10. For a perfectly competitive firm,
    a. P = AR at all levels of output
    b. P = AR at the profit-maximizing quantity only
    c. P > AR at all levels of output
    d. P < AR at the profit-maximizing quantity only
    e. P < AR at all levels of output

11. A firm in perfectly competitive industry is maximizing profit at Q = 3,000. Then its fixed cost increases. The profit-maximizing output is now
    a. greater than 3,000 and profit decreases
    b. less than 3,000 and profit decreases
    c. greater than 3,000 and profit is unchanged
    d. equal to 3,000 and profit decreases
    e. equal to 3,000 and profit increases

12. Which of the following does *not* characterize a perfectly competitive firm that has shut down in the short run?
    a. total revenue equals zero
    b. variable costs equal zero
    c. the firm suffers a loss
    d. fixed cost is positive
    e. fixed cost is zero

13. At its present rate of output, Barrel O' Biscuits, a perfectly competitive firm, finds that its marginal cost exceeds its marginal revenue and price exceeds average variable cost. To maximize profit, the firm should
    a. lower the price
    b. raise the price
    c. increase output
    d. reduce output
    e. maintain its current rate of output

14. A firm is currently producing 100 hair dryers and sells them in a perfectly competitive market at a price of $10 each. The marginal cost of producing the 100th hair dryer is $9 and the marginal cost of producing the 101st hair dryer is $10. To maximize profit, the firm should produce:
    a. 100 hair dryers
    b. Fewer than 100 hair dryers
    c. 101 hair dryers
    d. More than 101 hair dryers
    e. 0 hair dryers

15. Claude's Copper Clappers sells clappers for $40 each in a perfectly competitive market. At its present rate of output, Claude's marginal cost is $39, average variable cost is $45, and average total cost is $60. To improve his profit/loss situation, Claude should
    a. increase output
    b. reduce output but not to zero
    c. maintain the present rate of output
    d. shut down
    e. raise the price

16. Suppose a price-taking firm produces 400 units at its optimal output level. At that output rate marginal cost is $200, average total cost is $240, and average variable cost is $170. What can you determine about the market price that would force the firm to shut down in the short run?
    a. It equals $200.
    b. It is between $170 and $240.
    c. It is less than $170.
    d. It is between $170 and $200.
    e. It equals $240.

17. A perfectly competitive firm producing 100 units of output per period finds that:
    Average total cost is $20;
    Average variable cost is $12;
    Marginal cost is $18 and increasing;
    Price of the product is $15.
    This firm should
    a. produce more output
    b. raise the price of its product
    c. reduce production without shutting down
    d. shut down (reduce output to zero)
    e. do nothing (it is currently maximizing profit)

18. Mary Ann and Don provide catering services in a perfectly competitive market. When they started in business, the going rate was $50 per person per meal. After the price increased to $60, they became willing to supply more meals. Their response to the price change is shown by
    a. a rightward shift of the market supply curve
    b. a leftward shift of the market supply curve
    c. movement up along their firm's marginal cost curve
    d. movement down along their firm's marginal cost curve
    e. a rightward shift in their demand for jobs

19. If a perfectly competitive firm is operating in long-run equilibrium and market demand suddenly falls, the *short-run* result will be
    a. greater economic profit
    b. a normal profit
    c. lower average total cost
    d. lower average variable cost
    e. an economic loss

20. A constant-cost industry is distinguished by the fact that
    a. firms' long-run average cost curves are horizontal
    b. firms' short-run marginal cost curves are horizontal
    c. firms' short-run average total costs are horizontal
    d. the short-run industry supply curve is perfectly elastic
    e. the long-run industry supply curve is perfectly elastic

Answers

1. b 2. e 3. d 4. b 5. c 6. e 7. e 8. b 9. b 10. a
11. d 12. e 13. d 14. c 15. d 16. c 17. c 18. c 19. e 20. e

Long Answer Questions

LO1 Define a perfectly competitive market and explain its effect on demand

1.1. *(Market Structure)* Define market structure. What factors are considered in determining the market structure of a particular industry?

1.2. *(Demand Under Perfect Competition)* What type of demand curve does a perfectly competitive firm face? Why?

LO2 Explain how firms maximize profit in the short run

2.1. *(Short-Run Profit Maximization)* A perfectly competitive firm has the following fixed and variable costs in the short run. The market price for the firm's product is $150.

Output	FC	VC	TC	TR	Profit/ Loss
0	$100	$ 0	____	____	____
1	$100	$100	____	____	____
2	$100	$180	____	____	____
3	$100	$300	____	____	____
4	$100	$440	____	____	____
5	$100	$600	____	____	____
6	$100	$780	____	____	____

a. Complete the table.
b. At what output rate does the firm maximize profit or minimize loss?
c. What is the firm's marginal revenue at each positive level of output? Its average revenue?
d. What can you say about the relationship between marginal revenue and marginal cost for output rates below the profit-maximizing (or loss-minimizing) rate? For output rates above the profit-maximizing (or loss-minimizing) rate?

LO3 Identify ways firms minimize short-run losses

3.1. *(Minimizing Loss in the Short Run)* Explain the different options a firm has for minimizing losses in the short run.

LO4 Explain how firms manage short-run supply

4.1. *(The Short-Run Firm Supply Curve)* Use the following data to answer the questions below:

Q	VC	MC	AVC
1	$10	____	____
2	$16	____	____
3	$20	____	____
4	$25	____	____
5	$31	____	____
6	$38	____	____
7	$46	____	____
8	$55	____	____
9	$65		____

a. Calculate the marginal cost and average variable cost for each level of production.

b. How much would the firm produce if it could sell its product for $5? For $7? For $10?
c. Explain your answers.
d. Assuming that its fixed cost is $3, calculate the firm's profit at each of the production levels determined in part (b).

4.2. *(The Short-Run Firm Supply Curve)* Each of the following situations could exist for a firm in the short run. In each case, indicate whether the firm should produce in the short run or shut down in the short run, or whether additional information is needed to determine what it should do in the short run.
a. Total cost exceeds total revenue at all output levels.
b. Total variable cost exceeds total revenue at all output levels.
c. Total revenue exceeds total fixed cost at all output levels.
d. Marginal revenue exceeds marginal cost at the current output level.
e. Price exceeds average total cost at all output levels.
f. Average variable cost exceeds price at all output levels.
g. Average total cost exceeds price at all output levels.

LO5 Describe how taking the long-run view affects economic factors

5.1. *(The Long-Run Industry Supply Curve)* A normal good is being produced in a constant-cost, perfectly competitive industry. Initially, each firm is in long-run equilibrium.
a. Graphically illustrate and explain the short-run adjustments for the market and the firm to a decrease in consumer incomes. Be sure to discuss any changes in output levels, prices, profits, and the number of firms.
b. Next, show on your graph and explain the long-run adjustment to the income change. Be sure to discuss any changes in output levels, prices, profits, and the number of firms.

5.2. *(Long-Run Industry Supply)* Why does the long-run industry supply curve for an increasing-cost industry slope upward? What causes the increasing costs in an increasing-cost industry?

LO6 Describe how different cost structures influence an industry's long-run supply curve

6.1. *(Perfect Competition in the Long Run)* Draw the short and long-run cost curves for a competitive firm in long-run equilibrium. Indicate the long-run equilibrium price and quantity.
a. Discuss the firm's short-run response to a reduction in the price of a variable resource.
b. Assuming that this is a constant-cost industry, describe the process by which the industry returns to long-run equilibrium following a change in market demand.

6.2. *(The Long-Run Industry Supply Curve)* The following graph shows possible long-run market supply curves for a perfectly competitive industry. Determine which supply curve indicates a constant-cost industry and which an increasing-cost industry.
a. Explain the difference between a constant-cost industry and an increasing cost industry.
b. Distinguish between the long-run impact of an increase in market demand in a constant-cost industry and the impact in an increasing-cost industry.

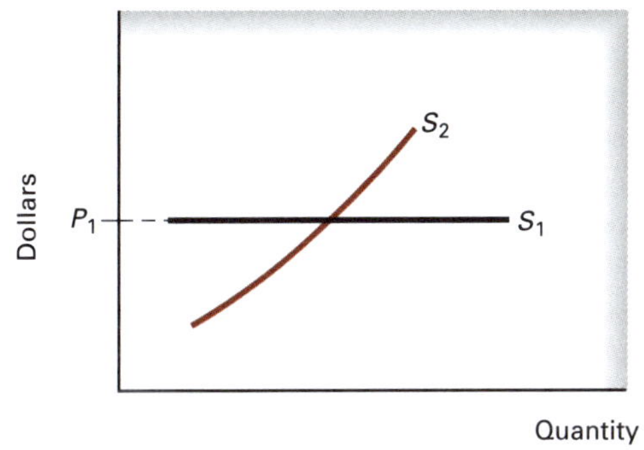

LO7 Identify how concepts of efficiency are used to judge market performance

7.1. *(What's So Perfect About Perfect Competition)* Use the following data to answer the questions.

Quantity	Marginal Cost	Marginal Benefit
0	—	—
1	$ 2	$10
2	$ 3	$ 9
3	$ 4	$ 8
4	$ 5	$ 7
5	$ 6	$ 6
6	$ 8	$ 5
7	$10	$ 4
8	$12	$ 3

a. For the product shown, assume that the minimum point of each firm's average variable cost curve is at $2. Construct a demand and supply diagram for the product and indicate the equilibrium price and quantity.
b. On the graph, label the area of consumer surplus as *f*. Label the area of producer surplus as *g*.
c. If the equilibrium price were $2, what would be the amount of producer surplus?

LO1 to LO6 (mixed)

1. Using graphs indicate equilibrium point (best level of output) in the Short-run and Long-run for a firm in perfect competition.
2. Answer the following questions:
   a. Should a company ever produce an output if the managers know it will lose money over the period? Explain.
   b. Does it imply the firm is in long-run equilibrium if it has short-run equilibrium? Does vice-versa hold true?
3. Comment whether the following statement is *true* or *false*. Give reasons for your answer.
   "The rising portion of the firm's MC curve above the firm's AVC curve is the competitive firm's short run supply curve of the product".
4. Despite operating at the profit maximizing level of output, the producer ends up making a loss. Is his decision rationale if he decides to continue producing or should he shut down?
5. Firms in a perfectly competitive market do not have to compete with the other individual firms in the market. True or false? Explain.

NUMERICAL QUESTIONS

1. The average variable cost function of a firm producing sewing machines has been found to be $AVC = 8 - 0.04Q + 0.0003Q^2$. The total fixed cost incurred by the firm is $400. Assuming that the market in which the firm operates is competitive:
   a. Compute the marginal cost function of the firm.
   b. How many sewing machines should the firm produce in the short-run?
   c. The firm has a new manager who wants to set the price of each machine at $8. Determine the profit/loss earned by the firm.
2. Assume the industry demand for an agricultural product is: $P = 1{,}000 - 20Q$. Assume that the marginal cost of product is $10 per unit. Calculate what the output and price shall be under the condition of pure competition.
3. A firm in a perfectly competitive industry which happens to be in long run equilibrium, charges $5 for its product. Its Average Cost is given by:

$$AC = 50 - 6Q + 0.2Q^2$$

   a. How much economic profit is the firm earning? Explain.
   b. How many units of output is the firm producing?
6. A firm in a perfectly competitive industry has the following short run total cost:
   $TC = 1000Q - 30Q^2 + Q^3$, where Q is the number of units produced by the firm. Below what price should the firm shut down its operations?
7. Determine the best level of output for a firm that sells its product at

$$P = \text{Rs. } 4$$

   And faces the total cost function as

$$TC = 0.04Q^3 - 0.9\,Q^2 + 10Q + 5$$

   Will the firm produce this level of output? Why?

PERFECT COMPETITION

Chapter in Review

KEY TERMS

market structure important features of a market, such as the number of firms, product uniformity across firms, firms' ease of entry and exit, and forms of competition

perfect competition a market structure with many fully informed buyers and sellers of a standardized product and no obstacles to entry or exit of firms in the long run

commodity a standardized product, a product that does not differ across producers, such as bushels of wheat or an ounce of gold

price taker a firm that faces a given market price and whose quantity supplied has no effect on that price; a perfectly competitive firm that decides to produce must accept, or "take," the market price

marginal revenue (MR) the firm's change in total revenue from selling an additional unit; a perfectly competitive firm's marginal revenue is also the market price

golden rule of profit maximization to maximize profit or minimize loss, a firm should produce the quantity at which marginal revenue equals marginal cost; this rule holds for all market structures

average revenue total revenue divided by quantity, or $AR = TR/q$; in all market structures, average revenue equals the market price

short-run firm supply curve a curve that shows how much a firm supplies at each price in the short run; in perfect competition, that portion of a firm's marginal cost curve that intersects and rises above the low point on its average variable cost curve

short-run industry supply curve a curve that indicates the quantity supplied by the industry at each price in the short run; in perfect competition, the horizontal sum of each firm's short-run supply curve

long-run industry supply curve a curve that shows the relationship between price and quantity supplied by the industry once firms adjust in the long run to any change in market demand

constant-cost industry an industry in which each firm's long-run average cost curve does not shift up or down as industry output changes

LO1 Define a perfectly competitive market and explain its effect on demand.

Market structures describe important features of the economic environment in which firms operate. A firm's decisions about how much to produce or what price to charge depend on the structure of the market. Perfect competition is the most basic of market structures; if it exists, an individual buyer or seller has no control over the price. Price is determined by market demand and supply.

Market Equilibrium and a Firm's Demand Curve in Perfect Competition

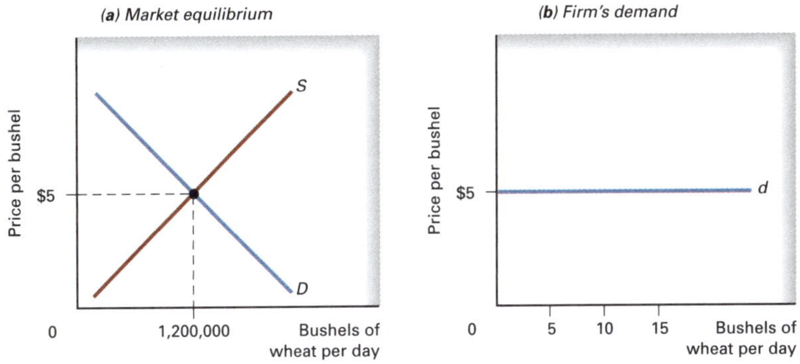

LO2 Explain how firms maximize profit in the short run.

All firms try to maximize economic profit, which is any profit above normal profit, by controlling their rate of output. Subtracting total cost from total revenue is one way to find the profit-maximizing output. Another way to find the profit-maximizing rate of output is to focus on marginal revenue and marginal cost. On a perfectly competitive firm's demand curve, market price, marginal revenue, and average revenue are all equal.

Short-Run Profit Maximization

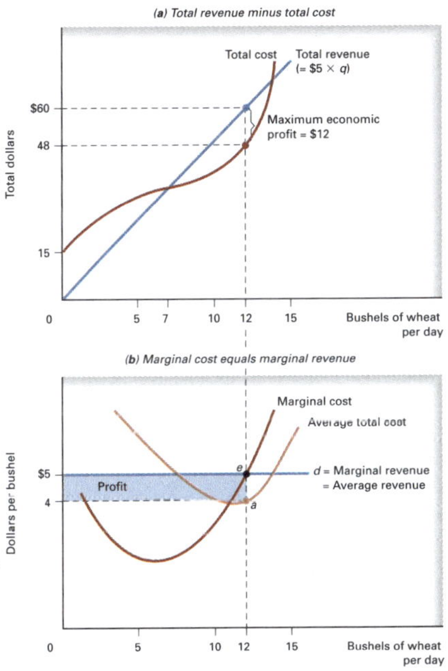

LO3 Identify ways firms minimize short-run losses.

Firms that have not identified a profitable level of output can either operate at a loss or shut down. In the short run, even a firm that shuts down keeps productive capacity intact by continuing to pay fixed costs, which are sunk regardless. For a firm to produce in the short run, rather than shut down, the market price must at least cover the firm's average variable cost.

Short-Run Loss Minimization

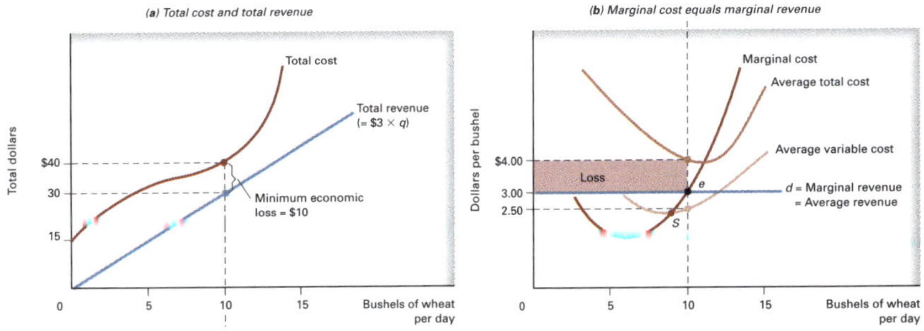

increasing-cost industries industries in which firms encounter higher average costs as industry output expands in the long run

productive efficiency the condition that exists when production uses the least-cost combination of inputs; minimum average cost in the long run

allocative efficiency the condition that exists when firms produce the output most preferred by consumers; marginal benefit equals marginal cost

producer surplus a bonus for producers in the short run; the amount by which total revenue from production exceeds variable cost

social welfare the overall well-being of people in the economy; maximized when the marginal cost of production equals the marginal benefit to consumers

CHAPTER EQUATIONS

Marginal benefit = Marginal cost

$$TR = q \times p$$

$$AR = TR/q$$

$$\text{Economic Profit or Loss} = TR - TC$$

Market price = Marginal revenue = Average revenue

LO4 Explain how firms manage short-run supply. If price exceeds average variable cost, the firm produces the quantity at which marginal revenue equals marginal cost. A firm changes the rate of output if the market price changes. As long as the price covers average variable cost, the firm supplies the quantity at which the upward-sloping marginal cost curve intersects the marginal revenue, or demand, curve. Individual firm supply curves can be summed to yield the market, or industry supply curve. A perfectly competitive firm supplies the short-run quantity that maximizes profit or minimizes loss. When confronting a loss, a firm either produces an output that minimizes that loss or shuts down temporarily. Given the conditions for perfect competition, the market converges toward the equilibrium price and quantity.

Summary of Short-Run Output Decisions

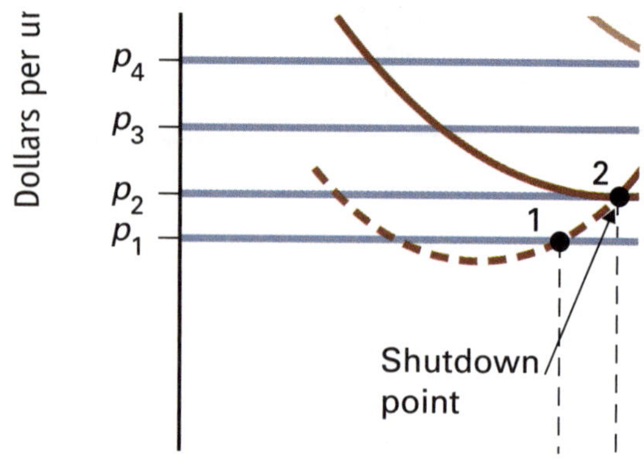

LO5 Describe how taking the long-run view affects economic factors. In the long run, firms enter and leave the market, adjust the scale of operations, and experience no distinction between fixed and variable cost. Short-run economic profit attracts new entrants in the long run and may cause existing firms to expand. Market supply thereby increases, driving down the market price until economic profit disappears. When market demand decreases, firms incur short-run losses and may go out of business in the long run. This results in lower market output and reduced operational scale that increases each remaining firm's long-run average cost.

Long-Run Equilibrium for a Firm and the Industry

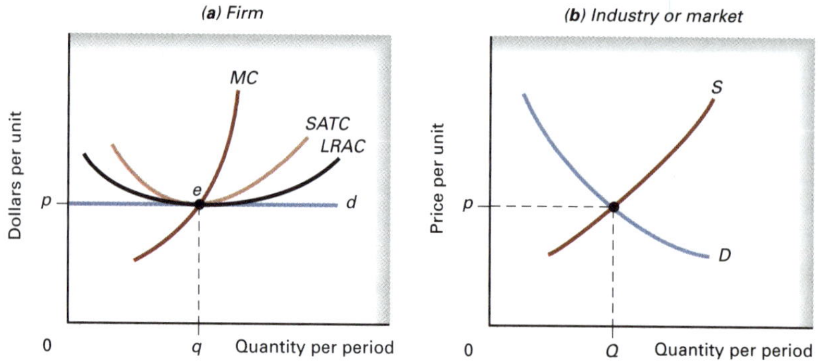

LO6 Describe how different cost structures influence an industry's long-run supply curve. In a constant-cost industry, each firm's long-run average cost curve does not shift up or down as industry output changes; each firm's per-unit costs are independent of the number of firms in the industry. The firms in some industries encounter higher average costs as industry output expands in the long run. Expanding output bids up the prices of some resources or otherwise increases per-unit production costs, and these higher costs shift up each firm's cost curves.

LO7 Identify how concepts of efficiency are used to judge market performance. Perfectly competitive markets exhibit both productive efficiency (because output is produced using the most efficient combination of resources available) and allocative efficiency (because the goods produced are those most valued by consumers). In equilibrium, a perfectly competitive market allocates goods so that the marginal cost of the final unit produced equals the marginal value that consumers attach to that final unit.

CHAPTER

10

Monopoly

Learning Outcomes

LO 1 List and describe barriers to market entry

LO 2 Explain sources of revenue for the monopolist

LO 3 Describe a firm's costs and its opportunities for profit maximization

LO 4 Explain monopoly and the allocation of resources

LO 5 Describe the problems that interfere with estimating the deadweight loss of a monopoly

LO 6 Describe conditions that create price discrimination

“How has China monopolized the world market for pandas?”

How can a firm monopolize a market? Why aren't most markets monopolized? Why don't most monopolies last? Why don't monopolies charge the highest possible price? How has China monopolized the world market for pandas? Why is the head of Starbucks worried about his coffee becoming a commodity? Do student and senior discounts come from corporate generosity? Why are there so many air fares for the same flight? These and other questions are answered in this chapter, which looks at our second market structure—monopoly.

What do you think?

Firms should be highly regulated to prevent monopolies from forming.

Strongly Disagree					*Strongly Agree*	
1	2	3	4	5	6	7

Monopoly is derived from the Greek, meaning “one seller.” In some parts of the United States, monopolists sell electricity, cable TV service, and local phone service. Monopolists also sell postage stamps, hot dogs at sports arenas, some patented products, some prescription drugs, and other goods and services with no close substitutes. You have probably heard about the evils of monopoly. You may have even played the board game *Monopoly* on a rainy day. Now we sort out fact from fiction.

Like perfect competition, pure monopoly is not as common as other market structures. But by understanding monopoly, you grow more familiar with market structures that lie between the extremes of perfect competition and pure monopoly. This chapter examines the sources of monopoly power, how a monopolist maximizes profit, differences between monopoly and perfect competition, and why a monopolist sometimes charges different prices for the same product.

Topics discussed in Chapter 10 include:

- Barriers to entry
- Price elasticity and marginal revenue
- Profit maximization and loss minimization
- Monopoly and resource allocation
- Welfare cost of monopoly
- Price discrimination
- The monopolists's dream

LO1 Barriers to Entry

As noted in Chapter 3, a *monopoly* is the sole supplier of a product with no close substitutes. Why do some markets come to be dominated by a single supplier? A monopolized market is characterized by barriers to entry, which are restrictions on the entry of new firms into an industry. Because of barriers,

barrier to entry any impediment that prevents new firms from entering an industry and competing on an equal basis with existing firms

© KEREN SU/STONE/GETTY IMAGES

new firms cannot profitably enter that market. Let's examine three types of entry barriers: legal restrictions, economies of scale, and control of an essential resource.

Legal Restrictions

One way to prevent new firms from entering a market is to make entry illegal. Patents, licenses, and other legal restrictions imposed by the government provide some producers with legal protection against competition.

Patents and Invention Incentives

In the United States, a **patent** awards an inventor the exclusive right to produce a good or service for 20 years from the date the patent is filed with the patent office. Originally enacted in 1790, patent laws encourage inventors to invest the time and money required to discover and develop new products and processes. If others could simply copy successful products, inventors would be less interested in incurring the up-front costs of invention. Abraham Lincoln said that "the patent system added the fuel of interest to the fire of genius." Patents also provide the stimulus to turn inventions into marketable products, a process called **innovation**.

Licenses and Other Entry Restrictions

Governments often confer monopoly status by awarding an individual firm the exclusive right to supply a particular good or service. Government licenses give certain firms the right to broadcast radio and TV signals. State in the U.S. authorize suppliers of medical care, plumbing, and legal advice. A license may not grant a monopoly, but it does block entry and often gives firms the power to charge prices above the competitive level. Thus, a license can serve as an effective barrier against new competitors. Governments also grant monopoly rights to sell hot dogs at civic auditoriums, collect garbage, provide bus and taxi service, and supply other services ranging from electricity to cable TV. Sometimes the government itself may claim that right by outlawing competitors. For example, many state governments sell liquor and lottery tickets, and the U.S. Postal Service has the exclusive right to deliver first-class mail to your mailbox.

patent
a legal barrier to entry that grants the holder the exclusive right to sell a product for 20 years from the date the patent application is filed

innovation
the process of turning an invention into a marketable product

Economies of Scale

A monopoly sometimes occurs naturally when a firm experiences *economies of scale,* as reflected by the downward-sloping, long-run average cost curve shown in Exhibit 1. In such instances, a single firm can supply market demand at a lower average cost per unit than could two or more firms, each producing less. Put another way, market demand is not great enough to allow more than one firm to achieve sufficient economies of scale. Thus, a single firm emerges from the competitive process as the only supplier in the market. For example, even though electricity *production* has become more competitive, electricity *transmission* still exhibits economies of scale. Once wires are strung throughout a community, the cost of linking an additional household to the power grid is relatively small. Consequently, the average cost of delivering electricity declines as more and more households are wired into an existing system.

A monopoly that emerges from the nature of costs is called a *natural monopoly,* to distinguish it from the artificial monopolies created by government patents, licenses, and other legal barriers to entry. A new entrant cannot sell enough to experience the economies of scale achieved by an established natural monopolist. Therefore, market entry is naturally blocked. A later chapter gets into the regulation of natural monopolies.

Control of Essential Resources

Sometimes the source of monopoly power is a firm's control over some resource critical to production.

© JW BURKEY/THE IMAGE BANK/GETTY IMAGES

Exhibit 1

Economies of Scale as a Barrier to Entry

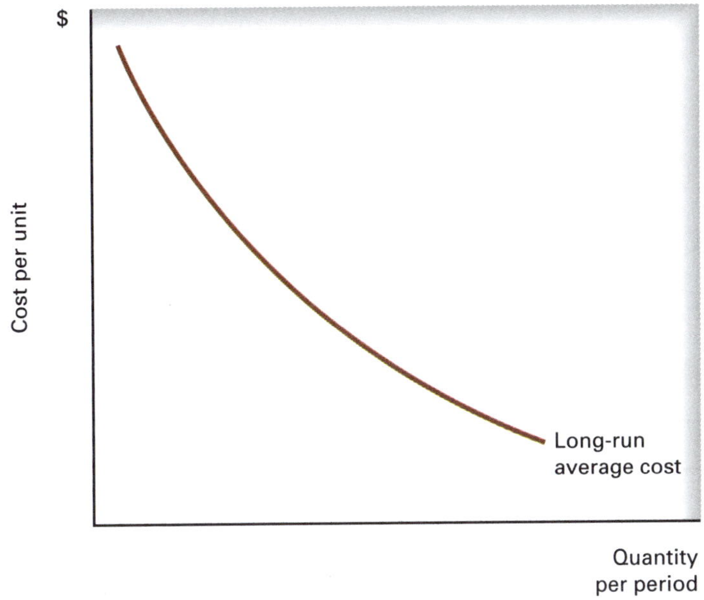

Here are some examples: Alcoa was the sole U.S. maker of aluminum from the late 19th century until World War II. Its monopoly power initially stemmed from production patents that expired in 1909, but for the next three decades, it controlled the supply of bauxite, the key raw material. Professional sports leagues try to block the formation of competing leagues by signing the best athletes to long-term contracts and by seeking the exclusive use of sports stadiums and arenas. China is a monopoly supplier of pandas to the world's zoos. The National Zoo in Washington, D.C., for example, rents its pair of pandas from China for $1 million a year. Other cities have similar arrangements. To control the supply, China stipulates that any offspring becomes China's property.[1] Finally, for decades, the world's diamond trade was controlled primarily by De Beers Consolidated Mines, which mined diamonds and also bought most of the world's supply of rough diamonds.

Local monopolies are more common than national or international monopolies. In rural areas, monopolies may include the only grocery store, movie theater, restaurant, or gas station for miles around. These are natural monopolies for products sold in local markets. But long-lasting monopolies are rare because economic profit attracts competitors. Also, over time, technological change tends to break down barriers to entry. For example, the development of wireless transmission of long-distance calls created competitors to AT&T. Wireless transmission is erasing the monopoly held by local cable TV providers and even local phone service. Likewise, text messaging, e-mail, the Internet, and firms such as FedEx and UPS now compete with the U.S. Postal Service's monopoly.

LO2 Revenue for the Monopolist

Because a monopoly, by definition, supplies the entire market, the demand for a monopolist's output is also the market demand. The demand curve therefore slopes downward, reflecting the law of demand—price and quantity demanded are inversely related. Let's look at demand, average revenue, and marginal revenue.

Demand, Average Revenue, and Marginal Revenue

Suppose De Beers controls the diamond market. Exhibit 2 shows the demand curve for 1-carat diamonds. De Beers, for example, can sell three diamonds a day at $7,000 each. That price-quantity combination yields total revenue of $21,000 (= $7,000 × 3). Total revenue divided by quantity is the *average revenue per diamond,* which also is $7,000. Thus, the monopolist's price equals the average revenue per unit. To sell a fourth diamond, De Beers must lower the price to $6,750. Total revenue from selling four diamonds is $27,000 (=

1. D'Vera Cohn, "Zoos Find Pandas Don't Make the Cash to Cover the Keep," *Washington Post,* 7 August 2005.

Exhibit 2

A Monopolist's Gain and Loss in Total Revenue from Selling One More Unit

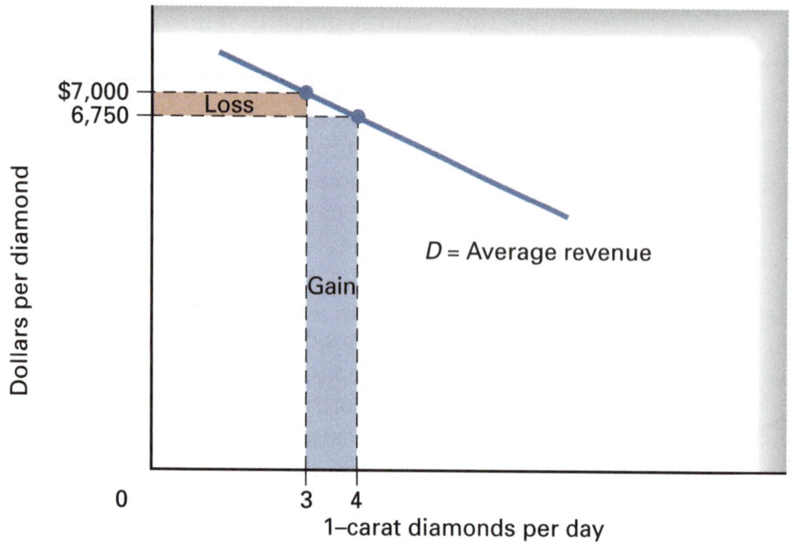

$6,750 × 4) and average revenue is $6,750. All along the demand curve, price equals average revenue. Therefore, *the demand curve is also the monopolist's average revenue curve,* just as the perfectly competitive firm's demand curve is that firm's average revenue curve.

What's the marginal revenue from selling a fourth diamond? When De Beers drops the price from $7,000 to $6,750, total revenue increases from $21,000 to $27,000. Thus, *marginal revenue*—the change in total revenue from selling one more diamond—is $6,000, which is less than the price, or average revenue, of $6,750. *For a monopolist, marginal revenue is less than the price, or average revenue.* Recall that for a perfectly competitive firm, marginal revenue equals the price, or average revenue, because that firm can sell all it supplies at the market price.

The Gains and Loss from Selling One More Unit

A closer look at Exhibit 2 reveals why a monopolist's marginal revenue is less than the price. By selling another diamond, De Beers gains the revenue from that sale. For example, De Beers gets $6,750 from the fourth diamond, as shown by the blue-shaded vertical rectangle marked "Gain." But to sell that fourth unit, De Beers must sell all four diamonds for $6,750 each. Thus, to sell a fourth diamond, De Beers must sacrifice $250 on each of the first three diamonds, which could have been sold for $7,000 each. This loss in revenue from the first three units totals $750 (= $250 × 3) and is identified in Exhibit 2 by the pink-shaded horizontal rectangle marked "Loss." The net change in total revenue from selling the fourth diamond—that is, the marginal revenue from the fourth diamond—equals the gain minus the loss, which equals $6,750 minus $750, or $6,000. So marginal revenue equals the gain minus the loss, or the price minus the revenue forgone by selling all units for a lower price. Because a monopolist's marginal revenue equals the price minus the loss, you can see why the marginal revenue is less than the price.

Incidentally, this analysis assumes that all units are sold at the market price; for example, the four diamonds are sold for $6,750 each. Although this is usually true, later in the chapter you learn how some monopolists try to increase profit by charging different customers different prices.

Revenue Schedules

Let's flesh out more fully the revenue schedules behind the demand curve of Exhibit 2. Column (1) of Exhibit 3 lists the quantity of diamonds demanded per day, and column (2) lists the corresponding price, or average revenue. Together, the two columns are the demand schedule for

Just Another Cup of Coffee?

Monopoly profits often arise from offering something that other producers can't match. For example, Starbucks over the years has built up a unique "experience" for the customer, including baristas who know customer orders by heart and a comfortable atmosphere that encourages patrons to relax and linger. That uniqueness had given Starbucks the market power to grow and to charge a premium price that rocketed the company's stock price more than fortyfold since 1992. But the company chairman has warned that pressure to grow could "commoditize" Starbucks, making it more vulnerable to competition from other coffee shops and even from fast-food chains. In addition, even monopoly power could not protect Starbucks from losing sales during the recession that started in December 2007. As consumers cut back on spending, foot traffic in Starbucks stores declined.

SOURCES: Janet Adamy, "Starbucks Chairman Says Trouble May Be Brewing," *Wall Street Journal,* 24 February 2007; Melissa Allison, "Starbucks Closing 5 Percent of U.S. Stores," *The Seattle Times,* 2 July 2008 (http://seattletimes.nwsource.com); Paul Ziobro, "Starbucks, After Years of Froth, Seen on a Cost-Cutting Grind," CNNMoney.com, 2 December 2008 (http://money.cnn.com).

© SUZANNE PLUNKETT/BLOOMBERG NEWS/LANDOV / © IMAGE SOURCE

Exhibit 3

Revenue for De Beers, a Monopolist

To sell more, the monopolist must lower the price on all units sold. Because the revenue lost from selling all units at a lower price must be subtracted from the revenue gained from selling another unit, marginal revenue is less than the price. At some point, marginal revenue turns negative, as shown here when the price is reduced to $3,500.

(1) 1-Carat Diamonds per Day (*Q*)	(2) Price (average revenue) (*p*)	(3) Total Revenue ($TR = p \times Q$)	(4) Marginal Revenue ($MR = \Delta TR/\Delta Q$)
0	$7,750	0	—
1	7,500	$ 7,500	$7,500
2	7,250	14,500	7,000
3	7,000	21,000	6,500
4	6,750	27,000	6,000
5	6,500	32,500	5,500
6	6,250	37,500	5,000
7	6,000	42,000	4,500
8	5,750	46,000	4,000
9	5,500	49,500	3,500
10	5,250	52,500	3,000
11	5,000	55,000	2,500
12	4,750	57,000	2,000
13	4,500	58,500	1,500
14	4,250	59,500	1,000
15	4,000	60,000	500
16	3,750	60,000	0
17	3,500	59,500	−500

1-carat diamonds. The price in column (2) times the quantity in column (1) yields the monopolist's *total revenue* schedule in column (3). So TR = p × Q. As De Beers sells more, total revenue increases until quantity reaches 15 diamonds.

$TR = p \times Q$

Marginal revenue, the change in total revenue from selling one more diamond, appears in column (4). In shorthand, MR = ΔTR/ΔQ, or the change in total revenue divided by the change in quantity. Note in Exhibit 3 that after the first unit, marginal revenue is less than price. As the price declines, the gap between price and marginal revenue widens. As the price declines, the loss from selling all diamonds for less increases (because quantity increases) and the gain from selling another diamond decreases (because the price falls).

$MR = \Delta TR/\Delta Q$

Revenue Curves

The schedules in Exhibit 3 are graphed in Exhibit 4, which shows the demand and marginal revenue curves in panel (a) and the total revenue curve in panel (b). Recall that total revenue equals price times quantity. Note that *the marginal revenue curve is below the demand curve and that total revenue reaches a maximum where marginal revenue is zero.* Please take a minute now to study these relationships—they are important.

Again, along the demand curve price equals average revenue, so the demand curve is also the monopolist's average revenue curve. In Chapter 5 you learned that the price elasticity for a straight-line demand curve declines as you move down the curve. When demand is elastic—that is, when the percentage increase in quantity demanded more than offsets the percentage decrease in price—a decrease in price increases total revenue. Therefore, *where demand is elastic, marginal revenue is positive, and total revenue increases as the price falls.* On the other hand, where demand is inelastic—that is, where the percentage increase in quantity demanded is less than the percentage decrease in price—a decrease in price reduces total revenue. In other words, the loss in revenue from selling all diamonds for the lower price overwhelms the gain in revenue from selling more diamonds. Therefore, *where demand is inelastic, marginal revenue is negative, and total revenue decreases as the price falls.*

From Exhibit 4, you can see that marginal revenue turns negative if the price drops below $3,750, indicating inelastic demand below that price. A *profit-maximizing monopolist would never expand output to the inelastic range of demand because doing so would reduce total revenue.* It would make no sense to sell more if total revenue drops in the process. Also note that demand is unit elastic at the price of $3,750. At that price, marginal revenue is zero and total revenue reaches a maximum.

LO3 The Firm's Costs and Profit Maximization

In perfect competition, each firm's choice is confined to quantity because the market has already determined the price. The perfect competitor is a *price taker.* The monopolist, however, can

Exhibit 4

Monopoly Demand, Marginal Revenue, and Total Revenue

(a) Demand and marginal revenue

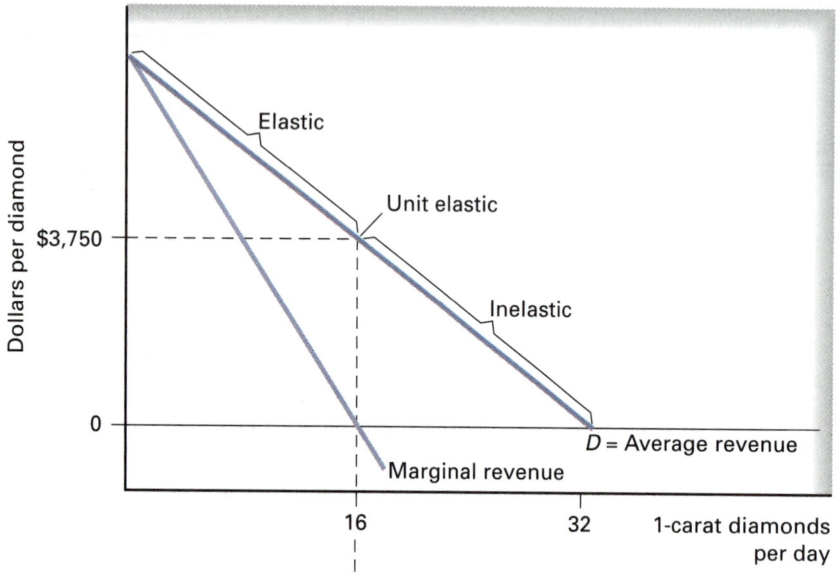

(b) Total revenue

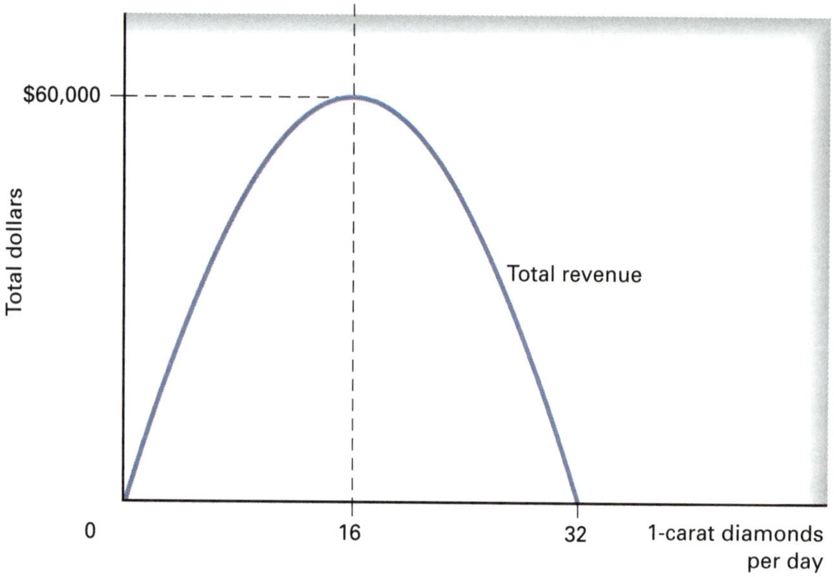

choose either the price or the quantity, but choosing one determines the other—they come in pairs. For example, if De Beers decides to sell 10 diamonds a day, consumers would demand that many only at a price of $5,250 per diamond. Alternatively, if De Beers decides to sell diamonds for $6,000 each, consumers would demand 7 a day. Because the monopolist can choose any price-quantity combination on the demand curve, we say the monopolist is a **price maker**. More generally, any firm that has some control over what price to charge is a price maker.

price maker
a firm with some power to set the price because the demand curve for its output slopes downward; a firm with market power

Profit Maximization

Exhibit 5 repeats revenue schedules from Exhibits 3 and 4 and also includes a short-run cost schedule similar to those already introduced in the two previous chapters. Please take a little time now to become familiar with this table. Then ask yourself this question: which price-quantity combination should De Beers select to maximize profit? As was the case with perfect competition, the monopolist can approach profit maximization in two ways—the total approach and the marginal approach.

Total Revenue Minus Total Cost

The profit-maximizing monopolist employs the same decision rule as the competitive firm. *The monopolist supplies the quantity at which total revenue exceeds total cost by the greatest amount.* Economic profit appears in column (8) of Exhibit 5. As you can see, maximum profit is $12,500 per day, which occurs at 10 diamonds per day. At that quantity, total revenue is $52,500 and total cost is $40,000.

Marginal Revenue Equals Marginal Cost

De Beers, as a profit-maximizing monopolist, increases output if it adds more to total revenue than to total cost. So De Beers expands output as long as marginal revenue, shown in column (4) of Exhibit 5, exceeds marginal cost, shown in column (6). But De Beers stops short of producing where marginal cost exceeds marginal revenue. Again, profit is maximized at $12,500 when output is 10 diamonds per day. For the tenth diamond, marginal revenue is $3,000 and marginal cost is $2,750. As you can see, if output exceeds 10 diamonds per day, marginal cost exceeds marginal revenue. An eleventh diamond's marginal cost of $3,250 exceeds its marginal revenue of $2,500.

> "The monopolist, however, can choose either the price or the quantity, but choosing one determines the other—they come in pairs."

For simplicity, we say that *the profit-maximizing output occurs where marginal revenue equals marginal cost,* (provided marginal cost curve cuts the marginal revenue curve from below) which, you will recall, is the golden rule of profit maximization.

Graphical Solution

The revenue and cost schedules in Exhibit 5 are graphed in Exhibit 6, with per-unit cost and revenue curves in panel (a) and total cost and revenue curves in panel (b). The intersection of the two marginal curves at point *e* in panel (a) indicates that profit is maximized when 10 diamonds are sold. Note that the marginal cost curve cuts the marginal revenue curve from below. At that quantity, we move up to the demand curve to find the profit-maximizing price of $5,250. Average total cost of $4,000 is identified by point *b*. The average profit per diamond equals

© COMSTOCK IMAGES/JUPITERIMAGES

the price of $5,250 minus the average total cost of $4,000. Economic profit is the average profit per unit of $1,250 multiplied by the 10 diamonds sold, for a total profit of $12,500 per day, as identified by the blue-shaded rectangle. *So the profit-maximizing rate of output is found where the marginal cost curve intersects the marginal revenue curve.* Further, the marginal cost curve cuts the marginal revenue curve from below.

In panel (b), the firm's profit or loss is measured by the vertical distance between the total revenue and total cost curves. De Beers expands output if the increase in total revenue from selling another diamond exceeds the increase in total cost. *The profit-maximizing firm produces where total revenue exceeds total cost by the greatest amount.* Again, profit is maximized where De Beers sells 10 diamonds per day.

Exhibit 5

Short-Run Costs and Revenue for a Monopolist

(1) Diamonds per Day (Q)	(2) Price (p)	(3) Total Revenue ($TR = p \times Q$)	(4) Marginal Revenue ($MR = \Delta TR/\Delta Q$)	(5) Total Cost (TC)	(6) Marginal Cost ($MC = \Delta TC/\Delta Q$)	(7) Average Total Cost ($ATC = TC/Q$)	(8) Total Profit or Loss ($= TR - TC$)
0	$7,750	0	—	$15,000	—		−$15,000
1	7,500	$7,500	$7,500	19,750	$4,750	$19,750	−12,250
2	7,250	14,500	7,000	23,500	3,750	11,750	−9,000
3	7,000	21,000	6,500	26,500	3,000	8,833	−5,500
4	6,750	27,000	6,000	29,000	2,500	7,250	−2,000
5	6,500	32,500	5,500	31,000	2,000	6,200	1,500
6	6,250	37,500	5,000	32,500	1,500	5,417	5,000
7	6,000	42,000	4,500	33,750	1,250	4,821	8,250
8	5,750	46,000	4,000	35,250	1,500	4,406	10,750
9	5,500	49,500	3,500	37,250	2,000	4,139	12,250
10	**5,250**	**52,500**	**3,000**	**40,000**	**2,750**	**4,000**	**12,500**
11	5,000	55,000	2,500	43,250	3,250	3,932	11,750
12	4,750	57,000	2,000	48,000	4,750	4,000	9,000
13	4,500	58,500	1,500	54,500	6,500	4,192	4,000
14	4,250	59,500	1,000	64,000	9,500	4,571	−4,500
15	4,000	60,000	500	77,500	10,500	5,167	−17,500
16	3,750	60,000	0	96,000	18,500	6,000	−36,000
17	3,500	59,500	−500	121,000	25,000	7,118	−61,500

Exhibit 6

Monopoly Costs and Revenue

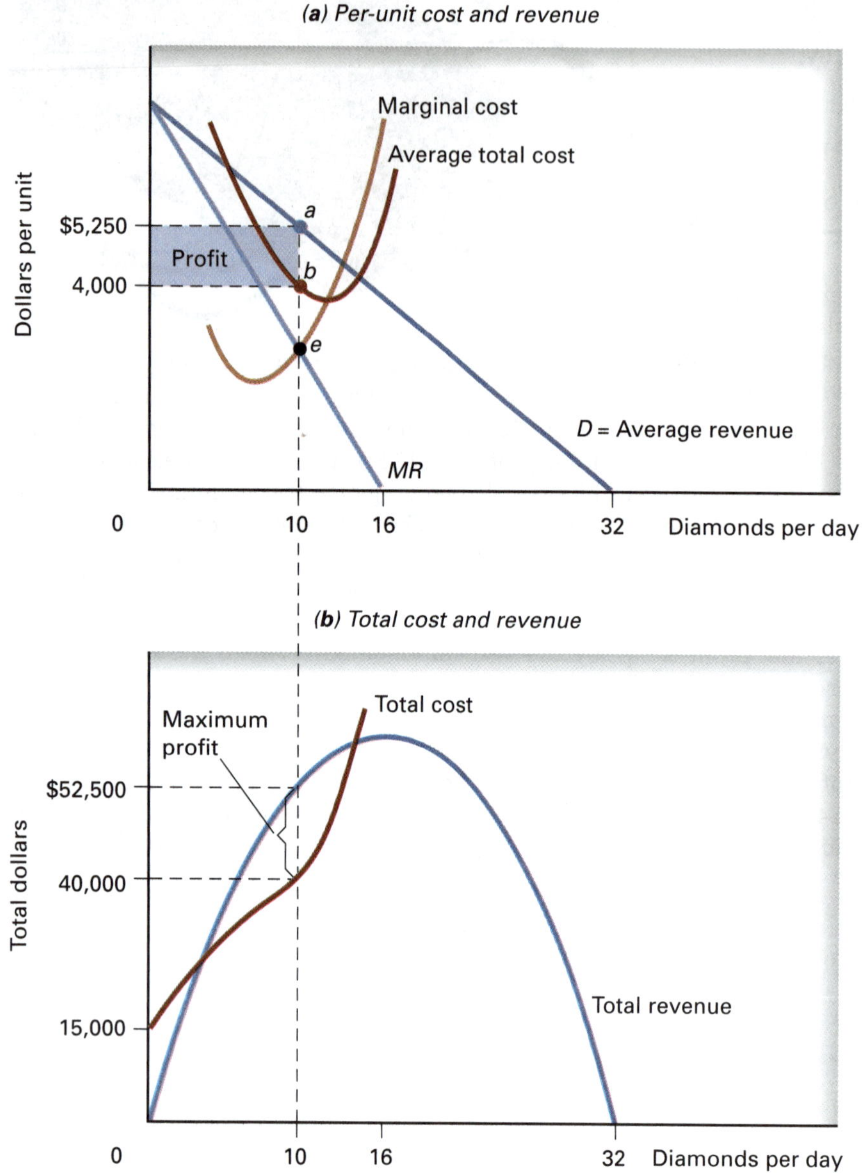

Total profit in panel (b) is measured by the *vertical distance* between the two total curves; in panel (a), total profit is measure by the shaded *area* formed by multiplying average profit per unit by the number of units sold.

One common myth about monopolies is that they charge the highest price possible. But the monopolist is interested in maximizing profit, not price. What the monopolist can charge is limited by consumer demand. De Beers, for example, could charge $7,500, but selling only one diamond would result in a big loss. Indeed, De Beers could charge $7,750 or more but would sell no diamonds. So charging the highest possible price is not consistent with maximizing profit. A monopolist may be able to set the price, but the quantity demanded at that price is determined by consumers. *Even the most powerful monopolist is subject to the law of demand.*

Short-Run Losses and the Shutdown Decision

A monopolist is not assured an economic profit. Although a monopolist is the sole supplier of a good with no close substitutes, the demand for that good may not generate economic profit in either the short run or the long run. After all, many new products are protected from direct competition by patents, yet most patents never turn into a profitable product. And even a monopolist that is initially profitable may eventually suffer losses because of rising costs, falling demand, or market entry of similar products. For example, Coleco, the original mass producer of Cabbage Patch dolls, went bankrupt after that craze died down. In the short run, the loss-minimizing monopolist, like the loss-minimizing perfect competitor, must decide whether to produce or to shut down. *If the price covers average variable cost, the monopolist produces, at least in the short run. If not, the monopolist shuts down, at least in the short run.*

Exhibit 7 brings average variable cost back into the picture. Recall from Chapter 7 that average variable cost and average fixed cost sum to average total cost. Loss minimization occurs in Exhibit 7 at point *e*, where the marginal revenue curve intersects the marginal cost curve. At the equilibrium rate of output, Q, price *p* is found on the demand curve at point *b*. That price exceeds average variable cost, at point *c*, but is below average total cost, at point *a*. Because price covers average variable cost and a portion of average fixed cost, this monopolist loses less by producing Q than by shutting down. The loss, identified

© MICKEY PFLEGER/TIME LIFE PICTURES/GETTY IMAGES

by the shaded rectangle, is the average loss per unit, *ab,* times the quantity sold, *Q*. The firm would shut down in the short run if the average variable cost curve is above the demand curve, or average revenue curve, at all output rates.

Recall that a perfectly competitive firm's supply curve is that portion of the marginal cost curve at or above the average variable cost curve. The intersection of a monopolist's marginal revenue and marginal cost curves identifies the profit-maximizing (or loss-minimizing) quantity, but the price is found up on the demand curve. Because the equilibrium quantity can be found along a monopolist's marginal cost curve but the equilibrium price appears on the demand curve, no single curve traces points showing unique combinations of both the price and quantity supplied. Because no curve reflects combinations of price and quantity supplied, *there is no monopolist supply curve.*

Long-Run Profit Maximization

For perfectly competitive firms, the distinction between the short run and the long run is important because entry and exit of firms can occur in the long run, erasing any economic profit or loss. For the monopolist, the distinction between the short run and long run is less relevant. *If a monopoly is insulated from competition by high barriers that block new entry, economic profit can persist into the long run.* Yet short-run profit is no guarantee of long-run profit. For example, suppose the monopoly relies on a patent. Patents last only so long and even while a product is under patent, the monopolist often must defend it in court (patent litigation has nearly doubled in the last decade). On the other hand, a monopolist may be able to erase a loss (most start-up firms lose money initially) or increase profit in the long run by adjusting the scale of the firm or by advertising to increase demand. A monopolist unable to erase a loss will, in the long run, leave the market.

Exhibit 7

The Monopolist Minimizes Losses in the Short Run

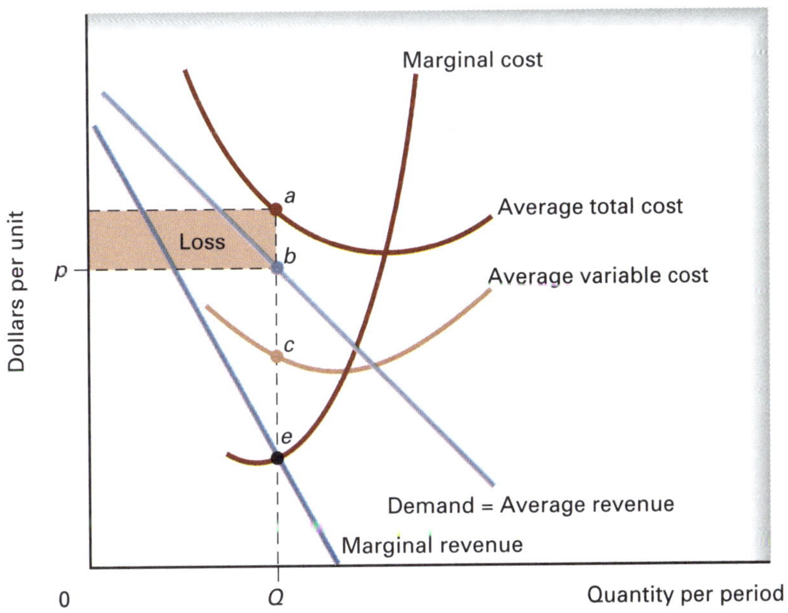

LO4 Monopoly and the Allocation of Resources

If monopolists are no greedier than perfect competitors (because both maximize profit), if monopolists do not charge the highest possible price (because the highest price would reduce quantity demanded to zero), and if monopolists are not guaranteed a profit (because demand for the product may be weak), then what's the problem with monopoly? To get a handle on the problem, let's compare monopoly with the benchmark established in the previous chapter—perfect competition.

Price and Output Under Perfect Competition

Let's begin with the long-run equilibrium price and output in a perfectly competitive market. Suppose the long-run market supply curve in perfect competition is horizontal, as shown by S_c in Exhibit 8. Because this is a constant-cost industry, the horizontal long-run supply curve also shows marginal cost and average total cost at each quantity. Equilibrium in perfect competition occurs at point c, where the market demand and market supply curves intersect to yield price p_c and quantity Q_c. Remember, the demand curve reflects the marginal benefit of each unit purchased. In competitive equilibrium, the marginal benefit of the final unit sold equals the marginal cost to society of producing that final unit. As noted in the previous chapter, when the marginal benefit that consumers derive from a good equals the marginal cost of producing that good, that market is said to be allocatively efficient and to maximize social welfare. There is no way of reallocating resources to increase the total value of output or to increase social welfare. Because consumers are able to purchase Q_c units at price p_c, they enjoy a net benefit from consumption, or a consumer surplus, measured by the entire shaded triangle, acp_c.

Price and Output Under Monopoly

With only one firm in the industry, the industry demand curve *D* in Exhibit 8 becomes the monopolist's demand curve, so the price the monopolist charges determines the market quantity. Because the monopolist's demand curve slopes downward, the marginal revenue curve also slopes downward and is beneath the demand curve, as is indicated by MR_m in Exhibit 8. Suppose the monopolist can produce at the same constant cost in the long run as can firms in the competitive industry. The monopolist maximizes profit by equating marginal revenue with marginal cost, which occurs at point *b*, yielding equilibrium price p_m and output Q_m. Again, the price shows the consumers' marginal benefit for unit Q_m. This marginal benefit, identified at point *m*, exceeds the monopolist's marginal cost, identified at point *b*. Because marginal benefit exceeds marginal cost, society would be better off if output expanded beyond Q_m. *The monopolist restricts quantity below what would maximize social welfare.* Even though the monopolist restricts output, consumers still derive some benefit, just not as much as with perfect competition. Consumer surplus is shown by the smaller triangle, amp_m.

THE MONOPOLIST RESTRICTS QUANTITY BELOW WHAT WOULD MAXIMIZE SOCIAL WELFARE.

Allocative and Distributive Effects

Consider the allocative and distributive effects of monopoly versus perfect competition. In Exhibit 8, consumer surplus under perfect competition is the large triangle, acp_c. Under monopoly, consumer surplus shrinks to the smaller triangle amp_m, which in this example is only one-fourth as large. The monopolist earns economic profit equal to the shaded rectangle. By comparing the situation under perfect competition with that under monopoly , you can see that the monopolist's economic profit comes entirely from what was consumer surplus under perfect competition. Because the profit rectangle reflects a transfer from consumer surplus to monopoly profit, this amount is not lost to society and so is not considered a welfare loss.

Exhibit 8

Perfect Competition and Monopoly Compared

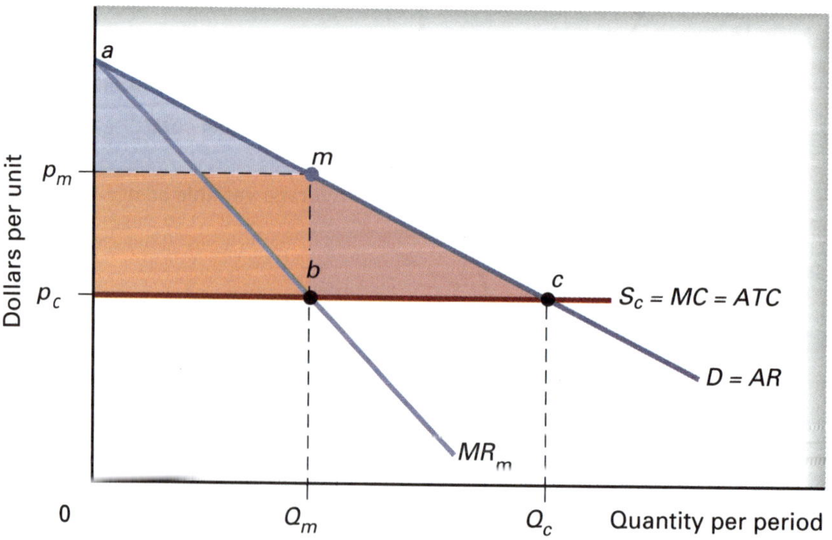

Notice, however, that consumer surplus has been reduced by more than the profit rectangle. Consumers also lose the triangle *mcb*, which is part of the consumer surplus with perfect competition. The *mcb* triangle is called the **deadweight loss of monopoly** because it is a loss to consumers but a gain to nobody. This loss results from the *allocative inefficiency arising from the higher price and reduced output of monopoly*. Again, society would be better off if output exceeded the monopolist's profit-maximizing quantity, because the marginal benefit of more output exceeds its marginal cost. Under monopoly, the price, or marginal benefit, always exceeds marginal cost. Empirical estimates of the annual deadweight loss of monopoly in the United States have ranged from about 1 percent to about 5 percent of national income. Applied to national income data for 2009, these estimates imply a deadweight loss of monopoly ranging from about $450 to $2,250 per capita—not a trivial amount.

© JUSTIN SULLIVAN/GETTY IMAGES

The Mail Monopoly

The U.S. Postal Service (USPS) was granted a monopoly in 1775 and has operated under federal protection ever since. USPS pays no taxes and is exempt from local zoning laws. It has a legal monopoly in delivering regular, first-class letters and has the exclusive right to use the space inside your mailbox. Other delivery services such as FedEx or UPS cannot use mail boxes or post office boxes.

Still, USPS has suffered in recent years because of rising costs and growing competition from new technologies. The price of a first-class stamp climbed from 6 cents in 1970 to 44 cents by 2009—a growth rate double that of inflation. New technologies such as email, ecards, online bill-payment, text messaging, and fax machines also displace USPS delivery services (email messages now greatly outnumber first-class letters). Because its monopoly applies only to regular first-class mail, USPS has lost chunks of other business to private firms offering lower rates and better service. The United Parcel Service (UPS), for example, is more mechanized and more containerized than the USPS and thus has lower costs and less breakage.

SOURCES: "Going Postal," *Wall Street Journal,* 13 April 2006; Katie Hafner, "Postal Service Finds a Friend in the Internet," *New York Times,* 2 August 2006; John McKinnon and Rick Brooks, "Mail Rates to Be Harnessed as Part of Postal-Overhaul Bill," *Wall Street Journal,* 11 December 2006; and the USPS home page at http://www.usps.com.

LO5 Problems Estimating the Deadweight Loss of Monopoly

The actual cost of monopoly could differ from the deadweight loss described so far. These costs could be lower or higher. Here's the reasoning.

Why the Deadweight Loss of Monopoly Might Be Lower

If economies of scale are substantial enough, a monopolist might be able to produce output at a lower cost per unit than could competitive firms. Therefore, the price, or at least the cost of production, could be lower under monopoly than under competition. The deadweight loss shown in Exhibit 8 may also overstate the true cost of monopoly because monopolists might, in response to public scrutiny and political pressure, keep prices below the profit maximizing level. Although monopolists would like to earn as much profit as possible, they realize that if the public outcry over high prices and high profit grows loud enough, some sort of government intervention could reduce or even erase that profit. For example, the prices and profit of drug companies, which individually are monopoly suppliers of patented medicines, come under scrutiny from time to time by elected officials who propose regulating drug prices or taxing "windfall profits." Drug firms might try to avoid such treatment by keeping prices below the level that would maximize profit. Finally, a monopolist might keep the price below the profit-maximizing level to avoid attracting competitors to the market. For example, some observers claim that Alcoa, when it was the only U.S. producer of aluminum, kept prices low enough to discourage new entry.

Why the Deadweight Loss Might Be Higher

Another line of reasoning suggests that the deadweight loss of monopoly might, in fact, be greater than shown in our simple diagram. *If resources must be devoted to securing and maintaining a monopoly position, monopolies may impose a greater welfare loss than simple models suggest.* For example, radio and TV broadcasting rights confer on the recipient the use of a particular band of the scarce broadcast spectrum. In the past, these rights have been given away by government agencies to the applicants deemed most deserving. Because these rights are so valuable, numerous applicants have spent millions

deadweight loss of monopoly net loss to society when a firm with market power restricts output and increases the price on lawyers' fees, lobbying expenses, and other costs associated with making themselves appear the most deserving. The efforts devoted to securing and maintaining a monopoly position are largely a social waste because they use up scarce resources but add not one unit to output. Activities undertaken by individuals or firms to influence public policy to directly or indirectly redistribute income to themselves are referred to as **rent seeking**.

The monopolist, insulated from the rigors of competition in the marketplace, might also grow fat and lazy—and become inefficient. Because some monopolies could still earn an economic profit even if the firm is inefficient, corporate executives might waste resources by creating a more comfortable life for themselves. Long lunches, afternoon golf, plush offices, corporate jets, and excessive employee benefits might make company life more pleasant, but they increase production costs and raise prices.

Monopolists have also been criticized for being slow to adopt the latest production techniques, being reluctant to develop new products, and generally lacking innovation. Because monopolists are largely insulated from the rigors of competition, they might take it easy. It's been said "The best of all monopoly profits is a quiet life."

Not all economists believe that monopolies manage their resources with any less vigilance than perfect competitors do. Some argue that because monopolists are protected from rivals, they are in a good position to capture the fruits of any innovation and therefore are more innovative than competitive firms are. Others believe that if a monopolist strays from the path of profit maximization, its share price will drop enough to attract someone who will buy a controlling interest and shape up the company. This market for corporate control is said to keep monopolists on their toes.

LO6 Price Discrimination

rent seeking
activities undertaken by individuals or firms to influence public policy in a way that increases their incomes

price discrimination
the charging of different prices for different quantities of the product, at different times to different customer groups or in different markets, when these price differences are not justified by cost differences

Price discrimination refers to the charging of different prices for different quantities of the product, at different times to different customer groups or in different markets, when these price differences are not justified by cost differences. In pure price discrimination, the seller charges each customer the maximum price that he or she is willing to pay.

© ISTOCKPHOTO.COM

However, in more common forms of price discrimination, the seller places customers in groups based on certain attributes and charges each group a different price. Price discrimination allows a company to earn higher profits than standard pricing because it allows firms to capture a greater part of the consumer's surplus. Price discrimination requires market segmentation and some means to discourage discount customers from becoming resellers and, by extension, competitors to the original seller.

Common Examples of Price Discrimination

Some common examples of price discrimination are medical doctors charging low prices from low-income patients (consumers) and higher price from high-income consumers; lower movie prices in the afternoon show and higher movie ticket price for the evening show; airline discounts for senior citizens; and the practice of charging different prices by the electric companies depending upon whether it is used for commercial or domestic purposes.

Few more examples of price discrimination are discussed in detail.

Air Travel Industry

For instance, an airline may apply differential pricing to "the same seat" over time, e.g., by discounting the price for an early or late booking (without changing any other fare condition). Customers booking early normally find lower prices if they are prepared to commit themselves to a flight by booking early. This gives the airline the advantage of knowing how full their flights are likely to be and a *source of cash-flow* in the weeks and months prior to the service being pro-

Conditions for Price Discrimination

1. Product demand curve must slope downward
2. At least two groups of consumers with different price elasticities
3. Charge each group a different price at low cost
4. Prevent those paying the lower price from reselling to those paying the higher price

vided. Closer to the date and time of the scheduled service, the price rises, on the simple justification that consumer's demand for a flight becomes more inelastic, the nearer to the time of the service. People who book late often regard travel to their intended destination as a necessity and they are therefore likely to be willing and able to pay a much higher price very close to departure. However, this could present an arbitrage opportunity in the absence of any restriction on reselling. Therefore, passenger name changes are typically prevented which makes this kind of price discrimination remain feasible.

Coupons

The use of coupons in retail is an attempt to distinguish customers by their reserve price. The assumption is that people who take the trouble of collecting coupons have greater price sensitivity than those who do not. Thus, making coupons available enables, for instance, breakfast cereal makers to charge higher prices to price-insensitive customers, while still make some profit off customers who are more price-sensitive.

Premium Pricing

For certain products, premium products are priced at a level (compared to "regular" or "economy" products) that is well beyond their marginal cost of production. For example, a coffee chain may price regular coffee at ₹50, but "premium" coffee at ₹150 (where the respective costs of production may be ₹25 and ₹40. Similar techniques are used in pricing business class airline tickets and premium alcoholic drinks.

Segmentation by Age Group and Student Status

Several amusement parks, tourist attractions, and other places have different admission prices per market segment: typical groupings are children, student, adult, and senior citizen. Each of these groups typically has a much different demand curve. For instance, children and senior citizens generally have much less disposable income, and thus the monopolist charges them a differential price.

International Price Discrimination

Pharmaceutical companies may charge customers living in wealthier countries (such as the United States) a much higher price for identical drugs than in poorer nations, as is the case with the sale of antiretroviral drugs in Africa. Since the purchasing power of African consumers is much lower, sales would be extremely limited without price discrimination. The ability of pharmaceutical companies to maintain price differences between countries is often reinforced by national drugs laws and regulations. Similarly, a producer who has monopoly power in the domestic market, but is more of a perfect competitor in the international market, charges differential pricing from the respective buyers: a higher price from domestic buyers and a lower price from the international buyer.

Dual Pricing

Even within a country, differentiated pricing may be established to ensure that citizens receive lower prices than non-citizens; this is known as dual pricing. For instance, many countries maintain separate admission charges for museums, national parks, and similar facilities, the usually professed reason being that citizens should be able to educate themselves and enjoy the country's natural wonders cheaply, but other visitors should pay the market rate. Similarly, many publicly run universities in several countries are subsidized by taxpayers of the state for their own citizens while outsiders pay a higher tuition fee.

Peak and Off-Peak Pricing

Peak and off-peak pricing is common in the telecommunications industry, leisure retailing, and in the travel sector. Telephone and electricity companies often separate markets by time. For instance, there are generally three rates for telephone calls: a daytime peak rate, an off-peak evening rate, and a cheaper weekend rate. Electricity suppliers also offer cheaper off-peak electricity during the night. At off-peak times, there is plenty of spare capacity and marginal costs of production are low (the supply curve is elastic). On the other hand, at peak times when demand is high, the short run supply curve becomes relatively inelastic as the supplier reaches capacity constraints. This raises *MC* of supply. A combination of higher demand and rising costs during peak hours, forces up the profit maximizing equilibrium price under price discrimination.

Wage Discrimination

Wage discrimination is when the price of equivalent labor is discriminated among different groups of workers. For instance, in several developing coun-

Office Model
(Faster—Higher Price)

Home Model
(Slower—Lower Price)

© RYAN MCVAY/PHOTODISC/GETTY IMAGES / © GEOSTOCK/PHOTODISC/GETTY IMAGES

tries women earn lower wages relative to males for similar kind of work.

Here are other examples of price discrimination: IBM wanted to charge business users of its laser printer more than home users. To distinguish between the two groups, IBM decided to slow down the home printer to 5 pages a minute (versus 10 for the business model). To do this, they added an extra chip that inserted pauses between pages.[2] Thus, IBM could sell the home model for less than the business model without cutting into sales of its business model. Intel offered two versions of the same computer chip; the cheaper version was the expensive version with some extra work done to reduce its speed. And Adobe stripped some features from its Photoshop CD to offer a cheaper version, Photoshop Elements. Major amusement parks, such as Disney World and Universal Studios, distinguish between local residents and out-of-towners when it comes to the price of admission. Out-of-towners typically spend substantial amounts on airlines and lodging just to be there, so they are less sensitive to the admission price than are local residents. The problem is how to charge a lower price to locals. The parks do this by making discount coupons available at local businesses, such as dry cleaners, which vacationers are less likely to visit. The Las Vegas monorail sorts out the locals from the visitors by charging $1 for those presenting a Nevada driver's license and $5 for those without one.

Types of Price Discrimination

Price discrimination could be of three kinds:

1. Price discrimination of degree one
2. Price discrimination of degree two
3. Price discrimination of degree three

We begin by discussing price discrimination of degree three.

Third Degree Price Discrimination: This refers to the charging of different prices for the same product in different markets until the marginal revenue of the last unit of the product sold in each market equals the marginal cost of producing the product. In third degree price discrimination, the monopolist divides the entire market into a few sub-markets and charges different prices for the same commodity in different sub-markets. The division here is generally among classes of consumers and not among individual consumers. The producer discriminates between prices as it increases his total revenue and profits as compared to the alternative situation with no price discrimination. Third degree price discrimination is possible if two conditions are met.

1. If various groups of customers have different elasticities of demand for the said commodity, and
2. If the classes of consumers can be kept separate. In other words, resale should not be possible.

Under price discrimination of degree three, the segment with a less elastic demand pays a higher price than the segment with a more elastic demand. This is the most common type of price discrimination. Third degree discrimination is linked directly to *consumers' willingness and ability to pay* for a good or service. It means that the prices charged may bear little or no relation to the cost of production. Price discrimination at movie theaters, railways, and museums are typical examples of this kind of price discrimination.

While discriminating between prices, the monopolist has to take two decisions, viz.

1. How much to produce, and
2. How to distribute in the sub-markets and at what price

2. Carl Shapiro and Hal Varian, *Information Rules: A Strategic Guide to the Network Economy* (Harvard Business School Press, 1999), p. 59.

Exhibit 9

Price Discriminating Monopolist

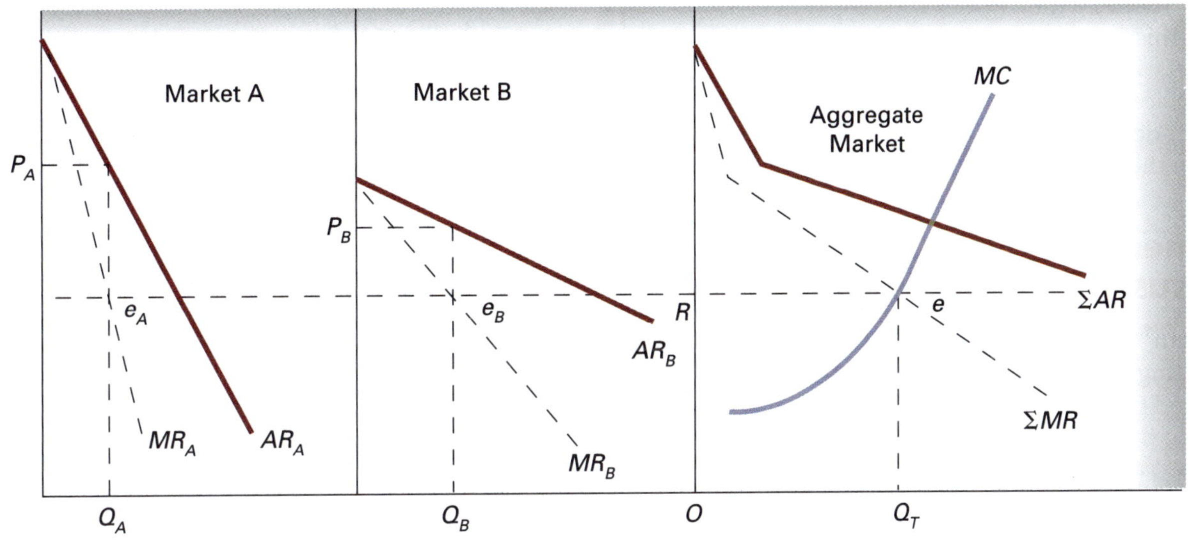

As a simple illustration, we assume there are two markets: Market A and Market B. Market A consists of consumers with a relatively inelastic demand while Market B consists of consumers with a relatively more elastic demand. The aggregate market demand is given by horizontal summation of the two sub-market demand curves.

The point where summation MR equals MC gives the equilibrium point "e". The optimal output that the monopolist needs to produce equals Q_T. MC of producing this output is OR (or eQ_T). To maximize profit in each of the sub-markets, the producer equates MC to MR_A in Market A and MC to MR_B in Market B (Note that MC is the same for the whole quantity produced, irrespective of the market in which it is going to be sold. MR in each market differs due to the difference in the elasticity of the two demand curves). Thus, the optimal distribution of output is when Q_A is distributed in Market A and Q_B in Market B. The reader must note that Q_A plus Q_B equals Q_T. The price charged in the two markets is P_A and P_B, respectively. It is clear that P_A is greater than P_B. This implies that lower the elasticity of demand, higher is the price charged.

Thus, in the first market, profit is maximized when:

$$MR_A = MC$$

In the second market, profit is maximized when:

$$MR_B = MC$$

Since MC is the same, the equilibrium condition becomes:

$$MR_A = MR_B = MC$$

If MR_A does not equal MR_B, it pays for the firm to re-distribute sales from the market in which MR is lower to the market where MR is higher. This re-distribution increases TR for the firm without changing its TC. Such re-distribution should continue until $MR_A = MR_B$.

Some of the examples of price discrimination of degree three are companies charging higher electricity prices from residential users than from commercial users in the United States. This is because commercial users, by having the option of generating their own electricity, have a higher price elasticity of demand. Resale is prohibited as buyers remain segmented since meters are installed either at offices or at homes, depending upon where it is consumed. Higher price charged by telephone companies during business hours than at other times of the day is another example of price discrimination of degree three.

Price Discrimination and Price Elasticity of Demand: Let us now generalize the relationship between price elasticity of demand and price discrimination. In general, lower the price elasticity of demand, higher will be the price charged.

We know that:

$$MR_1 = AR_1 (1 - 1/E_1)$$
$$MR_2 = AR_2 (1 - 1/E_2)$$

But AR = Price

Therefore,

$$MR_1 = P_1 (1 - 1/E_1)$$
$$MR_2 = P_2 (1 - 1/E_2)$$

Further, at equilibrium, $MR_1 = MR_2$

Thus,

$$P_1 (1 - 1/E_1) = P_2 (1 - 1/E_2)$$
$$\Rightarrow \quad P_1/P_2 = (1 - 1/E_1)/(1 - 1/E_2)$$

From the above, we can conclude the following:

If $E_1 = E_2$, then $P_1 = P_2$
If $E_1 < E_2$, then $P_1 > P_2$
If $E_1 > E_2$, then $P_1 < P_2$

From this we can see that if elasticity in both the markets is same, then price differentiation cannot take place. Further, with price discrimination, lower is the price elasticity of demand in a market, higher will be the relative price charged.

Numerical Illustration: Simple Versus Discriminating Monopoly

Problem 1: Given two isolated markets supplied by a single monopolist, let the two corresponding demand function be:

$$P_1 = 12 - Q_1 \quad \text{and} \quad P_2 = 20 - 3Q_2$$

Suppose the monopolist's TC function is:

$$C = 3 + 2(Q_1 + Q_2)$$

Calculate the equilibrium P, Q, and π under a regime of

1. Price discrimination
2. No price discrimination

Solution:

1. Price Discrimination: If the company was allowed to discriminate between prices, the π maximizing firm would set its quantities and prices in the two markets such that its total π is maximized. In order to do so, we first estimate the profit function and then set the first order derivatives with respect to Q_1 and Q_2 equal to zero. Setting the first order derivatives equal to zero yields the necessary condition for profit maximization.

$$\pi = P_1Q_1 + P_2Q_2 - C$$
$$\pi = 12\,Q_1 - Q_1^2 + 20Q_2 - 3Q_2^2 - 3 - 2(Q_1 + Q_2)$$
$$\pi = 10Q_1 - Q_1^2 + 18Q_2 - 3Q_2^2 - 3$$

Taking partial derivatives and equating them zero, we have:

$$\frac{\partial \pi}{\partial Q_1} = 10 - 2Q_1 = 0 \quad \text{or} \quad Q_1 = 5$$
$$\frac{\partial \pi}{\partial Q_2} = 18 - 6Q_2 = 0 \quad \text{or} \quad Q_2 = 3$$

The second order conditions (not shown here) are also met. Substituting these values in the demand function gives:

$$P_1 = 7 \quad \text{and} \quad P_2 = 11$$

perfectly discriminating monopolist a monopolist who charges a different price for each unit sold; also called the monopolist's dream

2. No Price Discrimination: If monopolist cannot discriminate, the objective would be to maximize π subject to the constraint $P_1 = P_2$.

i.e., $\quad 12 - Q_1 = 20 - 3Q_2$
or $\quad 8 - 3Q_2 + Q_1 = 0$

$$\phi_\lambda = 10\,Q_1 - Q_1^2 + 18Q_2 - 3Q_2^2 - 3 + \lambda\,[8 - 3Q_2 + Q_1]$$
$$\frac{\partial \phi}{\partial Q_1} = 10 - 2Q_1 + \lambda = 0$$
$$\frac{\partial \phi_\lambda}{\partial Q_1} = 18 - 6Q_2 - 3\lambda = 0$$
$$\frac{\partial \phi_\lambda}{\partial \lambda} = 8 + Q_1 - 3Q_2 = 0$$

Solving the three equations simultaneously gives:

$$Q_1 = 4, \quad Q_2 = 4, \quad \lambda = -2$$

Perfect Price Discrimination: The Monopolist's Dream

The demand curve shows the marginal value of each unit consumed, which is also the maximum amount consumers would pay for each unit. If the monopolist could charge a different price for each unit sold—a price reflected by the height of the demand curve—the firm's marginal revenue from selling one more unit would equal the price of that unit. Thus, the demand curve would become the firm's marginal revenue curve. A perfectly discriminating monopolist would charge a different price for each unit sold.

In Exhibit 10, again for simplicity, the monopolist is assumed to produce at a constant average and marginal cost in the long run. A perfectly discriminating monopolist, like any producer, would maximize profit by producing the quantity at which marginal revenue equals marginal cost. Because the demand curve is now the marginal revenue curve, the profit-maximizing quantity occurs where the demand, or marginal revenue, curve intersects the marginal cost curve, identified at point *e* in Exhibit 10. Price discrimination is a way of increasing profit. The area of the shaded triangle *aec* shows the perfectly discriminating monopolist's economic profit.

By charging a different price for each unit sold, the perfectly discriminating monopolist is able to convert every dollar of consumer surplus into economic profit. Although this practice may seem unfair to consumers, perfect price discrimination gets high marks based on allocative efficiency. Because such a monopolist does not have to lower the price to all customers to sell more, there is no reason to restrict output. In fact, because this is a constant-cost industry, Q is the same quantity produced in perfect competition (though in perfect competition, the triangle *aec* would be consumer surplus, not economic profit). As in the perfectly competitive outcome, the marginal benefit of the final unit produced and consumed just equals its marginal cost. And although perfect price discrimination yields no consumer surplus, the total benefit consumers derive from consuming this good just equals their total cost. Note also that because the monopolist does not restrict output, *there is no deadweight loss.* Thus, perfect price discrimination enhances social welfare when compared with

Exhibit 10

Perfect Price Discrimination

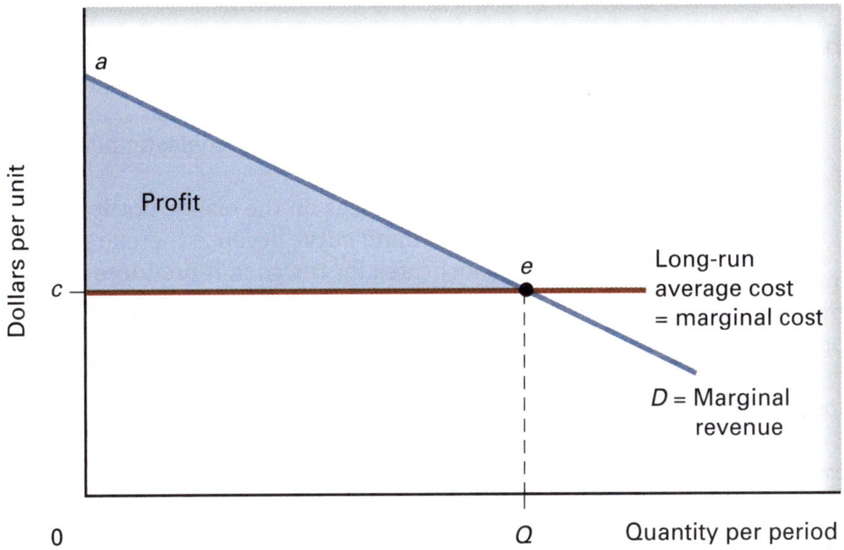

monopoly output in the absence of price discrimination. But the monopolist reaps all net gains from production, while consumers just break even on the deal because their total benefit equals their total cost.

However, in real world *Second Degree Price Discrimination* is more common than the first. Under second degree price discrimination, price varies according to quantity sold. Larger quantities are available at a lower unit price. By doing so, the producer is able to extract part, but not all, of the consumer's surplus. This is particularly widespread in sales to industrial customers, where bulk buyers enjoy higher discounts. Additionally, under second degree price discrimination, sellers are generally not able to differentiate between different types of consumers. Thus, the suppliers provide incentives for the consumers to differentiate themselves according to preference. As above, quantity "discount", or non-linear pricing, is a means by which suppliers use consumer preference to distinguish classes of consumers. This allows the supplier to set different prices to different groups and capture a larger portion of the total market surplus. While second degree price discrimination is more common than first degree price discrimination, it is nevertheless generally limited to cases where products and services are metered and thus measureable easily (as in kilowatt of electricity, cubic feet of water, number of copies duplicated, and so on). Thus, second degree price discrimination is often encountered in the pricing of electricity, gas, and water.

Examples of this are also found in the hotel and airline industries where spare rooms and seats are sold on a last minute *standby basis*. In these types of industry, the *fixed costs* of production are high. At the same time the *marginal or variable costs* are small and predictable. If there are unsold airline tickets or hotel rooms, it is often in the businesses best interest to *offload any spare capacity* at *discount prices*, subject to the condition that the cheaper price (that adds to revenue) at least covers the marginal cost of each unit.

The pricing of cell phone service reflects a firm's effort to capture more consumer surplus as profit. Pricing alternatives include (1) a per-minute price with no basic fee, (2) a flat rate for the month plus a price per minute, and (3) a flat rate for unlimited calls. These alternatives allow the company to charge those who use fewer minutes more per minute than those who call more. Such suppliers are trying to convert some consumer surplus into profit.

Final Word

Pure monopoly, like perfect competition, is not that common. Perhaps the best examples are firms producing patented items that provide unique benefits, such as certain prescription drugs. Some firms may enjoy monopoly power in the short run, but the lure of economic profit encourages rivals to hurdle seemingly high entry barriers in the long run. Changing technology also works against monopoly in the long run. For example, the railroad monopoly was erased by the interstate highway system. AT&T's monopoly on long-distance phone service crumbled as wireless technology replaced copper wire. The postal service's monopoly on first-class mail is being eroded by text messaging, e-mail, epayments, and private firms offering overnight delivery. De Beers has lost its grip on the diamond market. And cable TV is losing its local monopoly to technological breakthroughs in fiber-optics technology, wireless broadband, and the Internet.

Although perfect competition and pure monopoly are rare, our examination of them yields a framework to help understand market structures that lie between the two extremes. Many firms have some degree of monopoly power—that is, they face downward-sloping demand curves. The next chapter discusses the two market structures that lie in the gray region between perfect competition and monopoly.

Multiple Choice Questions

1. The demand curve faced by a firm with a patent on a marketable product
   a. is horizontal
   b. is vertical
   c. slopes upward
   d. slopes downward
   e. is nonexistent
2. If a monopolist must lower the price on all units in order to sell an additional unit,
   a. it is impossible for the monopolist to maximize profit
   b. the monopolist will always lose profit when it increases quantity
   c. the monopolist will always lose revenue when it increases quantity
   d. price will always be greater than marginal revenue
   e. price will always be less than marginal revenue
3. Suppose that a monopolist must choose between two points on its demand curve: it can sell 100 units for $3 each, or it can sell 140 units for $2 each. Which of the following is true?
   a. The monopolist is facing elastic demand.
   b. The monopolist is facing unit elastic demand.
   c. The monopolist is facing inelastic demand.
   d. The monopolist is facing perfectly elastic demand.
   e. The elasticity of demand cannot be determined with the information given.
4. Suppose it costs Minnie's Mini-Golf (a monopolist) not a penny more to let another person on the course. If Minnie's faces a linear (downward-sloping) market demand curve, it will maximize profit by choosing the point on the demand curve at which
   a. marginal revenue is greatest
   b. price elasticity is unit elastic
   c. price elasticity is inelastic
   d. price exceeds average total cost by the greatest amount
   e. price exceeds marginal cost by the greatest amount
5. A profit-maximizing monopolist
   a. never produces on the inelastic portion of the demand curve because it can increase profit by increasing output
   b. never produces on the inelastic portion of the demand curve because marginal revenue exceeds marginal cost
   c. always produces on the inelastic portion of the demand curve
   d. never produces on the elastic portion of the demand curve because there are no substitutes for the good it produces
   e. never produces on the inelastic portion of the demand curve because marginal revenue is negative there
6. Which of following is true of monopoly and not of perfect competition?
   a. Profit is maximized where marginal cost equals marginal revenue
   b. The industry demand curve is also the firm's demand curve
   c. Normal profits are made only if average total cost equals average revenue
   d. Profit is maximized in the elastic portion of the demand curve
   e. the firm has no control over the market price
7. Suppose Arf n' Barf restaurant has a monopoly on restaurant food in a certain small town. Their rent, which is one of several fixed costs they pay whether they sell food or not, has gone up. In the short run, the Arf n' Barf should
   a. pay the higher rent and increase menu prices
   b. pay the higher rent and leave menu prices unchanged
   c. pay the higher rent and lower prices
   d. go out of business
   e. shut down
8. Gilligan runs the only dry-cleaning business on a desert isle. If the cost of cleaning fluid falls, he can increase profit by
   a. raising price
   b. charging the highest price he can
   c. using less cleaning fluid
   d. lowering price
   e. charging a price equal to marginal cost
9. Suppose that at an output of 1,000 units, a monopolist has marginal cost of $40, marginal revenue of $30, average variable cost of $30, and average total cost of $50. In order to maximize profit or minimize loss in the short run, the firm should

a. shut down
b. continue to produce 1,000 units
c. produce fewer than 1,000 units but still operate
d. produce more than 1,000 units
e. increase its plant size to gain economies of scale

10. Suppose that the only maker of a particular type of horse hair clothing exits the industry because demand is too low. The correct analysis of this situation is that
    a. the producer's decision is irrational, since monopolies are not limited by the demand curve
    b. the producer's decision is irrational, since monopolies never go out of business
    c. the producer's decision is irrational, since it could simply raise the price
    d. the price received by the producer was lower than the marginal cost in the long run
    e. the price received by the producer was lower than the average total cost in the long run

11. A monopolist has no supply curve because
    a. as demand changes, each output level can be consistent with more than one profit-maximizing price
    b. monopolists tend to restrict output
    c. monopolists have no marginal cost curve
    d. monopolists can charge any price they want
    e. as demand changes, the firm's profit-maximizing choice of output may change

12. What is true at the profit-maximizing quantity for a nondiscriminating monopolist but *not* true of a perfectly competitive firm?
    a. Price equals marginal cost.
    b. Price is greater than marginal cost.
    c. Marginal revenue equals marginal cost.
    d. Marginal revenue is less than marginal cost.
    e. Marginal revenue is greater than average revenue.

13. Which of the following is *not* necessary in order for a firm to engage in price discrimination?
    a. The producer must face an inelastic demand curve.
    b. The producer must face a downward-sloping demand curve.
    c. There must be at least two identifiable classes of consumers with different price elasticities of demand.
    d. The producer must be able, at little cost, to distinguish between the different classes of buyers.
    e. It must be impossible for one buyer to resell to another.

14. Which of the following is a major criticism of a monopoly as a cause of allocative inefficiency?
    a. A monopolist fails to expand output to the level where the consumers' evaluation of an additional unit is just equal to its opportunity cost
    b. A monopolist has no incentive to produce efficiently, because even if it pays no attention to the costs of production, it will be guaranteed an economic profit
    c. A monopolist will always make profits therefore providing an incentive to keep prices at the level that maximizes consumer surplus
    d. A monopolist has an advantage because it can purchase the resources in a competitive market
    e. Consumer surplus would no longer be equal to producer surplus

15. Which of the following is true of marginal revenue for a monopolist that charges a single price?
    a. $P = MR$ because there are no close substitutes for the monopolist's product.
    b. $P > MR$ because the monopolist must decrease price on all units sold in order to sell an additional unit.
    c. $P < MR$ because the monopolist must decrease price on all units sold in order to sell an additional unit.
    d. $AR = MR$ because there are no close substitutes for the monopolist's product.
    e. $P = MR$ only at the profit-maximizing quantity.

16. If a monopolist must lower the price on all units in order to sell an additional unit,
    a. it is impossible for the monopolist to maximize profit
    b. the monopolist will always lose profit when it increases quantity
    c. the monopolist will always lose revenue when it increases quantity
    d. price will always be greater than marginal revenue
    e. price will always be less than marginal revenue

17. At the profit-maximizing quantity, the demand curve facing the firm in Exhibit 9-3 is
    a. perfectly elastic

b. price elastic
c. price inelastic
d. unit elastic
e. perfectly inelastic

18. The firm in Exhibit 11, which charges the same price to all customers, will produce where
    a. MR = 0 b. MR = MC
    c. MC < MR d. MC = ATC
    e. P = MC

Exhibit 11

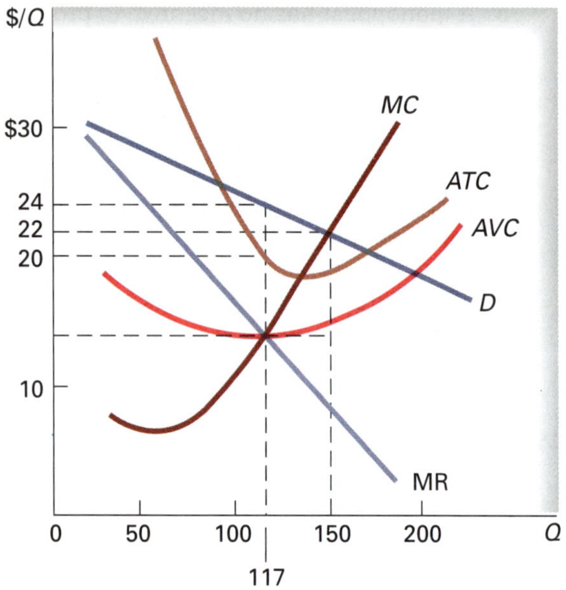

19. Suppose it costs Minnie's Mini-Golf (a monopolist) not a penny more to let another person on the course. If Minnie's faces a linear (downward-sloping) market demand curve, it will maximize profit by choosing the point on the demand curve at which
    a. marginal revenue is greatest
    b. price elasticity is unit elastic
    c. price elasticity is inelastic
    d. price exceeds average total cost by the greatest amount
    e. price exceeds marginal cost by the greatest amount

20. Irving R. Associates is granted a patent for a new product for which there are no close substitutes. Which of the following must be true at the profit-maximizing quantity?
    a. Price is equal to marginal cost.
    b. Average revenue is equal to marginal cost.
    c. Marginal revenue is positive.
    d. Marginal revenue is less than marginal cost.
    e. Price is greater than average revenue.

Answers

1. d	2. d	3. c	4. b	5. e	6. b	7. b	8. d	9. c	10. e
11. a	12. b	13. a	14. a	15. b	16. d	17. b	18. b	19. b	20. c

LONG ANSWER QUESTIONS

LO1 List and describe barriers to market entry

1.1. *(Barriers to Entry)* Explain how economies of scale can be a barrier to entry.

LO2 Explain sources of revenue for the monopolist

2.1. *(Monopoly)* Suppose that a certain manufacturer has a monopoly on the sorority and fraternity ring business (a constant-cost industry) because it has persuaded the "Greeks" to give it exclusive rights to their insignia.
   a. Using demand and cost curves, draw a diagram depicting the firm's profit-maximizing price and output level.
   b. Why is marginal revenue less than price for this firm?
   c. On your diagram, show the deadweight loss that occurs because the output level is determined by a monopoly rather than by a competitive market.
   d. What would happen if the Greeks decided to charge the manufacturer a royalty fee of $3 per ring?

LO3 Describe a firm's costs and its opportunities for profit maximization

3.1. *(Short-Run Profit Maximization)* Answer the following questions on the basis of the monopolist's situation illustrated in the following graph.
   a. At what output rate and price does the monopolist operate?
   b. In equilibrium, approximately what is the firm's total cost and total revenue?
   c. What is the firm's economic profit or loss in equilibrium?

3.2 Using graphs indicate equilibrium point (best level of output) in the Short-run and Long-run supply curves of a firm in monopoly

3.3 In the condition of monopoly, can a firm operate in the inelastic portion of the demand curve?

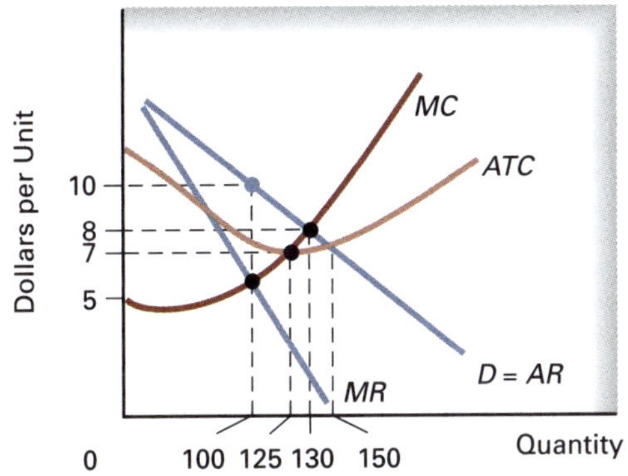

LO4 Explain monopoly and the allocation of resources

4.1. *(Monopoly and the Allocation of Resources)* What is the problem with monopoly? Compare monopoly to the benchmark of perfect competition established in the previous chapter. Use the exhibit below for reference.

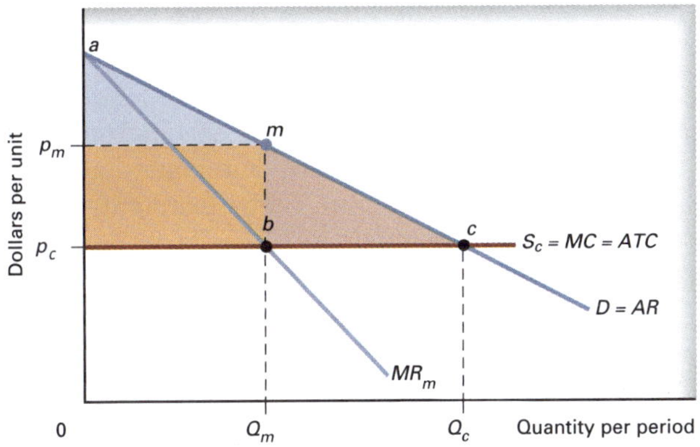

4.2. Under what conditions is perfect competition more efficient than a monopoly?

4.3. How is a dead-weight loss from monopoly affected by the slope of the demand curve?

LO5 Describe the problems that interfere with estimating the deadweight loss of a monopoly

5.1. *(Allocative and Distributive Effects)* Why is society worse off under monopoly than under perfect competition, even if both market structures face the same constant long-run average cost curve?

5.2. *(Welfare Cost of Monopoly)* Explain why the welfare loss of a monopoly may be smaller or larger than the loss shown in the exhibit above.

5.3. Do non-profit institutions, such as universities, ever engage in rent-seeking behavior? Explain.

LO6 Describe conditions that create price discrimination

6.1. *(Conditions for Price Discrimination)* List three conditions that must be met for a monopolist to price discriminate successfully.

6.2. *(Price Discrimination)* Explain how it may be profitable for South Korean manufacturers to sell new autos at a lower price in the United States than in South Korea, even with transportation costs included.

6.3. *(Perfect Price Discrimination)* Why is the perfectly discriminating monopolist's marginal revenue curve identical to the demand curve it faces?

NUMERICAL QUESTIONS

1. Assume the industry demand for an agricultural product is: $P = 1{,}000 - 20Q$. Assume that the marginal cost of product is \$10 per unit.
   a. Calculate what the output and price shall be under the condition of pure competition. If it is a pure monopoly, determine the price and output for the same (assume one price is charged to all clients).
   b. Can the lost gains from trade that result from having a monopoly be shown graphically?
2. The Regency Hotel is planning to use price discrimination between convention and general room rates. For a standard double room, its estimated demand curve for the general market is
   $Qg = 4{,}344 - 20Pg$
   For the convention market, its estimated demand curve is
   $Qc = 5{,}800 - 50Pc$
   In both equations, Q represents weekly quantity of rooms and P represents price per night. The hotel's weekly total cost is
   $TC = 112{,}000 + 40Q + 0.01Q^2$,
   Where Q is weekly total number of rooms rented ($Qg + Qc$).
   a. With price discrimination, how many rooms will be rented in each market? What price will the hotel charge in each market? What will be the hotel's weekly profit?
   b. Illustrate your results graphically.
   c. Compare the results from (a) with what the firm could obtain if it did not practice price discrimination.

MONOPOLY

Chapter in Review

KEY TERMS

barrier to entry
any impediment that prevents new firms from entering an industry and competing on an equal basis with existing firms

patent
a legal barrier to entry that grants the holder the exclusive right to sell a product for 20 years from the date the patent application is filed

innovation
the process of turning an invention into a marketable product

price maker
a firm with some power to set the price because the demand curve for its output slopes downward; a firm with market power

deadweight loss of monopoly
net loss to society when a firm with market power restricts output and increases the price

rent seeking
activities undertaken by individuals or firms to influence public policy in a way that increases their incomes

perfectly discriminating monopolist
a monopolist who charges a different price for each unit sold; also called the monopolist's dream

CHAPTER EQUATIONS

Total Revenue

$$TR = p \times Q$$

Marginal Revenue

$$MR = \Delta TR/\Delta Q$$

LO1 List and describe barriers to market entry. A monopolist sells a product with no close substitutes. Short-run economic profit earned by a monopolist can persist in the long run only if the entry of new firms is blocked. Three barriers to entry are (a) legal restrictions, such as patents and operating licenses; (b) economies of scale over a broad range of output; and (c) control over a key resource.

LO2 Explain sources of revenue for the monopolist. Because a monopolist is the sole supplier of a product with no close substitutes, a monopolist's demand curve is also the market demand curve. Because a monopolist that does not price discriminate can sell more only by lowering the price for all units, marginal revenue is less than the price. Where demand is price elastic, marginal revenue is positive and total revenue increases as the price falls. Where demand is price inelastic, marginal revenue is negative and total revenue decreases as the price falls. A monopolist never voluntarily produces where demand is inelastic because raising the price and reducing output would increase total revenue.

LO3 Describe a firm's costs and its opportunities for profit maximization. If the monopolist can at least cover variable cost, profit is maximized or loss is minimized in the short run by finding the output rate that equates marginal revenue with marginal cost. At the profit-maximizing quantity, the price is found on the demand curve.

Economies of Scale as a Barrier to Entry

A monopoly sometimes emerges naturally when a firm experiences economies of scale as reflected by a downward-sloping, long-run average cost curve. One firm can satisfy market demand at a lower average cost per unit than could two or more firms each operating at smaller rates of output.

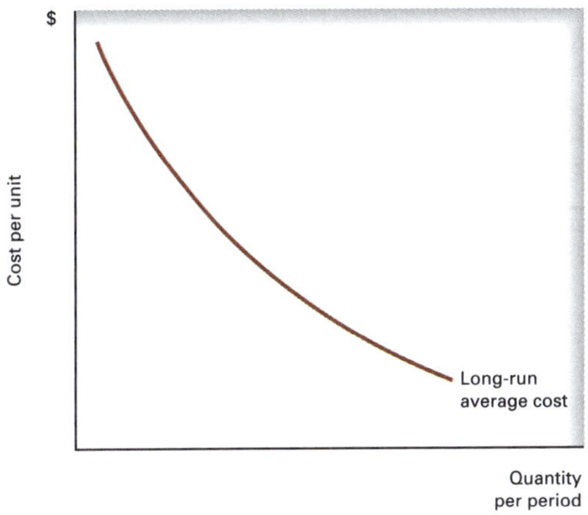

Monopoly Demand, Marginal Revenue, and Total Revenue

Where demand is price elastic, marginal revenue is positive, so total revenue increaes as the price falls. Where demand is price inelastic, marginal revenue is negative, so total revenue decreases as the price falls. Where demand is unit elastic, marginal revenue is zero, so total revenue is at a maximum, neither increasing nor decreasing.

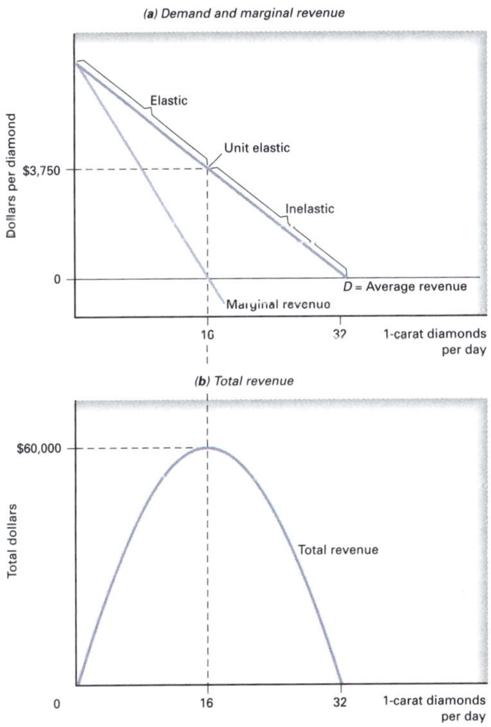

LO4 Explain monopoly and the allocation of resources. If costs are similar, a monopolist charges a higher price and supplies less output than does a perfectly competitive industry. Monopoly usually results in a deadweight loss when compared with perfect competition because the loss of consumer surplus exceeds the gains in monopoly profit.

LO5 Describe the problems that interfere with estimating the deadweight loss of a monopoly. Deadweight loss can be difficult to estimate. If economies of scale are substantial enough, a monopolist might be able to produce output at a lower cost per unit than could competitive firms. The price, or at least the cost of production, could be lower under monopoly than under competition, and deadweight loss may overstate the true cost of monopoly. Alternatively, the deadweight loss of monopoly might, in fact, be greater than shown in our simple diagram. If resources must be devoted to securing and maintaining a monopoly position, monopolies may impose a greater welfare loss than simple models suggest.

LO6 Describe conditions that create price discrimination. To increase profit through price discrimination, the monopolist must have at least two identifiable groups of customers, each with a different price elasticity of demand at a given price, and must be able to prevent customers charged the lower price from reselling to those charged the higher price. A perfect price discriminator charges a different price for each unit sold, thereby converting all consumer surplus into economic profit. Objectively, price discrimination is as efficient as perfect competition because the monopolist has no incentive to restrict output, so there is no deadweight loss.

The Monopolist Minimizes Losses in the Short Run

Marginal revenue equals marginal cost at point *e*. At quantity *Q*, price *p* (at point *b*) is less than average total cost (at point *a*), so the monopolist suffers a loss, identified by the pink rectangle. But the monopolist continues to produce rather than shut down in the short run because price exceeds average variable cost (at point *c*).

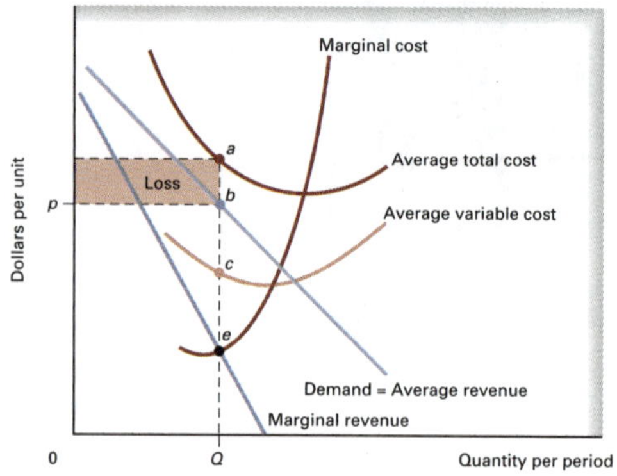

Perfect Competition and Monopoly Compared

A perfectly competitive industry would produce output Q_c, determined by the intersection of the market demand curve *D* and the market supply curve S_c. The price would be *pc*. A monopoly that could produce output at the same minimum average cost as a perfectly competitive industry would produce output Q_m, determined at point *b*, where marginal cost and marginal revenue intersect. The monopolist would charge price p_m. Thus, given the same costs, output is lower and price is higher under monopoly than under perfect competition.

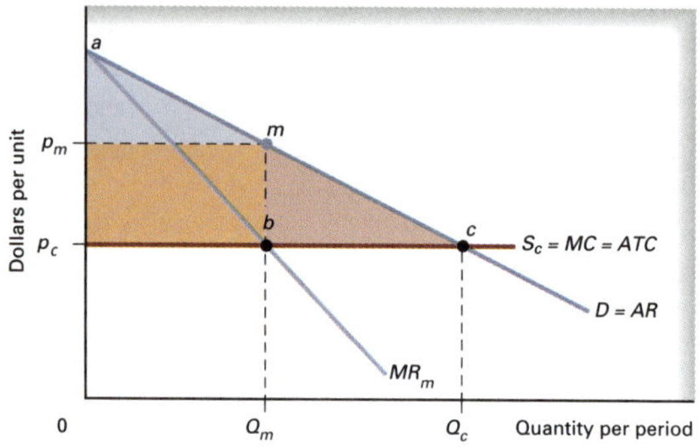

Perfect Price Discrimination

If a monopolist can charge a different price for each unit sold, it may be able to practice perfect price discrimination. By setting the price of each unit equal to the maximum amount consumers are willing to pay for that unit (shown by the height of the demand curve), the monopolist can earn a profit equal to the area of the shaded triangle. Consumer surplus is zero. Ironically, this outcome is efficient because the monopolist has no incentive to restrict output, so there is no deadweight loss.

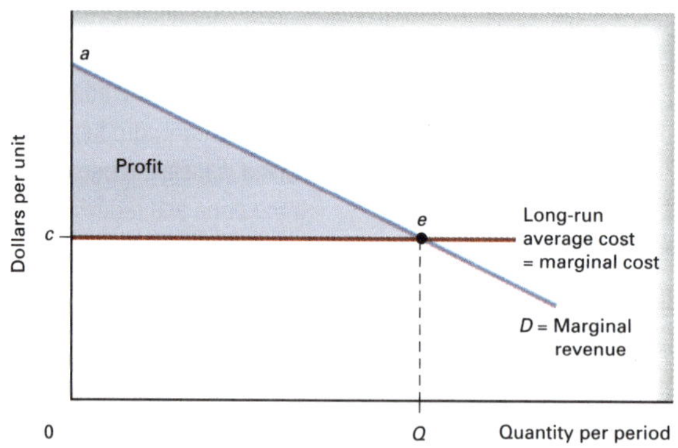

CHAPTER 11

Monopolistic Competition and Oligopoly

Learning Outcomes

LO[1] Discuss factors that lead to monopolistic competition

LO[2] Explain the concept of oligopoly

LO[3] Describe models of oligopoly

LO[4] Explain how game theory helps predict cartel behavior

LO[5] Compare oligopoly and perfect competition

“Why do some pizza makers deliver?”

© CREATAS IMAGES/JUPITERIMAGES

Why is Perrier water sold in green, tear-shaped bottles? Why are some shampoos sold only in salons? Why do some pizza makers deliver? Which market structure is like a golf tournament and which is like a tennis match? Why do airlines engage in airfare warfare? Why was the oil cartel, OPEC, created, and why has it met with spotty success? Why is there a witness protection program? To answer these and other questions, we turn in this chapter to the vast grey area that lies between perfect competition and monopoly.

Perfect competition and monopoly are extreme market structures. Under perfect competition, many suppliers offer an identical product and, in the long run, entry and exit erase economic profit. A monopolist supplies a product with no close substitutes in a market where natural and artificial barriers keep out would-be competitors, so a monopolist can earn economic profit in the long run. These polar market structures are logically appealing and offer a useful description of some industries observed in the economy.

But most firms fit into neither market structure. Some markets have many sellers producing goods that vary slightly, such as the many convenience stores that abound. Other markets consist of just a few sellers that in some industries produce essentially identical products, or commodities (such as oil), and in other industries produce differentiated goods (such as automobiles). This chapter examines the two remaining market structures that together include most firms in the economy.

What do you think?

I'm willing to pursue whatever option offers the greatest potential benefit, no matter what the risks.

Strongly Disagree 1 2 3 4 5 6 7 *Strongly Agree*

Topics discussed in Chapter 11 include:

- Monopolistic competition
- Product differentiation
- Excess capacity
- Oligopoly
- Collusion
- Prisoner's dilemma
- Concentration ratios
- Herfindahl index
- Lerner index
- Collusive oligopoly
- Non-Collusive oligopoly
- Cournot's model
- Kinked demand curve model
- Price leadership model

LO1 Monopolistic Competition

During the 1920s and 1930s, economists began formulating models that fit between perfect competition and monopoly. Two models of *monopolistic competition* were developed independently. In 1933 Edward Chamberlin of Harvard University published *The Theory of Monopolistic Competition*. Across the Atlantic that same year, Joan Robinson of Cambridge University published *The Economics of Imperfect Competition*. Although the theories differed, their underlying principles were similar. We discuss Chamberlin's approach.

Characteristics of Monopolistic Competition

As the expression **monopolistic competition** suggests, this market structure contains elements of both monopoly and competition. Chamberlin used the term to describe a market in which many producers offer products that are substitutes but are not viewed as identical by consumers. Because the products of different suppliers differ slightly—for example, some convenience stores are closer to you than others—the demand curve for each is not horizontal but slopes downward. Each supplier has some power over the price it can charge. Thus, the firms that populate this market are not *price takers,* as they would be under perfect competition, but are *price makers.* All price makers face a downward sloping demand curve.

Because barriers to entry are low, firms in monopolistic competition can, in the long run, enter or leave the market with ease. Consequently, there are enough sellers that they behave competitively. There are also enough sellers that each tends to get lost in the crowd. For example, in a large metropolitan area, an individual restaurant, gas station, drugstore, video store, dry cleaner, or convenience store tends to act *independently.* In other market structures, there may be only two or three sellers in each market, so they keep an eye on one another; they act *interdependently.* You will see the relevance of this distinction later in the chapter.

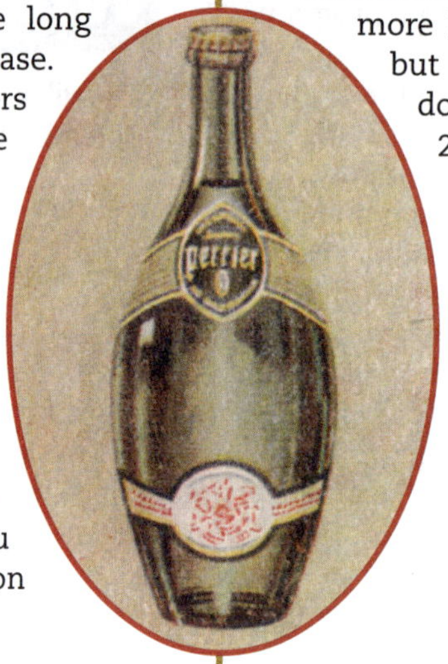

Product Differentiation

In perfect competition, the product is a commodity, meaning it's identical across producers, such as a bushel of wheat. In monopolistic competition, the product differs somewhat among sellers, as with the difference between one rock radio station and another, or one convenience store and another. Sellers differentiate their products in four basic ways.

monopolistic competition
a market structure with many firms selling products that are substitutes but different enough that each firm's demand curve slopes downward; firm entry is relatively easy

Physical Differences

The most obvious way products differ is in their physical appearance and their qualities. Packaging is also designed to make a product stand out in a crowded field, such as a distinctive bottle of water (Perrier) and instant soup in a cup (Cup-a-Soup). Physical differences are seemingly endless: size, weight, color, taste, texture, and so on. Shampoos, for example, differ in color, scent, thickness, lathering ability, and bottle design. Particular brands aim at consumers with dandruff and those with normal, dry, or oily hair.

Location

The number and variety of locations where a product is available are other ways of differentiation—*spatial differentiation.* Some products seem to be available everywhere, including online; finding other products requires some search and travel. If you live in a metropolitan area, you are no doubt accustomed to the many convenience stores that populate the region. Each wants to be closest to you when you need milk, bread, or nachos—thus, the proliferation of stores. As the name says, these mini grocery stores are selling *convenience.* Their prices are higher and selections more limited than at regular grocery stores, but they are usually closer to customers, don't have long lines, and some are open 24/7.

Services

Products also differ in terms of their accompanying services. For example, some products are delivered to your door, such as Domino's pizza and Amazon.com books; others are

© MARY EVANS PICTURE LIBRARY/ALAMY

>> Perrier's distinctive packaging helps it stand out in the crowded field of bottled water.

DiGiornonomics

© JB REED/BLOOMBERG NEWS/LANDOV

Is pizza delivery service actually worth the cost? Kraft Foods began a marketing campaign for its DiGiorno frozen pizzas comparing the price of its supreme pizza with the average price for an equivalent pizza delivered by one of three major chains. While a DiGiorno pizza costs $6.69, the delivered pizza costs $16.13. DiGiorno's competitors contend that the extra cost accounts for customization, fresh ingredients, and virtually zero investment of time and effort for the buyer. Kraft Foods, however, contends that even if you factor in the gas cost of driving to the store and the energy cost of cooking the pizza (both of which are almost negligible), pizza delivery is still almost twice the cost of a DiGiorno pizza. Are these basically the same product, or is this legitimate product differentiation?

SOURCE: Carl Bialik, "How Much Does Pizza Delivery Cost?" The Numbers Guy Blog, 8 December 2008. Available at http://blogs.wsj.com/numbersguy/how-much-does-pizza-delivery-cost-469/ (accessed 19 December 2008).

cash and carry. Some products are demonstrated by a well-trained sales staff; others are mostly self-service. Some products include online support and toll-free help lines; others come with no help at all. Some sellers provide money-back guarantees; others say "no refunds." The quality and range of accompanying services often differentiate otherwise close substitutes.

Product Image

A final way products differ is in the image the producer tries to foster in the buyer's mind. Producers try to create and maintain brand loyalty through product promotion and advertising. For example, suppliers of sportswear, clothing, watches, and cosmetics often pay for endorsements from athletes, fashion models, and other celebrities. Some producers emphasize the care and attention to detail in each item. For example, Banarasi sarees from Varanasi, one of the finest silk sarees in India, underscores the months of labor required to weave each piece by hand—as a way to justify the high price tag. Some producers try to demonstrate high quality based on where products are sold, such as Shahnaz Husain's ayurvedic beauty products sold only in salons. Some products tout their all-natural ingredients, such as Vadilal's ice cream, Meswak toothpaste, and Dabur's Real fruit Juice, or appeal to environmental concerns by focusing on organic products, such as the introduction of "Organic Herbal Gulal" by Organic India.

Short-Run Profit Maximization or Loss Minimization

Because each monopolistic competitor offers a product that differs somewhat from what others supply, each has some control over the price charged. This *market power* means that each firm's demand curve slopes downward. Because many firms offer close but not identical products, any firm that raises its price can expect to lose some customers to rivals. By way of comparison, a price hike would cost a monopolist fewer customers but would cost a perfect competitor *all* customers. Therefore, a monopolistic competitor faces a demand curve that tends to be more elastic than a monopolist's but less elastic than a perfect competitor's.

Recall that the availability of substitutes for a given product affects its price elasticity of demand. The price elasticity of the monopolistic competitor's demand depends on (1) the number of rival firms that produce similar products and (2) the firm's ability to differentiate its product from those of its rivals. *A firm's demand curve is more elastic the more substitutes there are and the less differentiated its product is.*

Marginal Revenue Equals Marginal Cost

From our study of monopoly, we know that a downward-sloping demand curve means the marginal revenue curve also slopes downward and lies beneath the demand curve. Exhibit 1 depicts demand and marginal revenue curves for a monopolistic competitor. The exhibit also presents average and marginal cost curves. Remember that the forces that determine the cost of production are largely independent of the forces that shape demand, so there is nothing special about a monopolistic competitor's cost curves. In the short run, a firm that can at least cover its variable cost increases output as long as marginal revenue exceeds marginal cost. A monopolistic competitor maximizes profit just as a monopolist does: the profit-maximizing quantity occurs where marginal revenue equals marginal cost; *the profit-maximizing price for that quantity is found up on the demand curve.* Exhibit 1 shows the price and quantity combinations that maximize short-run profit in panel (a), and minimize short-run loss in panel (b). In each panel, the marginal cost and marginal revenue curves intersect at point *e*, yielding equilibrium output *q*, equilibrium price *p*, and average total cost *c*. (Note that at point *e*, *MC* cuts *MR* from below.)

Maximizing Profit or Minimizing Loss in the Short Run

Recall that the short run is a period too brief to allow firms to enter or leave the market. The

Exhibit 1

Monopolistic Competitor in the Short Run

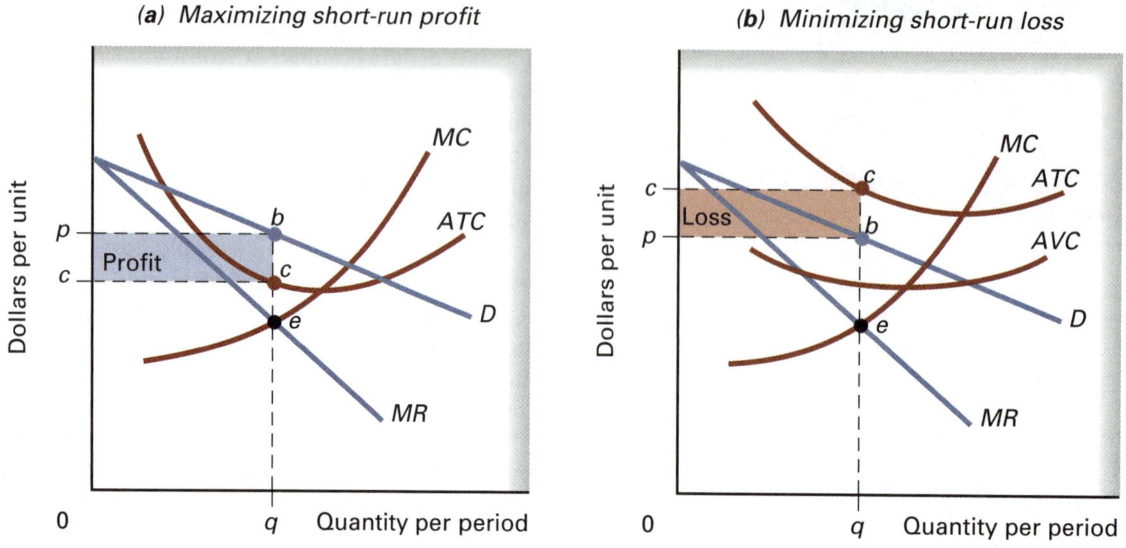

demand and cost conditions shown in panel (a) of Exhibit 1 indicate that this firm earns economic profit in the short run. At the firm's profit-maximizing quantity, average total cost, *c*, is below the price, *p*. Price minus average total cost is the firm's profit per unit, which, when multiplied by the quantity, yields economic profit, shown by the blue rectangle. Again, the profit-maximizing quantity is found where marginal revenue equals marginal cost; price is found up on the demand curve at that quantity. Thus, a monopolistic competitor, like a monopolist, has no supply curve—that is, *there is no curve that uniquely relates prices and corresponding quantities supplied*.

The monopolistic competitor, like monopolists and perfect competitors, is not guaranteed an economic profit. The firm's demand and cost curves could be as shown in panel (b), where the average total cost curve lies entirely above the demand curve, so no quantity allows the firm to escape a loss. In such a situation, the firm must decide whether to produce at a loss or to shut down in the short run. The rule here is the same as with perfect competition and monopoly: as long as price exceeds average variable cost, the firm in the short run loses less by producing than by shutting down. If no price covers average variable cost, the firm shuts down. Recall that the halt in production may be only temporary; shutting down is not the same as going out of business. Firms that expect economic losses to persist may, in the long run, leave the industry.

Short-run profit maximization in monopolistic competition is quite similar to that under monopoly. But the stories differ in the long run, as we'll see next.

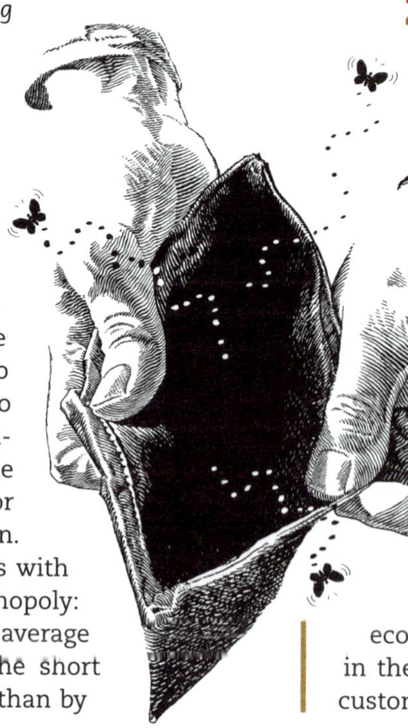

© DYNAMIC GRAPHICS/JUPITERIMAGES

Zero Economic Profit in the Long Run

Low barriers to entry in monopolistic competition mean that short-run economic profit attracts new entrants in the long run. Because new entrants offer similar products, they draw customers away from other firms in the market, thereby reducing the demand facing other firms. Entry continues in the long run until economic profit disappears. *Because market entry is easy, monopolistically competitive firms earn zero economic profit in the long run.*

On the other side of the ledger, economic losses drive some firms out of business in the long run. As firms leave the industry, their customers switch to the remaining firms, increasing

Exhibit 2

Long-Run Equilibrium in Monopolistic Competition

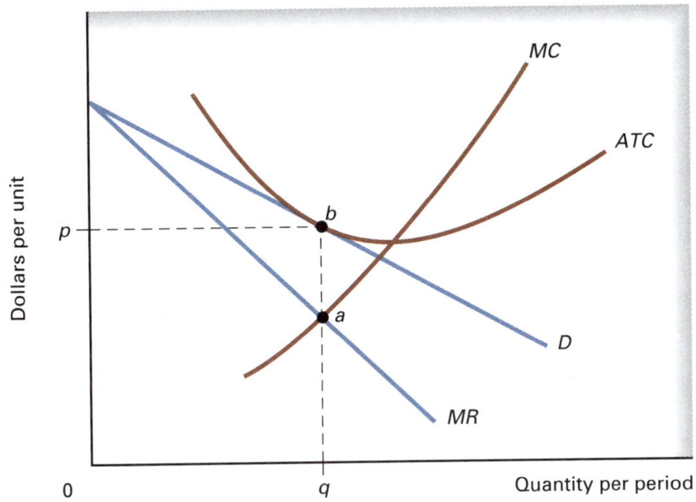

economic profit but does earn a normal profit (how do we know this?). At all other quantities, the firm's average total cost curve lies above the demand curve, so the firm would lose money by reducing or expanding production.

Thus, because entry is easy in monopolistic competition, short-run economic profit attracts new entrants in the long run. The demand curve facing each monopolistic competitor shifts left until economic profit disappears. A short-run economic loss prompts some firms to leave the industry in the long run until remaining firms earn just a normal profit. In summary, monopolistic competition is like monopoly in the sense that firms in each industry face demand curves that slope downward. *Monopolistic competition is like perfect competition in the sense that easy entry and exit eliminate economic profit or economic loss in the long run.*

the demand for those products. Firms continue to leave in the long run until the remaining firms have enough customers to earn normal profit, but not economic profit.

Exhibit 2 shows long-run equilibrium for a typical monopolistic competitor. In the long run, entry and exit shifts each firm's demand curve until economic profit disappears—that is, until price equals average total cost. In Exhibit 2, the marginal revenue curve intersects the marginal cost curve at point *a*. At the equilibrium quantity, *q*, the average total cost curve is tangent to the demand curve at point *b*. Because average total cost equals the price, the firm earns no

Monopolistic Competition and Perfect Competition Compared

How does monopolistic competition compare with perfect competition in terms of efficiency? In the long run, neither earns economic profit, so what's the difference? The difference traces to the demand curves facing individual firms in each of the two market structures. Exhibit 3 presents the long-run equilibrium price and quantity for a typical firm in each market structure, assuming each firm has identical cost

Exhibit 3

Perfect Competition Versus Monopolistic Competition in Long-Run Equilibrium

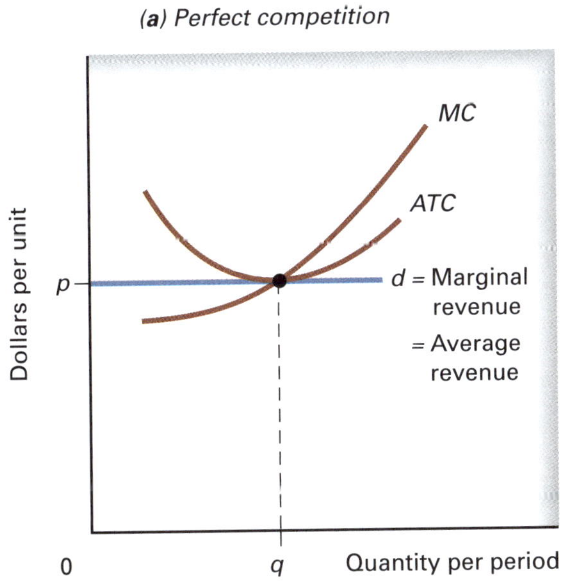

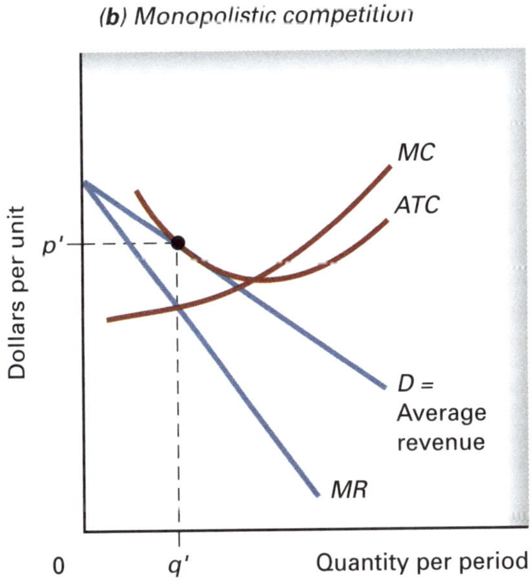

curves. In each case, the marginal cost curve intersects the marginal revenue curve at the quantity where the average total cost curve is tangent to the firm's demand curve.

A perfect competitor's demand curve is a horizontal line drawn at the market price, as shown in panel (a). This demand curve is tangent to the lowest point of the firm's long-run average total cost curve. Thus, a perfect competitor in the long run produces at the lowest possible average cost. In panel (b), a monopolistic competitor faces a downward-sloping demand curve because its product differs somewhat from those of other suppliers. In the long run, the monopolistic competitor produces less than required to achieve the lowest possible average cost. Thus, the price and average cost in monopolistic competition, identified as p' in panel (b), exceed the price and average cost in perfect competition, identified as p in panel (a). *If firms have the same cost curves, the monopolistic competitor produces less and charges more than the perfect competitor does in the long run, though neither earns economic profit.*

> The more similar the products, the greater the interdependence among firms in the industry.

Firms in monopolistic competition are not producing at minimum average cost. They are said to have **excess capacity**, because production falls short of the quantity that would achieve the lowest average cost. Excess capacity means that each producer could easily serve more customers and, in the process, lower average cost. *The marginal value of increased output would exceed its marginal cost, so greater output would increase social welfare.* Such excess capacity exists with gas stations, drugstores, convenience stores, restaurants, motels, bookstores, flower shops, and firms in other monopolistic competitive industries.

One other difference between perfect competition and monopolistic competition does not show up in Exhibit 3. Although the cost curves drawn in each panel of the exhibit are identical, firms in monopolistic competition spend more to differentiate their products than do firms in perfect competition, where products are identical. This higher cost of product differentiation shifts up the average cost curve.

Some economists have argued that monopolistic competition results in too many suppliers and in artificial product differentiation. The counterargument is that consumers are willing to pay a higher price for a wider selection. According to this latter view, consumers benefit from more choice among gas stations, restaurants, convenience stores, clothing stores, video stores, drugstores, textbooks, hiking boots, and many other goods and services. For example, what if half of the restaurants in your area were to close just so the remaining ones could reduce their excess capacity? Some consumers, including you, might be disappointed if a favorite closed.

Perfect competitors and monopolistic competitors are so numerous in their respective markets that an action by any one of them has little or no effect on the behavior of others in the market. Another important market structure on the continuum between perfect competition and monopoly has just a few firms. We explore this market structure in the balance of the chapter.

excess capacity
the difference between a firm's profit-maximizing quantity and the quantity that minimizes average cost; firms with excess capacity could reduce average cost by increasing quantity

oligopoly
a market structure characterized by so few firms that each behaves interdependently

undifferentiated oligopoly
an oligopoly that sells a commodity, or a product that does not differ across suppliers, such as an ingot of steel or a barrel of oil

LO2 An Introduction to Oligopoly

The final market structure we examine is *oligopoly,* a Greek word meaning "few sellers." When you think of "big business," you are thinking of **oligopoly**, an industry dominated by just a few firms. Perhaps three or four account for more than half the industry supply. Many industries, including steel, automobiles, oil, breakfast cereals, cigarettes, personal computers, and operating systems software, are *oligopolistic*. Because an oligopoly has only a few firms, each one must consider the effect of its own actions on competitors' behavior. Oligopolists are therefore said to be *interdependent*.

Varieties of Oligopoly

In some oligopolies, such as steel or oil, the product is identical, or undifferentiated, across producers. Thus, an **undifferentiated oligopoly** sells a commodity, such as an ingot of steel or a barrel of oil. But in other oligopolies, such as automobiles or breakfast cereals, the product is differentiated across producers. A **differentiated oligopoly** sells products that differ across producers, such as a Toyota Camry versus a Honda Accord.

The more similar the products, the greater the interdependence among firms in the industry. For example, because steel ingots are essentially identical, steel producers are quite sensitive to each other's pricing. A small rise in one producer's price sends customers to rivals. But with differentiated oligopoly, such as the auto industry, producers are not quite as sensitive about each other's prices. As with monopolistic competitors, oligopolists differentiate their products through (1) physical qualities, (2) sales locations, (3) services offered with the product, and (4) the image of the product established in the consumer's mind.

Because of interdependence, the behavior of any particular firm is difficult to predict. *Each firm knows that any changes in its product's quality, price, output, or advertising policy may prompt a reaction from its rivals. And each firm may react if another firm alters any of these features.* Monopolistic competition is like a professional golf tournament, where each player strives for a personal best. Oligopoly is more like a tennis match, where each player's actions depend on how and where the opponent hits the ball. Here's another analogy to help you understand the effects of interdependence: Did you ever find yourself in an awkward effort to get around someone coming toward you on a sidewalk? You each end up turning this way and that in a brief, clumsy encounter. You each are trying to figure out which way the other will turn. But since neither can read the other's mind, neither can work out the problem independently. The solution is for one of you to put your head down and just walk. The other then easily adjusts.

Why have some industries evolved into oligopolies, dominated by only a few firms? Although the reasons are not always clear, *an oligopoly can often be traced to some form of barrier to entry, such as economies of scale, legal restrictions, brand names built up by years of advertising, or control over an essential resource.* In the previous chapter, we examined barriers to entry as they applied to monopoly. Those same principles apply to oligopoly.

Economies of Scale

Perhaps the most important barrier to entry is economies of scale. Recall that the minimum efficient scale is the lowest output at which the firm takes full advantage of economies of scale. If a firm's minimum efficient scale is relatively large compared to industry output, then only a few firms are needed to satisfy industry demand. For example, an automobile plant of minimum efficient scale could make enough cars to supply nearly 10 percent of the U.S. market. If there were 100 auto plants, each would supply such a tiny portion of the market that the average cost per car would be higher than if only 10 plants manufacture autos. In the automobile industry, economies of scale create a barrier to entry. To compete with existing producers, a new entrant must sell enough automobiles to reach a competitive scale of operation.

Exhibit 4 presents the long-run average cost curve for a typical firm in the industry. If a new entrant sells only S cars, the average cost per unit, c_a, far exceeds the average cost, c_b, of a manufacturer that sells enough cars to reach the minimum efficient size, M. If autos sell for less than c_a, a potential entrant can expect to lose money, and this prospect discourages entry. For example, John Delorean tried to break into the auto industry in the early 1980s with a modern design featured in the *Back to the Future*

Exhibit 4

Economies of Scale as a Barrier to Entry

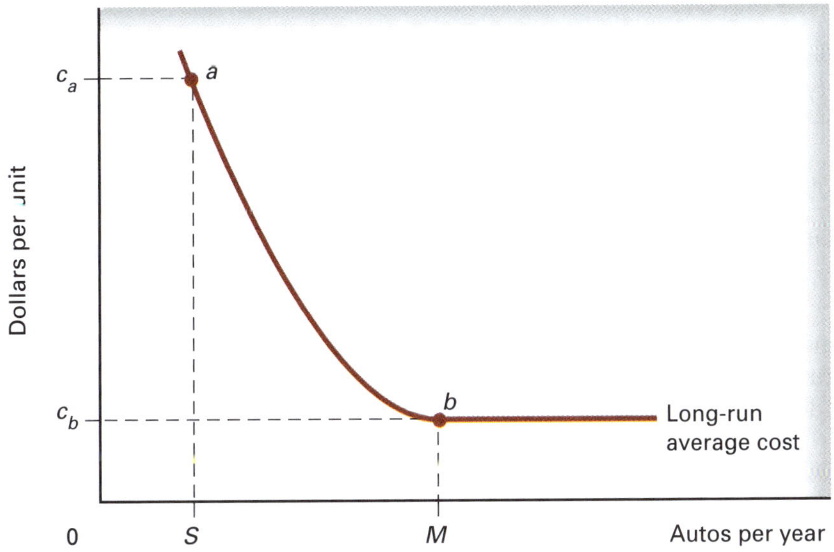

differentiated oligopoly
an oligopoly that sells products that differ across suppliers, such as automobiles or breakfast cereal

movies. But his company managed to build and sell only 8,583 Deloreans before going bankrupt.

The High Cost of Entry

Potential entrants into oligopolistic industries could face another problem. The total investment needed to reach the minimum efficient size is often gigantic. A new auto plant or new semiconductor plant can cost over $3 billion. The average cost of developing and testing a new drug exceeds $800 million (only 1 in 25 drug candidates identified by the industry ever makes it to market).[1] Advertising a new product enough to compete with established brands may also require enormous outlays.

High start-up costs and established brand names create huge barriers to entry, especially because the market for new products is so uncertain (four out of five new consumer products don't survive). An unsuccessful product could cripple an upstart firm. The prospect of such a loss discourages many potential entrants. That's why most new products come from established firms. For example, Colgate-Palmolive spent $100 million introducing Total toothpaste, as did McDonald's in its failed attempt to sell the Arch Deluxe. Unilever lost $160 million when its new detergent, Power, washed out.

Firms often spend millions and sometimes billions trying to differentiate their products. Some of these outlays offer consumers useful information and wider choice. But some spending seems to offer neither. For example, Pepsi and Coke spend billions on messages such "It's the Cola" or "Life is Good." *Regardless, product differentiation expenditures create a barrier to entry.*

© CORBIS/JUPITERIMAGES

Multiple products from the same brand dominate shelf space and attempt to crowd out new entrants.

Crowding Out the Competition

Oligopolies compete with existing rivals and try to block new entry by offering a variety of products. Entrenched producers may flood the market with new products in part to crowd out other new entries. For example, a few cereal makers offer more than a dozen products each. Many of these variations offer little that is new. One study of 25,500 new products introduced during one year found only 7 percent offered new or added benefits.[2]

"Multiple products from the same brand dominate shelf space and attempt to crowd out new entrants."

1. As reported in "Little Big Pharma," *Wall Street Journal*, 6 December 2006.
2. The study was carried out by Market Intelligence Service and was reported in "Market Makers," *The Economist*, 14 March 1998.

Oligopoly and Market Concentration

Many ratios and measures are used to determine whether the industry structure is oligopolistic or monopolistic. The degree by which an industry is dominated by a few large firms is measured by concentration ratios, the Herfindahl index or the Lerner index. One of the most popular measures is *concentration ratio*, which is given by the percentage of total industry output of a given number of large firms (usually 4, 8, or 12). It measures the extent to which the industry is dominated by the presence of a few large firms. For an industry in which the concentration ratio of top four firms is nearly 100, it is clearly oligopolistic. In fact, even if the ratio is above 50 or 60 percent, the industry is most likely to be oligopolistic. Both four-firm and eight-firm concentration ratios are widely used to determine the concentration levels in the industry.

The other common method of estimation is *Herfindahl index*. It measures the size of firms in relation to the industry and is an indicator of the amount of competition among them. It is defined as the sum of squared values of the market shares of all the firms in the industry. Hence, the Herfindahl index (*H*) is given by

$$H = \sum_{i=1}^{n} S_i^2$$

where, s_i = market share of the firm in industry, and n = number of firms in the industry.

If there is only 1 firm in the industry, its market share is 100 percent. The value of Herfindahl index in this case becomes H = 100^2 = 1,000. If there are 3 firms in the industry with market shares being 20 percent, 30 percent, and 50 percent, the Herfindahl index is estimated as H = $20^2 + 30^2 + 50^2$ = 3,800. A higher Herfindahl index value signifies decrease in competition along with increasing market power (lesser number of firms). The opposite is true if the value of the index is lower. The Herfindahl index is considered to be advantageous compared to concentration ratio as it takes all the firms into account. Also, by squaring the market share of each firm, the larger firms get a larger weight compared to the smaller firms.

However, according to the theory of contestable markets (when entry is free and exit is entirely costless), high concentration ratios or high Herfindahl index may not correctly capture the degree of monopoly power. In fact, if the markets are contestable, firms operate as if they are perfectly competitive and, thus, earn only normal profits, despite operating in an oligopolistic market.

Standard economic analysis suggests that in a market with strong competition among sellers, prices will tend to the level of the marginal cost of supply. Where there are no market failures due to externalities, this also corresponds to a condition for the optimum allocation of resources.

If prices are above this level because of lack of competition and the presence of market power over prices, there is a welfare loss to consumers. One measure of the degree of excessive pricing is the Lerner index, defined as the ratio of the margin (difference) between the price and the cost to the level of price, or (price – cost)/price. The *Lerner index* takes its lowest value of zero when the price is equal to marginal cost. As the price increases above the marginal cost, the Lerner index tends toward its maximum value of 1. The margin between monopoly prices and marginal costs is inversely related to the magnitude of the price elasticity of demand—the greater the price elasticity, the smaller the margin. Similarly, the Lerner index is equal to the inverse of the magnitude of the price elasticity of demand. The same results would apply to an industry made up of a few firms that are tacitly or explicitly colluding to maximize joint profits.

The Lerner index and the price-cost margin are positively related to the Herfindahl-Hirschman index (HHI) based on industry shares of the firms and inversely related to the magnitude of the industry elasticity of demand.

Analysis of market power links measures of industry concentration to the price-cost margin under assumptions about pricing strategies. The margin for firm "i" is conventionally defined by the Lerner index *Li*.

$$L_i = \frac{(P_i - C_i)}{P_i}$$

where P_i is the price charged and C_i is the marginal cost incurred by the ith firm. The index varies between zero and one. For a profit-maximizing monopoly, the Lerner index *LM* can be shown to be inversely related to the price elasticity of demand facing the firm (and the industry) by the equation.

$$L_M = \frac{-1}{\varepsilon}$$

(P – C)/C, the percentage markup over costs, and *P*/*C*, the price-cost ratio, can be similarly linked to the elasticity of demand:

$$\frac{(P - C)}{C} = \frac{-1}{(\varepsilon + 1)}; \quad \frac{P}{C} = \frac{\varepsilon}{(\varepsilon + 1)}$$

In an industry with several firms, the industry Lerner index is defined as:

$$L = \Sigma S_i Li$$

where s_i is the market share of the ith firm.

For a Cournot oligopoly, where each firm assumes in choosing its planned sales level that its rivals will not respond to its choice the Lerner index *LC* is equal to the HHI divided by the price elasticity of demand:

$$L_C = \frac{-H}{\varepsilon}; \quad \frac{(P - C)}{C} = \frac{-H}{(\varepsilon + H)}; \quad \frac{P}{C} = \frac{\varepsilon}{(\varepsilon + H)}.$$

The lower the concentration of the industry, the lower is the Lerner index and the price-cost margin. By contrast, in a Bertrand oligopoly, where each firm chooses its target price, in a one-shot game where firms do not consider more than the current situation, equilibrium price is equal to marginal cost and the value of L is zero.

LO3 Models of Oligopoly

Because oligopolists are interdependent, analyzing their behavior is complicated. No single model or single approach explains oligopolistic behavior completely. At one extreme, oligopolists may try to coordinate their behavior so they act collectively as a single monopolist, forming a cartel, such as OPEC. At the other extreme, oligopolists may compete so fiercely that price wars erupt, such as those that break out among airlines, tobacco companies, computer chip makers, and wireless service providers.

Several theories have been developed to explain oligopolistic behavior. As you will see, each has some relevance in explaining observed behavior, although none is entirely satisfactory as a general theory of oligopoly. Thus, *there is no general theory of oligopoly but rather a set of theories, each based on the diversity of observed behavior in an interdependent market.*

Based on the diversity of observed behavior, oligopoly can be collusive or non-collusive. A common characteristic of non-collusive oligopoly is that firms assume a certain reaction from competitors for any action undertaken by them. However, the firms are assumed to be naïve in the sense that they do not learn from their past experience. Thus, even if the competitor does not react in the way it was assumed to, the firm does not change its assumption and continues to assume that the initial assumption holds. Several models of non-collusive oligopoly exist. Few of them are Cournot's model, Bertrand's model, Chamberlin's model, and the kinked demand curve model. Each model is based upon an assumption related to the action-reaction behavior amongst duopolists/oligopolists. Collusive oligopoly is a way of reducing the uncertainty associated with oligopolistic interdependence. Under this, firms enter into collusive agreements. There are two main types of collusive agreements: price leadership and cartels. Cartels are typically of two forms: cartels that aim at joint profit maximization and cartels that aim at sharing of the market.

Cournot model an oligopoly model in which each firm assumes that the other keeps the output constant.

reaction curve the relationship between how a duopolist reacts to the other duopolist's action.

As stated, there are two types of collusive oligopoly:

i. **Price leadership or tacit collusion:** This occurs when one firm has a clear dominant position in the market and the firms with lower market shares follow the pricing changes driven by the dominant firm.
ii. **Overt collusion:** This occurs when firms openly agree on price, output, and other decisions aimed at achieving monopoly profits. Firms coordinate their activities through overt collusion by forming collusive coordinating mechanisms. Such a group of independent producers working in unison is called a **cartel**. When this happens the existing firms decide to engage in price fixing agreements or cartels. The aim of this is to maximize joint profits and act as if the market was a pure monopoly. But in reality the existence of the so called "perfect cartel" is quite rare. In most of the cases, cartels are found to be "loose" and in those cases, the distribution of profits and fixation of outputs of individual firms are not determined in a manner as perfect cartels do. Generally, a market sharing approach gets generated that operates in two different manners:
    - *Market Sharing by Non-Price Competition*: Here only a uniform price is set and the member firms are free to produce and sell amount of outputs which will maximize their individual profits. Here the firms are free to vary the style of their products and advertising expenditure to promote sales of their products.
    - *Market Sharing by Quota*: Here the member firms agree regarding the quota of output to be produced and sold by each of them at the agreed price.

Non-collusive Oligopoly

The models of non-collusive oligopoly are discussed here.

Cournot's Model

The **Cournot model** is an oligopoly model in which each firm assumes that the other keeps the output constant. This model was identified by an economist named Augustin Cournot (1838), and the equilibrium so arrived at is referred as Cournot equilibrium. This model is best explained with the help of reaction functions or reaction curves. We, thus, begin by explaining the concept of reaction curves. A **reaction curve** gives the relationship between how a duopolist reacts to the other duopolist's action.

Given the data about output levels of firm A, it is clear that firm A's output level is a decreasing schedule of what it assumes firm B will produce. It is called firm A's reaction curve. It plots the following combinations of A and B's output levels:

	Assuming firm B's Output level as	Output level of firm A will be
M	Zero Units	100 Units
N	100 Units	50 Units
T	150 Units	25 Units
R	200 Units	Zero Units

Exhibit 5

A's Reaction Curve

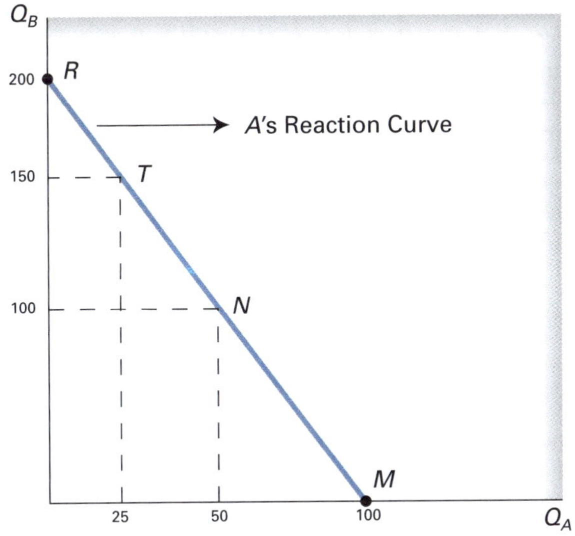

Similarly, firm B's reaction curve is obtained in a similar manner on the assumption that it also has same constant marginal cost of production (i.e., $MC_A = MC_B$).

Cournot's Equilibrium: Cournot's equilibrium occurs at point e_1 in Exhibit 6 where the two reaction curves intersect each other. In other words, both firms are simultaneously at the best response level because only then will neither firm have an incentive to deviate. At point e_1, each firm is producing that output level which maximizes its profit given what the rival firm is producing. It is a stable equilibrium. Cournot's equilibrium is a Nash equilibrium. The concept of Nash equilibrium, given by John Nash in 1951 states that in equilibrium, each firm is doing the best it can, given its competitor's behavior. In Cournot's equilibrium, each firm decides its own output that maximizes its profit given what its rival firm is producing. The firms have no incentive to change their output. Further, a Cournot player is a passive player taking the rival's output as given while working out one's best level of output. Cournot's equilibrium is a stable equilibrium provided that A's reaction curve is steeper than B's reaction curve, when output of player A is on the horizontal axis and output of player B is on the vertical axis. To understand why this is so, let us assume that oligopolist A produces output A_1 instead of A_e. Given that A produces A_1, B reacts by producing B_1. However, if B produces B_1, oligopolist A reacts by producing A_2. But when A produces A_2, B reacts by producing output equal to B_2. To this, A responds by producing A_3. This output adjustment continues, until A produces A_e and B produces B_e. Similar adjustment would follow, if we start the process from a point to the right of e_1.

It can be proved that if there are two firms then under Cournot equilibrium, each oligopolist firm sells one-third of the perfectly competitive product. It can also be shown that if there are three firms, then each produces 1/4th of the market. The total market supply thus will be ¾ (= 3∗1/4). In general, if there are n firms in the industry, each firm supplies $1/(n + 1)$ of the market, and the industry output, thus, will be $n/(n + 1)$.

To generalize:

$$Q_n = Q_c\,[n/(n + 1)]$$

where $n \geq 1$, and

Q_n = Total equilibrium output under Cournot oligopoly with n firms.

Q_c = Output resulting from a perfectly competitive market.

Thus, larger the number of firms, the closer is output and price under Cournot's model to the competitive output and price.

Exhibit 6

Cournot Equilibrium

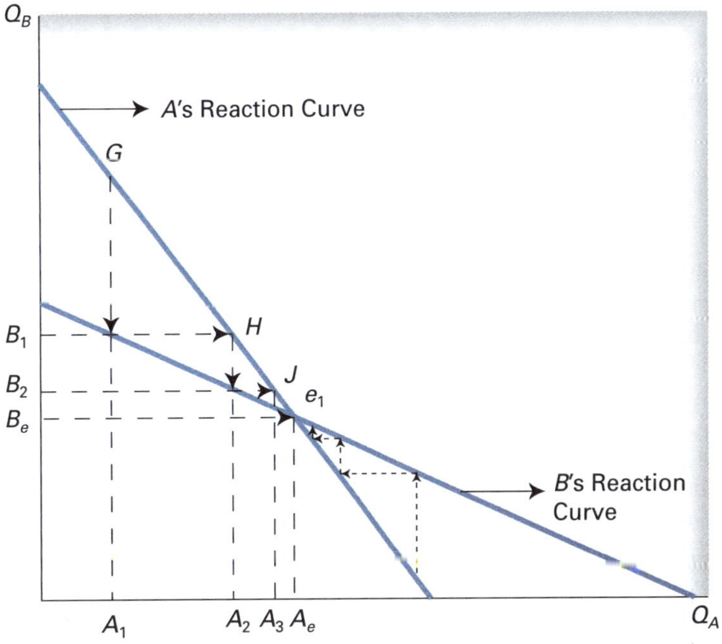

However, the Cournot's model has been criticized in several respects. These are as follows:

1. Firms do not learn from the past behavior pattern of the rival firms, and continue to assume that the competitor will keep the output constant. This implies that the behavioral pattern of firms is naïve.
2. Although each firm acts on the assumption that its competitor will not change its output, a quantity-war emerges which pushes the price down.
3. The model does not explain how long the adjustment period will take.
4. It is a "closed" model, i.e., entry is not allowed.

Mathematical Derivation: Cournot's Model and Cournot's Equilibrium

Assume that the market demand facing the duopolist is

$$P = a + b_X \quad b < 0$$

where X represents total output of the duopolists. That is

$$X = X_1 + X_2$$

Let the two duopolists have different costs

$$C_1 = f_1(X_1) \quad \text{and} \quad C_2 = f_2(X_2)$$

The first duopolist maximizes his profit by assuming that X_2 is constant, irrespective of his own decisions, while the second duopolist maximizes his profit by assuming that X_1 will remain constant.

The first-order condition for maximum profits of each duoplolist is:

$$\frac{\partial \Pi_1}{\partial X_1} = \frac{\partial TR_1}{\partial X_1} - \frac{\partial TC_1}{\partial X_1} = 0$$

$$\frac{\partial \Pi_2}{\partial X_2} = \frac{\partial TR_2}{\partial X_2} - \frac{\partial TC_2}{\partial X_2} = 0$$

Rearranging we have

$$\frac{\partial TR_1}{\partial X_1} = \frac{\partial TC_1}{\partial X_1}$$

$$\frac{\partial TR_2}{\partial X_2} = \frac{\partial TC_2}{\partial X_2}$$

Solving the first equation for X_1 we obtain X_1 as a function of X_2, that is, we obtain the reaction curve of firm A. It expresses the output which A must produce in order to maximize his profit for any given amount X_2 produced by his rival. Solving the second equation for X_2 gives X_2 as a function of X_1, that is, we obtain the reaction function of firm B. If we solve the two equations simultaneously, we obtain the Cournot equilibrium, the values of X_1 and X_2 which satisfy both equations; this is the point of intersection of the two reaction curves.

The second-order condition for equilibrium requires that

$$\frac{\partial^2 \Pi_i}{\partial X_i^2} = \frac{\partial^2 TR_i}{\partial X_i^2} - \frac{\partial^2 TC_i}{\partial X_i^2} < 0 \quad (i = 1, 2)$$

Or

$$\frac{\partial^2 TR_i}{\partial X_i^2} < \frac{\partial^2 TC_i}{\partial X_i^2}$$

That is each duopolist's *MR* must be increasing less rapidly than *MC*, that is, *MC* must cut *MR* from below for both the duopolists.

It can be further proved that if the duopolists are of unequal size, then one with the larger output will have the smaller *MR*. For this, let us assume that the market demand facing the duopolist is given by:

$$P = a + bX \quad b < 0$$

where X represents total output of the duopolists. That is

$$X = X_1 + X_2$$

With $X = X_1 + X_2$, we have:

$$\frac{\partial X}{\partial X_1} = \frac{\partial X}{\partial X_2} = 1$$

Now, $TR_i = PX_i$

$$P = a + b(X_1 + X_2) = f(X_1 + X_2)$$

Thus, $\dfrac{\partial TR_i}{\partial X_i} = P + X_i \dfrac{\partial P}{\partial X_i}$

But, $\dfrac{\partial P}{\partial X_1} = \dfrac{\partial P}{\partial X_2} = \dfrac{\partial P}{\partial X} = b$

Therefore, $\dfrac{\partial TR_i}{\partial X_i} = P + X_i \dfrac{\partial P}{\partial X} = P + (X_i)(b)$

Given that $P > 0$, and $b < 0$, it is clear that larger is X_i, the smaller will be *MR*.

Numerical Illustrations: Cournot's Model

Problem 1: Let the market demand and the total costs of the duopolists be as follows:

$$P = 100 - 0.5\,(X_1 + X_2)$$
$$C_1 = 5X_1$$
$$C_2 = 0.5X_2^2$$

Thereafter, the profit functions of the duopolists can be estimated as:

$$\Pi_1 = PX_1 - C_1 = [100 - 0.5(X_1 + X_2)]X_1 - 5X_1$$
$$\Pi_2 = PX_2 - C_2 = [100 - 0.5(X_1 + X_2)]X_2 - 0.5X_2^2$$

Solution: Opening of brackets yields:

$$\Pi_1 = 100X_1 - 0.5X_1^2 - 0.5X_1X_2 - 5X_1$$
$$\Pi_2 = 100X_2 - 0.5X_1X_2 - 0.5X_2^2 - 0.5X_2^2$$

Collecting terms we have

$$\Pi_1 = 95X_1 - 0.5X_1^2 - 0.5X_1X_2$$
$$\Pi_2 = 100X_2 - X_2^2 - 0.5X_1X_2$$

For profit maximization under the Cournot assumption, we equate $\frac{\partial \Pi_1}{\partial X_1}$ and $\frac{\partial \Pi_2}{\partial X_2}$ to zero. We thus have:

$$\frac{\partial \Pi_1}{\partial X_1} = 0 = 95 - X_1 - 0.5X_2$$

$$\frac{\partial \Pi_2}{\partial X_2} = 0 = 100 - 2X_2 - 0.5X_1$$

By equating the equations to zero, we get the two reaction functions as:

$$X_1 = 95 - 0.5X_2$$
$$X_2 = 50 - 0.25X_1$$

Solving the two equations simultaneously or by substitution, we get the solution as:

$$X_1 = 80$$

And $\quad X_2 = 30$

The total output produced by the duopolists is:

$$X = X_1 + X_2 = 120$$

Substituting the total output in the demand function yields the market price as:

$$P = 100 - 0.5X = 45$$

Solving for marginal revenue yields

$$MR_1 = \frac{\partial TR_1}{\partial X_1} = \frac{\partial (PX_1)}{\partial X_1} = P + X_1 \frac{\partial P}{\partial X}$$

$$MR_1 = 45 + 80\ (00.5)$$

$$MR_1 = 5$$

Further $MR_2 = 45 + 30\ (-0.5)$

$$MR_2 = 30$$

It may be noted that the firm with the larger output has the smaller marginal revenue. The profits of the duopolists are

$$\Pi_1 = 3200$$

And

$$\Pi_2 = 900$$

The second-order condition is also satisfied for both duopolists since the second derivative for both is negative:

$$\frac{\partial \Pi_1}{\partial X_1} = 95 - X_1 - 0.5X_2 \qquad \frac{\partial \Pi_2}{\partial X_2} = 100 - 2X_2 - 0.5X_1$$

$$\frac{\partial^2 \Pi_1}{\partial X_1^2} = -1 < 0 \qquad \frac{\partial^2 \Pi_2}{\partial X_2^2} = -2 < 0$$

We, thus, conclude that $X_1 = 80$ and $X_2 = 30$ are profit maximizing outputs for the Cournot duopolists.

Problem 2: Let there be two firms under Cournot's model having market demand curve as $P = 20 - X$, where X is the total production of the two firms 1 and 2. These firms are assumed to be producing under zero cost of production. Determine

a. Reaction curves of the two firms
b. Equilibrium level of output for both the firms
c. Equilibrium market price
d. Show graphically the Cournot's equilibrium, collusive equilibrium, and competitive equilibrium.

Exhibit 7

Equilibrium Under Cournot's Model

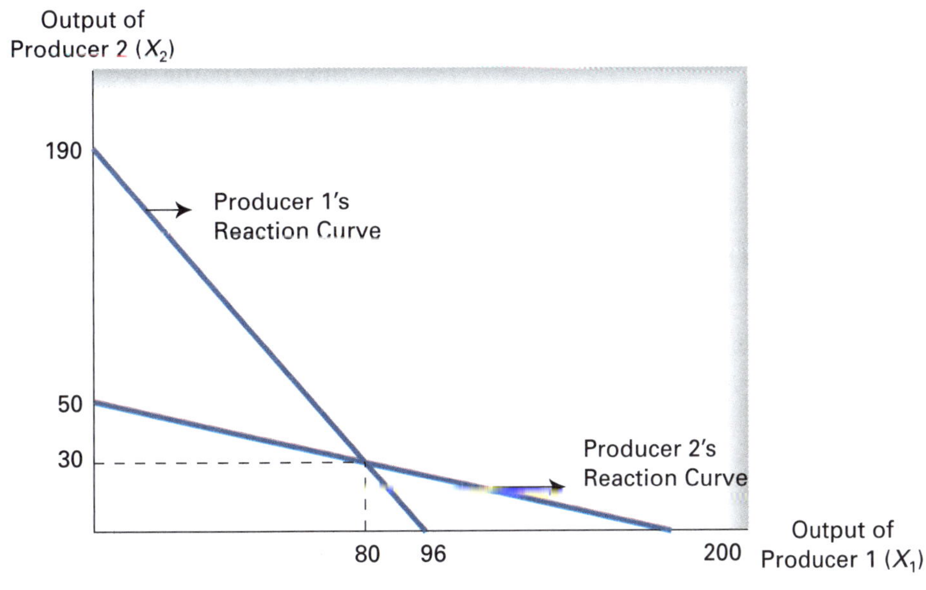

Solution:

a. Reaction curve for firm 1 is derived from the point where:

$$MR_1 = MC$$

$$TR_1 = P \cdot X_1 = (20 - X)X_1$$
$$= [20 - (X_1 + X_2)]X_1$$
$$= 20X_1 - X_1^2 - X_1X_2$$

$$MR_1 = \frac{\partial TR_1}{\partial X_1} = 20 - 2X_1 - X_2$$

Since $MR_1 = MC = 0$, we get:

$$2X_1 = 20 - X_2$$

Or $$\boxed{X_1 = 10 - \frac{1}{2}X_2} \quad (1)$$

This is firm 1's reaction curve.

Similiarly, firm 2's reaction curve is obtained where:

$$MR_2 = MC$$

$$TR_2 = P \,.\, X_2 = [20 - (X_1 + X_2)]X_2$$
$$= 20X_2 - X_1X_2 - X_2^2$$

$$MR_2 = \frac{\partial TR_2}{\partial X_2} = 20 - X_1 - 2X_2$$

Since $MR_2 = MC = 0$, we get:

$$2X_2 = 20 - X_1$$

Or $$\boxed{X_2 = 10 - \frac{1}{2}X_1} \quad (2)$$

This is firm 2's reaction curve.

b. Substituting (2) in (1) we can get equilibrium output as:

$$X_1 = 10 - \frac{1}{2}\left[10 - \frac{1}{2}X_1\right]$$

$$X_1 = 10 - 5 + \frac{1}{4}X_1$$

$$X_1 - \frac{1}{4}X_1 = 5$$

$$X_1 = \frac{20}{3}$$

Or $$\boxed{X_1 = 6.67} \quad (3)$$

Substituting (3) in (2), we get:

$$X_2 = 10 - \frac{1}{2} \times 6.67$$

$$\boxed{X_2 = 6.67} \quad (4)$$

Cournot's equilibrium:

$$X1 = X2 = 6.67$$

Thus, total quantity of X produced is:

$$X = X1 + X2$$
$$= 6.67 + 6.67 = 13.34$$

Equilibrium market price P is:

$$P = 20 - X$$
$$= 20 - 13.34$$
$$\therefore \quad P = 6.66$$

Exhibit 8

Collusive, Cournot's and Competitive Equilibrium

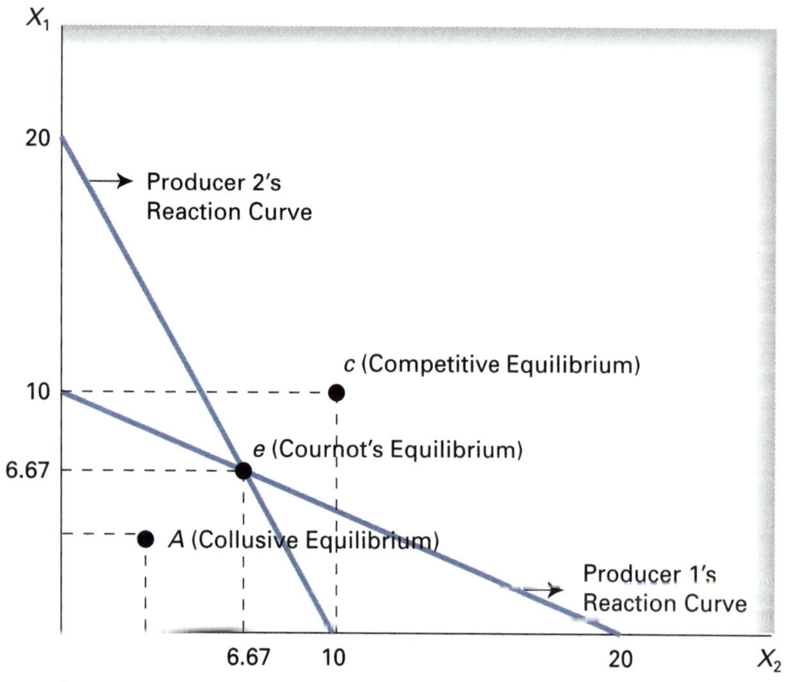

Let "e" be the point of intersection of two firm's reaction curves. It is Cournot's equilibrium point which gives $X_1 = X_2 = 6.67$. At this point each firm is maximizing its own profit, given the output of the other firm.

However, if the two firms collude and aim at joint profit maximization (which they then distribute equally) the equilibrium would be at Point A. The total profit will be maximum where

$$MR = MC$$
$$TR = P \cdot X = (20 - X)X = 20X - X^2$$

$$MR = 20 - 2X$$
$$MR = MC \text{ implies } 20 - 2X = 0$$
$$\text{(since } MC = 0\text{)}$$
$$\therefore \quad X = 10$$

Any combinations of X_1 and X_2 that gives output 10 will maximize profit and is called collusive equilibrium:

Perfectly competitive equilibrium point will occur where $P = MC$. This is shown by point C in Exhibit 8.

$$20 - X = 0$$
$$\therefore \quad X = 20$$

Kinked Demand Curve and Price Stability: Sweezy's Model

The kinked demand curve model developed by Paul M. Sweezy in 1939 is an attempt to explain price rigidity. The model has features common to most of oligopoly pricing models. This is the best known model explaining relatively more satisfactorily the behavior of the oligopolistic firms in maintaining price rigidity. Therefore, it is often referred to as the price rigidity model.

The kinked demand curve analysis does not deal with price and output determination. In fact, it assumes that prices are already determined. Thereafter, it tries to explain the tendency for prices to remain rigid, despite changing cost or market conditions. In other words, it seeks to establish that once a price-quantity combination has been determined by an oligopolist, an oligopoly firm will not find it profitable to change its price even in response to minor changes in cost of production or changing demand conditions. The logic behind this proposition is based upon the following assumption:

1. An oligopoly firm believes that if it reduces the price, other firms will follow suit by matching the price cuts, so that it does not stand to gain much, while
2. If it increases the price, other firms will not follow suit. In fact, the other firms might even indulge in price cutting, so that the price-raising firm stands to lose, at least a part of its share in the market.

This behavioral assumption is made by all the firms in respect of others. The oligopoly firms would therefore find it more desirable to maintain their price and output at the original level. The belief in this assumption by the oligopolists leads to a kink in the demand curve. The kink occurs at the existing price. The demand curve above the kink is flatter (more elastic) than the demand curve below the kink (less elastic). In this model, oligopolists recognize their interdependence but act without collusion in keeping their price constant. Thus, the oligopolists prefer to compete with others on the basis of non-price competition policies (after sales service, better quality or advertisement), rather than price policies. Graphically, price rigidity is shown in Exhibit 9.

Exhibit 9

Price Rigidity Under Kinked Demand Curve

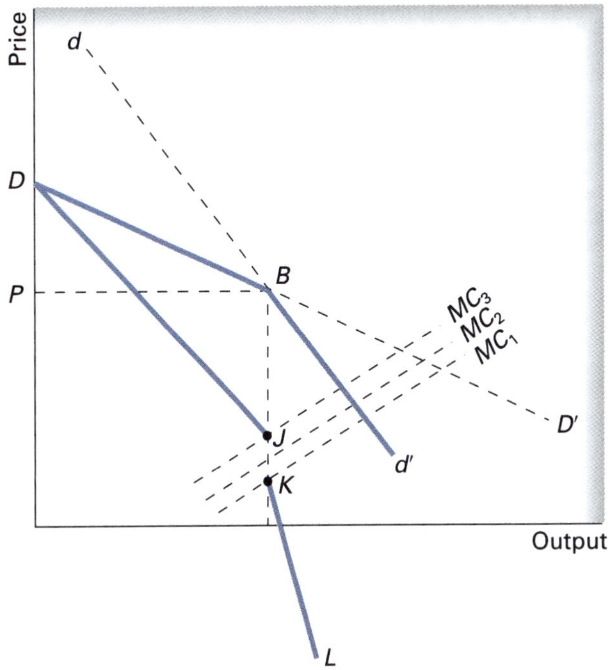

Let point B represent the current price-quantity combination of an oligopoly firm. Let us now introduce the assumption made: i.e., rival firms follow when an oligopolist reduces its price but do not follow when it increases its price. Now, the relevant demand curve facing the firm is *DBd′* which has a kink at point B (the prevailing price). Consider now the relationship between AR and MR. Given a kink in the demand curve (which is the *AR* curve), *MR* will have a discontinuity. We know that $MR = AR - AR/e$. If *MR* curve is drawn on the basis of this relationship, it will take a shape as shown by *DJKL* in Exhibit 9. The relevant *MR* for *DB* segment of the demand curve is given by *DJ*. For segment *Bd′* of the demand curve, the relevant *MR* is *KL*. Thus, the MR is discontinuous between point *J* and K. The discontinuity is at current output OQ. Suppose that the original marginal cost curve is given by MC_1, which intersects *MR* at point K. Since at output OQ, $MR = MC_1$ the firm makes maximum profit. Now, even if *MC* curve shifts upwards to MC_2 or any level between points *J* and *K*, its profit would not be affected. Therefore, it has no motivation for increasing (or decreasing) its price. It is always beneficial to stick to the current situation. Thus, both price and output are stabilized. This is what kinked demand curve analysis establishes. However, major criticism against this model is that it only explains the stabilization of output and price; it does not explain why and how the initial price is determined. Also, G. J. Stigler in 1947 criticized the model as he found no evidence that oligopolists generally matched price cuts but not price increases.

While constructing the graph, a note may be made of the following:

1. The kink in the *AR* curve causes a discontinuity in *MR*.
2. The gap in *MR* occurs directly below the kink.
3. The greater the variation in the slope of *AR* curve (above and below the kink), greater will be the discontinuity in the *MR* curve.
4. So long as changes in *MC* are confined to the gap in *MR*, there is no incentive for the oligopolist to change its price.
5. Only if the *MC* curve shifts above MC_3 or below MC_1, will the oligopolist be induced to increase its price (if shift is beyond MC_3) or decrease its price (if shift is below MC_1).
6. Even though no unique intersection between *MR* and *MC* curve takes place at point G, it nevertheless denotes profit maximizing equilibrium for the oligopolist. This is because, for outputs less than OQ, *MR* is greater than *MC* (motivating the oligopolist to enhance production), and for outputs greater than OQ, *MC* exceeds *MR* (motivating the oligopolist to reduce production). Thus, the producer is in equilibrium at output OQ.

Further, shifts in demand curve also may not motivate the oligopolist to change its price. With a rightward or leftward shift in the demand curve, while sales may increase or decrease, the oligopolist will keep the price constant as long as:

i. The kink on the demand curve remains at the same price, and
ii. The *MC* curve continues to pass through the discontinuous portion of the *MR* curve.

Numerical Illustration: Kinked Demand Curve Model

Suppose that the demand functions for price increases and for price cuts facing an oligopolist are, respectively,

$$Q_1 = 280 - 40P_1$$

or

$$P1 = 7 - 0.025Q_1$$

$$Q_2 = 100 - 10P_2$$

or

$$P2 = 10 - 0.1Q_2$$

where Q is output and *P* is price (in dollars).

Suppose that the firm's total cost function is

$$TC = 2Q + 0.025Q^2$$

collusion
an agreement among firms to increase economic profit by dividing the market and fixing the price

cartel
a group of firms that agree to coordinate their production and pricing decisions to earn monopoly profit

We can calculate MR_1, MR_2, and MC as follows:

$$TR_1 = P_1Q_1 = (7 - 0.025Q_1)Q_1 = 7Q_1 - 0.0250Q_1^2$$

$$MR_1 = \frac{d(TR_1)}{dQ_1} = 7 - 0.05Q_1$$

$$TR_2 = P_2Q_2 = (10 - 0.1Q_2)Q_2 = 10Q_2 - 0.1Q_2^2$$

$$MR_2 = \frac{d(TR_2)}{dQ_2} = 10 - 0.2Q_2$$

$$MC = \frac{d(TC)}{d(Q)} = 2 + 0.05Q$$

To find the kink or point of intersection of demand curves D_1 and D_2, we set $P_1 = P_2 = P$ or alternatively $Q_1 = Q_2 = Q$ and get:

$$7 - 0.025Q = 10 - 0.1Q$$

$$0.075Q = 3$$

$$Q = 40$$

and

$$P = 7 - 0.0075(40) = 6$$

The upper and lower limits of the *MR* gap are

$$MR_1 = 7 - 0.5(40) = 7 - 2 = 5$$

$$MR_2 = 10 - 0.2(40) = 10 - 8 = 2$$

Since

$$MC = 2 + 0.05(40) = 4$$

The *MC* curve passes through the vertical portion of the *MR* curve. The total profits (π) of the firm are

$$\pi = TR - TC = PQ - 2Q - 0.025Q^2$$

$$= 6(40) - 2(40) - 0.025(40)^2 = 120$$

The level of π could also have been found from

$$\pi = (P - ATC)q$$

$$ATC = \frac{TC}{q} = \frac{2Q + 0.025Q^2}{Q} = 2 + 0.025Q$$

$$= 2 + 0.025(40) = 3$$

So that

$$\pi = (6 - 3)(40) = 120$$

Collusion and Cartels

In an oligopolistic market, there are just a few firms, so to decrease competition and increase profits, these firms may try to *collude*, or conspire to rig the market. **Collusion** is an agreement among firms in the industry to divide the market and fix the price. A **cartel** is a group of firms that agree to collude so they can act as a monopoly to increase economic profit. Cartels are more likely among sellers of a commodity, like oil or steel. *Colluding firms, compared with competing firms, usually produce less, charge more, block new firms, and earn more profit. Consumers pay higher prices, and potential entrants are denied the opportunity to compete.*

Collusion and cartels are illegal in the United States. Still, monopoly profit can be so tempting that some U.S. firms break the law. For example, top executives at Archer Daniels Midland were convicted of conspiring with four Asian competitors to rig the \$650 million world market for lysine, an amino acid used in animal feed. Some other countries are more tolerant of cartels and a few even promote cartels, as with the 12 member-nations of OPEC. If OPEC ever met in the United States, its representatives could be arrested for price fixing. Cartels can operate worldwide because there are no international laws against them.

Perfect Cartels: Aiming at Joint Profit maximization

Suppose all firms in the industry formed a cartel with the objective of joint profit maximization. This situation is identical with that of a multi-plant monopolist who produces in two locations but has a common market in which it sells its produce. The aim of the cartel is to maximize joint profits. For simplicity, we assume that firms produce homogenous products (undifferentiated oligopoly). Further, there is a central agency which decides how much is to be produced, what price is to be charged, how the production is to be allocated among the producers and how the profits are to be distributed. We also assume that the central agency has all the information about firm costs and market demand. To illustrate the equilibrium graphically, let there be two firms A and B. The central agency then estimates the market (combined) MC of both the firms (by horizontal summation of individual MC curves). In order to maximize joint profits, the central agency determines the equilibrium price and output by equating ΣMC to MR. This occurs at point "e" (refer Exhibit 10). Equating MR to individual MCs yields corresponding equilibriums at e_A and e_B. Thus, firm A produces Q_A of output and firm B produces Q_B of output. The firm with lower costs ends up producing more of output. However, this does not mean that it will get a higher profit generated by it (= *PDWN*) as compared to the lower profit generated by firm *B* (= *PRST*). This is because distribution of profits between oligopolists is decided by the central agency. However, this is easier said than done.

Differences in Average Cost

If all firms have identical average cost curves, output and profit would be easily allocated across firms (each firm would produce the same amount), but if costs differ, as they usually do, problems arise. The greater the difference in average costs across firms, the greater the differences in economic profits among them. If cartel members try to equalize each firm's total profit, a high-cost firm would need to sell more than would a low-cost firm. But this allocation scheme would violate the cartel's profit-maximizing condition. Thus, *if average costs differ across firms, the output allocation that maximizes cartel profit yields unequal profit across cartel members*. Firms earning less profit could drop out of the cartel, thereby undermining it. Usually, the allocation of output is the result of haggling among cartel members. Firms that are more influential or more adept at bargaining get a larger share of output and profit. Allocation schemes are sometimes based on geography or on the historical division of output among firms. OPEC, for example, allocates output in proportion to each member country's share of estimated oil reserves. Cartel members of Norway's cement market base output on each firm's share of industry capacity.[3]

Exhibit 10

Cartels Aiming at Joint Profit Maximization

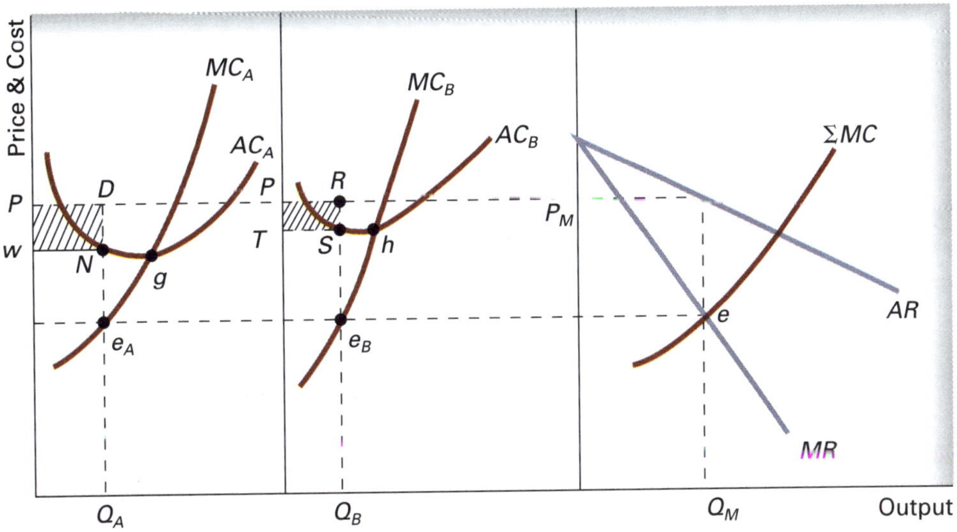

Number of Firms in the Cartel

The more firms in an industry, the more difficult it is to negotiate an acceptable allocation of output among

3. Lars-Hendrik Roller and Frode Steen, "On the Workings of a Cartel: Evidence from the Norwegian Cement Industry," *American Economic Review* 96 (March 2006), p. 322.

them. *Consensus becomes harder to achieve as the number of firms grows.* And the more firms in the industry, the more likely that some will become dissatisfied and bolt from the cartel.

New Entry into the Industry

If a cartel can't prevent new entry into the market, new firms will eventually force prices down, squeeze economic profit, and disrupt the cartel. The profit of the cartel attracts entry, entry increases market supply, and increased supply forces the price down. A cartel's success therefore depends on barriers that block the entry of new firms.

Cheating

Perhaps the biggest problem in keeping the cartel together is the powerful temptation to cheat on the agreement. Because oligopolists usually operate with excess capacity, some cheat on the price. By offering a price slightly below the fixed price, any cartel member can usually increase sales and profit. Even if cartel members keep an eagle eye on each firm's price, one firm can increase sales by offering extra services, secret rebates, or other concessions. Cartels collapse once cheating *becomes widespread*.

OPEC's Spotty History

The problems of establishing and maintaining a cartel are reflected in the spotty history of OPEC. Many members are poor countries that rely on oil as their major source of revenue, so they argue over the price and their market share. OPEC members also cheat on the cartel. In 1980, the price of oil exceeded $80 a barrel. During the 1990s, the price averaged $32 a barrel and dipped as low as $10 a barrel. Oil prices hit what was a record high of $145 a barrel in 2008, but then fell back to around $45 a barrel by the end of the year. Like other cartels, OPEC has difficulty with new entrants. The high prices resulting from OPEC's early success attracted new oil supplies from non-OPEC members operating in the North Sea, Mexico, and Siberia. The high price also made extraction from Canadian oil sands economical. As a result of new exploration and other oil sources, about 60 percent of the world's oil now comes from non-OPEC sources.

In summary: Establishing and maintaining an effective cartel is more difficult if (1) the product is differentiated among firms, (2) average costs differ among firms, (3) there are many firms in the industry, (4) entry barriers are low, or (5) cheating on the cartel agreement becomes widespread. Efforts to cartelize the world supply of a number of products, including bauxite, copper, tin, and coffee, have failed so far. Russia is trying to form a natural gas cartel with other gas exporters, but obstacles abound.

Dominant-Firm Price Leadership Model

Collusion can also take the form of price leadership. It represents a coordinated behavior on the part of the oligopolists whereby one producer sets the price and others follow the price decision. Price leadership can be of various types. However, three forms are most common: price leadership by a dominant firm; low cost price leadership model; and barometric price leadership model. Under dominant firm price leadership model, the firm with the largest market share is the price leader; under low cost price leadership model, the firm with the lowest cost of production is the price leader, while under barometric price leadership, generally the oldest or the most respected firm is the price leader. Here we explain how prices are determined by a dominant firm. Under dominant firm price leadership model, there is a dominant firm and several small firms. By virtue of being dominant (has considerable share of the total market), the larger firm sets the price and becomes the price leader, while other small firms become price followers. The model assumes that the dominant firm knows the overall market demand for the product. In addition, it also knows the marginal

© BOB SCOTT/ICONICA/GETTY IMAGES

Exhibit 11

Dominant Firm Price Leadership Model

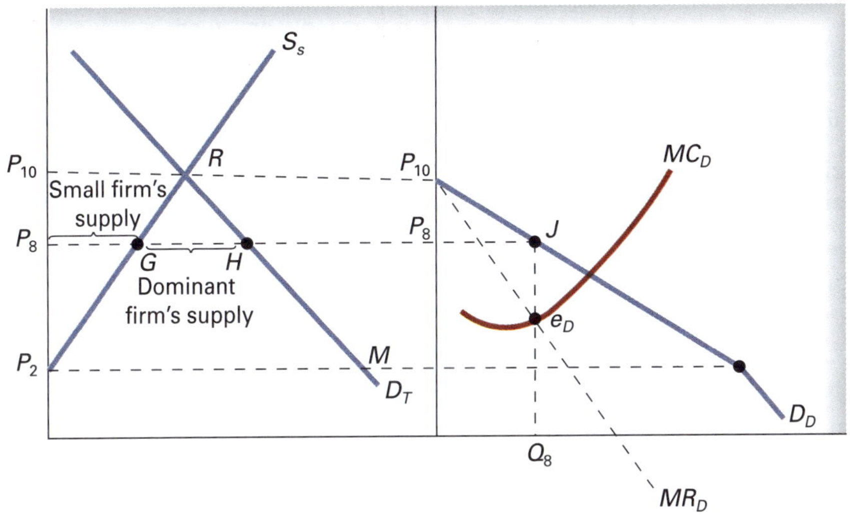

cost curves (supply curves) of the smaller firms. By horizontally adding up these curves, the dominant firm can estimate the total supply by the small firms at each price; given this knowledge, the dominant firm derives his own demand curve. He does so as follows. At each price, the larger firm will be able to supply the section of the total market not supplied by the smaller firms. That is, at each price the demand for the product of the leader will be the difference between total demand at that price and the total supply made by the small producers S_s. Thus, the dominant firm gets the residual demand. For example, at price P_{10}, the market demand equals the output supplied by the small producers. Therefore, at price P_{10}, the dominant firm has no market to supply. Correspondingly, the demand for the product of the leader will be zero. However, at prices below P_{10}, the demand for the leader's product becomes positive and keeps increasing with a fall in the price. For instance, at price of P_8, the total demand is P_8H; Of this, the small firms supply P_8G. The remaining GH is supplied by the leader. At P_2, the total demand is P_2M. At this price, the output supplied by the small firms is zero. Therefore, the entire output is supplied by the dominant firm. Thus, below P_2, the market demand coincides with the leader's demand curve.

Once the dominant firm has derived its demand curve D_D, it thereafter estimates its MR given by MR_D. Superimposing its MC curve, the dominant firm is in equilibrium at point e_D (where MR = MC and MC cuts MR from below). The price is set at P_8 and the profit maximizing output of the dominant firm is given by Q_8. At price P_8 the total market demand is P_8H. Of this P_8G is supplied by the small firms and the remaining GH (= P_8J) is supplied by the leader/dominant firm.

At this price, the dominant firm leader maximizes its profit by equating its MC to its MR, while the smaller firms are price-takers, and thus, may or may not maximize their profit, depending on their cost structure. However, if the leader is to maximize the profit, it must ensure that the small firms are not only price followers but also produce a quantity exactly equal to P_8G. In case, the small firms produce an amount greater or less than P_8G, the leader will not be able to maximize its profits.

To summarize, price leadership faces obstacles. Most importantly, the practice violates U.S. antitrust laws. Second, the greater the product differentiation among sellers, the less effective price leadership is as a means of collusion. Third, there is no guarantee that other firms will follow the leader. Firms that fail to follow a price increase take business away from firms that do. Fourth, unless there are barriers to entry, a profitable price attracts new entrants, which could destabilize the price-leadership agreement. And finally, as with formal cartels, some firms are tempted to cheat on the agreement to boost sales and profits.

Numerical Illustrations: Market Structures

Problem 1: Suppose that the functional relationship among profit, output, and advertising is given by the expression:

$$\pi = 1000 - 4Q - Q^2 + 2QA + 116A - 5A^2$$

Determine the profit maximizing rates of output and advertising expenditures.

Solution: The first step is to find the partial derivatives of π with respect to Q and A and set them equal to zero.

$$\frac{\partial \pi}{\partial Q} = -4 - 2Q + 2A = 0$$

$$\frac{\partial \pi}{\partial A} = 2Q + 116 - 10A = 0$$

Solving these two equations simultaneously gives Q = 12 and A = 14.

To prove that these values represent maximum π rather than minimum profit, we check to see that the second order conditions are met:

$$\frac{\partial^2\pi}{\partial Q^2} < 0; \frac{\partial^2\pi}{\partial A^2} < 0 \quad \text{and} \quad \left(\frac{\partial^2\pi}{\partial Q^2}\right)\left(\frac{\partial^2\pi}{\partial A^2}\right) > \left(\frac{\partial^2\pi}{\partial Q\partial A}\right)^2$$

Since

$$\frac{\partial^2\pi}{\partial Q^2} = -2; \frac{\partial^2\pi}{\partial A^2} = -10 \quad \text{and} \quad \frac{\partial^2\pi}{\partial Q\partial A} = 2$$

It is, thus, verified that the π maximizing output rate is 12 units and the profit (π) maximizing advertising outlay is ₹14 per period of time.

Problem 2: Given the following total revenue and total cost function:

$$TR = 24Q - Q^2$$
$$TC = 20 + 8Q + Q^2$$

Calculate the profit maximizing level of output and the break-even level of output.

Solution: *Profit Maximizing Level of Output*:

$$\pi = TR - TC$$
$$= 24Q - Q^2 - 20 - 8Q - Q^2$$
$$\pi = 16Q - 2Q^2 - 20$$

The first order partial derivative is to be equated to zero.

$$\frac{\partial\pi}{\partial Q} = 16 - 4Q = 0$$
$$Q = 4$$

The sufficient condition is also met,

since $\frac{\partial^2\pi}{\partial Q^2} = -4 < 0$

The break-even level of output:

The break-even level of output is given by the solution of equation $\pi = 0$ (*i.e.*, TR = TC)

$$16Q - 2Q^2 - 20 = 0 \quad \text{or} \quad Q^2 - 8Q + 10 = 0$$

$$Q = \frac{8 \pm \sqrt{64 - 40}}{2}$$

$$Q = 6.45 \quad \text{and} \quad Q = 1.55$$

Thus, there are two levels of output at which the firm breaks even.

Some other useful calculations are given here:

* $P = TR/Q = 24 - Q$
* $TFC = 20$
* $TVC = 8Q + Q^2$
* $AVC = TVC/Q = 8 + Q$
* Total contribution = TR – TVC
  $= 24Q - Q^2 - 8Q - Q^2$
  $= 16Q - 2Q^2$
* Average contribution = P – AVC
  $= 24 - Q - 8 - Q$
  $= 16 - 2Q$

Problem 3: Suppose the demand and supply conditions of a good are represented by the following equations:

Aggregate demand: $Q = 25 - 0.5P$
Aggregate supply: $Q = 10 + 1.0P$

And the *TC* of a particular firm is represented by:

$$C = 25 - 2q_1 + 4q_1^2$$

Determine the price-output equilibrium of the industry and equilibrium of the firm under conditions of pure competition.

Solution: The equilibrium price would be the one at which:

$$AD = AS$$

$$2.5 - 0.5P = 10 + 1.0P \quad \text{or} \quad P = 10$$

Industry output at P = 10 is obtained by substituting this price into either the demand or supply function:

$$Q = 25 - 0.5\ (10)$$
$$Q = 20$$

Thus equilibrium of a π maximizing firm would be represented by:

$$MR = MC = P$$

$$MC = \frac{\partial C}{\partial q_1} = -2 + 8q_1$$

$\therefore$ at equilibrium $-2 + 8q_1 = P$

$$q_1 = \frac{1}{8}(P + 2)$$

This is only if it is profitable for the firm to operate rather than shut down. To check on this, one needs to determine the firms shut down prices in the short and long run. In the short run, the shut-down point is equal to its minimum AVC. In the long-run, the shut-down point is equal to its minimum ATC.

$$TVC = -2q_1 + 4q_1^2$$
$$AVC = -2 + 4q_1$$

This is a linear function. Therefore, AVC has no minimum. The short-run supply would, therefore, be given by its unrestricted supply function:

$$q_1 = \frac{1}{8}(P + 2)$$
$$= \frac{1}{8}(10 + 2)$$
$$q_1 = 1.5$$

The firm would, thus, produce 1.5 units, sell at P = 10, have *TR* = 15, and *TC* = 31 and run into loss of 16. (Note that its loss of 16 is less than its fixed cost which equals 25).

To determine the firm's equilibrium in the long-run, we find its minimum ATC.

$$ATC = \frac{25}{q_1} - 2 + 4q_1$$

$$\frac{dATC}{dq_1} = \frac{-25}{q_1^2} + 4 = 0$$

or $$q_1 = 2.5$$

$$\frac{d^2ATC}{dq_1^2} = \frac{50}{q_1^3} > 0$$

Thus, ATC is minimum at $q_1 = 2.5$.

At $q_1 = 2.5$, $ATC = \frac{25}{2.5} - 2 + 4(2.5) = 18$

This means that the firm would supply positive output in the long-run if and only if P is greater than or equal to 18. However, since P = 10, it would leave the industry in the long-run.

Problem 4: Consider the firm's total cost function as:

$$C = q^3 - 14q^2 + 69q + 128$$

Find the supply function of the firm using the exact formula for marginal cost:

$$MC = 69 - 28q + 3q^2$$

Solution: The firm's supply curve is based on the rule MC = P, which implies $P = 69 - 28q + 3q^2$.

However, this equation is valid only for P ≥ minimum AVC.

We know that:

$$AVC = 69 - 14q + q^2$$

To find minimum of AVC, equate

$$\frac{dAVC}{dq} = 0 \quad \text{and} \quad \frac{d^2AVC}{dq^2} > 0$$

$$\frac{dAVC}{dq} = -14 + 2q = 0$$

$$\Leftrightarrow q = 7$$

$$\frac{d^2AVC}{dq^2} = 2 > 0$$

Hence, AVC is at its minimum, when $q = 7$.

When $q = 7$;

$$P = 69 - 28(7) + 3(7)^2$$
$$= 20$$

So the supply function can be written as:

$$P = 69 - 28q + 3q^2 \quad \text{for } P \geq 20$$
$$q = 0 \quad \text{for } P < 20$$

Problem 5: Assume that the market demand and the costs of the duopolists are

$$P = 100 - 0.5(Q_1 + Q_2)$$
$$C_1 = 5Q_1$$
$$C_2 = 0.5Q_2^2$$

Find out:

a. The equilibrium values of Q_1 and Q_2 making the Cournot's assumption.

b. The Stacklegerg's solution with 1 being the sophisticated leader.

Solution:

a. The profits of the duopolists are

$$\pi_1 = PQ_1 - C_1 = [100 - 0.5(Q_1 + Q_2)]Q_1 - 5Q_1$$

or $$\pi_1 = 100Q_1 - 0.5Q_1^2 - 0.5Q_1Q_2 - 5Q_1$$

$$\pi_2 = PQ_2 - C_2$$
$$= [100 - 0.5(Q_1 + Q_2)]Q_2 - 0.5Q_2^2$$

or $$\pi_2 = 100Q_2 - 0.5Q_2^2 - 0.5Q_1Q_2 - 0.5Q_2^2$$

so that

$$\pi_1 = 95Q_1 - 0.5Q_1^2 - 0.5Q_1Q_2$$
$$\pi_2 = 100Q_2 - Q_2^2 - 0.5Q_1Q_2$$

For profit maximization under the Cournot assumption:

$$\frac{d\pi_1}{dQ_1} = 0 = 95 - Q_1 - 0.5Q_2 \quad \Leftrightarrow \quad 95 - 0.5Q_2 = Q_1$$

$$\frac{d\pi_1}{dQ_2} = 0 = 100 - 2Q_2 - 0.5Q_1 \Leftrightarrow \quad 50 - 0.25Q_1 = Q_2$$

Solving the two reaction functions simultaneously gives:

$$Q_1 = 80 \qquad Q_2 = 30$$

b. Firm 1 will substitute 2's reaction function in own profit equation, which it will then maximize as if it were a monopolist.

$$\pi_1 = PQ_1 - C_1 = 95Q_1 - 0.5Q_1^2 - 0.5Q_1Q_2$$

Substitute

$$Q_2 = 50 - 0.25Q_1$$

Maximize $\pi_1 = 70Q_1 - 0.375Q_1^2$

$$\frac{d\pi_1}{dQ_1} = 70 - 0.75Q_1 = 0 \quad \text{or} \quad Q_1 = 93\frac{1}{3}$$

$$\frac{\partial^2\pi_1}{dQ_1^2} = -0.75 < 0$$

Firm 2 would be the follower. It would assume that 1 would produce 93.33 units. Thus, 2 would produce.

$$Q_1 = 50 - 0.25Q_1$$
$$= 50 - 0.25(93.33)$$
$$= 26.67$$

LO4 Game Theory

How do firms act when they recognize their interdependence but either cannot or do not collude? Because oligopoly involves interdependence among a few firms, we can think of interacting firms as players in a game. **Game theory** examines oligopolistic behavior as a series of strategic moves and countermoves among rival firms. This approach analyzes the behavior of decision makers, or players, whose choices affect one another. Game theory is not really a separate model of oligopoly but a general approach, an approach that focuses on each player's incentives to cooperate—say, through cartels or price leaders—or to compete, in ways to be discussed now.

To get some feel for game theory, let's work through the **prisoner's dilemma**, the most widely examined game. The game originally considered a situation in which two thieves, let's call them Raja and Veeru, are caught near the crime scene and brought to police headquarters, where they are interrogated in separate rooms. The police know the two guys did it but can't prove it, so they need a confession. Each thief faces a choice of confessing, thereby "squealing" on the other, or "clamming up," thereby denying any knowledge of the crime. If one confesses, turning state's evidence, he is granted immunity from prosecution and goes free, while the other guy is put away for 10 years. If both clam up, each gets only a 1-year sentence on a technicality (e.g. possession of stolen goods). If both confess, each gets 5 years.

What will Raja and Veeru do? The answer depends on the assumptions about their behavior—that is, what *strategy* each pursues. A **strategy** reflects a player's game plan. In this game, suppose each player tries to save his own skin—each tries to minimize his time in jail, regardless of what happens to the other (after all, there is no honor among thieves). Exhibit 12 shows the *payoff matrix* for the prisoner's dilemma. A **payoff matrix** is a table listing the rewards (or, in this case, the penalties) that Raja and Veeru can expect based on the strategy each pursues.

Raja's choices are shown down the left margin and Veeru's across the top. Each prisoner can either confess or clam up. The numbers in the matrix indicate the prison time in years each can expect based on the corresponding strategies. Raja's numbers are in red and Veeru's in blue. Take a moment now to see how the matrix works. Notice that the sentence each player receives depends on the strategy he chooses and on the strategy the other player chooses.

What strategies are rational assuming that each player tries to minimize jail time? For example, put yourself in Raja's shoes. You know that Veeru, who is being questioned in another room, will either confess or clam up. If Veeru confesses, the left column of Exhibit 12 shows the penalties. If you confess too, you both get 5 years in jail, but if you clam up, you

game theory an approach that analyzes oligopolistic behavior as a series of strategic moves and countermoves by rival firms

prisoner's dilemma a game that shows why players have difficulty cooperating even though they would benefit from cooperation

strategy in game theory, the operational plan pursued by a player

payoff matrix in game theory, a table listing the payoffs that each player can expect from each move based on the actions of the other player

Exhibit 12

The Prisoner's Dilemma Payoff Matrix (years in jail)

Raja \ Veeru	Confess	Clam up
Confess	Raja 5, Veeru 5	Raja 0, Veeru 10
Clam up	Raja 10, Veeru 0	Raja 1, Veeru 1

© COMSTOCK/THINKSTOCK

get 10 years and Veeru "walks." So, if you think Veeru will confess, you should too.

What if you believe Veeru will clam up? The right-hand column shows the two possible outcomes. If you confess, you do no time, but if you clam up too, you each get 1 year in jail. Thus, if you think Veeru will clam up, you're better off confessing. In short, whatever Veeru does, Raja is better off confessing. The same holds for Veeru. He's better off confessing, regardless of what Raja does. So each has an incentive to confess and each gets 5 years in jail. This is called the **dominant-strategy equilibrium** of the game because each player's action does not depend on what he thinks the other player will do.

But notice that if each crook could just hang tough and clam up, both would be better off. After all, if both confess, each gets 5 years, but if both clam up, the police can't prove otherwise, so each gets only 1 year in jail. If each could trust the other to clam up, they both would be better off. But there is no way for the two to communicate or to coordinate their actions. That's why police investigators keep suspects apart, that's why organized crime threatens "squealers" with death, and that's why the witness protection program tries to shield "squealers."

Price-Setting Game

The prisoner's dilemma applies to a broad range of economic phenomena including pricing policy and advertising strategy. For example, consider the market for gasoline in a rural community with only two gas stations, Texaco and Exxon. Here the oligopoly consists of two sellers, or a **duopoly**. Suppose customers are indifferent between the brands and focus only on the price. Each station posts its daily price early in the morning before learning about the other station's price. To keep things simple, suppose only two prices are possible—a low price or a high price. If both charge the low price, they split the market and each earns a profit of $500 per day. If both charge the high price, they also split the market, but profit jumps to $700 each. If one charges the high price but the other the low one, the low-price station gets most of the business, earning a profit of $1,000, leaving the high-price station with only $200.

Exhibit 13 shows the payoff matrix, with Texaco's strategy down the left margin and Exxon's across the top. Texaco's profit appears in red, and Exxon's in blue. Suppose you are running the Texaco station and are trying to decide what to charge. If Exxon charges the low price, you earn $500 charging the low price but only $200 charging the high price. So you earn more charging the low price. If, instead, Exxon charges the high price, you earn $1,000 charging the low price and $700 charging the high price. Again,

Exhibit 13

Price-Setting Payoff Matrix (profit per day)

		Exxon: Low price	Exxon: High price
Texaco	Low price	$500 / $500	$1,000 / $200
	High price	$200 / $1,000	$700 / $700

you earn more charging the low price. Exxon faces the same incentives. Thus, each charges the low price, regardless of what the other does.

The prisoner's dilemma outcome is an equilibrium because each player maximizes profit, given the price chosen by the other. Neither gas station can increase profit by changing its price, given the price chosen by the other firm. A situation in which a player chooses its best strategy given the strategies chosen by other firms is called a Nash equilibrium, named after Nobel Prize winner and former Princeton professor John Nash. He inspired the award-winning movie *A Beautiful Mind* starring Russell Crowe as Nash.

In this prisoner's dilemma, each charges the low price, earning $500 a day, although each would earn $700 charging the high price. Think of yourself as a member of the oil cartel discussed earlier, where the cartel determines the price and sets production quotas for each member. If you think other firms in the cartel will stick with their quotas, you can increase your profit by cutting your price and thereby increasing quantity sold. If you think the other firms will cheat on the cartel by cutting the price, then you should too—otherwise, you will get your clock cleaned by those cheaters. Either way, your incentive as a cartel member is to cheat on the quota. All members have an incentive to cheat, although all would earn more by sticking with the agreement that maximizes joint profit. Cheating is a **Nash equilibrium**, unless the cartel has

dominant-strategy equilibrium
In game theory, the outcome achieved when each player's choice does not depend on what the other player does

duopoly
a market with only two producers; a special type of oligopoly market structure

Nash equilibrium
a situation in which a firm, or a player in game theory, chooses the best strategy given the strategies chosen by others; no participant can improve his or her outcome by changing strategies even after learning of the strategies selected by other participants

real teeth to keep members in line—that is, unless cartel members have the strategy imposed on them.

This incentive to cut prices suggests why price wars sometimes break out among oligopolists. Even in industries with just two or three firms, competition often locks these rivals in a steel-cage death match for survival. For example, in late 2008, Toyota's Prius hybrid had a base price of $21,500. In response, Honda announced it would offer a new vehicle in 2009 that would undercut Toyota's price. Hyundai then followed with plans to release a Sonata in 2010 that would be even less expensive.[4] A bitter price war with Dell cut Hewlett-Packard's earnings on each $500 personal computer sold to a razor-thin $1.75.[5] Early profits in the animated movie business attracted entry, which over time cut profit and led to some bankruptcies. And just before a recent Thanksgiving weekend, a price war erupted in airfares. American Airlines first announced holiday discounts. Delta responded with cuts of up to 50 percent. Within hours, American, United, and other major carriers said they would match Delta's reductions. All these airlines were losing money at the time. So go the price wars.

The Indian aviation sector too has been exposed to intense competition with the advent of low-cost airlines. The success of Air Deccan, which entered the Indian market in 2003, spurred the entry of other Low Cost Carriers (LCCs) like SpiceJet, Indigo, Go Air and subsequently low fare offerings from Jet airways and Kingfisher airlines. As a result, the sector which was completely dominated by full-service airlines till a decade ago is now dominated by low-cost airlines. In fact the LCC market share increased from 1 percent in 2003–04 to 69 percent in 2010–11. However, longer term viability of LCCs models in India remains to be seen (Kingfisher exited the segment recently) as airport charges are same for Full Service Carrier's (FSC's) and LCCs in India.

The profitability margins of the Indian airlines industry has been severely impacted due to the combined impact of the following:

1. moderating passenger growth
2. lower profit margins due to excessive competitive environment
3. rising ATF prices
4. steep rupee depreciation
5. rising debt levels and interest costs

As per Centre for Asia Pacific Aviation (CAPA), Indian carriers posted staggering losses of $2.5 billion (₹ 12,500 crore) in 2011–12, worse than the losses of 2008–09 when traffic was declining and crude oil prices spiked to $150 per barrel.

Overall, the industry is bearing the brunt of aggressive price cuts, rising costs, expensive jet fuel, a weaker rupee, high interest payments and hence mounting losses. The government support required to bailout the loss making Air India has increased substantially; while the leading private players like Jet Airways and SpiceJet are making significant losses.

Cola War Game

As a final example of a prisoner's dilemma, consider the marketing strategies of Coke and Pepsi. Suppose each is putting together a promotional budget for the coming year, not knowing the other's plans. The choice boils down to adopting either a moderate budget or a big budget—one that involves multiple Super Bowl ads, showy in-store displays, and other marketing efforts aimed mostly at attracting customers from each other. If each adopts a big budget, their costly efforts will, for the most part, cancel each other out and limit each company's profit to $2 billion a year. If each adopts a moderate promotional budget, the money saved boosts profit for each to $3 billion a year. And if one adopts a big budget but the other does not, the heavy promoter captures a bigger market share and earns $4 billion, while the other loses market share and earns only $1 billion. What to do?

Exhibit 14 shows the payoff matrix for the two strategies, with Pepsi's choices listed down the left

Exhibit 14

Cola War Payoff Matrix (annual profit in billions)

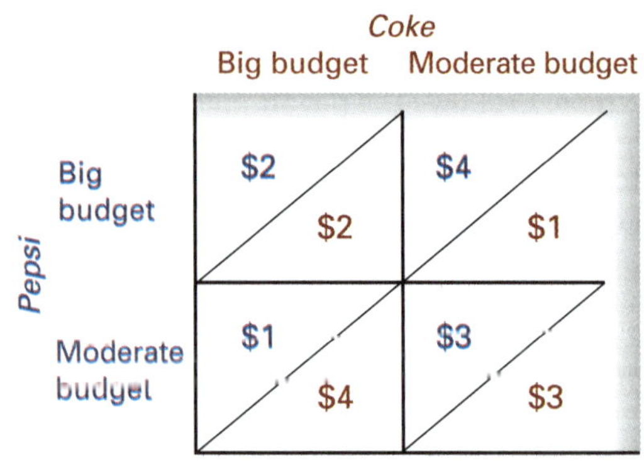

4. "Are We on the Brink of a Hybrid Price War?" BusinessGreen.com, 18 August 2008, (http://www.businessgreen.com/business-green/news/2224188/brink-hybrid-price-war); Edward Niedermeyer, "Hyundai Sonata Wades into Price War," The Truth About Cars, 22 August 2008, (http://www.thetruthaboutcars.com/hyundai-sonata-wades-into-hybrid-price-war/)

5. David Bank, "H-P Posts 10% Increase in Revenue," *Wall Street Journal,* 20 November 2003.

© C SQUARED STUDIOS/PHOTODISC/GETTY IMAGES

margin and Coke's across the top. In each cell of the matrix, Pepsi's profit appears in blue, and Coke's in red. Let's look at Pepsi's decision. If Coke adopts a big promotional budget, Pepsi earns $2 billion by doing the same but only $1 billion by adopting a moderate budget. Thus, if Coke adopts a big budget, so should Pepsi. If Coke adopts a moderate budget, Pepsi earns $4 billion with a big budget and $3 billion with a moderate one. Again, Pepsi earns more with a big budget. Coke faces the same incentives, so both adopt big budgets, earning $2 billion each in profit, even though each would have earned $3 billion with a moderate budget.

"The tit-for-tat strategy offers the other player immediate rewards for cooperation and immediate punishment for cheating."

One-Shot Versus Repeated Games

The outcome of a game often depends on whether it is a *one-shot game* or a *repeated game*. The classic prisoner's dilemma is a one-shot game. If the game is to be played just once, the strategy of confessing makes you better off regardless of what the other player does. Your choice won't influence the other player's behavior. But if the same players repeat the prisoner's dilemma, as would likely occur with the price-setting game, the cola war game, and the OPEC cartel, other possibilities unfold. In a repeated-game setting, each player has a chance to establish a reputation for cooperation and thereby may be able to encourage other players to do the same. After all, the cooperative solution—whether that involves clamming up, maintaining a high price, or adopting a moderate marketing budget—makes both players better off than if both fail to cooperate.

Experiments have shown that the strategy with the highest payoff in repeated games turns out to be the simplest—tit-for-tat. You begin by cooperating in the first round. On every round thereafter, you cooperate if the other player cooperated in the previous round, and you cheat if your opponent cheated in the previous round. In short, in any given round, you do whatever your opponent did in the previous round. The tit-for-tat strategy offers the other player immediate rewards for cooperation and immediate punishment for cheating. Some cartels seem to employ tit-for-tat strategies.

Coordination Game

In the coordination game, a Nash equilibrium occurs when each player chooses the same strategy. For example, you are driving on a country road and have to decide whether to drive on the right or the left side. Suppose you decide to drive on your left. If the driver coming from the opposite direction drives on his or her left, you pass each other without incident, so the cost to each of you is zero. But if the other player drives on the right-hand side, the probability of a crash increases. If, instead, you choose to drive on the right-hand side, you encounter no problems if the oncoming driver does the same, but face a greater likelihood of crashing if the other driver chooses the left-hand side. In this game, cost is minimized when both players choose to drive either on the left or on the right. And each strategy is a Nash equilibrium because no player can improve on that outcome, given the other player's choice. So if you choose the left-hand side and the other player chooses his or her left-hand side, then you can do no better and would do worse choosing the right-hand side.

Our discussion has given you some idea of game theory by focusing mostly on the prisoner's dilemma. Other games can be more complicated and involve more strategic interaction. Because firms are interdependent, oligopoly gives rise to all kinds of behavior and many approaches. Each approach helps explain certain behavior observed in oligopolistic markets. The *cartel*, or *collusion*, model shows why oligopolists might want to cooperate in fixing the market price; but that model also explains why a cartel is hard to establish and maintain. The *price-leadership* model explains why and how firms may charge the same price without explicitly establishing a formal cartel. Finally, *game theory*, expressed here mostly by the prisoner's

tit-for-tat
in game theory, a strategy in repeated games when a player in one round of the game mimics the other player's behavior in the previous round; an optimal strategy for getting the other player to cooperate

coordination game
a type of game in which a Nash equilibrium occurs when each player chooses the same strategy; neither player can do better than matching the other player's strategy

dilemma, shows how difficult a cooperative solution might be even though cooperation benefits both sides. Game theory is more an approach to oligopoly rather than a distinct model.

LO5 Comparison of Oligopoly and Perfect Competition

As we have seen, each approach explains a piece of the oligopoly puzzle. But each has limitations, and none provides a complete picture of oligopolistic behavior. Because there is no typical, or representative, model of oligopoly, "the" oligopoly model cannot be compared with the competitive model. We might, however, imagine an experiment in which we took the many firms that populate a competitive industry and, through a series of giant mergers, combined them to form, say, four firms. We would thereby transform the industry from perfect competition to oligopoly. How would firms in this industry behave before and after the massive merger?

Price Is Usually Higher Under Oligopoly

With fewer competitors after the merger, remaining firms would become more interdependent. Oligopoly models presented in this chapter suggest why firms may try to coordinate their pricing policies. *If oligopolists engaged in some sort of implicit or explicit collusion, industry output would be smaller and the price would be higher than under perfect competition.* Even if oligopolists did not collude but simply operated with excess capacity, the price would be higher and the quantity lower with oligopoly than with perfect competition. The price could become lower under oligopoly compared with perfect competition if a price war broke out among oligopolists. Two rivals, Intel and Advanced Micro Devices (AMD), together account for the entire market for a specific type of computer chip, yet these two are always at each other's throat, thereby keeping prices and profits down. Behavior also depends on whether there are barriers to entry. The lower the barriers to entry into the oligopoly, the more oligopolists act like perfect competitors.

Higher Profits Under Oligopoly

In the long run, easy entry prevents perfect competitors from earning more than a normal profit. With oligopoly, however, there may be barriers to entry, such as economies of scale or a way to differentiate a product such as with brand names, which allow firms in the industry to earn long-run economic profit. *With barriers to entry, we should expect profit in the long run to be higher under oligopoly than under perfect competition.* Profit rates do in fact appear to be higher in industries where a few firms account for a high proportion of industry sales. Some economists view these higher profit rates as troubling evidence of market power. But not all economists share this view. Some note that the largest firms in oligopolistic industries tend to earn the highest rate of profit. Thus, the higher profit rates observed in oligopolistic industries do not necessarily stem from market power per se. Rather, these higher profit rates stem from the greater efficiency arising from economies of scale in these large firms. An individual firm can also achieve greater market power and higher profit by differentiating its product.

Final Word

Firms in monopolistic competition and in oligopoly face a downward-sloping demand curve for their products. With monopolistic competition, there are so many firms in the market that each tends to get lost in the crowd. Each behaves independently. But with oligopoly, there are so few firms in the market that each must consider the impact its pricing, output, and marketing decisions will have on other firms. Each oligopolist behaves interdependently, and this makes oligopoly difficult to analyze. As a result, there are different models and approaches to oligopoly, several of which were discussed in this chapter.

The analytical results derived in this chapter are not as clear-cut as for the polar cases of perfect competition and monopoly. Still, we can draw some general conclusions using perfect competition as a guide. In the long run, perfect competitors operate at minimum average cost, while other types of firms usually operate with excess capacity. Therefore, given identical cost curves, monopolists, monopolistic competitors, and oligopolists tend to charge higher prices than perfect competitors do, especially in the long run. In the long run, monopolistic competitors, like perfect competitors, earn only a normal profit because entry barriers are low. Monopolists and oligopolists can earn economic profit in the long run if new entry is restricted. In a later chapter, we examine government policies aimed at increasing competition. *Regardless of the market structure, however, profit maximization prompts firms to produce where marginal revenue equals marginal cost.*

This chapter has moved us from the extremes of perfect competition and monopoly to the grey area inhabited by most firms. Exhibit 15 compares features and examples of the four market structures. Please take a moment now to review these key distinctions. Some of these issues are revisited later when we explore the government's role in promoting market competition.

Exhibit 15

Comparison of Market Structures

	Perfect Competition	Monopoly	Monopolistic Competition	Oligopoly
Number of firms	Many	One	Many	Few
Control over price	None	Complete	Limited	Some
Product differences	None	None	Some	None or some
Barriers to entry	None	Insurmountable	Low	Substantial
Examples	Wheat	Local electricity	Convenience stores	Automobiles

Multiple Choice Questions

1. In a monopolistically competitive market, all of the following are correct, except:
   a. Firms produce differentiated products
   b. There are several barriers to entry
   c. Firms have some control over the price they charge
   d. There are many firms in the market
   e. Firms can easily enter and exit the market
2. Monopolistic competition is best described as
   a. many firms with some control over price, and some product differentiation
   b. many firms with no control over price, producing identical products
   c. a few firms with some control over price, producing highly differentiated products
   d. a few firms with no control over price, producing similar products
   e. a single firm producing all of the output for the industry, with strong control over price
3. A monopolistic competitor's demand curve is
   a. perfectly elastic
   b. less elastic than a monopolist's or oligopolist's but more elastic than a perfect competitor's
   c. as elastic as an oligopolist's
   d. more elastic than a monopolist's or oligopolist's but less elastic than a perfect competitor's
   e. perfectly inelastic
4. A rise in demand for restaurant meals is likely to cause which of the following in the short run?
   a. economic losses for each restaurant
   b. a lower price for each restaurant meal
   c. fewer restaurants in the industry
   d. more restaurants in the industry
   e. economic profit for restaurants
5. If the firms in a monopolistically competitive industry are suffering short-run losses, which of the following will occur in the long run?
   a. Some firms will enter the industry.
   b. Customers of firms that leave the industry will switch to remaining firms.
   c. Firms that remain in the industry will face reduced demand.
   d. Firms will continue to incur losses.
   e. There will be no excess capacity.
6. An intersection known as Four Corners lies 300 miles from the nearest town. At this intersection are three independently owned gas stations and one small pharmacy. Which of the following is true?
   a. The firms are all perfectly competitive because of their size.
   b. It would be easier for all four firms to form a cartel than for only the gas stations to do so.
   c. The gas stations are monopolistically competitive because there are so few of them that they are almost monopolists.
   d. The gas stations are perfectly competitive; the pharmacy is not.
   e. The gas stations are oligopolists; the pharmacy is a monopolist.
7. There are multiple models of pricing behavior in oligopolistic markets because
   a. it is difficult to predict how rival firms will react to any pricing decision
   b. the demand curve slopes upward for these firms
   c. firms could earn profit in the long run unlike other markets
   d. price has a direct impact on profit for a firm in oligopoly
   e. the products are not identical in terms of quality, image, location
8. A brand name may contribute to oligopolists' economic profit by
   a. shifting the demand curve leftward
   b. shifting the supply curve leftward
   c. overcoming economies of scale
   d. acting as a barrier to entry
   e. reducing advertising costs
9. A cartel's profit-maximizing quantity occurs where the cartel's
   a. marginal cost equals marginal revenue
   b. marginal cost equals demand
   c. price is highest
   d. cost is lowest
   e. demand curve has a kink
10. During certain periods in the past few decades, if one of the three major breakfast cereal producers in the United States announced a price increase, the other two announced a similar price increase. This is a good example of
    a. monopolistic competition
    b. a cartel
    c. a pure monopoly

d. the kinked demand curve model of oligopoly
e. the price leadership model of oligopoly

11. Bank-with-us and First-Bank are the only two banks in GreenVillage, and they are trying to increase their profits by attracting more customers. Consumers are indifferent between banks; they are interested only in the interest rate they can earn on their savings. Assume that each bank can choose to offer a 2% or a 5% interest rate on savings. If both banks are offering 2% interest rate, they split the market and each earns $1.6 billion in profits. If both banks are offering 5% interest rate, they split the market and each earns $1.2 billion in profits. If one offers 2% and the other one offers 5%, the bank offering the higher interest rate earns $2 billion in profits, and the other bank earns only $1 billion. Which of the following statements is correct?
a. If Bank-with-us is offering 2% interest rate, then First-Bank is also offering 2% interest rate
b. If Bank-with-us is offering 2% interest rate, then First-Bank is offering 5% interest rate
c. First-Bank will offer 2% interest rate no matter what the other bank does
d. Bank-with-us will offer 2% interest rate only if First-Bank will offer 2%
e. Bank-with-us will offer 5% interest rate no matter what the other bank does

12. Bank-with-us and First-Bank are the only two banks in GreenVillage, and they are trying to increase their profits by attracting more customers. Consumers are indifferent between banks; they are interested only in the interest rate they can earn on their savings. Assume that each bank can choose to offer a 2% or a 5% interest rate on savings. If both banks are offering 2% interest rate, they split the market and each earns $1.6 billion in profits. If both banks are offering 5% interest rate, they split the market and each earns $1.2 billion in profits. If one offers 2% and the other one offers 5%, the bank offering the higher interest rate earns $2 billion in profits, and the other bank earns only $1 billion. What is the dominant strategy equilibrium?
a. Both banks offer 2% interest rate to maximize profits
b. Both banks offer 5% interest rate
c. Bank-with-us offers 2% no matter what the other bank does
d. Bank-with-us offers 2% and First-Bank offers 5%
e. Bank-with-us offers 5% and First-Bank offers 2%

13. Gin and Rummy, producers of skateboards, have to decide how much to charge for their boards. Assume that the strategies are to charge a low price ($200) or a high price ($400). The profits appear in the following payoff matrix:

		Rummy	
		Low price	High price
Gin	Low price	$400,000 / $400,000	$700,000 / $100,000
	High price	$100,000 / $700,000	$550,000 / $550,000

Which of the following statements is correct?
a. Gin charges the low price only when Rummy charges the low price
b. Gin charges the high price only when Rummy charges the high price
c. Gin charges the low price only when Rummy charges the high price
d. Gin charges the low price no matter the price charged by Rummy
e. Gin charges the high price no matter the price charged by Rummy

14. A prisoner's dilemma is a situation in which
a. a change in marginal cost may not lead to a change in price
b. a firm's competitors follow a price increase but ignore a price decrease
c. oligopolists behave irrationally
d. oligopolists attempt to maximize sales rather than profits
e. an oligopolists demand curve may become perfectly inelastic

15. The kinked demand curve model of oligopoly assumes that the elasticity of demand
a. is constant regardless of whether price increases or decreases
b. is perfectly elastic if price increases and perfectly inelastic if price decreases
c. in response to a price increase is less elastic than the elasticity of demand in response to a price decrease
d. in response to a price increase is more elastic than the elasticity of demand in response to a price decrease

16. A situation in which economic actors interacting with one another each choose their

best strategy given the strategies the others have chosen is called a(n)

a. socially optimal solution.
b. Nash equilibrium.
c. competitive equilibrium.
d. Dominant Strategy

17. If firms in a Cournot duopoly successfully collude to restrict output,
    a. Prices will drop
    b. Prices will remain unchanged
    c. The Industry will maximize profits
    d. Barriers to entry will no longer exist

18. Suppose the duopolists face the following market demand curve: $P = 30 - Q$, where Q is the total production of both firms, i.e. $Q = Q_1 + Q_2$. Also, both the firms have zero marginal cost. Find the Cournot Equilibrium in this case (Q_1, Q_2, P)
    a. 5, 5, 20
    b. 7.5, 7.5, 15
    c. 10, 10, 10
    d. 12.5, 12.5, 5

19. Suppose the duopolists face the following market demand curve: $P = 30 - Q$, where Q is the total production of both firms, i.e. $Q = Q_1 + Q_2$. Also, both the firms have zero marginal cost. Find the Collusive Equilibrium in this case (Q_1, Q_2, P)
    a. 5, 5, 20
    b. 7.5, 7.5, 15
    c. 10, 10, 10
    d. 12.5, 12.5, 5

20. Which of the following statements describes a move along the elastic portion of the kinked demand curve?
    a. When a firm increases its price, other firms will decrease theirs, so quantity will decrease by a large amount.
    b. When a firm increases its price, other firms will also increase theirs, so quantity will not decrease very much.
    c. When a firm increases its price, other firms will not change theirs, so quantity will decrease by a small amount.
    d. When a firm increases its price, other firms will not change theirs, so quantity will decrease by a large amount.

Answers

1. b 2. a 3. d 4. e 5. b 6. e 7. a 8. d 9. a 10. e
11. e 12. b 13. d 14. a 15. d 16. b 17. c 18. c 19. b 20. d

Long Answer Questions

LO1 Discuss factors that lead to monopolistic competition

1.1. *(Short-Run Profit Maximization)* A monopolistically competitive firm faces the following demand and cost structure in the short run:

Output	Price	FC	VC	TC	TR	Profit/ Loss
0	$100	$100	$0	___	___	___
1	90	___	50	___	___	___
2	80	___	90	___	___	___
3	70	___	150	___	___	___
4	60	___	230	___	___	___
5	50	___	330	___	___	___
6	40	___	450	___	___	___
7	30	___	590	___	___	___

a. Complete the table.
b. What is the highest profit or lowest loss available to this firm?
c. Should this firm operate or shut down in the short run? Why?
d. What is the relationship between marginal revenue and marginal cost as the firm increases output?

1.2. *(Monopolistic Competition and Perfect Competition Compared)* Illustrated below are the marginal cost and average total cost curves for a small firm that is in long-run equilibrium.
   a. Locate the long-run equilibrium price and quantity if the firm is perfectly competitive.
   b. Label the price and quantity p_1 and q_1.
   c. Draw in a demand and marginal revenue curve to illustrate long-run equilibrium if the firm is monopolistically competitive. Label the price and quantity p_2 and q_2.
   d. How do the monopolistically competitive firm's price and output compare to those of the perfectly competitive firm?
   e. How do long-run profits compare for the two types of firms?

1.3. Using graphs indicate equilibrium point (best level of output) in the Short-run and Long-run of a firm in monopolistic competition.

1.4. "Monopolistic Competition is the form of market organization in which there are many sellers of a differentiated product and entry into and exit from the industry are rather easy in the long run". While commenting on the same, also give the implications of each of the characteristic features of the monopolistic market.

LO2 Explain the concept of oligopoly

2.1. *(Varieties of Oligopolies)* Do the firms in an oligopoly act independently or interdependently? Explain your answer.

LO3 Describe models of oligopoly

3.1. *(Price Leadership)* Why might a price-leadership model of oligopoly not be an effective means of collusion in an oligopoly?

3.2. *(Collusion and Cartels)* Why would each of the following induce some members of OPEC to cheat on their cartel agreement?
  a. Newly joined cartel members are less-developed countries.
  b. The number of cartel members doubles from 11 to 22.
  c. International debts of some members grow.
  d. Expectations grow that some members will cheat.

3.3. Define Herfindahl index. Is it better than other measures of degree of market power like concentration ratio?

3.4. Do firms collude in a kinked demand curve model of oligopoly? Explain how the model accounts for price rigidity in oligopolistic market.

3.5. Differentiate between market-sharing cartel and centralized cartel. Is price leadership in an oligopoly an efficient way of tackling collusion among firms?

3.6. Explain the different models of oligopoly.

3.7. Firms in a cartel are often known to cheat. What is the motivation behind such a behavior? Is it possible to curtail cheating?

LO4 Explain how game theory helps predict cartel behavior

4.1. *(Collusion and Cartels)* Use revenue and cost curves to illustrate and explain the sense in which a cartel behaves like a monopolist.

4.2. *(Game Theory)* Suppose there are only two automobile companies, Ford and Chevrolet. Ford believes that Chevrolet will match any price it sets, but Chevrolet too is interested in maximizing profit. Use the following price and profit data to answer the following questions.

Ford's Selling Price	Chevrolet's Selling Price	Ford's Profits (millions)	Chevrolet's Profits (millions)
$ 4,000	$ 4,000	$ 8	$ 8
4,000	8,000	12	6
4,000	12,000	14	2
8,000	4,000	6	12
8,000	8,000	10	10
8,000	12,000	12	6
12,000	4,000	2	14
12,000	8,000	6	12
12,000	12,000	7	7

  a. What price will Ford charge?
  b. What price will Chevrolet charge once Ford has set its price?
  c. What is Ford's profit after Chevrolet's response?
  d. If the two firms collaborated to maximize joint profits, what prices would they set?
  e. Given your answer to part (d), how could undetected cheating on price cause the cheating firm's profit to rise?

4.3. *(Game Theory)* While grading a final exam, an economics professor discovers that two students have virtually identical answers. She is convinced the two cheated but cannot prove it. The professor speaks with each student separately and offers the following deal: Sign a statement admitting to cheating. If both students sign the statement, each will receive an "F" for the course. If only one signs, he is allowed to withdraw from the course while the other student is expelled. If neither signs, both receive a "C" because the professor does not have sufficient evidence to prove cheating.
  a. Draw the payoff matrix.
  b. Which outcome do you expect? Why?

4.4. What is meant by dominant strategy of a firm and a Nash Equilibrium? Is there any relation between the two?

4.5. How do the oligopolistic firms face the prisoner's dilemma? Explain the price competition in the presence of the dilemma in the case of a duopoly model.

LO5 Compare oligopoly and perfect competition

5.1. *(Market Structures)* Determine whether each of the following is a characteristic of perfect competition, monopolistic competition, oligopoly, and/or monopoly:
  a. A large number of sellers
  b. Product is a commodity
  c. Advertising by firms
  d. Barriers to entry
  e. Firms are price makers

Numerical Questions

1. Crystal Inc. produces quality television sets. Assume that the market for television sets is monopolistically competitive. It has been found that the inverse demand curve faced by Crystal (given its competitors' prices) can be expressed as $P = 5{,}000 - 0.2Q$ and Crystal's total costs can be expressed as $TC = 20{,}000{,}000 + .05Q^2$. Answer the following questions:
  a. Determine the price and quantity that Crystal will choose.
  b. Is the above value likely to be a long-run equilibrium for Crystal Inc.? Why or why not? If not, what is likely to happen in the market for television sets, and how will it affect Crystal?

2. Imagine two firms that have the demand curve as $P = 10 - Q$, where $Q = Q_1 + Q_2$. The firms' cost functions are given as $C_1(Q_1) = 4 + 2Q_1$ and $C_2(Q_2) = 3 + 3Q_2$.

a. Let us suppose that both firms have decided to enter the industry. Determine the joint profit-maximizing level of output that both firms can produce at. How much does each firm produce? If the assumption that the firms have entered the industry is removed, will the answer change?

b. Calculate each firm's equilibrium output and profit if they behave non-cooperatively using the Cournot model. Draw the firms' reaction curves and show the equilibrium.

c. How much should Firm 2 be willing to pay to purchase Firm 1 if collusion is considered illegal but the takeover is not?

3. The demand functions faced by two firms competing by choosing price are given as below:

$Q_1 = 20 - P_1 + P_2$ and $Q_2 = 20 + P_1 - P_2$

where P_1 and P_2 are the prices fixed by each firm respectively and Q_1 and Q_2 are the resulting demands of the products. Note that the demand for each good depends only on the difference in prices; if the two firms colluded and set the same price, they could make that price as high as they want, and earn infinite profits. Marginal costs are assumed to be zero.

a. Suppose the two firms set their prices at the same time. Find the resulting Nash equilibrium. What price will each firm charge, how much will it sell, and what will its profit be? (Hint: Maximize the profit of each firm with respect to its price.)

b. Suppose Firm 1 sets its price first and then Firm 2 sets its price. What price will each firm charge, how much will it sell, and what will its profit be?

c. Suppose you are one of these firms, and there are three ways you could play the game: (i) Both firms set price at the same time. (ii) You set price first. (iii) Your competitor sets price first. If you could choose among these options which would you prefer? Explain why.

4. Two firms A and B are known to produce premium handbags. Each firm has a cost function given by:

$$C(q) = 20q + q^2$$

The market demand for these handbags is represented by the inverse demand equation:

$$P = 200 - 2Q,$$

where $Q = q_1 + q_2$, total output.

a. Assume each firm acts towards profit maximization, taking output of its rival as given (i.e., the firms behave as Cournot oligopolists). Determine the equilibrium quantities selected by each firm. What is the value of total output, and what is the market price? What are the profits for each firm?

b. It occurs to the managers of the firms that there is a huge opportunity for profits by colluding. If the two firms decide to collude, what would be the output value for maximization of profit? Calculate the corresponding industry price as well. Also, give the output and the profit for each firm in this case.

c. Now, the managers of these firms realize that explicit agreements to collude are illegal. Each firm must decide on its own whether to produce the Cournot quantity or the cartel quantity. To aid in making the decision, the manager of A constructs a payoff matrix like the real one below. Fill in each box with the (profit of A, profit of B). Given this payoff matrix, what output strategy is each firm likely to pursue?

d. Suppose firm A can set its output level before firm B does. How much will firm A choose to produce in this case? How much will firm B produce then? What is the market price, and what is the profit for each firm? Is firm A better off by choosing its output first? Explain why or why not.

5. An oligopolist's demand curve is

$P = 30 - Q$ for Q smaller than 10, and

$P = 36 - 1.6Q$ for Q greater than or equal to 10.

Its Marginal Cost is 7. What is the firm's optimal output? Graph this kinked demand curve and the associated MR and MC curves. What if MC falls to 5?

6. Assuming a leader - follower residual market share model, determine the price – output equilibrium when the following information is given:

Industry's Demand Function: $Qi = 40000 - 0.2\,P$

Leader's Total Cost Function: $TC_L = 1{,}000 - 20{,}000\,Q_L + 3\,Q_L^2$

Each Follower's Total Cost Function:

$TC_F = 50 + 44{,}000\,Q_F + 20\,Q_F^2$

(Assume all firms to have identical cost functions)

7. Answer the following questions on the basis of the payoff matrix given below. The payoffs are the profits/losses of the two firms.

a. Determine if firm A has a dominant strategy

b. Determine if firm B has a dominant strategy

c. What is the optimal strategy for each firm

d. Calculate the Nash Equilibrium.

e. Indicate the condition in which the situation given in the payoff matrix is likely to occur.

		Firm B	
		Small Trucks	**Large Trucks**
Firm A	Small Trucks	(4,4)	(-2,-2)
	Large Trucks	(-2,-2)	(4,4)

8. Two water-polo players, John and Mark, are the best offensive players on the college team. If they cooperate and work together offensively – passing ball to each other, and screening other player etc. – they can each score 12 points. But, if one player tries to monopolize the offensive game, while the other player cooperates, the player who monopolizes the offensive game can score 18 points, while the other player can only score 2 points. However, they each score 8 points if both players try to monopolize the offensive game. Construct a payoff matrix for the players that captures the above situation of John and Mark and helps them decide whether they should cooperate or monopolize the offensive game. If the players play only once, what strategy can one expect the players to adopt? If the players expect to play in many games together, does the strategy adopted by players changes? Explain.

9. In the payoff matrix for two firms given below, answer the following questions:

		Firm B	
		Enter	**Don't Enter**
Firm A	Low Price	(3,-1)	(3,1)
	High Price	(4,5)	(6,3)

a. What is the best strategy for each firm?
b. As best as it may try, firm A cannot stop firm B from making an entry. Why?
c. How can firm A make its presence more dominant to restrict firm B from entering without increasing capacity?
d. Answer (c) above if capacity is allowed to expand for firm A.

MISCELLANEOUS QUESTIONS

1. What are the four types of market structures widely studied in managerial economics? Explain each one of them.
2. What do you understand by oligopoly? How is an oligopoly different from other market organizations? Give examples of oligopoly from context of Indian economy.
3. Explain the Cournot model of oligopoly. How is the equilibrium reached in case of a duopolistic Cournot model? Is Bertrand Model different from Cournot model? How?
4. Compare and contrast a monopolistically competitive firm's output and price in long-run equilibrium with the price and output if this firm was a perfect competitor.
5. A certain car manufacturer regards his business highly competitive because he is keenly aware of his rivalry with the other few car manufacturers in the market. Like the other car manufacturers, he undertakes vigorous advertising campaigns seeking to convince potential buyers of the superior quality and better style of his automobiles and reacts very quickly to claims of superiority by rivals. Is this meaning of perfect competition from an economics point of view? Explain.
6. How is Cournot equilibrium different from Nash Equilibrium?

MONOPOLISTIC COMPETITION AND OLIGOPOLY

Chapter in Review

11

KEY TERMS

monopolistic competition
a market structure with many firms selling products that are substitutes but different enough that each firm's demand curve slopes downward; firm entry is relatively easy

excess capacity
the difference between a firm's profit-maximizing quantity and the quantity that minimizes average cost; firms with excess capacity could reduce average cost by increasing quantity

oligopoly
a market structure characterized by so few firms that each behaves interdependently

undifferentiated oligopoly
an oligopoly that sells a commodity, or a product that does not differ across suppliers, such as an ingot of steel or a barrel of oil

differentiated oligopoly
an oligopoly that sells products that differ across suppliers, such as automobiles or breakfast cereal

Cournot model
an oligopoly model in which each firm assumes that the other keeps the output constant.

reaction curve
the relationship between how a duopolist reacts to the other duopolist's action.

collusion
an agreement among firms to increase economic profit by dividing the market and fixing the price

cartel
a group of firms that agree to coordinate their production and pricing decisions to earn monopoly profit

game theory
an approach that analyzes oligopolistic behavior as a series of strategic moves and countermoves by rival firms

prisoner's dilemma
a game that shows why players have difficulty cooperating even though they would benefit from cooperation

strategy
in game theory, the operational plan pursued by a player

payoff matrix
in game theory, a table listing the payoffs that each player can expect from each move based on the actions of the other player

dominant-strategy equilibrium
in game theory, the outcome achieved when each player's choice does not depend on what the other player does

LO1 Discuss factors that lead to monopolistic competition. Monopolistic competition describes a market in which many producers offer products that are substitutes but are not viewed as identical by consumers. Product differentiation allows each supplier some power over the price it can charge. Because barriers to entry are low, there are enough sellers that they behave competitively and act independently.

Monopolistic competition contains elements of both monopoly and competition. Monopolistic competition is like monopoly in the sense that firms in each industry face demand curves that slope downward. Monopolistic competition is like perfect competition in the sense that easy entry and exit eliminate economic profit or economic loss in the long run.

Monopolistic Competitor in the Short Run

The monopolistically competitive firm produces the level of output at which marginal revenue equals marginal cost (point *e*) and charges the price indicated by point b on the downward-sloping demand curve. In panel (*a*), the firm produces *q* units, sells them at price *p,* and earns a short-run economic profit equal to (*p* – *c*) multiplied by *q,* shown by the blue rectangle. In panel (*b*), the average total cost exceeds the price at the output where marginal revenue equals marginal cost. Thus, the firm suffers a short-run loss equal to (*c* – *p*) multiplied by *q,* shown by the pink rectangle.

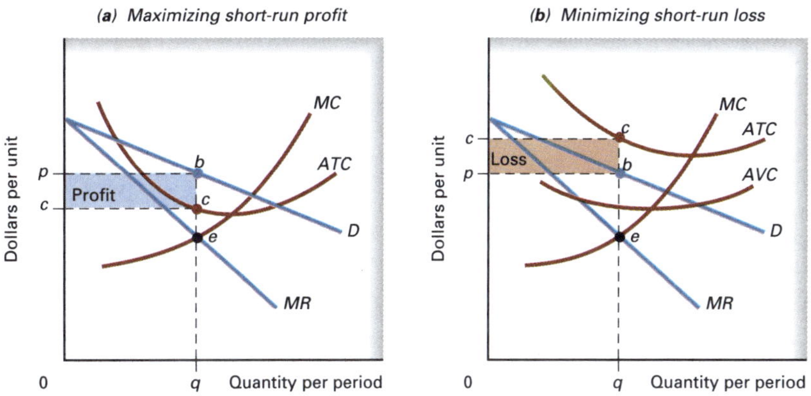

Long-Run Equilibrium in Monopolistic Competition

If existing firms earn economic profits in the short run, new firms will enter the industry in the long run. This entry reduces the demand facing each firm. In the long run, each firm's demand curve shifts leftward until marginal revenue equals marginal cost (point *a*) and the demand curve is tangent to the average total cost curve (point *b*). Economic profit is zero at output *q.* With zero economic profit, no more firms will enter, so the industry is in long-run equilibrium. The same long-run outcome occurs if firms suffer a short-run loss. Firms leave until remaining firms earn just a normal profit.

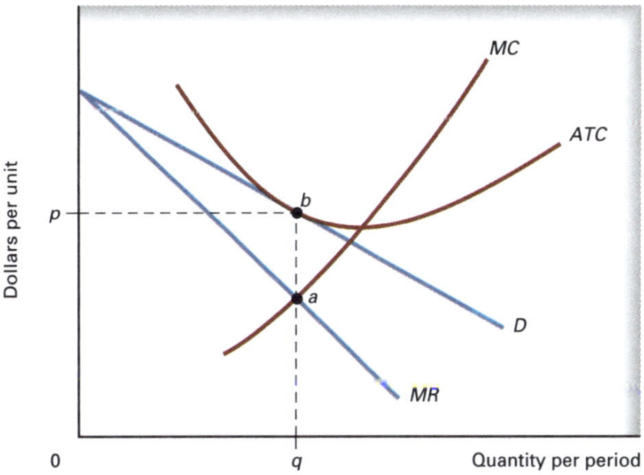

duopoly
a market with only two producers; a special type of oligopoly market structure

Nash equilibrium
a situation in which a firm, or a player in game theory, chooses the best strategy given the strategies chosen by others; no participant can improve his or her outcome by changing strategies even after learning of the strategies selected by other participants

tit-for-tat
in game theory, a strategy in repeated games when a player in one round of the game mimics the other player's behavior in the previous round; an optimal strategy for getting the other player to cooperate

coordination game
a type of game in which a Nash equilibrium occurs when each player chooses the same strategy; neither player can do better than matching the other player's strategy

Perfect Competition Versus Monopolistic Competition in Long-Run Equilibrium

Cost curves are assumed to be the same in each panel. The perfectly competitive firm of panel (a) faces a demand curve that is horizontal at market price *p*. Long-run equilibrium occurs at output *q*, where the demand curve is tangent to the average total cost curve at its lowest point. The monopolistically competitive firm of panel (b) is in long-run equilibrium at output *q*′, where demand is tangent to the average total cost curve. Because the demand curve slopes downward in panel (b), however, the tangency does not occur at the minimum point of average total cost. Thus, the monopolistically competitive firm produces less output and charges a higher price than does a perfectly competitive firm with the same cost curves. Neither firm earns economic profit in the long run. The firm in monopolistic competition has excess capacity, meaning that it could reduce average cost by increasing its rate of output.

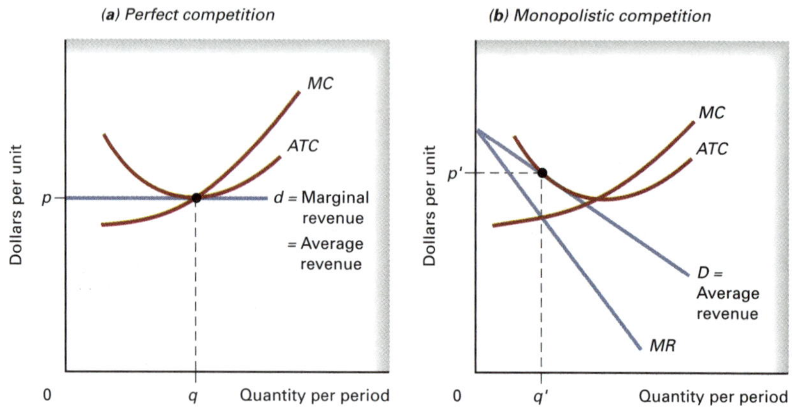

LO2 Explain the concept of oligopoly.

An oligolpoly is an industry dominated by just a few firms. Oligopolists are said to be interdependent since each one must consider the effect of its own actions on competitors' behavior. The formation of an oligopoly can often be traced to some form of barrier to entry, such as economies of scale, legal restrictions, brand names built up by years of advertising, or control over an essential resource.

Economies of Scale as a Barrier to Entry

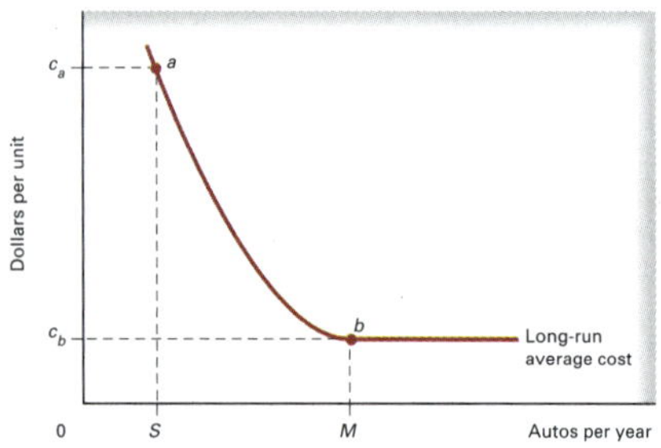

Cartel as a Monopolist

A cartel acts like a monopolist. Here, *D* is the market demand curve, *MR* the associated marginal revenue curve, and *MC* the horizontal sum of the marginal cost curves of cartel members (assuming all firms in the market join the cartel). Cartel profits are maximized when the industry produces quantity *Q* and charges price *p*.

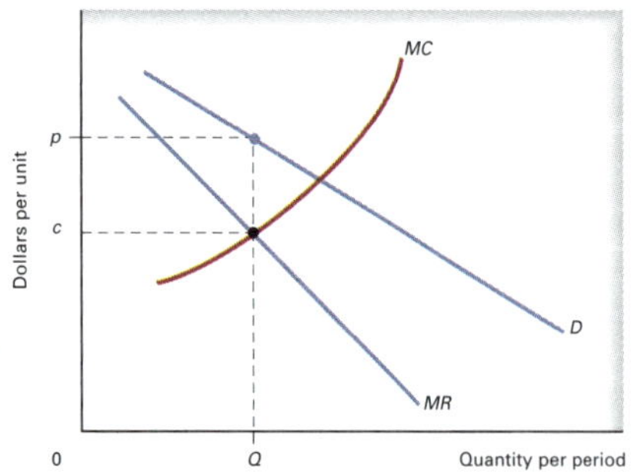

LO3 Describe models of oligopoly.

There is no general theory of oligopoly but rather a set of theories, each based on the diversity of observed behavior in an interdependent market. Some of the theories that are used to explain oligopoly behavior are collusion, price leadership, and game theory. These models identify formal and informal efforts to collude and the strategic decision making process that firms employ when collusion does not occur.

LO4 Explain how game theory helps predict cartel behavior.

Game theory examines oligopolistic behavior as a series of strategic moves and countermoves among rival firms. This approach analyzes the behavior of decision makers, or players, whose choices affect one another. While participation in a cartel would result in higher economic profits, game theory explains why the incentives to cheat are so great that firms often act in ways that result in lower profits.

The Prisoner's Dilemma Payoff Matrix (years in jail)

This matrix shows the years each prisoner can expect to spend in jail based on his actions and the actions of the other prisoner. Raja's payoff is in red and Veeru's in blue.

Raja \ Veeru	Confess	Clam up
Confess	Raja 5, Veeru 5	Raja 0, Veeru 10
Clam up	Raja 10, Veeru 0	Raja 1, Veeru 1

LO5 Compare oligopoly and perfect competition.

With monopolistic competition, there are so many firms in the market that each behaves independently. But with oligopoly, there are so few firms in the market that each must consider the impact its pricing, output, and marketing decisions will have on other firms. Each oligopolist behaves interdependently, and this makes oligopoly difficult to analyze. In general, price and profits are usually higher under oligopoly.

Comparison of Market Structures

	Perfect Competition	Monopoly	Monopolistic Competition	Oligopoly
Number of firms	Many	One	Many	Few
Control over price	None	Complete	Limited	Some
Product differences	None	None	Some	None or some
Barriers to entry	None	Insurmountable	Low	Substantial
Examples	Wheat	Local electricity	Convenience stores	Automobiles

CHAPTER

12

Decision Making *under* Certainty, Risk, *and* Uncertainty

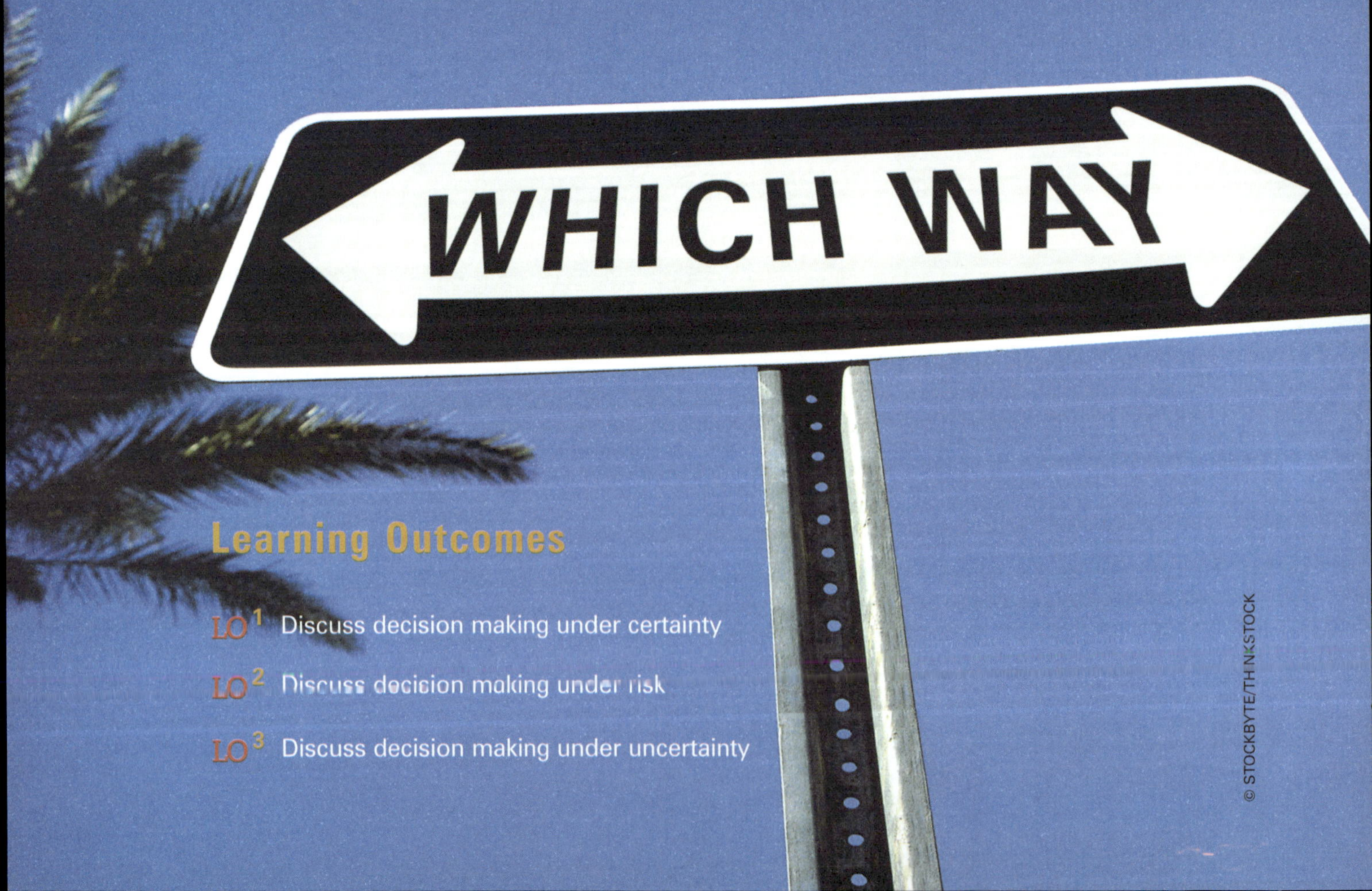

© STOCKBYTE/THINKSTOCK

Learning Outcomes

LO[1] Discuss decision making under certainty

LO[2] Discuss decision making under risk

LO[3] Discuss decision making under uncertainty

"Do business decisions usually consist of choices between courses of actions, or strategies?"

Is the ability to good decision making a key to success? Is decision making the same for all or can it be subjective? Do business decisions usually consist of choices between courses of actions, or strategies? Are these choices made under environment conditions over which the decision maker exercises limited or no control? Can we classify the decision makers' knowledge of possible states of nature as a state of certainty, risk, or uncertainty? Are gambling and insurance a contradiction? Can a person do both? Have you ever insured and gambled at the same time? Who are the risk-takers and how are they different from risk-avoiders? Answers to these and most such questions boil down to the decision-making process under certainty, risk, and uncertainty—the subject matter of this chapter.

What do you think?

A good manager's decision making should not be affected by his attitude towards risk, i.e., whether he is a risk lover; risk averse or risk neutral.

Strongly Disagree					*Strongly Agree*	
1	2	3	4	5	6	7

In this chapter, we shall deal with methods and approaches to decision making that decision makers may use under conditions of certainty, risk, and uncertainty. The distinctions among certainty, risk, and uncertainty reflect differences in the degree of knowledge enjoyed by the decision maker. The degree of knowledge declines gradually as we move from certainty to risk to uncertainty.

Each of these conditions of certainty, risk, and uncertainty are explained below.

Topics discussed in Chapter 12 include:

- Decision making under certainty
- Decision making under risk
- Decision trees
- Preference for risk
- Insurance and gambling
- Decision making under uncertainty

Certainty: It refers to the situation where there is only one possible outcome to a decision and this outcome is known precisely. For example, investing in Treasury bills leads to only one outcome (the amount of the yield), and this is known with certainty. The reason is that there is virtually no chance that the federal government will fail to redeem these securities at maturity or that it will default on interest payments. On the other hand, when there is more than one possible outcome to a decision, risk, or uncertainty is present.

Risk: It refers to a situation where there is more than one possible outcome to a decision and the probability of each specific outcome is known or can be estimated. Thus, risk requires that the decision maker knows all the possible outcomes of the decision and has some idea of the probability of each outcome's occurrence. For example, in tossing a coin, we can get either a head or/a tail. In the analysis of managerial

© PHOTOS.COM/THINKSTOCK

decision making involving risk, we will use such concepts as *strategy*, *states of nature*, and *payoff matrix*. A strategy refers to one of several alternative courses of action that a decision maker can take to achieve a goal. States of nature refers to conditions in the future that will have a significant effect on the degree of success or failure of any strategy, but over which the decision maker has little or no control. For example, the economy may be in boom period, in a normal period, or in a recession in the future. The decision maker has no control over states of nature that will prevail in the future but the future states of nature certainly affect the outcome of any strategy that he or she may adopt. A payoff matrix is a table that shows the possible outcomes or results of strategy under each state of nature. For example, a payoff matrix may show the level of profit that would result if the firm builds a large or a small plant and if economy will be booming, normal or in a recessionary state in the future.

Uncertainty: It is the case when there is more than one possible outcome to a decision and where the probability of each specific outcome is not known or even meaningful. This may be due to insufficient past information or instability in the structure of the variables. In extreme forms of uncertainty, not even the outcomes themselves are known. For example,drilling for oil in an unproven field carries with it uncertainty if the investor does not know either the possible outcomes or the probability of their occurrence.

Under conditions of *certainty*, the decision maker's task is to select the strategy that maximizes the payoff. Two powerful methods available for this task are the marginal analysis and linear programming tool. Under the condition of *risk*, the decision criterion for selecting the optimum strategy is the expected value. Expected value is defined as the weighted mean or average outcome, using probabilities for weights. The degree of risk is indicated by spread or variation of the probability distribution for each strategy or proposal. An accurate measurement of risk is provided by the coefficient of variation, which is simply the ratio of the standard deviation, to the mean, expressed as a percentage. When a sequential series of conditional decisions are to be made under risk, a decision tree enables the decision maker to visualize and evaluate all possible options for action. What a decision maker under risk actually decides depends largely upon his or her attitude towards risk. This may be expressed by a risk-return function or market indifference curve. Under conditions of *uncertainty*, the decision maker is faced with a state in which one or more alternatives result in a set of outcomes whose probabilities are unknown or meaningless. Several criteria for decision making under uncertainty prevail. Four of these, namely, the Wald or Maximin criterion, the Hurwicz alpha criterion, the Savage or minimax regret criterion, and the Laplace or Bayes criterion are discussed here. There are also methods for dealing with uncertainty in a non-quantitative way. These include referral to authority for guidance, attempts to control the environment, hedging, flexible investments, diversification, modification of goals, and the acquisition of additional information.

LO1 Decision Making Under Certainty

Under conditions of certainty, the decision maker has complete knowledge of the various states of nature (N_i) that are relevant to the decision and knows which one will occur. This effectively reduces the decision matrix to one

© ISTOCKPHOTO/THINKSTOCK

column. The decision maker simply chooses the strategy (S_i), course of action or project that yields the greatest payoff. A payoff matrix, also called a decision matrix, provides a useful tool to decision makers. An example of a payoff matrix is provided in Exhibit 1. In our example, let the four states of nature be represented by economic conditions of boom, stability, recession, and depression (N_1, N_2, N_3, and N_4, respectively). Further, let the five strategies be given by alternate advertising policies, such as

1. Advertising nationally through print, audio, and video media (S_1)
2. Advertising nationally through only print and TV media (S_2)
3. Advertising regionally through print, audio, and video media (S_3)
4. Advertising locally through only print and TV media (S_4)
5. No advertising (S_5)

Let the payoffs be in millions of rupees. The payoff matrix in Exhibit 1 shows that if strategy S_1 is adopted and the state of nature N_1 prevails, then the payoff is ₹12 million. Similarly, if strategy S_4 is adopted and the state of nature N_3 prevails, then the payoff is ₹20 million.

Exhibit 1
Payoff Matrix

Strategies	N_1	N_2	N_3	N_4
S_1	12	12	12	6
S_2	46	14	15	−8
S_3	40	35	15	−1
S_4	38	32	20	−3
S_5	35	30	25	−5

Under certainty, the decision depends upon which state of nature the decision maker is sure will occur. The possibilities are shown in Exhibit 2.

Exhibit 2
Possible Decisions under Conditions of Certainty

Certain State of Nature	Best Strategy	Payoff
N_1	S_2	46
N_2	S_3	35
N_3	S_5	25
N_4	S_1	6

In general, decision making under certainty requires that we find the largest payoff either by maximizing benefits (such as revenue, profit, or utility) or by minimizing costs. Some of the tools available to the decision maker for this purpose are marginal analysis and linear programming.

LO2 Decision Making Under Risk

Risk exists when the decision maker does not know in advance the specific outcome of a decision but is able to establish an objective probability distribution of payoffs, either *a priori* (i.e., by deduction) or *a posterior* (i.e., by empirical measurement). Under conditions of **risk**, the primary decision criterion is expected value, which is computed as:

$$E(X) = P_1X_1 + P_2X_2 + P_3X_3 + \ldots + P_nX_n = \Sigma P_iX_i$$

where

X_i = Value of the ith payoff

P_i = Probability of the ith payoff (which is equal to the probability of the ith state of nature)

To make a decision, the expected value is computed for each strategy and the one with the highest expected value is chosen. Taking the same example, let us suppose that the decision maker assumes a 25 percent chance of boom (N_1), a 50 percent chance of stability (N_2), a 20 percent chance of recession (N_3), and a 5 percent chance of depression (N_4). (Note that these probabilities add up to 100 percent.)

risk
under conditions of risk, the primary decision criterion is expected value

The expected value of each strategy is calculated and presented in Exhibit 3.

Exhibit 3
Expected Value Calculation

	$P = 0.25$	$P = 0.5$	$P = 0.2$	$P = 0.05$	P_1X_1	P_2X_2	P_3X_3	P_4X_4	Expected Value $E(X) = \Sigma P_iX_i$
Strategies	N_1	N_2	N_3	N_4	N_1	N_2	N_3	N_4	
S_1	12	12	12	6	3	6	2.4	0.3	11.7
S_2	46	14	15	−8	11.5	7	3	−0.4	21.1
S_3	40	35	15	−1	10	17.5	3	−0.05	30.45
S_4	38	32	20	−3	9.5	16	4	−0.15	29.35
S_5	35	30	25	−5	8.75	15	5	−0.25	28.5

© LIQUIDLIBRARY/THINKSTOCK

In the preceding example, there is a clear decision in favor of strategy S_3 because it has the highest expected value. But suppose that the expected values of alternative strategies are the same, then what? In this case, in order to choose between two or more strategies which have the same expected value, we must use some other yardstick. The yardstick is degree of risk, which is considered a secondary or auxiliary measure of expected value.

Coefficient of Variation (CV): Suppose a firm has an opportunity to invest in two different projects. One has an expected value of ₹500,000 with a standard deviation of ₹5,000. The other has an expected value of ₹100,000 with a standard deviation of ₹2,000. Which is riskier? If we use standard deviation as a measure of risk, we would have to conclude that the larger project is riskier. But considering the standard deviation in relation to the size of project, the relative risk is smaller for the larger project. Clearly, in order to compare the riskiness of projects with widely differing magnitudes of investments, payoffs, and expected values, a relative rather than an absolute measurement is necessary. Relative standard deviation is such a measurement, more commonly called the coefficient of variation.

coefficient of variation
the ratio of the standard deviation to the expected value, or mean

decision tree
graphic device that shows a sequence of strategic decisions and the expected consequences under each possible set of circumstances

The coefficient of variation is the ratio of the standard deviation to the expected value, or mean. When calculated as a percentage, it provides an index of the risk per rupee of return, and thus makes possible a comparison of strategies or projects of widely differing magnitude. The formula is

$$CV = \sigma/\mu * (100)$$

where,

σ = the standard deviation, and
μ = the expected or mean value

Sequential Decision Analysis Under Risk Using Decision Trees

A decision tree is a graphic device that shows a sequence of strategic decisions and the expected consequences under each possible set of circumstances. The construction and analysis of a decision tree is appropriate whenever a sequential series of conditional decisions must be made under condition of risk. By conditional decision, we mean a decision that depends upon circumstances or options that will occur at a later time.

Construction of the decision tree begins with the earliest decision and proceeds forward in time through a series of subsequent events and decisions. At each decision or event the tree branches out to depict each possible course of action, until finally all logical consequences and the resulting payoffs are depicted. An example of a decision tree is given in Exhibit 4.

It is important to note that in the construction of a decision tree, the branching out of squares represents strategies. Since the decision maker has full control over which strategy is chosen, these branches do not have probabilities. Branches of circles represent states of nature over which the decision maker has no control. Therefore, these branches have probabilities and the probabilities for all branches coming from any one circle must add upto 1.

Since each decision depends upon the evaluation of events that take place at a later time, the analysis of a decision tree begins at the end of the sequence and works backwards. We begin by constructing a decision tree from the left to the right. The basic decision to be made by the decision maker is whether to spend ₹50,000 to market a new product or to invest the money in a bank that guarantees a 10 percent return. The first decision, thus, is whether or not to market the product. Since this decision lies with the decision maker, these branches do not have a probability attached. Once the firm decides to market the product, two possibilities can occur: either the firm faces competition in the market in the near future or retains a monopoly position. Since the decision maker has no control over these events, the branches that emanate from the circle have a probability assigned next to them. In our example, the probability that the decision maker faces competition is given by 0.7. The probability that the decision maker retains a monopoly position is 0.3. In the likelihood that competition occurs, the decision maker can charge a high, medium, or a low price. Since this decision is made by the decision maker himself, no probabilities are assigned to these branches. Further, if the decision maker decides to charge a high price, the competitor in turn may charge a high, medium, or a low price. Since the decision maker has no control over the price charged by the competitor, these branches of high, medium, and low prices will have a probability assigned to each of them. In our example, the corresponding probabilities are assumed to be 0.5, 0.3, and 0.2, respectively. It may be noted yet again that the sum of probabilities emanating from the circle is one. In a similar way, we construct the entire decision tree. Once the decision tree has been constructed, the decision maker now has to take a decision. In order to do so, we need to move from right of the decision tree to the left of the decision tree.

Beginning in the upper right of graph, the analyst calculates the expected value if the firm's price is high and there is competition. The expected value is 20(0.5) + (–5)(0.3) + (–30)(0.2) = 2.5. This expected value is noted in or above the event circle. The expected values of medium and low price (8 and 8.8, respectively) are computed and noted in a similar manner. Since the low price gives the highest expected value, that value is noted in the decision box, and the other two branches are slashed to indicate they are non-optimal. In the alternative state of no competition, the only question is whether to charge a high, medium, or low price. The payoffs indicate that a high price is optimal, and thus the other two branches are slashed out.

At the first event point, that is the introduction of a competitive product the expected value is (8.8*0.7)+(60*0.3) = 24.16. The firm is now ready to make a decision. If it does not market, it gets ₹5.000. If it does market its product, there is an expected return of ₹24,160. It is clear that the firm should enter the market. The exhibit also gives a clear indication of the most profitable pricing strategy. The product should be initially marked at a high price. If competition develops, for which there is a 70 percent probability, the price should then be lowered to a low price in order to maximize the expected return.

Exhibit 4

Decision Tree: Construction and Analysis

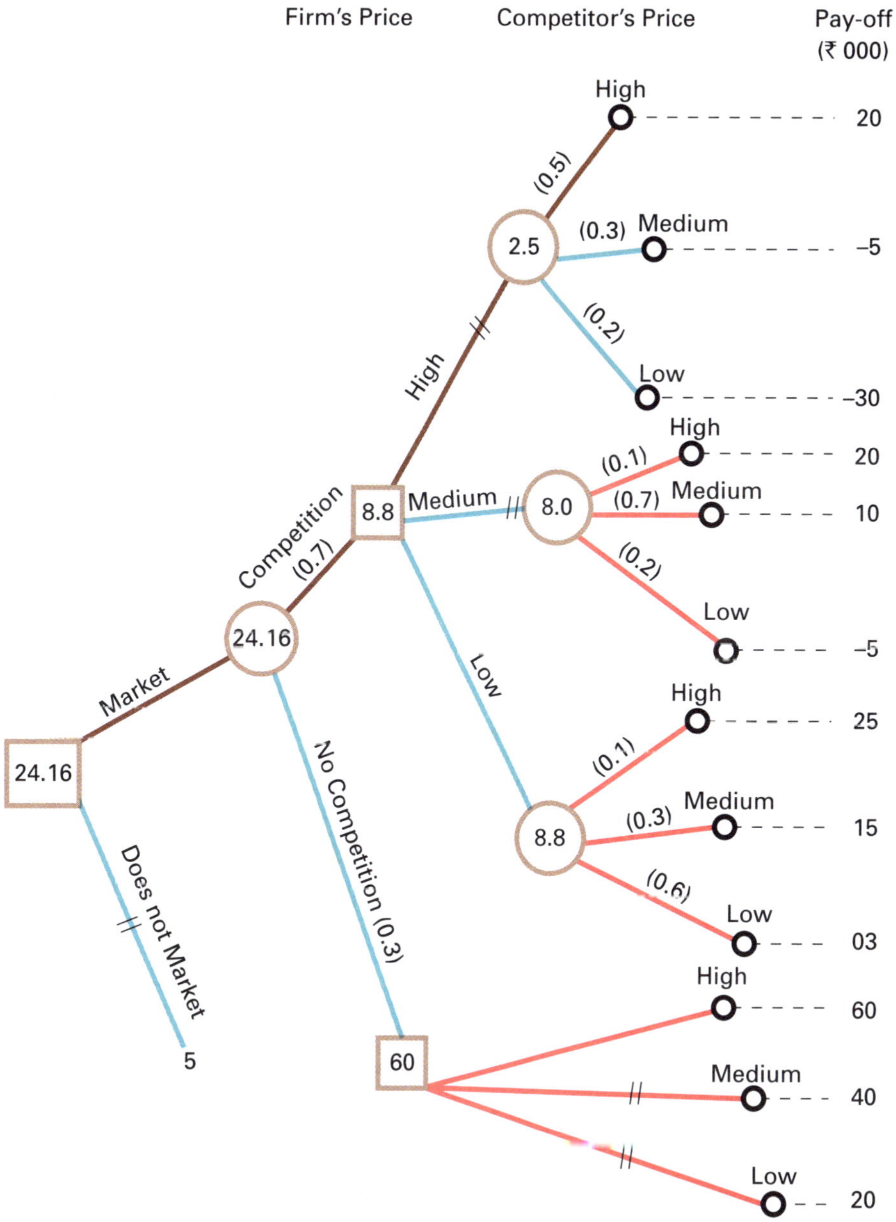

Numerical Illustration: Decision Tree

Frisp Inc. currently has assets worth $180,000 and wants to decide whether to market a new orange-flavored soda. The company has three alternatives:

Alternative 1: Test market the soda locally, then utilize the results of the market study to determine whether or not to market the soda nationally.

Alternative 2: Immediately (without test marketing) market the soda nationally.

Alternative 3: Immediately (without test marketing) decide not to market the soda nationally.

In the absence of a market study, Frisp Inc. believes that the soda has 60% chance of becoming a national success and 40% chance of being a national failure. If the soda is a national success, Frisp Inc.'s asset position will increase by $320,000 and if the soda is a national failure, Frisp Inc.'s asset position will decrease by $120,000.

If Frisp Inc. performs a market study (at a cost of $40,000), there is 54% chance of the study yielding favorable results (referred to as local success) and 46% chance that the study will yield unfavorable results (referred to as local failure). If a local success is observed, there is 80% chance that the soda will be a national success. If a local failure is observed, there is 85% chance that the soda will be a national failure. If Frisp Inc. is risk-neutral (wants to maximize its expected final asset position), what strategy should the company follow?

Solution

To draw a decision tree that represents the company's problem, we begin at the present and proceed towards future events and decisions. The decision tree is as shown in Exhibit 5.

The branches indicating *National failure* and *National success* are terminal branches of Frisp Inc.'s decision tree. A decision fork is drawn when Frisp Inc. has to make a decision. Here, the branches emanate from a square. An event fork, on the other hand, is drawn when outside forces determine which of the several random events will occur. The branches emanate from a circle in this case. Each of these branches has a probability assigned.

Since our aim is to maximize expected final asset position at each terminal branch, we must estimate

Exhibit 5

Decision Tree for Frisp Inc.

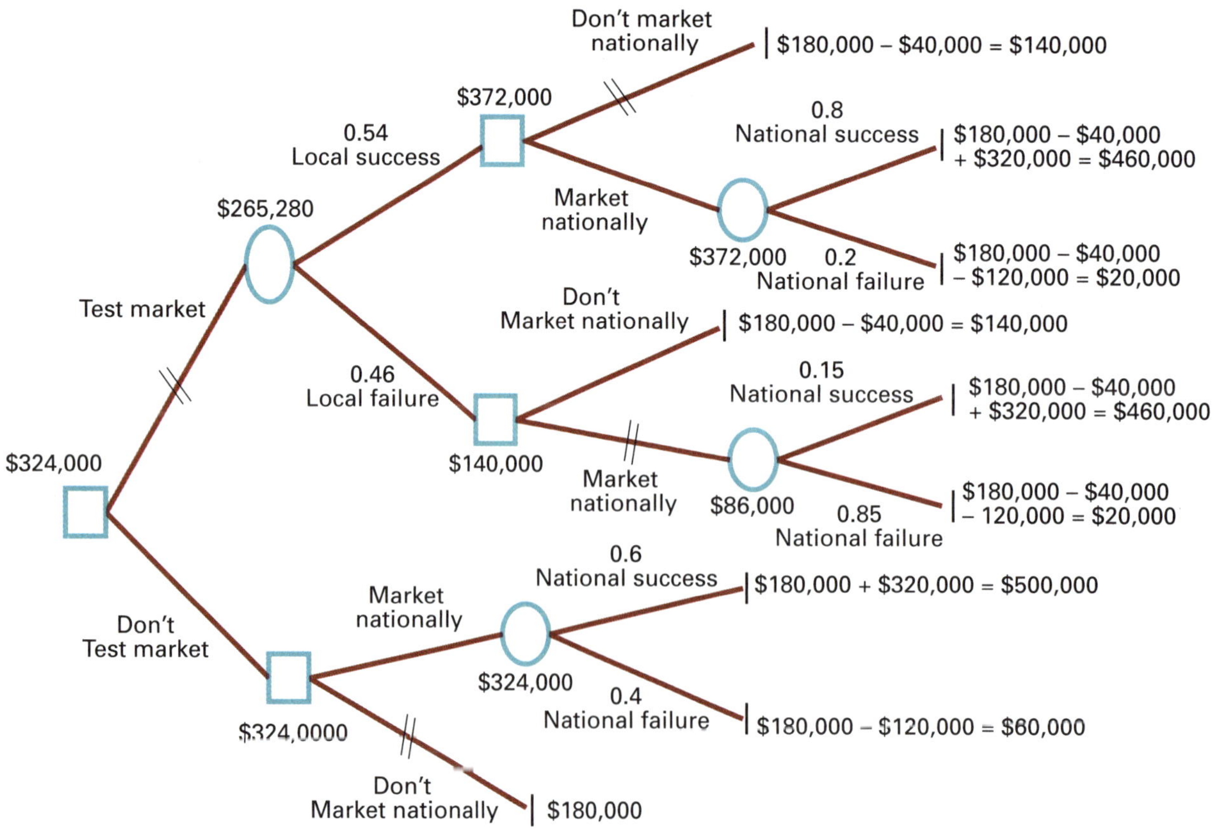

the final asset position that will result if the path leading to the given terminal branch occurs. For example, the terminal branch *National failure* that follows *Local failure* leads to a final asset position of \$180,000 − \$40,000 − \$120,000 = \$20,000. If we were to maximize expected revenues, we would enter revenues on each terminal branch.

To determine the decisions that will maximize Frisp Inc.'s final asset position, we work backwards from right to left. At each event fork, we calculate the expected final asset position.

We determine the expected final asset position for the following three event forks:

1. *Market nationally* after *Local success*. Here we have an expected final asset position of 0.8(\$460,000) + 0.2(\$20,000) = \$372,000
2. *Market nationally* after *Local failure*. Here we have an expected final asset position of 0.15(\$460,000) + 0.85(\$20,000) = \$86,000
3. *Market nationally* after *Don't test market*. Here we have an expected final asset position of 0.6(\$500,000) + 0.4(\$60,000) = \$324,000

We now evaluate the three decision forks:

1. Decision after *Local success*: *Market nationally* yields a larger expected final asset position than *Don'tmarket nationally*, so we select *Market nationally* and enter an expected final asset position of \$372,000. The other branch is slashed out.
2. Decision after *Local failure*: *Don't market nationally* yields a larger expected final asset position than *Market nationally*, so we select *Don't Market nationally* and enter an expected final asset position of \$140,000. The other branch is slashed out.
3. Decision for *Don't test market*: *Market nationally* yields a larger expected final asset position than *Don't market nationally*, so we select *Market nationally* and enter an expected final asset position of \$324,000. The other branch is slashed out.

We now evaluate the event fork emanating from the *Test market* decision. This event fork yields an expected final asset position of 0.54(\$372000) + 0.46(\$140,000) = \$265,280.

All that remains is to determine the correct decision at the decision fork *Test market* versus *Don't test market*. We have found that *Test market* yields an expected final asset position of \$265,280, and *Don't test market* yields an expected final asset position of \$324,000. Hence, we select the *Don't test market* value. This is the final value at the beginning of the tree (as shown in the leftmost square in the exhibit). Thus, the strategy of *Don't test market* and then *Market nationally* will yield maximum benefit.

Risk Preference

Generally, higher returns are associated with higher risk. Indeed, the essence of economics is making choices where there is a trade-off. Virtually all investment choices require giving up expected returns for higher risk, to taking more risk in the expectation of a greater expected return. Thus, any decision will reflect the manager's attitude or preference for risk, and these preferences differ substantially among individuals. For example, some investors are so averse to taking risk that they keep all their assets in bank deposits insured by the central government. On the other hand, others are willing to risk all they own, and can even borrow to finance extremely risky ventures (such as drilling oil wells). The reward for taking huge risk comes in the form of much higher returns.

We illustrate the concept of risk and risk preference through the following example. Consider the following gamble:

"I will toss a coin ten times. If a head appears each time, you must pay me ₹1,000. If tail appears one or more times, I will pay you a rupee."

Most people would reject this offer even though it is a fair game. That is, if the game were played many times, the amount lost would equal the amount won.

© LIQUIDLIBRARY/THINKSTOCK

However, the nature of the game is such that on any one trial the player could lose a large amount and stands to win only a small amount. The probability of a head appearing on ten consecutive tosses of a coin is given by $(1/2)^{10}$ or 0.001. The probability that there is at least one tail in ten tosses is 1 minus the probability that there would be ten heads or (1.0 – 0.001) = 0.999. These probabilities multiplied by their associated payoffs yield an expected value of zero; therefore, it is fair game.

In order to understand the concept of preference for risk, let us assume that individuals can associate satisfaction with money. More money usually means more satisfaction, although for many people each additional rupee brings less satisfaction than the previous rupee did. Economists use the term utility as a measure of satisfaction. Although an individual's satisfaction is virtually impossible to measure, it will be assumed that this can be done for a hypothetical individual. The assumption will make it easier to develop several important concepts. One such relationship between utility and money is shown in Exhibit 6a. The curve shows the relationship that has been just suggested, that is, utility increases as money increases but at a continually decreasing rate. Thus, the function is concave to the horizontal axis. A person having a concave utility function is said to be risk averse.

Suppose that this person has ₹10,000 and is offered the opportunity to bet ₹5,000 on the toss of a coin. If a head is tossed, she wins ₹5,000; if a tail is tossed, she loses ₹5,000. She now faces the choice of having ₹10,000 with certainty if she chooses not to bet (this option is called a certain prospect) or having ₹15,000 with probability 0.5 or ₹5,000 with probability 0.5. The latter option is called the uncertain prospect. The expected monetary value of the uncertain prospect is ₹10,000, that is:

$$E(X) = 0.5\,(₹5{,}000) + 0.5\,(₹15{,}000) = ₹10{,}000$$

This is the same as the rupee value of the certain prospect.

Now, consider the analysis in terms of the utility associated with each rupee payoff. For a risk-averse person, the rupee payoffs are translated into utility by using a function like that shown in Exhibit 6a. The certain prospect (i.e., having ₹10,000) is associated with a utility of 70. The expected value in utility of the uncertain prospect is determined as follows. A payoff of ₹5,000 corresponds to a utility value of 50, and an outcome of ₹15,000 is associated with a utility of 75. Thus, by substituting these utility values for the payoffs, the expected value in terms of utility is computed as:

$$E(X) = 0.5(50) + 0.5(75) = 62.5$$

This is less than the utility (70) associated with the certain prospect. Thus, this utility maximizing person prefers the certain prospect and chooses not to accept the bet. Note that an amount of ₹8,500 with certainty also would yield a utility level of 62.5. This amount is said to be the certainty equivalent of the gamble. The individual would pay up to ₹1,500 (i.e., the difference between the expected value of the gamble and the certainty equivalent) in order to avoid the gamble.

The case for a risk seeking person is depicted in Exhibit 6b. In this, the expected value of the utility associated with an uncertain prospect is greater than that of a certain prospect (55 vis. a vis. 40). Thus, here the certainty equivalent of the gamble (₹10,000) is less than the expected value of the gamble. This utility maximizing person, thus, prefers the uncertain prospect to the certain prospect and chooses to accept the bet. Note that an amount of ₹12,000 with certainty also would yield a utility level of 55. This amount is said to be the certainty equivalent of the gamble. The individual would thus be willing to pay up to ₹2,000 (i.e., the difference between the expected value of the gamble and the certainty equivalent) in order to gamble.

In the risk-neutral case depicted in Exhibit 6c, the expected value of the utility associated with an uncertain prospect is equal to that of a certain prospect where both have equal expected rupee values. The expected utility associated with the uncertain prospect is 100; that is, 0.5 (50) + 0.5 (150) =100. Thus, here the certainty equivalent of the gamble (₹10,000) equals the expected value of the gamble.

We can now formally define risk aversion, risk-seeking and risk-neutral as follows:

In general, if the certainty equivalent of the gamble is less than the expected rupee value of the gamble, the person is said to be risk averse.

Exhibit 6

Preference for Risk

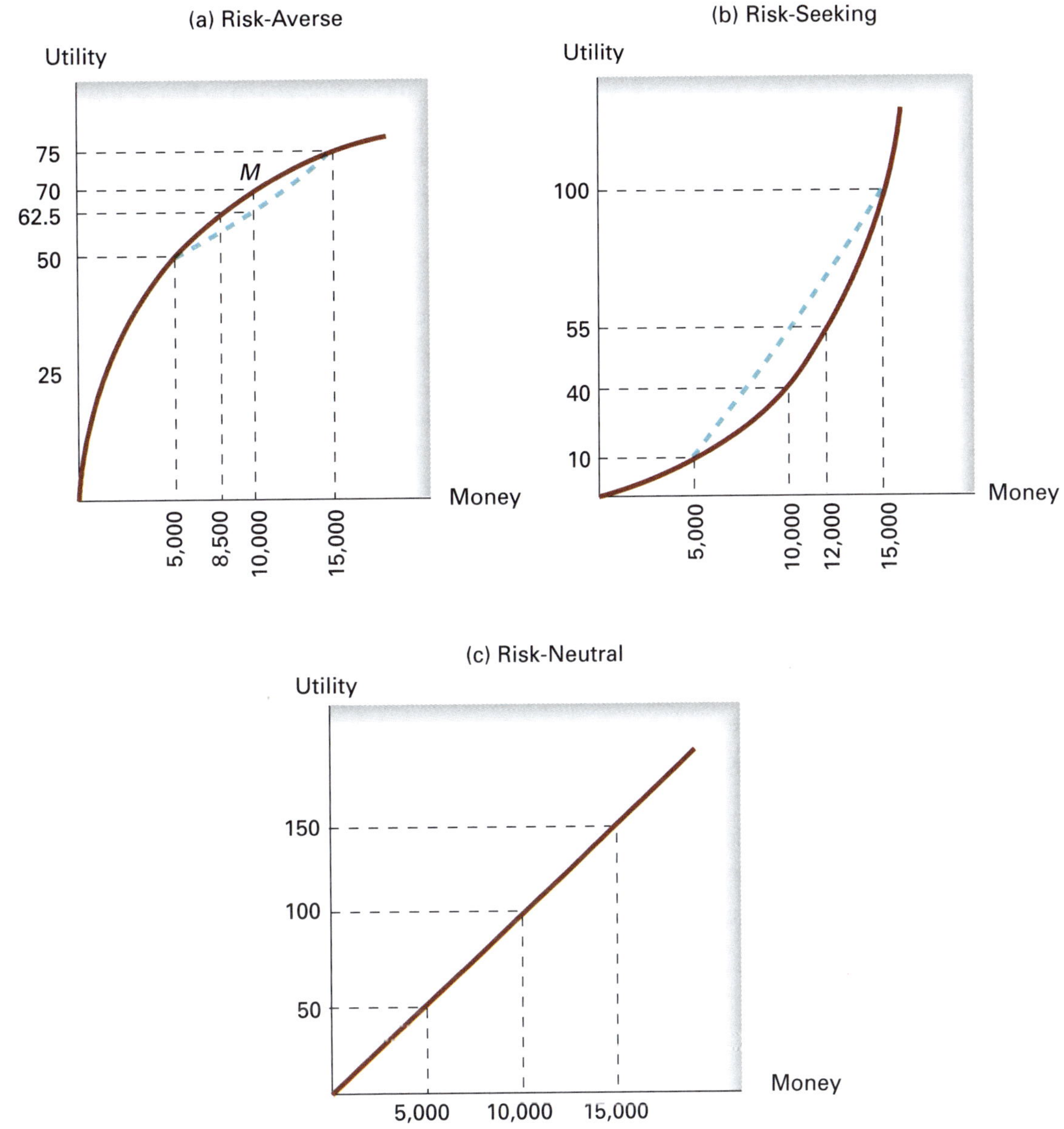

In general, if the certainty equivalent of the gamble is greater than the expected rupee value of the gamble, the individual is said to be risk seeking.

In general, if the certainty equivalent of the gamble equals the expected value of the gamble; the individual is said to be risk neutral.

We now formalize the concept of *preference for risk*. At any time, an individual has a given level of wealth, W, which is known with certainty. If the utility function is specified, the utility of that wealth is also known with certainty. Assume the initial level of wealth is \$100, and that the utility function for this person is given by the natural logarithm of wealth, i.e.,

$$U = \ln W$$

This function describes this individual's transformation of wealth into utility or satisfaction. The utility of the initial wealth of \$100 is 4.61 (i.e., ln(100) = 4.61). We now assume that the individual is faced with a gamble that has the following probability distribution.

Probability ()	Payoff ()
0.5	–80
0.5	+80

Since the expected outcome is zero, this is a fair game.

If the game is played and the individual wins, her wealth is \$180. In case she loses, her wealth is \$20.

The *expected wealth,* if the game is played, is given by

$$E(W) = 0.5(20) + 0.5(180) = \$100$$

which has a utility of 4.61, that is, the utility of expected wealth is

$$U[E(W)] = \ln[E(W)] = \ln(100) = 4.61$$

The *expected utility of wealth* is determined as

$$\begin{aligned} E[U(W)] &= 0.5[U(20)] + 0.5[U(180)] \\ &= 0.5[\ln(20)] + 0.5[\ln(180)] \\ &= 0.5(3.00) + 0.5\,(5.19) \\ &= 4.10 \end{aligned}$$

Now, the preference for risk can be formally defined.

Risk Aversion: An individual is said to be risk averse if, when faced with a gamble, the utility of expected wealth is greater than the expected utility of wealth, that is,

$$U[E(W)] > E[U(W)] \Rightarrow \text{Risk Aversion}$$

In the example just illustrated, the individual is thus found to be risk averse.

The case is shown in Exhibit 7. Here the utility function is considered as

$$U = \ln W.$$

The notion that $U[E(W)] > E[U(W)]$ simply states that this individual would prefer wealth of \$100 with certainty (with an associated utility of 4.61), to a gamble that had an expected wealth of \$100 (with an associated utility of 4.10). It is clear that for this individual the risk associated with the gamble has reduced utility.

Risk Seeking: An individual is said to be risk seeking if the utility of expected wealth is less than the expected utility of wealth, that is,

$$U[E(W)] < E[U(W)] \Rightarrow \text{Risk Seeking}$$

Risk Neutral: An individual is said to be risk neutral if the utility of expected wealth is equal to the expected utility of wealth, that is,

$$U[E(W)] = E[U(W)] \Rightarrow \text{Risk Neutrality}$$

Numerical Illustration: Risk Preference and Decision Making

Consider the problem facing a manager who must choose between two investments A and B each having an initial cost of ₹10 million. The probability distributions for the payoffs for each investment are

risk aversion
the utility of expected wealth is greater than the expected utility of wealth

risk seeking
if the utility of expected wealth is less than the expected utility of wealth

risk neutral
if the utility of expected wealth is equal to the expected utility of wealth

Exhibit 7

Utility Wealth Curve for $U = \ln W$

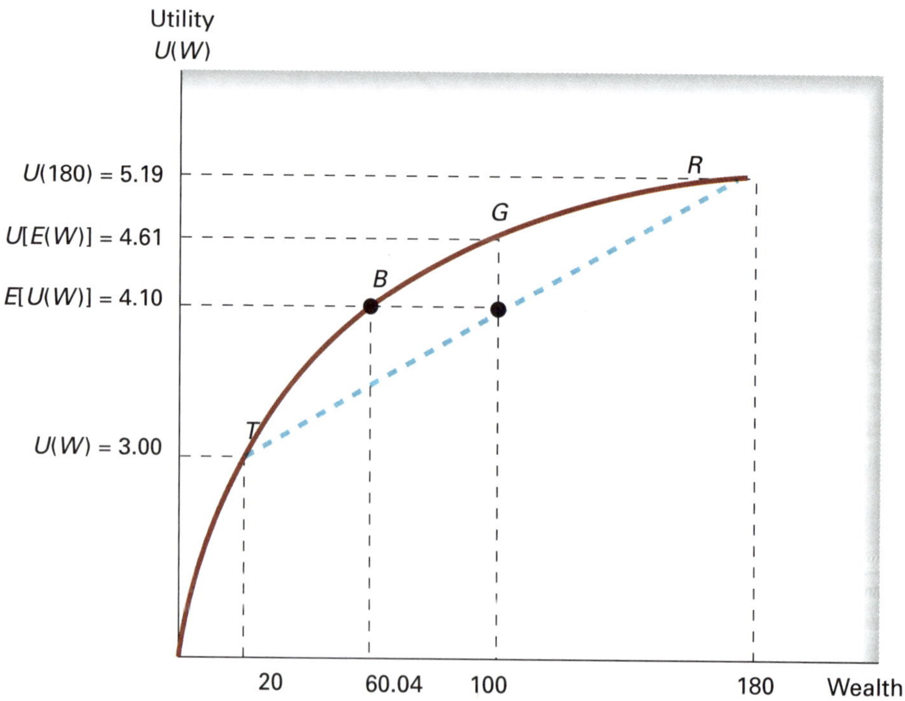

shown in Exhibit 8. Each payoff represents the present value of all future net profits.

Exhibit 8

Probability Distribution for the Payoffs

A		B	
Probability (P_i)	Payoff (X_i) (Million)	Probability (P_i)	Payoff (X_i) (Million)
0.20	–20	0.30	10
0.60	20	0.35	20
0.20	50	0.35	30

The decision maker's utility function is $\hat{u} = 100X - X^2$, where X is the rupee payoff in millions.

1. Would you characterize this decision maker as risk seeking, risk neutral, or risk averse? Explain.
2. If the objective is to maximize expected net present value, which investment is the better choice? (For the moment, disregard risk.)
3. Evaluate the risk associated with the rupee returns for each investment.
4. If the objective is utility maximization, which investment should be chosen?

Solution:

1. Based on the utility function, it is seen that the decision maker is risk averse. This can be shown in the following way. Select any two rupee payoffs, say, ₹20 million and ₹40 million, and arbitrarily assign them probabilities of occurrence, say, 0.4 and 0.6, respectively. The expected value of these payoffs is

   E (Rupees) = 0.4 (20) + 0.6 (40) = ₹32 million

   From the utility function the utilities associated with ₹20 million and ₹40 million are 1,600 and 2,400, respectively. Thus, the expected utility value is

   E (utility) = 0.4 (1,600) + 0.6 (2,400) = 2,080

   But if this person were offered ₹32 million with certainty (i.e., a certain prospect having the same value as the expected rupee value of the investments), the utility would be 2,176. Because the utility is higher for the certain prospect, the person is risk averse.

2. The expected returns for each investment are

   $$E\ (\text{Rupees})\ A = 0.20\ (-20) + 0.60\ (20) + 0.20\ (50) = 18$$

   $$E\ (\text{Rupees})\ B = 0.3\ (10) + 0.35\ (20) + 0.35\ (30) = 20.5$$

   Thus, B is the preferred choice because it has the higher expected value.

3. The evaluation statistics for risk and risk per rupee of expected return for both investments are

   Investment A:

   $$\sigma_A = \sqrt{0.20\ (-20 - 18)^2 + 0.60\ (20 - 18)^2 + 0.20\ (50 - 18)^2} = 496$$

   $$\upsilon_A = \frac{\sigma_A}{\upsilon_A} = \frac{496}{18} = 27.55$$

   Investment B:

   $$\sigma_B = \sqrt{0.30\ (10 - 20.5)^2 + 0.35\ (20 - 20.5)^2 + 0.35\ (30 - 20.5)^2} = 64.75$$

   $$\upsilon_B = \frac{\sigma_B}{\upsilon_B} = \frac{64.75}{20.5} = 3.158$$

   The risk is greater for A (σ_A = 496 compared to σ_B = 64.75) and the risk per rupee of expected return is also greater for A (υ_A = 27.55 compared to υ_B = 3.158).

4. To make the decision assuming the goal is utility maximization, the payoffs must be transformed from rupees into utility using the utility function $\hat{u} = 100X - X^2$. For example, the utility associated with a net payoff of –20 is

   $$\hat{u} = 100\ (-20) - 20^2 = -2{,}400$$

   repeating this for each outcome will yield two new probability distributions where the payoffs are in terms of utility.

Probability (P_i)	Payoff ($\hat{u}_i$)	Probability (P_i)	Payoff ($\hat{u}_i$)
0.20	–2,400	0.30	900
0.60	1,600	0.35	1,600
0.20	2,500	0.35	2,100

The expected utility returns are

$$E(u)_A = 0.20\ (-2400) + 0.60\ (1600) + 0.20\ (2500) = 980$$

$$E(u)_B = 0.30\ (900) + 0.35\ (1600) + 0.35\ (2100) = 1565$$

Hence, in terms of utility, investment B is the preferred alternative.

Insurance and Gambling: A Contradiction

Insurance is what one does to protect oneself against the risk of a loss. This includes insuring one's car, life, or home. Here a person is willing to pay a little bit now to avoid the risk of paying a lot more later. Gambling, on the other hand, is a lot like insurance, though in the reverse direction. With gambling one pays something now for the chance of getting even more later. We have traditional gambling like the games of casinos, state lotteries, and assorted legal and illegal betting on sports. Less obvious activities can also be forms of gambling. These include starting a business or playing in the stock market. Getting an education is also a form of gambling. Many of the less obvious ones are also different forms of investment: one pays something now in the hope of getting more later. Thus, investment is also a gamble.

So the question remains—are gambling and insurance a contradiction? Can a person do both? In fact, several people insure and gamble at the same time. This seems to contradict the typical behavior of a person who is either risk averse or a risk lover. However, according to Friedman and Savage (1948), a person's utility function might be convex for low levels of money involved and concave for higher levels of money involved (refer exhibit 9). Such a person becomes a risk lover at low levels of income and a risk averse for higher levels of money involved. Such a person would gamble (e.g., buy a lottery ticket) when money involved is less, while he would seek insurance when large amounts of money are involved (such as those associated with automobile theft or accident). Thus a utility function of this type makes a rational person to gamble and insure at the same time.

© ISTOCKPHOTO/THINKSTOCK

Numerical Illustration: When to Insure

Rita studies at Columbia University and uses a bicycle to get around. She is worried about having her bike stolen and therefore wants to insure her bicycle against theft. In case the bike is stolen she would have to buy a new one. A new cycle would cost her \$200. On survey, she finds out that 10 percent of bicycles in Columia are stolen every year. Her total savings are \$400 and her utility of money function is given by $U(x) = x^{1/2}$. Under what conditions would Rita take out insurance for a year? What if she has utility of money $U(x) = \ln(x)$.

If she takes out insurance she obtains utility $U(400 - R)$ where R is the premium. Without insur-

Exhibit 9

Gambling and Insuring: Not Necessarily a Contradiction

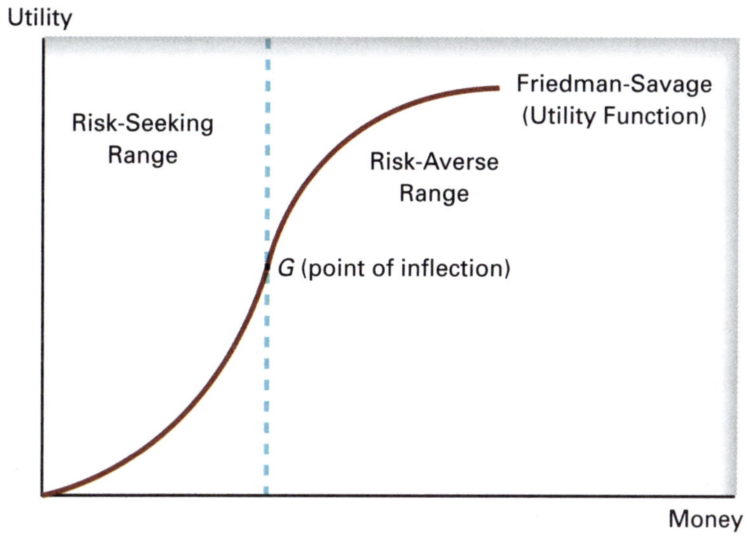

ance she gets (0.1) $U(200)$ + (0.9) $U(400)$. Equalizing these expected utilities and substituting $U(x) = x^{1/2}$, gives:

$$(0.1)\sqrt{200} + (0.9)\sqrt{400} = \sqrt{400 - R}$$

Or

$$R = 23.09$$

which means that insuring is the best decision as long as the premium does not exceed \$23.09. Similarly, if $U(x) = \ln(x)$, the maximum premium can be calculated as \$26.79.

LO3 Decision Making Under Uncertainty

Uncertainty is defined as the state in which one or more alternatives result in a set of possible specific outcomes whose probabilities are either unknown or meaningless. This means that decision making under uncertainty is always subjective. However, if the decision maker can identify the possible states of nature and estimate the resulting payoffs for each available strategy, then two basic approaches are available.

1. The decision maker may use the best available information and his or her own personal judgment and experience to assign subjective probabilities to the possible states of nature. This effectively converts the condition of uncertainty to a condition of risk for which expected value is the criterion of choice.
2. The decision maker may either disregard probability or treat them as equal, which amounts to the same thing. When this approach is taken, four decision criteria are available for evaluation of proposed strategies. These are as follows:
   a. The Wald decision criterion or Maximin criterion: Under this, the strategy that yields the best of the worst results is chosen.
   b. The Hurwicz alpha criterion: It allows the decision maker to inject optimism or pessimism into the decision process.
   c. The Savage decision criterion or minimax regret criterion: This seeks to minimize the opportunity cost of incorrect decisions.
   d. The Laplace decision criterion or Bayes criterion: This gives equal probability to each state of nature.

The Wald Decision Criterion

The **Wald or maximin decision criterion** is described by various authors as the criterion of pessimism, the criterion of extreme conservatism, and an attempt to maximize the security level. It envisions nature as perverse and malevolent with Murphy's Law fully operational. Therefore, the criterion says—"determine the worst possible outcome of each strategy and then pick the strategy yielding the best of the worst results."

As shown in Exhibit 10, the most dismal payoff from each row is chosen as the minimal security level associated with the strategy. The largest of these, a value of 6, implies that strategy S_1 is the best strategy under this criterion.

© ISTOCKPHOTO/THINKSTOCK

Exhibit 10

Decision Making under Wald Decision Criterion

	N_1	N_2	N_3	N_4	Maximin	Maximax
S_1	12	12	12	6	6*	12
S_2	46	14	15	–8	–8	46*
S_3	40	35	15	–1	–1	40
S_4	38	32	20	–3	–3	38
S_5	35	30	25	–5	–5	35

* Indicates best strategy under stated criterion

The strategy involves the smallest risks but at the same time promises the smallest return. It is up to the firm to decide just how a minimal level of return is to be weighted in the decision-making process and how much it can afford to risk if things turn for the worse. Because the criterion is fiscally conservative, it is particularly well suited to small business firms whose survival depends upon avoiding losses.

The Hurwicz Alpha Decision Criterion

The Hurwicz alpha decision criterion proposes to create a decision index (d) for each strategy, which is a weighted average of its extreme payoffs. The weighting factors are a coefficient of optimism (α), which is applied to the maximum payoff (M), and its complement ($1 - \alpha$), which is applied to the minimum payoff (m). The value of each strategy is thus:

$$d_i = \alpha M_i + (1 - \alpha)\, m_i$$

The strategy with the highest value for d_i is chosen as optimal.

Coefficient of optimism ranges from 0 to 1, enabling the decision maker to express his attitude toward risk-taking as a subjective degree of optimism. If the decision maker is completely pessimistic, he may decide that $\alpha = 0$. The result is the Wald or maximin criterion. If the decision maker is extremely optimist, for him $\alpha = 1$. In this case, the result would be the maximax criterion.

Suppose, for example, that the decision-maker is on the optimistic side and decides that $\alpha = 0.75$. His analysis of the current decision problem is shown below. It can be seen that the highest weighted average payoff results from selecting strategy S_3.

The decision indicated by the Hurwicz alpha criterion depends on the value of α, which in turn depends on the decision maker's own attitude toward risk. It is suitable for use by business firms; but if the decision maker's degree of optimism proves unfounded, substantial losses are likely. Therefore, due caution is advised.

Exhibit 11

Hurwicz Alpha Solution to Decision Problem

	Maximum (M_i)	Coefficient of Optimism (α)	Minimum (m_i)	Coefficient of Pessimism ($1-\alpha$)	Decision Index (d_i)
S_1	12	0.75	6	0.25	10.5
S_2	46	0.75	–8	0.25	32.5
S_3	40	0.75	–1	0.25	29.75
S_4	38	0.75	–3	0.25	27.75
S_5	35	0.75	–5	0.25	25

The Savage Decision Criterion

The Savage criterion, sometimes called the minimax regret criterion, examines "regret", which are the opportunity costs of incorrect decisions. Regret is measured as the absolute difference between the payoff for a given strategy and the payoff for the most effective strategy within the same state of nature.

This criterion is based on the assumption that the decision maker might experience *regret* after making the decision. This regret is also called as *Opportunity Loss*. Hence he will always try to minimize this regret. The working method is as follows:

Step I: From the given payoff matrix, develop an opportunity loss matrix or regret table as:

i. Find the best payoff corresponding to each state of nature, and

ii. Subtract all payoffs of that action from this best payoff.

Step II: Locate the maximum regret for each action.

Step III: Select that action as the best action which corresponds to the minimum of the above maximum regrets.

The rationale for measurement of regret is quite simple. If any particular state of nature occurs in the future, and if we have chosen the strategy that yields the maximum payoff for that state of nature, then we have no regret. But if we choose any other strategy, regret is the difference between what actually occurs and what we could have earned had we made the optimal decision.

After determining the maximum regret for each strategy, the strategy with the smallest maximum regret is chosen. This is shown in Exhibit 12.

Note that the decision maker who uses the Savage criterion explicitly abandons attempts to maximize payoff in favor of a strategy to achieve a satisfactory payoff with less risk. The Savage criterion is, therefore, particularly useful for evaluating a series of projects over a long span of time.

Exhibit 12

Decision Making Under Savage Criterion

					Regret Matrix				Maximum Regret
	N_1	N_2	N_3	N_4	N_1	N_2	N_3	N_4	
S_1	12	12	12	6	34	23	13	0	34
S_2	46	14	15	–8	0	21	10	14	21
S_3	40	35	15	–1	6	0	10	7	10
S_4	38	32	20	–3	8	3	5	9	9*
S_5	35	30	25	–5	11	5	0	11	11

* Indicates best strategy under stated criterion

The Laplace Decision Criterion

There is Bayesian postulate that if the probabilities of occurrences are unknown, they should be assumed equal. The Laplace criterion uses this postulate to calculate the expected value of each strategy; hence the Laplace criterion is also called the "Bayes Criterion". The strategy selected is the one with the greatest expected value that results from the assumed (subjective) probabilities.

For strategies S_1, S_2, S_3, S_4, and S_5, from our example, the expected values are 42∗1/4, 67∗1/4, 89∗1/4, 87∗1/4, and 85∗1/4, respectively. Thus, under the Laplace decision criterion, strategy S_3 would be selected.

Final Word

This chapter has dealt with methods and approaches to decision making that decision makers may use under conditions of certainty, risk, and uncertainty. Under conditions of certainty, the decision maker's task is to select the strategy that maximizes the payoff. Under the condition of risk, the decision criterion is to maximize the expected value. To calculate the expected value, the probabilities of states of nature are to be used as weights. The degree of risk is indicated by its coefficient of variation, which is simply the ratio of the standard deviation to the mean, expressed as a percentage. When a sequential series of conditional decisions are to be made under risk, a decision tree is to be constructed to evaluate the best option. What decision is finally made under risk depends upon the decision makers' attitude towards risk. Under conditions of uncertainty, the decision maker is faced with a state in which one or more alternatives result in a set of outcomes whose probabilities are unknown or meaningless. Several criteria for decision making under uncertainty prevail. Four of these, namely, the Wald or Maximin criterion, the Hurwicz alpha criterion, the Savage or minimax regret criterion, and the Laplace or Bayes criterion were discussed in this chapter.

MULTIPLE CHOICE QUESTIONS

Lee and Cody are competitors. Each is considering whether to take aggressive action against the other or to cooperate. Cody can observe Lee's decision. Their decision tree can be diagrammed as follows:

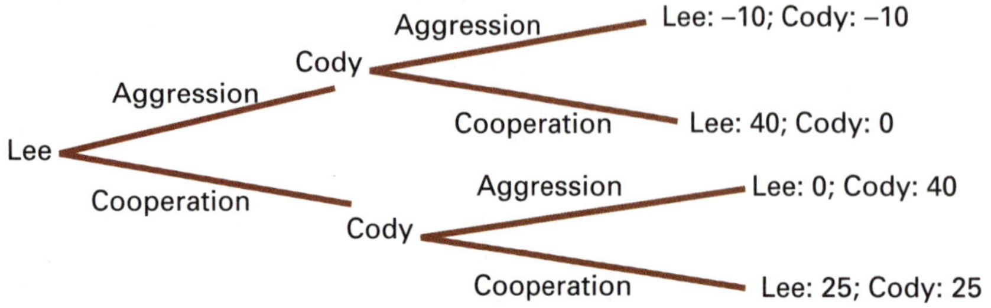

1. If Lee is aggressive, Cody will respond with _______ and if Lee cooperates, Cody will respond with _______.
   a. aggression; cooperation
   b. aggression; aggression
   c. cooperation; aggression
   d. cooperation; cooperation
2. Suppose Cody tells Lee that any aggression on Lee's part will be met with aggression, but that if Lee cooperates, Cody will respond cooperatively. Cody's statement is:
   a. a commitment device.
   b. a non-credible threat and promise.
   c. a description of the two equilibria for this game.
   d. a credible threat and promise.

Consider the decision problem of a firm described by the decision tree below:

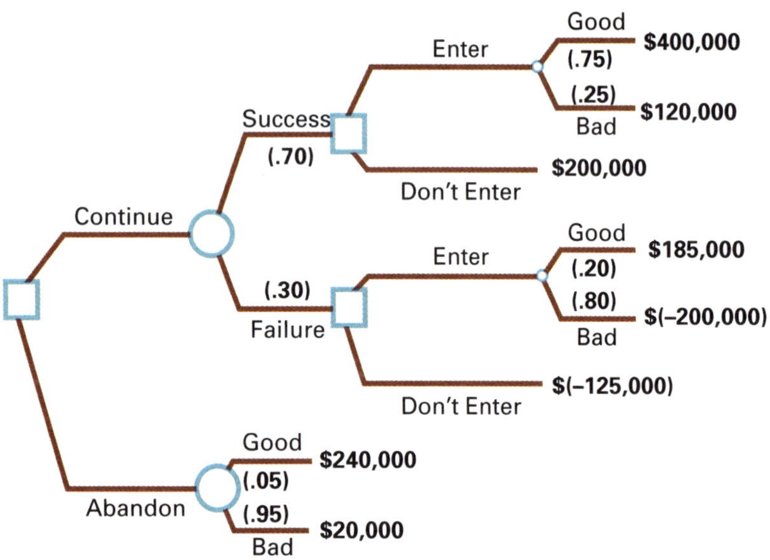

3. Suppose the firm initially chooses "Continue." Following this choice, if "chance" chooses "Failure," would the firm want to choose:
   a. Enter
   b. Don't Enter
   c. None of the above
   d. Cannot be determined

4. Suppose the firm initially chooses "Continue." Following this choice, if "chance" chooses "Success," would the firm want to choose:
   a. Enter
   b. Don't Enter
   c. None of the above
   d. Cannot be determined
5. The firm should initially choose:
   a. Continue
   b. Abandon
   c. None of the above
   d. Cannot be determined

Henry manages a firm that is going to start operating in a new market. He has the option of targeting either "high end" consumers or "low end" consumers. He has some uncertainty regarding actual market conditions in each of these two segments. Very loosely, he thinks that market conditions in each segment could be either "favorable" or "unfavorable." The probability of "favorable" versus "unfavorable" conditions in each market segment (along with his resulting profit in each case) is shown in the decision tree below:

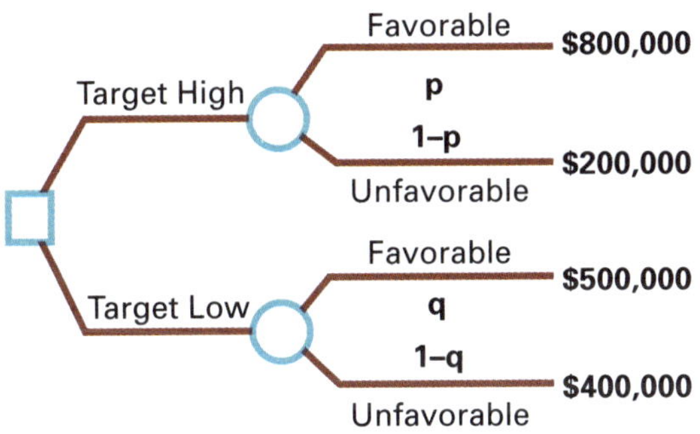

6. If p = 2/5 and q = 3/4 the segment that should be served is:
   a. High end
   b. Low end
   c. None of the above
   d. Cannot be determined
7. Suppose p = 2/5. For what range of values of q should he serve the "low end" consumers?
   a. $q < 0.4$ b. $q = 0.4$
   c. $q > 0.4$ d. None of the above
8. Suppose q = 3/4. For what range of values of p should he serve the "low end" consumers?
   a. $p > 0.46$ b. $p < 0.46$
   c. $p = 0.46$ d. None of the above
9. For what value of p should he serve the "high end" consumers (regardless of the value of q)?
   a. $p > 0.33$ b. $p < 0.5$
   c. $p > 0.5$ d. $p < 0.33$
10. For what value of p should he serve the "low end" consumers (regardless of the value of q)?
   a. $p > 0.33$ b. $p < 0.5$
   c. $p > 0.5$ d. $p < 0.33$

Acme steel fabricators has experienced booming business for the past five years. The company fabricates a wide range of steel products, such as railings, ladders, and light structural steel framing. The current manual method of materials handling is causing excessive inventories and congestion. Acme is considering the purchase of an overhead rail mounted hoist system or a forklift truck to increase capacity and improve manufacturing efficiency. The annual pre-tax payoff from the system depends on future demand. If demand stays at the current level, the probability of which is 0.50, annual savings from the overhead hoist will be $10,000. If demand rises, the hoist will save $25,000 annually because of operating efficiencies in addition to new sales. Finally, if demand falls, the hoist will result in an estimated annual loss of $65,000. The probability is estimated to be 0.30 for higher demand and 0.20 for lower demand. If the forklift is purchased, annual payoffs will be $5,000 if demand is unchanged, $10,000 if demand rises, and –$25,000 if demand falls. Calculate the expected payoffs for each alternative and answer the following questions:

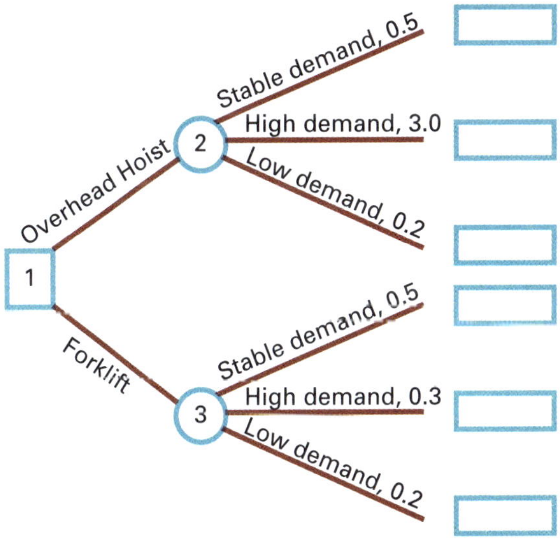

11. The value (in $) of payoff, if demand is stable and overhead hoist is used, is
   a. 10,000 b. 25,000
   c. 5,000 d. None of the above
12. The value (in $) of payoff, if demand is high and overhead hoist is used, is
   a. 10,000 b. 25,000
   c. 5,000 d. None of the above

13. The value (in $) of payoff, if demand is low and overhead hoist is used, is
   a. 10,000 b. 25,000
   c. –65,000 d. None of the above
14. The value (in $) of payoff, if demand is stable and forklift is used, is
   a. 10,000 b. 25,000
   c. 5,000 d. None of the above
15. The value (in $) of payoff, if demand is high and forklift is used, is
   a. 10,000 b. 25,000
   c. 15,000 d. None of the above
16. The equally *likely decision* criterion is also known as:
   (a) Bayes' (b) Minimax
   (c) Laplace (d) Hurwics
   (e) None of the above
17. Any problem that can be represented in a decision table can also be graphically illustrated in a:
   (a) utility curve. (b) Bayes' diagram.
   (c) decision tree. (d) Hurwicz diagram.
   (e) none of the above
18. One of the advantages of Bayes' Theorem is that:
   (a) it incorporates both initial estimates of probabilities and the information about the accuracy of the information source.
   (b) it allows the decision maker to know with certainty all probability values of major outcomes.
   (c) it is the optimal method for decision making under risk.
   (d) none of the above
19. Opportunity loss refers to:
   (a) the expected value of a bad decision.
   (b) the expected loss from a bad decision.
   (c) the difference between the actual payoff and the optimal payoff.
   (d) the regret from not having made a decision.
   (e) none of the above
20. The maximin criteria is a(n) ________ criteria.
   (a) optimistic
   (b) neutral
   (c) pessimistic
   (d) can be any one of the above depending on the problem
   (e) none of the above

Answers

1. **	2. **	3. a	4. a	5. a	6. b	7. c	8. b	9. c	10. d
11. a	12. b	13. c	14. c	15. a	16. c	17. c	18. a	19. c	20. c

Long Answer Questions

LO1 Discuss decision making under certainty

1.1 What is the difference between risk and uncertainty?

LO2 Discuss decision making under risk

2.1 What is a decision tree? What is its importance in decision-making and strategizing for managers?

2.2 How do decision trees help in making decisions under risk?

LO3 Discuss decision making under uncertainty

3.1 What are the different criterions to take decisions under uncertainty? Explain the Savage decision criteria of making decision under uncertainty.

Numerical Questions

1. Using decision tree, evaluate the following situation for two companies. Abel Corporation and Bain Corporation are the only competitors in the digital watch industry. Abel Corporation is considering an investment in technological research to improve its product. Abel can choose from three different investment levels: High, Medium, and Low. Following Abel's investment, Bain Corporation will have to choose between continuing to compete by selling its current product or undertaking an R&D project of its own. Bain can only choose one level of investment, so its choices are Invest or Not Invest. The net payoffs to Abel if it invests High, Medium, or Low given that Bain chooses to Invest would be $60, $50, and $40, respectively, and the corresponding net payoffs

to Bain would be \$5, \$10, and \$15. On the other hand, the net payoffs to Abel if it invests Low, Medium, or High given that Bain chooses to Not Invest would be \$60, \$80, and \$100, respectively, and the corresponding net payoffs to Bain would be \$20, \$15, and \$0. What must Abel choose to do in equilibrium, and what will Bain's response be?

2. Given the accompanying payoff matrix, which alternative would be selected by applying the various decision criteria under uncertainty? Assume that the coefficient of optimism is 0.75.

States of Nature

Strategy	N 1	N2	N3	N4
A	11	15	9	6
B	13	4	14	7
C	10	10	10	10
D	9	11	15	13
E	8	3	7	5

3. The Fitness World Sporting Company wants to move into a new sales region and must determine which of two plants to build. It can build a large plant that costs \$4 million or a small plant that costs \$2 million. The company estimated that the probability that the economy will be booming, normal, or in a recession is 30 percent, 40 percent, and 30 percent, respectively. The company also estimated the present value of net cash flows for each type of plant under each state of the economy to be as indicated in the following payoff matrix. Construct a decision tree for the firm to show which of the two plants the company should build. Assume that the company is risk neutral.

		Large Plant	Small Plant
Present value	Boom	\$10	\$4
Of net cash flows	Normal	6	3
(in millions)	Recession	2	2

Chapter in Review

KEY TERMS

risk
Under conditions of risk, the primary decision criterion is expected value

coefficient of variation
is the ratio of the standard deviation to the expected value, or mean

decision tree
graphic device that shows a sequence of strategic decisions and the expected consequences under each possible set of circumstances

risk aversion
the utility of expected wealth is greater than the expected utility of wealth

risk seeking
if the utility of expected wealth is less than the expected utility of wealth

risk neutral
if the utility of expected wealth is equal to the expected utility of wealth

LO1 **Discuss decision making under certainty.** Under conditions of certainty, the decision maker has complete knowledge of the various states of nature (N_i) that are relevant to the decision and knows which one will occur. This effectively reduces the decision matrix to one column. The decision maker simply chooses the strategy (S_i), course of action or project that yields the greatest payoff. In general, decision making under certainty requires that we find the largest payoff either by maximizing benefits (such as revenue, profit, or utility) or by minimizing costs. Some of the tools available to the decision maker for this purpose are marginal analysis and linear programming.

LO2 **Discuss decision making under risk.** A decision tree is a graphic device that shows a sequence of strategic decisions and the expected consequences under each possible set of circumstances. The construction and analysis of a decision tree is appropriate whenever a sequential series of conditional decisions must be made under condition of risk. By conditional decision, we mean a decision that depends upon circumstances or options that will occur at a later time.

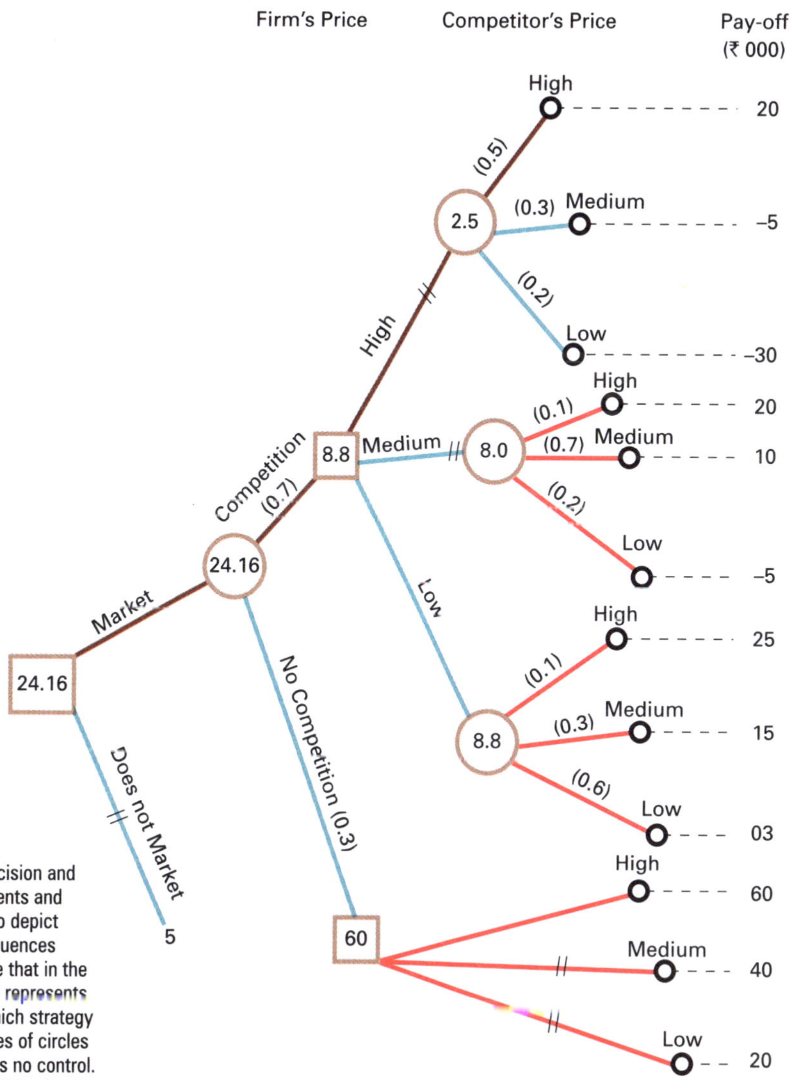

Construction of the decision tree begins with the earliest decision and proceeds forward in time through a series of subsequent events and decisions. At each decision or event the tree branches out to depict each possible course of action, until finally all logical consequences and the resulting payoffs are depicted. It is important to note that in the construction of a decision tree, the branching out of squares represents strategies. Since the decision maker has full control over which strategy is chosen, these branches do not have probabilities. Branches of circles represent states of nature over which the decision maker has no control. Therefore, these branches have probabilities and the probabilities for all branches coming from any one circle must add upto 1.

LO3 **Discuss decision making under uncertainty.** Uncertainty is defined as the state in which one or more alternatives result in a set of possible specific outcomes whose probabilities are either unknown or meaningless. This means that decision making under uncertainty is always subjective. However, if the decision maker can identify the possible states of nature and estimate the resulting payoffs for each available strategy, then two basic approaches are available.

1. The decision maker may use the best available information and his or her own personal judgment and experience to assign subjective probabilities to the possible states of nature. This effectively converts the condition of uncertainty to a condition of risk for which expected value is the criterion of choice.
2. The decision maker may either disregard probability or treat them as equal, which amounts to the same thing. When this approach is taken, four decision criteria are available for evaluation of proposed strategies. These are as follows:
   a. The Wald decision criterion or Maximin criterion: Under this, the strategy that yields the best of the worst results is chosen.
   b. The Hurwicz alpha criterion: It allows the decision maker to inject optimism or pessimism into the decision process.
   c. The Savage decision criterion or minimax regret criterion: This seeks to minimize the opportunity cost of incorrect decisions.
   d. The Laplace decision criterion or Bayes criterion: This gives equal probability to each state of nature.

CHAPTER 13

Learning Outcomes

LO1 Identify examples of resource demand and supply in daily life

LO2 Explain resource supply and demand

LO3 Define opportunity cost and economic rent

LO4 Analyze the factors influencing resource demand

Resource Markets

© LESTER LEFKOWITZ/PHOTOGRAPHER'S CHOICE/GETTY IMAGES

“Why do truck drivers in the United States earn at least 20 times more than bicycle-rickshaw drivers in India?”

Why do surgeons earn twice as much as general practitioners? Why do truck drivers in the United States earn at least 20 times more than bicycle-rickshaw drivers in India? Why are buildings taller in downtown Chicago than those in the city's suburbs? To answer these and other questions, we turn to the demand and supply of resources.

You say you've been through this demand-and-supply drill already? True. But the earlier focus was on the product market—that is, on the market for final goods and services. Goods and services are produced by resources—labor, capital, natural resources, and entrepreneurial ability. Demand and supply in resource markets determine the price and quantity of resources. And the ownership of resources determines the distribution of earnings throughout the economy.

Because your earnings depend on the market value of your resources, you should find a study of resource markets particularly relevant to your future. Certainly one consideration in your career choice is the expected earnings associated with alternative careers. The next three chapters examine how demand and supply interact to establish market prices for various resources.

What do you think?

I'd be willing to work more hours for an increased hourly wage.

Strongly Disagree						*Strongly Agree*
1	2	3	4	5	6	7

LO1 The Once-Over

Just to prove you already know more about resource markets than you may think, try answering the questions that arise in the following examples of resource demand and supply.

Topics discussed in Chapter 13 include:

- Demand and supply of resources
- Oportunity cost and economic rent
- Marginal revenue product
- Marginal resource cost
- Changes in resource demand

Resource Demand

Let's begin with the demand for labor. The manager of Wal-Mart estimates that hiring another sales clerk would increase total revenue by \$500 per week but increase total cost by \$400 per week. Should Wal-Mart hire another sales clerk? Sure, because profit would increase by \$100 per week. *As long as the additional revenue from employing another worker exceeds the additional cost, the firm should hire that worker.*

What about capital? Suppose that you run a lawn service during the summer, getting an average of $50 per lawn. You have all the business you can handle. You mow about 15 lawns a week, for total revenue of $750 a week. You are thinking of upgrading to a larger, faster mower called the Lawn Monster, but it would cost you an extra $500 per week. The bigger mower would cut your time per lawn in half, enabling you to mow 30 lawns per week, so your total revenue would double to $1,500. Should you make the switch? Because the additional revenue of $750 exceeds the additional cost of $500, you should move up to the Monster.

What about natural resources? A neighbor offers Farmer Jones the chance to lease 100 acres of farmland. Jones figures that farming the extra land would cost $70 per acre but would yield $60 per acre in additional revenue. Should Jones lease the extra land? What do you think? Because the additional cost of farming that land would exceed the additional revenue, the answer is no.

These examples show that a *producer demands another unit of a resource as long as its marginal revenue exceeds its marginal cost.*

Resource Supply

You likely also understand the logic behind resource supply. Suppose you are trying to decide between two jobs that are identical except that one pays more than the other. Is there any question which one you'll take? If the working conditions are equally attractive, you would choose the higher-paying job. Now let's say your choice is between two jobs that pay the same. One has normal 9-to-5 hours, but the other starts at 5 A.M., an hour when your body tends to reject conscious activity. Which would you choose? You would pick the one that suits your tastes.

People supply their resources to the highest-paying alternative, other things constant. Because other things are not always constant, people must be paid more for jobs less suited to their tastes. Your utility depends on both monetary and nonmonetary aspects of the job. Generally, people must be paid more for jobs that are dirty, dangerous, dull, exhausting, illegal, low status, have no future, have no benefits, and involve inconvenient hours than for jobs that are clean, safe, interesting, energizing, legal, high status, have bright prospects, have good benefits, and involve convenient hours.

LO2 The Demand and Supply of Resources

In the market for goods and services—that is, in the product market—households are the demanders and firms are suppliers. Households demand the goods and services that maximize utility, and firms supply the goods and services that maximize profit. In the resource market, roles are reversed: Firms are demanders and households are suppliers. Firms demand resources to maximize profit, and households supply resources to maximize utility. *Any differences between the profit-maximizing goals of firms and the utility-maximizing goals of households are sorted out through voluntary exchange in markets.*

Exhibit 1 presents the market for a particular resource—in this case, carpenters. As you can see, the demand curve slopes downward and the supply curve slopes upward. *Like the demand and supply for final goods and services, the demand and supply for resources depend on the willingness and ability of buyers and sellers to engage in market exchange.* This market converges to the equilibrium wage, or the market price, for this type of labor.

© eSTOCK PHOTO/ALAMY

The Market Demand for Resources

Why do firms employ resources? Resources produce goods and services, which firms try to sell for a profit. A firm values not the resource itself but the resource's ability to produce goods and services. Because the value of any resource depends on what it produces, the demand for a resource is said to be a derived demand—arising from the demand for the final product. For example, a carpenter's pay derives from the demand for the carpenter's output, such as a cabinet or a new deck. A professional baseball player's pay derives from the demand for ballgames. A truck driver's pay derives from the demand for transporting goods. The derived nature of resource demand helps explain why professional baseball players usually earn more than professional hockey players, why brain surgeons earn more than tree surgeons, and why drivers of big rigs earn more than drivers of delivery vans. Derived demand also explains why, in the face of a global financial crisis, some financial industry executives accepted deep cuts in bonuses and salaries.[1]

The market demand for a particular resource is the sum of demands for that resource in all its different uses. For example, the market demand for carpenters adds together the demands for carpenters in residential and commercial construction, remodeling, cabinetmaking, and so on. Similarly, the market demand for timber sums the demand for this resource as lumber, railway ties, furniture, pencils, toothpicks, paper products, firewood, and so on. The demand curve for a resource, like the demand for the goods produced by that resource, slopes downward, as depicted in Exhibit 1.

As the price of a resource falls, producers are more willing and able to employ that resource. Consider first the producer's greater willingness to hire resources as the resource price falls. In developing the demand curve for a particular resource, we assume the prices of other resources remain constant. So if the price of a particular resource falls, it becomes cheaper compared with other resources that could produce the same output. Firms therefore are more willing to hire this resource rather than hire other, now relatively more costly, resources. Thus, we observe *substitution in production*—carpenters for masons, coal for oil, security alarms for security guards, and backhoes for grave diggers, as the relative prices of carpenters, coal, security alarms, and backhoes fall.

A lower price for a resource also increases a producer's *ability* to hire that resource. For example, if the wage of carpenters falls, home builders can hire more carpenters for the same total cost.

Exhibit 1

Resource Market for Carpenters

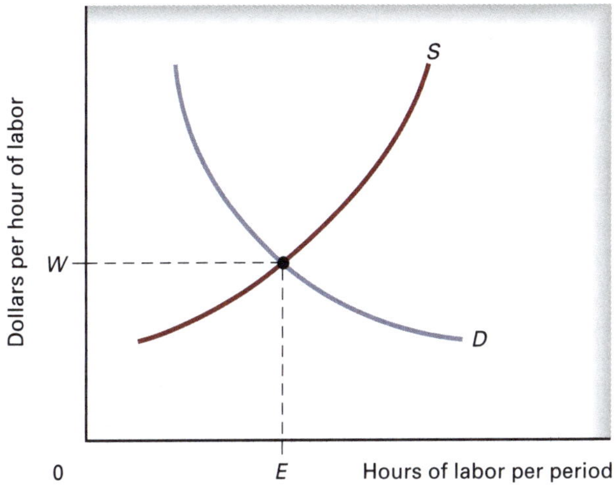

Fast Facts—World's Best Paid Athletes

The following list details the athletes with the top estimated earnings (including endorsements) from June 2007 to June 2008. Notice there are no athletes from the National Football League or Major League Baseball on this list. What does this tell you about the global market demand for football or baseball players versus the types of athletes on the list? What do you think this list would look like if it were restricted to American athletes?

Athlete	Nationality	Sport	Estimated Earnings
Tiger Woods	American	Golf	$115 million
David Beckham	British	Soccer	$50 million
Michael Jordan	American	Basketball	$45 million
Phil Mickelson	American	Golf	$45 million
Kimi Raikkonen	Finnish	Auto-Racing	$44 million
Kobe Bryant	American	Basketball	$39 million
LeBron James	American	Basketball	$38 million
Ronaldinho	Brazilian	Soccer	$37 million
Valentino Rossi	Italian	Motorcycle Racing	$35 million
Roger Federer	Swiss	Tennis	$35 million

SOURCES: Lacey Rose, "The World's Best Paid Male Athletes," *Forbes*, 8 August 2008. Available at http://www.forbes.com/sportsbusiness/2008/08/05/woods-beckham-jordan-biz-sports-cx_lr_0806athletes.html. Tom Van Riper and Kurt Badenhausen, "Top-Earning Female Athletes," *Forbes*, 22 July 2008. Available at http://www.forbes.com/2008/07/22/women-athletes-endorsements-biz-sports-cx_tvr_kb_0722athletes.html.

© JOHN WALTON/PA PHOTOS/LANDOV

1. "Wachovia CEO Joins Ranks of Execs Forgoing Bonuses," *BusinessWeek*, 9 December 2008. Available at http://www.businessweek.com/ap/financialnews/D94VHIL01.htm.

derived demand
demand that arises from the demand for the product the resource produces

The lower resource price means the firm is *more able* to employ the resource.

The Market Supply of Resources

The market supply curve for a resource sums all the individual supply curves for that resource. Resource suppliers are more *willing* and more *able* to increase quantity supplied as the resource price increases, so the market supply curve slopes upward, as in Exhibit 1. Resource suppliers are more *willing* because a higher resource price, other things constant, means more goods and services can be purchased with the earnings from each unit of the resource supplied. Resource prices are signals about the rewards for supplying resources. A high resource price tells the resource owner, "The market will reward you more for what you supply." Higher prices draw resources from lower-valued uses, including leisure. For example, as the wage for carpenters increases, the quantity of labor supplied increases. Some carpenters give up leisure to work more.

The second reason a resource supply curve slopes upward is that resource owners are more *able* to increase the quantity supplied as the resource price increases. For example, a higher carpenter's wage means more apprentices can undergo the extensive training to become carpenters. A higher wage *enables* resource suppliers to increase their quantity supplied. Similarly, a higher timber price enables loggers to harvest trees in less accessible forests, a higher gold price enables miners to extract the metal from lower grade ore, and a higher oil price enables producers to drill deeper and explore more remote parts of the world.

Temporary and Permanent Resource Price Differences

People have a strong interest in selling their resources where they are valued the most. *Resources tend to flow to their highest-valued use.* If, for example, carpenters can earn more building homes than making furniture, they shift into home building until wages in the two areas are equal. Because resource owners seek the highest pay, *other things constant*, earnings should tend toward equality across the different uses. For example, suppose carpenters who build homes earn \$25 per hour, which is \$5 more than carpenters who make furniture. This difference is shown in Exhibit 2 by an initial wage of \$25 per hour in panel (a) and an initial wage of \$20 per hour in panel (b). This gap encourages some carpenters to move from furniture making into home building, pulling up the wage in furniture making and driving down the wage in home building. Carpenters migrate into home building until wages equalize. In Exhibit 2, labor supply shifts leftward for furniture making and rightward for home building until the wage reaches \$24 in both

Exhibit 2

Market for Carpenters in Alternative Uses

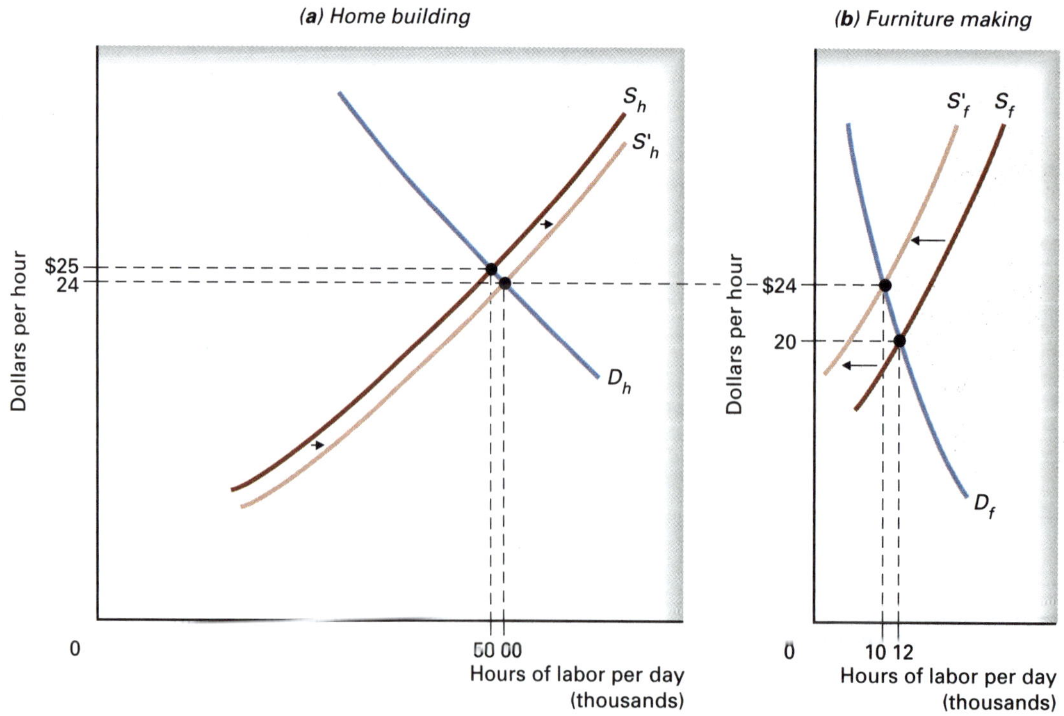

markets. Note that 2,000 hours of labor per day shift from furniture making to home building. *As long as the nonmonetary benefits of supplying resources to alternative uses are identical and as long as resources are freely mobile, resources adjust across uses until they earn the same in different uses.*

Sometimes earnings appear to differ between seemingly similar resources. For example, corporate economists on average earn more than academic economists, and land in the city goes for more than land in the country. As you will now see, these differences also reflect the workings of demand and supply.

Temporary Differences in Resource Prices

Resource prices might differ temporarily across markets because adjustment takes time. For example, sometimes wage differences occur among workers who appear equally qualified. As you have seen, however, a difference between the prices of similar resources prompts resource owners and firms to make adjustments that drive resource prices toward equality, as with the carpenters in Exhibit 2. The process may take years, but when resource markets are free to adjust, price differences trigger the reallocation of resources, which equalizes earnings for similar resources.

Permanent Differences in Resource Prices

Not all resource price differences cause reallocation. For example, land along New York's Fifth Avenue sells for as much as $36,000 a *square yard!* For that amount, you could buy several acres in Upstate New York. Yet such a difference does not prompt upstaters to supply their land to New York City—obviously that's impossible. Likewise, the price of farmland itself varies widely, reflecting differences in the land's fertility and location. Such differences do not trigger shifts of resource supply. Similarly, certain wage differentials stem in part from the different costs of acquiring the education and training needed to perform particular tasks. This difference explains why brain surgeons earn more than tree surgeons, why ophthalmologists earn more than optometrists, and why airline pilots earn more than truck drivers.

Differences in the nonmonetary aspects of similar jobs also lead to pay differences. For example, other things constant, most people would require higher pay to work in a grimy factory than in a pleasant office. Similarly, academic economists earn less than corporate economists, in part because academic economists typically have more freedom in their daily schedules, their attire, their choices of research topics, and even in their public statements.

Some price differences are temporary because they spark shifts of resource supply away from lower-paid uses and toward higher-paid uses. Other price differences cause no such shifts and are permanent. Permanent price differences are explained by a *lack of resource mobility* (urban land versus rural land), *differences in the inherent quality of the resource* (fertile land versus scrubland), *differences in the time and money involved in developing the necessary skills* (certified public accountant versus file clerk), or *differences in nonmonetary aspects of the job* (lifeguard at Malibu Beach versus prison guard at San Quentin).

© NBAE/GETTY IMAGES / © DON FARRALL/PHOTODISC/GETTY IMAGES

LO3 Opportunity Cost and Economic Rent

Shaquille O'Neal earned about $20 million in 2009 playing basketball plus at least $10 million

more from product endorsements, including his sneaker deal. But he would probably have been willing to play basketball and endorse products for less. The question is, how much less? What is his best alternative? Suppose his best alternative is to become a full-time rap artist, something he now does in his spare time (as of 2009, he had released six rap albums). Suppose, as a full-time rapper, he could earn $1 million a year, including endorsements. And suppose, aside from the pay gap, he's indifferent between basketball and rap, so the nonmonetary aspects of the two jobs even out. Thus, he must be paid at least $1 million to remain in basketball, and this represents his opportunity cost. *Opportunity cost is what that resource could earn in its best alternative use.*

The amount O'Neal earns in excess of his opportunity cost is called *economic rent.* **Economic rent** is that portion of a resource's earnings that exceeds the amount necessary to keep the resource in its present use. Economic rent is, as the saying goes, "pure gravy." In O'Neal's case, economic rent is $29 million. Economic rent is producer surplus earned by resource suppliers. The *division* of earnings between opportunity cost and economic rent depends on the resource owner's elasticity of supply. *In general, the less elastic the resource supply, the greater the economic rent as a proportion of total earnings.* To develop a feel for the difference between opportunity cost and economic rent, let's consider three resource markets.

economic rent
portion of a resource's total earnings that exceeds its opportunity cost; earnings greater than the amount required to keep the resource in its present use

Resource Market A:

All Earnings Are Economic Rent

If the supply of a resource to a particular market is perfectly inelastic, that resource has no alternative use. Thus, there is no opportunity cost, and all earnings are economic rent. For example, scrubland in the high plains of Montana has no use other than for grazing cattle. The supply of this land is depicted by the red vertical line in panel (a) of Exhibit 3, which indicates that the 10 million acres have no alternative use. Because supply is fixed, the rent paid to graze cattle on this land has no effect on the quantity of land supplied. *The land's opportunity cost is zero, so all earnings are economic rent, shown by the blue-shaded area.* Here, fixed supply determines the equilibrium quantity of the resource, but demand determines the equilibrium price.

Resource Market B:

All Earnings Are Opportunity Cost

At the other extreme is the market in which a resource can earn as much in its best alternative use as in its present use. This situation is illustrated by the perfectly elastic supply curve in panel (b) of Exhibit 3, which shows the market for janitors in the local school system. Here, janitors earn $10 an hour and supply 1,000 hours of labor per day. If the school system paid less than $10 per hour, janitors could find jobs elsewhere, perhaps in nearby factories, where

Exhibit 3

Opportunity Cost and Economic Rent

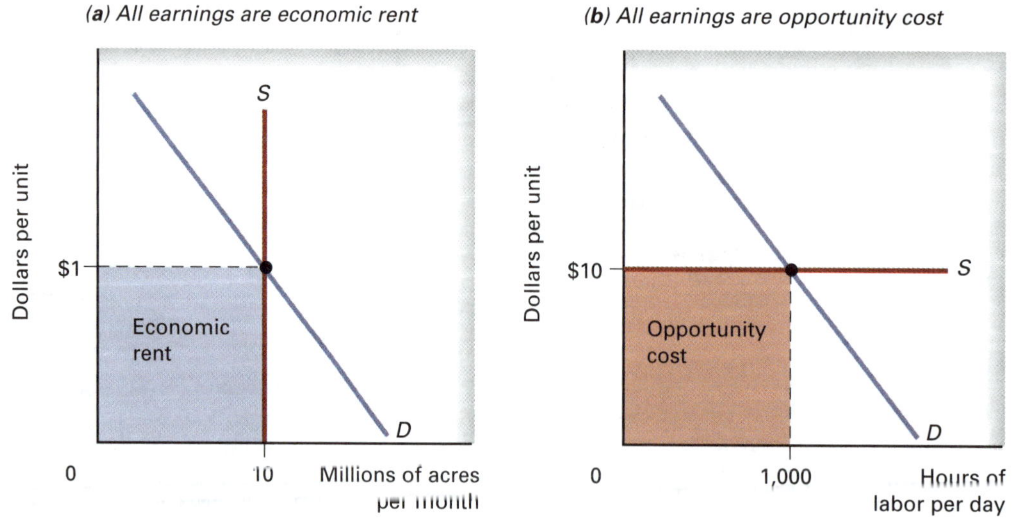

the wage is $10 per hour. *All earnings reflect opportunity cost*. There is no economic rent. In this resource market, the horizontal supply curve determines the equilibrium wage, but demand determines the equilibrium quantity.

Resource Market C:

Earnings Include Both Economic Rent and Opportunity Cost

If the supply curve slopes upward, most resource suppliers earn economic rent in addition to their opportunity cost. For example, if the market wage for unskilled work in your college community increases from $8 to $16 per hour, the quantity of labor supplied would increase, as would the economic rent earned by these workers. This market occurs in panel (c) of Exhibit 3, where the pink shading identifies opportunity cost and the blue shading, economic rent. If the wage increases from $8 to $16 per hour, the quantity supplied increases by 5,000 hours. For those who were willing to work for $8 per hour, the difference between $8 and $16 is economic rent. *When resource supply slopes upward, as it usually does, earnings consist of both opportunity cost and economic rent*. In the case of an upward-sloping supply curve and a downward-sloping demand curve, both demand and supply determine equilibrium price and quantity.

Note that specialized resources tend to earn a higher proportion of economic rent than do resources with alternative uses. Thus, Shaquille O'Neal earns a greater *proportion* of his income as economic rent than does the janitor who cleans his team's locker room.

Exhibit 3, cont.

Opportunity Cost and Economic Rent

(c) Earnings divide between economic rent and opportunity cost

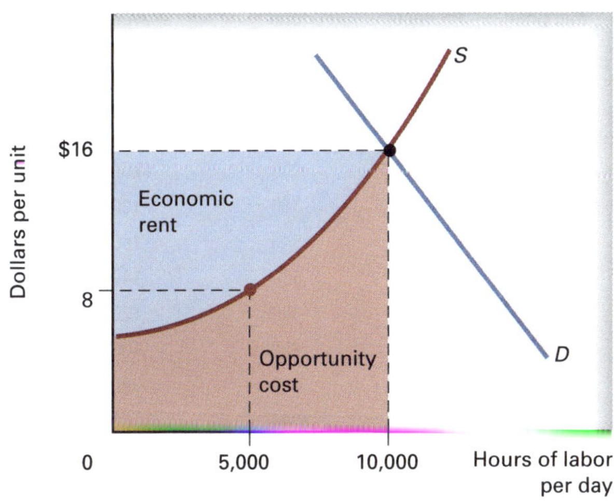

O'Neal would take a huge pay cut if he didn't play professional basketball, but the janitor could probably find another semiskilled job that would pay nearly as much.

To review: Given a resource demand curve that slopes downward, when the resource supply curve is vertical (perfectly inelastic), all earnings are economic rent; when that supply curve is horizontal (perfectly elastic), all earnings are opportunity cost; and when that supply curve slopes upward (an elasticity greater than zero but less than infinity), earnings divide between economic rent and opportunity cost. Remember, *the opportunity cost of a resource is what that resource could earn in its best alternative use. Economic rent is earnings in excess of opportunity cost.* Economic rent to a resource holder is like economic profit to the firm.

> "Economic rent is earnings in excess of opportunity cost."

This completes our introduction to resource demand and supply. In the balance of this chapter, we take a closer look at resource demand. The determinants of resource demand are largely the same whether we are talking about labor, capital, or natural resources. The supply of different resources, however, has certain peculiarities depending on the resource, so the supply of resources is taken up in the next chapter.

LO4 A Closer Look at Resource Demand

Although production usually involves many resources, we cut the analysis down to size by focusing on a single resource, assuming that employment of other resources remains constant. As usual, we assume that firms try to maximize profit and households try to maximize utility.

The Firm's Demand for a Resource

You may recall that when production costs were first introduced, we considered a moving company, where

© ISTOCKPHOTO/THINKSTOCK

labor was the only variable resource in the short run. We examined the relationship between the quantity of labor employed and the amount of furniture moved per day. The same approach is used in Exhibit 4, where only one resource varies. Column (1) lists possible employment levels of the variable resource, here measured as workers per day. Column (2) lists the amount produced, or total product, and column (3) lists the marginal product. The *marginal product* of labor is the change in total product from employing one more unit of labor.

With only one worker, total product is 10 units as is the marginal product. The marginal product of a second worker is 9 units. Notice in this example that diminishing marginal returns set in immediately—that is, right after the first worker.

Although labor is the variable resource here, we could examine the marginal product of any resource. For example, we could consider the number of lawns cut per week by varying the quantity of capital. We might start off with very little capital—imagine cutting grass with scissors—and then move up to a push mower, a power mower, and the Lawn Monster. By holding labor constant and varying the quantity of capital employed, we could compute the marginal product of capital. Likewise, we could compute the marginal product of natural resources by examining crop production for varying amounts of farmland, holding other inputs constant.

Marginal Revenue Product

The important question is: what happens to the firm's *revenue* when additional workers are hired? The first three columns of Exhibit 4 show how output changes with more workers. The *marginal revenue product* of labor indicates how much total revenue changes as more labor is employed, other things constant. The **marginal revenue product** of any resource is the change in the firm's total revenue resulting from employing an additional unit of the resource, other things constant. You could think of the marginal revenue product as the firm's "marginal benefit" from hiring one more unit of the resource. *Marginal revenue product depends on how much additional output the resource produces and at what price that output is sold.*

Selling Output in Competitive Markets

The calculation of marginal revenue product is simplest when the firm sells in a perfectly competitive

Exhibit 4

Marginal Revenue Product When a Firm Sells in a Competitive Market

(1) Workers per Day	(2) Total Product	(3) Marginal Product	(4) Product Price	(5) Total Revenue (5) = (2) × (4)	(6) Marginal Revenue Product (6) = (3) × (4)
0	0	—	$20	$ 0	—
1	10	10	20	200	$200
2	19	9	20	380	180
3	27	8	20	540	160
4	34	7	20	680	140
5	40	6	20	800	120
6	45	5	20	900	100
7	49	4	20	980	80
8	52	3	20	1040	60

© RYAN MCVAY/PHOTODISC/GETTY IMAGES

marginal revenue product the change in total revenue when an additional unit of a resource is hired, other things constant market, which is the assumption underlying Exhibit 4. An individual firm in perfect competition can sell as much as it wants at the market price. The marginal revenue product, listed in column (6) of Exhibit 4, is the change in total revenue that results from hiring an additional unit of the resource. For the perfectly competitive firm, the marginal revenue product is simply the marginal product of the resource multiplied by the product price of $20. Notice that because of diminishing returns, the marginal revenue product falls steadily as the firm employs more of the resource.

Selling Output with Some Market Power

If the firm has some market power in the product market—that is, some ability to set the price—the demand curve for that firm's output slopes downward. To sell more, the firm must lower its price. Exhibit 5 reproduces the first two columns of Exhibit 4. But column (3) now shows the price at which that output can be sold. Total output multiplied by the price yields the firm's total revenue, which appears in column (4).

The marginal revenue product of labor, which is the change in total revenue from adding another worker, appears in column (5). For example, the first worker produced 10 units per day, which sell for $40 each, yielding total revenue and marginal revenue of $400. Hiring the second worker adds 9 more units to total product, but to sell 9 more units, the firm must lower the price from $40 to $35.20. Total revenue increases to $668.80, which means the marginal revenue product from hiring a second worker is $268.80. For firms selling with some market power, the marginal revenue product curve slopes downward both because of diminishing marginal returns and because additional output can be sold only if the price falls.

Again, *marginal revenue product is the additional revenue from hiring another worker*. A profit maximizing firm is willing and able to pay as much as the marginal revenue product for an additional unit of the resource. Thus, *the marginal revenue product curve can be thought of as the firm's demand curve for that resource.* You could think of the marginal revenue product curve as the marginal benefit to the firm of hiring each additional unit of the resource.

To review: Whether a firm sells its product in a competitive market or sells with some market power, the marginal revenue product of a resource is the change in total revenue resulting from a 1-unit change in that resource, other things constant. The marginal revenue product curve of a resource is also the demand curve for that resource—it shows the most a firm would be willing and able to pay for each additional unit of the resource. For firms selling in competitive markets, the marginal revenue product curve slopes downward only because of diminishing marginal returns to the resource. For firms selling with some market power, the marginal revenue product curve slopes downward both because of diminishing marginal returns and because additional output can be sold only if the price falls. *For all types of firms, the marginal revenue product is the change in total revenue resulting from hiring an additional unit of the resource.*

© RYAN MCVAY/PHOTODISC/GETTY IMAGES

Exhibit 5

The Marginal Revenue Product When a Firm Sells with Market Power

(1) Workers per Day	(2) Total Product	(3) Product Price	(4) Total Revenue (4) = (2) × (3)	(5) Marginal Revenue Product
0	0	—	—	—
1	10	$40.00	$ 400.00	$400.00
2	19	35.20	668.80	268.80
3	27	31.40	847.80	179.00
4	34	27.80	945.20	97.40
5	40	25.00	1000.00	54.80
6	45	22.50	1012.50	12.50
7	49	20.50	1004.50	−8.00
8	52	19.00	988.00	−16.50

Marginal Resource Cost

If we know a firm's marginal revenue product, can we determine how much labor that firm should employ to maximize profit? Not yet, because we also need to know how much labor costs the firm. Specifically, what is the **marginal resource cost**—what does another unit of labor cost the firm? The typical firm hires such a tiny fraction of the available resource that its hiring decision has no effect on the market price of the resource. Thus, each firm usually faces a given market price for the resource and decides only on how much to hire at that price.

For example, panel (a) of Exhibit 6 shows the market for factory workers, measured as workers per day. The intersection of market demand and market supply determines the market wage of $100 dollars per day. Panel (b) shows the situation for the firm. The market wage becomes the firm's marginal resource cost of labor. The *marginal resource* cost curve is the horizontal line drawn at the

marginal resource cost
the change in total cost when an additional unit of a resource is hired, other things constant

$100 level in panel (b); this is the labor supply curve to the firm. Panel (b) also shows the marginal revenue product curve, or resource demand curve, based on the schedule presented in Exhibit 4. The marginal revenue product curve indicates the additional revenue the firm gets from adding another worker.

Given a marginal resource cost of $100 per worker per day, how much labor should the firm employ to maximize profit? *The firm hires more labor as long as doing so adds more to revenue than to cost—that is, as long as the marginal revenue product exceeds the marginal resource cost.* The firm stops hiring more labor once the two are equal. If marginal resource cost is a constant $100 per worker, the firm hires six workers per day because the marginal revenue product from hiring a sixth worker equals $100. Thus, the firm hires additional resources until

Marginal revenue product = Marginal resource cost

This equality holds for all resources employed, whether the firm sells in competitive markets or sells with some market power. Profit maximization occurs where labor's marginal revenue product equals the market wage. Based on data presented so far, we can't yet determine the firm's actual profit because we don't yet know about the firm's other costs. We do know, however, that in Exhibit 6, a seventh worker would add $100 to cost but would add less than that to revenue, so hiring a seventh worker would reduce the firm's profit (or increase its loss).

Exhibit 6

Market Equilibrium for a Resource and the Firm's Employment Decision

***(a)** Market*

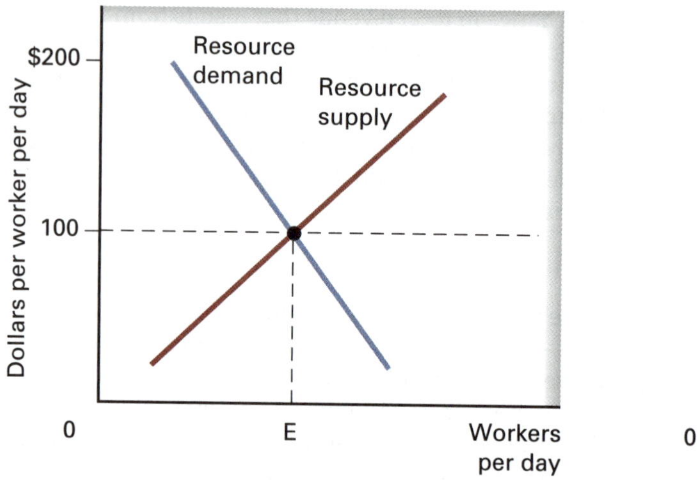

Whether a firm sells in competitive markets or with some market power, the profit-maximizing level of employment occurs where the marginal revenue product of labor equals its marginal resource cost. Similarly, profit-maximizing employment of other resources, such as natural resources and capital, occurs where their respective marginal revenue products equal their marginal resource costs. Each unit of a resource must "pull its own weight"—that is, each unit must bring in additional revenue that at least equals the additional cost.

> "Maximum profit (or minimum loss) occurs where the marginal revenue from an *input* equals its marginal resource cost."

© DYNAMIC GRAPHICS/JUPITERIMAGES

In earlier chapters, you learned how to find the profit-maximizing level of output. Maximum profit (or minimum loss) occurs where the marginal revenue from *output* equals its marginal cost. Likewise, maximum profit (or minimum loss) occurs where the marginal revenue from an input equals its marginal resource cost. Although the first rule focuses on output and the second on input, the two are equivalent ways of deriving the same principle of profit maximization.

Exhibit 6, cont.

Market Equilibrium for a Resource and the Firm's Employment Decision

(b) Firm

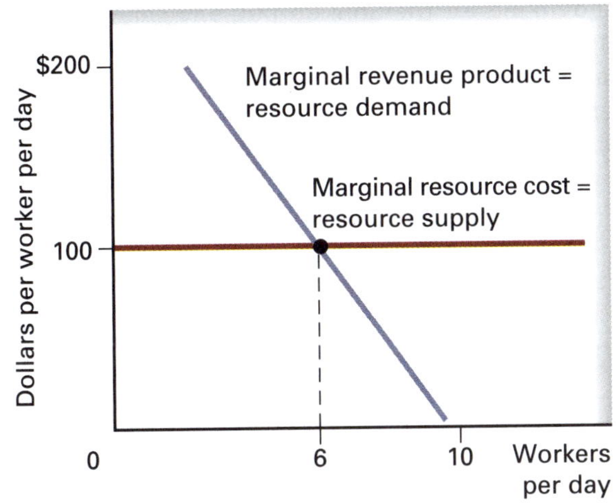

For example, in Exhibit 6, the firm maximizes profit by hiring six workers when the market wage is $100 per day. Exhibit 4 indicates that a sixth worker adds five units to output, which sell for $20 each, yielding labor's marginal revenue product of $100. The *marginal revenue* of that output is the change in total revenue from selling another unit of output, which is $20. The *marginal cost* of that output is the change in total cost, $100, divided by the change in output, 5 units; so the marginal cost of output is $100/5, or $20. Thus, *in equilibrium, the marginal revenue of output equals its marginal cost.* Now that you have some idea of how to derive the demand for a resource, let's discuss what could shift the resource demand curve.

Changes in Resource Demand

As we have seen, a resource's marginal revenue product depends on the resource's marginal product and the price at which that product is sold. Two things can change a resource's marginal product: (1) a change in the amount of other resources employed and (2) a change in technology. Only one thing can change the price of the product: a change in demand for the product. Let's consider first changes that could affect marginal product, then changes that could affect demand for the product.

Change in Other Resources Employed

Although our focus so far has been on a single input, in reality the marginal product of any resource depends on the quantity and quality of other resources used in production. Sometimes resources are *substitutes*. For example, coal substitutes for oil in generating electricity. And ATMs substitute for tellers in handling bank transactions. If two resources are **substitutes**, an increase in the price of one increases the demand for the other. An increase in the price of oil increases the demand for coal, and an increase in the market wage of tellers increases the demand for ATMs.

Sometimes resources are *complements*—trucks and truck drivers, for example. If two resources are **complements**, a decrease in the price of one leads to an increase in the demand for the other. If the price of tractor-trailers decreases, the quantity demanded increases, which increases the demand for truck drivers. More generally, any increase in the quantity and quality of a complementary resource, such as trucks, raises the marginal productivity of the resource in question, such as truck drivers, and so increases the demand for that resource. A bigger and better truck makes the driver more productive. One big reason a truck driver in the United States earns much more than a bicycle-rickshaw driver in India is the truck.

> TWO THINGS CAN CHANGE A RESOURCE'S MARGINAL PRODUCT: (1) A CHANGE IN THE AMOUNT OF OTHER RESOURCES EMPLOYED AND (2) A CHANGE IN TECHNOLOGY.

Changes in Technology

Technological improvements can boost the productivity of some resources but make other resources obsolete. The introduction of computer-controlled machines increased the demand for computer-trained machinists but reduced the demand for machinists without computer skills. The development of synthetic fibers, such as rayon and Orlon, increased the demand for acrylics and polyesters but reduced the demand for natural fibers, such as cotton and wool. Breakthroughs in fiber-optic and satellite telecommunication increased the demand for fiberglass and satellites and reduced the demand for copper wire.

resource substitutes resources that substitute in production; an increase in the price of one resource increases the demand for the other

resource complements resources that enhance one another's productivity; an increase in the price of one resource decreases the demand for the other

Computer programs are changing job prospects in fields such as law, medicine, accounting, and architecture. For example, Quicken's WillMaker software has written more wills than any lawyer alive. In medicine, software such as Skyscape's 5-Minute Clinical Consult helps doctors diagnose more than a thousand medical and surgical conditions. In accounting, software such as TurboTax completes tax forms with ease. And in architecture, three-dimensional modeling programs such as 3D Home Architect help configure all aspects of a structure. As software and hardware get cheaper, better, and easier to use, the demand for some professional services declines.

Changes in the Demand for the Final Product

Because the demand for a resource is *derived* from the demand for the final output, any change in the demand for output affects resource demand. For example, an increase in the demand for automobiles increases their market price and thereby increases the marginal revenue product of autoworkers.

In summary: The demand for a resource depends on its marginal revenue product, which is the change in total revenue resulting from employing one more unit of the resource. Any change that increases a resource's marginal revenue product increases resource demand.

The Optimal Use of More Than One Resource

As long as marginal revenue product exceeds marginal resource cost, a firm can increase profit or reduce a loss by employing more of that resource. Again, the firm hires more of a resource until the marginal revenue product just equals the marginal resource cost. This principle holds for each resource employed. The opening paragraph asked why buildings in downtown Chicago are taller than those in the suburbs. Land and capital, to a large extent, substitute in the production of building space. Because land is more expensive downtown than in the suburbs, builders downtown substitute capital for land, building up instead of out. Hence, buildings are taller closer to the center of the city and are tallest in cities where land is most expensive. Buildings in Chicago and New York City are taller than those in Salt Lake City and Tucson, for example.

The high price of land in metropolitan areas has other implications for the efficient employment of resources. For example, in New York City, as in many large cities, food vending carts seem to be on every corner. New York City

Increased demand for synthetic fibers reduced demand for natural fibers.

© PHOTOLINK/PHOTODISC/GETTY IMAGES

© DAMIR FRKOVIC/MASTERFILE

has more than 3,000 of them. Why are these carts so popular? Consider the resources used to supply sidewalk food: land, labor, capital, entrepreneurial ability, plus food. Which of these do you suppose is most expensive in New York City? Retail space along Madison Avenue's Golden Mile can rent for an average $800 a year per square foot. Because operating a vending cart requires about 6 square yards (or 54 square feet), renting that space could cost as much as $43,000 a year. Aside from the necessary public permits, however, space on the public sidewalk is free to vendors. Profit-maximizing street vendors substitute public sidewalks for costly commercial space. (Incidentally, does free public space mean sidewalk vendors earn long-run economic profit?)

Final Word

A firm hires each resource until the marginal revenue product of that resource equals its marginal cost. The objective of profit maximization ensures that to produce any given level of output, firms employ the least-cost combination of resources and thereby use the economy's resources most efficiently. Although our focus has been on the marginal productivity of each resource, we should keep in mind that an orchestra of resources combines to produce output, so the marginal productivity of a particular resource depends in part on the amount and quality of other resources employed.

Multiple Choice Questions

1. The resource market is different from the product market because
   a. in the resource market, firms don't maximize profit
   b. in the resource market, households don't maximize utility
   c. in the resource market, firms are demanders and households are suppliers
   d. supply and demand do not apply in the resource market
   e. supply and demand do not apply in the product market
2. As the price of land decreases along its demand curve, the relative price of land
   a. increases because the prices of other resources have also decreased
   b. decreases because the prices of other resources have also decreased
   c. increases because the prices of other resources have increased
   d. decreases because the prices of other resources are held constant
   e. remains constant because the prices of other resources also increase
3. Along the supply curve of lifeguards at local public pools,
   a. the wage paid to lifeguards is held constant
   b. the number of lifeguards is held constant
   c. the wage paid to lifeguards at private clubs is held constant
   d. the demand for lifeguards is assumed constant
   e. the admission price to these public pools rises as the wage rate for lifeguards increases
4. Other things equal, similar resources in alternative uses will be paid
   a. different amounts based on their different uses
   b. different amounts based on the alternative uses
   c. different amounts if resources are mobile
   d. similar amounts if resources are not mobile
   e. similar amounts if resources are mobile
5. Suppose that the wage for drive-thru clerks is $7 an hour at Burger King and $6.50 at McDonald's. The jobs are alike in all other respects. We would expect
   a. an increase in the supply of and demand for drive-thru clerks at Burger King
   b. an increase in the supply and a decrease in the demand for drive-thru clerks at Burger King
   c. a decrease in the supply of drive-thru clerks at Burger King but no change in demand
   d. an increase in the supply of drive-thru clerks at Burger King but no change in demand
   e. a decrease in the supply of and demand for drive-thru clerks at Burger King
6. We see permanent price differentials in land because
   a. the demand for land is high
   b. land has few uses
   c. location is the inherent quality that often determines its value
   d. real estate brokers are inefficient
   e. land is not traded in free markets
7. Which of the following is an example of a temporary price differential in a resource market?
   a. land downtown is more expensive than land in the suburbs
   b. a superstar professional basketball player is paid more than the average professional player
   c. cable television installers have a higher wage than telephone installers
   d. an airline pilot is paid more than a flight attendant
   e. a worker in a toxic waste plant earns more than a teacher
8. If all of the returns to a resource are in the form of economic rent,
   a. the price of that resource is determined exclusively by supply
   b. the price of that resource is determined exclusively by demand
   c. the price and quantity of that resource are determined exclusively by supply
   d. the price and quantity of that resource are determined exclusively by demand
   e. the equilibrium price is zero
9. If all of the income paid to a resource is opportunity costs,
   a. the price and quantity of that resource are determined exclusively by supply

b. the price and quantity of that resource are determined exclusively by demand
c. the quantity of that resource is determined exclusively by supply
d. the price of that resource is determined exclusively by demand
e. the quantity of that resource is determined exclusively by demand

10. Consider two resource markets in which the demand curves slope downward. In market A, the supply curve is horizontal, equilibrium price is $6, and 100 units of the resource are hired. In market B, the supply curve is vertical, equilibrium price is $20, and 30 units of the resource are hired. Which of the following is true?
    a. Total resource earnings are the same in both markets.
    b. Total resource earnings are greater in market A.
    c. Total resource earnings are greater in market B.
    d. There is more economic rent in market A.
    e. There is derived demand in market A, but not in market B.

11. Consider two resource markets in which the demand curves slope downward. In market A, the supply curve is horizontal, equilibrium price is $6, and 100 units of the resource are hired. In market B, the supply curve is vertical, equilibrium price is $20, and 30 units of the resource are hired. Which of the following is true?
    a. All of the resource earnings in market A are economic rent.
    b. All of the resource earnings in both markets are economic rent.
    c. All of the resource earnings in market B are economic rent.
    d. None of the resource earnings in either market is an opportunity cost.
    e. None of the resource earnings in either market is economic rent.

12. Consider two resource markets in which the demand curves slope downward. In market A, the supply curve is horizontal, equilibrium price is $10, and 90 units of the resource are hired. In market B, the supply curve is vertical, equilibrium price is $30, and 40 units of the resource are hired. Which of the following is correct?
    a. In market A, total earnings = $900, economic rent = $450, opportunity cost = $450
    b. In market A, total earnings = $900, economic rent = $0, opportunity cost = $900
    c. In market A, total earnings = $900, economic rent = $900, opportunity cost = $0
    d. In market B, total earnings = $1,200, economic rent = $300, opportunity cost = $900
    e. In market B, total earnings = $1,200, economic rent = $0, opportunity cost = $1,200

13. Which resource earns the highest economic rent as a proportion of total earnings?
    a. a resource specialized in one task
    b. a nonspecialized resource
    c. a resource with inelastic demand
    d. a resource in low demand
    e. a resource with elastic demand

14. For a firm hiring a resource in a perfectly competitive resource market, its demand curve for the resource is its
    a. marginal product curve
    b. marginal revenue product curve
    c. marginal resource cost curve
    d. marginal revenue curve
    e. total revenue curve

15. Under certain conditions, the slope of the marginal revenue product curve reflects the combined effects of diminishing marginal returns and a declining price of the product the firm sells. What are these conditions?
    a. The firm must be a price searcher in both the product market and the resource market.
    b. The firm must be a price searcher in the product market, regardless of whether it is a resource price searcher.
    c. The firm must be a price searcher in the product market but not necessarily in a perfectly competitive resource market.
    d. The firm must be a price searcher in a perfectly competitive product market.
    e. The firm must operate in a decreasing-cost industry.

16. If the marginal product of the second worker hired by a firm is 14 units and the price of a unit of output is $7 regardless of the quantity of output sold, then the marginal revenue product of the second worker is
    a. $98
    b. $14
    c. $7
    d. $2
    e. $21

17. Ten cases of spring water are sold for $6 each, and the marginal product of the last unit of labor is 5. If the price of a case increases from $6 to $8, then the marginal revenue product of the last unit of labor would
    a. decrease by $10
    b. increase by $40
    c. decrease by $30
    d. increase by $10
    e. not change
18. If the wage is below the marginal revenue product, then a profit-maximizing firm will
    a. employ more workers
    b. employ fewer workers
    c. see an increase in its demand for labor
    d. see an increase in its supply of labor
    e. see a fall in its demand for labor
19. Suppose a firm is a price searcher in the product market and hires labor in a perfectly competitive labor market. The firm hires four workers, the marginal product of the fourth worker is 4, and the wage rate is $40. The firm produces 100 units of the product, which sell for a price of $10 each. This firm is
    a. maximizing profit when it hires four workers
    b. not maximizing profit and should hire more workers to increase profit
    c. not maximizing profit and should hire fewer workers to increase profit
    d. maximizing profit when it produces 100 units of the product
    e. not maximizing profit when it produces 100 units of the product and should increase production to increase profit
20. Using free public space means that sidewalk vendors earn long-run economic profits.
    a. True
    b. False

Answers

1. c	2. d	3. c	4. e	5. d	6. c	7. c	8. b	9. e	10. a
11. c	12. b	13. a	14. b	15. b	16. a	17. d	18. a	19. c	20. b

Long Answer Questions

LO1 Identify examples of resource demand and supply in daily life

1.1. *(Resource Demand)* How do firms and individuals determine if it's worth it to (a) invest in capital improvements, (b) hire additional workers, or (c) decide where to work?

LO2 Explain resource supply and demand

2.1. *(Resource Demand and Supply)* Answer each of the following questions about the labor market:
    a. Which economic decision makers determine the demand for labor? What is their goal, and what decision criteria do they use in trying to reach that goal?
    b. Which economic decision makers determine the supply of labor? What is their goal and what decision criteria do they use in trying to reach that goal?
    c. In what sense is the demand for labor a derived demand?

LO3 Define opportunity cost and economic rent

3.1. *(Opportunity Cost and Economic Rent)* Define economic rent. In the graph below, assume that the market demand curve for labor is initially D_1.

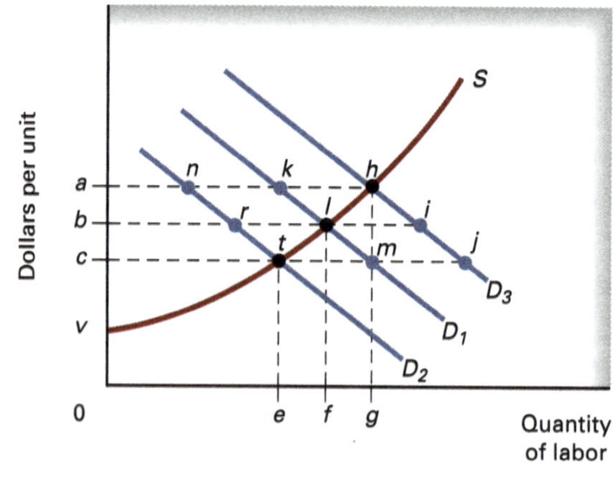

a. What are the equilibrium wage rate and employment level? What is the economic rent?
b. Next assume that the price of a substitute resource increases, other things constant. What happens to demand for labor? What are the new equilibrium wage rate and employment level? What happens to economic rent?
c. Suppose instead that demand for the final product drops, other things constant. Using labor demand curve D_1 as your starting point, what happens to the demand for labor? What are the new equilibrium wage rate and employment level? Does the amount of economic rent change?

LO4 Analyze the factors influencing resource demand

4.1. *(Firm's Demand for a Resource)* Use the following data to answer the questions that follow. Assume a perfectly competitive product market.

Units of Labor	Units of Output
0	0
1	7
2	13
3	18
4	22
5	25

a. Calculate the marginal revenue product for each additional unit of labor if output sells for $3 per unit.
b. Draw the demand curve for labor based on the above data and the $3-per-unit product price.
c. If the wage rate is $15 per hour, how much labor will be hired?
d. Using your answer to part (c), compare the firm's total revenue to the total amount paid for labor. Who gets the difference?
e. What would happen to your answers to parts (b) and (c) if the price of output increased to $5 per unit, other things constant?

4.2. *(Shifts of Resource Demand)* A local pizzeria hires college students to make pizza, wait on tables, take phone orders, and deliver pizzas. For each situation described, determine whether the demand for student employees by the restaurant would increase, decrease, or remain unchanged. Explain each answer.
a. The demand for pizza increases.
b. Another pizzeria opens up next door.
c. An increase in the minimum wage raises the cost of hiring student employees.
d. The restaurant buys a computer system for taking phone orders.

4.3. *(Selling Output as a Price Taker)* If a competitive firm hires another full-time worker, total output increases from 100 units to 110 units per week. Suppose the market price of output is $25 per unit. What is the maximum weekly wage at which the firm would hire that additional worker?

RESOURCE MARKETS

13 Chapter in Review

KEY TERMS

derived demand
demand that arises from the demand for the product the resource produces

economic rent
portion of a resource's total earnings that exceeds its opportunity cost; earnings greater than the amount required to keep the resource in its present use

marginal revenue product
the change in total revenue when an additional unit of a resource is hired, other things constant

marginal resource cost
the change in total cost when an additional unit of a resource is hired, other things constant

resource substitutes
resources that substitute in production; an increase in the price of one resource increases the demand for the other

resource complements
resources that enhance one another's productivity; an increase in the price of one resource decreases the demand for the other

LO1 Identify examples of resource demand and supply in daily life. A producer demands another unit of a resource as long as its marginal revenue exceeds its marginal cost. Conversely, people supply their resources to the highest-paying alternative, other things constant. People also consider utility when determining to whom to supply their resources.

Resource Market for Carpenters

The intersection of the upward-sloping supply curve of carpenters with the downward-sloping demand curve determines the equilibrium wage, *W,* and the level of employment, *E*.

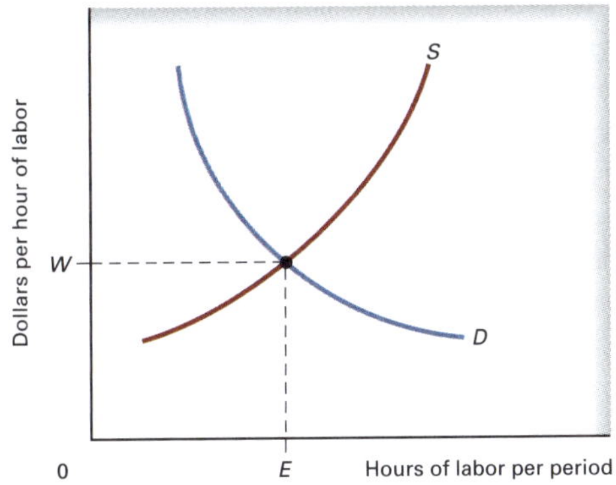

LO2 Explain resource supply and demand. A producer demands another unit of a resource as long as its marginal revenue exceeds its marginal cost. People supply their resources to the highest-paying alternative, other things constant. Because other things are not always constant, people must be paid more for jobs less suited to their tastes. Your utility depends on both monetary and nonmonetary aspects of the job.

LO3 Define opportunity cost and economic rent. Opportunity cost is what a resource could earn in its best alternative use. Economic rent is the portion of a resource's earnings that exceeds the amount necessary to keep the resource in its present use. In other words, economic rent is earnings in excess of opportunity cost.

Opportunity Cost and Economic Rent

In panel (a), the resource supply curve is vertical, indicating that the resource has no alternative use. The price is demand determined, and all earnings are economic rent. In panel (b), the resource supply curve is horizontal at $10 per hour, indicating that the resource can also earn that much in its best alternative use. Employment is demand determined, and all earnings are opportunity costs. Panel (c) shows an upward-sloping resource supply curve. Earnings are partly opportunity costs and partly economic rent. Both demand and supply determine the equilibrium price and quantity.

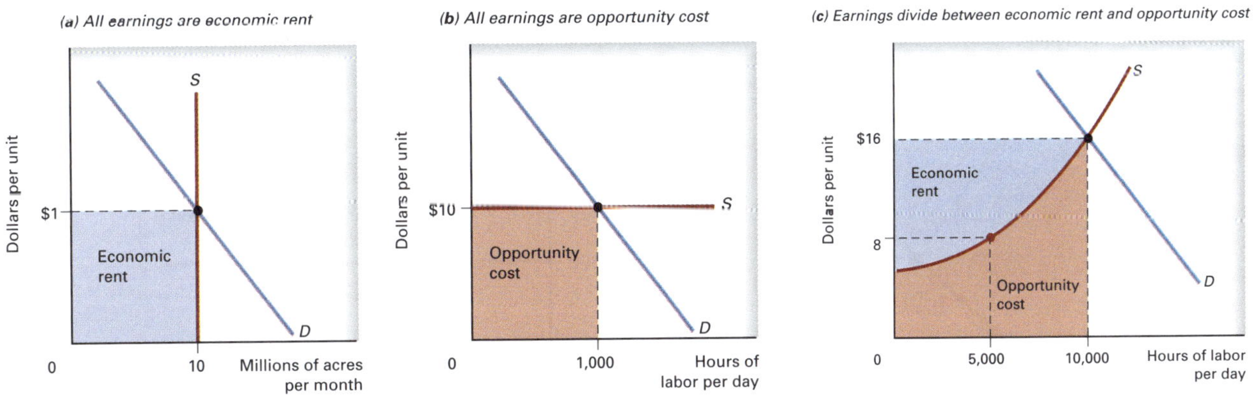

LO4 Analyze the factors influencing resource demand. The marginal revenue product of any resource is the change in the firm's total revenue resulting from employing an additional unit of the resource, other things constant. The marginal resource cost is what an additional unit of a resource will cost the firm. The profit-maximizing level of resource employment occurs where the respective marginal revenue products equals the marginal resource costs. A resource's marginal revenue product depends on the resource's marginal product and the price at which that product is sold. Two things can change a resource's marginal product: (1) a change in the amount of other resources employed and (2) a change in technology. Only one thing can change the price of the product: a change in demand for the product.

Marginal Revenue Product When Firm Sells in a Competitive Market

(1) Workers per Day	(2) Total Product	(3) Marginal Product	(4) Product Price	(5) Total Revenue (5) = (2) × (4)	(6) Marginal Revenue Product (6) = (3) × (4)
0	0	—	$20	$ 0	—
1	10	10	20	200	$200
2	19	9	20	380	180
3	27	8	20	540	160
4	34	7	20	680	140
5	40	6	20	800	120
6	45	5	20	900	100
7	49	4	20	980	80
8	52	3	20	1040	60

The Marginal Revenue Product When a Firm Sells with Market Power

(1) Workers per Day	(2) Total Product	(3) Product Price	(4) Total Revenue (4) = (2) × (3)	(5) Marginal Revenue Product
0	0	—	—	—
1	10	$40.00	$ 400.00	$400.00
2	19	35.20	668.80	268.80
3	27	31.40	847.80	179.00
4	34	27.80	945.20	97.40
5	40	25.00	1000.00	54.80
6	45	22.50	1012.50	12.50
7	49	20.50	1004.50	−8.00
8	52	19.00	988.00	−16.50

Market Equilibrium for a Resource and the Firm's Employment Decision

Market demand and supply of a resource, in panel (a), determine that resource's market wage and quantity. In panel (b), an individual firm can employ as much as it wants at the market wage, so wage becomes the firm's marginal resource cost. The marginal resource cost curve also is the supply curve of that resource to the firm. In panel (b), a resource's marginal revenue product is the firm's demand curve for that resource. The firm maximizes profit (or minimizes its loss) by hiring a resource up to the point where the resource's marginal revenue product equals its marginal resource cost, which is six workers per day in this example.

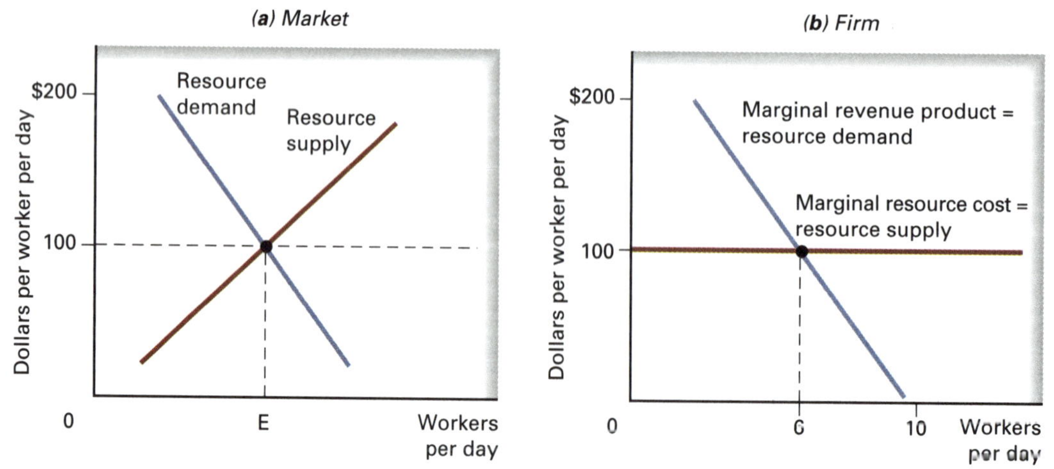

CHAPTER 14

Labor Markets *and* Unions

Learning Outcomes

LO[1] Discuss issues affecting labor supply and utility maximization LO[2] Explain the market supply factors that lead to differing wages LO[3] Describe unions and their collective bargaining strategies LO[4] Describe the relationship between union wages and employment

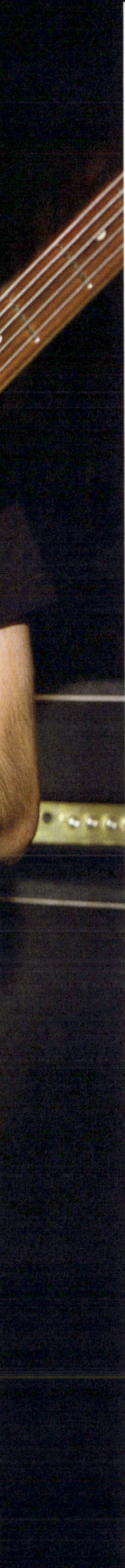

© DYNAMIC GRAPHICS/CREATAS IMAGES/JUPITERIMAGES

“Why do unknown rock bands play hours for peanuts, while famous bands play much less for much more?”

How do you divide your time between work and leisure? Why do many people work less if the wage increases enough? For example, why do unknown rock bands play hours for peanuts, while famous bands play much less for much more? Why are butchers more likely than surgeons to mow their own lawns? What determines the wage structure in the economy? What else besides the wage affects your labor supply? In what sense have labor unions become the victims of their own success? This chapter digs deeper into labor markets and wage determination.

What do you think?

Time is money.

Strongly Disagree 1 2 3 4 5 6 7 *Strongly Agree*

You can be sure of one thing: demand and supply play a central role in all this. You have already considered the demand for resources. Demand depends on a resource's marginal revenue product. The first half of this chapter focuses on the supply of labor, then brings demand and supply together to arrive at the market wage. The second half considers the role of labor unions. We examine the economic impact of unions and review recent trends in union membership.

LO1 Labor Supply

As a resource supplier, you have a labor supply curve for each of the many possible uses of your labor. To some markets, your quantity supplied is zero over the realistic range of wages. The qualifier "over the realistic range" is added because, for a high enough wage (say, $1 million per hour), you might supply labor to just about *any* activity. In most labor markets, your quantity supplied may be zero either because you are *willing* but *unable* to perform the job (professional golfer, airline pilot, novelist) or because you are *able* but *unwilling* to do so (soldier of fortune, prison guard, P.E. instructor). You have as many individual supply curves as there are labor markets, just as you have as many individual demand curves as there are markets for goods and services. Your labor supply to each market depends, among other things, on

Topics discussed in Chapter 14 include:

- Theory of time allocation
- Backward-bending labor supply curve
- Nonwage factors in labor supply
- Why wages differ
- Unions and collective bargaining
- Union wages and employment

your abilities, your taste for the job, and the opportunity cost of your time. Your supply to a particular labor market assumes that wages in other markets are constant, just as your demand for a particular product assumes that other prices are constant.

Labor Supply and Utility Maximization

Recall the definition of economics: *the study of how people use their scarce resources in an attempt to satisfy their unlimited wants*—that is, how people use their scarce resources to maximize their utility. Two sources of utility are of special interest in this chapter: the consumption of goods and services and the enjoyment of leisure. The utility derived from consumption serves as the foundation of demand. Another valuable source of utility is leisure—time spent relaxing with friends, sleeping, eating, watching TV, and in other recreation. Leisure is a normal good that, like other goods, is subject to the law of diminishing marginal utility. Thus, the more leisure time you have, the less you value an additional hour of it. Sometimes you may have so much leisure that you "have time on your hands" and are "just killing time." As that sage of the comic page Garfield the cat once lamented, "Spare time would be more fun if I had less to spare." Or as Shakespeare wrote, "If all the year were playing holidays, to sport would be as tedious as to work." Leisure's diminishing marginal utility explains why some of the "idle rich" may grow bored in their idleness.

© RYAN MCVAY/PHOTODISC/GETTY IMAGES

Three Uses of Time

Some of you are at a point in your careers when you have few resources other than your time. Time is the raw material of life. You can use your time in three ways. First, you can undertake **market work**—selling your time in the labor market. In return for a wage, you surrender control of your time to the employer. Second, you can undertake **nonmarket work**—using time to produce your own goods and services. Nonmarket work includes the time you spend doing your laundry, making a sandwich, or cleaning up after yourself. Nonmarket work also includes the time spent acquiring skills and education that enhance your productivity. Although studying and attending class may provide little immediate payoff, you expect that the knowledge and perspective so gained will enrich your future. Third, you can spend time in **leisure**—using your time in nonwork pursuits.

market work
time sold as labor

nonmarket work
time spent getting an education or on do-it-yourself production for personal consumption

leisure
time spent on nonwork activities

Work and Utility

Unless you are among the fortunate few, work is not a pure source of utility, as it often generates some boredom, discomfort, and aggravation. In short, time spent working can be "a real pain," a source of *disutility*—the opposite of utility. And work is subject to *increasing marginal disutility*—the more you work, the greater the marginal disutility of working another hour. In the extreme, you could feel burned out from overwork. You may work nonetheless, because your earnings buy goods and services. You expect the utility from these products to more than offset the disutility of work. Thus, the *net utility of work*—the utility of the consumption made possible through earnings minus the disutility of the work itself—usually makes some amount of work an attractive use of your time. In the case of market work, your income buys goods and services. In the case of nonmarket work, either you produce goods and services directly, as in making yourself a sandwich, or you invest your time in education with an expectation of higher future earnings and higher future consumption. The additional utility you expect from the sandwich and better future consumption possibilities resulting from education are the marginal benefits of nonmarket work.

Utility Maximization

Within the limits of a 24-hour day, seven days a week, you balance your time among market work, nonmarket work, and leisure to maximize utility. As a rational consumer, *you attempt to maximize utility by allocating your time so that the expected marginal utility of the last unit of time spent in each activity is identical*. Thus, in the course of a week or a month, the expected marginal utility of the last hour of leisure equals the expected net marginal utility of the last hour of market work, which equals the expected net marginal utility of the last hour of nonmarket work. In the case of time devoted to acquiring more human capital, you must consider the marginal utility expected from the future increase in earnings that result from your enhanced productivity.

Maybe at this point you are saying, "Wait a minute. I don't know what you're talking about. I don't allocate my time like that. I just sort of bump along, doing what feels good." Economists do not claim that you are even aware of making these marginal calculations. But as a rational decision maker, you allocate your scarce time trying to satisfy your unlimited wants, or trying to maximize utility. And utility maximization, or "doing what feels good," implies that you act *as if* you allocated your time to derive the same expected net marginal utility from the last unit of time spent in each alternative use.

You probably have settled into a rough plan for meals, work, entertainment, study, sleep, and so on—a plan that fits your immediate objectives. This plan is probably in constant flux as you make expected and unexpected adjustments in your use of time. For example, last weekend you may have failed to crack a book, despite good intentions. This morning you may have overslept because you were up late. Over a week, a month, or a year, however, your use of time is roughly in line with an allocation that maximizes utility as you perceive it at the time. Put another way, if you could alter your use of time to increase your utility, you would do so. Nobody's stopping you! You may emphasize immediate gratification over long-term goals, but, hey, that's your choice and you bear the consequences. *This time-allocation process ensures that at the margin, the expected net utilities from the last unit of time spent in each activity are equal.*

Because information is costly and because the future is uncertain, you sometimes make mistakes. You don't always get what you expect. Some mistakes are minor, such as going to a movie that turns out to be a waste of time. But other mistakes can be costly. For example, some people are now studying for a field that will grow crowded by the time they graduate, or some people may be acquiring skills that new technology will soon make obsolete.

Implications

The theory of time allocation described thus far has several implications for individual choice. First, consider the choices of market work, nonmarket work, and leisure. The higher your market wage, other things constant, the higher your opportunity cost of leisure and nonmarket work. For example, those who earn a high wage spend less time in nonmarket work, other things constant. Surgeons are less likely to mow their lawns than are butchers. And among those earning the same wage, those more productive in nonmarket work—handy around the house, good cooks—do more for themselves. Conversely, those who are all thumbs around the house and have trouble boiling water hire more household services and eat out more frequently.

By the same logic, the higher the expected earnings right out of high school, other things constant, the higher the opportunity cost of attending college. Most young, successful movie stars do not go to college, and many even drop out of high school, as noted earlier. Promising athletes often turn professional right after high school or before completing college. But the vast majority of people, including female basketball stars, do not face such a high opportunity cost of higher education. As one poor soul lamented, "Since my wife left me, my kids joined a cult, my job is history, and my dog died, I think now might be a good time to go back for an MBA."

Wages and Individual Labor Supply

To breathe life into the time-allocation problem, consider your choices for the summer. If you can afford to, you can take the summer off, spending it entirely on leisure, perhaps as a fitting reward for a rough academic year. Or you can supply your time to market work. Or you can undertake nonmarket work, such as cleaning the garage, painting the house, or attending summer school. As a rational decision maker, you select the combination of leisure, market work, and nonmarket work that you expect will maximize your utility. And the optimal combination is likely to involve allocating time to each activity. For example, even if you work, you might still take one or two summer courses.

Suppose the only summer job available is some form of unskilled labor, such as working in a fast-food restaurant or for the municipal parks department. For simplicity, let's assume that you view all such jobs as equally attractive (or unattractive) in terms of their nonmonetary aspects, such as working conditions, working hours, and so on. (These nonmonetary aspects are discussed in the next section.) If there is no difference among these unskilled jobs, the most important question for you in deciding how much market labor to supply is: What's the market wage?

Suppose the wage is $6 per hour. Rather than working at a wage that low, you might decide to work around the house, attend summer school, take a really long nap, travel across the country to find yourself, or perhaps pursue some combination of these. In any case, you supply no market labor at such a low wage. The market wage must rise to $7 before you supply any market labor. Suppose at a wage of $7, you supply 20 hours per week, perhaps taking fewer summer courses and shorter naps.

As the wage increases, the opportunity cost of time spent in other activities rises, so you substitute market work for other uses of your time. You decide to work 30 hours per week at a wage of $8 per hour, 40 hours at $9, 48 hours at $10, and 55 hours at $11. At a wage of $12 you go to 60 hours per week; you are starting to earn serious money—$720 a week. If the wage hits $13 per hour, you decide to cut back to 58 hours per week. Despite the cutback, your pay rises to $754, which is more than when the wage was $12. Finally, if the wage hits $14, you cut back to 55 per week, earning $770. To explain why you may eventually reduce the quantity of labor supplied, let's consider the impact of wage increases on your time allocation.

Substitution and Income Effects

An increase in the wage has two effects on your use of time. First, because each hour of work now buys more goods and services, a higher wage increases the opportunity cost of leisure and nonmarket work. Thus, as the wage increases, you substitute market work for other activities. This is the **substitution effect of a wage increase**. Second, a higher wage means a higher income for a given number of hours. This higher income increases your demand for all normal goods. Because leisure is a normal good, a higher income increases your demand for leisure, thereby reducing your allocation of time to market work. The **income effect of a wage increase** tends to reduce the quantity of labor supplied to market work.

substitution effect of a wage increase a higher wage encourages more work because other activities now have a higher opportunity cost

income effect of a wage increase a higher wage raises a worker's income, increasing the demand for all normal goods, including leisure, so the quantity of labor supplied to market work decreases

backward-bending supply curve of labor as the wage rises, the quantity of labor supplied may eventually decline; the income effect of a higher wage increases the demand for leisure, which reduces the quantity of labor supplied enough to more than offset the substitution effect of a higher wage

As the wage increases, the substitution effect causes you to work more, but the income effect causes you to work less and demand more leisure.

In our example, the substitution effect exceeds the income effect for wages up to $12 per hour, resulting in more labor supplied as the wage increases. When the wage reaches $13, however, the income effect exceeds the substitution effect, causing you to reduce the quantity of labor supplied.

Backward-Bending Labor Supply Curve

The labor supply curve just described appears in Exhibit 1. As you can see, this slopes upward until a wage of $12 per hour is reached; then it bends backward. The **backward-bending supply curve** gets its shape because the income effect of a higher wage eventually dominates the substitution effect, reducing the quantity of labor supplied as the wage increases. We see evidence of a backward-bending supply curve particularly among high-wage individuals, who reduce their work and consume more leisure as their wage increases. For example, entertainers typically perform less as they become more successful. Unknown musicians play for hours for hardly any money; famous musicians play much less for much more. The income effect of rising real wages helps explain the decline in the U.S. workweek from an average of 60 hours in 1900 to less than 40 hours today.

Flexibility of Hours Worked

The model we have been discussing assumes that workers have some control over the number of hours they work. Opportunities for part-time work

Exhibit 1

Individual Labor Supply Curve for Unskilled Work

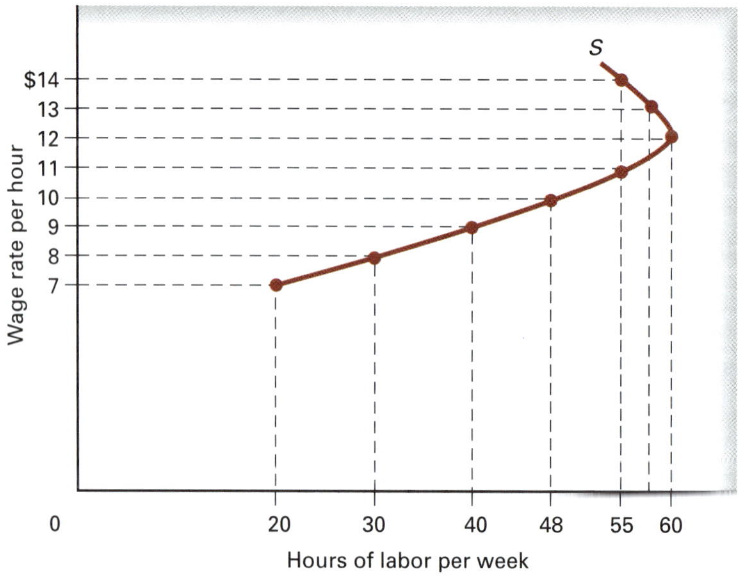

and overtime allow workers to put together their preferred quantity of hours. Workers also have some control over the timing and length of their vacations. More generally, individuals can control how long to stay in school, when to enter or leave the workforce, and when to retire. Thus, they actually have more control over the number of hours worked than you might think if you focused simply on the benchmark of, say, a 40-hour workweek.

All else equal, you are more inclined to take a position that provides valuable job experience.

Nonwage Determinants of Labor Supply

The supply of labor to a particular market depends on a variety of factors other than the wage, just as the demand for a particular good depends on factors other than the price. As we have already seen, the supply of labor to a particular market depends on wages in other labor markets. What nonwage factors shape a college student's labor supply for the summer?

Other Sources of Income

Although some jobs are rewarding in a variety of nonmonetary ways, the main reason people work is to earn money. Thus, the willingness to supply labor depends on income from other sources, including from family, savings, student loans, and scholarships. A student who receives a generous scholarship, for example, faces less pressure to work in the summer or during the college term. More generally, wealthy people have less incentive to work. For example, multimillion-dollar lottery winners often quit their jobs. And those who inherit a large sum are more likely to retire early.[1]

Nonmonetary Factors

Labor is a special kind of resource. Unlike capital or natural resources, which can be supplied regardless of the whereabouts of the resource owner, the supplier of labor must be where the work is performed. Because individuals must usually be physically present to supply labor, such *nonmonetary factors* as the difficulty of the job, the quality of the work environment, and the status of the position become important to labor suppliers. For example, deckhands on crab boats in the icy waters off Alaska can earn over $10,000 for five days of work, but the job is dangerous, winter temperatures seldom exceed zero, and daily shifts allow only three hours of sleep.

Consider the different working conditions you might encounter. A campus job that lets you study on the job is more attractive than one allowing no study time. Some jobs offer flexible hours; others have rigid schedules. Is the workplace air-conditioned, or do you have to sweat it out? The more attractive the working conditions, the more labor you supply to that market, other things constant. Finally, some jobs convey more status than others. For example, the president of the United States earns less than one-tenth that of corporate heads, but there is no shortage of applicants for the job. Similarly, U.S. Supreme Court justices typically take a huge pay cut to accept the job.

The Value of Job Experience

All else equal, you are more inclined to take a position that provides valuable job experience. Serving as the assistant treasurer for a local business during the summer provides better job experience and looks better on a résumé than serving mystery meat at the college cafeteria. Some people are willing to accept relatively low wages now for the promise of higher wages in the future. For example, new lawyers are eager to fill clerkships for judges, though the pay is low and the hours long, because these positions offer experience and contacts future

© CHRISTOPHER PILLITZ/REPORTAGE/GETTY IMAGES

1. As found in research by Jeffrey Brown, Courtney Coile, and Scott Weisbenner, "The Effect of Inheritance Receipt on Retirement," *NBER Working Paper 12386,* July 2006.

employers value. Likewise, athletes who play in the minor leagues for little pay believe that experience will help them get to the major leagues. Thus, *the more a job enhances future earning possibilities, the greater the supply of labor, other things constant.* Consequently, the pay is usually lower than for jobs that impart less valuable experience. Sometimes the pay is zero, as with some internships.

Taste for Work

Just as the taste for goods and services differs among consumers, the taste for work also differs among labor suppliers. Some people prefer physical labor and hate office work. Some become surgeons; others can't stand the sight of blood. Some become airline pilots; others are afraid to fly. Teenagers prefer jobs at Starbucks and Gap to those at McDonald's and Burger King.[2] Many struggling writers, artists, actors, and dancers could earn more elsewhere, but prefer the creative process and the chance, albeit slim, of becoming rich and famous in the arts (for example, the 120,000 members of the Screen Actors Guild earn less than $10,000 a year on average from their professional work). Some people have such strong preferences for certain jobs that they work for free, such as auxiliary police officers or volunteer firefighters. Likewise, most computer hackers earn nothing beyond the twisted satisfaction they get from spreading viruses and causing digital mayhem.

As with the taste for goods and services, economists do not try to explain how work preferences develop. They simply argue that your preferences are relatively stable and you supply more labor to jobs you like. Based on taste, workers seek jobs in a way that tends to minimize the disutility of work. This is not to say that everyone ends up in his or her most preferred position. The transaction costs of job information and of changing jobs may prevent some matchups that might otherwise seem desirable. But in the long run, people tend to find jobs that suit them. We are not likely to find tour guides who hate to travel, zookeepers who are allergic to animals, or garage mechanics who hate getting their hands dirty.

2. Dirk Johnson, "For Teenagers, Fast Food Is a Snack, Not a Job," *New York Times*, 8 January 2001.

LO2 Market Supply of Labor

In the previous section, we considered those factors, both monetary and nonmonetary, that influence individual labor supply. *The supply of labor to a particular market is the horizontal sum of all the individual supply curves.* The horizontal sum at each particular wage is found by adding the quantities supplied by each worker. If an individual supply curve of labor bends backward, does this mean that the market supply curve for labor also bends backward? Not necessarily. Because different individuals have different opportunity costs and different tastes for work, the bend in the supply curve occurs at different wages for different individuals. And, for some individuals, the labor supply curve may not bend backward over the realistic range of wages. Exhibit 2 shows how just three individual labor supply curves sum to yield a market supply curve that slopes upward.

Why Wages Differ

Just as both blades of scissors contribute equally to cutting paper, both labor demand and labor supply determine the market wage. Exhibit 3 shows average hourly wages for more than 130 million U.S. workers.

Exhibit 2

Deriving the Market Labor Supply Curve from Individual Labor Supply Curves

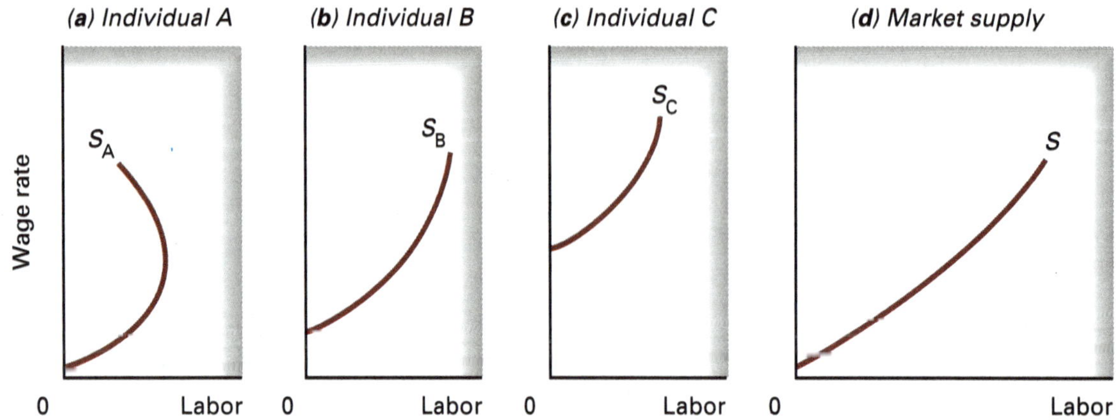

Exhibit 3

Average Hourly Wage by Occupation in the United States as of May 2007

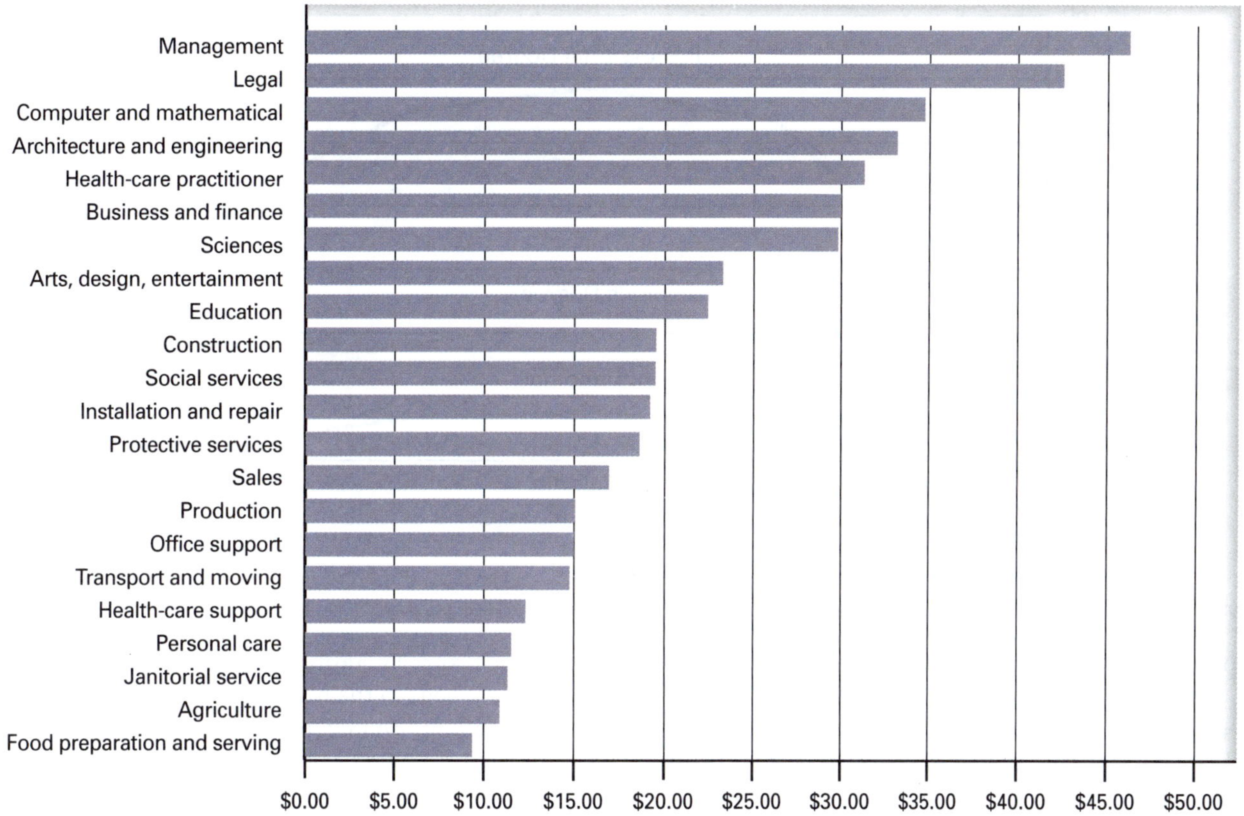

SOURCE: Developed from "Occupational Employment and Wages, May 2007," *U.S. Department of Labor News,* Chart 1, 17 May 2008, also available at http://www.bls.gov/news.release/pdf/ocwage.pdf.

Workers are sorted into 22 occupations from the highest to the lowest wage as of May 2007. Management earns the highest wage, at $46.22 an hour. The lowest is the $9.35 an hour averaged by workers preparing and serving food. Wage differences across labor markets trace to differences in labor demand and in labor supply, as you will see. The previous chapter discussed the elements that influence the demand for resources and examined labor in particular. In brief, *a profit-maximizing firm hires labor up to the point where labor's marginal revenue product equals its marginal resource cost*—that is, where the last unit employed increases total revenue enough to cover the added cost. Because we have already discussed what affects the demand for labor—namely, labor's marginal revenue product—let's focus more on labor supply.

Differences in Training, Education, Age, and Experience

Some jobs pay more because they require a long and expensive training period, which reduces market supply because few are willing to incur the time and expense required. But such training increases labor productivity, thereby increasing demand for the skills. Reduced supply and increased demand both raise the market wage. For example, chartered accuntants (CAs) earn more than file clerks because the extensive training of CAs limits the supply to this field and because this training increases the productivity of CAs compared to file clerks.

Exhibit 4 shows how education and experience affect earnings. Age groups are indicated on the horizontal axis and average annual earnings on the vertical axis. To standardize things, pay is for the highest level of education achieved. The relationship between income and education is clear. At every age, those with more education earn more. For example, among those ages 45 to 54, workers with professional degrees earned more than twice those with bachelor's degrees and nearly six times those without high school diplomas.

Age itself also has an important effect on income. Earnings tend to increase as workers acquire job experience and get promoted. Among educated workers, experience pays more. For example, among those with professional degrees, workers in the 45–54 age

Exhibit 4

Age, Education, and Pay

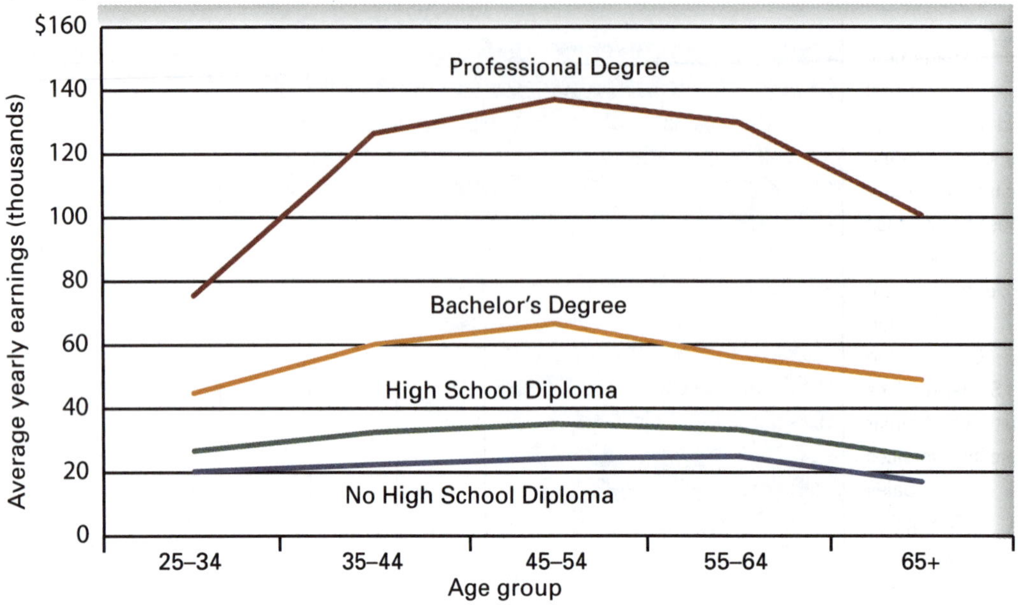

SOURCE: U.S. Census Bureau. http://www.census.gov. Figures are average earnings in 2005 based on the highest degree earned.

group earned on average 81 percent more than those in the 25–34 age group. But among those without high school diplomas, workers in the 45–54 age group earned on average only 20 percent more than those in the 25–34 age group. Differences in earnings reflect the normal workings of resource markets, whereby workers are rewarded according to their marginal productivity.

Differences in Ability

Because they are more able and talented, some earn more than others with the same training and education. For example, two lawyers may have identical educations, but earnings differ because of differences in underlying ability. Most executives have extensive training and business experience, but only a few get to run large corporations. In professional sports such as basketball and baseball, some players earn up to 50 times more than others. From lawyers to executives to professional athletes, pay differences reflect differing abilities and different marginal productivities.

Each year *Forbes* magazine lists the multimillion-dollar earnings of top entertainers and professional athletes. Entertainment and pro sports have come to be called **winner-take-all labor markets** because a few key individuals critical to the overall success of an enterprise are richly rewarded. In professional golf tournaments, attendance and TV ratings are significantly higher with Tiger Woods in the mix. Top performers generate a high marginal revenue product.[3]

winner-take-all labor markets markets in which a few key employees critical to the overall success of an enterprise are richly rewarded

The "star" treatment now extends to such fields as management, law, banking, finance, even academia. Consider, for example, corporate pay. In 1980, the chief executive officers (CEOs) of the 200 largest U.S. corporations earned about 42 times more than the average production worker. Now, this multiple tops 200. Comparable multiples are much lower in Germany and Japan.

© H + S IMAGES/IMAGE SOURCE

Differences in Risk

Research indicates that jobs with a higher probability of injury or death, such as coal mining, usually pay more, other things constant. Russians working at the partially disabled nuclear power plant, Chernobyl, earned 10 times the national

3. Bill Livingston, "LeBron," *Cleveland Plain Dealer,* 6 May 2007; Russell Adams, "The Real Most Valuable Players," *Wall Street Journal,* 14 April 2007; Economic Report of the President, February 2007, at http://www.gpoaccess.gov/eop/.

Gender Inequalities in Wages

One of the most visible examples of gender inequality is in wages. As seen from the table, there are significant disparities in the wage rates for men and women in agricultural and non-agricultural sectors. The difference in wages earned by men and women is on account of differences in productive skills and/or due to unexplained differences arising from gender discrimination in the work place. Controlling for occupational differences, women on average earn around 50 percent of what men earn in South Asian countries. For India, it is estimated that 55 percent of the wage gap between men and women cannot be explained by productivity and endowments. In rural labor markets in Bangladesh, 70 percent of the gender wage gap was due to discrimination at work place. For the rural areas of Bangladesh, 43 percent of the wage differential between men and women was on account of gender discrimination.

In Philippines, Thailand, and Vietnam, economic growth has led to a narrowing of the rural gendered pay gap. However, by decomposing this pay gap into an explained part (that is attributable to different levels of human capital among workers) and an unexplained part (that is due to gender bias or gender based discrimination), it is surmised that gender inequalities in earnings may actually be significantly higher than what is generally thought to be the case. The persistence of an unexplained gendered wage gap, which is much larger than the explained part, suggests the presence of systematic gender-based discrimination in pay which has no basis in the relative education, productivity or skill of workers.

Ratio of Female Wage Rate to Male Wage Rate in Selected Asia-Pacific Countries

Country	In Agricultural Wage Employment (%)	In Non Agricultural Wage Employment (%)
Afghanistan (2003)	50	20-30
Bangladesh (2006)	64 (in agro-processing)	—
India (2004/2005)	69 (casual); 79 (regular)	65 (casual), 57 (regular)
Pakistan (2001)	50 (in sugar)	—
Vietnam (1997/98)	73 (hourly wages)	—

SOURCE: Agriculture-Pathways to Prosperity in Asia and the Pacific, Asia and the Pacific Division, International Fund for Agricultural Development, March 2011, also available at http://www.ifad.org/pub/apr/pathways.pdf.

average, but workers face continued health risk from radiation exposure. Sex workers in Mexico earn 23 percent more for unprotected sex.[4] Truck drivers for American contractors in Iraq earn over $100,000 a year, but the job is dangerous. Workers also earn more, other things constant, in seasonal jobs such as construction, where the risk of unemployment is greater.

Geographic Differences

People have a strong incentive to sell their resources in the market where they earn the most. For example, the U.S. National Basketball Association attracts talent from around the world. About 20 percent of players come from abroad. Likewise, thousands of foreign-trained physicians migrate to the United States each year for the high pay. The flow of labor is not all one way. Some Americans seek their fortune abroad, with American basketball players going to Europe and baseball players to Japan. Workers often face migration hurdles. Any reduction in these hurdles would reduce wage differentials across countries.

Discrimination

Sometimes wage differences stem from racial or gender discrimination in the job market. Although such discrimination is illegal, history shows that certain groups—including African Americans, Hispanics, and women—have systematically earned less than others of equal ability.

Union Membership

Other things equal, members of organized labor earn more than nonmembers. The balance of this chapter discusses the effects of unions on the market for labor.

LO3 Unions and Collective Bargaining

Few aspects of labor markets make news more than labor unions. Labor negotiations, strikes, picket lines, confrontations between workers and employers—all fit TV's "action news" format. Despite media attention, only about one in eight U.S. workers is a union member and nearly all union agreements are reached without a strike. But labor unions are more important than their current membership indicates. Let's examine the tools that unions

4. See Paul Gertler et al., "Risky Business: The Market for Unprotected Commercial Sex," *Journal of Political Economy*, vol. 113, no. 3, 2005: pp. 518–550.

use to seek higher pay and better benefits for their members.

Collective Bargaining, Mediation, and Arbitration

Collective bargaining is the process by which representatives of union and management negotiate a mutually agreeable contract specifying wages, employee benefits, and working conditions. A tentative agreement, once reached, goes before the membership for a vote. If the agreement is rejected, the union can strike or can continue negotiations.

If negotiations reach an impasse and the public interest is involved, government officials may ask an independent mediator to step in. A mediator is an impartial observer who listens to each side separately and then suggests a resolution. If each side still remains open to a settlement, the mediator brings them together to work out a contract, but the mediator has no power to impose a settlement. In certain critical sectors, such as police and fire protection, where a strike could harm the public interest, differences are sometimes settled through binding arbitration. A neutral third party evaluates each position and issues a ruling that both sides must accept. Some disputes skip the mediation and arbitration steps and go directly from impasse to strike.

The Strike

A major source of union power is a strike, which is a union's attempt to withhold labor to stop production, thereby hoping to force the firm into accepting the union's position. But strikes are also risky for workers, who earn no pay or benefits during the strike and could lose their jobs. Union funds and, in some states, unemployment benefits, may aid strikers some, but incomes still fall substantially. *Although neither party usually wants a strike, both sides, rather than concede on key points, usually act as if they could endure one.* Unions usually picket to prevent or discourage so-called strikebreakers, or "scabs," from crossing the picket lines to work. But the targeted firm, by hiring temporary workers and nonstriking union workers, can sometimes continue production.

collective bargaining the process by which union and management negotiate a labor agreement

mediator an impartial observer who helps resolve differences between union and management

binding arbitration negotiation in which union and management must accept an impartial observer's resolution of a dispute

strike a union's attempt to withhold labor from a firm to halt production

> ALTHOUGH NEITHER PARTY USUALLY WANTS A STRIKE, BOTH SIDES, RATHER THAN CONCEDE ON KEY POINTS, USUALLY ACT AS IF THEY COULD ENDURE ONE.

LO4 Union Wages and Employment

Union members, like everyone else, have unlimited wants. But because resources are scarce, choices must be made. A menu of union desires includes higher wages, more benefits, greater job security, better working conditions, and so on. To keep the analysis manageable, let's focus on a single objective, higher wages, and consider three ways unions might increase wages: (1) by forming an inclusive, or industrial, union; (2) by forming an exclusive, or craft, union; and (3) by increasing the demand for union labor.

Inclusive, or Industrial, Unions: Negotiating a Higher Industry Wage

The market demand and supply curves for a particular type of labor are labeled *D* and *S* in panel (a) of Exhibit 5. In the absence of a union, the market wage is *W* and industry employment is *E*. At the market wage, each firm faces a horizontal, or perfectly elastic, supply of labor, as depicted by *s* in panel (b) of Exhibit 5. Thus, each firm can hire as much labor as it wants at the market wage of *W*. The firm hires workers up to the point where labor's marginal revenue product equals its marginal resource cost, resulting in *e* units of labor in panel (b). As we saw earlier, in equilibrium, labor is paid a wage just equal to its marginal revenue product.

With the *inclusive, or industrial,* approach, the union tries to negotiate industry-wide wages for each class of labor. Suppose the union negotiates a wage above the market-clearing level. Specifically, suppose the negotiated wage is *W′* in panel (a), meaning that no labor is supplied at a lower wage. In effect, the market supply of labor is perfectly elastic at the union wage out to point *a*. To the right of point *a*, however, the wage floor no longer applies; *aS* becomes the relevant portion of the labor supply curve. For an industry facing a wage floor of *W′*, the entire labor

Exhibit 5

Effects of Labor Union's Wage Floor

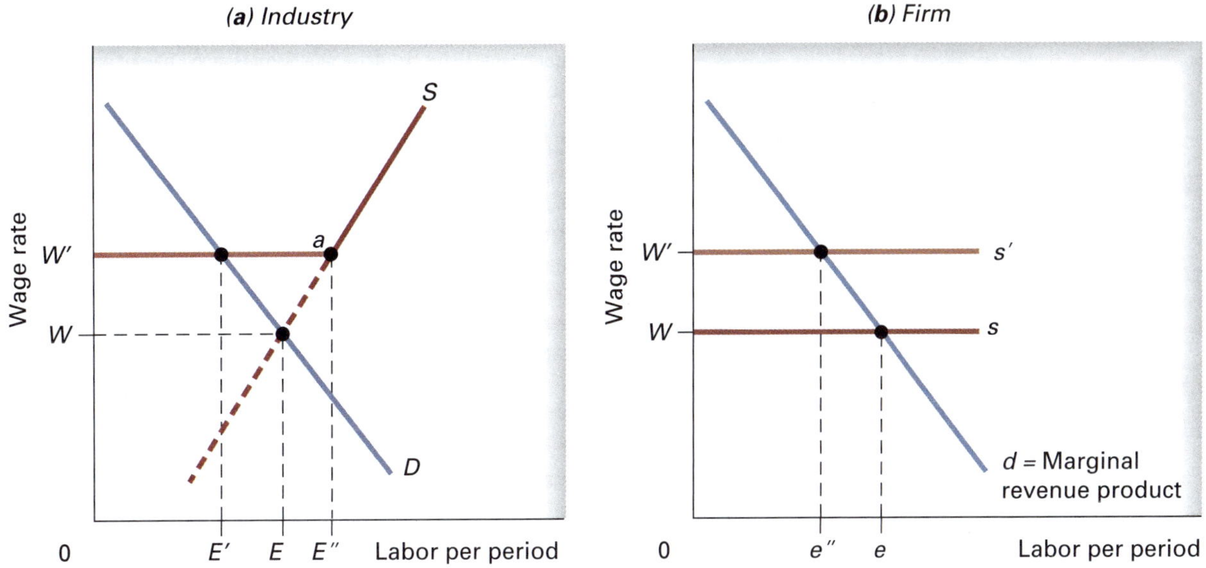

supply curve becomes W′aS, which has a kink where the wage floor joins the upward-sloping portion of the original labor supply curve.

Once this wage floor is established, each firm faces a horizontal supply curve of labor at the collectively bargained wage, W′. Because the union wage is higher than the market-clearing wage, each firm hires less labor. Consequently, the higher wage leads to a reduction in employment; the quantity of labor demanded by the industry drops from E to E′ in panel (a). At wage W′ workers in the industry would like to supply, E″, which exceeds the labor demanded, E′. Ordinarily this excess quantity supplied would force the wage down. But because union members agree collectively to the union wage, individual workers can't work for less, nor can employers hire them for less. *With the inclusive, or industrial, union, which negotiates with the entire industry, the wage is higher and employment lower than they would be in the absence of a union.*

The union must somehow ration the limited jobs available, such as by awarding them based on worker seniority, personal connections within the union, or lottery. Those who can't find union jobs must turn to the nonunion sector. *This increases the supply of labor in the nonunion sector, which drives down the nonunion wage.* So wages are relatively higher in the union sector first, because unions bargain for a wage that exceeds the market-clearing wage, and second, because those unable to find union jobs crowd into the nonunion sector. Studies show that union wages average about 15 percent above the wages of similarly qualified nonunion workers. Exhibit 6 compares median weekly earnings of union and nonunion workers. Note that unions are less successful at raising wages in more competitive sectors. For example, unions have less impact on manufacturing and service indus-

Exhibit 6

Median Weekly Earnings Are Higher for Union Than Nonunion Workers

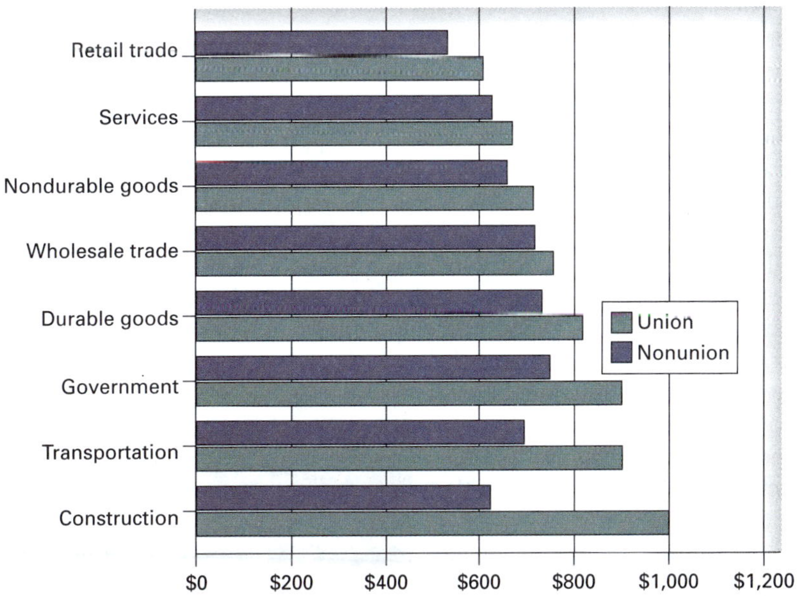

SOURCE: U.S. Bureau of Labor Statistics, "Union Member Summary," 25 January 2008, Table 4, at http://www.bls.gov/news.release/union2.t04.htm. Figures are for full-time workers in 2007.

© AP IMAGES

A Tale of Three Automakers

One factor in the recent troubles of the Detroit automakers has been their relations with the United Auto Workers labor union. During the 1940s, Ford, General Motors, and Chrysler established themselves as the cream of the market for automobiles in America; however, after losing several labor disputes in the late 1930s, they found themselves saddled with the UAW's monopoly over their labor force. Over the years this relationship has left them with high labor costs and cumbersome production processes, which Japanese carmakers were able to avoid as they began building factories in the United States in the 1980s. With increasing competition, the Big Three ultimately found themselves able to make profits on only their truck and SUV lines. When oil prices began to skyrocket in 2005 and 2006, Detroit's trucks and SUVs could not compete against the Japanese cars in fuel-efficiency, and their sales suffered. Their woes compounded as the economic recession in 2008 hit auto sales across the board.

SOURCE: Paul Ingrassia, "How Detroit Drove Into a Ditch," *Wall Street Journal*, 25 October 2008. Available at http://online.wsj.com/article/SB122488710556068177.html.

tries, where product markets tend to be competitive. Unions have greater success in government, transportation, and construction—sectors that tend to be less competitive. When there is more competition in the product market, employers cannot easily pass along higher union wages as higher product prices. New, nonunion, firms can enter the industry, pay market wages, and sell the product for less.

> Studies show that union wages average about 15 percent above the wages of similarly qualified nonunion workers.

Exclusive, or Craft, Unions: Reducing Labor Supply

One way to increase wages while avoiding an excess quantity of labor supplied is to somehow reduce the supply of labor, shown in Exhibit 7 as a leftward shift of the labor supply curve in panel (a). This supply reduction increases the wage and reduces employment. Successful supply restrictions of this type require that the union first limit its membership and second force all employers in the industry to hire only union members. The union can restrict membership with higher initiation fees, longer apprenticeship periods, tougher qualification exams, more restrictive licensing requirements, and so on. But even if unions restrict membership, they still have difficulty unionizing all firms in the industry.

Whereas wage setting is more typical of industrial unions, restricting supply is more typical of craft unions, such as unions of carpenters, plumbers, or bricklayers. Professional groups—doctors, lawyers, and accountants, for instance—also impose entry restrictions through education, examination, and licensing requirements. These restrictions, usually defended as protecting the public, are often little more than self-serving attempts to increase wages by restricting labor supply.

Increasing Demand for Union Labor

A third way to increase wages is to increase the demand for union labor by somehow shifting the labor demand curve outward as from *D* to *D*″ in panel (b) of Exhibit 7. This is an attrac-

© CHRISTINE BALDERAS/ISTOCKPHOTO.COM

Exhibit 7

Effect of Reducing Labor Supply or Increasing Labor Demand

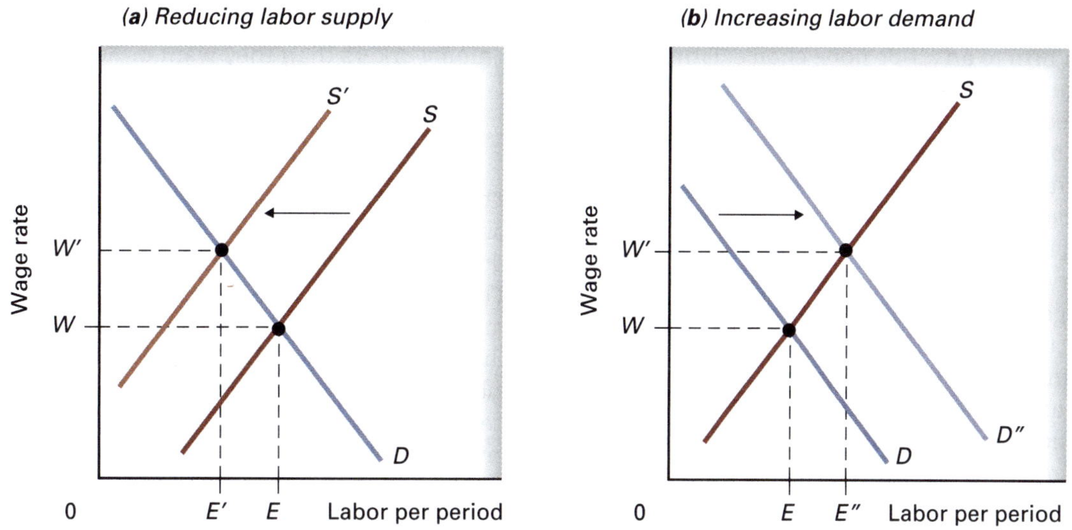

tive alternative *because it increases both the wage and employment*, so there is no need to restrict labor supply or to ration jobs among union members. Here are some ways unions try to increase the demand for union labor.

© ISTOCKPHOTO.COM

Increase Demand for Union-Made Goods

The demand for union labor may be increased through a direct appeal to consumers to buy only union-made products. Because the demand for labor is a derived demand, increasing the demand for union-made products increases the demand for union labor.

Restrict Supply of Nonunion-Made Goods

Another way to increase the demand for union labor is to restrict the supply of products that compete with union-made products. This approach relies on the derived nature of labor demand. The United Auto Workers, for example, has supported restrictions on imported cars. Fewer imported cars means greater demand for cars produced by U.S. workers, who are mostly union members. This strategy has become less effective as foreign automakers, such as Toyota, establish nonunion plants in the United States.

Increase Productivity of Union Labor

Some observers claim union representation improves labor-management relations. According to this theory, unions increase worker productivity by minimizing conflicts, resolving differences, and at times even straightening out workers who goof off. In the absence of a union, a dissatisfied worker may simply quit, increasing job turnover. Turnover is costly to the firm because the departing worker leaves with company-specific, on-the-job training that increases worker productivity. With a union, however, workers can resolve matters through union channels. Quit rates are in fact significantly lower among union workers (although this could also be due to the higher pay). If unions increase the productivity of workers, the demand for union labor increases.

Featherbedding

Yet another way unions try to increase union employment is by **featherbedding**, which makes employers hire more labor than they demand. For example, union rules require that each Broadway theater have a permanent "house" carpenter, electrician, and property manager. Once the play opens, these workers show up only on payday. The union may require that the box office be staffed by three people.

featherbedding union efforts to force employers to hire more workers than demanded at a particular wage

Featherbedding does not create an increase in demand, in the sense of shifting the demand curve to the right. Instead, it forces an employer to a point to the right of its labor demand curve. The union tries to limit a firm to an all-or-none choice: Either hire so many workers for the job, or we'll strike. Thus, with featherbedding, *the union attempts to dictate not only the wage but also the quantity that must be hired at that wage, thereby moving employers to the right of their labor demand curve.*

To review: We have examined three ways that unions try to raise members' wages: (1) by negotiating a wage floor above the equilibrium wage for the industry then somehow rationing the limited jobs among union members, (2) by restricting the supply of labor, and (3) by increasing the demand for union labor. Unions try to increase the demand for union labor in four ways: (1) through a direct public appeal to buy only union-made products, (2) by restricting the supply of products made by nonunion labor, (3) by reducing labor turnover and thereby increasing labor's marginal productivity, and (4) through featherbedding, which forces employers to hire more union workers than they want or need.

Final Word

The first half of this chapter focused on labor supply and explained why wages differ across occupations and among individuals within an occupation. The interaction of labor demand and supply determines wages and employment. The second half of the chapter explored the effect of unions on the labor market. At one time unions dominated some key industries. But as global competition intensifies, employers have a harder time passing higher union labor costs along to consumers.

Multiple Choice Questions

1. The amount of time an individual is willing to offer for a wage depends on the
   a. all of the following
   b. value of time devoted to leisure activities
   c. boredom, discomfort, and aggravation associated with work
   d. value of time devoted to nonmarket work
   e. satisfaction gained from goods purchased with the wages
2. Which of the following is an example of leisure?
   a. Sam mows his lawn
   b. Daniel babysits his nephews
   c. Jackie cooks for her family
   d. Brian sits by the pool
   e. Tom mows Sam's lawn for $30
3. People who can earn higher market wages
   a. have a greater net utility associated with nonmarket work
   b. supply more hours to market work than people with lower wages
   c. are less likely to perform nonmarket work
   d. are more likely to view leisure as an inferior good
   e. experience less disutility associated with market work
4. After reading an economics textbook about labor supply and utility maximization, Amelia Ruiz said, "I don't allocate my time like that." Her professor replied,
   a. "You caught us. Economists do not know what they are talking about."
   b. "This proves that you will always choose to spend your time in nonmarket work."
   c. "You act *as if* you allocated your time to derive the same expected net marginal utility from the last unit of time spent in each alternative use."
   d. "Don't you want to use your unlimited resources to satisfy your finite wants?"
   e. "It is obvious that labor supply is a derived demand based on marginal revenue product."
5. A college student working in a minimum-wage job has a _____ opportunity cost of _____ than a college dean.
   a. lower; market work
   b. lower; leisure
   c. higher; market work
   d. higher; nonmarket work
   e. higher; leisure
6. The individual supply curve of labor is backward bending because the substitution effect offsets the income effect at higher wage rates.
   a. True
   b. False
7. If leisure is a normal good, then a decrease in income _____ the time allocated to _____.
   a. decreases; market work
   b. decreases; leisure
   c. decreases; nonmarket work
   d. increases; leisure
   e. increases; market work, nonmarket work, and leisure time
8. Because leisure is a normal good, an increase in income
   a. decreases the demand for leisure time and reduces the amount of time allocated to market work
   b. decreases the demand for leisure time and increases the amount of time allocated to market work and/or nonmarket work
   c. increases the demand for leisure time and reduces the amount of time allocated to market work and nonmarket work
   d. increases the demand for leisure time and increases the amount of time allocated to market work and nonmarket work
   e. has no impact on the demand for leisure time
9. By itself, the substitution effect of an increase in the wage rate will
   a. always lead to an increase in the quantity of labor supplied
   b. always lead to a decrease in the quantity of labor supplied
   c. lead to an increase in the quantity of labor supplied only if leisure is like a normal good
   d. lead to an increase in the quantity of labor supplied only if leisure is not a normal good
   e. lead to an increase in the quantity of labor supplied only if the income effect works in the same direction

10. Sharon wants a career as an accountant. During the summer she turns down a job painting houses at $6 an hour to work in an accounting office for $4 an hour. Which of the following would *not* explain her choice?
   a. Accounting is more prestigious.
   b. The summer accounting job will help her get a full-time job in accounting when she graduates.
   c. She prefers to work inside.
   d. She would face the law of diminishing marginal utility if she had more goods.
   e. She dislikes the messiness of painting.
11. Bob and Mary each have a Ph.D. in economics. Bob has a job in private industry at which he earns $90,000 a year. Mary earns half that much as a college professor. Which of the following could *not* explain Mary's career choice?
   a. She experiences diminishing marginal utility.
   b. She enjoys the flexibility of her schedule.
   c. She enjoys teaching.
   d. She enjoys the informal atmosphere of a college.
   e. She likes having her summers free to do research.
12. Jobs that pay higher salaries must be riskier than lower-paying professions.
   a. True
   b. False
13. Which of the following could explain an increase in demand for labor?
   a. additional training that increases the productivity of each unit of labor in this market
   b. an increase in the amount of risk associated with this job
   c. a decrease in the amount of risk associated with this job
   d. an improvement in the working conditions associated with this job
   e. a decline in the working conditions associated with this job
14. A labor union is a group of
   a. employees who join together to improve their working conditions
   b. firms that join together to hire workers
   c. firms that work together to negotiate better prices in the market
   d. farmers who work together to receive better prices for their agricultural products
   e. workers and firm owners who join together to improve working conditions
15. The process by which union and management representatives negotiate a mutually agreeable contract specifying wages, benefits, and working conditions is called
   a. collective bargaining
   b. mediation
   c. arbitration
   d. striking
   e. litigation
16. In order for a strike to be successful, the union must decrease the supply of both union and non-union labor.
   a. True
   b. False
17. If union demands result in a surplus of labor in some industries, the resulting
   a. increased demand for labor in the nonunion sector drives nonunion wages up
   b. decreased demand for labor in the nonunion sector drives nonunion wages down
   c. increased supply of labor in the nonunion sector drives nonunion wages down
   d. increased supply of labor in the nonunion sector drives nonunion wages up
   e. decreased supply of labor in the nonunion sector drives nonunion wages up
18. If a professional association restricts membership and firms cannot employ nonassociation workers, the equilibrium wage will increase.
   a. True
   b. False
19. Which of the following may be used by a plumber's union or a medical professional association to restrict membership?
   a. all of the following are correct
   b. long apprenticeship periods
   c. difficult qualification exams
   d. stringent education standards
   e. high initiation fees
20. Which of the following is an example of featherbedding?
   a. a craft union's restricting entry into its profession
   b. a union-imposed wage floor
   c. an increase in labor productivity that results from a decrease in quit rates
   d. attempts to reduce the sale of nonunion goods
   e. a construction workers union's requiring an unnecessarily large number of workers to do a particular job

Answers

1. a 2. d 3. c 4. c 5. b 6. b 7. b 8. c 9. a 10. d

11. a 12. b 13. a 14. a 15. a 16. a 17. c 18. a 19. a 20. e

Long Answer Questions

LO1 Discuss issues affecting labor supply and utility maximization

1.1. *(Market Supply of Labor)* The following table shows the hours per week supplied to a particular market by three individuals at various wage rates. Calculate the total hours per week (Q_T) supplied to the market.

Hourly Wage	Q_1	Q_2 (Hours per Week)	Q_3	Q_T
$ 5	20	0	0	____
6	25	0	0	____
7	35	10	0	____
8	45	25	10	____
9	42	40	30	____
10	38	37	45	____

Which individuals, if any, have backward-bending supply curves in the wage range shown? Does the market supply curve bend backward in the wage range shown in the table?

1.2. *(Substitution and Income Effects)* Suppose that the cost of living increases, thereby reducing the purchasing power of your income. If your money wage doesn't increase, you may work *more* hours because of this cost-of-living increase. Is this response predominantly an income effect or a substitution effect? Explain.

1.3. *(Nonwage Determinants of Labor Supply)* Suppose that two jobs are exactly the same except that one is performed in an air-conditioned workplace. How could you measure the value workers attach to such a job amenity?

LO2 Explain the market supply factors that lead to differing wages

2.1. *(Why Wages Differ)* Why might permanent wage differences occur between different markets for labor or within the same labor market?

LO3 List types of unions and describe their collective bargaining strategies

3.1. *(Craft Unions)* Both industrial unions and craft unions attempt to raise their members' wages, but each goes about it differently. Explain the difference in approaches and describe the impact these differences have on excess quantity of labor supplied.

LO4 Describe the relationship between union wages and employment

4.1. *(Industrial Unions)* Review the logic underlying the exhibit below. Then determine the effect, on the industry and a typical firm, of an increase in the demand for industry output. Show your conclusions on a graph. Does the magnitude of the increase in demand make a difference?

Effects of Labor Union's Wage Floor

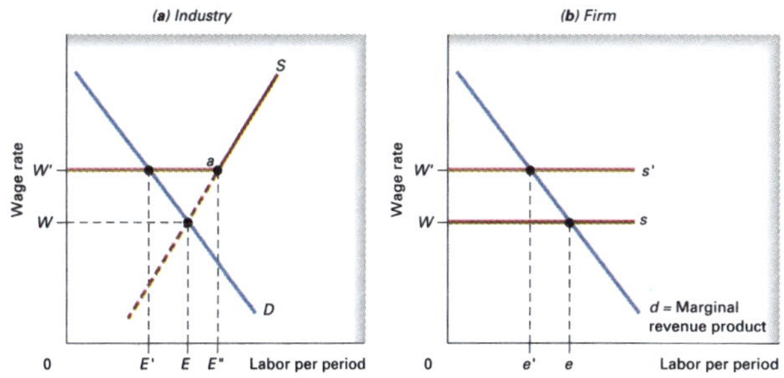

4.2. *(The Strike)* Why might firms in industries with high fixed costs be inclined to prevent strikes or end strikes quickly?

4.3. *(Industrial Unions)* Why are unions more effective at raising wages in oligopolistic industries than in competitive industries?

LABOR MARKETS AND LABOR UNIONS

Chapter in Review

14

KEY TERMS

market work
time sold as labor

nonmarket work
time spent getting an education or on do-it-yourself production for personal consumption

leisure
time spent on nonwork activities

substitution effect of a wage increase
a higher wage encourages more work because other activities now have a higher opportunity cost

income effect of a wage increase
a higher wage raises a worker's income, increasing the demand for all normal goods, including leisure, so the quantity of labor supplied to market work decreases

backward-bending supply curve of labor
as the wage rises, the quantity of labor supplied may eventually decline; the income effect of a higher wage increases the demand for leisure, which reduces the quantity of labor supplied enough to more than offset the substitution effect of a higher wage

winner-take-all labor markets
markets in which a few key employees critical to the overall success of an enterprise are richly rewarded

labor union
a group of workers who organize to improve their terms of employment

craft union
a union whose members have a particular skill or work at a particular craft, such as plumbers or carpenters

industrial union
a union of both skilled and unskilled workers from a particular industry, such as all autoworkers or all steelworkers

collective bargaining
the process by which union and management negotiate a labor agreement

mediator
an impartial observer who helps resolve differences between union and management

binding arbitration
negotiation in which union and management must accept an impartial observer's resolution of a dispute

LO1 Discuss issues affecting labor supply and utility maximization. People allocate their time to maximize utility. There are three uses of time: market work, nonmarket work, and leisure. A person attempts to maximize utility by allocating time so that the expected marginal utility of the last unit of time spent in each activity is identical.

The higher the wage, other things constant, the more goods and services can be purchased with that wage, so a higher wage encourages people to substitute market work for other uses of their time. But a higher wage also increases income, increasing the demand for all normal goods, including leisure. The net effect of a higher wage on the quantity of labor supplied depends on both the substitution effect and the income effect.

Individual Labor Supply Curve for Unskilled Work

When the substitution effect of a wage increase outweighs the income effect, the quantity of labor a worker supplies increases with the wage. Above some wage, shown here at \$12 per hour, the income effect dominates. Above that wage, the supply curve bends backward. Further increases in the wage reduce the quantity of labor supplied.

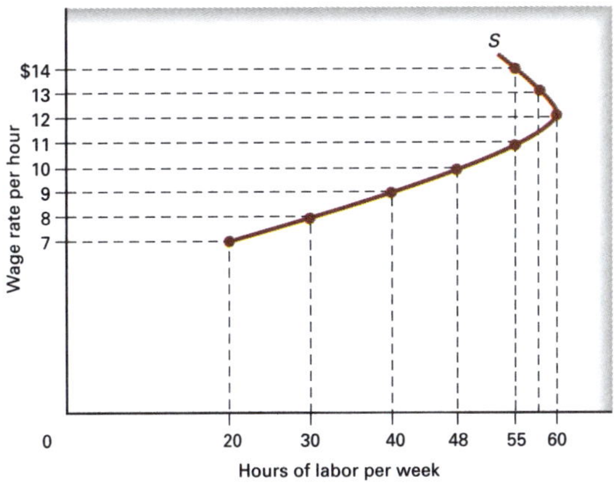

LO2 Explain the market supply factors that lead to differing wages. The intersection of labor demand and labor supply curves determines the market wage and market employment. The supply of labor depends not only on the wage, but on other factors, including (a) other sources of income, (b) job amenities, (c) the value of job experience, and (d) worker tastes. Market wages differ because of (a) differences in training and education; (b) differences in the skill and ability of workers; (c) risk differences, both in terms of the workers' safety and the chances of getting laid off; (d) geographic differences; (e) racial and gender discrimination; and (f) union membership.

Deriving the Market Labor Supply Curve from Individual Labor Supply Curves

The individual labor supply curve in panel (a) bends backward. The market supply curve, however, may still slope upward over the relevant range of wages.

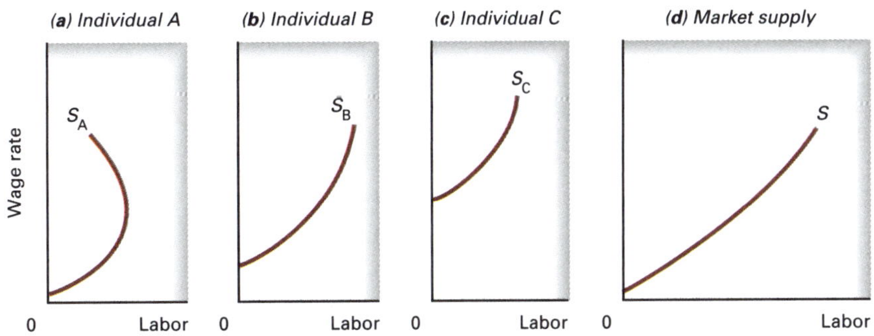

strike
a union's attempt to withhold labor from a firm to halt production

featherbedding
union efforts to force employers to hire more workers than demanded at a particular wage

right-to-work states
states where workers in unionized companies do not have to join the union or pay union dues

LO3 List types of unions and describe their collective bargaining strategies.

Unions can broadly be classified as either craft unions (people with a particular skill, or craft) or industrial unions (unskilled, semiskilled, and skilled workers in a particular industry). Unions and employers try to negotiate a labor contract through collective bargaining. A major source of union power has been the threat of a strike, which is an attempt to withhold labor from the firm.

LO4 Describe the relationship between union wages and employment.

Inclusive, or industrial, unions attempt to establish a wage floor that exceeds the competitive, or market-clearing, wage. A union wage above the market-clearing level creates an excess quantity of labor supplied, so the union must somehow ration the limited jobs among its members. Exclusive, or craft, unions try to raise union wages by restricting the supply of labor. Another way to raise union wages is to increase the demand for union labor.

Union membership as a percentage of the labor force has been falling for half a century. Reasons for the decline include right-to-work laws, growing global competition, a shift in employment from goods to services, a greater willingness to hire replacements for striking workers, a greater willingness of union members and others to work during strikes, and less political support for the labor movement.

Age, Education, and Pay

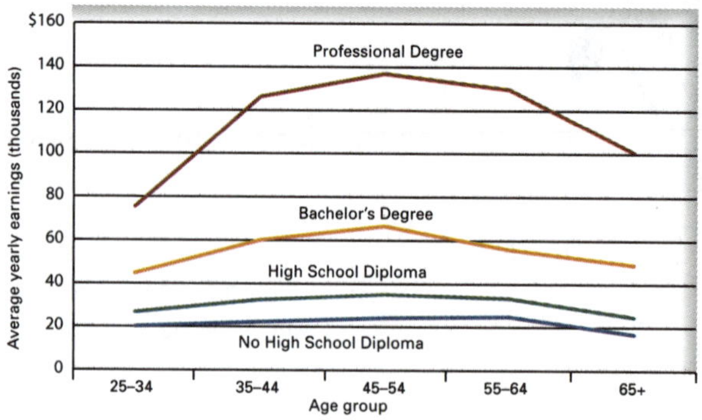

Effects of Labor Union's Wage Floor

Without a labor union, the market wage is *W* in panel (a). At that wage, each firm can hire as much labor as it wants. The individual firm in panel (b) hires more labor until the marginal revenue product equals the market wage, *W*. Each firm hires *e* units of labor, and industry employment is *E*. If a union negotiates a wage *W*′, which is above the market wage *W*, the supply curve facing the firm shifts up from *s* to *s*′. Each firm hires less labor, *e*′, so industry employment falls to *E*′. At the union wage there is now an excess quantity of labor supplied equal to *E*″ – *E*′.

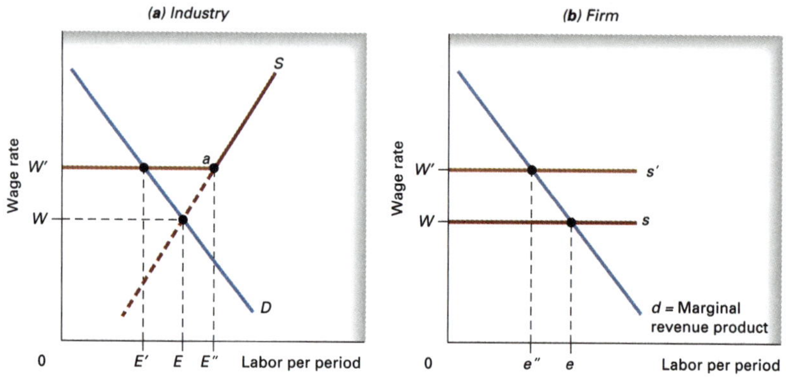

Effect of Reducing Labor Supply or Increasing Labor Demand

If a union can successfully restrict labor supply in an industry, the supply curve shifts to the left from *S* to *S*′, as in panel (a). The wage rises from *W* to *W*′, but at the cost of reducing employment from *E* to *E*′. If a union can increase the demand for union labor, as in panel (b), the demand curve shifts right from *D* to *D*″, raising both the wage and employment.

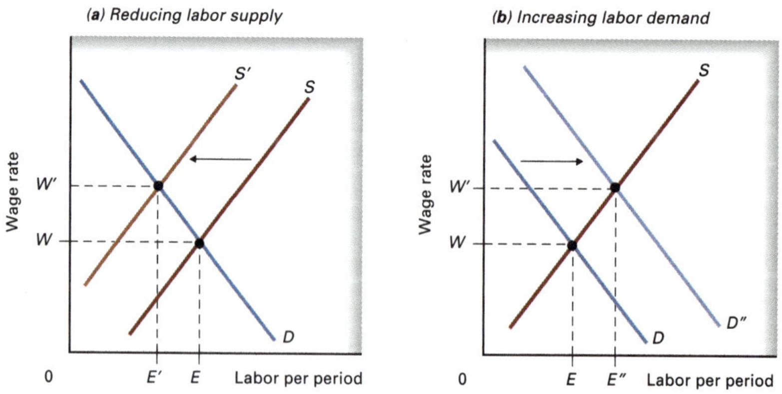

CHAPTER

15

Capital, Interest, *and* Corporate Finance

Learning Outcomes

LO[1] Discuss the role of time in production and consumption

LO[2] Describe the factors that determine optimal investment

LO[3] Explain present value and discounting

LO[4] Analyze different corporate finance strategies

“What’s seed money and why can’t Farmer Jatin grow a thing without it?”

Why is a movie rental only half the price of a movie ticket? Why do you burn your mouth eating pizza? What’s seed money and why can’t Farmer Jatin grow a thing without it? What’s the harm in pirated software, music, and DVDs? Why are state lottery jackpots worth much less than the advertised millions? These and other questions are answered in this chapter, which examines capital and investment.

So far, our discussion of resources has focused primarily on labor markets. This emphasis is appropriate because labor generates most income—more than two-thirds of the total. The rewards to labor, however, depend in part on the amount and quality of the other resources employed, particularly capital. A farmer plowing a field with a tractor is more productive than one scraping the soil with a stick. This chapter looks at the role of capital in production—its cost and its expected return. You will learn about the optimal use of capital and how firms finance their investments.

What do you think?

I think of myself as a saver.

Strongly Disagree						*Strongly Agree*
1	2	3	4	5	6	7

LO1 The Role of Time in Production and Consumption

Time is important in both production and consumption. In this section, we first consider the role of time on the production decision, then show why firms borrow household savings. Next, we consider the role of time in the consumption decision and show why households are rewarded for saving, or deferring consumption. By bringing together borrowers and savers, we find the market interest rate.

Topics discussed in Chapter 15 include:

- Production, saving, and time
- Consumption, saving, and time
- Optimal investment
- Loanable funds market
- Present value and discounting
- Corporate finance
- Stocks, bonds, and retained earnings

Production, Saving, and Time

Suppose Jatin is a primitive farmer in a simple economy. Isolated from any neighbors or markets, he literally scratches out a living on a plot of land, using only some crude sticks. While his crop is growing, none of it is available for current consumption. Because production takes time, to survive, Jatin must rely on food saved from prior

© ISTOCKPHOTO/THINKSTOCK

harvests. The longer the growing season, the more Jatin must save. Thus, even in this simple example, it is clear that *production cannot occur without prior saving.*

With his current resources, consisting of land, labor, seed corn, fertilizer, and some crude sticks, Jatin grows about 200 bushels of corn a year. He soon realizes that if he had a plow—a type of investment good, or capital—his productivity would increase. Making a plow in such a primitive setting, however, is time consuming and would keep him away from his fields for a year. Thus, the plow has an opportunity cost of 200 bushels of corn. He could not survive this drop in production without enough saved from previous harvests.

The question is: Should he invest his time in the plow? The answer depends on the cost and benefit of the plow. We already know that the plow's opportunity cost is 200 bushels—the forgone output. The benefit depends on how much the plow increases crop production and how long it lasts. Jatin figures that the plow would boost annual yield by 100 bushels and would last his lifetime. In making the investment decision, he compares the current cost to the future benefit. Suppose he decides that adding 100 bushels a year outweighs the one-time cost of 200 bushels to make the plow.

In making the plow, Jatin engages in *roundabout production*. Rather than working the soil with his crude sticks, he produces capital to increase his productivity. More roundabout production in an economy means more capital, so more goods can be produced in the future. Advanced industrial economies are characterized by much roundabout production and thus abundant capital accumulation.

positive rate of time preference
consumers value present consumption more than future consumption

You can see why production cannot occur without prior saving. *Production requires saving because both direct and roundabout production take time—time during which goods and services are not available from current production.* Now let's modernize the example by introducing the ability to borrow. Many farmers visit the bank each spring to borrow enough "seed money" to get by until the harvest. Likewise, other businesses often borrow at least a portion of the start-up funds needed to get going. Thus, in a modern economy, producers need not rely just on their own prior saving. Banks and other financial institutions serve as *intermediaries* between savers and borrowers. Financial markets for stocks and bonds also help channel savings to producers.

Let's take a look at the incentive to save.

Consumption, Saving, and Time

Did you ever burn the roof of your mouth eating a slice of pizza? Have you done this more than once? Why do you persist in such self-mutilation? You persist because that bite of pizza is worth more to you now than the same bite a minute from now. In fact, you are willing to risk burning your mouth rather than wait until the pizza has lost its destructive properties. In a small way, this phenomenon reflects the fact that you and other consumers value *present* consumption more than *future* consumption. You and other consumers are said to have a **positive rate of time preference**.

> "Production requires saving because both direct and roundabout production take time."

© BRIAN HAGIWARA/BRAND X PICTURES/JUPITERIMAGES / © BARBARA PEACOCK/THE IMAGE BANK/GETTY IMAGES

Exhibit 1a

Marginal Rate of Return per Year on Investment in Farm Equipment

(1) Farm Equipment	(2) Total Product (bushels)	(3) Marginal Product (bushels)	(4) Marginal revenue Product (4) = (3) x ₹4	(5) Marginal Resource Cost	(6) Marginal Rate of Return (6) = (4) / (5)
No equipment	200	—	—	—	—
Tractor-tiller	1,200	1,000	₹4,000	₹10,000	40%
Combine	2,000	800	3,200	10,000	32
Irrigator	2,600	600	2,400	10,000	24
Harrow	3,000	400	1,600	10,000	16
Crop sprayer	3,200	200	800	10,000	8
Post-hole digger	3,200	0	0	10,000	0

© RYAN MCVAY/PHOTODISC/GETTY IMAGES

Because you value present consumption more than future consumption, you are willing to pay more to consume now rather than wait. And prices often reflect this greater willingness to pay. Consider the movies. You pay about twice as much for a movie ticket than to rent the DVD four months later. The same is true for books. By waiting for the paperback, you can save more than half the hardback price. Photo developers, dry cleaners, fast-food restaurants, convenience stores, cable news networks, and other suppliers tout the speed of their services, knowing that consumers prefer earlier availability. Thus, *impatience* is one explanation for a positive rate of time preference. Another is *uncertainty*. If you wait, something might prevent you from consuming the good. A T-shirt slogan captures this point best: "Life is uncertain. Eat dessert first."

Because people value present consumption more than future consumption, they must be rewarded to postpone consumption. By saving a portion of their incomes in financial institutions such as banks, people forgo present consumption for a greater ability to consume in the future. Interest is the reward for postponing consumption. The **interest rate** is the annual reward for saving as a percentage of the amount saved. For example, if the interest rate is 5 percent, the reward, or interest, is ₹5 per year for each ₹100 saved. The higher the interest rate, other things constant, the more consumers are rewarded for saving, so the more they save. You will learn more about this later in the chapter.

LO2 Optimal Investment

In a market economy characterized by specialization and exchange, Farmer Jatin no longer needs to produce his own capital, nor need he rely on his own saving. He can purchase capital with borrowed funds. Suppose he wants to buy some farm equipment. He estimates how each piece of equipment would affect his productivity. Column (1) in Exhibit 1a identifies six pieces of farm machinery that Jatin has ranked from most to least productive. The total product of the equipment is listed in column (2), and the marginal product of each piece is listed in column (3). Note that other resources are assumed to remain constant.

With just his crude sticks, Jatin can grow 200 bushels of corn per year. He figures that a tractor-tiller would boost the harvest to 1,200 bushels. Thus, the tractor-tiller would yield a marginal product of 1,000 bushels per year. Adding a combine would increase total output to 2,000 bushels, yielding a marginal product of 800 bushels. Note that in this example, diminishing marginal returns from capital set in with the combine. Marginal product continues to decrease as more capital is added, dropping to zero for a post-hole digger, which Jatin has no use for.

Suppose Jatin sells corn in a perfectly competitive market, so he can sell all he wants at the market price of ₹4 a bushel. The marginal product from column (3) multiplied by ₹4 yields capital's *marginal revenue product* listed in column (4). The marginal revenue product of machinery is its marginal product times the price of corn, or the change in total revenue resulting from adding another piece of farm equipment.

For simplicity, suppose farm equipment costs ₹10,000 each. Thus, the marginal resource cost is ₹10,000, as listed in column (5). Suppose also that the equipment is so durable that it is expected to last indefinitely, that operating expenses are negligible, and that the price of corn is expected to remain at ₹4 per bushel in the future. Farm equipment

interest rate
interest per year as a percentage of the amount saved or borrowed

increases revenue not only in the first year but every year into the future. The *optimal investment decision requires Jatin to take time into account*. He can't simply equate marginal resource cost with marginal revenue product, because the marginal cost is a one-time outlay this year, whereas the marginal product is an annual amount this year and each year in the future. As we will see, markets bridge time with the interest rate.

Jatin must decide how much to invest in farm equipment. His first task is to compute the *marginal rate of return* he expects to earn each year by investing in farm machinery. The **marginal rate of return on investment** is capital's marginal revenue product as a percentage of its marginal resource cost. For example, the tractor-tiller yields a marginal revenue product of ₹4,000 per year and has a one-time marginal resource cost of ₹10,000. The marginal rate of return Jatin could earn on this investment is ₹4,000/₹10,000, or 40 percent per year. Therefore, the tractor-tiller yields a *marginal rate of return* of 40 percent per year, as shown in column (6). The combine yields a marginal revenue product of ₹3,200 per year and has a marginal cost of ₹10,000, so its marginal rate of return equals ₹3,200/₹10,000, or 32 percent per year. Dividing the marginal revenue product of capital in column (4) by the marginal resource cost of that capital in column (5) yields the marginal rate of return in column (6) for each piece of equipment.

Given the marginal rate of return, how much should Jatin invest to maximize profit? Suppose he borrows the money, paying the *market interest rate*. Jatin buys more capital as long as its marginal rate of return exceeds the market interest rate. He stops before capital's marginal rate of return falls below the market interest rate. For example, if the market interest rate is 20 percent, Jatin invests ₹30,000 in three pieces of equipment. The marginal rate of return on the third item purchased, an irrigator, is 24 percent. Investing another ₹10,000 to buy a harrow would yield a marginal return of only 16 percent, a rate below his cost of borrowing. At a market interest rate of 10 percent, Jatin would invest in the harrow as well. An interest rate of 6 percent would lead Jatin to also invest in the crop sprayer.

Farmer Jatin should increase his investment as long as the marginal rate of return on that investment exceeds the market interest rate. The marginal rate of return is the marginal benefit of the investment, and the market interest rate is the marginal cost, so Jatin is simply maximizing profit (or minimizing loss) by investing until marginal benefit equals the marginal cost. The data in column (6) are depicted in Exhibit 1b as a step-like graph, where the solid lines reflect the amount Jatin invests at each interest rate. For example, if the market interest rate is between 32 percent and 40 percent, Jatin should invest in the tractor-tiller. Because the marginal rate of return shows how much should be invested at each interest rate, this step-like graph represents the farmer's demand for investment. This is a derived demand, based on the marginal productivity of each piece of equipment. The demand curve steps down to reflect the diminishing marginal productivity of capital.

Would the example change if Jatin saved enough to buy the equipment? Not as long as he can earn the market interest rate on his savings. For example, suppose Jatin saved ₹50,000, which is earning an interest rate of 10 percent per year. In that case, Jatin should invest ₹40,000 in capital, with the last piece purchased, the harrow, earning a marginal return of 16 percent. The 10 percent interest Jatin earns on his remaining savings of ₹10,000 exceeds the 8 percent he could earn by investing that amount in the crop sprayer. Thus, as long as he can borrow and save at the same interest rate, Jatin ends up investing in the same equipment whether he borrows funds or draws down his own savings. *Whether Jatin borrows*

marginal rate of return on investment the marginal revenue product of capital expressed as a percentage of its marginal cost

Exhibit 1b

Marginal Rate of Return per Year on Investment in Farm Equipment

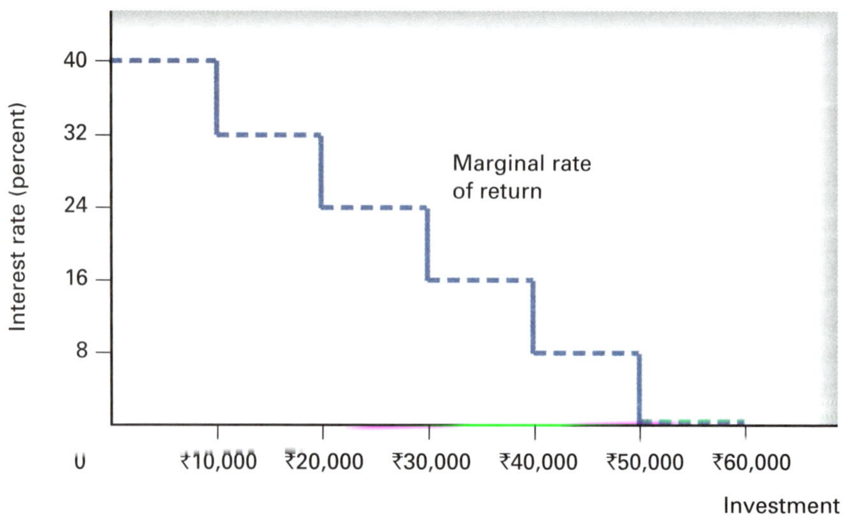

Steps to Determine the Optimal Amount of Investment

- Compute the marginal revenue product of capital
- Divide marginal revenue product by marginal resource cost to determine marginal rate of return
- Marginal rate of return curve = demand curve for investment
- Market interest rate = opportunity cost of investing, or the supply of investment funds
- If marginal rate of return > market interest rate, then invest more

the money or draws on his savings, the market interest rate represents his opportunity cost of investing.

Let's review the steps to determine the optimal amount of investment. First, compute the marginal revenue product of capital. Next, divide the marginal revenue product by the marginal resource cost to get the marginal rate of return. The marginal rate of return curve becomes a firm's demand curve for investment—that is, it shows the amount a firm is willing and able to invest at each interest rate. The market interest rate is the opportunity cost of investing either borrowed funds or savings and can be thought of as the supply of investment funds to the firm. A firm should invest more as long as the marginal rate of return on capital exceeds the market rate of interest.

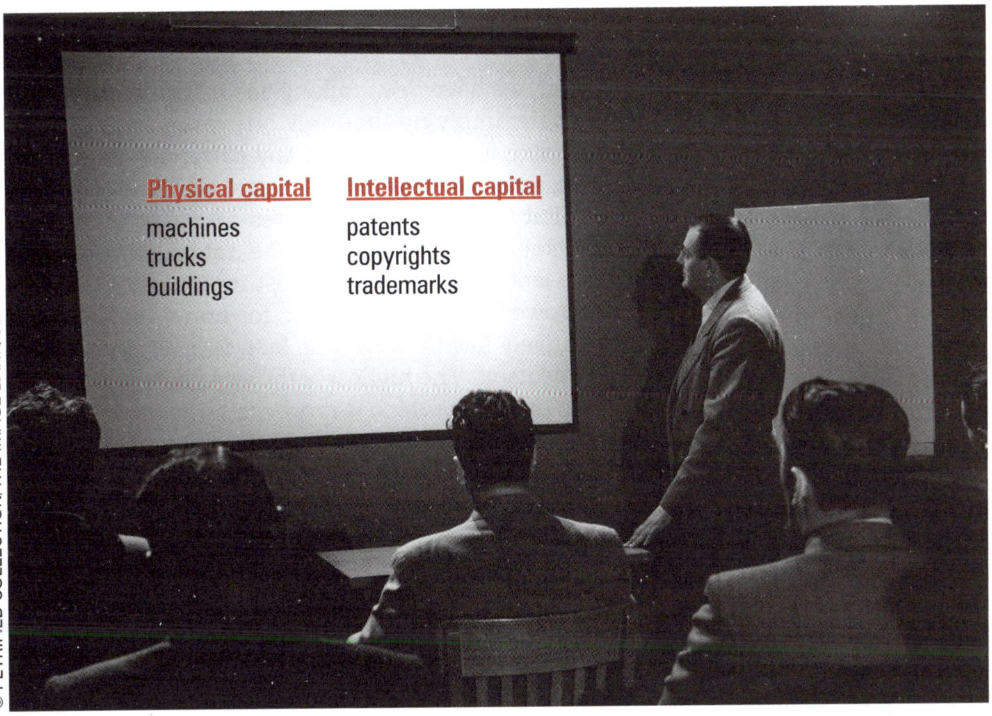

© PETRIFIED COLLECTION/THE IMAGE BANK/GETTY IMAGES

The Market for Loanable Funds

You learned earlier why producers are willing to pay interest to borrow money: *Money provides a command over resources, making both direct production and roundabout production possible.* The simple principles developed for Farmer Jatin can be generalized to other producers. The major demanders of loans are entrepreneurs who borrow to start firms and to invest in physical capital, such as machines, trucks, and buildings, and in intellectual capital, such as patents, copyrights, and trademarks. At any time, a firm has a variety of investment opportunities. The firm ranks these opportunities from highest to lowest, based on the expected marginal rates of return. The firm increases its investment until the expected marginal rate of return just equals the market interest rate. With other inputs held constant, as they were on the farm, the demand curve for investment slopes downward.

But entrepreneurs are not the only demanders of loans. As we have seen, households value present consumption more than future consumption; they are willing to pay extra to consume now rather than later. One way to ensure that goods and services are available now is to borrow for present consumption, as reflected by home mortgages, car loans, and credit card purchases. Some people also borrow to invest in their human capital, as reflected by college loans. The household's demand curve for loans, like the firm's demand for loans, slopes downward, indicating that consumers are more willing and able to borrow at lower interest rates, other things constant. The government sector and the rest of the world are also demanders of loans.

Demand for Loanable Funds

The **demand for loanable funds** curve shows the negative relationship between the market interest rate and the quantity of loans demanded,

demand for loanable funds
the negative relationship between the market interest rate and the quantity of loanable funds demanded, other things constant

other things constant. This curve is based on the expected marginal rate of return these borrowed funds yield when invested in capital. Each firm has a downward-sloping demand curve for loanable funds, reflecting a declining marginal rate of return on investment. With some qualifications, the demand for loanable funds of each firm can be summed horizontally to yield the market demand for loanable funds, shown as *D* in Exhibit 2. Factors assumed constant along this demand curve include the prices of other resources, the level of technology, and the tax laws.

Exhibit 2

Market for Loanable Funds

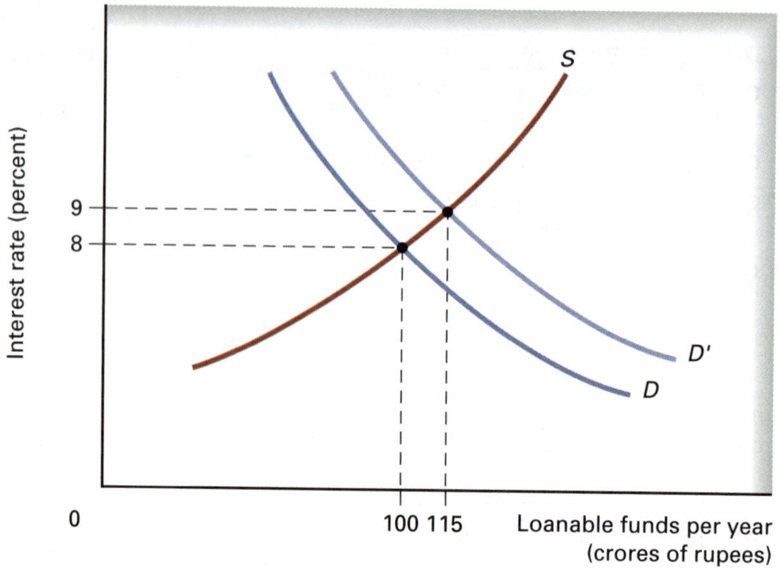

Supply of Loanable Funds

Banks are willing to pay interest on savings because they can, in turn, lend these savings to those who need credit, such as farmers, home buyers, college students, and entrepreneurs looking to start a new business or buy new capital. Banks play the role of *financial intermediaries* in what is known as the market for loanable funds. The higher the interest rate, other things constant, the greater the reward for saving. As people save more, the quantity of loanable funds increases. The **supply of loanable funds** curve shows the positive relationship between the market interest rate and the quantity of savings supplied, other things constant, as reflected by the usual upward-sloping supply curve shown as S in Exhibit 2.

supply of loanable funds the positive relationship between the market interest rate and the quantity of loanable funds supplied, other things constant

loanable funds market the market in which savers (suppliers of loanable funds) and borrowers (demanders of loanable funds) come together to determine the market interest rate and the quantity of loanable funds exchanged

prime rate the interest rate lenders charge their most trustworthy business borrowers

collateral an asset pledged by the borrower that can be sold to pay off the loan in the event the borrower defaults

Market Interest Rate

The **loanable funds market** brings together borrowers, or demanders of loanable funds, and savers, or suppliers of loanable funds, to determine the market interest rate. The demand and supply of loanable funds come together, as in Exhibit 2, to determine the market interest rate. In this case, the equilibrium interest rate of 8 percent is the only one that exactly matches the wishes of borrowers and savers. The equilibrium quantity of loanable funds is ₹100 crore per year. Any change in the demand or supply of loanable funds changes the market interest rate. For example, a major technological breakthrough that increases the productivity of capital increases its marginal rate of return, shifting the demand curve for loanable funds rightward, as shown in the movement from *D* to *D'*. Such an increase in the demand for loanable funds would raise the equilibrium interest rate to 9 percent and increase the market quantity of loanable funds to ₹115 crore per year.

Why Interest Rates Differ

So far, we have been talking about the market interest rate, implying that only one rate prevails in the loanable funds market. At any particular time, however, a range of interest rates coexist in the economy. Exhibit 3 shows interest rates for loans in various markets. The so-called **prime rate** is the interest rate lenders charge their most trustworthy business borrowers. The interest rate for home mortgages is relatively low because this loan is backed up by the home itself. The highest is the rate charged on credit card balances, which is more than double the rate on mortgages. Let's see why interest rates differ.

Risk

Some borrowers are more likely than others to default on their loans—that is, not to pay them back. Before a bank lends money, it usually requires a borrower to put up **collateral**, which is an asset pledged by the borrower that can be sold to pay off the loan in the event of a default. With business loans, any

Exhibit 3

Interest Rates Charged for Different Types of Loans

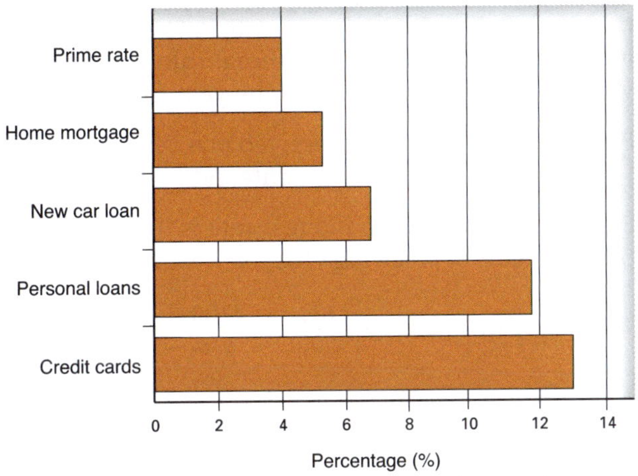

SOURCE: Federal Reserve Board; Bankrate.com; Moneycentral.msn.com. Interest rates are as of December 2008.

valuable asset—land, buildings, machinery—the firm owns can serve as collateral. With a home mortgage, the home itself becomes collateral. And with a car loan, the car becomes collateral. The more valuable the collateral backing up the loan, other things constant, the lower the interest rate charged on that loan. For example, the interest rate charged on car loans is usually higher than on home loans. A car loses its value more quickly than a home does, and a car can be driven away by a defaulting borrower, whereas a home usually increases in value and stays put. So a car offers worse collateral than a home—hence, the interest charged on a car loan is higher. Interest rates are higher still for personal loans and credit cards, because such borrowers usually offer no collateral.

Duration of the Loan

The future is uncertain, and the further into the future a loan is to be repaid, the more uncertain that repayment becomes. Thus, as the duration of a loan increases, lenders require a higher interest rate to compensate for the greater risk. The **term structure of interest rates** is the relationship between the duration of a loan and the interest rate charged. *The interest rate usually increases with the duration of the loan, other things constant.*

Administration Costs

The costs of executing the loan agreement, monitoring the loan, and collecting payments are called the *administration costs* of the loan. These costs, as a proportion of the loan, decrease as the size of the loan increases. For example, the cost of administering a ₹100,000 loan is less than 10 times the cost of administering a ₹10,000 loan. Consequently, that portion of the interest charge reflecting administration costs becomes smaller as the size of the loan increases, other things constant, thus reducing the interest rate for larger loans.

Tax Treatment

Differences in the tax treatment of different types of loans also affect the interest rate charged. For example, the interest earned on loans to state and local governments is not subject to federal income taxes. Because lenders focus on their after-tax rate of interest, state and local governments pay a lower interest rate than other borrowers pay.

To review: the demand and supply of loanable funds determine the market interest rate. At any given time, interest rates may differ because of differences in risk, maturity, administrative costs, and tax treatment. Now we move on to consider the value of some future benefit.

LO3 Present Value and Discounting

Because you value present consumption more than future consumption, present and future consumption cannot be compared directly. Someone who "eats like there's no tomorrow" apparently values present consumption much more than consumption tomorrow. A way of standardizing the discussion is to measure all consumption in terms of its present value. **Present value** is the current value of a payment or payments to be received in the future. For example, how much would you pay now to receive ₹100 one year from now? Put another way, what is the *present value* to you of receiving ₹100 one year from now?

Present Value of Payment One Year Hence

Suppose the market interest rate is 10 percent and you can either lend or borrow at that rate. One way to determine how much you would pay for the opportunity to receive ₹100 one year from now is to ask how much you would have to save now, at the market interest rate, to end up with ₹100 one year

term structure of interest rates the relationship between the duration of a loan and the interest rate charged; typically interest rates increase with the duration of the loan, because longer loans are considered more risky

present value the value today of income to be received in the future from now. Here's the problem we are trying to solve: What amount of money, if saved at an interest rate of, say, 10 percent, would accumulate to ₹100 one year from now? We can calculate the answer with a simple formula:

$$\text{Present value} \times 1.10 = ₹100$$

or:

$$\text{Present value} = \frac{₹100}{1.10} = ₹90.91$$

Thus, if the interest rate is 10 percent, ₹90.91 is the present value of receiving ₹100 one year from now; it is the most you would pay today to receive ₹100 one year from now. Rather than pay more than ₹90.91, you could simply deposit your ₹90.91 at the market interest rate of 10 percent and end up with ₹100 a year from now (ignoring taxes). Dividing the future payment by 1 plus the prevailing interest rate to express it in today's rupees is called **discounting**.

The present value of ₹100 to be received one year from now depends on the interest rate. The more that present consumption is preferred to future consumption, the higher the interest rate that must be offered savers to defer consumption. *The higher the interest rate, the more any future payment is discounted and the lower its present value.* Put another way, the higher the interest rate, the less you need to save now to yield a given amount in the future. For example, if the interest rate is 15 percent, the present value of receiving ₹100 one year from now is ₹100/1.15, which equals ₹86.96.

discounting
converting future rupees amounts into present value

On the other hand, the less present consumption is preferred to future consumption, the less savers need to be paid to defer consumption so the lower the interest rate. The lower the interest rate, the less the future income is discounted and the greater its present value. A lower interest rate means that you must save more now to yield a given amount in the future. As a general rule, the present value of receiving an amount one year from now is:

$$\text{Present value} = \frac{\text{Amount received one year from now}}{1 + \text{interest rate}}$$

For example, when the interest rate is 5 percent, the present value of receiving ₹100 one year from now is:

$$\text{Present value} = \frac{₹100}{1 + 0.05} = \frac{₹100}{1.05} = ₹95.24$$

Present Value for Payments in Later Years

Now consider the present value of receiving ₹100 two years from now. What amount of money, if deposited at the market interest rate of 5 percent, would yield ₹100 after two years? After one year, the value would be the present value times 1.05, which would then earn the market interest rate during the second year. After two years, the deposit would have accumulated to the present value times 1.05 times 1.05. Thus, we have the equation:

$$\text{Present value} \times 1.05 \times 1.05 = \text{Present value} \times (1.05)^2 = ₹100$$

Solving for the present value yields:

$$\text{Present value} = \frac{₹100}{(1.05)^2} = \frac{₹100}{1.1025} = ₹90.70$$

If the ₹100 were to be received three years from now, we would discount the payment over three years:

$$\text{Present value} = \frac{₹100}{(1.05)^3} = ₹86.38$$

If the interest rate is i, the present value of M rupees received t years from now is:

$$\text{Present value} = \frac{M}{(1 + i)^t}$$

Because $(1 + i)$ is greater than 1, the more times it is multiplied by itself (as determined by t), the larger the denominator and the smaller the present value. Thus, *the present value of a given payment is smaller the further into the future that payment is to be received.*

© RON CHAPPLE/THINKSTOCK IMAGES/JUPITERIMAGES

Present Value of an Income Stream

So far, we have figured out the present value of a single sum to be received in the future. Most investments, however, yield a stream of income over time. In cases where the income is received for a period of years, the present value of each receipt can be computed individually and the results summed to yield the present value of the entire income stream. For example, the present value of receiving ₹100 next year and ₹150 the year after is simply the present value of the first year's receipt plus the present value of the second year's receipt. If the interest rate is 5 percent:

$$\text{Present value} = \frac{₹100}{1.05} + \frac{₹150}{(1.05)^2} = ₹231.29$$

$$\text{Present value} = \frac{M}{(1+i)^t}$$

$$\text{Present value of receiving } M \text{ rupees each year forever} = \frac{M}{i}$$

Present Value of an Annuity

A given sum of money received each year for a specified number of years is called an **annuity**. Such an income stream is called a *perpetuity* if it continues indefinitely, as it would with indestructible farm machinery. The present value of receiving a certain amount forever seems like it should be a very large sum indeed. But because future income is valued less the more distant into the future it is to be received, the present value of receiving a particular amount forever is not much more than that of receiving it for, say, 20 years.

To determine the present value of receiving ₹100 a year forever, we need only ask how much money must be deposited in a savings account to yield ₹100 in interest each year. If the interest rate is 10 percent, a deposit of ₹1,000 will earn ₹100 per year. Thus, the present value of receiving ₹100 a year indefinitely when the interest rate is 10 percent is ₹1,000. More generally, the present value of receiving a sum each year forever equals the amount received each year divided by the interest rate.

$$\text{Present value of receiving M rupees each year forever} = \frac{M}{i}$$

The concept of present value is useful for investment decisions. Farmer Jatin, by investing ₹10,000 in the crop sprayer, expects to earn ₹800 more per year. So his marginal rate of return on that investment is 8 percent. At a market interest rate of 8 percent, the present value of a cash flow of ₹800 per year discounted at that rate would be ₹800/0.08, which equals ₹10,000. Thus, *Jatin is willing to invest capital until, at the margin, his investment yields a cash stream with a present value just equal to the marginal cost of the investment.* Jatin invests until marginal benefit equals marginal cost.

What about your decision to invest in human capital—to go to college? A chart in the previous chapter showed that those with at least a college degree earned nearly twice as much as those with just a high school diploma. We could compute the present value of an education by discounting earnings based on that level of education, then summing total earnings over your working life. Even without doing the calculations, we can say with reasonable certainty that the present value of at least a college education will be nearly twice that of just a high school education.

This discussion of present value and discounting concludes our treatment of capital and interest. We now have some tools to consider how firms, especially corporations, are financed.

LO4 Corporate Finance

During the Industrial Revolution, labor-saving machinery made large-scale production more profitable, but building huge factories filled with heavy machinery required substantial investments. The corporate structure became the easiest way to finance such outlays, and by 1920, corporations accounted for most employment and output in the U.S. economy. Back in Chapter 3, you learned about the pros and cons of the corporate form of business. Thus far, however, little has been said about corporate finance. As noted in Chapter 3, a corporation is a legal entity, distinct from its shareholders. The corporation may own property, earn a profit, sue or be sued, incur debt, even be found guilty of a crime. Stockholders, the owners of the corporation, are liable only to the extent of their investment in the firm. Use of the abbreviations Inc. or Corp. in the company name serves as a warning to potential creditors that stockholders will not accept personal liability for debts of the company.

annuity
a given sum of money received each year for a specified number of years

Corporate Stock and Retained Earnings

Corporations fund investment in three ways: by issuing stock, by retaining some of their profits, and by borrowing. Corporations issue and sell stock to raise money for operations and for new plants and equipment. Suppose you have developed a recipe for a hot, spicy chili that your friends have convinced you will be a best-seller. You start a company called Six-Alarm Chili. As the founder, you are that firm's entrepreneur. Recall that an entrepreneur is a profit-seeking decision maker who organizes an enterprise and assumes the risk of operation. An entrepreneur pays others for the opportunity to use their resources in the firm. The entrepreneur need not actually manage the firm's resources as long as he or she has the power to hire and fire the manager—that is, as long as the entrepreneur controls the manager.

Your company meets with early success, but you find that to remain competitive, you need to achieve economies of scale, which means the firm must grow fast. To fund that growth, you decide to incorporate. The newly incorporated company issues 1,000,000 shares of stock. You take 100,000 shares yourself as your *owner's equity* in the corporation. The rest are sold to the public for ₹10 per share, which raises ₹9 million for the company. You, in effect, pay for your shares with the "sweat equity" required to found the company and get it rolling. The initial sale of stock to the public is called an **initial public offering**, or **IPO**. A *share* of **corporate stock** is a claim on the net income and assets of a corporation, as well as the right to vote on corporate directors and on other important matters. A person who buys 1 percent of the 1,000,000 shares issued thereby owns 1 percent of the corporation, is entitled to 1 percent of any profit, and gets to cast 1 percent of the votes on important corporate decisions.

initial public offering (IPO)
the initial sale of corporate stock to the public

corporate stock
certificate reflecting part ownership of a corporation

dividends
after-tax corporate profit paid to stockholders rather than retained by the firm and reinvested

retained earnings
after-tax corporate profit reinvested in the firm rather than paid to stockholders as dividends

bond
certificate reflecting a firm's promise to pay the lender periodic interest and to repay the borrowed sum of money on the designated maturity date

Corporations must pay corporate income taxes on any profit. After-tax profit is either paid as **dividends** to shareholders or reinvested in the corporation. Reinvested profit, or **retained earnings**, helps the firm fund expansion. Stockholders usually expect dividends, but the corporation is not required to pay dividends. Once shares are issued, their price tends to fluctuate directly with the firm's profit prospects. People buy stock because of the dividends and because they hope the share price will appreciate, or increase.

Corporate Bonds

Again, your corporation can acquire funds by issuing stock, by retaining earnings, or by borrowing. To borrow money, the corporation can go to a bank for a loan or it can issue and sell bonds. A **bond** is the corporation's promise to pay back the holder a fixed sum of money on the designated *maturity date* plus make interest payments until that date. For example, a corporation might sell for ₹1,000 a bond that promises to make an annual interest payment of, say, ₹100 for 20 years and to repay the ₹1,000 at the end of 20 years.

The payment stream for bonds is more predictable than that for stocks. Unless this corporation goes

The Securities and Exchange Board of India

The Securities and Exchange Board of India (SEBI) is the regulator for the securities market in India. It was established on 12th of April 1992 through the Securities and Exchange Board of India Act, 1992. SEBI is headquartered in Mumbai, and has Northern, Eastern, Southern, and Western regional offices in New Delhi, Kolkata, Chennai, and Ahmadabad.

Controller of Capital Issues was the regulatory authority before SEBI came into existence; it derived authority from the Capital Issues (Control) Act, 1947.

Initially SEBI was a non statutory body without any statutory power. However in 1995, the SEBI was given additional statutory power by the Government of India through an amendment to the Securities and Exchange Board of India Act, 1992. In April, 1998 the SEBI was constituted as the regulator of capital markets in India under a resolution of the Government of India.

The SEBI is managed by six members, i.e. by the chairman who is nominated by central government and two members, i.e. officers of central ministry, one member from the RBI and the remaining two are nominated by the central government.

SEBI has to be responsive to the needs of three groups, which constitute the market:

- The issuers of securities
- The investors
- The market intermediaries

SEBI has three functions rolled into one body: quasi-legislative, quasi-judicial, and quasi-executive. It drafts regulations in its legislative capacity, it conducts investigation and enforcement action in its executive function, and it passes rulings and orders in its judicial capacity.

SOURCE: http://en.wikipedia.org/wiki/Securities_and_Exchange_Board_of_India.

Stock Exchanges in India

Though a number of other exchanges exist, the National Stock Exchange (NSE) and the Bombay Stock Exchange (BSE) are the two most significant stock exchanges in India and between them are responsible for the vast majority of share transactions. While both have similar total market capitalization (about USD 1.6 trillion), share volume in NSE is typically two times that of BSE.

The National Stock Exchange: The National Stock Exchange (NSE) is stock exchange located at Mumbai, India. It is in the top 20 largest stock exchanges in the world by market capitalization and largest in India by daily turnover and number of trades, for both equities and derivative trading. NSE has a market capitalization of around USD1 trillion and over 1,652 listings as of July 2012. The NSE's key index is the S&P CNX Nifty, known as the NSE NIFTY (National Stock Exchange Fifty), an index of fifty major stocks weighted by market capitalization.

Bombay Stock Exchange: BSE Limited formerly known as Bombay Stock Exchange (BSE) is a stock exchange located in Mumbai and is the oldest stock exchange in Asia. The equity market capitalization of the companies listed on the BSE was USD 1 trillion as of December 2011, making it the 6th largest stock exchange in Asia and the 14th largest in the world. The BSE has the largest number of listed companies in the world. As of March 2012, there are over 5,133 listed Indian companies and over 8,196 scrips on the stock exchange. The Bombay Stock Exchange has a significant trading volume. The BSE SENSEX, also called "BSE 30," is a widely used market index in India and Asia.

SOURCES: http://en.wikipedia.org/wiki/National_Stock_Exchange_of_India; http://en.wikipedia.org/wiki/Bombay_Stock_Exchange.

bankrupt, it must pay bondholders as promised. In contrast, stockholders are last in line when resource suppliers get paid, so bondholders get paid before stockholders. Investors usually consider bonds less risky than stocks, although bonds involve risks as well. Risks include corporate bankruptcy and higher market interest rates. For example, suppose you buy a bond that pay 6 percent interest. Soon after that purchase, the market interest rate increases, so newly issued bonds pay 8 percent interest. Your 6 percent bond is less attractive than the new bonds, so the market value of your bond declines. The value of your bond declines until bond buyers are indifferent between buying your 6 percent bond and buying an 8 percent bond.

Securities Exchanges

Once stocks and bonds have been issued and sold, owners of these securities are free to resell them on *securities exchanges*. In the United States, the *Securities and Exchange Commission (SEC)* is the federal body that regulates securities markets. The largest securities market is the New York Stock Exchange, which trades the securities of about 2,800 major corporations from all over the world. Altogether about 10,000

© STEPHEN HILGER/BLOOMBERG NEWS/LANDOV

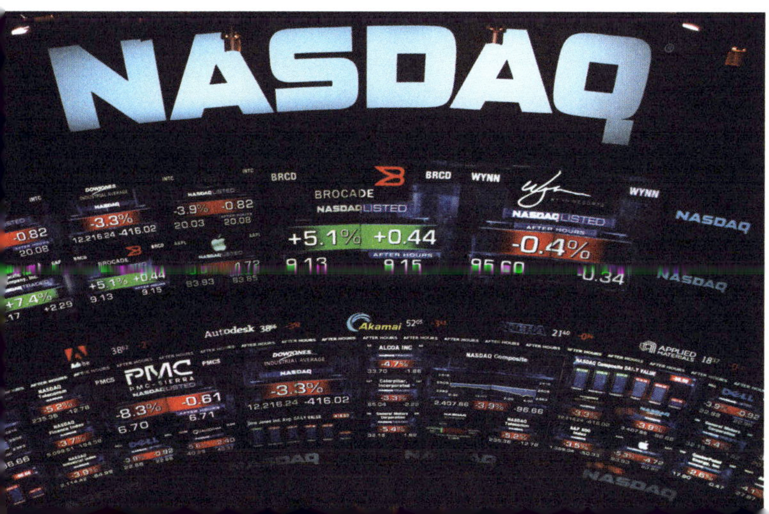

corporations trade on various U.S. exchanges. These are called publicly traded companies, to be distinguished from privately owned companies. Although privately owned companies, such as sole proprietors and partnerships, make up the overwhelming share of U.S. businesses in terms of numbers, corporations account for the overwhelming share of employment and sales.

Nearly all the securities traded each business day are *secondhand securities* in the sense that they have already been issued by the corporation. So the bulk of daily transactions does not finance firms in need of investment funds. Most money from daily trading goes from a securities buyer to a securities seller. *Institutional investors*, such as banks, insurance companies, and mutual funds, account for over half the trading volume on major exchanges. By providing a *secondary market* for securities, exchanges enhance the *liquidity* of securities—that is, the exchanges make the securities more readily sold for cash and thus more attractive to own. Of growing importance in securities exchanges are *hedge funds*, which often follow complex strategies to invest for institutions and wealthy clients.

The secondary markets for stocks also determine the current market value of the corporation. The market value of a firm at any given time can be found by multiplying the share price by the number of shares issued. Because the share price fluctuates throughout the trading day, so does the value of the corporation. In theory, the share price reflects the present value of the discounted stream of expected profit. Just to give you some idea, ExxonMobil, the top-valued U.S. corporation, had a market value of $334 billion at the close of the trading day on July 2, 2009. The 2,300 U.S. corporations traded on the New York Stock

Exchange had a combined market value of about $10 trillion, nearly 40% less than the year before because of the global financial crisis.

Securities prices give corporate management some indication of the wisdom of raising investment funds through retained earnings, new stock issues, or new bond issues. The greater a corporation's expected profit, other things constant, the higher the value of shares on the stock market and the lower the interest rate that would have to be paid on new bond issues. Securities markets usually promote the survival of the fittest by allocating investment funds to those firms able to make the most profitable use of them. *Thus, securities markets allocate funds more readily to successful firms than to firms in financial difficulty.* Some firms may be in such poor shape that they can't issue new securities.

One final point: When economists talk about investing, they have in mind purchases of new capital, such as new machines and new buildings. When the media talk about investing, they usually mean buying stocks and bonds. To an economist, Farmer Jatin is investing only when he buys new farm machinery, not when he buys stocks. As noted already, the overwhelming share of stock transactions are in secondary markets, so the money goes from buyers to sellers and does not go toward new capital purchases.

Final Word

This chapter introduced you to capital, interest, and corporate finance. Capital is a more complicated resource than this chapter has conveyed. For example, the demand curve for investment is a moving target, not the stable relationship drawn in Exhibit 1b. An accurate depiction of the investment demand curve calls for knowledge of the marginal product of capital and the price of output in the future. But capital's marginal productivity changes with breakthroughs in technology and with changes in the employment of other resources. The future price of the product can also vary widely. Consider, for example, the dilemma of a firm contemplating an investment in oil-drilling rigs in recent years when the price of crude oil fluctuated between $10 and $145 per barrel, as it has in the last decade.

MULTIPLE CHOICE QUESTIONS

1. The production of capital goods, which are then used to produce consumer goods, is called
   a. efficient production
   b. intermediation
   c. time preferences
   d. roundabout production
   e. derived production

2. Most companies that sell CDs by mail deliver in 1 to 2 weeks. Mosey Music, Inc., takes 4 weeks to deliver CDs. We should expect that Mosey Music
   a. will lose all its customers
   b. will not lose customers because the good in question is CDs, not the delivery date
   c. will have to charge more for its CDs to make up for the business it loses through slow delivery
   d. will have to charge less for its CDs to compete with firms that deliver CDs faster
   e. will be able to charge the same amount for its CDs as other firms do, as long as the CD quality is the same

3. If the annual interest rate is 4 percent, a consumer who spends ₹100 today
   a. will have to pay back ₹104 to the bank
   b. would have to pay ₹104 next year to get the same goods
   c. will receive ₹96 from the bank next year
   d. would have to pay ₹96 next year to get the same goods
   e. is giving up the ability to spend ₹104 on goods next year

4. All types of capital
   a. are forms of resources that can be used in future production
   b. require a physical existence
   c. earn an economic rent
   d. yield profits for their owners
   e. require obtaining more education and job skills

5. Exhibit 4 shows data gathered by Memo Co. as it prepares to purchase personal computers for its sales offices. Given the data in Exhibit 4, Memo Co.
   a. must be a perfectly competitive seller of output
   b. must be a monopoly seller of output
   c. must be a perfectly competitive buyer of personal computers
   d. cannot be a perfectly competitive buyer of personal computers
   e. may or may not be a perfectly competitive buyer of personal computers

6. Exhibit 4 shows data gathered by Memo Co. as it prepares to purchase personal computers for its sales offices. Given the data in Exhibit 4, the price of personal computers must be
   a. ₹5,000 each
   b. ₹500 each
   c. ₹250 each
   d. ₹200 each
   e. increasing as Memo Co. purchases more personal computers

7. Exhibit 4 shows data gathered by Memo Co. as it prepares to purchase personal computers for its sales offices. Assume that the personal computers are expected to last indefinitely, that operating expenses are negligible, and that the price of Memo's output is expected to remain constant in the future. As the number of personal computers Memo Co. might purchase increases to 120, the marginal rate of return on that kind of capital will
   a. decrease from 24 percent and eventually become negative

Exhibit 4

Personal computers	Marginal revenue product	Total resource cost	Marginal resource cost of 20 machines	Marginal rate of return	Marginal rate of interest
20	—	₹5,000	—	—	
40	₹1,200	10,000	₹5,000	24%	9%
60	960	15,000	5,000		9%
80	720	20,000	5,000		9%
100	480	25,000	5,000		9%
120	240	30,000	5,000		9%

b. rise from 24 percent
c. decrease from 24 percent but never become negative
d. remain constant because the price of personal computers is constant
e. remain constant because the increments being considered are constant

8. Exhibit 4 shows data gathered by Memo Co. as it prepares to purchase personal computers for its sales offices. Assume that the personal computers are expected to last indefinitely, that operating expenses are negligible, and that the price of Memo's product is expected to remain constant in the future. The marginal rate of return on 60 personal computers is closest to
a. 19 percent
b. 24 percent
c. 30 percent
d. 52 percent
e. 520 percent

9. A firm's marginal rate of return on investment curve shows the amount
a. saved by the firm at each alternative interest rate
b. invested by the firm at each alternative interest rate
c. saved by the firm at each alternative rate of time preference
d. invested by the firm at each alternative marginal resource cost
e. saved by the firm at each alternative marginal revenue product of investment

10. If financial intermediaries charge a higher rate of interest to lenders than they pay to borrowers, then
a. investing with borrowed funds involves a higher opportunity cost than investing with savings
b. investing with saving involves a higher opportunity cost than investing with borrowed funds
c. a firm is charged less interest to borrow than it can earn on savings
d. the opportunity cost of investing with borrowed funds equals the opportunity cost of investing with savings
e. a firm does not consider the market rate of interest when it makes investment decisions

11. As defined by economists, interest is
a. only the amount earned by productive capital as a resource
b. only the amount earned by land as a resource
c. only the amount earned by lending money
d. both the amount earned by productive capital as a resource and the amount earned by lending money
e. both the amount earned by land as a resource and the amount earned by lending money

12. Which of the following would cause a fall in the market interest rate?
a. an increase in the risk cost of investment
b. an increase in the inflation rate
c. an increase in the marginal rate of return on investment
d. a decrease in the marginal product of capital
e. none of the above

13. The interest rate charged on a home mortgage is lower than the interest rate charged on a credit card because:
a. The administration costs are higher on credit cards
b. The administration costs are lower on mortgages
c. A home mortgage is less risky than a credit card because the home becomes collateral
d. The mortgage loan amount is lower than the credit on a credit card
e. A home mortgage is riskier than a credit card

14. If the interest rate is 6%, the present value of receiving ₹300 next year is approximately:
a. ₹383
b. ₹306
c. ₹283
d. ₹260
e. ₹63

15. You buy a bond for ₹1,000 from the federal government, which guarantees that you will receive ₹70 a year forever. Thus, 7 percent was the market rate of interest when you bought the bond. Suppose that immediately after you buy the bond, the market rate of interest goes to 10 percent. The market value of your bond
a. could be more or less than ₹1,000
b. will be less than ₹1,000
c. will be more than ₹1,000
d. will remain unchanged
e. will be ₹1,000

16. The Great Homebody Nationwide Sweepstakes promises its winners a choice between ₹200,000 now or ₹120,000 now and ₹100,000

next year. The winners should take the ₹200,000 now

a. no matter what the interest rate is
b. no matter what the interest rate is, if their rate of time preference is high
c. no matter what the interest rate is, if their rate of time preference is low
d. only if the interest rate is above 25 percent
e. only if the interest rate is below 25 percent

17. A given sum of money received each year for a specific number of years is called a(n)
    a. bond
    b. perpetuity
    c. debt
    d. discount
    e. annuity

18. Congratulation, you just won the ₹1 lakh grand prize in the state lottery. You have to choose how to receive your prize. You can either get a lump sum of ₹350,000 today, or you can get ₹50,000 each year forever. You should choose the lump sum if the interest rate is:
    a. 10.5 percent
    b. Less than 10.5 percent
    c. More than 10.5 percent
    d. Less than 14.3 percent
    e. More than 14.3 percent

19. Corporations can acquire funds for investment projects through
    a. both c and e
    b. all of the following
    c. borrowing (e.g., from banks)
    d. issuing bonds
    e. issuing stock

20. Other things constant, the more profitable a corporation is,
    a. the lower the value of its shares on the stock market and the lower the interest rate that would have to be paid on new bond issues
    b. the higher the value of its shares on the stock market and the higher the interest rate it would have to pay on new bond issues
    c. the higher the value of its shares on the stock market and the lower the interest rate that would have to be paid on new bond issues
    d. the lower the value of its shares on the stock market and the higher the interest rate that would have to be paid on new bond issues
    e. the lower the interest rate that would have to be paid on new bond issues; the value of its shares on the stock market does not vary

Answers

1. d 2. d 3. e 4. a 5. c 6. c 7. c 8. a 9. b 10. a
11. d 12. d 13. c 14. c 15. b 16. d 17. e 18. e 19. b 20. c

Long Answer Questions

LO1 Discuss the role of time in production and consumption

1.1. *(Role of Time)* Complete the following sentences with a word or a phrase:
  a. If Bryan values current consumption more than future consumption, he has a(n) ___________.
  b. The reward to households for forgoing current consumption is ___________.
  c. Producing capital goods rather than producing final goods is known as ___________.

1.2. *(Consumption, Saving, and Time)* Explain why the supply of loanable funds curve slopes upward to the right.

LO2 Describe the factors that determine optimal investment

Marginal Rate of Return per Year on Investment in Farm Equipment

(1) Farm Equipment	(2) Total Product (bushels)	(3) Marginal Product (bushels)	(4) Marginal revenue Product (4) = (3) x ₹4	(5) Marginal Resource Cost	(6) Marginal Rate of Return (6) = (4) / (5)
No equipment	200	—	—	—	—
Tractor-tiller	1,200	1,000	₹4,000	₹10,000	40%
Combine	2,000	800	3,200	10,000	32
Irrigator	2,600	600	2,400	10,000	24
Harrow	3,000	400	1,600	10,000	16
Crop sprayer	3,200	200	800	10,000	8
Post-hole digger	3,200	0	0	10,000	0

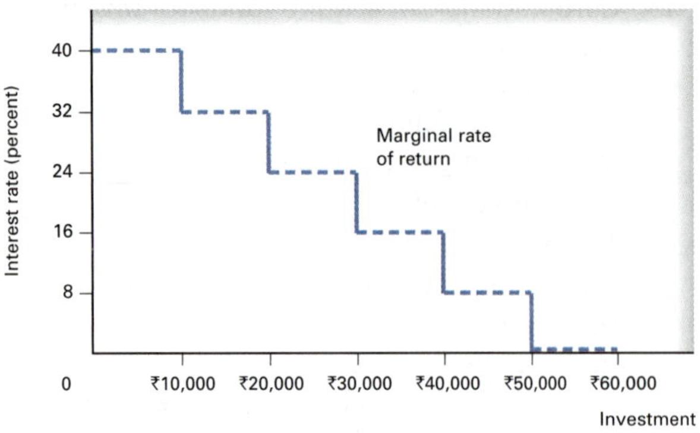

2.1. *(Optimal Investment)* Look back at the exhibit above. If the marginal resource cost rose to ₹24,000 what would be the optimal investment at a market interest rate of 10 percent? If the interest rate then rose to 16.6 percent, what would be the optimal level of investment?

2.2. *(Market for Loanable Funds)* Using the demand-supply for loanable funds diagram, show the effect on the market interest rate of each of the following:

a. An increase in the marginal resource cost of capital
b. An increase in the marginal productivity of capital
c. A shift in preferences toward present consumption and away from future consumption

LO3 Explain present value and discounting

3.1. *(Present Value)* Calculate the present value of each of the following future payments. (For some of these problems you may wish to use the online calculator available at http://www.moneychimp.com/articles/finworks/fmpresval.htm.)

a. A $10,000 lump sum received 1 year from now if the market interest rate is 8 percent
b. A $10,000 lump sum received 2 years from now if the market interest rate is 10 percent
c. A $1,000 lump sum received 3 years from now if the market interest rate is 5 percent
d. A $25,000 lump sum received 1 year from now if the market interest rate is 12 percent
e. A $25,000 lump sum received 1 year from now if the market interest rate is 10 percent
f. A perpetuity of $500 per year if the market interest rate is 6 percent

3.2. *(Present Value of an Income Stream)* Suppose the market interest rate is 10 percent. Would you be willing to lend $10,000 if you were guaranteed to receive $1,000 at the end of each of the next 12 years plus a $5,000 payment 15 years from now? Why or why not?

LO4 Analyze different corporate finance strategies

4.1. *(Securities Exchanges)* What role do securities exchanges play in financing corporations?

CAPITAL, INTEREST, AND CORPORATE FINANCE

15 Chapter in Review

KEY TERMS

positive rate of time preference consumers value present consumption more than future consumption

interest rate interest per year as a percentage of the amount saved or borrowed

marginal rate of return on investment the marginal revenue product of capital expressed as a percentage of its marginal cost

demand for loanable funds the negative relationship between the market interest rate and the quantity of loanable funds demanded, other things constant

supply of loanable funds the positive relationship between the market interest rate and the quantity of loanable funds supplied, other things constant

loanable funds market the market in which savers (suppliers of loanable funds) and borrowers (demanders of loanable funds) come together to determine the market interest rate and the quantity of loanable funds exchanged

prime rate the interest rate lenders charge their most trustworthy business borrowers

collateral an asset pledged by the borrower that can be sold to pay off the loan in the event the borrower defaults

term structure of interest rates the relationship between the duration of a loan and the interest rate charged; typically interest rates increase with the duration of the loan, because longer loans are considered more risky

present value the value today of income to be received in the future

discounting converting future rupee amounts into present value

annuity a given sum of money received each year for a specified number of years

initial public offering (IPO) the initial sale of corporate stock to the public

LO1 Discuss the role of time in production and consumption. Time is important to both production and consumption. Production cannot occur without savings, because both direct production and roundabout production require time—time during which the resources required for production must be paid. Because people value present consumption more than future consumption, they must be rewarded to defer consumption. Interest is the reward to savers for forgoing present consumption and the cost to borrowers for being able to spend now.

LO2 Describe the factors that determine optimal investment. Participants in a market economy characterized by specialization and exchange do not need to produce their own capital, nor rely on their own saving. They can purchase capital with borrowed funds. The demand and supply of loanable funds determine the market interest rate. At any given time, interest rates may differ because of differences in risk, maturity, administrative costs, and tax treatment. Choosing the profit-maximizing level of capital is complicated because capital purchased today yields a stream of benefit for years into the future. The marginal rate of return on capital equals the marginal revenue product of that capital as a percent of its marginal resource cost. The profit-maximizing firm invests up to the point where its marginal rate of return on capital equals the market rate of interest. The market interest rate is the opportunity cost of investment.

Marginal Rate of Return per Year on Investment in Farm Equipment

The marginal rate of return, shown in column (6), equals the marginal revenue product of farm equipment divided by its marginal resource cost.

(1) Farm Equipment	(2) Total Product (bushels)	(3) Marginal Product (bushels)	(4) Marginal revenue Product (4) = (3) x ₹4	(5) Marginal Resource Cost	(6) Marginal Rate of Return (6) = (4) / (5)
No equipment	200	—	—	—	—
Tractor-tiller	1,200	1,000	₹4,000	₹10,000	40%
Combine	2,000	800	3,200	10,000	32
Irrigator	2,600	600	2,400	10,000	24
Harrow	3,000	400	1,600	10,000	16
Crop sprayer	3,200	200	800	10,000	8
Post-hole digger	3,200	0	0	10,000	0

Marginal Rate of Return per Year on Investment in Farm Equipment

The marginal rate of return curve consists of line segments showing the relationship between the market interest rate and the amount invested in farm equipment. This curve shows the farmer's demand for investment.

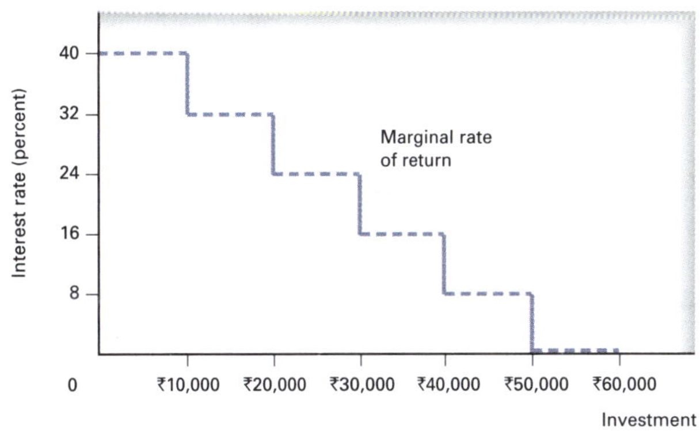

corporate stock
certificate reflecting part ownership of a corporation

dividends
after-tax corporate profit paid to stockholders rather than retained by the firm and reinvested

retained earnings
after-tax corporate profit reinvested in the firm rather than paid to stockholders as dividends

bond
certificate reflecting a firm's promise to pay the lender periodic interest and to repay the borrowed sum of money on the designated maturity date

CHAPTER EQUATIONS

Present Value

$$\text{Present value} = \frac{\text{Amount received one year from now}}{1 + \text{interest rate}}$$

$$\text{Present value} = \frac{M}{(1 + i)^t}$$

$$\text{Present value of receiving M rupees each year forever} = \frac{M}{i}$$

Market for Loanable Funds

Because of the declining marginal rate of return on capital, the quantity of loanable funds demanded is inversely related to the interest rate. The equilibrium rate of interest, 8 percent, is found where the demand for loanable funds intersects the supply of loanable funds. An increase in the demand for loanable funds from *D* to *D′* raises the equilibrium interest rate from 8 percent to 9 percent and increases the market quantity of loanable funds from ₹100 crore to ₹115 crore.

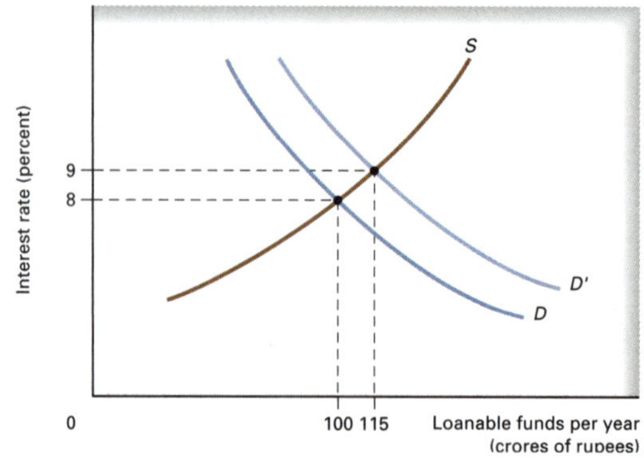

Interest Rates Charged for Different Types of Loans

Interest rates are higher for riskier loans. Rates for home mortgages and new cars are relatively low because these loans are backed up by the home or car as collateral. Personal loans and credit card balances face the highest rates, because these loans are riskier—that is, the likelihood borrowers fail to repay the loans is greater and the borrower offers no collateral.

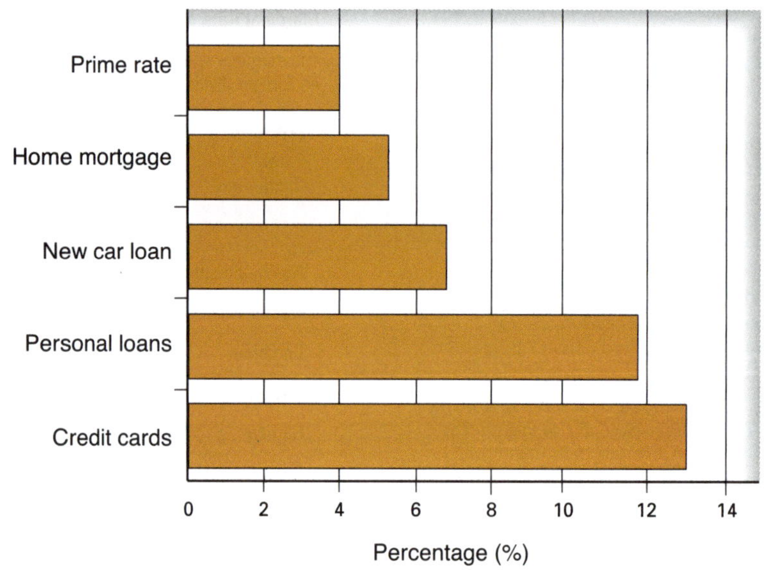

LO3 Explain present value and discounting. The current value of future payments is the present value. The process of translating future payments into present value is called discounting. The present value of a given payment is smaller the further into the future that payment is to be received. A given sum of money received each year for a specified number of years is called an annuity. The present value of receiving a sum each year forever is the amount received each year divided by the market interest rate.

LO4 Analyze different corporate finance strategies. Corporations fund new investment from three main sources: new stock issues, retained earnings, and borrowing (either directly from a bank or by issuing bonds). Once new stocks and bonds are issued, they can then be bought and sold on securities markets. The value of corporate stocks and bonds tends to vary directly with the firm's profit prospects. More profitable firms have more ready access to funds needed for expansion.

CHAPTER 16

Transaction Costs, Imperfect Information, and Market Behavior

Learning Outcomes

LO[1] Explain the rationale for the firm and describe its scope of operation

LO[2] Discuss the ways in which imperfect information influences market behavior

LO[3] Explain how asymmetric information affects product markets

LO[4] Describe the way asymmetric information influences labor markets

© IMAGE99/IMAGE100/JUPITERIMAGES

"Why is buying a used car such a gamble?"

Why do some firms, such as Domino's Pizza, specialize in a single product, while other firms, such as General Electric, make hundreds of different products? Why stop at hundreds? Why not thousands? In fact, why doesn't a giant firm make everything? Why is proper spelling important on your résumé? Why is buying a used car such a gamble? Why do some winners of online auctions end up losers? Answers to these and other seemingly unrelated questions are addressed in this chapter, which digs deeper into assumptions about firms and the information required for competitive markets.

What do you think?

It's important to do extensive research before making a purchase.

Strongly Disagree					*Strongly Agree*	
1	2	3	4	5	6	7

In the first half of this chapter, we step inside the firm to reconsider some simplifying assumptions about how firms work. We ask: Why do firms exist? How do they decide what to make themselves and what to buy from other firms? These steps toward realism move us beyond the simple depiction of the firm employed to this point. In the second half of this chapter, we challenge some simplifying assumptions about the information available to market participants. We ask: How does the lack of certain information affect behavior and shape market outcomes? Overall, this chapter should help you develop a more realistic view of how firms and markets work.

Topics discussed in Chapter 16 include:

- Transaction costs
- Vertical integration
- Economies of scope
- Optimal search
- Winner's curse
- Asymmetric information
- Adverse selection
- Principal-agent problem
- Moral hazard
- Signaling and screening

LO1 Rationale for the Firm and Its Scope of Operation

The competitive model assumes that all participants in the market know everything they need to about the price and availability of all inputs, outputs, and production processes. The firm is assumed to be headed by a brilliant decision maker with a computer-like ability to calculate all the relevant marginal products. This individual knows everything necessary to solve complex production and pricing problems. The irony is that if the marginal products of all inputs could be measured easily and if prices for all inputs could be easily determined, there would be little reason for production to take place in firms. In a world characterized by perfect competition, perfect information, constant returns to scale, and costless exchange, the consumer could bypass the firm to deal directly with resource suppliers, purchasing inputs in the appropriate amounts. Someone who wanted a table could buy timber, have it milled, contract with a carpenter, contract with a painter, and end up with a finished product. The consumer could carry out transactions directly with each resource supplier.

The Firm Reduces Transaction Costs

So why is production carried out within firms? About 70 years ago, in a classic article entitled "The Nature of the Firm," Nobel Prize winner Ronald Coase asked the question, "Why do firms exist?"[1] Why do people organize in the hierarchical structure of the firm and coordinate their decisions through a manager rather than simply rely on market exchange? His answer would not surprise today's students of economics: *Organizing activities through the hierarchy of the firm is usually more efficient than market exchange because production requires the coordination of many transactions among many resource suppliers.* In short, firms are superior to markets when production is complicated.

Consider again the example of purchasing a table by contracting directly with all the different resource suppliers—from the logger to the painter who applied the finishing varnish. Using resource markets directly involves (1) the cost of determining what inputs are needed and how they should be combined and (2) the cost of reaching an agreement with each resource supplier over and above the direct costs of the timber, nails, machinery, paint, and labor required to make the table. Where inputs are easily identified, measured, priced, and hired, production can be carried out through a price-guided "do-it-yourself" approach using the market. For example, getting your house painted is a relatively simple task: You can buy the paint and brushes and hire painters by the hour. You become your own painting contractor, hiring inputs in the market and combining them to do the job.

Where the costs of identifying the appropriate inputs and negotiating for each specific contribution are high, the consumer minimizes transaction costs

> "The more complicated the task, the greater the ability to economize on transaction costs through specialization and centralized control."

by purchasing the finished product from a firm. For example, although some people serve as their own contractor when painting a house, fewer do so when building a house; most buy a home already built or hire a building contractor. *The more complicated the task, the greater the ability to economize on transaction costs through specialization and centralized control.* For example, attempting to buy a car by contracting with the thousands of suppliers required to assemble one would be time consuming, costly, and impossible for most anyone. What type of skilled labor should be hired and at what wages? How much steel, aluminum, plastic, glass, paint, and other materials should be purchased? How should resources be combined and in what proportions? Anyone without a detailed knowledge of auto production couldn't do it. (Ford, for example, deals with some 30,000 suppliers.) That's why consumers buy assembled cars rather than contract separately with each resource supplier.

© DIMITRI VERVITSIOTIS/PHOTOGRAPHER'S CHOICE RF/GETTY IMAGES

At the margin, some activities could go either way, with some consumers using firms and some hiring resources directly in markets. The choice depends on each consumer's skill and opportunity cost of time. For example, some people may not want to be troubled with hiring all the inputs to get their house painted. Instead, they simply hire a firm for an agreed-on price—they hire a painting contractor. As you will see later in the chapter, however, hiring a contractor may give rise to other problems of quality control.

The Boundaries of the Firm

So far, the chapter has explained why firms exist: *Firms minimize the transaction costs and the production costs of economic activity.* The next question is: What are the efficient boundaries of the firm? The theory

1. *Economica* 4 (November 1937): 386–405.

of the firm described in earlier chapters is largely silent on the boundaries of the firm—that is, on the appropriate degree of vertical integration. Vertical integration is the expansion of a firm into stages of production earlier or later than those in which it specializes. For example, a steel company may decide (1) to integrate backward to mine iron ore or even mine the coal used to smelt iron ore or (2) to integrate forward to fashion raw steel into various components. A large manufacturer employs an amazing variety of production processes, but on average about half of the cost of production goes to purchase inputs from other firms. For example, Ford spends over $50 billion a year on parts, materials, and services. The total exceeds the annual output of many economies of the world.

© AP IMAGES

Putting the Pieces in Place

During 2008, Apple's activity indicated it intended to expand the scope of its operations. Apple bought the microprocessor design firm PA Semiconductor, which Apple CEO Steve Jobs suggested would be used for hardware design in Apple's iPods and iPhones. In the past, Apple had used both more specialized IBM and Motorola processors as well as Intel's more common processors. Then, in November, Apple hired former IBM executive Mark Papermaster, an expert in high-performance computing systems and processor design, to replace the head of its departing senior vice president of the company's iPod division (Papermaster was later sued by IBM for breaching a noncompete clause in his contract with IBM). Having its own design team in place would help Apple reduce costs with more efficient models specifically for the iPod and iPhone and eliminate reliance on outside chip suppliers. On the other hand, in purchasing PA Semiconductor, Apple may have expanded a little further than it wanted, as it now has to honor contracts that PA had with the Defense Department, which uses PA's chips in military weapons systems.

SOURCES: John Markoff, "Apple Hires I.B.M. Veteran as Device Engineer," *New York Times*, 4 November 2008. Available at http://www.nytimes.com/2008/11/05/technology/companies/05apple.html?scp=3&sq=apple%20papermaster&st=cse (accessed 23 December 2008); Ashlee Vance, "New iPhone Chip Will Cost an ARM and a Missile," Bits Blog, 15 September 2008. Available at http://bits.blogs.nytimes.com/2008/09/15/new-iphone-chip-will-cost-an-arm-and-a-missile/?scp=1&sq=pa%20semi%20inc&st=cse (accessed 23 December 2008).

How does the firm determine which activities to undertake and which to purchase from other firms? Should Dell manufacture its own computer chips or buy them from another firm? The answer depends on the benefits and costs of internal production versus market purchases. The point bears repeating: *Internal production and market purchases are alternative ways of organizing transactions.* The choice depends on which is a more efficient way of carrying out the transaction in question. Keep in mind that market prices coordinate transactions *between* firms, whereas managers coordinate activities *within* firms. The market coordinates resources by meshing the independent plans of separate decision makers, but a firm coordinates resources through the conscious direction of the manager.

The usual assumption is that transactions are organized by market exchange unless markets pose problems. Market exchange allows each firm to benefit from specialization and comparative advantage. For example, Dell can specialize in making computers and buy chips from Intel, a specialist. Computer chips are a standard product, but sometimes the input is not standardized or the exact performance requirements are hard to specify. For example, suppose one firm wants to hire another firm to supply research and development services. The uncertainty involved in such a nonspecific service makes it difficult to write, execute, and enforce a purchase agreement covering all possible contingencies that could arise. What if the R&D supplier, in the course of fulfilling the agreement, makes a valuable discovery for a different application? Who would have the right to that discovery—the firm that paid for the R&D service or the firm that came up with it? And who would determine if the application is different? Because incomplete contracts create potentially troublesome situations, conducting research and development *within the firm* usually involves a lower transaction cost than purchasing it in the market. At this point, it might be useful to discuss specific criteria firms consider when deciding whether to purchase a particular input from the market.

Bounded Rationality of the Manager

To direct and coordinate activity in a conscious way in the firm, a manager must understand how all the

vertical integration
the expansion of a firm into stages of production earlier or later than those in which it specializes, such as a steel maker that also mines iron ore

pieces of the puzzle fit together. As the firm takes on more and more activities, however, the manager may start losing track of details, so the quality of managerial decisions suffers. The more tasks the firm takes on, the longer the lines of communication between the manager and the production workers who must implement the decision. One constraint on vertical integration is the manager's **bounded rationality**, which limits the amount of information a manager can comprehend about the firm's operation. As the firm takes on more and more functions, coordination and communication become more difficult. The firm can experience diseconomies similar to those it experiences when it expands output beyond the efficient scale of production. The solution is for the firm to reduce its functions to those it does best. Such cutbacks occurred when automakers increased the proportion of parts they purchased from other firms.

bounded rationality the notion that there is a limit to the information that a firm's manager can comprehend and act on

Exhibit 1

Minimum Efficient Scale and Vertical Integration

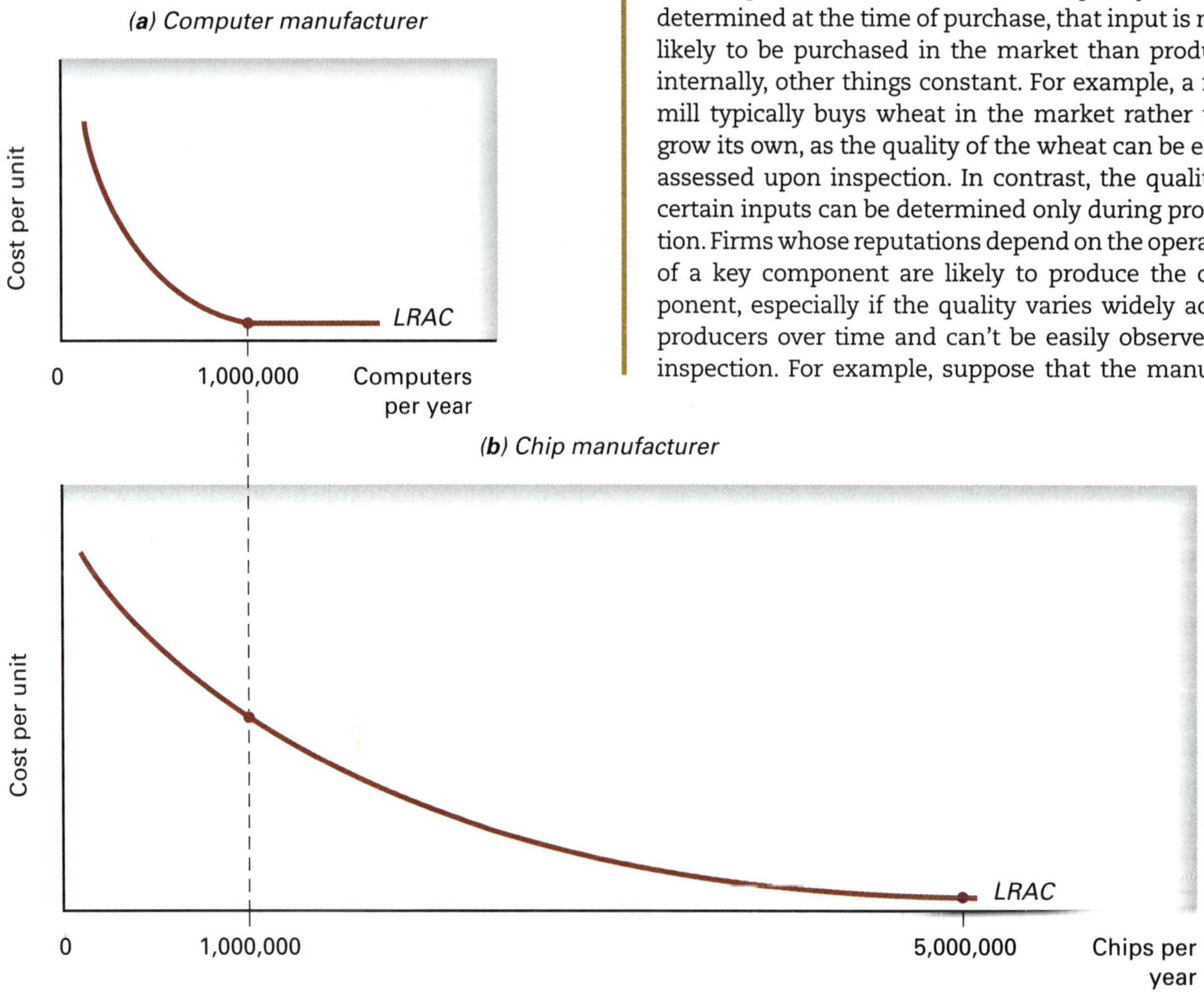

Minimum Efficient Scale

As noted when firm costs were introduced, the *minimum efficient scale* is the minimum rate of output at which economies of scale are fully exploited. For example, suppose that minimum efficient scale in the production of personal computers is 1 million per year, as shown by the firm's long-run average cost curve in panel (a) of Exhibit 1. Suppose this also turns out to be the amount that maximizes profit. Because the computer chip is an important component in a personal computer, should the PC maker integrate backward into chip production? What if the minimum efficient scale in chip production is 5 million per year? As you can see in panel (b) of Exhibit 1, the average cost of producing 1 million chips is much higher than the average cost at the minimum efficient scale of chip production. The PC manufacturer therefore minimizes costs by buying chips from a chip maker of optimal size. More generally, *other things constant, a firm should buy an input if the market price is below what it would cost the firm to make.*

Easily Observable Quality

If an input is well defined and its quality is easily determined at the time of purchase, that input is more likely to be purchased in the market than produced internally, other things constant. For example, a flour mill typically buys wheat in the market rather than grow its own, as the quality of the wheat can be easily assessed upon inspection. In contrast, the quality of certain inputs can be determined only during production. Firms whose reputations depend on the operation of a key component are likely to produce the component, especially if the quality varies widely across producers over time and can't be easily observed by inspection. For example, suppose that the manufacturer of a sensitive measuring instrument requires a crucial gauge, the quality of which can be observed only as the gauge is assembled. If the firm produces the gauge itself, it can closely monitor quality.

Producers sometimes integrate backward so they can offer consumers a guarantee about the quality of the components or ingredients in a product. For example, some chicken suppliers such as Tyson and Perdue can advertise the upbringing of their chickens because they raise their own. KFC, however, omits this family background because the company makes no claim about raising them, focusing instead on how well it cooks the chicken.

Many Suppliers

A firm wants an uninterrupted source of components. If there are many suppliers of that component, a firm is more likely to buy it than make it, other things constant. Not only do abundant suppliers ensure a dependable source of components, competition among these suppliers keeps the price down. But a firm that cannot rely on a consistent supply of components may make its own components to ensure a reliable supply.

The Trend Toward Outsourcing

Outsourcing occurs when a firm buys products, such as auto parts, or services, such as data processing, from outside suppliers. A firm relies on the division of labor and the law of comparative advantage to focus on what it does best, what it considers its **core competency**. Firms, particularly manufacturing firms, have long purchased some components from other firms, but the outsourcing movement extends this practice to a broader range of products and activities that typically were produced internally. Japanese firms pioneered outsourcing to reduce production costs and enhance quality. In the United States, outsourcing blossomed in manufacturing during the 1980s then spread to virtually every industry.

To review: If a firm relies on market purchases of inputs rather than on vertical integration, it can benefit from the specialization and comparative advantage of individual suppliers. Other things constant, the firm is more likely to buy a component rather than produce it if (1) buying the component is cheaper than making it, (2) the component is well defined and its quality easily observable, and (3) there are many suppliers of the component.

Economies of Scope

So far we have considered issues affecting the optimal degree of vertical integration in producing a particular product. Even with outsourcing, the focus is on how best to produce a particular product, such as an automobile or a computer. But some firms branch into product lines that do not have a vertical relationship. **Economies of scope** exist when it's cheaper to produce two or more different items in one firm than to produce them in separate firms. For example, General Electric produces hundreds of different products ranging from light bulbs to jet engines to NBC Universal. By spreading outlays for research and development and marketing (the company's motto is "Imagination at work") over different products, GE can reduce those costs per unit. Or consider economies of scope on the farm. A farm family often grows a variety of crops and raises different farm animals—animals that recycle damaged crops and food scraps into useful fertilizer. With economies of *scale*, the average cost per unit of output falls as the *scale* of the firm increases; *with economies of scope, average cost per unit falls as the firm supplies more types of products—that is, as the scope of the firm increases.* The cost of some fixed resources, such as specialized knowledge, can be spread across product lines.

Our focus has been on why firms exist, why they often integrate vertically, why they outsource, and why they sometimes produce a range of products. These steps toward realism move us beyond the simple picture of the firm created earlier. The rest of the chapter challenges some simplifying assumptions about the amount of information available to market participants.

LO2 Market Behavior with Imperfect Information

For the most part, our analysis of market behavior has assumed that market participants have full information about products and resources. For consumers, full information involves knowledge about a product's price, quality, and availability. For firms, full information includes knowledge about the marginal productivity of various resources, about the appropriate technology for combining them, and about the demand for the firm's product. In reality, *reliable information is often costly for both consumers and producers.* This section examines the impact of less-than-perfect information on market behavior.

outsourcing
a firm buys inputs from outside suppliers

core competency
area of specialty; the product or phase of production a firm supplies with greatest efficiency

economies of scope
average costs decline as a firm makes a range of different products rather than specializes in just one product

Optimal Search with Imperfect Information

Suppose you want to buy a new computer. You need information about the quality and features of each model and the prices at various retail outlets and online sites. To learn more about your choices, you may talk with friends and experts, read promotional brochures and computer publications, and visit online sites. Once you narrow your choice to one or two models, you may visit the mall, or let your fingers do the walking through the *Yellow Pages*, computer catalogs, online search engines, newspaper ads, and the like. Searching for the lowest price for a particular model involves a cost, primarily the opportunity cost of your time. This cost obviously varies from individual to individual and from item to item. Some people actually enjoy shopping, but this "shop 'til you drop" attitude does not necessarily carry over to all purchases. *For most of us, the process of gathering consumer information can be considered nonmarket work.*

Marginal Cost of Search

In your quest for product information, you gather the easy and obvious information first. You may check on the price and availability at the few computer stores at the mall. But as your search widens, the *marginal cost* of information increases, both because you may have to travel greater distances to check prices and services and because the opportunity cost of your time increases as you spend more time acquiring information. Consequently, the marginal cost curve for information slopes upward, as is shown in Exhibit 2. Note that a certain amount of information, I_f, is common knowledge and is freely available, so its marginal cost is zero.

Exhibit 2

Optional Search with Imperfect Information

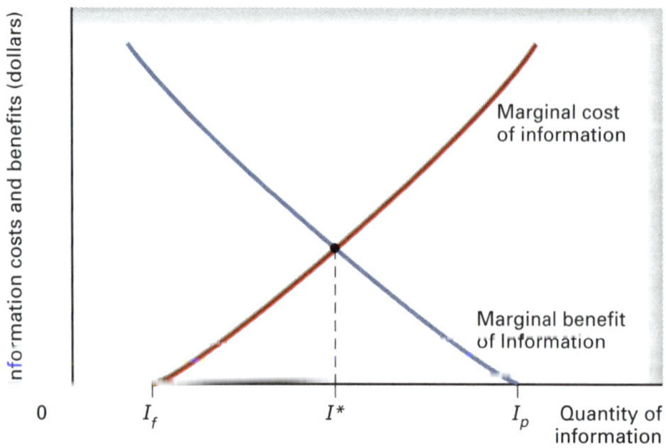

Marginal Benefit of Search

The *marginal benefit* from acquiring additional information is a better quality for a given price or a lower price for a given quality. The marginal benefit is relatively large at first, but as you gather more information and grow more acquainted with the market, additional information yields less and less marginal benefit. For example, the likelihood of uncovering valuable information, such as an added feature or a lower price, at the second store or Web site visited is greater than the likelihood of finding this information at the twentieth store or Web site visited. Thus, the marginal benefit curve for additional information slopes downward, as is shown in Exhibit 2.

Optimal Search

Market participants continue to gather information as long as the marginal benefit of additional information exceeds its marginal cost. *Optimal search occurs where the marginal benefit just equals the marginal cost,* which in Exhibit 2 is where the two marginal curves intersect. Notice that at search levels exceeding the equilibrium amount, the marginal benefit of additional information is still positive but below marginal cost. Notice also that at some point the value of additional information reaches zero, as identified by I_p on the horizontal axis. This level of information could be identified as *full information*. The high marginal cost of acquiring I_p, however, makes it impractical to become fully informed. Thus, firms and consumers, by gathering the optimal amount of information, I^*, have less-than-perfect information about the price, availability, and quality of products and resources.

Implications

This search model was developed by Nobel laureate George Stigler, who showed that the price of a product can differ among sellers because some consumers are unaware of lower prices offered by some sellers.[2] Thus, *search costs result in price dispersion, or different prices for the same product.* Some sellers call attention to price dispersions by claiming to have the lowest prices around and by promising to match any competitor's price. *Search costs also lead to quality differences across sellers, even for identically priced products, because consumers find the expected marginal cost of finding a higher quality product outweighs the expected marginal benefit.*

2. George Stigler, "The Economics of Information," *Journal of Political Economy* (June 1961): 213–225.

There are other implications of Stigler's search model. The more expensive the item, the greater the price dispersion in dollar terms, so the greater the expected marginal benefit from shopping around. You are more likely to shop around for a new car than for a new toothbrush. Also, as earnings increase, so does the opportunity cost of time, resulting in less searching and more price dispersion. On the other hand, any technological change that reduces the marginal cost of information lowers the marginal cost curve in Exhibit 2, increasing the optimal amount of information and reducing price dispersion. For example, some online sites, like mySimon.com, identify the lowest prices for books, airfares, automobiles, computers, and dozens of other products. And some online sellers, like Buy.com, maintain the lowest prices on the Web as a way of attracting customers who undertake such searches. Thus, by reducing search costs, the Internet reduces price dispersion.

The Winner's Curse

In 1996, the federal government auctioned off leases to valuable space on the scarce radio spectrum. The space was to be used for cell phones, wireless networks, and portable fax machines. The bidding was carried out in the face of much uncertainty about what were then new markets. Bidders had little experience with the potential value of such leases. At the time, 89 companies made winning bids for 493 licenses totaling $10.2 billion. But by 1998, it became clear that many of the winning bidders couldn't pay, and many went bankrupt.[3] The auction eventually collected only half the amount of the winning bids. (It will be interesting to see if similar results develop from the 2008 wireless spectrum auction, which raised $19.6 billion.) In auctions for products of uncertain value, such as wireless communications licenses, why do so many "winners" end up losers?

© RUBBERBALL/JUPITERIMAGES

When bids were submitted, the true value of space on the radio spectrum could only be estimated. Suppose the average bid for a license was $10 million, with some higher and others lower. Suppose also that the winning bid was $20 million. The winning bid was not the average bid, which may have been the most reliable estimate of the true value, but the highest bid, which was the most optimistic estimate. Winners of such bids are said to experience the **winner's curse** because they often lose money after winning the bid, paying the price of being overly optimistic.

The winner's curse applies to all cases of bidding in which the true value is unknown at the outset. For example, movie companies often bid up the price of screenplays to what some argue are unrealistic levels (only about 5 percent of screenplays studios purchase ever become movies). Likewise, publishers get into bidding wars over book manuscripts and even book proposals that are little more than titles. Team owners bid and often overpay for athletes who become free agents. CBS lost money on the 1998 Winter Olympics. And NBC may have overbid by offering $2.3 billion for the rights to broadcast the Olympics in 2002, 2006, and 2008; at the time of the bid, Olympic cities had not even been selected. Online auctions, like eBay, often sell items of unknown value.

With perfect information about market value, potential buyers would never bid more than that market value. *But when competitive bidding is coupled with imperfect information, the winning bidder often ends up an overly optimistic loser.*

LO3 Asymmetric Information in Product Markets

We have considered the effects of costly information and limited information on market behavior. But the issue becomes more complicated when one side of the market knows more than the

3. Scott Ritter, "FCC Says Several Bidders to Return Wireless Licenses," *Wall Street Journal*, 18 June 1998.

winner's curse
the plight of the winning bidder who overestimates an asset's true value

other side does, a problem of **asymmetric information**. There are two types of information that a market participant may want but lack: information about a product's *characteristics* and information about *actions* taken by the other party to the transaction. This section examines several examples of asymmetric information in the product market and the effects on market efficiency.

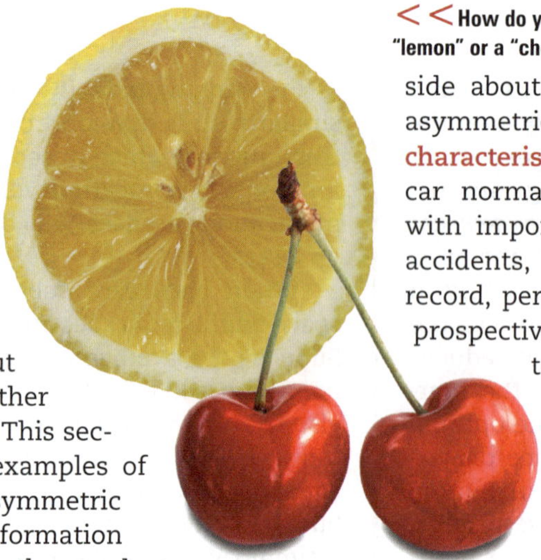

<< **How do you know if the used car you're buying is a "lemon" or a "cherry"?**

asymmetric information one side of the market has better information about the product than does the other side

hidden characteristics one side of the market knows more than the other side about product characteristics that are important to the other side

Hidden Characteristics: Adverse Selection

When one side of the market knows more than the other side about important product characteristics, the asymmetric information problem involves **hidden characteristics**. For example, the seller of a used car normally has abundant personal experience with important *characteristics* of that car, such as accidents, breakdowns, gas mileage, maintenance record, performance in bad weather, and so on. A prospective buyer can only guess at these characteristics based on the car's appearance and perhaps a test drive. The buyer cannot really know how well the car performs without driving it under varying traffic and weather conditions.

To simplify the problem, suppose there are only two types of used cars for sale: good ones and bad ones, or "lemons." A buyer who is certain about a car's type would be willing to pay $10,000 for a good used car but only $4,000 for a lemon. Again, only the seller knows which type is for sale. Prospective buyers believe that half the used cars on the market are good ones and half are lemons and are willing to pay, say, $7,000 for a car of unknown quality (the average expected value of cars on the market). Would $7,000 become the market price of used cars?

© STOCKBYTE/GETTY IMAGES / © MAXIMILLIAN STOCK LTD./FOODPIX/JUPITERIMAGES

George Akerlof's "The Market for Lemons"

"The Market for Lemons: Quality Uncertainty and the Market Mechanism" is a 1970 paper by the economist George Akerlof. It discusses information asymmetry, which occurs when the seller knows more about a product than the buyer. A lemon is an American slang term for a car that is found to be defective only after it has been bought. Akerlof's paper uses the market for used cars as an example of the problem of quality uncertainty.

Uncertainty in the market for used cars exists because many important mechanical parts and other elements are hidden from view and not easily accessible for inspection. Thus, the buyer of a car does not know beforehand whether it is a cherry (good used car) or a lemon (defective used car). So the buyer's best guess for a given car is that the car is of average quality; accordingly, he will be willing to pay only the price of a car of known average quality for buying this car. This means that the owner of a well-maintained, good used car will be unable to get a high enough price to make selling that car worthwhile. Therefore, owners of good cars will not place their cars on the used car market. The withdrawal of good cars from the market reduces the average quality of cars on the market, causing buyers to revise downward their expectations for any given car. This, in turn, motivates the owners of moderately good cars not to sell, and so on. This is sometimes referred to as "the bad driving out the good" in the market.

Brief Publication History

The paper "The Market for Lemons: Quality Uncertainty and the Market Mechanism" was first sent to *The American Economic Review* for publication, where it was rejected. The editor stated that the journal did not publish papers on subjects of such triviality. Thereafter, the paper was submitted to *The Review of Economic Studies,* where it was again rejected on the grounds that the *The Review* did not publish papers on topics of such triviality. Not quite disheartened, Akerlof submitted the paper to the *Journal of Political Economy,* where yet again it was rejected. The fourth time the paper was sent to the *Quarterly Journal of Economics,* where it was finally accepted!

It may be mentioned that Akerlof, Michael Spence, and Joseph Stiglitz jointly received the Nobel Memorial Prize in Economic Sciences in 2001 for their research related to asymmetric information.

SOURCE: George A. Akerlof, "The Market for Lemons: Quality Uncertainty and the Market Mechanism," *Quarterly Journal of Economics*, Vol. 84, No. 3 (The MIT Press, 1970): 488–500.

So far, the analysis has ignored the actions of potential sellers, who know which type of car they have. Because sellers of good cars can get only $7,000 for cars they know to be worth $10,000 on average, many will keep their cars or will sell them only to friends or relatives. But sellers of lemons will find $7,000 an attractive price for a car they know to be worth only $4,000. As a result, the proportion of good cars on the market will fall and the proportion of lemons will rise, reducing the average value of used cars on the market. As buyers come to realize that the mix has shifted toward lemons, they will reduce what they are willing to pay for cars of unknown quality. As the market price of used cars falls, potential sellers of good cars become even more reluctant to sell at such a low price, so the proportion of lemons increases, leading to still lower prices. The process could continue until few good cars are for sale on the open market. More generally, *when sellers have better information about a product's quality than buyers do, lower-quality products dominate the market.*

When those on the informed side of the market self-select in a way that harms the uninformed side of the market, the problem is one of **adverse selection**. In our example, car sellers, the informed side, self-select—that is, they decide whether or not to offer their cars for sale—in a way that increases the proportion of lemons for sale. Because of adverse selection, those still willing to buy on the open market often get stuck with lemons.

Hidden Actions: The Principal-Agent Problem

A second type of problem occurs when one side of a transaction can pursue an unobservable action that affects the other side. Whenever one side of an economic relationship can take a relevant action that the other side cannot observe, the situation is described as one of **hidden actions**. In this age of specialization, there are many tasks we do not perform for ourselves because others do them better and because others have a lower opportunity cost of time. Suppose your car isn't working and you have no clue how to fix it. The mechanic you hire may have other objectives, such as maximizing on-the-job leisure or maximizing the garage's profit. But the mechanic's actions are hidden from you. Although your car's problem may be only a loose electrical wire, the mechanic could inflate the bill by charging you for work not needed or not performed. This asymmetric information problem occurs because one side of a transaction can pursue *hidden actions* that affect the other side. When buyers have difficulty monitoring and evaluating the quality of goods or services purchased, some suppliers may substitute poor-quality resources or exercise less diligence in providing the service.

The problem that arises from hidden actions is called the **principal-agent problem**, which describes a relationship in which one party, known as the **principal**, contracts with another party, known as the **agent**, in the expectation that the agent will act on behalf of the principal. *The problem arises when the goals of the agent are incompatible with those of the principal and when the agent can pursue hidden actions.* For example, you are the principal and the garage mechanic is your agent. You could also confront a principal-agent problem when you deal with a doctor, lawyer, stockbroker, plumber, or building contractor, to name a few. Any employer-employee relationship could become a principal-agent problem, with the employer as the principal and the employee as the agent. Again, the problem arises because the agent's objectives are not the same as the principal's and because the agent's actions are hidden. Not all principal-agent relationships pose a problem. For example, when you hire someone to cut your hair or your lawn, there are no hidden actions, so you can judge the results for yourself.

Asymmetric Information in Insurance Markets

Asymmetric information also creates problems in insurance markets. For example, from an insurer's point of view, the ideal candidate for health insurance is someone who leads a long, healthy life, then dies peacefully while sleeping. But many people are poor risks for health insurers because of hidden characteristics (bad genes) or hidden actions (smoking and drinking excessively, getting exercise only on trips to the refrigerator, and thinking that a balanced meal consists of beef jerky and a six-pack of beer). In the insurance market, it is the buyers, not the sellers, who have more information about the characteristics and actions that predict their likely need for insurance in the future.

adverse selection
those on the informed side of the market self-select in a way that harms those on the uninformed side of the market

hidden actions
one side of an economic relationship can do something that the other side cannot observe

principal-agent problem
the agent's objectives differ from those of the principal's, and one side can pursue hidden actions

principal
a person or firm who hires an agent to act on behalf of that person or firm

agent
a person or firm who is supposed to act on behalf of the principal

© KIM WHITE/ADAM ROUNTREE/DANIEL ACKER/JIN LEE/TOM STARKWEATHER/CHRIS RATCLIFFE/JB REED/MIKE MERGEN/BLOOMBERG NEWS/LANDOV

If the insurance company has no way of distinguishing among applicants, it must charge those who are good health risks the same price as those who are poor ones. This price is attractive to poor risks but not to good ones, some of whom will not buy insurance. The insured group becomes less healthy on average, so rates must rise, making insurance even less attractive to healthy people. *Because of adverse selection, insurance buyers tend to be less healthy than the population as a whole.* Adverse selection has been used as an argument for national health insurance.

The insurance problem is compounded by the fact that once people buy insurance, their behavior may change in a way that increases the probability that a claim will be made. For example, those with health insurance may take less care of their health, and those with theft insurance may take less care of their valuables. This incentive problem is referred to as *moral hazard*. **Moral hazard** occurs when an individual's behavior changes in a way that increases the likelihood of an unfavorable outcome. More generally, *moral hazard is a principal-agent problem because it occurs when those on one side of a transaction have an incentive to shirk their responsibilities because the other side is unable to observe them.* The responsibility could be to repair a car, maintain one's health, or safeguard one's valuables. Both the mechanic and the insurance buyer may take advantage of the ignorant party. In the car-repair example, the mechanic is the agent; in the insurance example, the policy buyer is the principal. Thus, moral hazard arises when someone—either the agent or the principal, depending on the situation—can undertake hidden action.

moral hazard a situation in which one party, as a result of a contract, has an incentive to alter their behavior in a way that harms the other party to the contract

Moral hazard was a frequent topic of debate each time the federal government decided to bail out or not bail out a company or industry during the 2008 global financial crisis. For example, if an investment bank was rescued from its past risky behavior, would such banks be more inclined to take similar risks in the future?

Coping with Asymmetric Information

There are ways of reducing the consequences of asymmetric information. An incentive structure or an information-revealing system can be developed to reduce the problems associated with the lopsided availability of information. For example, all states now have "lemon laws" that offer compensation to buyers of new or used cars that turn out to be lemons. Used-car dealers may also offer warranties to reduce the buyer's risk of getting stuck with a lemon. Most garages provide written estimates before a job is done, and some return the defective parts to the customer as evidence that the repair was necessary and was carried out. People often get multiple estimates for major repairs.

Insurance companies deal with adverse selection and moral hazard in a variety of ways. Most require applicants to undergo a physical exam and to answer questions about their medical history and lifestyle (false information can block benefits). Preexisting medical conditions are not usually covered. To avoid adverse selection, an insurer often covers all those in a group, such as all company employees, not just those who would otherwise self-select. Insurers reduce moral hazard by making the policyholder pay, say, the first $250 of a claim as a "deductible" and by requiring the policyholder to co-pay a percentage of a claim. Also, as more claims are filed, insurance premiums go up and the policy could be canceled. Property insurers reduce premiums for those who install security systems, smoke alarms, sprinkler systems, and who take other safety precautions.

In equilibrium, each worker in a particular labor market is assumed to be paid the same wage, a wage equal to the marginal revenue product of the last unit of labor hired.

LO4 Asymmetric Information in Labor Markets

Our market analysis for particular kinds of labor typically assumes that workers are more or less interchangeable. In equilibrium, each worker in a particular labor market is assumed to be paid the same wage, a wage equal to the marginal revenue product of the last unit of labor hired. But what if ability differs across workers? Differences in ability present no particular problem as long as these differences can be readily observed by the employer. If the productivity of each worker is easily quantified through measures such as crates of oranges picked, quantity of garments sewn, or number of cars sold, these can and do serve as the basis for pay. And such incentives seem to affect output. For example, when the British National Health Service changed the pay basis of dentists from "contact hours" with patients to the number of cavities filled, dentists found more cavities and filled them in only a third of the time they took under the contact-hour pay scheme.[4]

Because production often requires a team effort, the employer may not be able to attribute specific outputs to particular workers. When information about each worker's marginal productivity is hard to come by, employers usually pay workers by the hour. Sometimes the pay combines an hourly rate and incentive pay linked to a measure of productivity. For example, a sales representative typically receives a base salary plus a commission tied to sales. At times, the task of evaluating performance is left to the consumer. Workers who provide personal services, such as waiters, barbers, beauticians, pizza deliverers, and bellhops, rely partly or mostly on tips. These services are "personal" and visible, so customers are usually in the best position to judge the quality and timeliness of service and to tip accordingly.

Adverse Selection in Labor Markets

Suppose an employer wants to hire a program coordinator for a new project. The job requires imagination, organizational skills, and the ability to work independently. The employer would like to attract the most qualified person available, but the qualities demanded are not directly observable. The employer offers the going wage for such a position. Individual workers are able to evaluate this market wage in light of their own abilities and opportunities. Talented people find the wage too low and are less inclined to apply for the job. Less-talented people, however, find this wage attractive and are more inclined to seek the position. Because of this adverse selection, the employer ends up with a pool of applicants of below-average ability.

A job applicant's true abilities—motivation, work habits, skills, ability to get along with others, and the like—are, to a large extent, *hidden characteristics*. In a labor market with hidden characteristics, employers might be better off offering a higher wage. The higher the wage, the more attractive the job is to more-qualified workers. Paying a higher wage also encourages those who are hired not to goof off or otherwise jeopardize an attractive job. Paying above-market wages to attract and retain more productive workers is called paying **efficiency wages**, something that Henry Ford did.

Signaling and Screening

The person on the side of the market with hidden characteristics and hidden actions has an incentive to say the right thing. For example, a job applicant might say, "Hire me because I am hardworking, reliable, prompt, highly motivated, and just an all-around great employee." Or a manufacturer might say, "At Ford, quality is job one." But such claims appear self-serving and thus are not necessarily believable. To cut through this fog, both sides of the market try to develop credible ways of communicating reliable information about qualifications.

Signaling is the attempt by the informed side of the market to communicate information that the other side would find valuable. Consider signaling in the job market. Because some jobs require abilities that are unobservable on a résumé or in an interview, job applicants offer proxy measures, such as years of education, college grades, and letters of recommendation. A proxy measure is called a *signal,* which is an observable indicator of some hidden characteristic. A signal is sent by the informed side of the market to the uninformed side and is useful because less-qualified applicants have trouble sending the same signal.

To identify the best workers, employers try to *screen* applicants. **Screening** is the attempt by the uninformed side of the market to uncover the relevant but hidden char-

© TONY ROBINS/ANTHONY BLAKE PHOTO LIBRARY/PHOTOLIBRARY

efficiency wage theory the idea that offering high wages attracts a more talented labor pool and encourages those hired to perform well so as to keep their jobs

signaling using a proxy measure to communicate information about unobservable characteristics; the signal is more effective if more-productive workers find it easier to send than do less-productive workers

screening the process used by employers to select the most qualified workers based on observable characteristics such as a job applicant's level of education and course grades

4. John Pencavel, "Piecework and On-the-Job Screening," *Working Paper,* Stanford University, June 1975.

acteristics of the informed party. An initial screen might check each résumé for spelling and typographical errors. Although not important in themselves, such errors suggest a lack of attention to detail—which could reduce labor productivity. The uninformed party must identify signals that less-productive individuals have more difficulty sending. A signal that can be sent with equal ease by all workers, regardless of their productivity, does not provide a useful way of screening applicants. But if, for example, more-productive workers find it easier to graduate from college than do less-productive workers, a college degree is a measure worth using to screen workers. In this case, education may be valuable, not so much because of its direct effect on a worker's productivity, but simply because it enables employers to distinguish between types of workers. In fact, the actual pay increase from a fourth year of college that results in graduation is several times the pay increase from just a third year of college. This finding is consistent with the screening theory of education.

To summarize: Because the potential productivity of job applicants cannot be measured directly, an employer must rely on proxy measures to screen applicants. The most valuable proxy is a signal that can be sent more easily by more productive workers and also is a good predictor of future productivity.

Final Word

The firm has evolved through a natural selection process as the form of organization that minimizes both transaction and production costs. The economic system selects for efficient production organizations. Attributes that yield an economic profit will thrive, and those that do not will fall away. The form of organization selected might not be optimal in the sense that it cannot be improved, but it is the most efficient of those that have been tried. If there is a way to organize production that is more efficient, some entrepreneur will stumble on it eventually, earning greater profit. The improvement may not always be the result of conscious design. Once a more efficient way of organizing production is uncovered, others will imitate it.

In conventional demand-and-supply analysis, trades occur in impersonal markets, and the buyer has no special concern about who is on the sell side. But with asymmetric information, the mix and characteristics of the other side of the market become important. When the problem of adverse selection is severe enough, some markets may cease to function. Market participants try to overcome the limitations of asymmetric information by signaling, screening, and trying to be explicit and transparent about the terms of the transaction.

Multiple Choice Questions

1. If the production of a sofa requires the purchase of 3 types of inputs and the production of a harp requires the purchase of 30 types of inputs,
   a. the harp-producing firm will buy the sofa-producing firm
   b. the sofa-producing firm will buy the harp-producing firm
   c. harp production is more likely to be done by firms than sofa production is
   d. sofa production is more likely to be done by firms than harp production is
   e. both harp and sofa production will always be done by firms because there is more than one input involved in each
2. Suppose that you can either buy a radio from a firm for \$50 or find and purchase the components yourself and then either assemble them yourself or hire someone to do so. You should
   a. buy the radio because it's possible to do so
   b. assemble the radio yourself because it's possible to do so
   c. assemble the radio yourself only if you know how to do so
   d. assemble the radio yourself only if the total price of all the components is less than \$50
   e. assemble the radio yourself only if the total price of all the components plus the value of your own time is less than \$50
3. According to Coase, firms emerge when
   a. transaction costs in the market are less than the cost of hierarchical control
   b. transaction costs in the market are more than the cost of hierarchical control
   c. prices in the market are less than the cost of hierarchical control
   d. prices in the market are more than the cost of hierarchical control
   e. implicit contracts in the market can be made explicit in a firm
4. Ronald Coase's study, "The Nature of the Firm," argued that
   a. market exchange is less costly than hierarchical exchange
   b. markets are more efficient than hierarchies
   c. firms are formed to take advantage of situations in which hierarchies are more efficient than markets
   d. the role of the entrepreneur is primarily to deal with central authority
   e. markets tend to be less competitive over time
5. In his article, "The Nature of the Firm," Ronald Coase
   a. suggested that monopolies may be more innovative than competitive firms
   b. argued that the economy should be organized into one large firm
   c. provided an answer to the question, "Why do firms exist?"
   d. focused on the concept of adverse selection
   e. analyzed concentration in U.S. industry
6. The more complicated a production process is,
   a. the lower the transactions cost of using markets
   b. the lower the cost of production
   c. the more likely the market will be used to organize production
   d. the more likely that transaction costs decrease through centralized control of production
   e. the more likely that transaction costs decrease through use of markets
7. Vertical integration is
   a. the expansion of a firm into earlier or later stages of production
   b. an attempt by a firm to allow market prices to coordinate more transactions
   c. an attempt by a firm to minimize shirking
   d. an attempt by a firm to minimize the need to coordinate transactions within its boundaries
   e. a way for a firm to accumulate information about its competitors
8. Wendy's must decide whether to grow its own potatoes for French fries. Growing potatoes is a very different process from running a fast-food restaurant. Based on this information *alone*, should Wendy's grow its own potatoes?
   a. No, because Wendy's managers have bounded rationality.
   b. Yes, because Wendy's managers have bounded rationality.
   c. No, because there is a small number of potato suppliers.
   d. Yes, because there is a small number of potato suppliers.

e. No, because it is easy to observe the quality of potatoes.

9. The McDonald's restaurants in Russia grow their own potatoes to guarantee that they are grown correctly. Growing potatoes is very different from running a fast-food restaurant. One could say of McDonald's decision to grow its own potatoes for the Russian franchise that
   a. the bounded rationality criterion outweighs the need for quality control
   b. the bounded rationality criterion is outweighed by the need for quality control
   c. both bounded rationality and the need for quality control are factors that make it rational for McDonald's to grow its own potatoes
   d. growing potatoes is irrational
   e. there must not be many potato suppliers in Russia

10. One reason many people make their own pickles rather than buy them is that
   a. they can maintain control over the quality during production
   b. the total cost of ingredients is the same as the price of store-bought pickles
   c. firms do not make high-quality pickles
   d. people place a high value on their time
   e. firms do not produce goods that can be made at home

11. If a firm experiences economies of scope,
   a. its average cost falls as it increases output
   b. its average cost rises as it increases output
   c. average production costs fall when it produces more than one kind of product
   d. it should integrate vertically
   e. average production costs rise as it produces more kinds of products

12. For most consumers, the process of learning about the efficiency and durability of various brands of refrigerators can be considered
   a. irrational
   b. unproductive
   c. a vocation
   d. nonmarket work
   e. costless

13. "It doesn't hurt to get more information . . ." is good advice
   a. especially when the opportunity cost of acquiring the information is high
   b. when information is less than perfect
   c. only if the marginal benefit of information is greater than the marginal cost of information
   d. only if the marginal benefit of information is equal to the marginal cost of information
   e. only if the marginal benefit of information is less than the marginal cost of information

14. The winner's curse is more likely when the value of a good at auction is uncertain.
   a. True
   b. False

15. Frank wants to buy a used car from Adam. Adam knows the car is a lemon, but he doesn't tell Frank. This is an example of:
   a. Natural selection
   b. Moral hazard
   c. Hidden actions
   d. Open-access resources
   e. Adverse selection

16. The lemons problem is that when there are hidden characteristics known only to the seller of a used car,
   a. the ratio of lemons to high-quality cars is likely to be high
   b. the ratio of lemons to high-quality cars is likely to be low
   c. good used cars will sell for more than their market value
   d. no lemons will be offered on the market
   e. the price of lemons will be below their market value

17. Copious Corp. is owned by 2 million stockholders who elect a board of directors that selects a management team responsible for hiring workers to serve customers by selling and repairing computer mice. Which of the following statements is true?
   a. In the principal-agent relationship between workers and customers, the customers are the agents.
   b. In the principal-agent relationship between workers and managers, the managers are the agents.
   c. In the principal-agent relationship between the stockholders and the board of directors, the stockholders are the agents.
   d. In the principal-agent relationship between the stockholders and the customers, the stockholders are the agents.
   e. In the principal-agent relationship between management and the board of directors, the managers are the agents.

18. Principal-agent problems are less likely to arise
    a. if it is easy for principals to know agents' actions and if there is less conflict between their goals
    b. if it is difficult for principals to know agents' actions and if there is less conflict between their goals
    c. if it is easy for principals to know agents' actions and if there is some difference in their goals
    d. if it is difficult for principals to know agents' actions and if there is some difference in their goals
    e. if agents have higher incomes
19. Which of the following is *not* an example of moral hazard?
    a. People with health insurance take poor care of themselves.
    b. Reckless drivers own the safest cars.
    c. Banks make risky loans because deposit insurance protects them.
    d. People give more to charity just because it is tax deductible.
    e. A quarterback holds on to the ball longer before passing because he has a good offensive line.
20. Adverse selection is more likely when
    a. a job requires specific training
    b. a job requires intangible or unmeasurable abilities
    c. the wage offered is above the average of all wages in the market
    d. the wage is based on true marginal revenue products
    e. performance can be monitored closely

Answers

1. c 2. e 3. b 4. c 5. c 6. d 7. a 8. a 9. b 10. a
11. c 12. d 13. c 14. a 15. e 16. a 17. e 18. a 19. d 20. b

Long Answer Questions

LO1 Explain the rationale for the firm and describe its scope of operation

1.1. *(Bounds of the Firm)* Ashland Oil buys its crude oil in the market. Larger oil refiners, such as Texaco, drill for their own crude oil. Why do some oil companies drill for their own crude oil and others buy crude oil in the market?

1.2. *(Economies of Scope)* Distinguish between economies of scale and economies of scope. Why do some firms produce multiple product lines, while others produce only one?

LO2 Discuss the ways in which imperfect information influences market behavior

2.1. *(Search with Imperfect Information)* The following questions concern the accompanying graph.
   a. Identify the two curves shown on the graph, and explain their upward or downward slopes.
   b. Why does curve *A* intersect the horizontal axis?
   c. What is the significance of quantity *d*?
   d. What does *e* represent?
   e. How would the optimal quantity of information change if the marginal benefit of information increased—that is, if the marginal benefit curve shifted upward?

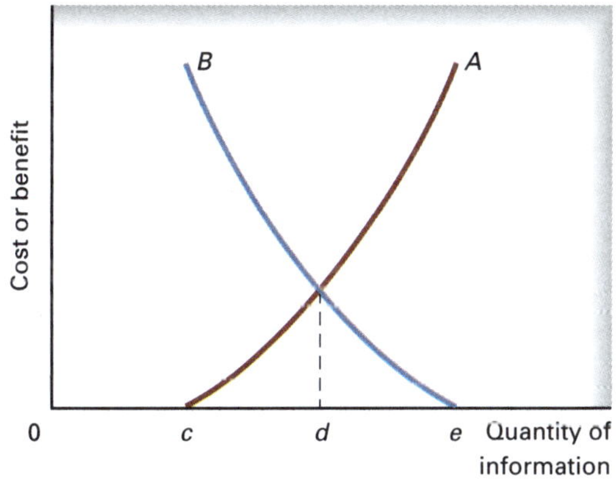

2.2. *(Search with Imperfect Information)* Determine the effect of each of the following on the optimal level of search.
   a. The consumer's wage increases.
   b. One seller guarantees to offer the lowest price on the market.
   c. The technology of gathering and transmitting market information improves.

LO3 Explain how asymmetric information affects product markets

3.1. *(Asymmetric Information)* Define asymmetric information. Distinguish between hidden characteristics and hidden actions. Which type of asymmetric information contributes to the principal-agent problem?

3.2. *(The Principal-Agent Problem)* Discuss the nature of the principal-agent problem. Determine which is the principal and which is the agent in each of the following relationships:
   a. A firm that produces export goods and the export management company that helps market its goods overseas
   b. The management of a firm and its stockholders
   c. A homeowner and the plumber hired to make repairs
   d. A dentist and a patient
   e. An employee-pension management firm and the company using its services

3.3. *(Adverse Selection and Moral Hazard)* Describe the problems faced by health insurance companies as a result of adverse selection and moral hazard. How do insurance companies try to reduce these problems?

LO4 Describe the way asymmetric information influences labor markets

4.1. *(Signaling)* Give an example of signaling in each of the following situations:
   a. Choosing a doctor
   b. Applying to graduate school
   c. Filling out a form for a dating service

Chapter in Review

KEY TERMS

vertical integration
the expansion of a firm into stages of production earlier or later than those in which it specializes, such as a steel maker that also mines iron ore

bounded rationality
the notion that there is a limit to the information that a firm's manager can comprehend and act on

outsourcing
a firm buys inputs from outside suppliers

core competency
area of specialty; the product or phase of production a firm supplies with greatest efficiency

economies of scope
average costs decline as a firm makes a range of different products rather than specializes in just one product

winner's curse
the plight of the winning bidder who overestimates an asset's true value

asymmetric information
one side of the market has better information about the product than does the other side

hidden characteristics
one side of the market knows more than the other side about product characteristics that are important to the other side

adverse selection
those on the informed side of the market self-select in a way that harms those on the uninformed side of the market

hidden actions
one side of an economic relationship can do something that the other side cannot observe

principal-agent problem
the agent's objectives differ from those of the principal's, and one side can pursue hidden actions

principal
a person or firm who hires an agent to act on behalf of that person or firm

agent
a person or firm who is supposed to act on behalf of the principal

moral hazard
a situation in which one party, as a result of a contract, has an incentive to alter their behavior in a way that harms the other party to the contract

LO1 **Explain the rationale for the firm and describe its scope of operation.** Firms arise when production is more efficient using the hierarchy of the firm than using market transactions. Because production requires elaborate coordination of many resources, all this activity can usually be carried out more efficiently under the direction of a firm's manager than by having a consumer negotiate detailed performance contracts with many resource suppliers. One way firms establish efficient boundaries is through vertical integration. Other things constant, the firm is more likely to buy a component rather than produce it if (a) it's cheaper to buy it than make it, (b) the item is well defined and its quality easily determined, and (c) there are many suppliers of the item. Economies of scope exist when it is cheaper to produce two or more different products in one firm than to produce them in separate firms.

Minimum Efficient Scale and Vertical Integration

The manufacturer in panel (a) is producing at the minimum efficient scale of 1,000,000 computers per year. That output requires 1,000,000 computer chips. If the manufacturer produced its own chips, the cost would be much higher than if it buys them from a chip manufacturer operating on a much larger scale. As panel (b) shows, economies of scale in chip production are far from exhausted when 1,000,000 chips a year are produced.

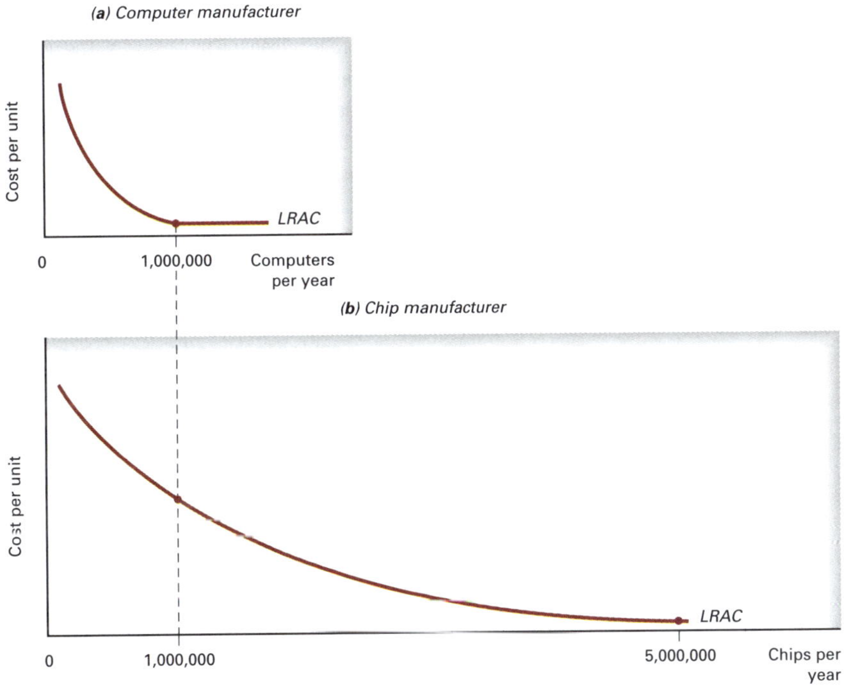

LO2 **Discuss the ways in which imperfect information influences market behavior.** A buyer searches for product information as long as the marginal benefit of search exceeds its marginal cost. Because information is costly, product prices may differ across suppliers. Search costs also lead to quality differences across sellers, even for identically priced products, because consumers find the expected marginal cost of finding a higher quality product outweighs the expected marginal benefit. A new technology, such as the Internet, that reduces search costs will increase the amount of search and reduce price differences for the same good.

efficiency wage theory the idea that offering high wages attracts a more talented labor pool and encourages those hired to perform well so as to keep their jobs

signaling using a proxy measure to communicate information about unobservable characteristics; the signal is more effective if more productive workers find it easier to send than do less-productive workers

screening the process used by employers to select the most qualified workers based on observable characteristics such as a job applicant's level of education and course grades

Optimal Search with Imperfect Information

When information is not free, additional information is acquired as long as its marginal benefit exceeds its marginal cost. Equilibrium, or optimal search, occurs where marginal benefit equals marginal cost. I* is the optimal quantity of information.

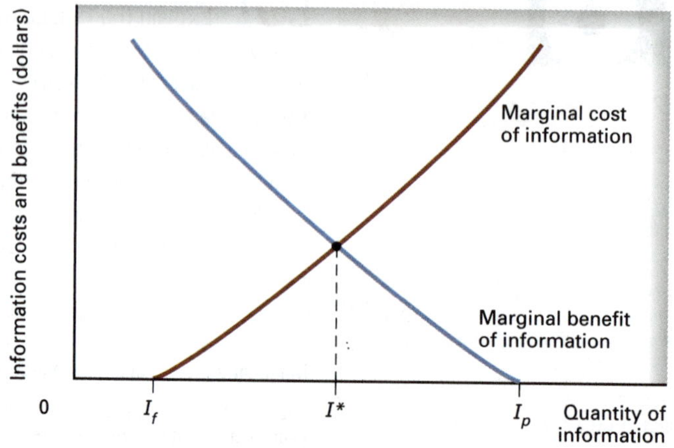

LO3 Explain how asymmetric information affects product markets.

Asymmetric information occurs when one side of the market is better informed about a product than the other side is. The uninformed side may not know about hidden characteristics or about hidden actions. Because of adverse selection, those on the uninformed side of the market may find they are dealing with exactly the wrong people. An incentive structure or an information-revealing system can be developed to reduce the problems associated with the lopsided availability of information.

LO4 Describe the way asymmetric information influences labor markets.

Asymmetric information occurs in labor markets when managers cannot attribute specific outputs to particular workers. If productivity is easy to measure, workers are paid according to their efficiency, as in piece work. If marginal productivity is harder to quantify, employers pay workers by the hour. Inability to quantify productivity also affects the hiring process and the salaries employers offer. Setting above-market wages to attract top talent may result in adverse selection. Highly qualified people may not consider the wage commensurate with their abilities and not apply, whereas less qualified applicants may find the wage attractive and apply in droves. To overcome this asymmetry, employers can screen applicants based on some signal, such as the level of education or college grades, that more-productive workers can send more easily than can less-productive workers.

CHAPTER 17

Economic Regulation *and Antitrust Policy*

Learning Outcomes

- LO 1 Describe the different types of government regulation
- LO 2 Explain why and how natural monopolies are regulated
- LO 3 Explain why producers are interested in economic regulation
- LO 4 Discuss antitrust policy and its enforcement
- LO 5 Describe the relationship between public policy and merger activity

© COMSTOCK IMAGES/JUPITERIMAGES

"Who benefits most when government regulates monopoly?"

If the "invisible hand" of competition yields such desirable results for the economy, why does the government need to regulate business? Is monopoly ever better than competition? Who benefits most when government regulates monopoly? Answers to these and other questions are addressed in this chapter, which discusses government regulation of business.

What do you think?

Government regulation provides essential protection for consumers.

Strongly Disagree						Strongly Agree
1	2	3	4	5	6	7

Businesspeople praise competition but they love monopoly. They praise competition because it harnesses the diverse and often conflicting objectives of various market participants and channels them into the efficient production of goods and services. Competition does this as if by "an invisible hand." Businesspeople love monopoly because it provides the surest path to economic profit in the long run—and, after all, profit is the name of the game for any business. The fruits of monopoly are so tempting that a firm might try to eliminate competitors or conspire with them to raise prices. As Adam Smith remarked more than two centuries ago, "People of the same trade seldom meet together, even for merriment or diversion, but the conversation ends in a conspiracy against the public, or in some contrivance to raise prices."

The tendency of firms to seek monopolistic advantage is understandable, but monopoly usually harms consumers and other producers. Public policy can play a role by promoting competition in those markets where competition seems desirable and by reducing the harmful effects of monopoly in those markets where the output can be most efficiently supplied by one or a few firms.

Topics discussed in Chapter 17 include:

- Regulating natural monopolies
- Theories of economic regulation
- Deregulation
- Antitrust policy
- Per se illegality
- Rule of reason

LO1 Types of Government Regulation

You'll recall that a monopolist supplies a product with no close substitutes, so a monopolist can charge a higher price than would prevail with competition. When only a few firms serve a market, those firms are sometimes able to coordinate their actions, either explicitly or implicitly, to act like a monopolist. The ability of a firm to raise the price without losing all its sales to rivals is called market power. Any firm facing a downward-sloping demand curve has some control over the price and thus some market power. The presumption is

market power the ability of a firm to raise its price without losing all its customers to rival firms that a monopoly, or a group of firms acting as a monopoly, restricts output to charge a higher price than competing firms would charge. With output restricted, the marginal benefit of the final unit sold exceeds its marginal cost, so expanding output would increase social welfare. By failing to expand output to the point where marginal benefit equals marginal cost, firms with market power produce less of the good than would be socially optimal.

Other distortions have also been associated with monopolies. For example, some critics argue that because a monopoly is insulated from competition, it is not as innovative as aggressive competitors would be. Worse still, because of their size and economic importance, monopolies may influence public choices to protect and enhance their monopoly power.

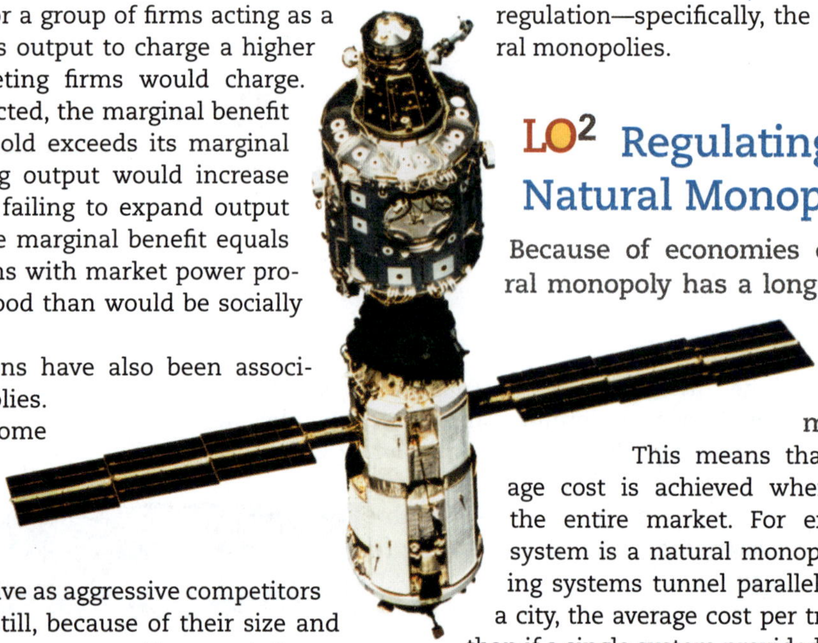

© STOCKBYTE/GETTY IMAGES

Three kinds of government policies are designed to alter or control firm behavior: social regulation, economic regulation, and antitrust policy. Social regulation tries to improve health and safety; for example, by controling unsafe working conditions and dangerous products. Social regulation has economic consequences, but we will not discuss social regulation in this chapter. Economic regulation aims to control the price, output, the entry of new firms, and the quality of service *in industries in which monopoly appears inevitable or even desirable*. Government controls over *natural monopolies*, such as local electricity transmission, local phone service, and a subway system, are examples of economic regulation. Several other industries, such as land and air transportation, have also been regulated in the past. Federal, state, and local governments carry out economic regulation. Antitrust policy outlaws attempts to monopolize, or cartelize, markets in which competition is desirable. Antitrust policy is pursued in the courts by government attorneys and by individual firms that charge other firms with violating antitrust laws. Economic regulation and antitrust policy are examined in this chapter. Let's turn first to economic regulation—specifically, the regulation of natural monopolies.

social regulation
government regulations aimed at improving health and safety

economic regulation
government regulation of natural monopoly, where, because of economies of scale, average production cost is lowest when a single firm supplies the market

antitrust policy
government regulation aimed at preventing monopoly and fostering competition in markets where competition is desirable

LO² Regulating a Natural Monopoly

Because of economies of scale, a natural monopoly has a long-run average cost curve that slopes downward over the range of market demand. This means that the lowest average cost is achieved when one firm serves the entire market. For example, a subway system is a natural monopoly. If two competing systems tunnel parallel routes throughout a city, the average cost per trip would be higher than if a single system provided this service.

Unregulated Profit Maximization

Exhibit 1 shows the demand and cost conditions for a natural monopoly, in this case a metropolitan subway system. A natural monopoly usually faces huge initial capital costs, such as those associated with digging a subway system, building a natural gas pipeline, launching a communications satellite, or wiring a city for electricity or for cable TV. Once capital is in place, average cost falls as output increases, so the average cost curve slopes downward over a broad range of output. In this situation, average cost is lowest when a single firm supplies the market.

An unregulated monopolist, like any other firm, chooses the price-quantity combination that maximizes profit. In Exhibit 1, the monopolist—in this case, the operator of a subway system—maximizes profit by producing where marginal revenue equals marginal cost—that is, where 50 million riders per month pay $4 per trip. The monopolist reaps the profit identified by the blue-shaded rectangle. The *abc* triangle, which is the area below the demand curve and above the $4 price, measures the consumer surplus—consumers' net gain from riding the subway. The problem with letting the monopolist maximize profit is that the resulting price-output combination is inefficient in terms of social welfare. Consumers pay a price that far exceeds the marginal cost of providing the service. *The marginal value of additional output exceeds its marginal cost, so social welfare would increase if output expanded.*

Exhibit 1

Regulating a Natural Monopoly

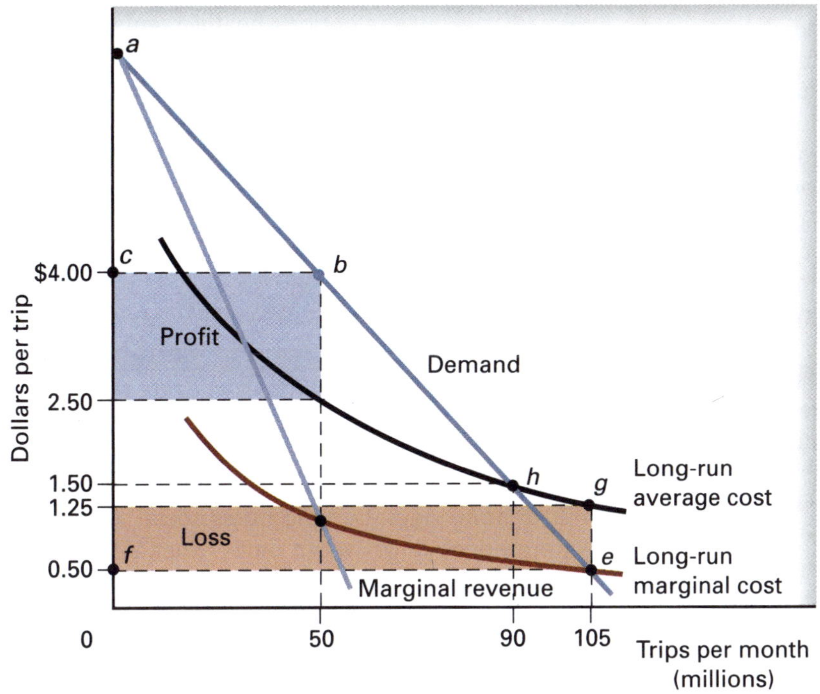

One option for government is to allow the monopolist to maximize profit. But government can increase social welfare by forcing the monopolist to lower the price and expand output. To accomplish this, government can either operate the monopoly itself, as it does with most urban transit systems, or government can *regulate* a privately owned monopoly, as it does with some urban transit systems, local phone services, cable TV service, and electricity transmission. Government-owned or government-regulated monopolies are called public utilities. Here we focus on government regulation, though the issues discussed are similar if the government chose to own and operate the monopoly.

Setting Price Equal to Marginal Cost

Many facets of a natural monopoly have been regulated, but the price-output combination gets the most attention. Suppose government regulators require the monopolist to produce the level of output that is efficient—that is, where the price, which also measures the marginal benefit to consumers, equals the marginal cost of the good. This price-output combination is depicted in Exhibit 1 as point *e*, where the demand curve, or the marginal benefit curve, intersects the marginal cost curve, yielding a price of $0.50 per trip and quantity of 105 million trips per month. Consumers clearly prefer this price to the $4 charged by the unregulated monopolist. The consumer surplus from riding the subway jumps from triangle *abc* without regulation to triangle *aef* with regulation.

Notice, however, that the monopolist now has a problem. The average cost of supplying each of the 105 million trips per month is $1.25, identified by point *g* on the average cost curve. This is more than double the regulated price of $0.50. Rather than earning a profit, the monopolist suffers a loss—in this case, $0.75 per trip, for a total loss of $79 million a month, identified by the pink-shaded rectangle. *Forcing a natural monopolist to produce where price equals marginal cost results in an economic loss to the monopolist.* In the long run, the monopolist would go out of business rather than endure such a loss.

Subsidizing the Natural Monopolist

How can regulators encourage the monopolist to stay in business yet still produce where price equals marginal cost? The government can cover the loss—*subsidize* the firm so it earns a normal profit. Bus and subway fares are typically set below the average cost of providing the service, with the difference made up by a government subsidy. For example, government susidies pay more than 40 percent of the Washington, D.C., Metro subway system. Amtrak requires a federal subsidy covering about a third of its operating budget, totalling more than $30 billion over the last three decades. One drawback with the subsidy solution is that, to provide the subsidy, the government must raise taxes or forgo public spending in some other area. Thus, the subsidy has an opportunity cost and could easily result in inefficiencies elsewhere in the economy.

public utilities
government-owned or government-regulated monopolies

Setting Price Equal to Average Cost

Although some public utilities are subsidized, most are not. Instead, regulators try to establish a price that provides the monopolist with a "fair return." Recall that the average cost curve includes a normal profit. Thus, *setting price equal to average cost* provides a normal, or "fair," profit for the monopolist. In Exhibit 1, the demand curve intersects the average cost curve at point *h*, yielding a price of $1.50 per trip and a quantity of 90 million trips a month. This price-output combination allows the monopolist to stay in business without a subsidy.

Setting price equal to average total cost enhances social welfare compared to the unregulated situation. The monopolist would prefer an economic profit but will accept a normal profit to stay in business. After all, a normal profit is the most this firm could expect if resources were redirected to their best alternative uses. But note that the marginal benefit of the 90 millionth trip exceeds its marginal cost. Therefore, expanding output beyond 90 million trips per month would increase social welfare.

The Regulatory Dilemma

Setting price equal to marginal cost yields the *socially optimal* allocation of resources because *the consumers' marginal benefit from the last unit sold equals the marginal cost of producing that last unit*. In our example, setting the price at $0.50 equates marginal benefit and marginal cost, but the monopolist faces losses unless government provides a subsidy. These losses disappear if price equals average cost, which in our example is $1.50. The higher price ensures a normal profit, but output falls 15 million trips short of the socially optimal level.

Thus, the dilemma facing the regulator is whether to set price equal to marginal cost, which is socially optimal but requires a government subsidy, or to set a break-even price even though output falls short of the socially optimal level. There is no right answer. Compared with the unregulated profit-maximizing price of $4, both reduce the price, increase output, erase economic profit, increase consumer surplus, and increase social welfare. Although Exhibit 1 lays out the options neatly, regulators usually face a cloudier picture. Demand and cost curves can only be estimated, and the regulated firm may withhold or distort information. For example, a utility may overstate costs so it can charge more.

© BRAND X IMAGES/JUPITERIMAGES

LO3 Alternative Theories of Economic Regulation

Why do governments regulate certain industries? Why not let market forces allocate resources? There are two views of government regulation. The first has been implicit in the discussion so far—namely, economic regulation is in the *public interest*. Economic regulation promotes social welfare by keeping prices down when one or just a few firms serve a market. A second, darker, view is that economic regulation is not in the public interest but is in the *special interest* of producers. According to this view, *well-organized producer groups expect to profit from economic regulation and persuade public officials to impose restrictions that existing producers find attractive, such as limiting entry into the industry or preventing competition among existing firms*. Individual producers have more to gain or to lose from regulation than do individual consumers. Producers typically are also better organized and more focused than consumers and are therefore better able to bring about regulations that favor producers.

Producers' Special Interest in Economic Regulation

To understand how and why producer interests could influence public regulation, think back to the last time you had your hair cut. Most states regulate the training and licensing of barbers and beauticians. If any new regulation affecting the profession is proposed, who do you suppose has more interest in that legislation, you or those who cut hair for a living? *Producers have an intense interest in matters that affect their livelihood, so they try to shape such legislation*. Those who cut hair for a living often try to restrict entry by requiring thousands of hours of instruction. At any public hearings on haircut regulations, industry officials provide self-serving testimony, while consumers largely ignore the whole thing.

As a consumer, you do not specialize in getting haircuts. You purchase haircuts, cold cuts, hardware, software, underwear, and thousands of other goods and services. You have no *special interest* in haircuts. Some economists argue that because consumers ignore such matters, business regulations often favor producer interests. Well-organized producer groups, as squeaky wheels in the legislative machinery, get the most grease in the form of favorable regulations. Such regulations are usually introduced under the guise of advancing consumer interests or protecting the public. Producer groups may argue that unbridled competition in their industry would hurt consumers. For example, the alleged problem of "cutthroat" competition among taxi drivers led to regulations that eliminated price competition and restricted the number of taxis in most large metropolitan areas. New York City has 10,000 fewer taxis now than it did 70 years ago. As a result, taxis are harder to find and fares are higher. To operate a cab in New York City, someone must purchase a "medallion." The purchase price reflects the market value to taxi owners of regulations that restrict entry and set fares above the competitive level. The average price of a taxi medallion increased from $27,000 in 1968 to more than $500,000 in 2008. Regulation gives medallion owners an abiding interest in blocking entry. If market entry and taxi fares were deregulated, cabs would become more plentiful, fares would fall to competitive levels, and medallions would become worthless.

We now give an example whereby regulations have been imposed on the number of vehicles allowed, yet several vehicles ply illegally on the roads. Such a regulation is neither in the interest of the supplier nor the consumer. We cite an example of cycle-rickshaw pullers in Delhi, India where a plethora of regulations exist. Existing laws allow only 99,000 cycle-rickshaws to ply in the city. But Delhi has up to eight lakh rickshaws, with just one out of every eight plying legally. A few years back, the Municipal Corporation of Delhi had mandated that rickshaw pullers have to be licensed and only 50,000 licenses were given out. At that time, Delhi had approximately two hundred thousand cycle-rickshaws providing an affordable and available service compared to buses or auto-rickshaws. Thus in one sweep, three-fourths of cycle-rickshaws suddenly became illegal. Another irrational rule was that the holder of the cycle-rickshaw had to ply his cycle-rickshaw himself, the owner and the driver must be the same person. This meant that while you can own multiple taxies or auto rickshaws or buses, you could not own more than one of the cheapest means of transport—the cycle-rickshaw. The law basically says one person can own only one cycle-rickshaw: No room for growth for individual owners in the cycle-rickshaw business. Fortunately, this ruling changed recently. Now, there is likely to be no cap on the number of cycle-rickshaws plying on Delhi's roads, though pullers will have to register themselves to obtain an identity card to work. A government task force has proposed this as part of an upcoming law. The proposed draft allows a person to operate multiple cycle-rickshaws after getting the vehicles registered. Though the proposed legislation bans unregistered cycle-rickshaws from plying, it does away with the current norm of authorities impounding rickshaws that flout the existing rules. In case a rickshaw-puller is caught flouting rules or a rickshaw is found to be unregistered, authorities will have to release the vehicle once the defaulter pays the prescribed fine.

Regulation may be introduced under the guise of quality control, such as keeping "quacks" out of certain professions. But entry restrictions usually reduce competition and increase prices. The special-interest theory may be valid even when the initial intent of the legislation was in the consumer interest. Over time, the regulatory machinery may shift toward the special interests of producers, who, in effect, "capture" the regulating agency. This **capture theory of regulation** was discussed by George Stigler, the Nobel laureate mentioned in the previous chapter. He argued that "as a general rule, regulation is acquired by the industry and is designed and operated for its benefit."[1]

The course of regulation and deregulation raises questions about the true objectives of regulation. Recall the alternative views of regulation: one holds that regulation is in the public, or consumer, interest; the other holds that regulation is in the special, or producer, interest. In the airline industry, regulation appeared more in accord with producer interests, and producer groups fought deregulation, which benefited consumers. On the other hand, investment banks and hedge funds have resisted regulation of their financial operations. Congress and the Obama administration are in the

capture theory of regulation
producers' political power and strong stake in the regulatory outcome lead them, in effect, to "capture" the regulating agency and prevail on it to serve producer interests

1. George Stigler, "The Theory of Economic Regulation," *Bell Journal of Economics and Management Science* (Spring 1971): 3.

process of regulating this industry to protect investors and promote stability in financial markets, but the ultimate effect of such regulation remains to be seen.

This concludes the discussion of economic regulation, which tries to reduce the harmful consequences of monopolistic behavior in those markets where the output can be most efficiently supplied by one or a few firms. We now turn to antitrust policy, which tries to promote competition in those markets where competition seems desirable.

LO4 Antitrust Policy and Enforcement

Although competition typically ensures the most efficient use of the nation's resources, an individual competitor would rather be a monopolist. If left alone, a firm might try to create a monopoly by driving competitors out of business, by merging with competitors, or by colluding with competitors. *Antitrust policy* is the government's attempt to reduce anticompetitive behavior and promote a market structure that leads to greater competition. *Antitrust policy attempts to promote socially desirable market performance.*

Origins of Antitrust Policy

Economic developments in the last half of the nineteenth century created bigger firms serving wider markets. Perhaps the two most important developments were (1) technological breakthroughs that led to a larger optimal plant size in manufacturing and (2) the rise of the railroad which reduced transport costs. *Economies of scale and cheaper transport costs extended the geographical size of markets,* so firms grew larger to serve this bigger market.

trust
any firm or group of firms that tries to monopolize a market

per se illegal
in antitrust law, business practices deemed illegal regardless of their economic rationale or their consequences

rule of reason
before ruling on the legality of certain business practices, a court examines why they were undertaken and what effect they have on competition

Sharp declines in the national economy of the United States in 1873 and in 1883, however, panicked large manufacturers. Because their heavy fixed costs required large-scale production, they cut prices in an attempt to stimulate sales. Price wars erupted, creating economic turmoil. Firms desperately sought ways to stabilize their markets. One solution was for competing firms to form a *trust* by transferring their voting stock to a single board of trustees, which would vote in the interest of the industry. Early trusts were formed in the sugar, tobacco, and oil industries. Although the impact of these early trusts is still debated today, they allegedly pursued anticompetitive practices to develop and maintain a monopoly advantage. Gradually the word **trust** came to mean any firm or group of firms that tried to monopolize a market.

Trusts provoked widespread criticism and their creators were dubbed "robber barons." Farmers, especially, were hurt by these early trusts, for while farm prices were pushed down by technological change in agriculture, the prices farmers paid for supplies were often higher because of trusts. Farmers accounted for 40 percent of the U.S. workforce at the time and thus had political clout. Some states, primarily agricultural, enacted *antitrust* measures in the 1880s, outlawing trusts. But these were largely ineffective because a trust could simply move to a state without such restrictions.

Antitrust Enforcement

Any law's effectiveness depends on the vigor and vigilance of enforcement. The pattern of antitrust enforcement goes something like this.

Per Se Illegality and the Rule of Reason

The courts have interpreted antitrust laws in essentially two different ways. One set of practices has been declared **per se illegal**—that is, illegal regardless of the economic rationale or consequences. For example, under the Sherman Act, all agreements among competing firms to fix prices, restrict output, or otherwise restrain competition are viewed as per se illegal. To prove guilt under a per se rule, the government need only show that the offending practice took place. Thus, the government need only examine the firm's *behavior.*

Another set of practices falls under the **rule of reason**. Here the courts take into account the facts surrounding the particular offense—namely, the reasons why the offending practice was adopted and its effect on competition. The rule of reason was first set forth in 1911, when the Supreme Court held that Standard Oil had illegally monopolized the petroleum refining industry in the United States. Standard Oil allegedly had come to dominate 90 percent of the market by acquiring more than 120 former rivals and by practicing predatory pricing to drive remaining rivals out of business—for example, by temporarily selling below marginal cost or dropping the price only in certain markets. In finding Standard Oil guilty, the Court focused on both the company's *behavior* and the *market structure* that resulted from that behavior. Based on this approach, the Court found that the company had behaved *unreasonably* and ruled that the monopoly should be broken up.

But in 1920, the rule of reason led the Supreme Court to find U.S. Steel not guilty of monopolization. In that case, the Court ruled that not every contract or combination in restraint of trade is illegal—only those that "unreasonably" restrained trade violated antitrust laws. The Court said that *mere size is not an offense.* Although U.S. Steel clearly possessed market power, the company, in the Court's view, had not violated antitrust laws because it had not unreasonably used that power. The Court switched positions in 1945, ruling that although Alcoa's conduct might be reasonable and legal, its mere possession of market power—Alcoa controlled 90 percent of the aluminum ingot market—violated antitrust laws per se. Here the Court was using *market structure* rather than firm *behavior* as the test of legality.

Competition Policy in India

For years after India's independence in 1947, India followed the strategy of planned economic development. The broad policy objectives were achieving self-reliance and promoting social justice. Self-reliance, over time came to mean import substitution. There were government-imposed controls over entry and exit in the market. Plant and firm size were subject to statutory limitations, and imports and foreign investment were restricted. Government-owned businesses enjoyed protections and preferences and dominated the "commanding heights of the economy" in various sectors. These policies were reflected in many of the state's economic policies, including its industrial policy, financial policy, trade policy, and exchange rate policy. In this system, there was little place for competition policy. In fact during this period (known as the pre-reform period or pre-1991 period), various restraints to competition existed. Some of these are listed as:

1. investment restraints (licensing);
2. control over acquisition of economic power through Monopolies and Restrictive Trade Practices Act (MRTP);
3. public sector reservation for infrastructure and other industries creating monopolies in various areas;
4. product reservation for the small-scale sector;
5. government procurement policies favoring public and small-scale sectors;
6. trade restrictions and high tariffs; and
7. restrictions on foreign direct investment.

However, since 1991, all these restraints (protective measures as well as controls) have been or are being relaxed now. The new economic policies (NEP) progressively widened the space for market forces and reduced the role of government in business. It was also recognized that a new competition law was called for because the existing Monopolies and Restrictive Trade Practices Act, 1969 (MRTP Act) had become obsolete in certain respects and there was a need to shift the focus from curbing monopolies to promoting competition. Need was thus felt to

1. enact a new competition law, called the Competition Act,
2. establish a competition authority, known as the Competition Commission of India,
3. repeal the MRTP Act, and
4. wind up the MRTP Commission.

As a result, The Competition Act, 2002 was passed by the Parliament in the year 2002, to which the President accorded assent in January, 2003. It was subsequently amended by the Competition (Amendment) Act, 2007. In accordance with the provisions of the Amendment Act, the Competition Commission of India and the Competition Appellate Tribunal have been established. The Competition Commission of India is now fully functional with a Chairperson and six members. The provisions of the Competition Act relating to anti-competitive agreements and abuse of dominant position were notified on May 20, 2009.

Competition Commission of India (CCI): Competition Commission of India is a body of the Government of India responsible for enforcing The Competition Act, 2002 throughout India and for preventing activities that have an adverse effect on competition in India. It was established on October 14, 2003. The Competition Act, 2002, as amended by the Competition (Amendment) Act, 2007, follows the philosophy of modern competition laws. The Act prohibits:

predatory pricing
pricing tactics employed by a dominant firm to drive competitors out of business, such as temporarily selling below marginal cost or dropping the price only in certain markets

1. anti-competitive agreements,
2. abuse of dominant position by enterprises, and
3. regulates combinations (acquisition, acquiring of control, and M&A), which causes or is likely to cause an appreciable adverse effect on competition within India.

The objectives of the Act are sought to be achieved through the Competition Commission of India. It is the duty of the Commission to eliminate practices having adverse effect on competition, promote and sustain competition, protect the interests of consumers and ensure freedom of trade in the markets of India. The Commission is also required to give opinion on competition issues on a reference received from a statutory authority established under any law and to undertake competition advocacy, create public awareness, and impart training on competition issues.

The objectives of Competition Law have been further highlighted in a recent judgment delivered by Honorable Supreme Court as:

"The main objective of competition law is to promote economic efficiency using competition as one of the means of assisting the creation of market responsive to consumer preferences. The advantages of perfect competition are three-fold: allocative efficiency, which ensures the effective allocation of resources, productive efficiency, which ensures that costs of production are kept at a minimum and dynamic efficiency, which promotes innovative practices."

(Judgment in Civil Appeal No. 7999 of 2010 pronounced on 9th September, 2010)

Herfindahl-Hirschman Index (HHI)
a measure of market concentration that squares each firm's percentage share of the market then sums these squares

LO5 Mergers and Public Policy

Some firms have pursued rapid growth by merging with other firms or by acquiring other firms. Much of what the Antitrust Division in the U.S. Justice Department and the Federal Trade Commission's (FTC) Bureau of Competition do is approve or deny proposed mergers and acquisitions. In determining possible harmful effects that a merger might have on competition, one important consideration is its impact on the share of sales accounted for by the largest firms in the industry. If a few firms account for a relatively large share of sales, the industry is said to be *concentrated.* As a measure of sales concentration, the Justice Department uses the **Herfindahl-Hirschman Index**, or **HHI,** which is found by squaring the percentage of market share of each firm in the market and then summing those squares. For example, if the industry consists of 100 firms of equal size, the HHI is 100 [$= 100 \times (1)^2$]. If the industry is a pure monopoly, its index is 10,000 [$= (100)^2$], the largest possible value. The more firms in the industry and the more equal their size, the smaller the HHI. This index gives greater weight to firms with larger market shares, as can be seen for the three examples presented in Exhibit 2. Each industry has 44 firms, but, for ease of exposition, only the market share of the top 4 firms differs across industries. Note that the index for Industry III is nearly triple that for each of the two other industries. Please take a minute now to work through the logic of the exhibit.

The Justice Department's guidelines sort all mergers into one of two categories: *horizontal mergers,* which involve firms in the same market, and *nonhorizontal mergers,* which include all other types of mergers. Of greatest interest for antitrust purposes are horizontal

Exhibit 2

Herfindahl-Hirschman Index (HHI) Based on Market Share in Three Industries

	Industry I		Industry II		Industry III	
Firm	Market Share (percent)	Market Share Squared	Market Share (percent)	Market Share Squared	Market Share (percent)	Market Share Squared
A	23	529	15	225	57	3,249
B	18	324	15	225	1	1
C	13	169	15	225	1	1
D	6	36	15	225	1	1
Remaining 40 firms	1 each	40	1 each	40	1 each	40
HHI		1,098		940		3,292

© MARIE-FRANCE BELANGER/ISTOCKPHOTO.COM

mergers, such as a merger between competing oil companies like Exxon and Mobil. The Justice Department generally challenges any merger in an industry that meets two conditions: (1) the post-merger HHI exceeds 1,800 and (2) the merger increases the index by more than 100 points. Mergers in an industry that would have a post-merger index of less than 1,000 are seldom challenged.[2] Other factors, such as the ease of entry into the market and gains in efficiency, are considered for indexes between 1,000 and 1,800.

Problems with Antitrust Policy

Despite the publicity and hoopla surrounding the Microsoft antitrust case (there was even a thinly disguised movie about Microsoft called *Antitrust*), there is growing doubt about the economic value of the lengthy antitrust cases pursued in the past. A case against Exxon, for example, was in the courts for 17 years before the company was cleared of charges in 1992. Another case began in 1969 when IBM, with nearly 70 percent of domestic sales of electronic data-processing equipment, was accused of monopolizing that market. IBM responded that its large market share was based on its innovative products and on its economies of scale. The trial began in 1975, the government took nearly three years to present its case; litigation dragged on for four more years. In the meantime, many other computer makers emerged both in this country and abroad to challenge IBM's dominance. In 1982, the government dropped the case, noting that the threat of monopoly had diminished enough that the case was "without merit." The U.S. case against Microsoft took nearly six years to resolve and it dragged on in state courts years longer.

2. Merger guidelines are laid out by the U.S. Department of Justice at http://www.usdoj.gov/atr/public/guidelines/hmg.htm.

Competition May Not Require That Many Firms

Joseph Schumpeter argued 60 years ago that competition should be viewed as a dynamic process, one of "creative destruction." Firms are continually in flux—introducing new products, phasing out old ones, trying to compete for the consumer's dollar in a variety of ways. In light of this, antitrust policy should not necessarily aim at increasing the *number* of firms in each industry. In some cases, firms grow large because they are better than rivals at offering what consumers want. Accordingly, firm size should not be the primary concern. Moreover, as noted in the chapter on perfect competition, economists have shown through market experiments that most of the desirable properties of perfect competition can be achieved with relatively few firms.[3] For example, the two leading chip makers, Intel and Advanced Micro Devices, have been locked in a price war for years, as each fights for market share. Likewise, Boeing, the only U.S. maker of commercial jets, competes fiercely with Europe's Airbus for every new contract.

3. See, for example, Vernon Smith, "Markets as Economizers of Information: Experimental Examinations of the 'Hayek Hypothesis,'" *Economic Inquiry* 20 (1982); and Douglas Davis and Charles Holt, *Experimental Economics* (Princeton, N.J.: Princeton University Press, 1993).

Microsoft on Trial

© GOH SENG CHONG/BLOOMBERG NEWS/LANDOV

The U.S. Justice Department and 20 state attorneys general filed lawsuits in 1998 alleging that Microsoft tried to protect its operating-system monopoly and to extend that monopoly into Internet software. Microsoft disputed the charges and said the government was interfering with its right to create new products that benefit consumers. Still, after months of proceedings, the judge ruled against Microsoft, maintaining that the company had attempted to monopolize the Web browser market by unlawfully "tying" Internet Explorer with Windows. As a remedy, he proposed restricting Microsoft's business practices and dividing the firm into two companies. Microsoft appealed the decision, arguing that it did not hold a monopoly and had not engaged in anticompetitive practices. Microsoft eventually reached an out-of-court settlement that gave personal-computer makers greater freedom to install non-Microsoft software on new machines. It also banned retaliation against companies that take advantage of these freedoms, prohibited exclusive contracts, and required Microsoft to disclose design information to hardware and software makers so they can build competing products that run smoothly with Windows.

SOURCES: Marc Ferranti, "Iowa Judge Approves Microsoft Class-Action Settlement," *PC World,* 18 April 2007; David Lawsky, "EU Considers New Kind of Microsoft Antitrust Action," *Scientific American,* 23 April 2007.

Abuse of Antitrust

Parties that can show injury from firms that violate antitrust laws can sue the offending company and recover three times the damages sustained. These so-called *treble damage* suits increased after World War II. More than 1,000 are filed each year. Courts have been relatively generous to those claiming to have been wronged. Even foreign firms have started suing in U.S. courts. And, in an unusual twist, foreign firms are now suing other foreign firms using U.S courts, laws, and lawyers. But studies show that such suits can be used to intimidate an aggressive competitor or to convert a contract dispute between, say, a firm and its supplier into treble damage payoffs. The result can have a chilling effect on competition. Many economists now believe that the anticompetitive costs from this abuse of treble damage suits may exceed any competitive benefits of these laws.

Growth of International Markets

Finally, a standard approach to measuring the market power of a firm is its share of the market. With greater international trade, however, the local or even national market share becomes less relevant. General Motors may still dominate U.S. auto manufacturing, accounting for nearly 40 percent of national sales by U.S. firms. But when Japanese and European producers are included, GM's share of the U.S. auto market falls to only about 20 percent of all sales. GM's share of world production has declined steadily since the mid-1950s. And throughout 2008 GM and Toyota were in a virtual tie to lead the world in global sales. Indeed, GM's very survival came into question in 2009 as GM and Chrysler sought and received federal aid to help the companies survive bankruptcy. *Where markets are open to foreign competition, antitrust enforcement that focuses on domestic producers makes less economic sense.* In response to the global nature of markets, antitrust policy is starting to take an international approach. The U.S. government has signed cooperative agreements with some other governments, including Japan and the European Union, to promote antitrust enforcement and reduce conflicting decisions. For example, antitrust investigators from the United States, the European Union, Japan, and Canada simultaneously raided 14 companies in 5 countries in a price fixing probe of the polyvinyl chloride market. Through the International Competition Network, more than 100 nations discuss antitrust procedures and policies. Such discussions have thrown light on anticompetitive regulations in place around the world. Many countries for decades have sheltered firms in some politically powerful industries. For example, until recently, regulations in India restricted entry into the hotel business. As a result, there were fewer hotel rooms in all of India, a country with more than a billion people, than in New York City with less than 1 percent that population.

Bailing Out Troubled Industries

The collapse of housing prices in 2008 caused mortgage defaults and led to rising unemployment. The federal government responded by offering financial assistance to affected industries, especially financial institutions and the big three automakers. The intent was to promote financial stability and keep the economy from sinking further. But the effect of such market intervention on competition remains to be seen.

Final Word

Competition has been growing in recent decades because of changing technology, greater international trade, industry deregulation, and antitrust

policy. Consumers benefit as firms compete by offering lower prices, better products, and new services to keep existing customers and attract new ones. Competition also ensures that the economy's resources find their most efficient uses. Through the process of creative destruction, competition promotes the survival of the fittest. Market forces continuously pressure firms to innovate—that is, to develop new and better products, services, methods of doing business, and technologies.

© BORIS ROESSLER/DPA/LANDOV

Multiple Choice Questions

1. Which of the following occurs if firms are able to restrict output and raise price?
   a. resources are misallocated
   b. wealth is shifted from consumers to government
   c. wealth is shifted from producers to consumers
   d. P = MC
   e. P = minimum LRAC
2. Which of the following is *not* a criticism of monopolies?
   a. They restrict output.
   b. They set price above the perfectly competitive level.
   c. They tend to be less innovative than firms in a competitive market.
   d. They exert a disproportionate amount of political influence.
   e. They reduce allocative efficiency through perfect price discrimination.
3. Economic regulation of business is justified if, by intervening, government can
   a. improve the allocation of resources in society
   b. create economic rents for special interest groups
   c. reduce output and increase prices for an industry
   d. increase tax revenue from the regulated industry
   e. force firms to increase their costs of production
4. The three kinds of government regulation designed to alter or control firm behavior are:
   a. Antitrust policy, lobbying, and social regulation
   b. Economic regulation, antitrust policy, and lobbying
   c. Social regulation, lobbying, economic regulation
   d. Social regulation, economic regulation, and antitrust policy
   e. Social regulation, antitrust policy, fiscal policy
5. Government controls of price, output, entry of new firms, and quality of service in industries where monopoly appears desirable are known as
   a. antitrust regulation
   b. economic regulation
   c. social regulation
   d. antimerger regulation
   e. consumer advocacy regulation
6. If a firm has a downward-sloping long-run average cost curve over the entire range of market demand, it is a
   a. local monopoly
   b. resource monopoly
   c. monopsony
   d. output monopoly
   e. natural monopoly
7. Most local phone companies
   a. face a horizontal demand curve
   b. are regulated
   c. are called public utilities
   d. have tremendous economies of scale
   e. are natural monopolies
8. The rail system in Metropolis is a natural monopoly. If the government regulates the system by setting the fare equal to marginal cost, which of the following will be true?
   a. Price and output will be higher than if the monopoly were unregulated.
   b. Price and output will be lower than if the monopoly were unregulated.
   c. Price will be lower and output higher than if the monopoly were unregulated.
   d. Price will be higher and output lower than if the monopoly were unregulated.
   e. Profit will be lower than if the monopoly were unregulated, but price and output could either increase or decrease.
9. The rail system in Metropolis is a natural monopoly. If the government regulates the system by setting the fare equal to marginal cost, which of the following will be true?
   a. Profit will be zero under regulation.
   b. Only normal profit will be earned under regulation.
   c. Accounting profit will be zero under regulation.
   d. Economic loss will occur under regulation.
   e. Profit will be higher than if the monopoly were unregulated.
10. Watt Power and Light, an electric company, will suffer an economic loss
    a. even at its profit-maximizing output because marginal cost is always less than average cost

b. even at its profit-maximizing output because average cost is always less than marginal cost
c. if regulators insist that it produce where price equals marginal cost because marginal cost is less than average cost
d. if regulators insist that it produce where price equals marginal cost because average cost is always less than marginal cost
e. if regulators insist that it produce where price equals average cost because average cost is always less than marginal cost

11. If a regulator sets the price equal to the natural monopolist's marginal cost,
    a. the monopoly will experience a loss
    b. the monopoly will earn a profit
    c. the monopoly will earn zero profit
    d. consumers will be worse off than they would be if the firm's profit maximization activities were unregulated
    e. the monopoly will be better off than it would be if its profit maximization activities were unregulated

12. Production by a monopoly would result in the socially optimal allocation of resources if
    a. price is set equal to marginal cost
    b. marginal revenue is set equal to price
    c. marginal revenue is set equal to marginal cost
    d. price is set equal to average total cost
    e. marginal revenue is set equal to average total cost

13. The rail system in Metropolis is a natural monopoly. If the government regulates the system by setting the fare equal to marginal cost, which of the following will be true?
    a. The managers of the rail system will be allowed to adjust marginal cost so that they can get a normal rate of return on capital.
    b. The managers of the rail system will be allowed to adjust marginal cost so that they can get a fair profit.
    c. The rail system will earn economic profit at that fare.
    d. If the government doesn't give the rail system a subsidy to supplement revenue from fares, the system will face continuous economic losses.
    e. If the government doesn't give the rail system a subsidy to supplement revenue from fares, fare increases will push marginal cost upward.

14. Which of the following is true of a natural monopoly?
    a. If regulated, the firm will have a higher level of output than an unregulated firm, whether the regulation is based on average cost, marginal cost, or normal profit.
    b. If regulated, the firm will have a lower level of output than an unregulated firm, whether the regulation is based on average cost, marginal cost, or normal profit.
    c. If regulated, the firm that is only allowed a normal profit will be allowed to charge a price in excess of its average cost.
    d. If regulated, the firm that is only allowed a normal profit will be allowed to produce more than a firm that must set a price equal to its marginal cost.
    e. If regulated, the firm that is only allowed a normal profit will be allowed to produce more than a firm that must set a price equal to its average cost.

15. The capture theory of regulation, espoused by George Stigler, asserts that
    a. consumers "capture" regulatory agencies so that regulation favors consumers
    b. producers "capture" regulatory agencies so that regulation favors producers
    c. regulators "capture" producers and limit their market power
    d. consumers "capture" some consumer surplus lost to monopoly
    e. consumers and producers work together to "capture" regulatory agencies in order to achieve more desirable regulation

16. According to the special interest theory,
    a. economic regulation is designed to promote social welfare
    b. producers may be able to influence regulators to impose restrictions favorable to producers
    c. groups of consumers with special interests may be able to control a regulatory agency to their own benefit
    d. foreign lobbyists may be able to control a regulatory agency to their own benefit
    e. the fighting between special interest groups over economic regulation may cancel out effects of such regulation

17. A camera manufacturer will sell its cameras only to retailers who agree to buy its brand of film. This is an example of
    a. price discrimination
    b. exclusive dealing

c. a tying contract
d. interlocking directorates
e. a trust

18. The "rule of reason"
    a. applies to business practices that are illegal regardless of their economic rationale or their consequences
    b. applies to business practices that are legal, regardless of their consequences
    c. means that business practices cannot be proven to be illegal, and a consent decree is required to halt the practices
    d. considers why a certain business practice was adopted and what the effects on competition are, before determining whether the practice is illegal
    e. focuses on market structure rather than on the behavior of firms in determining whether antitrust violations have occurred

19. Which of the following *most accurately* describes the type of mergers that the antitrust laws are intended to prohibit?
    a. mergers that tend to reduce competition
    b. horizontal mergers
    c. both vertical and horizontal mergers
    d. conglomerate mergers
    e. vertical mergers

20. If a firm with a 10 percent market share merges with a firm with 15 percent of the market, by how much will the Herfindahl index change? The other firms have 40 percent, 15 percent, 10 percent, and 10 percent shares.
    a. It rises by 100.
    b. It rises by 300.
    c. It falls by 200.
    d. It falls by 250.
    e. It rises by 25.

Answers

1. a 2. e 3. a 4. d 5. b 6. e 7. e 8. c 9. d 10. c
11. a 12. a 13. d 14. a 15. b 16. b 17. c 18. d 19. a 20. b

Long Answer Questions

LO1 Describe the different types of government regulation

1.1. *(Business Behavior and Public Policy)* Define market power, and then discuss the rationale for government regulation of firms with market power.

LO2 Explain why and how natural monopolies are regulated

2.1. *(Regulating Natural Monopolies)* The following graph represents a natural monopoly.

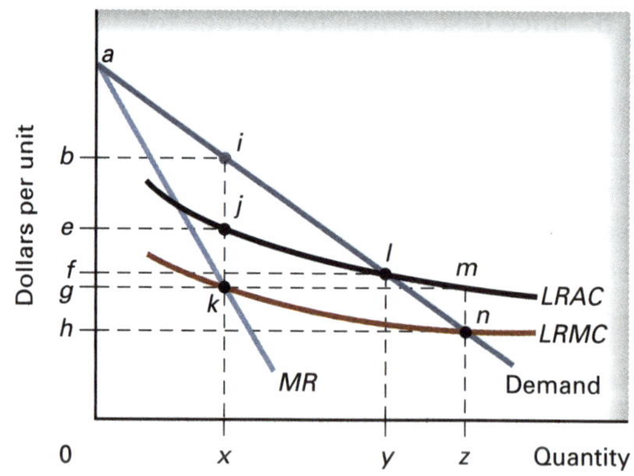

   a. Why is this firm considered a natural monopoly?
   b. If the firm is unregulated, what price and output would maximize its profit? What would be its profit or loss?
   c. If a regulatory commission establishes a price with the goal of achieving allocative efficiency, what would be the price and output? What would be the firm's profit or loss?
   d. If a regulatory commission establishes a price with the goal of allowing the firm a "fair return," what would be the price and output? What would be the firm's profit or loss?
   e. Which one of the prices in parts (b), (c), and (d) maximizes consumer surplus? What problem, if any, occurs at this price?

LO3 Explain why producers are interested in economic regulation

3.1. *(Theories of Regulation)* Why do producers have more interest in government regulations than consumers do?
   a. Compare and contrast the public-interest and special-interest theories of economic regulation. What is the capture theory of regulation?
   b. Which of these theories best describes the case of airline deregulation? Which best explains the government's case against Microsoft?

LO4 Discuss antitrust laws and their enforcement

4.1. *(Origins of Antitrust Policy)* Identify the type of anticompetitive behavior illustrated by each of the following:

a. A university requires buyers of season tickets for its basketball games to buy season tickets for its football games as well.

b. Dairies that bid on contracts to supply milk to school districts collude to increase what they charge.

c. The same individual serves on the boards of directors of General Motors and Ford.

d. A large retailer sells merchandise below cost in certain regions to drive competitors out of business.

e. A producer of carbonated soft drinks sells to a retailer only if the retailer agrees not to buy from the producer's major competitor.

LO5 Describe the relationship between public policy and merger activity

5.1. *(Mergers and Public Policy)* Calculate the Herfindahl-Hirschman Index (HHI) for each of the following industries. Which industry is the most concentrated?

a. An industry with five firms that have the following market shares: 50 percent, 30 percent, 10 percent, 5 percent, and 5 percent

b. An industry with five firms that have the following market shares: 60 percent, 20 percent, 10 percent, 5 percent, and 5 percent

c. An industry with five firms, each of which has a 20 percent market share

ECONOMIC REGULATION AND ANTITRUST POLICY

17 Chapter in Review

KEY TERMS

market power
the ability of a firm to raise its price without losing all its customers to rival firms

social regulation
government regulations aimed at improving health and safety

economic regulation
government regulation of natural monopoly, where, because of economies of scale, average production cost is lowest when a single firm supplies the market

antitrust policy
government regulation aimed at preventing monopoly and fostering competition in markets where competition is desirable

public utilities
government-owned or government-regulated monopolies

capture theory of regulation
producers' political power and strong stake in the regulatory outcome lead them, in effect, to "capture" the regulating agency and prevail on it to serve producer interests

trust
any firm or group of firms that tries to monopolize a market

per se illegal
in antitrust law, business practices deemed illegal regardless of their economic rationale or their consequences

rule of reason
before ruling on the legality of certain business practices, a court examines why they were undertaken and what effect they have on competition

predatory pricing
pricing tactics employed by a dominant firm to drive competitors out of business, such as temporarily selling below marginal cost or dropping the price only in certain markets

Herfindahl-Hirschman Index (HHI)
a measure of market concentration that squares each firm's percentage share of the market then sums these squares

LO1 Describe the different types of government regulation. When only a few firms serve a market, they are sometimes able to coordinate efforts and act like a monopolist and exercise significant market power. The three government policies designed to mitigate that power are social regulations, economic regulations, and antitrust policy. This chapter examined in detail only two forms of government regulation of business: (a) economic regulation, such as the regulation of natural monopolies, and (b) antitrust policy, which promotes competition and prohibits efforts to monopolize, or cartelize, an industry.

LO2 Explain why and how natural monopolies are regulated. Governments regulate natural monopolies so that output is greater and prices lower than if the monopolist was allowed to maximize profits. One problem with regulation is that the price that maximizes social welfare results in an economic loss, whereas the price that allows the firm to earn a normal profit does not maximize social welfare.

LO3 Explain why producers are interested in economic regulation. There are two views of economic regulation, which tries to reduce the harmful consequences of monopolistic behavior in markets where output can be most efficiently supplied by one or two firms. The first is that economic regulation is in the public, or consumer, interest because it controls natural monopolies where production by one or just a few firms is most efficient. A second view is that regulation is more in the special interest of producers who use regulations to fix the price, block entry, and increase profits.

Regulating a Natural Monopoly

With a natural monopoly, the long-run average cost curve slopes downward where it intersects the demand curve. The unregulated firm maximizes profit by producing where marginal revenue equals marginal cost, in this case, 50 million trips per month at a price of $4.00 per trip. This outcome is inefficient because price, or marginal benefit, exceeds marginal cost. To achieve the efficient output rate, regulators could set the price at $0.50 per trip. The subway would sell 105 million trips per month, which would be an efficient outcome. But at that price, the subway would lose money and would require a subsidy to keep going. As an alternative,regulators could set the price at $1.50 per trip. The subway would sell 90 million trips per month and would break even (because price equals average cost). Although the subway would earn a normal profit, social welfare could still be increased by expanding output as long as the price, or marginal benefit, exceeds marginal cost, but that would result in an economic loss, requiring a subsidy.

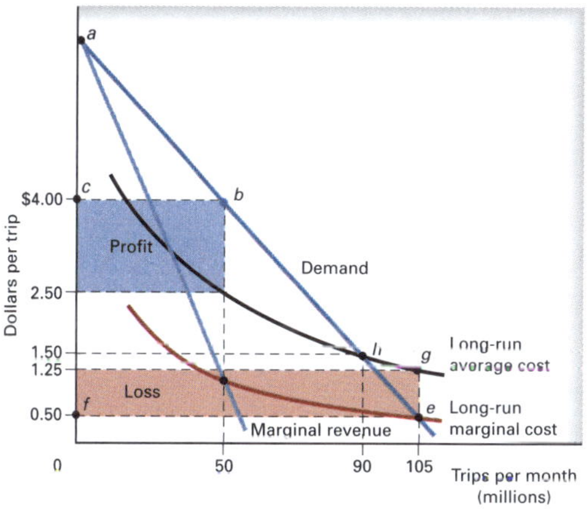

LO4 Discuss antitrust policy and its enforcement. Antitrust laws are aimed at promoting competition and prohibiting efforts to cartelize, or monopolize, an industry. The Sherman, Clayton, and FTC Acts provide the legal and institutional framework for antitrust enforcement in the United States. The Competition Commision of India is the concerned authority to oversee competition issues in India.

LO5 Describe the relationship between public policy and merger activity. To provent mergers from trending toward creating monopolies, the U.S. Justice Department uses the Herfindahl-Hirschman Index (HHI) to determine the sales concentration in an industry and the legality of a merger. (The higher the HHI for market, the more monopolistic it is.) Mergers in the United States have occurred in four waves since 1887.

Herfindahl-Hirschman Index (HHI) Based on Market Share in Three Industries

Each of the three industries shown has 44 firms. The HHI is found by squaring each firm's market share then summing the squares. Under each industry, each firm's market share is shown in the left column and the square of the market share is shown in the right column. For ease of exposition, only the market share of the top four firms differs across industries. The remaining 40 firms have 1 percent market share each. The HHI for Industry III is nearly triple that for each of the other two industries.

	Industry I		Industry II		Industry III	
Firm	Market Share (percent)	Market Share Squared	Market Share (percent)	Market Share Squared	Market Share (percent)	Market Share Squared
A	23	529	15	225	57	3,249
B	18	324	15	225	1	1
C	13	169	15	225	1	1
D	636	15225	1	1		
Remaining 40 firms	1 each	40	1 each	40	1 each	40
HHI		1,098		940		3,292

CHAPTER 18

Learning Outcomes

- LO[1] Define public goods
- LO[2] Discuss the role of public choice in representative democracy
- LO[3] Describe the underground economy
- LO[4] Explain bureaucracy and its role in representative democracy

Public Goods *and* Public Choice

© PHOTOS.COM/JUPITERIMAGES

“How do public goods differ from private goods?”

How do public goods differ from private goods? Why do most people remain largely ignorant about what's happening in the public sector? Why is it so difficult to interest the public in the public interest? Why is voter turnout so low? Why do some politicians express concern for average Americans, but vote for special interests? Why are incumbents more likely than challengers to support campaign spending limits? Answers to these and related questions are discussed in this chapter, which focuses on the public sector—both the rationale for public goods and public choices about those goods.

What do you think?

What one person views as wasteful spending, could be viewed by another as a worthwhile investment.

Strongly Disagree					*Strongly Agree*	
1	2	3	4	5	6	7

The effects of government are all around us. Stitched into the clothes you put on this morning are government-required labels providing washing instructions. Government subsidies affect the price of your Cheerios and the milk and sugar you put on them. Governments regulate the motor vehicle you travel in as well the speed and the sobriety of the driver. Taxpayers subsidize your education in a variety of ways. Yes, government plays a major role in the economy.

The role of government has been discussed throughout this book. For the most part, we assumed that government makes optimal adjustments to the shortcomings of the private sector—that is, when confronted with market failure, government adopts and implements the appropriate program to address the problem. But, just as there are limits to the market's effectiveness, there are limits to government's effectiveness. In this chapter, we look at the pros and cons of government activity. We begin with public goods, discuss the decision-making process, and then examine the limitations of that process.

Topics discussed in Chapter 18 include:

- Private versus public goods
- Representative democracy
- Rational ignorance
- Special-interest legislation
- Rent seeking
- The underground economy
- Bureaucratic behavior
- Private versus public production

LO1 Public Goods

Throughout most of this book, we have been talking about *private goods,* such as pizzas and haircuts. As noted in Chapter 3, private goods have two important features. First, they are *rival* in consumption, meaning that the amount consumed by one person is unavailable for others to consume. For example, when you and friends share a pizza, each slice others eat is one less available for you (which is why you usually eat a little faster when sharing). A second key feature of private goods is that suppliers can easily *exclude* those who don't pay. Only paying customers get pizzas. Thus, private goods are said to be *rival* and *exclusive.*

Private Goods, Public Goods, and In Between

In contrast to private goods, *public goods,* such as national defense, the National Weather Service, the Centers for Disease Control, or a local mosquito-control program, are *nonrival* in consumption. One person's consumption does not diminish the amount available to others. Once produced, such goods are available to all in equal amount; the good can be supplied to an additional consumer for zero marginal cost. But once a public good is produced, suppliers cannot easily deny it to those who don't pay. There are no vending machines for public goods. For example, if a firm sprays a neighborhood for mosquitoes, all those in the neighborhood benefit. The firm can't easily exclude those who fail to pay. Thus, the mosquito spraying is *nonexclusive*—it benefits all those in the neighborhood. Some people figure, "Since I can enjoy the benefits without paying, why bother paying?" As a consequence, for-profit firms can't profitably sell public goods. In this case of market failure, the government comes to the rescue by providing public goods and paying for them through enforced taxation. Sometimes nonprofit agencies also provide public goods, funding them through contributions and other revenue sources.

But the economy consists of more than just the polar cases of private and public goods. Some goods are *nonrival* but *exclusive.* For example, additional households can watch a TV show without affecting the reception of other viewers. It's not as if there is only so much TV signal to go around. Television signals are nonrival in consumption. Yet the program's producers, should they choose to, could charge each household for reception, as with cable TV, so the TV signal is nonrival but exclusive. A good that is nonrival but exclusive is called a *natural monopoly,* a term already introduced. Along the same lines, short of the point of congestion, additional people can benefit from a golf course, swimming pool, rock concert, or highway without diminishing the benefit to other users. These goods, when not congested, are nonrival. Yet producers can, with relative ease, exclude those who don't pay the greens fee, pool admission, ticket price, or road toll. These uncongested goods are both nonrival and exclusive and are therefore natural monopolies. Once congestion sets in, however, these goods become rival—space is scarce on a backed-up golf course, in a crowded swimming pool, at a jam-packed concert, or on a bumper-to-bumper highway. Once congestion sets in, these natural monopolies morph into private goods—both rival and exclusive.

open-access good a good such as ocean fish that is rival in consumption but nonpayers cannot be excluded easily

Some other goods are *rival* but *nonexclusive.* The fish in the ocean are rival in the sense that every fish caught is not available for others to catch; the same goes for migratory game, like geese. But ocean fish and migratory game are nonexclusive in that it would be costly if not impossible for a firm to prevent access to these goods. A good that is rival but nonexclusive is called an **open-access good**. We'll examine problems that arise with open-access goods in the next chapter.

Exhibit 1 sorts out the four categories of goods. Across the top, goods are classified as either *rival* or *nonrival,* and along the left margin, goods are either *exclusive* or *nonexclusive.* Private goods are usually provided by the private sector. Natural monopolies are sometimes provided by the private sector, as

Congested public highways may make less-busy (private) toll roads a more attractive option for some commuters.

© WALTER HODGES/BRAND X PICTURES/JUPITERIMAGES

Exhibit 1

Categories of Goods

	Rival	Nonrival
Exclusive	1. Private Goods —Pizza —Crowded swimming pool 	2. Natural Monopolies —Cable TV —Uncrowded swimming pool 
Nonexclusive	3. Open-Access Goods —Ocean fish —Migratory birds 	4. Public Goods —National defense —Mosquito control 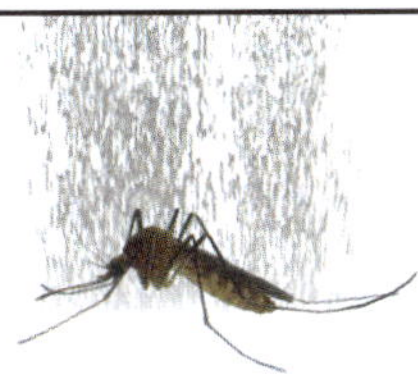

© THINKSTOCK IMAGES/JUPITERIMAGES / © RYAN MCVAY/PHOTODISC/GETTY IMAGES / © A. MESSERSCHMIDT/GETTY IMAGES / © JUDD PLISSOF/FOODPIX/JUPITERIMAGES / © FRANK GREENAWAY/DORLING KINDERSLEY/GETTY IMAGES

with a private golf course, and sometimes provided by government, as with a municipal golf course. Open-access goods are usually regulated by government, as you will see in the next chapter. And public goods are usually provided by government.

Optimal Provision of Public Goods

Because private goods are rival in consumption, the market demand for a private good at a given price is the sum of the quantities demanded by each consumer. For example, the market quantity of pizza demanded when the price is $10 is the quantity demanded by Alan plus the quantity demanded by Maria plus the quantity demanded by all other consumers in the market. The market demand curve for a private good is the *horizontal* sum of individual demand curves, an idea developed in Exhibit 7 of Chapter 6. The efficient quantity of a private good occurs where the market demand curve intersects the market supply curve.

But a public good is nonrival in consumption, so that good, once produced, is available in that amount to all consumers. For example, the market demand for a given level of mosquito control reflects the marginal benefit that Alan gets from that amount plus the marginal benefit that Maria gets plus the marginal benefit that all others in the community get from that amount of the good. Therefore, the market demand curve for a public good is the *vertical* sum of each consumer's demand for the public good. To arrive at the efficient level of the public good, we find where the market demand curve intersects the marginal cost curve—that is, where the sum of the marginal valuations equals the marginal cost.

Suppose the public good in question is mosquito control in a neighborhood, which, for simplicity, has only two households, one headed by Alan and the other by Maria. Alan spends more time in the yard than does Maria and thus values a mosquito-free environment more than she does. Their individual demand curves are shown in Exhibit 2 on the next page as D_a and D_m, reflecting the marginal benefits that Alan and Maria enjoy at each rate of output. Quantity is measured here as hours of mosquito spraying per week. By vertically summing marginal valuations at each rate of output, we derive the neighborhood demand curve, *D*, for mosquito spraying. For example, when the town sprays two hours a week, Maria values the second hour at $5 and Alan values it at $10. To get the market demand for the second hour of spraying, we simply add each resident's marginal benefit to get $15, as identified by point *e*.

How much mosquito spraying should the government provide? Suppose the marginal cost of spraying is a constant $15 an hour, as shown in Exhibit 2. The efficient level of output is found where the marginal benefit to the neighborhood equals the marginal cost, which occurs where the neighborhood demand curve intersects the marginal cost curve. In our example, these curves intersect where quantity is two hours per week.

Exhibit 2

Market for Public Goods

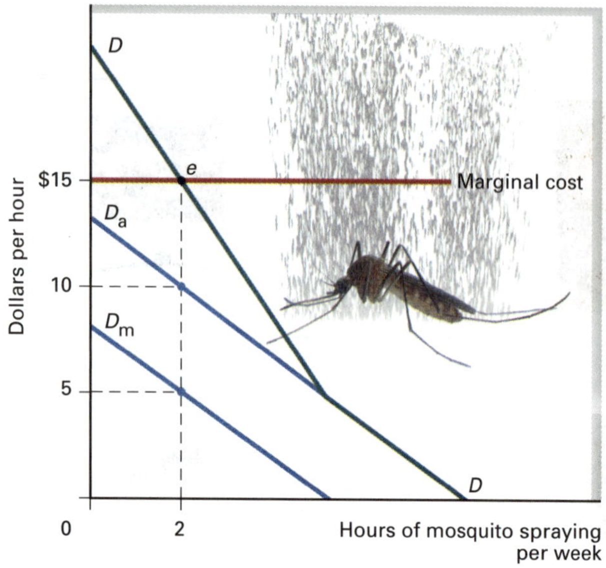

© FRANK GREENAWAY/DORLING KINDERSLEY/GETTY IMAGES

Paying for Public Goods

Suppose the government pays for the mosquito spray through taxes. The efficient approach would be to impose a tax on each resident equal to his or her marginal valuation. Simple enough, but there are at least two problems with this. First, once people realize their taxes are based on government estimates of how much they value the good, people tend to understate their true valuation. Why admit you really value the good if, as a result, you get socked with a higher tax bill? After all, people in the neighborhood can enjoy mosquito abatement whether or not they pay for it. So taxpayers tend to understate their true valuation of public goods. This creates the **free-rider problem**, which occurs because people try to benefit from the public good without paying for it.

But even if the government has accurate information about everyone's marginal valuations, some households have a greater ability to pay taxes than others. In our example, Alan values mosquito control more because he spends more time in the yard than does Maria. What if Alan is around more because he can't find a job? Should his taxes be double those of Maria, who has, say, a high-paying job? *Taxing people according to their marginal valuations of the public good may be efficient, but it may not be fair if the ability to pay differs.*

free-rider problem because a person cannot be easily excluded from consuming a public good, some people may try to reap the benefits of the good without paying for it

median-voter model under certain conditions, the preferences of the median, or middle, voter will dominate other preferences

Once the public good is produced, only that quantity is available, such as two hours of mosquito spraying per week. With private goods, each consumer can buy any quantity he or she demands and each can purchase a different amount. Thus, *public goods are more complicated than private goods in terms of what goods should be provided, in what quantities, and who should pay.* These decisions are thrashed out through public choices, which we explore in the balance of this chapter.

LO2 Public Choice in Representative Democracy

Government decisions about public goods and taxes are *public choices*. In a democracy, public choices usually require approval by a majority of voters. About 60 percent of the world's 200 independent nations are democracies. Thus, issues raised in this section about majority rule apply to most of the world, including India, all of Western Europe and nearly all of the Americas.

Median-Voter Model

As it turns out, we can usually explain the outcome of majority rule by focusing on the preferences of the median voter. The *median voter* is the one whose preferences lie in the middle of all voters' preferences. For example, if the issue is the size of the government budget, half the voters prefer a larger budget than the median voter and half prefer a smaller one. The **median-voter model** predicts that under certain conditions, the preference of the median, or middle, voter will dominate other choices. Here's an example. Suppose you and two roommates have just moved into an apartment, and the three of you must decide on furnishings. You agree to share common expenses equally and to make choices by majority rule. The issue at hand is whether to buy a TV and, if so, of what size. You each have a different preference. Your studious roommate considers a TV an annoying distraction and would rather go without; otherwise, the smaller, the better. Your other roommate, an avid TV watcher, prefers a 48-inch screen but would settle for a smaller one rather than go without. A 27-inch screen is your first choice, but you would accept the 48-inch screen rather than go without. What to do, what to do?

You all agree to make the decision by voting on two alternatives at a time, then pairing the winner against the remaining alternative until one choice dominates the others. When the 27-inch screen is paired with the no-TV option, the 27-inch screen gets both your vote and the TV fan's vote. When the 27-inch screen is then paired with the 48-inch screen, the 27-inch screen wins again, this time because your studious roommate sides with you rather than voting for the super screen.

Majority voting in effect delegates the public choice to the person whose preference is the median for the group. As the median voter in this example, you get your way. You have the votes for any choice between no TV and a 48 incher. Similarly, *the median voter in an electorate often determines public choices. Political candidates try to get elected by appealing to the median voter.* This is why candidates focus their rhetoric on "middle-class Indian families," or "middle-class American families." They are targeting the median voter. This is one reason why candidates often seem so much alike. Note that under majority rule, only the median voter gets his or her way. Other voters must go along with the median choice. Thus, other voters usually end up paying for what they consider to be either too much or too little of the public good. On the contrary, in private markets people get whatever amount they are willing and able to buy.

People vote directly on issues at New England town meetings and on the occasional referendum, but *direct democracy* is not the most common form of public choice. When you consider the thousands of choices made in the public sector—from the number of teachers to hire to what software to use for municipal records—it becomes clear that direct democracy for all public choices through referenda would be unwieldy and impractical. Rather than make decisions by direct referenda, voters elect *representatives,* who, at least in theory, make public choices that reflect their constituents' views. Under certain conditions, the resulting public choices reflect the preferences of the median voter. Some complications of representative democracy are explored next.

Special Interest and Rational Ignorance

We assume that consumers maximize utility and firms maximize profit, but what about governments? As noted in Chapter 3, there is no common agreement about what, if anything, governments try to maximize or, more precisely, what elected officials try to maximize. One theory that stems from the rational self-interest assumption of economic behavior is that elected officials try to *maximize their political support.*

To maximize political support, elected officials may cater to special interests rather than serve the interest of the public. The possibility arises because of the asymmetry between special interest and public interest, an idea introduced in the previous chapter. Consider only one of the thousands of decisions elected representatives make each year: funding an obscure federal program that subsidizes U.S. wool production. Under the wool-subsidy program, the federal government guarantees that a floor price is paid to sheep farmers for each pound of wool they produce, a subsidy that have cost taxpayers over $75 million since 2000. During deliberations to renew the program, the only person to testify before Congress was a representative of the National Wool Growers Association, who claimed that the subsidy was vital to the nation's economic welfare. Why didn't a single taxpayer challenge the subsidy? Why were sheep farmers able to pull the wool over taxpayers' eyes?

Households consume so many different public and private goods and services that they have neither the time nor the incentive to understand the effects of public choices on every product. What's more, voters realize that each of them has only a tiny possibility of influencing public choices. And even if an individual voter is somehow able to affect the outcome, the impact on that voter is likely to be small. For example, if a taxpayer could have successfully staged a grassroots campaign in 2000 to eliminate the wool subsidy, the average taxpayer would have saved, about 50 cents since then in federal income taxes. Therefore, unless voters have a special interest in the legislation, they adopt a stance of **rational ignorance**, which means that they remain largely oblivious to most public choices. The cost to the typical voter of acquiring information about each public choice and acting on it usually exceeds any expected benefit. It's not easy to interest the public in the public interest.

In contrast, consumers have much more incentive to gather and act on information about market decisions because they benefit directly and immediately from such information. *Because information and the time required to acquire and digest it are scarce, consumers concentrate on private choices rather than public choices. The payoff in making better private choices is usually more immediate, more direct, and more substantial.* For example, a consumer in the market for a new car has an incentive to examine the performance records of different models, test-drive a few, and check prices at dealerships and online. That same person has less incentive to examine the performance records of candidates for public office because that single voter has virtually no chance of deciding the elec-

rational ignorance
a stance adopted by voters when they realize that the cost of understanding and voting on a particular issue exceeds the benefit expected from doing so

tion. What's more, because candidates aim to please the median voter anyway, they often take positions that are similar.

Distribution of Benefits and Costs

Let's turn now to a different topic—how the benefits and costs of public choices are spread across the population. Depending on the issue, particular legislation may benefit only a small group or much of the population. Likewise, the costs of that legislation may be imposed only on a small group or on much of the population. The combinations of benefits and costs yield four possible categories of distributions: (1) widespread benefits and widespread costs, (2) concentrated benefits and widespread costs, (3) widespread benefits and concentrated costs, and (4) concentrated costs and concentrated benefits.

Traditional public-goods legislation, such as for national defense, a justice system, or cancer research, involves widespread benefits and widespread costs—nearly everyone benefits and nearly everyone pays. Traditional public-goods legislation usually has a positive impact on the economy because total benefits exceed total costs.

With **special-interest legislation**, benefits are concentrated but costs widespread. For example, as you'll see shortly, price supports for dairy products benefit a small group—dairy farmers. To benefit dairy farmers, a special interest, the program spreads costs across nearly all taxpayers and consumers. Legislation that caters to special interests usually harms the economy, on net, because total costs often exceed total benefits. Special-interest legislation benefitting a narrow geographical interest is called **pork-barrel spending**. To boost their reelection prospects, members of Congress "bring home the bacon" by delivering pork-barrel programs for their constituents. For example, a recent federal budget appropriated $50,000 for a tattoo removal program in San Luis Obispo, California; $150,000 to restore the Augusta Historic Theater in Georgia; and $2 million for a statue of a Roman god in Birmingham, Alabama.[1] **Populist legislation** involves widespread benefits but concentrated costs. Populist legislation usually has a tough time getting approved because the widespread group that benefits typically remains rationally ignorant about the proposed legislation, so these voters provide little political support. But the concentrated group who would get whacked by the taxes objects strenuously. Most economists agree that tort-reform legislation, for example, would benefit the economy as a whole by limiting product liability lawsuits, reducing insurance costs, and bringing some goods to the market that, because of liability suits, have all but disappeared, such as personal aircraft. But trial lawyers, the group that would be most harmed by such limits, have successfully blocked reforms for years. Because the small group that bears the cost is savvy about the impact of the proposed legislation but those who would reap the benefits remain rationally ignorant, populist legislation has little chance of approval. The only way such measures get approved is if some political entrepreneur raises enough visibility about the issue to gather public attention and votes. For example, a candidate for governor may run against high electric bills. The key is to somehow get the issue on voters' radar screens.

Finally, **competing-interest legislation** involves both concentrated benefits and concentrated costs, such as labor unions versus employers, or steel makers versus steel-using industries. These are the fierce political battles because both sides have a heavy stake in the outcome.

Exhibit 3 arrays the four categories of distributions. Across the top, benefits of legislation are either *widespread* or *concentrated,* and along the left margin, costs are either *widespread* or *concentrated*. Box 1 shows *traditional public-goods legislation,* such as national defense, with

traditional public-goods legislation legislation that involves widespread costs and widespread benefits—nearly everyone pays and nearly everyone benefits

special-interest legislation legislation with concentrated benefits but widespread costs

pork-barrel spending special-interest legislation with narrow geographical benefits but funded by all taxpayers

populist legislation legislation with widespread benefits but concentrated costs

competing-interest legislation legislation that confers concentrated benefits on one group by imposing concentrated costs on another group

1. Robert Novak, "Senate Sneaks Preserve Pork," *New York Post,* 19 April 2007.

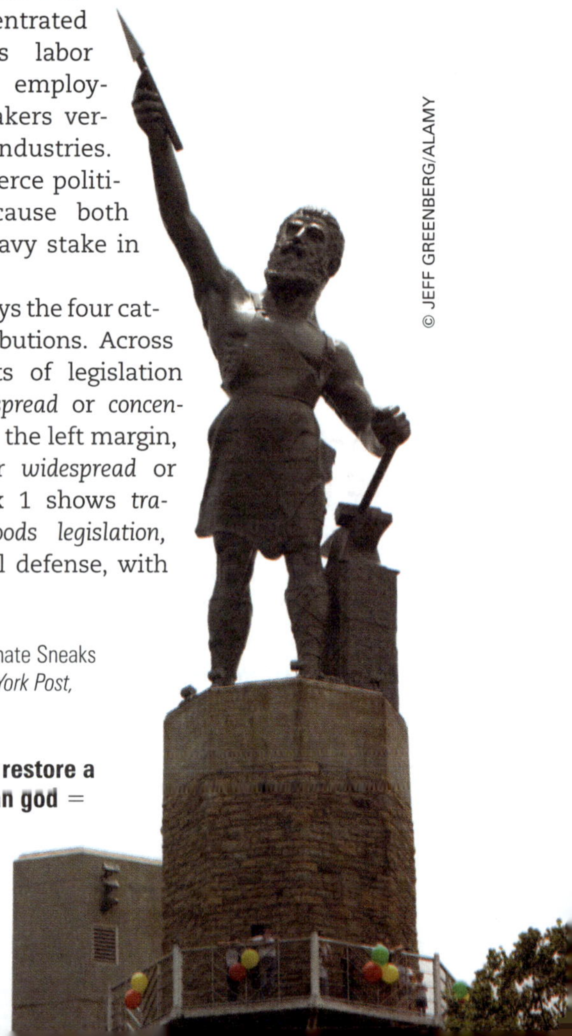

© JEFF GREENBERG/ALAMY

>> $2 million to restore a statue of a Roman god = pork barrel spending

© DIETER SPEARS/ISTOCKPHOTO.COM / © BRIAN HAGIWARA/BRAND X PICTURES/JUPITERIMAGES / ©THINKSTOCK IMAGES/JUPITERIMAGES / © RYAN MCVAY/PHOTODISC/GETTY IMAGES

Exhibit 3

Categories of Legislation Based on the Distribution of Costs and Benefits

		Distribution of Benefits	
		Widespread	**Concentrated**
Distribution of Costs	**Widespread**	1. Traditional Public Goods —National defense 	2. Special interest —Farm subsidies 
	Concentrated	3. Populist —Tort reform 	4. Competing interest —Labor union issues 

both widespread benefits and widespread costs. Box 2 shows *special-interest legislation,* such as farm subsidies, with concentrated benefits but widespread costs. Box 3 shows *populist legislation,* such as tort reform, with widespread benefits but concentrated costs. And box 4 shows *competing-interest legislation,* such as labor union issues, with both concentrated benefits and concentrated costs.

"Most economists agree that tort-reform legislation would benefit the economy as a whole... but trial lawyers, the group that would be most harmed by such limits, have successfully blocked reforms for years."

Rent Seeking

An important feature of representative democracy is the incentive and political power it offers interest groups to increase their wealth, either through direct transfers or through favorable public expenditures and regulations. Special-interest groups, such as dairy farmers, trial lawyers, and other producers, seek from government some special advantage or some outright transfer or subsidy. Such benefits are often called *rents* because they exceed what the producer would require to supply the product. Thus, rents represent earnings that exceed opportunity cost. The activity that interest groups undertake to secure these special favors from government is called *rent seeking,* a term already introduced.

The government frequently bestows some special advantage on a producer or group of producers, and abundant resources are expended to acquire these advantages. For example, *political action committees,* known more popularly as PACs, contribute millions to congressional campaigns. About 4,000 PACs try to shape federal legislation. The top contributors recently included the tobacco lobby and the American Trial Lawyers Association. Tobacco interests would like to influence cigarette legislation, and lawyers fear reforms that would limit liability lawsuits.

To the extent that special-interest groups engage in rent seeking, they shift resources from productive endeavors that create output and income to activities that focus more on transferring income to their special interests. *Resources employed to persuade government to redistribute income and wealth to special interests are unproductive because they do nothing to increase total output and usually end up reducing it.* Often many firms compete for the same government advantage, thereby wasting still more resources. If the advantage conferred by govern-

"Resources employed to persuade government to redistribute income and wealth to special interests are unproductive because they do nothing to increase total output and usually end up reducing it."

Farm Subsidies

In much of America, milk prices are the most regulated of farm products. Explaining the intricacies of the price support program for milk takes up three volumes of the *Code of Federal Regulations*. Interpreting and administering regulations employ hundreds of people at the U.S. Department of Agriculture—more than oversee the entire federal budget in the Office of Management and Budget.

Exhibit 4 presents the market for milk. Without government intervention, suppose the market price of milk would average \$1.50 per gallon for a market quantity of 100 million gallons per month. In long-run equilibrium, dairy farmers would earn a normal profit in this competitive industry. Consumer surplus is shown by the blue-shaded area. Recall that consumer surplus is the difference between the most that consumers would be willing to pay for that quantity and the amount they actually pay.

Now suppose the dairy lobby persuades Congress that milk should not sell for less than \$2.50 per gallon. The higher price encourages farmers to increase their quantity supplied to 150 million gallons per month. Consumers, however, reduce their quantity demanded to 75 million gallons per month. To make the floor price of \$2.50 stick, the government must buy the 75 million gallons of surplus milk generated by the floor price or somehow get dairy farmers to cut output to only 75 million gallons per month. For example, to reduce supply, the government could buy dairy cows from farmers (as occurred in the 1980s).

The dairy industry is supported by other legislation. Some states ensure even higher price floors than those imposed by the federal government. Foreign imports of liquid milk are tightly restricted. Other laws promote the consumption of dairy products more generally. For example, some states prohibit restaurants from serving margarine instead of butter unless the customer specifically asks for margarine.

The profound long-run problem for dairy farmers is that technological breakthroughs, such as genetically engineered hormones that stimulate milk production, have increased the milk yield per cow, making each farmer far more productive. Yet, despite the widely advertised "Got milk?" and milk-mustache campaigns, milk consumption remains flat. The combination of increased supply and stagnant demand puts downward pressure on the price.

SOURCES: "Farm Subsidies: Uncle Sam's Teat," *Economist,* 7 September 2006; Juliane Von Reppert-Bismark, "Europe Faults U.S. Farm Proposal," *Wall Street Journal,* 2 February 2007; "Washington Harvest," *Economist,* 27 March 2007; and the U.S. Department of Agriculture's dairy policy site at http://www.ers.usda.gov/Briefing/Dairy/Policy.htm.

© DON MASON/BRAND X PICTURES/JUPITERIMAGES /
© TETRA IMAGES/JUPITERIMAGES

Exhibit 4

Effects of Milk Price Supports

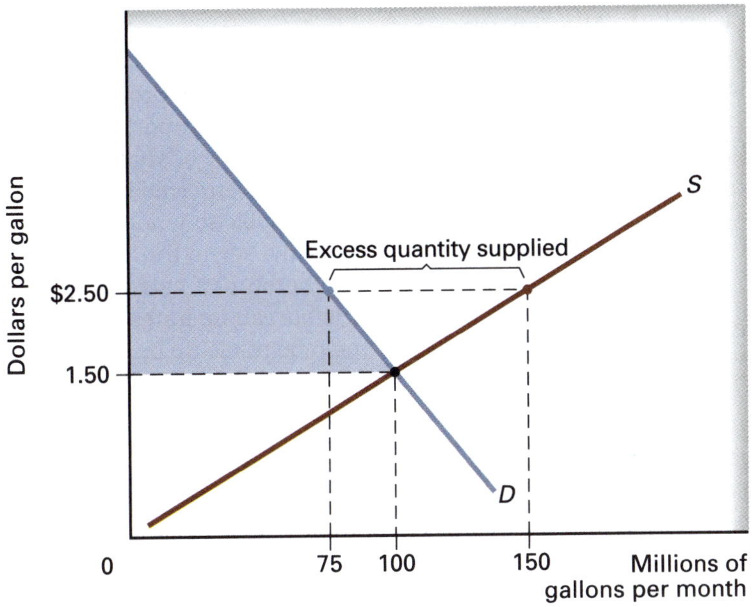

ment on some special-interest group requires higher income taxes, the earnings people expect from working and investing fall, so they may work less and invest less. If this happens, productive activity declines.

As a firm's profitability relies more and more on decisions made in Washington, resources are diverted from productive activity to rent seeking, or lobbying efforts. One firm may thrive because it secured some special government advantage at a critical time; another firm may fail because its managers were more concerned with productive efficiency than with rent seeking.

Think of the economy's output in a particular period as depicted by a pie. The pie represents the total value of goods and services produced. In answering the what, how, and for whom questions introduced in Chapter 2, policy makers have three alternatives: (1) they can introduce reforms that increase the size of the pie (that is, positive-sum changes); (2) they can decide simply to carve up the existing pie differently (redistribute income); or (3) they can start fighting over how the pie is carved up, causing some of it to end up on the floor (negative-sum changes).

Special-interest groups have little incentive to make the economy more efficient. In fact, they usually support legislation that transfers wealth to them even if the economy's overall efficiency declines. For example, suppose that the American Trial Lawyers Association is able to change product liability laws in a way that boosts lawyers' annual incomes by a total of $1 billion, or about $1,800 for each of the 550,000 lawyers in private practice. Suppose, too, that this measure drives up insurance premiums, raising the total cost of production by, say, $2 billion per year. Lawyers themselves have to bear part of this higher cost, but because they account for only about 1 percent of the spending in the economy, they bear only about 1 percent of the $2 billion in higher costs, or about $20 million. This amounts to $36 per lawyer per year. Thus, the legislation is a good deal for lawyers because their annual incomes grow about $1,800 each but their annual costs increase only about $36 each, resulting in the net average gain of $1,764 per lawyer in private practice. Much special-interest legislation leads to a net reduction in social welfare. For example, some of the nation's best minds are occupied with devising schemes to avoid taxes or divert income to favored groups at the expense of market efficiency.

There are hundreds of special-interest groups representing farmers, physicians, lawyers, teachers, manufacturers, barbers, and so on.

LO3 The Underground Economy

A government subsidy promotes production, as we saw in the case study on milk price supports. Conversely, a tax discourages production. Perhaps it would be more accurate to say that when government taxes productive activity, less production gets *reported*. If you ever worked as a waitress or waiter, did you faithfully report all your tip income to the Internal Revenue Service? If not, your unreported income became part of the underground economy. The **underground economy** describes all market activity that goes unreported either to avoid taxes or because the activity itself is illegal. Income arising in the underground economy ranges from unreported tips to the earnings of drug dealers.

Taxing productive activity has two effects. First, resource owners may supply less of the taxed resource because the after-tax wage declines. Second, to evade taxes, some people shift from the formal, reported economy to an underground, "off the books" economy. Thus, when the government taxes market exchange and the income it

underground economy
an expression used to describe market activity that goes unreported either because it is illegal or because those involved want to evade taxes

generates, less market activity and less income get reported.

We should take care to distinguish between tax *avoidance* and tax *evasion*. Tax avoidance is a *legal* attempt to arrange one's economic affairs to pay the least tax possible, such as buying municipal bonds because they yield interest free of federal income taxes. Tax evasion, on the other hand, is *illegal*; it takes the form of either failing to file a tax return or filing a fraudulent return by understating income or overstating deductions. Research around the world indicates that the underground economy grows more when (1) government regulations increase, (2) tax rates increase, and (3) government corruption is more widespread.[2]

The U.S. Commerce Department estimates that official figures capture only about 90 percent of U.S. income. And an Internal Revenue Service survey estimates that only about 90 percent of taxable income gets reported on tax returns. These studies suggest an underground economy of about $1.4 trillion in 2009.

Those who pursue rent-seeking activity and those involved in the underground economy view government from opposite sides. Rent seekers want government to become actively involved in transferring wealth to them, but those in the underground economy want to avoid government contact. *Subsidies and other advantages bestowed by government draw some groups closer to government; taxes drive some others underground.*

LO4 Bureaucracy and Representative Democracy

Elected representatives approve legislation, but the task of implementing that legislation is typically left to **bureaus**, which are government departments and agencies whose activities are financed by appropriations from legislative bodies.

bureaus government agencies charged with implementing legislation and financed by appropriations from legislative bodies

2. For a summary of these studies, see Simon Johnson et al., "Regulatory Discretion and the Unofficial Economy," *American Economic Review* 88 (May 1998): 387–392.

Ownership and Funding of Bureaus

We can get a better feel for government bureaus by comparing them to corporations. Stockholders own a corporation and share any profit or loss. Stockholders also get to vote on important corporate matters based on the number of shares owned. Corporate shares can be bought and sold in the stock market: ownership is *transferable* to whomever buys the shares. Taxpayers are in a sense the "owners" of government bureaus. If the bureau earns a "profit," taxes may decline; if the bureau operates at a "loss," as most do, this loss must be made up by taxes. Each taxpayer has just one vote, regardless of the taxes he or she pays. Ownership in the bureau is surrendered only if the taxpayer dies or moves out of the jurisdiction, but ownership is not transferable—it cannot be bought or sold directly.

Whereas corporations cover their costs if enough people purchase their products, bureaus are usually financed by government appropriation. Most funding comes from taxpayers. Bureaus do not have to meet a market test. Some bureaus get revenue through user charges, such as admission fees to state parks or tuition at state colleges, but even these bureaus typically rely on taxes for part of their revenue. Because of these differences in the forms of ownership and in the sources of funding, bureaus have different incentives than do for-profit firms, so they are likely to behave differently, as we'll see next.

Ownership and Organizational Behavior

A central assumption of economics is that people behave rationally and respond to economic incentives. The more tightly compensation is linked to individual incentives, the more people behave in accordance with those incentives. For example, if a letter carrier's pay is based on customer satisfaction, the carrier will make a greater effort to deliver mail promptly and intact.

> A central assumption of economics is that people behave rationally and respond to economic incentives.

A private firm receives a steady stream of consumer feedback. If the price is too high or too low to clear the market, surpluses or shortages become obvious. Not only is consumer feedback abundant, but the firm's owners have a profit incentive to act on that information to satisfy consumer wants. The promise of profits also creates incentives to produce output at the least cost. Thus, the firm's owners stand to gain from any improvement in customer satisfaction or any reduction in cost.

Because public goods and services are not sold in markets, government bureaus receive less consumer feedback and have less incentive to act on any feedback they do receive. There are usually no prices and no obvious shortages or surpluses. For example, how would you know whether there was a shortage or a surplus of police protection in your community? Not only do bureaus receive less consumer feedback than firms do, bureaus have less incentive to act on the information available. If a corporation is run poorly, someone could buy most of the shares, improve performance, then reap the benefits of a higher share price. Because the ownership of bureaus is not transferable, there is less incentive to eliminate waste and inefficiency.

Voters could pressure their elected representatives to make bureaus more responsive. But this discipline is rather crude. Most voters remain rationally ignorant about government performance in part because each voter has little impact on the outcome and each stands to gain so little from any increase in efficiency. For example, suppose that you are one of a million taxpayers in a city and you learn that by having FedEx Offices do all public copying, the city could save $1 million a year. If, through letters to the editor and calls to local officials, you somehow convince the city to adopt this cost-saving measure, you, as a typical taxpayer, would save yourself about a dollar a year in taxes.

Voters can leave a jurisdiction if they believe government is inefficient. This mechanism, whereby people "vote with their feet," does promote some efficiency and consumer satisfaction at the state and local levels, but it's also crude. What if you like some public programs but not others? Moreover, voters dissatisfied with the biggest spender and taxer, the federal government, cannot easily vote with their feet. Even if you were to move abroad, you, as a U.S. citizen, must still pay U.S. federal taxes on your worldwide income (nearly all other countries tax only domestic income of those living abroad).

> **BUREAUS ARE MONOPOLY SUPPLIERS OF PUBLIC GOODS, AND ELECTED OFFICIALS SOMETIMES HAVE ONLY LIMITED ABILITY TO CUT THAT BUDGET.**

Because of differences between public and private organizations—in the owners' ability both to transfer ownership and to appropriate profits—we expect bureaus to be less concerned with satisfying consumer demand or with minimizing costs than private firms are. A variety of empirical studies compares costs for products that are provided by both public bureaus and private firms, such as garbage collection. Of those studies that show a difference, most find private firms are more efficient.

Bureaucratic Objectives

Assuming that bureaus are not simply at the beck and call of the legislature—that is, assuming that bureaucrats have some autonomy—what sort of objectives do *they* pursue? The traditional view is that bureaucrats are "public servants," who try to serve the public as best they can. No doubt many public employees do just that, but is this a realistic assumption for bureaucrats more generally? Why should we assume self-sacrificing behavior by public-sector employees when we make no such assumption about private-sector employees?

One widely discussed theory of bureaucratic behavior claims that bureaus try to *maximize their budget,* for along with a bigger budget come size, prestige, amenities, staff, and pay—all features that are valued by bureaucrats.[3] According to this view, bureaus are monopoly suppliers of their output to elected officials. Rather than charge a price per unit, bureaus offer the entire amount as a package deal in return for the requested appropriation. This theory assumes that the elected officials have only limited ability to dig into the budget and cut particular items. If elected officials do try to cut the bureau's budget, the bureau may threaten to make those cuts as painful to constituents as possible. For example, if city officials attempt to slow the growth of the school budget, school bureaucrats, rather than increase teaching loads or reducing pay raises, may threaten to eliminate kindergarten, abolish the high school football team, disband the school band, or cut textbook orders. If such threats force elected officials to back off, the government budget turns out to be larger than the public would prefer. *Budget maximization results in a larger budget than that desired by the median voter.* The key to this argument is that bureaus are monopoly suppliers of public goods and elected officials have only limited ability to cut that budget. If taxpayers have alternatives in the private sector or if elected officials can dig

3. William A. Niskanen Jr., in *Bureaucracy and Representative Government* (New York: Aldine-Atherton, 1971).

into the budget, the monopoly power of the bureau is diminished.

Private Versus Public Production

Simply because some goods and services are *financed* by the government, this does not mean that they must be *produced* by the government. Elected officials may contract directly with private firms to produce public output. For example, city officials may contract with a private firm to collect garbage for the city. In some jurisdictions, for-profit firms now provide everything from fire protection to prisons. Elected officials may also use a combination of bureaus and firms to produce the desired output. For example, the Pentagon, a giant bureau, hires and trains military personnel yet contracts with private firms to develop and produce various weapon systems. State governments typically hire private contractors to build roads but employ state workers to maintain them. The mix of firms and bureaus varies over time and across jurisdictions, but the trend is toward increased *privatization*, or production by the private sector, of public goods and services.

When governments produce public goods and services, they are using *the internal organization of the government*—the bureaucracy—to supply the product. When governments contract with private firms to produce public goods and services, they are using *the market* to supply the product. While private firms have more incentives to be efficient than bureaus do, public officials sometimes prefer dealing with bureaus. Public officials may have more control over the bureau than over a private firm. Bureaus may also offer public officials more opportunities to appoint friends and political supporters to government jobs.

In situations where it would be difficult to specify a contract for the public good in question, a bureau may be more responsive to public concerns than a for-profit firm would be. Suppose the service provided by social workers is put out for bid. The firm that wins the bid may be tempted to skimp on quality, particularly if quality can be determined only by direct observation at the time the service is provided. The government would have difficulty monitoring the quality provided by a private contractor. The services of social workers might be better provided by a government bureau. Because profit is not its goal, a bureau may be less inclined to minimize cost by reducing quality. For example, one study found that privately-operated juvenile correction facilities in Florida had lower costs but experienced higher rates of recidivism than state-operated juvenile correction facilities. The lower costs of privately operated facilities were more than offset by the increased recidivism, making state operation the better choice.[4]

Ownership Versus Competition: The Debate

Does Ownership Matter: For publicly owned firms the task of monitoring managerial performance is entrusted to the government. Compared to private ownership, the most obvious differences in the relationship between managers and their immediate principals arise from the fact that:

1. the principals do not typically seek to maximize profits,
2. there are no marketable ordinary shares, and
3. there is no direct equivalent to the bankruptcy constraint on financial performance.

Given a welfare maximizing government, and assuming that monitoring of management is equally effective under both types of ownership (public and private), it is obvious that public ownership has some potential advantages over the private alternative:

1. In particular, it provides government with additional policy instruments to correct any deviations between social and private returns that arise from failures in goods and factor markets.
2. Government monitoring does not encounter the public good problems associated with dispersed shareholdings. In contrast with a shareholder who owns only a small fraction of the outstanding shares, government departments can directly intervene in managerial decision making or can set appropriate incentive structures for the managers of publicly owned firms.

Therefore, the loss of some instruments of control (e.g. takeover and bankruptcy threats) that result from public ownership does not necessarily imply that monitoring is made less effective.

Unfortunately, however, *monitoring* by public officials is not very effective. Regarding monitoring activities, it is interesting to note that two distinct groups are involved: politicians and civil servants. The full monitoring hierarchy is made up of the general public, its elected political representatives, non-elected civil servants, and the managers of the publicly owned firms. Hence, it is necessary to analyze a number of separate principal-agent problems.

4. Patrick Bayer and David Pozen, "The Effectiveness of Juvenile Correction Facilities: Public Versus Private Management," *Journal of Law and Economics* 48 (October 2005): 549–89.

Competition, Contestable Markets and Efficiency

A contestable market (Baumol and Willig, 1986; Brock, 1983; Schwartz, 1986; Sharkey, 1982; Shephard, 1984 and Spence, 1983) is one in which existing firms are vulnerable to hit and run entry. All firms—actual and potential—have access to the same production methods, and hence their cost functions are identical. Moreover, it involves no sunk costs; i.e., a firm can enter the market without making irrecoverable expenditures, and so there are no barriers to exit. Therefore, even a very temporary profit opportunity need not be neglected by a potential entrant, for he can go in, and, before prices change, collect his gains and then exit. In such a situation there will be no inefficiency in production and *price* = *Average cost* = *Marginal cost*. In such a situation industry output will be produced at minimum cost (internal efficiency) and since *price* = *marginal cost*; there is allocative efficiency as well, except possibly in a natural monopoly.

However, empirical applicability of contestability theory rarely exists due to the inevitable sunk nature of many costs (Schwartz and Reynolds, 1983; Dasgupta and Stiglitz, 1985). In such situations direct regulation of the dominant firm is then required. Even in the absence of sunk costs, potential competition need not act as a threat due to strategic entry deterrence policies adopted by the incumbent firm. The likely instruments of entry deterrence could be those that affect costs (the incumbent's and/or the rival's) and those that affect demand. As to the former, Dixit (1980) showed how the incumbent's choice of capacity could deter entry. Similarly, Salop and Scheffman (1983) argued that the incumbent by raising the wage rates in the industry might deter entry. Pre-emptive patenting (Gilbert and Newbery, 1982) could also deter entry. On the demand side the incumbent firm could deter entry by strategic advertising or by brand proliferation (Schmalensee, 1978, 1983).

Consider first the relationship between the general public and its elected representatives. As a useful starting point one can hypothesize that politicians take decisions with a view to maximizing the probability of electoral success. This does not necessarily imply that politicians will seek to achieve economic efficiency from the publicly owned firms. This is because voters are not well informed about the decisions made on their behalf and also on the eventual consequences of those decisions. In reality considerable informational asymmetries between politicians and voters exist. Since the election is usually concerned with a wide range of issues, not just the performance of a particular public enterprise coupled with the fact that any single voter faces an almost zero probability of influencing the outcome of the election; the average voter has very little incentive to acquire costly information. This implies that politicians may no longer derive electoral benefits from improvement of economic efficiency. In fact, there may be situations where efficiency improvements could lead to a worsening of electoral prospects[5].

Turning to the question of effective monitoring of the civil servants by the politicians, there are reasons for believing that the results will not be entirely satisfactory. Two such reasons being;

1. Effective monitoring by politicians is unlikely to have much of an impact on electoral prospects.
2. Factors that increase the welfare of civil servants may also have positive effects on the welfare of ministers.

Regarding the analogy to the *takeover market*, the only way the political market could replicate the market for corporate control is by initiating the takeover process, i.e. by threatening privatization. But such a threat must be credible. Conventional wisdom states that privatization is most likely to succeed if employees are offered bribes to ensure minimum opposition. The greater the inefficiency of a public firm, the greater would be the bribe offered. In such circumstances, rational employees will continue to perform inefficiently, i.e. retain as much managerial slack as possible. They cannot lose. If they are not privatized they continue to enjoy their "higher slacks." If they are privatized, they are likely to receive the capitalized value of the slack. Thus even the privatization threat may fail to improve the efficiency of public enterprises.

Thus judged in terms of public interest criteria, we can identify several potential sources of sub optimality in the framework of control for publicly owned industries. These are:

1. Displacement of social objectives by political objectives which may not necessarily imply economic efficiency. In fact, at times, it may lead to not only redundant costs (X-inefficiency) but also rising costs.
2. Internalities and private goals that lead to non-market failures such as budget growth (more is better) and employment growth.
3. Distributional inequity that is often based more on power than on income and wealth. Further

5. This will happen when political action to encourage managers to reduce costs would be observed by workers who suffer materially as a consequence, while the benefits in the form of lower prices or lower taxes may be spread over such a large population, that the benefits may not be visible to the recipients.

"rent seeking" or directly "unproductive" activities give rise to resource mis-allocations, so that even on the grounds for promoting allocative efficiency, public ownership may not necessarily be better than private ownership.

Does Competition Matter: The next step in our analysis is to consider how competitive markets influence company behavior under public and private ownership. Although there is no logical connection between public enterprise and the absence of competition, there are reasons why the two have often gone together. Two of them are cited: *First*, public ownership is one of the main solutions to the problems of market failure that arises in industries where competition is impossible or undesirable, or where major externalities exist or where conditions of natural monopoly exist. *Second*, managers of public sector enterprises and concerned civil servants and politicians try to resist the advent of effective competition, in order to enjoy the benefits related to a monopoly market environment (such as rent seeking or quiet life).

One of the major benefits of competitive forces on performance of the public enterprises is that competitive forces break the "monopoly of information" about industry conditions. In such a situation the greater the degree of competition, the greater is the enhancement of internal efficiency of the firm. Even though actual competition may not exist, even the threat of entry can have a major influence on industry conduct. For instance, *n* firms surrounded by insurmountable entry barriers are likely to behave very differently from *n* firms facing entry threats from potential competitors. It is partly for this reason that the liberalization of entry conditions has been so central to the debate on economic reforms related to privatization.

Several studies, notably by Hart (1983), show how product market competition can influence the nature of incentive contracts between the shareholders and managers of firm. For instance, if the unit costs of a firm depend on managerial effort and upon some exogenous cost characteristics of firms in the industry, then competition between them reveals information about manager's effort rates. Being better informed about managerial effort, shareholders can make managerial reward more sensitive to effort, and slack can, therefore, be reduced. Rewards can be based, in part on relative performance, and so managers are effectively in competition with each other. Thus, there is a theoretical underpinning to the idea that competition promotes efficiency within the firm, as well as efficient behavior in product markets.

Conclusion: We commenced the section with the question: does ownership matter? The analysis was concerned with the effects of ownership on allocative and internal efficiency of firms. We conclude that the allocation of property rights does matter because it determines the objective of the owner's of the firm and the systems of monitoring managerial performance. Public and private ownership differ in both respects. As a result, changes in property right should materially affect the incentive structures, and hence the behavior of managements.

However, the efficiency implications of these changes in incentives will depend very much upon the competitive environment in which a firm operates. Indeed, it may be so that the degree of competition in the product market along with an effective regulatory policy may have large effects on performance than ownership *per se*. Thus when market power is significant (as in the case of natural monopolies like electric utilities and water), and particularly when company behavior is subject to detailed regulation, there may be little empirical justification for a general presumption in favor of private sector. A case-by-case evaluation of the various trade-offs is thus necessary.

Further, in markets where competition in product markets is effective, and provided that other allocative inefficiencies associated with market failures are not substantial, available evidence supports either a presumption in favor of private enterprises (on both internal efficiency grounds and social welfare grounds) or no difference in efficiency between public and private enterprises. *Thus more than ownership, what matters for efficiency, is the degree of competition.*

Final Word

Governments attempt to address market failures in the private economy. But simply turning problems of perceived market failure over to government may not always be the best solution, because government has limitations and failings of its own. Participation in markets is based on voluntary exchange. Governments, however, have the legal power to enforce public choices. We should employ at least as high a standard in judging the performance of government, where allocations have the force of law, as we do in judging the private market, where allocations are decided by voluntary exchange between consenting parties. In other words, we should scrutinize a system that is compulsory at least as much as we scrutinize a system that is voluntary. After all, nobody is forcing you to buy tofu, but if you refuse to pay taxes to fund public programs you may not like, you could go to prison.

Multiple Choice Questions

1. Generally, people are more satisfied with private market outcomes than with public voting outcomes because
   a. each consumer in the private market can choose the quantity he or she desires
   b. most people are near the median
   c. the prices are lower
   d. markets are involuntary
   e. there are too many choices to make in the public sector
2. A public good, such as a community's emergency warning sirens, typically
   a. imposes benefits on only a few individuals but imposes costs on many people
   b. imposes both benefits and costs on relatively few individuals
   c. imposes benefits on many individuals but imposes the costs on relatively few people
   d. imposes both benefits and costs on many individuals
   e. only imposes costs on individuals when logrolling is prevalent in the government
3. A good that is nonrival but exclusive is called
   a. a private good
   b. a public good
   c. a quasi-private good
   d. an external good
   e. a normal good
4. A good that is rival but nonexclusive is called
   a. a private good
   b. a public good
   c. a quasi-private good
   d. an external good
   e. an open access good
5. A good that is both rival and exclusive is called
   a. a private good
   b. a public good
   c. a quasi-private good
   d. an external good
   e. an open access good
6. The market demand curve for a public good
   a. is the horizontal sum of all individual demand curves
   b. is the vertical sum of all individual demand curves.
   c. is upward sloping
   d. is horizontal
   e. does not exist
7. The efficient level of public good provision is determined
   a. where the market demand curve intersects the marginal cost curve
   b. where the sum of individual valuations equals the sum of marginal costs
   c. without regard to economic factors
   d. where marginal revenue product equals marginal factor cost
   e. at the minimum point of the average total cost curve
8. Public choice theory suggests that political candidates try to get elected by
   a. appealing to conservatives
   b. appealing to liberals
   c. appealing to senior citizens
   d. appealing to the median voter
   e. raising taxes
9. Special-interest legislation usually
   a. has widespread benefits and costs
   b. has concentrated benefits and costs
   c. has concentrated benefits but widespread costs
   d. concerns the provision of public goods
   e. concerns the provision of private goods
10. Special-interest legislation is characterized by
    a. concentrated costs and concentrated benefits
    b. concentrated benefits and widespread costs
    c. widespread benefits and widespread costs
    d. widespread benefits and concentrated costs
    e. zero costs
11. General Motors benefits from tariffs on imported automobiles. Companies that use many automobiles, such as rental agencies, want to get them cheaply. In this case, the issue of tariff legislation involves
    a. a simple majority because it promises concentrated costs and benefits
    b. competing interests because it promises concentrated costs and benefits
    c. a simple majority because it promises concentrated benefits and widespread costs
    d. competing interests because it promises concentrated benefits and widespread costs

e. competing interests because it promises concentrated costs and widespread benefits

12. Environmentalists, worried about sulfur dioxide in the air, pressure the government to require bus manufacturers to modify exhaust systems in buses. In this situation,
    a. benefits of the proposed requirements are more widespread than costs
    b. benefits and costs of the proposed requirements are equally widespread because producers of buses will pass cost increases on to bus companies who will increase fares
    c. pressure for government regulation is unnecessary because those who use buses will stop riding buses if they don't have cleaner emissions
    d. bus riders are more likely to lobby against the proposal than are bus producers
    e. bus riders are more likely to lobby against the proposal than are bus workers

13. Attempts by special-interest groups to gain favorable treatment from government are called
    a. utility maximizing
    b. profit seeking
    c. rent seeking
    d. profit maximizing
    e. rent minimizing

14. A payment over and above that necessary to call forth a resource is called
    a. profit
    b. rent
    c. taxes
    d. salary
    e. welfare

15. Rent seeking
    a. is the attempt to find apartments in a rent-controlled city
    b. only makes sense in a monopolistically competitive industry
    c. is a zero-sum game because the public's loss is the rent seeker's gain
    d. is the expenditure of resources to obtain favorable treatment from government
    e. occurs because of cyclical majority

16. The term *underground economy* refers to
    a. the coal-mining industry
    b. all ore mining
    c. the subway system
    d. purely illegal activity
    e. market activity not reported to the government

17. A tax on productive activity tends to
    a. increase formal market activity because it decreases prices
    b. decrease formal market activity because it increases work incentives
    c. decrease formal market activity because it lowers the return on such activity
    d. decrease activity in the underground economy because people are afraid of being connected with tax fraud
    e. increase activity in the underground economy because people are afraid of being connected with tax fraud

18. If bureaus are monopoly suppliers of public goods and elected officials have only limited ability to cut that budget, budget maximization results in a larger budget than that desired by the median voter.
    a. True
    b. False

19. Which of the following is *not* a typical goal of bureaucrats?
    a. increasing the size of their bureaus
    b. gaining prestige
    c. increasing the size of their staffs
    d. increasing their bureaus' budgets
    e. achieving greater efficiency

20. If the quality or quantity of a particular public service is very difficult to monitor, government is more likely to
    a. produce the service itself
    b. contract with private firms to supply the service
    c. take over private corporations to produce the service
    d. refuse to provide the service
    e. raise the price to consumers of the service

Answers

1. a 2. d 3. c 4. e 5. a 6. b 7. a 8. d 9. c 10. b
11. b 12. a 13. c 14. b 15. d 16. e 17. c 18. a 19. e 20. a

LONG ANSWER QUESTIONS

LO1 Define public goods

1.1. *(Optimal Provision of Public Goods)* Using at least two individual consumers, show how the market demand curve is derived from individual demand curves (a) for a private good and (b) for a public good. Once you have derived the market demand curve in each case, introduce a market supply curve and then show the optimal level of production.

1.2. *(Private and Public Goods)* Distinguish among private goods, natural monopolies, open-access goods, and public goods. Provide examples of each.

LO2 Discuss the role of public choice in representative democracy

2.1. *(Distribution of Costs and Benefits)* Suppose that the government decides to guarantee an above-market price for a good by buying up any surplus at that above-market price. Using a conventional supply-demand diagram, illustrate the following gains and losses from such a price support:

a. The loss of consumer surplus
b. The gain of producer surplus in the short run
c. The cost of running the government program (assuming no storage costs)
d. What is the total cost of the program to consumers?
e. Are the costs and benefits of the support program widespread or concentrated?

2.2. *(Median Voter Model)* In a single-issue majority vote, such as the TV example in this chapter, does the median voter always get his or her most preferred outcome?

2.3. *(Representative Democracy)* Major political parties typically offer "middle of the road" platforms rather than take extreme positions. Is this consistent with the concepts of the median voter and rational ignorance discussed in this chapter?

LO3 Describe the underground economy

3.1. *(Rent Seeking)* Explain how rent seeking can lead to a drop in production of goods and services. What role might the underground economy play in lessening the drop in productive activities?

LO4 Explain bureaucracy and its role in representative democracy

4.1. *(Bureaucracy and Representative Democracy)* How do the incentives and feedback for government bureaus differ from those for profit-making firms?

4.2. *(Bureaucracy and Representative Democracy)* A firm is described as combining managerial coordination with market exchange in order to produce its good or service. Does similar behavior occur in government bureaus? Explain.

PUBLIC GOODS AND PUBLIC CHOICE

18 Chapter in Review

KEY TERMS

open-access good
a good such as ocean fish that is rival in consumption but nonpayers cannot be excluded easily

free-rider problem
because a person cannot be easily excluded from consuming a public good, some people may try to reap the benefits of the good without paying for it

median-voter model
under certain conditions, the preferences of the median, or middle, voter will dominate other preferences

rational ignorance
a stance adopted by voters when they realize that the cost of understanding and voting on a particular issue exceeds the benefit expected from doing so

traditional public-goods legislation
legislation that involves widespread costs and widespread benefits—nearly everyone pays and nearly everyone benefits

special-interest legislation
legislation with concentrated benefits but widespread costs

pork-barrel spending
special-interest legislation with narrow geographical benefits but funded by all taxpayers

populist legislation
legislation with widespread benefits but concentrated costs

competing-interest legislation
legislation that confers concentrated benefits on one group by imposing concentrated costs on another group

underground economy
an expression used to describe market activity that goes unreported either because it is illegal or because those involved want to evade taxes

bureaus
government agencies charged with implementing legislation and financed by appropriations from legislative bodies

LO1 Define public goods. Private goods are rival and exclusive, such as a pizza. Public goods are nonrival and nonexclusive, such as national defense. Goods that are in between public and private goods include natural monopolies, which are nonrival but exclusive, such as cable TV, and open-access goods, which are rival but nonexclusive, such as ocean fish. Because private-sector producers cannot easily exclude nonpayers from consuming a public good, public goods are typically provided by government, which has the power to enforce tax collections.

Categories of Goods

	Rival	Nonrival
Exclusive	1. Private Goods —Pizza —Crowded swimming pool 	2. Natural Monopolies —Cable TV —Uncrowded swimming pool 
Nonexclusive	3. Open-Access Goods —Ocean fish —Migratory birds 	4. Public Goods —National defense —Mosquito control 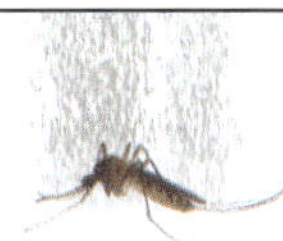

Market for Public Goods

Because public goods, once produced, are available to all in identical amounts, the demand for a public good is the vertical sum of each individual's demand. Thus, the market demand for mosquito spraying is the vertical sum of Maria's demand, D_m, and Alan's demand, D_a. The efficient level of provision is found where the marginal cost of mosquito spraying equals its marginal benefit. This occurs at point *e* where the marginal cost curve intersects the market demand curve, *D*.

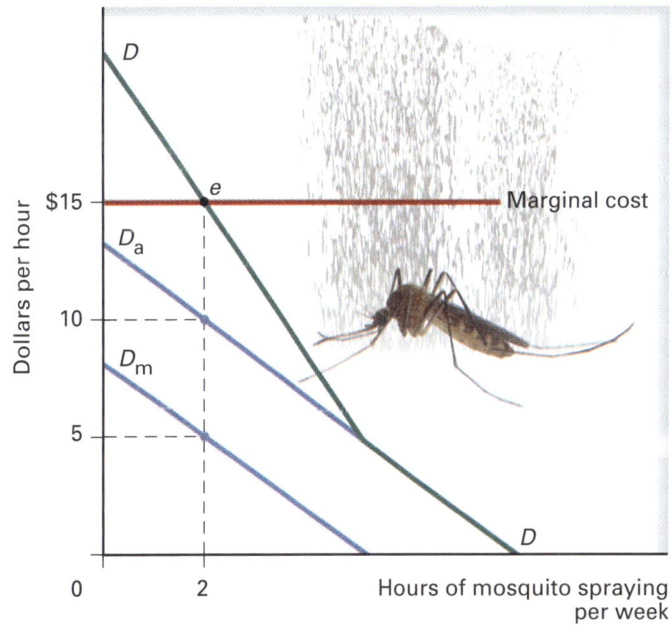

LO2 Discuss the role of public choice in representative democracy.

Public choice based on majority rule usually reflects the preferences of the median voter. Costs and benefits of public choices are spread throughout the democracy. The combinations of benefits and costs yield four possible categories of distributions: (1) widespread benefits and widespread costs (traditional public-goods legislation), (2) concentrated benefits and widespread costs (special-interest legislation), (3) widespread benefits and concentrated costs (populist legislation), and (4) concentrated costs and concentrated benefits (competing-interest legislation). An important feature of representative democracy is the incentive and political power it offers interest groups to increase their wealth, either through direct transfers or through favorable public expenditures and regulations.

Categories of Legislation Based on the Distribution of Costs and Benefits

Distribution of Costs	Distribution of Benefits: Widespread	Distribution of Benefits: Concentrated
Widespread	**1.** Traditional Public Goods —National defense 	**2.** Special interest —Farm subsidies 
Concentrated	**3.** Populist —Tort reform 	**4.** Competing interest —Labor union issues 

Effects of Milk Price Supports

In the absence of government intervention, the market price of milk is $1.50 per gallon, and 100 million gallons are sold per month. If government establishes a floor price of $2.50 per gallon, then the quantity supplied increases and the quantity demanded decreases. To maintain the higher price, the government must buy the excess quantity supplied at $2.50 per gallon.

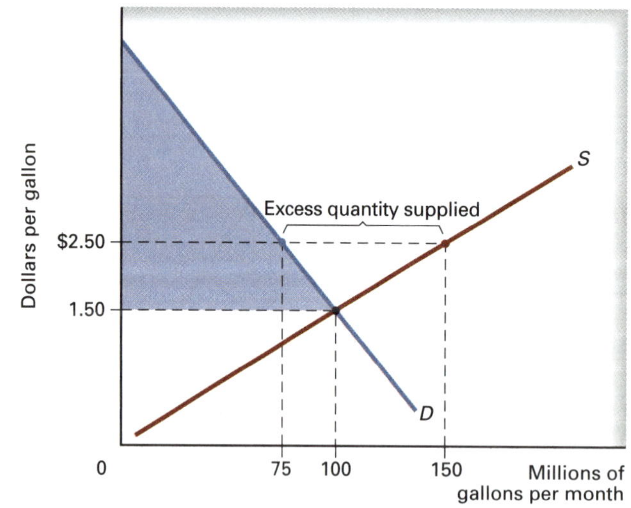

LO3 Describe the underground economy.

A government subsidy promotes production; conversely, a tax discourages production. When government taxes productive activity, less production gets reported and unreported income becomes part of the underground economy. The underground economy describes all market activity that goes unreported either to avoid taxes or because the activity itself is illegal.

LO4 Explain bureaucracy and its role in representative democracy.

Bureaus differ from firms in the amount of consumer feedback they receive, in their incentives to minimize costs, and in the transferability of their ownership. Because of these differences, bureaus may not be as efficient or as sensitive to consumer preferences as for-profit firms are.

CHAPTER 19

Learning Outcomes

- LO 1 Define externalities and explain the common-pool problem
- LO 2 Explain the optimal level of pollution
- LO 3 Assess the role of environmental problems in the economy
- LO 4 Describe positive externalities
- LO 5 Discuss the role of government in poverty alleviation and equity considerations
- LO 6 Identify the double market failure criterion

Externalities, Poverty, *and* Public Policy

© ISTOCKPHOTO/THINKSTOCK

“*Environmental problems are all negative externalities, which result from the actions of producers or consumers that affect many others.*”

The rivers in Jakarta, Indonesia, are dead—killed by acid, alcohol, and oil. Coral reefs in the South Pacific are being ripped apart by dynamite fishing. The tropical rainforest is shrinking because of slash-and-burn claims on the land's resources. The build up of greenhouse gases threatens to warm the oceans and near-surface air. Some streams in Colorado are still considered toxic from gold mining that ended more than a century ago. What does all this have to do with economics? These environmental problems are all negative externalities, which result from the actions of producers or consumers that affect many others. Markets can allocate resources efficiently only as long as property rights are well defined and can be easily enforced. But property rights to clean water, air, and soil, to fish in the ocean, to peace and quiet, and to scenic vistas are hard to establish and enforce. This lack of property rights to some resources results in externalities.

What do you think?

There are some resources that are impossible to effectively regulate.

Strongly Disagree					*Strongly Agree*	
1	2	3	4	5	6	7

Externalities may be either negative, such as air and water pollution, or positive, such as the general improvement in the civic climate that results from better education. This chapter discusses externalities and explores how public policies can reduce negative externalities and increase positive externalities. In addition to those instances where the market fails to provide a Pareto efficient allocation of resources, the government may have a role because of poverty considerations or because the resulting distribution of income and wealth is objectionable. However, in order to decide the question whether public intervention should be in the shape of direct production/provision of certain goods by the government or through other policies, it is prudent to use the “double market failure criterion.”

Topics discussed in Chapter 19 include:

- Exhaustible resources
- Renewable resources
- Common-pool problem
- Private property rights
- Optimal pollution
- Marginal social cost
- Marginal social benefit
- Coase theorem
- Markets for pollution rights
- Environmental protection
- Poverty alleviation
- Equity considerations
- Double market failure criterion

LO[1] Externalities and the Common-Pool Problem

Let's begin by distinguishing between exhaustible resources and renewable resources. An **exhaustible resource**, such as oil or coal, does not renew itself and so is available in a finite amount. Technology may improve the ability to extract these resources, but each gallon of oil burned is gone forever. Sooner or later, all oil wells will run dry. The world's oil reserves are *exhaustible*.

© JUDD PLISSOF/FOODPIX/JUPITERIMAGES

Renewable Resources

A resource is **renewable** if, when used conservatively, it can be drawn on indefinitely. Thus, timber is a renewable resource if trees are cut at sustainable rates and replaced with seedlings. The atmosphere and rivers are renewable resources to the extent that they can absorb and neutralize a certain level of pollutants. More generally, biological resources like fish, game, forests, rivers, grasslands, and agricultural soil are renewable if managed appropriately.

Some renewable resources are also open-access resources, an idea introduced in the previous chapter. An open-access resource is rival in consumption, but exclusion is costly. Fish caught in the ocean, for example, are not available for others to catch, so fish are rival in consumption. Yet it would be difficult, if not impossible, for a person or a firm to "own" fish still swimming in the open ocean and to prevent others from catching them, so ocean fish are nonexclusive. An open-access good is often subject to the **common-pool problem**, which results because people harvest a resource as long as marginal benefit exceeds marginal cost. For example, people will fish the oceans as long as the marginal benefit of catching more fish exceeds the marginal cost. Practically speaking, people will fish until the oceans become "fished out." Open-access goods are overfished, overhunted, overharvested, and overused. Because the atmosphere is an open-access resource, it's used as a dump for unwanted gases. Air pollution is a negative externality imposed on society by polluters. The problem is that people exploit any resource as long as their personal marginal benefit exceeds their personal marginal cost. As we'll see, personal marginal cost ignores costs imposed on others.

In a market system, specific individuals usually own the rights to resources and therefore have a strong interest in using those resources efficiently. *Private property rights*, a term introduced in Chapter 2, allow individuals to use resources or to charge others for their use. Private property rights are defined and enforced by government, by informal social actions, and by ethical norms. But because defining and enforcing property rights to open-access resources, such as the air, are quite costly or even impossible, these resources usually are not owned as private property.

Pollution and other negative externalities arise because there are no practical, enforceable, private property rights to open-access resources, such as the air. Market prices usually fail to include the costs that negative externalities impose on society. For example, the price you pay for a gallon of gasoline does not reflect the costs imposed by the greenhouse gases, sootier air, and the greater traffic congestion your driving creates. Electric rates do not reflect the negative externalities, or external costs, caused by fossil-fueled power plants. Note that externalities are unintended side effects of actions that are themselves useful and purposeful. Electricity producers, for example, did not go into business to pollute.

Resolving the Common-Pool Problem

Users of the atmosphere, waterways, wildlife, or other open-access resources tend to ignore the

exhaustible resource
a resource in fixed supply, such as crude oil or coal

renewable resource
a resource that regenerates itself and so can be used indefinitely if used conservatively, such as a properly managed forest

common-pool problem
unrestricted access to a resource results in overuse; use stops only when the marginal benefit drops to zero

1. Elisabeth Rosenthal, "Tuna Vanishing from Mediterranean," *International Herald Tribune*, 8 June 2006.

impact of their use on the resource's renewal ability. As quality and quantity diminish from overuse, the resource grows scarcer and could disappear. For example, Georges Bank, located off the New England coast, long one of the world's most productive fishing grounds, became so depleted by overfishing that by the 1990s the catch was down 85 percent from peak years. Tuna, once abundant in the Mediterranean, now faces extinction there.[1] The United Nations reports that 11 of the world's 15 primary fishing grounds are seriously depleted.

By imposing restrictions on resource use, government regulations may reduce the common-pool problem. Output restrictions or taxes could force people to use the resource at a rate that is socially optimal. For example, in the face of the tendency to overfish and to catch fish before they are sufficiently mature, the U.S. government has imposed a variety of restrictions on the fishing industry. The laws limit the total catch, the size of fish, the length of the fishing season, the equipment used, and other aspects of the business.

More generally, when imposing and enforcing private property rights would be too costly, government regulations may improve allocative efficiency. For example, stop signs and traffic lights allocate the scarce space at intersections, minimum size restrictions control lobster fishing, hunting seasons control the stock of game, and enforced study hours may calm the din in the college dormitory.

But not all regulations are equally efficient. For example, fishing authorities sometimes limit the total industry catch and allow all firms to fish until that total is reached. Consequently, when the fishing season opens, there is a mad scramble to catch as much as possible before the industry limit is reached. Because time is of the essence, fishing boats make no effort to fish selectively. And the catch reaches processors all at once, creating congestion throughout the supply chain. Also, each firm has an incentive to expand its fishing fleet to catch more in those precious few weeks. Thus, large fleets of technologically efficient fishing vessels operate for a few weeks until the limit is reached and then sit in port for the rest of the year. Each operator is acting rationally, but the collective effect of the regulation is grossly inefficient in terms of social welfare.

Ocean fish remain a common-pool resource because firms have not yet been able to establish and enforce rights to particular schools of fish. But advances in technology may some day allow the creation of private property rights to ocean fish, migrating birds, and other open-access resources. Establishing property rights to cattle on the Great Plains once seemed impossible, but the invention of barbed wire allowed ranchers to fence the range. In a sense, barbed wire tamed the Wild West.

LO2 Optimal Level of Pollution

Though the science is not fully resolved, fossil fuel used to power the likes of automobiles and electricity generators produces carbon dioxide, which mixes with other greenhouse gases that contribute to global warming. Electricity production from fossil fuels, therefore, involves the external cost of using the atmosphere as a gas dump. This section considers a way to analyze such externalities.

External Costs with Fixed Technology

Suppose *D* in Exhibit 1 depicts the demand for electricity. Recall that a demand curve reflects consumers' marginal benefit of each quantity. The lower horizontal line reflects the marginal private cost of electricity using fossil fuels. If producers base their

Exhibit 1

Negative Externalities: The Market for Electricity in the Midwest

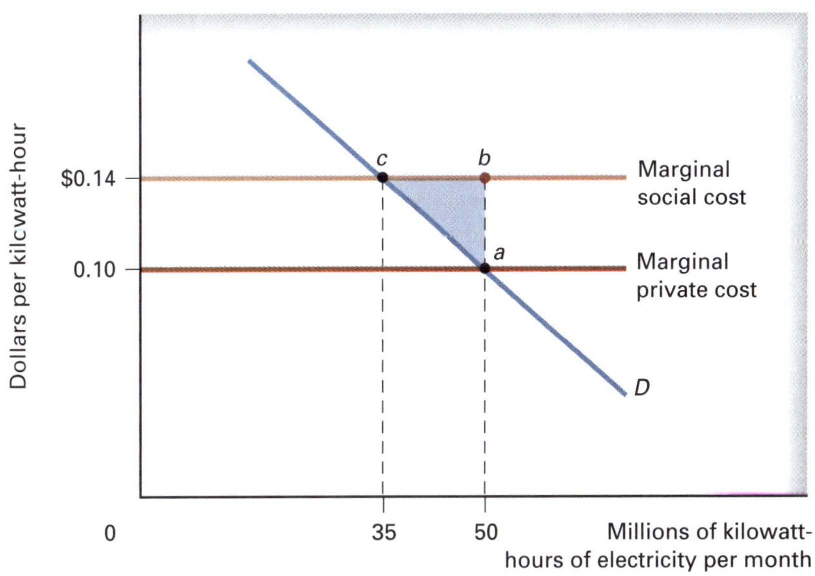

pricing and output decisions on their private marginal costs, the equilibrium quantity per month is 50 million kilowatt-hours and the equilibrium price is $0.10 per kilowatt-hour. At that price and quantity, identified by point *a*, the marginal private cost of production just equals the marginal benefit enjoyed by consumers of electricity.

Electricity production involves not only the private cost of the resources employed but also the external cost of using the atmosphere as a dump for greenhouse gases. Suppose that the marginal external cost imposed on the environment by the generation of electricity is $0.04 per kilowatt-hour. If the only way to cut emissions is to reduce electricity production, then the relationship between electricity production and pollution is fixed; the pollution in this case occurs with **fixed-production technology**.

The vertical distance between the marginal private cost curve and the marginal social cost curve in Exhibit 1 shows the marginal external cost of $0.04 per kilowatt-hour. The **marginal social cost** includes both the marginal private cost and the marginal external cost that production imposes on society. Because the marginal external cost here is assumed to be a constant $0.04 per kilowatt-hour, the two cost curves are parallel. Notice that at the private-sector equilibrium output level of 50 million kilowatt-hours, the marginal social cost, identified at point *b*, exceeds society's marginal benefit of electricity, identified on the demand curve at point *a*. The 50-millionth kilowatt-hour of electricity costs society $0.14 but yields only $0.10 of marginal benefit. Because the marginal social cost exceeds the marginal benefit, too much electricity is produced.

fixed-production technology
occurs when the relationship between the output rate and the generation of an externality is fixed; the only way to reduce the externality is to reduce the output

marginal social cost
the sum of the marginal private cost and the marginal external cost of production or consumption

variable technology
occurs when the amount of externality generated at a given rate of output can be reduced by altering the production process

marginal social benefit
the sum of the marginal private benefit and the marginal external benefit of production or consumption

The efficient quantity of 35 million kilowatt-hours is found where the demand, or marginal benefit, curve intersects the marginal social cost curve. This intersection is identified at point *c*. How could output be restricted to the socially efficient amount? If regulators knew the demand and marginal cost curves, they could simply limit production to 35 million kilowatt-hours, the efficient quantity. Or, on each kilowatt hour produced, they could impose a tax equal to the marginal external cost of $0.04. Such a pollution tax would lift the marginal private cost curve up to the marginal social cost curve. Thus, the tax would bring private costs in line with social costs.

With a tax of $0.04 per kilowatt-hour, the equilibrium combination of price and output moves from point *a* to point *c*. The price rises from $0.10 to $0.14 per kilowatt-hour, and output falls to 35 million kilowatt-hours. Setting the tax equal to the marginal external cost results in the efficient level of output. At point *c*, the marginal social cost of production equals the marginal benefit. Notice that greenhouse gas emissions are not eliminated at point *c*, but the utilities no longer generate electricity for which marginal social cost exceeds marginal benefit. The total social gain from reducing production to the socially optimal level is shown by the blue-shaded triangle in Exhibit 1. This triangle also measures the total social cost of allowing firms to ignore the external cost of production. Although Exhibit 1 offers a tidy solution, the external costs of greenhouse gases often cannot be easily calculated or taxed. At times, government intervention may result in more or less production than the optimal solution requires.

External Costs with Variable Technology

The previous example assumes that the only way to reduce greenhouse gases is to reduce output. But power companies, particularly in the long run, can usually change their resource mix to reduce emissions for any given level of electricity. If pollution can be reduced by altering the production process rather than by simply adjusting the quantity, these externalities are said to be produced under conditions of **variable technology**. With variable technology, the idea is to find the optimal level of pollution for a given quantity of electricity.

Let's look at Exhibit 2. The horizontal axis measures greenhouse gas emissions for a given level of electricity production. Emissions can be reduced by adopting cleaner production technology. Yet the production of cleaner air, like the production of other goods, is subject to diminishing returns. Cutting emissions of the most offensive greenhouse gases may involve simply changing the fuel mix, but further reductions call for more sophisticated and more expensive processes. Thus, the marginal social cost of reducing greenhouse gases increases, as shown by the upward-sloping marginal social cost curve in Exhibit 2.

The **marginal social benefit** curve reflects the additional benefit society derives from green-

Exhibit 2

The Optimal Reduction in Greenhouse Gas Emissions

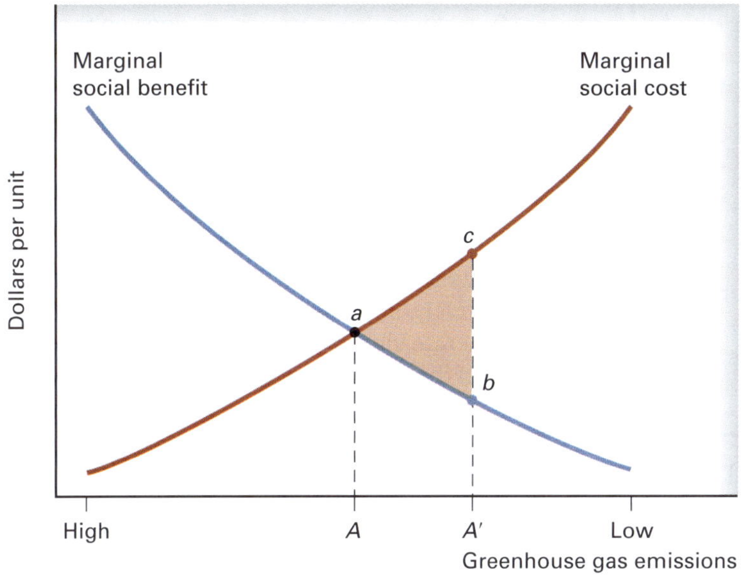

house gas reductions. When emissions are high, an improvement can save lives and thus is valued by society more than when emissions are low. Cleaner air, like other goods, has a declining marginal benefit to society (though the total benefit still increases). The marginal social benefit curve from cleaner air therefore slopes downward, as shown in Exhibit 2.

The optimal level of air quality for a given quantity of electricity is found at point *a*, where the marginal social benefit of cleaner air equals the marginal social cost. In this example, the optimal level of greenhouse gas emissions is A. If firms made their production decisions based simply on their private cost—that is, if the emission cost is external to the firm—then firms would have no incentive to search for production methods that reduce greenhouse gas emission, so too much production would result.

What if government regulators decree that greenhouse gas emission levels should be no higher than A′? For example, suppose a law establishes A′ as the maximum acceptable level of emissions. The marginal social cost, identified as *c*, of achieving that level of air quality exceeds the marginal social benefit, identified as *b*. The total social waste associated with imposing a greater-than-optimal level of air quality is shown by the pink-shaded triangle, *abc*. This area is the total amount by which the additional social costs of cleaner air (associated with a move from A to A′) exceed the additional social benefits. Improving air quality benefits society only as long as the marginal social benefit of cleaner air exceeds its marginal social cost.

What would happen to the optimal level of emissions if either the marginal cost curve or the marginal benefit curve shifted? For example, suppose some technological breakthrough reduces the marginal cost of cutting greenhouse gas emissions. As shown in panel (a) of Exhibit 3, the marginal social cost curve of reducing emissions would shift downward to *MSC*′, thereby reducing the optimal level of emissions from A to A′. *The simple logic is that the lower the marginal cost of reducing greenhouse gases, other things constant, the lower the optimal level of such emissions.*

An increase in the marginal benefit of air quality would have a similar effect. For example, suppose research indicates that the effects of a one degree increase in Earth's average temperature would be much more devastating than previously believed. This finding would increase the perceived benefits of reducing greenhouse gases. Thus, the marginal benefit of cleaner air would increase, as reflected in panel (b) of Exhibit 3 by an upward shift of the marginal social benefit curve to *MSB*′. As a result, the optimal level of air quality would increase. *The greater the marginal benefit of reducing greenhouse gases, other things constant, the lower the optimal level of emis-*

Exhibit 3

Effect of Changes in Costs or Benefits of Reducing Greenhouse Gas Emissions

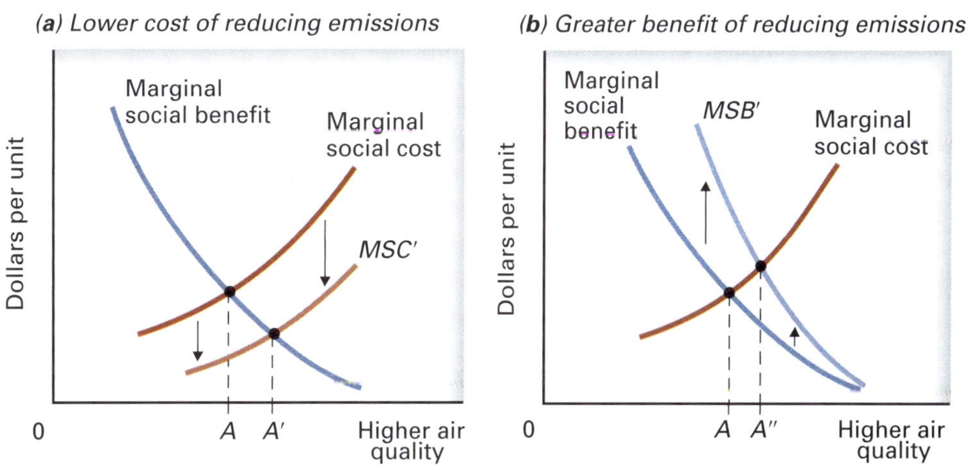

sions. As another example, recent research indicates that deaths from heart and lung disease would decrease 0.7 percent in large U.S. cities if suspended particulates in the air decrease by just 1/100,000th of a gram per cubic meter of air.[2] This finding increases the perceived benefits of cleaner air, leading to an increase in the optimal quality of clean air.

The Coase Theorem

The traditional analysis of externalities assumes that market failures arise because people ignore the external effects of their actions. For example, suppose a manufacturer of heavy machinery is next door to a research laboratory that tests delicate equipment. The vibrations caused by the manufacturing process throw off the delicate equipment next door. Professor Ronald Coase, who won the Nobel Prize in 1991, would argue that the negative externality in this case is not necessarily imposed by the heavy machinery—rather, it arises from the incompatible activities of the two firms. The externality is the result of both vibrations created by the factory *and* the location of the testing lab next door. Solutions might include modifying the factory, moving the factory, making the test equipment more shock resistant, or moving the testing lab.

According to Coase, the efficient solution depends on which party can avoid the externality at the lower cost. Suppose it would cost ₹2 million for the factory to reduce vibrations enough for the lab to function normally. On the other hand, if the factory makes no changes, the lab can't insulate equipment enough to operate accurately, so the lab would have to relocate at a cost of ₹1 million. Based on this information, the least-cost solution would be for the testing lab to relocate at a cost of ₹1 million. Coase argues that, as long as transaction costs are low, the parties will reach the efficient solution if one party is assigned the property right. And here's Coase's special insight: *This efficient solution will be achieved regardless of which party gets the property right.*

Coase theorem as long as bargaining costs are low, an efficient solution to the problem of externalities is achieved by assigning property rights to one party or the other, it doesn't matter which

2. Jonathan M. Samet et al., "Fine Particulate Air Pollution and Mortality in 20 U.S. Cities, 1987–1994," *New England Journal of Medicine*, 14 December 2000.

Suppose the testing lab is granted the right to operate free of vibrations from next door, so the testing lab can force the factory to reduce its vibration. Rather than cut vibrations at a cost of ₹2 million, the factory can pay the lab to relocate. Any payment greater than ₹1 million but less than ₹2 million makes both sides better off, because the lab would receive more than its moving cost and the factory would pay less than its cost of reducing vibrations. Thus, the lab will move, which is the efficient outcome.

Alternatively, suppose the factory is granted the right to generate vibrations in its production process, regardless of the impact on the testing lab. For the factory, this means business as usual. Because the minimum payment the factory would accept to reduce vibrations is ₹2 million, the lab would rather relocate at a cost of ₹1 million. Thus, whether property rights are granted to the lab or to the factory, the lab will move, which is the efficient, or least-cost, solution.

> "The traditional analysis of externalities assumes that market failures arise because people ignore the external effects of their actions."

The **Coase theorem** says that as long as bargaining costs are small, merely assigning the property right will generate an efficient solution to an externality problem regardless of which party is assigned that right. A particular assignment determines which side bears the externality costs but does not affect the efficient outcome.

Inefficient outcomes do occur, however, when the transaction costs of arriving at a solution are high. For example, an airport located in a populated area would have difficulty negotiating noise levels with all the affected residents. Or peasants contemplating clearing a portion of the tropical rainforest would be unable to negotiate with the millions, and perhaps, billions, of people ultimately affected by that decision. *When the number of parties involved in the transaction is large, Coase's solution of assigning property rights may not be enough.*

Markets for Pollution Rights

According to the Coase theorem, the assignment of property rights is often sufficient to resolve the market failure typically associated with externalities. Additional government intervention is not necessary. If pollution can be easily monitored and polluters easily identified, the government may be able to achieve an efficient solution to the problem of pollution simply by assigning the right to pollute. To see how this could work, let's look at an example. Firms that dump into a river evidently value the ability to discharge waste in this way. For them, the river provides a low-cost outlet for by-products that otherwise would have to be disposed of at greater cost. The river provides a disposal service, and the demand curve for that service slopes downward, just like the demand for other resources.

THE BEAUTY OF THIS SYSTEM IS THAT PRODUCERS WHO VALUE THE DISCHARGE RIGHTS THE MOST ULTIMATELY END UP WITH THEM.

The demand for the river as a discharge system is presented as *D* in Exhibit 4. The horizontal axis mea-sures the tons of discharge dumped into the river per day, and the vertical axis measures firms' marginal benefits of disposing of their waste in this way. The demand curve thus measures the marginal value to firms of using the river as a disposal service. With no restrictions on river pollution—that is, if all firms were free to dump waste into the river—dumping would continue as long it provided firms some marginal benefit. This marginal benefit falls to zero in Exhibit 4 when 250 tons per day are discharged.

The river, like the atmosphere and the soil, can absorb and neutralize a certain amount of discharge per day without deteriorating in quality. What if voters make the public choice that the river should remain clean enough for swimming and fishing? Suppose engineers determine this level of water quality can be maintained as long as no more than 100 tons are discharged per day. Thus, the "supply" of the discharge service provided by the river is fixed at 100 tons per day, shown by the vertical supply curve, *S*, in Exhibit 4.

If government regulators can easily identify polluters and monitor their behavior, authorities can allocate permits to discharge 100 tons per day. If polluters are simply given these permits (that is, if the price of permits is zero), there will be an excess demand for them, because the quantity supplied is 100 tons but the quantity demanded at a price of zero would be 250 tons. An alternative is to sell permits for 100 tons of pollution at the market-clearing price. The intersection of supply curve *S* and demand curve *D* yields a permit price of ₹2,500 per ton, which is the marginal value of discharging the 100th ton into the river each day. To most permit buyers, the marginal value of a permit exceeds ₹2,500 per ton.

The beauty of this system is that producers who value the discharge rights the most ultimately end up with them. Producers who attach a lower marginal value apparently have cheaper ways of resolving their waste problems, including changing production techniques. And if conservation groups want a higher river quality than the government's standard, such as water clean enough to drink, they can purchase pollution permits but not exercise them.

Exhibit 4

Optimal Allocation of Pollution Rights

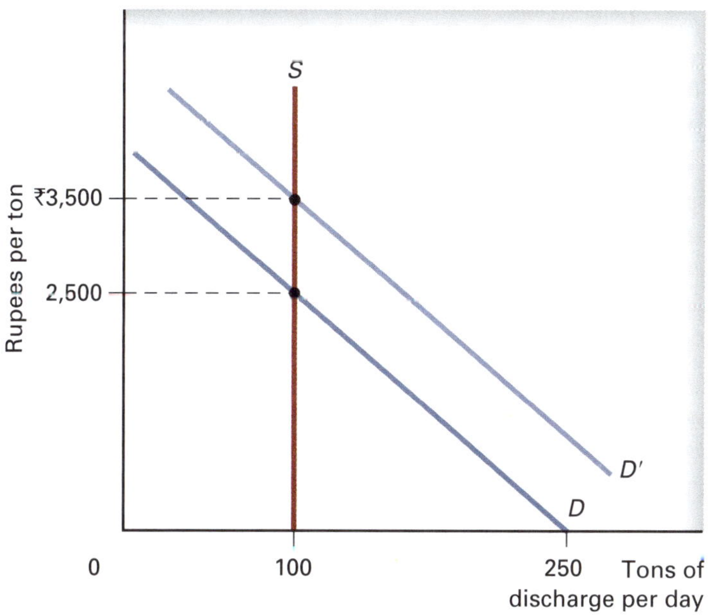

What if additional firms spring up along the river and are willing to pay more than ₹2,500 per ton for pollution rights? This greater demand is reflected in Exhibit 4 by *D*′. This increase of demand would bid up the market price of pollution permits to, say, ₹3,500 per ton. Some existing permit holders would sell their rights to those who value them more. Regardless of the comings and goings of would-be polluters, the total quantity of discharge rights is restricted to 100 tons per day, so the river's quality will be maintained. Thus, *the value of pollution permits, but not the total amount of pollution, may fluctuate over time.*

If the right to pollute could be granted, monitored, and enforced, then what had been a negative externality problem could be solved through market allocation. Historically, the U.S. government had relied on setting discharge standards and fining offenders. But in 1989, a pollution rights market for fluorocarbon emis-

© MONTY BRINTON/CBS/LANDOV

sions was established and was followed in 1990 by a market for sulfur dioxide. During the 1990s, sulfur dioxide emissions in the nation fell by more than half, exceeding the goals of the authorizing legislation. The "cap-and-trade" proposal from President Obama in 2009 aimed to create a market for greenhouse gas emissions. So the market for pollution rights is alive and growing.[3] Some companies and even celebrities are using a variant of pollution rights to become "carbon neutral"—that is, by estimating their carbon emissions then offsetting this impact by paying for projects to neutralize, or "sop up," equivalent emissions.[4] For example, Delta Air Lines allows online ticket buyers to pay an extra $5.50 for domestic flights or $11 for international flights for tree plantings to help offset flight emissions. And the band Coldplay funded 10,000 mango trees in India to help sop up emissions related to the release of the band's CD, *A Rush of Blood to the Head*.[5]

command-and-control environmental regulations
an approach that required polluters to adopt particular technologies to reduce emissions by specific amounts; inflexible regulations based on engineering standards that ignore each firm's unique ways of reducing pollution

economic efficiency approach
an approach that offers each polluter the flexibility to reduce emissions as cost-effectively as possible, given its unique cost conditions; the market for pollution rights is an example

3. For a discussion of the market for sulfur dioxide emissions, see Paul Joskow, Richard Schmalensee, and Elizabeth Bailey, "The Market for Sulfur-Dioxide Emissions," *American Economic Review* 88 (September 1998): 669–685.

4. See Andrew Revkin, "Carbon-Neutral Is Hip, But Is It Green?" *New York Times*, 29 April 2007.

5. Michael Hill, "Can Planting a Tree Absolve Your Eco-Sins?" *Arizona Republic*, 28 May 2007.

Pollution Rights and Public Choice

Unfortunately, legislation dealing with pollution is affected by the same problems of representative democracy that trouble other public policy questions. Big polluters have a special interest in government proposals relating to pollution, and they fight mea-sures to reduce pollution. But members of the public remain rationally ignorant about pollution legislation. So pollution regulations may be less in accord with the public interest than with the special interests of polluters. To win their cooperation, a portion of pollution permits are often *given* to existing firms or offered at below market prices. For example, under the sulfur dioxide program, the nation's 101 dirtiest power plants were granted credits equal to between 30 and 50 percent of the pollution they emitted before the program began. Because they received something of value, polluters were less inclined to oppose the legislation. Once permits were granted, some recipients found it profitable to sell their permits to other firms that valued them more. Thus, a market emerged that led to an efficient allocation of pollution permits. According to some analysts, the sulfur dioxide program saves up to $3 billion annually compared with the old system. More generally, a system of marketable pollution rights can reduce the cost of pollution abatement by as much as 75 percent.

Before 1990, **command-and-control environmental regulations** were the norm—an approach that required polluters, such as electric utilities, to introduce particular technologies to reduce emissions by specific amounts. These regulations were based on engineering standards and did not recognize unique circumstances across generating plants, such as plant design, ability to introduce scrubbers, and the ease of switching to low-sulfur fuels. But the market for pollution rights reflects an **economic efficiency approach** that offers each electric utility the flexibility to reduce emissions in the most cost-effective manner, given its unique operation. Firms with the lowest costs of emission control have an incentive to implement the largest reduction in emissions and then sell unused pollution permits to those with greater control costs.

Now that you know something about the theory of externalities, let's turn to an important application of the theory—environmental protection.

LO3 Environmental Protection

There have been efforts to address greenhouse gases on an international scale. A report by the Intergovernmental Panel on Climate Change, a group sponsored by the United Nations, was approved in May 2007 by more than 120 nations.[6] The study says, to fight global warming, the world must cut emissions of carbon dioxide and other greenhouse gases by (1) sharply improving energy efficiency in buildings, vehicles, and machines; (2) shifting from fossil fuels to nuclear, wind, solar, and other renewable energy sources; (3) preserving forests as absorbers of carbon dioxide, or as "carbon sinks"; and (4) capping agricultural emissions. The United States and China, which account for more than 40 percent of the world's emissions, approved the report but offered no indication that they would reverse their opposition to mandatory emission reductions. The report said that such reforms would require lifestyle changes, increased prices for some basics including gasoline and electricity, and greater investment in research and development.

Water Pollution

Two major sources of water pollution are sewage and chemicals. For decades, U.S. cities had an economic incentive to dump their sewage directly into waterways rather than clean it up first. Water current or tides would carry off the waste to become someone else's problem. Although each community found it rational, based on a narrow view of the situation, to dump into waterways, the combined effect of these local choices was water pollution, a negative externality imposed by one community on other communities. Federal money over the years has funded thousands of sewage treatment plants, which cut water pollution substantially. Nearly all U.S. cities now have modern sewage control systems. Hundreds of once-polluted waterways have been cleaned up enough for swimming and fishing.

Chemicals are another source of water pollution. Chemical pollution may conjure up an image of a pipe spewing chemicals into a river, but only about 10 percent of chemical pollution in the water comes from point pollution—pollution from factories and other industrial sites. About two-thirds come from nonpoint pollution—mostly runoff from agricultural

6. For panel reports, go to http://www.ipcc.ch/.

{Redrawing the Map}

With as much press as the green movement and eco-friendly initiatives are getting, one equally pressing issue is the prospect of global shortages of clean water. According to estimates by the United Nations, two-thirds of the global population could experience periodic and severe water shortages by 2025. Americans should not think themselves exempt either: 36 states estimate significant shortages in the next decade.

In January 2008, Georgia drew up a resolution to redraw the border between it and Tennessee along the 35th parallel. Originally this was the border proposed by Congress, but surveyors, using inaccurate equipment, marked the line roughly a mile south of where it should be. What's the big deal with this boundary? The 35th parallel runs through a bend in the Tennessee River, which Georgia could use to provide water to rapidly growing Atlanta. Many neighboring states, however, have complained that Georgia has not taken sufficient conservation measures. Such disputes are becoming more common. At the same time, the Supreme Court was reviewing a similar dispute between North and South Carolina. Would a change in the border create a positive or a negative externality?

© ISTOCKPHOTO.COM / © VISIONSOFAMERICA/JOE SOHM/DIGITAL VISION/GETTY IMAGES

SOURCES: Shaila Dewan, "Georgia Claims a Sliver of the Tennessee River," *New York Times*, 22 February 2008. Available at http://www.nytimes.com/2008/02/22/us/22water.html (accessed 23 December 2008); Adam Bluestein, "Blue Is the New Green," *Inc.*, November 2008, pp. 116–128.

pesticides and fertilizer. Congress has been reluctant to limit the use of pesticides, although pesticides pollute water and contaminate food. Industrial America seems an easier target than Old MacDonald's farm.

As the cost of solid waste disposal increases, some state and local governments are economizing, charging households by the pound for trash pickups, and requiring more recycling and returnable bottles. **Recycling** is the process of converting waste products into reusable materials.

Some recycling is clearly economical—such as aluminum cans, which are a relatively cheap source of

recycling
the process of converting waste products into reusable material

India's Voluntary Actions on Sustainable Development Strategy

India has taken a number of actions on voluntary basis in pursuance of a sustainable development strategy. As per India's GHG Emissions Profile: Results of Five Climate Modeling Studies, a report published in 2009, India's per capita GHG emissions in 2030–31 would be between 2.77 tons and 5.00 tons of CO_2 eq. Four of the five studies estimated that even in 2031, India's per capita GHG emissions would stay under 4 tons of CO_2 eq. which is lower than the global per capita emissions of 4.22 tons of CO_2 eq. in 2005. This means that even two decades from now, India's per capita GHG emissions would be well below the global average of 25 years earlier. Important measures taken by India are as follows:

India has adopted the National Action Plan on Climate Change (NAPCC) in 2008 which has both mitigation and adaptation measures. The eight National Missions which form the core of the NAPCC represent multi-prolonged, long-term, and integrated strategies for achieving key goals in the context of climate change. Adaptation is the focus of the NAPCC. At the same time, Missions on Solar Energy and Energy Efficiency are geared to mitigation.

India has announced a domestic goal of reducing the emission intensity of its GDP by 20–25 percent of the 2005 level by 2020. Apart from the NAPCC, all the Indian states have also been asked to prepare state-level action plans. These plans are envisioned as extensions of the NAPCC at various levels of governance, aligned with the eight National Missions.

SOURCE: Government of India (2012), Economic Survey 2011–12, Chapter 12.

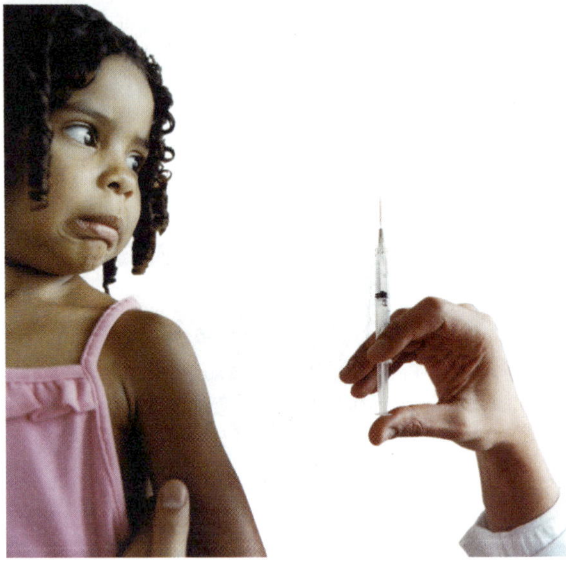

© WIDE GROUP/STONE/GETTY IMAGES

aluminum compared to producing raw aluminum. About two out of three aluminum cans now get recycled, though only 11 states require returnable deposits. Still, returnable deposit laws increase recycling. Incentives matter.

Recycling paper and cardboard is also economical and occurred long before the environmental movement. Such old standbys as paper drives, drop-off bins, and redemption centers collect more tonnage than curbside programs. Most recycling results from salvaging scrap material from business and industry, a practice that dates back decades.

Governments have tried to stimulate demand for recycled material—for example, by requiring newspapers to use a certain amount of recycled newsprint. Other recycled products are not in such demand. In fact, some recycled products have become worthless and must be hauled to landfills. Recycling imposes its own environmental cost. Curbside recycling requires fleets of trucks that pollute the air. Newsprint must

LIBRARY OF CONGRESS, LC-USZ62-119240

Blanket Ban on Plastic Bags in Delhi

In a significant decision to rid the city of plastic bags, Delhi government in 2011 imposed a blanket ban on their manufacture, sale, storage, and use of plastic bags in the national capital of India. This has been a long pending demand of the green groups.The ban has been imposed under the Environment (Protection) Act, 1986 under which the violators could face imprisonment up to five years and fine of up to ₹1 lakh or both.

Following a Delhi High Court order, the government had in January, 2009 also imposed a ban on the use (not manufacture) of plastic bags in various markets, shopping malls, hotels, and hospitals. However, this ban had not been very effective. The government, exercising provisions of Delhi Degradable Plastic Bags (Manufacturing, Sales, and Usage) and Garbage (Controlled) Act–2000, had forbidden sales, storage, and use of all kinds of plastic bags in certain notified places. The notified places included luxury hotels, hospitals, restaurants, all fruits and vegetable outlets of Mother Dairy, liquor vends, shopping malls, local shopping centers and all retail and wholesale outlets of branded chain of outlets selling different consumer products including fruits and vegetables.

SOURCE: http://articles.timesofindia.indiatimes.com/2011-04-04/delhi/29379740_1_sales-and-usage-fruits-and-vegetable-outlets-blanket-ban first be de-inked, creating a sludge that must be disposed of. But greater environmental awareness has made consumers more receptive to more efficient packaging. For example, liquid laundry detergent now comes in a concentrated "ultra" form, which cuts volume in half, and Unilever's brand All Small & Mighty cuts volume by two-thirds. Labels for all kinds of products proudly identify the recycled content of the packaging.

LO4 Positive Externalities

To this point, we have considered only negative externalities. But externalities are sometimes positive, or beneficial. Positive externalities occur when consumption or production benefits other consumers or other firms. For example, people who get inoculated against a disease reduce their own likelihood of contracting the disease, but they reduce the risk of transmitting the disease to others. Inoculations thus provide external benefits. Likewise, society as a whole receives external benefits from education because those who acquire more education become better citizens, can read road signs, are better able to support themselves and their families, and are less likely to require public assistance or to resort to violent crime for income. Researchers found that more schooling significantly reduces the probability of incarceration.[7] Thus, your education provides personal benefits but it also benefits others.

The effect of external benefits is illustrated in Exhibit 5, which presents the demand and supply of education. The demand curve, *D*, represents the private demand for education, which reflects the marginal private benefit for those who acquire the education. More education is demanded at a lower price than at a higher price.

The benefit of education, however, spills over to others in society. If we add this positive externality, or marginal external benefit, to the marginal private benefit of education, we get the marginal social benefit of education. The marginal social benefit includes all the benefits society derives from education, both private and external. The marginal social benefit curve is above the private demand curve in Exhibit 5. If education were a strictly private decision, the amount purchased would be determined by the intersection of the private demand curve *D* with supply curve *S*. The supply curve reflects the marginal cost of producing each unit of the good. This intersection at point *e* yields education level *E*, where

Exhibit 5

Education and Positive Externalities

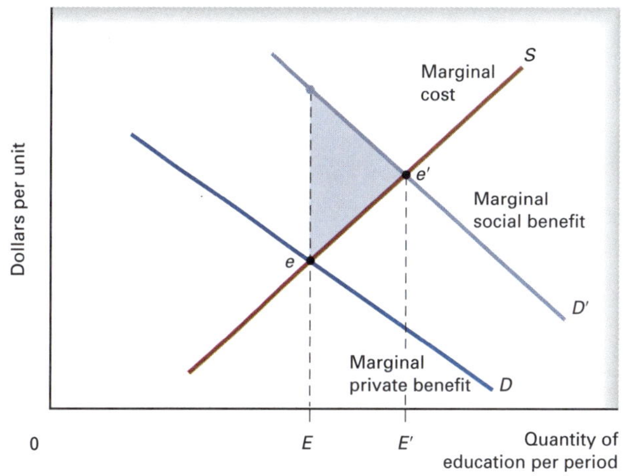

the marginal private benefit of education equals its marginal cost, as reflected by the supply curve. But at level *E*, the marginal social benefit exceeds the marginal cost. Social welfare would increase if education expands beyond *E*. As long as the marginal social benefit exceeds the marginal cost, social welfare increases as education expands. Social welfare is maximized at point *e′* in Exhibit 5, where *E′* units of education are provided—that is, where the marginal social benefit equals the marginal cost. The blue-shaded triangle identifies the increase in social welfare that results from increasing education from *E*, the private optimum, to *E′*, the social optimum.

Thus, society is better off if the level of education exceeds the private equilibrium. With positive externalities, decisions based on private marginal benefits result in less than the socially optimal quantity of the good. Thus, like negative externalities, positive externalities typically point to market failure, which is why government often gets into the act. When there are external benefits, public policy aims to increase quantity beyond the private optimum. For example, governments try to increase education by providing free primary and secondary education, by requiring students to stay in school until they reach 16 years of age, by subsidizing public higher education, and by offering tax breaks for some education costs.

LO5 Poverty Alleviation, Equity Considerations, and Government

In addition to those instances where the market fails to provide a Pareto efficient allocation of resources,

7. Lance Lochner and Enrico Moretti, "The Effects of Education on Crime: Evidence from Prison Inmates," *American Economic Review* 94 (March 2004): 155–189.

Government Initiated Anti-Poverty Programs in India

Home to the world's largest hungry population, India has a record on hunger that is worse than that of nearly 25 sub-Saharan African countries. India is ranked 66th among 88 vulnerable countries in the Global Hunger Index prepared by the International Food Policy Research Institute, and none of its states is categorized under "low hunger" or "moderate hunger category"[8]. In addition, past few years have seen rising food prices. Spiraling food price inflation and nutritional deprivation has affected millions of households in India.

To combat poverty, India has several social safety net programs. The National Rural Employment Guarantee Scheme (NREGS) and the Targeted Public Distribution Scheme (TPDS) are two of its flagship programs. Briefly, the *National Rural Employment Guarantee Scheme* is an Indian job guarantee scheme that was enacted by legislation on August 25, 2005. The scheme provides a legal guarantee for one hundred days of employment in every financial year to adult members of any rural household willing to do unskilled manual work. The work is performed at the statutory minimum wage of about USD 2.7 per day at 2009 prices. The Central Government's outlay for the scheme in fiscal year 2010-11 was ₹400 billion (USD 8.92 billion). The *Public Distribution System* (PDS), on the other hand, is a national food security system that distributes subsidized food to India's poor. Major commodities distributed include wheat, rice, sugar, and kerosene. PDS has a network of about 478,000 Fair Price Shops (FPS), perhaps the largest distribution network of its type in the world, operated by the Central and State Governments. The Central Government, through the Food Corporation of India, has assumed the responsibility for procurement, storage, transportation, and bulk allocation of food grains to the State Governments. The operational responsibility, including allocation within State, identification of families below the poverty line, issue of Ration Cards and supervision of the functioning of FPS, rests with the State Governments.

In addition to TPDS, the Indian government has initiated or strengthened a number of schemes to further assist the very poor in the form of cheaper grains. In December 2000, the *Antyodaya Anna Yojana* (AAY: grain scheme for the poorest of the poor) was launched. It seeks to identify the ten million poorest households out of the 65 million BPL families, and to provide them with 25 kg of foodgrains per family per month at a low price of ₹2/kg for wheat and ₹3/kg for rice. The *Annapurna Scheme*, commenced in 2000-01, provides 10 kg of food grains per person per month free to indigent senior citizens above the age of 65 but who are not drawing pension under the national old age pension scheme. In August 2001, the *Sampoorna Gramin Rozgar Yojana* (integrated rural employment scheme) was announced, under which states are provided with five million tons of food grains annually for undertaking work programs. Other existing welfare programs were also strengthened to provide food grains to benefit the poor. These include the mid-day meal scheme, wheat based nutrition program, and scheme for supply of food grains to scheduled caste/scheduled tribe/other backward classes. These schemes are used primarily (i) to make the PDS more focused and targeted towards the poor, (ii) to increase the employment opportunities of the poor, and (iii) to help reduce the overstock of food grains in the central reserves.

Despite the noble intention of targeting subsidized food grains to *"poor in all areas,"* unlike the erstwhile system which laid stress on *"all in poor areas,"* the TPDS is plagued with controversies. A study by Planning Commission (GOI, 2005) finds that about 58 percent of the subsidized food grains issued from the Central pool do not reach BPL families because of identification errors, non-transparent operations, and unethical practices in the implementation of TDPS. Apart from substantial leakages, the high cost of handling food grains implies that for one rupee worth of income transfer to the poor, the Government spends ₹3.65, indicating that one rupee of budgetary consumer subsidy is worth only 27 paisa to the poor. In a recent study, Khera (2010) too shows that 67 percent of the wheat meant for poor is directed elsewhere. In other words, for every 1 kg of wheat that reaches the poor household, the government directs 3 kgs of wheat at them.

the government may have a role because of poverty considerations or because the resulting distribution of income and wealth is objectionable.

A free and open market, we all know, tends to pay productive agents the value of what they produce. The income of an individual depends on the unit price of productive services times the number of units which he owns (including both capital goods and their own labor power). The number of units of productive services which they own depends on inheritance, effort, and luck, which are not equally distributed in the existing social order. But inevitability does not justify inequality. This inequality of wealth and income can be modified by suitable government policies. But here too, our views of the role of the government/State have changed markedly in the last two decades or so. The Second Fundamental Theorem of Welfare Economics provides a remarkable result: it argues that if the distribution of income was not socially optimal, then "all that" the government needs to do is to re-distribute the initial endowments. Having done that, the market would ensure efficient outcomes. There is, in effect, a complete dichotomy between efficiency and distributive issues and government's role was limited to the latter.

However, this view has been qualified in two important respects. *Firstly*, we know that equity and efficiency issues are not separate. In full perspective, the relation between equality and productivity doubtless runs as follows: if wealth and income were very unequally distributed, there is a range over which the community would probably achieve both higher output and more equality by re-distributing resources from rich to poor. If re-distribution contin-

8. To make matters worse there has been a decline in the per capita calorie consumption in recent years (Rao 2005; Meenakshi and Viswanathan 2005; Ray and Lancaster 2005; Patnaik 2004, 2007).

ued, a point of maximum productivity and moderate equality would be reached. Thereafter, additional degrees of equality could be purchased only at the expense of some sacrifice of productivity. These sacrifices would be small at first, but would increase steadily till, at the limit, complete equality would be reached only by a very considerable sacrifice of total output. That is, equality and productivity become competitive values beyond a certain point because of two reasons. One is the adverse incentive effect of progressive taxation on initiative, risk taking, and enterprise development. Second is the adverse incentive effect of receiving income without expending effort. Here, in brief, is the central problem of any government—how much more (or less) equality do we want in terms of the sacrifice (or gain) in productivity involved in moving towards it.

Secondly, the kind of lump sum re-distribution envisaged in the second fundamental theorem of Welfare Economics is not in general feasible. Accordingly, redistribution essentially always involves some distortions and given these distortions, it is not obvious that the kind of passive role for the government called for by the Second Welfare Theorem is desirable.

Thus, on the basis of the old Welfare Theorems, the rationale for government intervention is based on either the allocation of resources not being efficient, or if efficient, the distribution of income generated, not being socially acceptable. Thus, according to the traditional literature, decentralized markets would lead to an efficient allocation (except when market failures occur) of resources. Therefore, in their view, the role of State is limited.

However, sometimes non-market activities, whether intended to overcome the distributional inequities of market outcomes or to remedy other inadequacies in the market's performance, may themselves generate distributional inequities. The resulting inequities are often indexed on power rather than income or wealth. The government in order to carry out its activities either of direct production of public goods or of regulating the industry because of externalities or increasing returns has to place authority/power in the hands of some to be exercised over others. This redistribution of power provides opportunities for inequity and abuse by giving rise to "rent seeking" or "directly unproductive activities." What is relevant is the fact that economic costs of many policies such as minimum wage legislation, import licensing, industrial licensing, and credit rationing, are far greater when rent seeking takes place than traditional welfare cost analysis would suggest. In some instances, policies that might otherwise be desirable to meet non-economic objectives, or even to correct market failures, may result in a situation even less satisfactory than that prevailing before the policy was put in place.

Non-market activities may also result in distributional inequities indexed on income rather than power. For example, although provision of infrastructure is often proposed as a means of re-distributing resources from higher-income household to poor, yet its effectiveness depends on whether subsidies actually reach the poor, on the administrative costs associated with such targeting, and on the scope for allocating budgetary resources to this purpose without sacrificing other socially beneficial public expenditures. Unfortunately, very often price subsidies to infrastructure almost always benefit the non-poor disproportionately more. Moreover, targeting is also often not optimal in case of several of anti-poverty programs.

Thus systems, private as well as public, are marked by imperfections. The fact that in remedying market failures or redistributing income, some income gets re-distributed to the well-off, and some inefficiencies get created, does not necessarily mean that the government programs should be eliminated. It only means that there is an added "cost" to the program which needs to be taken into account in judging whether it is worthwhile.

LO6 The Double Market Failure Criterion

It has been said earlier that the presence of an endemic market failure may call for public intervention in some form but not necessarily through government production/provision of the relevant goods. In order to decide the question whether public intervention should be in the shape of direct production/provision of certain goods by the government or through other policies, it is prudent to use the so-called "double market failure criterion" (Minhas,1991; Kaur, 2003)[9]. First, one must establish sound evidence of market failure or a consensus for the acceptance of some distributional goal. Second, one must also search for evidence that a less intrusive policy cannot be utilized, or effective contracts for private production of public goods cannot be devised. Whenever double market failure criterion is fulfilled, the case for public sector production/provision of such goods is usually strong.

9. Kaur, Simrit, *Privatization and Public Regulation*, (Macmillan India Ltd., 2003); and Minhas, B.S., "Public versus Private Sectors: Neglect of Lessons of Economics in Indian Policy Formulation," *Arth Yojana* March 1991, Vol. 33: 1-11.

The need for public sector production is more or less well established when moral hazards and opportunistic/strategic behavior are strongly indicated. The most common examples of double market failure and opportunistic behavior arise in the production of public goods, defence (which is itself a public good), collection of taxes, printing of money, administration of justice, enforcement of contracts, etc. To illustrate the meaning of opportunistic behavior, one can easily conceive of private armies. In fact, private armies have been raised in the course of history and many such armies were involved in the thirty year war in Europe. The difficulty with the private armies is precisely the opportunistic behavior of the soldiers. Private armies cannot be trusted to carry out the contracts because the governments do not have an independent mechanism of enforcement of such contracts. Soldiers can be lured from one side to another because of, say, higher wages. Notice that the failure here is the failure of the market twice over: one's enjoyment of security from a given level of defence is not diminished by the enjoyment of security by millions of others. Defence, as a public good, is non-competitive and non-excludable among the citizens. It is almost impossible to envisage price-market arrangements for national security and further the contracts between the private armies and governments are unenforceable.

According to Stiglitz (1989)[10], there are two distinguishing features of the government/State, from which most of the other differences between the State and other economic organizations follow:

1. State is the one organization membership of which is universal, and
2. State has powers of compulsion not given to other economic organizations.

The very fact that membership is compulsory gives the State a power of compulsion which other organizations do not have. Thus, if in any transaction between the government and an individual, the individual becomes worse off, the individual has no right to exit. The right of exit is a distinct feature of any other economic organization, i.e., other than the State. Important examples of where the government uses its economic powers of compulsion are in the areas of power to tax (e.g. by taxing activities which have net negative externalities), power to proscribe certain activities, e.g., through licensing and power to make citizens participate in the social security system. In some countries, it uses its powers of compulsion more broadly than in others.

10. Stiglitz, J.E. (1989), ed., Arnold, J., The Economic Role of The State, Basil Blackwell Ltd., Heertje, 1989.

Final Word

Population pressure coupled with a lack of incentives to conserve open-access resources results in deforestation, dwindling fish stocks, and polluted air, land, and water.

Ironically, because of the tighter pollution controls in industrial countries, these countries are less polluted than developing countries, where there is more pollution from what little industry there is. Most developing countries have such profound economic problems that environmental quality is not a priority. For example, when India's Supreme Court tried to close some polluting factories in New Delhi, thousands of workers torched buses, threw stones, and blocked major roads, demanding the factories stay open. Although New Delhi's pollution masks any trace of a blue sky, workers believe their jobs are more important. Here's one account of New Delhi's air quality:

> *In the heat of the afternoons, a yellow-white mixture hung above the city, raining acidic soot into the dust and exhaust fumes. At night the mixture condenses into a dry, choking fog that envelops the headlights of passing cars, and creeps its stink into even the tightest houses. The residents could do little to keep the poison out of their lungs or the lungs of their children, and if they were poor, they could not even try.*[11]

Market prices can direct the allocation of resources only as long as property rights are well defined. Pollution arises not so much from the greed of producers and consumers as from the fact that open-access resources are subject to the common-pool problem.

In addition to those instances where the market fails to provide a Pareto efficient allocation of resources, the government may have a role because of poverty considerations or because the resulting distribution of income and wealth is objectionable. However, in order to decide the question whether public intervention should be in the shape of direct production/provision of certain goods by the government or through other policies, it is prudent to use the double market failure criterion. Double market failure occurs when two conditions hold: First, one must establish sound evidence of market failure or a consensus for the acceptance of some distributional goal. Second, one must also search for evidence that a less intrusive policy cannot be utilized, or effective contracts for private production of public goods cannot be devised.

11. William Langewiesche, "The Shipbreakers," *Atlantic Monthly* (August 2000): 42.

Multiple Choice Questions

1. When consumption of a good or service produces benefits or costs that are not reflected in the market price for the good, this is known as a(n)
   a. externality
   b. common pool problem
   c. nonexcludable resource
   d. public good
   e. renewable resource
2. All of the following are examples of negative externalities *except one*. Which is the exception?
   a. water pollution
   b. your roommate going on a diet
   c. second-hand smoke
   d. loud conversation in the workplace
   e. your neighbor building a bomb shelter on her front lawn
3. Property rights can be defined and enforced
   a. only by the government
   b. only by ethical norms
   c. by the government and by ethical norms
   d. only through constant renegotiation
   e. by government, by informal social actions, and by ethical norms
4. In the village of Axiok, any farmer can allow its cattle to graze on the common grassland. Which of the following statements is incorrect?
   a. Each farmer will allow their cattle to graze as long as the marginal benefit exceeds the marginal cost
   b. The grassland is a renewable resource, if managed appropriately
   c. The village's grassland will suffer from overgrazing
   d. One farmer has property rights to the grassland
   e. The grassland is subject to the common-pool problem
5. The common pool problem
   a. occurs whenever goods are not rivals in consumption
   b. is an example of adverse selection
   c. arises whenever property rights are well defined
   d. is usually caused by government intervention into private markets
   e. is one in which resources to which access is unrestricted will tend to be overused
6. Government restrictions on the use of an open-access resource
   a. may improve efficiency
   b. will decrease efficiency
   c. are unnecessary
   d. contribute to pollution of the resource
   e. contribute to depletion of the resource
7. Economists view pollution as an economic problem that arises because
   a. private enterprise always minimizes the amount of pollution produced
   b. profitable firms rarely pollute
   c. as the economy grows, the level of pollution declines
   d. firms that pollute do not pay the full social cost of producing their output
   e. pollution costs are borne by the consumer
8. In the production of electricity with fixed-production technology, the socially efficient price is \$2 and the socially efficient level of output is 400 units; the market equilibrium price is \$1.50 and the market equilibrium quantity is 600 units. The total social gain from producing the socially efficient output rather than the private equilibrium output is:
   a. \$50
   b. \$200
   c. \$400
   d. \$600
   e. There is not enough information to calculate it
9. Firms that emit toxins into the air tend to
   a. underproduce because the private cost of production exceeds the social cost
   b. overproduce because the social cost of production exceeds the private cost
   c. produce the same as nonpolluting firms
   d. produce at the socially optimal amount
   e. cover pollution costs in the product's price
10. When competitive market equilibrium determines a level of output for which the marginal social cost exceeds the marginal social benefit, the private equilibrium results in
   a. a positive externality
   b. a Coase equilibrium
   c. underproduction of the product
   d. a market failure
   e. external benefits

11. The socially efficient level of output is determined where
    a. marginal social cost equals marginal social benefit
    b. marginal private cost equals marginal social benefit
    c. average social cost equals average social benefit
    d. average private cost equals average social benefit
    e. total social cost equals total social benefit
12. When using the traditional command-and-control approach to environmental regulation, the government attempts to
    a. set a minimum requirement and then allows the firm to determine the most efficient method for achieving this requirement
    b. determine the most efficient method for different industries
    c. make allowances for differences across industries and between firms
    d. set engineering standards that are applicable to all situations and does not recognize unique circumstances
    e. set a maximum requirement and they allows the individual firm the latitude of choosing the most efficient method
13. When using the economic efficiency approach to controlling air and water pollution, the government
    a. forces each firm to produce emissions in the most cost efficient manner irrespective of its cost structure
    b. offers each firm the flexibility to reduce emissions in the most cost effective manner, given its unique cost structure
    c. offers each firm the option of choosing between the cost minimizing emission level and the profit maximizing emission level
    d. provides each firm with some fixed rules and then requires them to maximize profits given these fixed rules
    e. offers each firm the option of using marginal cost pricing and average cost pricing when determining the optimum emissions levels
14. A meditation class meets on the second floor of a building; the first floor is a nightclub. The loud music from the club disturbs the classes. The club could be soundproofed for a cost of $5,000 or move at a cost of $8,000. The class can't soundproof enough to overcome the music, but could be moved for $4,000. According to Coase,
    a. the club should be soundproofed so both businesses can stay open
    b. the club should be soundproofed because it is the one generating the externality
    c. the club should move rather than be soundproofed because eliminating an externality is better than compensating for it
    d. the class should move because it can eliminate the externality at a lower cost than can the nightclub
    e. whichever business has been there longer has the overriding property right; the other should adjust
15. The Coase theorem says that, if the appropriate property right is assigned to _____, an efficient solution to an externality problem will be achieved.
    a. the party causing the externality
    b. the victim of the externality
    c. the party that can avoid the externality at the higher cost
    d. the party that can avoid the externality at the lower cost
    e. either one of the parties involved
16. The 'Nuts & Bolts' factory is located next to the movie set for 'The silent man'. The noise coming from the factory makes the movie production close to impossible. The factory can be sound-proofed for $2 million or it can be moved for $4 million. The movie set can be moved for $1.5 million. Assume that the factory has the property right. What would be the optimal solution to this problem?
    a. The factory should pay for its own sound-proofing
    b. The movie producers should pay for the sound-proofing of the factory
    c. The movie producers should pay to move the movie set
    d. The factory should pay to move the movie set
    e. The factory should pay to move the factory
17. A metal-stamping factory moves next to a day care center. Noise from the factory makes it impossible for the kids to nap. It would cost the factory $5 million to move; it would cost $1 million for the day care center to move. Sound insulation for the factory costs $1 million; insulation for the day care center costs $200,000. The court initially determines that the day care center has the property right and

orders the factory to purchase insulation for the day care. But on appeal the factory is awarded the property right. How would the optimal solution to this problem change after the appeals court decision?

a. The insulation would still be bought, but it would be bought by the day care center, a result consistent with the Coase theorem.
b. Insulation for the factory would be bought instead of insulation for the day care center, a result consistent with the Coase theorem.
c. Insulation for the day care center would still be bought, but it would be bought by the factory, a result consistent with the Coase theorem.
d. Insulation for the factory would be bought instead of insulation for the day care center, a result inconsistent with the Coase theorem.
e. The day care center would move instead of buying insulation, a result consistent with the Coase theorem.

18. Other things equal, if the government increased the quantity of pollution rights to be sold,
    a. pollution would not be affected
    b. the price of pollution rights would rise, and the amount of pollution would decrease
    c. the price of pollution rights would fall, and the amount of pollution would decrease
    d. the price of pollution rights would fall, and the amount of pollution would increase
    e. the price of pollution rights would rise, and the amount of pollution would increase

19. When consuming a good creates positive externalities,
    a. private demand increases
    b. private demand decreases
    c. the private demand curve overstates the marginal social benefit of the good
    d. the private demand curve understates the marginal social benefit of the good
    e. the equilibrium quantity increases without government intervention

20. In order to increase society's well-being, a process that produces a positive externality might be
    a. taxed to discourage production
    b. subsidized to encourage production
    c. taxed to encourage production
    d. subsidized to discourage production
    e. provided without government intervention

Answers

1. a 2. b 3. e 4. d 5. e 6. a 7. d 8. a 9. b 10. d
11. a 12. d 13. b 14. d 15. e 16. c 17. a 18. d 19. d 20. b

LONG ANSWER QUESTIONS

LO1 Define externalities and explain the common-pool problem

1.1. *(Negative Externalities)* Suppose you wish to reduce a negative externality by imposing a tax on the activity that creates that externality. When the amount of the externality produced per unit of output increases as output increases, the correct tax can be determined by using a demand-supply diagram; show this. Assume that the marginal private cost curve slopes upward.

1.2. *(Externalities)* Complete each of the following sentences:
   a. Resources that are available only in a fixed amount are ________ resources.
   b. The possibility that a open-access resource is used until the net marginal value of additional use equals zero is known as the ________.
   c. Resources for which periodic use can be continued indefinitely are known as ________ resources.

1.3. *(Resolving the Common-Pool Problem)* Why have authorities found it so difficult to regulate the fishing catch in the open ocean to allow for a sustainable yield?

LO2 Explain the optimal level of pollution

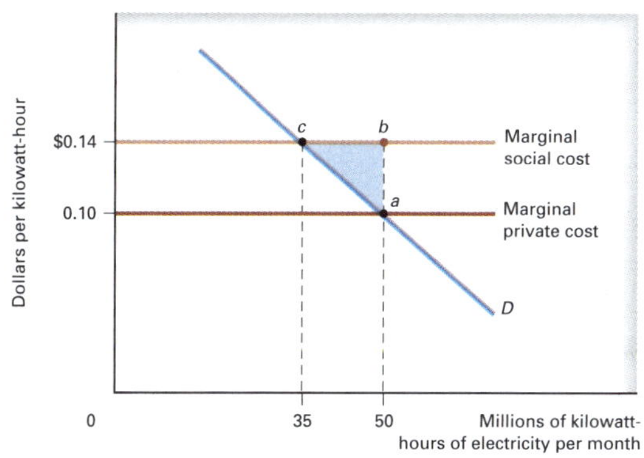

2.1. *(External Costs with Fixed-Production Technology)* Review the situation illustrated in the graph above. If the government sets the price of electricity at the socially optimal level, why is the net gain equal to triangle *abc*, even though consumers now pay a higher price for electricity? What would the net gain be if the government set the price above the optimal level?

2.2. *(External Costs)* Use the data in the table below to answer the following questions.

a. What is the external cost per unit of production?
b. What level is produced if there is no regulation of the externality?
c. What level should be produced to achieve economic efficiency?
d. Calculate the dollar value of the net gain to society from correcting the externality.

Quantity	Marginal Private Benefit (demand)	Marginal Private Cost (supply)	Marginal Social Cost
0	—	$0	$0
1	$10	2	4
2	9	3	5
3	8	4	6
4	7	5	7
5	6	6	8
6	5	7	9
7	4	8	10
8	3	9	11
9	2	10	12
10	1	11	13

2.3. *(External Costs with Variable Technology)* Think of an industry that pollutes the water and has access to variable technology for reducing that pollution. Graphically illustrate and explain the impact of each of the following, other things constant, on the optimal level of water quality:

a. New evidence is discovered about a greater risk of cancer from water pollution.
b. The cost of pollution-control equipment increases.
c. A technological improvement reduces the cost of pollution control.

2.4. *(Market for Pollution Rights)* The following graph shows the market for pollution rights.

a. If there are no restrictions on pollution, what amount is discharged?
b. What is the quantity supplied and the quantity demanded if the government restricts the amount of discharge to Q* but gives the permits away?
c. Where is market equilibrium if the government sells the permits? Illustrate this on the graph.
d. What happens to market equilibrium if the gvernment reduces the amount of discharge permitted to Q**? Illustrate this on the graph.

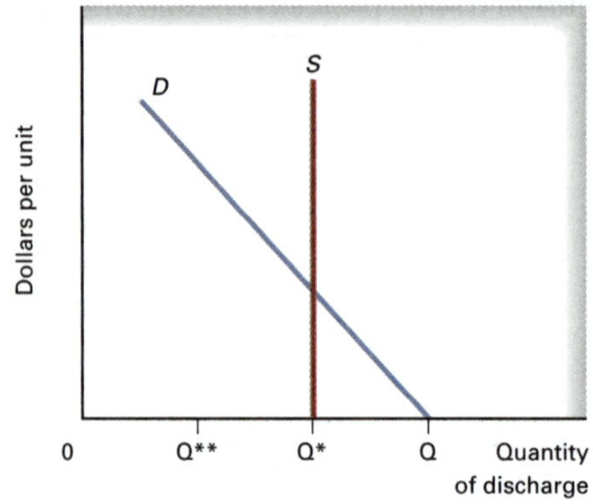

LO3 Assess the role of environmental problems in the economy

3.1. Comment on the efforts that have been taken to address greenhouse gases on an international scale.

3.2 Discuss the steps taken by India on voluntary basis towards sustainable development strategy?

LO4 Describe positive externalities

4.1. *(Positive Externalities)* The value of a home depends in part on how attractive other homes and yards in the neighborhood are. How do local zoning ordinances try to promote land uses that generate external benefits for neighbors?

LO5 Discuss the role of government in poverty alleviation and equity considerations

5.1. What kind of role do governments have to play in poverty alleviation? Is perfect equity always desirable?

LO6 Identify the double market failure criterion

6.1. What do you understand by double market failure criterion? What is the most common example of double market failure?

19 Chapter in Review

KEY TERMS

exhaustible resource
a resource in fixed supply, such as crude oil or coal

renewable resource
a resource that regenerates itself and so can be used indefinitely if used conservatively, such as a properly managed forest

common-pool problem
unrestricted access to a resource results in overuse; use stops only when the marginal benefit drops to zero

fixed-production technology
occurs when the relationship between the output rate and the generation of an externality is fixed; the only way to reduce the externality is to reduce the output

marginal social cost
the sum of the marginal private cost and the marginal external cost of production or consumption

variable technology
occurs when the amount of externality generated at a given rate of output can be reduced by altering the production process

marginal social benefit
the sum of the marginal private benefit and the marginal external benefit of production or consumption

Coase theorem
as long as bargaining costs are low, an efficient solution to the problem of externalities is achieved by assigning property rights to one party or the other

command-and-control environmental regulations
an approach that required polluters to adopt particular technologies to reduce emissions by specific amounts; inflexible regulations based on engineering standards that ignore each firm's unique ways of reducing pollution

economic efficiency approach
an approach that offers each polluter the flexibility to reduce emissions as cost-effectively as possible, given its unique cost conditions; the market for pollution rights is an example

recycling
the process of converting waste products into reusable material

LO1 Define externalities and explain the common-pool problem. An exhaustible resource is available in fixed supply, such as crude oil or coal. A renewable resource can regenerate itself if used conservatively, such as a properly managed forest. Some resources suffer from a common-pool problem because unrestricted access leads to overuse. Production that generates negative externalities results in too much output. Production that generates positive externalities results in too little output. Public policy should tax or otherwise limit production that generates negative externalities and should subsidize or otherwise promote production that generates positive externalities.

LO2 Explain the optimal level of pollution. The optimal amount of environmental quality occurs where the marginal social benefit of an improvement equals its marginal social cost. An upward shift of the marginal benefit curve of environmental quality or a downward shift of its marginal cost curve increases the optimal level of environmental quality. The Coase theorem argues that as long as bargaining costs are low, assigning property rights to one party leads to an efficient solution to the externality problem. The market for pollution permits reflects the Coase theorem in action.

Negative Externalities: The Market for Electricity in the Midwest

If producers base their output on marginal private cost, 50 million kilowatt-hours of electricity are produced per month. The marginal external cost of electricity is the cost of pollution imposed on society. The marginal social cost curve includes both the marginal private cost and the marginal external cost. If producers base their output decisions on marginal social cost, only 35 million kilowatt-hours are produced, which is the optimal output. The total social gain from basing production on marginal social cost is reflected by the blue-shaded triangle.

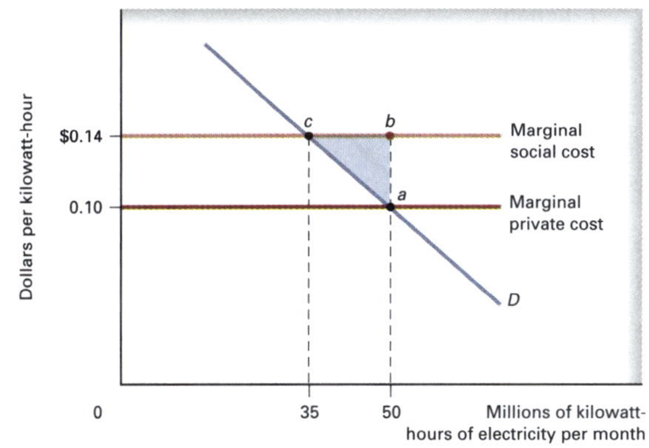

The Optimal Reduction in Greenhouse Gas Emissions

The optimal level of greenhouse gas emissions is found at point *a*, where the marginal social benefit of reducing such emissions equals the marginal social cost. If some lower level of emissions were dictated by the government, the marginal social cost would exceed the marginal social benefit, and social waste would result. The total social waste resulting from a lower than optimal level of emissions is shown by the pink-shaded triangle.

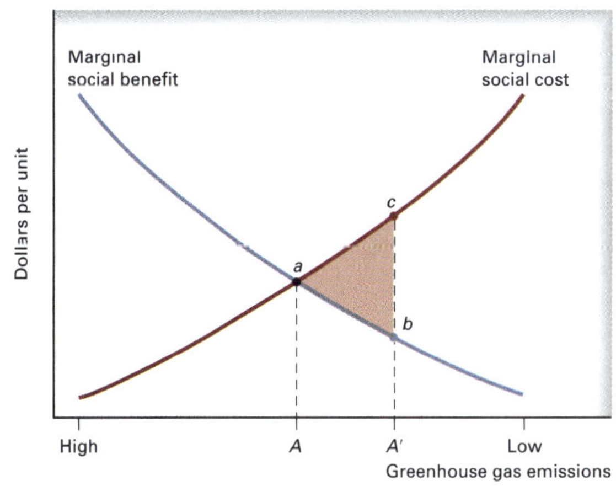

Effect of Changes in Costs or Benefits of Reducing Greenhouse Gas Emissions

Either a reduction in the marginal social cost of cleaner air, as shown in panel (a), or an increase in the marginal social benefit of cleaner air, as shown in panel (b), increases the optimal level of air quality.

(a) Lower cost of reducing emissions

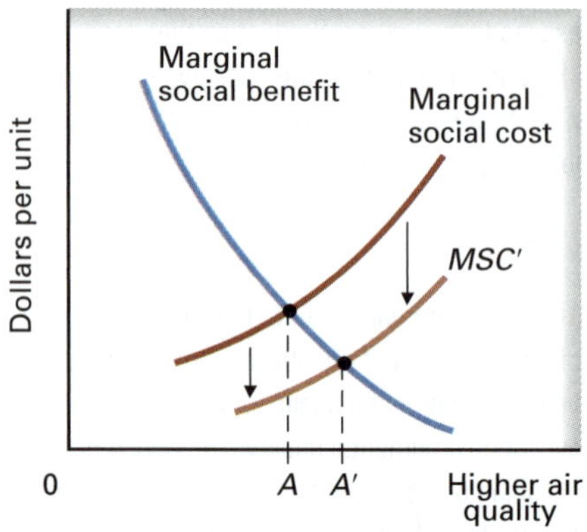

(b) Greater benefit of reducing emissions

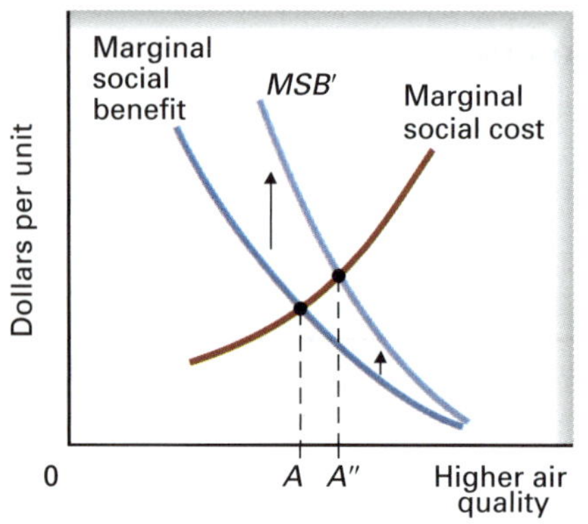

Optimal Allocation of Pollution Rights

Suppose the demand for a river as a discharge service is *D*. In the absence of any environmental controls, polluters dump 250 tons per day, where the marginal benefit of discharge is zero. If regulatory authorities establish 100 tons as the maximum daily level of discharge and then sell the rights, the market for these pollution rights clears at $25 per ton. If the demand for pollution rights increases to *D′* the market-clearing price of pollution rights rises to $35 per ton.

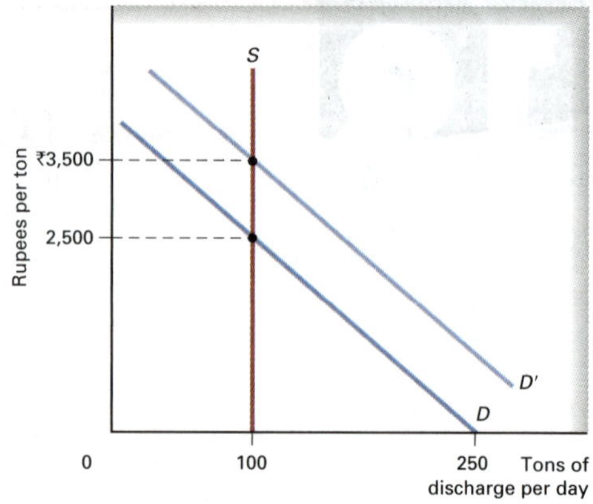

LO3 **Assess the role of environmental problems in the economy.** Here we primarily discuss what steps have been taken to address greenhouse gases internationally. There have been efforts to address greenhouse gases on an international scale. A report by the Intergovernmental Panel on Climate Change, a group sponsored by the United Nations, was approved in May 2007 by more than 120 nations. The study says, to fight global warming, the world must cut emissions of carbon dioxide and other greenhouse gases by (1) sharply improving energy efficiency in buildings, vehicles, and machines; (2) shifting from fossil fuels to nuclear, wind, solar, and other renewable energy sources; (3) preserving forests as absorbers of carbon dioxide, or as "carbon sinks"; and (4) capping agricultural emissions. The United States and China, which account for more than 40 percent of the world's emissions, approved the report but offered no indication that they would reverse their opposition to mandatory emission reductions. The report said that such reforms would require lifestyle changes, increased prices for some basics including gasoline and electricity, and greater investment in research and development.

LO4 **Describe positive externalities.** Positive externalities occur when consumption or production benefits other consumers or other firms. Aside from greenhouse gases, air and waterways are getting cleaner. The air is cleaner because of stricter emissions standards for motor vehicles, and waterways are cleaner because of billions spent on sewage treatment plants. Toxic waste sites do not pose as great a health threat as other forms of pollution such as smog and pesticide residue, but toxic waste often gets more media and political attention.

Education and Positive Externalities

In the absence of government intervention, the equilibrium quantity of education is *E*, where the marginal private benefit of education equals the marginal cost as reflected by the supply curve. Education also confers a positive externality on the rest of society, so the social benefit exceeds the private benefit. At quantity *E*, the marginal social benefit exceeds the marginal cost, so more education increases social welfare. In this situation, government tries to increase education to *E′*, where the marginal social benefit equals the marginal cost.

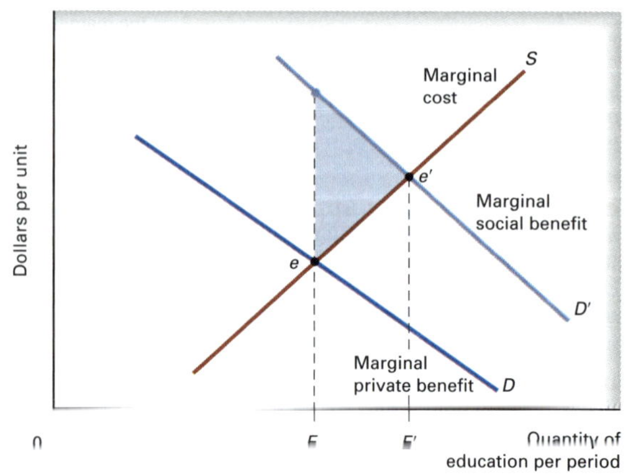

LO5 **Discuss the role of government in poverty alleviation and equity considerations.** Here we primarily discuss if equity and efficiency issues are separate or inter-dependant. Equity and efficiency issues are indeed interdependent for essentially two reasons. *Firstly*, we know that equity and efficiency issues are not separate. In full perspective, the relation between equality and productivity doubtless runs as follows: if wealth and income were very unequally distributed, there is a range over which the community would probably achieve both higher output and more equality by re-distributing resources from rich to poor. If re-distribution continued, a point of maximum productivity and moderate equality would be reached. Thereafter, additional degrees of equality could be purchased only at the expense of some sacrifice of productivity. These sacrifices would be small at first, but would increase steadily till, at the limit, complete equality would be reached only by a very considerable sacrifice of total output. That is, equality and productivity become competitive values beyond a certain point because of two reasons. One is the adverse incentive effect of progressive taxation on initiative, risk taking, and enterprise development. Second is the adverse incentive effect of receiving income without expending effort. Here, in brief, is the central problem of any government—how much more (or less) equality do we want in terms of the sacrifice (or gain) in productivity involved in moving towards it.

Secondly, the kind of lump sum re-distribution envisaged in the second fundamental theorem of Welfare Economics is not in general feasible. Accordingly, re-distribution essentially always involves some distortions and given these distortions, it is not obvious that the kind of passive role for the government called for by the Second Welfare Theorem is desirable.

LO6 **Identify the double market failure criterion.** It has been said earlier that the presence of an endemic market failure may call for public intervention in some form but not necessarily through government production/provision of the relevant goods. In order to decide the question whether public intervention should be in the shape of direct production/provision of certain goods by the government or through other policies, it is prudent to use the so-called "double market failure criterion" (Minhas, 1991; Kaur, 2003). First, one must establish sound evidence of market failure or a consensus for the acceptance of some distributional goal. Second, one must also search for evidence that a less intrusive policy cannot be utilized, or effective contracts for private production of public goods cannot be devised. Whenever double-market failure criterion is fulfilled, the case for public sector production/provision of such goods is usually strong.

CHAPTER

20

Learning Outcomes

LO[1] Describe the gains that trade brings

LO[2] Discuss the reasons for international specialization

LO[3] Explain trade restrictions and welfare loss

LO[4] Describe ways countries have reduced or eliminated trade barriers

LO[5] List and describe the arguments in favor of trade restrictions

LO[6] Explain how the balance of payments works

LO[7] Discuss foreign exchange rates and markets

LO[8] Define fixed and flexible exchange rates

International Trade *and* Finance

© ARTPARTNER-IMAGES/PHOTOGRAPHER'S CHOICE/GETTY IMAGES

“If the United States is such a rich and productive country, why does it import so many goods and services?”

Pulling a Levi’s jeans from Mexico, pulling a Benetton sweater from Italy over your head, and lacing up your Timberland boots from Thailand; after a breakfast that included coffee from Brazil, you climbed into your Volvo from Sweden and headed for a lecture by a visiting professor from Hungary; this is a routine morning scene in the United States. If the United States is such a rich and productive country, why do they import so many goods and services? Why don’t they produce everything themselves? And why do some producers try to restrict foreign trade? Answers to these and other questions are addressed in this chapter.

What do you think?

The U.S. government should eliminate all trade restrictions.

Strongly Disagree 1 2 3 4 5 6 7 *Strongly Agree*

The world is a giant shopping mall, and Americans are big spenders. For example, the U.S. population is less than 5 percent of the world’s population, but Americans buy more than half the Rolls Royces and diamonds sold around the world. Americans also buy Japanese cars, French wine, European vacations, Chinese products galore, and thousands of other goods and services from around the globe. Foreigners buy U.S. products too—grain, aircraft, movies, software, trips to New York City, and thousands of other goods and services. In this chapter, we examine the gains from international trade and the effects of trade restrictions on the allocation of resources. The analysis is based on the familiar tools of demand and supply.

Topics discussed in Chapter 20 include:

- Gains from trade
- Absolute and comparative advantage revisited
- Tariffs
- Quotas
- Welfare loss from trade restrictions
- Arguments for trade restrictions
- Balance of payments
- Trade deficits and surpluses
- Foreign exchange markets
- Purchasing power parity
- Flexible exchange rates
- Fixed exchange rates

LO1 The Gains from Trade

A family from Virginia that sits down for a meal of Kansas prime rib, Idaho potatoes, and California string beans, with Georgia peach cobbler for dessert, is benefiting from interstate trade. You already understand why the residents of one state trade with those of another. Back in Chapter 2, you learned about the gains arising from specialization and exchange. You may recall how you and your roommate could maximize output when you each specialized. The law of comparative advantage says that the individual with the lowest opportunity cost of producing a particular good should specialize in that good. Just as individuals benefit from specialization and exchange, so do states and, indeed, nations. To reap the gains that arise from specialization, countries engage in international trade. *Each country specializes in making goods with the lowest opportunity cost.*

A Profile of Exports and Imports

Just as some states are more involved in interstate trade than others, some nations are more involved in international trade than others. For example, exports account for about one-quarter of the gross domestic product (GDP) in the United Kingdom; about one-third of GDP in Canada; and about half of GDP in Germany, Switzerland, and Sweden. Despite the perception that Japan has a huge export sector, exports make up only about one-seventh of its GDP.

U.S. Exports and India's Exports

U.S. exports of goods and services amounted to \$1.6 trillion, or about 12 percent of GDP in 2007. The left panel of Exhibit 1a shows the composition by major category. The largest category is services, which accounted for 30.2 percent of U.S. exports. U.S. service exports include transportation, insurance, banking, education, consulting, and tourism. Capital goods ranked second at 27.2 percent of exports in 2007. Capital goods include high-tech products, such as computers and jet aircraft. Third most important are industrial supplies, at 19.2 percent of the total. Capital goods and industrial supplies help foreign producers make stuff and accounted for nearly half of U.S. exports. Consumer goods (except food, which appears separately) accounted for only 10.9 percent of exports. Consumer goods include entertainment products, such as movies and recorded music.

India's exports of principal components amounted to \$254,402 million in 2010–11. Panel (a) of Exhibit 1b shows the composition by major category. The highest category is that of manufactured goods, at 66 percent, followed by re-exports of petroleum products, which stand at 16 percent. The services sector has emerged as an independent entity only recently. The three broad categories of commercial services include transport, travel, and other commercial services. In 2009, India ranked among the first five countries in the export of other commercial services, which include computer and information services; communication services; and personal, cultural, and recreational services.

U.S. Imports and India's Imports

U.S. imports of goods and services in 2007 totaled \$2.3 trillion, or about 17 percent relative to GDP. The right panel of Exhibit 1a shows the composition of U.S. imports. The most important category, at 27.1 percent, is industrial supplies, such as crude oil from Venezuela and raw metals, including lead, zinc, and copper, from around the world. Whereas consumer goods accounted for only 10.9 percent of U.S. exports, they were 23.4 percent of imports. Imported consumer goods include electronics from Taiwan, shoes from Brazil, and all kinds of products from China. Ranked third in importance is capital goods, at 18.9 percent, such as printing presses from Germany. Note that services, which accounted for 30.2 percent of U.S. exports, were only 16.1 percent of imports.

India's import of principal components amounted to \$352,575 million in 2010–11. Panel (b) of Exhibit 1b shows the composition of India's imports. The most important category is petroleum crude and products, to the tune of 30 percent, followed by capital goods, which make up 20 percent of the total imports. In commercial services imports, India moved from 13th position in 2005 and 2008 to 12th position in 2009, with a 2.5 percent share.

Exhibit 1a

Composition of U.S. Exports and Imports in 2007

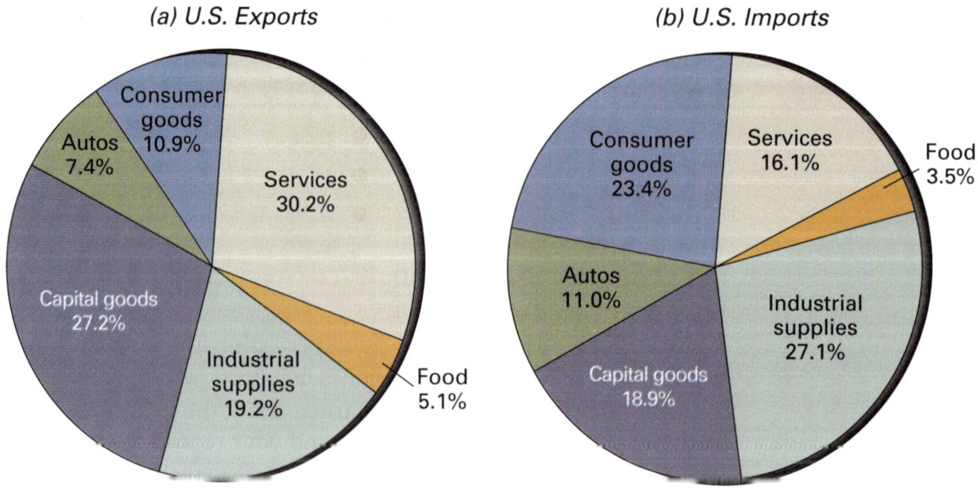

SOURCE: Based on government estimates in "International Data," *Survey of Current Business* 88 (December 2008), Table F, p. D-58.

Exhibit 1b

Composition of India's Exports and Imports in 2010–11

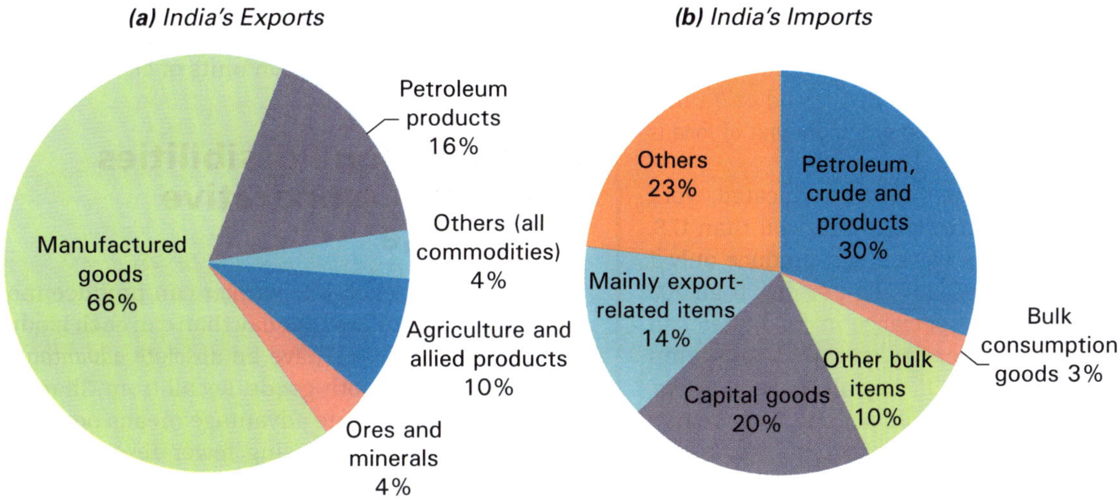

SOURCE: Handbook of Statistics on Indian Economy 2010-11, www.rbi.org.in.

Trading Partners

India's major trading partners are EU countries, U.S., U.A.E, and China. To give you some feel for America's trading partners, here are the top 10 destinations for merchandise exports in 2007: Canada, the European Union, Mexico, China, Japan, South Korea, Taiwan, Singapore, Brazil, and Hong Kong. The top 10 sources of merchandise imports are the European Union, China, Canada, Mexico, Japan, South Korea, Taiwan, Venezuala, Saudi Arabia, and Nigeria.

Production Possibilities Without Trade

The rationale behind most international trade is obvious. The United States grows little coffee because the climate is not suited to coffee. More revealing, however, are the gains from trade where the comparative advantage is not so obvious. Suppose that just two goods—food and clothing—are produced and consumed and that there are only two countries in the world—the United States, with a labor force of 100 million workers, and the mythical country of Izodia, with 200 million workers. The conclusions derived from this simple model have general relevance for international trade.

Exhibit 2 presents production possibilities tables for each country, based on the size of the labor force and the productivity of workers in each country. The exhibit assumes that each country has a given technology and that labor is efficiently employed. If no trade occurs between countries, Exhibit 2 also represents each country's *consumption possibilities* table. The production numbers imply that each worker in the United States can produce either 6 units of food or 3 units of clothing per day. If all 100 mil-

Exhibit 2

Production Possibilities Schedules for the United States and Izodia

(a) United States

Production Possibilities with 100 Million Workers (millions of units per day)

	U_1	U_2	U_3	U_4	U_5	U_6
Food	600	480	360	240	120	0
Clothing	0	60	120	180	240	300

(b) Izodia

Production Possibilities with 200 Million Workers (millions of units per day)

	I_1	I_2	I_3	I_4	I_5	I_6
Food	200	160	120	80	40	0
Clothing	0	80	160	240	320	400

© IMAGE SOURCE

lion U.S. workers produce food, they make 600 million units per day, as shown in column U_1 in panel (a). If all U.S. workers make clothing, they turn out 300 million units per day, as shown in column U_6. The columns in between show some workers making food and some making clothing. Because a U.S. worker can produce either 6 units of food or 3 units of clothing, *the opportunity cost of 1 more unit of food is 0.5 units of clothing.*

Suppose Izodian workers are less educated, work with less capital, and farm less fertile soil than U.S. workers, so each Izodian worker can produce only 1 unit of food or 2 units of clothing per day. If all 200 million Izodian workers specialize in food, they can make 200 million units per day, as shown in column I_1 in panel (b) of Exhibit 2. If they all make clothing, total output is 400 million units per day, as shown in column I_6. Some intermediate production possibilities are also listed in the exhibit. Because an Izodian worker can produce either 1 unit of food or 2 units of clothing, *their opportunity cost of 1 more unit of food is 2 units of clothing.*

We can convert the data in Exhibit 2 to a production possibilities frontier for each country, as shown in Exhibit 3. In each diagram, the amount of food produced is measured on the vertical axis and the amount of clothing on the horizontal axis. U.S. combinations are shown in the left panel by U_1, U_2, and so on. Izodian combinations are shown in the right panel by I_1, I_2, and so on. Because we assume for simplicity that resources are perfectly adaptable to the production of each commodity, each production possibilities curve is a straight line. The slope of this line differs between countries because the opportunity cost of production differs between countries.

Exhibit 3 illustrates possible combinations of food and clothing that residents of each country can produce and consume if all resources are efficiently employed and there is no trade between the two countries. **Autarky** is the situation of national self-sufficiency, in which there is no economic interaction with foreign producers or consumers. Suppose that U.S. producers maximize profit and U.S. consumers maximize utility with the combination of 240 million units of food and 180 million units of clothing—combination U_4. This is called the *autarky equilibrium*. Suppose also that Izodians are in autarky equilibrium, identified as combination I_3, of 120 million units of food and 160 million units of clothing.

autarky
national self-sufficiency; no economic interaction with foreigners

Exhibit 3

Production Possibilities Frontiers for the United States and Izodia Without Trade (millions of units per day)

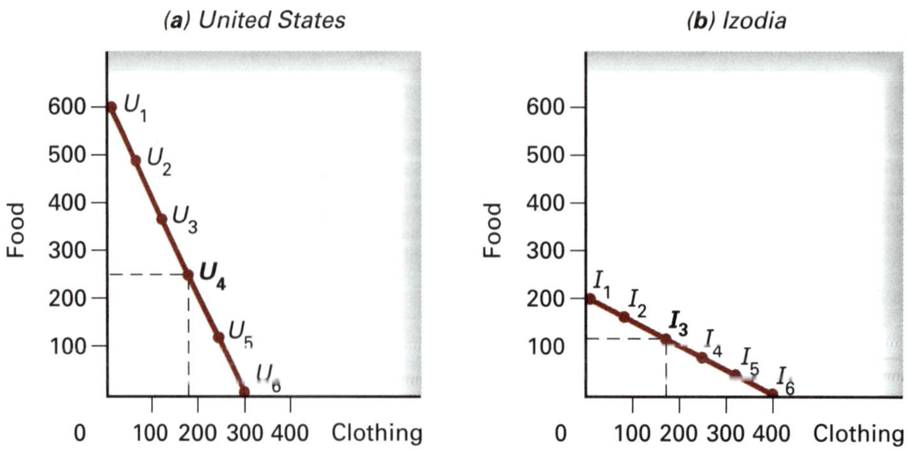

Consumption Possibilities Based on Comparative Advantage

In our example, each U.S. worker can produce more clothing and more food per day than can each Izodian worker, so Americans have an *absolute advantage* in the production of both goods. Recall from Chapter 2 that having an absolute advantage means being able to produce something using fewer resources than other producers require. Should the U.S. economy remain in autarky—that is, self-sufficient in both food and clothing productions—or could there be gains from specialization and trade?

As long as the opportunity cost of production differs between the two countries, there are gains from specialization and trade. *According to the law of comparative advantage, each country should specialize in producing the good with the lower opportunity cost.* The opportunity cost of producing 1 more unit of food is 0.5 units of clothing in the United States compared with 2 units of clothing in Izodia. Because the opportunity cost of producing food is lower in the United States than in Izodia, both countries gain if the United States specializes in food and exports some to Izodia, and Izodia specializes in clothing and exports some to the United States.

Before countries can trade, however, they must agree on how much of one good exchanges for another—that is, they must agree on the **terms of trade**. As long as Americans can get more than 0.5 units of clothing for each unit of food produced, and as long as Izodians can get more than 0.5 units of food for each unit of clothing produced, both countries will be better off specializing. Suppose that market forces shape the terms of trade so that 1 unit of clothing exchanges for 1 unit of food. Americans thus trade 1 unit of food to Izodians for 1 unit of clothing. To produce 1 unit of clothing themselves, Americans would have to sacrifice 2 units of food. Likewise, Izodians trade 1 unit of clothing to Americans for 1 unit of food, which is only half what Izodians would sacrifice to produce 1 unit of food themselves.

Exhibit 4 shows that with 1 unit of food trading for 1 unit of clothing, Americans and Izodians can consume anywhere along their blue consumption possibilities frontiers. *The consumption possibilities frontier* shows a nation's possible combinations of goods available as a result of specialization and exchange. (Note that the U.S. consumption possibilities curve does not extend to the right of 400 million units of clothing, because Izodia could produce no more than that.) The amount each country actually consumes depends on the relative preferences for food and clothing. Suppose Americans select combination *U* in panel (a) and Izodians select point *I* in panel (b).

Without trade, the United States produces and consumes 240 million units of food and 180 million units of clothing. With trade, the Americans specialize to produce 600 million units of food; they eat 400 million units and exchange the rest for 200 million units of Izodian clothing. This consumption combination is reflected by point U. Through exchange, Americans increase their consumption of both food and clothing.

Without trade, Izodians produce and consume 120 million units of food and 160 million units of clothing. With trade, Izodians specialize to produce 400 million units of clothing; they wear 200 million and exchange the rest for 200 million units of U.S. food. This consumption combination is shown by point *I*. Through trade, Izodians, like Americans, are able to increase their consumption of both goods. How is this possible?

Because Americans are more efficient in the production of food and Izodians are more efficient in the production of clothing, total output increases when each specializes. Without specialization, total world production was 360 million units of food and 340 million units of clothing. With specialization, food increases to 600 million units and clothing to 400 million units. Thus, both countries increase consumption with trade. *Although the United States has an absolute advantage in both goods, differences in the opportunity cost of production between the two nations ensure that specialization and exchange result in mutual gains*. Remember that comparative advantage, not absolute advantage, creates gains from specialization and trade. The only constraint on trade is that, for each good, *total world production must equal total world consumption*.

We simplified trade relations in our example to highlight the gains from specialization and exchange. We assumed that each country would completely specialize in producing a particular good, that resources were equally adaptable to the production of either good, that the costs of transporting goods from one country to another were inconsequential, and that there were no problems in arriving at the terms of trade. The world is not that simple. For example, we don't expect a country to produce just one good. Regardless, specialization based on the law of comparative advantage still leads to gains from trade.

Exhibit 4

Production (and Consumption) Possibility Frontiers with Trade (millions of units per day)

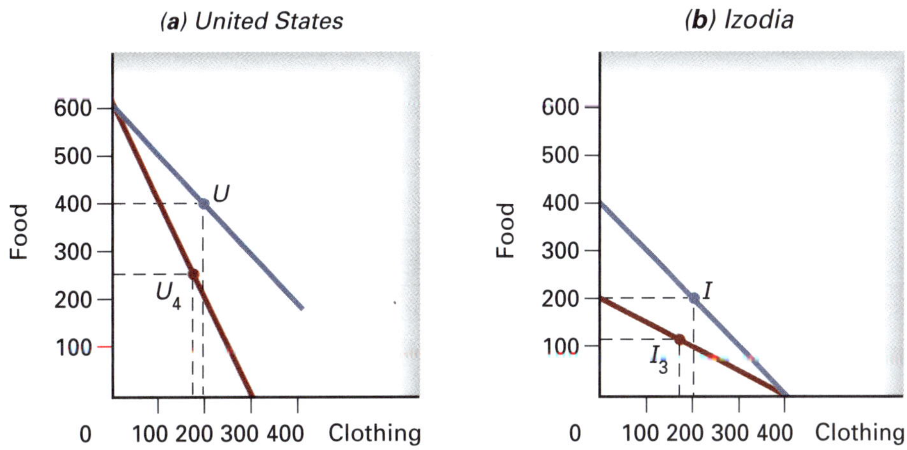

terms of trade how much of one good exchanges for a unit of another good

LO2 Reasons for International Specialization

Countries trade with one another—or, more precisely, people and firms in one country trade with those in another—because each side expects to gain from exchange. How do we know what each country should produce and what each should trade?

Differences in Resource Endowments

Differences in resource endowments often create differences in the opportunity cost of production across countries. Some countries are blessed with an abundance of fertile land and favorable growing seasons. The United States, for example, has been called the "breadbasket of the world" because of its rich farmland ideal for growing corn. Coffee grows best in the climate and elevation of Colombia, Brazil, and Jamaica. Honduras has the ideal climate for bananas. Thus, the United States exports corn and imports coffee and bananas. Seasonal differences across countries also encourage trade. For example, in the winter, Americans import fruit from Chile, and Canadians travel to Florida for sun and fun. In the summer, Americans export fruit to Chile, and Americans travel to Canada for camping and hiking.

Resources are often concentrated in particular countries: crude oil in Saudi Arabia, fertile soil in the United States, copper ore in Chile, rough diamonds in South Africa. The United States grows abundant supplies of oil seeds such as soybeans and sunflowers, but does not have enough crude oil to satisfy domestic demand. Thus, the United States exports oil seeds and imports crude oil. More generally, *countries export products they can produce more cheaply in return for products that are unavailable domestically or are cheaper elsewhere.* Remember, trade is based on comparative advantage, which is the ability to produce something at a lower opportunity cost than other producers face.

Exhibit 5 on the next page shows, for 12 key commodities, U.S. production as a percentage of U.S. consumption. If production falls short of consumption, this means the United States imports the difference. For example, because America grows coffee only in Hawaii, U.S. production is only 1 percent of U.S. consumption, so nearly all coffee is imported. The exhibit also shows that U.S. production falls short of consumption for oil and for metals such as lead, zinc, copper, and aluminum. If production exceeds consumption, the United States exports the difference.

Exhibit 5

U.S. Production as a Percentage of U.S. Consumption for Various Commodities

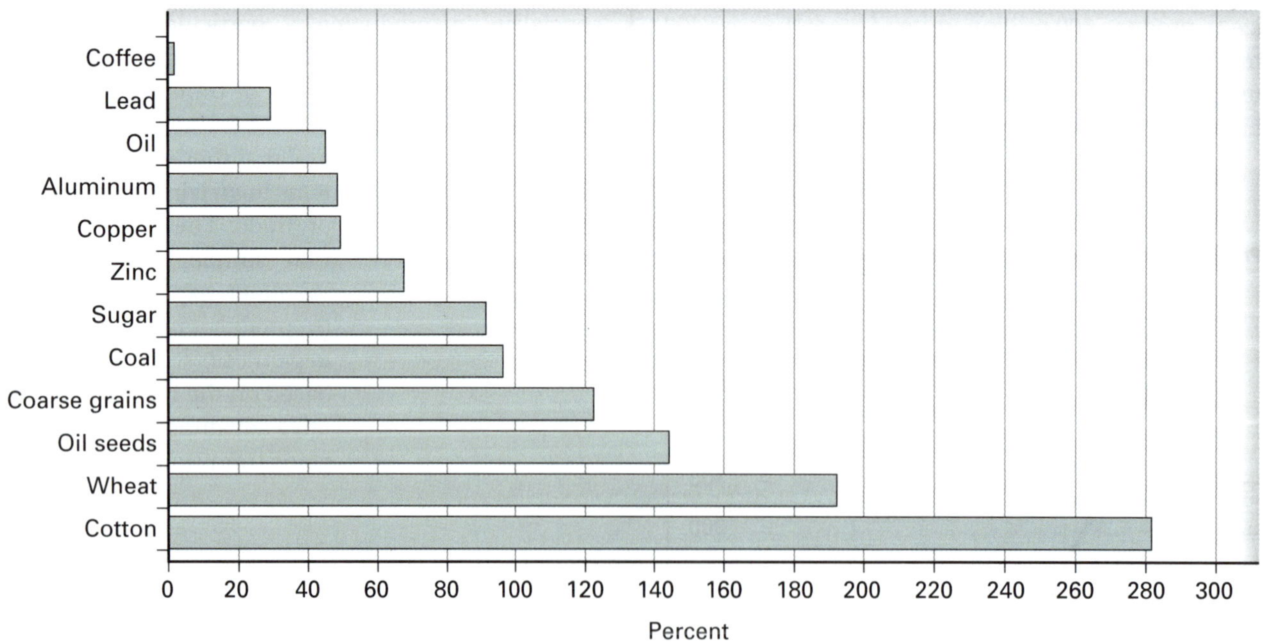

SOURCE: Based on annual figures from *The Economist World in Figures: 2007 Edition* (London: Profile Books, 2007).

For example, U.S.-grown cotton amounts to 281 percent of U.S. cotton consumption, so most U.S. grown cotton is exported. U.S. production also exceeds consumption for other crops, including wheat, oil seeds, and coarse grains (corn, barley, oats). In short, when it comes to basic commodities, the United States is a net importer of oil and metals and a net exporter of farm crops.

Economies of Scale

If production is subject to *economies of scale*—that is, if the long-run average cost of production falls as a firm expands its scale of operation—countries can gain from trade if each nation specializes. Such specialization allows firms in each nation to produce more, which reduces average costs. The primary reason for establishing the single integrated market of the European Union was to offer producers there a large, open market of now more than 500 million consumers. Producers could thereby achieve economies of scale. Firms and countries producing at the lowest opportunity costs are most competitive in international markets. For example, 60 percent of the world's buttons come from a single Chinese city.

Differences in Tastes

Even if all countries had identical resource endowments and combined those resources with equal efficiency, each country would still gain from trade as long as tastes differed among countries. Consumption patterns differ across countries and some of this results from differences in tastes. For example, the Czechs and Irish drink three times as much beer per capita as do the Swiss and Swedes. The French drink three times as much wine as do Australians. The Danes eat twice as much pork as do Americans. Americans eat twice as much chicken as do Hungarians. Soft drinks are four times more popular in the United States than in Europe. The English like tea; Americans, coffee. Algeria has an ideal climate for growing grapes (vineyards there date back to Roman times). But Algeria's population is 99 percent Muslim, a religion that forbids alcohol consumption. Thus, Algeria exports wine.

LO3 Trade Restrictions and Welfare Loss

Despite the benefits of exchange, nearly all countries at one time or another erect trade barriers, which benefit some domestic producers but harm other domestic producers and all domestic consumers. In this section, we consider the effects of trade barriers and the reasons they are imposed.

Consumer Surplus and Producer Surplus from Market Exchange

Before we explore the net effects of world trade on social welfare, let's develop a framework showing

>> Different tastes result in different consumption patterns, which affect trade.

or

?

© BRAND X PICTURES/THINKSTOCK / © ISTOCKPHOTO/THINKSTOCK

Exhibit 6

Consumer Surplus and Producer Surplus

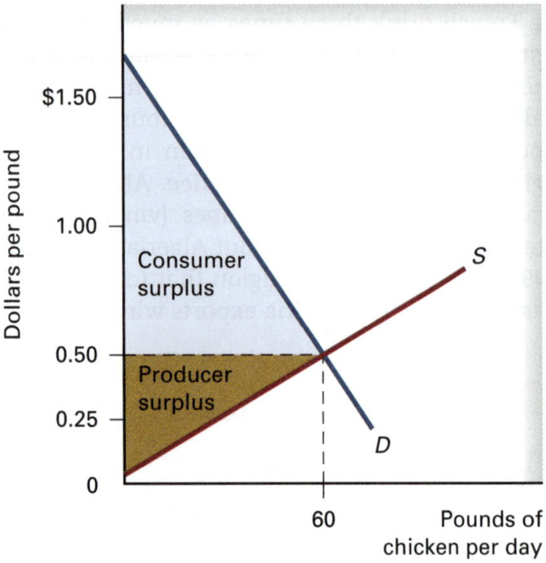

the benefits that consumers and producers get from market exchange. Consider a hypothetical market for chicken, shown in Exhibit 6. As discussed way back in Chapter 4, the height of the demand curve shows what consumers are willing and able to pay for each additional pound of chicken. In effect, the height of the demand curve shows the *marginal benefit* consumers expect from that pound of chicken. For example, the demand curve indicates that some consumers in this market are willing to pay $1.50 or more per pound for the first few pounds of chicken. But every consumer gets to buy chicken at the market-clearing price, which here is $0.50 per pound. Most consumers thus get a bonus, or a surplus, from market exchange.

The blue-shaded triangle below the demand curve and above the market price reflects the *consumer surplus* in this market, which is the difference between the most that consumers would pay for 60 pounds of chicken per day and the actual amount they do pay. We all enjoy a consumer surplus from most products we buy.

Producers usually derive a similar surplus. The height of the supply curve shows what producers are willing and able to accept for each additional pound of chicken. That is, the height of the supply curve shows the expected *marginal cost* from producing each additional pound of chicken. For example, the supply curve indicates that some producers face a marginal cost of $0.25 or less per pound for supplying the first few pounds of chicken. But every producer gets to sell chicken for the market-clearing price of $0.50 per pound. The gold-shaded triangle above the supply curve and below the market price reflects the *producer surplus,* which is the difference between the actual amount that producers receive for 60 pounds of chicken and what they would accept to supply that amount.

world price
the price at which a good is traded on the world market; determined by the world demand and world supply for the good

The point is that market exchange usually generates a surplus, or a bonus, for both consumers and producers. In the balance of this chapter, we will continue to look at the gains from international trade and how trade restrictions affect consumer and producer surplus.

Tariffs

A *tariff,* a term first introduced in Chapter 3, is a tax on imports. (Tariffs can apply to exports, too, but we will focus on import tariffs.) A tariff can be either *specific,* such as a tariff of $5 per barrel of oil, or *ad valorem,* such as 10 percent on the import price of jeans. Consider the effects of a specific tariff on a particular good. In Exhibit 7 on the next page, D is the U.S. demand for sugar and S is the supply of

Exhibit 7

Effect of a Tariff

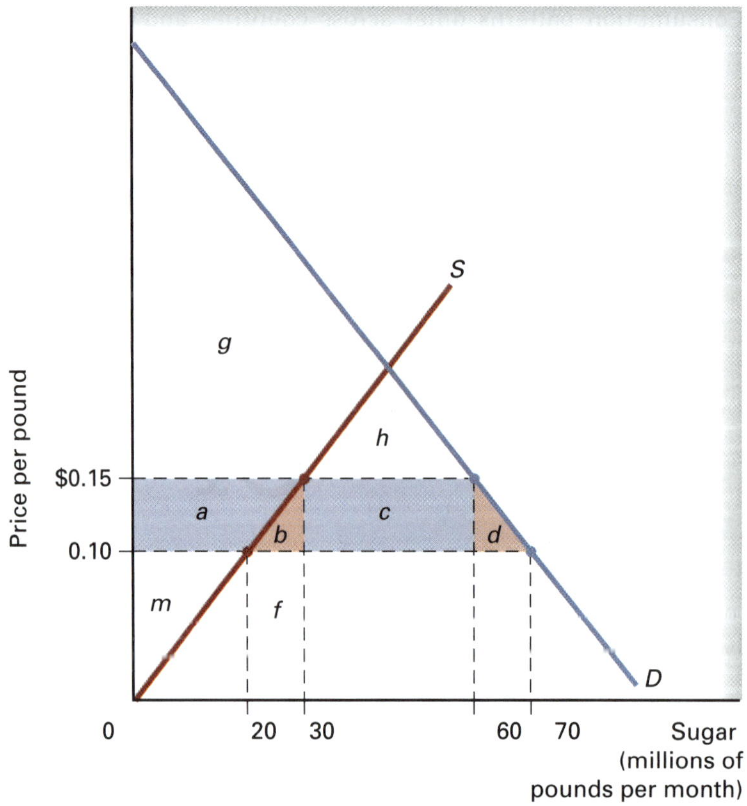

sugar from U.S. growers (there were about 10,000 U.S. sugarcane growers in 2007). Suppose that the world price of sugar is $0.10 per pound, as it was in June 2007. The **world price** is determined by the world supply and demand for a product. It is the price at which any supplier can sell output on the world market and at which any demander can purchase output on the world market.

With free trade, any U.S. consumers could buy any amount desired at the world price of $0.10 per pound, so the quantity demanded is 70 million pounds per month, of which U.S. producers supply 20 million pounds and importers supply 50 million pounds. Because U.S. buyers can purchase sugar at the world price, U.S. producers can't charge more than that. Now suppose that a specific tariff of $0.05 is imposed on each pound of imported sugar, raising its price from $0.10 to $0.15 per pound. U.S. producers can therefore raise their own price to $0.15 per pound as well without losing business to imports. At the higher price, the quantity supplied by U.S. producers increases to 30 million pounds, but the quantity demanded by U.S. consumers declines to 60 million pounds. Because quantity demanded has declined and quantity supplied by U.S. producers has increased, U.S. imports fall from 50 million to 30 million pounds per month.

Because the U.S. price is higher after the tariff, U.S. consumers are worse off. Their loss in consumer surplus is identified in Exhibit 7 by the combination of the blue- and pink-shaded areas. Because both the U.S. price and the quantity supplied by U.S. producers have increased, their total revenue increases by the areas *a* plus *b* plus *f*. But only area *a* represents an increase in producer surplus. Revenue represented by the areas *b* plus *f* merely offsets the higher marginal cost U.S. producers face in expanding sugar output from 20 million to 30 million pounds per month. Area *b* represents part of the net welfare loss to the domestic economy because those 10 million pounds could have been imported for $0.10 per pound rather than produced domestically at a higher marginal cost.

Government revenue from the tariff is identified by area *c*, which equals the tariff of $0.05 per pound multiplied by the 30 million pounds imported, for tariff revenue of $1.5 million per month. Tariff revenue is a loss to consumers, but because the tariff goes to the government, it can be used to lower taxes or to increase public services, so it's not a loss to the U.S. economy. Area *d* shows a loss in consumer surplus because less sugar is consumed at the higher price. This loss is not redistributed to anyone else, so area *d* reflects part of the net welfare loss of the tariff. Therefore, areas *b* and *d* show the domestic economy's net welfare loss of the tariff; *the two triangles measure a loss in consumer surplus that is not offset by a gain to anyone in the domestic economy.*

In summary: Of the total loss in U.S. consumer surplus (areas *a*, *b*, *c*, and *d*) resulting from the tariff, area *a* goes to U.S producers, area *c* becomes government revenue, but areas *b* and *d* are net losses in domestic social welfare.

The table below compares economic welfare when trade is unrestricted and when trade is restricted with a tariff. Letters refer to the regions marked in Exhibit 7. The area *b* + *d* shows the fall in total surplus and represents the dead weight loss of the tariff.

	Before Tariff	After Tariff	Change
Consumer Surplus	$g + h + a + b + c + d$	$g + h$	$-(a + b + c + d)$
Producer Surplus	m	$m + a$	$+ a$
Government Revenue	None	c	$+ c$
Total Surplus	$g + h + a + b + c + d + m$	$g + h + m + a + c$	$(b + d)$

The area *b* + *d* shows the fall in total surplus and represents the dead weight loss of the tariff

© PETER SZEKELY/ALAMY

Import Quotas

An *import quota* is a legal limit on the amount of a commodity that can be imported. Quotas usually target imports from certain countries. For example, a quota may limit furniture from China or shoes from Brazil. To have an impact on the domestic market, a quota must be set below what would be imported with free trade. Consider a quota on the U.S. market for sugar. In panel (a) of Exhibit 8, *D* is the U.S. demand curve and *S* is the supply curve of U.S. sugar producers. Suppose again that the world price of sugar is $0.10 per pound. With free trade, that price would prevail in the U.S. market as well, and a total of 70 million pounds would be demanded per month. U.S. producers would supply 20 million pounds and importers, 50 million pounds. With a quota of 50 million pounds or more per month, the U.S. price would remain the same as the world price of $0.10 per pound, and quantity would be 70 million pounds per month. In short, a quota of at least 50 million pounds would not raise the U.S. price above the world price because 50 million pounds were imported without a quota. A more stringent quota, however, would cut imports, which, as we'll see, would raise the U.S. price.

Suppose U.S. trade officials impose an import quota of 30 million pounds per month. As long as the U.S. price is at or above the world price of $0.10 per pound, foreign producers will supply 30 million pounds. So at prices at or above $0.10 per pound, the total supply of sugar to the U.S. market is found by adding 30 million pounds of imported sugar to the amount supplied by U.S. producers. U.S. and foreign producers would never sell in the U.S. market for less than $0.10 per pound because they can always get that price on the world market. Thus, the supply curve that sums domestic production and imports is horizontal at the world price of $0.10 per pound and remains so until the quantity supplied reaches 50 million pounds.

Again, for prices above $0.10 per pound, the new supply curve, S′, adds horizontally the 30-million-pound quota to S, the supply curve of U.S. producers. The U.S. price is found where this new supply curve, S′, intersects the domestic demand curve, which in the left panel of Exhibit 8 occurs at point *e*. *By limiting imports, the quota raises the domestic price of sugar above the world price and reduces quantity below the free trade level.* (Note that to compare more easily the effects of tariffs and quotas, this quota is designed to yield the same equilibrium price and quantity as the tariff examined earlier.)

Panel (b) of Exhibit 8 shows the distribution and efficiency effects of the quota. As a result of the quota, U.S. consumer surplus declines by the combined blue and pink areas. Area *a* becomes producer surplus and thus involves no loss of U.S. welfare. Area c shows the increased economic profit to those permitted by the quota to sell Americans 30 million pounds for $0.15 per pound, or $0.05 above the world price. If foreign exporters rather than U.S. importers reap this profit, area c reflects a net loss in U.S. welfare.

Area *b* shows a welfare loss to the U.S. economy, because sugar could have been purchased abroad for $0.10 per pound, and the U.S. resources employed to increase sugar production could have been used more efficiently producing other goods. Area *d* is also a welfare loss because it reflects a reduction in consumer surplus with no offsetting gain to anyone. Thus, areas *b* and *d* in panel (b) of Exhibit 8 measure the minimum U.S. welfare loss from the quota. If the profit from quota rights (area c) accrues to foreign producers, this increases the U.S. welfare loss.

Quotas in Practice

The United States has granted quotas to specific countries. These countries, in turn, distribute these quota rights to their exporters through a variety of

Exhibit 8

Effect of a Quota

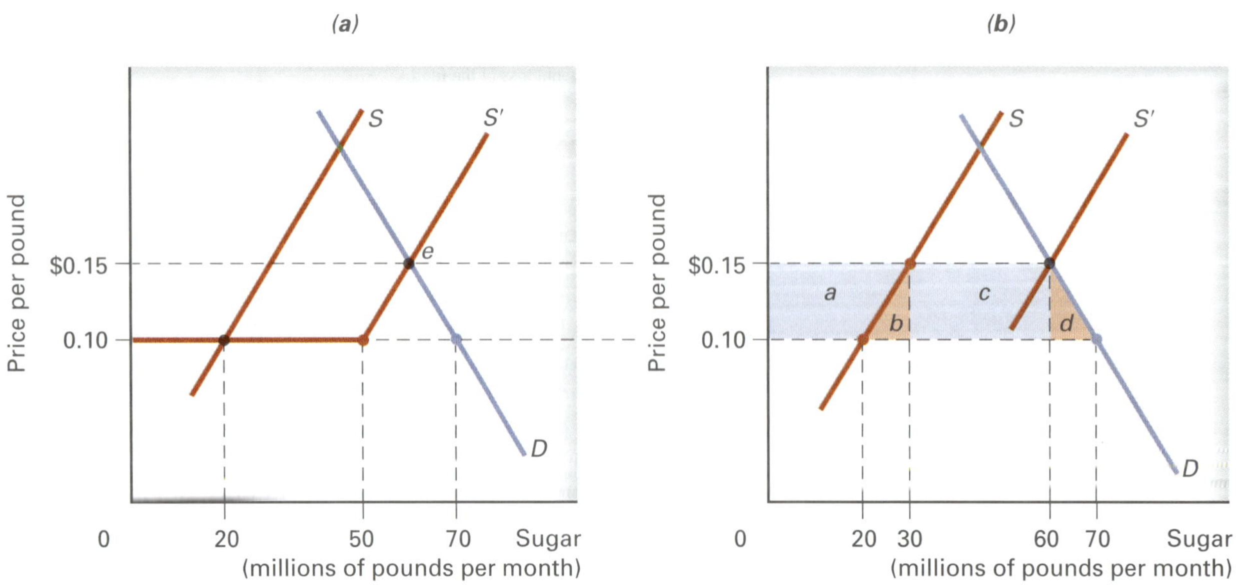

means. *By rewarding domestic and foreign producers with higher prices, the quota system creates two groups intent on securing and perpetuating these quotas.* Lobbyists for foreign producers work the halls of Congress, seeking the right to export to the United States. This strong support from producers, coupled with a lack of opposition from consumers (who remain rationally ignorant for the most part), has resulted in quotas that have lasted decades. For example, sugar quotas have been around more than 50 years. In January 2009, the world price of sugar was about $0.12 a pound, but U.S. businesses that need sugar to make products, such as candy, paid more than $0.20 a pound, costing consumers an extra $2 billion annually. Sugar growers, who account for only 1 percent of U.S. farm sales, have accounted for 17 percent of political contributions from agriculture since 1990.[1]

Some economists have argued that if quotas are to be used, the United States should auction them off to foreign producers, thereby capturing at least some of the difference between the world price and the U.S. price. Auctioning off quotas would not only increase federal revenue but would reduce the profitability of quotas, which would reduce pressure on Washington to perpetuate them. American consumers are not the only victims of sugar quotas. Thousands of poor farmers around the world miss out on an opportunity to earn a living growing sugarcane for export to America.

Tariffs and Quotas Compared

Consider the similarities and differences between a tariff and a quota. Because both have identical effects on the price in our example, they both lead to the same change in quantity demanded. In both cases, U.S. consumers suffer the same loss of consumer surplus, and U.S. producers reap the same gain of producer surplus. The primary difference is that the revenue from the tariff goes to the U.S. government, whereas the revenue from the quota goes to whomever secures the right to sell foreign goods in the U.S. market. *If quota rights accrue to foreigners, then the domestic economy is worse off with a quota than with a tariff.* But even if quota rights go to domestic importers, quotas, like tariffs, still increase the domestic price, restrict quantity, and thereby reduce consumer surplus and economic welfare. Quotas and tariffs can also raise production costs. For example, U.S. candy manufacturers face higher production costs because of sugar quotas, making them less competitive on world markets. Finally, and most importantly, *quotas and tariffs encourage foreign governments to retaliate with quotas and tariffs of their own, thus shrinking U.S. export markets, so the loss is greater than shown in Exhibits 7 and 8.*

1. Michael Schroeder, "Sugar Growers Hold Up Push for Free Trade," *Wall Street Journal,* 3 February 2004.

Other Trade Restrictions

Besides tariffs and quotas, a variety of other measures limit free trade. A country may provide *export subsidies* to encourage exports and *low-interest loans* to foreign buyers. Some countries impose *domestic content requirements* specifying that a certain portion of a final good must be produced domestically. Other requirements concerning health, safety, or technical standards often discriminate against foreign goods. For example, European countries once prohibited beef from hormone-fed cattle, a measure aimed at U.S. beef. Purity laws in Germany bar many non-German beers. Until the European Community adopted uniform standards, differing technical requirements forced manufacturers to offer as many as seven different versions of the same TV for that market. Sometimes exporters will voluntarily limit exports, as when Japanese automakers agreed to cut exports to the United States. The point is that *tariffs and quotas are only two of many devices used to restrict foreign trade.*

Recent research on the cost of protectionism indicates that international trade barriers slow the introduction of new goods and better technologies. So, rather than simply raising domestic prices, trade restrictions slow economic progress.

LO4 Reduction of Trade Barriers

In recent decades, countries have worked to reduce trade barriers and increase the flow of international trade. Let's examine multilateral agreements, the World Trade Organization, and common markets more closely.

Freer Trade by Multilateral Agreement

Mindful of how high tariffs cut world trade during the Great Depression, the United States, after World War II, invited its trading partners to negotiate lower tariffs and other trade barriers. The result was the

General Agreement on Tariffs and Trade (GATT), an international trade treaty adopted in 1947 by 23 countries, including the United States. Each GATT member agreed to (1) reduce tariffs through multinational negotiations, (2) reduce import quotas, and (3) treat all members equally with respect to trade.

Trade barriers have been reduced through trade negotiations among many countries, or "trade rounds," under the auspices of GATT. Trade rounds offer a package approach rather than an issue-by-issue approach to trade negotiations. Concessions that are necessary but otherwise difficult to defend in domestic political terms can be made more acceptable in the context of a package that also contains politically and economically attractive benefits. Most early GATT trade rounds were aimed at reducing tariffs. The Kennedy Round in the mid-1960s included new provisions against dumping, which is selling a commodity abroad for less than is charged in the home market or less than the cost of production. The Tokyo Round of the 1970s was a more sweeping attempt to extend and improve the system.

The most recently completed round was launched in Uruguay in September 1986 and ratified by 123 participating countries in 1994. The number of signing countries now exceeds 140. This so-called Uruguay Round, the most comprehensive of the eight postwar multilateral trade negotiations, included 550 pages of tariff reductions on 85 percent of world trade. The Uruguay Round also created the World Trade Organization (WTO) to succeed GATT.

General Agreement on Tariffs and Trade (GATT) an international tariff-reduction treaty adopted in 1947 that resulted in a series of negotiated "rounds" aimed at freer trade; the Uruguay Round created GATT's successor, the World Trade Organization (WTO)

dumping selling a product abroad for less than charged in the home market or for less than the cost of production

Uruguay Round the final multilateral trade negotiation under GATT; this 1994 agreement cut tariffs, formed the World Trade Organization (WTO), and will eventually eliminate quotas

World Trade Organization (WTO) the legal and institutional foundation of the multilateral trading system that succeeded GATT in 1995

The World Trade Organization

The World Trade Organization (WTO) now provides the legal and institutional foundation for world trade. Whereas GATT was a multilateral agreement with no institutional foundation, the WTO is a permanent institution in Geneva, Switzerland. A staff of about 500 economists and lawyers helps shape policy and resolves trade disputes between member countries. Whereas GATT involved only merchandise trade, the WTO also covers services and trade-related aspects of intellectual property, such as books, movies, and computer programs. The WTO will eventually phase out quotas, but tariffs will remain legal. As a result of the Uruguay Round, average tariffs fell from 6 percent to 4 percent of the value of imports (when GATT began in 1947, tariffs averaged 40 percent).

Whereas GATT relied on voluntary cooperation, the WTO settles disputes in a way that is faster, more automatic, and less susceptible to blockage than the GATT system was. The WTO resolved more trade disputes in its first decade than GATT did in nearly 50 years. Since 2000, developing countries have filed 60 percent of the disputes. But the WTO has also become a lightning rod for globalization issues.

Common Markets

Some countries looked to the success of the U.S. economy, which is essentially a free trade zone across 50 states, and have tried to develop free trade zones of their own. The largest and best known is

© V. BUDNIK/COLE GROUP/PHOTODISC/GETTY IMAGES

{No Dumping!}

The Bush Administration was often accused of being soft on China regarding trade, but on December 19, 2008, the United States filed a broad petition with the WTO alleging that China was using subsidies and cheap loans to provide Chinese exporters an unfair advantage. China has frequently been accused of dumping by American manufacturers, particularly steel makers. Between April 2008 and the end of the year, China's monthly steel exports to the United States nearly tripled, while U.S. steel mills had reduced production to 43% of capacity. China currently produces about 40% of global steel, though only six years before, it barely produced any. And while controversial, in many cases it is yet to be seen whether China's policies have actually been illegal.

SOURCE: Pete Engardio, "China: An Early Test for Obama," *Business Week,* 12 January 2008. pp.19–20.

© LEE JAE-WON/REUTERS/LANDOV

the European Union, which began in 1958 with a half dozen countries and expanded by 2007 to 27 countries and about 500 million people. The idea was to create a barrier-free European market like that of the United States in which goods, services, people, and capital are free to flow to their highest-valued use. Seventeen members of the European Union have also adopted a common currency, the *euro,* which replaced national currencies in 2002.

The United States, Canada, and Mexico have developed a free trade pact called the North American Free Trade Agreement (NAFTA). Through NAFTA, Mexico hopes to attract more U.S. investment by guaranteeing companies that locate there duty-free access to U.S. markets, which is where over two-thirds of Mexico's exports go. Mexico's 110 million people represent an attractive export market for U.S. producers, and Mexico's oil reserves could ease U.S. energy problems. The United States would also like to support Mexico's efforts to become more market oriented, as is reflected, for example, by Mexico's privatization of its phone system and banks. Creating job opportunities in Mexico also reduces pressure for Mexicans to cross the U.S. border illegally. After more than a decade of NAFTA, agricultural exports to Mexico have doubled, as has overall trade among the three nations, but Americans still buy much more from Mexicans and Canadians than the other way around.

Free trade areas are springing up around the world. The United States and other countries signed a free trade agreement with the Dominican Republic and five Central American countries, called DR-CAFTA. Five Latin American countries form Mercosur. These are Argentina, Brazil, Paraguay, Uruguay, and Venezuela. Full membership for Venezuela became effective on July 31, 2012, after the suspension of Paraguay on June 22, 2012 for the violation of the Democratic Clause of Mercosur. Bolivia, Chile, Colombia, Ecuador, and Peru currently have associate member status. In southeast Asia, ten nations have come together to form ASEAN, the Association of Southeast Asian Nations. And South Africa and its four neighboring countries form the Southern African Customs Union. Regional trade agreements require an exception to WTO rules because bloc members can make special deals among themselves and thus discriminate against outsiders. Under WTO's requirements, any trade concession granted one country must usually be granted to *all other* WTO members.

India's Trade Agreements[2]

India views regional trading arrangements (RTAs) as "building blocks" toward the overall objective of trade liberalization. Some of the main ones that India has signed with other countries include the following:

1. Agreement on South Asia Free Trade Area (SAFTA) is signed by all the member states of the South Asian Association for Regional Co-operation (SAARC) and came into force in 2006. Its members include Bangladesh, Bhutan, India, Maldives, Nepal, Pakistan, and Sri Lanka.
2. Asia-Pacific Trade Agreement (APTA), formerly known as the Bangkok Agreement, was signed on 31st July 1975 as an initiative of the United Nations Economic and Social Commission for Asia and the Pacific (ESCAP). It is a preferential tariff arrangement that aims at promoting intra-regional trade through exchange of mutually agreed concessions by the members (developing country) of the ESCAP region. The original signatories to the Agreement were Bangladesh, India, Lao People's Democratic Republic, the Republic of Korea, and Sri Lanka. Lao PDR has not issued customs notification on the tariff concessions granted, and hence to this extent, is not an effective participating member. China's accession to the Agreement was accepted at the Sixteenth Session of the Standing Committee of the Bangkok Agreement in April 2000.
3. BIMSTEC (Bay of Bengal Initiative for Multi-Sectoral Technical and Economic Cooperation), a sub-regional economic cooperation grouping was formed in Bangkok in June 1997. Its members are Bangladesh, India, Myanmar, Sri Lanka, and Thailand. Myanmar joined the grouping

2. http://business.gov.in/trade/trade_agreements.php.

in 1997. Bhutan and Nepal have also joined in 2004. Since its members belong to both ASEAN and SAARC, it is visualized as a "bridging link" between the two major groups. The chairmanship of BIMSTEC rotates among the member countries in alphabetical order. The immediate priority of the grouping is consolidation of its activities and making it attractive for economic cooperation.

4. India is also engaged with the Association of South East Asian Nations (ASEAN) since 1991. ASEAN was established on 8th August 1967 in Bangkok by the five original member countries, namely, Indonesia, Malaysia, Philippines, Singapore, and Thailand. Now, it has a membership of 10 countries namely Brunei Darussalam, Cambodia, Indonesia, Lao PDR, Malaysia, Myanmar, Philippines, Singapore, Thailand, and Vietnam. India is one of the four "Summit level Dialogue Partners" of ASEAN. A Framework Agreement on Comprehensive Economic Cooperation between ASEAN and India was signed in 2003. The key elements of the Agreement cover FTA in goods, services, and investment, as well as areas of economic cooperation. The Agreement also provided for an Early Harvest Programme (EHP), which covers areas of Economic Cooperation and a common list of items for exchange of tariff concessions as a confidence building measure.
5. India has also signed a framework agreement with Mercosur in 2003. The aim of this preferential trade agreement is to expand and strengthen the existing relations between Mercosur and India and promote the expansion of trade by granting reciprocal fixed tariff preferences with the ultimate objective of creating a free trade area between the parties. Mercosur is a trading bloc in Latin America formed in 1991. It was formed with the objective of facilitating the free movement of goods, services, capital, and people among the member countries. It is the fourth largest integrated market after the European Union (EU), North American Free Trade Agreement (NAFTA), and ASEAN.

LO5 Arguments for Trade Restrictions

Trade restrictions are often little more than handouts for the domestic industries they protect. Given the loss in social welfare that results from these restrictions, it would be more efficient simply to transfer money from domestic consumers to domestic producers. But such a bold transfer would be politically unpopular. Arguments for trade restrictions avoid mention of transfers to domestic producers and instead cite loftier goals. As we shall now see, none of these goals makes a strong case for restrictions, but some make more sense than others.

National Defense Argument

Some industries claim they need protection from import competition because their output is vital for national defense. Products such as strategic metals and military hardware are often insulated from foreign competition by trade restrictions. Thus, national defense considerations outweigh concerns about efficiency and equity. How valid is this argument? Trade restrictions may shelter the defense industry, but other means, such as government subsidies, might be more efficient. Or the government could stockpile basic military hardware so that maintaining an ongoing productive capacity would become less essential. Still, technological change could make certain weapons obsolete. Because most industries can play some role in national defense, instituting trade restrictions on this basis can get out of hand. For example, many decades ago U.S. wool producers secured trade protection at a time when some military uniforms were made of wool.

Infant Industry Argument

The infant industry argument was formulated as a rationale for protecting emerging domestic industries from foreign competition. In industries where a firm's average cost of production falls as output expands, new firms may need protection from imports until these firms grow enough to become competitive. Trade restrictions let new firms achieve the economies of scale necessary to compete with mature foreign producers.

But how do we identify industries that merit protection, and when do they become old enough to look after themselves? Protection often fosters inefficiencies. The immediate cost of such restrictions is the net welfare loss from higher domestic prices. These costs may become permanent if the industry never realizes the expected economies of scale and thus never becomes competitive. As with the national defense argument, policy makers should be careful in adopting trade restrictions based on the infant industry argument. Here again, temporary production subsidies may be more efficient than import restrictions.

Antidumping Argument

As we have noted already, *dumping* is selling a product abroad for less than in the home market or less than the cost of production. Exporters may be able to sell the good for less overseas because of export subsidies, or firms may simply find it profitable to sell for less in foreign markets where consumers are more sensitive to prices. But why shouldn't U.S. consumers pay as little as possible? If dumping is persistent, the increase in consumer surplus would more than offset losses to domestic producers. *There is no good reason why consumers should not be allowed to buy imports for a persistently lower price.*

An alternative form of dumping, termed *predatory dumping,* is the *temporary* sale abroad at prices below cost to eliminate competitors in that foreign market. Once the competition is gone, so the story goes, the exporting firm can raise the price in the foreign market. The trouble with this argument is that if dumpers try to take advantage of their monopoly position by sharply increasing the price, then other firms, either domestic or foreign, could enter the market and sell for less. There are few documented cases of predatory dumping.

Sometimes dumping may be *sporadic,* as firms occasionally try to unload excess inventories. Retailers hold periodic "sales" for the same reason. Sporadic dumping can be unsettling for domestic producers, but the economic impact is not a matter of great public concern. Regardless, all dumping is prohibited in the United States by the Trade Agreements Act of 1979, which calls for the imposition of tariffs when a good is sold for less in the United States than in its home market or less than the cost of production. In addition, WTO rules allow for offsetting tariffs when products are sold for "less than fair value" and when there is "material injury" to domestic producers. For example, U.S. producers of lumber and beer often accuse their Canadian counterparts of dumping.

> There is no good reason why consumers should not be allowed to buy imports for a persistently lower price.

Jobs and Income Argument

One rationale for trade restrictions that is commonly heard in the United States, and is voiced by WTO protestors, is that they protect U.S. jobs and wage levels. Using trade restrictions to protect domestic jobs is a strategy that dates back centuries. One problem with such a policy is that other countries usually retaliate by restricting *their* imports to save *their* jobs, so international trade is reduced, jobs are lost in export industries, and potential gains from trade fail to materialize. That happened big time during the Great Depression, as high tariffs choked trade and jobs.

Wages in other countries, especially developing countries, are often a small fraction of wages in the United States. Looking simply at differences in wages, however, narrows the focus too much. Wages represent just one component of the total production cost and may not necessarily be the most important. Employers are interested in the labor cost per unit of output, which depends on both the wage and labor productivity. Wages are high in the United States partly because U.S. labor productivity remains the highest in the world. High productivity can be traced to better education and training and to the abundant computers, machines, and other physical capital that make workers more productive. U.S. workers also benefit greatly from a stable business climate.

But what about the lower wages in many developing countries? Low wages are often linked to workers' lack of education and training, to the meager physical capital available to each worker, and to a business climate that is less stable and hence less attractive for producers. But once multinational firms build plants and provide technological know-how in developing countries, U.S. workers lose some of their competitive edge, and their relatively high wages could price some U.S. products out of the world market. This has already happened in the consumer electronics and toy industries. China makes 80 percent of the toys sold in the United States. Some U.S. toy sellers, such as the makers of Etch A Sketch, would no longer survive if they had not outsourced manufacturing to China.

Domestic producers do not like to compete with foreign producers whose costs are lower, so they often push for trade restrictions. But if restrictions negate any cost advantage a foreign producer might have, the law of comparative advantage becomes inoperative and domestic consumers are denied access to the lower priced goods.

Over time, as labor productivity in developing countries increases, wage differentials among countries will narrow, much as wage differentials narrowed between the northern and southern United States. As technology and capital spread, U.S. workers, particularly unskilled workers, cannot expect to maintain wage levels that are far above those in other countries. So far, research and development has kept U.S. producers on the cutting edge of technological developments, but staying ahead in the technological race is a constant battle.

Declining Industries Argument

Where an established domestic industry is in jeopardy of closing because of lower-priced imports, could there be a rationale for *temporary* import restrictions? After all, domestic producers employ many industry-specific resources—both specialized labor and specialized machines. This human and physical capital is worth less in its best alternative use. If the extinction of the domestic industry is forestalled through trade restrictions, specialized workers can retire voluntarily or can gradually pursue more promising careers. Specialized machines can be allowed to wear out naturally.

© HEMERA TECHNOLOGIES/PHOTOOBJECTS.NET/JUPITERIMAGES

Thus, in the case of declining domestic industries, trade protection can help lessen shocks to the economy and can allow for an orderly transition to a new industrial mix. But the protection offered should not be so generous as to encourage continued investment in the industry. Protection should be of specific duration and should be phased out over that period.

The clothing industry is an example of a declining U.S. industry. The 22,000 U.S. jobs saved as a result of one trade restriction were paid an average of less than $30,000 per year. But a Congressional Budget Office study estimated that the higher domestic clothing prices resulting from trade restrictions meant that U.S. consumers paid two to three times more than apparel workers earned. Trade restrictions in the U.S. clothing and textile industry started phasing out in 2005 under the Uruguay Round of trade agreements.

Free trade may displace some U.S. jobs through imports, but it also creates U.S. jobs through exports. When people celebrate a ribbon-cutting ceremony for a new software company, nobody credits free trade for those jobs, but when a steel plant closes, everyone talks about how those jobs went overseas. What's more, many foreign companies have built plants in the United States and employ U.S. workers. For example, a dozen foreign television manufacturers and all major Japanese automakers now operate plants in the United States.

The number of jobs in the United States has more than doubled in the last four decades. To recognize this job growth is not to deny the problems facing workers displaced by imports. Some displaced workers, particularly those in blue-collar jobs in steel and other unionized industries, are not likely to find jobs that will pay nearly as well as the ones they lost. As with infant industries, however, the problems posed by declining industries need not require trade restrictions. To support the affected industry, the government could offer wage subsidies or special tax breaks that decline over time. The government has also funded programs to retrain affected workers for jobs that are in greater demand.

Problems with Trade Protection

Trade restrictions raise a number of problems in addition to those already mentioned. First, protecting one stage of production usually requires protecting downstream stages of production as well. Protecting the U.S. textile industry from foreign competition, for example, raised the cost of cloth to U.S. apparel makers, reducing their competitiveness. Thus, when the government protected domestic textile manufacturers, the domestic garment industry also needed protection. Second, the cost of protection includes not only the welfare loss from the higher domestic price but also the cost of the resources used by domestic producer groups to secure the favored protection. The cost of *rent seeking*—lobbying fees, propaganda, and legal actions—can sometimes equal or exceed the direct welfare loss from restrictions. A third problem with trade restrictions is the transaction costs of enforcing the myriad quotas, tariffs, and other trade restrictions. These often lead to smuggling and black markets. A fourth problem is that economies insulated from foreign competition become less innovative and less efficient. The final and biggest problem with imposing trade restrictions is that other countries usually retaliate, thus shrinking the gains from trade. Retaliation can set off still greater trade restrictions, leading to an outright trade war.

>> This kiosk is the gateway to New York City's garment district, an area that continues to be severely affected by low-price competition from overseas markets.

© AP IMAGES

LO6 Balance of Payments

A country's gross domestic product, or GDP, measures the economy's income and output during a given period. To account for dealings abroad, countries must also keep track of international transactions. A country's *balance of payments,* as introduced in Chapter 3, summarizes all economic transactions during a given period between residents of that country and residents of other countries. *Residents* include people, firms, organizations, and governments.

International Economic Transactions

The balance of payments measures economic transactions between a country and the rest of the world, whether these transactions involve goods and services, real and financial assets, or transfer payments. The balance of payments measures a *flow* of transactions during a particular period, usually a year. Some transactions do not involve actual payments. For example, if *Time* magazine ships a new printing press to its Australian subsidiary, no payment is made, yet an economic transaction involving another country has occurred. Similarly, if CARE sends food to Africa or the Pentagon provides military assistance to the Middle East, these transactions must be captured in the balance of payments. So remember, although we speak of the *balance of payments,* a more descriptive phrase would be the *balance of economic transactions.*

Balance-of-payments accounts are maintained according to the principles of *double-entry bookkeeping.* Some entries are called *credits,* and others are called *debits.* As you will see, the balance of payments consists of several individual accounts. An individual account may not balance, but a deficit in one or more accounts must be offset by a surplus in the other accounts. Because total credits must equal total debits, there is a *balance* of payments—hence, the name. During a given period, such as a year, the inflow of receipts from the rest of the world, which are entered as credits, must equal the outflow of payments to the rest of the world, which are entered as debits.

The first of two major categories in the balance of payments is the current account. The current account records *current* flows of funds into and out of the country, including imports and exports of goods and services, net income earned by a country's residents from foreign assets, and net transfer payments from abroad. These are discussed in turn.

The Merchandise Trade Balance

The *merchandise trade balance,* a term introduced in Chapter 3, equals the value of merchandise exports minus the value of merchandise imports. The merchandise account reflects trade in goods, or tangible products (stuff you can put in a box), like French wine or U.S. computers, and is often referred to simply as the *trade balance.* The value of Indian merchandise exports is a credit in the Indian balance-of-payments account because Indian residents get *paid* for the exported goods. The value of Indian merchandise imports is a debit in the balance-of-payments account because Indian residents *pay* foreigners for imported goods.

If merchandise exports exceed merchandise imports, the trade balance is in *surplus.* If merchandise imports exceed merchandise exports, the trade balance is in *deficit.* The merchandise trade balance, which is reported monthly, influences foreign exchange markets, the stock market, and other financial markets. The trade balance depends on a variety of factors, including the relative strength and competitiveness of the domestic economy compared with other economies and the relative value of the domestic currency compared with other currencies. Strong economies with growing incomes tend to buy more of everything, including imports.

Because per capita income in the United States is the highest in the world, the United States imports more goods from each of the world's major economies than it exports to them. Exhibit 9 shows the U.S. merchandise trade deficit with major economies or regions of the world in 2008. The $246 billion trade deficit with China was by far the largest, triple that with Japan, Canada, or the European Union. The large trade deficit with the OPEC nations represents the high price of oil in mid-2008. The Chinese bought $66 billion in U.S. goods in 2008, but Americans bought $313 billion in Chinese goods, or about $2,700 per U.S. household. So China sells America five times more than it buys from America. Chances are, most of the utensils in your kitchen were made in China; most toys are also Chinese made. The United States does not have a trade surplus with any major economy in the world and is the world's biggest importer.

Balance on Goods and Services

The merchandise trade balance focuses on the flow of goods, but services are also traded internationally. *Services* are intangibles, such as transportation, insurance, banking, education, consulting, and tourism. Services are often called "invisibles" because they are not tangible. The value of U.S. service exports, as when an Irish tourist visits New York City, is listed as a credit in the U.S. balance-of-payments account because U.S. residents get paid for these services. The value of U.S. service imports, like computer programming outsourced to India, is listed as a debit in the balance-of-payments account because U.S. residents must pay for the imported services.

Because the United States exports more services than it imports, services have been in surplus for the last three decades. The **balance on goods and services** is the export value of goods and services minus the import value of goods and services, or *net exports*, a component of GDP.

Net Investment Income

Indian residents earn investment income, such as interest and dividends, from assets owned abroad. This investment income flows to India and is a credit in the balance-of-payments account. On the other side, foreigners earn investment income on assets owned in India, and this payment flows out of the country. This outflow is a debit in the balance-of-payments account. **Net investment income from abroad** is India's investment earnings from foreign assets minus foreigners' earnings from their assets in India.

Unilateral Transfers

Unilateral transfers consist of government transfers to foreign residents, foreign aid, money workers

balance on goods and services
the portion of a country's balance-of-payments account that measures the value of a country's exports of goods and services minus the value of its imports of goods and services

net investment income from abroad
investment earnings by Indian residents from their foreign assets minus investment earnings by foreigners from their assets in India

Exhibit 9

U.S. Merchandise Trade Deficits in 2008 by Country or Grouping

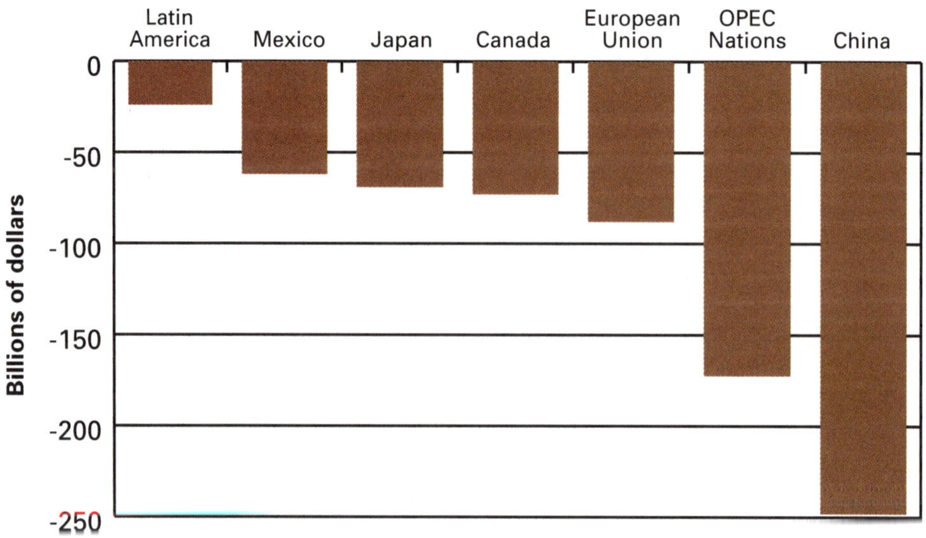

SOURCE: Developed from data in "Exports, Imports, and Balance of Goods by Selected Countries and Areas—2008," Exhibit 14, U.S. Bureau of Economic Analysis, 13 January 2009, at http://www.bea.gov/newsreleases/international/trade/2009/pdf/trad1108.pdf.

send to families abroad, personal gifts to friends and relatives abroad, charitable donations, and the like. Money sent out of the country is a debit in the balance-of-payments account. For example, immigrants to the Gulf countries often send money to families back home. **Net unilateral transfers abroad** equal the unilateral transfers received from abroad by Indian residents minus unilateral transfers sent to foreign residents by Indian residents.

The United States places few restrictions on money sent out of the country. Other countries, particularly developing countries, strictly limit the amount that may be sent abroad. More generally, many developing countries, such as China, restrict the convertibility of their currency into other currencies.

When we add net unilateral transfers to net exports of goods and services and net income from assets owned abroad, we get the **balance on current account**, which is reported quarterly. Thus, *the current account includes all international transactions in currently produced goods and services, net income from foreign assets, and net unilateral transfers.* It can be negative, reflecting a current account deficit; positive, reflecting a current account surplus; or zero.

The Financial Account

The current account records international transactions in goods, services, asset income, and unilateral transfers. The **financial account** records international purchases of assets, including financial assets such as stocks, bonds, and bank balances, and real assets such as land, housing, factories, and other physical assets. For example, U.S. residents purchase foreign securities to earn a higher return and to diversify their portfolios. Money flows out when Americans buy foreign assets or build factories overseas. Money flows in when foreigners buy U.S. assets or build factories here. The international purchase or sale of assets is recorded in the financial account.

Deficits and Surpluses

Nations, like households, operate under a budget constraint. Spending cannot exceed income plus cash on hand and borrowed funds. We have distinguished between *current* transactions, which include exports, imports, asset income, and unilateral transfers, and *financial* transactions, which reflect purchases of foreign real and financial assets. Any surplus or deficit in one account must be offset by deficits or surpluses in other balance-of-payments accounts.

Exhibit 10 presents India's balance-of-payments statement for 2010-11. A *statistical discrepancy* is required to balance the payments. Think of the statistical discrepancy as the official "fudge factor" that (1) measures the error in the balance of payments and (2) satisfies the double-entry bookkeeping requirement that total debits must equal total credits.

Exhibit 10

India's Balance of Payments for 2010–11 (millions of dollars)

Current Accounts	
1. Merchandise—exports f.o.b	250,468
2. Merchandise—imports, c.i.f	380,935
3. Trade balance (1-2)	–130,467
4. Invisibles, net	86,186
5. Current account balance (3+4)	–44,281
Capital Accounts	
6. Foreign investment	54,835
7. External assistance, net	4,965
8. Commercial borrowings, net	11,599
9. Rupee debt service	–69
10. NRI deposits, net	3,239
11. Other capital	–17,238
12. Capital account balance (6 to 11)	57,331
13. Overall balance (5+6)	13,050

SOURCE: Handbook of statistics on Indian Economy 2010–11, www.rbi.org.in.

Foreign exchange is the currency of another country needed to carry out international transactions. A country runs a deficit in its current account when the amount of foreign exchange received from exports, from holding foreign assets, and from unilateral transfers falls short of the amount needed to pay for imports, pay foreigners for their Indian assets, and make unilateral transfers. If the current account is in deficit, the necessary foreign exchange must come from a net inflow in the financial account. Such an inflow in the financial account could stem from borrowing from foreigners, selling domestic stocks and bonds to foreigners, selling a steel plant in Pittsburgh or a ski lodge in Aspen to foreigners, and so forth.

If a country runs a current account surplus, the foreign exchange received from exports, from holding

net unilateral transfers abroad
the unilateral transfers (gifts and grants) received from abroad by Indian residents minus the unilateral transfers Indian residents send abroad

balance on current account
the portion of the balance-of-payments account that measures that country's balance on goods and services, net investment income from abroad, plus net unilateral transfers abroad

financial account
the record of a country's international transactions involving purchases or sales of financial and real assets

assets abroad, and from unilateral transfers exceeds the amount needed to pay for imports, to pay foreign holders for U.S. assets, and to make unilateral transfers. If the current account is in surplus, this excess foreign exchange results in a net outflow in the financial account through lending abroad, buying foreign stocks and bonds, buying a shoe plant in Italy or a villa on the French Riviera, and so forth.

When all transactions are considered, accounts must always balance, though specific accounts usually don't. A deficit in a particular account should not necessarily be viewed as a source of concern, nor should a surplus be a source of satisfaction.

LO7 Foreign Exchange Rates and Markets

Now that you have some idea about international flows, we can take a closer look at the forces that determine the underlying value of the currencies involved. Let's begin by looking at exchange rates and the market for foreign exchange.

Foreign Exchange

Foreign exchange, recall, is foreign money needed to carry out international transactions. The **exchange rate** is the price measured in one country's currency of buying one unit of another country's currency. Exchange rates are determined by the interaction of the households, firms, private financial institutions, governments, and central banks that buy and sell foreign exchange. The exchange rate fluctuates to equate the quantity of foreign exchange demanded with the quantity supplied. Typically, foreign exchange is made up of bank deposits denominated in the foreign currency. When foreign travel is involved, foreign exchange often consists of foreign paper money.

exchange rate the price measured in one country's currency of purchasing 1 unit of another country's currency

currency depreciation with respect to the dollar, an increase in the number of dollars needed to purchase 1 unit of foreign exchange in a flexible rate system

currency appreciation with respect to the dollar, a decrease in the number of dollars needed to purchase 1 unit of foreign exchange in a flexible rate system

The foreign exchange market incorporates all the arrangements used to buy and sell foreign exchange. This market is not so much a physical place as a network of telephones and computers connecting financial centers all over the world. Perhaps you have seen pictures of foreign exchange traders in New York, Frankfurt, London, or Tokyo in front of computer screens amid a tangle of phone lines. The foreign exchange market is like an all-night diner—it never closes. A trading center is always open somewhere in the world.

© PETER GRIFFIN/ALAMY

We will consider the market for the euro in terms of the dollar. But first, a little more about the euro. For decades the nations of Western Europe have tried to increase their economic cooperation and trade. These countries believed they would be more productive and more competitive with the United States if they acted less like many separate economies and more like the 50 United States, with a single set of trade regulations and one currency. Imagine the hassle involved if each of the 50 states had its own currency.

In 2002, euro notes and coins entered circulation in the 12 European countries adopting the common currency. The big advantage of a common currency is that Europeans no longer have to change money every time they cross a border or trade with another country in the group. Again, the inspiration for this is the United States, arguably the most successful economy in world history.

So the euro is the common currency of the *euro area*, or *euro zone*, as the now 17-country region is usually called. The price, or exchange rate, of the euro in terms of the dollar is the number of dollars required to purchase one euro. An increase in the number of dollars needed to purchase a euro indicates weakening, or **depreciation**, of the dollar. A decrease in the number of dollars needed to purchase a euro indicates strengthening, or **appreciation**, of the dollar. Put another way, a decrease in the number of euros needed to purchase a dollar is a depreciation of the dollar, and an increase in the number of euros needed to purchase a dollar is an appreciation of the dollar.

Because the exchange rate is usually a market price, it is determined by demand and supply: The equilibrium price is the one that equates quantity demanded with quantity supplied. To simplify the analysis, suppose that the United States and the euro area make up the entire world, so the demand and supply for euros in international finance is the demand and supply for foreign exchange from the U.S. perspective.

The Demand for Foreign Exchange

Whenever U.S. residents need euros, they must buy them in the foreign exchange market, which could include their local banks, paying for them with dollars. Exhibit 11 depicts a market for foreign exchange—in this case, euros. The horizontal axis shows the quantity of foreign exchange, measured here in millions of euros. The vertical axis shows the price per unit of foreign exchange, measured here in dollars per euro. The demand curve *D* for foreign exchange shows the inverse relationship between the dollar price of the euro and the quantity of euros demanded, other things assumed constant. Assumed constant along the demand curve are the incomes and preferences of U.S. consumers, expected inflation in the United States and in the euro area, the euro price of goods in the euro area, and interest rates in the United States and in the euro area. People have many reasons for demanding foreign exchange, but in the aggregate, the lower the dollar price of foreign exchange, other things constant, the greater the quantity of foreign exchange demanded.

Exhibit 11

The Foreign Exchange Market

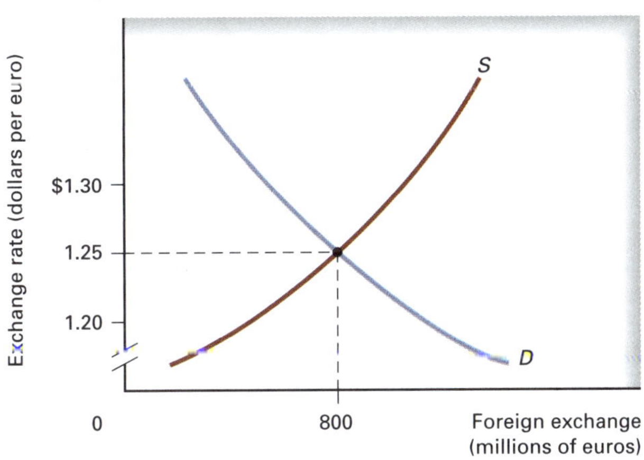

A drop in the dollar price of foreign exchange, in this case the euro, means that fewer dollars are needed to purchase each euro, so the dollar prices of euro area products (like German cars, Italian shoes, tickets to Euro Disney, and euro area securities), which list prices in euros, become cheaper. The cheaper it is to buy euros, the lower the dollar price of euro area products to U.S. residents, so the greater the quantity of euros demanded by U.S. residents, other things constant. For example, a cheap enough euro might persuade you to tour Rome, climb the Austrian Alps, wander the museums of Paris, or crawl the pubs of Dublin.

The Supply of Foreign Exchange

The supply of foreign exchange is generated by the desire of foreign residents to acquire dollars—that is, to exchange euros for dollars. Euro area residents want dollars to buy U.S. goods and services, acquire U.S. assets, make loans in dollars, or send dollars to their U.S. friends and relatives. Euros are supplied in the foreign exchange market to acquire the dollars people want. An increase in the dollar-per-euro exchange rate, other things constant, makes U.S. products cheaper for foreigners because foreign residents need fewer euros to get the same number of dollars. For example, suppose a Dell computer sells for $600. If the exchange rate is $1.20 per euro, that computer costs 500 euros; if the exchange rate is $1.25 per euro, it costs only 480 euros. The number of Dell computers demanded in the euro area increases as the dollar-per-euro exchange rate increases, other things constant, so more euros will be supplied on the foreign exchange market to buy dollars.

The positive relationship between the dollar-per-euro exchange rate and the quantity of euros supplied on the foreign exchange market is expressed in Exhibit 4 by the upward-sloping supply curve for foreign exchange (again, euros in our example). The supply curve assumes that other things remain constant, including euro area incomes and tastes, expectations about inflation in the euro area and in the United States, and interest rates in the euro area and in the United States.

Determining the Exchange Rate

Exhibit 11 brings together the demand and supply for foreign exchange to determine the exchange rate. At a rate of $1.25 per euro, the quantity of

If the exchange rate is allowed to adjust freely, or to float, in response to market forces, the market will clear continually, as the quantities of foreign exchange demanded and supplied are equated.

© DON FARRALL PHOTOGRAPHER'S CHOICE RF/GETTY IMAGES

euros demanded equals the quantity supplied—in our example, 800 million euros. Once achieved, this equilibrium rate will remain constant until a change occurs in one of the factors that affect supply or demand. If the exchange rate is allowed to adjust freely, or to *float,* in response to market forces, the market will clear continually, as the quantities of foreign exchange demanded and supplied are equated.

What if the initial equilibrium is upset by a change in one of the underlying forces that affect demand or supply? For example, suppose higher U.S. incomes increase American demand for all normal goods, including those from the euro area. This shifts the U.S. demand curve for foreign exchange to the right, as Americans buy more Italian marble, Dutch chocolate, German machines, Parisian vacations, and euro area securities.

This increased demand for euros is shown in Exhibit 12 by a rightward shift of the demand curve for foreign exchange. The demand increase from *D* to *D′* leads to an increase in the exchange rate per euro from \$1.25 to \$1.27. Thus, the euro increases in value, or appreciates, while the dollar falls in value, or depreciates. An increase in U.S. income should not affect the euro supply curve, though it does increase the *quantity of euros supplied*. The higher exchange value of the euro prompts those in the euro area to buy more American products and assets, which are now cheaper in terms of the euro.

arbitrageur someone who takes advantage of temporary geographic differences in the exchange rate by simultaneously purchasing a currency in one market and selling it in another market

To review: Any increase in the demand for foreign exchange or any decrease in its supply, other things constant, increases the number of dollars required to purchase one unit of foreign exchange, which is a depreciation of the dollar. On the other hand, any decrease in the demand for foreign exchange or any increase in its supply, other things constant, reduces the number of dollars required to purchase one unit of foreign exchange, which is an appreciation of the dollar.

Arbitrageurs and Speculators

Exchange rates between two currencies are nearly identical at any given time in markets around the world. For example, the dollar price of a euro is the same in New York, Frankfurt, Tokyo, London, Zurich, Hong Kong, Istanbul, and other financial centers. **Arbitrageurs**—dealers who take advantage of any difference in exchange rates between markets by buying low and selling high—ensure this equality. Their actions help to equalize exchange rates across markets. For example, if one euro costs \$1.24 in New York but \$1.25 in Frankfurt, an arbitrageur could buy, say, \$1,000,000 worth of euros in New York and at the same time sell them in Frankfurt for \$1,008,060, thereby earning \$8,060 minus the transaction costs of the trades.

Because an arbitrageur buys and sells simultaneously, little risk is involved. In our example, the arbi-

Exhibit 12

Effect on the Foreign Exchange Market of an Increased Demand for Euros

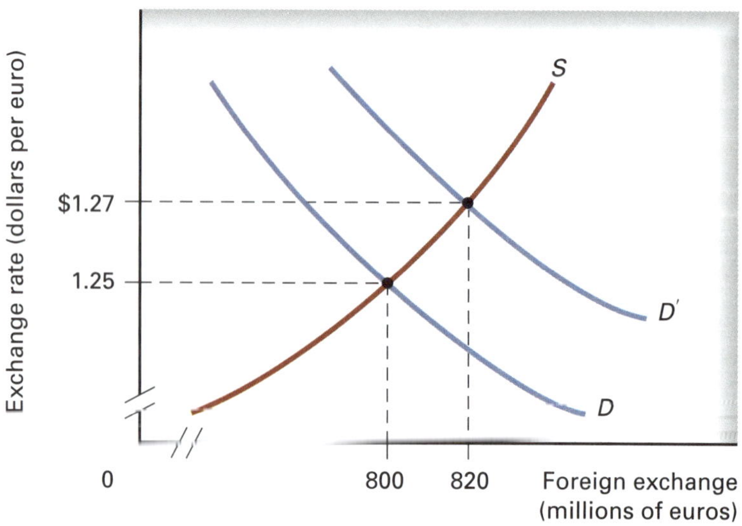

trageur increased the demand for euros in New York and increased the supply of euros in Frankfurt. These actions increased the dollar price of euros in New York and decreased it in Frankfurt, thereby squeezing down the difference in exchange rates. Exchange rates may still change because of market forces, but they tend to change in all markets simultaneously.

The demand and supply of foreign exchange arises from many sources—from importers and exporters, investors in foreign assets, central banks, tourists, arbitrageurs, and speculators. **Speculators** buy or sell foreign exchange in hopes of profiting by trading the currency at a more favorable exchange rate later. By taking risks, speculators aim to profit from market fluctuations—they try to buy low and sell high. In contrast, arbitrageurs take less risk, because they *simultaneously* buy currency in one market and sell it in another.

Finally, people in countries suffering from economic and political turmoil, such as occurred in Russia, Indonesia, and the Philippines, may buy *hard* currency as a hedge against the depreciation and instability of their own currencies. The dollar has long been accepted as an international medium of exchange. It is also the currency of choice in the world markets for oil and illegal drugs. But the euro eventually may challenge that dominance, in part because the largest euro denomination, the 500 euro note, is worth about six times the largest U.S. denomination, the $100 note. So it would be six times easier to smuggle euro notes than U.S. notes of equal value.

Purchasing Power Parity

As long as trade across borders is unrestricted and as long as exchange rates are allowed to adjust freely, the **purchasing power parity (PPP) theory** predicts that the exchange rate between two currencies will adjust in the long run to reflect price differences between the two currency regions. *A given basket of internationally traded goods should therefore sell for about the same around the world (except for differences reflecting transportation costs and the like).* Suppose a basket of internationally traded goods that sells for $10,000 in the United States sells for 8,000 euros in the euro area. According to the purchasing power parity theory, the equilibrium exchange rate should be $1.25 per euro. If this were not the case—if the exchange rate were, say, $1.20 per euro—then you could exchange $9,600 for 8,000 euros, with which you buy the basket of commodities in the euro area. You could then sell that basket of goods in the States for $10,000, yielding you a profit of $400 minus any transaction costs. Selling dollars and buying euros will also drive up the dollar price of euros.

The purchasing power parity theory is more of a long-run predictor than a day-to-day indicator of the relationship between changes in the price level and the exchange rate. For example, a country's currency generally appreciates when inflation is low compared with other countries and depreciates when inflation is high. Likewise, a country's currency generally appreciates when its real interest rates are higher than those in the rest of the world, because foreigners are more willing to buy and hold investments denominated in that high-interest currency. As a case in point, the dollar appreciated during the first half of the 1980s, when real U.S. interest rates were relatively high, and depreciated during 2002 to 2004, when real U.S. interest rates were relatively low. The dollar was expected to depreciate during 2009 because of historically low real interest rates, recession, and high government borrowing.

Because of trade barriers, central bank intervention in exchange markets, and the fact that many products are not traded or are not comparable across countries, the purchasing power parity theory usually does not explain exchange rates at a particular point in time that well. For example, if you went shopping in London tomorrow, you would soon notice a dollar does not buy as much there as it does in the United States.

LO8 Fixed and Flexible Exchange Rates

Flexible Exchange Rates

For the most part, we have been discussing a system of **flexible exchange rates**, with rates determined by demand and supply. Flexible, or *floating*, exchange rates adjust continually to the myriad forces that buffet foreign exchange markets. Consider how the exchange rate is linked to the balance-of-payments accounts. Debit entries in the current or financial accounts increase the demand for for-

speculator someone who buys or sells foreign exchange in hopes of profiting from fluctuations in the exchange rate over time

purchasing power parity (PPP) theory the idea that the exchange rate between two countries will adjust in the long run to equalize the cost between the countries of a basket of internationally traded goods

flexible exchange rate rate determined in foreign exchange markets by the forces of demand and supply without government intervention

The Resilience of Gold

Despite the breakdown of the gold standard, most countries still hold a substantial gold reserve, and gold has often been considered a safe haven for investment in volatile markets. However, during the economic crisis of 2008, even gold was affected by market turmoil. In March, gold had reached a record high of \$1,003.20 per troy ounce, leaving the metal in line with many other assets such as oil, stocks, and grain commodities. A rising dollar pushed gold down further, where it hit a low of \$712 in November. It managed a slight recovery, closing 2008 around \$870, leaving it up only 4% for the year, though it still outperformed most other asset classes, such as the S&P 500-stock index—down 41%—and crude oil—down 61%. Gold remained volatile at the start of 2009, passing \$1000 again in late February but slipping to \$930 by early July.

SOURCE: David Gaffen, "Gold, Not So Golden in 2008, Loses Chance to Be Market Star," *Wall Street Journal,* 29 December 2008. Available at http://online.wsj.com/article/SB123052519180239011.html (accessed 29 December 2008). Matt Whittaker, "Gold Tumbles 2.7% as Optimism Grows," *Wall Street Journal,* 6 April 2009. Available at http://online.wsj.com/article/SB123906170679495133.html (accessed 7 April 2009).

© STOCKBYTE/GETTY IMAGES

eign exchange, resulting in a depreciation of the dollar. Credit entries in these accounts increase the supply of foreign exchange, resulting in an appreciation of the dollar.

Fixed Exchange Rates

When exchange rates are flexible, governments usually have little direct role in foreign exchange markets. But if governments try to set exchange rates, active and ongoing central bank intervention is often necessary to establish and maintain these **fixed exchange rates**. Suppose the European Central Bank selects what it thinks is an appropriate rate of exchange between the dollar and the euro. It attempts to *fix*, or to *peg,* the exchange rate within a narrow band around the particular value selected. If the euro threatens to climb above the maximum acceptable exchange rate, monetary authorities must sell euros and buy dollars, thereby keeping the dollar price of the euro down. Conversely, if the euro threatens to drop below the minimum acceptable exchange rate, monetary authorities must sell dollars and buy euros. This increased demand for the euro will keep its value up relative to the dollar. Through such intervention in the foreign exchange market, monetary authorities try to stabilize the exchange rate, keeping it within the specified band.

fixed exchange rate
rate of exchange between currencies pegged within a narrow range and maintained by the central bank's ongoing purchases and sales of currencies

currency devaluation
an increase in the official pegged price of foreign exchange in terms of the domestic currency

currency revaluation
a reduction in the official pegged price of foreign exchange in terms of the domestic currency

If monetary officials must keep selling foreign exchange to keep the value of their domestic currency from falling, they risk running out of foreign exchange reserves. Faced with this threat, the government has several options for eliminating the exchange rate disequilibrium. First, the pegged exchange rate can be increased, which is a **devaluation** of the domestic currency. (A decrease in the pegged exchange rate is called a **revaluation**.) Second, the government can reduce the domestic demand for foreign exchange directly by imposing restrictions on imports or on financial outflows. Many developing countries do this. Third, the government can adopt policies to slow the domestic economy, increase interest rates, or reduce inflation relative to that of the country's trading partners, thereby indirectly decreasing the demand for foreign exchange and increasing the supply of foreign exchange. Several Asian economies, such as South Korea and Indonesia, pursued such policies to stabilize their currencies. Finally, the government can allow the disequilibrium to persist and ration the available foreign reserves through some form of foreign exchange control.

This concludes our introduction to the theories of international finance. Let's examine international finance in practice.

Exchange Rate Policy in India[3]

India's exchange rate policy has evolved with the new economic reforms since 1991. It has shifted from a par value system to a basket-peg and further to a managed float exchange rate system. Between 1947–1971, India followed the par value system of the exchange rate, whereby the rupee's external par value was fixed at 4.15 grains of fine gold. The RBI maintained the par value of the rupee within the permitted margin of ±1% using pound sterling as the intervention currency. The devaluation of the rupee in September 1949 and June 1966 in terms of gold resulted in the reduction of the par value of rupee in terms of gold. With the breakdown of the Bretton Woods System in December 1971, the rupee was linked with pound sterling. Sterling being fixed in terms of the U.S. dollar under the Smithsonian Agreement of 1971, the rupee also remained stable against the dollar. In order to overcome the weaknesses associated with a single currency peg and to ensure stability of the exchange rate, the rupee, with effect from September 1975, was pegged to a basket of currencies. However, by the late eighties and the early nineties, it was recognized that both macroeconomic policy and structural factors had contributed to balance of payment difficulties.

In 1991, a two step downward exchange rate adjustment was undertaken, which also effectively brought to a close the period of pegged exchange rate. In March 1992, the Liberalised Exchange Rate Management System (LERMS) was put in place involving dual exchange rate system in the interim period. The dual exchange rate system was replaced by unified exchange rate system in March 1993.

RBI has started to intervene actively in the forex market to reduce the volatility in the market due to demand-supply mismatch in the domestic foreign exchange market. After 2002–03, following the Asian crisis, the Reserve Bank made direct interventions in the market through purchases and sales of the U.S. dollars in the forex market and sterilized the dollar's impact on monetary base. Empirical evidence in the Indian case has generally suggested that in the present day managed float regime of India, intervention has served as a potent instrument in containing the magnitude of exchange rate volatility of the rupee and the intervention operations do not influence as much the level of rupee. It is, however, pertinent to note that Reserve Bank's intervention in the foreign exchange market has been relatively small in terms of volume (less than 1 percent during last few years), except during 2008–09. The Reserve Bank's gross market intervention as a percent of turnover in the foreign exchange market was highest in 2003–04 though in absolute terms the highest intervention was $84 billion in 2008–09. During October 2008 alone, when the contagion of the global financial crisis started affecting India, the RBI sold $20.6 billion in the foreign exchange market. This was the highest intervention till date during any particular month.

For the period as a whole, 1993–94 to 2007–08, the Indian rupee has depreciated against the dollar. The rupee has also depreciated against other major international currencies. Another important feature has been the reduction in the volatility of the Indian exchange rate during last few years. Among all currencies worldwide, which are not on a nominal peg, and certainly among all emerging market economies, the volatility of the rupee-dollar rate has remained low. Moreover, the rupee in real terms generally witnessed stability over the years despite volatility in capital flows and trade flows. The various episodes of volatility of exchange rate of the rupee have been managed in a flexible and pragmatic manner.

Final Word

International trade arises from voluntary exchange among buyers and sellers pursuing their self-interest. Since 1950, world output has risen eightfold, while world trade has increased nearly twentyfold. World trade offers many advantages to the trading countries: access to markets around the world, lower costs through economies of scale, the opportunity to utilize abundant resources, better access to information about markets and technology, improved quality honed by competitive pressure, and, most importantly, lower prices for consumers. Comparative advantage, specialization, and trade allow people to use their scarce resources most efficiently to satisfy their unlimited wants.

Despite the clear gains from free trade, restrictions on international trade date back centuries, and pressure on public officials to impose trade restrictions continues today. Domestic producers (and their resource suppliers) benefit from trade restrictions in their markets because they can charge domestic consumers more. Trade restrictions insulate domes-

3. Pami Dua and Rajiv Ranjan "Exchange Rate Policy and Modelling in India," Study No. 33, Development Research Group, Reserve Bank of India, www.rbi.org.in.

tic producers from the rigors of global competition, in the process stifling innovation and leaving the industry vulnerable to technological change from abroad. With trade quotas, the winners also include those who have secured the right to import goods at the world prices and sell them at the domestic prices. Consumers, who must pay higher prices for protected goods, suffer from trade restrictions, as do the domestic producers who import resources. Other losers include U.S. exporters, who face higher trade barriers as foreigners retaliate with their own trade restrictions.

Producers have a laser-like focus on trade legislation, but consumers remain largely oblivious. Consumers purchase thousands of different goods and thus have no special interest in the effects of trade policy on any particular good. Congress tends to support the group that makes the most noise, so trade restrictions often persist, despite the clear and widespread gains from freer trade.

Multiple Choice Questions

1. In determining comparative advantage, cost is measured in terms of
   a. foreign currency
   b. domestic currency
   c. gold only
   d. units of weight and measure
   e. opportunities forgone

2. For each watch Denmark produces, it gives up the opportunity to make 50 pounds of cheese. Germany can produce one watch for every 100 pounds of cheese it produces. Which of the following is true with regard to opportunity costs in the two countries?
   a. The opportunity cost of producing watches is higher in Denmark.
   b. The opportunity cost of producing cheese is higher in Denmark.
   c. The opportunity cost of producing cheese is identical in both countries.
   d. It is impossible to compare opportunity costs because the two countries use different currencies.
   e. In both countries combined, the opportunity cost of one watch is 150 pounds of cheese.

3. For each watch Denmark produces, it gives up the opportunity to make 50 pounds of cheese. Germany can produce one watch for every 100 pounds of cheese it produces. Which of the following is true concerning production possibilities curves in both countries?
   a. The slopes of the countries' production possibilities frontiers cannot be determined unless the number of workers in each country is known.
   b. The countries' production possibilities frontiers have the usual bowed-out shape.
   c. On a graph with cheese on the vertical axis, the slope of Germany's production possibilities frontier is everywhere equal to 1/100.
   d. On a graph with cheese on the vertical axis, the slope of Germany's production possibilities frontier is steeper than Denmark's.
   e. On a graph with cheese on the vertical axis, the slope of Germany's production possibilities frontier is everywhere equal to negative 1/100.

4. For each bow the Romans are producing, they give up the opportunity to make 10 arrows. The Dacians are giving up producing 2 bows for every 40 arrows they are producing. Which of the following is true regarding comparative advantage?
   a. The Romans have comparative advantage in producing arrows
   b. The Romans have comparative advantage in producing bows
   c. The Romans have comparative advantage in producing arrows and bows
   d. The Dacians have comparative advantage in producing arrows and bows
   e. The Dacians have comparative advantage in producing bows

5. Which of the following is *not* a basis for trade between two nations?
   a. different skill levels of the labor forces
   b. one nation's absolute advantage
   c. a difference in tastes between countries
   d. economies of scale
   e. different capital stocks

6. Which of the following is true?
   a. International trade makes it possible for a country's consumption possibilities to exceed its production possibilities.
   b. International trade requires that a country's production possibilities exceed its consumption possibilities.
   c. A country's production possibilities always equal its consumption possibilities.
   d. A country's consumption possibilities can never equal its production possibilities because of leakages in the system.
   e. As long as there is full employment of resources, a country's production possibilities will exceed its consumption possibilities even with trade.

7. As a result of international trade,
   a. the gain to producers in the importing country exceeds the loss to consumers in the importing country
   b. the loss to producers in the importing country is less than the gain to consumers in the importing country caused by a decrease in price
   c. the loss to producers in the importing country exceeds the gain to consumers in the importing country caused by an increase in price

d. the loss to producers in the importing country is equal to the gain to consumers in the importing country because price increases and equilibrium quantity decreases
e. the loss to producers in the importing country is equal to the gain to consumers in the importing country because price decreases and equilibrium quantity increases

8. As a result of a tariff on imports, consumers in the importing country
   a. purchase more domestically produced goods and fewer foreign goods, resulting in the consumption of fewer total goods than without the tariff
   b. purchase more domestically produced goods and fewer foreign goods, resulting in the consumption of more total goods than without the tariff
   c. purchase more domestically produced goods and more foreign goods, resulting in the consumption of fewer total goods than without the tariff
   d. purchase fewer domestically produced goods and fewer foreign goods, resulting in the consumption of more total goods than without the tariff
   e. cease importing any goods at all

9. The difference between a specific tariff and an ad valorem tariff is that a specific tariff
   a. is a set amount of money per unit of a product, while an ad valorem tariff is a set percentage of product price
   b. is a set percentage of product price, while an ad valorem tariff is a set amount of money per unit of a product
   c. names a particular good to which the tariff applies, while an ad valorem tariff applies to large classes of products
   d. applies only to imports, while an ad valorem tariff applies only to exports
   e. sets a strict quota limit on the amount one individual can purchase, while an ad valorem tariff sets no such limit

10. To be effective, an import quota must
   a. reduce the price and increase the quantity of imports
   b. set the price of the imported good higher than the domestic equilibrium price
   c. restrict imports to less than would be imported under free trade
   d. restrict imports to less than exports in trade with that particular country
   e. be directed at the product of a specific country

11. Which of the following is *not* an argument in favor of restricting trade?
   a. to preserve national security
   b. to prevent dumping
   c. to increase consumer surplus
   d. to protect infant industries
   e. to protect declining industries

12. Which of the following is *not* true of declining industries?
   a. Job loss is not a problem in a declining industry because the workers can easily find jobs in expanding industries.
   b. Jobs may be lost by declining industries but new jobs are created in expanding industries.
   c. One way to solve the problems posed by declining industries is for the government to fund programs to retrain workers for jobs that are in greater demand.
   d. One way to solve the problems posed by declining industries is for the government to offer wage subsidies or special tax breaks that decline over time.

13. The balance of payments summarizes the transactions that occur during a given time period between
   a. the government of one country and the government of another country
   b. the national government and local governments in the same country
   c. individuals, firms, and government of one country and individuals, firms, and governments throughout the rest of the world
   d. individuals, firms, and governments of two countries
   e. non-government residents (individuals and firms) of two countries

14. Which of the following is *not* classified as a service in the current account?
   a. transportation
   b. insurance
   c. tourist expenditures
   d. income earned from foreign investments
   e. unilateral transfers

15. Which one of the following is *not* true?
   a. An exchange rate is the price of one currency in terms of another.

b. An exchange rate is the means by which the price of a good in one country is translated into the price to the buyer in another country.
c. The cost of a foreign good in dollars will depend on the current exchange rate.
d. The exchange rate will affect the willingness of foreign buyers and sellers to trade with each other.
e. The exchange rate is the price of a currency in terms of another currency for exchanges of goods and services but not for financial transactions.

16. If on Tuesday you can buy 125 yen per U.S. dollar and on Wednesday you can buy 120 yen per U.S. dollar,
   a. both the U.S. dollar and the yen have appreciated
   b. both the U.S. dollar and the yen have depreciated
   c. the U.S. dollar has appreciated and the yen has depreciated
   d. the U.S. dollar has depreciated and the yen has appreciated
   e. the yen has appreciated and the U.S. dollar has remained constant

17. If the U.S. dollar depreciates, it means that
   a. the value of the U.S. dollar has increased
   b. the value of foreign exchange has decreased
   c. fewer U.S. dollars are required to purchase foreign exchange
   d. more U.S. dollars are required to purchase foreign exchange
   e. exports will immediately fall

18. Which of the following best describes a graph showing the supply and demand for foreign exchange?
   a. The quantity of foreign exchange is on the horizontal axis and the quantity of the domestic currency is on the vertical axis.
   b. The quantity of the domestic currency is on the horizontal axis and the quantity of foreign exchange is on the vertical axis.
   c. The quantity of foreign exchange is on the horizontal axis and the price of foreign exchange in terms of the domestic currency is on the vertical axis.
   d. The quantity of foreign exchange is on the vertical axis and the price of foreign exchange in terms of the domestic currency is on the horizontal axis.
   e. The quantity of the domestic currency is on the horizontal axis and the price of foreign exchange in terms of dollars is on the vertical axis.

19. Foreign exchange rates tend toward equality around the world because of the actions of
   a. central banks
   b. stock markets
   c. commodity markets
   d. the World Bank
   e. arbitrageurs

20. The theory that changes in the exchange rate reflect only changes in the price levels of two countries is called
   a. the floating exchange rate theory
   b. the fixed exchange rate theory
   c. the flexible exchange rate theory
   d. purchasing power parity
   e. the managed exchange rate theory

Answers

1. c	2. b	3. d	4. b	5. b	6. a	7. b	8. a	9. a	10. c
11. c	12. a	13. c	14. e	15. e	16. d	17. d	18. c	19. e	20. d

Long Answer Questions

LO1 Describe the gains that trade brings

1.1. *(Comparative Advantage)* Suppose that each U.S. worker can produce 8 units of food or 2 units of clothing daily. In Fredonia, which has the same number of workers, each worker can produce 7 units of food or 1 unit of clothing daily. Why does the United States have an absolute advantage in both goods? Which country enjoys a comparative advantage in food? Why?

1.2. *(Comparative Advantage)* The consumption possibilities frontiers shown in the following exhibit assume terms of trade of 1 unit of clothing for 1 unit of food. What would the consumption possibilities frontiers look like if the terms of trade were 1 unit of clothing for 2 units of food?

Production (and Consumption) Possibility Frontiers with Trade (millions of units per day)

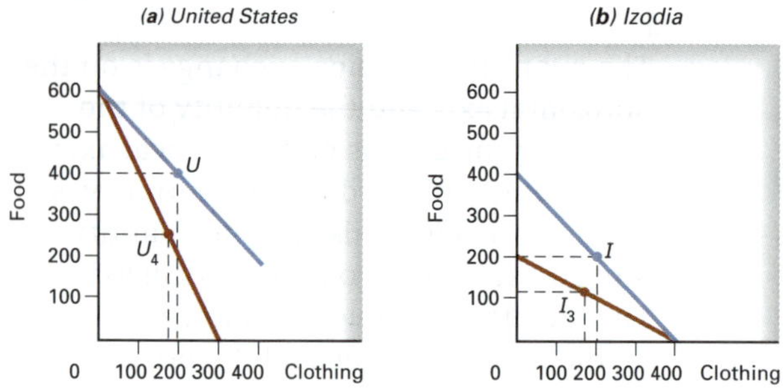

LO2 Discuss the reasons for international specialization

2.1. *(Reasons for International Specialization)* What determines which goods a country should produce and export?

LO3 Explain trade restrictions and welfare loss

3.1. *(Import Quotas)* How low must a quota be in effect to have an impact? Using a demand-and-supply diagram, illustrate and explain the net welfare loss from imposing such a quota. Under what circumstances would the net welfare loss from an import quota exceed the net welfare loss from an equivalent tariff (one that results in the same price and import level as the quota)?

3.2. *(Trade Restrictions)* Suppose that the world price for steel is below the U.S. domestic price, but the government requires that all steel used in the United States be domestically produced.

a. Use a diagram like the one that follows to show the gains and losses from such a policy.
b. How could you estimate the net welfare loss (deadweight loss) from such a diagram?
c. What response to such a policy would you expect from industries (like automobile producers) that use U.S. steel?
d. What government revenues are generated by this policy?

Effect of a Tariff

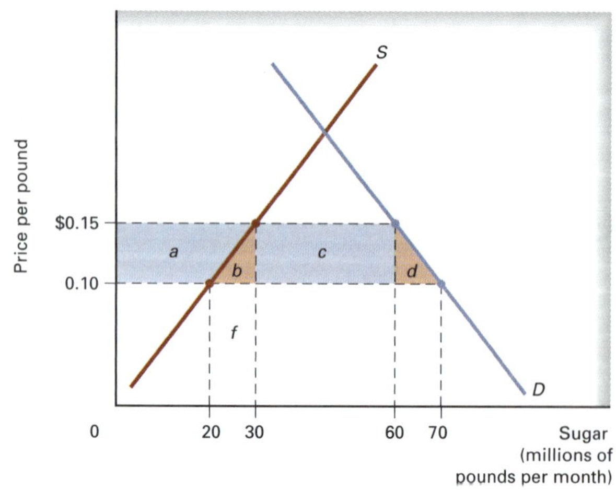

Effect of a Quota

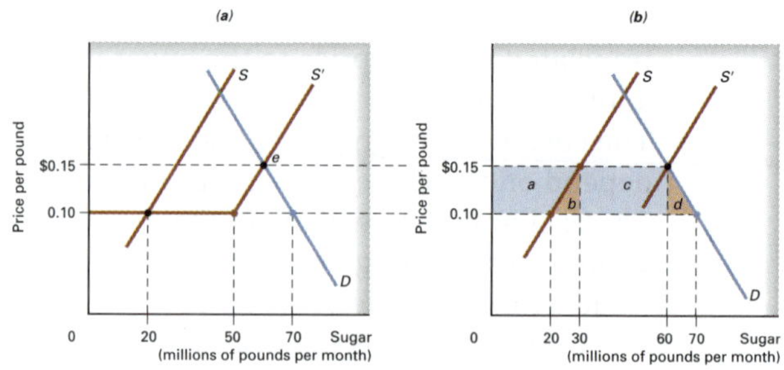

3.3. *(Trade Restrictions)* The previous three graphs show net losses to the economy of a country that imposes tariffs or quotas on imported sugar. What kinds of gains and losses would occur in the economies of countries that export sugar?

LO4 Describe ways countries have reduced or eliminated trade barriers

4.1. *(The World Trade Organization)* What is the World Trade Organization (WTO) and how does it help foster multilateral trade? (Check the WTO Web site at http://www.wto.org/.)

LO5 List and describe the arguments in favor of trade restrictions

5.1. *(Arguments for Trade Restrictions)* Explain the national defense, declining industries, and infant industry arguments for protecting a domestic industry from international competition.

5.2. *(Arguments for Trade Restrictions)* Firms hurt by cheap imports typically argue that restricting trade will save U.S. jobs. What's wrong with this argument? Are there ever any reasons to support such trade restrictions?

LO6 Explain how the balance of payments works

6.1. *(Balance of Payments)* The following are hypothetical data for the U.S. balance of payments. Use the data to calculate each of the following:

a. Merchandise trade balance
b. Balance on goods and services
c. Balance on current account
d. Capital account balance
e. Statistical discrepancy

	Billions of Dollars
Merchandise exports	350.0
Merchandise imports	2,425.0
Service exports	170.0
Service imports	2,145.0
Net income and net transfers	221.5
Outflow of U.S. capital	245.0
Inflow of foreign capital	70.0

6.2. *(Balance of Payments)* Explain where in the U.S. balance of payments an entry would be recorded for each of the following:
   a. A Hong Kong financier buys some U.S. corporate stock.
   b. A U.S. tourist in Paris buys some perfume to take home.
   c. A Japanese company sells machinery to a pineapple company in Hawaii.
   d. U.S. farmers make a gift of food to starving children in Ethiopia.
   e. The U.S. Treasury sells a bond to a Saudi Arabian prince.
   f. A U.S. tourist flies to France on Air France.
   g. A U.S. company sells insurance to a foreign firm.

LO7 Discuss foreign exchange rates and markets

7.1. *(Determining the Exchange Rate)* Use these data to answer the following questions about the market for British pounds:

Pound Price (in $)	Quantity Demanded (of pounds)	Quantity Supplied (of pounds)
$4.00	50	100
3.00	75	75
2.00	100	50

   a. Draw the demand and supply curves for pounds, and determine the equilibrium exchange rate (dollars per pound).
   b. Suppose that the supply of pounds doubles. Draw the new supply curve.
   c. What is the new equilibrium exchange rate?
   d. Has the dollar appreciated or depreciated?
   e. What happens to U.S. imports of British goods?

LO8 Define fixed and flexible exchange rates

8.1. *(Exchange Rates)* Discuss the differences between a flexible exchange rate and a fixed exchange rate. What measures can the government take to maintain fixed exchange rates?

INTERNATIONAL TRADE

Chapter in Review

20

KEY TERMS

autarky national self-sufficiency; no economic interaction with foreigners

terms of trade how much of one good exchanges for a unit of another good

world price the price at which a good is traded on the world market; determined by the world demand and world supply for the good

General Agreement on Tariffs and Trade (GATT) an international tariff-reduction treaty adopted in 1947 that resulted in a series of negotiated "rounds" aimed at freer trade; the Uruguay Round created GATT's successor, the World Trade Organization (WTO)

dumping selling a product abroad for less than charged in the home market or for less than the cost of production

Uruguay Round the final multilateral trade negotiation under GATT; this 1994 agreement cut tariffs, formed the World Trade Organization (WTO), and will eventually eliminate quotas

World Trade Organization (WTO) the legal and institutional foundation of the multilateral trading system that succeeded GATT in 1995

balance on goods and services the portion of a country's balance-of-payments account that measures the value of a country's exports of goods and services minus the value of its imports of goods and services

net investment income from abroad investment earnings by Indian residents from their foreign assets minus investment earnings by foreigners from their assets in India

net unilateral transfers abroad the unilateral transfers (gifts and grants) received from abroad by Indian residents minus the unilateral transfers Indian residents send abroad

balance on current account the portion of the balance-of-payments account that measures

LO1 Describe the gains that trade brings.

The law of comparative advantage says that the individual with the lowest opportunity cost of producing a particular good should specialize in that good. Just as individuals benefit from specialization and exchange, so do states and, indeed, nations. To reap the gains that arise from specialization, countries engage in international trade. Each country specializes in making goods with the lowest opportunity cost. Before countries can trade, however, they must agree on how much of one good exchanges for another (i.e., the terms of trade).

Production Possibilities Frontiers for the United States and Izodia Without Trade (millions of units per day)

Panel (a) shows the U.S. production possibilities frontier; its slope indicates that the opportunity cost of an additional unit of food is 1/2 unit of clothing. Panel (b) shows production possibilities in Izodia; an additional unit of food costs 2 units of clothing. Food is produced at a lower opportunity cost in the United States.

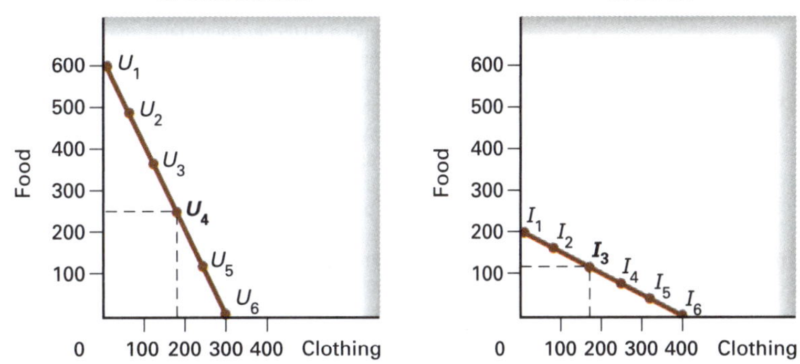

Production (and Consumption) Possibility Frontiers with Trade (millions of units per day)

If Izodia and the United States can trade at the rate of 1 unit of clothing for 1 unit of food, both can benefit. Consumption possibilities at these terms of trade are shown by the blue lines. The United States was previously producing and consuming U_4. By trading with Izodia, it can produce only food and still consume combination U, which has more food and more clothing than U_4. Likewise, Izodia can attain preferred combination I by trading its clothing for U.S. food. Both countries are better off as a result of international trade.

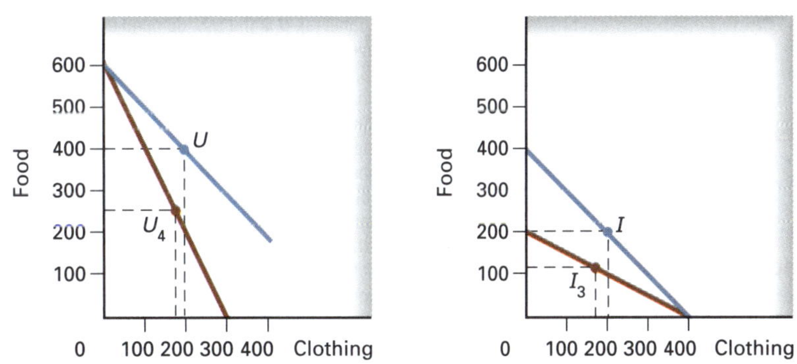

LO2 Discuss the reasons for international specialization.

Countries export products they can produce more cheaply in return for products that are unavailable domestically or are cheaper elsewhere. If production is subject to economies of scale (i.e., if the long-run average cost of production falls as a firm expands its scale of operation), countries can gain from trade if each nation specializes. Consumption patterns differ across countries, and some of this results from differences in tastes, a situation that allows countries to gain from trade.

that country's balance on goods and services, net investment income from abroad, plus net unilateral transfers abroad

financial account
the record of a country's international transactions involving purchases or sales of financial and real assets

exchange rate
the price measured in one country's currency of purchasing 1 unit of another country's currency

currency depreciation
with respect to the dollar, an increase in the number of dollars needed to purchase 1 unit of foreign exchange in a flexible rate system

currency appreciation
with respect to the dollar, a decrease in the number of dollars needed to purchase 1 unit of foreign exchange in a flexible rate system

arbitrageur
someone who takes advantage of temporary geographic differences in the exchange rate by simultaneously purchasing a currency in one market and selling it in another market

speculator
someone who buys or sells foreign exchange in hopes of profiting from fluctuations in the exchange rate over time

purchasing power parity (PPP) theory
the idea that the exchange rate between two countries will adjust in the long run to equalize the cost between the countries of a basket of internationally traded goods

flexible exchange rate
rate determined in foreign exchange markets by the forces of demand and supply without government intervention

fixed exchange rate
rate of exchange between currencies pegged within a narrow range and maintained by the central bank's ongoing purchases and sales of currencies

currency devaluation
an increase in the official pegged price of foreign exchange in terms of the domestic currency

currency revaluation
a reduction in the official pegged price of foreign exchange in terms of the domestic currency

U.S. Production as a Percentage of U.S. Consumption for Various Commodities

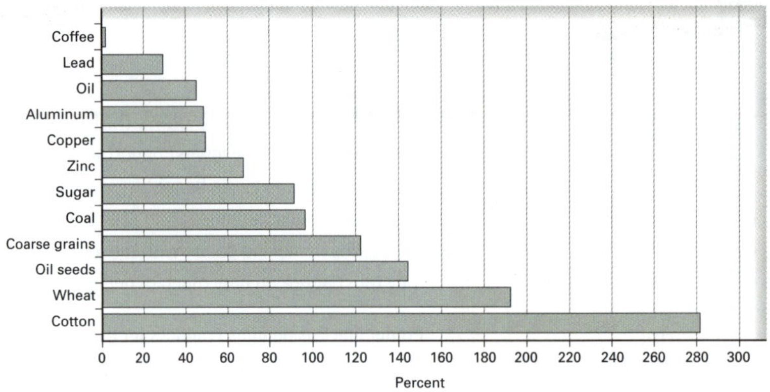

Effect of a Tariff

At a world price of $0.10 per pound, U.S. consumers demand 70 million pounds of sugar per month, and U.S. producers supply 20 million pounds per month; the difference is imported. After the imposition of a $0.05 per pound tariff, the U.S. price rises to $0.15 per pound. U.S. producers increase production to 30 million pounds, and U.S. consumers cut back to 60 million pounds. Imports fall to 30 million pounds. At the higher U.S. price, consumers are worse off; their loss of consumer surplus is the sum of areas *a, b, c,* and *d.* Area *a* represents an increase in producer surplus; this area is transferred from consumers to producers. Area *b* reflects the higher marginal cost of domestically producing sugar that could have been produced more cheaply abroad; thus *b* is a net U.S. welfare loss. Area *c* shows government revenue from the tariff. Area *d* reflects the loss of consumer surplus resulting from the drop in consumption. The net welfare loss to the U.S. economy consists of areas *b* and *d.*

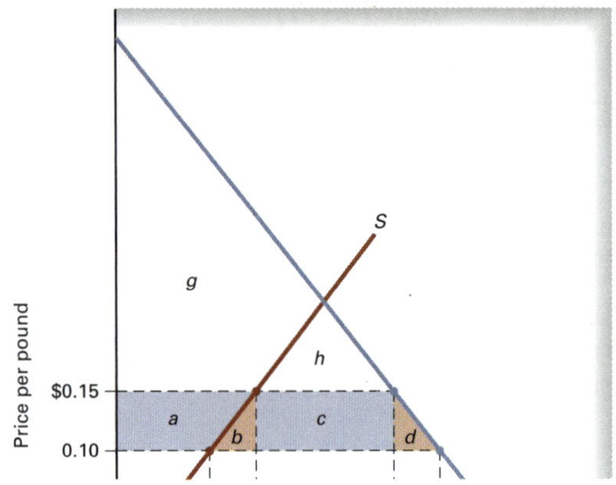

Effect of a Quota

In panel (a), *D* is the U.S. demand curve and *S* is the supply curve of U.S. producers. When the government establishes a sugar quota of 30 million pounds per year, the supply curve from both U.S. production and imports becomes horizontal at the world price of $0.10 per pound and remains horizontal until the quantity supplied reaches 50 million pounds. For higher prices, the supply curve equals the horizontal sum of the U.S. supply curve, *S*, and the quota. The new U.S. price, $0.15 per pound, is determined by the intersection of the new supply curve, *S'*, with the U.S. demand curve, *D.* Panel (b) shows the welfare effect of the quota. As a result of the higher U.S. price, consumer surplus is cut by the shaded area. Area *a* represents a transfer from U.S. consumers to U.S. producers. Triangular area *b* reflects a net loss; it represents the amount by which the cost of producing an extra 10 million pounds of sugar in the United States exceeds the cost of buying it from abroad. Rectangular area *c* shows the gain to those who can sell foreign-grown sugar at the higher U.S. price instead of the world price. Area *d* also reflects a net loss—a reduction in consumer surplus as consumption falls because of the price increase. Thus, the blue-shaded areas illustrate the loss in consumer surplus that is captured by domestic producers and those who are permitted to fulfill the quota, and the pink-shaded triangles illustrate the net welfare cost of the quota on the U.S. economy.

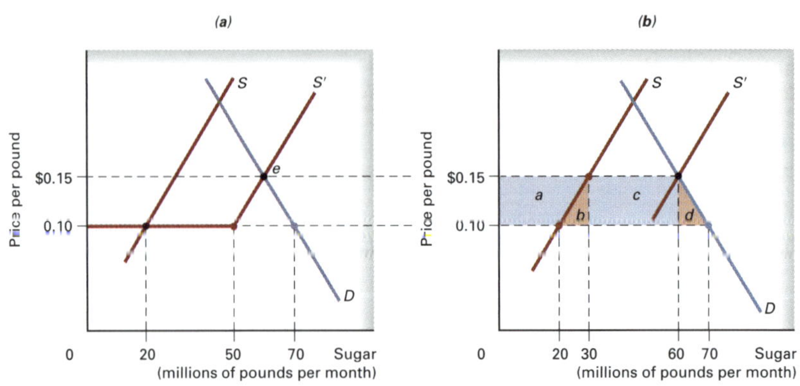

LO3 Explain trade restrictions and welfare loss. Market exchange usually generates a surplus, or a bonus, for both consumers and producers. Governments try to regulate surpluses by imposing tariffs (either specific or *ad valorem*) and import quotas, granting export subsidies, or extending low-interest loans to foreign buyers. Loss in U.S. consumer surplus resulting from tariffs is divided three ways: a portion goes to domestic producers; a portion becomes government revenue; and the last portion represents net losses in domestic social welfare. Welfare loss occurs when consumers must pay a higher price for products that could have been imported and sold at a lower price.

LO4 Describe ways countries have reduced or eliminated trade barriers. Trade restrictions impose a variety of strains on the economy besides the higher costs to consumers, so countries have worked to create free trade agreements and common markets to reduce or eliminate trade barriers. The General Agreement on Tariffs and Trade (GATT) was an international treaty ratified in 1947 to reduce trade barriers. Subsequent negotiations lowered tariffs and reduced trade restrictions. The Uruguay Round, ratified in 1994, lowered tariffs, phased out quotas, and created the World Trade Organization (WTO) as the successor to GATT.

LO5 List and describe the arguments in favor of trade restrictions. Arguments used by producer groups to support trade restrictions include promoting national defense, nurturing infant industries, preventing foreign producers from dumping goods in domestic markets, protecting domestic jobs, and allowing declining industries time to wind down and exit the market.

LO6 Explain how the balance of payments works. The balance of payments reflects all economic transactions between one country and the rest of the world. The current account measures flows from (a) goods; (b) services, including consulting and tourism; (c) income from holdings of foreign assets; and (d) unilateral transfers, or public and private transfer payments to and from foreign residents. The financial account measures international transactions in real and financial assets.

India's Balance of Payments for 2010–11 (millions of dollars)

Current Accounts	
1. Merchandise—exports f.o.b	250,468
2. Merchandise—imports, c.i.f	380,935
3. Trade balance (1-2)	–130,467
4. Invisibles, net	86,186
5. Current account balance (3+4)	–44,281
Capital Accounts	
6. Foreign investment	54,835
7. External assistance, net	4,965
8. Commercial borrowings, net	11,599
9. Rupee debt service	–69
10. NRI deposits, net	3,239
11. Other capital	–17,238
12. Capital account balance (6 to 11)	57,331
13. Overall balance (5+6)	13,050

U.S. Imports Have Topped Exports Since 1976, and the Trade Deficit Has Widened

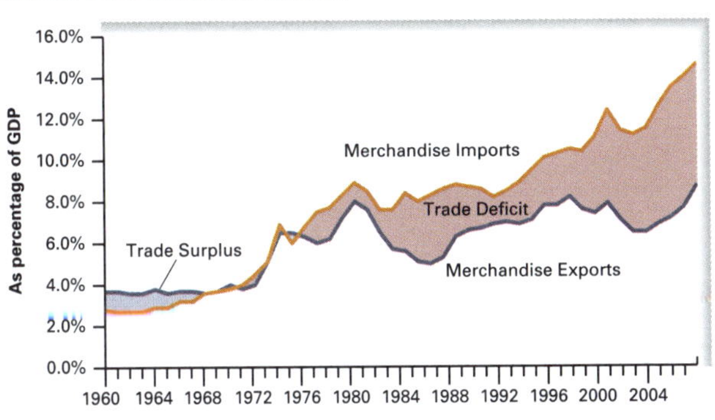

U.S. Merchandise Trade Deficits in 2008 by Country or Grouping

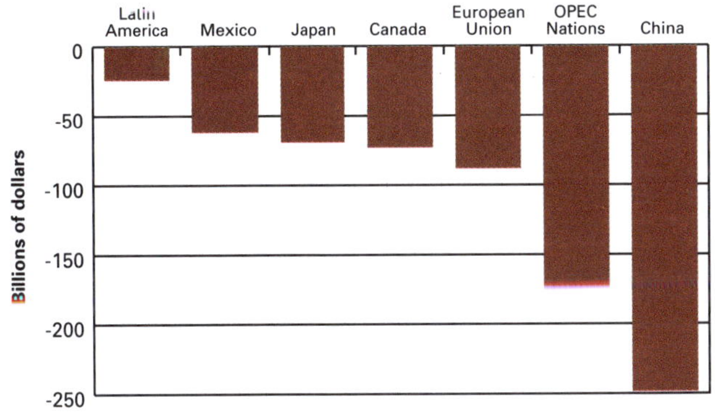

LO7 **Discuss foreign exchange rates and markets.** Under a system of fixed exchange rates, monetary authorities try to stabilize the exchange rate, keeping it between a specified ceiling and floor value. A country may try to hold down the value of its currency, so that exports will be cheaper to foreigners and imports will cost more to domestic consumers. One objective here is to increase domestic production and employment.

The Foreign Exchange Market

The fewer dollars needed to purchase 1 unit of foreign exchange, the lower the price of foreign goods and the greater the quantity of foreign goods demanded. The greater the quantity of foreign goods demanded, the greater the quantity of foreign exchange demanded. Thus, the demand curve for foreign exchange slopes downward. An increase in the exchange rate makes U.S. products cheaper for foreigners. The increased demand for U.S. goods implies an increase in the quantity of foreign exchange supplied. The supply curve of foreign exchange slopes upward.

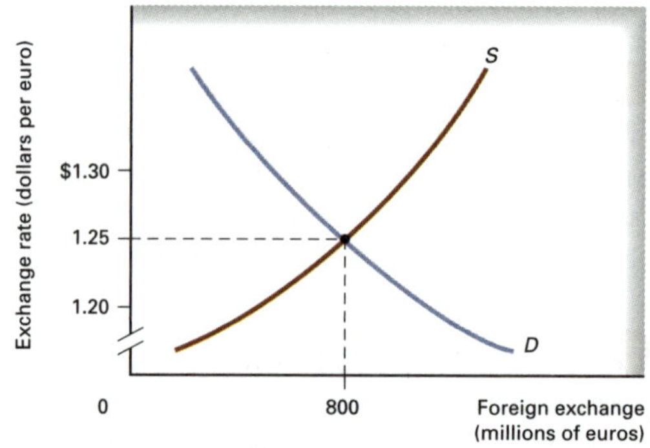

Effect on the Foreign Exchange Market of an Increased Demand for Euros

The intersection of the demand curve for foreign exchange, *D*, and the supply curve for foreign exchange, *S*, determines the exchange rate. At an exchange rate of $1.25 per euro, the quantity of euros demanded equals the quantity supplied. An increase in the demand for euros from *D* to *D′* increases the exchange rate from $1.25 to $1.27 per euro.

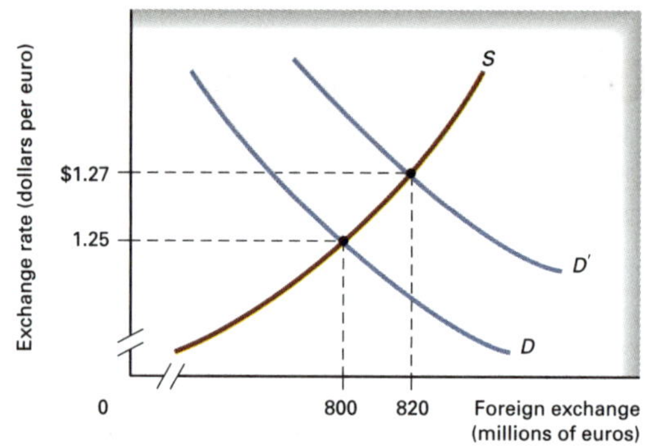

LO8 **Define fixed and flexible exchange rates.** Under a system of flexible, or floating, exchange rates, the value of the dollar varies inversely with respect to changes in the demand for foreign exchange and directly with respect to changes in the supply of foreign exchange. If governments, however, try to impose fixed exchange rates, active and ongoing central bank intervention is often necessary to establish and maintain them.

CHAPTER 21

Economic Development

Learning Outcomes

LO 1 Describe the worldwide variation in economic vitality

LO 2 Explain why productivity is the key to development

LO 3 Discuss international trade and development

LO 4 Describe the role of foreign aid in economic development

© STEPHEN DOREY/ALAMY

"How might subsidized food and used clothing programs for poor countries retard their economic development?"

Why are some countries so poor while others are so rich? What determines the wealth of nations? Why do families in low-income countries have more children than those in higher-income countries? And how might programs that send subsidized food and used clothing to poor countries have the unintended consequence of retarding economic development there? People around the world face the day under quite different circumstances. Even during a national recession, most Americans rise from a comfortable bed in a nice home, select the day's clothing from a wardrobe, choose from a variety of breakfast foods, and drive to school or to work in one of the family's personal automobiles. But some of the world's 6.9 billion people have little housing, clothing, or food. They have no automobile and no formal job. Their health is poor, as is their education. Many cannot read or write. A billion people need eyeglasses but can't afford them.

In this chapter, we sort out rich nations from poor ones and try to explain the difference. We discuss sources of economic development, and weigh the pros and cons of foreign aid.

What do you think?

Poverty is a self-perpetuating cycle.

Strongly Disagree					*Strongly Agree*	
1	2	3	4	5	6	7

Topics discussed in Chapter 21 include:

- Developing countries
- The key to development
- Privatization
- The poorest billion
- Foreign trade and development
- Foreign aid and development

LO1 Worlds Apart

Differences in economic vitality among countries are huge. Countries are classified in a variety of ways based on their economic development. The yardstick most often used to compare living standards across nations is the amount an economy produces per capita, or *output per capita*. The World Bank, an economic development institution affiliated with the United Nations (UN), estimates income per capita to classify economies. The measure begins with *gross national income (GNI)*, which is the market value of all goods and services produced by resources supplied by the countries' residents and firms, regardless of the location of the resource. For example, U.S. GNI includes profit earned by an American factory in Great Britain but excludes profits earned by a Japanese factory in Kentucky.

GNI measures both the value of output produced and the income that output generates. The World Bank computes the GNI per capita, then adjusts figures across countries based on the purchasing power of that income in each country. Using this measure, the World Bank sorts countries around the world into three major groups: *high-income economies, middle-income economies,* and *low-income economies.*

Data on world population and world output are summarized in Exhibit 1. High-income economies in 2009 made up only 16 percent of the 6.9 billion people on Earth, but accounted for 72 percent of world output. So high-income economies, *with only about one-sixth of the world's population, produced nearly three-quarters of the world's output.* Middle-income economies made up 71 percent of the world's population, but accounted for 27 percent of the world output. And low-income countries made up 13 percent of the world's population, but account for only 1 percent of world output.

developing countries
Nations typified by high rates of illiteracy, high unemployment, high fertility rates, and exports of primary products; also known as low-income and middle-income economies

industrial market countries
Economically advanced capitalist countries of Western Europe, North America, Australia, New Zealand, and Japan; also known as developed countries and high-income economies

Developing and Industrial Economies

The low- and middle-income economies are usually referred to as **developing countries**. Most high-income economies are also referred to as **industrial market countries**. So low- and middle-income economies, what are called developing countries, made up 84 percent of the world's population in 2009 but produce only 28 percent of the output. Compared to industrial market countries, developing countries usually have higher rates of illiteracy, higher unemployment, faster population growth, and exports consisting mostly of agricultural products and raw materials.

On average, about half of the labor force in developing countries works in agriculture versus only about 3 percent in industrial market countries. Because farming methods are relatively primitive in developing countries, farm productivity is low and some households barely subsist. Industrial market countries or *developed countries* are primarily the economically advanced capitalist countries of Western Europe, North America, Australia, New Zealand, and Japan. They were the first to experience long-term economic growth during the 19th century.

Exhibit 2 presents income per capita in 2010 for a sample of high-, middle-, and low-income economies. Because most countries in the sample have large populations, together they account for 56 percent of the world population. Countries are listed from top to bottom in descending order based on income per capita. Again, figures have been adjusted to reflect the actual purchasing power of the local currency in its respective economy. The bars in the chart are color-coded, with high-income economies in blue, middle-income economies in orange, and low-income economies in red. Per capita income in the United States, the exhibit's top-ranked country, was six times that of China, a middle-income economy. But per capita in China, in turn, was about seven times that of Ethiopia and 25 times that of the Democratic Republic of the Congo, both, poor African nations. Residents of China likely feel poor relative to America, but they appear well off compared to the poorest nations. U.S per capita income was 47 times that of Ethiopia, and 158 times that of the Congo, one of the poorest nations on Earth. Thus, there is a tremendous range of per capita income around the world. Exhibit 2 looks at income per capita, but neither income nor population is always measured accurately, especially in the poorest countries.

Exhibit 1

Share of World Population and World Output From High-, Middle-, and Low-Income Economies as of 2009

*(**a**) Share of world population from high-, middle-, and low-income economies*

*(**b**) Share of world output from high-, middle-, and low-income economies*

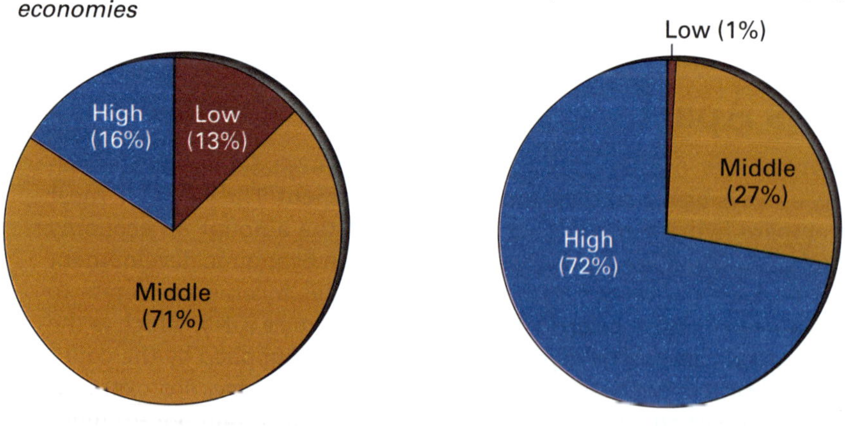

SOURCE: Based on population and output estimated from the World Bank's *World Development Report: 2011*, Table 1 at http://wdr2011.worldbank.org/sites/default/files/Complete%202011%20WDR%20Conflict%2CSecurity%20and%20Development_0.pdf. Find the World Bank at http://web.worldbank.org.

Exhibit 2

Per Capita Income for Selected Countries in 2010

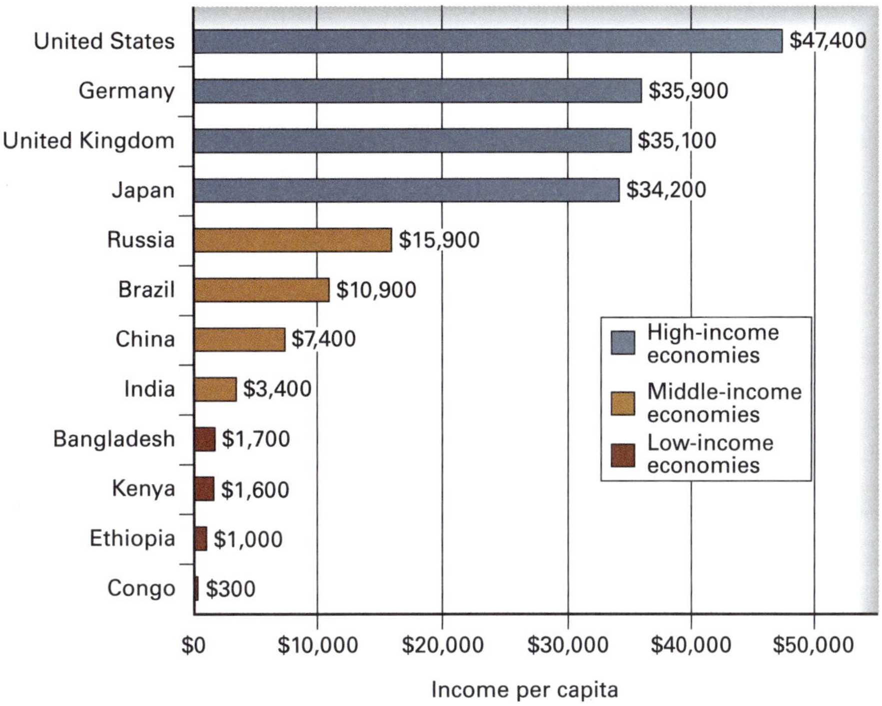

SOURCE: Developed from estimates from the Central Intelligence Agency's *World Factbook: 2011* at www.cia.gov/ library/ publications/the-world-factbook/index.html. Figures are based on the purchasing power of each country's currency.

Health and Nutrition

Differences in stages of development among countries are reflected in a number of ways besides per capita income. For example, many people in developing countries suffer from poor health as a result of malnutrition and disease. AIDS is devastating some developing countries, particularly those in sub-Saharan Africa. In 2009, about 150 of every 1,000 people ages 15 to 49 in South Africa, Zambia, and Zimbabwe had HIV, compared to only 3 of every 1,000 among those in high-income economies. In sub-Saharan Africa, life expectancy at birth averaged 52 years versus 80 years in high-income economies, 69 years in middle-income economies, and 59 years in all low-income economies.

Malnutrition

Those in the poorest countries consume only half the calories of those in high-income countries. Even if an infant survives the first year, malnutrition can turn normal childhood diseases, such as measles, into life-threatening events. The World Health Organization cites malnutrition as the biggest single threat to the world's public health. Malnutrition is a primary or contributing factor in more than half of the deaths of children under the age of 5 in low-income countries. Diseases that are well controlled in the industrial countries—malaria, whooping cough, polio, dysentery, typhoid, and cholera—can become epidemics in poor countries. Many of these diseases are water borne, as safe drinking water is often hard to find. In low-income countries, about 28 percent of children under the age of 5 suffered from malnutrition in 2008. Among middle-income countries the figure was 22 percent. Among high-income countries, it was 3 percent.

Infant Mortality

Health differences among countries are reflected in child mortality. Child mortality rates are much greater in low-income countries than in high-income countries. As of 2009, the mortality rate for children up to 5 years of age was 7 per 1,000 live births in high-income economies, 51 in middle-income econo-

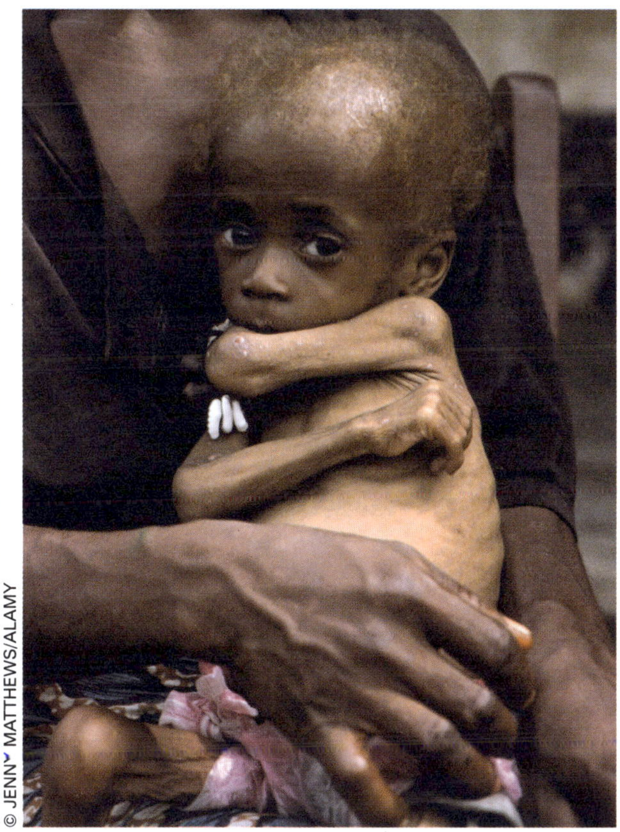

© JENNY MATTHEWS/ALAMY

Exhibit 3

Child Mortality Rates per 1,000 Live Births as of 2009

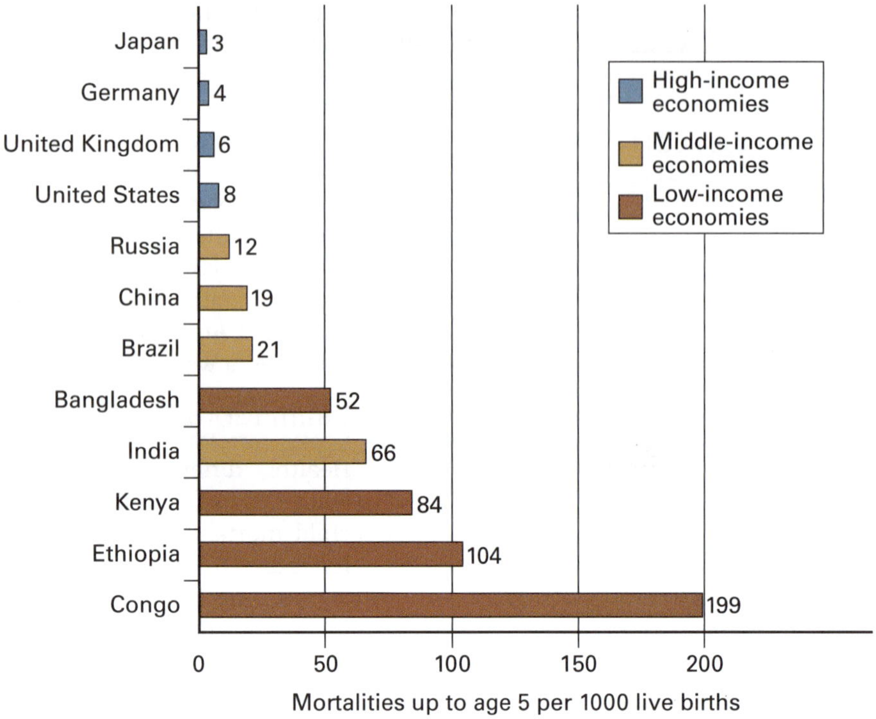

SOURCE: Based on figures from the World Bank's *World Development Report: 2011*, Table 3. Find the World Bank at http://www.worldbank.org.

mies, and 118 in low-income economies. Rates for our representative sample of high-, medium-, and low-income economies appear in Exhibit 3. Again, high-income economies appear as blue bars, middle-income as orange bars, and low-income as red bars. Among the dozen countries shown, child mortality was highest in the sub-Saharan African nations of Congo, Ethiopia, and Kenya. Child mortality among all 48 sub-Saharan African countries averaged 19 times that in high-income countries.

High Birth Rates

Developing countries are identified not only by their low incomes and high mortality rates but also by their high birth rates. This year, more than 80 million of the 90 million people added to the world's population will be born in developing countries. In fact, the birth rate is one of the clearest ways of distinguishing between industrial and developing countries. Very few low-income economies have a fertility rate below 2.2 births per woman, but none of the industrial market economies has a fertility rate above that level.

This year, more than 80 million of the 90 million people added to the world's population will be born in developing countries.

Exhibit 4 presents total fertility rates per woman for selected countries as of 2011. Ethiopia, the second-poorest nation on the list, has among the world's highest fertility rates at 6.0. This means each woman on average gives birth to 6.0 children during her lifetime. Note that the four low-income economies, shown as red bars, have the highest fertility rates. Historically, families tend to be larger in poor countries because children are viewed as a source of farm labor and as economic and social security as the parents age. Most developing countries have no pension or social security system for the aged. The higher child mortality rates in poorer countries also engender higher birth rates, as parents strive to ensure a sufficiently large family.

Sub-Saharan African nations are the poorest in the world and have the fastest-growing populations. Because of high fertility rates in the poorest countries, children under 15 years old make up 43 percent of the population there. In high-income countries, children make up only 18 percent of the population. Italy, a high-income economy, became the first country in history with more people over the age of 65 than under the age of 15. Germany, Greece, Spain, Portugal, Japan, Hungary, Switzerland, and the United Kingdom have since followed. An aging population poses fiscal problems, because these same countries typically offer generous health and pension benefits to the elderly.

In some developing countries, the population growth rate has exceeded the growth rate in total production, so the standard of living as measured by per capita output has declined. Still, even in the poorest of countries, attitudes about family size are changing. According to the United Nations, the birth rate during a typical woman's lifetime in a developing country has fallen from six children in 1965 to under three

Exhibit 4

Average Number of Births During a Woman's Lifetime as of 2011

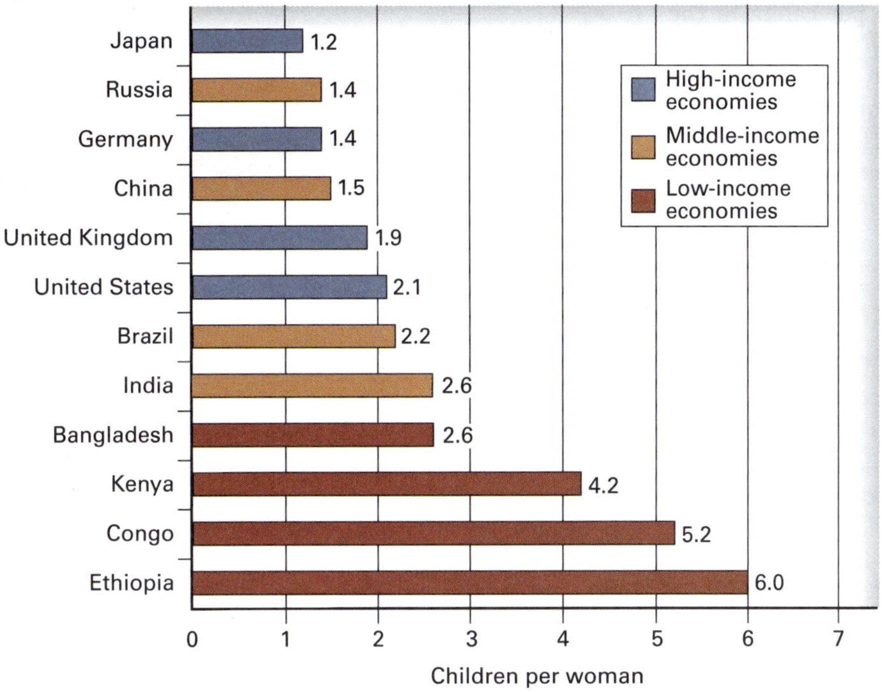

SOURCE: Developed from estimates from the Central Intelligence Agency's *World Factbook: 2011* at www.cia.gov/library/publications/the-world-factbook/index.html.

children today. Evidence from developing countries more generally indicates that when women have employment opportunities outside the home, fertility rates decline. And as women become better educated, they earn more and tend to have fewer children.

Women in Developing Countries

Throughout the world, the poverty rate is higher for women than men, particularly women who head households. The percentage of households headed by women varies from country to country, but nears 50 percent in some areas of Africa and the Caribbean. Because women often must work in the home as well as in the labor market, poverty can impose a special hardship on them. In many cultures, women's responsibilities include gathering firewood and carrying water, tasks that are especially burdensome if firewood is scarce and water is far from home.

Women in developing countries tend to be less educated than men. In the countries of sub-Saharan Africa and South Asia, for example, only half as many women as men complete high school. In Ethiopia, among those ages 15 and older, half the males can read and write, but only one third of females can. Women have fewer employment opportunities and earn lower wages than men do. For example, northern Sudan's Muslim fundamentalist government bans women from working in public places after 5:00 P.M. In Algeria, Egypt, Jordan, Libya, and Saudi Arabia, women account for only about one-quarter of the workforce. Women are often on the fringes of the labor market, working long hours in agriculture. They also have less access to other resources, such as land, capital, and technology.

WOMEN IN DEVELOPING COUNTRIES TEND TO BE LESS EDUCATED THAN MEN.

LO2 Productivity: Key to Development

We have examined some signs of poverty in developing countries, but not why poor countries are poor. At the risk of appearing simplistic, we might say that poor countries are poor because they do not produce many goods and services. In this section, we examine why some developing countries experience such low productivity.

Low Labor Productivity

Labor productivity, measured in terms of output per worker, is by definition low in low-income countries. Why? Labor productivity depends on the quality of the labor and on the amount of capital, natural resources, and other inputs that combine with labor. For example, one certified public accountant with a computer and specialized software can sort out a company's finances more quickly and more accurately than can a thousand high school–educated file clerks with pencils and paper.

One way a nation raises its productivity is by investing more in human and physical capital. This investment must be financed by either domestic savings or foreign funds. Income per capita in the poorest countries is often too low to support much investment. In poor countries with unstable governments, the wealthy minority frequently invests in more stable foreign economies. This leaves less to invest domestically in either human or physical capital; without sufficient capital, workers remain less productive.

© SUSAN LIEBOLD/ALAMY

Technology and Education

What exactly is the contribution of education to the process of economic development? Education helps people make better use of resources. If knowledge is lacking, other resources may not be used efficiently. For example, a country may be endowed with fertile land, but farmers may lack knowledge of irrigation and fertilization techniques. Or farmers may not know how to rotate crops to avoid soil depletion. In low-income countries, 34 percent of those 15 and older were illiterate in 2008, compared to 17 percent in middle-income countries, and only 2 percent in high-income countries. Many in developing countries drop out of school because the family can't afford it or would rather put the child to work. Child labor in developing countries obviously limits educational opportunities.

Education also makes people more receptive to new ideas and methods. Countries with the most advanced educational systems were also the first to develop. In the 20th century, the leader in schooling and economic development was the United States. In Latin America, Argentina was the most educationally advanced nation 100 years ago, and it is one of the most developed Latin American nations today. The growth of education in Japan during the 19th century contributed to a ready acceptance of technology and thus to Japan's remarkable economic growth in the 20th century.

Inefficient Use of Labor

Another feature of developing countries is that they use labor less efficiently than do industrial nations. Unemployment and underemployment reflect inefficient uses of labor. *Underemployment* occurs when skilled workers are employed in low-skill jobs or when people are working less than they would like—a worker seeking full-time employment may find only a part-time job. *Unemployment* occurs when those willing and able to work can't find jobs.

Unemployment is measured primarily in urban areas, because in rural areas farm work is usually an outlet for labor even if many workers are underemployed there. The unemployment rate in developing nations on average is about 10 percent to 15 percent of the urban labor force. Unemployment among young workers—those aged 15 to 24—is typically twice that of older workers. In developing nations, about 30 percent of the combined urban and rural workforce is either unemployed or underemployed. In Zimbabwe, the unemployment rate was 95 percent in 2010; it's no surprise why Zimbabwe is the poorest nation in the world—even poorer than the Congo.

Although more than half the labor force in developing countries works in agriculture, only about one-third of output in these countries stems from agriculture.

In some developing countries, the average farm is as small as two acres. Productivity is also low because few other inputs, such as capital and fertilizer, are used. *Although more than half the labor force in developing countries works in agriculture, only about one-third of output in these countries stems from agriculture.* In the United States, where farmers account for only 2 percent of the labor force, a farmer with modern equipment can farm hundreds or even thousands of acres (the average U.S. farm is about 500 acres). In developing countries, a farmer with a hand plow or an ox-drawn plow can farm maybe 10 to 20 acres. U.S. farmers, though only one-fiftieth of the labor force, grow enough to feed a nation and to lead the world in farm exports. The average value added per U.S. farm worker is about 75 times that of farm workers in low- and middle-income countries.

Low productivity obviously results in low income, but low income can, in turn, affect worker productivity. Low income means less saving and less saving means less investment in human and

"Low income and low productivity may reinforce each other in a cycle of poverty."

physical capital. Low income can also mean poor nutrition during the formative years, which can retard mental and physical development. These difficult beginnings may be aggravated by poor diet and insufficient health care in later life, making workers poorly suited for regular employment. Poverty can result in less saving, less education, less capital formation, a poor diet, and little health care—all of which can reduce a worker's productivity. Thus, *low income and low productivity may reinforce each other in a cycle of poverty*.

Natural Resources

Some countries are rich in natural resources. The difference is most striking when we compare countries with oil reserves and those without. The Middle East countries of Bahrain, Kuwait, Qatar, Saudi Arabia, and the United Arab Emirates are classified as high-income economies because they were lucky enough to be sitting atop huge oil reserves. But oil-rich countries are the exception. Many developing countries, such as Chad and Ethiopia, have little in the way of natural resources. Most developing countries without oil reserves are in trouble whenever oil prices rise. Since oil must be imported, higher oil prices drain oil-poor countries of precious foreign exchange.

Oil-rich countries also show us that an abundant supply of a natural resource is not in itself enough to create a modern industrial economy. On the other hand, Japan has one of the most developed economies in the world, yet has few natural resources. Connecticut is consistently the most productive of the United States measured in per capita income, but the state has little in the way of natural resources (its main natural resource is gravel). In fact, many researchers believe that reliance on resource wealth can be something of a curse for a nation.

© BARRY VERSON/ALAMY

Financial Institutions

Another requirement for development is an adequate and trusted system of financial institutions. An important source of funds for investment is the savings of households and firms. People in some developing countries have little confidence in their currency because some governments finance a large fraction of public outlays by printing money. This practice results in high inflation and sometimes very high inflation, or hyperinflation, as has occurred recently in Zimbabwe, where annual inflation was just about incalculable. High and unpredictable inflation discourages saving and hurts development.

Developing countries have special problems because banks are often viewed with suspicion. At the first sign of economic problems, many depositors withdraw their funds. Because banks cannot rely on a continuous supply of deposits, they cannot make loans for extended periods. If financial institutions fail to serve as intermediaries between savers and borrowers, the lack of funds for investment becomes an obstacle to growth. During the global financial crisis of 2008, banks in industrial market countries also suffered from depositors' sagging confidence. One measure of banking presence is the credit provided by banks as a percent of that nation's total output. This percentage is more than five times greater in high-income countries than in low-income countries.

Capital Infrastructure

Production and exchange depend on a reliable infrastructure of transportation, communication, sanitation, and electricity. Roads, bridges, airports, harbors, and other transportation facilities are vital to commercial activity. Reliable mail service, telephone communications, Internet connections, clean water, and electricity are also essential for advanced production techniques. Imagine how difficult it would be to run even a personal computer if the supply of electricity and access to the Internet were unavailable or continually interrupted, as is often the case in many developing countries.

Exhibit 5

Fixed and Mobile Phone Lines per 1,000 People for 2009

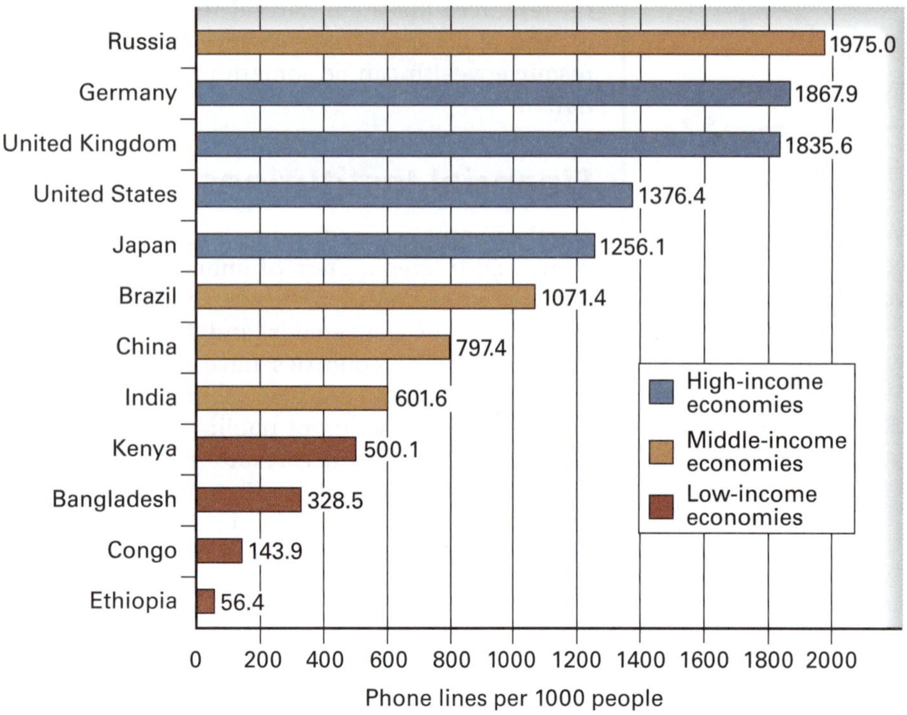

SOURCE: Computed based on fixed and mobile line estimates from the Central Intelligence Agency's *World Factbook: 2011* at www.cia.gov/library/publications/the-world-factbook/index.html.

Some developing countries have serious deficiencies in their physical infrastructures. As just one measure, Exhibit 5 shows the number of fixed and mobile telephone lines per 1,000 people in 2009 for the 12 countries examined earlier. The high-income economies have about 6 times more phones per 1,000 people than the bottom four countries, which are low-income economies. Russia, the top rated in this category, had 1,975 phone lines per 1,000 people. Bottom-ranked Ethiopia had just 56 phone lines per 1,000 people. Still, more than half the world's population had cell phones in 2009.[1]

Phone lines help knit together an economy's communications network. Countries without reliable phone service have difficulty not only communicating but reaping the benefits of other technology advances, such as the Internet. Exhibit 6 shows Internet users as a percent of the population in 2009 for our sample countries. There is an unmistakable digital divide between high-income and low-income economies. In the four high-income economies, an average 79 percent of the population used the Internet. In low-income economies, just 3 percent used the Internet on average. Even in India, which has a reputation as computer savvy, what with all the online support centers and software companies we read about, only 5 percent of the population were Internet users.

© LH IMAGES/ALAMY

Entrepreneurship

An economy can have abundant supplies of labor, capital, and natural resources, but without entrepreneurship, the other resources will not be combined efficiently to produce goods and services. Unless a country has entrepreneurs who are able to bring together resources and take the risk of profit or loss, develop-

1. "Father of the Cell Phone," *The Economist*, 6 June 2009.

Exhibit 6

Internet Users as Percent of Population for 2009

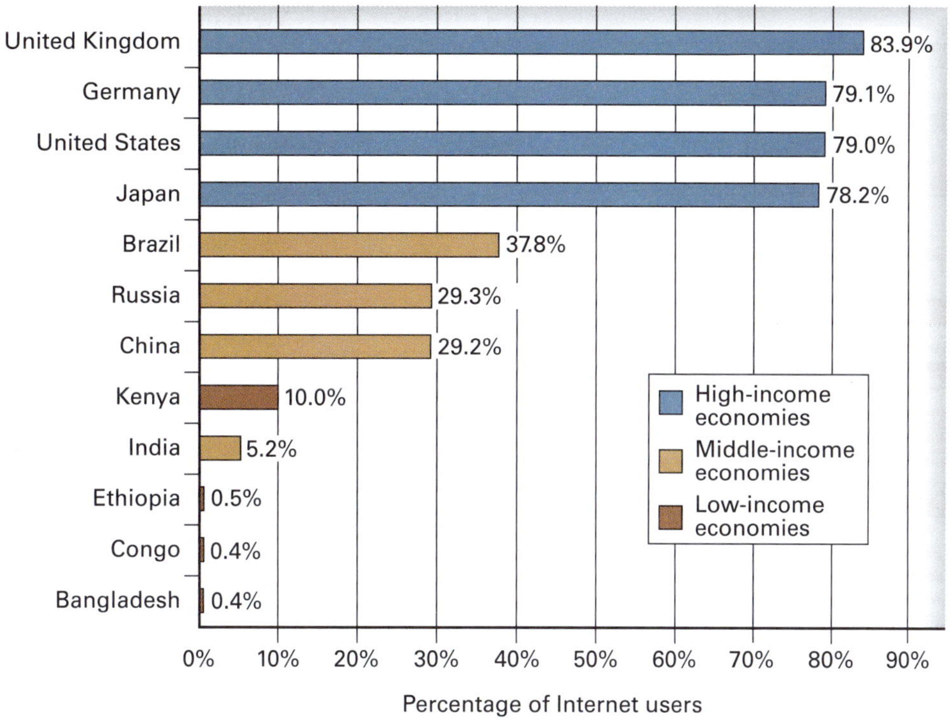

SOURCE: Computed from user estimates in the Central Intelligence Agency's *World Factbook: 2011* at www.cia.gov/library/publications/the-world-factbook/index.html.

ment may never get off the ground. Many developing countries were once under colonial rule, a system of government that offered the local population fewer opportunities to develop entrepreneurial skills.

One source of entrepreneurial experience for developing countries comes from McDonald's and other international franchises. For example, by providing management training, McDonald's stimulates entrepreneurship directly through its franchises and indirectly by showing competitors how a business is run. Such franchises also demonstrate to customers what they should come to expect in the way of service, cleanliness, quality, and the like.[2]

Government officials sometimes decide that entrepreneurs are unable to generate the kind of economic growth the country needs. State enterprises are therefore created to do what government believes the free market cannot do. But state-owned enterprises may have objectives other than producing goods efficiently—objectives that could include providing jobs for friends and relatives of government officials.

Rules of the Game

Finally, in addition to human capital, natural resources, financial institutions, capital infrastructure, and entrepreneurship, a successful economy needs reliable *rules of the game*. Perhaps the most elusive ingredients for development are the formal and informal institutions that promote production and exchange: the laws, customs, conventions, and other institutional elements that sustain an economy. A stable political environment with well-defined property rights is important. Little private-sector investment will occur if potential investors believe their capital might be appropriated by government, destroyed by civil unrest, blown up by terrorists, or stolen by thieves.

Under capitalism, the rules of the game include private ownership of most resources and the coordination of economic activity by the price signals generated by market forces. Market coordination answers the questions of what to produce, how to produce it, and for whom to produce it. Under socialism, the rules of the game include government ownership of most resources and the allocation of resources through central plans. For example, countries such as Cuba and North Korea carefully limit the private ownership of resources like land and capital. More generally, personal freedom is limited in centrally planned economies (for example, in North Korea, people need a government permit just to travel outside their own town).[3]

Although there is no universally accepted theory of economic development, around the world markets have been replacing central plans in many once-socialist countries. **Privatization** is the pro-

2. Adrian Tschoegli, "McDonald's—Much Maligned, But an Engine of Economic Development," *Global Economy Journal*, 7(Issue 4 2007) at http://www.bepress.com/gej/vol7/iss4/5/.

3. Peter Wonacott, "The Mystery of North Korean Fans," *The Wall Street Journal*, 26 June 2010.

privatization
The process of turning government enterprises into private enterprises

Exhibit 7

GDP per Capita for Developing Economies in 2010

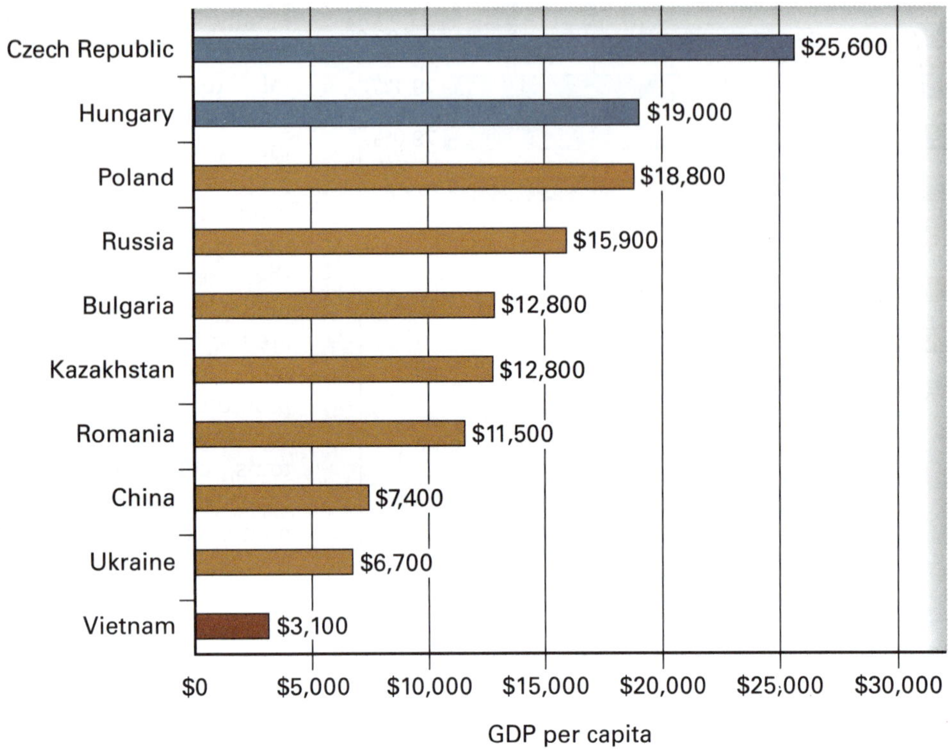

SOURCE: Computed from estimates in the Central Intelligence Agency's *World Factbook: 2011* at www.cia.gov/library/publications/the-world-factbook/index.html. Figures are based on the purchasing power of the local currency.

cess of turning government enterprises into private enterprises in these developing economies. Privatization is the opposite of *nationalization* (what Hugo Chávez has been doing in Venezuela). For example, Russian privatization began in 1992 with the sale of municipally owned shops. Exhibit 7 presents, for 10 developing economies, the gross domestic product (GDP) per capita in 2010 based on the purchasing power of the domestic currency. Notice the dramatic differences across these economies, with GDP per capita in the Czech Republic eight times greater than that in Vietnam. Russia's GDP per capita was midway between those two. The Czech Republic and Hungary, identified with blue bars, have joined the ranks of high-income economies. Seven of the 10 countries are middle-income economies, and are identified with orange bars. Vietnam, the red bar, is a low-income economy that still reflects vestiges of central planning. For example, banks there are more likely to lend to businesses that are politically connected than to those that are the most profitable. Thus, the most profitable Vietnamese firms tend to avoid banks and rely instead on reinvested earnings and informal loans.[4]

social capital
The shared values and trust that promote cooperation in the economy

High-income economies have developed a reliable and respected system of property rights and customs and conventions that nurture productive activity. These successful economies have also cultivated the social capital that helps the economy run more smoothly. **Social capital** consists of the shared values and trust that promotes cooperation in the economy. At the national level, social capital could be reflected in a sense of common purpose. For example, despite the troubling recession, polls show that Americans remain among the most patriotic people in the world. In a 2010 survey, 83 percent said they were "extremely" or "very" proud to be Americans.[5] At the local level, social capital could be expressed by a neighborhood crime watch, and there is evidence that such efforts help reduce property crime.[6] Low-income economies typically have poorly defined property rights, less social capital, and in the extreme, customs and conventions where bribery is commonplace and government corruption is an everyday practice. Worse still, civil wars have ravaged some of the poorest countries on Earth. Such violence and uncertainty make people less willing to invest in their own future or in the future of their country.

4. Edmund J. Malesky and Markus Taussig, "Where Is Credit Due? Legal Institutions, Connections, and the Efficiency of Bank Lending in Vietnam," *Journal of Law, Economics, and Organization*, 25 (October 2009): 525–578.
5. Lexington, "Where Has All the Greatness Gone," *The Economist*, 17 July 2010.
6. Paolo Buonanno, "Does Social Capital Reduce Crime," *Journal of Law and Economics*, 52 (February 2009): 145–170.

Income Distribution Within Countries

Thus far the focus has been on income differences across countries, and these differences can be vast. But what about income differences within a country? Are poor countries uniformly poor or are there sizable income differences among that nation's population? One way to measure inequality across households is to look at the share of national income going to the poorest fifth of the population. As a point of reference, in the unlikely event that income in an economy were evenly distributed across all households, then the poorest fifth would also receive exactly one fifth, or 20 percent, of national income. More realistically, the poorest fifth receives less than 20 percent of the income, but how much less? Is the percentage of income going to the poorest fifth higher for low-income countries than for high-income countries? In other words, is income more evenly distributed among poor countries than among rich countries? Not necessarily. Among our 12 nations, the poorest fifth of the population got an average of 7.7 percent of the income in the high-income countries, 5.6 percent in middle-income countries, and 7.2 percent in low-income countries. So, at least in this sample, income was less evenly distributed among middle-income countries than in high- or low-income countries.

LO3 International Trade and Development

Developing countries need to trade with developed countries to acquire the capital and technology that will increase labor productivity on the farm, in the factory, in the office, and in the home. To import capital and technology, developing countries must first acquire the funds, or foreign exchange, needed to pay for imports. Exports usually generate more than half of the annual flow of foreign exchange in developing countries. Foreign aid and private investment make up the rest.

> "Exports usually generate more than half of the annual flow of foreign exchange in developing countries."

Trade Problems for Developing Countries

Primary products, such as agricultural goods and other raw materials, make up the bulk of exports from developing countries, just as manufactured goods make up the bulk of exports from industrial countries. About half the merchandise exports from low-income countries consist of raw materials, compared to only 20 percent among high-income countries. A problem for developing countries is that the prices of primary products, such as coffee, cocoa, sugar, and rubber, fluctuate more widely than do the prices of finished goods, because crop supplies fluctuate with the weather.

When developing countries experience trade deficits, they often try to restrict imports. Because imported food is critical to survival, developing countries are more likely to cut imports of capital goods—the very items needed to promote long-term growth and productivity. Thus, many developing countries cannot afford the modern machinery that will help them become more pro-

© AFTYP_KOK/SHUTTERSTOCK.COM

ductive. Developing countries must also confront industrial countries' trade restrictions, such as tariffs and quotas, which often discriminate against primary products. For example, the United States strictly limits sugar imports and has done so for more than half a century. Such restrictions are one reason the Doha Round of trade agreements has not gone smoothly.

Migration and the Brain Drain

Migration plays an important role in the economies of developing countries. A major source of foreign exchange in some countries is the money sent home by migrants who find jobs in industrial countries. According to the World Bank, migrants sent home about $416 billion in 2009. Thus migration provides a valuable safety valve for poor countries. But there is a downside. Often the best and the brightest professionals, such as doctors, nurses, and engineers, migrate to developed countries. For example, every year thousands of nurses migrate from countries such as Kenya and the Philippines to the United States, where half the world's nurses are employed. The financial attraction is powerful: A nurse in the Philippines would start there at less than $6,000 a year, compared with at least $36,000 in the United States.

The Philippines economy benefits from the billions sent home by overseas workers. So the upside of the brain drain for the poor country is the money sent home by overseas workers. Still, a nation is hurt when its best and brightest leave for opportunities elsewhere. Some African countries are demanding compensation for educating the doctors and nurses who move to high-income economies.

Import Substitution Versus Export Promotion

An economy's progress usually involves moving up the production chain from agriculture and raw material to manufacturing then to services. If a country is fortunate, this transformation occurs gradually through natural market forces. For example, in 1850 most U.S. jobs were in agriculture. Now most jobs are in the service sector. Sometimes governments try to speed up the evolution. Many developing countries, including Argentina and India, pursued a strategy called **import substitution**, whereby domestic manufacturers would make products that until then had been imported. To insulate domestic manufacturers from foreign competition, the government imposed stiff tariffs and quotas. This development strategy became popular for several reasons. First, demand already existed for these products, so the "what to produce" question was easily answered. Second, import substitution provided infant industries a protected market. Finally, import substitution was popular with those who supplied resources to the favored domestic industries.

import substitution
A development strategy that emphasizes domestic manufacturing of products that were imported

export promotion
A development strategy that concentrates on producing for the export market

Like all trade protection, however, import substitution erased the gains from specialization and comparative advantage among countries. Often the developing country replaced low-cost foreign goods with high-cost domestic versions of those same goods. And domestic producers, shielded from foreign competition, usually failed to become efficient. Worse still, other countries often retaliated with their own trade restrictions.

Critics of import substitution claim that export promotion is a surer path to economic development. **Export promotion** concentrates on producing for the export market. This development strategy begins with relatively simple products, such as textiles. As a developing country builds its technological and educational base—that is, as the developing economy learns by doing—producers can then make more complex products for export. Economists favor export promotion over import substitution because the emphasis is on comparative advantage and trade expansion rather than on trade restriction. Export promotion also forces producers to grow more efficient in order to compete on world markets. Research shows that facing global competition boosts domestic efficiency.[7] What's more, export promotion requires less government intervention in the market than does import substitution.

Of the two approaches, export promotion has been more successful around the world. For example, the newly industrialized countries of East Asia have successfully pursued export promotion, while Argentina, India, and Peru have failed with their import-substitution approach. In 1965, the newly industrialized economies of Hong Kong, South Korea, Singapore, and Taiwan had an average income only 20 percent that of high-income countries. Now these four are themselves high-income countries.

7. See Martin Baily and Hans Gersbach, "Efficiency in Manufacturing and the Need for Global Competition," in *Brookings Papers on Economic Activity: Microeconomics*, M. Baily, P. Reiss, and C. Winston, eds. (Washington, D.C.: Brookings Institution, 1995): 307–347.

Most Latin American nations, which for decades had favored import substitution, are now pursuing free trade agreements with each other and with the United States. Even India is dismantling trade barriers, with an emphasis on importing high-technology capital goods.

Trade Liberalization and Special Interests

Although most people would benefit from freer international trade, some would be worse off. Consequently, governments in developing countries often have difficulty pursuing policies conducive to development. Often the gains from economic development are widespread, but the beneficiaries, such as consumers, do not recognize their potential gains. On the other hand, the losers tend to be concentrated, such as producers in an industry that had been sheltered from foreign competition, and they know quite well the source of their losses. So the government often lacks the political will and support to remove impediments to development, because the potential losers fight reforms that might harm their livelihood while the potential winners remain largely unaware of what's at stake. What's more, consumers have difficulty organizing even if they become aware of what's going on. A recent study by the World Bank suggests a strong link in Africa between governments that cater to special-interest groups and low rates of economic growth.

Nonetheless, many developing countries have been opening their borders to freer trade. People around the world have been exposed to information about the opportunities and products available on world markets. So consumers want the goods and firms want the technology and capital that are available abroad. Both groups want government to ease trade restrictions. Studies by the World Bank and others have underscored the successes of countries that have adopted trade liberalization policies.

LO4 Foreign Aid and Economic Development

We have already seen that because poor countries do not generate enough savings to fund an adequate level of investment, these countries often rely on foreign financing. Private international borrowing and lending are heavily restricted by the governments of developing countries. Governments may allow residents to purchase foreign exchange only for certain purposes. In some developing countries, different exchange rates apply to different categories of transactions. Thus, the local currency is not easily convertible into other currencies. Some developing countries also require foreign investors to find a local partner who must be granted controlling interest. All these restrictions discourage foreign investment. In this section, we will look primarily at foreign aid and its link to economic development.

Foreign Aid

Foreign aid is any international transfer made on *concessional* (that is, especially favorable) terms for the purposes of promoting economic development. Foreign aid includes grants, which need not be repaid, and loans extended on more favorable repayment terms than the recipient could normally secure. Concessional loans have lower interest rates, longer repayment periods, or grace periods during which repayments are reduced or even waived (similar to some student loans). Foreign aid can take the form of money, capital goods, technical assistance, food, and so forth.

> FOREIGN AID CAN TAKE THE FORM OF MONEY, CAPITAL GOODS, TECHNICAL ASSISTANCE, FOOD, AND SO FORTH.

Some foreign aid is granted by a specific country, such as the United States, to another specific country, such as the Philippines. Country-to-country aid is called *bilateral* assistance. Other foreign aid goes through international bodies such as the World Bank. Assistance provided by organizations that use funds from a number of countries is called *multilateral*. For example, the World Bank provides loans and grants to support activities that are viewed as prerequisites for development, such as health and education programs or basic development projects like dams, roads, and communications networks. And the International Monetary Fund extends loans to countries that have trouble with their balance of payments.

During the last four decades, the United States has provided the developing world with over $400 billion in aid. Since 1961, most U.S. aid has been coordinated by the U.S. Agency for International Development (USAID), which is part of the U.S. Department of State. This

foreign aid An international transfer made on especially favorable terms for the purpose of promoting economic development agency concentrates primarily on health, education, and agriculture, providing both technical assistance and loans. USAID emphasizes long-range plans to meet the basic needs of the poor and to promote self-sufficiency. Foreign aid is a controversial, though relatively small, part of the federal budget. Since 1993, official U.S. aid has been less than 0.2 percent of U.S. GDP, compared to an average of 0.3 percent from 21 other industrialized nations.

Does Foreign Aid Promote Economic Development?

In general, foreign aid provides additional purchasing power and thus the possibility of increased investment, capital imports, and consumption. But it remains unclear whether foreign aid *supplements* domestic saving, thus increasing investment, or simply *substitutes* for domestic saving, thereby increasing consumption rather than investment. What is clear is that foreign aid often becomes a source of discretionary funds that benefit not the poor but their leaders. Historically, more than 90 percent of the funds distributed by USAID have gone to governments, whose leaders assume responsibility for distributing these funds.

© HUNG CHUNG CHIH/SHUTTERSTOCK.COM

Much bilateral funding is tied to purchases of goods and services from the donor nation, and such programs can sometimes be counterproductive—they have unintended consequences. For example, in the 1950s, the United States began the Food for Peace program, which helped sell U.S. farm products abroad, but some recipient governments turned around and sold that food to finance poorly conceived projects. Worse yet, the availability of low-priced food from abroad drove down farm prices in the developing countries, hurting poor farmers there. The same holds for clothing. Used clothing donated to thrift shops and charitable organizations in industrialized countries typi cally winds up for sale in Africa, where the low price discourages local production of clothing.[8] Before used clothing swamped the continent, Africa had a textile industry, but no more. Textiles are often the first rung on the ladder to developing a broader manufacturing base.

Foreign aid may have raised the standard of living in some developing countries, but it has not necessarily increased their ability to become self-supporting at that higher standard of living. Many countries that receive aid are doing less of what they had done well. Their agricultural sectors have suffered. For example, though we should be careful when drawing conclusions about causality, per capita food production in Africa has fallen since 1960. Outside aid has often insulated government officials from their own incompetence and from the fundamental troubles of their own economies. No country receiving U.S. aid in the past 25 years has moved up in status from developing to industrial. And most countries today that have achieved industrial status did so without foreign aid. Development success typically takes time and involves gradual movements toward freer markets.

Because of disappointment with the results of government aid, the trend is toward channeling funds through private nonprofit agencies such as CARE. More than half of foreign aid now flows through private channels. The privatization of foreign aid follows a larger trend toward privatization in developing economies around the world.

8. Garth Frazer, "Used-Clothing Donations and Apparel Production in Africa," *Economic Journal*, 118 (October 2008): 1764–1784.

Final Word

Because no single theory of economic development has become widely accepted, this chapter has been more descriptive than theoretical. We can readily identify the features that distinguish developing from industrial economies. Education is key to development, both because of its direct effect on productivity and because those who are more educated tend to be more receptive to new ideas. A physical infrastructure of transportation and communication systems and utilities is needed to link economic participants. And trusted financial institutions help link savers and borrowers. A country needs entrepreneurs with the vision to move the economy forward. Finally, the most elusive ingredients are the laws, manners, customs and ways of doing business that nurture economic development. Economic history is largely a story of economies that have failed to produce a set of economic rules of the game that lead to sustained economic growth. Some transitional economies and some newly emerging industrial countries in Asia show that economic development continues to be achievable.

Multiple Choice Questions

1. The yardstick most often used to compare living standards across nations is
   a. average production cost per unit
   b. sales revenue per month
   c. utility per capita
   d. output per capita
   e. imports per year
2. GDP (gross domestic product) measures the market value of all goods and services produced by resources supplied by the countries' residents and firms, regardless of the location of the resource.
   a. True
   b. False
3. Compared to industrial market countries, developing countries usually have
   a. exports consisting mostly of agricultural products and raw materials
   b. faster population growth
   c. higher unemployment
   d. higher rates of illiteracy
   e. All of the answers are correct
4. Which of the following is not a country or region most likely to be among industrial market countries?
   a. Western Europe
   b. North American
   c. Australia
   d. South Asia
   e. Japan
5. A trend in developing countries is that
   a. the birth rate during a typical woman's lifetime has increased from three to six children
   b. attitudes toward family size are changing
   c. when women have employment opportunities outside the home, fertility rates increase
   d. as women become better educated, they earn less
   e. as women become less educated, they tend to have fewer children
6. Labor productivity depends on the
   a. quality of the labor
   b. the amount of capital
   c. the amount of natural resources
   d. the amount of other inputs, such as technology
   e. All of the answers are correct
7. The country of Yipi can raise its productivity by investing more in
   a. both human and physical capital
   b. human capital only
   c. physical capital only
   d. stable foreign economies
   e. stocks and bonds
8. Poor countries are poor because of all of the following except:
   a. Do not produce many goods and services
   b. Have reliable rules of the game
   c. Have low labor productivity
   d. Have low education levels
   e. Have serious deficiencies in the physical infrastructure
9. If Varun is a skilled worker employed in a low-skill job, he is
   a. underemployed
   b. unemployed
   c. overemployed
   d. fully employed
   e. All the answers are correct
10. Which of the following statements best serves as a summary of the other statements?
    a. Low income can mean poor nutrition during the formative years, which can retard mental and physical development
    b. Low income and low productivity may reinforce each other in a cycle of poverty
    c. Low productivity obviously results in low income
    d. Low income means less saving and less saving means less investment in human and physical capital
    e. Poverty can result in less education, less capital formation, a poor diet, and little health care
11. A requirement for development is
    a. an unreliable system of financial institutions
    b. a lack of saving by households and firms
    c. low confidence in domestic currency
    d. low and predictable inflation that encourages saving
    e. None of the answers is correct
12. In developing countries, it is not true that
    a. banks are often viewed with suspicion
    b. at the first sign of economic problems, many bank depositors withdraw their funds

c. because banks cannot rely on a continuous supply of deposits, banks cannot make loans for extended periods
d. if financial institutions fail to serve as intermediaries between savers and borrowers, the lack of funds for investment will make growth rates double
e. the credit provided by banks as a percent of total output is one fifth that in high-income countries

13. Which of the following resources is necessary to combine efficiently the other resources to produce goods and services?
a. natural resources
b. capital
c. labor
d. entrepreneurial ability
e. financial institutions

14. Sjen Mavago, the economics minister of the country of X-Marks-the-Spot, has concluded that entrepreneurs are unable to generate the kind of growth the country needs. Her decision to create state enterprises might be motivated by the desire to
a. earn profit
b. provide jobs for friends and relatives of government officials
c. take risks
d. encourage a free market
e. limit government's role in the economy

15. Laws, customs, conventions, and other institutional elements that sustain an economy fall under the category of
a. rules of the game
b. human capital
c. natural resources
d. financial institutions
e. capital infrastructure

16. A problem for developing countries is that the prices of primary products fluctuate more widely than do the prices of finished goods because
a. crop supply changes very little despite the weather
b. crop supply fluctuates with the weather
c. weather never varies
d. crops go in and out of fashion as new diets are developed
e. crop demand fluctuates with the weather

17. When a developing country relies on import substitution,
a. it sacrifices the gains from specialization and comparative advantage
b. replaces low-cost foreign goods with high-cost domestic goods
c. domestic producers, shielded from foreign competition, usually fail to become efficient
d. other countries often retaliate with their own trade restrictions
e. All of the answers are correct

18. When a developing country relies on export promotion:
a. It concentrates on producing for the export market
b. The emphasis is on comparative advantage and trade expansion
c. It forces producers to become more efficient
d. It requires less government intervention in the market
e. All of the answers are correct

19. A World Bank study suggests a strong link in Africa between governments that _____ special-interest groups and _____ rates of economic growth.
a. cater to, high
b. cater to, moderate
c. cater to, low
d. ignore, low
e. ignore, moderate

20. Soft budget constraints will lead to
a. inefficiency
b. quick responses to changes in supply and demand
c. good investment decisions
d. high product quality
e. managers eager to satisfy consumer demand rather than production quotas

Answers

1. d	2. b	3. e	4. d	5. b	6. e	7. a	8. b	9. a	10. b
11. d	12. d	13. d	14. b	15. a	16. b	17. e	18. e	19. c	20. a

LONG ANSWER QUESTIONS

LO1 Describe the worldwide variation in economic vitality

1.1. *(Worlds Apart)* Per capita income most recently was about 158 times greater in the United States than in the Democratic Republic of the Congo. Suppose per capita grows an average of 3 percent per year in the richer country and 6 percent per year in the poorer country. Assuming such growth rates continue indefinitely into the future, how many years would it take before per capita income in the Congo exceeds that of the United States? (To simplify the math, suppose at the outset per capita income is $158,000 in the richer country and $1,000 in the poorer country.)

LO2 Explain why productivity is the key to development

2.1. *(Import Substitution Versus Export Promotion)* Explain why domestic producers who supply a good that competes with imports would prefer an import-substitution approach to trade policy rather than an export-promotion approach. Which policy would domestic consumers prefer and why?

LO3 Discuss international trade and development

3.1. *(International Trade and Development)* From the perspective of citizens in a developing country, what are some of the benefits and drawbacks of international trade?

LO4 Describe the role of foreign aid in economic development

4.1. *(Foreign Aid and Economic Development)* Foreign aid, if it is to be successful in enhancing economic development, must lead to a more productive economy. Describe some of the problems in achieving such an objective through foreign aid.

21 Chapter in Review

KEY TERMS

developing countries
nations typified by high rates of illiteracy, high unemployment, high fertility rates, and exports of primary products; also known as low-income and middle-income economies

industrial market countries
economically advanced capitalist countries of Western Europe, North America, Australia, New Zealand, and Japan; also known as developed countries and high-income economies

privatization
the process of turning government enter-prises into private enterprises

social capital
the shared values and trust that promote cooperation in the economy

import substitution
a development strategy that emphasizes domestic manufacturing of products that had been imported

export promotion
a development strategy that concentrates on producing for the export market

foreign aid
an international transfer made on especially favorable terms for the purpose of promoting economic development

LO1 Describe the worldwide variation in economic vitality. The most common measure of comparison of standards of living between different countries is output per capita. Developing countries are distinguished by low output per capita, poor health and nutrition, high fertility rates, and poor education.

Share of World Population and Output from High-, Middle-, and Low-Income Economies as of 2009

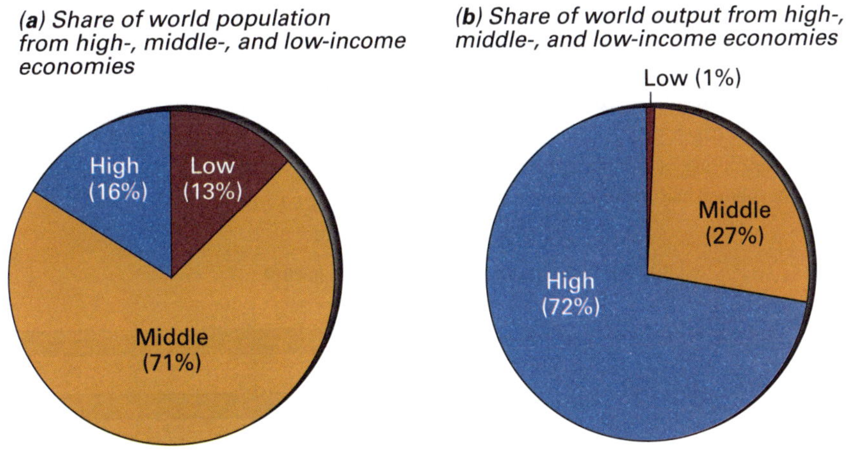

Per Capita Income for Selected Countries in 2010

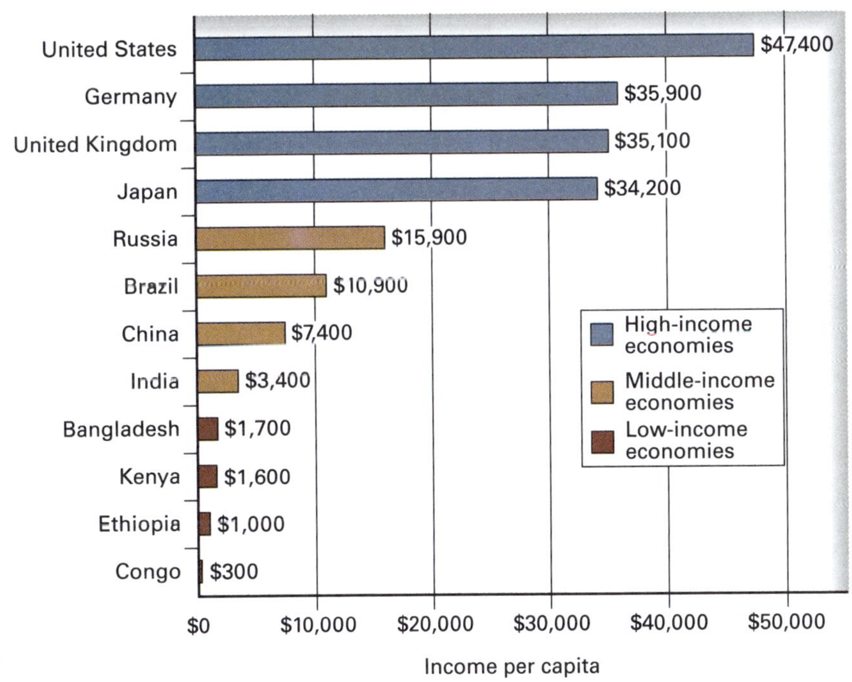

LO2 **Explain why productivity is the key to development.** Labor productivity, measured in terms of output per worker, is by definition low in low-income countries, as it depends on the quality of the labor and other inputs that combine with labor, such as capital and natural resources. The key to a rising standard of living is increased productivity. To foster productivity, developing nations must stimulate investment, support education and training programs, provide sufficient infrastructure, and foster supportive rules of the game.

LO3 **Discuss international trade and development.** Developing countries need to trade with developed countries to acquire the capital and technology that will increase labor productivity. Exports usually generate more than half of the annual flow of foreign exchange in developing countries. Foreign aid and private investment make up the rest. Developing countries often use either import substitution or export promotion strategies to improve production. With import substitution, domestic manufacturers make products that had previously been imported and the government supports them with tariffs and quotas. Export promotion concentrates on producing for the export market. Export promotion has proven generally more successful.

LO4 **Describe the role of foreign aid in economic development.** Foreign aid has been a mixed blessing for most developing countries. In some cases, aid has helped countries build the roads, bridges, schools, and other capital infrastructure necessary for development. In other cases, foreign aid has simply increased consumption and insulated government from painful but necessary reforms. Worse still, subsidized food from abroad has undermined domestic agriculture, hurting poor farmers.

GDP Per Capita for Developing Economies in 2010

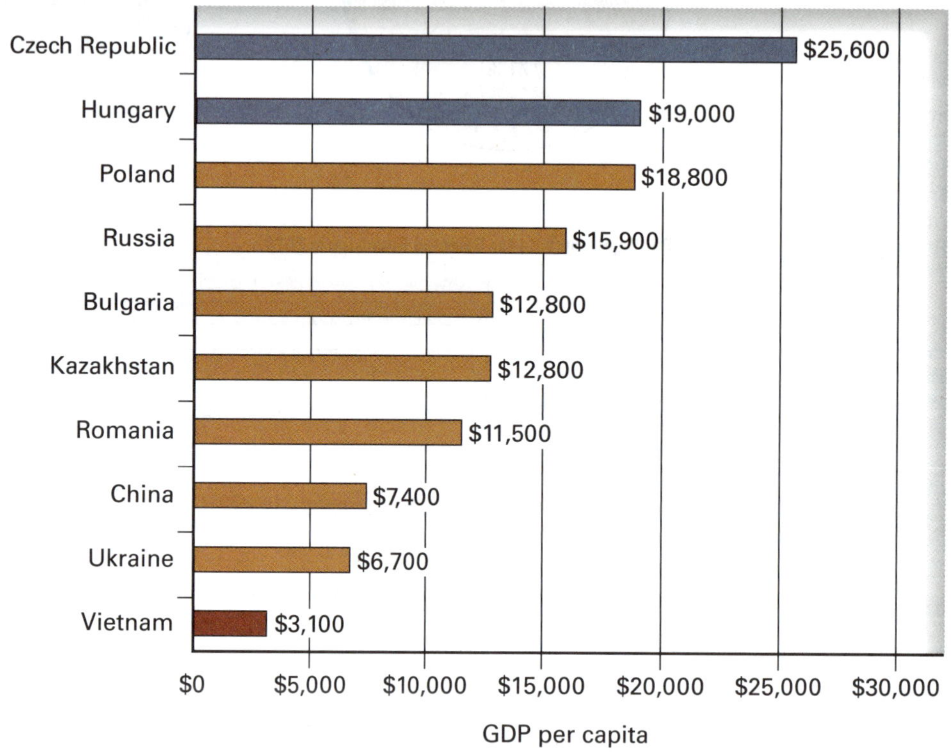

Case Study

The Opportunity Cost of College (Chapter 2)

What is your opportunity cost of attending college full time this year? What was the best alternative you gave up? If you held a full-time job, you have some idea of the income you gave up to attend college. Suppose you expected to earn $20,000 a year, after taxes, from a full-time job. As a full-time college student, you plan to work part time during the academic year and full time during the summer, earning a total of $10,000 after taxes. Thus, by attending college this year, you gave up after-tax earnings of $10,000 (= $20,000 – $10,000).

There is also the direct cost of college itself. Suppose you are paying $6,000 this year for in-state tuition, fees, and books at a public college (paying out-of-state rates would add another $6,000 to that, and attending a private college would add about $15,000). The opportunity cost of paying for tuition, fees, and books is what you and your family could otherwise have purchased with that money.

How about room and board? Expenses for room and board are not necessarily an opportunity cost because, even if you were not attending college, you would still need to live somewhere and eat something, though these could cost more in college. Likewise, whether or not you attended college, you would still buy goods such as CDs, clothes, and toiletries, and services such as laundry, haircuts, and DVD rentals. Your spending for such products is not an opportunity cost of attending college but the personal cost that arises regardless of what you do. So for simplicity, assume that room, board, and personal expenses are the same whether or not you attend college. The forgone earnings of $10,000 plus the $6,000 for tuition, fees, and books yield an opportunity cost of $16,000 this year for a student paying in-state rates at a public college. Opportunity cost jumps to about $22,000 for students paying out-of-state rates and to about $31,000 for those at private colleges. Scholarships, but not loans, would reduce your opportunity cost (why not loans?).

This analysis assumes that other things remain constant. But if, in your view, attending college is more of a pain than you expected your next best alternative to be, then the opportunity cost of attending college is even higher. In other words, if you are one of those people who find college difficult, often boring, and in most ways more unpleasant than a full-time job, then the cost in money terms understates your opportunity cost. Not only are you incurring the expense of college, but you are also forgoing a more pleasant quality of life. If, on the other hand, you believe the wild and crazy life of a college student is more enjoyable than a full-time job would be, then the dollar figures overstate your opportunity cost, because your next best alternative involves a less satisfying quality of life.

Apparently, you view college as a wise investment in your future, even though it's costly and perhaps even painful. College graduates on average earn about twice as much per year as high school graduates, a difference that exceeds $1 million over a lifetime. These pay gains from college encourage a growing fraction of college students to pile up debts to finance their education.

Still, college is not for everyone. Some find the opportunity cost too high. For example, Bill Gates and Paul Allen dropped out of college to cofound Microsoft (Gates was the second richest person on earth in 2007; Allen ranked 19th). Tiger Woods, once an economics major at Stanford, dropped out after two years to earn his fortune in professional golf. And Paula Creamer, who skipped college to play golf, won her first $1 million sooner than any LPGA player in tour history. High school basketball players who believe they are ready for the pros also skip college, as do most tennis pros. Many actors even drop out of high school to pursue their craft, including Jim Carrey, Tom Cruise, Johnny Depp, Robert DeNiro, Cameron Diaz, Colin Farrell, Nicole Kidman, Jude Law, Demi Moore, Keanu Reeves, Kiefer Sutherland, Hilary Swank, Charlize Theron, and Kate Winslet.

SOURCES: "Tuition and Fees, 2006–7," *Chronicle of Higher Education Facts and Figures*, http://chronicle.com/stats/tuition/; Hillary Chura, "Cracking the Books for Financial Aid to College," *New York Times*, 27 January 2007; "The World's Billionaires," *Forbes*, 3 July 2007; and "College Board Connect to College Success" at http://www.collegeboard.com/.

THINK ABOUT IT

During the Vietnam War, colleges and universities were overflowing with students. Was this bumper crop of students caused by a greater expected return on a college education or by a change in the opportunity cost of attending college? Explain.

*Remember

There are more case studies to illustrate economic concepts at 4ltrpress.cengage.com/econ.

Case Study

User-Generated Products (Chapter 3)

In a market economy, new products and processes are usually developed by profit-seeking entrepreneurs, but sometimes sheer curiosity and the challenge of solving problems lead to new and better ways of doing things. For example, loose communities of computer programmers have been collaborating for decades. By the early 1990s, they formed a grass roots movement known as "open source," which was fueled by the Internet. In 1991, Linus Torvalds, a student at the University of Helsinki in Finland, wrote the core for what would become known as the Linux operating system. He posted his program online and invited anyone to tinker with the coding. Word spread, and computer aficionados around the world began spending their free time making Linux better.

Other software has developed in the open-source arena. For example, from the University of Illinois came web server software named Apache, and Swedish researchers developed database software called MySQL. The *Free Software Directory* lists more than 6,000 free software packages. The term *free* refers not only to the dollar cost of the software, which is zero, but to what you can do with the software—you can examine it, modify it, and redistribute it to anyone. Free user-generated software now includes the second most popular desktop operating system (Linux), web browser (Firefox), and office suite (OpenOffice), and the most widely used web server (Apache).

But most software sold is copyrighted to prevent redistribution, and buyers usually cannot even see the code, let alone tinker with it. Some for-profit start-up companies are piggybacking on user-generated products to create new software. For example, the developers of Zimbra email software drew from more than 40 open-source programs, including Apache and MySQL, to build the basics of their email system. Those 40 programs had been tested and improved by users over many years. Once Zimbra took shape, the company posted it online as open-source software for fine-tuning. Software junkies helped debug and improve it. The company now sells Zimbra online for much less than Microsoft charges for its email system.

Other user-generated products include some familiar names—Wikipedia, MySpace, Facebook, and YouTube. Wikipedia is a free online encyclopedia written and edited by volunteers. The idea is that collaboration over time will improve content much the way that open-source software has evolved. Wikipedia claims to be one of the most visited online sites. Founder Jimmy Wales says he spent a half million dollars getting Wikipedia going, but now the project relies on volunteers and donations.

MySpace and Facebook are social networking sites that allow users to post personal profiles, blogs, photos, music, videos, and more. So the main attraction of the sites is material provided by users. The companies simply provide the software and hardware framework to support the network. MySpace, founded in July 2003, was sold in July 2005 for about $330 million. Facebook was started by a college sophomore in 2004; in 2006 that founder turned down a $1 billion offer from Yahoo.

YouTube is an online video site that allows users to post their own videos and to view those posted by others. Searching for particular subjects is easy. For example, "comparative advantage" turned up "KaratEconomics Lesson 1." When YouTube was sold to Google in October 2006, YouTube had only 67 employees and no profit. Still, because visitors were viewing more than 100 million videos a day, all those eyeballs gave YouTube tremendous advertising potential. Google paid $1.65 billion for a company with no profit. Google still has its own video site; so does Yahoo.

User-generated products are not new. Radio call-in shows have been making money off callers for decades. But the Internet has increased opportunities for users to create new products and to improve existing products. Most of the users are just having fun. The more users involved, the more valuable that product is to each user. That's why networking and video sites are trying to dominate their markets.

SOURCES: Robert Guth, "Trolling the Web for Free Labor, Software Upstarts Are a New Force," *Wall Street Journal,* 13 November 2006; Pui-Wing Tam, "Google's YouTube Pact Spawns Big Payday," *Wall Street Journal,* 8 February 2007; and Robert Guth, "Linux Starts to Find Home on Desktops," 13 March 2007. The Free Software Directory is found at http://directory.fsf.org/.

THINK ABOUT IT

Why are users willing to help create certain products even though few, if any, users are paid for their efforts?

***Remember**

There are more case studies to illustrate economic concepts at 4ltrpress.cengage.com/econ.

Case Study

The Marginal Value of Free Medical Care (Chapter 6)

Certain Americans, such as the elderly and those on welfare, receive government-subsidized medical care. State and federal taxpayers spend more than $600 billion a year providing medical care to 88 million Medicare and Medicaid recipients, or more than $6,800 per beneficiary. Medicaid is the largest and fastest growing spending category in most state budgets. Beneficiaries pay only a tiny share of Medidaid costs; most services are free.

The problem with giving something away is that a beneficiary consumes it to the point where the marginal value reaches zero, although the marginal cost to taxpayers can be sizeable. This is not to say that people derive no benefit from these programs. Although beneficiaries may attach little or no value to the final unit consumed, they likely derive a substantial consumer surplus from all the other units they consume. For example, suppose that Exhibit 8 represents the demand for health care by Medicaid beneficiaries. If the price they face is zero, each beneficiary consumes health care to the point where the demand curve intersects the horizontal axis—that is, where his or her marginal valuation is zero. Although they attach little or no value to their final unit of Medicaid-funded health care, their consumer surplus is the entire area under the demand curve.

One way to reduce the cost to taxpayers without significantly harming beneficiaries is to charge a token amount—say, $1 per doctor visit. Beneficiaries would eliminate visits they value less than $1. This practice would yield significant savings to taxpayers but would still leave beneficiaries with abundant health care and a substantial consumer surplus (measured in Exhibit 8 as the area under the demand curve but above the $1 price). As a case in point, one Medicaid experiment in California required some beneficiaries to pay $1 per visit for their first two office visits per month (after two visits, the price of additional visits reverted to zero). A control group continued to receive free medical care. The $1 charge reduced office visits by 8 percent compared to the control group. Medical care, like other goods and services, is also sensitive to its time cost (a topic discussed in the next section). For example, a 10 percent increase in the average travel time to a free outpatient clinic reduced visits by 10 percent. Similarly, when the relocation of a free health clinic at one college increased students' walking time by 10 minutes, visits dropped 40 percent.

Market Demand and Consumer Surplus

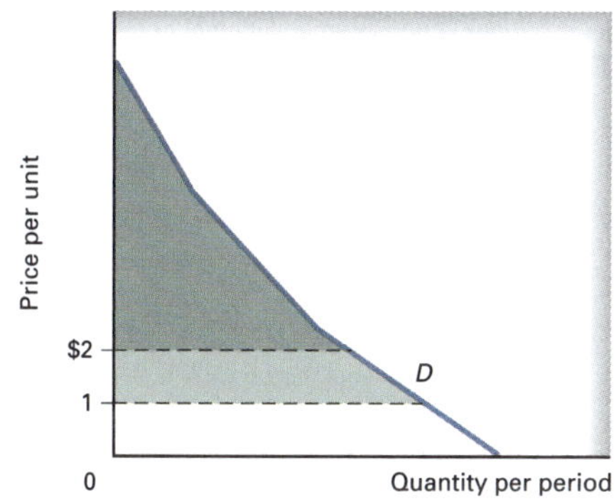

Another problem with giving something away is that beneficiaries are less vigilant about getting honest value, and this may increase the possibility of waste, fraud, and abuse. People won't tolerate padded bills and fake claims if they have to pay their own bills. Another source of inefficiency is the tendency of recipients to use the emergency room for nonemergency care (an emergency room visit usually costs the government much more than a visit to the doctor's office). Finally, program beneficiaries have less incentive to pursue healthy behavior themselves through a good diet, sufficient exercise, and the like. This doesn't mean certain groups don't deserve heavily subsidized medical care. The point is that when something is free, people consume it until their marginal value is zero, they pay less attention to getting honest value, they overuse costly alternatives, and they take less personal responsibility.

Some Medicare beneficiaries visit one or more medical specialists most days of the week. Does all this medical attention improve their health care? Not according to a long-running Dartmouth Medical School study. Researchers there found no apparent medical benefit and even some harm from such overuse. As one doctor lamented, "The system is broken. I'm not being a mean ogre, but when you give something away for free, there is nothing to keep utilization down."[2] Even a modest money cost or time cost would reduce utilization, yet would still leave beneficiaries with quality health care and a substantial consumer surplus.

As a result of 2006 federal legislation, states are beginning to require a small payment for some Medicaid services, such as $1 to fill a generic drug prescription and $2 for an office visit (children and pregnant women are exempt). Ohio now requires a $3 payment for using the emergency room for nonemergency care (doctor visits in Ohio remain free of charge). None of these requirements could be considered excessively burdensome on beneficiaries, but they might help slow government spending on what has become the largest and fastest growing item in state and federal budgets.

SOURCES: Dave Dhaval and Robert Kaestner, "Health Insurance and Ex Ante Moral Hazard: Evidence from Medicare," National Bureau of Economic Research Working Paper 12764 (December 2006); Elliot Fisher et al., "The Implications of Regional Variation in Medicare Spending," *Annals of Internal Medicine,* 18 February 2003; Gina Kolata, "Patients in Florida Lining Up for All That Medicare Covers," *New York Times,* 13 September 2003; Timothy Williams, "City to Hire Investigators to Pursue Providers' Medicaid Fraud," *New York Times,* 30 December 2006; and Steven Rhoads, "Marginalism," in *The Fortune Encyclopedia of Economics,* edited by D. R. Henderson (New York: Warner, 1993), pp. 31–33. For more on Medicare and Medicaid, go to http://www.cms.hhs.gov/.

THINK ABOUT IT

Medicare recipients pay a monthly premium for coverage, must meet an annual deductible, and have a copayment for doctors' office visits. President George W. Bush introduced some coverage of prescription medications (prior to that, there was none). What impact would an increase in the monthly premium have on their consumer surplus? What would be the impact of a reduction in copayments? What is the impact on consumer surplus of offering some coverage for prescription medication?

*Remember

There are more case studies to illustrate economic concepts at 4ltrpress.cengage.com/econ.

Case Study

Timely Fashions Boost Profit for Zara (Chapter 10)

One way a firm can increase market power is to offer a differentiated product. Zara, the largest fashion retailer in Europe, has been described as "possibly the most innovative and devastating retailer in the world." The company makes nearly all its clothing in its own workshops and factories, including designing, fabric dyeing, tailoring, and ironing. Just about all the clothing is produced in Arteixo, Spain, where Zara operates 14 factories connected by tunnels to a giant distribution center. In a matter of hours, that center fills up with clothing.

Zara's retail shops and clothing factories communicate through a sophisticated feedback mechanism for gathering market intelligence and putting it to work. Sales associates carry personal digital assistants to relay information on fashion trends and customer demand back to the company's team of 200 designers in Spain. Real-time sales data allow the factory to increase production of items that are selling and to bring out similar designs. By doing everything in house, Zara avoids the delay involved with manufacturing in a low-cost country such as China. Direct shipments from factory to shops also eliminate the need for costly warehouses.

Zara takes as little as two weeks to develop a new item and deliver it to one of its more than 1,000 retail stores. The industry average is nine months. The company launches about 10,000 new designs a year, making new items in small batches at first so if something doesn't sell, there is not much left over. But if something catches on, stores can restock in a few days, so Zara doesn't miss out on a fashion wave. Thus, shops never have to wait long for fresh stock or to get an order filled. Whereas traditional stores such as the Gap may get new fashions twice a season, Zara distributes them twice a week. And in perhaps its most unusual of strategies, the company advertises little, relying instead on prime store location and word of mouth.

In short, Zara believes that making its own apparel rather than outsourcing production to a lower-cost country, reduces delays, exploits customer feedback, maintains flexibility, and ensures quality This ready supply of new clothing lines and continuous supply of popular items help Zara differentiate its products. Amancio Ortega, Zara's founder, opened his first store in 1975. His wealth in 2007 reached an estimated $24 billion, ranking him the 8th richest person on the planet. The market rewards successful innovation.

SOURCES: Rachel Tiplady, "Zara: Taking the Lead in Fast Fashion," *Business Week,* 2 April 2006; Vanessa O'Connell, "How Fashion Makes Its Way from the Runway to the Rack," *Wall Street Journal,* 8 February 2007; Eric Wilson, "OK Knockoffs, This Is War," *New York Times,* 30 March 2006; and "The World's Billionaires," *Forbes*, 8 March 2007.

THINK ABOUT IT

Firms earn economic profit by offering a differentiated product. How does Zara differentiate its clothing?

***Remember**

There are more case studies to illustrate economic concepts at 4ltrpress.cengage.com/econ.

Index

Q

R

U

V

W

X

Y

Z